THE COLONIAL ERA

AN EYEWITNESS HISTORY

THE COLONIAL ERA

Faith Jaycox

Facts On File, Inc.

The Colonial Era

Copyright © 2002 by Faith Jaycox

Maps © 2002 by Facts On File

Facts On File, Inc.
132 West 31st Street
New York, NY 10001

Library of Congress Cataloging-in-Publication Data
Jaycox, Faith.
    The colonial era : an eyewitness history / Faith Jaycox.
        p. cm.
    Includes bibliographical references (p.) and index.
    ISBN 0-8160-4138-5 (acid-free paper)
    1. United States—History—Colonial period, ca. 1600–1775. 2. United States—History—
Colonial period, ca. 1600–1775—Biography. 3. United States—History—Colonial period, ca.
1600–1775—Sources. I. Title.
    E188 .J39 2002
    973.2—dc21   2001033565

Facts On File books are available at special discounts when purchased in bulk quantities for businesses, associations, institutions or sales promotions. Please call our Special Sales Department in New York at (212) 967-8800 or (800) 322-8755.

You can find Facts On File on the World Wide Web at
http://www.factsonfile.com

Text design by Joan M. Toro

Jacket design by Cathy Rincon

Maps by Dale Williams

NOTE ON PHOTOS

Many of the illustrations and photographs used in this book are old, historical images. The quality of the prints is not always up to modern standards, as in many cases the originals are from glass negatives or the originals are damaged. The content of the illustrations, however, made their inclusion important despite problems in reproduction.

Printed in the United States of America.

VB FOF 10 9 8 7 6 5 4 3 2 1

This book is printed on acid-free paper.

For my many-times-great colonial grandparents,
who helped "write" this chronicle:
my maternal grandparents, James Mackall,
who arrived in Maryland in ca. 1655,
and John Calvin, who arrived in 1669, both from Scotland;
my paternal grandparents, Johannes and Susanna Lau Joho,
born in Alsace, who joined the Palatine migration to Philadelphia
in 1738 before moving on to the Virginia backcountry;
and my grandparent-in-law Thomas Jeacockes, born in Stratford-on Avon,
who with his brothers Francis and William joined the Great Migration
to Connecticut, soon forsaking it for Long Island.
And especially for my ancestress Sarah Kirby (Allen),
born in America in 1638. Under the influence of Quaker beliefs,
she spoke publicly in a religious meeting at Sandwich, for which act,
in March 1657, she was sentenced by Plymouth Colony officials
to be whipped for "opposing and abusing" the male minister.

CONTENTS

AUTHOR'S NOTE

Many sources dating from the colonial period use archaic or highly individual conventions of spelling, making them difficult for most contemporary readers to understand easily. When selecting "eyewitness testimony" from these sources, I have modernized the spelling with the goal of aiding the reader's comprehension. To give the reader some sense of the "flavor" of these documents, I have retained the original capitalization, punctuation, and spelling of names and place names. However, when selecting from sources that have been recently republished, I have reproduced them exactly, without further changes. I have included a very small number of selections that most readers will unfortunately find difficult; they are worth the additional effort, I believe, because they have a unique value. Throughout the "eyewitness testimony" selections, I have inserted occasional bracketed, *italicized* comments to clarify a point. Bracketed comments that are not italicized are reproduced from the source from which the selection was taken.

No "eyewitness testimony," of course, tells the "whole truth," even about the person who has written it. All are opinions, points of view, personal experiences, arguments, or pleas designed to win a point or influence others. Some, indeed, are very obviously and highly opinionated. They have been included specifically to give the reader a sense of the wide range of viewpoints and experiences that existed among literate people in the colonial era.

PREFACE

The Colonial Era chronicles the founding and growth of European settlements in North America, from the mid–1500s to 1776. During those years, neither the nation of the United States of America nor of Canada had yet come into being. There were English colonies, of course, 13 of which declared independence from Great Britain on July 4, 1776. But other English colonies existed as well, remaining loyal to Britain during the American war for independence. Several were in modern Canada and two were in Florida, whose western boundary at the time stretched to the Mississippi River. In addition, colonies that were *not* English also existed in North America. Spanish settlements dotted the Southwest from the Mississippi to California; and French-speaking settlements, abandoned to English or Spanish rulers less than 15 years earlier, stretched from New Orleans up the Mississippi and into Canada, where the largest was then called British North America (modern Quebec).

As is well known, the brash Thirteen Colonies eventually grew to dominate North America as the United States. This chronicle focuses on their development, but it also tells the story of the French, Spanish, and other English colonies that shared a vast continent with them for 200 years. The English were actually latecomers to North America; before they arrived, both France and Spain had sent their first settlers. When those two nations later retreated from the continent, their settlements—and usually the people who had settled there—remained in place, to be later absorbed into the United States and Canada. Although the political and legal institutions of the modern North American nations developed primarily from English colonial foundations, many aspects of modern North America cannot be properly appreciated if the colonies founded by other nations are ignored.

To the explorer or colonist of the 16th and 17th century, the North American continent was a vast and uncharted land. The entire continent appeared to European eyes—blind to the claims of the Native Americans who inhabited the entire continent with varying degrees of density—as an open field to claim, to exploit, and to settle. Maps did not show modern political boundaries—those dividing the United States from Canada on the north and from Mexico on the south—because they did not exist. The history of the colonial era, from one perspective, is the history of why and how modern boundaries emerged from two centuries of contest among the major powers of Europe, the colonial systems they established, and their Indian allies. That sense of contest and choice is difficult to recapture by looking only for the "roots" of modern political systems, for past outcomes have a way of appearing inevitable from the perspective of the present.

During the colonial era, considerable cultural diversity existed in North America. Even within the English colonies themselves, more ethnic and religious heterogeneity existed than is sometimes recognized. While this diversity is interesting in itself, it is more important for what it reveals about the earliest experiences of North Americans. A constant feature of colonial life for most colonists—both European and African—was contact with people who were culturally or religiously different. Their experiences often involved cross-cultural exchange as well, both with each other and with the indigenous Native Americans. These exchanges were not always even, of course, a fact that highlights the importance of factors that establish and transmit the dominance of one group over another. Nor did the parties to such exchanges always recognize and value them, although at times they did both. Most European denizens of the colonial era were unabashedly and even aggressively sure of the superiority of their own way of life. Many came to the New World for the purpose of preserving their own cultural and religious integrity and had no qualms about forcing those within their reach to join them in the process. Nonetheless, as often as not, the realities of the New World involved them in a learning process. While tolerance, ideologically speaking, was rarely valued and sometimes suspect, it was often necessary in practice and usually proved its worth. The major European colonial cultures were not, in fact, ever totalitarian. Many examples exist of toleration as well as cultural accommodation, incorporation, and blending.

In colonial history, a chronicle of the founding and growth of European settlements always contains within itself an opposite story: the destruction of the traditional ways of life of the Native Americans, whom the Europeans displaced. In the early years of colonization, many Indian groups welcomed the Europeans. Frequently, they even maneuvered with each other to establish advantageous trading and political relationships with the newcomers to the continent. Native Americans wanted to obtain European trade goods, which they believed would enhance their lives. Tribes saw an opportunity to form political alliances with new groups, as they often did with each other, to increase their own status or to strengthen their position against enemies. Few, of course, volunteered to embrace the strange European way of life, and most were bemused that the newcomers believed themselves to be superior. All the same, for two centuries many Native Americans forged contacts with colonial people, exchanging visits, attending ceremonies, and fighting alongside their soldiers.

Native Americans were all too soon aware that they were being overpowered by the numbers and land-consuming lifestyle of Europeans, as well as by their diseases. Nonetheless, in approaching the Indians throughout this text, I have attempted meet them on their own terms—that is, as intentional historical actors who tried to advance what they believed to be their own best interests. While *The Colonial Era* chronicles important events in relations between Native Americans and colonists, it does not attempt to treat in detail the myriad Indian cultures that predated and coexisted with early European settlement.

INTRODUCTION
The Age of Exploration

At the opening of the 16th century, less than a decade after Christopher Columbus's first voyage in 1492, no European understood how vast the North American continent really was. Many, in fact, did not yet actually believe in its existence. Most geographers had theorized for some time that the world was, in fact, round. Unaware of North America, however, they greatly underestimated the earth's size and circumference. Columbus found the West Indies at almost exactly the spot where they calculated Asia to be located on the globe. Like many others of his day, he believed to the end of his life that he had reached large islands off Asia's coast, and he logically called their residents Indians.

As the 16th century progressed and knowledge of the Americas' vastness accumulated, the continents were for some time considered far more a barrier to trade than an opportunity to establish a new European world. Explorers, as historians have long pointed out, were seeking not a new world but an old one. Specifically, they were searching for a westward sea route to the rich trading centers of India, Asia, and the Orient.

By the opening of the 16th century, a new merchant class had developed in Europe. These traders and bankers were a new "middle" class, sandwiched between the nobility on one side and the commoners (many still peasants or serfs) on the other. Ambitious for wealth and the status and power that it made possible, the merchant class developed its resources by brokering the importation and sale of spices, textiles, and other goods—first from the Middle East, then from India, China, and other Asian ports. Highly valued in Europe, these goods included silks and damasks; colorful dyes; perfumes; jewels; foods like oranges and figs; steel; medicinal herbs; and spices like cinnamon, clove, and pepper. Some were luxuries for the rich, as they remain today. The item most in demand, however, was the most mundane: spices, which were one of the very few ways 16th century people, whether wealthy or ordinary, had of preserving food.

The extreme difficulty of importing goods from the Far East, however, blocked the aspirations of merchants and the desires of their prospective customers. Existing routes were partly by sea and partly by land; the land route in particular was both expensive and very hazardous. Goods traveled by caravan through perhaps hundreds of small, local, effectively independent municipalities, each of which could and did tax or regulate trade. Merchants were forced to rely on personal contacts with scores of individual traders along the route, each of whom charged a middleman's fee. Trading caravans braved the ever present of possibilities of fraud, theft, and outright hostility in Middle Eastern lands with long memories of the brutal Crusades. Once through the Middle Eastern land route, they arrived in Italy to embark by sea on the final leg of their journey to western and northern Europe. First, however, they paid fees to the city-states of Italy, whose advantageous location in the Mediterranean enabled them to exercise a virtual monopoly on eastern trade.

European merchants hoped to find a way to avoid paying both the Italians and the Middle Eastern middlemen, and that meant finding a sea route to Asia. The new middle class of merchants was not the only European group interested in exploration, however. Kings and queens, who during the Middle Ages had shared power with feudal lords, quickly saw that they could improve their positions by allying with commercial interests. Monarchs oversaw voyages of exploration as royal sponsors and often as personal investors, granting patents and eventually offering military support. Throughout Europe, Crown-sponsored exploration and trading networks generated wealth for merchants *and* for monarchs, who were usually entitled to a "royal fifth," or 20 percent of the profit. Slowly, monarchs used the wealth to consolidate their power, and unified nations emerged from a decentralized maze of medieval lords and manors. Where Crowns saw the opportunity for power, the Church saw the opportunity to spread Christianity. After it became clear that the New World was populated by vast, unconverted populations, the Roman Catholic Church gave its blessing and sometimes its encouragement to exploratory ventures. In doing so it strengthened the resolve of the politically and personally ambitious as well as the truly spiritual, who now foresaw eternal blessings for opening new and "heathen" lands. Other Europeans were inspired less by the spirit than by the intellectual ferment of the Renaissance. Scholars rediscovered classical and Middle Eastern knowledge, spurring the development of highly skilled mathematicians and scientists; they in turn made available theories and methods for exploration. To all other motives for exploration, of course, was added human curiosity.

The first European nation to explore systematically by sea was Portugal, well positioned at the tip of the Iberian peninsula to launch its ships into uncharted waters. The Portuguese were aided by the fortuitous development of the caravel, a fast and maneuverable new ship, and by tools promoted by Prince Henry the Navigator (1394–1460) at his navigational school at Sagres. Like other Europeans, the Portuguese knew that there were two possible sea routes to Asia: the first down and around the known African continent, the second a pioneering journey west across the uncharted Atlantic Ocean. Although captains of Portuguese birth later sailed west for other nations, the Portuguese crown itself chose the African route. By the end of the 15th century, Portuguese sailors had discovered the Azores, explored the length of the African coast, and finally rounded the Cape of Good Hope to sail on to Asia. They had established permanent, militarily fortified trading settlements known as "factories" along the coast of Africa—especially on the "gold coast" of Guinea, which was widely believed to be abundant in gold. The Portuguese had also entered the human slave trade, probably for the first time in 1441.

For many centuries before the arrival of the Portuguese in Africa, an extensive overland African slave trade had flourished under the control of Arabic and Berber peoples on the north coast and to the west of Africa. Slave trading had also existed among some European peoples. Germanic tribes had been especially active in enslaving Slavs, from whose name the word slavery derives, but recent political changes had effectively ended the trade. (Slavs were, however, the first slave laborers in Portugal's early sugar colony on Madeira.)

After the Portuguese entered the slave trade, African captives began to be diverted from old routes bound northward across the desert to new east–west routes bound for coastal ports. Portuguese traders began to send African captives back to Portugal and Spain along with gold, ivory, and other commodities. A few of these early captives accompanied the first Spanish and Portuguese to the New World as explorers, even before large numbers of Africans were brought to labor there.

Portugal's early success in establishing and dominating the sea route down the African coast reduced the sea-going options of other European nations searching for a sea route to Asia. Some began to sail west across the Atlantic. John Cabot, an Italian sailing for England, reached Newfoundland in the late 1490s. Balboa, sailing for Spain, saw the Pacific from the Isthmus of Panama in 1513. In 1519, Magellan sailed south around South America. After he died en route, his surviving crew eventually continued around the tip of Africa and back up its west coast to return to Europe. In the 1520s and 1530s, both the French and Portuguese explored the Atlantic coast of North America, and in 1542 Juan Cabrillo explored the Pacific coast, claiming it for Spain. Until the 1800s, in fact, European explorers continued to search for a Northwest Passage, the hoped-for (but nonexistent) water route across North America to the trading markets of eastern Asia.

Meanwhile, Spain, the first nation to reach the New World by sailing west in 1492, began to build a colonial empire. In 1496, the Spanish under Christopher Columbus founded their first settlement on Hispaniola (now the Dominican Republic). By the middle of the 16th century the Spanish had subjugated the indigenous peoples of South and Central America. They had founded fabulously profitable mining operations, sending plundered New World gold and silver back to Europe. They had also discovered that the indigenous people of the Americas, no matter how brutally exploited, did not make satisfactory labor for Spain's New World sugar plantations. Having brought the first Africans to Hispaniola in 1505, the Spanish began to import slaves in ever-increasing numbers after the middle of the century, their destination the Indies and South and Central America. Eventually, Portugal and Spain were joined in slave trading by other European nations. Together they brought at least 10 million Africans to the New World, about five percent of whom came to North America.

Spain quickly dominated European conquest of the New World, gaining such tremendous wealth that it consequently began to dominate Europe. It subjugated Portugal in 1580 and obtained control over the Netherlands in 1579. Partly in response to Spain's success, other European nations began to develop an interest in founding colonies. No single, universal cause led nations to found colonies in the New World, however. Politics, ambition, religion, and human adventurousness went hand in hand. Economic opportunism—both of individuals and groups—played a large role. Some believed that Mediterranean and Near Eastern products like silk, oil, wine, and sugar could be provided by colonies in the New World, thus ending the need for certain foreign trade altogether. Some saw indigenous populations as new, limitless markets for European manufactured goods. Some distressed nobility or "younger sons" (who under inheritance law called primogeniture received little of their fathers' estates) saw a chance to recoup wealth and feudal grandeur. At the other extreme, some officials saw a perfect disposal site for the displaced or restive poor, for troublesome individuals of all kinds, and for outright convicts.

Many others were led to the New World in part or in whole for religious reasons. Some were missionary clergy with sincere spiritual motives, although their effects on the indigenous populations have in modern times come to be seen as mixed at best. Others were small groups or individuals seeking the religious and civil rights they were denied in Europe. Some were dissenting or persecuted groups, whose numbers had greatly increased during the 16th century as Christianity splintered under the influence of the Reformation. Under the same influence, however, heads of state also came to see themselves as important instruments for the triumph of whatever religious affiliation their nations embraced. They claimed and settled land in the New World for their national faith.

Historians often describe individual decisions to emigrate as a combination of push-pull factors; while some factors "push" people out of their native country, others "pull" or attract them to a new land. From the beginning, one "pull" factor for many individuals who arrived in North America was the great human appeal of a fresh start in the New World. Some were spurred on by a sense of adventure. A few were simply romantics, who imagined they were entering a new and unspoiled Eden. Few, however, intended to establish an egalitarian new social order in North America, absent the hierarchies and inequities of the Old World. Many early colonists were conscripted from the lowest orders of European society and were treated accordingly. Another large group, the Africans, arrived against their will and enslaved. The majority of ordinary settlers who followed the explorers, however, were "pulled" to the New World by a simple desire to improve their lives. Many, called indentured servants, sold their labor for several years in order to pay for the trip.

The investors and colonists involved in early ventures to settle North America were as varied as their motives and their often conflicting goals. Almost every one of them, however, greatly underestimated how much European support, and how much human struggle, would be required before new colonies could flourish in the New World.

PART I

PRELUDE TO COLONIAL NORTH AMERICA

1

European Settlement of North America
to 1607

THE EMPIRE OF NEW SPAIN

In 1565, Spain founded the first permanent European settlement in North America at St. Augustine, Florida.

Before successfully founding St. Augustine, Spain had made at least six other attempts to establish colonies in North America. As early as 1526, Lucas Vázquez de Ayllón sailed from Santo Domingo, Hispaniola (modern Dominican Republic and Haiti), to an area the Spanish called *Chicora* (modern South Carolina and Georgia). He was accompanied by Dominican priests, some 500 men, and about 100 women and children; approximately 100 of the group were probably African slaves. The supply ship was wrecked, and the would-be colonists were struck by malaria, a disease of the Southern Hemisphere to which most Europeans had no resistance. Three months later, 150 returned to Santo Domingo. Many of the others, including Ayllón, had died. Some of the Africans, historians believe, remained behind and joined local Guale Indian society.

In 1528, another colonization effort was made, by way of the ruthlessly destructive expedition carried out by Pánfilo de Narváez. Narváez landed more than 600 men and women at Tampa Bay. After disease, Indian retaliation, and seafaring disasters had taken their toll, only four men survived. Before being rescued, they wandered through the American Southwest for eight years. The group included Estéban (or Estavanico), an African and former slave who later guided a Spanish expedition to New Mexico; and Álvar Núñez Cabeza de Vaca, whose famous *Relation* describing their adventures was published in 1542.

Although Spain did not succeed immediately in North America, it already possessed a thriving colonial empire, called New Spain, in the Southern Hemisphere of the New World. As early as 1496, the first permanent settlement in New Spain had been founded, at Santo Domingo on the island of Hispaniola. By 1511, the other major islands of the West Indies—Puerto Rico, Cuba, and Jamaica—had been subjugated. Hernán Cortés had conquered Mexico by 1521 and Francisco Pizarro had conquered Peru by 1535. By 1550, Spanish colonial towns dotted the Caribbean West Indies and the coasts of Central and South America; in some of them, theaters, printing presses, and universities flourished.

Back in Spain, the king's treasury flourished as well, receiving one-fifth of all private profit extracted from colonies in the New World. With this wealth, Spain had become the strongest power in Europe.

Well before St. Augustine was founded, therefore, Spanish patterns of colonial development had been established in the New World. The vanguards were conquistadores—semi-independent military adventurers seeking wealth, power, and renown, who left a particularly violent and brutal legacy. Following the conquistadores were well-born Spanish settlers, lusting to claim *encomiendas,* or large grants of land much like feudal estates. From the Native American inhabitants of that land, the *encomendero,* or grantee, was entitled by Spanish law to extract unpaid labor. In Central and South America, encomenderos forced Native Americans to mine gold and great deposits of silver ore or maintain large ranches or farms. In the West Indies, the Spanish forced the indigenous peoples to labor on lucrative sugar plantations. This pattern of colonial development resulted in catastrophic losses of indigenous populations throughout New Spain, brought on by overwork, European disease, and probably despair. The Spanish government

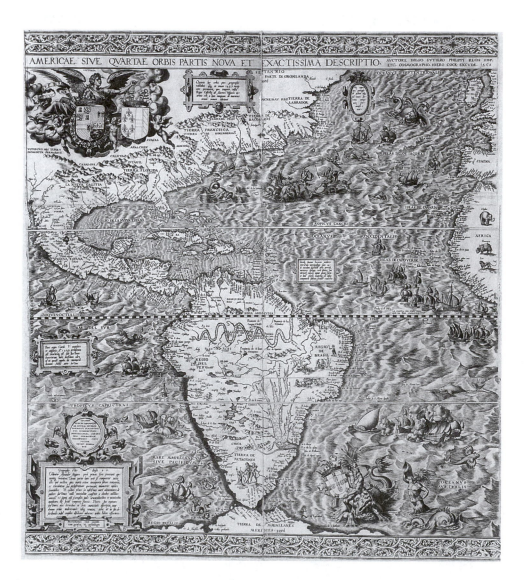

Map of America, 1562, by Diego Guitiérrez *(Library of Congress)*

repeatedly issued decrees intended to limit the exploitation of its native New World subjects, but with little success. The Church sent missionaries, who complained at length about the situation. Unfortunately, their complaints were used to justify the substitution of African slaves for Indian laborers. Soon the Spanish began importing slaves, beginning the involuntary migration of 10 million Africans to the New World.

With its empire flourishing, the Spanish crown favored expanding into North America, for two reasons. First, Spain wanted to secure the territory claimed by Juan Ponce de León in 1513. Called La Florida, the claim stretched westward from the Atlantic to New Mexico and northward at least as far as the Chesapeake (modern Virginia). Second, Spain needed military bases on the Florida coast to protect its shipping routes. Spanish ships left ports on the gulf coast of Mexico and the north coast of South America, carrying gold and silver mined by slaves and headed for the treasury of Spain, crossed the Gulf of Mexico, and sailed through the Straits of Florida, then up the Atlantic coast before heading across the Atlantic. After 1550, the treasure fleet was increasingly attacked by pirates from Spain's European rivals—or, as pirates were termed if they were commissioned by a rival nation, privateers. It had become clear to other nations that Spain's power in Europe depended on New World wealth, and they intended to disrupt its flow and obtain a share for themselves.

FRANCE STAKES A CLAIM IN THE NEW WORLD

Spain's most powerful rival in Europe was France. In 1524, powerful French merchants funded an expedition by Italian navigator Giovanni de Verrazzano, probably with the approval of King Francis I of France, to explore the New World and search for a passage to Asia. Verrazzano found no passage, but he did establish for the first time that Spanish Florida and modern Canada were parts of the same continuous landmass. Verrazzano named the north Atlantic coastline Arcadia. Mapmakers altered it to La Cadie and eventually Acadia.

Unfortunately for French ambitions, Spain's exclusive right to the New World had been affirmed by Pope Alexander VI in the 1493 bull (or official edict) *Inter Caetera*. King Francis was quite willing to defy Spain but reluctant to alienate the Vatican. In 1533, however, he persuaded Pope Clement VII that *Inter Caetera* applied only to territory Spain had specifically claimed *before* the bull was written. Having forestalled Vatican censure, in 1534 Francis commissioned Jacques Cartier to explore Acadia for France.

Cartier, an experienced navigator from the Breton fishing port of Saint-Malo, reached the Gulf of St. Lawrence in May. On the Gaspé Peninsula, he erected a cross hung with the arms of France—although he referred to the area in his journals as "the land which God gave to Cain." When suspicious Indians protested the cross, Cartier told them it was only a marker for future explorers. He sailed back to France in September, taking with him two young Indian men to be trained as interpreters. The following May, he returned with the two men, a large crew, and a fleet of three ships. Sailing up the St. Lawrence River, he visited the Indian village at Stadacona (the site of modern Quebec) and continued on to Hochelaga, a palisaded Indian village with a population of 2,000. He named the site Mont Real (present-day Montreal); the nearby impassable rapids he named La Chine (China), in the hope that he had found the entryway to the Northwest Passage to Asia.

Near Stadacona, Cartier's men constructed winter quarters. Because the site is at almost the same latitude as Paris, he had not anticipated the severity of the St. Lawrence winter. Scurvy struck, and many of his men died. Finally, Indians taught them to make a medicinal tea from white cedar trees. (Scurvy is caused by a deficiency of vitamin C, which the extract contained.) In the spring, Cartier captured five Stadaconans, including the chief, Donnacona, and sailed back to France. In his journals, Cartier called the Stadaconans Canadians; "Canada" was probably an Iroquoian word meaning "village," which he did not fully understand. From Cartier's journals, the name passed to mapmakers.

War between France and Spain delayed further French exploration until 1541. At that time Francis appointed a lieutenant general of Canada to organize a colonizing expedition, with Cartier as captain. His appointee was Jean François de la Roque, sieur de Roberval, a courtier, Huguenot (French Protestant), and pirate. Cartier departed first, with five ships. Eight miles up the St. Lawrence from Stadacona, his men constructed a village he named Charlesbourg Royal. Relations with the Indians were tense throughout the winter, primarily because Cartier had failed to return Chief Donnacona or his other captives, all of whom had died in Europe. In June, with no sign of Roberval, Cartier prepared to return to France. At St. John's Harbor, Newfoundland, he met 200 colonists and Roberval, who ordered him to disembark and remain in Canada. Cartier declined. He returned to France with pyrite and quartz, which he believed to be gold and diamonds. They were soon known as "fool's gold" and "Canadian diamonds."

Roberval rebuilt Charlesbourg Royal. The colony was an odd mixture of gentlemen's families and minor criminals. The gentlemen believed that with large land grants they would be a wealthy aristocracy; the convicts had been furloughed from French prisons when enough volunteers to settle the colony could not be found. The group was beset by hunger, disease, and quarreling. About one-third died over the winter, most of scurvy, the remedy for which had apparently been lost. Roberval turned tyrannical, whipping colonists and ordering one hanged for thievery.

In summer 1543, Cartier made his final voyage to Canada, to rescue the remaining colonists. For half a century, France sent no additional expeditions to Acadia. Nonetheless, Cartier's voyages and Roberval's unsuccessful colony produced written records and maps that maintained a French claim to the North Atlantic seaboard and kept the idea of a New France alive.

FORT CAROLINE AND ST. AUGUSTINE

In 1562, France issued a direct challenge to Spain and its treasure fleet. On February 16, a French colonizing expedition set sail from Dieppe, led by Jean Ribaud (or Ribault) and bound for Florida. On board were several stone pillars engraved with the arms of the French throne.

At the time, France was torn by religious strife between Catholics and Protestants and by related political strife between powerful nobles and the crown. Ribaud himself, like most of his group of 150 men, was a Huguenot (French Protestant). Although Ribaud's expedition had been organized by Gaspard de

Coligny, the admiral of France and Huguenot leader, it was also supported by high-ranking Catholics. Both groups hoped to profit from investments in the New World, and both agreed on the need to weaken Spain.

Ribaud's expedition landed on May 1 at the mouth of the St. Johns River, near modern Jacksonville. Greeted by friendly Timucua Indians, Ribaud planted a stone pillar. He then sailed north to a large harbor on the coast of present-day South Carolina, where his men constructed a small log fort. Ribaud named it Charlesfort, in honor of young King Charles IX, and returned to France for supplies, leaving 26 men behind. Unfortunately, civil unrest in France prevented his immediate return. By the following spring, the men at Charlesfort were desperate for food and supplies. They constructed a vessel, using moss for caulking and shirts for the sail, and shoved off for France. Before the vessel was rescued by a passing English ship, at least one colonist had been killed and cannibalized.

In 1564, Coligny organized a second expedition, again primarily Huguenot. It was led by René Laudonnière, who had accompanied Ribaud on the first voyage. Three ships carried more than 100 sailors and a similar number of soldiers, as well as craftsmen, an apothecary, gentlemen adventurers, at least four women, and an artist named Jacques Le Moyne. Laudonnière proceeded to Ribaud's stone column on the St. Johns River. There his group built a triangular fort, with a galleried house for the officers. They named it Fort Caroline, in honor of the French royal dynasty.

The demands of colonizing the wilderness soon threatened to overwhelm the small settlement. The originally friendly Indians became hostile after Laudonnière mishandled relations with them. Even with mild winter weather and abundant fish and wildlife, the group did not plant or hunt sufficient food. Some seized weapons and vessels and turned to piracy. In 1565, while on a slaving voyage, the famed English captain Sir John Hawkins put in at Fort Caroline; the colonists agreed to evacuate with his fleet. Before they embarked, however, Jean Ribaud arrived with seven ships filled with supplies and new colonists, including women and children.

The revitalization of Fort Caroline was short-lived. Ribaud arrived on August 28; on the same day, the Spanish fleet of Pedro Menéndez de Avilés landed 40 miles to the south. Menéndez had been sent by King Philip II of Spain with orders to oust the French and establish a Spanish settlement. Menéndez and his 800 Spanish settlers and soldiers were greeted by Timucua Indians. While the Timucua watched, the priests who accompanied the expedition said mass and named the site San Agustín in honor of St. Augustine, whose feast day it was. The Timucuan *cacique* (or chief), Seloy, offered his longhouse for Menéndez's shelter. The Spanish fortified Seloy's village forthwith, fearing that the French might attack them first.

Indeed, upon learning of the arrival of the Spanish from an Indian courier, Ribaud did set sail with most of Fort Caroline's soldiers to attack the Spanish by sea. Storms forced his fleet ashore, however, near modern Cape Canaveral. Meanwhile, Menéndez marched 500 men overland, guided by Indians and by three pirates from Caroline whom he had found in a Cuban jail. Although continuous rains drenched the troops as they marched through swamps and humid Florida forests, Menéndez reached Fort Caroline. He attacked at dawn on September 21, catching most of the garrison in nightclothes. Because most of the French soldiers had accompanied Ribaud's fleet, the fort was easily overpowered.

Menéndez slaughtered the Huguenot men but spared a few Catholics. Fifty women and children (including some infants born in Florida) were taken prisoner by the Spanish and sent to Santo Domingo, Hispaniola. Twenty-six French settlers escaped, including Laudonnière and at least one woman, and returned to France in three small ships. Among the escapees was the artist Jacques Le Moyne. From memory he later drew scenes of Florida and its inhabitants; published in 1591, they remain the most extensive extant record of North American Indian life before European settlement.

Menéndez renamed Caroline, dubbing it San Mateo, in honor of St. Matthew, on whose feast day the battle occurred. Leaving a garrison of soldiers, he returned to St. Augustine. In the following weeks, he searched out Ribaud and his grounded fleet. Pretending to offer amnesty, he murdered most of them, sparing only a few Catholics and skilled workers. The site, at the mouth of a river, was named Mantanzas, or "Place of the Slaughters."

THE FLORIDA COLONY TO 1608

In Spanish minds, the colony called Florida was extensive, stretching north to the Chesapeake (modern Virginia) and west to Mexico. Most activity in the colony during the 16th century, however, occurred within the boundaries of modern Florida, Georgia, and South Carolina. Menéndez, the colony's head, was an experienced sea captain, military officer, and trader. He came to Florida as an *adelantado,* an official who invested and risked his own financial resources to settle a colony under authorization from the crown. In return, adelantados received inheritable titles and offices, extensive authority, and the hope of future wealth. Usually, they also received military support and religious personnel from Spain.

Having founded St. Augustine in 1565, in 1566 Menéndez founded Santa Elena on the coast of modern South Carolina (the site of modern Port Royal) to be the capital city of the Florida colony. In 1570, he moved his family there, and during his lifetime Santa Elena was wealthier and larger than St. Augustine. Menéndez also established small garrisons along the west coast of Florida and up the Atlantic coastline to protect Spanish shipping and establish relations with the Indians. He recruited Castilian farming families for the colony and brought slaves of African descent from Cuba for agricultural and construction labor.

Between 1565 and Menéndez's death in 1574, however, the Florida colony struggled to survive. Food shortages were a constant problem. Colonists were dissatisfied with the difficult conditions and attempted mutiny in 1566 and 1570. In 1568, a French-led expedition sent to revenge the slaughter at Fort Caroline arrived at San Mateo and burned it. Indians attacked several times. Menéndez, like many European colonial administrators who followed him, expected to requisition food from the Indians whenever needed (as military leaders customarily did from the European populace). He also attempted to choose their tribal officials. He was unable to understand the Indians' hostility to these intrusions, but the Spanish Crown consistently refused his requests to exterminate them. After Menéndez's death, his Florida lands and titles were divided between his two daughters. Their husbands quarreled, and in 1576 one of them fled back to Spain, taking the Florida treasury with him. The Council of the Indies, the Spanish body that oversaw all New World colonies, decided to terminate the adelantado agreement and make Florida a crown, or royal, colony under direct control of the king. The council sent a new governor to restore order.

A new disaster arrived in 1586, when English pirate Sir Francis Drake attacked with 2,000 men. They destroyed St. Augustine, carrying off gold, cannon, tools, furnishings, and even doors, as well as many black slaves, to whom Drake offered freedom. Spanish colonists, however, hid in the woods during the attack, and returned later to rebuild the city. After the attack, Santa Elena was abandoned and its residents consolidated at St. Augustine, but no new Spanish settlers arrived for the remainder of the century. Typhus epidemics broke out in 1570, 1586, and 1592. A hurricane caused extensive damage in 1599. In all, the fort at St. Augustine was destroyed and rebuilt nine times in the first half-century of its existence. On the ninth occasion, in 1604, masonry-and-stone construction was finally substituted for wood, making the fort less susceptible to attack, fire, and rot.

At the opening of the 17th century, St. Augustine was little more than a struggling military garrison. But it clung to life, the only surviving European settlement in North America.

Missions in Florida

In the view of the Catholic Church, as expressed in *Inter Caetera,* Spain's territorial claims were justified by the duty to spread the Catholic faith, and the Spanish crown was under special obligation to do so. Throughout New Spain, Catholic missionaries accompanied Spanish settlers. The missionaries' role was twofold: to convert Indians to Christianity and to secure their loyalty to the protector of the faith, the king of Spain.

This task proved extremely difficult in the early years of the Florida colony. The Jesuits who originally accompanied Menéndez abandoned Florida after a group of them were murdered in the Chesapeake area in 1571. In 1573, the Franciscans arrived. Their first mission, Nombre de Dios (Name of God), was established among the Timucua at the north end of St. Augustine. The Franciscans were less successful among the Calusa on Florida's west coast, the Cusabo near Elena, and the Guale in modern Georgia. All three groups particularly valued individual liberty and resisted sedentary farming and European social morality.

Secular authorities hoped the missions would establish political control over the Florida Indians, making travel safe among its far-flung outposts. Authorities also saw the missions as sites for extracting food or goods from the natives. At times, secular and religious motives collided. In 1597, the Guale along the Georgia coast revolted, killing five Franciscans. In retaliation, the governor, Gonzales Menéndez de Canzo, destroyed their villages and enslaved them. The remaining friars, however, insisted that the Guale be released and the exorbitant Spanish demands for food reduced. After the intercession of the Spanish crown, both their goals were accomplished.

Soon, the Franciscans became an important factor in the colony's survival. In 1602, the Council of the Indies set up a commission of inquiry to determine whether the Florida colony had outlasted its strategic purpose. Many were concerned by its cost and its failure to flourish. However, the Franciscan missionaries did not want to abandoned their new converts. In 1606, they arranged a visit to Florida by the bishop of Cuba, Don Juan Cabezas Altamirano, who officiated at mass confirmations. Impressed by such spiritual success, the Council of the Indies agreed to maintain the colony.

Life in the Florida Colony

The town of St. Augustine was laid out according to a plan, with house lots of a standard size. Most buildings were wood, and roofs thatch, although *coquina* (a local stone composed of shells and coral) was also used. As in Spain, city officials regulated trade and held court. Surviving court records indicate, for example, that a tailor sued the governor of Santa Elena for calling him a Lutheran, the Spanish term for all Protestants.

Florida colonists reproduced the hierarchical society of 16th-century Spain, although some upward mobility was possible. Most common crafts, occupations, and professions were represented in the colony, including moneylenders, tavern keepers, and prostitutes. Well-born emigrants from Spain brought luxurious clothing, furnishings, rugs, and household accessories (including a Ming dynasty wine ewer, remnants of which were discovered on an archaeological dig). According to ships' inventories, the wealthy imported delicacies to eat and livery for their servants. Ordinary soldiers, on the other hand, had few possessions.

By the end of the 16th century, the ethnic makeup of St. Augustine was diverse. Many more men than women emigrated from Spain, and Spanish men were encouraged to marry Indian women. By 1600, at least half the women in St. Augustine were Indian and many residents were of mixed ethnicity. The population also included people of African descent, both slave and free. The Florida colony had citizens of other nationalities as well. In a 1607 report, Governor Pedro de Ybarra listed 56 naturalized citizens: 28 Portuguese, some probably of Jewish descent; 20 French, 6 Germans, and 2 Flemings.[1]

OÑATE FOUNDS NEW MEXICO FOR SPAIN

By 1550, conquistadores had explored the Gulf and Pacific coasts of North America, and Francisco Vásquez de Coronado had explored the Southwest. For 40 years after these expeditions, however, no major attempts were made to settle the area. Unlike Florida, the Southwest had no strategic importance to Spain. None of the expeditions found gold and silver, although the Spanish never completely lost hope. Moreover, in 1573 the Crown forbade expeditions into new lands without formal royal permission, hoping to curtail the violence of earlier explorers. The Crown's Comprehensive Orders for New Discoveries also substituted the term *pacification* for the conquest of Native Americans and reemphasized the religious purpose of settlement.

In 1583, King Philip II ordered the viceroy of Mexico to colonize the territory north of New Spain, known as New Mexico, for the purpose of converting its Indian inhabitants to Christianity. Soon, several expeditions of priests and adventurers were scouting the area, with both religious and secular motives. They discovered a string of independent pueblos, or villages, extending up the Rio Grande. Their 40,000 inhabitants were sedentary and peaceful, providing the priests with a promising field for missions. The viceroy was slow to act on their report, however, and in 1590 Gaspar Castano de Sosa, lieutenant governor

Acoma Pueblo, a Native American structure that predates European settlement *(Photo by Ferenz Fedor, Courtesy Museum of New Mexico, Neg. No. 100364)*

of a Mexican province, set out for New Mexico without permission. His 170 colonists settled at a pueblo he named Santo Domingo, but Sosa was soon arrested and returned to Mexico.

Finally, the viceroy appointed Don Juan de Oñate governor of the new province of New Mexico. Oñate was a successful military leader, born in New Spain to a prominent family that had grown wealthy by exploiting the silver mines of Zacatecas. His wife was a descendant of both Cortés and the Aztec emperor Montezuma. As an adelantado, Oñate financed the expedition. The Crown sent friars to accompany him and provided military supplies.

Between 400 and 500 people left Santa Barbara, Mexico, on January 26, 1598: 130 men with wives, children, and servants, and 10 Franciscan friars. The group included Spaniards, Africans, Mexican Indians, and many people of mixed race. In tow were livestock, 83 wagons, and mining equipment. In April 1598, near the present site of El Paso, Oñate took possession of New Mexico. As the Crown required of all conquistadores and adelantados, he gathered the indigenous people and read the *Requerimiento,* which summarized Christian history and ordered the audience to submit to church, pope, and king. If they did not, it proclaimed, "The resultant deaths and damages shall be your fault and not the monarch's or mine or the soldiers." Ceremonies included a play written by one of the officers, portraying the conversion of the Indians to Christianity. (Unfortunately, it has not survived.) At least six times en route along the Rio Grande, Oñate repeated the ceremony and recorded in his journal that the Indians had agreed to become subjects of Spain.

The group advanced north to a pueblo called Ohke, 20 miles north of modern Sante Fe. Oñate renamed the site San Juan de los Caballeros (San Juan of the Gentlemen), perhaps because his adelantado agreement required the Crown to grant the status of hidalgo, or gentleman, to many of his settlers. The colonists confiscated Ohke, forcing out the Indians and requisitioning food, clothing, and labor. A few months later, the group moved to a nearby pueblo, which they named San Gabriel de Charma. There they built a church and planted crops.

Relations with the closest pueblos did not turn hostile. The pueblo at Acoma, however, quickly tired of demands the settlers made under threat of torture, murder, and rape. In 1598, the inhabitants of Acoma attacked and killed a small Spanish military party that included Oñate's nephew. In January 1599, Oñate retaliated. The Spanish force of under 100 men was victorious over a much larger group of Indians. Eight hundred Acoma men, women, and children were slaughtered. About 80 men and 500 women and children were taken prisoner and brought to trial. Adults over the age of 25 were sentenced to 20 years' slavery for the Spanish; adult males also had one foot cut off. Boys under the age of 12 were placed in care of the church; girls were sent to Mexican convents.

Oñate's settlement at San Gabriel did not thrive. Winters were harsh, and summers were hot. Food shortages were common, as were bedbugs and vermin. No precious metals were discovered, and disorder increased. In 1601, Oñate returned from an expedition to find that most colonists had returned to Mexico. In 1607, he was forced to resign.

After Oñate's resignation, the Spanish Crown considered abandoning New Mexico. As in Florida, the arguments of the Franciscans proved decisive, although their missions had progressed slowly. In 1608, the same year that St. Augustine was reprieved, the Franciscans received authorization to remain in New Mexico. A year later, New Mexico was officially made a Crown Colony.

ENGLAND STAKES A CLAIM IN THE NEW WORLD

In the 16th century, England's interest in North America focused on Newfoundland and the present-day maritime provinces of Canada. Some historians believe that fishermen from Bristol, a port on England's west coast, may have reached the outer banks of the modern maritime provinces even before Christopher Columbus's voyage in 1492. In any case, in 1497 John Cabot (Giovanni Caboto), an Italian navigator with close ties to Bristol shipowners, sailed for the New World with a patent from King Henry VII of England. (A patent, sometimes called *letters patent,* was a document granting its holder certain rights in certain territories.) Cabot explored what were probably the coastlines of modern Newfoundland, Cape Breton Island, and Nova Scotia, staking a claim for England, Cabot did not find the route to Asia he sought, but he did find rich fishing banks that held an astonishing abundance of cod, other fish, and sea mammals like seal and whale.

Cabot's return excited great interest at court and among merchants. Bristol shipowners were delighted with his report that fish "can be taken not only with the net but in baskets let down with a stone." Fish was an important staple of the European diet. Few other foods could be preserved, but dried fish could be kept for long periods of time and was crucial for military and seagoing expeditions. Catholics, in addition, observed an average of three meatless days per week. The fishing industry could produce great wealth for its investors. Between 1503 and 1506, the Company of Adventurers into the Newfound Land, composed of both Bristol and Portuguese traders, sent several expeditions to the area. Throughout the 16th century, fishermen of England, Portugal, Spain, and France shared the waters. As many as 400 vessels visited the banks in the summer months, usually returning to Europe in the fall, but few left records. Unlike voyages of exploration, fishing voyages were commonplace; in addition, fishermen guarded their secrets.

In the second half of the 16th century, an expansionist party in England began to promote colonization, first in Ireland and then in the New World. English expansionism fed on hatred of Spain, on the desire to increase trade, and on the fear that "surplus population" in England threatened civil peace. After 1575, England's relations with Spain deteriorated and the influence of expansionists increased. Queen Elizabeth I could not officially send expeditions to Spanish-occupied lands without risking war. She could, however, defend the English claim to territory visited by Cabot. In 1578, Elizabeth granted Sir Humphrey Gilbert a patent to explore "such remote heathen and barbarous lands countries and territories not actually possessed of any Christian prince or people" and to settle them with English subjects.

Gilbert's first voyage, in 1578–79, was unsuccessful. His second voyage, in 1583, was better financed and better organized. It was partially supported by a group of English Catholics who could practice their religion openly in England only if they paid a special and exorbitant tax. Merchants and crown ministers also invested. Gilbert arrived at St. John's Harbor, Newfoundland, on August 3, 1583, with 260 men. The group included craftsmen, "mineral men" and refiners to seek valuable ores, and musicians to amuse the colonists and the Indians. When Gilbert arrived, 36 fishing vessels were in port. The international village created by the fishermen was self-governing. Every fortnight, the officers elected one of the captains as "admiral" to mediate disputes, occasionally with the assistance of a jury.

Gilbert called the fishermen together on August 5, 1583, and claimed Newfoundland for England. He read the patent from the queen, which established English law in the territory, guaranteed certain rights to English citizens residing there, and declared the Church of England to be the established church of the land. These principles would be repeated in subsequent English colonial charters over the next 200 years.

By August 20, so much discontent was riddling Gilbert's group that they sailed for home, planning to return the following year. Gilbert's ship was lost at sea, however, and he perished. His death ended England's interest in colonizing Canada for almost four decades, until 1610.

The First English Settlement at Roanoke

After Gilbert's death, the cause of North American colonization was taken up by his more worldly and practical half-brother, Sir Walter Raleigh. Raleigh, a poet and a veteran of the brutal Irish wars, was Queen Elizabeth's favorite courtier. In 1584, she granted him a valuable patent for all colonization ventures south of Newfoundland. Raleigh quickly sent two ships on a voyage of reconnaissance, captained by Philip Amandas and Arthur Barlow. In July they reached Roanoke Island, situated between the coast of modern North Carolina and the coastal islands and sandbars called the Outer Banks. At first glance, the location appeared ideal. Close enough to Spanish shipping routes to serve as a base for English privateers, it was also hidden from the coast. When the expedition returned to England, Barlow gave Raleigh an extremely positive report. Barlow described the indigenous people as friendly, hospitable, intelligent, and dignified. He brought with him two young Indian men, Manteo and Wanchese, to be taught English and serve as interpreters for future colonizing voyages. Raleigh publicized the report enthusiastically. The queen knighted him and gave him permission to call the land Virginia in her honor; her sobriquet, as an unmarried sovereign, was the "virgin queen."

In 1585, Raleigh organized a second expedition, headed by Sir Richard Grenville, his cousin and a privateer. The expedition landed at Roanoke Island in June. Unfortunately Barlow's report had omitted an important fact. Roanoke was surrounded by shallow waters and a treacherous shoreline, and the expedition lost most of its supplies when the flagship ran aground in shallow water. Grenville oversaw the construction of a fort, where he left 107 men when he returned to England in August. On the voyage home, he engaged in piracy, as was the custom, producing a handsome profit for Raleigh's investors.

The fort at Roanoke was left under the command of Ralph Lane, a military officer recalled from the Irish wars. His group had men of several nationalities, including Irish servants, Germans miners, and Joachim Gans, the "mineral expert," a Jewish metallurgist born in Prague. Lane did not direct his men to plant crops or even to do extensive hunting or fishing. He expected the Indians to supply them with food, and his soldiers raided fields and fishing weirs when they did not. The "hospitable" Indians described by Barlow soon disappeared into the forests they knew intimately. The winter of 1585–86 was difficult for the small garrison. Two relief ships, delayed by worsening relations with Spain, finally reached Roanoke in late summer 1586. They found a deserted colony. In June, English pirate Sir Francis Drake had arrived, having recently destroyed St. Augustine. Drake had offered his countrymen a choice of reinforcements and supplies or passage back to England. They had chosen the latter.

Drake's offer of reinforcements included as many as 350 African slaves captured from the Spanish and 300 Indians, most of them women. Their fate is unknown, although historians believe that some were left on the Carolina Banks with the supplies taken from St. Augustine. Three members of Lane's expedition, who were away from the fort exploring, were also left behind; in addition, the relief ships left 15 new men at the deserted fort to maintain the English claim to the island. Their fate also is unknown.

Lane's short-lived colony at Roanoke—the first English settlement in the boundaries of the modern United States—left two legacies. The first was a permanent trove of knowledge about the New World. Accompanying the expedition were two men named Thomas Hariot and John White. Hariot was an Oxford mathematician; he had taught Manteo and Wanchese English and learned Algonquian from them. Upon his return to England, he wrote *A brief and true report of the new found land of Virginia,* providing great detail about Native Americans and about resources and agriculture—including maize, or corn (previously unfamiliar to the English but soon to be the staple food of colonists), and tobacco. White, a surveyor and skilled artist, drew illustrations of the land, plant and animal life, and Native American customs. The drawings appeared in engraver Theodore De Bry's *America* (1590), which became a best seller in four languages. De Bry revised White's figures of Native Americans to conform to European notions of the human form and beauty; White's originals were not rediscovered until the 20th century.

The second legacy, unfortunately for the colonists who were to follow, was the hostility of local Native Americans. Grenville's men had destroyed an Indian village, supposedly in retaliation for a theft. Lane's men had ambushed the Roanoke tribe at what the Englishmen mistakenly believed to be a war council, killing several chieftains friendly to the English.

The "Lost Colony" of Roanoke

Raleigh soon organized another voyage. In 1587, a new group of men, women, and children set out for the New World. Raleigh had learned from past mistakes. Soldiers or mercenaries would not endure the hardships of establishing an English colony. Almost all the new Roanoke colonists were family groups and had invested in the voyage. The colonists understood the need to produce their own food, and each was to receive 500 acres of land. John White, returning as governor, had 12 assistants among the colonists to serve as a board of directors. None were above middle-class rank; most were craftsmen. Raleigh, however, purchased coats of arms for all the assistants, in order to provide the colony with an aristocracy. The colonists, not counting the sailors who brought them, numbered 89 men, 17 women, and nine children, all boys. No clergyman accompanied them, but two recently convicted thieves, furloughed from prison, did. Also accompanying them were two Indians previously taken to England, including Manteo, a Hatteras Indian from their village on Croatoan Island.

The new colony, to be named the City of Raleigh, was to be located north of Roanoke in the more navigable and fertile Chesapeake area. The captain of the fleet, however—a privateer who had also piloted Grenville—landed at Roanoke and refused to take the colonists elsewhere. Lane's fort was still standing and usable after minor repairs. Nearby, White's colonists built small houses, a storehouse, and a jail. Within a week of the colonists' arrival, however, relations with local Indians were badly established. An English settler had been killed by suspicious Roanoke Indians (who probably remembered experiences with earlier groups). The English made a retaliatory raid, but the group they mistook for Roanoke and attacked were actually friendly Hatteras, Manteo's people, and included women and children. Although a truce was made, relations remained uneasy.

At the end of August, Governor White returned to England to obtain more supplies. He left behind more than 100 colonists, including his new granddaughter, born August 18 to Elinor White Dare and promptly named Virginia. Unfortunately for White and his colony, he arrived in England in November 1587, when war with Spain threatened. The Crown forbade any English ship to leave port, fearing attack by the Spanish Armada. White could not obtain passage back to his colony until March 1590, at which time he accompanied three privateering ships. They arrived in Roanoke in August to find the fort deserted and overgrown with weeds. A palisade had been erected, although the houses had been dismantled. The cannon and iron bars lay about. Three chests of

White's belongings, which the colonists had buried, had been dug up, opened, and scattered.

The colonists had, from the beginning, intended eventually to move on to the Chesapeake. White had an agreement with them: Should they move while he was gone, they were to carve their destination in a tree and to add a cross if they left under attack. White found the word CROATOAN carved, without a cross, and assumed that their destination had been nearby Croatoan Island (modern Cape Hatteras). Unfortunately for the historical record, a storm blew up, and White's fleet headed out to sea to avoid the treacherous shoreline. They returned to England without visiting Croatoan. Raleigh and White made no further attempts to find the "Lost Colony," as it came to be known, nor was its fate ever determined. The Spanish, on the other hand, searched for the English colony for many years, but found only the ruins at Roanoke. When English settlers arrived at Jamestown in 1608, they found no Europeans nearby.

What happened to the Roanoke colonists? The question has remained unanswered for four centuries. Some believe that the colonists joined the Hatteras from Croatoan Island, their joint descendants becoming a tribe today known as the Lumbee. Most historians believe that the group split up after White's departure and theorize that most of them moved north to the Chesapeake as planned; they were probably killed, however, when the powerful Virginia chief Powhatan, head of a large confederacy, massacred the Chesapeake Indian tribe shortly before settlers arrived at Jamestown. It is also theorized that a smaller group remained behind to await White on Croatoan Island.

THE FUR TRADE BEGINS IN FRENCH ACADIA

The fur trade began as a result of casual trading between Indian trappers and unknown, early-16th-century European fishermen visiting the North Atlantic. The Native Americans who greeted Jacques Cartier's first expedition in 1534 were already familiar with fur trading, historians believe, although no earlier written records of trade exist. The Indians met Cartier bearing furs and offered a formal welcoming ceremony, which included secreting their young women in the woods. After the middle of the 16th century, fishing expeditions began to carry more and more furs back to Europe. The felt made from durable, waterproof beaver pelts had long been a popular material for expensive hats in Europe; around 1580, however, beaver felt suddenly gained popularity for a wide variety of ordinary and military headgear. (Its popularity lasted more than 200 years; even the tricornered hat worn by the American Revolutionary soldier, for example, was made from it.) After 1580, trade intensified and French merchants organized voyages for the sole purpose of fur trading.

The fur trade demanded an economic partnership between the French and the Indians. It required relations with Native Americans that were different, and in many ways better, than Indian-European relations elsewhere on the continent. Nonetheless, the fur trade had far-reaching consequences for Native American cultures. Some tribes attempted to extend their hunting grounds or to monopolize trade, leading to intertribal wars. By 1600, the agricultural Iroquoian-speaking Indians from the towns of Hochelaga and Stadacona who had met Cartier in the 1530s had completely disappeared from the St. Lawrence valley.

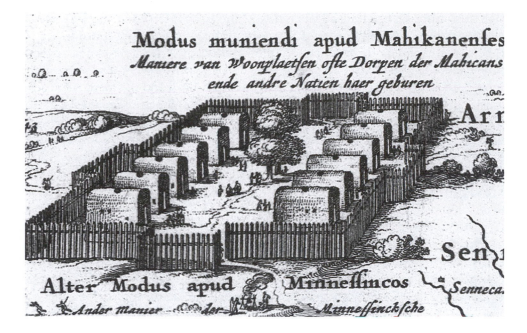

A palisaded Indian village, similar to those built by St. Lawrence–area tribes, detail from a map by Nicholaes Visscher (1685) *(Library of Congress)*

Regular trading sites developed along the St. Lawrence and eventually became trading posts. More and more merchants sent ships, competition for furs increased, and the Indians became increasingly astute traders. Some French merchants, seeking a way to reduce their costs, attempted permanent settlements. In 1598, Troilus de la Roche left a group of 250 colonists on Sable Island, 100 miles off present-day Halifax. Most were pardoned criminals; 50 were female. Each year, Roche sent supplies and reinforcements, and he was sent furs in return. The supply ship failed to arrive in 1602, and the colonists mutinied. The following spring, the 11 living colonists returned to France by the supply boat, where they were pardoned by the king. In 1600, Chauvin de Tonnetuit, a French nobleman backed by merchants from Rouen, attempted to found a small colony at the mouth of the Saguenay River, called Tadoussac. The 16 colonists did not survive the winter, but the site continued as a summer trading post.

Champlain and Port Royal

In 1603, Pierre de Gua, sieur de Monts, received a royal patent from King Henry IV of France to establish colonies in North America. He also received a 10-year monopoly on the fur trade. (A monopoly was the right to be the sole legal supplier, distributer, or producer of a product. Individual traders were required to sell their goods to the monopolist, who distributed them at a profit.) De Monts enlisted Samuel de Champlain, a seaman and commoner then in his 20s, to accompany an expedition to Acadia. The king appointed De Monts lieutenant general, or governor, from the 46th to the 40th parallels (modern Cape Breton to Philadelphia). He appointed Champlain, who was probably trained in surveying and mapmaking, as royal geographer.

De Monts, Champlain, and 78 men sailed in 1604. They established St. Croix on an island at the mouth of the St. Croix River (the boundary of modern New Brunswick and Maine). The group included artisans such as blacksmiths, carpenters, and stonemasons; at least one surgeon and apothecary;

Croatian miners; De Monts's black servant; and both a Catholic and Protestant cleric—who, according to legend, were later buried in the same grave to see if they would continue their violent disputes after death. A few gentlemen adventurers accompanied them, including Jean de Biencourt de Poutrincourt, who soon returned to France with furs. The winter was harsh and the men had insufficient food or fresh water. Scurvy raged. By spring, 35 had died and 20 more were ill, although neither Champlain nor De Monts was affected. The Indians brought food in March, and three months later Poutrincourt returned from France with supplies and 40 new colonists. Dismantling the buildings, they moved to a site on the Bay of Fundy in modern Nova Scotia, which they named Port Royal (now Annapolis Royal). The second winter was easier; only a few died.

Poutrincourt and De Monts sailed to France to defend their fur-trading monopoly, which was under attack from other merchants. In July 1606, Poutrincourt returned as lieutenant governor; de Monts remained in France. Poutrincourt brought his 14-year-old son Charles de Biencourt, livestock, and additional colonists. Among them was apothecary Louis Hébert, later a founder of Quebec; and Marc Lescarbot, a lawyer whose *Histoire de la nouvelle France* (*The History of New France,* 1609) recorded extensive information about the colony. Lescarbot also wrote and staged a play, *The Theatre of Neptune in New France,* with Greek gods and Native Americans as characters.

The Port Royal colony maintained exceptionally good relations with the nearby Micmac, who visited daily. The colonists successfully grew grains, vegetables, herbs, hemp, and flax; they also built a grist mill, enabling them to make European-style bread, which they often traded with the Indians for game meat. Often, Micmac chiefs dined with Champlain's famous Ordre de Bon-Temps (Order of Good Cheer). A kind of early men's club, complete with regalia for the day's "chief steward," it required the 15 officers of the colony to take turns hosting feasts for themselves.

In spring 1607, the supply ship brought bad news. The king had ended de Monts's monopoly in the fur trade, under pressure from other merchants and hatmakers who disliked the price rise it caused. Without the monopoly profits, however, de Monts and his investors could not fund the costs of the colony—the supplies, wages, ships. De Monts ordered the colonists to return to France. Membertou, the Micmac *sagemore* (chief), agreed to keep watch over the site; Poutrincourt sailed to seek new financing, with which he would resume the colony in 1610.

CHRONICLE OF EVENTS

Before 1492
Fisherman from Bristol, England, may have reached the Newfoundland fishing banks; evidence is not conclusive.

1492
Christopher Columbus makes landfall in the present-day Bahamas and Haiti. He is searching for a western route from Spain to the trading centers of Asia.

1493
Pope Alexander VI issues the papal bull *Inter Caetera*. It confirms Spain's claim to most of the New World and instructs the Crown to convert the indigenous people to Christianity.

1496
Santo Domingo is founded on the island of Hispaniola; it is the first permanent settlement in New Spain.

1497–98
John Cabot, an Italian sailing in the pay of England, explores the coast of the modern Canadian maritime provinces, where he discovers rich fishing banks. The discovery causes great interest in Europe and later justifies England's claim to North America.

After 1500
As many as 400 European fishing ships frequent the Newfoundland banks each year. Individual fishermen begin to trade with the Indians for furs. Year-round European settlements may have existed; evidence is not conclusive.

Spanish trade routes, detail of a map by Robert Sayer (1750) *(Library of Congress)*

1511

All major islands of the West Indies are now part of New Spain.

1513

Juan Ponce de León explores for Spain territory that he names La Florida. Until his second expedition in 1521, he believes it to be an island of the West Indies.

1521

The subjugation of Mexico by Hernán Cortés is complete; it is now part of New Spain.

1522

Survivors of Ferdinand Magellan's voyage, who have circumnavigated the globe by sailing west, return to Europe. European explorers will now begin a long search for a route through the middle of North America, which they call the Northwest Passage—and which will later be proven not to exist.

1524

Giovanni de Verrazzano explores the Atlantic coastline for France. He names the northern coastline Arcadia (later Acadia) and provides France with a claim to the New World.

1526

Lucas Vázquez d'Ayllón makes the first Spanish attempt to colonize North America, a short-lived settlement in present-day Georgia. Some people of African descent who accompanied him are believed to have remained in North America.

1528

Pánfilo de Narváez lands 600 men and women at Tampa Bay. The venture meets many disasters; only four men survive.

1533

French king François I convinces Pope Clement VII that *Inter Caetera* applies only to territory claimed prior to 1493. The way is cleared for other European nations to claim New World territory without fear of alienating the papacy.

1534

Jacques Cartier makes his first voyage to Canada for France, exploring the Gulf of St. Lawrence.

1535

Cartier makes his second voyage, sailing down the St. Lawrence River to the site of present-day Montreal.

1540–42

Francisco Vásquez de Coronado explores the North American Southwest for Spain.

1541

Cartier makes his third voyage, a colonizing expedition organized by Jean François de la Roque, sieur de Roberval. Cartier builds and winters at Charlesbourg Royal.

1542

Roberval and 200 colonists arrive in May; Cartier declines to remain in Canada and sails for France.

1543

Cartier makes his final voyage to Canada to rescue the Roberval colonists who have survived the harsh winter.

1562

Jean Ribaud leads a French Huguenot expedition to the St. Johns River in Florida. The men return to France the following spring.

1564

The second French Huguenot expedition, led by René de Laudonnière, founds Fort Caroline at the mouth of the St. Johns River.

1565

August 28: Ribaud returns to Florida with reinforcement for Fort Caroline. On the same day, Pedro Menéndez de Avilés lands 40 miles south, under orders to oust the French and found a colony for Spain. He names his site St. Augustine; it will become the first permanent European settlement in North America.

September 20: The Spanish attack and destroy Ft. Caroline. Menéndez slaughters most male settlers.

After 1565

Slaves of African descent are known to be in the Florida colony.

1566

Menéndez founds Santa Elena on the coast of present-day South Carolina.

1571

A group of Spanish Jesuit missionaries is murdered by Indians in the Chesapeake Bay area; the Jesuits leave Florida.

1573

Franciscans arrive to take over missionary work in Florida.

Spain issues the Comprehensive Orders for New Discoveries; it substitutes the term *pacification* for conquest, elevates the role of religious missionaries, and forbids unapproved expeditions into new lands.

1576

St. Augustine is declared a royal colony.

1578

Sir Humphrey Gilbert is granted a charter by Queen Elizabeth I of England to found a colony in New-foundland.

1580

In Europe, headgear made from beaver pelts becomes popular. French merchants quickly step up fur-trading voyages to Canada.

1583

August 5: Gilbert claims Newfoundland, establishing the laws of England there. On his return voyage in August, he is lost at sea.

1584

Queen Elizabeth grants Sir Walter Raleigh a patent to territory south of Newfoundland. He sends an exploratory voyage; it lands at Roanoke Island and returns with an enthusiastic report. The queen gives Raleigh permission to call the land Virginia in her honor.

1585

April: An expedition of 100 men, headed by Sir Richard Grenville, builds a fort at Roanoke Island.

1586

English pirate Francis Drake attacks and burns St. Augustine. Spanish colonists hide in the woods and later rebuild the city. Drake sails on to Roanoke; colonists there return to England with him.

1587

July: Raleigh's second group of English colonists, headed by Governor John White, arrives at Roanoke Island.

August: White returns to England for supplies. Impending war with Spain prevents his immediate return.

1587

Colonists at Santa Elena, Florida, destroy the settlement and move to St. Augustine.

1588

The English navy defeats the Spanish Armada. Spain's domination of the seas ends and England's era as a great sea power begins.

1590

August: White finally returns to Roanoke to discover that his colonists have disappeared. Their fate is never conclusively determined; they are known to history as the "Lost Colony."

1597

The Guale in Georgia revolt, killing five Franciscan missionaries.

1598

Don Juan de Oñate founds the settlement of San Gabriel, New Mexico, for Spain.

Troilus de la Roche leaves colonists at Sable Island off present-day Halifax; the survivors return to France in 1603.

1599

January: Oñate attacks Acoma Pueblo, killing 800 and taking more than 500 prisoners.

February: The Acoma prisoners are tried; adults are enslaved, and children placed under care of the church.

1602

Spain's Council of the Indies calls a Commission of Inquiry to determine the fate of the Florida colony. Franciscan missionaries argue for its maintenance.

1604

Pierre de Gua, sieur de Monts, and Samuel de Champlain sail to Acadia; they establish a French colony on the St. Croix River.

1605

Champlain moves the colony to Port Royal in modern Nova Scotia.

1606

Poutrincourt arrives in Port Royal as lieutenant governor of Acadia.

The bishop of Cuba, Don Juan Cabezas Altamirano, visits the Florida missions.

1607

The Port Royal colonists are ordered to return to France; Oñate is forced to resign as governor of New Mexico. Spain considers abandoning the colony, but Franciscan missionaries argue for its maintenance.

EYEWITNESS TESTIMONY

Upon the 25 of the month, we caused a fair high Cross to be made of the height of thirty foot, which was made in the presence of many of them [*the Indians*], upon the point of the entrance of the said haven [*Gaspé Bay*], in the midst whereof we hung up a Shield with three Fleur de Lis in it, and in the top was carved in the wood with Antique letters this poesy, Vive le Roy de France. Then before them all we set it upon the said point. They with great heed beheld both the making and setting of it up. So soon as it was up, we altogether kneeled down before them, with our hands toward Heaven, yielding God thanks; and we made signs unto them, showing them the Heavens, and that all our salvation depended only on him which in them dwells: whereat they showed a great admiration, looking first one at another, and then upon the Cross. And after we were returned to our ships, their Captain clad with an old Bear's skin, with three of his sons, and a brother of his with him, came unto us in one of their boats, but they came not so near us as they were wont to do: there he made a long Oration unto us, showing us the cross we had set up, and making a cross with two fingers, then did he show us all the Country about us, as if he would say that all was his, and that we should not set up any cross without his leave. . . . Then did we show them with signs, that the cross was but only set up to be as a light and leader which ways to enter into the port, and that we would shortly come again, and bring good store of iron wares and other things, but that we would take two of his children with us, and afterward bring them to the said port again. . . . After these were gone, and had told the news unto their fellows, in the afternoon there came to our ships six boats of them, with five or six men in every one, to take their farewells of those two we had detained to take with us, and brought them some fish, uttering many words which we did not understand, making signs that they would not remove the cross we had set up.

> *Jacques Cartier, "First Relation of Jacques Cartier of S. Malo," 1534, in Burrage, ed.,* Early English, *pp. 24–26.*

In the month of December . . . the said unknown sickness [*scurvy*] began to spread itself amongst us after the strangest sort that ever was either heard of or seen, insomuch as some did lose all their strength, and could not stand on their feet, then did their legs swell, their sinews shrink as black as any coal. Others also had all their skins spotted with spots of blood of a purple color: then did it ascend up to their ankles, knees, thighs, shoulders, arms, and neck: their mouth became stinking, their gums so rotten, that all the flesh did fall off, even to the roots of the teeth, which did also almost fall out. With such infection did this sickness spread itself in our three ships, that about the middle of February, of a hundred and ten persons that we were, there were not ten whole, so that one could not help the other. . . . Our Captain seeing this our misery, and that the sickness was gone so far, ordained and commanded, that every one should devoutly prepare himself to prayer, and in remembrance of Christ, caused His Image to be set upon a tree, about a flight shot from the fort amidst the ice and snow, giving all men to understand, that on the Sunday following, service should be said there, and that whosoever could go, sick or whole, should go thither in Procession. . . . Phillip Rougemont, born in Amboise, died, being 22 years old, and because the sickness was to us unknown, our Captain caused him to be ripped [*autopsied*] to see if by any means possible we might know what it was, and so seek means to save and preserve the rest of the company: he was found to have his heart white, but rotten, and more than a quart of red water about it: his liver was indifferent fair, but his lungs black and mortified, his blood was altogether shrunk about the heart, so that when he was opened great quantity of rotten blood issued out from about his heart: his milt [*spleen*] toward the back was somewhat perished, rough as it had been rubbed by a stone. . . . Sometimes we were constrained to bury some of the dead under the snow, because we were not able to dig any graves for them the ground was so hard frozen, and we so weak. Besides this, we did greatly fear that the people of the country would perceive our weakness and misery, which to hide, our Captain, whom it pleased God always to keep in health, would go out with two or three of the company, some sick and some whole, whom when he saw out the Fort, he would throw stones at them and chide them, feigning that so soon as he came again, he would beat them, and then with signs show the people of the country that he caused all his men to work and labor in the ships, some in caulking them, some in beating of chalk, some in one thing, and some in another, and that he would not have them come forth until their work was done. And to make his tale seem true and likely, he would make all his men whole and sound to make a great noise with knocking sticks, stones, hammers, and other things together. . . .

> *Jacques Cartier, winter 1535–36, "Short and Brief Narration," in Burrage, ed.,* Early English, *pp. 72–75.*

. . . . he arrived in the said County, accompanied with two hundred persons, soldiers, mariners, and common people, with all furniture necessary for a Fleet. The said General at his first arrival built a fair Fort, near and somewhat Westward above Canada, which is very beautiful to behold, and of great force, situated upon a high mountain, wherein there were two courts of buildings, a great Tower, and another of forty or fifty foot long: wherein there were diverse Chambers, a Hall, a Kitchen, houses of office, Cellars high and low, and near unto it were an Oven and Mills, and a stove to warm men in, and a Well before the house. And the building was situated upon the great River of Canada, called France prime, by Monsieur Roberval. There was also at the foot of the mountain another lodging, part whereof was a great Tower of two stories high, two courts of good building, where at the first all of our victuals, and whatsoever was brought with us was sent to be kept: and near unto that Tower there is another small river. In these two places above and beneath, all the meaner sort was lodged. . . .

Monsieur Roberval used very good justice, and punished every man according to his offense. One whose name was Michael Gallion, was hanged for his theft. John of Nantes was laid in irons, and kept prisoner for his offence, and others also were put in irons, and diverse were whipped, as well men as woman: by which means they lived in quiet.

> *Jean François de la Roque, sieur de Roberval (writing about himself), 1542, "The Voyage of John Francis de la Roche, Knight, Lord of Roberval," in Hakluyt,* Principal Navigations, *vol. 8, pp. 285–86.*

For his meaning was to take two Indians of this place to bring them into France, as the Queen had commanded him . . . we came to the self same place where at the first we found the Indians, from thence we took two Indians by the permission of the king, which thinking that they were more favored that the rest, thought themselves very happy to stay with us. But these two Indians seeing we made no show at all that we would go on land, but rather that we followed the midst of the current, began to be somewhat offended,

and would by force have leaped into the water, for they are so good swimmers that immediately they would have gotten into the forests. . . . A few days after they began to bear so good will toward me, that, as I think, they would rather have perished with hunger & thirst, than have taken their refection [*nourishment*] at any man's hand but mine. Seeing this their good will, I sought to learn some Indians words, & began to ask them questions, showing them the thing whereof I desired to know the name, how they called it. They were very glad to tell it to me, and knowing the desire that I had to learn their language, they encouraged me afterwards to ask them every thing. So that putting down in writing the words and phrases of the Indian speech, I was able to understand the greatest part of their discourses.

> *René Laudonnière, 1562, "A Notable History," in Hakluyt,* Principal Navigations, *vol. 8, pp. 464–66.*

M. de Laudonnière . . . replied that he had been sent by a most powerful ruler, called the King of France, to offer a treaty to him by which the King of France would become [*Timucua chief*] Saturiba's friend, and the friends of his allies, and an enemy to their enemies. The chief was greatly pleased. After we had exchanged gifts in pledge of our perpetual friendship Saturiba came closer to our forces and was greatly impressed by our arms, particularly by the harquebuses.

When he reached the ditch around our fort, he took all its measurements, both inside and out, and seeing that the earth was being taken from the ditch and formed into a rampart, he asked what our purpose was. He was told that we were making an enclosure large enough to hold us all and that we were going to erect many small houses inside it. Saturiba was filled with admiration and said he hoped to see our work finished as quickly as possible. We asked him for some of his men to help us in the building. He agreed to this and sent us eighty of the strongest; they were of the greatest help to us in completing the fort and the huts.

Every one of us—noblemen, soldiers, workmen, sailors—worked hard to get our post ready to shelter us from the weather and protect us against enemies. And every man was also making sure, through much private trading of gifts, that he would become rich.

> *Jacques le Moyne describes June 1564, "Brief Narrative," in Lorant,* The New World, *p. 40.*

Wherefore I sent to all the kings my neighbors [*Indian chieftains*] to pray them, that if there were any Christian dwelling in their counties, they would find means that he might be brought unto me, and that I would make them double recompense. They which love rewards, took so much pain, that the two men, whereof we have spoken, were brought unto the fort unto me. They were naked, wearing their hair long unto their hams [*thighs*] as the Savages use to do, and were Spaniards born, yet so well accustomed to the fashion of the country that at the first sight they found our manner of apparel strange. After that I had questioned of certain matters with them, I caused them to be appareled, and to cut their hair; which they would not lose, but lapped it up in a linen cloth, saying that they would carry it into their country to be a testimony of the misery that they had endured in the Indies. In the hair of one of them was found a little gold hidden, to the value of five and twenty crowns, which he gave unto me. And examining them of the places where they had been, and how they came thither, they answered me that fifteen years past, three ships, in one of which they were, were cast away over against a place named Calos [*West Florida*] . . . and that the king of Calos recovered the greatest part of the riches which were in the said ships, traveling in such sort that the greatest part of the people was saved, and many women; among which number there were three or four women married, remaining there yet, and their children also, with this king of Calos.

René Laudonnière, 1564–65, "An Oration," in Hakluyt,
Principal Navigations, *vol. 9, pp. 49–50.*

. . . [*Fort Caroline settlers*] had now had made the inhabitants [*the Indians*] weary of them by their daily craving of maize, having no wares left to content them with withal, and therefore were inforced to rob them, and to take away their victual perforce, which was the occasion that the Floridians (not well contented therewith) did take certain of their company in the woods and slew them; whereby there grew great wars betwixt them and the Frenchmen: and therefore they being but a few in number durst not venture abroad, but at such times as they were inforced thereunto for want of food do the same: and going twenty harquebusiers in a company, were set upon by eighteen kings, having seven or eight hundred men, which with one of their bows slew one of their men, and hurt a dozen, & drove them all down to their boats; whose policy in fight was to be

marveled at: for having shot at diverse of their bodies which were armed, and perceiving that the arrows did not prevail against the same, they shot at their faces and legs, which were the places that the Frenchmen were hurt in.

John Sparkes, a sailor, August 1565, "The Voyage Made by M. John Hawkins Esquire," in Hakluyt,
Principal Navigations, *vol. 10, p. 55.*

. . . my Lord Admiral [*Coligny*] took it very evil that I had carried a woman with me [*to Florida*] . . . Whereunto I answered, that the woman was a poor chambermaid, which I had taken up in an Inn, to oversee my household business, to look to an infinite sort of diverse beasts, as sheep and poultry which I carried over with me to store the country withall: that it was not meet to put a man to attend this business: likewise, considering the length of time that I was to abide there, me thought it should not offend anybody to take a woman with me, as well to help my soldiers in their sicknesses, as in mine own, whereunto I felt afterward. And how necessary her service was for us, each one at that time might easily perceive: That all my men thought so well of her, that at one instant there were six or seven which did demand her of me in marriage; as in very deed one of them had her after our return.

Laudonnière, 1564, "A Letter of the Lord Admiral,"
in Hakluyt, Principal Navigations, *vol. 9, p. 86.*

On Wednesday, the 5th, two hours before sunset, we saw four French ships at the mouth of a river [*St. Johns, Florida*]. When we were two leagues from them, the first galley joined the rest of the fleet, which was composed of four other vessels. The general concerted a plan with the captains and the pilots, and ordered the flag-ship, the *San Pelayo,* and a chaloupe to attack the French flag-ship, the *Trinity,* while the first galley and another chaloupe would attack the French galley, both of which vessels were very large and powerful. All the ships of our fleet put themselves in good position; the troops were in the best of spirits, and full of confidence in the great talents of the captain-general. They followed the galley; but as our general is a very clever and artful officer, he did not fire, not seek to make any attack on the enemy. He went straight to the French galley, and cast anchor about eight paces from her. The other vessels went to the windward, and very near the enemy. During the maneuvers, which lasted until about two hours

Menéndez de Avilés *(Courtesy St. Augustine Historical Society)*

de San Vincente, who is a very distinguished gentleman. They were very well received by the Indians, who gave them a large house belonging to a chief, and situated near the shore of the river. Immediately Captain Patino and Captain San Vincente, both men of talent and energy, ordered an intrenchment to be built around this house, with a slope of earth and fascines, these being the only means of defense possible in that country, where stones are nowhere to be found. Up to to-day we have disembarked twenty-four pieces of bronze guns of different calibers, of which the least weighed fifteen hundred weight. . . .

On Saturday, the 8th, the general landed with many banners spread, to the sound of trumpets and salutes of artillery. As I had gone ashore the evening before, I took a cross and went to meet him, singing the hymn *Te Deum laudamus.* The general marched up to the cross, followed by all who accompanied him, and there they all kneeled and embraced the cross. A large number of Indians watched these proceedings and imitated all they saw done. The same day the general took formal possession of the country in the name of his Majesty, and all the captains took the oath of allegiance to him, as their general and governor of the country.

Father Grajales describes the Spanish taking possession of Florida at St. Augustine, September 8, 1565, in French, ed., Historical Collections, *pp. 217–19.*

after sunset, not a word was said on either side. Never in my life have I known such stillness. Our general inquired of the French galley, which was the vessel nearest his, "Whence does this fleet come?" They answered, "From France." "What are you doing here?" said the Adelantado. "This is the territory of King Philip II. I order you to leave directly; for I neither know who you are nor what you want here." The French commander then replied, "I am bringing soldiers and supplies to the fort of the King of France." He then asked the name of the general of our fleet, and was told, "Pedro Menendez de Aviles, Captain-General of the King of Spain, who have come to hang all Lutherans [*Protestants*] I find here."

Francisco Lopez de Mendoza Grajales, chaplain of the Menéndez expedition, September 4, 1565, "Memoir," in French, ed., Historical Collections, *pp. 210–11.*

Two companies of infantry now disembarked; that of Captain Andres Soyez Patino, and that of Captain Juan

Our captain arose early in the morning to refresh himself after the bad weather of the night before. He opened the gate of the fort an hour before sunrise, while most of us were sound asleep in our beds. By then the Spaniards had crossed the woods, ditches, and rivers, guided by the natives. Early on this day—Monday, September 20, a cloudy and rainy morning—they entered the fort with no resistance. They made a horrible, tragic slaughter of our forces, so great was the anger and hatred they had for our nation. They vied with one another to see who could best cut the throats of our people—healthy and sick, women and children. It was a piteous, grievous sight. . . .

The Spanish nearly captured me while I was on my way to work, tools in hand. They met me as I came out of my cabin. I could think of no way of escaping but to turn tail and run as fast as I was able. A pikeman chased me, but by the grace of God my strength was doubled—poor old man that I am, and gray-headed. I leaped over the rampart, which I could not have done if I had thought about it, for it was eight or nine feet high. Once over, I raced toward the forest.

Nicolas le Challeux, a carpenter at Fort Caroline, September 20, 1565, "True and Perfect Narrative of the Last Voyage . . . of Captain Jean Ribaut," in Lorant, The New World, p. 100.

The French gentleman . . . returned within an hour with the message from Captain Ribault to the Adelantado, accepting his guarantee of safety. He then crossed over with eight gentlemen, whom the Adelantado received cordially, for they were all distinguished persons, and he offered them refreshments with wine and preserves. Captain Ribault said that he was grateful for so kind a reception, but their hearts were sorrowful on account of hearing of the death of their companions, that they could not partake of their hospitality, except to take some wine and preserves. . . . Thereupon, the Adelantado ordered Captain Diego Florio de Valdez, Admiral of the fleet, to bring them over in boats, ten at a time, and distribute them among the bushes behind the sand-hills, with their hands tied behind their backs, and afterwards marched them four leagues by land at night, taking with them Captain Ribault and his officers, with their hands tied behind their backs. Before they set out for *St. Augustine,* the Adelantado asked Captain Ribault if they were Lutherans or Roman Catholics, and he replied that they were Lutherans, and commenced to sing a psalm, *"Domine memento mei,"* and, after they finished it, he remarked that "they were made of earth, and to earth they must return, and that twenty years, more or less, were of no consequence." Then the Adelantado ordered all of them to be put to death, except the fifers, drummers, trumpeters, and four others who were Catholics. . . .

Don Solis de las Meras, 1565, in French, ed., Historical Collections, pp. 216–22.

A few days after the Adelantado arrived, some Indians came to him at *St. Augustine,* to inform him that there were a great many Christians four leagues distant . . . whereupon he took with him forty men in boats, to reconnoiter the country, and arrived on the bank of the river after midnight, where he halted until morning; and after hiding his soldiers among the bushes and trees, he surveyed the country from the top of a tree, and saw many people on the opposite side of the river with banners flying; and thinking how he should prevent them from crossing over he drew so near to them

that he could count them. Presently he saw a Frenchman swimming over the river, and as he approached the Adelantado, he called out that the people on the other side were Frenchmen who had been shipwrecked in a hurricane. The Adelantado asked him how many were on the opposite side? He replied, about two hundred followers of Captain Ribault, Viceroy and Captain-General for the King of France (Charles IX).

. . . The Adelantado replied that . . . as they were Lutherans, he looked upon them as enemies, and would wage war against them with fire and sword, whether on sea or land, for the King; "as I have come here to establish the Holy Roman Catholic faith in Florida. But if you will surrender yourselves and arms, and trust to my mercy, you may do so, and I will act towards you as God may prompt me; otherwise, do as you please, for I will not make any truces or treaties with you."

. . . Thereupon the Frenchman returned to his people; and in less than an hour after he came back, and said to the Adelantado "that all the Frenchmen would trust to his mercy and surrender on his terms," and brought back in his boat all their flags, arquebuses, pistols, swords, buckles, helmets, and breast-plates.

. . . the Adelantado asked if there were any Roman Catholics among them. Eight of them said they were Roman Catholics, and he had them put into a boat and sent to *St. Augustine,* but the remainder, who were Lutherans he ordered, after giving them something to eat, to be marched to *St. Augustine* to be put to death.

Don Solis de las Meras, Menéndez's brother-in-law, 1565, "Narrative," in French, ed., Historical Collections, pp. 216–22.

. . . I would that you should well understand that the Indians shall be governed in good faith and prudently, that those who may be weak in the faith, being newly converted, be strengthened and confirmed, and the idolaters may be converted and received the faith of Christ; that the first may praise God, knowing benefits of His divine mercy, and the others, who are yet infidels, by the example and imitation of those who are already freed from blindness, may be led to the knowledge of the faith.

But there is one thing more important for the conversion of the Indian idolaters which is, to endeavor, by every means possible, that they shall not be scandalized by the vices and bad habits of those who pass from our western shores to those parts. This is the key of this holy enterprise, in which are included all things requisite. Well understand, most noble man, that I declare to you that a great opportunity is offered to you in the carrying-out and management of these matters, which shall redound, on the one hand, to the service of God, and, on the other, to the increase of the dignity of your King, esteemed of men as well as loved and rewarded by God.

Pope Pius V to Florida governor Menéndez, August 1, 1569, in French, ed., Historical Collections, *pp. 222–23.*

. . . many perquisites were promised to all those who should come to settle these provinces . . . all manner of cattle, twelve head with the bull; establishing us on good soil, and giving us allotments of lands for farming and raising cattle. And nothing of all this has been fulfilled to us, unless it be to keep us on an island surrounded by sea water . . . the larger part of which island, at every period of spring tides, is overflowed by the sea; . . . and we have no other assistance save our own arms, although by doing some hoeing we have broken up a little land which we sow with maize to sustain our children; because the soil is not of the quality for sowing any other . . . as a little wheat and barley has been planted here by hoeing and after having headed badly, there is nothing to it but the husk. Besides which, even if the soil were rich and fertile, it has not the climate nor is the earth very dry, unless it be with the frosts and extreme cold caused therein by the winter, which comes in December and January; for in the months of April and May . . . it does nothing but rain all that time, which is when we are sowing and gathering the maize; and so we have suffered and so suffer great hardships. . . . [W]e came well supplied, having been farmers in Spain . . . and so here we feel ourselves lost, and old, and weary, and full of sickness.

Alonzo Martin, Santa Elena colonist, to Governor Hernando de Miranda, February 27, 1576, in Quinn, ed., New American World, *vol. 5, pp. 15–16.*

Upon Monday being the fifth of August the General [*Sir Humphrey Gilbert*] caused his tent to be set up on the side of a hill in the view of all the fleet of English men and strangers, which were in number between thirty and forty sail; then, being accompanied by all his Captains, Masters, Gentlemen and Soldiers he caused all, the Masters and principal officers of the ships as well Englishmen as Spaniards Portugals and all other nations to repair into his tent and then and there in the presence of them all he did cause his commission under the great seal of England to be openly and solemnly read . . .

The effect whereof being signified unto the strangers by an interpreter he took possession of the said land in the right of the Crown of England by digging up a turf and receiving the same with a hazel wand delivered unto him after the manner of the law and custom of England.

Then he signified unto the company both strangers and others than from thenceforth they were to live in that land as the territories appertaining unto the Crown of England and to be governed by such laws as by good advice should be set down which in all points (so near as might be) should be agreeable to the Laws of England and for to put the same in execution presently he ordained and established three laws:

1. Establishment of the Church of England.
2. Any attempt prejudicial to Her Majesty's rights in the territory to be punished as in a case of High Treason.
3. Anyone uttering words of dishonor to Her Majesty should lose his ears and have his goods and ship confiscated.

All men did very willingly submit themselves to these laws.

Then he caused the Queen's Majesties arms to be engraved and set upon a pillar of wood nor far from the ten with great solemnity.

Edward Hayes's narrative, August 5, 1583, qtd. in Prowse, History of Newfoundland, *pp. 71–72.*

The second of July, we found shoal water, where we smelled so sweet, and so strong a smell, as if we had been in the midst of some delicate garden abounding with all kind of odoriferous flowers, by which we were assured, that the land could not be far distant: and keeping good watch, and bearing but slack sail, the fourth of the same month we arrived upon the coast, which we supposed to be a continent and firm land . . . and after thanks given to God for our safe arrival thither, we manned our boats, and went to view the land next adjoining, and "to take possession of the same, in the right of the Queen's most excellent Majesty, as rightful Queen, and Princess of the same." . . . Which being performed, according to the ceremonies used in such enterprises, we viewed the land about us, being, whereas we first landed, very sandy and low towards the water's side, but so full of grapes, as the very beating and surge of the Sea overflowed them, of which we found such plenty, as well there as in all places else, both on the sand and on the green soil on the hills, as in the plains, as well on every little shrub, as also climbing towards the tops of high Cedars, that I think in all the world the like abundance is not to be found: and my self having seen those parts of Europe that most abound, and such difference as were incredible to be written.

Arthur Barlow's report to Sir Walter Raleigh, 1584, in Hakluyt, Principal Navigations, *vol. 8, pp. 298–99.*

The next day there came unto us diverse boats, and in one of them the King's brother, accompanied with forty or fifty men, very handsome and goodly people, and in their behavior as mannerly and civil as any of Europe. His name was Granganimeo, and the king [*of the Roanoke Indians*] is called Wingina, the country Wingandacoa, and now by her Majesty Virginia. . . .

After we had presented this his brother with such things as we thought he liked, we likewise gave somewhat to the others that sat with him on the mat: but presently he arose and took all from them and put it in his own basket, making signs and token, that all things ought to be delivered unto him, and the rest were but his servants, and followers. A day or two after this, we fell to trading with them, exchanging some things that we had, for Chamois, Buff, and Deer skins: when we showed him all our packet of merchandise, of all things he saw, a bright tin dish most pleased him, which he presently took up and clasped it before his breast, and after making a hole in the brim thereof and hung it about his neck making signs that it would defend him against his enemies arrows: for those people maintain a deadly and terrible war, with the people and King adjoining. We exchanged our tin dish for twenty skins, worth twenty Crowns or twenty Nobles: and a copper kettle for fifty skins worth fifty Crowns. They offered us good exchange for our hatchet, and axes, and for knives, and would have given anything for swords, but we would not depart with any. . . .

The King's brother had great liking of our armor, a sword, and diverse other things which we had: and offered to lay a great box of pearl in gauge for them: but we refused it for the time, because we would not

make them know, that we esteemed thereof, until we had understood in what places of the country the pearl grew. . . .

Arthur Barlow's report, 1584, in Hakluyt, Principal Navigations, *vol. 8, pp. 301–03.*

. . . corn, which is very white, faire and well tasted, and grows three times in five months: in May they sow, in July they reap: in June they sow, in August they reap: in July they sow, in September they reap: only they cast the corn into the ground, breaking a little of the soft turf with a wooden mattock, or pickax.

Arthur Barlow's report, the earliest known English description of corn cultivation, 1584, in Hakluyt, Principal Navigations, *vol. 8, p. 304.*

Franciscan Fathers, so you have come
From the distant parts of the East
To settle this poor and barren nest
Where the sun's fair face is hid.
What humbly now I beg you all
Is to teach these western tribes
Who look upon Satan as their friend
But their Maker, God, regard as foe.

Florida governor Pedro Menéndez Marques, ca. 1585, quoted in Caruso, The Southern Frontier, *p. 117.*

The 13th. we passed by water to Aquascoc005ke.

The 15th. we came to Secotan and were well entertained there of the Savages.

The 16. we returned thence, and one of our boats with the Admiral was sent to Aquascococke to demand a silver cup which one of the Savages had stolen from us, and not receiving it according to his promise, we burned, and spoiled, their corn, and Town, all the people being fled.

Anonymous journal keeper, "The Voyage Made by Sir Richard Greenvile [sic]," 1585, in Hakluyt, Principal Navigations, *vol. 8, p. 316.*

[When] Your Majesty made me the grant of being treasurer here eight years ago I decided to establish myself in this corner of the world, and not finding many suitable to my quality I married Sofia Petronila de Estrada Manrique, only daughter of Captain Rodrigo de Junco, factor of these provinces. If Your Majesty finds it inconvenient for father-in-law and son-in-law to be royal officials I shall gladly [accept a] transfer. But the limitations of the land are such that not only are the royal officials related by blood and marriage, but the governors as well.

Juan de Cevadilla, St. Augustine official, to the Spanish king, October 10, 1585, quoted in Bushnell,
The King's Coffer, p. 46.

The grain is about the bigness of our ordinary English peas, and not much different in form and shape: but of diverse colors: some white, some red, some yellow, and some blue. All of them yield a very white and sweet flour: being used according to his kind, it makes a very good bread. We made of the same in the country some malt, whereof was brewed as good ale as was to be desired. So likewise by help of hops, thereof may be made as good beer. It is a grain of marvelous great increase: of a thousand, fifteen hundred, and some two thousand fold. There are three sorts, of which two are ripe in eleven and twelve weeks at the most, sometimes in ten, after the time they are set, and are then of height in stalk about six or seven foot. The other sort is ripe in fourteen, and is about ten foot high, of the stalks, some bear four heads, some three, some one, and some two: every head containing of five, six, or seven hundred grains, with a few more or less. Of these grains, besides bread, the inhabitants made victual, either by parching them, or seething them whole until they be broken of boiling the flower with water into a pap.

Thomas Hariot describes corn, 1585–86, "A Brief and
True Report of the New Found Land of Virginia,"
in Hakluyt, Principal Navigations, vol. 8,
pp. 363–64.

There is an herb which is sowed apart by itself, and is called by the inhabitants Uppowoc: in the West Indies it has diverse names, according to the several places and countries where it grows, and is used: the Spaniards generally call it Tobacco. The leaves thereof being dried and brought into powder: they use to take the fume or smoke thereof, by sucking it through pipes made of clay, in to their stomach and head: from whence it purges superfluous flem and other gross humors, and opens all the pores and passages of the body: by which means the use thereof not only preserves the body from obstructions, but also (if any be, so that they have not been of too long continuance) in short time breaks them: whereby their bodies are notably preserved in health, and know not many grievous diseases, wherewithal we in England are oftentimes afflicted.

This Uppowoc is of so precious estimation amongst them, that they think their gods are marvelously delighted therewith: whereupon sometime they make hallowed fire, and cast some of the powder therein for a sacrifice: being in a storm upon the waters, to pacify their gods, they cast some up into the air and into the water: so a weir for fish being newly set up, they cast some therein and into the air: also after an escape of danger, they cast some into the air likewise. . . .

We ourselves during the time we were there, used to suck it after their manner, as also since our return, and have found many rare and wonderful experiments of the virtues thereof: of which the relation would require a volume by itself: the use of it by so many late men and women of great calling as else, and some learned Physicians also, is sufficient witness.

Thomas Hariot describes tobacco, 1585–86, in Hakluyt,
Principal Navigations, vol. 8, pp. 363–64.

It was the last of May, 1586, when all [Pemisapan's] own savages began to make their assembly at Roanoke. . . . [I]n truth they, privy to their own villainous purposes against us, held as good espial upon us, both day and night, as we did upon them.

. . . the king did abide my coming to him, and finding myself amidst 7. or 8. of his principal Weroances, & followers, (not regarding any of the common sort) I gave the watchword agreed upon (which was Christ our victory,) and immediately those his chief men, and himself, had by the mercy of God for our deliverance, that which they had purposed for us. The king himself being shot through by the Colonel with a pistol lying on the ground for dead, & I looking as watchfully for the saving of Manteo's friends, as others were busy that none of the rest should escape, suddenly he started up, and ran away as through he had not been touched, insomuch as he overran all the company, being by the way shot athwart the buttocks by my Irish boy with my Petronell [*handgun*]. In the end an Irish man serving me, one Nugent and the deputy provost undertook him, and following him into the woods overtook him, and I in some doubt least we had lost both the king, and my man by our own negligence to have been intercepted by the Savages, we met him returning out of the woods with Pemisapan's head in his hand.

Ralph Lane, "An Account of the Particularities of the
Employments of the English Men Left in Virginia,"
May 1586, in Hakluyt, Principal Navigations,
vol. 8, p. 297.

Francisco Hernández, ensign of the fort at San Augustin . . . being duly sworn . . . stated that on Friday on Friday after Corpus Christi, on the sixth of the present month of June, certain vessels appeared at sea off the port. They anchored at the entrance at the bar, and, according to three negroes who deserted from the English, these were 23 large ships and many pinnaces and boats, to a total of more than 50 sail in all. . . .

Saturday morning at dawn boats and frigates and pinnaces put in, to land men. Twenty pinnaces and boats landed troops which deponent estimates at a thousand men.

They marched in formation with six flags flying, all red, without any other colour whatsoever. As they advanced a piece was fired from the fort, at which they paused and took shelter behind certain sand dunes. Other pieces were fired, which sank two pinnaces which were off the coast with seamen aboard.

As soon as the English discovered the fort, its position, and where they could plant artillery, they informed the English commander, who was on board the ships outside the bar. Thereupon, with twenty additional boatloads of men, the English commander came ashore with all his music. He brought four pieces of artillery and these were set up on land and began to batter the fort. The enemy so busied himself until nightfall on Saturday. The exchange of artillery fire continued until night fell. . . .

He signed his name and is about 40 years old. . . .

Francisco Hernández's deposition on Drake's attack, June 1586, in Quinn, ed., New American World, *vol. 5, pp. 42–43.*

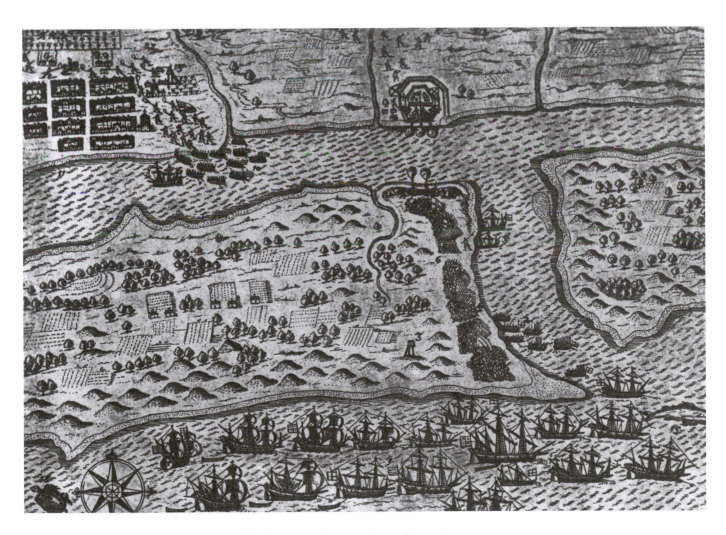

Drawing of Drake's attack on St. Augustine, 1586 *(Courtesy St. Augustine Historical Society)*

Your lordship bids me report whether the English have made any settlement on the Florida coast, which extends towards the Newfoundland Banks. . . . Pedro Menendez Marquez wrote me in reply to my inquiries . . . saying that 150 leagues beyond Santa Elena . . . there was a settlement of the English [*at Roanoke*] who in September, two year ago, passed by these ports of Florida. . . .

I have been unable to learn anything further or more definite since, except from certain negroes who ran away from Francis Drake. In Saint Augustine they deposed that all the negroes, male and female, the enemy had with him and certain other equipment which he had taken in Santo Domingo and at Cartagena, were to be left in the fort and settlement which they say exists on that coast. . . .

Up to the present nothing more is known nor have I been able to learn anything further, but I am certain that the enemy has an establishment there because it is so suitable a position from which to sally upon these Indies wherever they may desire, for they say they are settled directly west of Bermuda and so, because this would make them such close neighbours, I am as worried as though I knew certainly that they were there. Even if they are not, nothing is lost by being vigilant. . . .

Diego Fernández de Quiñones to the Casa de Contratacion (Spanish House of Trade), March 22, 1587, in Quinn, ed., New American World, *vol. 5, pp. 58–59.*

The two and twentieth of July, we arrived safe at Hatorask, where our ship and pinnace anchored: The Governor [*White himself*] went aboard the pinnace, accompanied with forty of his best men, intending to pass up to Roanoke forthwith, hoping there to find those fifteen Englishmen, which Sir Richard Grenville had left there the year before, with whom he meant to have conference, concerning the state of the Country, and Savages, meaning after he had so done, to return again to the fleet, and pass along the coast, to the Bay of Chesapeake, where we intended to make our seat and fort. . . . [B]ut as soon as we were put with our pinnace from the ship, [*the captain*] called to the sailors in the pinnace, charging them not to bring any of the planters back again, but leave them in the Island, except the Governor, & two or three such as he approved, saying that the Summer was far spent, wherefore he would land all the planters in no other place. . . . [I]t booted not the Governor to contend

with them, but passed to Roanoke, and the same night, at sunset, went aland on the Island, in the place where our fifteen men were left, but we found none of them, not any sign, that they had been there, saving only we found the bones of one of those fifteen, which the Savages had slain long before.

John White's "The Fourth Voyage Made To Virginia," July 22, 1587, in Hakluyt, Principal Navigations, *vol. 8, p. 391.*

Our boats and all things fitted again, we put off from Hatorask, being the number of 19 persons in both boats: but before we could get to the place, where our planters were left, it was so exceeding dark, that we overshot the place a quarter of a mile: there we espied towards the North end of the Island the light of a great fire through the woods, to the which we presently rowed: when we came right over against it, we let fall our Grapnel near the shore, & sounded with a trumpet a Call, & afterwards many familiar English tunes of Songs, and called to them friendly; but we had no answer, we therefore landed at daybreak, and coming to the fire, we found the grass & sundry rotten trees burning about the place. From hence . . . we came to the place where I left our Colony in the year 1586. In all this way we saw in the sand the print of the Savages' feet of 2 or 3 sorts trodden the night, and as we entered up the sandy bank upon a tree, in the very brow thereof were curiously carved these fair Roman letters CRO: which letters presently we knew to signify the place, where I should find the planters seated, according to a secret token agreed upon between them & me at my last departure from them, which was, that in any ways they should not fail to write or carve on the trees or post of the doors the name of the place where they should be seated; for at my coming away they were prepared to remove from Roanoke 50 miles into the main. Therefore at my departure from them in Anno 1587 I willed them, that if they should happen to be distressed in any of those places, that then they should carve over the letters or name, a Cross in this form [*a maltese cross*], but we found no such sign of distress. . . . [W]e found the houses taken down, and the place very strongly enclosed with a high palisade of great trees, with cortynes and flankers very Fort-like, and one of the chief trees or posts at the right side of the entrance had the bark taken off, and 5 foot from the ground in fair Capital letters was graven CROATOAN without any cross or sign of distress; this done, we entered into the palisade, where we found many bars of Iron, two pigs of Lead, four iron fowlers, Iron sacker-shot, and such like heavy things, thrown here and there, almost overgrown with grass and weeds. . . . Presently Captain Cooke and I went to the place, which was in the end of an old trench, made two years past by Captain Amadas: where we found five Chests, that had been carefully hidden of the Planters, and of the same chests three were my own, and about the place many of my things spoiled and broken, and my books torn from the covers, the frames of some of my pictures and Maps rotten and spoiled with rain, and my armor almost eaten through with rust. . . .

John White, "The Fift[h] Voyage of M. John White," August 17, 1590, in Hakluyt, Principal Navigations, vol. 8, pp. 416–18.

Offer of Don Juan de Oñate for the Conquest

First, I offer to take at least two hundred men, furnished with everything necessary, including provisions sufficient to reach the settlements and even more, this all at my cost and that of the soldiers, his majesty not being obligated to pay them any wages besides what I may willingly give from my estate. Further:

Fifteen hundred pesos in flour and maize.
Five hundred pesos in wheat for sowing.
Five hundred pesos in jerked beef.
One thousand head of cattle.
Three thousand sheep.
One thousand rams.
One hundred head of black cattle.
One hundred and fifty colts.
One hundred and fifty mares.
Two pairs of bellows with equipment for the blacksmith's trade.
Four pairs of bellows for mines, in case there should be any.
Two thousand pesos in iron for horseshoes, with the necessary nails, five hundred pesos of this sum to be in extra nails.
Five hundred pesos in footgear.
Five hundred pesos in medicines.
Six hundred pesos in iron tools such as plowshares, bars, picks, wedges, hoes, sledge hammers, adzes, augers, chisels, saws, and sickles.
Six hundred pesos in unmanufactured iron.
Five hundred pesos in articles to trade and to use as gifts for the Indians.

Two hundred pesos in paper.
Five hundred pesos in frieze and sackcloth.

All of these things I offer to take in addition to supplies and food for the soldiers in the amount needed until the settlements are reached. . . .

Don Juan de Oñate's adelantado agreement, 1595, in Hammond and Rey, eds., Don Juan, vol. 1, pp. 44–45.

Your main purpose shall be the service of God our Lord, the spreading of His Holy Catholic faith, and the reduction and pacification of the natives of the said provinces. . . .

. . . Under all circumstances they must treat the Indians well; they must humor and regale them so that they come in peace and not in war. They must not harm or annoy them nor set them a bad example. This is very important for the success of such an important undertaking.

. . . the Spaniards will attract the Indians, by good treatment and pay, to their homes to help with the indispensable tasks. The natives must not be compelled to serve against their will, as they resent very much the imposition of personal service.

Viceroy of Mexico Luis de Velasco's instructions to Oñate, October 2, 1595, in Hammond and Rey, eds, Don Juan, vol. 1, pp. 65–67.

At this time, the cart train was in trouble, both on account of dissention among those in charge, and of lack of water, and the governor had to return to them. He smoothed everything by his tact and came back to this place on June 12 and brought some provisions. His visit gave us new life. During this time two negroes, Luis and Manuel, got lost and their straying cost them their lives.

On the 14th we traveled three leagues, stopping always in open country. We halted for the night opposite Teypana, the pueblo which we called Socorro, because it furnished us with much maize. Its chieftain, named Letoc, gave us a very accurate and truthful account of the pueblos of the country, as we later learned by experience. We found people only at this pueblo, and at the first and second; all the others we found deserted. . . .

We traveled . . . to the pueblo of San Juan Bautista, newly built, but deserted because of our coming. Here we found a large quantity of maize, and so many painted idols that in two rooms alone I counted sixty.

We remained at this place on the feast day of Saint John the Baptist, and many Indians from different places came to visit us. . . . [T]hey seemed like spies. . . .
Don Juan de Oñate's journal, June 1598, in Hammond and Rey, eds., Don Juan, vol. 1, p. 318.

He [*Oñate*] told them that he had come to this land to bring them to the knowledge of God our Lord, on which depended the salvation of their souls, and to live peaceable and safely in their countries, governed justly, safe in their possessions, protected from their enemies, and that he had not come to cause them any harm.

They should know, therefore, that there was only one God almighty, creator of heaven and earth, rewarder of the upright and punisher of the wicked. Thus God had heaven for the glory of the former, reserved for the good, and hell for the punishment of the latter, reserved for the bad. This God and lord of us all had two servants on earth through whom He ruled. One was in charge of spiritual matters relating to the soul; this was the pope, Roman pontiff, high priest, and head of the church, whose representative in this land was the most reverend father commissary, who was present. They should respect and honor him, as well as all the priests, as ministers and men of the house of God. The other one, who governed the world in temporal matters, was the most Christian king, Don Philip, our lord, sole defender of the church, king of Spain and the Indies, whose representative in this land was his lordship, the governor. They must obey and respect him, because it was fitting that they should render obedience and vassalage to God and the King, and in their stead, to the most reverend father commissary in spiritual matters, and to the governor in temporal matters and those relating to the government of their republics.

. . . The Indian captains of these kingdoms rose and knelt before the governor and the father commissary and kissed their hands as a sign of obedience and vassalage, as they had been instructed.
"Act of Obedience and Vassalage" administered to the Indians of San Juan Bautista by Oñate, September 9, 1598, in Hammond and Rey, eds., Don Juan, vol. 1, pp. 342–44.

. . . I am informed that there are above 100. sail of Spaniards that come to take Cod [*in Newfoundland*] (who make all wet, and do dry it when they come home) besides 20. or 30. more than come from Biscayne to kill Whale. . . . These be better appointed for shipping and furniture of munition, than any nation saving the Englishmen, who commonly are lords of the harbors where they fish, and do use all strangers' help in fishing if need require, according to an old custom of the country, which thing they do willingly, so that you take nothing from them more than a boat or a twain of salt, in respect of your protection of them against rovers or other violent intruders, who do often put them from good harbor, and &. As touching their tonnage, I think it may be near five or six thousand ton. But of Portugals there are not lightly above 50. sail, and they make all wet in like sort, whose tonnage may amount to three thousand tons, and not upward. Of the French nation and Bretons, are about one hundred and fifty sails, the most of their shipping is very small, not past forty tons, among which some are great and reasonably well appointed, better than the Portugals, and not so well as the Spaniards, and the burden of them may be some 7000 tons.
Anthony Parkhurst to Richard Hakluyt the elder, November 13, 1598, in Hakluyt, Principal Voyages, vol. 8, p. 9.

The interpreter said that this Indian was named Caoma, a native of the pueblo of Acoma. . . . Not being a Christian he was not asked to take an oath. He explained through the interpreter that he was not present at Acoma when they killed the maese de campo and the others, as he had gone to the country. When he returned on the night of the day they were killed, the Indians at the Pueblo told him how the maese de campo and his men came to the pueblo and asked the natives to furnish them with the maize and flour which they needed, and because they asked for such large amounts they killed them. He said he was very sorry for what the Indians had done and denounced them for it. Then the governor asked him to explain why it was that when the sargento major and the soldiers went to his pueblo to summon them to peace, the Indians, instead of submitting, attacked with arrows, stones, and clubs. He replied that they refused to come down peacefully and to be friends because they had already killed the Spaniards, but he urged the Indians, both men and women, all of whom hurled stones, to submit peacefully, but they refused.

. . . This is the truth and what he knows. He gave this testimony in the presence of Captain Alonso

Gomez, his defense attorney, who signed it, together with the governor.

Caoma's statement at trial of Acoma Indians, February 9, 1599, in Hammond and Rey, eds., Don Juan, *vol. 1, pp. 470–71.*

. . . From below the pueblo, through the interpreter Don Tomas, they offered the Indians peace and friendship three times, but they replied that they had already killed the Spaniards and did not want peace but wanted to kill them all, including the Indians of the pueblos, for their failure to kill the Spaniards. He saw that while they were watering their horses near the rock on which the pueblo is situated, about thirty Indians appeared and killed two horses with arrows and refused absolute to make peace. In view of this the sargento major ordered war without quarter.

The battle started in the afternoon . . . and continued until night when a strong point near the houses outside the pueblo was taken and held through the night. The fight was renewed in the morning, and about four o'clock in the afternoon the sargento major, seeing that he was killing many natives and also that six or seven Spaniards had been wounded, one of whom was this witness who to this day is bedridden from the wounds, again sent them word to accept peace and be friends, saying that all he wanted was to investigate their killing of the Spaniards, and that he would show them justice. They replied through the interpreter that all they wanted was to die there with their women and children.

Spanish soldier Alférez Vitoria Carabajal's statement at the trial of the Acoma Indians, February, 1599, in Hammond and Rey, eds., Don Juan, *vol. 1, pp. 472–73.*

The males who are over twenty-five years of age I sentence to have one foot cut off and to twenty years of personal servitude.

The males between the ages of twelve and twenty-five I sentence likewise to personal servitude.

The women over twelve years of age I sentence likewise to twenty years of personal servitude.

Two Indians from the province of Moqui who were present at the pueblo of Acoma and who fought . . . , I sentence to have the right hand cut off and to be set free in order that they convey to their land the news of this punishment.

All of the children under twelve year of age I declare free and innocent of the grave offense for which I punish their parents. . . . I place the girls under the care of our father commissary . . . in order that he . . . may distribute them in this kingdom or elsewhere in monasteries or other places where he thinks that they may attain the knowledge of God and the salvation of their souls.

The boys under twelve years of age I entrust to . . . my sargento major, in order that they may attain the same goal.

The old men and women, disabled in the war, I order freed and entrusted to the Indians of the province of the Querechos. . . .

I order that all of the Indian men and women who have been sentenced to personal servitude shall be distributed among my captains and soldiers . . . who may hold and keep them as their slaves. . . .

Don Juan de Oñate sentences the Acoma Indians, February 12, 1599, in Hammond and Rey, eds., Don Juan, *vol. 1, pp. 477–78.*

But I will relate that, for to keep us merry and cleanly concerning victuals, there was an order established at the table of the said Monsieur de Poutrincourt, which was named *"L'Ordre de bon temps"* (the order of good time, or the order of mirth), at first invented by Monsieur Champlain, wherein they (who were of the same table) were every one of his turn and day (which was in fifteen days once) steward and caterer. Now his care was that we should have good and worshipful fare, which was so well observed that . . . we have ordinarily had there as good cheer as we could have at La Rue aux Ours, and at far lesser charges. For there was none but (two days before his turn came) was careful to go a-hunting or fishing, and brought some dainty thing, besides that which was of our ordinary allowance. So well, that at breakfast we never wanted some modicum or other of fish flesh; and, at the repast of dinners and suppers, yet less; for it was the great banquet, where the Governor of the feast or Steward (whom the savages do call *atoctegic*), having made the cook to make all things ready, did march with his napkin on his shoulder and his staff of office in his hand, with the collar of the order about his neck, which was worth above four crowns, and all of them of the order following of him, bearing every one a dish. The like also was also at the bringing in of the fruit, but not with so great a train. And at night, after grace was said, he resigned the collar of the order, with a cup of wine, to his successor in that charge, and they drank to another. I have heretofore said that we had abundance of fowl, as mallards, outards [*bustards*], geese, grey and white, partridges, and other birds: item, of elans (or stag-flesh) [*moose*], of caribou (or deer), beavers, otters, bears, rabbits, wild-cats (or leopards), and such like, which the savages did take, wherewith we made as good dishes of meat as in the cook's-shops that be in La Rue aux Ours (Bear Street) and greater store; for of all meats none is so tender as elan's flesh (whereof we made good pasties), nor so delicate as the beaver's tail. . . . In such actions we had always twenty or thirty savages, men, women, girls, and boys, who beheld us doing our offices. Bread was given to them gratis, as we do here to the poor. But as for the Sagamos Membertou and other Sagamos (when any came to us), they sat at table eating and drinking as we did; and we took pleasure in seeing them, as contrariwise their absence was irksome unto us. . . .

Marc Lescarbot, 1604–07, Nova Francia,
pp. 117–19.

We found there some little pieces of copper of the thickness of a sou, and others still thicker embedded in grayish and red rocks. The miner accompanying us, whose name was Master Jacques, a native of Sclavonia, a man very skillful in searching for minerals, made the entire circuit of the hills to see if he could find any gangue [the matrix in which an ore is found] but without success. Yet he found, some steps from where we had taken the pieces of copper, before mentioned, something like a mine, which, however, was far from being one. He said that, from the appearance of the soil, it might prove to be good, if it were worked, and that it was not probable that there could be pure copper on the surface of the earth, without there being a large quantity of it underneath.

Samuel de Champlain, "Voyages of 1604–07,"
in Voyages, *p. 80.*

Continuing with the said confirmations, His Excellency went to . . . Nombre de Dios, on the 2nd of April of the same year. Its chief is Doña Maria: she is married to a Spaniard, a soldier of this garrison. It is said that this chief has more than three thousand Indians in her district: although they are not all Christian, they are friendly: they are divided among many other towns. It is said that Doña Maria takes a very real interest in the affairs of this garrison and the Spaniards in it. She was confirmed, and two legitimate children of hers, and also two hundred and thirteen natives and a few Spaniards, probably as many as twenty.

. . . His Excellency baptized the chief of Tuquepi, and confirmed him with the catechism, because it was and is understood that his conversion is of great significance since he is chief of a nation of Indians called the Salchiches. They are warlike people, and not Christian, as is known. With the conversion of the chief is understood their conversion also, and so that they should not change their mind the Bishop speeded up the proceedings, with the baptism and confirmation in the said manner: His Excellency baptized and confirmed him himself, and the wife of the chief also, who wanted to become Christian too. There were also confirmed two hundred and eight people. . . .

Description of bishop of Cuba Don Juan Cabezas
Altamirano's visit to Florida, March–June 1606,
from a document in the Archives General de Indias in
Quinn, ed., New American World,
vol. 5, pp. 131–32.

PART II

FOUNDINGS:
1607 TO 1670

2

New Spain, New France, and Acadia
1607–1670

SPAIN'S NORTH AMERICAN COLONIES

Although Spain's power in Europe declined during the 17th century, its colonial empire continued to flourish. Its two colonies in North America, however, were exceptions. Located on the northern border of New Spain, Florida and New Mexico grew slowly but remained struggling frontier communities. By 1670, the colony of New Mexico had only one town, at Santa Fe. The colony of Florida had only one civilian settlement, at St. Augustine. Spanish emigrants continued to prefer more prosperous areas of New Spain.

Although important differences existed between Florida and New Mexico in the 17th century, they had much in common. Both colonies were maintained to satisfy the European principle of claim by occupation: Nations asserted rights to New World territory, usually with loosely defined boundaries, by maintaining a settlement there. St. Augustine enabled Spain to claim part of the Atlantic seaboard. Santa Fe enabled Spain to claim the vast western half of North America, only partially explored. Unlike Spain's colonies in the West Indies and South and Central America, however, neither Florida nor New Mexico contributed to the wealth of the mother country. To the contrary, both had to be supported by the *situado,* funds transferred to them from the Spanish treasury. These funds paid soldiers and officials and supported missionaries. The recipients, in turn, depended on the money to purchase whatever trade goods they needed.

Both Florida and New Mexico experienced a wave of mission building during the 17th century. In both colonies, Native Americans periodically rebelled against Spanish religious and cultural impositions. By 1600, Spain had developed a body of law—not always enforced—to protect its Indian subjects from abuses by Spanish settlers. Nonetheless, the law still recognized two institutions of compulsory labor by Indians. *Encomiendas,* or grants of territory, enabled private persons to collect *tribute,* a kind of tax, from the indigenous subjects who resided there. By law, tribute was defined as a set amount of goods like corn, which the *encomendero,* or grantee, could sell for his own profit. Often, however, encomenderos extracted direct labor from the Indians instead. The second form of compulsory labor was *repartimiento.* It required rotating groups of Indians to work on public works projects. The groups often included women as well as men. *Repartimiento* law required payment for the labor and a limitation on its length, but both requirements were often disregarded.

SANTA FE BECOMES NEW MEXICO'S CAPITAL

On November 1, 1609, New Mexico became a royal colony under direct control of the Spanish Crown. Soon afterward, Don Pedro de Peralta, the first royal governor, arrived at the colony's only settlement, San Gabriel. He was accompanied by a group of Franciscans and some 50 soldiers, artisans, and their families. Peralta was under orders to find a new location for the colonial capital. In spring 1610, he chose the site of Santa Fe, near the geographical middle of the missions along the Rio Grande. For the colony's ecclesiastical headquarters, the Franciscans chose the pueblo of Santo Domingo.

Using conscripted Indian labor, Santa Fe was constructed as a fortified *villa,* or town. Its buildings were adjoined to form an enclosed plaza. Part of the structure was the *casa real,* or government building. A block within a block, the casa reale had its own interior patio and included the governor's home, administrative areas, and quarters for soldiers. (Later known as the Palace of the Governors, it is the oldest surviving European building in the modern United States.) Outside Santa Fe's walls, Spanish settlers built their homes. Each was entitled to two lots, adjoining fields for gardening, and additional acreage farther from town. A separate section for Tlascalan Indians from Mexico who accompanied the settlers, called the Barrio Analco, was built.

New Mexico was very isolated in the 17th century. The colony was supported in part by a Spanish-financed supply caravan that arrived approximately every three years from Mexico. The 1,500-mile round trip took six months each way. Four-wheeled wagons, pulled by ox or mule teams, carried metal tools, religious supplies, household items, cloth, and some food for the colony. It returned to Mexico with trade goods sent by the missionaries or influential

Palace of the Governors (El Palacio Real), Santa Fe, the oldest surviving European colonial building in continuous use in the modern United States *(Historical American Building Survey)*

settlers—and sometimes with Indian slaves. The caravan had a military guard, and new settlers, officials, and clergy traveled in its train.

In 1623, Friar Alonso de Benavides became the first *custodio* of the New Mexican missions. (The *custodio* was the head Franciscan administrator, usually translated as custodian or commissary.) In a 1630 report, Benavides noted that the population of Santa Fe was 250 Spanish and 700 Indians and people of mixed race; the colony as a whole had, in addition, 25 missions, 60 priests, 90 pueblos, and 60,000 Indians. By 1680, the Spanish population in New Mexico had reached approximately 3,000.

FORCED PUEBLO LABOR IN NEW MEXICO

When the first Spanish arrived in the Rio Grande valley, they named the prosperous, town-dwelling indigenous peoples the Pueblo Indians. (In Spanish, *pueblo* means "small town.") From the Spanish perspective, the peaceful, settled, and compact living arrangements of the Pueblo made them particularly suitable for conquest, or "pacification," and conversion to Christianity. In fact, the inhabitants of the approximately 75 independent pueblos were not one tribe and were divided into several mutually unintelligible language groups. The Pueblo did share a general culture, with similar architecture, highly developed agricultural skills, and polytheistic religious beliefs that pervaded daily life. Religious rituals varied, however, as did social and political institutions.

Encomiendas were quickly established in New Mexico—and extensively abused. In 1640, the Crown limited their number to 35. Tribute was set by law at one and a half bushels of corn and one woven blanket or hide per Indian person per year. Despite the law, *encomendero* families frequently demanded domestic or agricultural labor from the Pueblo. The *repartimiento* was also widely abused. Some governors established workshops where Indians were forced to manufacture or decorate objects for sale in Mexico. Individual Spanish families used the repartimiento Indians as personal servants and for agricultural work, the production of items for export, and porterage. Of all forms of forced labor, Indians most hated porterage. Porters were required to carry trade goods on their backs over long distances, leaving their homes and families for long periods of time. Evidence also exists that under conditions of forced labor Indian women were often sexually assaulted.[1] The Pueblo grew increasingly resentful of forced labor as the 17th century progressed.

The use of Indian slaves was also common among the Spanish settlers of New Mexico; most households had at least one. Slavery was an established tradition among many Native American groups in the area, who enslaved tribal war captives; settlers sometimes purchased these captives. However, they also conducted slave raids among outlying tribes or provoked them into attack in order to take their own captives. They also seized orphaned Pueblo children, although the Pueblo lacked the concept of orphanhood and cared for them within the extended family. The condition of slavery, however, was not passed on to the Indian slave's children.

STRUGGLE BETWEEN CHURCH AND STATE

In all of Spain's colonies in the New World, the civil and religious motives for colonization often clashed. In New Mexico, the conflict was especially intense and bitter in the 17th century. In effect, two separate and competing governments existed in the colony. The civil government at Santa Fe consisted of the governor; a town council, or *cabildo,* of four (sometimes elected, sometimes appointed); and two alcaldes, or magistrates, to adjudicate disputes for the small Spanish community. Civil officials were responsible for military defense and for economic development. The ecclesiastical government at Santo Domingo was headed by the Franciscan custodio, who was unusually powerful because New Mexico had no bishop until 1680. The Franciscans claimed full authority over all indigenous peoples, as well as ordinary ecclesiastical authority over the Spanish settlers. They maintained that religious goals overrode all civil considerations.

Civil and religious leaders continually struggled against each other's control. Some 25 governors were assigned to the colony between 1610 and 1680. Some were incompetent; all were poorly funded and used their appointments as a means to increase personal wealth. Few were personally devout and several were openly contemptuous of the Franciscans and church authority. Most Franciscans assigned to New Mexico were undoubtedly sincere missionaries of the church and its beliefs. However, they also proved ambitious for power and were quarrelsome, litigious, and at times quite as capable as the governors of engaging in disreputable tactics. More than once both the governor and the presiding Franciscan were jointly recalled to Mexico City.

Civil and ecclesiastical authorities often clashed over the misuse of forced Indian labor. The friars expected their converts to labor in the construction of the mission itself, as well as in the production of the mission's food supply and some items for trade. They believed that these activities were justified because they supported spiritual life. Unfortunately for the Pueblo, the only wealth the Spanish settlers could extract from New Mexico also depended on the exploitation of the Indians' labor.

Conflict first arose under Governor Pedro de Peralta (1610–14). Friar Isidro Ordóñez arrived in 1612, determined to subjugate civil authority to that of the church. He ordered the governor to cease using Indian labor to build Santa Fe and forbade the collection of tribute at some pueblos. Before the viceroy recalled both men, Peralta had shot at Ordóñez (he missed, but hit another friar), while Ordóñez had excommunicated Peralta twice and imprisoned him on authority of the Inquisition. (The Spanish Inquisition, a tribunal devoted to discovering and persecuting heresies against the Catholic faith, was established elsewhere in New Spain in the 1570s and in New Mexico in the 1620s.)

The most serious conflict occurred during the tenure of Custodio Juan de Salas and Governor Luis de Rosas (1637–41), a former military officer not friendly to compromise. Rosas replaced *cabildo* members who opposed him, installed a renegade priest at Santa Fe, and physically beat two Franciscans who came to negotiate peace. Although Rosas had the support of some wealthy Santa Fe families, military officials sided with the friars. They fortified ecclesiastical headquarters at Santo Domingo and, together with the friars, brought the colony to the brink of civil war. Orders came from Madrid to remove both governor and clergy.

The dispute between church and state intensified again under Governor Bernardo López de Mendizábal (1659–60) and Custodio Friar Juan Ramírez. The two arrived together with the same supply train from Mexico City; on the journey, they fought so much that 10 other Franciscans turned back to Mexico. Mendizábal permitted the Pueblo to resume traditional ceremonial dancing and accused both the military and the clergy of misusing their labor. He and his wife were both arrested under the authority of the Inquisition. The governor died (or was murdered) in prison before he could be tried; his wife, Teresa de Aguilera, was tried "on suspicion of being a Jew," but her case was eventually dismissed. Mendizábal was replaced by Governor Don Diego de Peñalosa (1661–64), an adventurer of high birth but exceedingly low behavior. He too was brought before the Spanish Inquisition (the charges took two days to read) and banished to Europe, where he tried unsuccessfully to interest both England and France in attacking New Mexico.

Missions in New Mexico

Missions in New Mexico were usually founded at established pueblos, with Spanish soldiers stationed nearby. Eventually, a church would be built close outside the preexisting pueblo walls; the pueblo itself was usually not modified.

To church and crown of the 17th century, Christian religious belief could not be separated from "civilized," or European, social behavior and lifestyle. Indians who violated these expectations were punished, often by flogging. (By tradition, Franciscans also flogged themselves to atone for sins.) Missionaries expected and required the Pueblo to adopt clothing that fully covered their bodies; to practice monogamy; and most importantly to abandon their traditional religious rituals, which the Church believed to be devil worship. Objects sacred to the Indians were destroyed, and traditional Pueblo religious leaders were often persecuted. The friars did not eradicate Pueblo religious beliefs and practices, however, but rather drove them underground. Many Pueblo apparently combined the rituals and beliefs of Catholicism with those of their traditional religion.

Pueblo acceptance of Christianity in the early decades of the 17th century gave way to increasing dissatisfaction and, finally rebellion. The most important reason, of course, was anger at the suppression of their own culture and religion, and at the imposition of forced labor. But there were other reasons as well. Many probably perceived the missionaries as powerful shamans, like those of their traditional religion. When disastrous events occurred, they believed that the friars had lost their powers to intercede with natural or supernatural forces. Such events included a smallpox epidemic that occurred in the 1640s and a drought in the 1660s, which brought crop failures and starvation to both the Indians and the Spanish. Rebellions occurred at Zuni Pueblo in 1632, at Jemez in 1644 and 1647; and in Tewa villages in 1650. In 1639–40, Pueblo Indians at Taos burned the church, killed two priests, and escaped to what is now Kansas. Spanish soldiers put down the revolts and sold the leaders into slavery. Some historians believe that extant records may, in fact, greatly understate the frequency of rebellion.

In some ways, of course, the missions in New Mexico improved the life of the Indians. The friars provided metal tools, established animal herds, and introduced new European plants, like winter wheat, to lengthen the growing season. They certainly protected the Pueblo from what would surely have been far worse exploitation and possibly extinction at the hands of the Spanish settlers.

LIFE IN 17TH-CENTURY NEW MEXICO

Unfortunately, most day-to-day records of life in New Mexico were destroyed in the Pueblo Revolt of 1680. Despite the lost records, the colony is known to have been peopled primarily by emigrants from Mexico, not directly from Spain. People of African descent are known to have arrived with early groups of settlers; a few French and Portuguese are also known to have lived in the colony. By 1670, many people had a mixed ethnic heritage, primarily due to unions between Spanish men and Indian women. Except for the colony's officials, most men were farmers or soldiers. Social distinctions were very important; some colonists prospered and were able to acquire large, productive landholdings. The formal education level was low and illiteracy markedly high. The only schools were at the missions, and usually only Indians attended. Although New Mexico produced the characteristic two-wheeled cart called a *carreta,* the population was unable to move about freely. Settlers needed an official permit to leave their land.

Spanish settlers and missionaries in New Mexico adopted and adapted the distinctive adobe architecture of the Pueblo Indians, blending it with Spanish form. Often, adobe mission churches reached more than 30 feet in height. Adobe, made from clay mixed with straw or manure, was traditionally produced by Pueblo women. The Spanish introduced large wooden forms in which abode could be formed into bricks or blocks weighing about 50 to 60 pounds and conscripted Pueblo men to build with them. Roofs were constructed using the distinctive *vigas,* large logs that usually projected from the tops of the walls. In some unforested locations, such logs must have been hauled from great distances.

To the church's consternation, Spanish settlers eagerly adopted many folk rituals and spells of the Indians. During the 1630s, the Office of the Inquisition investigated many claims of witchcraft, although the Indians themselves were exempt from religious prosecution. At the other extreme of spirituality, a great religious legend developed during the century, that of María de Jésus de Agreda, the Lady in Blue. María was a cloistered abbess at a Spanish convent who believed she could practice mystical bilocation. According to legend, she appeared to Indians throughout the Southwest over a period of 25 years, urging them to seek conversion. Indians apparently were able to identify her picture; María (who never left Spain and died in 1665) apparently was able to give detailed descriptions of the Southwest. Friar Alfonso de Benavides accepted her claims, although most clerics did not. The legend survived for many years.

SPANISH FLORIDA AND ST. AUGUSTINE

St. Augustine remained the capital and primary settlement of Florida. Small military garrisons and Franciscan missions also dotted the royal colony, which included territory in modern Georgia, the Carolinas, and Alabama. St. Augustine's Spanish population grew slowly, from 300–500 in 1607 to approximately 1,000 by the century's end. The Native American population in Florida, however, suffered a disastrous decline. At least 925,000 Indians are believed to have inhabited Florida when the Spanish first arrived. By 1617, that figure had been reduced to a mere 36,750, and to 10,000 by the 1660s. Most remaining in 1660 were Apalachee; the Timucua around St. Augustine, the Guale to the north, and the Calusa to the south were decimated. In Florida, as in other parts of the New World, much of the decline in

Native American population was due to epidemics of diseases, almost all of which originated in Europe or Africa. Diseases such as smallpox, syphilis, typhus, yellow fever, and malaria were imported or spread by European explorers, traders, and settlers and by African slaves. Epidemics struck Europeans and Africans as well as Native Americans, of course. Most newcomers, however, had some resistance to some of the diseases. The Indian population had no resistance to any and was struck by one after the other.[2]

In Florida, the use of forced Indian labor was much less extensive than in New Mexico. *Encomiendas* were never well established, and regular tribute was not collected, although goods were demanded when needed. The repartimiento was used, however, especially for agricultural work and freight transport. As missions spread out across the Florida territory, Indian porters were forced to carry supplies from St. Augustine, returning in the opposite direction with trade goods produced at the missions. The majority of Florida house servants, however, were not Indians but slaves of African descent. Slaves also supplemented the repartimiento labor force, especially for the continual repair of the fort at St. Augustine.

Between 1608 and 1670, 20 different governors served the colony. There was no representative government, although families with wealth and status exerted public influence. Profiteering and graft were common. Although the colony struggled financially, it managed to grow its own food. Colonists traded with the Indians for tobacco, pottery, and wild turkey, fish, and game. Most had great difficulty, however, trading with merchants for imported European goods like cloth or metal items. The colony produced very little surplus for trade, and the salaries provided by the *situado* were paid irregularly. In 1628, for example, Dutch pirate Piet Heyn captured the entire Spanish treasure fleet as it made its way through the Caribbean with Florida's situado. Hard times among the Spanish also affected the Indians adversely, because more demands for labor and food were made. In 1629, the Eastern Timucua rebelled, led by a *cacica* (female chief). She was hanged, and her followers were shipped to Havana as slaves. In the 1640s, large-scale cattle ranching began in the grasslands of central Florida, where the Native American population had declined significantly. Governor Francisco Menéndez Márquez granted grazing rights to settlers and to some Indian chiefs, who erected *estancias,* or buildings and corrals.

Throughout the 17th century, Florida was frequently under threat of attack. Pirates roamed the Caribbean and the Atlantic seaboard. Indians revolted periodically and also conducted intertribal warfare, sometimes obligating the Spanish to participate. In 1650, England captured the Spanish possession of Jamaica and used it, the Spanish believed, as a base for piracy. In 1668, British pirate Robert Searles sacked St. Augustine, capturing all persons who appeared to be African or Indian for sale as slaves. In 1670, the English founded a settlement as far south as modern Charleston in territory Spain claimed as its own. Now alarmed, the Crown sent new officials and resources to Florida. Preparations were laid to build a large and permanent fortress to protect the Spanish claim.

THE MISSIONS OF FLORIDA

Franciscan missions grew significantly after 1607. In 1612, Friar Francisco de Peraja's first Spanish-Timucuan catechism was published in Mexico City. That work, and several that followed, preserved considerable knowledge of Indian cultures. By the 1620s, 20 new missions had been established as far north as present-day Savannah. Unlike friars in the Southwest, Florida missionaries were not usually accompanied by soldiers.

By 1630, the severe decline in Indian population had caused a marked labor shortage in the colony. Because Spanish policy required new groups of Indians to be conquered, or "pacified," by voluntary conversion, labor shortages often brought increased support for missionary activities. Not unexpectedly, between 1630 and 1670, the Franciscans received a large increase in manpower and resources to extend their missions westward. By mid-century, 70 missionaries attended more than 35 missions. After 1630, the Franciscans expanded into Apalachee territory in the Florida panhandle. The mission of San Luis de Tali-mali, near modern Tallahassee, quickly became a successful port for trade with St. Augustine and Havana. The Apalachee supplied new labor for the Spanish, but serious rebellions occurred in 1638 and 1647. In 1656, a Timucua rebellion took place.

In the 17th century, missionaries did not attempt to replace the traditional Native American political structure as they had in the 16th century. The missionaries did insist upon acceptance of aspects of European civilization that they believed to be inseparable from the religious tenets of Christianity. Indians were required to cut their traditionally long hair, to take Spanish names upon baptism, and to adopt clothing that covered their bodies. Forbidden were ritual dancing, traditional burial practices, and in particular the popular intertribal ball games (which originally had a ceremonial or religious association). Nonetheless, some Indian leaders were receptive to missionaries. Some probably saw the friars as allies against their traditional enemies or as a means to establish trade for European goods. Some may have been receptive to conversion because their traditional religion had not protected them from diseases—or from Europeans.

Mission centers were usually established in preexisting Indian villages, which had traditional round or oval residences built around a public space. In this space, a square or rectangular church and a residence for the friars was constructed. Most of the Florida Indians among whom the missionaries worked were at least seasonally agricultural and sedentary. The friars introduced dairy farming and other animal husbandry, new varieties of plants, double planting, and metal tools. Often these changes enabled mission Indians to create an agricultural surplus for trade.

LIFE IN ST. AUGUSTINE

Social distinctions were important in the Florida colony. At the top were the Spanish hidalgos—men of status analogous to English gentlemen. All hidalgos had some official capacity or title in the government or military. Because shop-keeping disqualified a man from claiming hildago status, merchants and traders were usually French or Portuguese, the latter probably of Jewish background. Spanish commoners worked as soldiers, farmers, and craftsmen. At the bottom of the social structure were slaves of African descent as well as some free blacks, many of whom were brought from Cuba. Usually they spoke Spanish and were baptized Catholics who had taken Spanish names. In the 17th century, marriages between Spanish men and Indian women were no longer encouraged.

Friars, in fact, tried to segregate Indian communities from the other settlers, believing they were corrupted by the Spanish, African, and mixed-race populations.

During the 17th century, houses in Florida increased in size and relative importance. Houses, often constructed by Indian labor, were located in town, with larger tracts of farmland farther out. Homes of the wealthy usually had walled grounds extensive enough to contain orchards, grape vines, and vegetable gardens. Among the wealthy, households were large and extended (rather than nuclear) and often included dependent kinsmen, servants, and slaves. Elaborate clothing was very important to colonists of high status. They imported linens, velvets, silks, taffetas, and fine laces for men's dress clothing as well as women's. The wealthy even imported water from a spring on Anastasia Island. Ordinary colonists had far fewer and cheaper houses, goods, and food. Their pottery, soaps, oil, and candles were domestically produced rather than imported. They sometimes adopted the Indian use of leather for clothing.[3] It was rare for girls to receive any formal education, but boys often received a basic education from the friars.

THE FOUNDING OF QUEBEC

In 1607, France had only one settlement in North America: Port Royal on the Bay of Fundy in Acadia (modern Nova Scotia). Founded by Pierre de Gua, sieur de Monts, the tiny fur-trading settlement was abandoned in 1608 when De Monts lost his fur trade monopoly.

Back in France, De Monts successfully obtained a renewal of his monopoly for one year. His associate, Samuel de Champlain, recommended founding a new colony in a new location. Champlain preferred a site near the former Stadacona and Cartier-Roberval settlement, on the St. Lawrence River. He believed this location at *kébec,* the "place where the river narrows" in Algonquin, would enable them to dominate the fur trade by controlling access to the St. Lawrence valley. On July 3, 1608, Champlain arrived at Quebec with 28 workmen. They constructed a cluster of three buildings, connected by an upper floor walkway and surrounded by a palisade, which Champlain named the Habitation.

After a first winter marked by scurvy and dysentery, only eight men were alive to greet the colonists who arrived in June 1609. For a decade, Quebec remained a fur-trading settlement primarily peopled by young men who depended on supply ships for existence. In 1617, Louis Hébert, a Paris apothecary turned farmer, arrived from Acadia with his wife and daughters. They received the first grant of land and remained as the first farming family.

NATIVE AMERICAN ALLIANCES IN NEW FRANCE

By 1608 the St. Lawrence Iroquoian-speaking Indians, whom Jacques Cartier had called the Stadaconans and Hochelagans, had entirely disappeared from the St. Lawrence valley. In their place were two large and rival groups, the Iroquois Confederacy, or League of the Five Nations (Seneca, Oneida, Onondaga, Cayuga, and Mohawk), and the Huron Alliance (also called the Huron confederacy). Increased opportunities for fur trading after 1580 had intensified a long-standing conflict between the two groups. By the time Champlain arrived, they were bitter rivals for territory, trade, and power in the area.

The Iroquois, who numbered approximately 30,000 in the early 17th century, were located south of the St. Lawrence River, centering on the north-central area of modern New York State. The Huron, who numbered 20,000, lived north of the St. Lawrence, centering on the Georgian Bay area of Lake Huron. They were allied with other tribes to the north, especially the Montagnais and Algonkin. Both the Huron and Iroquois confederacies were trading and agricultural peoples; both were politically skilled members of the Iroquoian language group. Both had traded with Europeans since the early 16th century. Before Champlain's arrival, however, the Huron-allied northern tribes had established trading relations with the French at Tadoussac. In return, the French had agreed to support the Huron Alliance against the Iroquois Confederacy. When Champlain arrived in 1608, he inherited the agreement.

In 1609, Champlain accompanied members of the Huron Alliance to make war on the Iroquois tribes. They surprised a group of Mohawk at the large lake to which Champlain gave his name, near modern Ticonderoga, New York. Champlain's victory, along with several others during the Iroquois wars of 1609–15, established the supremacy of European firearms over traditional Native American weapons. It also cemented the French partnership with the northern tribes and enabled them to control the St. Lawrence fur trade. The Iroquois Confederacy was forced to establish a new trade route to the south and a trading partnership with the Dutch who visited the Hudson River. The legacy of the Iroquois conflict, however, had long-lasting consequences for New France.

NEW FRANCE UNDER THE 100 ASSOCIATES

Champlain wanted to expand the settlement at Quebec, and in 1618 he presented an ambitious plan to King Louis XIII of France. By 1627, however, the population of Quebec was still under 100, only about 10 of them women. In that year, the king's chief minister, the powerful French cardinal Armand de Plessis, duc de Richelieu, took interest in Champlain's colony. Richelieu completely reorganized support for New France, forming the Company of the 100 Associates (also called the Company of New France). This group of wealthy and well-connected aristocrats and merchants was granted a 15-year monopoly on all trade except fishing and whaling. In return, it was required to send at least 200 settlers yearly, and clergy as needed.

In 1628, the Associates dispatched supplies and 400 settlers to Canada. Unfortunately, war had broken out with England; English privateer David Kirke was raiding Acadian settlements and had obtained an English commission to capture Quebec. Kirke blockaded the St. Lawrence and turned back the Associates' ships. Without supplies, Quebec suffered a terrible winter. The following year, Kirke returned and obtained Quebec's surrender to the English on July 19, 1629.

When Champlain arrived in France, he promoted negotiations to regain the colony. In 1632, the Treaty of Saint-Germain-en-Laye restored all France's North American settlements. About 40 French, including three Jesuits, arrived in Quebec soon afterward and Champlain returned in 1633. Although the English had

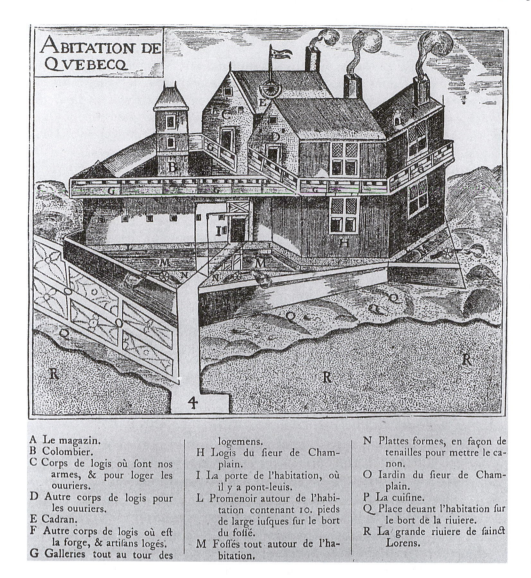

ABITATION DE QVEBECQ

A Le magazin.
B Colombier.
C Corps de logis où font nos armes, & pour loger les ouuriers.
D Autre corps de logis pour les ouuriers.
E Cadran.
F Autre corps de logis où est la forge, & artisans logés.
G Galleries tout au tour des logemens.
H Logis du sieur de Champlain.
I La porte de l'habitation, où il y a pont-leuis.
L Promenoir autour de l'habitation contenant 10. pieds de large iusques sur le bort du fossé.
M Fossés tout autour de l'habitation.
N Plattes formes, en façon de tenailles pour mettre le canon.
O Iardin du sieur de Champlain.
P La cuisine.
Q Place deuant l'habitation sur le bort de la riuiere.
R La grande riuiere de sainct Lorens.

The Habitation of Quebec, drawn by Samuel de Champlain *(National Archives of Canada, C-005750)*

burned the settlement before leaving, within a year Champlain had overseen its reconstruction and started a new settlement at Trois-Rivières. The 100 Associates sent colonists regularly after 1632, but population grew slowly. Although the original backers of the colony had included both Huguenots and Catholics, only Catholics were permitted to immigrate to New France. Most came as *engagés*—workmen who contracted for three years' labor, passage, room, and board. At the end of service, many returned to France. In 1634, the Associates granted the first *seigneurie,* a large tract of land. The seigneur acted as a landlord, in turn leasing plots called *rotures* to farmers, whom he was required to recruit. Seigneuries were not limited solely to persons of high birth; some were granted to the Church and to individuals who had performed services for the colony.

On Christmas day, 1635, Champlain died. His funeral was attended by hundreds of Indians as well as the French settlers. Although neither a nobleman nor a wealthy merchant, he had crossed the Atlantic 20 times in the service of his colony and produced three volumes of writings and maps describing it. Never elevated to governor in his lifetime, he was afterward called the "father of New

France." Champlain was replaced by Charles Huault de Montmagny, the first official governor general.

By 1645, the 100 Associates were almost bankrupt from the expenses of the colony. They ceded fur-trade rights to an organization of New France businessmen whose behavior soon elicited many complaints. As a result, in 1647 the Crown established the Council of Quebec, composed of the governors of Quebec and Montreal, the head of the Jesuits, and two elected representatives. Only a few residents, however, actually qualified to vote or hold office.

In 1635, with financial backing from wealthy Frenchmen and -women, a Jesuit college was opened in Quebec. Gradually, it developed the classical college curriculum of the era, and by 1655 it had four Jesuit instructors and 20 students. In 1639, two orders of nuns founded convents in Quebec: the Ursulines to teach French and Indian girls and the Hospitalières to tend the ill at the Hôtel Dieu, a hospital founded in 1637. By 1640–41, the Ursulines had almost 50 pupils. In 1659, the first bishop of New France, the 36-year-old nobleman François de Laval, arrived in Quebec (the position was not confirmed by Rome until 1674). A powerful man—some said power-mad—he exerted great influence in civil and religious life. Laval made few friends but firmly established the centrality of the Catholic Church in the life of New France. In 1668, he founded a seminary at Quebec to train Canadian-born priests.

THE FOUNDING OF MONTREAL

In 1642, Montreal was founded on an island in the St. Lawrence River, the site of the former Indian village Hochelega. It was sponsored by the Société de Notre-Dame de Montréal, a group of French religious mystics who wished to covert the Indians to Christianity. Over the next quarter-century, wealthy Frenchmen, inspired by a religious revival in France, contributed large sums of money to the project.

The 60 original settlers included farmers and craftsmen, a few soldiers, six women, and children. They were led by Paul de Chomedy, sieur de Maisonneuve, a military officer. Among the group were Jeanne Mance and Marie-Madelaine de La Peltrie, the benefactress of the Ursuline convent in Quebec, who planned to found a hospital. The colonists built a palisaded village they named Ville-Marie de Montréal; it was surrounded by a moat and had a chapel, gardens, and dwellings. Friendly Huron confederacy Indians visited in July, and in August more settlers arrived with supplies and livestock.

In June 1643, Iroquois ambushed a group of six settlers, beginning two decades of skirmishes with Montreal residents. Attacks intensified in the 1650s. Quebec, a trade-dominated colony never enthusiastic about Montreal's religious purpose, piety, or location, urged colonists to evacuate. Instead, buildings were refortified many times. Dogs were trained to guard the settlement. Farmers worked the fields under armed guard; the hospital, which provided medical care to both French settlers and Indians, installed a cannon. Despite the difficulties, new settlers continued to arrive. In 1657, the Sulpicians of Paris founded a seminary. In 1658, Marguerite Bourgeoys, a nun, opened a school for girls in a converted stable; in 1659, she established the Congrégation de Notre-Dame, the first religious community founded in Canada.

MISSIONS IN NEW FRANCE

The first missionaries to the Native Americans of New France were Recollects, a branch of the Franciscans, who arrived in 1615. In 1625, they were replaced by Jesuits. In 1634, Father Jean de Brébeuf led a small party into the wilderness, and within a few years many more missionaries had followed him. Although the Jesuits endured many physical hardships, they met little success in the first half of the 17th century. Many Huron were strongly opposed both to religious conversion and to any attempt to modify Indian social and sexual practices. In 1639, Father Jérôme Lalemant began construction of Ste.-Marie, a mission village far into the Canadian interior on Georgian Bay. The community also included traders, soldiers, and *donneés,* laymen (some of high birth) who gave years of service to the missions as farmers or artisans. In 1648, Ste.-Marie and other missions were attacked by the Iroquois. Father Lalemant, Father Brébeuf, and others suffered the traditional fate of Iroquois prisoners of war—death by torture. Missions collapsed, but Jesuits, to whom martyrdom had great spiritual meaning, now had martyrs for New France. In the 1660s, missions began to be established once again, on the Great Lakes in present-day Wisconsin and New York State.

Madame de la Peltrie, founder of the Ursuline convent *(National Archives of Canada, C-117820)*

The *Jesuit Relations,* the yearly reports of missionaries in New France, was published annually in France from 1632 to 1673. The *Relations* spread awareness of New France and raised extensive financial support for the Jesuits.

NEW FRANCE BECOMES A ROYAL COLONY

After 1660, the Mohawk and other Iroquois began attacks on all French settlements in New France. The fur trade suffered, and agricultural productivity declined; some workers and settlers returned to France. In 1663, King Louis XIV and his minister Jean-Baptiste Colbert, in response to requests from officials and clerics, made New France a royal colony. Royal attention to colonial policy and generous royal financing soon followed. In 1665, the Crown sent the Régiment de Carignan-Salières to the besieged colony. Numbering more than 1,000, they achieved peace with the Iroquois by 1667. After the treaty, New France entered two peaceful decades of growth. The regiment was decommissioned, but its members were strongly encouraged to remain in New France as colonists. Many did, some taking a prominent place in political and social life.

To govern the royal colony, the Crown appointed a governor general, usually of noble birth, to oversee military and diplomatic relations with the Indians and the British. An *intendant* was also appointed. Usually a minor aristocrat, the intendant was the civil administrator of the colony responsible for economic issues and the system of justice; the first was Jean Talon, who arrived in 1665. A council, the Conseil Souverain, was appointed to serve as the colony's high court. In 1666, the first census of New France was conducted. It counted

3,215 French; about one-half in Quebec, 625 in Montreal, and 455 in the third settlement, at Trois-Rivières. The population also included a few Indian women married to Frenchmen and a few immigrants from other European countries. Men outnumbered women by two to one, however. The Crown was determined to see the population increase. France began recruiting female settlers as *filles du roi* (the king's daughters). More than 700 young women arrived in New France over the next decade, their passages and dowries paid by the Crown. Almost all quickly entered into marriages. In 1669, payments were established for families with more than 10 children; in 1670 the parents of unmarried young men over 20 and young women over 16 were fined. By 1670, the population of New France had increased to more than 6,000, primarily by natural increase.

By 1663, 70 seigneuries reached from Quebec to Montreal. In theory, the seigneuries were modeled on the feudal system. The seigneur was to build a large manor on the land as well as a church and other communal buildings, hold court and administer justice, and see to public works and a militia. In practice, few manors were built, and many of the landlords lived in Europe. Landholding was linked to social and political power, however, and was a means of social mobility for some grantees.

For the proprietors of family farms on *rotures,* who were called *habitants,* the seigneurial system had drawbacks. It required them to make yearly payments for their land (called *cens et rentes,* a yearly tax or tribute plus rent) and to provide unpaid labor for public works projects. However, land was abundant. Farmers usually leased 60 arpents of woodland (an arpent is a little less than an acre), clearing a small amount more each year. Wheat was the staple crop. Most farms were self-sufficient, with gardens and livestock for the family's personal use, but they usually produced little surplus. Habitants, or French Canadian farmers, married young and produced large families. Rural children received little education, and literacy actually decreased rapidly during the period.

FUR TRADING IN NEW FRANCE

The economy of New France was based on the fur trade. Unfortunately, European disease followed the French to the New World, and epidemics of measles and smallpox struck their Huron trading partners during the 1630s. Huron numbers were reduced dramatically, probably by half. In the 1640s, the Iroquois began a series of raids and attacks on the northern tribes that lasted more than a decade and resulted in the defeat of the Huron Alliance. By the end of the 1650s, most Huron who had not been killed had been dispersed to other parts of present-day Canada and the United States.

After the defeat of the Huron, certain Iroquois tribes became middlemen to the French, transporting furs from tribes far inland. Fur trade was so vital to New France, however, that French traders also increased their efforts to contact Indian trappers directly. Young men called *coureurs de bois* (literally, runners or couriers of the woods) traveled woodland routes seeking furs. The government strongly discouraged these activities. The term *coureur de bois* originally connoted a semi-illegal trader and was used in the uncomplimentary sense that *gun runner* is used today. Nonetheless, by 1670 coureurs had replaced much of the Indian-organized transport of furs.

In 1654, Médard Chouart des Groseilliers, one of the earliest coureurs de bois, made a voyage across the Michigan peninsula and up the western shore of Lake Michigan. In 1659, at the height of the Iroquois wars, he and Pierre-Espirt Radisson made a successful trading voyage to western Lake Superior. Officials of New France did not welcome their efforts, even fining them, and strongly discouraged their argument that the future of the fur trade lay in Hudson's Bay. Like many New World traders, Groseilliers and Radisson were less interested in political loyalty than in profits. They went to the English, who were eager to expand their fur-trading activities. In 1670, when King Charles II of England granted a royal charter to the Company of Adventurers Trading into Hudson's Bay, the group included Groseilliers and Radisson.

ACADIAN SETTLEMENTS

The territory called Acadia (modern Nova Scotia, Prince Edward Island, New Brunswick, and part of Maine) was strategically located near both the entry to fur-trade country and the Newfoundland fishing banks. Lying between New France and New England, it was claimed by both the French and the British throughout the 17th century.

In 1610, Jean Biencourt de Poutrincourt returned to the abandoned French colony of Port Royal with new financing. Accompanying him were his son Charles Biencourt; Father Jossu La Flèche, a priest whose presence he hoped would forestall Jesuits missionaries; and Claude and Charles de Saint-Etienne de La Tour, a father and son destined to play major roles in Acadia. Poutrincourt was greeted by his old Micmac associate Membertou and found his abandoned settlement, furnishings, and gardens intact. Membertou permitted La Flèche to baptize him and his family, probably as a show of goodwill.

Despite Poutrincourt's objections, the Jesuits soon arrived to establish missions at Port Royal. A power struggle began immediately and concluded with Poutrincourt transported back to France and imprisoned. Meanwhile, a wealthy financial supporter of the Jesuits, the marquise de Guércheville, offered to fund a mission at St.-Saveur on the coast of modern Maine. The Jesuits departed in 1613. Within weeks of their arrival in Maine, Virginia officials sent Captain Samuel Argall to oust the French Catholic intruders, on grounds the territory was within the original Virginia grant. Argall destroyed the mission, killing a priest and several settlers; the rest he imprisoned. Incidentally, he learned of Port Royal—which he also looted and burned. Poutrincourt, released from jail in France, sailed back to Port Royal to find his colony in ruins. He returned permanently to France. His son Biencourt and Charles La Tour remained in Acadia but did not rebuild the settlement. Biencourt died in 1623; La Tour and his Indian wife presided alone over a prosperous fur-trading fort he established at the mouth of the St. John River.

The French claim to Acadia notwithstanding, in 1621 King James I of England made a proprietary grant of territory north of the St. Croix River (the boundary between modern Maine and Canada) to the Scotsman William Alexander. Alexander, later earl of Stirling, named the land Nova Scotiae, or New Scotland. He sent expeditions in 1622 and 1623 and sold the title baronet of Nova Scotia to anyone who agreed to send settlers. In 1627, Alexander's son and the privateer David Kirke established a settlement at the old site of Port

Royal. (Kirke then carried La Tour's father, Claude, back to England, where he married an Englishwoman and obtained the title baronet.) In 1631, however, the Scots settlers were ordered to leave, in accordance with terms of the pending Treaty of Saint-Germain-en-Laye.

In 1632, Isaac de Razilly, a cousin of Richlieu, was sent to repossess Acadia for France, although the Crown had also granted Charles La Tour rights to remain on the St. John River at Fort La Tour. Razilly recruited men, women, children, and Capuchin friars to reestablish Port Royal and communities at La Hève and Penobscot (on the coasts of modern Nova Scotia and Maine). After his death in 1636, his successor, Charles de Menou, sieur d'Aulnay de Charnisay, plunged into a lengthy rivalry with La Tour. La Tour was an adaptable trader; d'Aulnay was a haughty aristocrat. Both, however, were equally ambitious to control the fur trade. In 1638, the French Crown divided Acadia between them. Each man was granted his own settlement; confusingly, each was also granted land surrounding the other's settlement.

La Tour and d'Aulnay continued to battle. La Tour lobbied the newly created Massachusetts colony for military assistance. His remarkable second wife, Françoise-Marie Jacqueline, traveled to France to obtain help. When the French imprisoned her, she escaped to England, raised a ship and supplies, and then sued the English captain of the ship in Boston. She won, sold the captain's cargo, and used funds to buy supplies for Fort La Tour. Finally, she led the soldiers at Fort La Tour when, in her husband's absence, d'Aulnay attacked and overpowered the fort in 1645. d'Aulnay recanted on the terms of surrender and hanged all her soldiers in her presence. Françoise-Marie Jacqueline died d'Aulnay's captive a few months later.

D'Aulnay drowned in 1650. By 1653, La Tour had reobtained the French monopoly on the Acadian fur trade. He had also married d'Aulnay's widow and heir, combining their interests. In 1654, however, New Englanders recaptured Acadia from the French. La Tour sailed to England, where he claimed his father's baronetcy and land grant in Nova Scotia. In 1667, England returned Acadia to France in treaty negotiations—although Acadia still had no definite boundaries.

NEWFOUNDLAND SETTLEMENTS

The idea of an English colony in Newfoundland had remained alive among merchants in London since Gilbert's unsuccessful attempt to found one in 1583. The merchants and fishermen of western England, on the other hand, opposed colonization. Their seasonal fishing voyages were very profitable and attracted almost no interference from the government. They feared that colonization would increase competition and control over the industry. Conflict between London and West Country interests dominated Newfoundland throughout the 17th century. Meanwhile, its rich fishing banks continued to attract fishermen of several nations.

In 1610, John Guy of Bristol brought a group of 38 settlers to Newfoundland, sponsored by a London company. Avoiding the heavily visited harbors, Guy's colonists settled at Cuper's Cove (now Cupids) on the Avalon Peninsula in the southeast corner of the island. The indigenous Beothuk, known for their avoidance of Europeans, moved inland. Although women and children arrived at

Cod fishing in Newfoundland, detail
of a map by Herman Moll (1715)
(Library of Congress)

the colony, the English company apparently lost interest. No records of it exist
after the 1620s.

Several other colonization attempts were made, including one by Sir George
Calvert, later Lord Baltimore, at Ferryland in the 1620s. None prospered, primarily because of continuing hostility from western England fishing interests.
Under their influence, King Charles I issued the Western Charter in 1634. It prohibited permanent settlement within six miles of Newfoundland's shoreline and
gave the captain of the first ship to arrive at harbor authority over all residents
that season. Disregarding his own decree, in 1638 Charles made a grant to David
Kirke, who attempted to renew the settlement at Ferryland. It, too, failed.

Settlers remained in Newfoundland, however, in opposition to royal policy
and without English aid. By midcentury, as many as 2,000 inhabitants, 350 families among them, lived in some 40 communities. No organized government
existed. In the 1660s, after the restoration of Charles II to the throne of England, following the English Civil War Kirke requested a renewal of his grant
while the west England interests asked for a renewal of the Western Charter.
Meanwhile, France founded a settlement at Placentia in 1662.

CHRONICLE OF EVENTS

1607

Pierre de Gua, sieur de Monts, evacuates Port Royal, Acadia, the only existing French settlement in North America, when his fur-trade monopoly is canceled.

1608

The Council of the Indies announces that Florida and New Mexico are to be maintained as Spanish colonies.

De Monts obtains a renewal of his monopoly. Samuel de Champlain suggests founding a colony at Quebec.

July 3: Samuel de Champlain arrives at Quebec with 28 workmen.

1609

July 30: Champlain accompanies the Huron Alliance to make war on the Iroquois Confederacy. At Lake Champlain they engage the Mohawk, who probably have never seen European firearms in battle. Champlain wins a decisive victory, gaining the enmity of the Iroquois.

November 1: New Mexico becomes a royal colony under direct control of the Spanish crown. Governor Don Pedro de Peralta arrives at San Gabriel with settlers and Franciscan missionaries.

1610

Peralta founds Santa Fe. The Franciscans establish ecclesiastical headquarters at Santo Domingo.

Jean Biencourt de Poutrincourt and his son Charles Biencourt reestablish Port Royal.

John Guy of Bristol founds Cuper's Cove (Cupids) in Newfoundland, which lasts through the 1620s.

1612

New Franciscan missionaries arrive in Florida; soon, 20 new missions are established. Father Francisco de Pereja's first book written in the Timucuan language is published in Mexico.

The defeat of the Iroquois, 1609, drawn by Samuel de Champlain *(National Archives of Canada, C-009711)*

Struggles for power between civil and ecclesiastical authorities begin in New Mexico; they will continue through the 1670s.

1613

French Jesuits found a mission at St.-Saveur, Maine. Within weeks, Samuel Argall, commissioned by the English governor of Virginia, attacks and destroys it as well as Port Royal. Poutrincourt will return permanently to France; Biencourt remains in Acadia.

1615

Recollect friars initiate missionary activity in New France.

1620s

The Iroquois intensify their trade with the Dutch in the Hudson Valley, obtaining firearms from them.

1621

King James I of England grants part of Acadia to Scotsman William Alexander, which he names Nova Scotiae, or New Scotland.

1623

Biencourt dies; Charles La Tour presides over French Acadia and its fur trade.

Sir George Calvert, later Lord Baltimore, obtains a charter from King James I to found a settlement in Newfoundland.

1625

Father Alonso de Benavides arrives in New Mexico as the Franciscan custodio. He will publish a famous report about the Spanish settlements, conduct the Inquisition, and investigate Indian claims of the appearance of María de Agreda, the Lady in Blue.

Jesuits replace the Recollects in New France.

1627

The Company of 100 Associates is organized by French minister Cardinal Richelieu to oversee the management of New France.

Alexander's son establishes a settlement at Nova Scotiae.

1628

Dutch pirate Piet Heyn captures the Spanish treasure fleet in the Caribbean.

English privateer David Kirke arrives at St. Lawrence River and turns back ships carrying new settlers and supplies for Quebec.

George Calvert, Lord Baltimore, arrives in Newfoundland but soon abandons his settlement.

1629

The Timucua rebel in eastern Florida.

Champlain surrenders his starving colony at Quebec to the English.

1630s

Franciscans begin a new wave of mission building, extending into Apalachee territory in western Florida in 1633.

1631

English king Charles I orders Scots settlers to leave Nova Scotiae.

1632

By the treaty of Saint-Germain-en-Laye, England returns New France and Acadia to France. Settlers and Jesuits return to Quebec. Isaac de Razilly is sent to Acadia; Charles La Tour is also granted fur-trade rights.

The annual *Jesuit Relations* begins publication in France.

1632

A rebellion at Zuni Pueblo in New Mexico marks the beginning of two decades of sporadic rebellion in several pueblos.

1634

The first seigneurie, or large semifeudal land grant, is made in New France.

Father Brébeuf and other Jesuits begin missionary work in the Canadian wilderness.

Under pressure from English fishermen, King Charles I issues the Western Charter, prohibiting settlement in Newfoundland within six miles of the shore.

1635

The Jesuits open a college in Quebec.

December 25: Champlain dies.

1636

Sieur d'Aulnay replaces Razilly in Acadia and begins a struggle for power with La Tour.

1637

A struggle for power between Governor Luis de Rosas and Franciscan custodio Juan de Salas brings New Mexico to the brink of civil war.

1638

The Apalachee rebel in Florida.

The French Crown divides Acadia and its fur trade between La Tour and D'Aulnay.

1639

At Taos Pueblo, Indians begin a rebellion in which two priests are killed and the church is burned. Many Indians later escape to modern Kansas.

Two orders of nuns, the Ursulines and the Hospitalières, arrive in Quebec.

Father Lalement builds Ste.-Marie, a Huron mission on Georgian Bay.

1640s

Cattle ranching begins in central Florida.

The Iroquois begin attacks on the Huron; within a decade, the Huron are defeated and dispersed.

1642

Montreal is founded by the Society of Notre Dame, a group of French religious mystics.

1643

Iroquois begin attacks on Montreal, which will last until the 1660s.

1644

In New Mexico, a rebellion occurs at Jemez Pueblo.

1645

In Acadia, D'Aulnay attacks and captures La Tour's settlement.

1647

In New Mexico, a second rebellion occurs at Jemez Pueblo.

The Apalachee rebel again in Florida.

The Council of Quebec is established with two elected representatives.

1648

Ste.-Marie is attacked and destroyed by the Iroquois; Fathers Lalement and Brébeuf and others suffer death by torture. Missions in New France are abandoned until the 1660s.

1650s

Coureurs de bois begin to increase in number in New France, searching for sources of fur. By 1670, they will have replaced much Indian-organized transport of furs.

1650

In New Mexico, rebellions occur in Tewa pueblos.

The English capture Jamaica from the Spanish.

In Acadia, D'Aulnay dies; La Tour again obtains the French fur-trade monopoly.

1654

New Englanders recapture Acadia for England.

1656

The Timucua rebel in Florida.

1657

England returns Acadia to France.

1659

François de Laval, the first bishop of New France, arrives; he will exert great influence in civil and religious life.

Marguerite Bourgeoys establishes the Congrégation de Notre-Dame in Montreal; the order of nuns is the first new religious community to be established in Canada.

1660s

New Mexico suffers a serious drought.

The Mohawk and other Iroquois begin attacks on all French settlements in New France.

1662

The French establish a settlement at Placentia, Newfoundland.

1663

New France is made a royal colony by King Louis XIV.

1665

The Régiment de Carignan-Salières arrives in Quebec with more than 1,000 troops to protect the colony from the Iroquois. The *filles du roi,* marriageable young women, also begin arriving.

1666

The first official census of New France is taken; the French population is 3,215.

1667

The Iroquois agree to a peace treaty with New France, opening two decades of growth for the colony.

Acadia is returned to France by the Treaty of Breda.

1668

English pirate Robert Searles sacks St. Augustine; the Spanish Crown soon sends officials and workers to prepare for building a new fort to protect Florida from the English.

In New France Bishop Laval founds a seminary to train priests; it will become a university.

1669

To encourage the increase of population in New France, monetary bonuses are granted for large families.

1670

The English found Charleston, South Carolina, well into territory the Spanish consider to be part of Florida.

English king Charles II grants a royal charter to the Hudson's Bay Company for a large area of northern Canada.

Parents of unmarried men (over 20) and women (over 16) are fined in New France to encourage marriage and population growth.

EYEWITNESS TESTIMONY

After arming ourselves with light armor, we each took an arquebus and went on shore. I saw the enemy [*the Iroquois*] go out of their barricade, nearly two hundred in number, stout and rugged in appearance. They came at a slow pace toward us, with a dignity and assurance which greatly amused me, having three chiefs at their head. Our men also advanced in the same order, telling me that those who had three large plumes were the chiefs . . . and that I should do what I could to kill them. . . .

As soon as we had landed, they began to run for some two hundred paces toward their enemies, who stood firmly. . . . I marched some twenty paces in advance of the rest, until I was within about thirty paces of the enemy, who at once noticed me and, halting, gazed at me, as I did also at them.

When I saw them making a move to fire at us, I rested my musket against my cheek and aimed directly at one of the three chiefs. With the same shot, two fell to the ground; and one of their men was so wounded that he died soon after. . . .

The Iroquois were greatly astonished that two men had been so quickly killed, although they were equipped with armor woven from cotton thread and with wood which was proof against their arrows. This caused great alarm among them.

. . . they lost courage, and took to flight, abandoning their camp and fort, and fleeing into the woods.

Samuel de Champlain describes the battle at Lake Champlain, July 1609, in Norman, Discoverers, *pp. 256–57.*

Upon your first arrival there [*Newfoundland*] the sooner to operate our patent and to prevent ye murmuring of suspicious and jealous persons that perhaps will not [fail] to spread abroad that this enterprise will be to the prejudice of ye fishermen as well of our nation as others. We do hold it expedient that you call an assembly of all the fishermen that shall be here thereabouts and there in their presence openly and distinctly cause to be read the grant under the King's Majesties great seal which you shall have along with you, that by the tenor of it they may be satisfied that there is no intent of depriving them of their former right of fishing which being done you shall declare in the presence of them all that you enter upon that place to take actual seizin and possession (never by grace and assistance of God to be discounted) in ye name of the whole country comprehended within the said grant. . . .

"Instructions to John Guy from the Associates of His Company," 1610, quoted in Prowse, History *p. 95.*

As to the country [*Acadia*], I have never seen anything so beautiful, better, or more fertile; and I can say to you, truly and honestly, that if I had three or four labourers with me now, and the means of supporting them for one year, and some wheat to sow in the ground tilled by their labour alone, I should expect to have a yearly trade in Beaver and other Skins amounting to seven or eight thousand livres, with the surplus which would remain to me after their support. . . . I assure you it is delightful to engage in trade over here and to make such handsome profits. If you wish to take a hand in it, let me know your intentions by the bearer, who desires to return and traffic here in pursuance of what he has seen.

Sieur Bertrand, letter to his brother in France, 1610, quoted in Jones, Gentlemen and Jesuits, *p. 146.*

Now, for the present, there is no need of any learned Doctors [*Jesuits*] who may be more useful in combating vices and heresies at home. Besides, there is a certain class of men in whom we cannot have complete confidence, who are in the habit of censuring everything that is not in harmony with their maxims, and wish to rule wherever they are. It is enough to be watched from abroad without having these fault-finders, from whom even the greatest Kings cannot defend themselves, come near enough to record every movement of our hearts and souls.

Marc Lescarbot, La conversion des Sauvages, *1610, quoted in Jones,* Gentlemen and Jesuits, *p. 157.*

The city of St. Augustine lies near the sea at the water's edge; it contains over 300 Spanish residents, who are all married soldiers living there as a garrison. The city is well built of stone, with friars, who are almost all evangelizing the Indians in their villages. There is a hospital to care for the indigent sick, a shrine to Santa Barbara, and a fort with some 25 excellent bronze cannon. His Majesty appoints a Governor, who is Captain General, and two Royal Officials.

The city lies full 30° N.; its climate is like that of Spain, with winter and summer; the country is fertile, level, and wooded, with some swamps. Spanish fruit trees bear with great abundance, as of cereals, garden truck, and vegetables; they grow excellent quinces, pomegranates, pears, and other kinds of fruit, and marvelous melons. There are many districts converted to the Faith; the Indians are very good Christians and devout. One league from the city lies the village of San Sebastián, and there are other villages, like Ais, Moloa, Matacumba, and others. . . .

Antonio Vasquez Espinosa, Compendium and Description of the West Indies, *1612, in Quinn,* North American Discovery, *pp. 182–83.*

Do not be deceived. Let no one persuade himself with vain words that I do not have the same power and authority that the Pope in Rome has, or that if his Holiness were here in New Mexico he could do more than I. Believe you that I can arrest, cast into irons, and punish as seems fitting to me any person without exception who is not obedient to the commandments of the church and mine. What I have told you, I say for the benefit of a certain person [the governor] who is listening to me who perhaps raises his eyebrows.

Father Isidro Ordóñez to the congregation at Santa Fe, July 1613, quoted in Kessell, Kiva, *p. 97.*

But most unexpectedly, by some hazard or other (for a hazard it certainly was, and not a premeditated plan), some English from Virginia [*Argall's men*] were driven upon our shores, who attacked our ships with the utmost fury, at a time when nearly all its defenders were occupied on land. Resistance was nevertheless made for a time, but we were soon obliged to surrender. In the struggle, two of the French were killed, four were wounded; and in addition our brother Gilbert Duthet received a mortal wound. He made a most Christian end, the following day, under my ministration.

Our ships having been captured and everything pillaged, it was a great concession to us,—that is, to us priests and Jesuits,—that we were not killed. And yet this sparing of our lives, if considered in itself only, would have been worse than any death. For what were we to do in an absolutely desert and barren region [*St. Saveur, Maine*] despoiled and destitute of everything? The savages, indeed, used to come to us stealthily and by night; and with great generosity and devotion commiserated our misfortune, and promised us whatever they could. Truly the condition of things was such that either death itself or a more calamitous misfortune, everywhere threatened us. There were in all thirty of us in these distressing circumstances. One consideration

rendered the English less severe, namely, that one of our boats had escaped, in spite of their watchfulness; and as they had no doubt that it would bear witness to the violence done us, they were obliged to spare our lives, for they feared reprisals and dreaded our king.

Father Pierre Baird, letter to Rome, May 26, 1614, in Tyler, ed., Narratives, *pp. 228–29.*

With ease many [*Florida*] Indian men and women have learned to read in less than two months, and they write letters to one another in their own language.

Father Luís de Oré describes the effect of Pareja's dictionary, 1616, quoted in Gannon, Cross, *p. 53.*

1. That those of the Plantations there [*settlers in Newfoundland*] have put sundry of the Petitioners from the chiefest places of fishing there and disposed of the same to such as pleased them.

2. That they have taken away great quantities of salt, casks, boats, stages [*frames for drying fish*] and other provisions there let by the Petitioners and converted the same to their own use.

3. That they have denied . . . the Petitioners from taking birds upon the Island of Baccaleau, the flesh of which birds the Petitioners have heretofore used for bait. . . .

4. That in the chiefest time of fishing those in the said Plantation have summoned a Court of Admiralty and exacted fees of train [*oil from sea mammals*] and fish for not appearing.

5. That those of said Plantation have harbored pirates there and dealt with them which hath been the means to induce them to frequent that place to the great prejudice and hindrance of the Petitioners.

Petition of West Country fishermen to the Crown, December 1618, in Prowse, History, *p. 100.*

I have noticed that before the anathema was read to this simple folk they did not have the fear concerning the use of these powders and herbs which they now so truly show. Their hearts are agitated, and they are afraid.

Father Estéban de Perea, agent of the New Mexico Inquistion, 1620s, quoted in Scholes, "First Decade," New Mexico Historical Review, *vol. 19, p. 217.*

For addition of building [*at Ferryland*], we have at this present a Parlor of fourteen foot besides the chimney, and twelve foot broad, of convenient height, and a lodging chamber over it; to each a chimney of stone work with stairs and a stairs case, besides a tenement of two rooms, or a story and a half, which serves for a store house till we are other wise provided. The Forge hath been finished this five weeks: the Salt-works is now almost ready. Notwithstanding this great task for so few hands, we have both Wheat, Barley, Oates, Peas, and Beans about the quantity of two acres. Of Garden room about half an acres: the corn though late sown is now in earing; the Beans and the goodliest Peas that I ever saw, have flourished in their blooms this twenty days. We have a plentiful kitchen garden of Lettice, Raddish, Carrots, Coleworts, Turnips and many other things. We also have at this present a flourishing meadow of at least three Acres, with many hay-cocks of exceeding good hay. . . . We have also broken ground for a Brew-house and other Tenements. We have a wharf in good forwardness towards the low water mark.

Edward Wynne to Sir George Calvert, July 28, 1622, in Prowse, History, p. 128.

Those flies seem to have a great power and authority upon all loitering people that come to the Newfoundland; for they have the property, that when they find any such lying lazily, or sleeping in the Woods, they will presently be more nimble to seize upon them, than any Sergeant will be to arrest a man for debt; neither will they leave stinging or sucking out the blood of such sluggards, until like a beadle they bring him to his Master, where he should labor; in which time of loitering those flies will so brand such idle persons in their faces, that they may be known from others as the Turks do their slaves.

Sir Richard Whitbourne, 1623, Discourse, quoted in Prowse, History, pp. 117–18.

Permit for Juan Fulano to take one orphan from wherever he finds him, provided that he treats him well and teaches him the Christian catechism.

Full text of a vale, *or permit, to seize an orphaned Pueblo child, signed by New Mexico governor Don Juan de Eulate, December 1623, quoted in Kessell, Kiva, p. 107.*

Trees all in bud, cherries leafed out, and wheat a span high. The raspberries put forth their leaves, the chevril is ready to cut; in the woods, sorrel two inches high many be seen. . . .

The birches open their leaves, and the other trees follow them close; the oak buds swell and the apple trees transplanted from France and the wild plums bud out; cherry trees have quite large leaves, grapevines budding and flowering; sorrel ready to cut. . . . Violets white and yellow are in flower, maize being sown, wheat a little over a span high. Most of the plants and herbs are above ground; some days of the month were very hot. . . .

Strawberries begin to blossom, and the oaks to unfurl their leaves.

Samuel de Champlain's nature journal, May 15, 18, and 29, 1624, in Morison, Champlain, p. 182.

I have become a teacher in Canada: the other day I had a little Savage on one side of me, and a little Negro or Moor on the other, to whom I taught their letters. After so many years of teaching, behold me at last returned to the A, B, C., with so great content and satisfaction that I would not exchange my two pupils for the finest audience in France. This little Savage is the one who will soon be left entirely with us. The little Negro was left by the English with this French family which is here. We have taken him to teach and baptize, but he does not yet understand the language well: therefore we shall wait some time yet. When we talked to him about baptism, he made us laugh. His mistress asking him if he wanted to be a Christian, if he wanted to be baptized and be like us, he said "yes;" but he asked if he would not be skinned in being baptized. I think he was very much frightened, for he had seen those poor Savages skinned. As he saw that they laughed at his questions, he replied in his patois, as best he could: "You say that by baptism I shall be like you: I am black and you are white, I must have my skin taken off then in order to be like you." There upon all began to laugh more than ever, and, seeing that he was mistaken, he joined in and laughed with the others. . . .

Jesuit Father Paul Le Jeune teaches the first known African slave sold in Canada, 1632, in Thwaites, ed., Jesuit Relations, vol. 5, pp. 63–65.

1st. If any man kill another or steal to value of forty shillings to be brought to prison to England & if proved by two witnesses—delinquent to suffer death.

2. No ballast to be thrown out to prejudice of harbor.

3. That no person deface or spoil any stage [*platform for drying fish*], Cookroom &c.

4. That such ship as first entereth a harbor shall be admiral—wherein for time being he shall reserve only so much beach & flakes [*drying frame*] as is needful for number of boats as he shall use, with overplus only for one boat, as privilege for his first coming, after content themselves with what he shall have use for with keeping more to the prejudice of others next coming—any that possess several places in several harbors with intent to keep all before they can resolves which to choose shall be bound to resolve and send advice to such aftercomers & within 48 Hours if the weather so serve, said aftercomers may likewise choose—so none receive prejudice by others delays. . . .

6. That no person steal any fish, train [*oil*], or salt or any other provision belonging to fishing ships.

7. That no person set fire to the woods or rind the trees except for Cookrooms. . . .

9. That no person rob the net of others out of any drift boat.

10. That no person set up any tavern for selling wine, beer, strong waters, cider, or tobacco.—by such means fishermen neglect their labors, and spend wages upon which their wives and children depend they are likewise hurtful in many other way—men make themselves hurtful by purloining and stealing from others.

11. On Sunday Divine service to be said by some of the Masters of ships, such prayers as are in Book of Common prayer.

Charles I's Newfoundland fishing regulations, January 22, 1633, in Prowse, History, *p. 154.*

But we soon noticed that the great care and solicitude with which the Xumana Indians came to us every summer to plead for friars to go and baptize them must have been through inspiration from heaven. . . . We called them to the convent and asked them their motive in coming every year to ask for baptism with such insistency. Gazing at a portrait of Mother Luisa in the convent, they said: A woman in similar garb wanders among us over there, always preaching, but her face is not old like this, but young." Asked why they had not told us before, they answered, "Because you did not ask us, and we thought she was around here, too." . . .

The friars, although they did not see the nun [*María de Jesús, the Lady in Blue*] there, learned accurately from all the Indians how she had appeared visibly to everyone and had instructed them in their own tongue and reproved them for being lazy because they did not come to seek us. At that very moment, there came ambassadors from other neighboring nations, such as the Quiviras and Xapies, also pleading for baptism, because the same nun had preached to them. . . .

When I arrived in Spain in 1630, the most reverend general of the order . . . gave me a special permit to visit her personally at Agreda. . . . She convinced me absolutely by describing to me all the things in New Mexico as I have seen them myself. . . . Consequently, I have no doubts in this matter whatsoever.

Father Alonso de Benavides, 1634, Revised Memorial, *pp. 94–95.*

It is requested that the Spanish governors [*of New Mexico*] be forbidden to issue warrants or permits to take Indian boys or girls from the pueblos on the pretext that they are orphans, and take them to serve permanently in the houses of the Spaniards where they remain as slaves. As a matter of fact, the orphans are well cared for at the homes of their grandparents or other relatives where they are brought up as if they were their own children. In case there should be any one without a home, the governor should not issue warrants without the consent of the ecclesiastical minister, who lives alone with the Indians and knows their needs and relieves them as much as he is able. This must be done so that the destitute Indian orphans may live freely with their relatives. The governors often take from the Spaniards some Indians who are serving the Spaniards well, in order to keep them for themselves. They take them without compensation, or, in payment, give them a permit to go to the pueblos to look for other boys and girls and to take them by force.

It is requested that the Indians taken in wars, whatever their nation, may not be given as slaves or sentenced to personal service outside of New Mexico. . . . On the contrary, they should be placed in convents of the friars or in houses of Spaniards or Indians of exemplary conduct so that they may be taught our holy Catholic faith with all kindness. . . .

Father Alonso de Benavides to the king of Spain; the royal order was issued January 30, 1635, in Benavides, Revised Memorial, *p. 171.*

The friars suffer greatly in this mission field [*Florida*]. They must walk barefoot in this cold land when going about from mission to mission. The Indians are very widely scattered about in forty-four doctrinas. For this great number there are only thirty-five religious [*friars*].

Many times it is necessary for a missionary to walk eight or ten leagues to hear a confession. All of which sufferings are augmented by the fact that the missionaries get very little aid in the form of assistants who might lighten some of their burdens. Some of the priests, being so overburdened with work and seeing so many Indians without hope of converting them, become discouraged and return to Spain.

Father Francisco Alonzo de Jesús to the king of Spain, 1635, quoted in Gannon, Cross, p. 54.

From the moment he [*Francisco de la Mora Ceballos*] became governor [*of New Mexico*] he had attended only to his own profit, causing grave damage to all these recently converted souls. He has commanded them to weave and paint great quantities of mantas and hangings. Likewise he had made them seek out and barter for many tanned skins and haul quantities of piñon nuts. As a result he has now loaded eight carretas with what he has amassed and is taking them and as many men from here to drive them to new Spain, thwarting everything His Majesty has ordered in his royal ordinance.

New Mexico, detail of a map by Philip Lea (1685) *(Library of Congress)*

Thus, not since this governor took office, has a single pueblo been baptized, He has refused to lend support to the Faith. Instead he has sought in every way to insult with the ugliest words every minister His Majesty employs here in his royal service converting the natives. Likewise he has sought by force and violence to use the citizens of the villa of Santa Fe and its cabildo, because they are poor people, to make utterly untrue reports against the religious of these provinces solely to discredit us with Your Excellency.

Antonio de Ibargaray, a Franciscan messenger, to the Viceroy of Mexico, November 1636, quoted in Scholes, Church and State, pp. 287–88.

. . . the religious [*Franciscans*] are masters of the resources of the land and they proceed without a civil judge. The ecclesiastical one they do have here is for throwing the cloak over their faults. The faults they possess in this kingdom are not heard beyond this land, and they are not punished with more than a reprimand, if by chance one is handed down, and that does not hurt them in the slightest. In this way they are masters of the land and of its assets.

Francisco Gómez, a wealthy New Mexican settler, to the viceroy of Mexico, October 1638, quoted in Kessell, Kiva, p. 159.

I have also been informed that the said Kerqs [*David Kirke and his brothers*] have a patent from the King of Great Britain to collect something on the cod fishery and that they propose to take this not only from British subjects but also from all who go there to fish. This will be contrary to all justice and to the freedom which has been enjoyed there up to this time. I surmise that the King of Britain does not know what has been done and that no one but his own subjects will submit to this.

Pompone de Bellièvre, Seigneur de Grignon, French ambassador to King Charles I, May 16, 1639, quoted in Prowse, History, p. 148.

. . . a narrative of New France, which spoke forcibly of the Isle of Montreal as being the best place in the country for the establishment of a mission and meeting place for the savages, . . . fortunately came into the hands of M. de la Dauversière, a person of outstanding piety, who was in the first place much touched in reading it, and was later even more affected, since God gave him so plain a picture of this place that he described it to everyone in a way that left no doubt that there was something extraordinary in it. . . . He described the beauty and richness of its soil, the length and breadth of its different parts. Finally he talked so familiarly about it that . . . the reverend Father Chauveau . . . told him that God had caused him to know this island, revealing it to him as the scene of the work to which he ought to devote his efforts, and thus aid in the conversion of the savages, by the means of a fine French colony which could give them a taste of a more civilised life. Yet whilst he saw what he ought to do, he wished the Father to say whether he believed it was from God or no. This father, enlightened from above, and convinced by what he had heard, replied: "Have no doubts on the subject; work at it in earnest."

François Dollier de Casson, a Sulpician missionary in Canada, before 1642, History of Montreal, *pp. 62–63.*

About thirty-five persons of condition have joined together to labor for the conversion of the poor Savages of New France, and to endeavor to gather a goodly number of them on the Island of Montreal, which they have chosen as a suitable place for their object. Their intention is to have houses built, in which to lodge them; to till the soil, in order to feed them; to establish Seminaries for their instruction, and a Hotel-Dieu for succoring their sick. All these Gentlemen and Ladies met together one Thursday, toward the end of the month of February of this year, 1642, at ten o'clock in the morning, in the Church of Notre Dame at Paris, before the Altar of the Blessed Virgin. . . . They also consecrated themselves, and joined in a participation of prayers and good works; so that, being animated by one and the same spirit, they may labor more sincerely for the glory of God and for the salvation of those poor peoples. . . .

Jesuit Father Barthélemy Vimont, 1642, in Thwaites, ed., Jesuit Relations, *vol. 22, p. 209.*

On the fifteenth of August was celebrated the first Festival of this Holy Isle [*Montreal*], the day of the glorious and triumphant Assumption of the Blessed Virgin. The fine tabernacle sent out by the Gentlemen was placed upon the Altar of a Chapel which, as yet, is built only of bark, but which is none the less valuable. . . . After the instruction given to the Savages, there was a fine Procession after Vespers, in which those good people took part,—quite astonished at seeing so pious a ceremony, at which we did not omit to pray to God for

the King, for the Queen, for their little Princes, and for the whole of their Empire. This the Savages did with much affection. And thus did we unite our desires with all those of France.

After the Festival, we visited the great forest which covers this Island; and when we had been led to the mountain from which it takes its name, two of the chief Savages of the band stopped on its summit, and told us that they belonged to the nation of those who had formerly dwelt on this Island. Then, stretching out their hands towards the hills that lie to the East and South of the mountain. "There," said they, "are the places where stood Villages filled with great numbers of Savages. The Hurons, who then were our enemies, drove our Forefathers from this country."

Father Barthélemy Vimont, 1642, in Thwaites, ed., Jesuit Relations, *vol. 22, pp. 203–215.*

The governor and assistants [*of Massachusetts*] met at Boston, to consider what might lawfully be done for saving La Tour and his fort out of the hands of D'Aulnay. . . . So soon as we were met, word was brought to us, that a vessel sent by some merchants to carry provisions to La Tour was fallen into the hands of D'Aulnay, who had made prize of her, and turned the men upon an island, and kept them there ten days, and then gave them an old shallop (not above two tons) and some provisions to bring them home, but denied them their clothes, etc. . . . and any guns or compass, whereby it was justly conceived that he intended they should perish, either at sea, or by the Indians (who were at hand, and chased them next day, etc.). Upon this news we presently dispatched away a vessel to D'Aulnay with letters, wherein we expostulated with him about this act of his, complaining of it as a breach of the articles of our peace, and required the vessel and goods to be restored, or satisfaction for them. We gave answer also to some charges he laid upon us in a very high language, as if we had hired the ships which carried home the lady La Tour . . . which caused us to answer him accordingly, that he might see we took notice of his proud terms, and were not afraid of him. And whereas he oft threatened us with the king of France his power, etc., we answered that we did acknowledge him to be a mighty prince . . . yet New England had a God, who was able to save us, and did not use to forsake his servants.

John Winthrop's journal, 1645, in Winthrop, History, *vol. 2, p. 267.*

To say . . . that they were Merchants of London, whom you cannot hinder from trading with whom they please, this were good, if we did not well know, that La Tour, being worth nothing, and altogether unknown to your said Merchants, they would never trust such persons, if you (or) other Gentlemen were not his security. Moreover, that persons who desire peace with their Neighbors, as you say you do, would have hindered such proceedings if they had pleased, it being easily done in such places, as we are in. . . . . To say that your English, who have done such acts of hostility, were not sent by you; pardon me, Sir, if you please, if I will tell you this is the mocking of a Gentleman to render such answers.

Charles, sieur d'Aulnay complains to Massachusetts officials, March 1645, quoted in Mahaffie, Land of Discord, *p. 80.*

During the first war with the Hiroquois, there was in Montreal a [female dog], which never failed to go scouting every day, taking her little ones with her; and if any one of them acted stubbornly, she would bite it, to make it go on. Nay, more, if one of the pups turned back in the midst of its run, she would fall upon it at her return, as if by way of punishment. Moreover, if she scented, while on the patrol, some Hiroquois, she would turn short, moving directly homeward, barking, and announcing that the enemy was not far, away. Her natural inclination was for hunting squirrels; but her constancy in making the round every day as faithfully as men, beginning now on one side, now on the other; her perseverance in directing her little ones, and in punishing them when they failed to follow; and her fidelity in turning short, when the scent of the enemies caught her sense of smell,—all these caused astonishment.

Father Jérôme Lalemant, Jesuit Relation of 1647, in Thwaites, ed., Jesuit, *vol. 32, pp. 27–28.*

As soon as they were taken captive, they were stripped naked, and some of their nails were torn out—, and the welcome which they received upon entering the village of St. Ignace was a hail-storm of blows with sticks upon their shoulders, their loins, their legs, their breasts, their bellies, and their faces,—there being no part of their bodies which did not then endure its torment. Father Jean de Brebeuf, overwhelmed under the burden of these blows, did not on that account lose care for his flock; seeing himself surrounded with Christians

whom he had instructed, and who were in captivity with him, he said to them: "My children, let us lift our eyes to Heaven at the height of our afflictions; let us remember that God is the witness of our sufferings, and will soon be our exceeding great reward. Let us die in this faith; and let us hope from his goodness the fulfillment of his promises. I have more pity for you than for myself; but sustain with courage the few remaining torments. They will end with our lives; the glory which follows them will never have an end." "Echon," they said to him (this is the name which the Hurons gave the father), "our spirits will be in Heaven when our bodies shall be suffering on earth. Pray to God for us, that he may show us mercy; we will invoke him even until death."

Some Huron infidels—former captives of the Iroquois, naturalized among them, and former enemies of the Faith—were irritated by these words, and because our Fathers in their captivity had not their tongues captive. They cut off the hands of one, and pierced the other with sharp awls and iron points; they apply under their armpits and upon their loins hatchets heated red in the fire, and put a necklace of these about their necks in such a way that all the motions of their bodies gave them a new torture. For, if they attempted to lean forward, the red-hot hatchets which hung behind them burned the shoulders every where; and if they thought to avoid that pain, bending back a little, their stomachs and breasts experienced a similar torment; if they stood upright, without leaning to one side or the other, these glowing hatchets, touching them alike on all sides, were a double torture to them. They put about them belts of bark, filled with pitch and resin, to which they set fire, which scorched the whole of their bodies.

At the height of these torments, Father Gabriel Lallemant lifted his eyes to Heaven, clasping his hands from time to time, and uttering sighs to God, whom he invoked to his aid. Father Jean de Brebeuf suffered like a rock, insensible to the fires and the flames, without uttering any cry, and keeping a profound silence, which astonished his executioners themselves; no doubt, his heart was then reposing in his God. Then, returning to himself, he preached to those Infidels, and still more to many good Christian captives, who had compassion on him.

Those butchers, indignant at his zeal, in order to hinder him from further speaking of God, girdled his mouth, cut off his nose, and tore off his lips; but his blood spoke much more loudly than his lips had done; and, his heart not yet being torn out, his tongue did not fail to render him service until the last sign, for blessing God for these torments, and for animating the Christians more vigorously than he had ever done.

Father Paul Ragueneau, March 1649, in Thwaites, ed.,
Jesuit Relations, vol. 34, pp. 141–46.

A lay sister novice who had charge of making the bread [*at the Ursuline convent in Quebec*], fearing that the dough might freeze, had put lighted coals in the bread trough and then carefully covered it. Since this was not customary, no one was aware of what she had done. This poor girl who had intended to remove the charcoal forgot about it so that at midnight, the fire having kindled the wood in the trough, which was made of pine, a highly flammable substance, spread everywhere, even into the cellars which in this country are not vaulted.

The bakery was in one of these and our offices were just above it. Our provisions for the whole year were down these, both those which had come from France—lard, oil, butter, brandy for our servants—and domestic products such as fish, etc. When the fire had consumed everything down there, it rose to the ceilings which were double with earth packed between them. Had not one of the mistresses of the children been sleeping in this area and heard the crackling and noise of the fire, we would all have been destroyed by the fire within half an hour. The fire had already broken through and the place was collapsing and about to fall. She woke the children—there was a sizable number of them—then came to the sister's dormitory, then ran back to the children whom she and some other sisters had difficulty in saving. The sisters saved themselves for the most part only half dressed, not having had time to take along their footwear.

I was only able to throw out the window some community papers that had been in my keeping along with some little boxes I found at hand. The few minutes it took me to do this saved my life. I was already on my way upstairs to my office to throw a bolt of fabric out that window, sure that my sisters had left their habits in their cells in order to save themselves, when I thought better of it. Had I gone up there I would surely have perished, for in less time than it takes to say a *Miserere* all the corridors were aflame. I was the last one to leave the house, caught between two fires. I had hardly left my room which was situated right under the convent bell, when the bell crashed. As I tried to save myself, the fire swept after me. I escaped, as had some others who preceded me, through the grille which fortunately, being constructed of wood, had been broken. Our parlor was at the end of our dormitory. As I emerged, I was bewildered to see the danger we had run—another sister and I. The whole length of the rood was on fire, for in this country all the boards are made of pine while the framework is constructed of dry wood and gum.

I found our poor community in the snow, as quiet and controlled as though nothing had happened, gazing at this pitiful sight as they prayed. Some were standing in the snow in bare feet. Those who had shoes or slippers insisted on giving them to their companions. It was a moving sight. Someone who was watching the sisters said aloud that either they must be crazy or they must have a profound love of God to be so detached in losing everything, seeing ourselves within a few minutes reduced to nothing in the snow. This good

Mère Marie of the Incarnation *(National Archives of Canada, C-008070/C-139973)*

man did not understand the strength of the grace with which our good Jesus filled our hearts.

Mother Marie describes the convent fire of 1650, "Relation of 1654," in Marie de l'Incarnation, Mère, Marie of the Incarnation, *Mahoney, ed., pp. 163–64.*

The hostility of the Iroquois is not what holds us back. There are some who consider this country to be lost, but I do not see that we have so much to fear on that score as, I am told from France, people of our sex and condition have to fear from French soldiers. I tremble at what I have been told. The Iroquois are barbarians, but they certainly do not deal with persons of our sex as I am told the French have done. Those who have lived among them have told me that they never resort to violence and that they leave free those who do not want to consent to them.

Mother Marie to her son, September 9, 1652, in Marie de l'Incarnation, Mère, Marie of the Incarnation, *Mahoney, ed., pp. 247–248.*

Seigneur de la Tour, knight of the king's orders, and his lieutenant general in Acadie, a country of New France, of the one part, and the lady Jeane Motin, widow of the late monsieur Charles de Menou, knight, seigneur d'Aulnay, in his lifetime, also lieutenant general for the king, in all the said country of Acadie, of the other part. Firstly, the said seigneur chevalier de la Tour shall take for his wife and lawful spouse, madame d'Aulnay, with all her rights and effects, which rights the said seigneur, the future husband, consents shall be separated from their future community . . . until the entire payment of debts created in the lifetime of the said late seigneur d'Aulnay, and since his decease until the present hour . . . after which payment and the last sou of all the debts, she shall take her part of the property of the association at *pro rata* of that which shall belong to her, and which she shall have thereto contributed of her rights and pretensions, which shall then come into their said future community. . . . Thereof Monsieur de la Tour now declares that he will not receive, or interfere with anything of the said rights and property of the said madame d'Aulnay, his future wife, until the full payment of the general debts of the society. . . . The said seigneur de la Tour has endowed, and does endow the said lady, his future spouse, for her lifetime only, with the property of the said fort and habitation of the river St. John, in all its extent, all as the said seigneur the future husband possesses it, without reserving or diminishing anything, with all the rights of trading, fruits, revenues, emoluments thence proceeding, as well within the said river as from the islands and shores adjacent, which the said seigneur promises to improve.

Marriage contract of Charles La Tour and Jeane Motin, widow of Charles, Sieur d'Aulnay, February 24, 1653, in Murdoch, History, *pp. 120–21.*

We have some Huron pupils whom the Fathers have thought appropriate to raise in the French manner, for since all the Hurons are presently converted and dwell near the French, it is felt that in time it would be possible for the French to marry these Huron girls. This could not take place unless the girls were French not only in language but also in custom. . . .

In the peace treaty it was proposed to the Iroquois that they should bring us some of their girls and that Father Le Moyne, when he returned from their country, should bring with him five daughters of their women captains [*chiefs*], but this time conditions were not favorable. These women captains are important women among the savages with a deliberative voice in their councils, reaching conclusions just like the men. It was even they who delegated the first ambassadors to make a peace treaty.

Mother Marie to her son, September 24, 1654, in Marie de l'Incarnation, Mère, Marie of the Incarnation, *Mahoney, ed., pp. 252–53.*

It was a terrible job to bring that [*colonial financial records*] up to date. Eight persons worked on it, and every book had over 400 folios covering the infantry and the friars. Since there is only one supplier of clothing and staples, and the outlet for merchandise is the royal warehouse, where everything necessary to life is dispensed against [the soldiers'] salaries—everything for women and children as well as themselves—the treasury and presidio are in total confusion. No one knows what he is owed nor what he owes, not even the royal officials, and the usual thing is to give people more than is owed them.

St. Augustine auditor, November 20, 1655, quoted in Bushnell, The King's Coffer, *p. 132.*

Sir, these Indians are very jealous and they are excited beyond measure when someone approaches their wives, daughters, or sisters. And the lieutenant and the soldiers who are there are men and by that fact weak.

And it does not surprise us that some restlessness of this sort should be encountered among them [*the Spanish soldiers*], but it does weigh on us because of the offense against God and because this conversion is new and also because of seeing them offended. And if their presence here continues, we do not doubt that their irritation will reach the point that is feared, for they did not have nearly as much reason for the rebellion that they staged some years past.

Franciscans at San Luis de Talimali to the Florida governor, 1657, quoted in Henderson, Spanish Pathways, *p. 160.*

He heard it said that the Indians in the pueblo of La Isleta went out to perform these dances, and while they were dancing them the minister of the pueblo, who was then Father Friar Salvador de Guerra, not being able to restrain them in any other way, went throughout the pueblo with a cross upon his shoulders, a crown of thorns, and a rope about his neck, beating his naked body, in order that they might stop the dance. When he reached a certain part of the pueblo they came after him weeping, saying that they were not to blame, because the governor had commanded them to do as they were doing.

Father Benito de la Navidad's declaration against Governor Mendizábal, May 17, 1661, in Hackett, ed., Historical Documents, *p. 184.*

. . . the Indians of this *doctrina* came to the governor, Don Bernardo Lopez de Mendizábal, who had come to visit the pueblo, and asked permission to perform certain dances called the *catzinas*. The governor gave the permission freely and without any objection. The deponent said to him that he ought to take notice that these *catzinas* had been performed in the pueblos in the vicinity of the villa of Santa Fe, and that the rest of the kingdom had been scandalized at them, because they had never been seen before, and they were held to be idolatrous and diabolical. To this it governor replied that people did not know what they were talking about; that the *zarambeque* and other dances which the Spaniards dance were not prohibited, and that he had not observed that there were any superstitions connected with the *catzinas*. . . . Thereupon the Indians went out to dance. . . . The Indians went out wearing various evil costumes; one of them especially had an ugly costume, like a devil, with horns on the head, and a bear skin which he dangled by two fingers thrust through the eye-socket—a horrible thing. They sang

something which sounded like "Hu-hu-hu," at which the governor said "Look there, this dance contains nothing more than 'Hu-hu-hu,' and these thieving friars say that it is superstitious."

Thomé Domínguez, deposition against New Mexican governor, May 21, 1661, in Hackett, ed., Historical Documents, *pp. 177–78.*

As soon as the governor reached these provinces, he ordered the natives to make nine wagons, and for the purpose of drawing these he has taken nearly two hundred oxen and three-year-olds [*cattle*] from the haciendas of the Spaniards and from the cattle of the convents, by virtue of his power as governor. For the purpose of loading the nine wagons, he obliged the Indians of the six pueblos of Las Salinas to carry the salt on their shoulders and on their own animals as far as the hacienda of Captain Don Diego de Guadalajara, which is distant from the said pueblos twenty-four, twenty-eight, and thirty leagues, one way only, without giving any pay either to the carpenters or to those who carried the salt. He oppressively and violently commanded them to do it, and did not even furnish them with food.

Capt. Andrés Hurtado, testimony against Governor Mendizábal, September, 1661, in Hackett, ed., Historical Documents, *p. 187.*

In 1662 a great French ship full of men and women put into Grand Placentia, where she landed a great number of soldiers and passengers who fortified the Harbour with 18 pieces of ordinance as one Issac Dethick who was there affirmed.

Dethick saw the Governor's Commission under the great seal of France for the command of the whole country of Newfoundland, and the following year was forced to remove from his Plantation and settle at the Bay of Ards [*Bay de Verds*] where deponent found him and took from him an account of the proceedings which he sent for England by Mr. Robert Prowse to be presented to the King.

John Raynor's deposition of 1662, in Prowse, History, *pp. 178–79.*

[*Charles Aubert de La Chesnaye*] has granted in consideration of seiguerial *cens et rentes* payable annually on All Saints Day, November 1, to Claude Bouchard, his heirs, and assigns, an area of three arpents of land on the great St. Lawrence River . . . the said Bouchard promises and obliges himself to pay each year on All Saints Day the sum of twenty *sols* of nonredeemable *rente* for each *arpent* of frontage on the great St. Lawrence River a *cens* of three *sols* for the entire concessions, and three live capons also payable annually and without fraud on All Saints Day at the seigneurial manor of Beaupré.... The lessee will also be obligated to clear his land without delay and to build a house on it within a year from this day at the latest, and to continue to cultivate it in the following years.... Failing this the seigneur will be entitled to recover full title to the land.... The said Bouchard will also be obliged to allow a road fifteen feet wide along the river for the benefit of navigation and to bring his grain to the seigneurial mill to have it ground there. To maintain friendly relations with his neighbors, he will be obliged to fence in his land as he clears it, failing which he will not be entitled to claim compensation for the damage his neighbors; cattle may cause.... The lessee will enjoy full possession of the concession and will use and dispose of it as he, his heirs and assigns will think fit....

Contract for a roture on a seigneurie, Quebec, 1662, in Zoltvany, ed., French Tradition, pp. 89–90.

[He says that Mendizábal] has done and said, and has seen done and committed, many things which are against our holy Catholic faith ... performing and using Jewish ceremonies, as for instance dressing himself carefully on Fridays in clean clothes, first causing his feet to be washed. This he does, being a descendant of Juan Nuñez de León, who was sentenced by this Holy Office and abjured vehemently suspicions against him of Judaism, as appears in his trial process. The accused accompanies these ceremonies with great repugnance to and depreciation of religion, showing a scandalous spirit opposed to religion, and great hatred of the ministers of the holy gospel. For these reasons, and because he utters heretical statements which are irreligious and scandalous [and opposed] to the free privilege of the church; [his loyalty to] our holy faith is greatly suspected....

Don Juan de Ortega Montáñez to the New Mexican Inquisition, March 14, 1662, in Hackett, ed., Historical Documents, p. 176.

As for the winter season, although it lasts five months, during which the ground is covered with snow, and the cold is rather severe, still it is not disagreeable; the cold is exhilarating, and on most days the weather is calm and fine, and one does not find oneself at all inconvenienced by the cold. We go all about on the snow, by the aid of certain foot gear, made by the Indians, which we call snow-shoes, and which are very convenient. In truth the snow is less troublesome here than the mud is in France.

Pierre Boucher, 1664, Canada, pp. 19–20.

The people best fitted for this country are those who can work with their own hands in making clearings, putting up buildings and otherwise for as men's wages are very high here, a man who does not take care and practice economy will be ruined; but the best way is always to begin by clearing land and making a good farm, and to attend to other things only after that has been done, and not to do like some whom I have seen, who paid out all their money for the erection of fine buildings which they had to sell afterwards for less than the cost....

I would advise a man having money enough to bring two laboring men with him, or even more if he has the means, to clear his land; this is in answer to the question whether a person having three thousand or four thousand francs to employ here could do so with advantage; such a person could get himself into very easy circumstance & in three or four years if he choose to practice economy, as I have already said.

Pierre Boucher, 1664, Canada, pp. 79–81.

Most of our settlers are persons who came over in the capacity of servants and who, after serving their masters for three years, set up for themselves. They had not worked for more than a year before they had cleared land on which they got more than enough grain for their food. They have but little, generally when they set up for themselves, and marry wives who are no better off than they are; yet, if they are fairly hard working people you see them in four or five years in easy circumstances, and well fitted out for persons of their condition in life.

Poor people would be much better off here than they are in France, provided they are not lazy; they could not fail to get employment and could not say, as they do in France, that they are obliged to beg for their living because they cannot find any one to give them work; in one word, no people are wanted, either men or women, who cannot turn their hands to some work, unless they are very rich....

Women's work consists of household work and of feeding and caring for the cattle; for there are few female servants, so that wives are obliged to do their own house work; nevertheless those who have the means employ valets who do the work of maidservants.

Pierre Boucher, 1664, Canada, p. 81.

To this Gen. don Diego de Peñalosa replied, "if the custos [*custodio*] excommunicated me, I would hang him or garrote him immediately, and if the Pontiff came here and wanted to excommunicate me or actually did so, I would hang the Pontiff, because in this kingdom I am the prince and the supreme magistrate, and there is no one who may excommunicate the prince and supreme magistrate."

Franciscan custodio Alonso de Posadas, Inquisition testimony, May 1664, quoted in Kessell, Kiva, p. 201.

The King cannot concur with you in the whole of your reasoning as to the means of rendering Canada a great and powerful State, perceiving many obstacles thereto which cannot be overcome except by a long lapse of time; because, even though he should have no other business and could direct both his application and power to that object, it would not be prudent to depopulate his kingdom, which he should do to people Canada. Besides this consideration, which will appear important to you, there remains yet another, namely, that if his Majesty removed thither a greater number of men than what the land now cleared could feed, 'tis certain that if they did not all perish at once they would at least suffer great privations. . . . The true means of strengthening that Colony is to cause justice to reign there, to establish a good police, to preserve the inhabitants in safety, and to discipline them against all sorts of enemies; because all these things, which constitute the basis and foundation of all settlements, being well attended to, the country will get filled up insensibly, and in the course of a reasonable time many become very considerable. . . .

Jean-Baptiste Colbert to Intendant Talon, April 5, 1666, in Brodhead, Documents, vol. 9, p. 39.

The before named lord, the king of Great Britain, shall restore and give up unto the above named lord, the most Christian king, or to those who shall have charge and authority on his part, sealed in good form with the great seal of France, the country called Acadie, situated in North America, which the most Christian

king has formerly enjoyed; and to execute this restitution, the above named king of Great Britain, immediately after the ratification of the present treaty, shall furnish to the above named most Christian king all the acts and authorities, expedited duly and in good form, necessary to that effect, or shall cause them to be furnished to those of his ministers or officers who shall be delegated by him.

Treaty of Breda, Article 10, July 1667, in Murdoch, History, p. 140.

I pray you to commend it to the consideration of the whole people, that their prosperity, their subsistence, and all that is dear to them, depend on a general resolution, never to be departed from, to marry youths at eighteen or nineteen years and girls at fourteen or fifteen; since abundance can never come to them except through the abundance of men [*population*]. . . . Those who seem to have absolutely renounced marriage should be made to bear additional burdens, and be excluded from all honors; it would be well even to add some marks of infamy.

Jean-Baptiste Colbert to Intendant Talon, February 20, 1668, quoted in Parkman, Old Regime, p. 1261.

. . . these savage languages are difficult and one must have great constancy to conquer them. My task during the winter mornings is to teach them to the young sisters. Some of them have succeeded in learning the rules and in analyzing the parts of speech, provided that I translate the savage language into French. But to learn by heart a number of words from the dictionary—this is difficult for them and very thorny. . . . I am determined before my death to leave as many writings as possible. From the beginning of Lent to the Ascension I wrote a big book in Algonquin on sacred history and other holy things, along with a dictionary and a catechism in Iroquois, which is a treasure. Last year I wrote a big Algonquin dictionary with a French alphabet and another with the alphabet used by the savages.

Mother Marie to her son, August 9, 1668 (the works mentioned have not survived), in Marie de l'Incarnation, Mère, Marie of the Incarnation, Mahoney, ed., p. 270.

. . . in future all inhabitants of the said country of Canada who shall have living children to the number of ten, born in lawful wedlock, not being priests, monks, or nuns, shall each be paid out of the moneys sent by his Majesty to the said country a pension of three hundred livres a year, and those who shall have twelve children, a pension of four hundred livres; and that, to this effect, they shall be required to declare the number of their children every year in the months of June or July to that intendant of justice, police, and finance, established in the said country, who, having verified the same, shall order the payment of said pensions, one-half in cash, and the other had at the end of the year.

French decree, 1669, quoted in Parkman, Old Regime,
pp. 1262–63.

... this kingdom [*New Mexico*] is seriously afflicted, suffering from two calamities, cause enough to finish it off, as is happening with the greatest speed.

The first of these calamities is that the whole land is at war with the very numerous nation of the heathen Apache Indians, who kill all the Christian Indians they encounter. No road is safe. One travels them all at risk of life for the heathens are everywhere. They are a brave and bold people. They hurl themselves at danger like people who know not God, not that there is a hell.

The second calamity is that for three years no crop had been harvested. Last year, 1668, a great many Indians perished of hunger, lying dead along the roads, in the ravines, and in their hovels. There were pueblos, like Las Humanas, where more than four hundred and fifty died of hunger. The same calamity still prevails, for, because there is no money, there is not a fanega of maize or wheat in all the kingdom. As a result the Spaniards, men as well as women, have sustained themselves for two years on the cowhides they have in their houses to sit on. They roast them and eat them. And the greatest woe of all is that they can no longer find a bit of leather to eat, for their livestock is dying off.

Father Juan Bernal, April 1669, quoted in Scholes,
Troublous Times, *pp. 320–21.*

3

The Founding of Virginia, New England, and New Netherland
1607–1630

ENGLISH COLONIZATION REVIVES

In 1603, King James I ascended the throne of England. Like his predecessor, Queen Elizabeth I, James believed that absolute royal authority was his divine right. He ruled with the aid of a Privy Council, an appointed group of nobles responsible only to him. James and his son Charles I, however, were destined to reign during an era of unprecedented demands for political and religious reform in England. Parliament—more specifically, the House of Commons—struggled to increase its power relative to the Crown and Privy Council. Religious dissenters—Independents, Separatists, non-Conformists, Puritans—struggled for religious toleration or reform of the established Church of England, of which the king was head.

During the same years, the English renewed their interest in North American colonization. Although religious dissenters later became the best-remembered colonizers, colonization efforts were originally led by English commercial interests. English merchants had profited significantly from privateering and illicit trading in the New World during almost 20 years of war with Spain, finally concluded in 1604. In the treaty ending the war, however, England failed to win rights for English merchants to participate legally in the lucrative trade. Merchants and others, however, remained eager to challenge Spain's commercial monopoly. They commissioned new voyages of exploration to the North American coast south of Newfoundland. Explorers returned with glowing reports of timber, furs, and, farther south, valuable medicinal herbs. Many began to think that colonization would be the most efficient means to engage in trade and to increase England's power.

THE VIRGINIA COMPANY

In the revival of English colonization efforts, two groups of wealthy merchants and aristocrats took the lead. One centered in London and included some associates of the 16th-century Roanoke venture. The second centered in West Country port towns like Plymouth, Bristol, and Exeter. The two groups were competitors; they united, nonetheless, to petition the Crown for a charter to form a new joint-stock company. A joint-stock company was a semiprivate organization that reduced risk by pooling capital. Unlike a modern corporation, however, it was formed for a limited and specific venture. Joint-stock companies originated to fund the costs of distant, overseas trading ventures; in doing so, however, they supported exploration and settlement of newly discovered areas. Their charters usually granted some political authority as well economic rights in the lands where they were to operate.

The charter sought by the London and West Country groups was for the purpose of colonizing Virginia, as Sir Walter Raleigh had named the vast territory south of Newfoundland and north of Spanish Florida. The charter, which was granted in 1606, was written by Sir Edward Coke, the famed jurist, but strongly influenced by Sir John Popham, the lord chief justice and a West Country partisan. The charter established the Virginia Company, as it was officially known, but divided it into two groups. The London Company was granted the right to operate in the southern portion of the Virginia territory between 34 and 41 degrees north latitude (modern North Carolina to New York City). The Plymouth Company was to operate between 38 and 45 degrees north latitude (the Potomac River to modern Bangor, Maine). The territory overlapped between 38 and 41 degrees; in this area, neither company could settle within 100 miles of the other.

According to the charter, the overall management and direction of the Virginia enterprise was left to a Council of Virginia. Its 13 members were appointed by the king and resided in England (in practice, many were also Virginia Company investors). In addition, both the London and Plymouth companies were ordered to establish a council in their respective colonies. Colony councils would choose a president and officials, enact local law, hold court, and grant land. Company members, called adventurers because they adventured, or invested, their capital, were to provide financing and settlers. They had the right to trade freely and to mine gold, silver, and copper, with one-fifth of the precious metals reserved for the king. Trade duties were suspended for seven years. The Church of England was to be established in new settlements and its beliefs proselytized to the Native Americans. Colonists were guaranteed the same legal rights "as if they had been abiding and born within this our Realm of England, or any other of our said Dominions." These rights included common law, trial by jury, and personal and property rights. Because colonists were ruled by a company-appointed council, however, they did not have the same political rights as people residing in England—the right to vote, for example.

The Plymouth Company prepared ships to sail to the northern half of Virginia territory. In summer 1607, Sir Ferdinando Gorges sent 100 men to the mouth of the Sagadahoc River (modern Kennebec in Maine). The group was led by Raleigh Gilbert, Sir Humphrey Gilbert's son, and George Popham, who was related to Sir John Popham. They constructed Fort St. George, a church, and 15 dwellings, and then left 44 men to winter. The following summer, the survivors returned home, dismayed by the weather, the hostility of the Indians, and the lack of precious metals. Most of the investors in the Plymouth division of the Virginia Company were discouraged, and many placed their capital with the London division.

THE FOUNDING OF JAMESTOWN

While the Plymouth Company prepared to settle the Sagadahoc River area, the London Company immediately laid plans to establish a colony in the southern half of Virginia territory. Their exploratory expedition was captured by the Spanish, but in December 1606 three ships—the *Susan Constant, Goodspeed,* and *Discovery*—sailed under Captain Christopher Newport. They carried four boys and 140 men, including gentlemen adventurers, craftsmen, soldiers, and a minister. Before they reached Virginia, 39 had died and Captain John Smith, the military officer for the settlement, had been put in irons for threatened mutiny. The group carried a locked metal box containing the London Company's instructions and list of council appointees. When they arrived and opened it, Smith was listed as one of seven colony council members. The other members promptly voted to make Edward Wingfield president and to expel Smith from the council.

In April 1607, the ships arrived at a bay the Indians called K'tchisipik, or Great Water. After a month's search up the five rivers that feed Chesapeake Bay, the settlers selected a site 30 miles inland on the Powhatan River for their settlement. They renamed the river the James and named their settlement James Cittie, later known as Jamestown, in the king's honor. The site, located on a peninsula (now an island), could be easily defended, had a deep harbor, and allowed access to Indian trade. Unfortunately, it was also swampy, unhealthy, and located in the territory of a powerful Indian confederacy, the same group that had driven Spanish Jesuits from the area in the 1570s.

As instructed by the company, the settlers immediately divided into three groups to carry out clearing, construction, and exploration. The explorers went as far as modern Richmond, where they met the Pamunkey chief Wahunsonakok, known as Powhatan, head of the confederacy. The construction group built a triangular log fort, storehouse, dwellings, and small church. The clearing

Jamestown and surrounding Indian villages, detail of a 1624 map by Captain John Smith (*Library of Congress*)

group, however, cleared only four acres and planted no early crop. Among the colonists, none had listed his occupation as farmer; more than one-third listed gentleman.

Jamestown's first year was one of extreme suffering from famine, disease, and Indian hostility. Never welcoming to the settlers, local Indians first attacked in May 1607, as the English were scouting the bay. Summer that year was hot, and malaria-carrying mosquitoes infested the area. The council began quarreling; President Wingfield was deposed. The observant Powhatan curtailed trade with the colonists, making it difficult for them to obtain sufficient food.

In January 1608, when Captain Newport returned to the colony with supplies and 120 new men (called the First Supply) from England, only 38 of the original colonists remained alive. Five days later, a fire destroyed almost every building at Jamestown and most of the supplies and ammunition. Colonists survived the winter with only three habitable houses. When summer arrived, Captain John Smith left the settlement to explore, returning in September with food obtained from the Indians. The colonists, who had once again foregone clearing and planting during the summer in order to search for gold, promptly made him the council president in appreciation.

Smith immediately took charge of the unpromising situation, imposing strict discipline and announcing that each settler must "work or starve." Smith's leadership enabled the colony to survive. He organized the immediate clearing and planting of 40 acres and the care of livestock, marching men to their tasks under guard when necessary.

In October 1608, Captain Newport returned again, this time with the Second Supply—70 new settlers, including Polish and German experts in the manufacture of glass. Also on board were the first two female residents of Jamestown.

Jamestown's Early Struggles

Thanks to Smith's efforts, only a few colonists died during the winter of 1608–09. In July 1609, Captain Samuel Argall arrived at Jamestown with supplies—and news of a new charter. Dismayed by reports from the colony, the London Company had launched a campaign to rescue it. It successfully requested the Crown to grant the Second Charter, which enabled participants to share in potential profits by investing either money or labor. A planter (as colonists were called) who emigrated and invested labor received shares in the company, just as adventurers did for their investment of capital. All stock—and all the land—was to be held in a common pool for seven years until 1616, when cleared land was to be divided among the settlers and profits to be distributed to all. In the meantime, all settlers were to work common grounds, contribute to the common store, and draw from the store for necessary food and supplies. The council and president were replaced by a governor with full authority to direct the colony. Thomas West, lord de la Warr, was chosen first governor and captain general, although he did not emigrate immediately.

The company also made extensive and successful efforts to raise both money and settlers. The venture into Virginia was heavily publicized as a patriotic undertaking and popular enthusiasm grew. More than 650 individuals contributed money, about 100 of whom were merchants and another 100 members of Parliament. Another 600 men, women, and children agreed to emigrate. Nine ships sailed for Virginia. One sank in a hurricane and another, carrying the deputy governor Thomas Gates, was wrecked on Bermuda (coincidentally allowing England to claim the island). The remaining ships arrived in Jamestown with 400 settlers. No housing or food had been prepared for them. John Smith, whose presidential authority had been ended by the Second Charter, sailed for England and never again returned to Jamestown.

The following winter, 1609–10, was termed the "starving time" by the Jamestown colonists. The new colonists were weakened by the voyage, inadequate food and shelter, unaccustomed climate, and diseases. Powhatan's warriors prevented the colonists from venturing outside their palisade and killed their livestock. By spring, the population had declined from 500 to 60. For food, colonists had resorted to eating horses, rats, dogs, snakes, and at least one human carcass. They had given up farming altogether in favor of gathering roots, nuts, and berries. When Deputy Governor Gates arrived with the Bermuda survivors in May 1610, he was so shocked that he loaded the 60 colonists onto his ship and set sail. Before reaching the bay, however, they met Governor de la Warr and his fleet, carrying supplies and 150 new settlers.

De la Warr immediately sent a ship back to Bermuda for a load of wild hogs and dispatched Gates and Captain Newport to England to discuss matters with the company. Virginia was reorganized as a military outpost and ruled by martial law. Forts Charles and Henry were established at the mouth of the James River, and Jamestown was repaired and rebuilt. The starving time ended, although more colonists died from disease. De la Warr returned to England in March 1611 but remained governor in law through 1618.

During these early years, constant fear of a Spanish attack was added to the threat of starvation and the hostility of the Powhatan Confederacy. Spain regarded Jamestown as an intrusion into its territory of Florida and a threat to its fleets. Alarmed by England's popular enthusiasm for the colony, the Spanish ambassador sent worried communiques to his king. Spanish expeditions reconnoitered the village in 1609 and 1611 and engaged Indians to spy on the colonists. King Philip III of Spain, however, declined to order the attack that would doubtless have ended the Virginia venture, probably believing reports that it could not survive on its own.

After De la Warr's departure, the colony was governed by deputy governors Gates (1611–14) and Thomas Dale (1614–16). In 1612 the company received another new charter, which gave it more authority. The governors imposed the so-called Dale's Laws, and the Virginia settlement slowly stabilized. The *Lawes and Orders Divine, Politique, and Martial for the Colony of Virginia* (1612), the first legal code written in the English colonies, was extremely severe; its strict enforcement, however, established order and forced all to contribute to the colony's survival. Dale organized food production by fencing in fields, assigning a garden plot to each male settler, and assigning guards to livestock. Dale also modified the communal nature of the Virginia enterprise. In 1613–14, he leased three acres of cleared land to each settler. Each could retain the products or profits from it in exchange for two and one-half barrels of grain per year and one month's labor on communal projects.

A year earlier, in 1612, colonist John Rolfe had finally discovered a much-desired money crop for the colony: tobacco. Tobacco smoking had become quite common in England (much to King James I's personal disapproval), but English tastes preferred the sweeter Spanish West Indian tobacco to the native Virginia variety. Rolfe domesticated tobacco from Trinidad and the Orinoco River valley. His experiment was so successful that tobacco quickly became the colony's only export. Soon, settlers were planting so much tobacco that they had to be required by law to plant two of every three acres in food crops, in order to prevent new food shortages. From the first four barrels of Rolfe's tobacco sent to England, exports grew to 20,000 pounds by 1617, 60,000 pounds by 1622, and 500,000 pounds by 1628.[1]

When Dale returned to England in 1616, Virginia's English population had grown to 351, including 60 women and children. Colonists had spread out to Henrico (modern Hampton) and other settlements. However, in 1617, when Samuel Argall returned as the new governor, he discovered that settlers had lapsed into their old and disorderly lifestyle. He therefore again imposed Dale's Laws.

THE GREAT CHARTER AND THE FIRST COLONIAL ASSEMBLY

Communal profit pooling was to end—but no profits yet existed to be divided among the Virginia company planters and adventurers. Company members in England knew that change was imperative, but they disagreed about how to obtain it. The court party wanted martial rule in the colony; the reform, or Parliamentarian, party wanted to extend political rights to the colonists. The reform party, led by Sir Edwin Sandys, prevailed. In 1619, Sir George Yeardley arrived as the new governor of Virginia, bringing with him another new charter. Subsequently known as the Great Charter, it extended land grants and representative government to the Virginia settlers.

The Great Charter established a unicameral General Assembly, or House of Burgesses, which was to follow the general procedure of the English House of Commons. It was composed of the governor and his six-member council as well as 22 burgesses (two from each of 11 settlements). The first legislative assembly in English North America met in the Jamestown church on July 30, 1619, and lasted six days, with John Pory elected as speaker. Laws were passed regarding public conduct, church attendance, and the promotion of industries. The assembly forbade the sale of firearms to Indians and denounced provoking them. Burgesses also voted themselves a salary, taxing each male colonist one pound of tobacco to pay it. Although the assembly was not democratic, or even representative in the modern sense, it marked the beginnings of political community in Virginia.

The Great Charter also revised land distribution. Colonists who were currently freemen (rather than indentured servants) received a "first division" of 100 acres, plus another 100 for each share of stock held in the venture. Indentured settlers were to receive 100 acres on completion of service. New emigrants received 50 acres, known as a headright, plus an additional 50 acres for each adult family member and servant accompanying them. Very large tracts were granted to prominent colony officials and were made available to groups who agreed to send out settlers. Some tracts were retained by the company to be tilled by tenants, and a large grant near Henrico was set aside for a future Indian college. These land grants significantly affected future development in the colony by encouraging colonists to spread out rather than settle towns; some of the larger grants became the foundation of future plantations.

The Great Charter opened a period of growth in Virginia. Encouraged by Sandys and his colleagues, more than 3,000 new settlers arrived within the next three years, most of them indentured servants. Among them were chaperoned young women, sent by the company in 1620 and 1621, who became known as tobacco brides. Upon marriage, the groom was required to reimburse the cost of his bride's passage—120 pounds of tobacco. Also arriving in 1619 were the first convicted felons and 100 destitute boys to be apprenticed. In an attempt to diversify the colony's economy, Sandys also sent a variety of craftsmen, including ironworkers, German sawyers, Italian glassmakers, French shipbuilders, and tenants to experiment with new crops on company-owned property. King James I himself furnished silkworm cocoons, hoping to domesticate the production of silk.

In August 1619 the first people of African descent arrived in the colony on a Dutch ship with an English pilot. The "twenty and odd Negroes" were probably from the West Indies. They were purchased by Governor George Yeardley and Abraham Piersey, who paid in provisions for the sailors' journey home. Historical evidence suggests that the Africans were probably treated much like white indentured servants when they first arrived. In official Virginia documents, black servants would not be distinguished from white until the 1640s, nor slavery written into law until the 1660s.

Between 1619 and 1623, the English Crown and the company began a dispute over the regulation and taxation of tobacco imports. The solution of Virginia farmers was to send their entire crop to Holland. After several compromises proved unsatisfactory, in 1623 the colonists were granted exclusive import rights in England in return for payment of a duty, but the tobacco duty issue was destined to continue long into Virginia's future.

INDIAN RELATIONS AND THE MASSACRE OF 1622

When the first English settlers arrived in Virginia in 1607, Powhatan, a powerful Pamunkey chief, presided over an Algonquian empire. His relatives or lieutenants were installed as *werowances* (chiefs) of most of the 30 nearby Algonquian tribes. Powhatan probably did not believe that the English seriously threatened his dominance.[2] He commanded 14,000 people, 3,200 of whom were warriors. Shortly before the arrival of the first settlers, he had eliminated the semi-independent Chesapeake tribe (and possibly Roanoke Colony survivors living among them).

In November 1608, Powhatan halted trade with the English when they also began trade with his enemies the Monacan. Desperate for food, Captain John Smith raided a Pamunkey village and forced the ransom of its werowance, Opechancanough (Powhatan's relative), an act that would have repercussions for many years.

The following year, 1609, marked the beginning of the first war between the English and the Powhatan. Jamestown leaders conducted numerous raids on Indian villages, killing the residents and confiscating crops. The small band of Indians of Paspahegh, whose traditional land included Jamestown, were exterminated; the werowance's children were taken captive and transferred to a ship,

Powhatan, detail from a 1624 map by Captain John Smith (*Library of Congress*)

from which they were thrown overboard and shot in the water. In 1613, Thomas Dale and Samuel Argall captured Powhatan's daughter Matoaka, known as Pocahontas, who had long befriended the colonists and according to Captain John Smith had once saved his life. In spring 1614, the first Powhatan war ended—not in a truce or a victory for either side but in the marriage of Pocahontas to Englishman John Rolfe. Powhatan representatives attended the Christian ceremony, and Jamestown entered a period of relative peace with its Native American neighbors.

Peaceful coexistence became increasingly fragile, however, as the production of tobacco increased. Because tobacco cultivation quickly depleted the soil, it required extensive amounts of land to enable crop rotation. As the English spread out, the potential of open conflict with the Indians increased. In 1618, Powhatan died and was succeeded by Opechancanough. Slowly and carefully, Opechancanough orchestrated a plan with werowances throughout the confederacy. On the morning of March 22, 1622, Indians made seemingly ordinary and friendly visits to spread-out English settlements—then attacked. Of the 1,240 English colonists resident in Virginia, 347 men, women, and children were killed within a few hours. Among them was John Rolfe. (Pocahontas had died in England in 1617.) Livestock was killed and buildings were burned. After the 1622 massacre, Virginia colonists retreated behind stockades and no longer attempted to coexist peacefully with the Powhatan. Until 1632, when the second Powhatan war ended, intermittent skirmishes and crop destruction occurred.

News of the massacre dealt a final blow to the nearly bankrupt London Company. King James I personally detested its Parliamentarian leader, Sir Edwin Sandys, and the public was dismayed at the astonishing death rate in Virginia. More than 7,250 settlers had been sent out since 1607; only 1,250 remained alive. The King's Privy Council took over the company and sent a commission to Virginia to investigate. In 1624, the company's charter was declared void. Virginia ceased life as a proprietary, for-profit venture and became a royal colony under direct control of the Crown. Undistributed land reverted from the company to the king, although existing private ownership was not challenged. The king made no provision to continue the Virginia Assembly, but in 1625 Francis Wyatt, the first royal governor, informally reconvened the burgesses.

LIFE IN JAMESTOWN

Early immigration to Virginia had distinctive characteristics. It included an unusually large proportion of male settlers who called themselves gentlemen and undoubtedly lacked manual skills as well as enthusiasm for manual labor. (Many historians now believe, however, that continuing malnutrition was equally responsible for the early colonists' inability to clear land and farm successfully.) After 1619, most new colonists arrived as indentured servants—men and women who signed voluntary contracts to work for a certain number of years in return for passage, food, clothing, and housing. These contracts, and thus the labor of the servant, could be bought and sold without the servant's consent. Historical evidence indicates that treatment of these servants was often severe and abusive, more so than would have been permitted in England at the time.[3]

Settlers migrated to Virginia individually, not in groups, and as a whole the colony was less community- and family-oriented than New England settlements. Prior to 1630, no social organization existed other than the church, and there was no designated place for new settlers to stay when they arrived. The proportion of men to women remained high. Women, little attracted by the harsh conditions and primitive material culture of the settlement, were nonetheless in high demand as settlers—and brides. The assembly ruled on several breach of promise cases when prospective grooms found themselves jilted.

Early ministers were Anglicans. Little piety existed among the general population, and little missionary activity occurred, although some Indians did convert to Christianity. Prior to 1622, some Indian families lived in English settlements, and during especially difficult years, some settlers lived with the Indians. After the 1622 massacre, the English specifically discouraged friendly exchanges, believing that familiarity had lured them into a false sense of security. Marriages between Englishmen and Indian women were never encouraged as they were in Spain's colonies; despite the example of John Rolfe and Pocahontas, such marriages were in fact extremely rare.

When the London Company was dissolved in 1624, a muster list, or census, was compiled in a house-to-house survey. It reported 1,218 people—934 men and 270 women (a few were not identified by gender). Of these, 23 were of African descent. Only 334 were married (one married couple was African), and the number of children per family was small. Of the total population of 1,218, 507 were servants, including 22 of the 23 blacks and two Indians.[4] By 1630, one-half of the servants in the colony were attached to only 14 households with large land grants; two households had more than 35 servants.

THE COUNCIL FOR NEW ENGLAND

Many investors abandoned the moribund Plymouth division of the Virginia Company after the failure of its 1607 settlement at Sagadahoc. Sir Ferdinando Gorges did not. He sent several expeditions to the north Atlantic coast, including one by John Smith in 1614. Smith's resulting *Description of New England* (1616) gave the area its name.

As a precaution, Gorges and others secured another charter from the Crown to maintain their Virginia Company claim. The new charter of 1620 created a group called the Council for New England, granting them rights from modern Philadelphia to Newfoundland. The council was primarily composed of aristocrats like Gorges rather than merchants; it also included Sir William Alexander, who would soon attempt to settle present-day Nova Scotia. The council's purpose was not to establish colonies but rather to make large land grants while profiting from trade and fishing in the area. Under its auspices, numerous small settlements were founded on the north Atlantic seaboard, sometimes accompanied by a minister who dissented from the Church of England, but they remained isolated fishing and trading posts.

RELIGIOUS DISSENT IN ENGLAND

At the beginning of the 17th century, England was home to many kinds of Protestant dissenters as well as conforming Anglicans and Catholics. The Church of England, or Anglican Church, had been separated from Catholicism and the pope's authority by King Henry VIII. Under his daughter Queen Elizabeth I, it had been firmly established as the national church, which meant that the church and state were mutually dependent. The church and clergy were supported by taxes or other government money, and the appointment of church officials was influenced by the monarch, who was the church's official head. The state enforced the acquiescence of its citizens to the established church, all of whom were assumed to be members of the local parish. The church, for its part, could be counted on to enforce acquiescence to government authority.

By 1600, many clergy and individuals in England believed that the Anglican Church had not sufficiently altered or reformed the ritual and organization of the Catholic Church. A small group of these dissenters, called Separatists, rejected the identification of church with state and favored both a vastly simplified ritual and a democratic organization. They believed each congregation should be independent from higher ecclesiastical authorities, like bishops, and should have the power to choose its own minister. The majority of dissenters, however, wished to remained within the Anglican Church and to "purify" it. This large and disparate group became known as the Puritans.

The early Puritans were neither prudes, fanatics, nor hypocrites. Many did not object to the idea of an established church. Few favored outright religious liberty. Like other dissenters, they opposed the Anglican policy of allowing the unregenerate in the church membership and the morally lax in the clergy. (Clerical appointments were often based less on religious commitment than family position.) Dissenters believed that church membership was only for true believers and carried an obligation to live according to its moral precepts.

In 1603, 1,000 dissenters signed a petition supporting further reformation of the Church of England and presented it to King James I. Its effect was to antagonize him. He feared the democratic influence of "presbyterianism," or the election of church officials by the congregation rather than appointment by higher officials; as he put it, "No Bishop, No King."

"I will make them conform themselves, or else I will harry them out of the land, or else do worse," the king proclaimed. In 1604, all clergy were ordered to conform their services and teachings to the established Church of England or surrender their posts. English citizens who did not attend Anglican services, Catholics as well as dissenting Protestants, could be imprisoned or even expelled from the country.

The Separatists Migrate

In 1606, in the rural community of Scrooby in north central England, a group of Separatists withdrew from the Anglican Church and founded their own congregation. They were led by William Brewster, a financially comfortable member of the gentry with close connections to Edwin Sandys of the Virginia Company. Such congregations were illegal; the group was harassed and some were jailed. In 1608, many left for the Netherlands, which tolerated many forms of Protestantism. Although relations with their Dutch neighbors were good, city life in Amsterdam and Leyden disconcerted them. They feared their children would intermarry with the Dutch and their religious community would cease to exist. Worse, Catholic Spain was threatening to reassert control over the Netherlands. The Separatists determined to migrate again.

At the same time, Brewster's friend Sandys was promoting his Virginia venture. Under the Great Charter of 1619, his company could grant large tracts of land to groups of settlers. Sandys gave one such grant to Brewster, to be located near the Hudson River, the northern boundary of the London company's territory. The Separatists organized a joint-stock company, making a soon-regretted alliance with London merchants headed by Thomas Weston. Prospective colonists agreed to pool their resources and their labor, draw from the common store of food and supplies, and at the end of seven years divide the land and profits—ignoring Virginia's lack of success with a similar communal arrangement. As at Jamestown, the arrangement was not adopted for religious reasons; it was designed to share profit from the resources of the New World. The Separatists also attempted to obtain James I's royal sanction, but they had to be satisfied with an oral guarantee that he would "not molest them, provided they carried themselves peaceable."

A ship fitted out by the Separatists, the *Mayflower,* left London on September 16, 1620, under Captain Christopher Jones. A second ship, clearly unseaworthy, had to turn back and had delayed the intended spring departure. The *Mayflower* had 102 passengers. None were of aristocratic birth, but several were gentry of reasonably substantial means. William Bradford, their leader, spoke of them as "saints" (those who were Separatists) and "strangers" (those who were not). The saints numbered 41: 17 men, 10 women, and 14 children. More than 60 of the passengers were strangers: some recruited by Weston, some indentured servants, some hired for specific skills, some destitute children. Among the strangers, however, were several future leaders of the colony. They included Miles Standish, the ship's military officer and a professional soldier (the Separatists had declined Captain John Smith's offer to accompany them); and John Alden, a cooper who maintained the beer barrels. Also on board were provisions, tools, seed, and probably pigs, goats, and chickens (but no cattle, horses, or sheep). Later, in his written history of Plymouth Plantation, Bradford referred to the *Mayflower* passengers as "pilgrims." They have been known by that name ever since.

The voyage took nine weeks. One passenger died, and one infant was born. The *Mayflower* reached the tip of Cape Cod on November 11—probably due to navigational error, since their intended destination was the Hudson River. The Pilgrims landed in territory to which they had no grant, with no charter from the king to form a legal basis of government. In hopes of effectively governing themselves, 41 of the adult men signed the Mayflower Compact on November 21 in the ship's cabin. Not a constitution but an agreement to organize a government and enact laws for the good of all, the Mayflower Compact was the first "plantation," or social, covenant in the New World. Like the church covenants of the Separatists, it stated that the group consented to be governed and that government would exist because the group consented to it.

THE PILGRIMS FOUND PLYMOUTH

Despite their November landing, the Pilgrims spent one month searching for a site to build their colony. Meanwhile, they lived on board ship. They met small parties of Nauset Indians and found Indian corn buried in the sand, which they took as a sign of God's providence. (In later years, according to William Bradford, they compensated the Indians for the corn.) On December 21, 1620, they moved to their chosen site directly across the bay from the tip of Cape Cod and named it Plymouth. They constructed a common house and a platform on which they placed the ship's four small cannon. By lot, each of 19 families received land to build its own house; unmarried men, who were not permitted to live alone, were assigned to families.

The early years of the Plymouth settlement, like those of other colonial ventures, were marked with hardship and death. Four died before the Plymouth site was chosen, and little more than 50 survived the winter. The ship's crew wintered with them, also losing about half its number to scurvy, pneumonia, and tuberculosis. In January, fire destroyed the storehouse. With the coming of spring, conditions improved. Illness lessened. Two English-speaking Indians approached and offered assistance. They were Samoset, a transplanted Abenaki of the Pemaquid band; and Squanto (Tisquantum), a Narragansett who had been kidnapped, taken to England, and eventually returned. The bilingual pair brokered political and trade negotiations, and Squanto taught the colonists how to cultivate corn.

The Pilgrims had established their settlement within Wampanoag Indian territory near the abandoned village of Pautuxet. They established relations with the Native Americans that were very different from those at Jamestown, because conditions differed. In the decade before the Pilgrims arrived, a severe smallpox epidemic had struck the Algonquian peoples of the area. The Wampanoag on the cape alone had previously been more numerous than the Powhatan in Virginia; the epidemic wiped out 90 percent of their population. Many villages were completely abandoned. The sachem, or esteemed chief, Massasoit found his position reduced and his power threatened. Massasoit needed an ally against the Narragansett to the north—and the Pilgrims needed land. In March 1621, Massasoit and the Pilgrims signed a peace treaty. In October, when the Pilgrims gathered to give thanks for their first harvest, Massasoit and his warriors attended, contributing several deer to the first Thanksgiving. Because of their mutual needs, relative peace was maintained for half a century.

As was the case in Virginia, the system of working land in common and drawing from a common store met with little success at Plymouth. In November 1621, 35 new colonists arrived, sent by London investor Thomas Weston with no additional supplies whatsoever. (Their ship, the *Fortune,* was sent back to impatient company investors loaded with lumber and furs but was captured by French privateers.) In 1623, with severe food shortages looming, 90 more new settlers arrived. Some were "particulars," who paid their own way (or came "on their own particular") and according to company instructions were to be given

A modern reconstruction of a "wigwam," one form of temporary shelter built by the first English colonists *(Collection of the House of the Seven Gables)*

their own land, since they did not participate in the profit-sharing arrangement. Nor did they share the religious and political community of the Pilgrims. Facing a colony with twice as many strangers as saints, Governor Bradford allotted an acre of land to each family for its individual cultivation. Although the grants were contrary to the contract with the company, they successfully alleviated the food shortage; a year later, they were made permanent.

In summer 1622, more than 60 men sent by Weston arrived at Plymouth, and then moved north to Wessagusset (Weymouth). Their settlement soon became noted for its civil disorder. They aggravated the nearby Massachuset Indians; Massasoit saw his advantage and urged the Pilgrims to "prevent war" by attacking. Miles Standish led a small group to take control of the settlement, murdering several Massachuset. Most of Weston's men, fearing reprisals, opted for passage home. In 1625, a new group of indentured men arrived, led by a Captain Wollaston, to establish a new trading post on the site. The following year it was seized by Thomas Morton, another investor, when Wollaston was in Virginia. Morton, a well-connected Englishman, renamed the settlement Ma-re Mount. (*Ma-re* is a pun on the Latin word for "sea".) It soon became known as Merry Mount, however, for its hedonistic lifestyle. The Pilgrims believed that both their own community and their peace with the Native Americans was threatened—as was their control of the fur trade, which had begun as early as 1621. The final outrage was a tall maypole erected by Morton, which the people of Plymouth viewed as a pagan symbol. In 1628, under Captain Standish, the Plymouth colonists attacked the settlement and sent its leader back to England.

Four years earlier, in 1624, the Anglican minister John Lyford had arrived at the colony, causing great dissension by supporting discontented "particulars." The Pilgrims banished him. Lyford's complaints, however, provided Weston's company of merchants and "adventurers" in England with a convenient reason to withdraw its financial support from the colony. In 1627, Plymouth Colony sent Issac Allerton to London to buy out the remaining investors. The financial obligation was assumed by a group of eight men known as the Undertakers because they "undertook" the debt. In return, the colony gave the men a six-year monopoly on Plymouth fur trade. The colony also divided all property among the settlers, including indentured servants, and private ownership of land completely replaced the communal system. Cattle were imported from England, and the colony was soon exporting corn surpluses. In 1629 and 1630, additional Pilgrims arrived from the Netherlands and the population reached 300. Trading stations were founded in the Sagadahoc and Penobscot regions of modern Maine and on Cape Cod. The Pilgrims also established trade and diplomatic relations with the nearby Dutch settlement, New Netherland.

Plymouth Colony was governed by a governor and seven assistants, chosen annually by a vote of the freemen. It also held meetings of the 41 original signers of the Mayflower Compact, known as the General Court. Almost all adult male landowners in Plymouth were admitted to the status of freeman and voter. Upward mobility was soon evident. Some of the 20 indentured servants who arrived on the *Mayflower* prospered and even assumed leadership roles. In 1621, the tenuous legal status of the colony was partially resolved when it received a patent from the Council for New England, in whose territory it had actually settled. That grant, however, was in the name of the London merchants; in 1630,

Bradford and the colony itself received a second and more definitive document. Plymouth never received a royal charter, however, and its Mayflower Compact was not binding on the king. Colonists nonetheless carefully conducted official business as loyal English subjects.

THE DUTCH AND NEW NETHERLAND

In the early decades of the 17th century, the largest and most successful trading fleet in Europe belonged not to England, France, or Spain but to the Netherlands. The Netherlands struggled for almost 80 years (1569–1648) to obtain complete independence from Spain, which considered the area part of the Spanish Empire. During this time, however, its people achieved the highest standard of living in Europe. Their prosperity was built on secular economic activity and trade, protected by state-funded warships. They also enjoyed extensive religious toleration. Because of these factors, the Netherlands served as a haven for refugees from all over Europe, as it had for the Pilgrims.

In 1602, the Dutch East India Company was chartered by the States General, or assembly, to trade with Asia. The company did so immediately, sailing ships south and east around Africa's Cape of Good Hope. In 1609, the group determined to search for a shorter, western route to Asia—the fabled Northwest Passage. It hired English explorer Henry Hudson, who had already made several unsuccessful searches on England's behalf. In his ship, the *Halve Maen* (*Half Moon*), Hudson explored the Atlantic coast from Newfoundland to Virginia. He visited Delaware Bay, which he determined was not a route to Asia, then entered modern New York Harbor and sailed up the river now named for him, as far as modern Albany. Traveling through the heart of Iroquois Confederacy lands, he entertained chiefs and established the basis for Dutch–Indian trade. He determined that the Hudson River was not the Northwest Passage. It was, however, the site of the largest potential fur trade south of French Canada.

On its return to the Netherlands, Hudson's ship put in at England. Desirous of learning what he knew, the English refused to allow Hudson's ship to continue to Amsterdam, until the following summer. The Dutch East India Company was disappointed that he had not located the Northwest Passage, but other Dutch merchants were pleased with what he did discover. During the next decade, they made many trading voyages to the rich fur country Hudson had explored. In 1614, the States General gave the name New Netherland to the territory Hudson had explored between the Hudson and Delaware Rivers, which the Dutch called the North and South Rivers. In the same year, the New Netherland Company was formed by 13 merchants. The company built Fort Nassau (at modern Albany), which was used until 1617.

The Hudson Valley fur trade brought the Dutch, like the French, into contact with both the Huron Alliance and the Iroquois, or Five Nations, Confederacy. Dutch traders, however, successfully avoided being drawn into the conflict between the two. The territory they claimed as New Netherland was controlled by the Iroquois, and in 1618 the Dutch concluded a treaty with them. The treaty gave the Iroquois access to European tools and weapons, including firearms. Trade with the Dutch enabled the Iroquois Confederacy to significantly increase its power over the next half-century, with serious consequences for the French and deadly consequences for the Huron.

In 1621, the Dutch West India company was chartered, with extensive political authority to establish colonies. England objected strongly to the notion of a Dutch colony in New Netherland, even sending its ambassador to protest to the States General. In fact, the Dutch West India Company's primary goal was not to found a colony in North America but to challenge Spain's empire in Africa, the Caribbean, and South America. Ironically, the English protest convinced the company of the need to establish a "claim by occupation" in the wedge-shaped territory between the Delaware and Hudson Rivers that separated New England and Virginia. In 1623, New Netherland was designated a province of the Dutch West India Company, and in 1624, a plan of government drawn up. The company had extensive power to appoint officials, make laws (which could not conflict with those of the Netherlands), and administer justice, although the States General appointed the director general, or governor. Freedom of conscience was established for the colony, although public church services had to to follow Dutch Reformed convention. The company retained control of trade. Its primary goal was to establish a settlement of resident traders, farmers, and other supply personnel to service trading ships that called at port.

The Founding of New Amsterdam

In spring 1624, the *Nieu Nederlandt,* captained by Cornelius Jacobsen Mey (or May), brought the first group of 30 families to New Netherland. Most were French-speaking Protestants from the southern Netherlands (modern Belgium) called Walloons. Eighteen families journeyed up the Hudson to construct Fort Orange at the site of old Fort Nassau. Some settled at Governor's Island and some on the Delaware River at a new Fort Nassau (in modern New Jersey). A few of Mey's families may also have settled on Manhattan Island, although the historical evidence is unclear. In May 1625, an expedition arrived under Willem Verhulst, accompanied by a council of Dutch ship captains, more settlers, supplies, livestock, and an engineer to design a fort and town. These settlers constructed some 30 homes on the west side of lower Manhattan to found the town of New Amsterdam.

New Netherland was governed by its director general, a few other appointed officials, and an appointed council composed of merchants and visiting sea captains as available. In 1626, Peter Minuit (probably pronounced *minnewit*), also a Walloon, replaced Verhulst as director general. Minuit's instructions were to make a contract immediately with the Indians and to obtain title to the land on which the settlers resided. Minuit soon oversaw the purchase of Manhattan Island for goods worth 60 guilders, or about $24. Some historians maintain that this famous price was closer to the actual value of the land at the time than it now seems. In any case, the Native Americans with whom the Dutch dealt doubtless considered the price a rent or tribute for use, not purchase; they did not believe land could be owned, bought, or sold in the same way Europeans did. Although different understandings of land purchase eventually caused difficulties, relations with the small agricultural tribes in the immediate area were generally peaceable in the first decade of New Amsterdam's existence.

Under Minuit's direction, Fort Amsterdam was constructed at Manhattan's tip (now called the Battery) and a stone counting house built nearby. Minuit moved most of the settlers from the Hudson and Delaware Rivers to Manhattan, in part due to deteriorating relations between the Mohawk and Mahican Indians near Fort Orange. The company sent generous supplies and livestock. Consequently, New Amsterdam never experienced a starving time as the English colonies had, although it did experience similar problems stemming from unrealistic expectations among both investors and colonists. Dutch colonists, consumed by hopes of wealth from the fur trade, neglected to provide food and shelter for themselves, sometimes even trading scarce provisions. The labor shortage for farm work and construction soon led to the decision to import African slaves; the first group of 11 men arrived in 1626.

New Netherland progressed far more slowly than the company had hoped, and the costs of supporting it were high. As other nations had done, the company decided to transfer part of the costs of colonization to private investors. In 1629, the patroon system was established. The Charter of Privileges to Patroons (or Charter of Freedoms and Exemptions) offered an 18-mile tract of land on any navigable river to any man who would bring 50 settlers over the age of 14. The patroon was to govern like the lord of a manorial estate, establishing laws and holding courts. By 1630, five patroonships had been granted, but only one, the Van Rensselaer at Albany, was successful. The Charter of Privileges also provided for smaller grants of land, "as much as they can comfortably work," which in later years attracted more individual colonists.

In 1627, Peter Minuit sent the colony's secretary, Isaac de Raisieres, to Plymouth to establish relations with the English. Soon, the Dutch introduced the Plymouth settlers to wampum trade. The Dutch had needed a currency in their thriving trade with the Indians, but like all North American colonists, they lacked a supply of European coin. The Indians offered wampum, or *sewant*. Wampum strings or belts of various sizes, made of beads laboriously cut from coastal shells, were universally prized among both Algonquian and Iroquois tribes. Both used wampum for ceremonial and diplomatic purposes and for personal adornment. Somewhat analogous to gold and silver among Europeans, wampum originally denoted status; as more became available, however, it became a common currency. The Algonquian Indian communities on Long Island, or Sewanhacky (shell land), manufactured much of the local wampum. First the Dutch, then the English, began to participate in its trade and introduced European tools to its manufacture. Soon it was legal tender in both New Netherland and New England.

By 1630, New Netherland was home to only about 300 colonists, but its diversity already contrasted with other North American settlements. The Walloons clung to the French language, and few Dutch settlers spoke French. No minister arrived until 1628, although two comforters (lay officials of the Dutch Reformed Church) performed church sacraments. When Dominie Jonas Michaelius arrived he had difficulty establishing a church, not only because of language differences but because the settlers were not interested in religion.

THE MASSACHUSETTS BAY COMPANY

In March 1628, an English group called the Dorchester Company obtained a patent from the Council for New England for land between the Merrimac and Charles Rivers (modern Massachusetts). Although it had been encouraged by the Reverend John White, a dissenting minister, its stated purposes were primarily commercial; its members numbered both Puritans and conforming Anglicans. In September 1628, the company sent 60 men to establish a trading post and develop fisheries at Naumkeug. The settlement's governor, John Endicott, changed Naumkeug's name to Salem and staked out a claim to the deserted Merry Mount (and chopped down the maypole). In March 1629, the company successfully obtained a royal charter to form a colonial government, although both Thomas Morton and the Gorges family objected. The Company of Massachusetts Bay in New England, as it was termed in the charter, was to provide a governor, deputy, and 18 assistants, elected annually by the freemen. Freemen were to form a General Court to control the admittance of new members or freemen; the court was also to enact laws, providing they did not conflict with the laws of England. On June 27, 1629, about 400 settlers arrived in Salem. The leaders were merchants; many of the others were indentured servants.

While the Massachusetts Bay Company was organizing its venture, however, the political situation for religious dissenters in England deteriorated significantly. Their taxes were increased during an economic downturn, causing distress and rioting. In 1628, Parliament reacted by forcing the king to sign a Petition of Right; it guaranteed all Englishmen freedom from arbitrary arrest and no taxation without Parliament's consent. King Charles I in turn dissolved Parliament in 1629. The Puritans, who had formed a significant portion of the House of Commons, no longer had a voice in government.

In summer 1629, 12 prominent Puritans met at Cambridge. Led by John Winthrop, an attorney and squire, they pledged to take their families to New England. In August, in a secret meeting, Winthrop and others in effect bought out the original Massachusetts Bay Company, signing a document called the Cambridge Agreement. The Massachusetts Bay Company ceased existence as a commercial enterprise and became a company of Puritan dissenters. In June 1630, 11 ships of Puritan colonists arrived at Salem, prepared to remake Endicott's trading colony into a biblical commonwealth.

CHRONICLE OF EVENTS

1607

The Plymouth division of the Virginia Company sends 100 men to Sagadahoc (modern Maine); they construct a fort, church, and dwellings, leaving 44 men to winter there. The following year, the survivors will return to England.

April: Of 144 men and boys sent by the London division of the Virginia Company, 105 survivors reach Chesapeake Bay aboard the *Susan Constant, Goodspeed,* and *Discovery* under Captain Christopher Newport. A skirmish with Powhatan Confederacy Indians occurs as the men explore.

May 14: Having sailed farther up the James River, the men land to begin building Jamestown. The men fail to plant adequate crops, and disease is rampant.

1608

A Separatist group later known as the Pilgrims leaves England for the Netherlands.

January: Captain Newport returns to the Jamestown colony with supplies and 120 new men (called the First Supply); only 38 colonists remain alive. Five days later, a fire destroys the settlement. Colonists survive the winter in three houses.

September: Jamestown settlers have again failed to plant adequate crops; Captain John Smith is made governor and institutes strict reforms, telling the colonists they must "work or starve."

October: The first two women colonists arrive in Jamestown.

1609

The London Company receives a new charter, allowing Virginia colonists to share in profits; for seven years, they will cultivate communal land and draw from a communal store. The company launches a publicity campaign in England and 600 new colonists embark for Jamestown.

The Dutch East India Company hires English explorer Henry Hudson to search for a western route to Asia. Hudson explores the coast of North America and sails up what is later named the Hudson River to the site of present-day Albany, through the heart of Iroquois Confederacy lands, discovering rich fur-trading country.

winter of 1609–10: Jamestown endures the "starving time." By spring, only 60 of 500 colonists remain alive. Skirmishes begin the first Powhatan war, which will continue until 1614.

1610s

An epidemic decimates Wampanoag and other populous Indian tribes in the Massachusetts area; this decline will facilitate English settlement in the area.

Dutch merchants establish fur trading in the Hudson and Delaware valleys.

1610

May: Deputy Governor Thomas Gates arrives at Jamestown and loads the surviving colonists on his ship. They meet Governor de la Warr's fleet and new settlers in the James River, and return.

1612

The *Laws and Orders Divine, Politique, and Martial,* called Dale's Laws, are written for Virginia. Through 1616, Deputy Governors Thomas Gates and Thomas Dale use the strict code to establish what amounts to martial law in an effort to revive the colony.

John Rolfe domesticates West Indian tobacco at Jamestown, establishing a much-desired money crop. Soon, it will be the colony's only export.

The London Company receives the Charter of 1612 for Virginia.

1613

Jamestown settlers are leased three acres of land to cultivate for their own profit.

Captain Samuel Argall helps Jamestown soldiers capture Pocahontas, the daughter of Powhatan, then attacks French settlements in Maine and Acadia.

Adrien Block, a Dutch fur trader, builds the small Fort Nassau near modern Albany; it will be used for fur trading until 1617.

1614

April: John Rolfe marries Pocahontas in a Christian ceremony, and a truce is made with the Powhatan.

June: Rolfe ships his first tobacco to England.

The Dutch States General designates the name New Netherland for the area Hudson explored, between the Hudson (North) River and the Delaware (South) River.

1616

Governor Dale returns to England accompanied by John Rolfe and his wife Pocahontas. Pocahontas gives birth to a son but dies in England of smallpox in 1617.

1618

The great chief Powhatan dies and is succeeded by his relative Opechancanough.

1619

Virginia's new governor, Sir George Yeardley, arrives with the Great Charter. It establishes a General Assembly for the colonists, composed of the governor, his council, and 22 elected burgesses. It also establishes land grants for all existing colonists and headrights for future colonists. New settlers, many of them indentured servants, begin to arrive in the colony. One of the larger grants is given to William Bradford and his group of Separatists in the Netherlands, later called the Pilgrims. They form a joint-stock company with London merchants headed by Thomas Weston.

July 30: The General Assembly of Virginia convenes at the church in Jamestown. It is the first legislature to meet in the English North American colonies.

August: Twenty African slaves arrive at Jamestown.

1620

The Council of New England is created by King James I, composed of some members of the Plymouth Company of Virginia and others. Its purpose is to make land grants.

The London Company sends the first group of young women to Jamestown as "tobacco brides."

November 11: The Pilgrims reach Cape Cod, having been blown off course; their probable destination was the Hudson River area, then the northern boundary of Virginia.

November 21: The Mayflower Compact is signed by 41 male passengers of the *Mayflower.* It is a social compact that establishes government by the consent of the governed.

December 21: The Pilgrims establish their village at Plymouth.

1621

English-speaking Indians Samoset and Squanto appear and aid the Pilgrims in the spring. Chief Massasoit signs a treaty with the Pilgrims.

June: The Plymouth colony receives a patent (later called the Pierce patent) from the Council of New England for the land that it is occupying illegally.

The Dutch West India Company is formed to colonize New Netherland; it is given a monopoly on all trade to the New World and West Africa.

October: The Pilgrims hold the first feast of Thanksgiving. Massasoit and other Indians attend.

1622

March 22: The Powhatan massacre more than 300 Virginia colonists in a carefully planned and orchestrated attack led by Opechancanough. The attack marks the end of any attempt at peaceful coexistence between the colonists and Indians; skirmishes will continue throughout the decade.

May: Sixty men, sent by Thomas Weston, arrive at Plymouth. They establish a disorderly settlement at Wessagusset. Captain Miles Standish is sent to take control of the settlement, urged on by Massasoit. He murders some Massachuset Indians.

1623

Faced with a majority of colonists who do not belong to the Pilgrims' religious community, Governor Bradford gives all settlers an acre of land to cultivate for their own profit.

New Netherland is designated a province of the Dutch West India Company. The company provides blueprints for the design of New Amsterdam, which are eventually followed in some detail.

1624

The London division of the Virginia Company is almost bankrupt; officials and the public are alarmed at the death rate in the colony. The company's charter is declared void, and Virginia is made a royal colony. The General Assembly holds its last official meeting of the decade, although it will continue to meet informally.

A thorough census is conducted in Virginia; the population is 1,218.

Anglican minister John Lyford arrives in Plymouth. He will cause difficulty for the group in England when he complains of his treatment by the Pilgrims; Weston's investment group will withdraw financial support.

In the spring, the *Nieu Nederlandt,* captained by Cornelius Jacobsen Mey, drops off colonists in four locations in New Netherland, including present-day

Governor's Island, the new Fort Nassau on the Delaware River (in modern New Jersey), and Fort Orange (modern Albany).

1625

Charles I ascends the throne of England. He and Bishop William Laud will step up persecution of open dissenters from the Church of England.

Captain Wollaston takes over the Wessagusset site; Thomas Morton will seize control of it in Wollaston's absence and rename it Merry Mount, erecting a tall maypole, which enrages the Pilgrims.

Settlers arrive in New Amsterdam with Governor Willem Verhulst. They begin construction of the town of New Amsterdam on the west side of Manhattan Island.

1626

Peter Minuit becomes governor of New Netherland. He purchases the island of Manhattan from the Indians for 60 guilders. Fort Amsterdam, on the tip of Manhattan, is established.

Eleven African slaves are brought to New Amsterdam.

1627

Issac Allerton and others, called the Undertakers, buy out investors in Thomas Weston's former company. All land is divided among the settlers in Plymouth Colony.

New Netherland official Isaac de Raisieres travels to Plymouth to establish relations with the English. The Dutch will introduce Plymouth settlers to the wampum trade.

1628

Jamestown exports 500,000 pounds of tobacco.

Captain Miles Standish attacks Merry Mount and sends Morton back to England.

John Endicott and a group of settlers arrive at Salem, sent by a group named the Dorchester Company.

A minister of the Dutch Reformed Church arrives in New Netherland, the colony's first religious leader.

1629

King Charles I dissolves Parliament. Puritans, who had been well represented in the House of Commons, no longer have a voice in government.

The Charter of Privileges to Patroons is issued in New Netherland; any man bringing 50 settlers over the age of 14 is given an 18-mile tract on one side of the Hudson River, to be governed like a manorial estate.

The Dorchester Company receives a royal charter renaming it the Massachusetts Bay Company and authorizing it to found a colony. It is primarily a commercial enterprise.

August: John Winthrop and 11 other Puritan leaders agree to migrate. They sign the Cambridge agreement, secretly buying out the investors in the Massachusetts Bay Company, and begin preparations to found Puritan settlements in New England.

1630

Plymouth receives a new patent from the Council of New England (later called the "Old Charter"), naming Governor Bradford as grantee and establishing its boundaries.

June: The first Puritans arrive in Massachusetts Bay Colony.

Eyewitness Testimony

Sea Gull. Come boys, Virginia longs till we share the rest of her. . . .

Scape Thrift. But is there such treasure there, Captain . . . ?

Sea Gull. I tell thee, gold is more plentiful there than copper is with us; and for as much red copper as I can bring, I'll have thrice the weight in gold. Why, man, all their dripping pans are pure gold; and all the chains with which they chain up their streets are gold; all the prisoners they take are fettered in gold; and for rubies and diamonds they go forth on holidays and gather 'em by the seashore to hang on their children's coats, and stick in their children's caps. . . . Besides, there we shall no more law than conscience, and not too much of either.

British dramatist John Marston, Eastward Hoe!, *1605, in West, ed.,* Source Book, *p. 15.*

The same day we entered into the Bay of Chesapeake directly, without any let or hindrance. There we landed and discovered a little way. . . . At night, when we were going aboard, there came the Savages creeping upon all four, from the Hills, like Bears, with their Bows in their mouths, charged us very desperately in the faces, hurt Captain Gabrill Archer in both his hands, and a sailor in two places of the body very dangerous. After they had spent their Arrows, and felt the sharpness of our shot, they retired into the Woods with a great noise, and so left us.

George Piercy, a Jamestown military officer, describes the first night ashore, 1607, in Tyler, ed., Narratives, *p. 8.*

Our men were destroyed with cruel diseases, as Swellings, Fluxes, Burning Fevers, and by wars, and some deported suddenly, but for the most part they died of mere famine. There were never Englishmen left in a foreign Country in such misery as we were in this new discovered Virginia. We watched every three nights, lying on the bare cold ground, what weather soever came, [and] warded all the next day, which brought our men to be most feeble wretches. Our food was but a small Can of Barley sod in water, to five men a day, our drink cold water taken out of the River, which was at a flood very salty at a low tide full of slime and filth, which was the destruction of many of our men. Thus we lived for the space of five months in this miserable distress not having five able men to man our Bulwarks upon any occasion. If it had not pleased God to have put a terror in the Savages heart, we had all perished by those wild and cruel Pagans, being in that weak estate as we were; our men night and day groaning in every corner of the Fort most pitiful to hear. If there were any conscience in men, it would make their hearts to bleed to hear the pitiful murmurings and out-cries of our sick men without relief, every night and day, for the space of six weeks, some departing out of the World, many times three or four in a night; in the morning, their bodies trailed out of their Cabin like Dogs to be buried. In this sort did I see the mortality of divers of our people.

It pleased God, after a while, to send those people which were our mortal enemies to relieve us with victuals, as Bread, Corn, Fish, and Flesh in great plenty, which was the setting up of our feeble men, otherwise we had all perished.

George Piercy describes 1607–08 at Jamestown, in Tyler, ed., Narratives, *pp. 21–22.*

A modern recreation of the *Susan Constant,* which brought the first settlers to Jamestown *(Courtesy Jamestown Settlement and Yorktown Victory Center/Jamestown-Yorktown Foundation)*

Countrymen, the long experience of our late miseries, I hope is sufficient to persuade every one to a present correction of himself; and think not that either my pains, or the adventurers' purses, will ever maintain you in idleness and sloth; I speak not this to you all, for divers of you I know deserve both honor and reward, better then is yet here to be had: but the greater part must be more industrious, or starve, howsoever you have been heretofore tolerated by the authority of the Council from that I have often commanded you, yet seeing now the authority resteth wholly in my self, you must obey this for a law, that he that will not work shall not eat (except by sickness he be disabled) for the labors of 30 or 40 honest and industrious men shall not be consumed to maintain 150 idle varlets. Now though you presume the authority here is but a shadow, and that I dare not touch the lives of any, but my own must answer it; the letters patents each week shall be read to you, whose contents will tell you the contrary. I would wish you therefore without contempt seek to observe these orders set down: for there are now no more Councils to protect you, nor curb my endeavors. Therefore he that offendeth let him assuredly expect his due punishment.

John Smith's speech to Jamestown colonists, 1608, in Tyler, ed., Narratives, *p. 180.*

But 30 of us he [*Capt. Smith*] conducted down the river some 5 miles from Jamestown, to learn to make Clapboard, cut down trees, and in lay in the woods. Amongst the rest he had chosen Gabriel Beadle and John Russell, the only two Gallants of this last Supply, and both proper Gentlemen. Strange were these pleasures to their conditions; yet lodging, eating, and drinking, working or playing, they were but doing as the President did himself. All these things were carried so pleasantly as with a week they became Masters: making it their delight to hear the trees thunder as they fell; but the Axes so oft blistered their tender fingers that many times every third blow had a loud oath to drown the echo; for the remedy which sin, the President devised how to have every man's oaths numbered, and at night for every oath to have a can of water poured down his sleeve, with which every offender was so washed that a man should scarce hear an oath in a week.

Attributed to Anas Todkill, a Jamestown Carpenter, 1608, in West, Source Book, *pp. 36–37.*

The one and twentieth [*September 1609*] was faire weather, and the wind all southerly: we determined yet once more to go farther up into the river, to try what depth and breadth it did bear; but much people [*Indians*] resorted aboard, so we went not this day. Our carpenter went on land, and made a fore-yard. And our master and his mate determined to try some of the chief men of the country, whether they had any treach-

ery in them. So they took them down into the cabin, and gave them so much wine and *aqua vita,* that they were all merry: and one of them had his wife with them, which sat so modestly, as any of our country women would do in a strange place. In the end one of them was drunk, which had been aboard of our ship all the time that we had been there: and that was strange to them; for they could not tell how to take it. The canoes and folk went all on shore: but some of them came again, and brought straps of beads: some had six, seven, eight, nine, ten; and gave him. So he slept all night quietly. . . .

The second [*October 1609*], fair weather. At break of day we weighted, the wind being at north-west, and got down seven leagues; then the flood was come strong, so we anchored. Then came one of the savages that swam away from us at our going up the river with many others, thinking to betray us. But we perceived their intent, and suffered none of them to enter our ship. Whereupon two canoes full of men, with their bows and arrows shot at us after our stern: in recompense whereof we discharged six muskets, and killed two or three of them. Then above an hundred of them came to a point of land to shoot at us. There I shot a falcon [*cannon*] at them, and killed two of them: whereupon the rest fled into the woods. Yet they manned off another canoe with nine or ten men, which came to meet us. So I shot at it also a falcon and shot it through, and killed one of them. Then our men with their muskets killed three or four more of them. So they went their way; within a while after we got down two leagues beyond that place, and anchored in a bay, clear from all danger of them on the other side of the river, where we saw a very good piece of ground: and hard by it there was a cliff, that looked of the color of a white green, as though it were either copper or silver mine: and I think it to be one of them, by the trees that grow upon it. For they be all burned, and the other places are green as grass; it is on that side of the river that is called Manna-hata [*Manhattan*]. There we saw no people to trouble us and rode quietly all night; but had much wind and rain.

Journal of Robert Juet, Henry Hudson's mate, in Levermore, ed., Forerunners, *pp. 416, 420–21.*

Where they Unto their labour fall,
    as men that meane to thrive:
Let's pray that heaven may blesse them all
    and keep them long alive.

Those men that *Vagrants* liv'd with us,
   have there deserved well:
Their Governour writes in their praise,
   as divers Letters tel.

And to th'Adventurers thus he writes,
   be not dismayd at all,
For scandall cannot doe us wrong
   God will not let us fall.
Let England knowe our willingnesse,
   for that our worke is good,
Wee hope to plant a Nation,
   where none before hath stood.

    English poet Richard Rich's promotional verse,
    "News from Virginia," *1610, in Silverman, ed.,*
    Colonial American Poetry, *pp. 15–17.*

3. That no man blaspheme God's holy name upon pain of death, or use unlawful oaths, taking the name of God in vain, curse, or bane upon pain of severe punishment for the first offense so committed and for the second to have a bodkin thrust through his tongue; and if he continue the blaspheming of God's holy name, for the third time so offending, he shall be brought to a martial court and there receive censure of death of his offense....

6. ... no man or woman shall dare to violate or break the Sabbath by any gaming, public or private abroad or at home ... As also every man and woman shall repair in the morning to the divine service and sermons preached upon the Sabbath day and in the afternoon to divine service and catechizing, upon pain for the first fault to lose their provision and allowance for the whole week following, for the second to lose the said allowance and also to be whipped, and for the third to suffer death....

9. No man shall commit the horrible and detestable sins of sodomy, upon pain of death; and he or she that can be lawfully convicted of adultery shall be punished with death. No man shall ravish or force any woman, maid, or Indian, or other, upon pain of death....

25. Every man shall have an especial and due care, to keep his house sweet and clean, as also so much of the street, as lies before his door, and especially he shall so provide, and set his bedstead whereon he lies, that it may stand three foot at least from the ground, as he answer the contrary at a martial court....

31. What man or woman soever shall rob any garden, public or private, being set to weed the same, or

willfully pluck up therein any root, herb, or flower, to spoil and waste or steal the same, or rob any vineyard, or gather up the grapes, or steal any ears of the corn growing, whether in the ground belonging to the same fort or town where he dwells, or in any other, shall be punished with death....

    Dale's Laws, 1611, in Strachey, ed.,
    For the Colony, *pp. 1–27.*

There is nothing so generally spoken of in the Court [*of Spain*] as their intent to remove Our Plantation from Virginia. And, for mine own part, I am of the belief that the Spaniards will serve us as they did the Frenchmen [*at Fort Caroline*] unless we undertake the business much more thoroughly and roundly than hitherto we have done.

    English ambassador to Spain John Digby writing to King
    James I, September 22, 1612, in West,
    Source Book, *p. 49.*

... with my capture and the extraordinary occurrences following it His Majesty [*the King of Spain*] will have opened his eyes and seen this new Algiers of America, which is coming into existence here.... His Majesty will have been able to determine what is most important and that is to stop the progress of a hydra in its infancy, because it is clear that its intention is to grow and encompass the destruction of all the West, as well by sea as by land and that great results will follow I do not doubt, because the advantages of this place make it very suitable for a gathering-place of all the pirates of Europe, where they will be well received. For this nation [*England*] has great thought of an alliance with them. And this nation by itself will be very powerful because as soon as an abundance of wheat shall have been planted and there shall be enough cattle, there will not be a man of any sort whatever who will not alone or company with others fit out a ship to come here and join the rest, because as Your Lordship knows this Kingdom abounds in poor people who abhor peace—and of necessity because in peace they perish–and the rich are so greedy and selfish that they even cherish a desire for the Indies and the gold and silver there....

    Don Diego de Molina, held prisoner in Jamestown as a
    Spanish spy, to the Spanish king, 1613, in Tyler, ed.,
    Narratives, *pp. 218–19.*

Let me tell you all at home this one thing, and I pray remember it,—if you give over this country and lose it, you with your wisdoms will leap such a gudgeon as our state hath not done the like since they lost the Kingdom of France. Be not gulled with the clamorous reports of base people. . . . [I]f the glory of God hath no power with them, and the conversion of these poor Infidels, yet let the rich Mammon's desires egg them on to inhabit these countries. I protest unto you by the faith of an honest man, the more I range the Country, the more I admire it.

Governor Thomas Dale to the London Company, 1613, in West, Source Book, *p. 17.*

. . . the Towne its selfe by care and providence . . . is reduced into a handsome forme, and has in it two fair rowes of howses, all of Framed Timber, two stories, and an upper Garret, or Corne loft high, besides three large and substantiall Storehouses, joined together in length some hundred and twenty foot; and this town hath been lately newly, and strongly impaled, and a fair Platforme for Ordenance in the west Bulwarke raised; there are also without this town in the Island some very pleasant and beautiful howses. . . .

Ralph Hamor, soldier at Jamestown, describes Henrico, 1614, quoted in Bridenbaugh, Jamestown, *p. 132.*

Let therefore this my well advised protestation, which here I make between God and my own conscience, be a sufficient witnesses at the dreadful day of judgement (when the secret of all men's hearts shall be opened) to condemn me herein, if my chiefest intent and purpose be not, to strive with all my power of body and mind, in the undertaking of so mighty a matter, no way led (so far forth as man's weakness may permit) with the unbridled desire of carnal affection: but for the good of this plantation, for the honor of our countries for the glory of God, for my own salvation, and for the converting to the true knowledge of God and Jesus Christ, an unbelieving creature, namely Pocahontas. To whom my heart and best thoughts are, and have a long time bin so entangled, and enthralled in so intricate a labyrinth, that I was even awearied to unwind my self thereout. But almighty God, who never faileth his, that truly invoke his holy name hath opened the gate, and led me by the hand that I might plainly see and diseem the safe paths wherein to tread.

John Rolfe to Governor Dale, 1614, in Tyler, ed., Narratives, *pp. 239–41.*

Pocahontas *(National Portrait Gallery, Smithsonian Institution; transfer from the National Gallery of Art; gift of Andrew W. Mellon, 1942)*

Appeared at the Assembly the Deputies from the United Company of Merchants who have discovered and found New Netherlands, situate in America between New France and Virginia, the sea coasts whereof lie in the Latitude of forty to forty five degrees. And who having rendered a Report of their said Discovery and finding, requesting, in consequence, the Grant promised by their High Mightinesses' published placard. Deliberation being had thereon, their High Mightinesses have granted and allowed, and hereby grant and allow, the Petitioners that they alone shall have the right to resort to, or cause to be frequented, the aforesaid newly discovered countries situate in America between New France and Virginia, the sea coasts whereof lie in the Latitude of from Forty to forty five degrees, now named New Netherlands . . . within the term of three years . . . to the exclusion of all others, either directly or indirectly sailing, resorting to, or frequenting the Said Newly discovered and found Countries, harbors, or places, from these United Netherlands, within the said three years, on pain of Confiscation of the ships and goods wherewith the attempt shall be made contrary hereunto. . . .

Act of the Dutch States General, October 11, 1614, in Brodhead, ed., Documents, *vol. 1, p. 10.*

About the latter end of August, a Dutch man of War of the burden of 160 tons arrived at Point-Comfort, its Commander's name Captain Jope, his pilot for the West Indies one Mr. Marmaduke an Englishman. They met . . . in the West Indies, and determined to hold consort ship hitherward, but in their passage lost one the other. He brought not any thing but 20. and odd Negroes, which the Governor and Cape Merchant bought for victual (whereof he was in great need as he pretended) at the best and easiest rate they could. He had a large and ample Commission from his Excellency to range and take purchase in the West Indies.

John Rolfe to Sir Edwin Sandys, 1619, in Kingsbury, ed., Records, *vol. 3, p. 243.*

All our riches for the present do consist in Tobacco, wherein one man by his own labor hath in one year raised to himself to the value of 200*l.* sterling; and another by the means of six servants hath cleared at one crop a thousand pound English. These be true, yet indeed rare examples, yet possible to be done by others. Our principal wealth (I should have said) consisteth in servants: But they are chargeable to be furnished with arms, apparel and bedding and for their transportation . . . both at sea, and for their first year commonly at land also: But if they escape [*survive*] they prove very hardy, and sound able men.

Now that your lordship may know, that we are not the veriest beggars in the world, our cowkeeper here of James Citty on Sundays goes accoutered all in fresh flaming silk; and a wife of one that in England had professed the black tie, not of a scholar, but of a collier of Croydon, wears her high beaver hat with a faire pearl hatband, and a silken suite thereto correspondent. But to leave the Populace, and to come higher; the Governor here, who at his first coming, besides a great deal of worth in his person, brought only his sword with him, was at his late being in London, together with his lady, out of his mere gettings here, able to disburse very near three thousand pound to furnish himself for his voyage. and once within seven years, I am persuaded (*absit invidia verbo*) that the Governor's place here may be as profitable as the lord Deputies of Ireland.

John Pory to Sir Dudley Carleton, 1619, in Tyler, ed., Narratives, *pp. 284–85.*

The other Council more general to be called by the Governor and yearly of Course and no oftener but for very extraordinary and Important occasions shall consist for present of the said Council of State and of Two Burgesses out of every town hund[red] and other particular plantation to be especially Chosen by the inhabitants. Which Council shall be called the general Assembly, wherein as also in the said Council of State, all matters shall be decided determined and ordered by the greater part of the voices then present, Reserving always to the Governor a negative voice, And this general assembly shall have free power, to treat Consult and conclude as well of all emergent occasions concerning the public weal of the said colony and every part thereof, as also to make ordinary and enact such general laws and orders for the behoof of the said colony and the good government thereof as shall time to time appear necessary or requisite.

Virginia's Great Charter, 1619, in Kingsbury, ed., Records, *vol. 3, pp. 483–84.*

The most convenient place we could find to sit in was the choir of the Church Where Sir George Yeardley, the Governor, being set down in his accustomed place, those of the Council of Estate [*the colonial council*] sat next to him on both hands, except only the Secretary then appointed Speaker, who sat right before him, John Twine, clerk of the General Assembly, being placed next to the Speaker, and Thomas Pierse, the Sergeant, standing at the bar, to be ready for any Service the Assembly should command him. But forasmuch as men's affairs do little prosper where God's service is neglected, all the Burgesses took their places in the Choir till a prayer was said by Mr. Bucke, the Minister, that it would please God to guide and sanctify all our proceedings to his own glory and the good of this Plantation. Prayer being ended, to the intent that as we had begun at God Almighty, so we might proceed with awful and due respect towards the Lieutenant, our most gracious and dread Sovereign, all the Burgesses were entreated to retire themselves into the body of the Church, which being done, before they were fully admitted, they were called in order and by name, and so every man (none staggering at it [*objecting to it*]) took the oath of Supremacy, and then entered the Assembly. . . .

These obstacles removed, the Speaker . . . delivered in brief to the whole assembly the occasions of their meeting. Which done, he read unto them the commission for establishing the Council of the Estate and the general Assembly, wherein their duties were described to the life. Having thus prepared them, he read over unto them the great Charter or commission of privileges, orders, and laws, sent . . . out of England. . . .

John Twine records the first Virginia Assembly, July 30, 1619, in West, ed., Source Book, *pp. 54–55.*

Captain William Powell presented a petition to the general Assembly against one Thomas Garnett, a[n *indentured*] servant of his, not only for extreme neglect of his business to the great loss and prejudice of the said Captain, and for openly and impudently abusing his house, in sight both of Master and Mistress, through wantonness with a woman servant of theirs, a widow, but also for falsely accusing him to the Governor both of Drunkenness and Theft, and besides for bringing all his fellow servants to testify on his side, wherein they justly failed him. It was thought fit by the general assembly (the Governor himself giving sentence), that he should stand four days with his ears nailed to the Pillory, viz: Wednesday, Aug. 4th, and so likewise Thursday, Friday, and Saturday next following, and every of those days should be publically whipped.

Virginia Assembly, August 3, 1619, in Tyler, ed., Narratives, *p. 268.*

Against excess in apparel, that every man be assessed in the church for all public contributions, if he be unmarried according to his own apparel, if he be married according to his own and his wife's or either of their apparel. . . .

That no man do sell or give any of the greater hoes to the Indians, or any English dog of quality, as a mastiff, greyhound, bloodhounds, land or water spaniel, or any other dog . . . whatsoever, of the English race, upon pain of forfeiting 5s sterling to the public uses of the Incorporation where he dwelleth. . . .

That no man do sell or give any Indian any piece shot or powder, or any other arms, offensive or defensive upon pain of being held a Traitor to the Colony, and of being hanged as soon as the facts is proved, without all redemption. . . .

That no man shall purposely go to any Indian towns, habitations or places or resorts without leave from the Governor or commander of that place where he liveth, upon pain of paying 40s to public uses as aforesaid. . . .

The Ministers and Churchwardens shall seek to present all ungodly disorders, the committers whereof if, upon good admonitions and mild reproof, they will not forbear the said scandalous offenses, as suspicions of whordoms, dishonest company keeping with women and such like, they are to be presented and punished accordingly. . . .

No maid or woman servant, either now resident in the Colony or hereafter to come, shall contract herself in marriage without either the consent of her parents, or of her Master or Mistress, or of the magistrate and minister of the place both together. And whatsoever minister shall marry or contracts any such persons without some of the foresaid consents shall be subject to the severe censure of the Governor and Council of Estate.

Acts of the first Virginia Assembly, August 4, 1619, in Tyler, ed., Narratives, *pp. 270–73.*

It is fully agreed at this general Assembly that in regard of the great pains and Labor of the Speaker of this Assembly . . . and likewise in respect of the diligence of the Clerk and sergeant, officers thereto belonging, That every man and man servant of above 16 years of age shall pay into the hands and Custody of the Burgesses of every Incorporation and plantation one pound of the best Tobacco, to be distributed to the Speaker and likewise to the Clerk and Sergeant of the Assembly, according to their degrees and ranks. . . .

Virginia Assembly, August 4, 1619, in Tyler, ed., Narratives, *pp. 276–77.*

The grains of our country do prosper very well there: Of Wheat they have great plenty: but their Maize, being the natural grain of that Country, doth far exceed in pleasantness, strength, and fertility. The Cattle which we have transported thither (being now grown near to five hundred) become much bigger of Body than the breed from which they came: the Horses also more beautiful, and fuller of courage. And such is the extraordinary fertility of that Soil, that the Does of the Deer yield two Fawns at a birth, and sometimes three. . . . To conclude, it is a Country, which nothing but ignorance can think ill of, and which no man but of a corrupt mind and ill purpose can defame.

Declaration of the London Company, 1620, in West, ed., Source Book, *pp. 64–65.*

. . . all great & honorable actions are accompanied with great difficulties, and must be both enterprised and overcome with answerable courages. It was granted the dangers were great, but not desperate; the difficulties were many, but not invincible. For though there were many of them likely, yet they were not certain; it might be sundry of the things feared might never befall; others by provident care & the use of good means, might in a great measure be prevented; and all of them, through the help of God, by fortitude and patience, might either be borne, or overcome. True it was, that such attempts were not to be made and undertaken without good ground & reason; not rashly or lightly as many have done for curiosity or hope of gain, &c. But their condition was not ordinary; their ends were good & honorable; their calling lawful, & urgent; and therefore they might expect the blessing of God in their preceding.

William Bradford on the Separatists' decision to migrate, 1620, Bradford's History, pp. 34–35.

Lastly, whereas you are become a body politic, suing amongst yourselves civil government, and are not furnished with any persons of special eminence above the rest, to be chosen by you into office, let your wisdom and godliness appear, not only in choosing such persons as do entirely love and will promote the common good, but also in yielding unto them all due honor and obedience . . . and this duty you may the more willing . . . perform, because you are at least for the present to have only them for your ordinary governors which your selves shall make choice of for that work.

Separatist minister John Robinson to the departing Pilgrims, ca. 1620, in West, ed., Source Book, *p. 116.*

And the time being come that they must depart, they were accompanied with most of their brethren out of the city, unto a town sundry miles off called Delfes-Haven, where the ship lay ready to receive them. So they left that goodly & pleasant city, which had been their resting place near 12 years; but they knew they were pilgrims [Heb. 3], & looked not much on those things, but lift up their eyes to the heaven, their dearest country, and quieted their spirits.

William Bradford describes the Separatists' departure, 1620, Bradford's History, p. 73.

We therefore . . . do . . . grant . . . that all Circuit, Continent, Precincts, and Limits in America, lying and being in Breadth from Forty Degrees of Northerly Latitude, from the Equinotical Line, the Forty-eight Degrees of the said Northerly Latitude, and in Length all the Breadth aforesaid throughout the Maine Land,

from Sea to Sea . . . shall be the Limits. . . . And to the End that Said Territories may forever hereafter be more particularly and certainly known and distinguished, our Will and Pleasure is that the same shall from henceforth be nominated, termed, and called by the Name of New-England, in America. . . .

Charter of the Council for New England, 1620, in West, ed., Source Book, *p. 110.*

Afterwards they [*the Pilgrims*] directed their course to come to the other shore, for they knew it was a neck of land they were to cross over, and so at length got to the sea-side, and marched to this supposed river, & by the way found a pond of clear fresh water, and shortly after a good quantity of clear ground where the Indians had formerly set corn, and some of their graves. And proceeding further they saw new-stubble where corn had been set the same year, also they found where lately a house had been, where some planks and a great kettle was remaining, and heaps of sand newly patted with their hands, which they, digging up, found in them diverse faire Indian baskets filled with corn, and some in ears, faire and good, of diverse colors, which seemed to them a very goodly sight, (having never seen any such before). . . . [T]hey returned to the ship, least they should be in fear of their safety; and took with them part of the corn, and buried up the rest, and so like the men from Eshcoll carried with them of the fruits of the land, & showed their brethren; of which, & their returns, they were marvelously glad, and their hearts encouraged.

After this, the shallop being got ready, they set out again for the better discovery of this place. . . . [T]here was also found 2 of their [*the Indians'*] houses covered with mats, & sundry of their implements in them, but the people were run away & could not be seen; also there was found more of their corn, & of their beans of various colors. The corn & beans they brought away, purposing to give them full satisfaction when they should meet with any of them (as about some 6. months afterward they did, to their good content). And here is to be noted a special providence of God, and a great mercy to this poor people, that here they got seed to plant them corn the next year, or else they might have starved, for they had none, nor any likelihood to get any till the season had been past (as the sequel did manifest).

The Pilgrims go ashore, November 11, 1620, Bradford's History, pp. 99–100.

We send you in this ship one widow and eleven maids for wives for the people in Virginia. There hath been especial care had in the choice of them, for there hath not any one of them been received but upon good commendations, as by a note herewith sent you may perceive. We pray you all therefore that at their first landing they may be housed, lodged, and provided for of diet till they be married, for such was the haste of sending them away, as that straitened with time, we had no means to put provisions aboard, which defect shall be supplied by the magazine ship. And in case they cannot be presently married, we desire they may be put to several householders that have wives till they can be provided of husbands. There are near fifty more which are shortly to come, are sent by our most honorable Lord and Treasurer, the Earl of Southampton and certain worthy gentlemen who taking into their consideration, that the plantation can never flourish till families be planted, and the respect of wives and children fix the people on the soil, therefore have given this fair beginning. For the reimbursing of whose charges, it is ordered that every man that marries them give 120 Y. weight of the best leaf tobacco for each of them, and in case any of them die, that proportion must be advanced to make it up upon those that survive.

The London Company sends tobacco brides to Virginia, 1621, in Kingsbury, ed., Records, *vol. 3, pp. 493–94.*

All this while the Indians came skulking about them, and would sometimes show them selves aloof of, but when any approached near them, they would run away. And once they stole away their tools where they had been at work, & were gone to dinner. But about the 16 of March a certain Indian came boldly amongst them, and spoke to them in broken English, which they could well understand, but marveled at it. At length they understood by discourse with him, that he was not of these parts, but belonged to the eastern parts, where some English ships came to fish, with whom he was acquainted, & could name sundry of them by their names, amongst whom he had got his language. He became profitable to them in acquainting them with many things concerning the state of the country in the east-parts where he lived, which was afterwards profitable unto them; as also of the people here, of their names, number, & strength; of their situation & distance from this place, and who was chief amongst them. His name was *Samaset,* he told them also of another Indian whose name was *Squanto,* a native of this place, who

had been in England & could speak better English than him self. Being, after some time of entertainments & gifts, dismissed, a while after he came again, & 5 more with him, & they brought again all the tools that were stolen away before, and made way for the coming of their great Sachem, called *Massasoyt;* who, about 4 or 5 days after, came with the chief of his friends & other attendants, with the aforesaid *Squanto.* With whom, after friendly entertainment, & some gifts given him, they made a peace with him (which hath now continued this 24 years) in these terms.

1. That neither he nor any of his, should injury or do hurt to any of their people.

2. That if any of his did any hurt to any of theirs, he should send the offender, that they might punish him.

3. That if any thing were taken away from any of theirs, he should cause it to be restored; and they should doe the like to this.

4. If any did unjustly war against him, they would aid him; if any did war against them, he should aide them.

5. He should send to his neighbors confederates, to certify them of this, that they might not wrong them, but might be likewise comprised in the conditions of peace.

6. That when their men came to them, they should leave their bows & arrows behind them.

William Bradford describes the peace treaty with Chief Massasoit, spring 1621, Bradford's History *pp. 114–15.*

Afterwards they (as many as were able) began to plant their corn, in which service Squanto stood them in great stead, showing them both the manner how to set it, and after how to dress & tend it. Also he told them except they got fish & set with it (in these old grounds) it would come to nothing, and he showed them that in the middle of April they should have store enough, come up the brook, by which they began to build, and taught them how to take it, and where to get other provisions necessary for them; all which they found true by trial & experience.

William Bradford describes Squanto's aid to the Pilgrims, spring 1621, Bradford's History, *p. 121.*

May 12 [*1621*] was the first marriage in this place, which, according to the laudable custom of the Low-Countries, in which they had lived, was thought most requisite to be performed by the magistrate, as being a civil thing, upon which many questions about inheritances do depend, with other things most proper to their cognisance, and most consonant to the scriptures, Ruth 4. and no where found in the gospel to be laid on the ministers as a part of their office....

William Bradford describes civil marriage among the Pilgrims, May 1621, Bradford's History, *p. 121.*

This indenture made the First Day of June, 1621, Between the President and Council of New England . . . and John Peirce Citizen and Clothworker of London and his Associates. . . . Witnesseth that whereas the said John Peirce and his Associates have already transported and . . . at their cost and charges themselves and diverse persons into New England and there to erect and build a Town and settle diverse Inhabitants for the advancement of the general Plantation of that Country of New England, Now the said President and Council, in consideration thereof and for the furtherance of the said plantation and encouragement of the said Undertakers, have agreed to grant, assign, allot, and appoint to the said John Peirce . . . one hundred acres of ground for every person so to be transported, besides diverse other privileges, Liberties, and commodities hereafter mentioned....

Grant of the Council of New England to the Pilgrims' company, June 1621, in West, ed., Source Book, *p. 118.*

. . . we have built seven dwelling-houses and four for the use of the plantation, and have made preparation for diverse others. We set the last spring some twenty acres of Indian corn, and sowed some six acres of barley and peas; and according to the manner of the Indians, we manured our ground with . . . shads, which we have in great abundance, and take with great ease at our doors. Our corn did prove well; and, God be praised, we had a good increase of Indian corn, and our barley indifferent good, but our peas not worth the gathering, for we feared they were too late sown....

Now because I expect your coming unto us . . . I thought it good to advertise you of a few things needful. . . . Trust not too much on us for corn at this time . . . bring good store of clothes and bedding with you. Bring every man a musket or fowling-piece. Let your piece be long in the barrel and fear not the weight of it, for most of our shooting is from stands. Bring juice of lemons, and take it fasting; it is of good use. For hot waters, aniseed water is the best; but use it sparingly. If you bring anything for the comfort in the country, but-

ter or salted oil, or both is very good. . . . Bring paper and linseed oil for your windows, with cotton yarn for your lamps. Let your shot be most for big fowls, and bring store of powder and shot.

Pilgrim Edward Winslow to a friend in England, December 1621, in West, ed., Source Book, *pp. 120–22.*

. . . as well on the Friday morning that fatal day being the two and twentieth of March, as also in the evening before, as at other times before, they [*the Powhatan*] came unarmed into our houses, with Deer, Turkeys, Fish, Fruits, and other provisions, to sell us: yea in some places, sat down at breakfast with our people, whom immediately with their own tools they slew most barbarously, not sparing either age or sex, man, woman or child; so suddenly in their cruel execution, that few or none discerned the weapon or blow that brought them to destruction. In which manner they also slew many of our people then at their several works in the fields, well knowing in what places and quarters each of our men were, in regard of their familiarity with us, for the effecting that great master-piece of works, their conversion: and by this means fell that fatal morning under the bloody and barbarous hands of that perfidious and inhumane people, three hundred forty seven men, women, and children; most by their own weapons; and not being content their lives, they fell again upon the dead bodies, making as well as they could, a fresh murder, defacing, dragging, and mangling their dead carcasses into many pieces, and carrying some parts away in derision, with base and brutish triumph.

John Smith, March 22, 1622, General History of Virginia, *in Tyler, ed.,* Narratives, *pp. 358–59.*

To lull them the better in security they sought no revenge till their Corn was ripe. Then they drew together three hundred of the best Soldiers amongst the Savages to surprise their Corn. Under the conduct of Sir George Yearley, being embarked in convenient shipping and all things necessary for the enterprise, they went first to Nandsamund, where the people set fire on their own houses and spoiled what they could, and then fled with what they could carry; so that the English did make no slaughter amongst them for revenge. Their Corn fields being newly gathered, they surprised all they found, burnt the houses [that] remained unburnt, and so departed....

Thence they sailed to Pamunkey, the chief seat of Opechancanough, the contriver of the massacre. The

Savages seemed exceeding fearful, promising to bring them Sara [Boys, a captive], and the rest of the English yet living, with all the Arms, and what they had to restore, much desiring peace, and to give them any satisfaction they could. Many such devices they feigned to procrastinate the time ten or twelve days, till they had got away their Corn from all the other places up the River, but that where the English kept their quarters. At last when they [the English] saw all those promises were but delusions, they seized on all the Corn there was, set fire on their houses. . . . Thus by this means the Savages are like as they report to endure no small misery this Winter and that some of our men are returned to their former plantations.

John Smith, 1622–23, General History, in Tyler, ed., Narratives, pp. 384–85.

The inhabitants of Wessagusset (having translated the name of their habitation from that ancient Savage name to Ma-re Mount and being resolved to have the new name confirmed for a memorial to after ages) did devise amongst themselves to have it performed in a solemn manner with Revels, & merriment after the old English custom: prepared to set up a Maypole upon the festival day of Philip and Jacob; & therefore brewed a barrel of excellent beer, & provided a case of bottles to be spent, with other good cheer, for all comers of that day. And because they would have it in a complete form, they had prepared a song fitting to the time and present occasion. And upon Mayday they brought the Maypole top the place appointed, with drums, guns, pistols, and other fitting instruments, for that purpose; and there erected it with the help of Savages, that came thither of purpose to see the manner of our Revels. A goodly pine tree of 80 foot long, was reared up, with a pair of buckshorns nailed on, somewhat near unto the top of it: where it stood as a fair sea mark for directions; how to find out the way to mine host of Ma-re Mount.

Thomas Morton, 1623, New English Canaan, pp. 132–33.

For when we go to Jamestown (that is 10 miles of us) there lie all the ships that come to land, and there they must deliver their goods. And when we went up to town [we would go], as it may be, on Monday at noon, and come there by night, [and] then load the next day by noon, and go home in the afternoon, and unload, and then away again in the night, and [we would] be up about midnight. Then if it rained or blowed never so

hard, we must lie in the boat on the water and have nothing but a little bread. For when we go into the boat we [would] have a loaf allowed to two men, and it is all [we would get] if we stayed there two days, which is hard; and [we] must lie all that while in the boat. But that Goodman Jackson pitied me and made me a cabin to lie in always when I [would] come up, and he would give me some poor jacks [*fish*] [to take] home with me, which comforted me more than peas or water gruel. Oh, they be very godly folks, and love me very well, and will do anything for me. And he much marveled that you would send me a servant to the Company; he saith I had been better knocked on the head. And indeed so I find it now, to my great grief and misery; and saith that if you love me you will redeem me suddenly [*buy my indenture*], for which I do entreat and beg. And if you cannot get the merchants to redeem me for some little money, then for God's sake get a gathering or entreat some good folks to lay out some little sum of money in meal and cheese and butter and beef. Any eating meat will yield great profit.

Jamestown indentured servant Richard Frethorne to his parents in England, 1623, in Kingsbury, ed., Records, vol. 4, pp. 60–61.

Whereas to the great contempt of the majesty of God and ill example to others, certain women within this colony have of late contrary to the laws ecclesiastical of the Realm of England contracted themselves to two several men at one time, whereby much trouble does grow between parties: and the Governor and Council of State, thereby much disquieted: to prevent the like offense in others hereafter, it is by the Governor and Council ordered in court, that every Minister give notice in his church to his parishioners, that what man or woman soever shall hereafter use any word or speech tending to contract of marriage unto two several persons at one time (though not precise and legal, yet so as may entangle and breed scruple in their consciences) shall for such their offense undergo either corporal punishment (as whipping etc.) or other punishment by fire, or otherwise, according to the quality of the person so offending.

Virginia Assembly, 1624, in Kingsbury, ed., Records, vol. 4, p. 487.

Known ye . . . that We reposing assured trust and confidence in the understanding, care, fidelity, experience, and circumspection of you . . . have nominated and assigned, and do hereby nominate and assign you the said Sir Francis Wyatt, to be the present Governor and you the said Francis West, Sir George Yeardley, and rest before mentioned, to be our present Council of and for the said Colony and Plantation in Virginia: Giving and granting unto you, and the great number of you, by this presents respectively, full power and authorities to perform and execute the places, powers, and authorities incident to a Governor and Council in Virginia, respectively, and to direct and govern, correct and punish our Subjects now inhabiting or being, or which hereafter shall inhabit or be in Virginia ... and to do, execute and perform all and every other matters and things concerning that Plantation, as fully and amply as any Governor and Council resident there, at any time within the space of five years now last past. ...

King James I's commission to the first royal officials of Virginia, 1624, in West, ed., Source Book, *pp. 81–82.*

Master Layford was at the Merchant's charge sent to Plymouth plantation to be their Pastor. But the Brethren, before they would allow of it, would have him first renounce his calling, to the office of the Ministry [*in the Anglican Church*], received in England, as heretical and papistical (so he confessed) and then to receive a new calling from them, after their fanatical invention which he refused, alleging and maintaining, that his calling as it stood was lawful, and that he would not renounce it; and so John Oldham his opinion was one the affirmative, and both together did maintain the Church of England to be a true Church ... and by this means canceled their good opinion, amongst the number of the Separatists, that stay they must not, lest they should be spies, and to fall foul on this occasion, the Brethren though it would betray their case, and make it fall under censure, therefore against Master Layford they had found out some scandal; to be laid on his former course of life, to blemish that, and so to conclude he was a spotted beast, and not to be allowed. ...

Thomas Morton, 1624, New England Canaan, *pp. 118–19.*

... and as soon as they [*the settlers at Ft. Orange*] had built hutts of Bark the Macikanders or River Indians, ye Maquaes: Oneydes: Onondagas, Cayouga & Sennekes with the Mahawawa or Ottawawaes Indians came and made covenants of friendship with the said Adrien Jorise there Commander Bringing him great Presents of Beaver or of Peltry & desired that they

might come & and have a Constant free Trade with them which was concluded upon. ...

Catelyn Trico, who arrived on the Nieu Nederlandt *in 1624, quoted in Edmonds,* Musket, *p. 161.*

The island of the Manhatas is full of trees, and, in the middle, rocky. On the north side, there is good land in two places, where two farmers, each with four horses, would have enough to do, without much clearing or grubbing at first. The grass is good in the forests and valleys; but when made into hay, it is not so nutritious for the cattle as the hay in Holland, in consequence of its wild state; yet it annually improves by cultivation. On the east side there rises a large level field, of about one hundred and sixty acres, through which runs a very fine fresh stream; so that land can be plowed without much clearing. It appears to be good. The six farms, four of which lie along the River Hell-gate [*the East River*], stretching to the south side of the island, have at least one hundred and twenty acres ready to be sown with winter seed, which, at the most, may have been plowed eight times.

Letter of Isaac De Rasieres to Samuel Blommaert, 1626, quoted in Brodhead, History, *pp. 167–78.*

Those great important works of suppressing the Indians, discoveries by sea and land, and Fortification against a foreign enemy, that they may be thoroughly and effectively performed, will require no less numbers than Five hundred soldiers, to be yearly sent over, for Certain years, with a full years provision of Victual, apparel, arms, Munition, tools, and all necessaries to which Worthy design the Colony will be always ready to yield their best furtherance and assistance, as they have been very forward since the Massacre, notwithstanding their great loss then sustained. And we Conceive so great expense, will have the better success, if the ordering thereof be referred to the Governor and Council here residing, with the advice (in special cases) of the General Assembly.

Virginia council to the king's Special Council for the Colony, April 1626, in West, ed., Source Book, *pp. 84–85.*

Yesterday, arrived here the Ship the Arms of Amsterdam, which sailed from New Netherlands, out of the River Mauritius, on the 23rd September. They report that our people are in good heart and live in peace there; the Women also have borne some children

t' Fort nieüw Amsterdam op de Manhatans

The earliest known view of New Amsterdam, drawn 1626–28 (*New York Public Library Print Collection, Print Collection, Miriam and Ira D. Wallach Division of Art, Prints, and Photographs; Astor, Lenox, and Tilden Foundations*)

there. They have purchased the Island Manhattes from the Indians for the value of 60 guilders; 'tis 11,000 morgens in size. They had all their grain sowed by the middle of May, and reaped by the middle of August. They send thence samples of summer grain; such as wheat, rye, barley, oats, buckwheat, canary seed, beans and flax.

The cargo of the aforesaid ship is: 7246 Beaver Skins; 675 Otter skins; 48 Mink skins; 36 Wild cat skins; 33 Minks; 34 Rat [*muskrat*] skins.

Peter Schagen to the Dutch States General, 1627, in Brodhead, ed., Documents, *vol. 1, p. 37.*

New Plymouth lies on the slope of a hill, stretching east toward the sea-coast, with a broad street about a cannon-shot of eight hundred [paces?] long leading down the hill, and with [another street] crossing in the middle, northward to the rivulet and southward to the land. The houses are constructed of hewn planks, with gardens also inclosed behind and at the sides with hewn timber; so that their houses and court-yards are arranged in very good order, with a stockade against a sudden attack. At the ends of the streets are three wooden gates. In the centre, on the cross street, stands the governor's house; before which is a square inclosure, upon which four swivels are mounted, so as to flank along the streets. Upon the hill they have a large square house with a flat roof, made of thick sawn plank, stayed with oak beams; upon the top of which they have six cannon, which shoot iron balls of four and five pounds weight, and command the surrounding country. The lower part they use for their church, where they preach on Sundays and the usual holidays. They assemble by beat of drum, each with his musket or fire-lock, in front of the captain's door. They have their cloaks on, and place themselves in order three abreast, and are led by a sergeant, without beat of drum. Behind comes the governor in a long robe. Beside him, on the right hand, comes the preacher, with his cloak on; and on the left hand the captain, with his side-arms and his cloak on, and with a small cane in his hand. And so they march in good order, and each sets his arms down near him. Thus they are constantly on their guard night and day.

Letter of Isaac de Raisieres, 1627, quoted in Brodhead, History, *pp. 178–79.*

Now though they had some untoward persons mixed amongst them from the first, which came out of England, and more afterwards by some of the adventurers, as friendship or other affections led them,—though sundry were gone, some for Virginia, and some to other places,—yet diverse were still mingled amongst them, about whom the Governor & council with other of their chief friends had serious consideration, how to settle things in regard of this new bargain or purchase made, in respect of the distribution of things both for the present and future. . . . Therefore they resolved, for sundry reasons, to take in all amongst them, that were either heads of families, or single young men, that were of ability, and free, (and able to govern them selves with meet discretion, and their affairs, so as to be helpful in the commonwealth,) into this partnership or purchase [*buying out Weston*]. First, they considered that they had need of men & strength both for defense and carrying on of businesses. 2, most of them had borne their parts in former miseries & wants with them, and therefore (in some sort) but equal to partake in a better condition, if the Lord he pleased to give it. But chiefly they saw not how peace would be preserved without so doing. . . .

So they called the company together, and conferred with them, and came to this conclusion, that the [*fur*] trade should be managed as before, to help to pay the debts; and all such persons as were above named should be reputed and enrolled for purchasers; single free men to have a single share, and every father of a family to be allowed to purchase so many shares as he had persons in his family; that is to say, one for himself, and one for his wife, and for every child that he had living with him, one. As for servants, they had none . . . and so every one was to pay his part according to his proportion towards the purchase, & all other debts, what the profit of the trade would not reach too; viz. a single man for a single share, a master of a family for so many as he had. This gave all good content.

William Bradford, 1627, Bradford's History, *pp. 257–59.*

The people, for the most part, are all free, somewhat rough, and loose, but I find in most all of them love and respect towards me. . . . As to the natives of this country, I find them entirely savage and wild, strangers to all decency, yea, uncivil and stupid as posts, proficient in all wickedness and godlessness; devilish men, who serve nobody but the devil, that is, the spirit which in their language they call manetto; under which title they comprehend everything that is subtle and crafty and beyond human skill and power. They have so much witchcraft, divination, sorcery, and wicked traits that they cannot be held in any bands or locks. . . .

The promises which the Lords Masters of the Company had made me of some acres of surveyed lands for me to make myself a home . . . is wholly of no avail. For their Honors well know that there are no horses, cows, or laborers to be obtained here for money. Every one is short in these particulars and wants more. . . .

. . . They are making a windmill to saw the wood, and we also have a grist-mill. They bake brick here, but it is very poor. There is good material for burning lime, namely, oyster-shells, in large quantities. The burning of potash has not succeeded; the master and his laborers are very disappointed. We are busy now in building a fort of good quarry stone, which is to be found not far from here in abundance. May the Lord only build and watch over our walls.

Dominie Jonas Michaelius to his superior in Holland, 1628, in Hart, ed., American History, *vol. 1, pp. 576–78.*

I, Francis Bright, of Roily, in Essex, clerk, have this present 2nd February, 1628, agreed with the Company of Adventurers for New-England, in America, to be ready with my wife, two children, and one maid-servant, by the beginning of March next, to take our passage to the Plantation at or near Massachusetts Bay, in New-England, as aforesaid; where I do promise, God sparing me life and health, to serve the said Company in the work of the Ministry, by my true and faithful endeavors, for the space of three years. For and in consideration whereof, these several particulars are this day agreed upon by the said Company, and by me accept, namely:

1. That £20 shall be forthwith paid me by the Company's treasurer towards charges of fitting myself with apparel and other necessaries for the voyage.

2. That £10 more shall be paid me by him towards providing of books; which said books, upon my death

or removal from the charge now intended to be transferred upon me, are to be and remain to such minister as shall succeed in my place for the said Company; and before my departure out of England, I am to deliver a particular of the said books.

3. That £20 yearly shall be paid me for three years, to begin from the time of my first arrival in New-England, and so to be accounted and paid at the end of each year.

4. That during the said time, the Company shall provide for me and my family aforementioned, necessaries of diet, housing, firewood, and shall be at the charge of the transportation of us into New-England; and at the end of the said three years, if I shall not like to continue longer there, to be at charges of transporting us back for England.

5. That in convenient time a house shall be built, and certain lands allotted thereunto; which, during my stay in the country and continuing in the ministry, shall be for my use, and after my death or removal, the same to be for succeeding ministers.

6. That at the expiration of the said three years, one hundred acres of land shall be assigned unto me, for me and my heirs forever.

7. That in case I shall depart this life in that country, the said Company shall take care for my widow, during her widowhood and abode in that country and Plantation; the like for my children whilst they remain on the said Plantation.

8. That the milk of two kine [*cows*] shall be appointed me toward the charge of diet for me and my family, as aforesaid, and half their increase during the said three years, to be likewise mine; but the said two kine and the other half of the increase to return to the Company at the end of the said three years. . . .

The Reverend Francis Bright's agreement with the Massachusetts Bay Company, 1629, in Young, ed., Chronicles, *pp. 207–09.*

That his Majesty will be pleased graciously to extend his favor to the planters, for a new confirmation of their lands and goods by charter under the great seal of England, and therein to authorize the Lords to consider what is fit to be done for the ratifying of the privileges formerly granted, and holding of a general assembly, to be called by the Governor upon necessary occasions, therein to propound laws and order for the good government of the people; and for that it is most reasonable that his majesty's subjects should be governed only by such laws as shall have their original from his majesty's royal approbation, it be therefore so ordered, that those laws, so there made, only stand as propositions, until his majesty shall be pleased, under his great seal or privy seal, or by the Lords of his noble privy council, to ratify the same.

Virginia governor Sir John Harvey to King Charles I, 1629, in West, ed., Source Book, *p. 86.*

For the better accommodation of businesses, we have divided the servants belonging to the Company into several families, as we desire and intend they should live together. . . .

Our earnest desire is that you take special care, in settling these families, that the chief in the family, at least some of them, be grounded in religion; whereby morning and evening family duties may be duly performed, and a watchful eye held over all in each family, by one or more in each family to be appointed thereto, that so disorders may be prevented, and ill weeds nipped before they take too great a head. It will be a business worthy your best endeavours to look unto this in the beginning, and, if need be, to make some exemplary to all the rest; otherwise your government will be esteemed as a scarecrow. Our desire is to use lenity, all that may be; but, in case of necessity, not to neglect the other, knowing that correction is ordained for the fool's back. . . . And we heartily pray you, that all be kept to labor, as the only means to reduce them to a civil, yea a godly life, and to keep youth from falling into many enormities, which by nature we are all too much inclined unto.

Massachusetts Bay Company to Governor Endicott, April 21, 1629, in Young, ed., Chronicles, *pp. 167–68.*

Whereas in our last we advised you to make composition with such of the savages as did pretend any title or lay claim to any of the land within the territories granted to us by his Majesty's charter, we pray you now be careful to discover and find out all such pretenders, and by advice of the Council there to make such reasonable composition with them as may free us and yourselves from any scruple of intrusion. . . .

And for the better governing and ordering of our people, especially such as shall be negligent and remiss in performance of their duties, or otherwise exorbitant, our desire is that a house of correction be erected and set up, both for the punishment of such offenders, and to deter others by their example from such irregular courses. . . .

As in our former, so now again we especially desire you to take care that no tobacco be planted by any of the new planters under your government, unless it be some small quantity of mere necessity and for physic, for preservation of their healths. . . .

And as we desire all should live in some honest calling and procession, so we pray you to be unpartial in the administration of justice, and endeavour that no man whatsoever, freeman or servant to any, may have just cause of complaint therein. . . .

We pray you to endeavour, though there be much strong waters sent for sale, yet so to order it as that the savages may not, for our lucre sake, be induced to the excessive use, or rather abuse of it; and at any hand take care our people give no ill example. . . .

Massachusetts Bay Company to Governor Endicott, June 3, 1629, in Young, ed., Chronicles, *pp. 182–90.*

I. Such participants of the Said Company as may be inclined to plant any colonies in New Netherlands shall be permitted to send, in the ships of this Company going thither three or four persons to inspect the situation of the country, provided that they . . . pay for board and passage, going and coming, six stivers a day (such as desire to mess in the cabin to pay 12 stivers) and agree to give assistance like others, in cases offensive and defensive. And if any ships be taken from the enemy [*pirated*], they shall received pro rata their portions with the ship's company, each accord to his quality, that is to say, the colonists messing outside the cabin shall be rated with the sailors and those messing in the cabin with those of the Company's servants messing at table who receive the lowest wages. . . .

III. All such shall be acknowledged patrons of New Netherlands as shall agree to plant there a colony of 50 souls, upwards of 15 years old, within the space of four years. . . . making together four years, to the full number of 50 persons. . . . But they are warned that the Company reserves to itself the island of the *Manhattes.* . . .

IX. Those who shall send over these colonies, shall furnish them with proper instructions in order that they may be ruled and governed comfortably to the rule of government, both as to administration and justice, made, or to be made by the Assembly of the Nineteen, which instructions they must first lay before the directors of the respective Chambers. . . .

XII. Inasmuch as it is the intention of the Company to people the island of the *Manhattes* first, this island shall be provisionally also be the staple port for all products and wares that are found on their North River [*the Hudson*] and lands thereabouts, before they are allowed to be sent elsewhere. . . .

XXI. And as to private persons who on their own accord . . . shall go thither and settle as freemen in smaller numbers than patrons, they may with the approbation of the director and council there, choose and take possession of as much land as they properly cultivate and hold the same in full ownership either for themselves or for their masters. . . .

XXVI. Whosoever shall settle any colonies out of the limits of *Manhattes* Island must satisfy the Indians of that place for the land and may enlarge the limits of their colonies if they settle a proportionate number of colonists thereon.

XXVII. The patrons and colonists shall in particular endeavor as quickly as possible to find some means whereby they may support a minister and a schoolmaster, that thus the service of God and zeal for religion may not grow cool and be neglected among them. . . .

XXX. The Company will endeavor to supply the colonists with as many blacks as it possible can, on the conditions hereafter to be made, without however being bound to do so to a greater extent or for a longer time than it shall see fit.

Charter of Freedoms and Exemptions, June 7, 1629, in New York State Library, Van Rensselaer, *pp. 137–53.*

Upon due consideration of the state of the Plantation now in hand for New-England, wherein we, whose names are hereunto subscribed, have engaged ourselves, and having weighed the greatness of the work in regard of the consequence, God's glory and the Church's good; as also in regard of the difficulties and discouragements which in all probabilities must be forecast upon the prosecution of this business; considering withal that this whole adventure grows upon the joint confidence we have in each other's fidelity and resolution herein, so as no man of us would have adventured it without assurance of the rest; now, for the better encouragement of ourselves and others that shall join with us in this action, and to the end that every man may without scruple dispose of his estate and affairs as may best fit his preparation for this voyage; it is fully and faithfully agreed amongst us, and every of us doth hereby freely and sincerely promise and bind himself, in the word of a Christian, and in the presence of God, who is the searcher of all hearts, that we will so really endeavour the prosecution of this work, as by God's assistance, we will be ready in our persons, and with such of our several families as are to go with us, and such provision as we are able conveniently to furnish ourselves withal, to embark for the said Plantation by the first of March next, at such port or ports of this land as shall be agreed upon by the Company, to the end to pass the seas, (under God's protection,) to inhabit and continue in New-England: Provided always, that before the last of September next, the whole government, together with the patent for the said Plantation, be first, by an order of Court, legally transferred and established to remain with us and others which shall inhabit upon the said Plantation....

Cambridge agreement, August 26, 1629, in Young, ed., Chronicles, *pp. 281–82.*

Now know ye that the said Council, by Virtue and Authority of his said late Majesty's Letters patents, and ...in consideration that William Bradford and his Associates have for these nine years lived in New-England ...and have there...planted a Town...at their own proper Costs...and now seeing that by the special Providence of God and their extraordinary Care and Industry, they have increased the Plantation to near three hundred People...have given...unto the said William Bradford...all that Part of New England.... Also it shall be lawful and free for the said William Bradford, his Associates, his Heirs and Assignees, at all times hereafter, to incorporate by some usual or fit Name and Title...with Liberty to them and their Successors, from time to time to frame and make Orders, Ordinances, and Constitutions...for the better Government of his or their People and Affairs in New England...provided that the said Laws and Orders be not repugnant to the Laws of England....

Grant of Council of New England to Plymouth Colony, January 1630, in West, ed., Source Book, *pp. 124–25.*

We, the director and council of New Netherlands, residing on the island the *Manahatas* and in Fort Amsterdam, ... do hereby testify and declare, that on this day the date underwritten, before us appeared and presented themselves their proper persons, *Kottamack, Mawanemit, Abantzeene, Sagiskwit,* and *Kanamoack,* owners and proprietors of their respective parcels of land extending up the [*Hudson*] river, south and north, from the said fort [*Fort Orange*] ... and declared freely and advisedly that for and on account of certain quantity of merchandise which they acknowledged to have received in their hands and possession before the execution hereof, by virtue and title of sale, they hereby convey, cede and make over to and for the behoof of the Hon. *Kiliaen van Rensselaer,* absent ... the respective parcels of lands herein before specified, with the timber, appurtenances and dependencies thereof, together with all the interests, rights and jurisdiction to them the grantors conjointly or severally belonging ... and at the same time giving him ... full, absolute, and irrevocable power, authority, and special command to hold, in quiet possession, cultivation, occupations, and use ... without the grantors holding in the least any part, right, interest or authority whether of property, command or jurisdiction, but on the contrary, hereby, desisting from, yielding, giving up and renouncing the same forever....

Certificate of purchase of Indian land, August 13, 1630, in New York State Library, Van Rensselaer, *pp. 166–68.*

4

Settlement Spreads in New England, the Chesapeake, and the Middle Atlantic

1630–1642

THE GREAT MIGRATION BEGINS

In 1630, a large movement of people from England to North America began; it was called the Great Migration. Before the Great Migration ended in 1642, 20,000 English colonists had arrived in New England.

In 1629, a group of English Puritans had bought out commercial investors in the Massachusetts Bay Company. Under the leadership of John Winthrop and Thomas Dudley, they had begun organizing to found a Puritan commonwealth

A modern reconstruction of a timber cottage, one kind of temporary housing built by early English settlers *(Collection of the House of the Seven Gables)*

in the New World. In June 1630, the first 11 ships arrived at Salem, carrying Winthrop, Dudley, and 1,000 colonists. A small settlement already existed there, led by fellow Puritan John Endicott, but Winthrop's group did not like the site. Almost immediately, they moved to Charlestown. From there, leaders soon took groups to Medford, Dorchester, Watertown, Roxbury, Lynn, and Shawmut. In September, the Shawmut settlement was renamed Boston in honor of the English town from which many of the group came. Its bay and harbor soon became the center of the colony.

By the end of 1630, six more ships had arrived. The first winter was predictably difficult. Some 200 died, and another 100 returned to England. Winthrop exerted firm leadership, however, purchasing food from nearby Plymouth Colony and the Indians. By the second winter, Massachusetts Bay Colony had stabilized.

The leaders of the Massachusetts Bay Company, like investors in all previous colonization ventures, hoped their colony would prosper economically. That goal, however, was subordinate to their religious and communal ends. Unlike previous colonizing companies, the Massachusetts Bay Company did not manage a distant colony in hope of future profit. All investors were also colonists. In effect, the company, or corporation (as it was called), and the colony were one and the same.

GOVERNMENT IN MASSACHUSETTS BAY

The charter of the Massachusetts Bay Company called for a governor, deputy governor, court (or council) of assistants, and freemen (voters who were male shareholders or investors in the company). Together, they were to function as a General Court, or assembly. The governor and assistants were to be elected yearly by the General Court; the assistants, also called magistrates, were to act as judges or justices of the peace, trying all major civil and criminal cases.

The first meeting of the General Court was held in October 1630. Only eight of the original 12 shareholders remained alive to vote as freemen. All eight were also assistants. However, at the assembly, more than 100 other Massachusetts men appeared and applied for admission to the corporation as voting freemen. The original investors postponed a ruling to consider if and how power was to be shared. At the General Court of May 1631, they announced that male property owners who were full members of a Puritan church could apply to the General Court for admission as voting freemen. However, they also announced (contrary to the actual charter) that assistants were to be elected for life; governors were to be elected by the assistants and from among their number only; and laws were to be passed only by the governor and assistants, not the court as a whole.

Three groups of men now existed in the colony: leaders, voting freemen, and nonvoters. The leaders, who have often been called the Puritan oligarchy, had power similar to that of proprietors in other colonies. Voting freemen had some power; however, their number was limited because full church membership was strictly controlled. By 1640, only about one-quarter of the population were church members; only about 300 men—or one-fifth of the adult male population—were admitted as freemen. Nonvoters, the remainder of the male colonists, could be either "free men" and landowners or indentured servants. They had no vote in the colony's government. Neither, of course, did women.

Although the corporation and colony were self-governing, neither was democratic, nor was democracy a goal. Almost immediately, however, the power of the Puritan oligarchy was challenged by voting freemen. In 1632, residents of Watertown protested a tax levied by the assistants. Spurred by the protest, the General Court voted to establish the election of two representatives from each town, to "advise" assistants on matters of taxation. In 1634, town representatives demanded to see the charter. The charter, of course, called for the yearly election of assistants and the participation of the General Court in lawmaking. The charter's policies were reinstated forthwith, along with other reforms. Henceforth, the May session of the General Court was open to all freemen. At the other three sessions, representatives from each town were to attend.

The General Court of 1634 also guaranteed colonists the right to trial by jury. After 1635, both regular and grand jury systems operated. However, no colonial code of laws yet existed, separate from English common law. (Common law derives from custom and cumulative judicial decisions, not from a specially composed code.) Originally, the colony's leaders believed that new colonial common law would develop just as common law had developed in England. In 1637, however, the General Court appointed a committee to draft a code of laws, but the committee took no action. Finally, in December 1641, the General Court approved a document called the Massachusetts Body of Liberties, written by the Reverend Nathaniel Ward. It named only 12 capital offenses (a much smaller number than most codes of the day) and specified the punishment for a given crime, curtailing the discretionary authority of judges. It also enumerated about 100 rights, or "liberties," including some for women, children, servants, foreigners, and even animals.

Back in England, neither King Charles I nor William Laud, the archbishop of Canterbury, was pleased by the independence and vigor of the Puritan colony in Massachusetts. They were particularly unhappy that Massachusetts had effectively disenfranchised members of the Church of England. In 1634, Charles appointed a Council for Foreign Plantations to supervise all colonies—and appointed Archbishop Laud as its head. The commission set about to review the terms of the Massachusetts Bay Company's charter, but discovered it was missing; Winthrop had carried it to New England with him. (In the 17th century, official documents were laboriously hand written then personally signed and sealed by the king or other officials; no quick way of making multiple copies existed.) Charles demanded its return; Massachusetts officials refused. In 1638, Charles began legal proceedings to rescind the charter entirely and ordered Massachusetts to send representatives to England. Again, the colonists refused him. Charles and the commission consequently drew up plans for royal government in Massachusetts. Agreeing among themselves to refuse any royal governor, colonists increased the militia and fortified Boston harbor.

In 1639, Charles appointed Sir Ferdinando Gorges royal governor of Massachusetts, but Gorges never reached New England. Growing political unrest was roiling England, and the crown quickly became too preoccupied to deal with its Puritan colony in America. Charles had not permitted Parliament to meet for a decade, since 1629. When he finally reconvened Parliament in 1640, he found it dominated by Puritans and Parliamentarians who strongly opposed him, Laud, and royal authority. In 1642, animosity erupted into the English Civil War. The beginning of the war effectively ended the Great Migration. But by then the

English population of New England had grown to more than 16,000. Twenty-two towns had been founded, and the largest, Boston, had a population of more than 2,000.

THE PURITAN WAY

John Winthrop's Puritans had a strong sense of mission and saw themselves as a chosen people led by God. They intended to found a community of the godly and a biblical commonwealth; that is, a state founded on divine intention as they believed it to be revealed in the Bible.

Puritanism was a way of life, based on the belief that the purpose of human life was to glorify God on earth. No aspect of everyday life was separable from that belief. Although they rejected ostentation, materialism, and sensuality for its own sake, the Puritans were not ascetics. They approved of living well, if plainly, providing that behavior was conducted within the bounds of their moral code and did not distract either individuals or the community from God. Even a person's "calling," or job on earth, had a religious end. The Puritan economic code required a just price and a fair wage, reasonable interest rates, and honest business dealings. The love of money was as much a sin as idleness; thrift was approved, but individual economic gain that hurt the community or its poor was not. The Puritans did not pursue happiness, they pursued godliness.

Puritans conceived of themselves as a community. They believed they had made an agreement, or covenant, with God not only as individuals but as a community. God's favor depended on the condition of the community as a whole as well as on the condition of individual souls. For that reason, behavior was regulated, often minutely and by law. The entire community was responsible for overseeing and correcting the behavior of each individual. The Puritan community, furthermore, was a collection of families. The family, to Puritans, was a little commonwealth that mirrored the structure of the state. Good order in the family, or family governance, was considered necessary to good order in the community. The father was the head of the family, responsible for maintaining order within it; the wife was subordinate; and children were held to strict obedience. Unmarried people, if young, were not permitted to live alone or even together with others of the same sex. They were assigned to a family and, along with servants and apprentices, integrated into its order.

The Puritans believed that because of original sin, humans were born depraved. They could not earn salvation by their behavior but could be saved by God's grace alone—a doctrine the Puritans called the Covenant of Grace. They also believed that God had predestined, or already selected at birth, those who were saved and those who were damned. Nonetheless, in each person a constant struggle took place between good and evil. Observant individuals engaged in unrelenting self-examination as well as a strenuous devotional life. Through psychological vigilance and spiritual effort, they hoped to learn if they had received grace, or been "elected" for salvation. Good behavior was a sign of those among the elect, although it neither earned nor guaranteed salvation.

The leaders of Massachusetts Bay Colony all shared similar religious beliefs and tolerated little dissent from them. Tax money was used to support individual churches, and laws were passed to enforce attendance. However, the church was not "established" like the Church of England, because an organized, hierarchical

Puritan church did not exist. Individual churches were founded on the covenant, or congregational, system. Church members agreed among themselves to be a church, and each church was independent, choosing its own minister. After 1634, however, the formation of new congregations required the approval of both civil officials and the ministerial synod, or assembly of ministers, in the colony. Although all residents of a given community were expected to participate in religious services as members of the congregation, far fewer were members of the church, or (as Puritans believed) the elect. After 1636, a lengthy conversion narrative, or description of the experience Puritans called election, was required for full church membership, restricting it even more.

In Puritan worship, traditional ritual and Christian sacraments were de-emphasized, but the importance of the sermon increased. It develop into a lengthy, literary form; it both exhorted its listeners to conversion and directed them in everyday matters large and small. Colonists not only listened to sermons at Sunday services, they also flocked to lectures (additional sermons by ministers) during the week. Prominent ministers like John Cotton of Boston's First Church drew listeners from miles around. Eventually, Boston's market day was established to coincide with Cotton's lecture day.

Historians continue to disagree about the extent to which religious leaders controlled the state and society in Massachusetts Bay Colony. The Puritans intended civil society to embody their religious beliefs. Accordingly, they believed that leaders of the church should also have political power. The clergy itself, however, could not hold office and had no official power in government. Ideally in the Puritan commonwealth, civil and religious authorities were of one mind and reinforced each other.

As time passed, minds differed. The rapid growth of Massachusetts Bay Colony inevitably challenged the ideal unity of the Puritan commonwealth. Heavy immigration brought people who had varying motives and were less sympathetic to the community's original goals. As early as 1635, the General Court found it necessary to pass an ordinance finding people who failed to attend Sunday church services. Economic growth and prosperity challenged the notion of a just community. Leaders disagreed among themselves. And the independence of all churches soon gave rise to religious dissent.

Religious Dissent and the Expansion of New England

The first prominent dissenter from the Puritan way was Roger Williams, a well-connected Cambridge graduate and theologian who arrived in Boston in 1631. A Separatist, he refused to accept a position as teacher or minister in Boston—the offer of which was intended as a high compliment—because the congregation had not formally separated from the Anglican Church. Instead, he ministered at Salem and Plymouth, where he lived among and studied the Indians. He concluded that the Massachusetts charter and subsequent land grants were invalid because the land belonged to the Indians, not to the English king. Williams also believed that the church and state should be separate. He denied that civil government had any right to persecute individuals for religious beliefs. He argued for "soul liberty," or liberty of conscience and the right of private judgment. He also argued for religious toleration, believing no one could know for certain what beliefs were true.

Williams's ideas alarmed Puritan leaders. The General Court refused to seat representatives from Salem while Williams preached there. In October 1635, Williams was banished from Massachusetts and threatened with deportation to England (where he might have been put to death). He fled to the Narragansett Indians and in June 1636, purchased land from them and founded the settlement of Providence. He was soon joined by other dissenters, and a new government was established that separated state and church. In 1640, colonists agreed to a governing body of five men, called disposers because they disposed of, or granted, the land. Freeholders could approve or deny their actions in general meetings.

Another dissenter was Anne Hutchinson, a midwife, mother of 13 children, and neighbor of Governor Winthrop. She began holding meetings for women in her home to discuss the sermons of Boston minister John Cotton and her brother-in-law, the Reverend John Wheelwright. In themselves, such meetings were not unusual. Soon, however, Hutchinson's reputation as a preacher grew, and even men began to attend. Hutchinson began to preach doctrines associated with the antinomian movement, which emphasized that God revealed himself directly to the devout. She believed that divine spirit existed in every true Christian and that salvation could not be influenced by moral instruction or regulation. These ideas were inherent in orthodox Puritanism, but their emphasis—and the fact that Hutchinson was a woman—threatened ministerial power.

Soon political power was also threatened. Hutchinson attained great popularity, and among her followers were many who disliked the political and economic authoritarianism of the colony's leaders. By 1636, Boston had split into two factions. Harry Vane, allied with the Hutchinsonians, defeated Winthrop for governor. After a bitter political quarrel, anti-Hutchinsonians returned Winthrop to office in 1637. A synod of ministers was soon convened to root out heresies. Hutchinson was tried before the General Court in November 1637 and again before the Church of Boston in March 1638. She was banished and excommunicated. She departed Massachusetts in spring 1638, going first to Williams's colony, then to Aquidneck (after 1644 called Rhode Island). Many followers joined her, founding Portsmouth and eventually Newport and Warwick. The settlements remained independent of each other and refuges for various dissenters or religious minorities. Hutchinson herself eventually moved to Long Island, where she and five of her children were killed in an Indian raid in 1643. She left no writings, but the transcripts of her two trials provide a record of her ideas.

Hutchinson's brother-in-law, the Reverend John Wheelwright, was also banished. He and his followers subsequently founded Exeter, New Hampshire. In 1638, the General Court, still displeased, charged New Hampshire with "unneighborly conduct" and the following year granted a group from Massachusetts permission to move there. In 1641, the four small English settlements in New Hampshire agreed to be governed by Massachusetts Bay Colony. English settlements also appeared on Long Island also claimed by New Netherland, and in Maine prior to 1642, peopled by migrants seeking a more liberal society or different economic opportunities. Most of these settlements, however, were made in lands still claimed by English proprietors. In 1635, the Council for New England had resigned its charter; rights to its grant were divided between the Gorges family, which received Maine and southern Massachusetts, and John Mason, who received New Hampshire and northern Massachusetts.

CONNECTICUT AND THE PEQUOT WAR

The colonists who spread into Connecticut from established Massachusetts settlements were not religious dissenters. Instead, they were attracted by the fertile land and active fur trade in the Connecticut River valley. In 1633, both Plymouth traders and the Dutch, who considered the area part of their New Netherland claim, built trading posts there. In 1634, English trader John Oldham began a small trading settlement at Wethersfield. In 1635, John Winthrop, Jr. (the governor's son), arrived from England to build a trading settlement on behalf of some English Puritans who also believed they had a legitimate grant to the Connecticut River valley. Soon after, the General Court granted permission for the residents of several towns to move as well, provided they did not separate politically from the Massachusetts Bay Colony. In 1636, the Reverend Thomas Hooker's congregation established Newton (later Hartford), and 800 colonists quickly spread among Windsor, Wethersfield, and Springfield, collectively called the "river towns." Soon the General Court set up a commission of eight members to oversee Connecticut settlements.

At first, English relations with the so-called River Indians of the Connecticut River valley were relatively peaceful. As the English expanded into the valley, they generally purchased the land from the Indians. As always, however, increasing settlement increased tensions. Rivalries already existed among the Pequot, Narragansett, and Mohegan over the wampum and fur trade. In 1633, a smallpox epidemic devastated the Pequot, reducing their numbers dramatically. They were unable to regain their former power and feared their enemies might ally against them. In 1634, they sought an alliance with Massachusetts Bay Colony against the Dutch and the Narragansett. Winthrop demanded tribute of skins and furs as a condition, but John Oldham, sent to collect it in 1636, was murdered at Block Island. John Endicott led a punitive raid against the Pequot; in retaliation, the Pequot raided English settlements in Connecticut in 1636 and 1637. Roger Williams convinced the Narragansett to ally with the English; the Mohegan did so, too. After a Pequot attack on Wethersfield in April 1637, the river towns united. Reinforced by troops from Massachusetts Bay, Captains John Mason and Robert Underhill led expeditions against Pequot strongholds in May and July. Pequot men, women, and children were slaughtered by the English and their Indian allies, and the tribe was decimated; many historians consider it the first English war of extermination against Native Americans. Indian captives were enslaved, with some sold to the West Indies and a few retained in New England. In 1638, Williams negotiated a peace settlement with the Narragansett and Mohegan that lasted almost half a century.

The removal of the Pequot encouraged additional English migration to the Connecticut River valley and the formal establishment of a government separate from Massachusetts. In 1637, an assembly of river town representatives convened at Hartford. Ostensibly meeting to deal with the growing Pequot crisis, they also established some governmental institutions. In January 1639, the Fundamental Orders of Connecticut, often called the first written colonial constitution, was adopted. It was a social compact, drawing its authority from the consent of the governed, rather than a royal document drawing authority from the Crown. Connecticut's structure was similar to that of Massachusetts, although the right to vote was more liberal and did not require church membership.

In 1638, John Davenport and Theophilus Eaton, strict Puritans, founded New Haven. While the site's harbor seemed ideal for trade, they also wanted to found an independent biblical commonwealth more orthodox than Massachusetts Bay. Unless they could find a biblical precedent, New Haven leaders disallowed practically everything, even venerable English institutions like trial by jury. Soon similar communities sprang up nearby, all of them resisting incorporation into the colony of Connecticut for many years.

PLYMOUTH COLONY

The growth of Massachusetts Bay Colony quickly overshadowed the small Pilgrim colony at Plymouth. Plymouth enjoyed economic prosperity between 1630 and 1642, however, as a supplier of meat and grain to the flood of new settlers in Massachusetts Bay. Plymouth colonists also continued fur trading.

The population grew from about 250 in 1630 to 1,800 in 1642. Many were migrants from Massachusetts Bay, attracted by Plymouth's less rigorous link between church and civil authority. Established Plymouth settlers also spread out. In 1636, representatives from the three largest settlements—Plymouth, Scituate, and Duxbury—developed a code of laws for civil and criminal offenses, inheri-

Fairbanks House, Dedham, Massachusetts, built 1636, the oldest surviving frame house in the United States *(Historic American Building Survey)*

tance (equal for all children), and other matters. It did not, however, include statutes regulating aspects of private life and behavior.

Admission to freemanship, or full voting citizenship, was generous in Plymouth and not limited to church members. Nonetheless, some men chose not to become freemen, probably because it demanded attendance at four assembly sessions per year. In 1638, the General Court voted to become representative. Deputies, elected from towns, were to attend three of the assemblies; the yearly election assembly, which determined the governor and his seven assistants, still required attendance by all freemen. The General Court also voted to allow all "settled" male heads of family in the colony, whether or not they were admitted freemen, to vote for the deputies. Only freemen, however, could hold office or vote for colonywide officials. In 1639, this new governmental organization was formalized as the Fundamentals of Plymouth.

In 1640, Governor Bradford turned over the Plymouth Company's patent, issued to him and the assistants in 1630, to the General Court. Control of undistributed land passed to the General Court; Bradford, six remaining English creditors, and 58 Old Purchasers among the original Pilgrims received large land grants in return.

LIFE IN NEW ENGLAND

Although the several New England settlements disagreed on some issues and often distrusted each other, by 1640 a way of life had developed that clearly contrasted with life in the Chesapeake colonies. New England experienced primarily a family and group migration. Extended families and even whole congregations arrived together. Puritans did not scatter to isolated farms and plantations; they moved as groups to settle new towns. The town or township, not the county, became the primary political division in New England.

Massachusetts Bay Colony controlled the formation of new towns within its grant, deciding location and boundaries. Legal permission to move was obtained from the General Court; the corporation granted land, usually 20–40 square miles. After purchasing it from the Indians, the corporation vested it in a group henceforth termed the town *proprietors*. For their part, proprietors agreed to hire a minister and settle a certain number of families. Usually, town settlement began with the laying out of a village plan, which included home lots, a commons, and outlying fields. On or near the commons, a church—or, as the Puritans called it, the meeting house—was built. Usually the town had a single main street, with narrow but long home lots. A home lot had space for a barn, a garden, and a small orchard; "strips" for crops were assigned farther out of town. Individual grants were not large, nor were they equal, but they were available to many people. Undistributed land continued to be held in common by the proprietors for future growth and later arrivals.

The meeting house was the center of local life, serving not only for church services but also for town meetings and occasionally as a schoolhouse. The town meeting was the characteristic form of government in New England settlements. Most settlements held town meetings once a month. Men were admitted to town citizenship by vote of existing citizens. Town citizenship was separate from colonywide freemanship and much more liberal, although most towns also had residents who did not vote. At town meetings, voters passed

Massachusetts and the Connecticut Valley, detail of a map by Nicholaes Visscher (1685) *(Library of Congress)*

local ordinances and elected officials, including the overseers, or selectmen, who acted as administrators and as judges in minor disputes. Colonywide officials did not appoint local officials in New England as they did in the Chesapeake colonies.

From 1630 until 1642, the New England economy was self-sustaining and prosperous. Reasonably well-financed new settlers continued to arrive, bringing items to trade for food and even houses, as established settlers moved to new locations or built more substantial homes. After 1640, as migration slowed, neither Massachusetts Bay Colony nor Plymouth farmers were able to sell their surpluses and cattle, and grain prices fell sharply. A brief depression followed, but by 1642 merchants had begun to find new markets overseas.

Puritan leaders tried to maintain control of both trade and wages, as their vision of a well-ordered biblical commonwealth required. In the fur trade, officials granted a few monopolies to men of "good character." Trade of all kinds quickly began to center on Boston, which had become the capital in 1632 and was the port at which most English goods entered the colony. As early as 1633, both retail and wholesale shops existed. By 1634, the assistants decreed a weekly market day, and in 1635 officials appointed one man from each town to purchase goods at dockside, in hopes of reducing disorder. The demand for both goods and labor, however, exceeded the supply. Many skilled workers, especially those in construction trades, commanded such high wages that some became as wealthy as the leaders. Puritan leaders found economic change to be almost as troubling as religious dissent, blaming it on ambitious merchants.

The majority of emigrants to New England were "middling" people (what would be called the middle class today). A few were minor gentry, but neither the very poor nor the very rich came in great numbers. A remarkably high proportion—higher than anywhere in England at the time—had university degrees, mostly from Cambridge.[1] Most New England settlers were small, diversified farmers; neither the land nor climate encouraged large plantations. Consequently, far fewer people arrived as indentured servants than in the Chesapeake, although some colonists worked for wages as hired hands or as servants. Indentured servants were free to join the church and were often entitled to land at the end of their term. The first slaves of African descent probably arrived in New England in the 1620s, although the first written records date from the 1630s. By 1642, some black slaves probably lived in most New England port towns.

Education in New England

The Puritans' religious beliefs demanded a literate citizenry, able to read the Bible. In 1635, Boston hired a schoolmaster; soon after, many other settlements established "free schools." Schools were the responsibility of town governments. Town overseers appointed a schoolmaster, subject to approval by the town meeting, and arranged for his salary, lodging, and schoolhouse. Free schools, despite their name, were not usually free—parents who were able usually paid a modest tuition. Schools received additional support from voluntary private contributions, but usually not from public funds. In 1639, Dorchester became the first community to establish a permanent tax on property to support its school. School attendance was voluntary and almost always limited to boys. In place of formal schooling, many children, both boys and girls, were "put out," or apprenticed, by parents or guardians—that is, they were contracted to another adult for a certain number of years, usually to learn a craft, trade, or domestic skills.

The first New England schools did not teach basic literacy; reading ability was a requirement for admittance. Many children, including girls, were taught to read in a household setting, either by their parents, by a neighbor who kept a "dame school" for young children, or (if apprenticed) by their masters.[2] Schoolmasters in the first free schools, in addition to their other duties, were expected to tutor willing boys in Latin grammar, the primary requirement for university admittance and study for the ministry; grammar schools concentrated on it and took their name from it. In 1636, wealthy citizens in Boston subscribed to maintain a school later named Boston Latin School (the first in the English colonies to operate continuously to the present day); a grammar school was established at Charlestown the same year.

In 1642, the Massachusetts General Court passed the first colonial law establishing the principle of compulsory education (although not compulsory school attendance). It required all children to be taught basic literacy, religious instruction, and knowledge of "capital law"—laws based in the Bible. For poor children, it also required apprenticeships to provide a means of self-support. The law held parents and masters responsible for the education of their children or apprentices and established fines for those who did not comply. Carrying out and enforcing the law was left to individual towns.

In 1636, the General Court ordered the establishment of the first institution of higher education in the English colonies, Harvard College. Modeled on England's Cambridge University, its stated purpose was to educate colonial ministers. Instruction probably began in 1638, the year the Reverend John Harvard left his estate to the college. That same year, Newtown, where the school was located, changed its name to Cambridge. Harvard's first master, Nathaniel Eaton, proved unsatisfactory, and in 1640 he was replaced by its first president, Henry Dunster. In 1642, Dunster oversaw graduation of the college's first nine students as well as the establishment of a set curriculum, which included liberal arts, classical languages, philosophy, and religion.

In 1638, the first printing press in the English colonies was established in Cambridge by Stephen Day. In 1640, Day printed his first book, the *Bay Psalm Book,* a new translation of the Psalms by a group of Puritan ministers led by the Reverend Richard Mather.

LORD BALTIMORE'S GRANT

George Calvert, a well-connected royalist and secretary of state to King James I, invested in several early English colonization ventures. In 1625, however, Calvert converted to Catholicism. Aware that non-Anglicans were politically suspect in England, he resigned his offices and sought a grant from the king, to establish his own colony. He received a grant and a title as well, becoming lord of the Irish barony of Baltimore. Calvert's first grant was in Newfoundland. He built a manor house there, but in 1629 he abandoned the site, taking his family to Virginia. Although royal governor John Harvey welcomed him, the Virginia Council did not; it was suspicious of Calvert's religion and his motives as a Royalist.

Calvert returned to England to seek his own grant within Virginia territory, whose boundaries stretched from modern North Carolina to the Hudson River. He requested land to the south of settlements. King Charles I, however, hoping to prevent expansion by the Dutch in New Netherland, issued a charter to Calvert for land north of Virginia settlements. It was to be named *terra mariae,* or Mary Land, after Charles's wife, Queen Henrietta Maria. Although the grant was relatively modest in size, the power given to Calvert by the Charter of 1632 was generously formulated. As the "True and Absolute Lords and Proprietors," he and his heirs were not delegates of the crown but rather owned the land outright. The king reserved the standard one-fifth of precious metals and the right to control trade. Otherwise, Calvert had absolute authority in the colony. He controlled all branches of government, and he alone could initiate legislation for the colony. His only limits were the laws of England and the legal rights of all English subjects, neither of which Maryland's laws could contradict.

George Calvert died two months before his charter passed the seals, or became law when the privy council affixed its seal. His sons, Cecilius and Leonard, took over the project. Both were reasonably tolerant and politically astute. They were also intelligent organizers who heeded the disastrous example of early Virginia. They published an extensive list of provisions that each colonist would need to bring, ranging from food to bedding to kitchen utensils. They offered generous individual land grants to attract settlers. To the very wealthy they offered large manors similar to the seignuries of New France or the patroonships of New Amsterdam: 2,000 acres for each five men transported to tenant the land. However, they also offered other settlers, both male and female, 100 acres for themselves and each adult who accompanied them plus 50 acres for each child. Modest quitrents were imposed on all. (A quitrent is a yearly payment, comparable to a tax, made to a private individual with proprietary rights over land.)

Cecilius and Leonard Calvert also established a policy of de facto religious toleration for Maryland. Their father had intended to provide a haven in which English Catholics could worship freely, without paying England's special, exorbitant tax on them. The Calverts, however, could not write laws for Maryland

A modern reconstruction of wattle-and-daub cottages, one form of temporary housing built by early English colonists *(Courtesy Jamestown Settlement and Yorktown Victory Center/Jamestown-Yorktown Foundation)*

that were directly contrary to laws in England—that is, they could neither disestablish the Anglican Church nor establish any other. They sidestepped the issue by omitting any law prohibiting or punishing the practice of religion. At no time, in fact, were Catholics ever a majority in the colony.

In February 1634, the *Ark* and *Dove* arrived at Point Comfort, Virginia. Aboard were 17 gentlemen and their families, mostly Catholics, and about 100 artisans and farmers, mostly Protestants. Also on board—probably without the knowledge of English officials—were two English Jesuits. They were accompanied by Governor Leonard Calvert. Cecilius, the second Lord Baltimore, remained in England to defend the Maryland claim against Virginia representatives who had come to protest it to the Crown.

Colonists aboard the *Ark* and *Dove* sailed up the Potomac River to a village of the Yaocomico, part of the Piscataway Indian Confederation. There they concluded an agreement to purchase approximately 30 miles of shoreline. On a bluff overlooking the river, they established the town of St. Mary's. From its inception, the colony experienced far fewer difficulties than previous European settlements to the south and north. The climate was moderate and healthful; in addition, the site the Indians sold them was already cleared and planted.

Maryland's First Decade

Almost immediately, a boundary dispute erupted. Virginian William Claiborne had been granted the Virginia fur trade monopoly while in England protesting Maryland's establishment. In 1634, he founded a trading village on Kent Island in Chesapeake Bay with about 100 settlers. The island was within Maryland's grant, and the Calverts hoped to enter the fur trade themselves. After a bitter dispute, which included a 1635 battle of sorts between ships belonging to Virginians and Marylanders, the Crown awarded the island to Maryland. Claiborne, in compensation, was made an official of Virginia for life—but his animosity would erupt again in the future.

The Calverts soon faced another challenge to their absolute power, this one within their own colony. The governor ruled with the assistance of a three-member appointed council; an assembly was to "advise and consent." The first assembly met in February 1635; it was unicameral and included the council, all gentlemen of the colony, and one commoner selected by the governor. The assembly ignored Lord Baltimore's right to be the sole initiator of legislation and passed several laws of local concern. Baltimore vetoed them from England and sent his own code of laws. The 1638 session of the assembly, led by council member Thomas Cornwallis, in turn rejected Calvert's code. A compromise was reached, and in 1639 Calvert agreed to limited powers of initiative for the assembly, reserving veto power for himself.

At all assemblies after the first, all freemen of the colony were required to cast a vote. This requirement, impossible to fulfill, led to a system of proxies. Attendees collected the votes of those who could not attend and voted for them. The proxy system enabled wealthy landowners, who had the leisure to attend the lengthy session, to dominate the assembly. In 1639, the system became formalized when five local divisions called hundreds were directed by Calvert to elect representatives, or burgesses, to the assembly.

Despite Maryland's religious toleration, religious disputes arose. The first was between the colony and the Jesuits. The two English Jesuits who accompanied the settlers, Fathers Andrew White and John Altman, received land grants like any other settlers for themselves and their servants. They worked to establish missions among the Indians; Father White converted some Piscataway (later called Conoy), completing a dictionary and catechism in their language. In 1637, the new head of the mission, Father Philip Fisher (also known as Thomas Copely), envisioned mission communities like those in Spanish colonies. He attempted to purchase additional land from the Indians on his own and refused to acknowledge that mission lands were subordinate to civil law. Calvert strongly opposed the establishment of autonomous Jesuit communities, and in 1641 he forbade them to own more land than was necessary for their own support. Eventually both the pope and the English crown acknowledged Calvert's policy. Other religious disputes arose between Protestant servants and Catholic masters. After 1640, the increasing migration of Puritans began to cause disruption. In 1641, an influential Catholic locked them out of the chapel at St. Mary's, which they also used for services. Soon after, the Puritans began to organize a church.

Throughout its first decade, Maryland enjoyed prosperity and population growth. Tobacco quickly became the main crop, although the Calverts established a law requiring two of every three acres to be planted in food crops. By 1640, the population had grown to about 700. Sixteen manors existed, the largest comprising 6,000 acres. Catholics were about one-quarter of the total population; however, they included most of the families who held large land grants, and they wielded considerable power. The manorial tenant system envisioned by George Calvert, however, was never successful, since colonists preferred to own their own land. Consequently, planters relied increasingly on unfree labor. By 1642, a large majority of Maryland colonists were white indentured servants and did not own land. Also by that date, some slaves of African descent are known to have been in the colony, although laws officially recognizing slavery were not passed until the 1660s.

In Maryland, Indian relations remained much more peaceable than in Virginia, although skirmishes increased in the 1640s as settlers claimed more and more land. Most nearby Indians were members of the Piscataway Confederation. Settlers, however, did not always distinguish these relatively friendly groups from their traditional tribal enemies, the hostile Susquehannock to the north.

GROWTH IN VIRGINIA

Between 1630 and 1642, the colony of Virginia experienced two kinds of growth, in population and in tobacco production. In 1630, the population was about 2,500. In 1635 alone, 1,600 new settlers arrived, and by 1642 the population was more than 15,000.[3] Most of the new settlers arrived as indentured servants. A few more slaves of African descent also arrived in the colony; as late as the 1650s, however, the total black population remained under 300.

Sir John Harvey, who took office as governor in 1630, encouraged agricultural diversification, as per the king's instructions. Soon Virginia grew enough corn to sell surpluses to New England. But tobacco remained the staple crop; from 500,000 pounds per year at the end of the 1620s, production increased to 4 million pounds per year by 1640. Governor Harvey attempted to limit production and require quality grading in order to raise and control prices, but the measures were not well enforced. During the 1630s, periodic gluts occurred in the English market, prices declined, and Virginia growers suffered.

War with the Powhatan, which had dragged on since the massacre of 1622, officially ended in 1632. The truce, negotiated by Governor Harvey, was not popular among Virginians. Almost no friendly interactions between colonists and Indians occurred during the next decade. Skirmishes continued as demands for land increased; Indian captives taken after the truce were usually shipped out of the country to be sold as slaves. After 1633, the colony erected a six-mile-long palisade from Jamestown to a fort on the York River, fencing off a large area of the James peninsula and excluding Native Americans from it. During tense times, the palisade was patrolled by local militias. The Powhatan were pushed northward as well; by 1642, settlers were claiming land along the York and Rappahannock Rivers.

During the decade, Virginia colonists made significant strides toward representative government and the limitation of arbitrary authority. The assembly continued to convene, although the Crown had not mentioned it when Virginia was made a royal colony in 1624. Assemblies petitioned the king repeatedly to acknowledge them, but their requests were simply ignored. The 1632 session of the assembly reaffirmed a resolution, passed at their last legal meeting in 1624, that the governor could not levy or collect taxes without their approval. As the political and financial difficulties of the English Crown increased during the 1630s, the royal governor, although appointed by the king, became more dependent on the assembly for financial support.

The Crown-appointed council, composed entirely of Virginia colonists and landholders, was also determined to curtail the royal governor's arbitrary power. In April 1635, the council deposed Governor Harvey, arrested him, and shipped him back to England. The king returned Harvey to Virginia in 1637, equally determined not to allow royal authority to be countermanded. In 1639, he sent former governor Francis Wyatt to replace him. With Governor Wyatt, King Charles I sent written instructions that the assembly was to meet "as formerly," thus confirming its legitimacy. The royal acknowledgment of representative government in Virginia in 1639 is considered an important milestone in colonial history. It implied that residents of English colonies had the same inherent political rights as residents of England, which the king could not invalidate or revoke.

In 1634, Virginia created eight counties, decentralizing many aspects of colonial administration and the judiciary. Each county was headed by a "magistrate and militia officer," usually appointed from among the county's gentry and later known as the justice of the peace. In addition to overseeing the organization of a militia, he heard minor legal cases. Convicted miscreants might be jailed, put in stocks or pillories, whipped, or in some cases required to make public confession in church. Periodically, courts composed of all county justices were held. Because Virginia had no colonywide written code of laws, decisions were based on English common law and local regulations. Appeals could be taken to a court composed of the governor and council, or to the assembly itself.

LIFE IN THE CHESAPEAKE

By 1642, a distinctive way of life had begun to take shape in the Chesapeake colonies of Virginia and Maryland. Tobacco planting influenced many of its characteristics. One was the pattern of landownership. Tobacco demanded large amounts of land, because it quickly depleted the soil in any one field; in addition, colonists wanted land on navigable rivers feeding into the bay, to lessen the expense of transporting tobacco to market. Consequently, colonists spread out to relatively isolated plantations, or farms; communal town life and government did not develop as they did in New England. Tobacco planting also demanded large numbers of unskilled laborers, most of whom were white male indentured servants. Servants' lives did improve; however, the death rate for servants remained higher than for free colonists, especially during the first, or seasoning, year, when newcomers often contracted new diseases. Since men continued to outnumber women, many did not marry and family life was less well established than in New England.

The Chesapeake frontier still offered opportunities for social mobility, although a local gentry was beginning to develop. Some arrived as minor English gentry, usually without significant wealth, and some were ordinary people. Both groups rose by acquiring large tracts of land, working them with unfree labor, succeeding as entrepreneurs, and securing various public offices. Records indicate that several single women achieved financial success in Maryland, which offered land grants to female as well as male heads of household. The women arrived with enough servants to claim substantial tracts—to the displeasure of male colonists who tried to amend the policy as early as 1634. Among indentured servants, approximately one-half of males who *survived* probably became landholders; a few achieved a pronounced rise in status and wealth.[4] A few black slaves gained freedom after an indenture-like period, and a few owned land.

Adam Thoroughgood House, Virginia, built ca. 1634, the oldest surviving English colonial brick house *(Historic American Building Survey)*

NEW NETHERLAND

In 1633, the Dutch West India Company sent Wouter van Twiller to replace Peter Minuit as director general of New Netherland. Van Twiller, known for his intemperance, was well connected but ill qualified. His administration was marked by continual disputes with New England and Virginia over rights to land. The company sent workers to rebuild New Amsterdam, but many had to be dispatched to the Connecticut River valley to protect the fur-trading post there. A scaled-down building project was completed over the next two years, largely by slaves of African descent. The fort was repaired, three windmills built, and several new buildings and a church erected. Nonetheless, the population rose from only about 300 in 1630 to 500 in 1638. The company's land policies were not generous, and Dutch emigrants could expect fewer rights and a lower standard of living than they enjoyed in the Netherlands. Most Dutch who emigrated were employees of the company, sent as officials, soldiers, or farmers for the bouwries, or company farms, north of New Amsterdam on Manhattan. Under Van Twiller, the colony also failed to thrive economically. Embezzlement by company officials and illegal fur trading by everyone was the rule. Van Twiller was removed in 1637, and Willem Kieft replaced him in 1638.

Kieft found the company farms deserted and much of New Amsterdam again in bad repair. He immediately instituted reforms. In 1638 and 1640, the company liberalized land and other policies. Settlers were granted some local self-government and the right to trade freely. The company recruited colonists from all over northern and western Europe and the population finally began to grow, reaching nearly 2,000 by 1643. The heterogeneity of the colony also increased. Of the 82 settlers who arrived at the patroonship of Rensselaerwyck during the decade, for example, some 30 were from England, Norway, or German-speaking countries rather than the Netherlands. Migrants from the English colonies also settled in New Netherland, among them religious dissenters attracted by its tolerance and escaping servants attracted by its lax law enforcement. By 1642, the English had become so numerous, especially on Long Island, that an English secretary was appointed to assist the governor. Slaves of African descent continued to be imported in small numbers by the company, primarily from South America and the Indies. They probably worked as farm laborers, stevedores, or soldiers. The first surviving map of New Amsterdam, dated 1639, shows a slave camp north of New Amsterdam. Records suggest that by 1640 some blacks were also freedmen and property owners.

Governor Kieft's tenure unfortunately marked the end of good relations with local Indians, in part because of changed conditions and in part because of his mismanagement. Near Fort Orange, active fur trade had depleted Mohawk hunting grounds, and the Mohawk began attacking other tribes. Kieft, who had forbidden the sale of firearms to other Indians, approved supplying them to the Mohawk. He hoped they would ally with the Dutch against the Raritan (a group living on Staten Island near the mouth of the Hudson) and other tribes near New Amsterdam, where greatly increased population and spreading settlement had increased tensions. Disputes arose over wandering European livestock (who invaded unfenced Indian cornfields) and marauding Indian dogs (who killed colonists' livestock). Kieft further angered nearby tribes by attempting to extract a tax or tribute to pay soldiers to patrol the area; he also accused the Raritan of attacking fur-trading vessels. In 1641, Indian raids began on outlying bouwries and threatened to escalate into full-scale war. Kieft called together the heads of white families, who elected a Committee of 12 to consult with him. The committee was the first representative political body in New Netherland.

Although Kieft dissolved the committee in 1642, it magnified political awareness among the colonists. New Netherland had been founded as a commercial venture, and the West India Company had made little effort to develop institutions of colonial government. No code of laws existed. The council, composed only of the governor and some subordinate company officials, controlled all executive and legislative functions. With the help of the *schout*, a combined sheriff and prosecutor, it also held court, but the justice it dispensed was not satisfactory to the colonists. By 1642, the expanding population of New Netherland was discontented, fractious, and often disorderly.

THE FOUNDING OF NEW SWEDEN

The Delaware River valley, claimed by both the Dutch and English, was rich in furs and well known to Dutch traders. In 1631, David Peter de Vries planted a small settlement at Zwaanendael, or Valley of the Swans (modern New Jersey). It was destroyed almost immediately by Indians and the land returned to the Dutch West India Company.

In the mid-1630s, some Dutch investors became disenchanted with the Dutch West India Company. They journeyed to Stockholm, where commercial life was closely tied to the Netherlands. Their goal was to convince the Swedes to organize a new company to plant a settlement in the Delaware River valley. Under King Gustavus Adolphus, Sweden had recently established itself as a new military power and protector of Lutheran Protestants against the Catholic Crowns. As the Dutch investors had accurately surmised, Swedish interests were receptive to flexing their new power by founding a colony in the New World.

In 1638, the New Sweden Company was authorized in the name of the Swedish Crown. One of the Dutch investors in the new enterprise was Peter Minuit, former director general of New Amsterdam. Forthwith, he and his Dutch crew were given command of two small vessels, the *Kalmar Nyckel* and the *Fogel Grip*. Minuit loaded them with trade goods, supplies, and two dozen Swedish and Finnish soldiers and colonists, and set sail. Under Sweden's flag, Minuit sailed into Delaware Bay and up the river in March. He landed at a natural stone wharf, the Rocks (modern Wilmington). At the time, the valley was inhabited by some 2,500 Lenni Lenape (or Lenape then known as Delaware). Peaceable and nonacquisitive, the Lenape were not organized to defend themselves. Previous trade with Europeans had already subjected them to attacks by their enemies the Susquehannock, whom the Lenape called Minqua (meaning "trecherous"); the Minqua wanted to control trade themselves. Almost immediately, Minuit met with five chiefs, or sachems, including at least one Minqua, to negotiate a land purchase. In obtaining deeds from the Indians, Minuit was interested in more than peaceful coexistence. He was also eager to secure the disputed valley from the claims of the Dutch and the English.

The purchase completed, Minuit's soldiers constructed Fort Christina near the mouth of the Christina River. Both were named after the 12-year-old Swedish queen, Gustavus's daughter and successor. Using native logs and 500 bricks carried with them on the voyage, they built a log palisade enclosing a communal dwelling and a storehouse. In June, the *Kalmar Nyckel* left the small band of settlers and returned to Holland loaded with furs. (During the voyage, Minuit lost his life in a West Indian hurricane.) The *Fogel Grip,* meanwhile, made a trading voyage to the West Indies; it returned with New Sweden's first slave of African descent. In 1640, the *Kalmar Nyckel* returned to New Sweden with Governor Peter Ridder, a Swedish naval officer of Dutch birth. Also on board were colonists, including women and children and the first Lutheran minister in North America, the Reverend Reore Torkillus. Later that year, a group of Dutch settlers also arrived. In 1641, Swedish investors—many of them high government officials—bought out the Dutch investors. After that date, the Swedish government itself, in effect, managed the colony. Johan Printz was appointed governor and dispatched to the tiny colony, arriving in 1643.

Life in New Sweden

At least half the early settlers of New Sweden were ethnic Finns. Many Finns had migrated to Sweden's northern frontier, where their distinct language and culture became increasingly irritating to their hosts. Upon the founding of New Sweden, the Finns were officially urged to emigrate. Ethnic Swedes, however, proved far more difficult to recruit as colonists. They suffered neither religious persecution, population pressure, nor economic distress, and emigration thus promised little material improvement.

Tiny New Sweden did not flourish because Sweden did not provide adequate support. Ironically, the Swedes and Finns who emigrated had skills particularly well suited to conditions in the New World. Unlike the urban Dutch and

This Swedish log cabin, Delaware County, Pennsylvania, built ca. 1650, is one of the oldest surviving log houses. *(Photo by Ian McLaughlin for Historic American Building Survey)*

Spanish or the English and French villagers who immigrated to North America, they were accustomed to a forested environment. They used wood to make many household objects, even shoes. They knew how to prepare and use various kinds of animal skins. They were familiar with an efficient method of clearing land called *svedjebruket;* trees were felled, then burned the next year where they lay, requiring minimum effort as well as refertilizing the ground.

The most important skill introduced to the New World by the colonists of New Sweden, however, was that of building log dwellings, later called log cabins. Log dwellings were widely used in rural Sweden and Finland but were unknown at the time in England, Holland, Spain, France, or among Native Americans in the New World. Log construction was particularly suitable for heavily forested frontiers. Materials were close at hand and easily obtained; construction required no special skills, no manufactured nails, and no tools except an axe. Logs, either round or roughly hewn, were notched at the ends on both the top and bottom, then stacked horizontally and interlocked at the corners. Using log construction, the colonists of New Sweden built not only homes but also storehouses, forts, barns, churches, and other one- or two-story buildings. Much remarked by visitors to New Sweden, log dwellings eventually became an icon of the colonial frontier.[5]

CHRONICLE OF EVENTS

1630

The Great Migration of English Puritans to New England begins.

June and July: The first 11 of 17 ships to arrive by the end of 1630 disembarks in Salem. Governor John Winthrop and more than 1,000 colonists are on board. The colonists go first to Charlestown then spread out into various settlements.

September: The settlement of Shawmut is renamed Boston, in honor of the town of origin of many Puritans. Governor Winthrop moves there in October.

October 29: The General Court of Massachusetts Bay Colony meets for the first time. More than 100 men apply for the status of freeman, or full voting citizen, which was originally restricted to investors in the Massachusetts Bay Company.

1631

The Massachusetts General Court agrees to admit male church members to the status of voting freeman. However, contrary to the colony's charter, the court also decrees that laws are to be passed only by the governor and his assistants, not the court as a whole.

Roger Williams arrives in Boston. His ideas of soul liberty, the separation of church and state, and the rights of Indians will cause the first major religious dispute in the Massachusetts Bay Colony.

Peter Minuit is recalled as director general of New Netherland.

David Peter de Vries plants a small Dutch settlement at Zwaanendael (modern New Jersey). It is destroyed almost immediately by Indians.

1632

Residents of Watertown, Massachusetts, protest taxation; the General Court votes to establish the election of two representatives from each town to advise the assistants (council members) in lawmaking.

Boston becomes the capital of Massachusetts Bay Colony.

George Calvert, Lord Baltimore, receives a charter from King Charles I of England, for a colony to be named Mary Land after the queen. One purpose is to found a haven for Catholics, who, like Puritans, cannot worship freely in England.

The second Powhatan war ends in Virginia. For the next decade, few friendly interchanges will occur, and skirmishes will continue.

The Virginia Assembly, which still meets without official sanction from King Charles I, reaffirms its resolution of 1624: No taxes can be levied in the colony without its consent.

1633

William Laud is elevated to archbishop of Canterbury and renews vigorous enforcement of laws against English Puritans.

New Netherland and Plymouth colonies both build trading posts in the Connecticut River valley.

Virginia settlers erect a six-mile-long palisade from Jamestown to the York River.

1634

King Charles I appoints the Council for Foreign Plantations to oversee all colonies, with Archbishop Laud as head. They discover that the Massachusetts Bay Colony charter is missing; Winthrop has taken it to New England with him. The colony refuses to return it. Massachusetts General Court representatives also demand to see the charter. They reinstate its original provisions, which call for yearly elections, general court participation in lawmaking, and other reforms. After this date, three of the four yearly court sessions will be attended by elected representatives.

Anne Hutchinson immigrates to Massachusetts and begins holding meetings in her home to discuss religious ideas. Soon she will gain a reputation as a popular preacher, a role forbidden to Puritan women.

Trader John Oldham builds a small settlement at Wethersfield in Connecticut.

A market is officially established at the Boston seaport.

Virginia creates a system of counties, headed by a magistrate who oversees the militia and decides minor legal matters.

Virginian William Claiborne founds a trading settlement of about 100 people on Kent Island in Chesapeake Bay.

February: The *Ark* and *Dove* reach Maryland with about 200 settlers and Governor Leonard Calvert.

March: Maryland colonists establish St. Mary's.

1635

The Council for New England resigns its charter; its lands are divided between the Gorges family, which receives Maine and southern Massachusetts, and John Mason, who receives New Hampshire and northern Massachusetts.

The Massachusetts General Court passes a resolution establishing fines for those who do not attend Sunday services.

John Winthrop, Jr., arrives to build a trading settlement in the Connecticut River valley.

Boston hires its first schoolmaster.

The Council of Virginia arrests and attempts to depose Governor John Harvey; he is sent back to England.

February: The first Maryland Assembly meets. Although they are not empowered to initiate legislation, they pass laws of local concern. Cecilius Calvert, Lord Baltimore, will veto them and send his own code.

Controversy over Kent Island continues between Virginian William Claiborne and Maryland leaders. In April and May, their ships engage in battle in the Chesapeake.

September 13: Roger Williams is sentenced to banishment by the Massachusettts General Court. He will proceed to Rhode Island and purchase lands from the Indians.

1636

New England Puritan churches begin to require conversion narratives, further restricting church membership, a requirement for voting rights.

Anne Hutchinson has caused a major religious and political dispute in Massachusetts Bay Colony, preaching that God reveals himself directly to the devout. The entire colony is divided; the faction that supports Hutchinson elects Harry Vane governor.

The Reverend Thomas Hooker's congregation founds Hartford. Colonists quickly spread out to other Connecticut settlements, called the river towns.

John Oldham is murdered by the Pequot Indians, who also begin raids on Connecticut settlements.

Plymouth Colony writes a code of laws.

Boston and Charlestown open grammar schools; the General Court votes to establish a college in Massachusetts.

June: Roger Williams founds Providence.

1637

John Winthrop regains the governorship of Massachusetts Bay Colony; he will serve until 1640. The ministerial synod convenes to begin taking action on religious heresies.

Connecticut river town representatives establish some governmental institutions separate from those of Massachusetts.

King Charles I returns Governor Harvey to Virginia.

English Jesuits in Maryland attempt to purchase land from the Indians and establish a community independent of civil law. Their efforts are strongly opposed by Lord Baltimore.

Willem Kieft becomes director general of New Netherland. Population growth will begin, but relations with the Indians will disintegrate under his leadership.

April: In Connecticut, the Pequot attack Wethersfield, setting off the Pequot War.

May to July: Captains John Mason and John Underhill attack Pequot strongholds. The Pequot are virtually exterminated.

November 17: Anne Hutchinson is tried before the Massachusetts General Court and sentenced to banishment.

1638

King Charles I begins legal proceedings to rescind the Massachusetts charter; colonists refuse to send representatives to England as he orders. He will begin drawing up plans for royal government in Massachusetts.

John Wheelwright, banished from Massachusetts for heresy, founds Exeter in modern New Hampshire.

Roger Williams negotiates a peace treaty with the Narragansett and Mohegan that will last half a century.

John Davenport and Theophilus Eaton found New Haven, with a more orthodox theocracy than Massachusetts Bay. Soon several similar settlements spring up; they resist union with other Connecticut settlements.

The General Court of Plymouth Colony votes to become representative. All settled male heads of families, not just freemen, are permitted to elect deputies.

John Harvard dies and leaves his estate to a proposed college. Instruction begins. Newtown is renamed Cambridge.

The Maryland Assembly vetoes Lord Baltimore's code of laws for the colony. Committees are formed to reach a compromise.

The Kent Island Controversy is finally settled; the island will belong to Maryland.

Land and trade policies are liberalized in New Netherland, and new settlers begin to arrive. The first schoolmaster arrives.

Dutch and Swedish investors establish a new company; the Swedish crown authorizes the settlement of New Sweden.

March: Scandinavian colonists, led by Peter Minuit, arrive in the Delaware River valley.

Anne Hutchinson is excommunicated by a synod of ministers; soon afterward she leaves the colony for Rhode Island. Many followers join her, founding several settlements.

1639

King Charles I appoints Sir Ferdinando Gorges royal governor of Massachusetts, but due to increasing political unrest in England, he never sets sail for New England.

River towns in Connecticut adopt the Fundamental Orders.

Dorchester, Massachusetts, establishes the first property tax to support a school.

Stephen Day establishes the first printing press in the English colonies at Cambridge.

Plymouth adopts the Fundamental Orders, which contain its laws and formalize its new representative structure of government.

Lord Baltimore agrees to allow the Maryland Assembly to initiate legislation. Five "hundreds," or divisions, are drawn and directed to send representatives to the assembly.

King Charles I appoints Sir Francis Wyatt governor of Virginia; he arrives with Charles's written acknowledgment of the Virginia Assembly's right to meet.

The first surviving map of New Amsterdam shows a slave camp at the north end of the settlement.

The first African slave arrives in New Sweden.

1640

The Long Parliament convenes in England, dominated by Puritans and Parliamentarians who strongly opposed the king, Archbishop Laud, and royal power.

Providence (Rhode Island) colonists agree to a government that separates church and state, with a governing body of five men.

Governor Bradford turns over the patent for Plymouth to the General Court; the court is now in charge of distributing land.

The *Bay Psalm Book* is published at Cambridge; it is the first book to be printed in the English colonies.

Prices for cattle and grain begin to decline, the beginning of a two-year economic depression in Massachusetts Bay and Plymouth Colonies.

Governor Peter Ridder arrives in New Sweden; with him is the first Lutheran minister in North America.

1641

The Massachusetts General Court adopts the first code of laws for the Bay colony, known as the Massachusetts Body of Liberties.

The four English settlements in modern New Hampshire agree to be governed by Massachusetts Bay.

Indian raids on New Netherland escalate. Director General Kieft calls colonists together; they elect a Committee of 12 to help manage the crisis. It is the first representative body in New Netherland.

Swedish interests buy out Dutch investors in New Sweden; the Swedish government virtually manages the colony after this date.

1642

The English Civil War begins, between royalist supporters of Charles I on one side and Puritans and Parliamentarians on the other.

The Great Migration ends. More than 20,000 colonists have arrived in New England; 22 towns have been founded. The population of New England is 16,000, of which more than 2,000 are in Boston and 1,800 in Plymouth Colony. Rhode Island and Connecticut settlements are governmentally separate from Massachusetts. English settlements exist in Maine, New Hampshire, and Long Island.

Massachusetts passes the first colonial law establishing the principle of compulsory education.

The population of Virginia is about 15,000; tobacco production is over 4,000,000 pounds per year. Settlers have begun to claim land on the York and Rappahannock Rivers.

An English secretary is appointed in New Netherland to help with the increasing number of English colonists. The population reaches about 2,000.

By this date, Scandinavian settlers have introduced log construction, later called the log cabin, to North America.

EYEWITNESS TESTIMONY

Thus stands the cause between God and us, we are entered into Covenant with him for this work. . . . Now If the Lord shall please to hear us, and bring us In peace to the place we desire, then hath he ratified this Covenant and sealed our Commission, (and) will expect a strict performance of the Articles contained In it, but if we shall neglect the observation of these Articles which are the ends we have propounded, and dissembling with our God shall fail to embrace this present world and prosecute our carnal intentions . . . the Lord will surely break out in wrath against us be revenged of such a perjured people and make us know the price of the breach of such a Covenant. . . .

We must delight In each other, make other's Conditions our own rejoice together, mourn together, labor, and suffer together, always having before our eyes . . . our Community as members of the same body. . . . [T]he Lord will be our God and delight to dwell among us, as his own people and will command a blessing upon us in all our ways . . . that men shall say of succeeding plantations: the lord make It like that of New England: for we must Consider that we shall be as a City upon a Hill, the eyes of all people are upon us; so that if we shall deal falsely with our god in this work we have undertaken and so cause him to withdraw his present help from us, we shall be made a story and a byword through the world. . . .

John Winthrop's shipboard speech, "A Model of Christian Charity," 1630, Winthrop Papers, *vol. 2, pp. 294–95.*

My Father was a God fearing Man, and in good esteem among God's faithful Servants: His outward Estate was not great. . . . I did desire my dear Father (my dear Mother being dead) that I might live abroad [*work*], which he consented to: So I first went for trial to live with a worthy Gentleman, Mr. William Southcot, who lived about Three Miles from the City of Exon. He was careful to keep a Godly Family. There being but a very mean Preacher in that Place, we went every Lord's Day into the City, where were many famous Preachers of the Word of God. I then took such a liking unto the Rev. Mr. John Warham, that I did desire to live near him: So I removed (with my Father's Consent) into the City. . . . With him I Covenanted. I never so much as heard of New England until I heard of many godly Persons that were going there, and that Mr. Warham was to go also. My Master asked me whether I would

go? I told him were I not engaged unto him I would willingly go: He answered me, that should be no hindrance.

Captain Roger Clap, 1630, in Young, Chronicles, *pp. 345–46.*

. . . we began to consult of the place of our sitting down; for Salem, where we landed, pleased us not. . . . [W]e were forced to change counsel, and for our present shelter to plant dispersedly. . . .

This dispersion troubled some of us; but help it we could not, wanting ability to remove to any place fit to build a town upon, and the time too short to deliberate any longer, lest the winter should surprise us before we had builded our houses. . . . Insomuch that the ships being now upon their return, some for England, some for Ireland, there was, as I take it, not much less than a hundred (some think many more,) partly out of dislike of our government, which restrained and punished their excesses, and partly through fear of famine, not seeing other means than by their labor to feed themselves, which returned back again; and glad were we so to be rid of them.

Thomas Dudley, letter to the Countess of Lincoln, 1630, in Young, Chronicles, *pp. 310–15.*

This year John Billington the elder (one that came with the first) [*on the Mayflower*] was arraigned, and both by grand and petit jury and found guilty of willful murder by plain and notorious evidence was for the same accordingly executed. This, as it was the first execution amongst them [*the Plymouth colonists*], so was it a mater of great sadness among them. They used all due means about his trial, and took the advice of Mr. Winthrop and other the ablest gentlemen in the Bay of the Massachusetts, that were then newly come over, who concurred with them that he ought to die, and the land to be purged from blood. He and some of his had been often punished for miscarriages before, being one of the profanest families among them. They came from London, and I know not by what friends shuffled into their company. His fact was, that he way-laid a young man, one John Newcomin, (about a former quarrel,) shot him with a gun, whereof he died. . . .

William Bradford, 1630, Bradford's History, *pp. 329–30.*

Hugh Davis to be soundly whipped, before an assembly of Negroes and others for abusing himself to the dishonor of God and the shame of Christians, by defiling his body in lying with a negro; which fault he is to acknowledge next Sabbath day.

Virginia Assembly, September 17, 1630, in Hening, comp., Statutes, vol. 1, p. 146.

So I pray, father, send me four or five yards of cloth to make us some apparel and loving father, though I be far distant from you yet I pray you remember me as your child, and we do not know how long we may subsist, for we cannot live here without provisions from old England. Therefore, I pray do not put away your shop stuff, for I think that in the end, if I live, it must be my living, for we do not know how long this plantation will stand. . . . I had thought to come home in this ship, for my provisions were almost all spent, but that I humbly thank you for your great love and kindness in sending me some provisions, or else I should and might have been half famished, but now, if it please God that I have my health, I will plant what corn I can, and if provisions be not cheaper between this and Michaelmas and that I do not hear from you what I was best to do, I propose to come home at Michaelmas.

William Pond of Watertown to his father in England, March 15, 1631, in Massachusetts Historical Society, Proceedings, 2nd ser., no. 3 (1894), pp. 472–73.

. . . It is ordered that Josias Plaistowe shall (for stealing 4 baskets of corn from the Indians) return them 8 baskets again, be fined five pounds, and hereafter to be called by the name of Josias, and not Mr., as formerly he used to be; and that William Buckland and Thomas Andrew shall be whipped for being accessory to the same offense.

Order of Massachusetts Bay Assistants, August 5, 1631, in West, Source Book, p. 185.

It is ordered, That there be a uniformity throughout this colony both in substance and circumstance to the cannons and constitution of the church of England as near as may be and that every person yield ready obedience unto them upon penalty of the pains and forfeitures in that case appointed. . . .

Virginia law, February 24, 1632, in Hening, comp., Statutes, vol. 1, p. 155.

First the aforesaid *Gerrit de Reux* shall bind himself by oath and on forfeiture of his stipulated wages and the goods which he may have in that country that neither he nor his men shall trade in prohibited furs, especially of otters or beavers . . . without express consent from the West India Company and his aforesaid patroon.

The patroon shall furnish *Gerrit de Retix* aforesaid, out of the animals which he has in that country if they are still alive and to be had: four horses . . . three cows . . . two heifer calves . . . also four sows. . . . The aforesaid *de Reux* shall further do his best with the assistance of the smiths and the carpenters of the Company that the aforesaid house may at the very first opportunity be erected, roofed and surrounded by wooden palisades. Also that he may be provided with wagon and plow by the wheelwright. . . .

Further, the aforesaid Gerrit shall be bound to engage here a good farm servant and a boy at the expense of the patroon, and on his arrival there still another servant shall be added if possible. The patroon shall pay the wages and board of the servants and boy till the first of May 1634 and shall pay him, *Gerrit de Reux,* 180 guilders a year, from the time of his arrival in that country till the first of January 1634. All the crops and increase of live stock, likewise milk and butter and all other profits till the first of January 1634 shall therefore be for the behoof of the patroon. . . .

The aforesaid *de Reux* shall raise as many sheep and hogs as possible, and of what he sells thereof one half the proceeds shall go to the patroon and the other half to himself. Of the winter wheat to be sown in the fall of 1633, one half shall be for the benefit of the aforesaid *Gerrit de Reux* on condition that the last year he deliver to the patroon, first of all, as much grain as he received the first year. . . .

Gerrit de Reux aforenamed shall also cause the yearly manure to be distributed over the land in the most advantageous manner, without wasting it. . . .

Contract between a patroon and a farmer, signed in Amsterdam, June 15, 1632, in New York State Library, Van Rensselaer, pp. 193–95.

Dear wife, and comfortable yoke-fellow,

If our heavenly Father be pleased to make our yoke more heavy than we did so soon expect, remember (I pray thee,) what we have heard, that our heavenly husband, the Lord Jesus, when he first called us to fellowship with himself, called us unto this condition, to deny ourselves and to take up our cross daily, to follow him. And truly, sweet heart, though this cup may be brackish at the first taste, yet a cup of God's mingling is doubtless sweet in the bottom to such as have learned to make it their greatest happiness to partake with Christ, as in his glory, so in the way that leadeth to it. . . .

Meanwhile, send me now by this bearer such linen as I am to use.

The Reverend John Cotton to his wife, Sarah, October 3, 1632, in Young, Chronicles, *p. 432.*

The scarcity of workmen had caused them to raise their wages to an excessive rate . . . and accordingly those who had commodities to sell advanced their prices sometime double to that they cost in England, so as it grew to a general complaint, which the court [*Massachusetts General Court*], taking knowledge of, as also of some further evils which were springing out of the excessive rates of wages, they made an order that carpenters, masons, etc., should take but 2 shilling the day, and laborers but 18 pence, and that no commodity should be sold at above 4 pence in the shilling more than it cost for ready money in England. . . .

The evils which were springing, etc., were: (1) Many spent much time because they could get as much in four days as would keep them a week. (2) They spent much in tobacco and strong waters, which was a great waste to the commonwealth. . . .

John Winthrop's journal, 1633, History, *vol. 1, p. 138.*

The 18th, arrived here [*New Netherland*] an Englishman, who came from New England to trade in the river. . . . This Englishman invited the governor to come and see him. I went with him, in company with a number of the officers, who became intoxicated, and got into such high words, that the Englishmen could not understand how it was that there should be such unruliness among the officers of the Company, and that a governor should have no more control over them; he was not accustomed to it among his countrymen.

David Pietersz de Vries, Voyages from Holland to America, *April 18, 1633, in Hart,* American History, *vol. 1, pp. 523–24.*

Robert Cowles is fined ten pounds, and enjoined to stand with a white sheet of paper on his back, wherein a *drunkard* shall be written in great letters, and to stand therewith so long as the Court thinks meet, for abusing himself shamefully with drink.

Order of Massachusetts Bay Assistants, September 13, 1633, in West, Source Book, *p. 185.*

An agreement made by the whole consent and vote of the Plantation made Monday 8th of October, 1633.

It is ordered that for the general good and well ordering of the affairs of the Plantation there shall be every Monday before the Court by eight of the clock in the morning, and presently upon the beating of the drum, a general meeting of the inhabitants of the Plantation at the meeting house, there to settle (and set down) such orders as may tend to the general good as aforesaid; and every man to be bound thereby without gainsaying or resistance. It is also agreed that there shall be twelve men selected out the Company that may or the greatest part of them meet as aforesaid to determine as aforesaid, yet so as it is desired that the more of the Plantation will keep the meeting constantly and all that are there although none of the Twelve shall have a free voice as any of the Twelve and that the greater vote both of the Twelve and the other shall be of force and efficacy as aforesaid. And it is likewise ordered that all things concluded as aforesaid shall stand in force and be obeyed until the next monthly meeting and afterwards if it be not contradicted, and otherwise ordered upon the said monthly meeting by the greatest parts of those that are present as aforesaid.

Initial organization of town government, Dorchester, Massachusetts, in West, Source Book, *pp. 188–89.*

1. His Lord requires his said Governor and Commissioners that in their voyage to Mary Land they be very careful to preserve unity and peace amongst all the passengers on Shipboard, and that they suffer no scandal nor offence to be given to any of the Protestants, whereby any just complaint may hereafter be made, by them, in Virginia or in England, and that for that end, they cause all Acts of Roman Catholic Religion to be done as privately as may be, and that they instruct all the Roman Catholics to be silent upon all occasions of discourse concerning matters of Religion; and that the said Governor and Commissioners treat the Protestants with as much mildness and favor as Justice will permit. And this to be observed at Land as well as at Sea. . . .

5. That they write a letter to Captain Claiborne . . . to give him notice of their arrival and of the Authority and charge committed to them by his Lord . . . and tell him . . . that he hath settled a plantation there within the precincts of his Lord's patent . . .

12. That they cause all the planters to employ their servants in planting of sufficient quantity of corn and

other provision of victual and that they do not suffer them to plant any other commodity whatsoever before that be done in a sufficient proportion which they are to observe yearly. . . .

15. That in fine they be very careful to do justice to every man without partiality, and that they avoid any occasion of difference with those of Virginia and to have as little to do with them as they can this first year. . . .

Cecilius Calvert, Lord Baltimore, instructions to Maryland colonists, November 13, 1633, in Hall, ed., Narratives, *pp. 16–23.*

II. Any married man that shall transport himself, his wife and children; shall have assigned unto him, his heirs and assignees for ever, in freehold, (as aforesaid) for himself 100 acres; and for his wife 100 acres; and for every child that he shall carry over, under the age of 16 years, 50 acres; paying for a quit rent 12 pence for every fifty acres.

III. Any woman that shall transport herself or any children, under the age of six years, shall have the like Conditions as aforesaid.

IV. Any woman that shall carry over any women servants, under the age of forty years, shall have for and in respect of every such woman servant, 50 acres; paying only a quit rent as aforesaid.

Lord Baltimore, on land grant policies, ca. 1633, "A Relation of Maryland," in Hall, ed., Narratives, *p. 92.*

To avoid all occasion of dislike, and Color of wrong, we bought the space of thirty miles of ground of them [*Piscataway Indians*], for axes, hoes, cloth and hatchets, which we call Augusta Carolina. It made them more willing to entertain us, for that they had wars with the Sasquasahannockes, who come sometimes upon them, and waste and spoil them and their country, for thus they hope by our means to be safe, God disposing things thus for those which were to come to bring the light of his holy law to these distressed, poor infidels, so that they do indeed like us better for coming so well provided, assuring themselves of greater safety, by living by us. Is not this miraculous, that a nation a few days before in general arms against us and our enterprise should like lambs yield themselves, glad of our company, giving us houses, land, and livings for a trifle. *Digitus dei est hic* [*this is the finger of God*] and some great good is meant toward this people.

Father Andrew White, "Brief Relation," 1634, in Hall, ed., Narratives, *p. 42.*

From hence the Governor [*Calvert*] went to Paschatoway . . . where he found many Indians assembled, and here he met with one Captain Henry Fleete an Englishman, who had lived many years among the Indians, and by that means spake the Country language very well, and was much esteemed of by the natives. Him our Governor sent a shore to invite the Werowance to a parley. . . .

To make his entry peaceable and safe, he thought fit to present the Werowance and the Wisoes [*chieftains*] of the Town with some English Cloth, . . . Axes, Hoes, and Knives which they accepted very kindly, and freely gave consent that he and his company should dwell in one part of their Town, and reserved the other for themselves; and those Indians that dwelt in that part of the Town, which was allotted for the English, freely left them their houses, and some corn that they had begun to plant: It was also agreed between them, that at the end of harvest they should leave the whole town; which they did accordingly: And they made mutual promises to each other, to live friendly and peaceably together, and if any injury should happen to be done on any part, that satisfaction should be made for the same and thus upon the 27 day of March, Anno Domini, 1634. the Governor took possession of the place, and named the Town Saint Mary's. . . .

They coming thus to seat upon an Indian Town, where they found ground cleared to their hands, gave them opportunity (although they came late in the year) to plant some Corn, and to make them gardens, which they sowed with English seeds of all sorts, and they prospered exceeding well. They also made what haste they could to finish their houses. . . .

Anonymous promotional tract, "A Relation of Maryland," March 1634, in Hall, ed., Narratives, *pp. 72–76.*

The River [*the Delaware*] aboundeth with beaver, otters, and other meaner furs. . . . The people [*Native Americans*] are for the most part very well proportioned, well featured, gentle, tractable and docible. The land is very good and fruitful and withall very healthful. The soil is sandy and produceth divers sorts of fruits, especially grapes, which grow wild in great quantity, of which I have eaten six several sorts, some of them as food as they are ordinarily in Italy, or Spain; and were they replanted I think they would be far better. Here also grows the fruit which in Italy they call lazarroli, plums, a divers sorts of berries and diverse other fruits not known in Europe. . . . The earth being fruitful is covered over with woods and stately timber, except only in those places, where the Indians had planted their corn. The Country is very well replenished, with deer and in some places store of Elk. The low grounds of which there is great quantity excellent for meadows and full of Beaver and Otter. The quantity of fowl is so great as can hardly be believed, we took at one time 48 partridges together, as they crossed the river, chased by wild hawks. I myself sprang in two hours 5 or 6 coveys in walking of a mile. There are infinite number of wild pigeons, black birds, Turkeys, Swans, wild geese, ducks, Teals, widgeons, brants, herons, cranes etc. of which there is so great abundance, as that the Rivers and creeks are covered with them in winter.

English Captain Thomas Young's "Brief Relation," 1634, in Streeter, ed., Papers, *p. 311.*

The Hollanders of Hudson's river having gotten some intelligence of our being here by the Indians, who in some places live not a day's journey from: them, overtook me here [*the Delaware River*]. . . . When they were come aboard of me, I sent for them into my cabin, and asked them what they made here. They answered me, they came to trade as formerly they had done. I asked them if they had any Commission from his Majesty to trade in the river or no. They answered they had none from the King of England; but from the Governor of New Netherlands they had. To which I replied, that I knew no such Governor, nor no such place as New Netherland. I told them that this Country did belong to the Crown of England; as well by ancient discovery as likewise by possession, lawfully take; and that his Majesty was no pleased to make more ample discovery of this river, and of other places also, where he would erect colonies; and that I was therefore sent hither with a Royal Commission under the Great Seal to take possession thereof. I perceived by their countenances that this news struck them cold at heart, and after a little pause they answered me, that they had traded in this river heretofore. I replied that therein they had done his Majesty and his subjects the greater injury.

Captain Thomas Young's "Brief Relation," 1634, in Streeter, ed., Papers, *p. 308.*

It is ordered that Robert Cowles, for drunkenness by him committed at Rocksbury, shall be disenfranchised, wear about his neck, and to hand upon his outward garment, a D, made of red cloth, and set upon white;

to continue this for a year, and not to leave it off at any time when he comes amongst company. . . .

Order of Massachusetts Bay Assistants, March 14, 1634, in West, Source Book, *p. 186.*

It was further ordered that it shall be lawful for the freemen of every plantation to choose two or three of each town before every General Court, to confer of and prepare such public business as by them shall be thought fit to consider of at the next General Court, and that such persons as shall be hereafter so deputed by the freemen of the several plantations, to deal in their behalf, in the public affairs of the common wealth, shall have the full power and voices of all the said freemen, derived to them for the making and establishing of laws, granting of lands, etc., and to deal in all other affairs of the commonwealth wherein the freemen have to do, the matter of election of magistrates and other officers only, excepted, wherein every freeman is to give his own voice.

General Court of Massachusetts, May 1634, in West, Source Book, *p. 193.*

When the Governor [*Harvey*] came first into this Country [*Virginia*], it was in great scarcity and want of victuals; in so much as tho' it abounded with tobacco, they starved for want of corn, Nay, they were forced yearly to expect from England great supplies of victuals; in so much as it was the custom to transport hither from England a whole year's provisions for every man they landed here. Though now, at this present, through his care and provident government, the country is not only able abundantly to support itself and 1500 persons more which have landed here this year, but it hath this very year also been able to, spare their zealous neighbors of New England 10,000 bushels of corn for their relief; besides good quantities of beans goats and hogs; whereof this country hath great plenty. And it is credibly reported that at this present there are above 5,000 head of beef here; whose increase the Governor takes great care to preserve and increase. . . . The swine here are excellent, and I never tasted better in Italy or Spain.

Captain Thomas Young to Sir Toby Matthew, July 13, 1634, in Streeter, Papers, *p. 295.*

At this time a French ship came with commission from the king of France, (as they pretended,) and took Penobscott, a Plimouth trading house, and sent away the men which were in it, but kept their goods and

Manhattan Island, a 1639 map by Joan Vinckeboons (Library of Congress)

gave them bills for them, and bade them tell all the plantations, as far as forty degrees, that they would come with eight ships, next year, and displant them all. But by a letter which the captain wrote to the governour of Plimouth, it appeared they had commission from Mons. Roselly [Razilly], commander at the fort near Cape Breton, called La Havre, to displant the English as far as Pemaquid, and by it they professed all courtesy to us here.

John Winthrop, 1635, History, *vol. 1, p. 198.*

These general grievances made some of the people meet in some numbers and in an unlawful manner, yet without any manifestation of bad intents, only desires to exhibit their complaints.... The governor [Harvey] having intelligence of this Petition grew enraged, and sent out his warrants to apprehend the complainants. ... [P]resently the council being called together he declared it necessary that Martial law should be executed upon the Prisoners, but it was desired they might have legal trial; soon growing into extreme choler and passion, after many passings and repassings to and fro, he at length sat down in the chair and with a frowning countenance bid all the council sit. After a long pause he drew a paper out of his pocket and reading it to himself said to the council; I am to propound a question unto you; I require every man, in his Majesty's name, to deliver his opinion in writing ... unto this proposition (which is this): What do you think they deserve that have gone about to persuade the people from their obedience to his Majesty's substitute.... And I begin with you Mr. Menefie; who answered, I am but a young Lawyer and dare not upon the sudden deliver my opinion.... Mr. Farrar begun to complain of that strong command, the governor cut off his speech saying in his Majesty's name I command you not to speak till your turn. Then myself replied, I conceive this a strange kind of proceeding; instantly in his Majesty's name he commanded me silence.... Then followed many bitter languages from him, till the sitting ended. The next meeting in a most stern manner he demanded the reason that we conceived of the country's Petition against him. Mr. Menefie made answer, the chiefest cause was the detaining of the Letters to his Majesty and the Lords. Then he rising in a great rage said to Mr. Menefie; and do you say so? He replied, yes: presently the governor in a fury went and striking him on the shoulder as hard as I can imagine he could said, I arrest you of suspicion of Treason to his Majesty. Then Captain Utie being near said, and we the like to you sir. Whereupon I seeing him in a rage, took him in my arms and said: Sir, there is no harm intended against you save only to acquaint you with the grievances of the Inhabitants and to that end I desire you to sit down in your chair.

Virginia Council member Samuel Matthews, 1635,
in Virginia Magazine *1 (1894), pp. 418–22.*

And that upon the 28 day of April last . . . the said Mathewes, Utye, Farrer, Pearce, Minefie and John Pott came all armed and brought with them about 50 Musketeers, and beset me in my own house, which was the place which I appointed for our meeting. That I and Mr. Kemp (his Majesty's Secretary there) were then sitting together expecting the council, when the said mutinous company entered the place, and John Utye in the presence of the rest gave me a very great and violent stroke upon the shoulder and said with a loud voice, I arrest you for treason; and thereupon Mathewes and the rest of the said company, came all about me, and laid hold on me, and there held me so as I was not able to stir from the place, and all of them said to me; you must prepare yourself to go for England, for you must and shall go, to answer the complaints that are against you.

That upon this Uproar John Pott, (who by the said company was placed at the door of said house) with his hand gave a sign and immediately the Musketeers which before that time lay hid, came presently running with their pieces presented towards my house. . . .

That to prepare their way to the meeting they caused guards to be set in all ways and passages, so that no man could travel or come from place to place, nor had I means or power to raise any force to suppress this meeting they having restrained me, and set a guard upon me.

Governor John Harvey to the Commission for Foreign
Plantations, 1635, Virginia Magazine *1 (1894),*
pp. 425–26.

. . . Father, I trust in Him who hath the hearts and the disposing of them in His hand that I have not provoked you to harbor so ill an opinion of me as my mother's letters do signify . . . that is to say, that I should abuse your goodness and be prodigal of your purse. . . .

For my habit, it is mean, for the most as many servants, and if I had not had money which I had for some things here, I might have wanted many necessaries which I could not have been without, . . . except I should have made you a score [*debt*] here, which I was not willing to do. I writ to my mother for lace not out of any prodigal or proud mind but only for some cross-clothes [*headbands*], which is the most allowable and commendable dressing here. She would have me wear dressings which I did so long as they would suffer me, whilst the elders with others entreated me to leave them off, for they gave great offence. . . . But for mine own part, since my sending for things gives such offence, I will be more sparing in that kind hereafter, but leave it to the Lord . . . to give me an heart to be content with my portion, knowing that nothing can befall me but that that He hath appointed. . . . Dear Father, I . . . submit myself in all duty and obedience as belongeth unto a child to yourself and my mother. . . .

Mary Downing, Boston, to her father in England,
November 27, 1635, in Emerson, Letters, *pp. 179–80.*

After God had carried us safe to New England, and we had builded our houses, provided necessaries for our livelihood, rear'd convenient places for God's worship, and settled the Civil Government: One of the next things we longed for, and looked after was to advance Learning, and perpetuate it to Posterity; dreading to leave an illiterate Ministry to the Churches, when our present Ministers shall lie in the dust. And as we were thinking and consulting how to effect this great Work; it pleased God to stir up the heart of one Mr. Harvard (a godly Gentleman and a lover of Learning, there living amongst us) to give the one half of his Estate . . . towards the erecting of a College, and all his Library.

Anonymous pamphlet, describing events of 1636–38,
"New England's First Fruits" (1642), in Hart, ed.,
American History, *vol. 1, p. 467.*

Obj[ection]. If it be said, there may be many carnal men whom God hath invested with sundry eminent gifts of wisdom, courage, justice, fit for government.

Ans[wer]. Such may be fit to be consulted with and employed by governors, according to the quality and use of their gifts and parts, but yet are men not fit to be trusted with place of standing power or settled authority. Ahitophel's wisdom may be fit to be heard (as an oracle of God) but not fit to be trusted with power of settled magistracy, lest he at last call for 12,000 men to lead them forth against David (11 Sam. 17:1–3). . . .

Obj. If it be said again, that then the Church estate could not be compatible with any commonwealth under heaven.

Ans. . . . Now, if it be a divine truth that none are so fit to be trusted with public permanent authority but godly men, who are fit materials for church fellowship, then from the same grounds it will appear that none are so fit to be trusted with the liberties of the Commonwealth as church members; for the liberties of the freemen of this Commonwealth are such as require men of faithful integrity to God and the state to preserve the same.

The Reverend John Cotton, sermon, 1636,
in Hutchinson, History, *p. 495.*

Democracy, I do not conceive, that ever God did ordain as a fit government either for Church or commonwealth. If the people be governors, who shall be governed?

The Reverend John Cotton, letter to Lord Say and Sele,
1636, in Hutchinson, History, *p. 497.*

He is to instruct the youth both on shipboard and on land, in reading, writing, ciphering, and arithmetic, with all zeal and diligence; he is also to implant the fundamental principles of true Christian religion and salvation, by means of catechizing; he is to teach them the customary forms of prayers and also to accustom them to pray; he is to give heed to their manners, and bring these as far as possible to modesty and propriety, and to this end he is to maintain good discipline and order, and further to do all that is required of a good, diligent and faithful schoolmaster.

Instructions to colonial schoolmasters from the Dutch
Reformed Church, 1636, in Finegan, ed.,
Free Schools, p. 16.

Mr. Winthrop, Governor: Mrs. Hutchinson, you are called here as one of those that have troubled the peace of the commonwealth and the churches here;

you are known to be a woman that hath a great share in the promoting and divulgings of those opinions that are causes of this trouble . . . you have spoken diverse things so we have been informed very prejudicial to the honor of the churches and ministers thereof, and you have maintained a meeting and an assembly in your house that hath been condemned by the general assembly as a thing not tolerable nor comely in the sight of God nor fitting for your sex, and notwithstanding that was cried down, you have continued the same. . . . Why do you keep such a meeting at your house as you do every week upon a set day?

Mrs. Hutchinson: It is lawful for me so to do, as it is all your practices, and can you find a warrant for yourself and condemn me for the same thing? . . . [I]t was in practice before I came. Therefore I was not the first. . . . There was never any man with us. . . . I conceive there lies a clear rule in Titus that the elder women should instruct the younger and then I must have a time wherein I must do it.

Gov: All this I grant you . . . but what is this to the purpose that you, Mrs. Hutchinson, must call a company together from their callings to come to be taught of you?

Mrs. H: Will it please you to answer me this and to give me a rule, for then I will willingly submit to any truth If any come to my house to be instructed in the ways of God, what rule have I to put them away?

Gov: But suppose that a . . . man should come and say "Mrs. Hutchinson, I hear that you are a woman that God hath given his grace unto and you have knowledge in the word of God, I pray instruct me a little," ought you not to instruct this man?

Mrs. H: I think I may. . . .

Gov: Your course is not to be suffered for, besides that we find such a course as this to be greatly prejudicial to the state . . . and your opinions being known to be different from the word of God may seduce many simple souls that resort to you . . . so that now they are flown off from magistrates and ministers. . . . We see not that any should have authority to set up any other exercises besides what authority hath already set up. . . .

Mrs. H: Sir, I do not believe that to be so.

Gov: Well, we see how it is. We must therefore put it away from you, or restrain you from maintaining this course.

Mrs. H: If you have a rule for it from God's word, you may.

Anne Hutchinson's trial before the General Court of Massachusetts, November, 1637, in Hart, ed., American History, *vol. 1, pp. 382–85.*

. . . Captain *Mason* entering into a Wigwam, brought out a fire-brand, after he had wounded many in the house, then he set fire on the West-side where he entered, my self set fire on the South end with a train of Powder, the fires of both meeting in the center of the Fort blazed most terribly, and burnt all in the space of half an hour; many courageous fellows [*Pequot Indians*] were unwilling to come out, and fought most desperately through the Palisadoes, so as they were scorched and burnt with the very flame, and were deprived of their arms, in regard the fire burnt their very bowstrings, and so perished valiantly: mercy they did deserve for their valor, could we have had opportunity to have bestowed it; many were burnt in the Fort, both men, women, and children, others forced out . . . which our soldiers received and entertained with the point of the sword; down fell men, women, and children, those that escaped us, fell into the hands of the Indians [*English allies*], that were in the rear of us; it is reported by

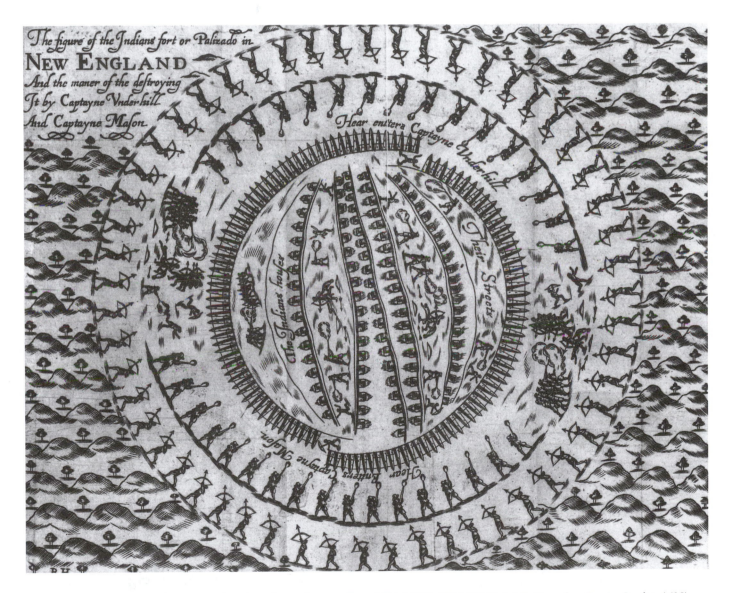

Captain John Underhill's drawing of the colonial attack on a Pequot village, 1637 *(NYPL, KC 1638, Underhill,* Newes from America, *London, 1638)*

themselves that there were about four hundred souls in this Fort, and not above five of them escaped out of our hands. Great and doleful was the bloody sight to the view of young soldiers that never had been in war to see so many souls lie gasping on the ground so thick in some places, that you could hardly pass along. It may be demanded, why should you be so furious (as some have said) Should not Christians have more mercy and compassion? But I would refer you to David's war, when a people is grown to such a height of blood, and sin against God and man and all confederates in the action, there he hath no respect to persons. . . . We had sufficient light from the word of God for our proceedings. . . .

Captain John Underhill describes the Pequot War, summer 1637, News from America, *in Hart, ed.,* American History, *vol. 1, pp. 443–44.*

The wife of one William Dyer, a milliner in the New Exchange, a very proper and fair woman, and both of them notoriously infected with Mrs. Hutchinson's errors, and very censorious and troublesome (she being of a very proud spirit, and much addicted to revelations,) had been delivered of a child some few months before, October 17, and the child buried, (being still-born,) . . . [S]ome rumor began to spread, that the child was a monster. . . .

The governour . . . caused the said monster to be taken up, and though it were much corrupted, yet most of those things were to be seen, as the horns, the claws, the scales, etc. When it died in the mother's body (which was about two hours before the birth,) the bed whereon the mother lay did shake, and withal there was such a noisome savor, as most of the women [*attendants*] were taken with extreme vomiting and purging, so as they were forced to depart. . . .

Another thing observable was, the discovery of it, which was just when Mrs. Hutchinson was cast out of the church.

John Winthrop, 1638, History, *vol. 1, pp. 313–16.*

Theocratic, or to make the Lord God our Governour, is the best Form of Government in a Christian Common-wealth, and which men that are free to choose (as in new Plantations they are) ought to establish. . . . The Assumption I prove thus:

That Form of Government where 1. The people that have the power of choosing their Governors are

in Covenant with God 2. Wherein the men chosen by them are godly men, and fitted with a spirit of Government: 3. In which the laws they rule by are the Laws of God: 4. Wherein Laws are executed, Inheritances allotted, and civil differences are composed, according to Gods appointment: 5. In which men of God are consulted with in all hard eases, and in matters of religion is the Form which was received and established among the people of Israel whil'st the Lord God was their Governour. . . .

The Reverend John Davenport's "Defense of Theocracy," 1638, in Hart, ed., American History, *vol. 1, p. 331.*

This year the reverend and judicious Mr. Joseph Glover . . . provided, for further completing the Colonies [*of Massachusetts Bay*] in Church and Commonwealth work, a Printer, which hath been very useful in many respects . . . [and] Master Ezekiel Rogers, who with a holy and humble people, made his progress to the North-Eastward, and erected a Town about 6 miles from Ipswich, called Rowly. . . . [T]hese people being very industrious every way, soon built many houses, to the number of about three-score families, and were the first people that set upon making of Cloth in this Western World; for which end they built a fulling-mill, and caused their little-ones to be very diligent in spinning cotton wool; many of them having been clothiers in England, till their zeal to promote the Gospel of Christ caused them to wander. . . .

Edward Johnson, 1638, Johnson's Wonder, *p. 183–84.*

The Second of *October,* about 9 of the clock in the morning, Mr. *Maverick's* Negro woman came to my chamber window, and in her own Country language, and tune sang very loud and shrill, going out to her, she used a great deal of respect towards me, and willingly would have expressed her grief in English; but I apprehended it by her countenance and deportment, whereupon I repaired to my host, to learn of him the cause, and resolved to entreat him in her behalf for that I understood before, that she had been a Queen in her own Country. . . . Mr. Maverick was desirous to have a breed of Negroes and therefore seeing she would not yield by persuasions to company with a Negro young man he had in his house; he commanded him will'd she nill'd she to go to bed to her, which was no sooner done but she kicked him out again, this she took in high disdain beyond her slavery, and this was the cause of her grief.

John Josselyn observes slavery near Boston, 1638,
"Account of Two Voyages to New England,"
in Massachusetts Historical Society, Collections,
3rd series, vol. 3 (1833), p. 231.

That it may be prevented that noe woman here vow chastety in the world, unlesse she marry within seven years after land shall fall to hir, she must either dispose away of hir land, or else she shall forfeite it to the nexte of kinne, and if she have but one Mannor, whereas she canne not alienate it, it is gonne unlesse she git a husband.

Maryland colonist's recommendation to Lord Baltimore,
1638, quoted in Spruill, Women's Life, *p. 11.*

Dorothy Talbye was hanged at Boston for murdering her own daughter, a child of three years old. She had been a member of the church of Salem, and of good esteem for godliness, etc., but falling at difference with her husband, through melancholy or spiritual delusions, she sometimes attempted to kill him, and her children, and herself, by refusing meat, saying it was so revealed to her, etc. After much patience, and diverse admonitions not prevailing, the church cast her out. Whereupon she grew worse; so as the magistrate caused her to be whipped. Whereupon she was reformed for a time, and carried herself more dutifully to her husband, etc.; but soon after she was so possessed with Satan, that he persuaded her (by his delusions, which she listened to as revelations from God) to break the neck of her own child, that she might free it from future misery. . . .

John Winthrop, 1638, History, *vol. 1, pp. 335–36.*

Amongst other enormities that fell out amongst them [*Plymouth colonists*], this year 3 men were, (after due trial) executed for robbery and murder which they had committed. . . . Arthur Peach was the chief of them, and the ring leader of all the rest. He was a lusty and a desperate young man, and had been one of the soldiers in the Pequot war, and had done as good service as the most there, and one of the forwardest in any attempt. And being now out of means, and loath to work, and failing to idle courses and company, he intended to go to the Dutch plantation; and had lured these 3, being other men's servants and apprentices, to go with him. . . . At length there came a Narragansett Indian by,

who had been in the Bay a trading, and had both cloth and beads about him. . . . Peach called him to drink tobacco with them, and he came and sat down with them. Peach . . . took a rapier and ran him through the body once or twice, and took from him 5 fathom of wampum, and 3 coats of cloth, and went their way, leaving him for dead. But he scrabbled away, when they were gone, and made shift to get home, (but died within a few days after,) by which means they were discovered; and by subtlety the Indians took them. . . . The Indians sent for Mr. Williams, and made a grievous complaint; his friends and kindred were ready to rise in arms, and provoke the rest thereunto. . . . But Mr. Williams pacified them, and told them they should see justice done upon the offenders. . . . Yet some of the rude and ignorant sort murmured that any English should be put to death for the Indians. . . . [T]hey all in the end freely confessed in effect all that the Indian accused them of . . . and so . . . were cast by the jury, and condemned, and executed for the same. And some of the Narragansett Indians . . . were present when it was done, which gave them and all the country good satisfaction.

William Bradford, 1638, Bradford's History,
pp. 432–35.

I make known to you, Peter Minuit, who call yourself commander in the service of her Royal Majesty of Sweden, that the whole South [*Delaware*] River, in New Netherland, has been many years in our [*Dutch*] possession, and has been secured by us with forts above and below, and sealed with our blood, which has happened during your own direction of New Netherland, as is well known to you. But as you now do make a beginning of a settlement between our forts, and are building there a fort, to our prejudice and disadvantage, which we shall never endure or tolerate, and as we are persuaded it never has been commanded by Her Swedish Majesty to build fortresses on our rivers and coasts, or to settle people on the adjoining lands, or to trade in peltries, or to undertake any other thing to our prejudice; now therefore, we protest against all evil consequences of such encroachments. And declare that, while we will not be answerable for any mishap, bloodshed, trouble, and disaster which you may hereafter suffer, we are resolved to defend out rights in all such manner as we deem proper.

Director-General Willem Kieft to Peter Minuit, 1638,
quoted in Brodhead, History, *p. 283.*

Let Inquest be made for the Lord Proprietor, if in the river of Potomac on the Eastern shore, on the three and twentieth day of April in the year of our Lord 1635. . . . Rateliff Warren, commonly known by the name of Lieutenant Warren, Richard Hancock, Robert Lake with divers others . . . not having the peace of God before their eyes, but being seduced by the malicious instigation of the devil, and of malice premeditated, in one pinnace belonging to William Claiborne of the Isle of Kent gent[leman], with force and arms, that is, with guns and pistons charged, swords, and other weapons, . . . feloniously, and as pirates and robbers an assault did make, and upon the said Thomas Cornwallis and his company diverse guns charged with powder and bullets did shoot and discharge . . . and one William Ashmore of St Mary's Apprentice . . . did shoot and wound in his breast on his left side . . . William Ashmore instantly died.

Maryland inquest, February 12, 1638,
in Streeter, Papers, pp. 33.

Forasmuch as you, Mrs. Hutchinson, have highly transgressed and offended, and forasmuch as you have so many ways troubled the Church with your Errors and have drawn away many a poor soul, and have upheld your Revelations: and forasmuch as you have made a Lie, and etc. Therefore in the name of our Lord Je[sus] Ch[rist] and In the name of the Church I do not only pronounce you worthy to be cast out, but I do cast you out and . . . I do deliver you up to Satan, that you may learn no more to blaspheme, to seduce and to lie, and I do account you from this time forth to be a Heathen and a Publican and so to be held of all the Brethren and Sisters, of this Congregation, and of others: therefore I command you . . . as a Leper to withdraw yourself out of the Congregation. . . .

Anne Hutchinson's excommunication from Boston's First
Church, March 1638, Massachusetts Historical Society,
Proceedings, 2nd ser., no. 4 (1889), pp. 189–91.

Be it known . . . that on the 29th of December in the year sixteen hundred and thirty-eight, appeared personally . . . the mate Michell Simonssen, from Sardam, about the age of fifty-four years; the gunner Johan Joachimssen, about the age of thirty years; the second mate, Jacob Evertssen Sandelin from Scotland, about the age of thirty-eight years; the upper boatswain, Peter Johanssen from the Bemster, about the age of twenty-seven years; all four of whom, in the abovementioned respective capacities, have lately served on the ship called

the Key of Calmar . . . related in what manner they, in this now ending year, sailed on the above-mentioned ship so far into the South [*Delaware*] River that they came to and by another river, the Minquas Kil, which they also in like manner sailed into. And they made their presence known with all kinds of signs, both by the firing of cannon and otherwise, and also sailed several miles into the same river, and went into the country, but neither found nor observed any sign or vestige of Christian people. . . . [W]hereupon the abovementioned Director Peter Minuit requested and caused the nations or people to whom the land really belonged to come before him, whom he then asked, if they wished to sell the river, with all the land lying about there, as many days' journeys as he would request. This they agreed to with the common consent of the nations. The parties were therefore agreed with one another, and thereupon, on the twenty-ninth of March of the above year; appeared and presented themselves before the abovementioned ship's council, in the name of their nations or people, five *Sachems or* princes, by the name of Mattahorn, Mitot Schemingh, Eru Packen, Mahamen, and Chiton, some being present [on behalf] of the Ermewormahi, the others on behalf of the Mante [*all Lenni Lenape*] and Minqua nations. And these sachems or princes . . . ceded, transported, and transferred all the land, as many days' journeys on all places and parts of the river as they requested; upwards and on both sides. Because, however, they did not understand our language, the abovementioned Andress Lucassen, who had before this lived long in the country and who knew their language, translated the same into their speech . . . and the country was called New Sweden.

"Affidavit of Four Men from the Kalmar Nyckel,"
March 1638, in Myers, Narratives, pp. 86–89.

Memorandum, that William Edwin, planter, acknowledges himself to owe unto the Lord Proprietor one thousand weight of merchantable tobacco, to be paid on demand, in case the said William Edwin hath precontracted himself to any other woman that Mary Whitehead (spinster) or in case there is any consanguinity affinity or other lawful impediment, to the knowledge of the said William Edwin, why he should not be married to the said Mary Whitehead.

March 26, A licence was granted to William Edwin to marry Mary Whitehead.

Maryland's first marriage license, March 26, 1638,
in Streeter, Papers, pp. 278–79.

Know all men by these presents that I Wehanownowit Sagamore of piskatoquake for good considerations me thereunto moving and for certain commodities which I have received have granted and sold unto John Wheelwright of piscatoquake . . . all the right title and interest in all such lands, woods, meadows, rivers, brooks, springs, as of right belongs unto me from Merimack river to the patents of piscatoquake bounded with the South East side of piscatoquake patents and so to go into the Country north West thirty miles as far as the east line, to have and to hold the same to them and their heirs for ever. only the ground w[hi]ch is broken up is excepted. and that it shall be lawful for the said Sagamore to hunt and fish and fowl in the said limits.

Indian bill of sale for Exeter, New Hampshire, April 3, 1638, in Hart, ed., American History, *vol. 1, p. 426.*

Sir, we have been long afflicted by a young man, boisterous and desperate, Philip Verin son of Salem, who, as he hath refused to hear the word with us (which we molested him not for) this twelve month, so because he could not draw his wife, a gracious and modest woman, to the same ungodliness with him, he hath trodden her under foot tyrannically brutishly: which she and we long bearing, though with his furious blows she went in danger of life, at the last the major vote of us discard him from our civil freedom, or disfranchise, and etc: he will have justice (as he clamors) at other Courts: I wish he might, for a foul and slanderous and brutish carriage, which God hath delivered him up unto. He will haul his wife with ropes to Salem, where she must needs be troubled and troublesome as differences yet stand. She is willing to stay and live with him or else where, where she may not offend and etc. I shall humbly request that this item be accepted, and he no way countenanced. . . .

Roger Williams to John Winthrop, May 22, 1638, in Williams, Letters, *pp. 95–96.*

At Providence also, the devil was not idle. For whereas, at their first coming thither, Mr. Williams and the rest did make an order, that no man should be molested for his conscience, now men's wives, and children, and servants, claimed liberty hereby to go to all religious meeting, though never so often, or though private, upon the week days; and because one Verin refused to let his wife go to Mr. Williams so oft as she was called for, they required to have him

censured. But there stood up one Arnold . . . telling them that, when be consented to that order, he never intended it should extend to the breach of any ordinance of God, such as the subjection of wives to their husbands, etc. . . . Some were of opinion, that if Verin would not suffer his wife to have her liberty, the church should dispose her to some other man, who would use her better.

John Winthrop, on the Verin case, 1638, History, *vol. 1, pp. 340–41.*

This is to give you notice of the abuses and scandalous reproaches which God and his ministers do daily suffer by William Lewis, of St. Mary's, who saith that our Ministers [*Protestants*] are the Ministers of the devil; and that our books are made by the instruments of the devil, and further saith that those servants which are under his charge, shall keep nor read any book which doth appertain to our religion within the house of the said William Lewis, to the great discomfort of those poor bondsmen which arc under his subjection, especially in this heathen country, where no godly minister is, to teach and instruct ignorant people in the grounds of religion. And as for people which cometh unto the said Lewis or otherwise to passe the week, the said Lewis taketh occasion to call them into his chamber, and there laboreth, with all vehemency, craft, and subtlety, to delude ignorant persons.

Protestant servants of William Lewis, a Catholic, petition the Maryland courts, July 1638, in Streeter, Papers, *pp. 212–13.*

And Mr. Secretary found him [*Lewis*] guilty of an offensive and indiscreet speech in calling the author of the book an instrument of the devil; but acquitted him from that . . . he used that speech touching Protestant ministers in general. He likewise found him guilty of a very offensive speech in calling the Protestant ministers, the ministers of the devil. He likewise found him to have exceeded, in forbidding them to read a book otherwise allowed and lawful to be read by the State of England; but he acquitted him of the accusation that he forbad his servants to have or use Protestant books in his house. And because these his offensive speeches and other his unseasonable disputations in point of religion tended to the disturbance of the public peace and quiet of the colony. . . . [T]herefore he fined him 500 weight of tobacco to the Lord of the Province. . . .

Maryland courts, July 3, 1638, in Streeter, Papers, *p. 216.*

Inventory of goods and chattels of Zachary Motter-shead, gentleman, late of St Mary's, deceased.
Item,

2 coats	100
3 shirts	60
4 towels and 1 pillowber	20
A double, 2 pr stockings, 2 linings	2
7 bands, 2 caps, 4 pair of cuffs,	
3 pr boothose And one handkerchief	40
2 brushes, 1 rule, 16 gold buttons	10
7 books	12
1 pr of boots and spurs	12
1 hat and cap	30
1 gun and 2 locks	60
1 bed, 2 pillows and 1 rug	80
1 waistcoat	8
1 chest	30
1 looking glass, 1 pewter pot,	
1 candlestick	6
1 shirt	16
1 suit of clothes	20

516 lbs of tobacco

Maryland estate valued in tobacco, August 29, 1638, in Streeter, Papers, p. 21.

At a General Court held at Boston, great complaint was made of the oppression used in the country in the sale of foreign commodities; and Mr. Robert Keane, who kept a shop in Boston, was notoriously above others observed and complained of; . . . he was charged with many particulars; in some, for taking above 6 pence in the shilling profit; in some above 8 pence; and, in some small things, above two for one; And being hereof convict (as appears by the records), he was fined. . . .

After the Court had censured him, the church of Boston called him also in question, where (as before he had done in the Court) he did, with tears, acknowledge and bewail his covetous and corrupt heart. . . . These things gave occasion to Mr. Cotton, in his public exercise the next lecture day, to lay open the error of such false principles, and to give some rules of direction in the case. Some false principles were these.

1. That a man might sell as dear as he can, and buy as cheap as he can. . . .

4. That, as a man may take the advantage of his own skill or ability, so he may of another's ignorance or necessity. . . . The rules for trading were these:

1. A man may not sell above the current price, i.e., such a price as is usual in the time and place. . . .
John Winthrop, 1639, History, vol. 1, pp. 377–81.

For their [*the students'*] breakfast, that it was not so well ordered, the flour not so fine as it might, nor so well boiled, or stirred, at all times that it was so, it was my sin of neglect, and want of that care that ought to have been in one that the Lord had intrusted with such a work. Concerning their beef, that was allowed them, as they affirm, which, I confess, had been my duty to have seen they should have had it, and continued to have had it, because it was my husband's command; but truly I must confess, to my shame, I cannot remember that ever they had it, nor that ever it was taken from them. . . . I must confess, that I have denied them cheese, when they have sent for it, and it have been in the house; for which I shall humbly beg pardon of them, and own the shame, and confess my sin. For the Moor [*the black servant*] his lying in Sam. Hough's sheet and pillow-bier, it hath truth in it. . . . And that they eat the Moor's crusts. . . . And for their wanting beer, betwixt brewings, a week or half a week together, I am sorry that it was so at any time. . . .
Mistress Eaton, wife of Harvard's first head, to the General Court, ca. 1639, quoted in Morison, Builders, pp. 191–92.

There were so many lectures now in the country, and many poor persons would usually resort to two or three in the week, to the great neglect of their affairs, and the damage of the public. The assemblies also were (in divers churches) held till night, so as such as dwelt far off could not get home in due season, and many weak bodies could not endure so long, in the extremity of the heat or cold, without great trouble, and hazard of their health. Whereupon the general court ordered, that the elders should be desired to give a meeting to the magistrates and deputies, to consider about the length and frequency of church assemblies. . . .

John Winthrop, 1639, History, vol. 1, p. 390.

Whereas the director general and council of New Netherland have observed that many persons, both servants of the Company and inhabitants, contrary to the orders and commands of the High and Mighty Lords the States General and the Chartered West India Company, have presumed to sell to the Indians in these parts, muskets, powder and lead, which has already caused much evil and will hereafter result in but greater evil if no means be adopted by us here to prevent the same; therefore every inhabitant of New Netherland, be his state, quality or condition what it may, is most expressly forbidden to sell any muskets, powder or lead to the Indians, on pain of being punished by death, and if any one shall inform against any person who shall violate this law, he shall receive a reward of 50 guilders.

Ordinance of New Netherland, 1639, in New York State Library, Van Rensselaer, p. 426.

It is likewise enacted that all masters of families shall use their best endeavors for the furnishing of themselves and all those of their families which shall be capable of arms (excepting negroes) with arms both offensive and defensive . . . upon such penalty as shall be thought fit by the Governor and council.

Virginia Assembly, 1640, William and Mary Quarterly, 2nd ser., 4 (1924), 147.

This year came over [*to Massachusetts*] . . . the reverend godly M. Peirson: This people finding no place in any of the former erected Colonies to settle in, to their present content, repaired to an Island, severed from the Continent of New-haven, with about 16 miles off the salt Sea, and called Long-Island, being about 120 miles in length, and yet but narrow: here this people erected a Town, and called it South Hampton. There are many Indians on the greatest part of this Island, who at first settling of the English there, did much annoy their Cattle with the multitude of Dogs they kept, which ordinarily are young wolves brought up tame, continuing of a very ravening nature.

Edward Johnson, 1640, Johnson's Wonder, p. 195.

If therefore the verses are not always so smooth and elegant as some may desire or expect; let them consider that God's Altar need not our polishings; Ex. 20. For we have respected rather a plain translation, than to smooth our verses with the sweetness of any paraphrase, and so have attended Conscience rather than Elegance, fidelity rather than poetry, in translating the hebrew words into english language, and David's poetry into english meter; that so we may sing in Zion the Lords songs of praise according to his own will; until he take us from hence, and wipe away all of tears,

and bid us enter into our masters joy to sing eternal Hallelujahs.

The Lord to me a shepherd is,
want therefore shall not I.
He in the folds of tender grass,
doth cause me down to lie:
To waters calm me gently leads
Restore my soul doth he:
He doth in paths of righteousness:
for his names sake lead me.

Preface and 23rd Psalm, Bay Psalm Book, 1640 [not paginated].

A negro maid, servant to Mr. Stoughton of Dorchester, being well approved by divers years experience, for sound knowledge and true godliness, was received into the church and baptized.

John Winthrop, 1641, History, vol. 2, p. 31.

Marvelous may be to see and consider how some kind of wickedness did grow and break forth here [*in Massachusetts*], in a land where the same was so much witnessed against, and so narrowly looked unto, and severely punished when it was known; as in no place more, or so much, that I have known or heard of; insomuch as they have been somewhat censured, even by moderate and good men, for their severity in punishments. And yet all this could not suppress the breaking out of sundry notorious sins . . . especially drunkenness and uncleanness; not only incontinency between persons unmarried, for which many both men and women have been punished sharply enough, but some married persons also. But that which is worse, even sodomy and buggery, (things fearful to name,) have broke forth in this land, oftener than once. . . . [O]ne reason may be, that the Devil may carry a greater spite against the churches of Christ and the gospel here, by how much the more they endeavor to preserve holiness and purity amongst them. . . .

William Bradford, 1642, Bradford's History, p. 459.

This Spring Cows and Cattle of that kind (having continued at an excessive price so long as any came over with estates to purchase them) fell of a sudden in one week from 22 *l.* the Cow, to 6, 7, or 8 *l.* the Cow at most, insomuch that it made all men admire how it came to pass, it being the common practice of those that had any store of Cattle, to sell every year a Cow or two, which clothed their backs, filled their bellies with more varieties than the Country of itself afforded, and put gold and silver in their purses beside.

Edward Johnson, 1642, Johnson's Wonder, *p. 209.*

It is ordered that the selectmen of every town, in the several precincts and quarters where they dwell, shall have a vigilant eye over their brethren and neighbors to see, first, that none of them shall suffer so much barbarism in any of their families as not to endeavor to teach, by themselves or others, their children and apprentices so much learning as may enable them to read the English tongue, and the capital laws; upon penalty of 20 shilling for each neglect therein.

Also that all masters of families do once a week (at the least) catechize their children and servants in the grounds and principles of religion. . . .

And further, that all parents and masters do breed and bring up their children and apprentices in some honest lawful calling, labor, or employment. . . .

Massachusetts school law, May 1642, in Charters and General Laws, *pp. 73–75.*

5

The English Colonies Meet in the Middle
1642–1670

THE ENGLISH COMMONWEALTH

In 1642, England plunged into civil war. The Royalists, also called Cavaliers, supported the king's absolute authority. The Parliamentarians, many of whom were Puritans, wanted to limit royal power or subordinate it to that of Parliament. In 1644 and 1645, the Parliamentarian troops won important victories. King Charles I attempted to escape to Scotland but was captured in 1646 and was beheaded on January 30, 1649. After Charles's execution, Parliament refused to allow his son, Charles II, to ascend the throne. Instead, in May 1649, Parliament voted to establish a commonwealth in England, with itself as the supreme power. In 1653, Oliver Cromwell was named lord protector, or head of the Commonwealth, for life. Cromwell died in 1658. In 1660, the Commonwealth was ended, the monarchy was restored, and Charles II was crowned king.

Because of the civil war, from 1642 to 1650 the English colonies in North America had considerable independence. Neither the king nor Parliament had sufficient power or energy to manage them. No colony became directly involved in the hostilities, and all remained officially neutral except the royal colony of Virginia, which supported the king. After the establishment of the Commonwealth, however, the new English leaders turned their attention to colonial affairs and the economic potential of England's empire. The largest English colonies at the time were in the West Indies, but the nine English colonies of North America had a combined population of 37,000. Commonwealth leaders did not find a completely effective way to manage the colonies, but after 1650 various Parliamentary committees attempted supervision.

During the Commonwealth, English merchant interests were very influential and the promotion of English trade was an official goal. In 1651, Parliament passed the first of a long series of Navigation Acts, designed to regulate and control trade. The Navigation Act of 1651 required all trade goods between England and her colonies, or among the colonies themselves, to be carried in English or colonial ships, and all trade goods between the colonies and other nations to be carried in English ships or the ships of the nation producing the merchandise. (The word *English* was meant to include colonial and Irish vessels.) The law was never effectively enforced, and colonial governments generally disregarded or evaded it. Nonetheless, it did intensify tension with the Dutch, then the strongest merchant marine and trading power in Europe. The Dutch manufactured few goods, but they monopolized the colonial carrying trade or hired ships that carried goods from one port to another. In 1652, the Netherlands declared war on England. England ordered Massachusetts to attack New Netherland, but peace was concluded in 1654 before they did so.

NEW ENGLAND CONFEDERATION

In 1642, when the Great Migration ended, New England had five independent colonies—Plymouth, Massachusetts Bay, Connecticut, New Haven, and Rhode Island—as well as organized settlements in New Hampshire and Maine. Their combined population was about 20,000. After 1642, a short depression occurred because the economy had come to depend on continual waves of new settlers. Immigration began again after 1650, however, and by 1660 the population had doubled. Settlements slowly began to join together, in part for protection and in part because they had common interests.

In May 1643, commissioners from Massachusetts, Plymouth, Connecticut, and New Haven met at Boston and signed a compact called the New England Confederation. They officially named themselves the United Colonies of New England. The confederation was the first attempt at voluntary unity among the English colonies in North America. It had no power to intervene in the internal affairs of its member colonies; its primary purpose was to conduct foreign relations with the French to the north, the Dutch to west, and the Native Americans all around. Members were concerned about the maintenance of religious orthodoxy, however, and excluded Rhode Island. The confederation was not representative in terms of population. Each of the four colonies had two commissioners. Six of the eight had to approve any policy, making it possible for the three small colonies to outvote the far larger Massachusetts Bay. Massachusetts, when its interests were seriously threatened, sometimes blocked or ignored joint decisions. Nonetheless, confederation members cooperated on the return of fugitives, the construction of roads, the support of Harvard College, and the promotion of missionary work. Most important, the confederation cooperated in maintaining relative peace with Native Americans, which neither the Chesapeake colonies nor New Netherland achieved during the period.

Massachusetts Bay Colony, 1642–1660

Civil war in England ended King Charles I's attempt to make Massachusetts a royal colony. Massachusetts Bay Colony continued to conduct itself independently, defining its own interests and acting to advance them. In 1651, it set up its own mint to overcome the shortage of coin. It welcomed all nations to trade in its harbors. It refused to grant freedom of conscience or to extend voting rights to men who were not members of a Puritan church, despite pressure from even the Puritan-dominated English Commonwealth government.

After Massachusetts recovered from the depression of the early 1640s, the colony entered a period of vigorous economic growth and diversification. Although it never successfully ended dependence on England for cloth or metal goods like plows, guns, and kettles, leaders encouraged domestic manufacturing. In 1643, John Winthrop, Jr., organized the Company of Undertakers for the Iron Works in New England, an English and American group of investors. They provided capital and a shipload of skilled ironworkers to found an integrated ironworks at Saugus. (An integrated mill processes ore, then converts it into finished products.) By 1650, the Saugus ironworks was producing a ton of iron per day. The colonial fishing industry also developed rapidly during the 1640s, when many of England's fishermen were pressed into military service. Most important of all were the expanded commercial activities of merchants. During the 1640s, merchants entered into a triangular trade with London and the island colonies of the Spanish Azores, the Canaries, and the West Indies. New England ships carried agricultural products to the islands and sugar from the islands to New England. In 1643, the first Boston vessel carried slaves from Africa to Barbados, beginning New England's involvement in the slave trade. Soon merchants began to expand their activities into shipbuilding and associated resources like timber. By the 1650s, merchants were the wealthiest economic group in the colony.

Commercial expansion and economic prosperity put increasing pressure on the original ideals of the Puritan colony. The ideal Puritan community was one in which religious and political institutions were very closely connected, the discretionary power of the Puritan leaders was not questioned, and individual gain was subordinate to the common good. Certainly these ideals still influenced the behavior of many New Englanders during the period, especially in small, self-governing communities. But the forces of change were clearly increasing. In 1649, population growth necessitated the founding of the Second Church of Boston, the first time in New England that town and church were no longer one body. In the 1650s, sumptuary laws were passed in response to the increasing prosperity of the middle and lower classes. (Sumptuary laws regulate who can wear certain types of clothing, to make their rank

A modern drawing based on historical research of the Saugus Iron Works, opened 1646 *(Courtesy Saugus Iron Works National Historic Site [NPS])*

A modern reconstruction of the administration/warehouse building at Saugus, the first iron works in the English colonies *(Courtesy Saugus Iron Works National Historic Site [NPS])*

in the social order clear to all.) Boston became a thriving harbor and metropolis, attracting many newcomers and increasing the colony's heterogeneity. In 1644, a Jewish merchant arrived from the Netherlands. (He was denied the right to settle by the Puritan authorities.) In 1652, the first large group of non-English immigrants arrived, Scots deported by Oliver Cromwell because they had supported King Charles. The General Court passed regulations requiring newcomers, or "strangers," as they were called, to register with magistrates and to take an oath of allegiance.

Merchants and others, concerned that economic growth would be hampered by restrictive policies, began to call for increased toleration and for broader voting rights. In 1646, Dr. Robert Child and others presented a Remonstrance and Petition to the General Court requesting that requirements for church membership (on which voting rights depended) be loosened. It was rejected, and the petitioners were imprisoned. A synod of ministers was convened to consider the matter of church membership, and in 1648 it issued the Cambridge Platform of Church Discipline. Rather than granting concessions, the document reinforced and even increased church authority.

Although the Puritan oligarchy retained control, the old order was slowly passing. Four towering figures died: John Winthrop in 1649; William Bradford in 1657; and the prominent ministers John Cotton and Thomas Hooker in 1647 and 1652, respectively. Change was signaled in institutional ways as well. Although the Massachusetts General Court was still far from a democratically elected body, the deputies became increasingly unhappy with the power of the assistants. In 1644, the General Court became bicameral. The deputies convened as one "house" and the assistants as another; the agreement of both bodies was required to pass legislation. The Massachusetts Body of Liberties was rewritten as the more detailed Laws and Liberties in 1648. Detailed written laws specified citizens' rights and thus reduced the discretionary or arbitrary power of the Puritan oligarchy. Among other provisions, the Laws and Liberties established standard judicial procedures.

On November 11, 1647, Massachusetts passed the first compulsory school law in the colonies. It required all towns of 50 families or more to establish a "petty" school to teach basic literacy. Towns of 100 families were required to establish a grammar school to prepare boys for the university. The influential law left financing and oversight to local decision. In some towns, taxes provided full or partial support, but in many more some combination of private contributions and tuition was used. The law did not make attendance compulsory, however, and small neighborhood "dame schools" and private grammar schools continued to exist.

During the 1640s, Puritan missionaries began extensive work among the Indians for the first time. Such work was difficult because Puritanism depended on literacy, community institutions, and proof of conversion so demanding that even many English colonists could not meet it. In 1649, however, Puritans in England organized the Company for the Propagation of the Gospel in New England to provide financial support. The most famous missionary was the Reverend John Eliot, who translated many Christian works into the Algonquian language. In 1651, he founded the first "Praying Town" at Natick, where Puritan churches, elementary schools, and town governments were established by and for converted Indians. Indian residents were required to adopt English dress and social behavior.

A modern reconstruction of the forge buildings at Saugus *(Courtesy Saugus Iron Works National Historic Site [NPS])*

In 1650, Harvard College received a charter from the General Court, making it an independent corporation, although the "overseers" (ministers and magistrates) also continued to exercise control. In the mid-1650s, an Indian College was established at Harvard. Very few Indians ever attended, and only one is known to have received a degree. The building set aside for it, however, housed a press to print John Eliot's Indian religious texts. In 1650, the first nontheological work of colonial literature was published in London: a book of poetry entitled *The Tenth Muse, Lately Sprung Up in America* by Anne Bradstreet.

July 1656 marked the arrival in Boston of Mary Fisher and Anne Austin, the first Quaker missionaries in the colonies. Quakerism was the last and most radical sect inspired by the movement to "purify" the Church of England. It was founded in England in 1649 by George Fox, a man of very modest birth. The core Quaker belief was the "inner light," or voice of God, in each human being, accessible through quiet contemplation. Quakerism emphasized the moral virtues of sobriety, honesty, and hard work, but it was egalitarian in the extreme. It denied the need for religious rituals, church organization, or a formally trained ministry; it forbade its adherents to swear oaths, pay taxes, fight wars, or remove their hats to those in authority. Early Quaker adherents were zealous missionaries who sometimes engaged in outrageously disruptive behavior. They were severely persecuted throughout England and its colonies—with the exception of Rhode Island—as well as in New Amsterdam.

Boston quickly jailed and deported Fisher and Austin, but many more Quaker missionaries immediately replaced them. In October 1656, Massachusetts instituted punishments for preaching or sympathizing with Quaker ideas; penalties quickly increased from imprisonment to whipping, bodily mutilation, and, in 1658, death by hanging. Persecution reached its height in 1659–61, when four Quakers were hanged. One was Massachusetts resident Mary Dyer, a former friend of Anne Hutchinson.

OTHER NEW ENGLAND COLONIES, 1642–1660

Both New Hampshire and Maine came increasingly under the control of the large and powerful Massachusetts Bay Colony. In New Hampshire, the town of Exeter became part of Massachusetts in 1643, the last settlement there to do so. (Rev. John Wheelwright, who had founded the town after being banished by Massachusetts, soon left to found a new community in Maine.) Massachusetts reorganized New Hampshire settlements as self-governing towns, with considerable local control. Major issues, however, were decided by the General Court in Boston. In 1651, Massachusetts also claimed jurisdiction over Maine, and in the following years it sent commissioners to evaluate every settlement. Most were fishing villages whose lack of civil organization and moral rectitude displeased the leaders of the Bay Colony. Settlements in southern Maine agreed to be under the jurisdiction of Massachusetts in 1653; those in the Casco Bay area in 1658.

Rhode Island colonists, however, took forceful steps to prevent annexation by Massachusetts. In 1642, Roger Williams set sail for England to obtain a separate charter for the colony. While there, he published an Indian lexicon, *Key into the Language of America,* which quickly brought him favorable public notice. His mission was successful despite the outbreak of the English Civil War. The charter that was granted on March 14, 1644, allowed Providence, Portsmouth,

Newport, and Warwick to unite and form a government. In May 1647, the first Rhode Island General Assembly met and drew up a constitution and code of laws. The assembly was composed of six representatives from each town; its presiding officer was termed a president. One assistant from each town helped the president carry out governmental duties and formed a circuit court. Initiative and referendum were introduced. Church and state were separated, and church membership was not a basis for citizenship. In the late 1650s, the colony was pressured by Massachusetts to expel the Quakers, whom even Roger Williams disliked. Rhode Island's assembly, however, steadfastly refused to outlaw their presence or preaching.

Connecticut both expanded and unified after 1642. The colony claimed Long Island and absorbed the Hamptons. A code of laws was drafted in 1650; age, property, and behavioral qualifications for freemanship and the lesser status of "admitted inhabitant" were enacted, as was compulsory schooling. The independent New Haven settlements unified and elected Theophilus Eaton governor in 1643, adopting Fundamental Orders that restricted suffrage to church members. In 1656, the New Haven colony drafted a code of laws that proscribed much personal behavior and became the prototype of New England's "blue laws" (so called because they were originally printed on blue paper).

VIRGINIA AND MARYLAND, 1642–1660

Like New England, the Chesapeake colonies took advantage of England's inattention in the 1640s to exercise self-government and to develop independently. In both Maryland and Virginia, colonists continued to concentrate on tobacco cultivation. Officials attempted to restrict planting and encourage diversification, but to little avail. Greek winemakers were brought to Virginia, for example, but by the 1650s, even they had ceased tending vineyards in order to grow tobacco.

In 1643, the county court system was established in Virginia. Not solely judicial courts in the modern sense, the county courts were also administrative offices with extensive governmental functions. They controlled land records, probates, manumissions, and indentured servitude records as well as weights and measures and other vital statistics. The county courts decentralized many of the governmental functions that were controlled by the central colonial government in New England colonies. The Virginia assembly also reformed tax law (the poll, or head, tax on every adult regardless of income, was eliminated), made the election of burgesses somewhat more democratic, and strengthened the role of the Anglican Church after three Puritan ministers arrived in 1643.

By the early 1640s, plantations in Virginia spread up both the James and Rappahannock Rivers, claiming more and more land of the former Powhatan Confederacy. The nearby Pamunkey were still headed by Opechancanough, the chief who had directed the massacre of 1622; he was now nearly 100 years old. When the English Civil War broke out, he thought it signaled a chance to evict the English from Virginia. Although the Indian population had been greatly reduced by the 1640s, Opechancanough revived the confederacy.

On April 18, 1644, Chesapeake area tribes attacked the outlying settlements of Virginia and massacred 500 settlers, beginning Opechancanough's War. Virginia responded immediately. Captain William Claiborne divided the colony into sections and distracted Opechancanough elsewhere while attacking

Pamunkey villages. As land was captured, a series of forts was constructed from the James to the York River. Captured Indians were sold into slavery in the West Indies. Nonetheless, the Powhatan could not be brought to terms. In 1646, the Virginia Assembly sent a force to capture Opechancanough. Personally led by Governor William Berkeley, the group captured the aged chief and carried him to Jamestown prison. While there, he was murdered by a guard.

His successor, Necotowance, agreed to a treaty in October 1646. Indians gave up all land between the York and James Rivers as far west of the falls of the James and Pamunkey Rivers, and they were prohibited from trespassing there under pain of death. In return, the assembly agreed that white settlers were not to enter lands beyond this frontier. Within two years, however, tremendous population growth in Virginia made the agreement unenforceable. By the early 1650s, three new counties had been formed in the Indian land. In 1653, Virginia developed a new Indian policy. Reservations were set aside for the Pamunkey and Chickahominy (members of the former Powhatan confederacy), and white settlers were required to leave. In 1656, the burgesses attempted to make the Indians individual property owners. Indians were granted head rights, or a certain number of acres per person, just as white settlers were. Few Indians gave up their traditional way of life, however, preferring to remain on land beyond the boundaries of white settlement.

When news reached Virginia of the beheading of Charles I in 1649, the Virginia Assembly proclaimed its loyalty to the young Charles II, then in exile at The Hague. The English Commonwealth government first attempted to subdue the colony with a trade embargo, but Dutch ships ignored it. In 1652, Comonweatlh officials sent a fleet and four commissioners to obtain Virginia's surrender. Although Governor Berkeley, an ardent Royalist, assembled more than 1,000 Virginia troops the burgesses agreed to submit peacefully. Governor Berkeley resigned the governorship but remained in the colony. The assembly became the chief governing body. One month later, it declared its own power to select the governor, choosing Richard Bennett, a Puritan. In 1658, the burgesses nonetheless defied their chosen governor when he ordered them to dissolve. They declared themselves in authority, then voted to reappoint Governor Berkeley.

After 1642, Virginia enjoyed both prosperity and exceptional population growth, from about 15,000 in 1642 to 40,000 in the 1660s. The majority of immigrants were either single young men who arrived as indentured servants or ordinary families fleeing English turmoil. Beginning in 1649, however, the migration also included many prominent royalists, or Cavaliers, some of whom some founded families that rose to great prominence in 18th-century colonial politics. Another significant group of immigrants were Scots, deported for their resistance when Commonwealth forces invaded Scotland in the 1650s. Despite Puritan rule in England, Anglican worship continued in Virginia without extensive opposition. Religious persecution was far milder than in New England, although by 1660 most dissenters, including Puritans, had been pressured to move to more tolerant Maryland.

Maryland mirrored the turbulence of England during the Civil War. The Calvert proprietors, Catholics and royalists, tried to keep the colony and its Protestant majority independent of the conflict. In 1644, however, the "time of troubles" began. While Governor Leonard Calvert was in England, Parliamentarian sympathizers lead by Richard Ingle seized control. In 1645, Ingle's followers attacked and pillaged estates and the Jesuit missions. The governor returned and reestablished his authority, but he soon died. In 1649, Lord Baltimore appointed the Protestant William Stone governor, hoping he could deal successfully with the new Puritan power in England. At Baltimore's request, Stone welcomed Puritans from Virginia led by Richard Bennett, who settled at the mouth of the Severn River (modern Annapolis). In 1649, again at Baltimore's suggestion, Maryland passed a religious toleration act, which formalized freedom of worship and set penalties for sectarian fighting. Although the Maryland Toleration Act extended freedom of conscience only to Christians, it was a significant milestone.

Despite Lord Baltimore's efforts, English Commonwealth officials did not distinguish clearly between defiant Virginia and cooperative Maryland when it sent the fleet and commissioners in 1652. One of the commissioners was Maryland's old foe William Claiborne of Kent Island. He helped remove Governor Stone and establish a Puritan civil government in Maryland, headed by Richard Bennett and himself. The Maryland Assembly of 1654 repudiated religious toleration and forbade Catholics to worship openly. In 1655, Stone, acting under Baltimore's orders, attempted to regain control of the colony by force but was defeated in the Battle of Severn River. In 1657, however, Oliver Cromwell restored Maryland to the Calvert proprietors. Maryland Puritans were granted amnesty; they in turn recognized religious toleration, and a heresy case against Jewish doctor Jacob Lumbrozo was dropped. In 1660, Governor Josias Fendell attempted a parliamentary revolt against the proprietors, but it was not successful.

Maryland political history is also distinguished by the 1648 request of Margaret Brent, a wealthy landowner, businesswoman, and executor of Leonard Calvert's estate, to vote and to sit in the assembly. Her request, the first by a woman to be recorded in the colonies, was made on the basis of her status as a large landowner and Calvert's representative; it was denied on the basis of her sex.

NEW NETHERLAND, 1642–1664

In 1643–44, Governor Willem Kieft's mismanagement of Indian relations finally led to war. Since 1640, periodic raiding and counter-raiding had occurred between the Dutch and the Raritan and other small neighboring Algonquian tribes. In 1643, however, the Algonquian groups moved closer to New Amsterdam after being attacked by Mohawk. In response Kieft, company employees, and settlers formed a militia. With the help of Captain John Underhill, the English leader in the Pequot War, they ruthlessly destroyed nearby Indian villages and fields. About 1,000 Indians of both genders and all ages were killed in hostilities. In 1645, with the mediation of the Mohawk, treaties were signed with several tribes, and the wars came to an end. During the hostilities, peace had been maintained in the Hudson Valley and fur trade with the Iroquois had not been seriously interrupted. Near New Amsterdam, however, colonists' crops were destroyed, settlements abandoned, and lives lost. One artifact of the war was a defensive wall built across the lower end of Manhattan; its location today is known as Wall Street.

During the war, Kieft had convened a Council of Eight Men. After the peace, the Eight Men appealed to the Netherlands States General, or assembly, to formalize popular representation. The States General ignored their request but did remove the unpopular Kieft. As the new director general, it appointed Peter Stuyvesant, distinguished by a silver-tipped peg leg he wore to replace the leg lost in military service. He arrived in 1647 and served New Netherland for its 17 remaining years as a Dutch colony.

To both the States General and the West India Company, decisions about New Netherland were business decisions, not matters for popular vote. To them, the colony's purpose was to maintain a commercial port in the strategically important wedge between the southern and northern English colonies. By 1647, however, with a discontented population of less than 2,000 (nearby New England had a population above 25,000), Stuyvesant recognized the need to introduce some representative government to the colony. Although he refused to convene a representative assembly, he ordered an election to choose 18 men, from which he and the company-appointed colony council selected nine (a Dutch institution called double election). The Council of Nine Men was to advise and assist and had the right eventually to nominate its own successors. Unfortunately its first act was to attempt a review of Kieft and company policy; it was firmly squelched, and the leaders were imprisoned.

The Nine Men continued to seek reform, however, and in 1652 they again asked the States General for more representative government, more colonists, the elimination of trade restrictions, and the settling of boundary disputes with New England. The Dutch government reduced the cost of passage for colonists and ordered Stuyvesant to establish a burgher, or municipal government, in New Amsterdam. In 1653, the municipality of New Amsterdam formally came into existence. A *schout* (a combination sheriff and prosecuting attorney), two *burgomasters* (equivalent to co-mayors), and five *schpens* (aldermen or magistrates who had both judicial and administrative authority) were appointed by Stuyvesant, together forming a municipal court. Nonetheless, colonists continued to press for more self-government and for schools. Several other settlements received town government on the Dutch model. Under Dutch rule, however, New Netherland never achieved colonywide self-government.

During Stuyvesant's tenure, the population finally began to grow. By 1664, New Amsterdam alone had increased to 1,600, and the colony as a whole to about 9,000—of whom 2,000 were English in Long Island and elsewhere. Trade also increased markedly, although the colony as a whole was not exceptionally prosperous. It was almost never politically peaceable. In part, fractiousness arose from New Amsterdam's exceptional heterogeneity. By 1658, all official edicts were issued in three languages: Dutch, French, and English. The English in New Netherland disliked Dutch political institutions. Dutch residents disliked the company. Added to the mix were Scandinavians on the Delaware River and French Huguenot settlements.

Religious heterogeneity added other conflicts. Dutch commercial interests preferred a policy of toleration, although the company officially sponsored Dutch Reformed clergy. Stuyvesant also supported the Reformed confession and was personally intolerant as well. In cooperation with Dominie Johannes Megapolensis and other clergy, he denied Lutherans the right to a minister in 1654, a dispute that dragged on for many years. In September 1654, a group of observant Jews from a former Dutch colony in Brazil arrived in New Amsterdam, the first such group to migrate to North America. Megapolensis favored sending them to Rhode Island, which he called "the sewer of New England."

Stuyvesant had to be ordered repeatedly by the States General to cease curtailing their rights and grant them freedom of worship. In 1657, Quakers began arriving in the colony. Like New England officials, Stuyvesant imprisoned, tortured, and attempted to ban them. Citizens of Flushing opposed these actions, signing a remonstrance in favor of religious toleration. Several Flushing residents were jailed, and the schout Tobias Feake, who drafted the document, was banished.

Nonetheless, Stuyvesant accomplished many things for what he perceived to be the public good. When he took office, New Amsterdam had an unfinished church, no schoolhouse, and 35 taverns. Stuyvesant repaired and remodeled it into a well-kept Dutch town, greatly increasing its fortifications. He established institutions of public order and safety, attempted to regulate alcohol consumption, and made other regulations intended to improve the colony's moral and civic order. By 1664, 11 of New Netherland's 12 villages had schools, including a Latin grammar school established in New Amsterdam in 1659 with an imported Lithuanian physician as its master. Partly in response to these changes, for the first time, families began arriving in the colony in greater numbers than single men. Settlement spread over Manhattan and Staten Islands and up both banks of the lower Hudson River.

Stuyvesant was less successful in maintaining peace with the Indians. Wars broke out again in 1655, 1659–60, and 1663–64, the latter two near the Hudson River village originally called Esopus (renamed Wiltwyck in 1661, and then finally Kingston in 1669). All were costly to both sides. After the war of 1663–64, the Lenni Lenape, Raritan, and Mahican Indians along the Hudson ceded all lands in the immediate area to the Dutch.

Stuyvesant also had limited success at settling disputes with his English neighbors. A brief respite occurred in 1650 when he traveled to New England to negotiate the Treaty of Hartford with the New England Confederation. The Dutch ceded part of their claim to Long Island and the Connecticut River valley; New Englanders acknowledged for the first time that their boundaries were not infinite. However, the treaty was disliked by New Netherlanders and never ratified by the English government, which refused in any way to acknowledge a Dutch right to North American land. In 1659, Massachusetts reneged on the Treaty of Hartford, and Connecticut did the same in 1662. Stuyvesant visited Boston in 1663 but could not negotiate a settlement. The following year, Connecticut claimed all of Long Island. These local boundary disputes, however, were not responsible for the loss of New Netherland to the English in 1664. That event was determined by growing Anglo-Dutch trade rivalries in Europe.

The Dutch West India Company opened slave trading to New Netherland colonists in 1648, and after 1654, the use of New Amsterdam as a slave trading port greatly increased. On September 15, 1655, slave trade directly with Africa began when the *Witte Paert* arrived with 300 Africans. Slave trading proved highly profitable for the colony, which levied a 10 percent tax on it. Most slaves who arrived in New Amsterdam were sold to Chesapeake colonists but in New Netherland, the Dutch West India Company itself was the largest slaveowner. Individual New Netherland colonists who owned slaves usually had only one or two who performed household or agricultural work. Most historians agree that slavery was less brutal in New Netherland than in other colonies at the time. Gender balance was more equal, and slaves had some personal rights. The company developed a status called half-freedom, in which slaves could travel, own property, and contract to work for private settlers when not employed by the company. It was not uncommon for slaves to be manumitted, or freed, after long service. By 1664, the black population was probably close to 700, the highest of any North American colony at the time.

NEW SWEDEN, 1642–1664

In 1643, Johan Printz arrived as the new governor of New Sweden's 200 settlers. A military officer of imposing size whom the Indians called Big Gut, he brought his wife, six children, a drummer, a trumpeter, and a hangman, as well as new colonists. New Sweden, like other European colonies, did not have exact boundaries; settlements existed in modern Pennsylvania and New Jersey as well as Delaware. Printz chose Tinicum Island (near modern Philadelphia) to build the colony's capital. He also built a two-story log mansion, complete with library, glass windows, and woodwork imported from Sweden.

The year he arrived, Printz imprisoned George Lamberton, the head of Connecticut English colonists who had migrated into the area as the Delaware Company of New Haven. Lamberton was tried in court, and his group forced to leave the area. Printz purchased additional land from the Indians, began the cultivation of tobacco, and oversaw construction projects. Among them was the first Lutheran chapel in America, built in 1643 at Tinicum Island, and a larger log church at Fort Christina in 1646. By 1646, Lutheran pastor Johan Campanius had translated Luther's Little Catechism into Lenape. New Sweden, however, faced an insurmountable difficulty: lack of interest from the Swedish Crown. Wars in Europe and the failure of the colony to produce immediate profits had dampened Swedish enthusiasm. During the years 1648 to 1653, not one ship arrived from Sweden with news, supplies, trade goods, or additional colonists.

New Netherland governor Peter Stuyvesant had been officially instructed by the Dutch to coexist with the Swedes, but he remained annoyed by their presence on the valuable fur-trading river. In 1651, aware that Printz had few resources and no support from Sweden, Stuyvesant sent a fleet to erect Fort Kasimir about six miles downstream from Christina. Stuyvesant settled Dutch families and soldiers at the fort and repurchased the land from the Indians in order to undermine the Swedish claim. In 1653, a new New Sweden governor, Johan Rising, captured Fort Kasimir from the Dutch and renamed it Fort Trinity. Two years later, Stuyvesant set sail for the Delaware Bay with a war fleet of seven ships carrying 600 men. New Sweden was surrendered to the Dutch with no shots fired. Sweden protested to the Netherlands but did not press the issue.

During the decade of Dutch rule, 1655–64, the former New Sweden was an appendage of New Netherland with no name of its own. The first Dutch administrator, Jean Paul Jaquet, moved the capital to Fort Kasimir and oversaw the building of New Amstel (modern New Castle) nearby. The town quickly became a center of trade and commerce, with merchant ships often anchored at the wharf and bark wigwams temporarily standing outside the fort's palisade. Nonetheless, for the remainder of the 1650s, the colony struggled periodically with food shortages and illness.

In the late 1650s, boundary disputes with Maryland resurfaced. To negotiate a settlement, Stuyvesant sent Augustine Herrman, a successful New Netherland trader, cartographer, and native of Prague, to meet with Philip Calvert. Although the dispute was not permanently resolved for a century, Calvert deeded Herrman an estate in Maryland. There, Herrman built Bohemia Manor and planned a cart road between Delaware settlements and Maryland. The road eventually became an important commercial route.

In 1659, when Alexander D'Hinoyossa became head of the colony, its population—which had once reached some 500—had again been reduced to 200. Many had died, some had moved to the more developed Chesapeake, but D'Hinoyossa determined to improve conditions. New settlers arrived, including additional Swedes and Finns, although hostilities between Five Nations tribes and the Lenni Lenape made settlers wary. Among new arrivals was a group of 41 Mennonites, a pacifist and antislavery group led by Peter Plockhoy. Near present-day Lewes they founded the first Mennonite settlement in North America. In August 1664, 72 African men and women arrived aboard the slave ship *Gideon*.

THE RESTORATION IN ENGLAND

In 1660, King Charles II was restored to the throne of England, where he ruled until 1685. This period, called the English Restoration, was marked by political authoritarianism, a reaction against the Puritans, low public and private morality, and significant growth in English sea power and commerce. It was an era of great colonial expansion and tightening imperial control.

When Charles II came to the throne, the population of the English North American colonies had grown to about 80,000. During the Commonwealth, no new colonies had been founded. Charles revived the concept of the proprietary colony, in which grantees owned the land outright and exercised extensive authority delegated from the Crown. He used these grants to repay debts to aristocrats who had supported the royal cause. Because proprietors were, in effect, landlords who received income from the settlers, they were anxious to encourage colonization. By the end of the decade, settlers began moving into proprietary lands in New Jersey and in the Carolinas as far south as Spanish Florida.

After Charles II was restored to the throne, haphazard oversight of England's growing empire came to an end and centralized management began. Although the king and Privy Council retained final authority, in 1660 a Council for Foreign Plantations was appointed, becoming in 1668 the Council for Trade and Plantations. Advisory subcommittees of "experts"—that is, merchants who could advise on trade issues—were periodically called into existence. Under Charles II, the economic value of colonies became the motive force of English policy. Like other European colonial powers of the day, England embraced the economic doctrines of mercantilism. Mercantilism held that colonies existed to strengthen the material welfare of the founding nation. A colony's purpose was to supply raw materials to the founding nation and to purchase the finished products manufactured there. Although prosperous colonies were desirable, dependent colonies were crucial. Under no circumstances were colonies to become manufacturing or trading competitors of the founding nation.

Before 1660 ended, a new Navigation Act was passed. Like the little enforced act of 1651, it aimed at weakening the still-flourishing carrying trade of England's Dutch rivals as well as enforcing the tenets of mercantilism. It repeated the provisions of the former act but added the requirement that ships have English captains and crews. The Navigation Act of 1660 also established the new principle of *enumeration;* that is, it named certain colonial products that could be sold and shipped only to England or its other colonies for processing. (New England's chief exports, lumber and fish, were not enumerated, although Chesapeake tobacco was.) An accompanying taxation act gave all import-export duties to Charles II as income. Thus, colonial trade with other nations was discouraged, English manufacturing was protected, and the royal treasury was guaranteed funds. The Staple Act, or Navigation Act of 1663, further required all foreign goods to be reloaded at English ports in English ships before being shipped to the colonies; other nations could no longer carry their own products there.

Historians still do not agree about the effect of the navigation acts on the colonies. In any case, colonial merchants and traders evaded them and engaged in outright smuggling, if necessary; colonial courts assisted by rarely convicting those accused of such crimes. In 1663, colonial governors were officially made responsible for enforcement of the acts but most proved lax in their duties. The acts did, however, hurt Dutch commerce and led to a second war between England and the Netherlands in 1664.

THE 1660S IN THE CHESAPEAKE

Within three weeks of the Restoration, Charles II confirmed the reappointment of William Berkeley to the Virginia governorship. In 1662, the House of Burgesses passed a revised code of laws, repealing any Commonwealth-era reform "which might keep in memory our enforced deviation from his majesty's obedience." They also formally adopted English common law, divided counties into precincts, and passed an act encouraging the establishment of schools and a college. No colonywide effort to establish schools was made during the decade, however, although some private schools probably existed.

Berkeley's second term, unfortunately, was far less successful than his first. Although Charles II referred to loyal, royalist Virginia as his "old dominion," he imposed harmful policies on the colony. The navigation acts brought economic distress to tobacco farmers, as the English market became glutted and prices declined. In May 1667, the Second Anglo-Dutch War brought Dutch warships to the James River, where they destroyed numerous colonial vessels. Worse, Charles made proprietary grants of Virginia land to several English nobles, threatening both the colony's jurisdiction and the rights of its citizens. Berkeley traveled to England to protest, and by 1670 most of the grantees had given up most rights over land specified in Virginia's charter, but disputes lingered into the next decade.

Berkeley himself became increasingly authoritarian and arbitrary, consolidating power in the hands of an elite minority and exhibiting poor judgment in the use of public funds. He appointed and dominated the council, declaring its members free from taxes and quitrents. He personally appointed most other officials as well, including the powerful county justices of the peace. He ordered a new poll tax to support the Anglican Church. After 1662, he refused for 14 years to call new elections for burgesses, denying representation to newly formed counties. Discontent increased among servants and the poor. In 1663, a planned uprising of indentured servants was discovered; in 1670, the assembly restricted the right to vote to male property holders, disenfranchising the landless. Relations with the Indians also worsened once again, particularly on the frontier. In 1666, a brief war erupted with the Doeg and Potomac (a Powhatan band).

Maryland grew steadily during the 1660s, primarily due to immigration. The population increased from about 8,000 in 1660 to more than 13,000 in 1670; many of the newcomers were indentured servants. Under Charles Calvert, who became governor in 1661, four new counties were organized on the Eastern Shore, and justices of the peace were appointed for all counties. In the newly bicameral legislature, established in law in 1650 and in fact in 1659, the upper house, or Governor's Council, was chosen from the elite of the colony. Most were related to each other and to the Calverts by blood, marriage, or economic interest. The lower house, or House of Burgesses, had four representatives from each county and two from St. Mary's city. Although burgesses were not necessarily among the colony's elite, they often had considerable power in their local communities. The assembly successfully retained the right to approve taxes set by the proprietors, which it had won during the Commonwealth. In December 1670, the governor issued a proclamation disenfranchising anyone with fewer than 50 acres of land or an estate of less than 40 pounds sterling.

The religious diversity of Maryland continued to increase during the 1660s. Quakers, who had been persecuted in the 1650s, began arriving again and met far less opposition. By 1670, Talbot County alone had four Quaker meetinghouses. Some Quakers were successful merchants, and some participated in Maryland politics as both burgesses and appointed officials. While other colonies required oaths of loyalty for political participation (oath-swearing was forbidden by Quaker belief), Maryland required only a "promise" of loyalty to the proprietor. Presbyterians also increased in number, particularly in Somerset County. Many were Scottish Presbyterians deported by the English for their religious nonconformity.

Cecil Calvert, Lord Baltimore, hands a map of Maryland to his grandson. Painting by Gerald Soest, ca. 1670 *(Courtesy of Maryland Department, Enoch Pratt Free Library)*

MASSACHUSETTS, 1660–1670

Massachusetts Bay, having exercised the most independence of any colony during the Commonwealth, offered the most resistance to English imperial control after the Restoration. Massachusetts officials quickly acknowledged Charles II but resisted many of his policies.

In 1661, upon advice of the Privy Council, Charles II ordered freedom of worship extended to Anglicans and suffrage extended to men "of good estate" regardless of church membership. Massachusetts ignored the former and evaded the latter by officially requiring "certification by a minister" rather than church membership. In 1664, the Privy Council responded by establishing a commission to examine all the northern colonies and to investigate Massachusetts in particular. The commissioners (who arrived in Boston accompanied by three English warships and 300 soldiers) received little cooperation and occasional defiance from Massachusetts officials. Although their report was critical, few reprisals followed. For the remainder of the decade, colony officials continued to restrict suffrage and freedom of worship, evade the trade laws, and extend control over New Hampshire and Maine.

Merchants, however, became increasingly aware of their common interests and of the conflict between those interests and the political goals of the Puritan oligarchy. Many merchants found ways to work with British interests and to profit from the new trade laws. Some signed a petition urging colony leaders to cooperate more willingly with the crown. According to one commissioner, only about one-quarter of Massachusetts merchants were church members. Indeed, many successful young men no longer sought to join the church, and in many towns church members were no longer in the majority. With good reason, Puritan leaders and clergy feared that political and social authority would soon slip from the hands of the religiously orthodox.

In 1662, the synod of ministers developed a solution known as the Half-Way Covenant, which established two levels of church membership. The children of full members could become official church members by confessing their belief but without offering proof of a conversion experience. They were required to live upright lives but could not participate in church governance. In effect, the Half-Way Covenant enabled the prosperous second- and third-generation sons of the original New England settlers to obtain the franchise. In the short term, some congregations refused to adopt it; however, by the end of the 17th century, the distinction between the two kinds of church membership had vanished.

Power in Massachusetts was slowly passing to those who favored economic individualism and held less strictly to the original Puritan codes of social behavior. To all of the clergy and many of the faithful, these signs of change in the original covenant were clearly portents of doom. In the 1660s and after, sermons and other literature termed *jeremiads* began to proliferate. (Jeremiads, or self-condemnations that warn of God's anger when people of the covenant forsake the godly path, are named after the biblical prophet Jeremiah, who condemned the Hebrews for similar sins.) One of the most famous jeremiads was the Reverend Michael Wigglesworth's long poem *The Day of Doom*. Published in 1662, it became an immediate best-seller; many adults and children memorized it in full.

Indian relations had been relatively peaceful since the Pequot War of 1637, but in the 1660s, tension increased. The economic interdependence of the Indians and the whites had decreased significantly due to the exhaustion of the fur trade in the area and the end of the wampum trade. Intertribal relations among the Narragansett, Wampanoag, and other Algonquian groups solidified, awakening English fears that a conspiracy was afoot.

In addition, many Indian leaders strongly disapproved of missionary efforts. The Wampanoag were particularly resistant, but missionaries increased their efforts despite Indian complaints. In 1663, the Reverend John Eliot published his completed Algonquian translation of the Bible, the so-called Indian Bible. New Praying Towns were founded; seven existed in 1660 and 14 by 1674. Deteriorating relations were of particular concern to the small Plymouth Colony. Massasoit, the Wampanoag leader with whom the first settlers had negotiated, died in 1661. In the 1660s, colonists sought more land, but Massasoit's son and successor Metacom (called King Philip by the English) refused to sell. Colonists ignored the chief, founding the town of Swansea in 1667 near his own village.

OTHER NEW ENGLAND COLONIES, 1660–1670

Both Connecticut and Rhode Island, more cooperative with the monarchy than Massachusetts, received new charters from King Charles II that not only recognized their existing governments but extended their rights of self-government.

Connecticut had no charter, and John Winthrop, Jr., the governor, personally went to England to obtain one. Winthrop was popular at court (he was the first colonial admitted to the Royal Society), and his efforts were successful. The new charter, granted in April 1662, made his colony entirely self-governing. It called for a governor with limited powers, a council of 12 magistrates, and an assembly with two deputies from each town, all elected yearly by freemen. It set Connecticut's boundaries to include part of Rhode Island and part of the Dutch territory in the Hudson Valley. More significantly, it extended Connecticut's jurisdiction to all of the New Haven colony settlements. The New Haven settlements resisted until December 1664; at that time they chose to be incorporated to avoid being annexed to England's new colony of New York. In 1670, the colony instituted a significant change in the method of voting: a system of sealed proxies, which enabled freemen to vote for colony officers without actually attending the yearly election court, an impossible task for many.

Rhode Island, determined not to be absorbed by Connecticut, was the first colony to acknowledged the newly restored king; officials then requested a new charter from him. In July 1663, the charter was granted and the boundary between Rhode Island and Connecticut was readjusted; however, boundary disputes continued into the 18th century. The charter created a corporation of freemen with rights to the land and power to admit new freemen and choose officials. Most important, the charter contained a clause granting freedom of conscience and another clause prohibiting other colonies from seizing Rhode Island citizens for heresy.

Rhode Island remained sparsely settled, growing from about 1,500 in 1660 to 2,000 in 1670. By 1660, Quaker worship had been organized on Aquidneck; soon afterward, a yearly meeting for Quakers from all over New England was established. Many Quakers occupied high civil offices during the decade.

NEW NETHERLAND BECOMES NEW YORK

As commercial rivalry escalated between the English and the Dutch, New Netherland's strategic position became an increasing concern to England. It prevented the geographical unity of New England and the Chesapeake, of course, but more important it enabled Dutch merchants to continue trading with England's colonies. New Amsterdam and ports on the Delaware River were used by both New England and Chesapeake merchants to evade the English Navigation Acts. New Amsterdam was also a main port for the slave trade, on which England was anxious to break the Dutch monopoly.

In the early 1660s, the duke of York founded the Company of Royal Adventurers to Africa, later the Royal African Company, to enable England to compete with the Dutch for the slave trade. In 1663, events along the African coast began the Second Anglo-Dutch War. In England, the Council for Foreign Plantations considered attacking and seizing New Netherland immediately. Charles's solution was simpler. England had never formally recognized the Dutch claim to North America. Charles simply granted his brother James, the duke of York, all land between the Connecticut and Delaware Rivers. The grant of March 12, 1664, included all of New Netherland, present-day New Jersey, New York, and Delaware, as well as western Connecticut and eastern Maine. Parliament approved the plan, and on April 2 the king appointed Colonel Richard Nicholls governor of the territory. Nicholls and a fleet of four warships sailed to New Amsterdam, anchoring off Coney Island in August and demanding that the colony surrender. The already discontented and now frightened New Netherland colonists probably assumed that English rule would be no worse than Dutch, and possibly better. Upon hearing the generous English terms, they refused to fight, and a delegation urged Stuyvesant to surrender at once. He did so, without bloodshed, on August 27, 1664.

That achieved, Nicholls sent two ships and 200 men down the coast to the Delaware River valley to demand the surrender of the former New Sweden. Delaware administrator D'Hinoyossa attempted to resist, and some 30 Dutch soldiers briefly exchanged fire with the English before New Sweden surrendered. According to a Dutch report, the English subsequently plundered the fort and town, taking 4,000 pounds sterling, livestock, tools, and food. They also destroyed the Mennonite colony, captured and sold more than 60 African slaves, and sold all Dutch soldiers into indentured servitude.

In 1667, the Treaty of Breda, which ended the Second Anglo-Dutch War, confirmed the conquest of New Netherland by England and gave new slave-trading rights to the English. Dutch colonization in North America had come to an end.

Nicholls, trained in law at Oxford University, proved to be an able governor for the diverse colony. Even Stuyvesant remained there until his death in 1672. Nicholls quickly changed the name of both New Netherland and New Amsterdam to New York. He gave the town a charter and appointed a mayor, aldermen, and sheriff. He also appointed four councillors and a secretary to serve as the colony's council. He prepared the so-called Duke's Laws, approved by representatives from each of the 13 English and four Dutch towns in March 1665. The laws were drawn from English, Dutch, and New England codes. Religious toleration was established, although each town had to build and maintain a church; under English rule, the Dutch Reformed Church actually expanded. The laws contained no provision for schools, however. Existing schools established by the Dutch became parochial schools, teaching the Dutch language and the Reformed religion. Other colonists relied on private schools. More girls continued to attend school in New York than in other colonies, however, carrying on a Dutch tradition. Although control of local issues was placed in the hands of local residents, the Duke's Laws contained no provision for a colonial assembly. To the increasing dissatisfaction of the colonists, New York in 1670 was the only English colony without one.

The seat of government for the Delaware settlements remained in New York. Captain John Carr was put in charge of them; he changed the name of New Amstel to New Castle but retained most local customs of governance, appointing a schout and a five-man council (3 Swedes, 2 Dutch) to advise him. Settlers from other English colonies began to arrive in earnest. Although English rule was relatively benign, not all of the old Scandinavian colonists welcomed it. In 1668, a rebellion was organized by Marcus Jacobsen, known as the Long Finn because of his height. Assisted by Englishman John Coleman and Lutheran pastor Lars Lock, he convinced many settlers to "assist" an imaginary Swedish invasion to recapture the colony. The plot was discovered; Jacobsen was found guilty of treason in October 1669 and sold as an indentured servant in Barbados. Many others were fined for their participation in Long Finn's Rebellion, one of whom was Armgant Printz, daughter of New Sweden's former governor.

THE FOUNDING OF NEW JERSEY

The duke of York quickly found his huge grant prohibitively expensive to manage. He granted the territory of modern New Jersey to a proprietary group that included Virginia governor William Berkeley and Sir George Carteret, governor of the English Channel island of Jersey. Confusion and controversy over jurisdiction immediately arose and continued for many years. New York governor Nicholls believed the area to be under his control because it included several Dutch settlements in the Bergen and Hoboken areas and Swedish settlements on the Delaware. He encouraged English settlers on Long Island to move there as well, where they founded Elizabeth. Under a special grant, groups of Quakers also settled at Shrewsbury and Middletown. In 1665, however, Philip Carteret, a relative of the proprietor, arrived as governor with a group of French-speaking colonists from the island of Jersey. He brought a document called the Concessions and Agreements, which offered liberal land grants, liberty of conscience, and a plan of government. Representatives were to be chosen by the freemen to aid the governor and his council, and a formal assembly was to be established when sufficient population existed. In 1666, many New Englanders migrated to found Newark and other settlements. When the first assembly was called in 1669, it was dominated by former New Englanders, who passed laws based on those of New Haven and restricted suffrage to church members. Governor Carteret, displeased, did not call another assembly for seven years. In 1670, when he attempted to collect taxes and quitrents, many settlers refused to pay.

John Winthrop, Jr., governor of Connecticut (*NYPL Emmet Collection 10490; Print Collection, Miriam and Ira D. Wallach Division of Arts, Prints, and Photographs, Astor, Lennox and Tilden Foundations*)

EXPANSION INTO THE CAROLINAS

In 1660, only one, small European settlement existed between Virginia and the Spanish town of St. Augustine. It had been founded by Virginia migrants in 1653 in the Albemarle Sound area. After the Restoration, Sir John Colleton, a Barbadian and member of Charles II's Privy Council, became interested in founding a Carolina colony. In 1663, Charles II granted a charter to Colleton, Virginia governor Berkeley and other English nobles for territory between the 31st and 36th parallels north latitude (modern Virginia to Florida). The charter gave the eight proprietors extensive, inheritable power and provided for freedom of conscience for the colonists. The proprietors hoped to populate the area with seasoned settlers from existing English colonies, especially Barbados. Barbados had many displaced small farmers and former indentured servants, created by the increasing domination of large sugar plantations worked by African slaves.

The proprietors issued "A Declaration and Proposal to All That Will Plant in Carolina," modified by the "Concessions and Agreements" in 1665. The agreements established three counties: Albemarle to the north, Clarendon in the Cape Fear area, and Craven, or modern South Carolina. The first attempts at settlement, however, were not successful. A group from Barbados arrived in Clarendon County in 1665 but abandoned the settlement in 1667. More settlers moved from Virginia to Albemarle, but it remained isolated. In 1669, Sir Ashley Cooper, the earl of Shaftesbury, revived the Carolina project. He enlisted the philosopher John Locke to draft the Fundamental Constitutions of Carolina. Locke produced an elaborate plan for a feudal-like colony with manorial lands, ranks of nobility, and strange official titles like "palatine" instead of governor. Ill-suited to a frontier settlement, few of its provisions were ever enacted. Nonetheless, colonists sailed from England. In April 1670, William Sayle and his small group reached the coast. There, on rivers they named the Ashley and the Cooper, they founded the settlement of Old Charles Town. The Spanish in Florida set sail to evict them but were driven back by bad weather. English relief ships soon arrived, and the colony survived its first year without a "starving time."

SLAVERY AND UNFREE LABOR, 1642–1670

The importation of large numbers of African slaves did not begin until after 1680. Prior to 1670, however, several important changes set the stage for later growth. One was the enforcement of mercantile policies. Throughout its colonies, England encouraged large-scale agriculture and, in turn, dependence on unfree labor. Another development was the entry of the English themselves into the slave trade. A third was the increasing recognition of slavery in colonial legal codes and the gradual restriction of the rights of blacks.

In all colonies, some people of African descent remained or became free. In 1645, for example, 11 black indentured servants and their wives were freed by order of New Netherland's council, whom they had petitioned, and awarded land in modern Greenwich Village for their long service. To some extent, free blacks could function like white settlers. Some owned land; a few instances are known of free blacks receiving head rights and even having servants and owning slaves themselves. Beginning in the 1640s, however, black and white servants began to be distinguished in court rulings. In the 1660s, specific legislation was passed. Virginia recognized slavery in 1661, although free blacks were not affected, and removed import duties on ships bringing slaves to the colony. In 1662, children of black women were declared slave or free depending on the status of their mothers. In 1667, conversion to Christianity was declared an insufficient basis for freedom, overruling a Christian scruple that forbade the enslavement of other Christians. In 1668, free blacks were denied equality in law, and in 1669 the murder of a slave by a master was removed from the list of felonies.

Beginning in the 1640s, many New England ships returning from the West Indies also carried a few slaves. Most of these slaves remained in the port cities, where women and children worked in households and men worked in ship-related occupations or agricultural work. Massachusetts and Connecticut barred blacks from military service in 1657 and 1660, respectively. In 1670, Massachusetts confirmed in law that children of slaves could be sold into slavery. In New York, slavery was specifically retained as a legal institution in the Duke's Laws of 1665.

Despite the increasing legal restrictions on blacks, prior to 1670 white indentured servants were far more common, numerous, and economically important than slaves. But the demand for white servants eventually exceeded the supply, and "forced indentures" began to arrive. They included convicts, the poor or vagrant, political prisoners, and victims of kidnapping. In England, the kidnapping, or "spiriting," of both children and adults had developed into an organized business, causing extensive public alarm. In 1645, Parliament passed the first law against "spirits," or kidnappers; by 1671, spiriting had become a capital offense. Probably at least five percent of all indentured servants were victims of the trade.

In the colonies, the public was more alarmed by the number of indentured convicts. England had more than 300 capital offenses in the 17th century, although an extensive system of pardons lessened the number of people put to death. After 1655, many were offered "conditional pardons," or pardons on condition of emigration to the colonies. In 1670, Virginia passed an act prohibiting convict importation. Other large groups of "forced indentures" were Irish people, including children, the poor, and Catholic priests, sent after the rebellion of 1641, and Scots rebels sent after Cromwell's invasion in 1651.

In the Chesapeake, slavery-like living conditions began to develop, endured by white servants as well as blacks who worked alongside them. Although white servants lived separately from black servants on large plantations, both groups were driven by overseers and punished by whipping. Food and clothing were usually insufficient. Beginning in the 1640s, however, the high death rate among white servants dropped, and more survived the period of indenture. A few prospered, but freed servants were less likely to acquire land than formerly and were disproportionately affected by the new property qualifications for voting enacted around 1670. Increasingly, established settlers viewed former white indentured servants as a disruptive underclass, composed of rootless young men who were difficult to control.

The Beginnings of Urban Life, 1642–1670

By 1670, a clear contrast had developed between life in outlying agrarian settlements and in the bigger towns, which were busy and bustling. Boston was the largest and most important town and port in the colonies. Timber and fish from the north, cattle from the west, sheep from Rhode Island, and grain from Connecticut arrived to be shipped out, while European goods landed at the 15 wharves existing by 1645. New Amsterdam, the second-largest city and port, received furs from outlying traders and meat and grain from nearby settlements. In 1648, a farmer's market was opened on the Strand; space around the fort became a cattle market for 40 days each fall. By the 1660s, the arrival of slave ships and informal slave markets were common sights.[1]

Issues of public safety were already concerns. Stuyvesant appointed fire wardens and forbade thatched roofs in 1653. Boston suffered a serious fire the same year and soon after adopted a fire code, purchasing long ladders and crooks to pull down burning houses. The New York Rattle Watch, forerunner of the police force, began in 1653 with a captain and eight men paid to walk New Amsterdam streets at night. Municipal garbage collection began. In 1662, Boston hired a "scavenger" to clear the streets of "carrion and matters of offensive nature"; in 1670, New York's cartmen were employed to collect garbage after many ordinances against throwing it into the streets proved ineffective. (Cartmen hired out their teams and wagons to carry goods about the city.) Traffic control began. In 1652, Stuyvesant forbade galloping and required horses to be led on all streets except Broadway. In 1662, the Massachusetts General Court was compelled to reinforce Boston's 1656 ordinance against "irregular riding," because fast-moving horses had become a threat to pedestrians and children.

CHRONICLE OF EVENTS

1642

The combined non-Indian population of the nine English colonies in North America is more than 37,000.

Civil war erupts in England between Royalists and Parliamentarians. King Charles I's attempt to make Massachusetts a royal colony comes to an end.

1643

John Winthrop, Jr., organizes the first American ironworks at Saugus, Massachusetts.

A Boston ship carries slaves from Africa to Barbados for the first time, beginning New England's direct involvement in the slave trade.

All New Hampshire settlements are now under the jurisdiction of Massachusetts Bay Colony.

The New Haven settlements unify and elect a governor.

Virginia adopts the county court system and passes laws strengthening the role of the Anglican Church.

War begins between New Netherland and neighboring Algonquian tribes.

Johan Printz arrives as governor of New Sweden. He expels Puritan settlers from Connecticut.

The first Lutheran chapel in America is built in New Sweden.

May 10: Commissioners from the settlements of Massachusetts Bay, Plymouth, Connecticut, and New Haven meet to form the New England Confederation for mutual defense and action. Rhode Island and settlements in Maine and New Hampshire are excluded. It is the first attempt at voluntary unity among the English colonies.

1644

In England, Parliamentarians win important victories over the Royalist troops. King Charles I attempts to escape to Scotland.

The Massachusetts General Court becomes bicameral, part of a long struggle by representatives to curtail the power of the Puritan oligarchy.

Rhode Island receives a charter from the English government; it can now legally form a separate government.

The "time of troubles" begins in Maryland; Parliamentarian sympathizers seize control of the government.

April 18: Opechancanough's War begins in Virginia when tribes of the revived Powhatan Confederacy attack, killing 500 colonists.

1645

Parliament passes the first of several laws prohibiting the kidnapping of indentured servants.

The New England Confederation negotiates a settlement with the Narragansett, avoiding an impending war.

In Maryland, Parliamentarian sympathizers attack Jesuit missions.

New Netherland signs treaties with surrounding Indian tribes, and hostilities end. All lands near New Amsterdam are ceded to the Dutch. More than 1,000 Indians have been killed, and much destruction has also occurred in the colony.

Fifteen wharves are in operation in Boston.

1646

King Charles I is captured by Parliamentarian forces.

Dr. Robert Child and others request that the Massachusetts General Court ease church membership restrictions on the franchise. The petitioners are imprisoned.

Virginia troops capture Indian chief Opechancanough; he is murdered while in custody. The Powhatan tribes agree to a treaty in October, giving up all land between the James and York Rivers as far as the falls.

Governor Leonard Calvert reestablishes his authority in Maryland.

1647

The first Rhode Island General Assembly meets.

Peter Stuyvesant arrives as governor of New Amsterdam. He orders an election to select an advisory Council of Nine Men.

The Reverend John Cotton dies.

November 11: Massachusetts passes the first compulsory school law, requiring all towns of 50 families or more to establish a public school.

1648

The Cambridge Platform of Church Discipline is adopted by the ministerial synod in Massachusetts, reinforcing church authority.

The Massachusetts Laws and Liberties are passed, reducing the discretionary power of the Puritan elite.

1649

The Company for the Propagation of the Gospel is organized by English Puritans to encourage missionary work among the Indians.

The Second Church of Boston is founded, marking the first New England community in which church and town are no longer one body.

Prominent Royalists, called Cavaliers, begin migrating to Virginia. Several will found distinguished colonial families.

William Stone, a Protestant, is appointed governor of Maryland. He welcomes Puritans to the colony.

Maryland passes the Religious Toleration Act, which affords freedom of conscience to all Christians.

John Winthrop dies.

January 30: King Charles I, tried for treason and found guilty, is beheaded. Virginia declares its loyalty to Charles II, in exile.

May: The English Commonwealth is officially established; Oliver Cromwell will be its head for life.

1650

The New England Confederation and Peter Stuyvesant negotiate a treaty. New England receives eastern Long Island and the Connecticut River valley and in return recognizes Dutch rights to New Netherland; the English Crown refuses to acknowledge the treaty.

Connecticut drafts a code of laws.

Maryland adopts a bicameral assembly, but records indicate the assembly does not meet in two houses until 1659.

Harvard receives a charter from the Massachusetts General Court, making it a corporation.

The Tenth Muse by Anne Bradstreet, the first book of poetry by an American colonist, is published in London.

1651

England passes the first Navigation Act, requiring all trade between the colonies and England to be carried in English or colonial ships. Although the act is not well enforced, it angers the Dutch, at whom it is directed.

The Reverend John Eliot founds the first Indian "Praying Town" at Natick, Massachusetts.

1652

The Dutch declare war on England, opening the First Anglo-Dutch War (1652–54).

"Scotch House," Saugus, Massachusetts, built 1651, quarters for Scottish indentured servants who worked in the iron mill *(Historic American Building Survey)*

Scots deported by Oliver Cromwell are the first large group of non-English immigrants to arrive in Boston.

England sends a fleet and commissioners to Virginia to demand its surrender to the Commonwealth government. Governor William Berkeley resigns, ending his first term. The commissioners establish a Puritan-controlled government in Maryland.

New Amsterdam is formally made a municipality; Stuyvesant forbids galloping horses on city streets.

1653

Settlements in southern Maine agree to be under the jurisdiction of Massachusetts.

Virginia sets aside reservations for Indians.

In New Amsterdam, Stuyvesant establishes fire wardens and the Rattle Watch, forerunners of a police force.

1654

Harvard's first president resigns, accused of unorthodox religious beliefs.

The Maryland Assembly repudiates religious toleration.

A group of observant Jews arrives in New York from Dutch colonies in South America, the first such group known to migrate to North America.

1655

Former governor William Stone attempts to regain control of Maryland but is defeated by Puritan forces.

New Netherland begins slave trading directly with Africa.

Stuyvesant and his troops capture New Sweden. It becomes an appendage of New Netherland.

England establishes "conditional pardons"; certain criminals will be pardoned if they emigrate to North America.

1656

The first Quakers arrive in Massachusetts. Persecution quickly begins.

New Haven adopts a code of laws proscribing much personal behavior, forerunner of New England's "blue laws."

Virginia grants head rights of land to Indians. Most prefer to maintain their traditional way of life.

1657

Cromwell restores Maryland to the Calvert family proprietors. Religious toleration is restored.

William Bradford dies.

1658

Cromwell dies and is succeeded by his son, whose leadership proves unsatisfactory.

In Maine, Casco Bay settlements agree to be under the jurisdiction of Massachusetts Bay Colony.

The Virginia Assembly, on the death of Cromwell, declares itself the supreme power in the colony and reappoints Governor Berkeley to a second term.

1659

Persecution of Quakers reaches its height over the next two years; four are hanged in New England.

1660

The English monarchy is restored; Charles II is crowned king.

Parliament passes a new Navigation Act, reaffirming that goods must be carried to and from the colonies in English ships; enumerated, or listed, items can be sold and shipped only to England.

The combined non-Indian population of the nine mainland English colonies is about 80,000.

1661

Charles II orders Massachusetts to extend voting rights to non-Puritan church members "of good estate"; the colony evades the law.

Wampanoag chief Massasoit dies. He is succeeded by his less accommodating son Metacom, whom the English call King Philip.

A Virginia statute recognizes the existence of slavery.

1662

The Massachusetts ministerial synod adopts the Half-Way Covenant, allowing children of church members to join without a conversion experience; thus, they will be able to vote.

The Reverend Michael Wigglesworth publishes his best-selling long poem *The Day of Doom.*

Connecticut receives a charter from Charles II, giving it jurisdiction over the New Haven colony.

Virginia declares black children slave or free depending on the status of their mothers.

Boston hires a scavenger to collect garbage; the general court reinforces ordinances against fast-moving horses in Boston.

1663

England passes the Staple Act, a navigation act requiring all goods headed for the colonies to be reloaded into English ships.

The Second Anglo-Dutch War begins on the African coast.

King Charles II grants a charter to a group of proprietors for the Carolina territory between Virginia and Spanish Florida.

Rhode Island receives a charter from Charles II; it specifically recognizes freedom of conscience.

A Maryland statute recognizes slavery.

The Reverend John Eliot publishes the *Indian Bible,* a translation into Algonquian.

1664

The Privy Council sends four commissioners to examine the New England colonies. Massachusetts extends little cooperation.

New Haven finally agrees to be under the jurisdiction of Connecticut.

March: Charles II grants his brother James, the duke of York, a large tract in North America that includes New Netherland.

August: English colonel Richard Nicholls arrives in New Amsterdam and obtains Stuyvesant's surrender without shots being fired. New Netherland is renamed New York. New Sweden also surrenders to the English.

1665

The Duke's Laws are established for New York. They grant local self-government but have no provision for a colonywide assembly. The laws also recognize slavery.

Philip Carteret, appointed governor by the proprietors of New Jersey, arrives with colonists and a plan of government. Several settlements already exist; Governor Nicholls of New York believes the area is under his jurisdiction.

1667

The Treaty of Breda ending the Second Anglo-Dutch War confirms the English conquest of New Netherland and grants slave-trading rights to the English.

Virginia declares that conversion to Christianity is not sufficient reason to free a slave.

1668

In Virginia, free blacks are denied equality in law.

In Delaware, settlers plan Long Finn's Rebellion in the false belief that Sweden intends to recapture the colony. They are discovered and the leaders punished.

1669

The first New Jersey Assembly meets. It is dominated by migrants from New England, who make church membership a prerequisite for voting.

In Virginia, the murder of a slave by a master is removed from the list of felonies.

1670

Massachusetts confirms in law that children of slaves can be sold.

Connecticut establishes a system of sealed proxies, enabling freemen to vote without traveling to the assembly.

The Virginia Assembly restricts voting rights to male property holders; previously most free male inhabitants could vote. In Maryland, Governor Charles Calvert disenfranchises settlers with fewer than 50 acres of land.

Settlers arrive in Carolina and found Old Charles Town (Charleston).

EYEWITNESS TESTIMONY

Give ear unto a Maid, that lately was betray'd,
And sent into Virginny, O:
In brief I shall declare, what I have suffer'd there,
When that I was weary, weary, weary,
    weary, O. . . .

I have play'd my part, both at Plow and Cart,
In the Land of Virginny, O;
Billets from the Wood, upon my back they load,
When that I was weary, weary, weary, weary, O. . . .

Popular English ballad "The Trappan'd [kidnapped] Maiden," ca. 1640s, in Firth, ed., American Garland, *pp. 251–53.*

Whereas there are divers loitering runaways in the colony who very often absent themselves from their master's service, And sometimes in two or three months cannot be found, whereby their said masters are at great charge in finding them, And many times even to the loss of their year's labor before they be had, Be it therefore enacted and confirmed that all runaways that shall absent themselves from their said master's service shall be liable to make satisfaction by service at the end of their times by indenture double the time of service so neglected. . . . And if such runaways shall be found to transgress the second time or oftener (if it shall be duly proved against them) that then they shall be branded in the cheek with the letter R and pass under the statute of incorrigible rogues.

. . . . .

. . . it should not be lawful under the penalty aforesaid for any popish priest that shall hereafter arrive to remain above five days after warning given for his departure by the Governor or commander of the place where he or they shall be, if wind and weather hinder not his departure. . . .

. . . . .

For the preservation of the purity of doctrine and unity of the church, It is enacted that all ministers whatsoever which shall reside in the colony are to be conformable to the orders and constitutions of the church of England, and the laws therein established, and not otherwise be admitted to teach or preach publically or privately, And that the Governor and Council do take care that all nonconformists upon notice of them shall

be compelled to depart the colony with all conveniency.

Virginia statutes, 1643, in Hening, Statutes, *vol. 1, pp. 254–55, 277.*

On the Island of Manhatte, and in its environs, there may well be four or five hundred men of different sects and nations: the Director General told me that there were men of eighteen different languages; they are scattered here and there on the river, above and below, as the beauty and convenience of the spot invited each to settle: some, mechanics, however, who ply their trade, are ranged under the fort; all the others were exposed to the incursions of the natives, who, in the year 1643, while I was there, actually killed some two score Hollanders, and burnt many houses and barns full of wheat. . . .

Shortly before I arrived there, three large ships of 300 tons each had come to load wheat; two found cargoes, the third could not be loaded, because the savages had burnt a part of their grain. These ships came from the West Indies, where the West India Company usually keeps up seventeen ships of war.

Father Isaac Jogues describes 1643, Narrative, *pp. 55–56.*

The lady Moodye, a wise and anciently religious woman, being taken with the error of denying baptism to infants, was dealt withal by many of the elders and others, and admonished by the church of Salem, (whereof she was a member,) but persisting still, and to avoid further trouble etc., she removed to the Dutch against the advice of all her friends. Many others infected with anabaptism, removed thither also. She was after excommunicated.

John Winthrop, 1643, History, *vol. 2, pp. 148–49.*

There arose a sudden gust at N. W. so violent for half an hour, as it blew down multitudes of trees. It lifted up their meeting house at Newbury, the people being in it. It darkened the air with dust, yet through God's great mercy it did no hurt, but only killed one Indian with the fall of a tree. It was straight between Linne and Hampton.

John Winthrop, 1643, History, *vol. 2, p. 149.*

It was agreed and concluded as a fundamental order not to be disputed or questioned hereafter, that none shall be admitted to be free burgesses in any of the plantations within this jurisdiction for the future, but such planters as are members of some or other of the approved churches in New England, nor shall any but such free burgesses have any vote in any election ... nor shall any power or trust in the ordering of any civil affairs, be at any time put into the hands of any other than such church members, though as free planters, all have right to their inheritance and to commerce, according to such grants, orders and laws as shall be made concerning the same.

Fundamental Orders of New Haven, November 6, 1643, in Macdonald, ed., Documentary Source Book, *pp. 51–52.*

I acknowledge that to molest any person, Jew or Gentile, for either professing doctrine, or practicing worship merely religious or spiritual, it is to persecute him, and such a person (what ever his doctrine or practice be true or false) suffereth persecution for conscience.

But withal I desire it may be well observed, that this distinction is not full and complete: for beside this that a man may be persecuted because he holdeth or practiseth what he believes in conscience to be a Truth, (as Daniel did, for which he was cast into the Lions' den, Dan. 6) and many thousands of Christians, because they durst not cease to preach and practice what they believed was by God commanded, as the Apostles answered (Acts 4. and 5) I say besides this a man may also be persecuted, because he dares to be constrained to yield obedience to such doctrines and worships as are by men invented and appointed.

Roger Williams, The Bloudy Tenent of Persecution, *1644, in Blau, ed.,* Cornerstones, *pp. 37–38.*

The Government among them [*the Iroquois*] consists of the oldest, the most sensible, the best-speaking and most warlike Men; these commonly resolve, and the young and war-like Men carry into Execution; but if the common People do not approve of the Resolution, it is left entirely to the judgment of the Mob. The Chiefs are generally the poorest among them, for instead of their receiving from the common People as among Christians, they are obliged to give to them; especially when any one is killed in War, they give great Presents to the next of Kin to the deceased, and if they take any Prisoners they present them to that Family whereof one has been killed, and the Prisoner is adopted by the Family into the Place of the Person who was killed. There is no Punishment here for Murder and other Villainies, but every one is his own

Avenger: The Friends of the deceased revenge themselves upon the Murderer until Peace is made by Presents to the next of Kin. But although they are so cruel, and have no Laws or Punishments, yet there are not half so many Villainies or Murders committed amongst them as amongst Christians, so that I sometimes think with astonishment upon the Murders committed in the Netherlands, notwithstanding their severe Laws and heavy Penalties.

The Reverend Johan Megapolensis, 1644, in Hart, ed., American History, *vol. 1, p. 528.*

But how hard the Puritans have lain upon my neck and yet do lay can be seen from the documents which are enclosed here. I believe that I shall hardly get rid of them in a peaceful manner, because they have sneaked into new Netherland also with their Pharisean practices. Now they are so strong there that they have chased the Hollanders from that place called Fort River [*Connecticut River*] and now keep with violence the land rightfully purchased by the Hollanders. ...

Nothing would be better than to send over here a couple of hundred soldiers, until we broke the necks of all of [*the Indians*] in this River. ... They are a lot of poor rogues. Then each one could be secure here at his work, and feed and nourish himself unmolested ... and also we could take possession of the places (which are the most fruitful) that the savages now possess. ...

Governor Johan Printz to the Swedish Crown, 1644, in Myers, ed., Narratives, *pp. 113, 116–18.*

... the divine service with its ceremony are here held just as in Old Sweden, in the good old Swedish language. Our pastor is bedecked with chausable and differs in all manners from the other sects hovering around us here. The great festivals and solemn prayer-days, Sundays and Apostle days, are all celebrated entirely according to our o[ld] Swedish form, on Fridays and Wednesdays, sermons and on all other days prayers, evening and morning. And as the pastor (for he is alone) cannot daily provide all places therewith, therefore I have at each settlement appointed one who can read, that this one daily holds evening and morning prayers and thus makes the people inclined to piety. All this the Savages have long watched and it is nothing new to them, as we have often tried to bring them to some hearing of God, have had them a few stay with us, but they have watched their opportunity and have run way again to the Savages. The Hollanders have taken young boys, let them be taught to read and to write, so that they in all things have been as clever as the Christians, but they have in like manner waited for an opportunity to run away, and are now in these wars the cleverest enemies and persecutors of the Hollanders, so that they can hardly be converted with kindness.

Governor Printz to Chancellor Brahe, July 1644, in Johnson, ed., Instruction, p. 164.

The said Narigansett and Niantick sagamores and deputies do hearby promise and covenant to keep and maintains a firm and perpetual peace, both with all the English United Colonies and their successors, and with Uncass, the Monhegen sachem, and his men; with Ossamequine, Pumham, Sokanoke, Cutshamakin, Shoanan, Passaconaway, and all other Indian sagamores, and their companies, who are in friendship with or subject to any of the English; hereby engaging themselves, that they will not at any time hereafter disturb the peace of the country, by any assaults, hostile attempts, invasions, or other injuries, to any of the United Colonies, or their successors; or to the aforesaid Indians; either in their persons, buildings, cattle, or goods, directly or indirectly; nor will they confederate with any other against them; and if they know of any Indians or others that conspire or intend hurt against the said English, or any Indians subject to or in friendship with them, they will without delay acquaint and give notice thereof to the English commissioners, or some of them.

Treaty between the New England Confederation and the Narragansett, 1645, in Bradford, History, pp. 522–23.

Diverse free schools were erected, as at Roxbury (for maintenance whereof every inhabitant bound some house or land for a yearly allowance forever) and at Boston (where they made an order to allow forever 50 pounds to the master and an house, and 30 pounds to an usher, who should also teach to read and write and cipher, and Indians' children were to be taught freely, and the charge to be by yearly contribution, either by voluntary allowance, or by rate of such as refused, etc., and this order was confirmed by the general court). Other towns did the like, providing maintenance by several means.

By agreement of the commissioners, and the motions of the elders in their several churches, every family in each colony gave one peck of corn or twelve pence to the college at Cambridge.

John Winthrop, 1645, History, vol. 2, pp. 264–65.

Mr. Hopkins, the governor of Hartford upon Connecticut, came to Boston, and brought his wife with him (a godly young woman, and of special parts,) who was fallen into a sad infirmity, the loss of her understanding and reason, which had been growing upon her divers years, by occasion of her giving herself wholly to reading and writing, and had written many books. Her husband, being very loving and tender of her, was loath to grieve her; but he saw his error, when it was too late. For if she had attended her household affairs, and such things as belong to women, and not gone out of her way and calling to meddle in such things as are proper for men, whose minds are stronger, etc., she had kept her wits, and might have improved them usefully and honorably in the place God had set her. He brought her to Boston . . . to try what means might be had here for her. But no help could be had.

John Winthrop, 1645, History, vol. 2, pp. 265–66.

It is wonderful in our eyes to understand by these two honest Indians what prayers Waaubon and the rest of them used to make, for he that preaches to them professes he never yet used any of their words in his prayers, from whom otherwise it might be thought that they had learned them by rote. One is this:

Amanaomen Jebovah tabassen metagb. (Take away Lord my stony heart.) Another: *Cbecbesom lebovab kekowbogkew.* (Wash Lord my soul.) . . . These are but a taste. They have many more, and these more enlarged than thus expressed, yet what are these but the sprinklings of the spirit and blood of Christ Jesus in their hearts?

The Reverend John Eliot, "The Day Breaking . . . with the Indians," 1646 in Massachusetts Historical Society, Collections, 3rd ser., vol. 3, p. 20.

And we plainly perceiving that the scope of their [*Massachusetts Bay Colony's*] doctrine was bent only to maintain that outward form of worship which they had erected to themselves, . . . our consciences could not close with them in such their practices, which they perceiving, denied us the common benefit of the Country, even so much as a place to reside in, and plant upon, for the maintenance and preservation of our selves, our wives and little ones;

as also proceeded against us, as they had done to others; yea with more severity, unto confinements, imprisonments, chains, fines, whippings, and banishment out of all their jurisdictions to wander in the wildernesses in extremity of winter, yea when the snow was up to the knee, and rivers to wade through up unto the middle, and not so much as one of the Indians to be found in that extremity of weather to afford us either fire, or any harbor, such as themselves had; being removed into swamps and thickets, where they were not to be found; in which condition, in the continuation of the weather we lay diverse nights together, having no victuals, but what we took on our backs, and our drink as the snow afforded unto us, whereupon we were constrained with the hazard of our lives to betake our selves into a part of the Country called the Narragansett Bay, buying several parcels of Land of the Indians there inhabiting; and sat down in, and near the place where Master Roger Williams was. . . .

Samuel Gorton's Simplicities Defence, *1646, in Hart, ed.,* American History, *vol. 1, p. 399.*

1. When any Scholar is able to Read Tully or such like classical Latin Author *ex tempore,* and make and speak true Latin in verse and prose *suo (ut aiunt) Marte,* and decline perfectly the paradigms of Nouns and verbs in the Greek tongue, then may he be admitted into the College, nor shall any claim admission before such qualifications. . . .

3. Seeing the Lord giveth wisdom, every one shall seriously by prayer in secret, seek wisdom of Him. Prov. 2.2, 3 etc. . . .

8. They shall be slow to speak, and eschew not only oaths, lies, and uncertain rumors, but likewise all idle, foolish, butter scoffing, frothy wanton words and offensive gestures.

9. None shall pragmatically intrude or intermeddle in other men's affairs. . . .

13. The Scholars shall never use their Mothertongue except that in public exercises of oratory or such like, they be called to make them in English. . . .

Harvard's regulations, ca. 1646, quoted in Morison, Founding, *pp. 333–335.*

We therefore desire that civil liberty and freedom be forthwith granted to all truly English, equal to the rest of their countrymen, as in all plantations is accustomed to be done, and as all freeborn enjoy in our native country. . . .

Whereas there are diverse sober, righteous and godly men, eminent for knowledge and other gracious gifts of the holy spirit, no ways scandalous in their lives and conversation, members of the church of England (in all ages famous for piety and learning) not dissenting from the latest and best reformation of England, Scotland, and etc. yet they and their posterity are detained from the seals of the covenant of free grace, because, as it is supposed, they will not take these churches' covenants, for which as yet they see no light in God's word; neither can they clearly perceive what they are, every church having their covenant differing from another's, at least in words. . . .

Dr. Robert Child to the Massachusetts General Court, May 1646, in Hart, ed., American History, *vol. 1, pp. 392.*

Great harm was done in corn (especially wheat and barley) in this month by a caterpillar like a black worm about an inch 1/2 long. They eat up first the blades of the stalk, then they eat up the tassels, whereupon the ear withered. It was believed by divers good observations that they fell in a great thunder shower, for divers yards and other bare places, where no one of them was to be seen an hour before, were presently after the shower almost covered with them. . . .

John Winthrop, July 1646, Journal, *pp. 299–300.*

Though this petition of Dr. Child was in a peaceable way presented, . . . the Elders . . . publicly used several Expressions . . . that it was a seditious Petition . . . subversive both to Church and Commonwealth, . . . some calling those that so Petitioned . . . Sons of Belial, Judases, Sons of Corah . . . which seemed not to arise from a Gospel Spirit . . . yea publicly exhorting Authority to lay hold upon those Petitioners, which the same night they did. Nor were the Magistrates . . . altogether silent, but spake in the same key. . . . They were fined . . . two of them had their trunks and Studies broke up, and their Papers taken away, and imprisoned close prisoners, and are in danger of their lives by reason of that Capital Law, "If any man . . . attempt the alteration . . . of our Frame of Polity or Government fundamentally, he shall be put to death."

Major John Child, "Relation of the Effects this Petition Produced," 1647, in Caldwell and Persinger, Source History, *pp. 62–63.*

It being one chief project of that old deluder Satan to keep men from the knowledge of the Scriptures, as in former times by keeping them in an unknown tongue, so in these latter times by persuading from the use of tongues, that so at least the true sense and meaning of the original might be clouded by false glosses of saint-seeming deceivers, that learning may not be buried in the grave of our fathers in the church and common-wealth, the Lord assisting our endeavors:

It is therefore ordered that every township in this jurisdiction, after the Lord has increased them to the number of 50 householders, shall then forthwith appoint one within their town to teach all such children as shall resort to him to write and read, whose wages shall be paid either by the parents or masters of such children the inhabitants in general, by way of supply, as the major part of those that order the prudentials of the town shall appoint, provided those that send their children be not oppressed by paying much more than they can have them taught for in other towns.

And it is further ordered that when a town shall increase to the number of 100 families or householders, they shall set up a grammar school, the master thereof being able to instruct youth so far as they may be fitted for the university. . . .

"Old Deluder Satan Law" (Massachusetts school law), 1647, in Shurtleff, ed., Records, vol. 2, p. 203.

He that is willing to tolerate any Religion, or discrepant way of Religion, besides his own, unless it be in matters merely indifferent, either doubts of his own, or is not sincere in it.

He that is willing to tolerate any unsound Opinion, that his own may also be tolerated, though never so sound, will for a need hang God's Bible at the Devil's girdle. . . .

That State that will give Liberty of Conscience in matters of Religion, must give Liberty of Conscience and Conversation in their Moral Laws, or else the Fiddle will be out of tune, and some of the strings crack. . . .

Experience will teach Churches and Christians, that it is far better to live in a State united, though a little Corrupt, than in a State, whereof some Part is incorrupt, and all the rest divided.

The Reverend Nathaniel Ward, The Simple Cobbler of Aggawam, 1647, in Hart, ed., American History, vol. 1, pp. 394–95.

The church is either triumphant or militant. Triumphant, the number of them, who are glorified in heaven; militant, the number of them, who are conflicting with their enemies upon earth. . . . A Congregational-church, is by the institution of Christ a part of the Militant-visible-church, consisting of a company of Saints by calling, united into one body, by a holy covenant, for the public worship of God, and the mutual edification one of another. . . . the doors of the churches of Christ upon earth, do not by God's appointment stand so wide open, that all sorts of people good and bad, may freely enter therein at their pleasure . . . but such as are admitted thereto, as members, ought to be examined and tried first, whether they be fit and meet to be received into church society. . . . The power and authority of magistrates is not for the restraining of churches . . . but for helping in and furthering thereof. . . .

Congregational synod, "Platform of Church Discipline," (The Cambridge Platform) 1648, in Caldwell and Persinger, Source History, p. 64.

Whitman House, Farmington, Connecticut, built 1664 *(Photo by Robert Fulton III for Historic American Building Survey)*

About the midst of this summer there arose a fly out of the ground about the bigness of the top of a man's little finger of brown color. They filled the woods from Connecticut to Sudbury with a great noise, and eat up the young sprouts of the trees but meddled not with the corn. . . . If the lord had not stopped them they had spoiled all our orchards. . . .

John Winthrop, August 1648, Journal, p. 343.

[Boston is] the Center Town and Metropolis of this Wilderness work. . . . Environed it is with the Brinish floods . . . two constant Ferries are kept for daily traffic thereunto. The form of this Town is like a heart, naturally situated for Fortifications, having two Hills . . . next the Sea, the one well fortified . . . with store of great Artillery well mounted, the other hath a very strong battery built of whole Timber, and filled with Earth. At the descent of the Hill in the extreme point thereof, betwixt these two strong arms lies a large Cove or Bay, on which the chiefest part of this Town is built, over-topped with a third Hill; all three . . . keep a constant watch . . . being furnished with a Beacon and loud babbling Guns. . . . The chief Edifice . . . is crowded on the Sea-banks, and wharfed out with great industry and cost, the buildings beautiful and large, some fairly set forth with Brick, Tile, Stone and Slate, and orderly placed with comely streets, whose continual enlargement presages some sumptuous City. . . . But now behold the admirable Acts of Christ; at this his peoples landing, the hideous Thickets in this place were such, that Wolfs and Bears nursed up their young . . . in those very places where the streets are full of Girls and Boys sporting up and down, with a continued concourse of people. Good store of Shipping is here yearly built, and some very fair ones: both Tar and Masts the Country affords from its own soil; also store of Victual both for their own and Foreigners-ships, who resort hither for that end: this Town is the very Mart of the Land, French, Portugals and Dutch come hither for Traffic.

Edward Johnson, ca. 1650, Johnson's Wonder, *pp. 70–71.*

I am obnoxious to each carping tongue
Who says my hand a needle better fits,
A poet's pen all scorn I should thus wrong,
For such despite they cast on female wits:
If what I do prove well, it won't advance,
They'll say it's stol'n, or else it was by chance.

Anne Bradstreet, "Prologue," 1650, Works, *p. 16.*

Reverend and dear friends, whom I unfeignedly love and respect:

It doth not a little grieve my spirit to hear what sad things are reported daily of your tyranny and persecutions in New England,—as that you fine, whip, and imprison men for their consciences. First, you compel such to come into your assembly as you know will not join with you in your worship, and when they shew their dislike thereof or witness against it, then you stir up your magistrates to punish them for such (as you conscience) their public affronts. Truly, friends, this your practice of compelling any in matters of worship to do that whereof they are not fully persuaded, is to make them sin; for so the apostle (Rom. 14 and 23) tells us; and many are made hypocrites thereby, conforming in their outward man for fear of punishment. We pray for you and wish you prosperity in every way, and hoped that the Lord would have given you so much light and love there that you might have been eyes to God's people here, and not to practice those courses in a wilderness you went so far to prevent.

Richard Saltonstall, a founder of Watertown, to Reverend John Cotton, ca. 1650, in West, ed., Source Book, *pp. 249–50.*

The bowl has been going round a long time for the purpose of erecting a common school and it has been built with words, but as yet the first stone is not laid. . . . According to the proclamations during the administration of Director Kieft, if we rightly consider and examine them all, we cannot learn or discover that any thing,—we say *any thing* large or small,—worth relating, was done, built or made, which concerned or belonged to the commonalty. . . . The negroes, also, who came from Tamandare were sold for pork and peas, from the proceeds of which something wonderful was to be performed, but they just dripped through the fingers. There are, also, various other negroes in this country, some of whom have been made free for their long service, but their children have remained slaves, though it is contrary to the laws of every people that any one born of a Christian mother should be a slave and be compelled to remain in servitude. . . .

Adriaen Van der Donck, "Of the Reasons . . . How New Netherland is So Decayed," 1650, in Hart, ed., American History, *vol. 1, p. 535.*

His [Stuyvesant's] first arrival . . . was like a peacock, with great state and pomp. The declaration of His Honor, that he wished to stay here only three years, with other haughty expressions. . . . The appellation of *Lord General,* and similar titles, were never before known here. . . . At one time, after leaving the house of the minister, where the consistory had been sitting and had risen, it happened that Arnoldus Van Herdenbergh related the proceedings relative to the estate of Zeger Teunisz, and how he himself, as curator, had appealed from the sentence; whereupon the Director, who had been sitting there with them as an elder, interrupted him and replied, "It may during my administration be contemplated to appeal, but if any one should do it, I *will make him a foot shorter,* and send the pieces to Holland, and let him appeal in that way." . . .

Adriaen Van der Donck, 1650, in Hart, ed., American History, *vol. 1, p. 535.*

. . . what is it can be hoped for in a change, which we have not already? Is it liberty? The sun looks not on a people more free than we are from all oppression. Is it wealth? Hundreds of examples show us that Industry and Thrift in a short time may bring us to as high of it as the country and our Conditions are yet capable of. Is it security to enjoy this wealth when gotten? Without blushing I will speak it, I am confident there lives not that person can accuse me of attempting the least act against any man's property. Is it peace? The Indians, God be blessed, round about us are subdued: we can only fear the Londoners, who would fain bring us to the same poverty, wherein the Dutch found and relieved us, would take away the liberty of our consciences, and tongues, and our right of giving and selling our goods to whom we please. But, Gentlemen, by the Grace of God, we will not so tamely part with our King, and all these blessings we enjoy under him. . . .

Governor Berkeley to the Virginia Assembly, 1651, in Hart, ed., American History, *vol. 1, pp. 233–34.*

First, It is agreed and consented that the plantation of Virginia, and all the inhabitants thereof, shall be and remain in due obedience and subjection to the commonwealth of England, according to the laws there established, And that this submission and subscription be acknowledged a voluntary act not forced nor constrained by a conquest upon the country, And that they shall have and enjoy such freedoms and privileges as belong to the free borne people of England, and that the former government by the commissions and instructions be void and null.

2dly. Secondly, that the Grand Assembly as formerly shall convene and transact the affairs of Virginia, wherein nothing is to be acted or done contrary to the government of the common wealth of England and the laws there established. . . .

8thly. That Virginia shall be free from all taxes, customs and impositions whatsoever, and none to be imposed on them without consent of the Grand Assembly. . . .

Governor Richard Bennett surrenders Virginia to Parliament 1652, in Hart, ed., American History, *vol. 1, pp. 235–36.*

He began the Sabbath at evening; therefore then performed Family-duty after supper, being larger then ordinary in Exposition, after which he Catechized his children and servants, and then returned into his Study. The morning following, Family-worship being ended, he retired into his Study, until the Bell called him away. Upon his return from Meeting, he returned again into his Study (the place of his labor and prayer) unto his private devotion where (having a small repast carried him up for his dinner) he continued till the tolling of the bell. The public service being over, he withdrew for a space to his prementioned Oratory for his sacred addresses unto God, as in the forenoon; then came down, repeated the Sermon in the family, prayed, after supper sung a Psalm, and towards bedtime betaking himself again to his Study, he closed the day with prayer. Thus he spent the Sabbath continually.

The Reverend John Norton memorializes the Reverend John Cotton, 1652, in Hart, ed., American History, *vol. 1, p. 338.*

It can be no less than a contradiction to affirm the Supreme power; which we take to be the General Courts of every jurisdiction Can be commanded by others to an absurdity in policy; That an Entire Government and jurisdiction should prostitute itself to the Command of Strangers; A Scandal in Religion that a general court of Christians should be obliged to act and engage upon the faith of six Delegates against their Conscience all which must be admitted In case we acknowledge ourselves bound to Undertake an offensive war upon the bare determination of the Commissioners who can not nor ever did challenge Authority over us or expect Subjection from us. . . .

Massachusetts General Court to New England Confederation, 1653, in Hart, ed., American History, *vol. 1, pp. 453–54.*

The Women are not (as is reported) put into the ground to work [*i.e., as field hands*], but occupy such domestic employments and housewifery as in England, that is dressing victuals, righting up the house, milking, employed about dairies, washing, sewing, etc. and both men and women have times of recreations, as much or more than in any part of the world besides. Yet some wenches that are nasty, beastly and not fit to be so employed are put into the ground, for reason tells us, that they must not at charge be transported and then maintained for nothing, but those that prove so awkward are rather burdensome than servants desirable or useful.

John Hammond describes the Chesapeake, 1656, in Hall, ed., Narratives, pp. 290–91.

In Maryland, during this year and the next preceding, Ours [*the Jesuits*] have escaped grievous dangers, but have had to contend it difficulties and straits, and have suffered many unthings as well from enemies as from our own people. English who inhabit Virginia made an attack on the colonists, themselves Englishmen too; and safety being guaranteed in conditions, received indeed the Governor of Maryland, with many others, in surrender. But in treacherous violation of the conditions, four of the captives, and three of them Catholics, out of extreme hatred of our religion were pierced with leaden balls. Rushing into our houses, they demanded for death the impostors, as they called them, intending inevitable slaughter to those who should be caught. But the Fathers, by the protection of God, unknown to them, carried from before their faces in a little boat; their books, furniture and whatever was in the house, fell a prey to robbers. With almost the entire loss of their property, private and domestic, together with great peril of life, they were secretly carried into Virginia; and in the greatest want of necessities, scarcely and with difficulty do they sustain life. They live in a mean hut, low and depressed, not much unlike a tern, or even a tomb, in which that great defender of the faith St. Athanasius, lay concealed for many years.

Annual Letter of the Maryland Jesuits to Rome, 1655–56, in Hall, ed., Narratives, pp. 141–42.

. . . We have here seen and learned with displeasure, that your Honors, against our apostille of the 15th of February, 1655, granted to the Jewish or Portuguese nation at their request, have forbidden them to trade at Fort Orange and South River, and also the purchase of real estate, which is allowed them here in this country without any difficulty, and we wish that this had not occurred but that your Honors had obeyed our orders which you must hereafter execute punctually and with more respect. Jews or Portuguese people, however, shall not be permitted to establish themselves as mechanics (which they are not allowed to do in this city), nor allowed to have open retail shops, but they may quietly and peacefully carry on their business as heretofore and exercise in all quietness their religion within their houses, for which end they must without doubt endeavor to build their houses close together in a convenient place on one or the other side of New Amsterdam— at their choice—as they have done here.

West India Company to Governor Stuyvesant, June 1656, American Jewish Historical Society, Publications 28 (1909).

You have been pleased to send up unto us a certain prohibition or command that we should not receive or entertain any of those people called Quakers because they are supposed to be by some, seducers of the people. For our part we cannot condemn them in this case, neither can we stretch out our hands against them, to punish, nbanish or persecute them. . . .

The law of love, peace and liberty in the States extending to Jews, Turks, and Egyptians, as they are considered the sons of Adam, which is the glory of the outward state of Holland, so love, peace and liberty, extending to all in Christ Jesus, condemns hatred, war and bondage. And because our Savior saith it is impossible but that offenses will come, but woe unto him by whom they cometh, our desire is not to offend one of his little ones, in whatsoever form, name or title he appears in, whether Presbyterian, Independent, Baptist or Quaker, but shall be glad to see anything of God in any of them. . . .

Therefore, if any of these said persons come in love unto us, we cannot in conscience lay violent hands upon them, but give them free egress and regress unto our Town, and houses, as God shall persuade our consciences.

Remonstrance of the inhabitants of Flushing to Governor Peter Stuyvesant, December 27, 1657, "Remonstrance of the Inhabitants of the Town of Flushing." Long Island: Our Story. URL: lihistory.com.

October 1, Wednesday. . . . We embarked and dismissed our four guides, but Sander Poeyer, with his Indian, accompanied us; shortly after we pushed off, the boat became almost half full of water, where upon we were obliged to land and turn the boat upside down; we caulked the seams somewhat with old linen, our people having left behind them the tow which had been given them for that purpose, and thus made it a little tighter, but one was obliged to sit continually and bail out the water. In that way, we came with the same tide a good league and a half down Elk River, and found ourselves at its east branch, where we built a fire in the woods, and proceeded with the night ebb on our journey with great labor, as the boat was very leaky, and we had neither rudder nor oar, but merely paddles.

October 2, Thursday. Having paddled down Elk River most the whole of the night, came about 8 o'clock to Sassafracx River, where we stopped during that tide at . . . the plantation of one Mr. Jan Turner. Here we found Abraham the Finn, a soldier who had run away from Christina, and also a Dutch woman [*an indentured servant*]. . . . We offered them the General's pardon, in case they would return to New Amstel within six months, and should they then be unwilling to stay there, they would be at liberty go to the Manhattans. The woman accepted these conditions, having three months more to serve, when she would return. But the soldier raised many objections.

Augustine Herrman's journal, 1659, in Hall, ed.,
Narratives, p. 315.

Be it enacted That in case any English servant shall run away in company with any negroes who are incapable of making satisfaction by addition of time, Be it enacted that the English so running away in company with them shall serve for the time of the said negroes absence as they are to do for their own by a former act.

. . . . .

Whereas the barbarous usage of some servants by cruel masters bring so much scandal and infamy to the country in general, that people who would willingly adventure themselves hither, are through fear thereof diverted, and by that means the supplies of particular men and the well seating of his majesties country very much obstructed, Be it therefore enacted that every master shall provide for his servants competent diet, clothing and lodging, and that he shall not exceed the bounds of moderation in correcting them beyond the merit of their offences; and that it shall be lawful for any servant giving notice to their masters (having just cause of complaint against them) for harsh and bad usage, or else of want of diet or convenient necessaries

to repair to the next commissioner to make his or their complaint. . . .

Virginia statutes, 1660, in Hening, Statutes,
vol. 2, pp. 26, 117–18.

12

Authority without wisdom is like a heavy axe without an edge: fitter to bruise than polish. . . .

39

A prudent mother will not clothe her little child with a long and cumbersome garment; she easily foresees what events it is like to produce, at the best, but falls and bruises or perhaps somewhat worse. Much more will the allwise God proportion His dispensations according to the stature and strength of the person He bestows them on. Large endowments of honour, wealth, or a healthful body would quite overthrow some weak Christian; therefore God cuts their garments short to keep them in such a trim that they might run the ways of His commandment. . . .

77

God hath by his providence so ordered that no one country hath all commodities within itself, but what it wants another shall supply that so there may be a mutual commerce through the world. As it is with countries so it is with men, there was never yet any one man that had all excellences, let his parts natural and acquired, spiritual and moral be never so large, yet he stands in need of something which another man hath (perhaps meaner than himself) which shows us perfection is not below, as also that God will have us beholden one to another.

Anne Bradstreet, "Meditations Divine and Moral,"
ca. 1660, Works, pp. 274, 279, 291.

1. You shall inform yourself by the best ways and means you can of the state and condition of all Foreign Plantations, and by what commissions or authorities they are and have been governed and disposed of; and are to procure either from such persons as have any grants thereof from the Crown, or from the records themselves, the copies of all such commissions and grants, to be transcribed and registered in a book provided for that purpose. . . .

5. You are to apply yourselves to all prudential means for the rendering those dominions useful to England and England helpful to them, and for bringing the several Colonies and Plantations, within themselves, into a more certain civil and uniform of

government and for the better order and distributing of public justice among them. . . .

8. You are to take especial care and enquire into the strict execution of the late Act of Parliament entitled An Act for the encouragement and increasing of Shipping and Navigation. . . .

10. You are most especially to take and effectual care of the propagation of the Gospel in the several Foreign Plantations. . . . And you are to consider how such of the Natives or such as are purchased by you from other parts to be servants or slaves may be best invited to the Christian Faith, and be made capable of being baptised thereunto; it being the honor of our Crown and of the Protestant Religion that all persons in any of our Dominions should be taught the knowledge of God, and be made acquainted with the mysteries of Salvation. . . .

King Charles II's instructions to Council for Foreign Plantations, 1660, in Hart, ed., American History, *vol. 1, pp. 184–86.*

2. Twelve Strangers [*Quakers*] in that Country [*Massachusetts*] but free-born of this Nation [*England*], received twenty-three Whippings, the most them being with a Whip of three Cords, with Knots at the ends, and laid on with as much strength as they could be by the Arm of their Executioner, the stripes amounting to Three hundred and Twenty. . . .

5. Two beaten with Pitched Ropes, the blows amounting to an hundred thirty nine, by which one of them was brought near unto death, much of his body being beat like unto a jelly, and one of their own Doctors, a Member of the Church, who saw him, said, It would be a Miracle if ever he recovered, he expecting the flesh should rot off the bones; who afterwards was banished upon pain of death. . . .

9. Five kept fifteen days (in all) without food, and fifty eight days shut up close by the Jailor. . . .

10. One laid neck and heels in irons for sixteen hours.

11. One very deeply burnt in the right hand with the letter H, after he had been whipt with above thirty stripes. . . .

12. One chained the most part of twenty days to a Log of wood in an open prison in the Winter-time. . . .

Edward Burrough to King Charles II, 1660, in Hart, ed., American History, *vol. 1, pp. 484–85.*

For the increase of shipping and encouragement of the Navigation of this Nation, wherein under the good providence and protection of God the Wealth Safety and Strength of this Kingdom is so much concerned Be it Enacted . . . That . . . from thence forward no Goods or Commodities whatsoever shall be Imported into or Exported out of any Lands Islands Plantations or Territories to his Majesty belonging or in his possession or which may hereafter belong unto or be in the possession of His Majesty His Heirs and Successors in Asia Africa or America in any other Ship or Ships Vessel or Vessels whatsoever but in such Ships or Vessels as do truly and without fraud belong only to the people of England or Ireland Dominion of Wales or Town of Berwicke upon Tweede, or are of the built of, and belonging to any of the said Lands Islands Plantations or Territories as the Proprietors and right Owners thereof and whereof the Master and three fourths of the Mariners at least are English under the penalty of the Forfeiture and Loss of all the goods and commodities. . . .

English Navigation Act, December 1, 1660, in Macdonald, ed., Documentary Source Book, *p. 56.*

The Souther-side or roundhead of the town is bounded with the arm of the sea. . . . Nearest the Wester-side of this head is a plot of ground a little higher than the other ground: on which stands a windmill: and a Fort four square, 100 yards on each side, at each corner flanked out 26 yards. . . . In this fort is the Church, the governor's house, and houses for soldiers, ammunition, etc. . . . Within the town, in the midway between the N.W. corner and N.E. gate the ground has a small descent on each side much alike, and so continues through the town into the arm of the water on the Easter-side of the Town; by the help of this descent they have made a (canal) almost through the town, keyed It on both sides with timber and boards as far in as the three small bridges; and near the coming into the (canal) they have built two firm timber bridges with rails on each side; at low water the (canal) is dry; at high water boats come into it, passing under the two bridges, and go as far as the three small bridges. . . .

"Description of Ye Towne of Manadens [Manhatten]," 1661, in O'Callaghan, Documentary, *vol. 2, p. 59.*

The Schout and Schepens of the Court of Breuckelen respectfully represent that they found it necessary that a Court Messenger was required for the Schepens'

Chamber, to be occasionally employed in the Village of Breuckelen and all around where he may be needed, as well to serve summons, as also to conduct the service of the Church, and to sing on Sundays; to take charge of the School, dig graves, etc., ring the Bell, and perform whatever else may be required. . . .

Brooklyn records, 1661, in Hart, ed., American History, *vol. 1, p. 585.*

Herewith very respectfully declare Emanuel Pieterson, a free Negro, and Reytory, otherwise Dorothy, Angola, free Negro woman, together husband and wife, the very humble petitioners of your noble honors, that she, Reytory, in the year 1643, on the third of August, stood as godparent or witness at the Christian baptism of a little son of one Anthony van Angola, begotten with his own wife named Louise, the which aforementioned Anthony and Louise were both free Negroes; and about four weeks thereafter the aforementioned Louise came to depart this world, leaving behind the aforementioned little son named Anthony, the which child your petitioner out of Christian affection took to herself, and with the fruits of her hands' bitter toil she reared him as her own child, and up to the present supported him, taking all motherly solicitude and care for him, without aid of anyone in the world . . . your petitioners . . . very respectfully address themselves to you, noble and right honorable lords, humbly begging that your noble honors consent to grant . . . approval of the above-mentioned adoption and nurturing, on the part of your petitioner, in behalf of the aforementioned Anthony with the intent [of declaring] that he himself, being of free parents, reared and brought up without burden or expense of the Company, or of anyone else than your petitioner, in accordance therewith he may be declared by your noble honors to be a free person: this being done, [the document] was signed with the mark of Anthony Pieterson.

Petition to the Director General of New Netherlands, 1661, in Aptheker, ed., Negro People, *vol. 1, pp. 1–2.*

That part of Virginia . . . is divided into several Counties and those Counties contain in all about Fifty Parishes, the Families whereof are dispersedly and scatteringly seated upon the sides of Rivers; some of which running very far into the Country, bear the English Plantations above a hundred Miles, and being very broad, cause the Inhabitants of either side to be listed in several Parishes. Every such Parish is extended many Miles in length upon the River's side, and usually not

above a mile in Breadth backward from the River, which is the common stated breadth of every Plantation belonging to each particular Proprietor, of which Plantations, some extend themselves half a mile, some a mile, some two miles, some three miles, and upward upon the sides of those Rivers, many of them are parted from each other by small Rivers and creeks, which small Rivers and Creeks are seated after the manner of the great Rivers. The families of such Parishes being seated after this manner, at such distances from each other, many of them are very remote from the House of God, though placed in the midst of them. Many Parishes as yet want both Churches and Glebes, and I think not above a fifth part of them are supplied with Ministers . . . the more remote Families being discouraged, by the length or tediousness of the way, through extremities of heat in Summer, frost and Snow in Winter, and tempestuous weather in both, do very seldom repair thither.

"R.G." to the Bishop of London, September, 1661, in Hart, ed., American History, *vol. 1, p. 295.*

Then were brought near with trembling fear,
a number numberless,
Of blind Heathen, and brutish men
that did God's Law transgress . . .
Whose wicked ways Christ open lays,
and makes their sins appear,
They making plans their case to ease,
if not themselves to clear.
"Thy written Word," say they, "good Lord,
we never did enjoy;
We ne'er refus'd, nor it abus'd,
Oh, do not us destroy!"

The Reverend Michael Wigglesworth, "The Day of Doom," 1662, in Massachusetts Historical Society, *Proceedings, vol. 12, pp. 83–84.*

Negro women's children to serve according to the condition of the mother.

. . . . .

Whereas some doubts have arisen whether children got by any Englishman upon a negro woman should be slave or free, Be it therefore enacted and declared by this present grand assembly, that all children borne in this country shall be held bond or free only according to the condition of the mother, And that if any christian shall commit fornication with a negro man or woman, he or she so offending shall pay double the fines imposed by the former act.

. . . . .

Whereas diverse persons purchase women servants to work in the ground [*fields*] that thereby they may avoid the payment of levies, Be it henceforth enacted by the authority aforesaid that all women servants whose common employment is working in the crop shall be reputed tithable, and levies paid for them accordingly. . . .

Virginia statutes, 1662, in Hening, Statutes,
vol. 2, pp. 170.

Now Know ye, that . . . we . . . Do Ordain, Constitute and Declare That they, the said John Winthrop, . . . and all such others as now are or hereafter shall be Admitted and made free of the Company and Society of our Colony of Connecticut in America, shall . . . be one Body Corporate and Politic in fact and name, by the Name of Governor and Company of the English Colony of Connecticut in New England in America; . . And further, we . . . Do Declare . . . that for the better ordering and managing of the affaires and business of the said Company and their Successors, there shall be one Governor, one Deputy Governor and Twelve Assistants, to be from time to time Constituted, Elected and Chosen out of the Freemen of the said Company for the time being. . . .

Charter of Connecticut, May 3, 1662, in Macdonald, ed.,
Documentary Source Book, *p. 61.*

. . . no Commodity of the Growth Production or Manufacture of Europe shall be imported into any Land Island Plantation Colony Territory or Place to His Majesty belonging, or which shall [belong hereafter] unto, or be in the Possession of His Majesty . . . in Asia Africa or America (Tangier only excepted) but what shall be bona fide and without fraud laden and shipped in England Wales [and] the Town of Berwicke upon Tweede and in English built Shipping. . . .

Staple Act, 1663, in Macdonald, ed., Documentary
Source Book, *p. 75.*

My Fathers and Brethren, this is never to be forgotten, that New-England is originally a plantation of religion, not a plantation of trade.

Let merchants and such as are increasing Cent per Cent remember this, Let others that have come over

since at several times understand this, that worldly gain was not the end and design of the people of New England, but Religion. And if any man amongst us make religion at twelve, and the world at thirteen, let such an one know he hath neither the spirit of a true New-England man nor yet of a sincere Christian.

John Higginson's Election Day sermon, "The Cause of
God . . . in New England," 1663, quoted in Bailyn,
New England, *p. 140.*

And whereas, in their humble address, they have freely declared, that it is much on their hearts (if they may be permitted), to hold forth a lively experiment, that a most flourishing civil state may stand and best be maintained, and that among our English subjects, with a full liberty in religious concernments; and that true piety rightly grounded upon gospel principles, will give the best and greatest security to sovereignty, and will lay in the hearts of men the strongest obligations to true loyalty: Now know ye, . . . because some of the people and inhabitants of the same colony cannot, in their private opinions, conform to the public exercise of religion, according to the liturgy, forms and ceremonies of the Church of England, or take or subscribe the oaths and articles made and established in that behalf; and for that the same, by reason of the remote distances of those places, will (as we hope) be no breach of the unity and uniformity established in this nation: . . . do hereby . . . declare, That our royal will and pleasure is, that no person within the said colony, at any time hereafter, shall be any wise molested, punished, disquieted, or called in question, for any differences in opinion in matters of religion, and do not actually disturb the civil peace of our said colony; but that all and every person and persons may, from time to time, and at all times hereafter, freely and fully have and enjoy his and their own judgments and consciences, in matters of religious concernments, throughout the tract of land hereafter mentioned; they behaving themselves peaceable and quietly, and not using this liberty to licentiousness and profaneness, nor to the civil injury or outward disturbance of others. . . .

Rhode Island Charter, July 15, 1663, in Macdonald, ed.,
Documentary Source Book, *pp. 68–69.*

In this Province there are but few Towns, and those much scattered as generally they are all throughout New England, They are rather farms than Towns but in this Province there is a Bay called Casko Bay in which are very many Islands, 2 Outlets to the Sea, many good Harbors, and great store of fish and Oysters, Crabs and Lobsters, In this Province as in all the rest there are great store of wild Ducks Geese and Deer in their Seasons, Strawberries, Raspberries, Gooseberries, Barberries, and several sorts of Bilberries, Several sorts of Oakes and Pines, Chestnut Trees, and Walnut Trees, sometimes for 4 Or 5 Miles together, the more Northerly the Country is, the better the Timber is accounted.

On the North East side of Kenebeck River, which is the bounds of the Province of Maine, upon Shipscot River, and upon Pemaquid 8 or 10 miles Asunder are 3 small Plantations belonging to his Royal highness the biggest of which hath not about 30 houses in it, and those very mean ones too and spread over 8 Miles of ground at least. The People for the most part are fishermen, and never had any Government amongst them, and most of them are such as have fled thither from other places to avoid justice, Some here are of Opinion, that as many men may share in a Woman, as they do in a Boat, and some have done so.

English Commissioners' report on Maine, 1665, in Hart, ed., American History, *vol. 1, pp. 429–30.*

The Company will, once more, in good faith, plead ignorance of there having been an insufficient supply of provisions, since it cannot imagine that, in a country so productive as New Netherland, any scarcity should exist in a year of such abundance as that of 1664. . . . Stuyvesant says: That the scarcity of provisions was caused, among other things, by the arrival of the ship *Gideon* with between three and four hundred Negroes. Truly, also, a flimsy excuse. For besides the number not being so large, one-fourth of them had been delivered to the officer of the city's Colony on the South river [*New Sweden*], who took his departure with them for the South river three days after the arrival of the frigates, because he saw the shape things were taking in New Netherland and around the government; and the remainder were sold shortly after, so that he had not to provide for them. . . .

Michael Ten Hove, "Reply of the West India Company," 1666, in Hart, ed., American History, *vol. 1, pp. 537–39.*

We do hereby Grant unto all persons who have already Adventured to the Province of New Cesaria or New Jersey or shall transport themselves or Servants before the first day of January which shall be in the year of our Lord 1665. These following proportions viz. to every freeman that shall go with the first Governor from the Port when he embarks (or shall meet him at the Rendevous he appoints) for the Settlement of a Plantation there; armed with a good Musket boare twelve bullets to the Pound, with Ten pounds of powder and Twenty pound of Bullets, with bandoleers and match convenient, and with six months provision for his own person arriving there 150 acres of Land English measure. And for every able man Servant that he shall carry with him armed and provided as aforesaid and arriving there, the like quantity of 50 acres of land English measure, And whoever shall send Servants at that time shall for every able man Servant he or she so sends armed and provided as aforesaid and arriving there the like quantity of 150 acres And for every weaker Servant or Slave male or female exceeding the age of fourteen years which any one shall send or carry arriving there 75 acres of Land And to every Christian Servant exceeding the age aforesaid after the expiration of their time of service 75 acres of Land for their own use.

"Concessions and Agreements of the Proprietors of East Jersey," 1665, in Hart, ed., American History, *vol. 1, pp. 564–65.*

. . . from an ancient Custom at the primitive seating of the place, the Son works as well as the Servant, (an excellent cure for untamed Youth) so that before they eat their bread, they are commonly taught how to earn it; which makes them by that time Age speaks them capable of receiving that which their Parents indulgency is ready to give them, and which partly is by their own laborious industry purchased, they manage it with such a serious, grave, and watching care, as if they had been Masters of Families, trained up in that domestic and governing power from their Cradles. These Christian Natives of the Land, especially those of the Masculine Sex are generally conveniently confident, reservedly subtle, quick in apprehending, but slow in resolving; and where they spy profit sailing towards them with the wings of a prosperous gale, there they become much familiar. The Women differ something in this point, though not much. They are extreme bashful at the first view, but after a continuance of time hath brought them acquainted, there they become discreetly familiar, and are much more talkative than men. All Complemental Courtships, dressed up in critical Rarities, are mere strangers to them, plain wit comes nearest their Genius; so that he that intends to Court a Mary-Land Girl, must have something more than the Tautologies of a long-winded speech to carry on his design, or else he may (for aught I know) fall under the contempt of her frown, and his own windy Oration.

George Alsop, "A Character of the Province of Maryland,"
1666, in Hart, ed., American History,
vol. 1, pp. 270–71.

Whereas some doubts have risen whether children that are slaves by birth, and by the charity and piety of their owners made partakers of the blessed sacrament of baptism, should by virtue of their baptism be made free; It is enacted and declared by this grand assembly, and the authority thereof, that the conferring of baptism doth not alter the condition of the person as to his bondage or freedom; that diverse masters, freed from this doubt, may more carefully endeavor the propagation of christianity by permitting children, though slaves, or those of greater growth if capable to be admitted to that sacrament.

Virginia statute, 1667, in Hening, Statutes, *vol. 2, p. 260.*

1st. That none shall be admitted freemen or free Burgesses within our Town upon Passaick River in the Province of New Jersey, but such Planters as are members of some or other of the Congregational Churches nor shall any but such be chosen to Magistracy or to Carry on any part of Civil judicature, or as deputies or assistants, to have power to Vote In establishing Laws, and making or Repealing them or to any Chief Military Trust or Office. Nor shall any But such Church Members have any Vote in any such elections; Tho' all others admitted to Be planters have Right to their proper Inheritance, and do and shall enjoy all other Civil Liberties and Privileges . . . (Deut. 1.25; Exod. 18.31; Deut. 17.15; Jer 36.21)
*Item—.*the Town agreed, that any Man that would take Pains to kill Wolves, he or they for their Encouragement should have 15s. For every grown Wolf that they kill, and this to be paid by the Town Treasury.

Town meeting, Newark, New Jersey, 1668, in Hart, ed.,
American History, *vol. 1, pp. 566–67.*

Be it enacted and declared by this grand assembly, if any slave resist his master (or other by his master's order correcting him) and by the extremity of the correction should chance to die, that his death shall not be accompted felony, but the master (or that other person appointed by the master to punish him) be acquit from molestation, since it cannot be presumed that prepensed malice (which alone makes murder felony) should induce any man to destroy his own estate.

Virginia statute, 1669, in Hening, Statutes, *vol. 2, p. 270.*

Nine. There shall be just as many landgraves as there are counties, and twice as many caziques, and no more. These shall be the hereditary nobility of the province, and by right of their dignity be members of parliament. Each landscape shall have four baronies, and each cazique two baronies, hereditarily and unalterably annexed to and settled upon the said dignity. . . .
Twenty-two. In every signiory, barony, and manor, all the leet-men shall be under the jurisdiction of the respective lords of the said signiory, barony, or manor, without appeal from him. Nor shall any leet-man or leet-woman have liberty to go off from the land of their particular lord and live anywhere else, without license obtained from their said lord, under hand and seal.
Twenty-three. All the children of leet-men shall be leet-men, and so to all generations.

John Locke, "Fundamental Constitutions of Carolina,"
1669, Avalon Project, URL: yale.edu/lawweb/avalon.

Upon the meeting of the commission let a proclamation be made by saying, O yes, O yes, O yes, [Oyez] Silence is commanded in the court while his Majesty's Commission are sitting upon pain of imprisonment....

After this let a jury of twelve good men be empaneled.

Then let the Long Finn prisoner in the Fort be called for and brought to the bar.

Upon which the jury is to be called over and numbered one, two, and etc., and if the prisoner have no exception against either of them let them be sworn as directed in the Book of Laws for Trial of criminals, and bid to look upon the prisoner at the Bar. . . .

Then proceed with the indictment as follows:

John Binckson, you stand here indicted . . . for that having not the fear of God before thine eyes but being instigated by the devil . . . at Christina and at several other times and places before thou did most wickedly, traitorously, feloniously and maliciously conspire and attempt to invade by force of arms this government settled under the allegiance and protection of His Majesty and also did most traitorously solicit and entice diverse and threaten other of his Majesty's good subjects to betray their allegiance to his Majesty the King of England, persuading them to revolt and adhere to a foreign prince, that is to say, to the King of Sweden. . . . John Binckson and etc. what hast thou to say for thyself, Are you guilty of the felony and treason laid to the charge or not guilty? If he say not guilty, then ask him By who will he be tried. If he say by God and his country, say, God send you a good deliverance.

Then call the witnesses and let them be sworn either to their testimony already given in, or to which they will then declare upon their oaths.

Upon which the Jury is to have their charge given them directing them to find the matter of fact according to evidence and then let them be called over as they go out to consult upon their verdict in which they must all agree.

When the Jury returns to deliver in their verdict to the court let them be called over again and then asked: Gentlemen, are you agreed upon your verdict in this case in difference between our sovereign Lord the King and the prisoner at the Bar. Upon their saying yes, ask who shall speak for you. . . . Then read the verdict and say: Gentlemen, this is your verdict upon which you are all agreed; upon their saying yes, call that the prisoner be taken from the bar and secured.

English form for holding court, December 16th, 1669, in Brodhead, Documents, *vol. 12, pp. 467–72.*

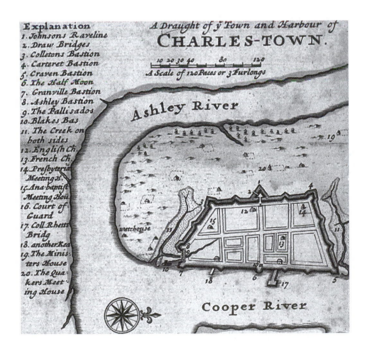

The fort at Charleston, detail of a map by Herman Moll, 1715 *(Library of Congress)*

The Lord foreseeing the defection of Israel after Moses his death, commands him to write that prophetical song recorded in Deuteronomy 32 as a testimony against them, wherein the chief remedy which he prescribes for the prevention and healing of their apostasy is their calling to remembrance God's great and signal love in manifesting himself to them in the wilderness, in conducting them safely and mercifully, and giving them possession of their promised inheritance (ver. 7–14). And when Israel was apostatized and fallen, the Lord, to convince them of their ingratitude and folly, brings to their remembrance his deliverance of them out of Egypt, his leading them through the wilderness for the space of forty years, and not only giving them possession of their enemies' land but also raising up even of their own sons, prophets . . . all of which were great and obliging mercies.

Samuel Danforth's Election Day address, "New England's Errand into the Wilderness," 1670, quoted in Bercovitch, American Jeremiad, *p. 15.*

What are all the contentions and wars of this world about, generally, but for greater dishes and bowls of porridge, of which, if we believe God's spirit in scripture, Esau and Jacob were types? . . . Besides Sir the matter with us is not about these children's toys of land, meadows, cattle, government, and etc. . . . the Most High and only wise hath in his infinite wisdom provided this country and this corner as a shelter for the poor and persecuted, according to their several persuasions. . . . Thus Sir, the King's Majesty . . . hath vouchsafed his royal promise under his hand and broad seal that no person in this Colony shall be molested or questioned for the matters of his conscience to God, so he be loyal and keep the civil peace. Sir, we must part with lands and lives before we part with such a jewel. . . .

I have offered . . . to discuss by disputation writing or printing . . . these three positions; first that forced worship stinks in God's nostrils. Second that it denies Christ Jesus yet to be come, and makes the church yet national, figurative and ceremonial. Third That in these flames about religion, as his Majesty his father and grandfather have yielded, there is no other prudent, Christian way of preserving peace in the world but by permission of differing consciences. . . .

Roger Williams to Major Mason, June 1670, Letters, *pp. 343–47.*

PART III

A DIVERSITY OF INTERESTS: 1670–1750

6

New France Expands and the Spanish Colonies Struggle
1670–1750

EUROPEAN POWERS REALIGN

In the second half of the 17th century, a century-long international struggle began in Europe, changing relationships among the colonial powers. Spain's influence declined, while King Louis XIV intrigued to make France the dominant power. Alliances shifted, and a long series of wars occurred. All of these conflicts arrived at the doorstep of the French, Spanish, and English colonies in North America. The colonies seized the occasions to do battle over local issues and control of trade. Their Indian allies and enemies usually participated in the hostilities as well, often to their own detriment. No matter what the colonists won or lost, however, final negotiations in Europe were governed by European considerations. In most cases, conquests in North America were canceled by treaty and the lands returned to their former European claimants.

NEW FRANCE: COMMERCE AND CONFLICT

For a hundred years under Louis XIV (ruled 1661–1715) and his great-grandson Louis XV (ruled 1715–74), the French Crown and ministers maintained the most centralized colonial administration and actively managed colonial policy of all the imperial powers. The system was first developed under the talented minister Jean-Baptiste Colbert (retired 1683). Colbert's office, called the Ministry of the Marine, oversaw both French finances and French colonies. Colbert, a devoted mercantilist, closely regulated the economic life of New France. He especially encouraged New France to export furs and to increase agricultural production, to supply food to slave-worked plantations in the French West Indies.

The fur trade flourished in New France after the Iroquois wars ended in the late 1660s. After 1670, however, the English began to compete with the French in the far north, establishing posts in Hudson's Bay under a charter from King Charles II of England. Colbert responded by encouraging expansion to the west. In 1673, Louis Joliet and Father Jacques Marquette explored the Great Lakes and upper Mississippi River. In 1682, René-Robert Cavelier de La Salle followed the Mississippi its entire length to the Gulf of Mexico. Claiming the whole Mississippi River valley for France, La Salle named it Louisiana in honor of the king. By the end of 1680s, a chain of small French posts had been founded along the Great Lakes and on the upper Mississippi and Illinois Rivers. The French also established posts in Hudson's Bay, where most remained all-male settlements dependent on imported supplies.

As the French moved west and north, they established many new Indian trading alliances. In response, tribes of the Iroquois Confederacy began attacking France's Indian allies in the western Great Lakes area, and in 1684 the Iroquois entered into a formal alliance with the English at Albany. In 1689, France and England declared war (the War of the League of Augsburg, called King William's War in the English colonies), giving the rival colonies themselves an opportunity for open conflict. With English assistance, Iroquois tribes attacked New France at Lachine (above Montreal), closing the entry to fur transport routes. Soon the attacks extended to farms near Montreal, where killing and destruction of building, crops, and livestock continued into the 1690s. In retaliation, in 1689 Governor Louis de Buade, comte de Frontenac, led the troops of New France and its Indian allies on raids of New York and New England towns and Onondaga and Oneida villages. Like the Iroquois, the French and Indians engaged in *petite guerre,* an Indian tactic of sudden, unexpected attack and destruction of undefended settlements, in which settlers were killed or taken captive. Successful French attacks on Newfoundland and on English forts in Hudson's Bay were led by Pierre le Moyne, sieur d'Iberville. In turn, the English captured Port Royal, Acadia, and planned but did not complete an attack on Quebec. In 1697, the Treaty of Ryswick returned France and England's prewar North American possessions. Nonetheless, the Iroquois made peace in 1701 with both the French and their allies, the so-called Western Tribes (some small Algonquian-speaking groups and Iroquoian-speaking groups not aligned with the Iroquois Confederacy). The Iroquois agreed to remain neutral in future contests between European colonists.

Hostilities did not severely interrupt the French fur trade. By 1696, the abundant supply of furs had caused a glut in the French market, and France attempted to close the trade by royal edict. Nonetheless, Minister of the Marine Louis de Pontchartrain decided to continue extending the French fur-trading frontier for political and strategic reasons. Military officers were assigned to western posts and given monopolies there. Pontchartrain established a crescent of forts stretching from the St. Lawrence River and Great Lakes down the Mississippi River to the Gulf of Mexico. This fortified crescent walled in the English to the east and the Spanish to the west while giving France control of interior waterways and an ice-free southern port.

To prevent incursions into the fur trade from the south and east, one fort Pontchartrain ordered constructed was on the waters connecting Lakes Huron and Erie. In 1701, Anthoine de la Mothe Cadillac founded the fortified town of Fort Pontchartrain du Detroit with 100 settlers and soldiers. (*Detroit* means "narrows.") Cadillac was made commandant, seigneur, and fur factor, or trader-monopolist. He convinced French allies among the Huron, Ottawa, and Potawatomi and numerous other groups to settle nearby. After the Fox arrived, intertribal rivalries erupted in a series of wars in the area. By 1750, Detroit had about 500 European or Métis (French-Indian) people, 33 Indian slaves, and about 75 small farms. In addition to fur trading, the settlers provisioned voyageurs.

In 1702, the War of Spanish Succession (called Queen Anne's War in the English colonies) led to renewed hostilities in New France and New England. Governor-General Philippe de Vaudreuil again authorized petite guerre; the most destructive attack occurred at Deerfield, Massachusetts, in 1703. The French also attacked Newfoundland; the English recaptured Acadia in 1710. In 1711, the English mounted a sea-and-land attack on Quebec but abandoned it when the war fleet was shipwrecked. In 1713, the Treaty of Utrecht acknowledged the English claim to Acadia (renamed Nova Scotia), Newfoundland, and Hudson's Bay. France received Île St-Jean (modern Prince Edward Island) and Île Royale (Cape Breton Island).

By the second decade of the 18th century, the fur glut had ended in France; demand revived and trade once again flourished. After 1681, when officials began issuing trading permits called *congés,* licensed western traders called *voyageurs* had increasingly replaced individual coureurs de bois. Now, large, eight-man canoes were built. Although the independence and endurance of voyageurs became legendary, most were actually employees of fur-trade companies. Especially after 1720, many married and established families with Native American women in the west. Their children became the distinct Métis people, combining both French and Indian cultures.

For 30 years after the Treaty of Utrecht, New France enjoyed relative peace. At the entryway to the St. Lawrence, the fortress and naval base of Louisbourg was constructed. Begun in 1720 and built over two decades, the massive fort enclosed 55 acres. By 1740, Louisbourg's population had grown to 5,000 and it was a busy fishing and shipping port in the triangular trade with the West Indies.

A typical "habitant house," built by French settlers at Cahokia, Illinois, 1737 *(Historic American Building Survey)*

Despite commercial rivalry with its English neighbors, Louisbourg also engaged in trade with New England. In 1740, war broke out again in Europe (the War of the Austrian Succession, called King George's War in the English colonies), with France and England on opposing sides. In 1745, New England forces sailed from Boston to attack Louisbourg. The fort was forced to surrender but was returned to France two years later by the Treaty of Aix-la-Chapelle. In 1749, New France laid claim to the Ohio River valley in response to the formation of an English enterprise called the Ohio Land Company.

Government and Society in New France

After New France became a royal colony in 1663, control over major decisions resided in Paris. Authority proceeded from the king down, and the officials of New France were accountable for their actions to the Crown, not to the people of New France. In North America, the king's representative was the governor-general, usually a noble and a military officer, who conducted both diplomatic relations and war. Administration of the colony was in the hands of the intendant, usually a minor noble, who oversaw public order, justice, and the colony's finances. Disputes between the two officials often disrupted colonial government prior to 1700. Over time, the Crown slowly restricted the arbitrary power of the governor general and increased the relative power of the intendant. Beneath the two were local governors or mayors, deputy intendants, and many lesser officials. All were appointed rather than elected, and all were on the royal payroll. In outlying districts, militias were organized under an appointed captain, an unpaid but prestigious position similar to the English colonies' justice of the peace. In addition, a regular military bureaucracy developed in New France. By 1750, waiting lists existed of well-born young men seeking appointments as officers in the regular Canadian Troupes de la Marine.

The colony's main governing body was the Sovereign Council (Conseil souverain), established by royal edict in 1663. It was composed of the governor, intendant, bishop, attorney-general, a clerk, and five appointed councilors. Although the colony operated under the body of French civil and criminal law called the Custom of Paris, the council enacted royal edicts, passed regulations of local concern, and also served as a court. In 1703, the number of councilors was increased to 12 and the group was renamed the Superior Council (Conseil supérieur). By 1750, the council's primary role was to act as a superior court; local law was written by the intendant. Local courts had also been established in Quebec, Trois-Rivières, and Montreal to hear cases and enact municipal regulations. The French legal system, however, was not adversarial like that of the English colonies; it was inquisitorial. Private lawyers were forbidden to practice in the colony; colonists represented themselves. Juries did not exist. Judges interrogated plaintiffs, defendants, and witnesses, on occasion using torture to extract information, then rendered a verdict. Several times in the early 18th century, the king sent instructions to New France that justice was to be rendered to all his subjects, regardless of status or wealth. The lack of impartial justice, however, was a recurring complaint in the colony. Officials had particular difficulty deciding how to treat Indians who became embroiled in criminal matters. As early as May 1679, the king decreed that any colonist who provided liquor to Indians would be held responsible for any illegal act subsequently committed. Usually, however, Indian crimes were treated as diplomatic issues.

Representative government and local control did not exist in New France as it did in the English colonies. Citizens were forbidden to assemble on their own to discuss public issues or to circulate petitions, although individuals were permitted to petition the Crown. Some consultative processes did exist. An institution called the public assembly was developed by officials and formalized in 1706 by order of the king. Public assemblies could be convened by officials only, to explain important issues or pending legislation to the citizens. All could speak on such occasions, and official records were kept of the opinions expressed. In outlying areas, the captains of the militia were expected to know and convey local opinion. After reviewing opinions the governor and intendant retained authority to render a decision. Chambers of commerce were established in Quebec in 1708 and in Montreal in 1717. Their function was to consult with officials on trade and economic issues. Despite the lack of self-government, there is little evidence of political discontent in New France comparable to that of the English colonies during the same period. Except for import-export duties, however, citizens of New France were not regularly taxed by the government.

The Catholic bishop of New France had considerable influence in the life of the colony. He wielded power over social and intellectual matters as well as any civil issue that he believed to affect morality. Particularly under the dominant personality of François de Montmorency Laval, bishop of Quebec (retired 1688), many conflicts occurred between church and civil authorities, as well as with the Jesuits. The relative importance of missions gradually declined due to continuing Indian hostility, and colonists themselves became the focus of ecclesiastical authorities. By 1750, ecclesiastical influence on civil matters had been reduced. Religious orthodoxy was strictly enforced, however, and New France remained a Catholic society. Protestant immigration, marriages, and religious ceremonies of any kind were forbidden, although a few Protestant residents were tolerated.

Few emigrants arrived after 1672. As a consequence, population growth was due almost entirely to natural increase. The population of New France increased from 10,000 in 1670 to 15,000 by 1700, and to more than 60,000 by 1760. The Crown used monetary rewards to encourage early marriages and large families. By the mid-18th century, the vast majority of New France's citizens were native-born and thought of themselves as *canadiens,* not French. European visitors to the colony also remarked on the distinct *canadien* culture. By 1750 three-quarters of the population was rural, although Quebec had grown to 8,000 people and Montreal to more than 4,000. Seigneuries stretching between the two cities were filled in with long, strip-shaped farms fronting the river; a second row was developing behind them.

Society in New France was very hierarchical. By 1750 a *canadien* aristocracy had developed. Government and military officials, a few wealthy merchants, and church officials of high birth formed an elite with close connections to Europe. Advancement in political influence and social status, and perhaps the attainment of a title for those who lacked one, depended on obtaining a position in the government or military bureaucracy. Titled residents of New France, unlike their European counterparts, had the Crown's permission to engage in trade and commerce, and many did. Unlike English colonial merchants, however, who usually reinvested much of their wealth and continued expanding, both nobles and ambitious commoners in New France usually spent their wealth to support an aristocratic lifestyle. Seigneuries were sought to enhance prestige more than wealth, which they rarely produced. In 1711, the Crown required seigneurs to give up vacant, unsettled land. Much of it was given to the church, which by the mid-18th century was landlord to more than one-third of the population. Education in New France was generally restricted to the elite, and the majority of the population remained illiterate in 1750. The colony had no printing press and little indigenous literature, although the elite supported arts like portrait painting and silver smithing.

Most domestic servants in New France were born there; the colony used indentured servitude to support orphans and the poor. Slavery was accepted in New France, although slaves were much less numerous than in the English Chesapeake colonies. Few were purchased for agricultural work; most did domestic work. Most black slaves arrived from the French Indies; however, many *canadiens* preferred Indian slaves, called *panis* (from *Pawnee,* although they came from many different tribes). In 1709, slavery was recognized by an official decree, and in 1736 all manumissions were required to be registered with the government. In 1734, Marie-Joseph Angelique, the black slave of a Montreal merchant, attempted to escape by setting a fire; it spread to almost 50 buildings, including the hospital. Marie-Joseph was captured, tortured, hanged, and burned.

The French Settle Louisiana

René-Robert Cavelier de La Salle, trained as a Jesuit but released from his vows, reached the mouth of the Mississippi River on April 6, 1682. The territory he claimed for France, like most European claims, had generous and indistinct boundaries. "Louisiana" encompassed all land drained by the Mississippi and its tributaries. It extended north to New France, east to the Appalachian Mountains, and west to the northern boundary of New Spain and the Rocky Mountains. Despite the territory's size, when La Salle returned by sea in January 1685 to found a colony at the mouth of the Mississippi, he missed his intended destination by some 400 miles and landed in Spanish territory. At Matagora Bay in modern Texas, his group of soldiers and families founded Fort St. Louis. Two years later, in March 1687, La Salle's own men murdered him. In 1689, the Spanish located the ruins of the fort and took the survivors, who were living with nearby Indians, to Mexico.

Despite La Salle's disaster, French officials continued to support the idea of a Louisiana colony to compete with the Spanish and English and to provide a port on the Gulf of Mexico. Support grew after the 1697 publication of *La Salle's Last Discoveries in America* by Henri de Tonti, a colorful trader who had accompanied the first expedition. Soon the English were rumored to be planning a settlement as well. In 1698 the *canadien* Pierre Le Moyne d'Iberville was chosen to found a royally supported military outpost in Louisiana. He sailed with his 18-year-old brother, Jean-Baptiste Le Moyne, sieur de Bienville; and 300 men, including Father Anatastase Douay, an explorer who spoke several Indian dialects. In January 1699, Iberville reached Pensacola—already claimed by the Spanish—and sailed on to explore Mobile Bay and the mouth of the Mississippi, meeting the Houma and Bayogoula Indians. He then ordered the construction of Fort Maurepas near modern Biloxi, Mississippi, and, in 1702, Fort St. Louis de la Mobile (in modern Alabama). Meanwhile, Bienville explored the Mississippi, where he encountered an English ship scouting a settlement site. The French turned the

English away and planted a small fort about 50 miles above the mouth of the river. Soon, Henri de Tonti arrived with fur cargoes, having successfully transported them from New France.

When Iberville died in France in 1706, Bienville became the commandant, or head, of the struggling Louisiana settlements. The soldier-colonists found the heat oppressive, the mosquitoes fierce, the alligators frightening, and the soil resistant to their grudging efforts to grow crops. The Spanish, the English, and their southern Indian allies were all hostile. The Jesuit missionaries met with little success. Bienville quarreled constantly with the commissary, or business manager, who had been sent from France, weakening official authority. France, distracted by the War of the Spanish Succession, did not send adequate provisions or funds. Tropical diseases and food shortages wracked the settlers.

Female immigrants remained difficult to recruit. The French believed that marriage encouraged settlers to take up farming, and in 1704 the bishop of Quebec sent 23 chaperoned young Canadian women to the Mobile settlement. Called Pelican girls after the ship in which they arrived, they were accompanied by Canadian families, two nuns, a midwife, and male settlers. Baptismal records indicate, however, that many children were born to French men and Indian women.

In 1712, displeased with the failure of the colony to support itself, the French Crown made Louisiana a proprietary colony. About 300 colonists resided in the Gulf settlements at the time, the majority in modern Mississippi. Louisiana's first proprietor was Antoine Crozat. His royal charter granted him military support, land, commercial control, a trade monopoly, and the sole right to import African slaves; in return, he was required to send colonists yearly.

Crozat removed Bienville and other officials. In May 1713, Anthoine de la Mothe Cadillac arrived from Detroit as the new governor, with his wife and 12 young women whom she chaperoned. Cadillac created a Superior Council to serve as an advisory body and a court. He instituted a legal code based on the Custom of Paris. He encouraged agriculture and sent the intrepid Quebec-born trader Louis Juchereau de Saint-Denis to New Spain, hoping to establish trade there. Saint-Denis also established a small garrison at Natchitoches in 1714, the first permanent settlement in the modern state of Louisiana. Official quarreling continued, however, especially between Cadillac and Bienville, who remained the military commandant.

Crozat's proprietary venture came to naught. He did not compete successfully for the Indian fur trade with the English, who offered better trade goods and higher prices. He did not establish legal trade with New Spain (although much illicit trading occurred). Although he offered free passage to settlers and more than 7,000 arrived during Cadillac's governorship, well over half died. In 1717, Crozat asked the Crown to release him from the proprietorship. The charter was transferred to Scotsman and French subject John Law. Law had accumulated a fortune in banking and business and had organized the Bank of France in 1716. Using the resources of the bank, he created a joint-stock company, the Company of the Indies, to fund the Louisiana venture.

Law promoted Louisiana throughout Western Europe, offering *concessions* (large grants to company directors and nobles, some of whom sent settlers) and *habitations* (farm-size grants). Law reappointed Bienville governor and in 1718 gave him permission to construct a town near the mouth of the Mississippi.

Bienville named the site New Orleans for the duc d'Orleans, regent of the young king of France, Louis XV. He immediately put 75 men, mostly slaves and prisoners, to work clearing and draining the land. The site was low and marshy; in the first three years it was regularly damaged by floods, storms, and seeping water. In 1721, a royal engineer, Adrien de Pauger, arrived and began a system of dikes and levees. Pauger also drew a city plan, composed of squares—11 arranged east to west and six north to south, for a total of 66 squares. (It became the present-day Vieux Carré or French Quarter). By 1721, New Orleans had 470 residents, including 172 black slaves, 21 Indian slaves, and 38 white indentured servants. It was made capital of the Louisiana colony and quickly became its most important commercial center.

In 1717, Law began shipping male and female convicts and their families to the colony, as well as orphans and the indigent; in 1720, the colony, displeased with its new residents, passed a law prohibiting further importation of criminals. Most immigrants who arrived, however, were farmers or craftsmen. Although the seasoning year was difficult, by 1721 the population had grown to about 5,000. In that year Law began sponsoring German-speaking emigrants from the Rhineland and Palatinate, many of whom were also arriving in English Pennsylvania at the time. More than 2,000 came to the Louisiana colony during the decade. Most settled in areas north of New Orleans, where they established successful farms and grew most of the city's food. German immigration continued throughout the first half of the 18th century.

In 1719, the Company of the Indies began large-scale importation of slaves to clear fields for rice, indigo, and sugar plantations. Many slaves arrived from Senegambia, sought for their rice-growing skills; others were brought from St-Domingue (present-day Haiti) for their experience with sugar agriculture. In 1724, the first Black Code, or Code Noir, was formulated. Adapted from the Code Noir of the French island colonies, it decreed that of children would be slave or free depending on the status of their mother. It also prohibited marriage between races and forbade slaves to own property, testify in court, or meet in groups. It required slaves to be instructed and married in the Catholic faith and encouraged the preservation of slave families (spouses and children under 14 were not to be sold separately). The Code Noir also expelled Jews from the colony.

Law's aggressive promotion of Louisiana in Europe had created extensive speculative investment in the venture. In the early 1720s, his bank failed; company stock became worthless; and the Mississippi Bubble, as it was called, burst. John Law fled France. The French government reorganized the Company of the Indies, appointed a commission to oversee it, and provided a partial subsidy. Bienville was again appointed governor and again quarreled with the new commissary, Jacques de la Chaise. Colonists began taking sides; the military and older families supported the governor and the merchants supported la Chaise. In 1724, Bienville and all his family members were removed from office. Etienne de Périer was appointed governor, with particular instructions to end official feuding in Louisiana.

Under Périer, the colony grew and developed. In 1725, the Capuchins founded the colony's first school for boys. In 1727, Ursuline nuns arrived. Provided with land and slaves, they took over the hospital and founded a school for girls. The Ursulines also had limited success establishing silk production, the undying colonial dream. In 1727, *filles à la cassette,* or casket girls, began arriving. (The *cassette,* translated casket, was a small piece of luggage containing clothing provided by the company.) Like the *filles du roi* of New France, they were sent to establish French colonial families. Soldiers who married them were discharged from the military and given land, a rifle, and a cow.

As the colony grew, Indian relations deteriorated. In 1716, Fort Rosalie had been built in Natchez territory (near modern Natchez, Mississippi) to enable the French to compete with the English for Indian trade. In 1729, the military commandant at the fort confiscated cultivated Indian lands nearby for use by the 450 white settlers and 200 black slaves on nearby rice, indigo, and tobacco plantations. In November, as was customary, Natchez came to the fort for seasonal employment as game hunters and were provided with weapons and ammunition. Without warning, they immediately attacked; they massacred nearly 300 people, destroyed the fort, and made captives of many slaves, women, and children. The French, allying with the Choctaw and smaller tribes, pursued the Natchez, devastating them. Some 500 were sold into slavery in the Caribbean, and the remnants joined the English-allied Chickasaw, although they maintained their own culture.

As a result of the hostilities, the Louisiana economy was disrupted, refugees crowded into New Orleans—and officials again quarreled. In January 1731, the Company of the Indies surrendered its charter. For the next 31 years, Louisiana was governed as a royal colony under direct control of the French king and his ministers. In 1733, Bienville was returned to the colony as governor once again. He reestablished public order in New Orleans, ordered refugees back to their farms, and rebuilt the military. In 1736, Bienville assembled a force to attack the Chickasaw and Natchez remnant. It included a separate company of 270 free and enslaved blacks, with black officers, whom the French recruited partially to prevent an Indian-black alliance. Bienville's troops, however, were ambushed and forced to retreat. In 1739, with extensive support from the French government, he again led 1,000 French soldiers, 300 blacks, colonials, and Indian allies against the Chickasaw. Although neither side was victorious, the Chickasaw agreed to a treaty in 1740. The destruction and losses incurred during the Chickasaw Wars, however, weighed heavily on Bienville. In May 1743, having begged for retirement, he was replaced by Pierre de Rigaud, marquis de Vaudreuil-Cavagnal, the son of the former governor of New France.

Vaudreuil brought stability to the colony of 3,000 white settlers, 800 soldiers, and some 4,000 slaves. Personally sophisticated and popular, he introduced court-like ceremony to government and society in New Orleans; some historians credit him with introducing Mardi Gras festivities. Vaudreuil reconciled colonial political factions. However, he was less successful at improving the economy, in part because English cemented a trade alliance with Indians on the Louisiana colony's eastern border. In 1748, the Chickasaw again began raiding and attacking settlers in outlying areas.

After 1721, Louisiana usually had a royal engineer or architect in residence. In the 1740s, Ignace-François Broutin revamped New Orleans. Stonemasons and woodcarvers embellished the buildings and began the tradition of elaborate cemetery memorials. In the city of New Orleans, musical events and dancing were popular, with taverns and gambling establishments already the subject of regulation by the 1740s. In outlying settlements, social life revolved around holy days and celebrations like weddings. As was the case in New France before 1750, education in Louisiana was restricted to the elite; the majority of the colonists were illiterate.

SPANISH POWER DECLINES

After 1670, Spain, led by the periodically deranged King Charles II until 1700, suffered political and economic decline. Spain was unable to supply its colonies adequately. Nonetheless, its ministers clung to mercantilism, discouraging manufacturing in the colonies and restricting trade to Spanish goods, Spanish ships, Spanish merchants, and a tiny number of Spanish ports. St. Augustine and later Pensacola were legal ports but none existed farther west on the Gulf coast. Goods sent to or from New Mexico had to be carried overland from Veracruz and guarded by a military escort. This policy greatly increased the cost of Spanish goods to colonists; as a consequence, well over half of trade was conducted illicitly with the French and English. Both the French and the English also traded more successfully with the Indians than did the Spanish, and both slowly chipped away at Spain's territorial claims. By the early 18th century, Spain, under King Philip V, thought of its North American settlements only as buffer colonies. Florida protected Spain's more valuable West Indian possessions, while New Mexico protected the rich silver mines of northern Mexico.

The Pueblo Revolt in New Mexico

At the opening of the 1670s, New Mexico was marked by hardship and conflict. Among the 2,900 Spanish, the struggle for power continued between the clergy and the civil authorities. Among the 17,000 Pueblo, restiveness grew over the religious and cultural impositions of the Spanish. From 1667 to 1672, a severe drought brought famine to both groups. In 1672, the Apache began a series of raids and attacks. Despite these conditions, Spanish demands for Indian labor continued. As conditions worsened, many Pueblo resumed or increased their traditional religious practices. The Spanish clergy, frustrated with their converts, asked the civil authorities to intervene. In 1675, Governor Juan Francisco de Treviño arrested 47 Pueblo medicine men for sorcery and witchcraft. Some were hanged; others were finally released at the request of a Tewa delegation united from several pueblos.

After release from Spanish custody, a San Juan Pueblo medicine man named Popé moved to Taos, the pueblo most distant from Santa Fe. There Popé and other leaders planned a unified offensive against the Spanish. Although the Pueblo had no tradition of united political action, most agreed to join. Popé sent runners over 200 miles to more than 25 pueblos, carrying knotted yucca cords to use as calendars. Each day one knot was untied and the residents of all the pueblos knew how many days remained until August 11, 1680. On August 9, however, two of the runners were captured by the Spanish, and secrecy was breached. The Pueblo sent messengers from village to village, and the uprising began at once on August 10.

Settlers in the Río Abajo (downriver from Santa Fe) evacuated to El Paso, where a small mission had been founded in 1659 among the Manso Indians south of the Rio Grande. The Río Arriba area (upriver) suffered far worse loss of life and destruction. By August 16, Governor Antonio de Otermín and some 1,000 Spanish huddled inside the walls of Santa Fe, surrounded and short of water. On August 19, Spanish soldiers surprised the Indians into temporary retreat. On August 20, Santa Fe refugees abandoned the city and headed south. The Pueblo watched from the hilltops but did not attack. New Mexico had become the only European colony ever reconquered by the Indians.

The Santa Fe survivors eventually reached El Paso. More than 400 settlers had been killed, including 21 of the 33 priests. A muster at El Paso counted 1,946 remaining. About 500 continued to Mexico, contrary to official orders. The others remained at El Paso for 12 years, during which time the Indian revolt spread to tribes and missions in northern Mexico. The New Mexicans established a temporary government but remained as fractious as ever. There were shortages of food and clothing and a particular shortage of labor, since no Indians could be requisitioned to perform it. During the 1680s, the New Mexicans made three unsuccessful attempts to recapture Santa Fe.

Meanwhile, the Pueblo reoccupied Santa Fe and Santo Domingo, destroying reminders of Spanish authority. Houses and churches were sacked and burned. Documents and religious objects were destroyed. Despite the hopes of Indian leaders, however, a complete return to traditional ways was not possible after 80 years of Spanish rule. The Apache and Navajo continued to attack, and harvests were poor. As the 1680s passed, Pueblo unity gave way to division.

The Reconquest of New Mexico

By 1690, the reconquest of New Mexico had become important to Spain. France had claimed the Mississippi River valley, and the English were encroaching on Florida. Officials appointed Don Diego de Vargas, a capable and intrepid nobleman, as governor and captain general. Vargas arrived in El Paso in February 1691. The settlers pleaded to be permitted to move south into Mexico. Instead, in fall 1692, Vargas led 60 Spanish soldiers and 100 Indian allies back into New Mexico. His seemingly quixotic plan was to repossess each pueblo peacefully by announcing that he had come to pardon the Indians and accept their return to the Catholic faith. Amazingly, his plan succeeded. Twenty-three pueblos pledged anew their allegiance to Spain, and mass baptisms followed. Vargas's success was celebrated jubilantly in Mexico City.

In October 1693, Vargas led 70 Spanish families, 18 clergymen, plus soldiers, Indian allies, and 4,000 head of livestock on a tortuous journey back to New Mexico. At Santa Fe, resident Pueblo renounced their agreement with Vargas and resisted reoccupation of the city. Vargas and Indians of Pecos Pueblo took the city by force, executing 70 Pueblo and enslaving the 400 who surrendered. Indians of many other pueblos also renounced the peace agreement; within a year, however, Vargas and his soldiers had subdued the colony.

After the *reconquista,* or reconquest, relations between the Indians and the Spanish were different than they had been before the Pueblo Revolt. *Encomiendas* were not reestablished. Settlers received land grants for small *ranchos,* or farmsteads, not the large *estancias* of the pre-revolt era. The Spanish continued to purchase Indian slaves from the nomadic tribes, but the Pueblo themselves were not again forced to labor for individuals. The clergy ceased attempting to eradicate all native religious practices. The Spanish recognized formal Indian title to their lands. Nonetheless, in 1694 the Indians of Jemez killed their priests and permanently relocated among the independent Hopi and Navajo. In 1696, another uprising, called the Second Pueblo Revolt, resulted in the death of six priests, but it was the last major revolt against the Spanish in New Mexico.

For many years, life in New Mexico remained difficult. Food shortages continued, and the clergy complained about colonists' treatment of the Indians. The governor and the cabildo (council) quarreled, and Vargas was imprisoned for three years. Nonetheless, Vargas established new towns in 1695 to reinforce Spanish occupation, at Cañada (north of Santa Fe) and at Bernalillo. In 1706, Governor Francisco de Cuervo y Valdés founded the town of Albuquerque, named for the duke of Albuquerque, viceroy of New Spain. It was the fourth official *villa* (incorporated town) of the colony; by 1720 it was the most populous. Albuquerque homesteads were spread out, contrary to the official Spanish pattern of compact settlement. After the church was constructed in 1720, however, some settlers built small second homes within the villa. Settlers raised sheep and wove woolen blankets and stockings, sending them along with piñon nuts to Mexico in the trading convoy that formed each fall.

Much to the displeasure of the Spanish Crown, French traders finally reached Santa Fe in 1739. Both the Spanish settlers and the Indians welcomed them, anxious to obtain their goods, and the governor requested legalization of the trade. The request was denied by Spanish officials, but trade proved so profitable to the French that it continued illicitly. The period was also marked by the arrival of the Comanche, who occasionally raided the pueblos and the Spanish settlements for captives and livestock.

By 1740, some 40 priests resided in New Mexico, and by 1752 more than 3,000 settlers of Spanish or multiethnic descent lived there. The Pueblo Indian population remained at about 10,000, one-quarter of what it had been before the Spanish arrived. By the mid-18th century, several folk arts and traditions had become well established. In September 1712, an annual fiesta began to honor Vargas's *reconquista*. Folk dramas reminiscent of medieval morality plays were frequently performed. During the Christmas season, for example, Las Posadas (the search of Mary and Joseph for housing) was reenacted by processions. Folk crafts also developed, notably woodworking and the carving of *santos,* or saints.

The Spanish Enter Arizona

In the late 17th century, the unrest among Indians in northern Mexico and the Southwest spurred Spanish authorities to fund additional missionary activity to secure the frontier. Jesuits were sent to La Pimería Alta (Land of the Upper Pima), or modern southern Arizona and northern Sonora province of Mexico. The Akimel O'odham (Pima) inhabitants of the region were a primarily sedentary and peaceable group, although the Spanish disliked and distrusted them. Jesuits in the area acted as diplomats as well as explorers and cartographers. The most influential was Father Eusebio Francisco Kino (born Chini in Italy), assigned to Pimería Alta in 1687. During his 40 years there, he began 24 missions and made 40 tours. In 1701, Father Kino established the first missions in modern Arizona—San Gabriel de Guevavi and San Xavier del Bac, the latter near present-day Tucson. Using constant diplomacy, he also maintained relative peace between the Akimel O'odham and the Apache, who roamed and sometimes raided in the Pimería Alta. Father Kino also drew a map of the Southwest that was used for two centuries and showed that California was not an island, as the Spanish had previously believed.

Father Kino died in 1711. Without his forceful personality, missions did not thrive in the Pimería Alta, although other Jesuits continued them. In the late 1720s, official Spanish interest in the area revitalized due to continuing incursions of Plains Indians and increasing worries that they had made French alliances. In 1730, the crown funded three new missions to the Indians. Church records indicate that some Spanish settlers had also moved into the area, although no formal villa was founded. In 1736, the discovery of silver southwest of Guevavi sparked a brief mining rush. Before the mines were closed by the Spanish government in 1741, thousands of Spanish had arrived. Some remained after the rush ended, and the mining camp, called Arizonac, gave the area its name.

Spanish Settlement in Texas

In the late 17th century, the occupation of Texas also became important to Spain. For more than a century, Spain had claimed the entire Gulf coast between Florida and Mexico. After La Salle's ill-fated colony at Matagora Bay, the Spanish decided to establish a presence in the Kingdom of Tejas, as they called East Texas. It was home to Caddo-speaking Indians, politically organized into three confederacies. In 1690, a small group of Franciscan missionaries and soldiers were sent to the Hasinai Confederacy in Tejas (*tejas* or *taychas* was the Hasinai Confederacy word for "ally" or "friend"). A mission was also established at San Antonio to serve as a way station on the route from Mexico. The Hasinai were prosperous, sophisticated, and relatively sedentary agriculturalists; they did not live in villages, however, but in scattered housing near their fields, making missionary work difficult. All the East Texas missions were abandoned in 1693.

In the second decade of the 18th century, Spanish interest in East Texas reawakened as French traders increasingly penetrated the plains. In July 1714, Louisiana trader Louis Saint-Denis reached the frontier presidio (fort or garrison) of San Juan Bautista, south of the Rio Grande, hoping to formally establish French trade with New Spain. Saint-Denis was put under house arrest while officials planned to reoccupy East Texas. In April 1716, some 75 people—soldiers, together with families, Franciscans, and Indian guides—assembled at the presidio. The versatile Saint-Denis—having married the granddaughter of the presidio's captain and become a Spanish subject—joined the group as an official. The soldiers advanced as far as Natchitoches, the westernmost French trading post. Immediately to the west of Natchitoches, the missionaries and settlers established new communities among the Caddo, building four small wooden churches and a presidio. Soon, officials in New Spain appointed Martín de Alarcón governor of Texas and instructed him to reestablish a way station on the San Antonio River. In 1718, the presidio San Antonio de Béxar, the mission San Antonio de Valero, and the civilian settlement Villa de Béxar were founded with 10 families.

In 1719, San Antonio's population increased when the East Texas colonists arrived, having been driven from their settlement by the Louisiana French in what is known as the Chicken War. (Settlers escaped when their chickens distracted the French.) In 1721 a Spanish-born nobleman, Marqués de Aguayo, personally financed and led an expedition to recapture East Texas. He established

Chapel at Mission San Jose y San Miguel, San Antonio, Texas, built 1720–21 *(Photo by Jet Lowe for Historic American Building Survey)*

three new presidios there, including Los Adaes, close to Natchitoches, and soon named the capital of the Texas province. En route, Aguayo delivered large herds of horses, cattle, and sheep to San Antonio, thus beginning ranching in Texas. Texas settlements did not thrive, however, and did not attract a large number of settlers, remaining dependent on illicit trade with the nearby French. Most Caddo resisted conversion. The one exception was at San Antonio, where five missions existed by 1731. That year, a small group of Spanish arrived from Tenerife, Canary Islands—farmers and fishermen who had been designated *hidalgos,* or gentlemen, for their willingness to emigrate. A municipal government was formed, but for some years it was marked by clashes between older San Antonians and the new arrivals. In 1738, San Antonians began building the Cathedral of San Fernando. By 1750, the total population of *tejanos*—those of Spanish descent—numbered about 500, and the missions counted about 1,000 Indian residents.

The Spanish Found Pensacola

After 1685 the Spanish sent 11 expeditions to search for La Salle's ill-fated French colony before locating its ruins in 1689. In the process, they rediscovered Pensacola Bay and its excellent harbor, the site of a failed attempt at Spanish settlement in the 16th century. In 1698, upon learning that the French were sending Pierre le Moyne d'Iberville and colonists to the Gulf of Mexico, they occupied the bay with troops from Havana. In November, Governor Andrés de Arriola arrived from Veracruz with 350 people, including an Austrian military engineer, and constructed a fort overlooking the harbor entrance. Many of the settlers had been conscripted from Mexican prisons and proved unsatisfactory colonists. Nonetheless, in January 1699 the Spanish successfully refused the French entrance to the harbor; the French continued on to Biloxi.

Luckily for the Pensacola settlement, relations with the Louisiana French remained good. For two decades, the Spanish relied on them for food, unable to grow their own. The French also helped the Spanish defend the fort from English and Indian attack during the War of the Spanish Succession. In 1719, however, during the War of the Quadruple Alliance, French soldiers attacked Pensacola. They transported its residents to Havana, where the Spanish governor ordered the French ships seized. The Spanish recaptured the city in August; the French captured it again in September and traded their Spanish prisoners for the French prisoners still in Havana. Despite the sound and fury, a European treaty signed in 1721 returned Pensacola to the Spanish.

The new governor, Alejandro Wauchope, a Scotsman by birth, began rebuilding the town. By 1723, it had a church, military barracks, homes, storehouses, and a 60-foot-high tower. In 1727, the English-allied Talapoosa attacked but withdrew when the French intervened. The small presidio remained an illicit trading site between the French and the Spanish.

Spanish Florida

While the French settled to the west of Spanish Florida, the far more numerous English threatened from the north. In 1670, the English founded the town of Charleston in territory formerly claimed by Spain. Hoping to halt the English advance, the Spanish signed the Treaty of Madrid, which set a new English-Spanish border near the southern boundary of modern South Carolina. Intermittent hostilities continued on the border, however.

In October 1672, ground was broken in St. Augustine for the construction of the Castillo de San Marcos, on the site of the city's nine previous forts. The Castillo, surrounded by a seawater moat, guarded both the harbor and land approaches to the city. It was designed to be self-sufficient and could house the entire population of the city within its 12-foot-thick coquina stone walls. It was built primarily by the labor of Indians and black slaves, many of whom became skilled stonemasons under the tutelage of craftsmen from Cuba.

In 1674, Gabriel Díaz Vara Calderón, bishop of Santiago de Cuba, visited the colony, the first visit by a bishop since 1606. He inspected every mission and left a detailed report of 13 near modern Tallahassee, 11 among the Timucua (near St. Augustine), and eight among the Guale (in modern Georgia), with more than 13,000 Hispanicized Indians. Although Florida had never been a popular assignment among Franciscans, after his visit new missionaries arrived. Unfortunately, during the 1680s the Carolina English also made inroads in Guale territory, not as priests but as traders. The English and their Indian allies soon began attacking Florida's northern mission frontier. The Guale missions were completely wiped out by 1690; the Franciscans did not attempt to reestablish them. By 1686, the English had also begun to attack missions in the Timucua and Apalachee areas.

In 1702, during the War of the Spanish Succession in Europe, Governor James Moore of Carolina attacked St. Augustine with a half-white, half-Creek force. They leveled the town as well as missions nearby. At Nombre de Dios, the oldest Florida mission, the friars' extensive library as well as the church and convent were completely destroyed. However, Moore failed to capture the castillo, where 1,500 residents had taken refuge under the leadership of Governor Joseph de Zúñiga. Moore, who lost the Carolina governorship for his failure, returned to Florida in 1704 to lead a vicious attack on the prosperous Apalachee missions. English troops were joined by the Yamassee and some mission Indians who were restive over the repression of their own culture and Spanish demands for labor. As was the case in New Mexico, churches were looted, and few loyal mission Indians survived. About 300 Apalachee became refugees at St. Augustine and a few migrated west, but most were enslaved by the English. Thereafter, the Apalachee gradually became absorbed by other tribes and eventually ceased to exist as a separate people.

After 1708, no missions existed beyond the immediate vicinity of St. Augustine. Florida's first bishop arrived in 1709, but finding few communicants, he left again in three weeks. After 1715, the Yamassee, themselves now in retreat from the English, sought a new alliance with the Spanish. Many settled near St. Augustine. In 1735, a new bishop, Francisco de San Buenaventura, arrived from Spain and revived religious activity. He confirmed 1,000 Spanish, Indians, and blacks and reopened a grammar school for boys, the first since the English invasions. He left in 1745, however, and was not replaced for a decade.

By 1683, enough free blacks lived in Florida to form a separate militia unit commanded by its own officers. The unit's participation in Spanish military excursions probably helped publicize opportunities to slaves in nearby English colonies. Slaves had some rights under Spanish colonial law (although not always in practice); for example, Catholic marriage was recognized and family preservation was encouraged. In 1687, eight men, two women, and a child held as slaves in Carolina escaped to Florida. Upon requesting baptism as Catholics, they were given sanctuary by the governor with consent of the Crown. Additional small groups of runaways arrived almost every year. In 1693, Spanish king Charles II issued a decree that all slave refugees from the British were to be freed. In Florida, officials unsuccessfully attempted to placate outraged English slave owners by offering monetary remuneration.

In 1738, the town of Gracia Real de Santa Theresa de Mose, or Fort Mose, was founded two miles north of St. Augustine. It was the first community of free blacks in North America. Its original population was about 100, and black military captain Francisco Menéndez was recognized by the Spanish as its "chief." Residents built a walled fort and homes, and a friar was assigned to the community.

On the Carolina border, the English continued to expand southward, beyond the line set by the Treaty of Madrid. After the English colony of Georgia was founded at Savannah in 1733, the land between the Savannah and St. Johns Rivers became the site of intermittent Spanish-English skirmishes. In 1739, the War of Jenkins' Ear began in the Caribbean between the two nations, melding in 1744 into King George's War (called the War of the Austrian Succession in Europe). The English took advantage of the formal declaration of war to invade Florida. In 1740, General James Oglethorpe of Georgia captured several forts north of St. Augustine, including Fort Mose. Again, however, the castillo proved unconquerable. Under Governor Manuel de Montiano, it held through 38 days of English attack, during which Spanish forces also retook Fort Mose. Oglethorpe, like Moore, was forced to withdraw. In 1742, Spanish troops sent from Cuba counterattacked English settlements on the Georgia coast, but the

Spanish in turn suffered a defeat. In 1748, however, the Treaty of Aix-la-Chapelle confirmed Georgia settlements as English possessions.

St. Augustine remained a garrison town. Much of the population depended on the *situado* for support, although a few small merchants lived in the colony and illegal trade with Carolina and New York also developed. Few new Spanish settlers arrived other than soldiers and officials. Conflict was constant between the *peninsulares,* or Spanish-born colonials, and the Florida-born criollos. The highest offices were usually reserved for the *peninsulares,* even among the Franciscans, because the Spanish Crown feared that criollo officials would weaken its authority. As in other Spanish colonies, most criollos were of multiethnic descent. The Spanish developed an elaborate vocabulary for describing multiethnic children, and after 1735 the *Book of the Pardos* (or persons of color) attempted to record all such births in Florida.

The Florida governor, who also headed the military and exercised both judicial and legislative authority, was appointed by the Crown. He was assisted by a small, appointed, and often contentious administrative staff. Except for a few brief periods, no *cabildo,* or town council, existed in Florida. By 1750, the population of Florida (not including "independent Indians") was about 2,000, residing almost entirely near St. Augustine. About 15–20 percent were blacks, probably about 15 percent free. Like other settlers, free black residents farmed, worked at various jobs, and received support from the *situado* as soldiers. Close by St. Augustine were a few small Indian villages with remnants of the Yamassee, Timucua, Guale, and Apalachee. By the same date, the non-Indian population of Carolina had reached 20,000, while the English colonies as a whole numbered more than 1 million.

CHRONICLE OF EVENTS

1670

The English establish the Hudson's Bay Company and begin building trading posts there.

The English establish Charleston in territory formerly claimed by Spain. The Treaty of Madrid demarcates a new boundary line south of Charleston between Carolina and Spanish Florida.

1672

At St. Augustine, construction begins on the Castillo de San Marcos.

1675

In New Mexico the governor arrests 47 Pueblo medicine men in an attempt to stamp out Indian religious practices. Three are hanged. Pueblo resentment increases.

1680

August 9: The Pueblo Revolt begins in New Mexico. Led by Popé, a San Juan medicine man, the Pueblo attack and kill more than 400 Spanish settlers.
August 21: Santa Fe is evacuated. Spanish settlers flee to a mission at El Paso, where they will remain for 12 years. The Pueblo occupy Santa Fe and destroy reminders of Spanish occupation.

1681

New France officials begin issuing *congés,* permits to individual fur traders; soon, licensed traders called *voyageurs* will replace coureurs de bois.

1682

April: René-Robert La Salle reaches the mouth of the Mississippi River and claims all territory drained by the river for France; he names it Louisiana.

1683

Free blacks in Florida found a militia unit commanded by their own officers.

1685

La Salle's colonizing expedition reaches the Gulf coast of Spanish Texas in error; the group founds a settlement at Matagora Bay.

1687

La Salle is murdered by his own men; his colonizing effort disintegrates.

Eleven black slaves escape from Carolina to Florida and are given sanctuary upon requesting confirmation as Catholics.

1690

King William's War (called the War of the League of Augsburg in Europe) opens in America; the French and Indians attack English settlers in New York and New England.

The English capture Port Royal, Acadia; the French retake it the following year.

Spanish missions are established in East Texas to prevent French expansion in the area.

1692

Don Diego de Vargas reconquers New Mexico by convincing Pueblo Indians at Santa Fe and elsewhere to surrender to Spanish authority.

1693

Spanish settlers reoccupy New Mexico. The Pueblo renege on their agreement, and Santa Fe must be taken by force.

The Spanish abandon missions in East Texas.

Castillo de San Marcos, begun 1672 *(Photo by Jack Boucher for Historic American Building Survey)*

Charles II of Spain decrees that slave refugees from the English colonies are to be freed in Florida upon conversion to Catholicism.

1696

France attempts to close the Canadian fur trade because of a glut in the European market.

The Second Pueblo Revolt occurs in New Mexico.

1697

The Treaty of Ryswick ends King William's War. All conquered lands in America are returned to their pre-war European claimants.

1698

The Spanish found Pensacola.

1699

Pierre Le Moyne, sieur d'Iberville, finds the mouth of the Mississippi River and constructs Fort Maurepas at modern Biloxi, Mississippi; it is the first French settlement in Louisiana territory.

1701

The Iroquois Confederacy makes peace with New France and many of its Indian allies; the Iroquois agree not to take sides in future conflicts between European colonies.

Anthoine de la Mothe Cadillac founds Detroit.

Father Eusebio Kino founds missions at Guevavi and Bac (near modern Tucson) in Arizona.

1702

The War of the Spanish Succession (called Queen Anne's War in America) begins.

The French found Mobile (in modern Alabama).

Governor James Moore of Carolina attacks St. Augustine; he fails to take the castillo but destroys the town and missions.

1704

Moore and his Indian allies destroy missions in Apalachee territory; many of the Apalachee are sold into slavery in the West Indies.

The English attack Acadia.

1706

Albuquerque is founded; by 1720, it will be the most populous town in New Mexico.

1709

April: By decree, New France formally acknowledges slavery.

1710

The English capture Port Royal, Acadia.

1711

England abandons plans to attack Quebec after its war fleet is shipwrecked.

1712

The French Crown makes Louisiana territory a proprietary colony and awards the charter to Antoine Crozat.

1713

The Treaty of Utrecht ending the War of the Spanish Succession gives Acadia (renamed Nova Scotia), Newfoundland, and Hudson's Bay to England; Île St-Jean (Prince Edward Island) and Île Royale (Cape Breton Island) go to the French.

Cadillac arrives in Louisiana as governor.

1714

The French establish a garrison at Natchitoches, the first settlement in modern Louisiana State. French trader Louis Saint-Denis reaches Santa Fe; he is imprisoned, and the Spanish decide to reoccupy East Texas.

1716

The French establish Fort Rosalie (modern Natchez).

The Spanish reestablish missions in East Texas as a buffer colony; they also establish a mission, presidio, and villa at San Antonio.

1717

Antoine Crozat resigns his Louisiana charter. It is awarded to John Law and his Company of the Indies.

1718

Jean-Baptiste Le Moyne, sieur de Bienville, founds New Orleans.

A civilian settlement at San Antonio and the mission San Antonio de Valero, later called the Alamo, are established.

1719

The War of the Quadruple Alliance begins in Europe; it will last until 1721.

The French invade East Texas; residents flee to San Antonio.

The French attack Pensacola; in the following years the fort will be recaptured by the Spanish and captured again by the French.

1720

The French begin building the massive fortress of Louisbourg on Île Royale.

1721

The European treaty ending the War of the Quadruple Alliance returns Pensacola to Spain.

Adrien de Pauger lays out the Vieux Carré in New Orleans; the city becomes Louisiana's capital.

The Spanish reoccupy East Texas, founding Los Adaes, which becomes the Texas capital.

1724

The Code Noir, or Black Code, is established in Louisiana. It regulates the behavior of slaves and blacks and expels Jews from the colony.

1729

The Natchez massacre 300 settlers at Fort Rosalie and take many slaves, women, and children captive. French retaliation sends many Natchez into slavery; a remnant joins the Chickasaw while others are dispersed.

1731

The French Company of the Indies surrenders its charter; Louisiana will be a royal colony for the next 31 years.

1733

The English colony of Georgia is founded south of the line demarcated by the Treaty of Madrid.

1736

In the Spanish Southwest, a silver rush begins at Arizonac; it will end in 1741 but gives the area its name.

Under Bienville, the French attack the Chickasaw, beginning the Chickasaw Wars. The French are forced to retreat.

1738

Fort Mose, the first community of free blacks in North America, is founded two miles north of St. Augustine.

1739

The Anglo-Spanish War, or the War of Jenkins' Ear, begins.

French traders reach Santa Fe; the Spanish king refuses to legalize French trade, but it continues illicitly.

1740

The Chickasaw agree to a treaty with Louisiana, although neither side has been victorious in the destructive wars.

Georgia governor James Oglethorpe invades St. Augustine but cannot capture the Castillo.

The War of the Austrian Succession begins in Europe. (It is called King George's War in America after 1744.)

1742

Spanish forces from Cuba attack sites on the Georgia coast.

1743

Philippe de Rigaud, marquis de Vaudreuil, arrives as governor of Louisiana. He reconciles factions and introduces elegant social life to New Orleans.

1745

New England forces capture Louisbourg.

1748

The Treaty of Aix-la-Chapelle ends the War of the Austrian Succession; Louisbourg is returned to France and Georgia settlements are confirmed as English territory.

The Chickasaw begin new raids on Louisiana settlements.

1749

The French claim the Ohio River valley.

EYEWITNESS TESTIMONY

There remains no more, except to speak of the Calumet [*sacred pipe*]. There is nothing more mysterious or more respected among them [Indians of the upper Mississippi]. . . . It seems to be the God of peace and of war, the Arbiter of life and of death. It has but to be carried upon one's person and displayed, to enable one to walk safely through the midst of Enemies—who, in the hottest of the Fight, lay down Their arms when it is shown. For that reason, the Illinois gave me one, to serve as a safeguard among all the Nations through whom I had to pass during my voyage. There is Calumet for peace, and one for war, which are distinguished solely by the Color of the feathers with which they are adorned; red is a sign of war. They also use it to put an end to Their disputes, to strengthen Their alliances, and to speak to Strangers. It is fashioned from a red stone, polished like marble, and bored in such a manner that one end serves as a receptacle for the tobacco, while the other fits into the stem; this is a stick two feet long, as thick as an ordinary cane, and bored through the middle. It is ornamented with the heads and necks of various birds, whose plumage is very beautiful. To these they also add large feathers. . . .

Father Jacques Marquette's narrative, 1674, in Thwaites, ed., Jesuit Relations, *vol. 59, pp. 130–32.*

Four leagues from Lake Ontario there is a cataract or waterfall unusual beyond belief. The river, here only an eighth of a league wide, is extremely deep in places. So swift is the current above the huge falls that none of the animals which try to cross there can withstand it. They are all swept away and plunged downward more than five hundred feet.

The Great Falls of Niagra consist of two sheets of water and a cascade with a shelflike island in the center. It is terrifying the way the water foams and boils, thundering unceasingly. When the wind is from the south, the roar can be heard for more than fifteen leagues.

Father Louis Hennepin, 1678–79, Description, *p. 21.*

On Tuesday, the thirteenth of the said month, at about nine o'clock in the morning, there came in sight of us in the suburb of Analco, in the cultivated field of the hermitage of San Miguel, and on the other side of the river of the villa, all the Indians of the Tanos and Pecos nations and the Querez of San Marcos, armed and giving war-whoops. As I learned that one of the Indians who was leading them was from the villa and had gone to join them shortly before, I sent some soldiers to summon him and tell him on my behalf that he could come to see me in entire safety, so that I might ascertain from him the purpose for which they were coming. Upon receiving this message he came to where I was, and, since he was known, as I say, I asked him how it was that he had gone crazy too—being an Indian who spoke our language, was so intelligent, and had lived all his life in the villa among the Spaniards, where I had placed such confidence in him—and was now coming as a leader of the Indian rebels. He replied to me that they had elected him as their captain, and that they were carrying two banners, one white and the other red, and that the white one signified peace and the red one war. Thus if we wished to choose the white it must be [upon our agreeing] to leave the country, and if we chose the red, we must perish, because the rebels were numerous and we were very few; there was no alternative, inasmuch as they had killed so many religious and Spaniards.

Letter of New Mexico governor Antonio de Otermín, September 1680, in Hackett, ed., Historical Documents, *pp. 330–31.*

On the next day, Saturday, they [*the Pueblo*] began at dawn to press us harder and more closely with gunshots, arrows, and stones, saying to us that now we should not escape them, and that besides their own numbers, they were expecting help from the Apaches whom they had already summoned. They fatigued us greatly on this day, because all was fighting, and above all we suffered from thirst, as we were already oppressed by it. At nightfall, because of the evident peril in which we found ourselves by their gaining the two stations where cannon were mounted, which we had at the doors of the casas reales, aimed at the entrances of the streets, in order to bring them inside it was necessary to assemble all the forces that I had with me, because we realized that this was their [the Indians'] intention. Instantly all the said Indian rebels began a chant of victory and raised war-whoops, burning all the houses of the villa, and they kept us in this position the entire night, which I assure your reverence was the most horrible that could be thought of or imagined, because the whole villa was a torch and everywhere were war chants and shouts. What grieved us most were the dreadful flames from

Niagara Falls and a beaver colony, detail from a 1715 map by Herman Moll *(Library of Congress)*

the church and the scoffing and ridicule which the wretched and miserable Indian rebels made of the sacred things, intoning the ablado and the other prayers of the church with jeers.

Governor Otermín, September 1680, in Hackett, ed.,
Revolt, *vol. 1, p. 102.*

On reaching the said pueblo [*Succoro*] it was found deserted and without people, the church and all the convent burned, and in the tower two bells with their clappers gone. . . . [A] large excavation which was in the presbytery in which they [the Spaniards] had buried some images when the rebellion broke out, had been opened by the apostates and the images

taken out. . . . [I]n the . . . sacristy was found a crown of twigs and two pieces of the arm of a holy image of Christ; and in the cloister were the skeletons of two dead persons. . . . On entering the plaza . . . there was found the entire thigh, leg, and foot of a holy image of Christ, in one piece, all the rest of the divine image being burned to charcoal and ashes; also, some bases of other images and many pieces of burned crosses. One large cross of pine which had been in the cemetery they had cut down at the base with axes and had burned the arms and most of the rest of it in the plaza of the said pueblo. . . .

Otermín's march to El Paso, November 1680, in Hackett,
Revolt, *vol. 2, p. 205.*

At last, after a navigation of about forty leagues, we arrived, on the sixth of April, at a point where the [*Mississippi*] river divides into three channels. The sieur de la Salle divided his party the next day into three bands, to go and explore them. He took the western, the sieur Dautray the southern, the sieur Tonty, whom I accompanied, the middle one. These three channels are beautiful and deep. The water is brackish; after advancing two leagues it became perfectly salt, and advancing on, we discovered the open sea, so that on the ninth of April, with all possible solemnity, we performed the ceremony of planting the cross and raising the arms of France. After we had chanted the hymn of the church, "Vexilla Regis," and the "Te Deum," the sieur de la Salle, in the name of his majesty, took possession of that river, of all rivers that enter it, and of all the country watered by them. An authentic act was drawn up, signed by all of us there, and amid a volley from all our muskets, a leaden plate inscribed with the arms of France, and the names of those who had just made the discovery, was deposited in the earth. The sieur de la Salle, who always carried an astrolabe, took the latitude of the mouth. . . .

> *Father Zenobius Membré, 1682, in Hart, ed.,*
> American History, *vol. 2, p. 143.*

We were still in want of Canoes. Monsieur de la Sale sent to the Camp of the Indians to barter for some, and they who went thither observ'd, that those People had made their Advantage of our Ship-wreck, and had some Bales of Normandy blankets, and they saw several Women had cut them in two and made Petticoats of them. They also saw Bits of Iron of the Ship that was cast away, and return'd immediately to make their Report to Monsieur de la Sale, who said we must endeavour to get some Canoes in Exchange, and resolv'd to send thither again the next Day. Monseieur de Hamel, Ensign to Monsr. De Beaujeau, offer'd to go up in his Boat, which Monsier de la Sale agreed to, and order'd . . . some others to bear him company.

No sooner were those Gentlemen, who were more Hot than Wise, landed, but they went up to the Camp of the Indians, with their Arms in their Hands, as if they had intended to force them, whereupon several of those People fled. Going into the Cottages, they found others, to whom Monsieur de Hamel endeavor'd to signify by Signs, that he would have the Blankets they had found restor'd; but the Misfortune was, that none of them understood one another. The Indians though

it their best Way to withdraw, leaving behind them some Blankets and Skins of Beasts, which those Gentlemen took away, and finding some Canoes in their Return they seiz'd two, and got in, to bring them away. . . .

Thus night came upon them, which oblig'd those unexperienc'd Canoe Men, being thoroughly tir'd, to go ashore to take some Rest, and the Weather being cold, they lighted a Fire, about which they laid them down and fell asleep; the Sentinel they had appointed doing the same. The Indians returning to their Camp, and perceiving our Men had carried away two Canoes, some skins and Blankets, took it for a Declaration of a War, resolv'd to be reveng'd, and discovering an unusual Fire, presently concluded that our men had halted there. A considerable number of them repaired to the Place, without making the least Noise, found our careless People fast asleep, wrap'd up in their Blankets, and shot a full Volley of their Arrows upon them all together of a Sudden, having first given their usual shout before they fall on.

> *Henri Joutel, February 1685,* Journal, *pp. 54–55.*

After proceeding about six leagues, I turned westnorthwest and saw a bay, *the best that I have seen in my life.* We put into it and found a depth of eight, nine, and ten fathoms in its mouth, which is not very wide. After steering northwest, north and northeast inside of it, I dropped anchor in seven fathoms. The entrance lies on an almost straight north and south line. This bay the Indians call *Panzacola.* After anchoring at a distance of about a cannon shot and a half within the bay, I climbed to the topmast. I did not see land to the north or northeast. With the Indian pilot we went in the longboat to the village of the Panzacolas. Upon arriving there on the seventh, the natives came forth to talk with our Indian interpreter, showing deep affection and good will. They led us to the hut of their chief where they brought forth a cross for us to kiss, and with deep devotion we did this upon our bended knees. Then, when we were all seated, we asked them if they had seen or heard of any white people. To this they answered only ten white men whom some native fishermen had found almost starved to death. The Indians had brought them to their village and had treated the strangers hospitably, considering their own relative poverty.

> *Juan de Reina, February 1686, in Leonard, trans.,*
> Spanish Approach, *pp. 13–14.*

As the recent [*Glorious*] Revolution in England will change the face of American affairs, it becomes necessary to adopt entirely new measures to secure Canada against the great dangers with which it is threatened. . . . The only means to avoid these misfortunes is to anticipate them by the expedition against Albany . . . on condition of negotiating eventually with [English] King for that Colony [*New York*], which is the only means of securing Canada, firmly establishing the Religion, Trade, and the King's authority throughout all North America. If the favorable opportunity which presents of becoming master of that Colony be neglected . . . it will destroy Canada in a little time. . . .

> *Montreal governor Louis-Hector, chevalier de Callières to French officials, 1689, in Caldwell and Persinger,* Source History, *p. 126.*

At this time the squads which were stationed at the sides and corners saw that a large host was approaching, some on horseback and others afoot, from the surrounding pueblos. Without doubt they had planned to hurl themselves upon us from the rear upon my arrival. Some Indian, or perhaps some of those who may have been in the corn fields and fortified towers they have there, must have gone to notify the said pueblos, whose warriors, as I say, were advancing rapidly, afoot and on horseback, and with their weapons. Most of them carried lances with long shafts. From what I later asked them, it seems that they have an Indian blacksmith who makes them for them. I ordered the captain of the presidio to go out with a squad from the said place and, without venturing any great distance from it, meet the said troop and prevent it from passing. The other squad was ordered to advance in like manner from the other side. I remained, holding the said position . . . with the soldiers of the third squad. . . . [T]he said rebels, who were aware of all that was taking place . . . repeated from the entrenchments that the troops were now coming to their aid . . . to which I answered them that they would not join forces, and that it was indeed a pity that they did not believe in the goodness of my heart, and what I had told them to the effect that they had been deceived by the devil. . . .

> *Don Diego de Vargas's campaign journal, 1692, in Espinosa, trans.,* First Expedition, *p. 85.*

"He who takes no risk to win an immortal name," said the intrepid General [*Vargas*], . . . "accomplishes nothing"; and so, piously invoking the aid of Most Holy Mary, he marched in. Unperturbed and even with great

dignity and composure he went on to the central square with the Father-President and six soldiers. . . . When the noise of the many people about it had quieted, he declared to them . . . "Since our Monarch and Lord, Charles II, their legitimate king, has overlooked the apostasy by which they had renounced the Catholic religion; the sacrilege in which they had murdered the missionaries, profaned the churches, broken the images, and desecrated the sacred vessels, and the treachery by which they had put the Spaniards to the

Don Diego de Vargas *(Courtesy Museum of New Mexico, Neg. No. 11409)*

knife without sparing the women and young children; the barbarity with which they had burned the ranch-houses of the latter and had ruined their towns, and all the results following such abominations, his Royal Highness was sending the General here with all his regal authority and with the sole purpose of restoring them to the fold of the Holy Church, which would receive them like a pious mother if they would penitently and tearfully seek this; the only condition attached was that they should swear allegiance to his Catholic Majesty as their legitimate king."

. . . after ordering the standard-bearer at his side to unfurl his banner, the General declared in clear and intelligible words: "[I now repossess] the City of Santa Fe, capital of the realm of New Mexico". . . .

Journal of Sigüenza y Góngora, 1692, in Leonard, trans.,
Mercurio Volante, *pp. 64–65.*

There is a Nation of Indians call'd the Yammasees, who formerly liv'd under the Spanish Government, but now live under the English, about 80 Miles from Charles-Town. Some of these Indians going a Hunting about 200 Miles to the Southward, met with some Spanish Indians that lived about Sancta Maria, not far from Augustine, the Seat of the Spanish Government; and taking them prisoners, brought them Home, designing to sell them for slaves to Barbadoes or Jamaica as was usual. . . . There were three Men and one Woman; they could speak Spanish, and I had a Jew for an Interpreter, so upon examination I found they profess'd the Christian Religion as the Papists do; upon which I thought in a most peculiar manner, they ought to be freed from Slavery; and thereupon order the King [chief] to carry them to Augustine, to the Spanish Governor. . . .

Carolina governor John Archdale, ca. 1695,
"New Description of that Fertile and Pleasant Province of
Carolina" [1707], in Salley, ed., Narratives, *p. 300.*

. . . an English vessel from Jamaica, bound to Carolina, was Cast-away to the Southward of Augustine amongst barbarous Indians, who in a wonderful manner were preserv'd from being murdered by them, so that they came at last to Augustine; and when the Spanish Governor heard of it he sent them all things necessary. . . . Two of these were called Robert Barrow and Edward Wardell, publick Friends [Quakers], Men of great Zeal, Piety, and Integrity.

Governor Archdale, ca. 1695–96, in Salley, ed.,
Narratives, *p. 301.*

The combat was not at all an equal one. Nevertheless, we made the English recognize that the [French] King's arms could be immortalized with as much honour and glory in the seas of ice [*i.e., Hudson's Bay*] as in the other remotest parts of the earth. . . . The *Hampshire,* seeing that she could not engage us between a shoal and their own two vessels . . . determined to run us down, and, for that purpose, tried to get to the windward of us (which she was unable to do), but we ran alongside of her, yard-arm to yard-arm. As we were so close to each other, I ordered a volley of musketry to be fired at her forecastle, where there were many sailors who called out for us to lead aboard. They immediately returned our volley with a discharge of grape which cut nearly all our rigging in pieces and wounded many of our men. As they ran along by our ship, we fired our batteries which were so well aimed that they proved most effective, for we were no sooner separated from one another than the *Hampshire* immediately foundered under sail. The *Dering,* which was close to us, sent us her broadside, but the encounter was a cruel catastrophe for the English, because the *Hudson's Bay* lowered her flag, and the Dering took to flight. . . . We had seven shots below the surface and the water came pouring in, not to speak of several shots which passed through from side to side.

Monsieur de la Potherie, September 5, 1697, in Tyrrell,
ed., Documents, *pp. 208–09.*

We continued to clear the trees away. I put ten men to squaring timber for the bastions, to be made of beams a foot and a half thick, laid one upon another and dovetailed at the corners. I had thirty men transported from the ship in my longboat. The work goes along slowly; I have no men who can use an ax; most of them take a day to fell one tree; but the trees are truly big ones, oak and hickory. I have had a forge set up to repair the axes. All of them break.

The 12th. My longboat brought from the ship the cows that belong to Surgère and me. We brought them from France. . . .

The 13th. My longboat brought the hogs and a bull. I had the woods burned and the site for the fort cleared.

The 14th. My longboat brought from the ship two pieces of cannon—eight pounders—and the gun-carriages and cannon balls. I sent men half a league from here to cut the stakes for the palisade. Every day the longboat brings eighty to a hundred of them. I am having an oven made and trenches dug for the palisade. The bastions are coming along. For two days I have kept twenty-five men busy sowing peas, corn, and beans. . . .

The 19th, 20th, and 21st. I had some pales squared and dressed down to 3 inches thick to floor the bastions, which I have built to a height of 9 feet. In them I put the cannon, with a parapet 4 feet high. . . .

Pierre le Moyne d'Iberville constructs Biloxi, April 1699, in Le Moyne, Iberville's Gulf Journals, *pp. 92–93.*

In the months of December and January, when the Rio del Norte is usually frozen over so thickly that laden carts cross upon the ice, eagles with white heads and necks come to its banks, and at sunrise perch on the trees near by. In a little while, circling in the air, they fly to a great height, whence they descend, head downward and wings drawn back, with the swiftness of a shooting star. The noise that they make is so great that it sounds like thunder, and while they are still more than a hundred yards away the ice makes loud cracking noises, and when they reach it a large hole is already open. The eagle enters by it and seizes in its claws a fish weighing four, five, or more pounds, which it eats upon the ice if no one prevents it. The most remarkable thing is that in a short space of time the ice is already closed up.

Don Noreiga, alcalde mayor of San Juan de Los Caballeros, early 1700s, in Hackett, ed., Historical Documents, *pp. 384–85.*

. . . regarding the establishment of Detroit. . . . It is an incontestable fact, that the strength of the savages lies in the remoteness of the French, and that ours increases against them with our proximity. For it is certain that, with a little Indian corn, these people have no difficulty in traversing two hundred leagues to come and take some one's life by stealth; and when we want to get to their lands, we are obliged to provide ourselves with stores of all kinds and to make great preparations, which involves the King in extraordinary expenses, and always with very little effect since it is like beating drums to catch hares. . . .

It is not advisable that I, any more than the other officers, soldiers and inhabitants, should do any trade with the savages, in order to take away from the people of the other established posts their cause for complaint, as to which they are very active. . . . But as it would be impossible for me to live without doing any

trading and with only the 1000 livres pay which I have, which will barely suffice for making the head men of the savages eat and drink at my table so as to attach them to our interests by this good treatment, I hope you will be so good to me as to inform M. de Pontchartrain of the indispensable necessity for increasing it, lest I should become absolutely unable to continue my services in the style due to His Majesty.

Antoine de la Mothe Cadillac, letter to Louis de Pontchartrain, October 18, 1700, in Holli, ed., Detroit, *pp. 12–14.*

On the 12th May [*1701*], eight Alibamon Chiefs arrived at Mobile to consult with M. de Bienville whether they should continue to war with the Chicachas, Tomes, and Mobilians. He advised them to make a peace, and gave them some presents for this purpose. On the 24th June, a Spanish shallop arrived from Pensacola, on board of which was Don José de Roblas, Captain of Infantry, and a son of the nurse of Count de Montezuma, bringing a letter from Francisco Martin, Governor of Pensacola, asking to be supplied with some provisions, which M. de Bienville granted.

On the 10th August, M. de Bienville was informed that M. St. Denis and some Canadians had invaded the territory of our allies to capture slaves, which he ordered to be restored.

On the 1st October, M. Davion, missionary, and Father Lirnoge, a Jesuit, arrived from the Mississippi; to give notice that one of their brethren and three Frenchmen had been murdered on the Yasous river, by two young Courois, who had acted as their guides.

On the 11th November, Don Francisco Martin arrived from Pensacola, with the news that France and Spain were at war with England, and asked for a supply of arms and powder, which was given him.

On the 28th, two shallops, with two Spanish officers, arrived at the fort from St. Augustine, Florida, and brought a letter from Don Joseph de Souniga y Serda, Governor of that place, informing M. de Bienville that it was besieged by fourteen English vessels and two thousand Indians. He further requested that a small vessel might be sent to the Viceroy of Mexico, informing him of what had happened. M. de Bienville sent him one hundred muskets and five hundred pounds of powder.

French officer Bénard de la Harpe, 1701, Historical Journal, *in Hart, ed.,* American History, *vol. 2, pp. 315–16.*

The reduction of Boston would infallibly draw after it the ruin of that country; were the grain of Long Island burnt, the settlers would be obliged to retire into Pennsylvania. . . . The abandonment of these parts would greatly weaken New York, and deprive it of the power of undertaking anything. . . . If the security of Canada depend on the capture of Boston, the establishment of Acadia is still more involved. . . .

Iberville to French officials, 1701, in Caldwell,
Source History, p. 127.

There's no difference between the Pirates that scour the Seas, and the Canada Merchants; unless it be this, that the former Sometimes enrich 'emselves all of a sudden by a good Prize; and that the latter can't make their fortune without trading for five or six years, and that without running the hazard of their Lives. I have known twenty little Pedlars that had not above a thousand Crowns stock when I arriv'd at Quebec, in the year 1683; and when I left that place, had got to the tune of twelve thousand crowns. 'Tis an unquestion'd truth, that they get fifty per Cent upon all the Goods they deal in, whether they buy 'em up upon the arrival of the Ships of Quebec, or have 'em from France by way of Commission; but over and above that, there are some little gaudy Trinkets, such as Ribbons, Laces, Embroideries, Tobacco-Boxes, Watches, and an infinity of other baubles of Iron Ware, upon which they get a hundred and fifty per Cent, all Costs clear. . . .

As soon as the French Ships arrive at Quebec, the Merchants of that City who have their Factors in the other Towns, load their Barques with Goods in order to transport 'em to their other towns. . . . If they pay for their Goods in Skins, they buy cheaper than if they made their payments in Money or Letters of Exchange; by reason that the Seller gets considerably by the Skins when he returns to France. Now, you must take notice, that all these Skins are bought up from the Inhabitants, or from the Savages, upon which the Merchants are considerable gainers. To give you an instance of this matter. A Person that lives in the Neighborhood of Quebec carries a dozen of Martins Skins, five or six Foxes Skins, and as many Skins of wild Cats, to a Merchant's House, in order to sell 'em for Woolen Cloth, Linen, Arms, Ammunition, &c. In the truck of these Skins, the Merchant draws a double profit, one upon the score of his paying no more for the Skins, than one half of what he afterwards sells 'em for in the lump to the Factors . . . and the other by the exorbitant rate he puts upon the Goods that the poor Planter takes in exchange for his Skins.

Louis-Armand de Lom d'Acre, baron de Lahontan, 1703,
New Voyages, vol. 1, pp. 374–76.

The Governour General [*of New France*] has the disposal of all Military Posts; He bestows Companies, Lieutenancies, and Under-Lieutenancies, upon who he pleases, with his Majesty's gracious Approbation; but he is not allow'd to dispose of particulate Governourships, or of the place of a Lord Lieutenant of a Province, or of the Major of any Town. He is impower'd to grant to the Gentry and the other Inhabitants, Lands and Settlements all over Canada; but there Grants must be given in concert with the Intendant. He is likewise authoris'd to give five and twenty Licences a year to whom he thinks fit, for trading with the Savage Nations of that vast Continent. He is invested with the power of upending the execution of Sentences against Criminals; and by virtue of this Reprieve, can easily procure 'em a Pardon, if he has a mind to favour 'em. But he can't dispose of the King's Money, without the consent of the Intendant, who is the only Man that can call it out of the hands of the Treasurer of the Navy.

Baron de Lahontan, 1703, New Voyages, vol. 1, p. 384.

. . . by the latest report from the deputy of Apalachee, the warnings so often given of the desire of the enemy [*the English*] to possess that province are seen justified. . . . The deputy set out with some foot soldiers and Christian Indians to oppose and dislodge the enemy. During the skirmish he was abandoned by those Indians who accompanied him, and who joined their own kind, whereupon those who were mounted fled, leaving behind those who were surrounded by the enemy. Twenty-two of the infantry, killed or captured, were lost. Among them were those who had come from Pensacola to drive back cattle for the subsistence [*of that place*], of which they are now deprived. The Indian alcaldes were barbarously burned alive, and sixteen Spaniards were killed. The remainder were ignominiously carried off naked. For each death of a wounded enemy Indian, they retaliated by burning a Spaniard or Indian. . . .

St. Augustine officials to the viceroy, July 1704,
in Boyd et al., eds., Here Once, p. 59.

. . . all of the English or Irish, Catholics or non-Catholics, who wish to come to these provinces from whatever parts, either by sea or land, will be admitted under the royal pledge of peace with good treatment and transported by available vessels to Havana or such other places they may choose, as was done with the Irish Catholic who on a recent occasion went to surrender at the blockhouse of Apalachee. . . .

[A]ll of the Negroes of Carolina, Christians or non-Christians, free or slave, who may wish to come, will be given the same treatment and granted their complete freedom, so that those who do not wish to remain in these parts may pass to others which appear better to them, with formal certificates of their freedom granted them under royal pledge.

Order of St. Augustine governor Joseph de Zúñiga, ca. 1704, in Boyd, et al., eds., Here Once, *p. 46.*

It has been proposed to His Majesty as a good thing to send ships from Canada to the islands of America [*West Indies*] to carry out a reciprocal trade in the products of the two colonies. On this point His Majesty wishes to explain . . . that since colonies must be considered only in relation to the kingdom, they must be carefully prevented from supplying each other with the merchandise that they are accustomed to draw from France.

French Crown to Canadian intendant, June 1705, in MacKirdy et al., eds., Changing Perspectives, *p. 6.*

The inhabitants of America in general, French as well as English, do not part with their blacks unless they know them to be bad or vicious. . . . If one wishes to follow what is practiced among the English, French ships must bring blacks to Louisiana and the settlers of this colony must be able to pay for them either in kind or in money.

French Ministry of the Marine to Bienville, 1708, quoted in Piersen, From Africa, *p. 45.*

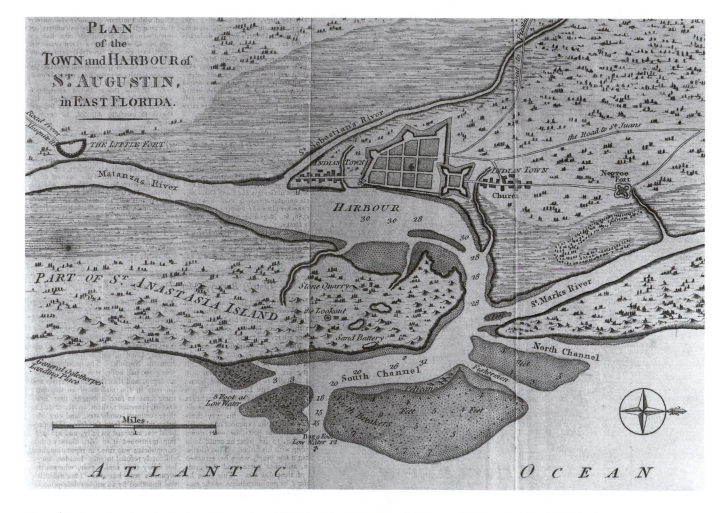

Map of St. Augustine, showing Indian settlements and "Negroe Fort" (Fort Mose) *(Courtesy St. Augustine Historical Society)*

Hence, in accordance with the wishes of His Majesty, we order that those who have bought or who will hereafter buy any Pani or Negro are to be granted complete ownership of that slave; that these Panis or Negroes are to be forbidden from leaving their Masters and that a fifty-pound fine is to be levied on anyone who incites slaves to leave their Masters.

Order of New France Intendant Jacques Raudot, April 1709, "Some Missing Pages: The Black Community in the History of Quebec and Canada," Quebec English Schools Network, URL: qesn.meb.bouv.qc.ca.

. . . I went . . . to examine the kivas [*ceremonial chambers*]. I found four in this form: One halfway between the two house blocks, subterranean. I entered it by the ladder placed in the square door of the roof. It had a hearth where they build a fire. On top of this kiva I found a holy cross of wood stained red which apparently they had just put in place a short time before. In the vicinity of the door near the ladder there was about a load of firewood which I ordered removed and the kiva destroyed. It was entirely closed up, unroofed, and filled with rock. There remained not a sign or a trace that there had been on that site and in that place any kiva at all. . . .

Captain Alfonso Rael de Aguilar, report on Pecos Pueblo, 1714, quoted in Kessell, Kiva, p. 314.

As Catholics the Indians are obliged to detest all heathen ceremony. However, in such a critical case, one must exercise the prudence of the serpent and the simplicity of the dove, because violence will result in more harm than one bargains for. Christ, our life, removed the weight of the Law and rendered it easy and light. *Jugum enim meum suave est, et onus meum leve.* [For my yoke is easy, and my burden is light. Mat., II: 30.1]

With a load so weightless, and of such ease, one must carry the natives (weak sheep) with the patience of the gardener cultivating a recently planted garden. Little by little he removes the weeds and through patience he comes to see the garden free of darnel. But to will that the new plant bear leaves, flowers, and fruit all at once is to will not to harvest anything.

Fray Antonio de Miranda of Acoma Pueblo, 1714, quoted in Kessell, Kiva, p. 319.

The Teja Indian approached them [*the Caocose of East Texas*] cautiously, making signs of peace by which he detained them to speak to them. . . . They made signs for us to leave. Nevertheless, they came closer. . . . They thus did as they were told, although very perturbed, and they embraced the governor. By this time the three religious [*clergymen*] and more soldiers had arrived, and going closer to the shore of the cove and alighting from our horses, we caressed them by embracing them and showed other customary signs of peace. Afterward, in the name of his Majesty, the said governor proceeded to distribute clothing and tobacco among the three who were present, and by means of the Indian guide who served as an interpreter, he told them to call the others who were in the canoe, who in all were four men, four women, and eight children, and to all of them he gave clothing and tobacco with which they were well pleased. . . . They were given to understand that the intention of the Spaniards was to come and settle the said bay, and that they should give notice of the peace and friendship that were shown them to all those of their nation, which is called Caocose and which is said to be very numerous and to inhabit the islets and shoals which surround the bay. They left very consoled. . . . [W]e, having returned to the place, in the name of his Majesty, whom God keep, the said governor took lawful possession of all the bay. . . .

Father Francisco Céliz, 1718–19, Diary, p. 66.

St. Augustine . . . is a garrison containing three hundred soldiers under pay and about one hundred familys, of inhabitants, that make near one hundred more men, besides women and children whose cheif support depends on the expence and pay of the soldiers. . . . The Spaniards of St. Augustine drive a trade with the Indians of Florida for ambergrise and wraked goods and with the other Indians for peltry.

The place being only a garrison there is but small trade there. What they formerly sent to the Havana was hides, tallow and the rows of fish especially mullets salted. The country produces pitch and tarr, which by the help of the Negroes plundered by the Indians from Carolina and bought by the Spaniards they begin to make a trade on, to our great detriment. In the open feilds there is orringe trees and in St. Augustine lemmon trees, citron trees, lime trees, besides peaches, figgs, pomgranates and some olive trees. . . .

The country is capable of a great many improvements but the place being as I said a garrison and the soldiers very raw lazy fellows being banditts banished from New Spain for crimes comitted there is no great matter can be expected from them. The town is unfortified containing about 200 houses and has a convent of Franciscan fryers, with two more churches some built with timber, some with stone.

Carolina governor Robert Johnson, January 1720,
in Merrens, ed., Colonial, *pp. 59–62.*

The Sieur de la Tour was no sooner arrived at the place [*New Orleans*], then consisting only of some unimportant houses, scattered here and there, formed by voyageurs, who had come down from Illinois, than he cleared a pretty long and wide strip along the river, to put in execution the plan he had projected. Then . . . he traced on the ground the streets and quarters which were to form the new town, and notified all who wished building sites to present their petitions to the council. To each settler who appeared they gave a plot ten fathoms from by twenty deep. . . . It was ordained that those who obtained these plots should be bound to inclose them with palisades, and leave all around a strip at least three feet wide, at the foot of which a ditch was to be dug, to serve as a drain for the river water in time of inundation. The Sieur de la Tour deemed these canals, communicating from square to square, not only absolutely necessary, but even to preserve the city from inundation, raised in front, near a slight elevation, running to the river, a dike or levée of earth, at the foot of which he dug a similar drain.

All were engaged in these labors, and several houses or cabins were already raised, when about the month of September a hurricane came on so suddenly, that in an instant it leveled houses and palisades. With this impetuous wind came such torrents of rains, that you could not step out a moment without risk of being drowned. . . . In fact, this tempest was so terrible that it rooted up the largest trees, and the birds, unable to keep up, fell in the streets. . . .

Monsieur Dumont, 1720–21, History of Louisiana
[1753], in French, ed., Historical Memoirs, *pp. 23–24.*

. . . The Lieutenant General extended his conference with the [French] commandant telling him that the objective behind the coming of the Governor was to occupy the land of the Adays as had already been done with the land of the Texas. He added [the Governor was] to re-establish the Mission of San Miguel [de los Adays] and construct a presidio on that frontier. . . .

The [French] commandant replied that he did not have specific orders to agree to this or to prevent it. [He added] that he knew of the truce which existed in Europe between the two crowns and that he would uphold it in America if his lordship agreed to it. With this [act] the conquest of that entire Province [*East Texas*] was completed. . . .

On September first the chief of the Adays came with many Indians all showing great merriment at the coming of the Spaniards. They were affectionately received by the Governor and given gifts as had been done with the other [Indian] captains of the Texas Indians. [The Chief] explained to the Spaniards that the great pleasure which he felt with their coming because all of the Indians of that country wanted to lived under their protection. They desired this because when the French invaded . . . they and the Nachitoches Indians displayed hostility towards them for lamenting the retreat of the Spaniards.

Father Juan de la Peña, diary, 1721, in Santos, trans.,
Aguayo Expedition, *pp. 69–70.*

It was about this time, that is 1722, that Indian hostilities broke out against the colonists. . . . This misfortune happened but too soon for Sergeant Riter . . . whose cabin was the more distant from the fort, and lay on a rising ground. While sleeping there one night with his wife, and a son some fifteen or sixteen years old, a party of ten or twelve Indians glided noiselessly by the clear moonlight into his cabin, the door of which was closed by a mere curtain. They did not get in so quietly as to avoid wakening the sergeant; he immediately put his hand out of bed, and seized his gun, and after calling several times, "Who goes there?" tried to fire when he received no answer. . . . [T]he Indians, seeing his arms useless, sprang on him . . . dragged him out of bed to the middle of his cabin, scalped him, and gave him in the back a blow, with a kind of tomahawk . . . which went right through him. While some were engaged in treating the poor fellow thus, others seized his wife, and took her out of the cabin to a ravine, intending to carry her off to their village as a slave. . . . [T]he sergeant's wife, when led to the ravine, seeing herself guarded only by two Indians, and believing her husband and son both massacred by the savages, resolved to avenge their death and expose herself to the fury of their murderers, rather than be carried off a slave. While leaving the cabin she had caught up a wood-cutter's knife, which she slipped up the sleeve of her chemise. At a moment when her guards least expected it, she drew it and dealt one so furious a blow that he fell dead at her feet; she drew it out and struck the other, but less successfully, giving him only a deep wound. At his cry, his companions ran up; and the brave woman fell, pierced with arrows.

Monsieur Dumont, 1722, in French, ed.,
Historical Memoirs, *pp. 43–44.*

. . . Since it appeared . . . that English might drive us away from Niagra and establish themselves there, we are determined to have two barks constructed at Fort Frontenac to be used in case of need against the English to drive them from the establishment, and also to be used for the transport of materials to build a stone fort at Niagra, which we believe is necessary to put that post in a defensible condition against the English, and even to maintain it against the Iroquois. . . .

I have had sent up for this reason, in the month of February last, two carpenters and four longsawmen. . . . I have also sent nine other carpenters and two blacksmiths. . . . M. De Joncauire at Fort Frontenac, who came from the Senecas and who is coming down to Montreal . . . was carrying two strings of wampum to M. de Vaudreuil on behalf of the Iroquois, who ask by one of these strings that nothing should be done at Niagra, and by the other that the barks should not be built.

As M. de Longueuil is convinced of the importance of fortifying himself at Niagra and of building these barks, he will be careful not to neglect anything in order to let the Iroquois know that they should not take offence, and that on the contrary, it is to their interest to agree to it. . . .

Canadian Intendant Bégon to French minister, June 10,
1725, in LaMontagne, ed., Royal Fort, *p. 216.*

The projects set on foot by the English, since the Treaty of Utrecht, indicate that Canada is the object of their constant jealousy and . . . it is more and more obvious that the English are endeavoring to interlope among all the Indian nations, and to attract them to themselves. They entertain constantly the idea of becoming masters of North America, persuaded that the European nation which will be possessor of that section [*i.e., Canada*], will in course of time, be also master of America.

French ministry document, August 1725, in Caldwell,
Source History, *pp. 128–29.*

At this juncture arrived [*in Louisiana*] a vessel sent from France loaded with young women, a necessary ship-

ment, without which it was impossible to make any solid establishment in the country. There were indeed on the island some married Canadians, who had children and even marriageable daughters, but they were old settlers, and looked upon as lords of the island, for they had risen to wealth by trade either with Crozat's vessels or the Spaniards. One especially, named Trudeau, had very pretty frame house, two stories high, covered with shingles.

As soon on the young women were landed they were lodged in the same house, with a sentinel at the door. Leave was given to see them by day and make a selection, but as soon as it was dark entrance to the house was forbidden to all persons. These girls were not long in being provided for and married and we may say that this first cargo did not suffice for the number of suitors who came forward, inasmuch as the one who remained last had nearly given rise to a very serious dispute between two young men, who wished to fight for her, although this Helen was anything but pretty, having the air of a guardsman than of a girl.

Monsieur Dumont, 1727, in French, ed.,
Historical Memoirs, *pp. 43–44.*

In 1738, altho' Peace subsisted . . . another Method was taken by the Spaniards to answer their Ends. Hitherto the Government of St. Augustine had not dared to acknowledge, much less to justify, the little Villainies and Violences offered to our Properties: But now an Edict of his Catholic Majesty himself, bearing Date in November 1733, was published by Beat of Drum round the Town of St. Augustine (where many Negroes belonging to English Vessels that carried thither Supplies of Provisions, &c., had the Opportunity of hearing it) promising Liberty and Protection to all Slaves that should desert thither from any of the English Colonies, but more especially from this [*South Carolina*]. And, lest that should not prove sufficient of itself, secret Measures were taken to make it known to our Slaves in general. In Consequence of which Numbers of Slaves did, from Time to Time, by land and Water desert to St. Augustine; And, the better to facilitate their Escape, carried off their Master's Horses, Boats, &c. some of them first committing Murder; and were accordingly received and declared free. Our present Lieutenant Governor, by Deputies sent from hence on that Occasion to Seignor Don Manuel de Montiano, the present Governor of St. Augustine, set forth the Manner in which those Slaves had escaped:

and re-demanded them pursuant to the Stipulation between the Two Governments, and to the Peace subsisting between the Crowns. Notwithstanding which, tho' that Governor acknowledged those Slaves to be there, yet producing the King of Spain's said Edict he declared that he could not deliver them up, without a positive Order for that purpose from the King, and that he should continue to receive all others that should resort thither.... The Success of those Deputies being too well known at their Return, Conspiracies were form'd and Attempts made by more Slaves to desert to St. Augustine....

South Carolina legislators, 1741, in Hart, ed.,
American History, vol. 2, p. 342.

It is true there is no want of wood to guard against the cold, which very soon becomes extreme, and encroaches greatly upon the spring, but it is, however sometimes extremely shocking not to be able to stir out of doors without being frozen, at least without being wrapt up in furs like a bear. Moreover, what a spectacle is it to behold one continued tract of snow, which pains the sight, and which hides from your view all the beauties of nature? No more difference between the rivers and the fields, no more variety, even the trees are covered with snowfrost, with large icicles descending from all their branches, under which you cannot pass with safety. What can a man think who sees the horses with beards of ice more than a foot long, and who can travel in a country, where, for the space of six months, the bears themselves dare not show their faces to the weather?

Pierre Charlevoix describes Canada, 1744,
Journal, vol. 1, pp. 253–54.

Our Creoles [*Canadian-born colonists*] are accused of great avidity in amassing, and indeed they do things with this in view, which could hardly be believed if they were not seen. The journeys they [*fur traders*] undertake; the fatigues they undergo; the dangers to which they expose themselves, and the efforts they make surpass all imagination. There are, however, few less interested, who dissipate with greater facility what has cost them so much pains to acquire, or who testify less regret at having lost it. Thus there is some room to imagine that they commonly undertake such painful and dangerous journeys out of a taste they have contracted for them. They love to breathe a free air, they are early accustomed to a wandering life; it has charms

for them, which make them forget past dangers and fatigues, and they place their glory in encountering them often.... I know not whether I ought to reckon amongst the defects of our Canadians the good opinion they entertain of themselves. It is at least certain that it inspires them with a confidence, which leads them to undertake and execute what would appear impossible to many others.... It is alleged they make bad servants, which is owing to their great haughtiness of spirit, and to their loving liberty too much to subject themselves willingly to servitude.

Pierre Charlevoix, 1744, Journal, vol. 1, pp. 264–65.

The Villa of Albuquerque and Village of Atrisco.... Both together have something more than a hundred families, who are employed in planting and weaving hose and blankets.... Cañada is thirty leagues to the south of the capital. This foundation is in a beautiful and fertile plain that may be entirely watered by the river. It has about fifty families of Spaniards, who are occupied in planting and are ministered to by the father of the mission of San Agustín de la Isleta.... [T]hey called it Cañada because in the year 1740 ten Frenchmen entered the kingdom by way of the mission of Taos. Because of having traveled on foot in thirty days, with an Indian as guide, from Cañada, a pueblo of New France, to the kingdom of New Mexico, where they settled in this place, they called it Cañada. Eight of the said Frenchmen returned in the same way that they came, but two remained in the kingdom. One practiced his trade as a barber or surgeon, and the other, his companion, for his grace and merit in having instigated the Indians to a new uprising, was ordered ... to be hanged, which will serve as a warning.

Father Miguel de Menchero's survey of New Mexico,
May 1744, in Hackett, ed., Historical
Documents, pp. 400–01.

Then came a resplendent triumphal chariot with the arms of Spain and an imperial crown and scepter. And riding in this chariot was a personage who acted in three different parts a very learned drama in praise of our King and Lord don Ferdinand the Sixth, to great acclamation by the people with many huzzas and "Long live our King and Lord don Ferdinand the Sixth."

Father Lorenzo Estremera describes a Santa Fe parade,
January 1748, quoted in Hazen-Hammond,
Short History, p. 34.

North America Divided into its III Principal Parts, a 1685 map by Philip Lea, shows California as an island. *(Library of Congress)*

Behold, then, the English far within our territory [*the Ohio Valley*]; and, what is more, they are under the protection of a crowd of savages whom they entice to themselves, and whose number increases every day. Their design is, without doubt, to establish themselves there; and, if efficacious measures be not taken as soon as possible to arrest their progress, we run great risk of seeing ourselves quickly driven from the upper countries, and of being obliged to confine ourselves to the limits which it may please those gentlemen to prescribe to us. . . .

Father Bonnecamp, The English on the Ohio, *1749, in Caldwell,* Source History, *p. 129.*

But one more thing I have to tell you, which is of great consequence to the province. And that is, the Spaniards, at St. Augustine, who, during the war, seduced and encouraged our negroes (or slaves) to desert from this province, and gave them freedom, continue that practice, now in peace, notwithstanding all the remonstrances made on that subject. And there is hardly a week but a dozen of them go off at a time in canoes.

Charleston resident "R.T.," letter, July 1749, in Merrens, ed., Colonial, pp. 173–74.

July 25th [*1749*]. The women in general are handsome here [*in Canada*]; they are well bred and virtuous, with an innocent and becoming freedom. They dress up very fine on Sundays . . . hair . . . is always curled and powdered and ornamented with glittering bodkins and aigrettes. Every day but Sunday they wear a little neat jacket, and a short petticoat [*skirt*] which hardly reaches half the leg, and in this particular they seem to imitate the Indian women. The heels of their shoes are high and very narrow, and it is surprising how they walk on them. In their knowledge of economy [*housekeeping*] they greatly surpass the English women in the plantations, who indeed have taken the liberty of throwing all the burden of housekeeping upon their husbands, and sit in their chairs all day with folded arms. The women in Canada on the contrary do not spare themselves, especially among the common people, where they are always in the fields, meadows, stables, etc. and do not dislike any work whatsoever. However, they seem rather remiss in regard to the cleaning of the utensils, and apartments, for sometimes the floors, both in the town and country, are hardly cleaned once in six months, which is a disagreeable sight to one who comes from amongst the Dutch and English, where the constant scouring and scrubbing of the floors is reckoned as important as the exercise of religion itself.

Peter Kalm, 1749, Travels, vol. 2, pp. 224–25.

August 1st . . . [*Montreal*] extends along the great branch of the river. On the other side it is furrowed with excellent corn fields, charming meadows and delightful woods. . . . It is pretty well fortified, and surrounded with a high and thick wall. On the east side it has the River St. Lawrence, and on all the other sides a deep ditch filled with water, which secures the inhabitants against all danger from sudden incursions of the enemy's troops. . . . The priests of the seminary of St. Sulpitius have a fine large house, where they live together. The college of the Franciscan Friars is likewise spacious, and has good walls, but it is not so mag-

nificent as the former. The college of the Jesuits is small, but well built. To each of these three buildings are annexed fine large gardens, for the amusement, health and use of the communities to which they belong. Some of the houses in the town are built of stone, but most of them are of timber, though very neatly built. Each of the better sort of houses has a door towards the street, with a seat on each side of it, for amusement and recreation in the morning and evening. . . .

Every Friday is a market day when the country people come to the town with provisions, and those who want them must supply themselves on that day, because it is the only market day in the whole week. On that day, likewise, a number of Indians come to town to sell their goods and buy others.

Peter Kalm, 1749, Travels, vol. 2, pp. 238–39.

August 2nd . . . All the farms in Canada stand separate from each other, so that each farmer has his possessions entirely separate from those of his neighbor. . . . The farmhouses hereabouts are generally all built along the rising banks of the river, either close to the water or at some distance from it, and about three or four arpents from each other. . . .

The farmhouses are generally built of stone, but sometimes of timber, and have three or four rooms. The windows are seldom of glass, but most frequently of paper. They have iron stoves in one of the rooms and chimnies [*fireplaces*] in the rest. The roofs are covered with boards. The crevices and chinks are filled up with clay. The other buildings are covered with straw. . . .

There are several crosses put up by the roadside, which is parallel to the shores of the river. These crosses are very common in Canada, and are put up to excite devotion in the travelers. They are made of wood, five or six yards high, and proportionally broad. In that side which looks toward the road is a square hole, in which they place an image of our Savior, the cross, or of the holy Virgin with the child in her arms, and before that they put a piece of glass, to prevent its being spoiled by the weather.

Peter Kalm, 1749, Travels, vol. 2, pp. 244–45.

August 3rd . . . Trois Rivieres is a little market town, which had the appearance of a large village. . . . On one side the river passes by, which is an English mile and a half broad. On the other side are fine corn-fields, though the soil is very much mixed with sand. In the town are two churches of stone, a nunnery, and a house for the friars of the order of St. Francis. This town is likewise the seat of the third governor in Canada, whose house is likewise of stone. Most of the other houses are of timber, a single story high, tolerably well built, and stand very much asunder, and the streets are crooked. . . . Its present inhabitants live chiefly by agriculture, though the neighboring ironworks may serve in some measure to support them.

Peter Kalm, 1749, Travels, *vol. 2, pp. 247–48.*

August 6th . . . Quebec, the chief city in Canada . . . is distinguished into the lower and the upper. The lower lies on the river . . . The upper city lies above the other on a high hill and takes up five or six times the space of the lower, though it is not quite so populous . . . the view from the palace of the lower city (part of which is immediately under it) is enough to cause a swimming of the head. There is only one easy way of getting to the upper city, and . . . [t]his road is very steep, although it is made winding. However, they go up and down it in carriages, and with wagons. Most of the merchants live in the lower city, where the houses are built very close together. The streets in it are rugged, very rough, and almost always wet. There is likewise a church, and a small, marketplace. The upper city is inhabited by people of quality, by several persons belonging to the different offices, by tradesmen, and others. . . .

The Palace is . . . a large building of stone, two stories high, extending north and south. . . . The palace is the lodging of the governor-general of Canada, and a number of soldiers mount the guard before it, both at the gate and in the courtyard. When the governor, or the bishop, comes in or goes out they must all appear in arms, and beat the drum.

Peter Kalm, 1749, Travels, *vol. 2, pp. 257–59.*

7

Expansion, Misrule, and Rebellion in the English Colonies
1670–1691

UNREST SIMMERS

As the 1670s opened, the English colonies appeared to be prospering. Under the surface, however, political, social, and economic unrest was gathering force. After 1675, all of the colonies experienced dissension that lasted for the remainder of the 17th century. Several experienced open rebellions. Disagreements with Crown officials sometimes occurred, but the colonial unrest during these years was not caused by a desire to separate from England. The unrest grew, instead, from a muddle of colonial issues, including heavy tax burdens that were perceived to be unfairly distributed, lack of representation and equal justice for ordinary citizens, and religious differences. Unrest was magnified by disagreement over Indian policies as the growing colonial population demanded more land and hostilities intensified. It was also magnified by fears of French invasion.

Much colonial discontent was related to the imposition of quitrents, or yearly payments some colonists were required to make to proprietors. After 1670, New York, New Jersey, Maryland, and the Carolinas continued as proprietary colonies, and Pennsylvania was founded by a proprietor in 1682. New proprietary privileges were also awarded in some existing colonies. In contrast, in most New England colonies, land was owned outright by the individual settlers to whom it was granted or sold. Although the government could tax them, they alone owned any profit from the land. In the proprietary colonies, however, a different form of landownership existed. Ultimately, the land was considered to be the Crown's. Proprietors had the king's authority to grant or sell the land to settlers as they wished, under the condition that the proprietors were entitled to set and collect yearly quitrents. The quitrent was analogous to a yearly property tax. However, instead of being paid directly to the government for public expenditures, as a tax would be, the quitrent was paid to the proprietor. It was the proprietor's personal profit or income, which he might use as he wished. The settlers who bought the land were still considered its owners; they were not renters as that term is understood today. Nor were they tenant farmers, who also existed in some colonies and who did not have any ownership claim to the land.

The 17th-century institutions of proprietorship and quitrents derived from the medieval manor. The lord of the manor provided military protection and governed peasant-tenants in a given area; tenants, in turn, gave their lord part of what they produced. English proprietorships, Spanish *encomiendas,* French seigneuries, and Dutch patroonships all developed from the manorial system of landownership. In the 17th century, quitrents (like taxes) were still usually paid in goods rather than cash.

BACON'S REBELLION IN VIRGINIA

During William Berkeley's second term as governor of Virginia, the sources of discontent were legion. Berkeley had grown increasingly arbitrary, appointing most officeholders himself and refusing to call for new elections of burgesses between 1660 and 1674. In 1670, the franchise itself was restricted to those who owned land. Taxes were heavy. Agricultural discontent rumbled in the colony, worsened by difficult weather and a severe epidemic that killed over half the colony's cattle. The price of tobacco remained extremely low, but duties were unaffected because they were tied to bulk rather than price. In 1673, a Dutch war fleet on its way to New York during the Third Anglo-Dutch War destroyed much of the tobacco fleet. On top of all this, in the same year King Charles II made new proprietary grants of all Virginia lands to Henry Bennet, lord Arlington, and Thomas, lord Culpeper, who increased the tax burden on colonists by demanding quitrents.

Underlying surface events, the social structure of Virginia was changing. The fastest growing segment of the population was former indentured servants who had reached the end of their servitude. A significant number of them moved about from place to place as tenants or laborers, with little discernable "stake in society"—at least from the point of view of better established colonists. Unfortunately, few former servants could find good land. All the land close to navigable rivers had already been claimed (although not necessarily cleared and planted) by the now-established elite. Governor Berkeley, to his credit, attempted to establish a land tax to encourage speculators holding large tracts to make them available; but instead the assembly voted to maintain poll, or per person, taxes. To obtain a farm many people were forced to move to the backcountry. The backcountry frontier, however, was also home to Indians pushed west by white settlement. Frontier farmers saw them not as victims but as enemies and rivals for the land.

In 1676, an armed disorder known as Bacon's Rebellion occurred. Its immediate cause was growing hostility between Indians and non-Indians in the backcountry. The Susquehannock had moved into the territory of the Doeg, the tribe closest to Virginia's frontier. Soon Indians were skirmishing with each other and with settlers, all of them rival land claimants. After the murder of a white overseer in 1675, a local militia attacked an innocent group of Indians. Reprisals and counterattacks began in earnest, and some 300 settlers were soon dead. Berkeley, however, refused to act until the assembly could meet, upon which it agreed, at Berkeley's insistence, to wage only a defensive war. Berkeley, like many other colonial leaders at the time, feared that local hostilities could develop into a larger and coordinated Indian uprising; by adopting a defensive strategy he hoped to avoid a large-scale war. Frontier forts were to be established and patrolled, but no attacks on Indians were to be permitted. Berkeley hoped the forts would restrain both Indians and backcountry farmers, whom he believed to be unruly and unscrupulous.

Many Virginians, not only those on the frontier, were incensed by the refusal to declare war. They believed that Berkeley had compromised the colony's safety to avoid disrupting the fur trade, from which he and other wealthy colonists profited. In the backcountry, a group gathered at an encampment to wage war on the Indians at its own expense.

Nathaniel Bacon, a powerful orator, soon emerged as their leader. The wealthy son of an English lord, 28-year-old Bacon was a member of the governor's council. Like his less fortunate backcountry neighbors, however, he made no distinction between friendly and hostile Indians, holding them all in contempt. Bacon and his force of about 300 volunteers attacked the Susquehannock in defiance of Berkeley's orders. Berkeley declared Bacon a rebel and suspended him from the council. Correctly sensing the general discontent, however, the governor called for new elections of burgesses; Bacon was elected in a

"Bacon's Castle," Surrey County, Virginia, built ca. 1655 and used as a garrison in the rebellion *(Historic American Building Survey)*

landslide in his own district. While Bacon was en route to the June 1676 session of the assembly at Jamestown, Berkeley captured him—then publically pardoned him and promised him a military commission to go against the Indians. When the commission was slow to be conferred, Bacon's backcountry volunteers marched to Jamestown to demand it. It was granted by the assembly, which also passed a series of reform measures known as Bacon's Laws. Many of these laws restricted the arbitrary power of appointed officials; the sale of Indian prisoners into slavery was also instituted.

With his commission in hand, Bacon assembled 1,300 men, some of them servants and slaves. Then, for reasons unclear to historians, Berkeley again declared him a rebel. In response, Bacon and his troops marched to Jamestown and took control of the colony. He next led his troops against the Indians—including the friendly Pamunkey, whom he hoped to enslave and sell. In Bacon's absence, Berkeley regained control of Jamestown. When Bacon returned in September, his followers burned the town and looted estates of the wealthy. Suddenly, however, Bacon was taken ill. He died on October 26, probably from dysentery. Without his leadership, his rebellion soon ended.

Berkeley's forces regained control of the colony without the help of the 11 ships and 1,000 troops belatedly sent by King Charles II. With the troops came commissioners to investigate the uprising and restore order. They also had orders to pardon the rebels, partly because English officials suspected that the Virginia elite was indeed profiting at the expense of the small farmer—and of royal revenues. Berkeley treated the commissioners poorly and the rebels harshly, hanging several of the leaders and forcing the assembly to repeal many of Bacon's Laws. He lengthened the indentures of all servants who had joined Bacon and returned the slaves to their masters.

Crown officials recalled Berkeley to England, where he died shortly after his arrival in 1677. He was replaced by Thomas, lord Culpeper. The Crown also replaced the volunteer Virginia militia with a paid force, correctly perceiving that many volunteers were as hostile to Virginia's government as to the Indians. As the commissioners recommended, several of Bacon's Laws were restored. Indian policies were revised and blockhouse patrols were established on the border to take aggressive rather than defensive action. The Susquehannock dispersed, eventually being absorbed into the Iroquois Confederacy. The remaining Pamunkey were granted reserved lands. For the rest of the century, few hostilities occurred, although settlers slowly pushed Indians who stayed in the area west of the Appalachian Mountains.

Historians agree that Bacon's Rebellion was significant but disagree vigorously over its correct interpretation. Many call it the first democratic uprising in America history, a battle by common people against abuses of power and special privilege. Many recent historians, however, also point out that Bacon redirected popular anger at legitimate grievances almost entirely onto the Indians. Some interpret the rebellion as a contest for control between two elite groups, since Bacon had many wealthy supporters. A few see the rebellion as the first American sectional conflict—a fight between those in settled or urban areas and those in frontier or rural areas. Still others focus on the unusually significant role women played in the rebellion, on both sides. Lady Berkeley, the much-younger second wife of the governor, was very active in the loyalist cause. On the rebel side, many women took an active role as "news wives," carrying news about events, plans, and actions throughout the backcountry. Whatever the interpretation, evidence clearly indicates that Bacon had substantial popular support—what Berkeley loyalists called a mob of "tag, rag, and bobtail." Folk literature continued to celebrate Bacon for years afterward.

KING PHILIP'S WAR IN NEW ENGLAND

Although relations between whites and Indians had been reasonably peaceable since the Pequot War of 1636, Indian hostilities also broke out in New England in 1675. They were not directly connected to those in Virginia, but they had the same root cause: the relentless desire of the growing colonial population to claim more and more Indian land. By 1675, the combined non-Indian population of the northern English colonies had grown to more than 50,000. The Algonquian tribes of New England, however, could not continue moving westward without intruding on the territory of their traditional enemies, the Iroquois.

By 1675, there were more than 1,000 Anglicized Indians in 14 "Praying Towns" established by Puritan missionaries. Many more Indians lived nearby and maintained their traditional culture, although they had adopted European manufactured goods and become economically interdependent with the English. New England authorities imposed their laws on those nearby Indians, who were sometimes arrested and brought to trial for disputes with colonists, crimes, or violations of laws such as the observance of the Sabbath. In 1671, Plymouth Colony jailed the Wampanoag chief Metacom, or King Philip, who had refused to sell the colony more land. The colony confiscated his band's guns and forced him to admit he was subject to English law.

In late 1674, John Sassamon, who had studied briefly at Harvard Indian College and was the minister at a Praying Town, warned the English that Metacom was preparing for war. In retaliation, Sassamon was murdered by Wampanoag, three of whom were tried for his murder at Plymouth and executed in June 1675. Within one week, a group of Wampanoag had murdered a family of settlers at Swansea, the settlement established in 1667 about four miles from Metacom's village.

Whether or not New Englanders actually sought an opportunity to subjugate nearby tribes and confiscate their land, once hostilities began they seized their chance to do so. Five companies of colonists were raised. Colonists, however, had not yet mastered the methods of wilderness warfare, and most of the early victories were Metacom's. The Wampanoag moved into a swampy area ruled by Weetamoo, a female Wampanoag chief of the Pocasset village. The swamp was even more daunting to the English than the woods and they chose to attack the Narragansett instead. Soon both the Narragansett and Nipmuc joined with the Wampanoag, and the war spread quickly throughout the Connecticut River valley. Throughout the winter of 1675–76, Indian forces continued to burn town after town on the frontier. In February 1676, Indians attacked Lancaster, Massachusetts, and leveled it, killing more than 50 people, and carrying away captives. By April they had attacked within 17 miles of Boston. Refugees poured into Boston and other coastal towns. Massachusetts and Connecticut both passed draft laws forbidding colonists to leave the colony to avoid military service.

Despite their early victories, Indian forces were unable to unite behind a single leader. By spring 1676, they were seriously weakened by food shortages, while the English obtained assistance by sea from other colonies. By summer bands of Indians began to surrender. King Philip himself was shot in August—by a Praying-Town Indian fighting on the English side. By summer's end, the war was over. The colonists had achieved their final victory over the Indians of southern New England.

About 3,000 Indians lost their lives in King Philip's War, and those who lived continued to suffer. Indian leaders were executed; for years, Metacom's head was displayed on a pike at Plymouth's fort. Captives, including Metacom's wife and son, were sold into slavery in the West Indies. Children under the age of 14 were enslaved within the colony until they turned 24, when they were freed. Wampanoag society was destroyed, but no tribe was completely exterminated. The few Wampanoag who remained in the area were confined to Praying Towns or worked as tenant farmers or servants. Other Algonquian tribes migrated west or north.

The colonial losses of life and property in the war were also extremely heavy; relative to population and resources, the war was probably the most costly ever fought in America. About 1,000 colonial civilians lost their lives. Plymouth was particularly devastated and struggled with debts from the war for many years. The New England Confederation ended, having proved unable to coordinate war efforts effectively.

New England ministers viewed the war as God's punishment for the errors to which the Puritans had succumbed. They continued to preach and write jeremiads. King Philip's War also gave birth to a new American literary form, the captivity narrative. Captivity narratives described a colonist's capture and suffering at the hand of Indians, and his or her eventual release by the grace of God. The first was written by Mary Rowlandson, abducted during the attack on Lancaster in 1676. Rowlandson's narrative, first published in 1682, went through four editions in its first year and continued as a bestseller for well over a century.

REBELLION IN MARYLAND AND CAROLINA

In Maryland, settlements were not as spread out or as exposed to attack as those in the Virginia backcountry. Economic conditions were very similar in the two colonies, however. The price of tobacco remained low; taxes and proprietary quitrents were high. Although Governor Charles Calvert was not as personally arbitrary as William Berkeley, colonists resented the control of council and government offices exerted by his appointees, many of whom were his relatives. Religious as well as political dissension continued between the elite Catholic minority and the Protestant majority, some of whom had also grown wealthy by 1670. Calvert restricted the franchise in 1670; after that date, he began to call partial assemblies to render his opponents ineffective.

In September 1676, the same month that Bacon burned Jamestown, William Davyes and John Pate attempted an insurrection in Maryland over taxes and the unrepresentative bodies that levied them. Calvert was in England at the time, but the acting governor, also alarmed by Bacon's Rebellion in Virginia, hanged them both. Discontent continued to simmer, and in 1681 another tax and quitrent protest was led by Josias Fendell and John Coode (pronounced Code).

They were quickly arrested, denounced as "rank Baconists," and banished—temporarily, in Coode's case.

In Carolina, the Albemarle settlement on the Chowen River (modern North Carolina) also rebelled against proprietary rule and taxes in the 1670s. Albemarle had been settled in the mid-1650s by emigrants from Virginia, prior to the 1663 proprietary grant of Carolina. An antiproprietary faction grew in the colony, led by precharter settlers who believed that proprietorship had worsened their situation.

When England passed the Plantation Duties Act in 1673, taxing trade between the individual colonies, Albemarle colonists refused to obey the law. Albemarle lacked a good coastal port, and tobacco farmers traded almost exclusively with shallow-draft New England vessels that could travel in the Outer Banks. When the proprietors attempted to enforce the new navigation act, Governor Peter Carteret was forced to flee the colony.

Pro- and antiproprietary forces continued quarreling. In 1677, acting governor and customs collector Thomas Miller seized goods traded illegally and imprisoned the ships' captains. Colonists rose in a revolt known as Culpeper's Rebellion. It was led by John Culpeper, a recent migrant from South Carolina (not to be confused with Lord Culpeper, governor of Virginia), and George Durant, a precharter settler. Rebels jailed Miller, elected an assembly, and chose John Culpeper governor. They sent armed men to prevent an appointed governor from crossing the Virginia border, although no confrontation took place. The proprietors, aware that the rebels had established a reasonably stable government, left it in place until 1683, when they sent Seth Sothel as the new governor. By that date, the settlement had more than 2,000 colonists. Most were small tobacco farmers, the majority of whom had far fewer indentured servants or African slaves than neighboring planters to the south.

At Charles Town (later called Charleston), founded in 1670, political discord broke out as well, particularly over the method of granting land. By 1672 about

Spreading settlement in South Carolina, detail from a 1682 map by Joel Gascoyne *(Library of Congress)*

a third of the 200 residents were relatively wealthy planters from Barbados. They quickly dominated the government. Just as quickly they acquired a reputation for aggressive self-interest—and behavior similar to that of pirates whom they permitted to use the city as a port. Almost immediately, the planters antagonized the nearby Indians and soon began enslaving them, despite the proprietors' instructions to the contrary. In 1677, the proprietors claimed a monopoly on trade with the Westo band. (The Westo were probably displaced Erie driven south by the Iroquois in 1657 and some Yuchi from Georgia.) The monopoly precipitated a war that resulted in the band's decimation. South Carolina also established an extensive triangular trade with England, other North American colonies, and the West Indies and began to import substantial numbers of black slaves.

In 1680, the Charles Town settlement moved to the site of modern Charleston at the confluence of the Ashley and Cooper Rivers. The proprietors sent instructions for a planned town with streets carefully laid out in a gridiron pattern. It grew more rapidly than Albemarle, in part because the proprietors launched a campaign to attract settlers. Groups of French Huguenots arrived almost immediately. In 1681, a group of Scots established Stuart's Town at old Port Royal, but it was destroyed by the Spanish in 1683. The proprietors also recruited English dissenters, hoping their moral strictness would balance the influence of the Barbadians. Instead they initiated several decades of political factionalism in the colony. In 1685, when the proprietors attempted to institute the Fundamental Constitutions, 12 members of the assembly, called the parliament, resigned in protest.

NEW YORK AND THE JERSEYS

In 1670, New York was the only English colony without a representative assembly. During the next 15 years, discontent deepened over arbitrary government and special privilege, economic monopolies, and taxation. On occasion, active protest occurred. Long Islanders began tax protests in 1670. They were briefly interrupted in 1673 when the Netherlands, with the cheerful if passive assistance of many Dutch New Yorkers, recaptured New York City during the Third Anglo-Dutch War. The Netherlands held the city for 15 months before the Treaty of Westminster returned it to the English in October 1674.

As governor the English Crown appointed Sir Edmund Andros (pronounced Andrews), a military officer well connected at court. Soon, Long Islanders were protesting to him and demanding a representative assembly. In 1674, the governor recommended to James, duke of York, that citizens be permitted to elect councilors, but the duke refused. Citizens, in turn, refused to pay customs duties in 1680, seizing the collector and shipping him back to England. When Andros was recalled to England soon afterward, he once again advised the duke that more representative government was imperative.

In 1683, Thomas Dongan, a military man and a Catholic, arrived as the new governor. He brought with him instructions from the duke to call an assembly, which he did promptly. On October 17, 1683, a council of six, plus 17 elected deputies, assembled. They passed the Charter of Liberties and Privileges, which was similar to a constitution. It made the representative assembly the supreme legislative authority and guaranteed English rights, English law, freedom of religion, and free elections. It allowed taxation only upon consent of the assembly. In 1684, Dongan, anxious to maintain the relationship the Dutch had established with the Iroquois Confederacy, met with them at a conference in Albany. The Iroquois agreed to become English subjects, and the English agreed to supply them with firearms and assistance against the French.

Colonists continued, however, to be restive about the colony's long-standing system of economic monopolies. New York City was the only legal port of entry; the city also held monopolies on Hudson River shipping, exporting, and flour-milling, the latter requiring every farmer in the colony to send his grain to New York City. Albany had a monopoly on the Indian fur trade. These monopolies enabled a small group of men to control and profit from an entire industry. Similar special privileges were won by artisans and craftsmen in certain industries, although the government proved far more willing to regulate artisans' guilds than the monopolies of the wealthy. In either case, each monopoly was resented by those who did not directly profit. Many colonists consequently engaged in smuggling or illicit trade.

In the Jersey grant of Sir George Carteret and others, confusion and controversy over jurisdiction and other matters continued after 1670. Jersey contained a disparate collection of settlers: Dutch along the Hudson, emigrants from New Haven in Newark, Quakers at Middletown and Shrewsbury, and a group of Barbadian planters in Bergen County who purchased huge tracts and brought slaves. In 1670, settlers resisted when Governor Philip Carteret attempted to collect quitrents and impose oaths of loyalty. In 1672, they met in an unauthorized assembly to discuss ways to avoid proprietary authority. The resistance was quelled after the duke of York announced that those who did not honor the proprietary claim might forfeit their lands and their franchise.

In 1674, Berkeley sold his share in Jersey to two English Quakers, Edward Byllynge and John Fenwick. Shortly after, the colony was divided into East Jersey, still under control of the Carterets, and West Jersey, under Quaker control. (The 1675 diagonal line between the two actually divided the colony into a northeastern section adjoining New York and a southwestern section adjoining the future colony of Pennsylvania.) The Quaker proprietors of West Jersey quarreled among themselves, however, and in 1676 William Penn and two other trustees were appointed to oversee the development of the colony. In 1677, Penn published the Laws, Concessions, and Agreements for West Jersey, the most progressive colonial constitution to date. Settlers were granted full rights to their land, with deeds recorded, and the right to elect an executive and a representative assembly annually. Freedom of religion, freedom of speech in the legislature, and public jury trial were established. English Quakers provided much assistance to the colony, which grew quickly. By 1681, 1,400 Quakers had arrived to join the Swedes, Finns, Dutch, and English in the Delaware River valley, the Quakers carefully purchasing their land from the Lenni Lenape.

In more populous East Jersey, the controversy over jurisdiction continued with the government of New York. After New York governor Andros arrested East Jersey governor Carteret in 1679, Carteret took the matter to the Crown. The claim of the East Jersey proprietors was confirmed. Nonetheless, many settlers, used to outright landownership, continued to resist paying quitrents. In 1682, after Carteret's death, a group of Quakers purchased his proprietary rights.

THE FOUNDING OF PENNSYLVANIA

English Quakers had long desired to establish a colony over which they would have complete control. In 1680, William Penn petitioned King Charles II for a grant along the Delaware River, where he hoped to found a colony based on Quaker principles. Although Penn had been expelled from Oxford and imprisoned several times for his Quaker beliefs, he was the son of a prominent English admiral and remained well connected at court. In 1681, the king made Penn a grant so generous that it caused boundary disputes with New York and Maryland for a century. Penn also asked for and received additional land west and south of the Delaware River, the former New Sweden. Because Pennsylvania was landlocked, Penn needed a harbor and wanted to control the river leading to it. This area, called the Lower Counties, eventually became the colony of Delaware.

Penn's grant was announced as satisfaction of a £16,000 debt owed to the admiral—probably to justify a royal grant to a Quaker. The king also privately told the Privy Council that he hoped to rid England of the most troublesome members of the Society of Friends, as the Quakers called themselves, then numbering about 60,000. Royal officials named the grant Pennsylvania (or Penn's Woods) in honor of Admiral Penn, although William objected to having the colony bear his name, lest it "be looked on as a vanity." Penn's grant gave him the right to decide the form of government in the colony. He was, however, ordered to enforce the Navigation Acts, to submit all laws for the king's approval, and to allow colonists to appeal from the highest courts to the king.

Penn intended his colony to be a "holy experiment," governed according to Quaker principles of toleration and freedom of conscience. Quakers believed in the innate equality of all people before God. They demonstrated this belief by permitting women to speak or preach in religious meetings and to assume some other kinds of authority—shocking ideas to members of other religious denominations. Although few Quakers questioned the existence of differences in worldly rank and wealth, they stressed honest, fair, and humane dealings with all people, regardless of status. Quakers dressed plainly and refused to show deference by removing their hats. They substituted "thee" and "thou," which were familiar and informal terms of address in the 17th century, for more formal or polite words. These Quaker beliefs were very unsettling to other people in the hierarchical and authoritarian world of the 17th century.

Upon obtaining his grant, Penn immediately sent letters to the Indians of the province and initiated a series of treaties to obtain title to the land. In his Conditions and Concessions of 1681, he established rules to prevent land speculation, decreed that "Indians shall have liberty to do all things . . . that any of the planters shall enjoy," and ordered that settlers preserve one wooded acre for each five cleared. For the remainder of his life, Penn maintained good relations with the Lenni Lenape in the east and the Susquehannock and others to the west. He apparently met with Indians unarmed, spoke partially in the Indian languages, and participated in ceremonial games or contests.

Penn planned his colony carefully. He hired a surveyor to design its main port, called Philadelphia, or the City of Brotherly Love. In 1682, he issued a Frame of Government. It provided for a council of 72 men elected by the freeholders (rather than appointed, as was usual) on a rotating basis, one-third each year. The council was to initiate legislation as well as oversee the system of justice and appoint lesser officials. The document also provided for a representative assembly that could reject bills sent by the council, although it could not initiate them. Many of the provisions outlawed certain kinds of behavior that Quakers believed to be offences against God, such as lying, drunkenness, and gambling. Penn's Frame of Government was vague on many other details, however, and was modified several times in succeeding years.

Pennsylvania was more widely advertised in the British Isles and on the continent than any other colony to date. By October 1682, when Penn himself finally arrived, the colony already had 4,000 settlers. The first Pennsylvania Council met on December 4, 1682. It formally united the Lower Counties (modern Delaware) and naturalized the Swedes, Finns, and Dutch living there. It also expanded the laws in the Frame of Government into the so-called Great Law. The Great Law established equal protection and voting rights for members of all religions (although atheists were excluded and only Christians could hold office), eliminated common brutal punishments like bodily mutilation, and eliminated the death penalty for any crime except murder or treason. By 1684, more than 50 shiploads of settlers had arrived from England, Ireland, Wales, Holland, and Germany. The population was already nearly 7,000, with more than 2,000 residing in Philadelphia. Although many Pennsylvania settlers quickly prospered, like residents of other colonies they disliked paying the modest quitrents Penn was entitled to collect.

In 1683, a group of Germans, mostly Quakers led by Mennonite Francis Pastorius, established the second settlement in Pennsylvania, at Germantown. The first Germantown colonists were skilled at cloth-making, and by 1685 they had opened a store in Philadelphia to sell their linen. Many Mennonites, followers of the Anabaptist Menno Simmons, soon immigrated. Early Pennsylvania settlers also included both indentured servants and slaves. Quakers did not reject servitude, although they did require fair treatment by masters. Many Quakers did disapprove of slavery, although Penn himself owned slaves. In February 1688, Pastorius and three other men submitted to the Friends' meeting at Germantown the first written protest against slavery in the English colonies.

THE DOMINION OF NEW ENGLAND

In 1674, the English Crown's advisory Council for Trade and Plantations was replaced by the Committee for Trade and Plantations, a permanent subcommittee of the Privy Council usually called the Lords of Trade. The Lords of Trade quickly began to centralize colonial administration and enforce the Navigation Acts, a duty at which colonial governors were notoriously remiss. In the North American colonies, their goal was to tighten royal control. They turned first to New England, and in particular Massachusetts. Complaints about the Bay Colony's independence, especially in matters of trade, had circulated since the Restoration. In 1676, the Lords of Trade dispatched Edward Randolph to investigate.

Randolph was received cooly, and the Crown's demand that agents be sent to London was rebuffed. Randolph in turn called New England leaders "inconsiderable mechanics." His reports detailed extensive illegal shipping, lack of compliance with royal orders, persecution of religious dissidents, and the annexation of Maine and New Hampshire. When Randolph returned to England, he presented a list of 24 "assumed powers" that the colony exercised without justification. He advised the Crown that royal authority would be welcomed by many in the colony, a questionable conclusion. The Lords of Trade demanded explanations from Massachusetts officials, none of which proved reassuring. In 1679, the Privy Council made New Hampshire a separate, royal colony. It also sent Randolph back to Massachusetts as collector of customs.

Within a year, Randolph had seized 10 ships for illegal trading; all 10 were found not guilty by Massachusetts juries. Massachusetts leaders, their Puritan commonwealth now clearly threatened, finally sent agents to London. They did not plead the colony's case successfully. In 1684, Massachusetts's charter was revoked and it was made a royal colony. In the interim, however, the Massachusetts General Court had repealed all tax laws.

The Lords of Trade viewed the revocation of the charter as the first step toward consolidating the northern colonies under one administration with one governor; it was to be called the Dominion of New England. Eventually, they hoped to unite all 11 of the existing English North American colonies. The lords' planning was interrupted, however, when King Charles II died in 1685 and his brother, the duke of York, ascended the throne as James II. The Lords of Trade quickly established a temporary government for the Dominion of New England, with Joseph Dudley of Massachusetts as acting president. A council of 17 was appointed, none of whom were orthodox Puritans; no representative assembly was provided for. The temporary government operated for about a year—albeit with considerable difficulty, since all tax laws had been repealed and none could be collected. Although the reign of the Puritan oligarchy had ended, the independence of Massachusetts colonists had not. They quickly began to use the ports of Connecticut and Rhode Island to avoid enforcement of the Navigation Acts in Massachusetts.

In England, the Lords of Trade wrote a new constitution for the colony, from which King James II struck the provision for a representative assembly. He allowed to stand, however, a provision for the imposition of quitrents on all landowners in the colony. On December 20, 1686, Sir Edmund Andros returned to America as the first royal governor of the Dominion of New England, which included New York, the Jerseys, and the New England colonies. He appointed a council with representatives from all the colonies, their numbers roughly proportional to population. It met weekly for administrative functions and quarterly to legislate, although attendance was usually small.

Andros was an aristocrat who during his term as governor of New York had been disliked by his constituents and distrusted by New Englanders. Upon his arrival, he immediately scandalized the Puritans by celebrating Christmas. (The Puritans believed Christmas celebrations to be a vestige of what they called "popery," or Catholicism.) By April 1689, when the Dominion of New England was overthrown, Andros had angered religious colonists by insisting that all marriages be performed with Anglican rites, all schoolmasters receive his personal approval, and all Puritan churches be used for Anglican services on alternate Sundays. He had angered the merchants by enforcing the trade laws. He had angered the freemen by revising local control over land distribution and requiring all to obtain new patents in the king's name. He had angered almost everyone by prohibiting more than one town meeting per year and establishing a new tax system, which led to the jailing of protesters. Andros, a military man, was more successful in rebuilding the defenses of the colonies ravaged in King Philip's War. He brought English soldiers to the colony (although the redcoats, as they were called, were not universally welcomed) and established better Indian relations. In 1688, he attacked the French at Penobscot, which unfortunately resulted in a series of retaliatory raids by the French and Abenaki in Maine and northern New England.

Andros's tenure was short, however, due to the Glorious Revolution in England. King James II had been unpopular, in part because he was a Catholic; he received grudging support because he had a Protestant daughter, Mary, from his first marriage to succeed him. In 1688, however, his young second wife (Mary of Modena), also a Catholic, gave birth to a son and new heir. Parliament invited James's daughter Mary and her husband, William of Orange, governor of the Netherlands, to assume the English throne at once. The pair arrived in England in November. Shortly thereafter, sensing the popular opinion against him, James escaped to France, an action Parliament regarded as abdication. In February 1689, Parliament confirmed the ascension of William and Mary to the throne; they were crowned king and queen in April that year.

To discontented colonists, the Glorious (and bloodless) Revolution was an opportunity to end the Dominion of New England. When news reached the colonies that William and Mary had been crowned, Andros was seized and jailed, as were Randolph and other appointed officials. (They remained in jail until February 1690, when the Crown ordered that they be returned to England.) The colonists in Massachusetts established a Council for the Safety and Preservation of the Peace and voted to resume government under the old charter. The Crown, however, would not restore the old charter and granted Massachusetts a new one in 1691. Under the new charter, the governor was appointed by the Crown, although the council was chosen by the assembly. A religious test for the franchise was not permitted, and appeals to the king from the high court were allowed. Plymouth was consolidated with Massachusetts Bay and ended its life as an independent colony. Maine was also put under the jurisdiction of Massachusetts, although New Hampshire remained a separate colony. Both Connecticut and Rhode Island, which had never surrendered their charters, continued to govern themselves as before. The Jerseys were quietly returned to the control of their proprietors.

LEISLER'S REBELLION IN NEW YORK

As much as New Englanders disliked the Dominion of New England, in New York sentiment was even stronger. King James II had refused to approve New York's Charter of Liberties and Privileges, passed in 1683, or a representative assembly for the colony. Having lost the power to set or approve taxes, the citizens increasingly protested tax policies. The always heterogeneous and fractious population divided into several factions, defined by regional economic differences, crosscut by ethnic differences, and crosscut again by religious differences. Tension existed between the older Dutch elite and the newer Anglo-Dutch establishment. Almost everyone resented the self-interested policies of the merchants and large landholders who controlled the council.

In early 1689, when news arrived of the Glorious Revolution, Deputy Governor Francis Nicholson did not immediately proclaim the new king and queen.

Rumors flew that he intended to turn the colony over to the French. Long Island residents replaced royally appointed officials immediately. In Manhattan, a revolt occurred under the leadership of Jacob Leisler, a successful merchant and German immigrant who had married into the older Dutch elite. On May 31, he and about 500 armed followers, primarily Dutch, seized the fort. Nicholson fled to England. Ignoring the appointed council, Leisler called a "convention" of freemen, which voted him "commander in chief." They proclaimed the new king and queen and shortly thereafter convened a legislature, although three counties refused to send delegates.

Meanwhile, the French and their Algonquian allies perceived an opportunity to gain control of the lucrative fur trade from the Iroquois and the English in Albany. They destroyed Schenectady in February 1690 and raided many other frontier towns. Leisler held a conference at Albany, while New England troops sailed to attack Port Royal, Acadia. Representatives planned an invasion of New France for the following summer, although it was never successfully launched. These hostilities were the American front of the War of the League of Augsburg (called King William's War in the English Colonies), which pitted England against the growing power of King Louis XIV's France.

Leisler had support from many factions, primarily small landowners and artisans but also some prominent Dutch families. Although the newer Anglo-Dutch establishment viewed his regime as mob rule, Leisler redressed many long-standing grievances. As months went by, his popularity was lessened somewhat by expenditures for hostilities against the French and Indians. In early 1691, the Crown sent two regiments of troops and a royal governor, Henry Sloughter, to New York. Leisler surrendered peacefully. Nonetheless, his enemies allied with the new administration, and Leisler and nine other rebels were arrested. Leisler and his son-in-law were found guilty of treason and hanged. The deep division and rivalry between pro- and anti-Leislerians continued for many years, however.

THE SOUTHERN COLONIES AFTER 1688

In Maryland, George Calvert, lord Baltimore, was also slow to acknowledge William and Mary as king and queen. As in New York, popular discontent multiplied. In April 1689, a Protestant Association was established, led by former Anglican minister John Coode and others. Their stated purpose was to gain the Catholic proprietor's recognition of the new Protestant monarchs of England, but they acted to take over the Maryland government. In July, about 250 armed men, led by Coode, seized the capital at St. Mary's and forced Governor William Joseph to surrender. The following month they convened a legislature. They also petitioned the crown to make Maryland a royal colony, publishing a list of grievances that included taxes, unrepresentative government, and various offenses related to religious differences. The Protestant Association governed moderately for two years, but in 1692 a new royal governor, Sir Lionel Copley, arrived. Lord Baltimore was deprived of all governmental control of the colony, although he retained the land titles and the quitrent revenue.

In Virginia, Lord Howard of Effingham, governor since 1684, quarreled with the assembly and dissolved it in May 1688; he did not reconvene it until April 1689. Although a small revolt was attempted upon the ascension of

Albemarle, detail of a 1682 map by
Joel Gascoyne (*Library of Congress*)

William and Mary (Effingham, like Calvert, was Catholic) it was not successful. Former New York governor Nicholson arrived as deputy governor in 1689 and contributed significantly to smoother political relations during the following two years. He toured the frontiers and made some progress in Indian relations. The assembly finally passed legislation for a free school and college, although they were not established immediately.

In the large Carlonina proprietary grant given to a group of eight English nobles in 1663 by King Charles II, popular discontent remained plentiful, but no effective leader emerged. In Albemarle (modern North Carolina), the corrupt administration of Seth Sothel, the first Carolina proprietor to come to America, was ended in 1689 when the legislature put him on trial and banished him. In Clarendon province (modern South Carolina), the English proprietors installed John Colleton of Barbados (a relative of proprietor Sir John Colleton) as governor in 1686. They apparently hoped he could manage the Carolina Barbadian faction—but their hopes were soon dashed. Colleton angered the colonists by forbidding a planned attack on the Spanish in Florida. Controversy over approval of the Fundamental Constitutions continued and the parliament, or assembly, demanded the right to initiate laws and govern according to the Concessions and Agreements of 1665. In response the proprietors ordered the assembly dissolved and all laws rescinded. By 1690, in the absence of any written law, Colleton governed by executive decree. At this juncture the banished Sothel arrived from Albemarle and assumed control of the government in Charleston. Colleton briefly summoned the militia, but Sothel gained the support of many citizens by immediately reconvening the assembly. He was grudgingly recognized by the other proprietors in England as the legitimate governor and Colleton was banished. Within a year, however, Sothel's fellow proprietors disallowed all legislation passed under his arbitrary administration. They replaced him with a new governor, Philip Ludwell, a Virginia landowner who had married the widow of late proprietor (and Virginia governor) Sir William Berkeley. Sothel retired to his extensive estate in North Carolina.

CHRONICLE OF EVENTS

1670

The estimated non-Indian population is in excess of 35,000 in Massachusetts Bay, 5,000 in Plymouth, 2,000 in Rhode Island, 2,000 in New Hampshire, 1,000 in Jersey, 45,000 in Virginia, and 13,000 in Maryland.

New York is the only English colony without a representative assembly.

Jersey residents refuse to pay quitrents to proprietor Sir George Carteret. Turmoil ensues for two years.

Property qualifications for voting are established in Virginia and Maryland.

Charles Town (modern South Carolina) is founded.[1]

1671

In Plymouth, Wampanoag chief Metacom, or King Philip, is arrested. His guns are confiscated, and he is forced to agree that the Wampanoag are subject to English law.

1672

Jersey colonists hold an unauthorized assembly, but James, duke of York, threatens to forfeit their land and disenfranchise them.

In Virginia, a law sets a bounty on the head of maroons, or slaves who form fugitive communities.

1673

In England, the Plantation Duty Act is passed. Customs are levied on enumerated items shipped from colony to colony.

The Third Anglo-Dutch War breaks out between England and the Netherlands. The Dutch destroy the tobacco fleet in Virginia. New York is captured and remains in Dutch hands for 15 months.

In Virginia, Lords Arlington and Culpeper are granted all of Virginia as a proprietary grant. They eventually relinquish governmental control but continue collecting quitrents.

1674

In England, the Committee for Trade and Plantations, called the Lords of Trade, takes over the administration of the colonies. It is a permanent committee of the Privy Council.

New York is recaptured by the English. Sir Edmund Andros is appointed governor. He informs the duke of York of the colonists' desire for a representative assembly, but James refuses to establish one.

A proprietary interest in Jersey is purchased by two Quakers, Edward Byllynge and John Fenwick. They quarrel, and William Penn is made arbiter. Byllynge transfers his interest to Penn and others.

1675

The estimated non-Indian population of Connecticut is 12,000.

In New England, King Philip's War begins with the Wampanoag, who are soon joined by the Nipmuc and Narragansett. The war spreads quickly up the Connecticut River valley.

Jersey is divided into East Jersey, under control of the Carteret proprietors; and West Jersey, under control of the Quakers. The Quaker migration to West Jersey begins.

In Virginia, skirmishes begin between Susquehannock, Doeg, and white settlers in the backcountry frontier.

1676

Edward Randolph arrives in Massachusetts, having been sent by the Lords of Trade to investigate the independent colony.

January: In Virginia, Indians kill the overseer of Nathaniel Bacon's farm. By March, 300 Virginians will have been killed. Governor William Berkeley refuses to attack and establishes a defensive policy.

February: As King Philip's War progresses, Indians attack Lancaster, Massachusetts; one of their captives is Mary Rowlandson. She will later write a narrative of her experiences that will become a colonial bestseller and start a new American genre of literature called the captivity narrative.

April: In Virginia, Nathaniel Bacon leads an expedition of 300 volunteers against the Pamunkey. In Massachusetts, Indians attack within 17 miles of Boston.

June: After Bacon arrives in Jamestown with armed supporters, Governor Berkeley commissions him to lead troops against Indians in the backcountry. The House of Burgesses passes many reforms known as Bacon's Laws.

July: Bacon and a force of 1,300 march on Jamestown and capture it.

August: Metacom, or King Philip, is killed by an Indian fighting with the English. The war in New England comes to an end. Many adult Indians are sold into slavery in the West Indies. Wampanoag society has been destroyed; colonists must recover from one of the most destructive wars in American history relative to the population engaged.

September: In Maryland, rebels attempt to capture the government; they fail and are hanged.

October: Bacon unexpectedly dies of dysentery. His rebellion dissipates, and Berkeley regains control.

1677

Randolph returns to England. He reports that Massachusetts has usurped royal authority through 24 "assumed powers" and advises that its independence be curbed.

William Penn publishes the Laws, Concessions, and Agreements, a progressive constitution for West Jersey.

Virginia governor Berkeley is recalled to England.

In Albemarle (modern North Carolina), Culpeper's Rebellion occurs over custom duties; the dissident colonists remain in power and John Culpepper, leader of the rebellion, is acquitted by the proprietors.

1679

New Hampshire is made a royal colony separate from Massachusetts Bay.

1680

In New York, citizens refuse to pay customs duties.

In Virginia, a law is passed forbidding slaves to carry arms.

In Carolina, the Charles Town settlement moves to the site of modern Charleston, South Carolina.

1681

William Penn receives a charter for Pennsylvania from the king; both the northern and southern borders of the generous grant will be disputed for many years. Penn also receives the Delaware settlements.

In Maryland, Josiah Fendell and John Coode lead a rebellion and are banished.

1682

Penn issues a Frame of Government for Pennsylvania. The site of Philadelphia is surveyed.

October: Penn arrives in Pennsylvania.

December: The first Pennsylvania Assembly meets. It passes the Great Law.

1683

Thomas Dongan arrives as the governor of New York. He brings orders from the duke of York to establish an assembly. The first New York Assembly meets in October and passes the Charter of Liberties and Privileges.

A group of Germans, mostly Quakers, founds Germantown, the second settlement in Pennsylvania.

1684

The Massachusetts charter is revoked; it becomes a royal colony.

New York governor Dongan makes a treaty with the Iroquois at Albany; they become English allies against other colonial powers.

1685

King Charles II dies and his Catholic brother, the duke of York, succeeds him as King James II of England.

1686

The Dominion of New England is established, with a temporary president and council but no popular assembly. It includes Massachusetts, New Hampshire, Maine, Connecticut, Rhode Island, Plymouth, and New York. In December, Edmund Andros arrives as the first governor.

1688

February: Quakers and Mennonites in Germantown, Pennsylvania, issue the first written protest against slavery in the English colonies.

November: In England, the Glorious Revolution begins. King James II flees, and his Protestant daughter, Mary, and her husband, William of Orange, become queen and king of England upon the invitation of Parliament.

1689

In Europe, the War of the League of Augsburg begins (called King William's War in the English colonies); England is allied against France.

February: William and Mary formally become king and queen of England, ending the Glorious, or "Bloodless," Revolution.

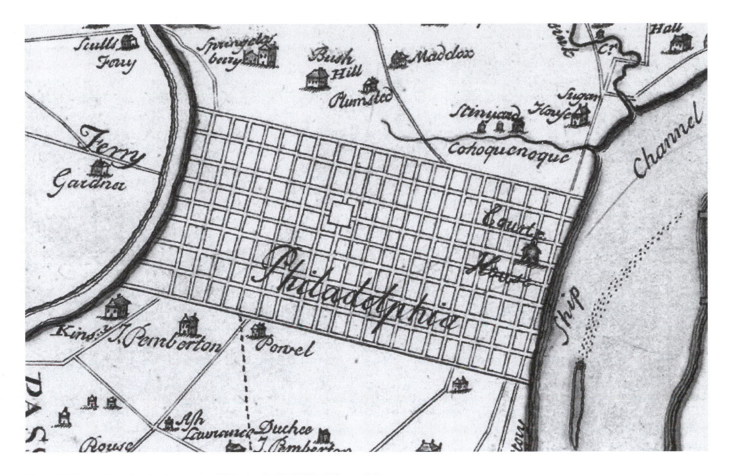

Plan of Philadelphia, detail of a map by Nicholas Scull (1752) *(Library of Congress)*

April: Boston insurgents jail Andros. The Dominion of New England comes to an end. The New England colonies reestablish charter government. In Maryland, the Protestant Association is formed, supposedly to proclaim the new king and queen of England.

May: Massachusetts votes to reestablish charter government. In New York, Jacob Leisler and his followers seize control of the government.

July: In Maryland, Coode's Rebellion occurs when protesters seize St. Mary's. They will rule moderately for two years.

1690

The estimated non-Indian population is in excess of 4,000 in both New Hampshire and Rhode Island, almost 50,000 in Massachusetts, 8,000 in the Jerseys, and more than 24,000 in Maryland.

In Carolina, the proprietors declare all laws void; Governor John Colleton governs by edict.

February: French and Indian allies destroy Schenectady, New York, and begin attacks on New England settlements.

May: New England forces capture Port Royal, Acadia. Representatives of the northern colonies meet in Albany and plan a joint invasion of Canada.

1691

Massachusetts is granted a new charter; religious affiliation is no longer a qualification for voting. Connecticut and Rhode Island resume their old charters. Plymouth is consolidated with Massachusetts Bay and ends its life as a separate colony.

March: Henry Sloughter arrives as royal governor of New York, and Jacob Leisler is hanged.

EYEWITNESS TESTIMONY

What course is taken about instructing the people within your government in the Christian religion . . . ?

Answer. The same course that is taken in England out of towns; every man according to his ability instructing his children. We have forty eight parishes, and our ministers are well paid, and by my consent should be better if they would pray oftener and preach less. But of all other commodities, so of this, the worst are sent us, and we had few that we could boast of, since the persecution in Cromwell's tyranny drove divers worthy men hither. But, I thank God, *there are no free schools nor printing,* and I hope we shall not have these hundred years; for learning has brought disobedience, and heresy, and sects into the world, and *printing* has divulged them, and libels against the best government. God keep us from both!

Governor William Berkeley to English officials, 1670, in Hart, ed., American History, *vol. 1, p. 241.*

Capital Laws

1. If any Man or Woman after legal conviction shall Have or Worship any other God but the Lord God, he shall be put to death, *Deu.* 13.6. 17, 21. *Ex.* 22.2.

2. If any person within this Colony shall Blaspheme the Name of God the Father, Son or Holy Ghost, with direct, express, presumptuous or high-handed Blasphemy, or shall Curse in the like manner, he shall be put to death, *Levit.* 24. 15, 16. . . .

11. If any person rise up by False Witness wittingly and of purpose to take away any man's life, he or she shall be put to death, *Deut.* 19. 16, 18, 19. . . .

14. If any Child or Children above *sixteen years old,* and of sufficient understanding, shall Curse or Smite their natural Father or Mother, he or they shall be put to death, unless it can be sufficiently testified, that the Parents have been very unchristianly negligent in the education of such Children, or so provoked them by extreme and cruel correction, that they have been forced thereunto to preserve themselves from death or maiming, *Exod.* 21. 17. *Levit.* 20.9. *Exod.* 21.15.

15. If any man have a stubborn or rebellious Son, of sufficient understanding and years, *viz. sixteen years of age,* which will not obey the voice of his Father, or the voice of his Mother, and that when they have chastened him, he will not hearken unto them; then may his Father or Mother, being his natural Parents lay hold on him, and bring him to the Magistrates assembled in Court . . . such a Son shall be put to death, *Deut.* 21.20. 21. . . .

Connecticut "Blue Laws," 1672, in Hart, ed., American History, *vol. 1, pp. 489–90.*

For so much of the said Commodities as shall be laded and put on board such Ship or Vessel these following rates and Duties, That is to say:

For Sugar White the hundred Weight containing one hundred and twelve pounds five shillings;

For Brown Sugar and Muscavadoes the hundred weight containing one hundred and twelve pounds one shilling [and] six pence;

For Tobacco the pound one penny;

For Cotton-wool the pound one half-penny;

For Indigo the pound, two pence;

For Ginger the hundred Weight containing one hundred and twelve pounds one shilling;

For Logwood the hundred Weight containing one hundred and twelve pounds, five pounds;

For Fusticke and all other Dying-wool the hundred Weight containing one hundred and twelve pounds six pence;

And also for every pound of Cacao-nuts one penny.

Plantation Duties Act, 1672, in Macdonald, ed., Documentary Source Book, *p. 79.*

Sarah Scott presented for Reviling and striking her Mother. Upon due hearing of the case, The Court Sentences her to stand upon a Block or Stoole of two foot high in the Markett place in Boston upon a thursday immediately after lecture with an inscription upon her breast in a faire character For undutiful abusive & reviling speeches & carriages to her naturall mother. . . .

County Court, Suffolk, Massachusetts, July 1673, in Cott, ed., Root, *p. 60, 61.*

Various are the reports and conjectures of the causes of [*King Philip's*] war. Some impute it to an imprudent zeal in the magistrates of Boston to Christianize those heathen before they were civilized and enjoining them the strict observation of their laws, which, to a people so rude and licentious, hath proved even intolerable. . . . [F]or that while the magistrates, for their profit, put the laws severely in execution against the Indians, the people, on the other side, for lucre and gain, entice and provoke the Indians to the breach thereof, especially to drunkenness. . . . Massachusetts having made a law that every Indian drunk should pay 10s. or be whipped. . . . [T]he magistrates finding much trouble and no profit to arise to the government by whipping, did change that punishment into 10 days work . . . which did highly incense the Indians.

Some believe there have been vagrant and Jesuitical priests, who have made it their businesses for some years past, to go from Sachem to Sachem, to exasperate the Indians against the English and to bring them into a confederacy, and that they were promised supplies from France and other parts to extirpate the English nation out of the continent of America. Others impute the cause to some injuries offered to the Sachem, Philip; for he being possessed of a tract of land called Mount Hope, a very fertile, pleasant and rich soil, some English had a mind to dispossess him thereof, who never wanting one pretense or other to attain their end, complained of injuries done by Philip and his Indians to their stock and cattle, whereupon Philip was often summoned before magistrate, sometimes imprisoned, and never released but upon with a considerable part of his land.

But the government of Massachusetts (to give it in their own words) do declare these are the great evils for which God hath given the heathen commission to rise against them: The woeful breach of the 5th commandment, in contempt of their authority, which is a sin highly provoking to the Lord: For men wearing long hair and periwigs made of women's hair; for women wearing borders of hair and for cutting, curling, and laying out the hair, and disguising themselves by following strange fashions in their apparel: For profaneness in the people not frequenting their meetings, and others going away before the blessing be pronounced: For suffering the Quakers to live amongst them . . . contrary to their old laws and resolutions.

Edward Randolph's report to the Crown, ca. 1675, in Hart, ed., American History, *vol. 1, pp. 458–59.*

"Gentlemen and Fellow Soldiers: . . . The Governor is now in Gloster County endeavoring to raise Forces against us, having Declared us Rebels and Traitors: if true, crimes indeed too great for Pardon; our consciences herein are our best witnesses, and theirs so conscious, as like cowards therefore they will not have the courage to face us. It is Revenge that hurries them on without regard to the People's Safety, and had rather we should be murder'd and our ghosts sent to our

Slaughter'd country-men by their actings, than we live to hinder them of their Interest with the heathen, and preserve the remaining part of our Fellow Subjects from their cruelties. Now then we must be forced to turn our swords to our own defense, or expose ourselves to their Mercies, or Fortune of the woods, whilst his majesty's country here lies in Blood and Wasting (like a candle) at both ends. How Incapable we may be made (if we should proceed) through Sickness, want of Provisions, Slaughter, wounds less or more, none of us is void of the Sense hereof. . . . To which they all cry'd "Amen, amen, we are all ready and will rather die in the Field than be hanged like Rogues, or Perish in the woods, expos'd to the Favors of the merciless Indians."

The Royal Commissioners report Bacon's speech, 1677, in Andrews, ed., Narratives, *pp. 119–20.*

I have much to write of lamentation over the work of Christ among our praying Indians . . . the poor Wameset Indians who in a fright fled into the woods until they were half starved the occasion of their flight was, because some ungodly and unruly youth, came upon them where they were ordered by Authority to be, called them forth their houses, shot at them, killed a child of godly parents wounded his mother and 4 more. . . . At another place there were a company . . . surprised by the Enemy and carried away captive and we cannot hear anything of them, what is become of them, whether any of them be martyred we cannot tell, we cannot say how many there be of them but more

Old Ship Meetinghouse (Congregational), Hingham, Massachusetts, built 1681 *(Photo by Dorthy Abbe for Historic American Building Survey)*

than an hundred and sundry of them right Godly, both men and women, Another great company of new praying Indians of the Niepmuk fled at the beginning of the Wars. . . .

The Reverend John Eliot to English supporters, October 1675, in Company for Propagation, Some Correspondence, *pp. 54–55.*

[*King Philip*] being hid in a Swamp on Mount Hope Neck, with his little Party, one of his *Indians* being discontented with him made an Escape from him, and came to Rhode-Island, and informed Capt. Church a Plymouth Captain of a Company. . . . [W]hereupon the said Captain and his Company with some Rhode-Island Men went in Pursuit and Search after him, taking an Indian Guide with them, and beset a Swamp where they heard he was, which was very miry, and the Ground so loose, that our Men sunk to the Middle in their Attempts to come at this skulking Company; but all in vain, the Passage was too difficult.

   While we were thus beset with Difficulties in this Attempt, the Providence of God wonderfully appeared, for by Chance the Indian Guide and the Plymouth Man, being together, the Guide espied an Indian and bid the Plymouth-man shoot, whose Gun went not off, only flashed in the Pan; with that the Indian looked about, and was going to shoot, but the Plymouth-man prevented him, and shot the Enemy through the Body, dead, with a Brace of Bullets; and approaching the Place where he lay, upon Search, it appeared to be King Philip, to their no small Amazement and great joy. This seasonable Prey was soon divided, they cut off his Head and Hands, and conveyed them to Rhode-Island, and quartered his Body, and hung it upon four Trees.

Richard Hutchinson, 1676, "The War in New-England Visibly Ended," in Hart, ed., American History, *vol. 1, p. 461.*

At which time the Susquo-hannan Indians (a known Enemy to that Country) having made an Insurrection, and killed divers of the English, amongst whom it was his [*Nathaniel Bacon's*] fortune to have a Servant slain; in revenge of whose death, and other damage(s) he received from those turbulent Susquo-hanians, without the Governor's consent he furiously took up Arms against them and was so fortunate as to put them to flight, but not content therewith; the aforesaid Governor hearing of his eager pursuit after the vanquished Indians, sent out a select Company of Soldiers to command him to desist; but he instead of listning thereunto, persisted in his Revenge, and sent to the Governor to entreat his Commission, at he might more cheerfully prosecute his design; which being denied him . . he notwithstanding continued to make head with his own Servants, and other English . . . against them. In this interim the people of Henrica had returned him Burgess of their County; and he in order thereunto, took his own Sloop and came down towards James Town, conducted by thirty odd Soldiers. . . . [I]t being perceived that he had lined the Bushes of the said Town with Soldiers, the governor thereupon ordered an alarm to be beaten through the whole town, which took so hot, that Bacon thinking himself not secure whilst remained there within reach of their Fort, immediately commanded his men aboard, and tow'd his Sloop up the River; which the Governor perceiving, ordered the Ships which lay at Sandy-point to pursue and take him . . . so that Mr. Bacon finding himself pursued both before and behind, after some capitulations, quietly surrendered himself Prisoner to the Governor's Commissioners. . . .

Anonymous, 1677, in Hart, ed., American History, *vol. 1, p. 243.*

I was at this time knitting a pair of white Cotton Stockings for my Mistress; and I had not yet wrought upon the Sabbath-day: when the Sabbath came, they bade me go to work; I told them it was Sabbath-day, and desired them to let me rest, and told them I would do as much more to-morrow; to which they answered me, they would break my face. And here I cannot but take notice of the strange providence of God in preserving the Heathen: They were many hundreds, old and young . . . and they travelled with all they had, bag and baggage, and yet they got over this River aforesaid; and on Monday they set their Wigwams on fire, and away they went: on that very day came the English Army after them to this River, and saw the smoke of their Wigwams; and yet this River put a stop to them. God did not give them courage or activity to go over after us; we were not ready for so great a mercy as victory and deliverance; if we had been, God would have found a way for the English to have passed this River, as well as for the Indians, with their Squaws and Children, and all their Luggage. —*Oh that my People had hearkened to me, and Israel had walked in my wayes, I should soon have sub-*

dued their Enemies, and turned my hand against their Adversaries, Psal. lxxxi: 13.14.

Mary Rowlandson's captivity narrative, 1677, in Andrews, ed., Journeys, *p. 40.*

Upon the 4th day of [*October*] 1677 . . . a parcel of men to the number of 30 or 40 of the precinct of Pasquotank . . . being set on by the foresaid [*John*] Culpeper . . . did without making any addresses complaint, or information to the deponent or any else in authority, and without any lawful warrant or order, with force and arms *vid.* swords, guns, and pistols, violently rush into the house where the deponent and 2 more of the Lords Proprietor's Deputies were present and seized us as their prisoners and then went to searching over the public records and other of the deponents writings. . . . [H]aving also in this action sent abroad up and down the Country their seditious libels drawn by the said Culpeper to put all in a flame, and on the said 4th of October a little after the deponent and the other 2 Deputies aforesaid were seized their prisoners. . . .

Affidavit of Thomas Miller, Carolina customs collector, October 1677, in Andrews, ed., Narratives, *pp. 152–53.*

Upon complaint made to this Court by Elizabeth Waters that her Husband William Waters doth refuse to allow her victuals clothing and fireing necessary for her Support or livelihood and hath acted many unkindnesses and cruelties towards her: The Court having sent for the said William Waters and heard both partys, do Order that the said Waters be admonish't for his cruelty and unkindness to his wife, and that he forthwith provide Suitable meate drinke and apparrell . . . or allow her five Shilling per weeke.

County Court, Suffolk, Massachusetts, July 1679, in Cott, ed., Root, *p. 63.*

. . . we leave every Man to walk as God shall persuade their hearts, and do actively and passively yield obedience to the Civil Magistrate and do not actively disturb the Civil peace and live peaceably in the Corporation as our Charter requires, and have liberty to frequent any meetings of worship for their better Instruction and information, but as for beggars and vagabonds we have none amongst us; and as for lame and impotent persons there is a due course taken. This may further humbly inform your Lordships that our predecessors about forty years since left their native country and comfortable settlements there because they could not in their private opinions conform to the Liturgy, forms and ceremonies of the Church of England, and transported themselves and families over the Ocean seas to dwell in this remote wilderness that they might enjoy their liberty in their opinions, which upon application to his gracious Majesty after his happy restoration did of his bountiful goodness grant us. . . .

Rhode Island governor Peleg Sandford to the Lords of Trade, 1680, in Hart, ed., American History, *vol. 1, p. 409.*

We started out to go to Cambridge, lying to the northeast of Boston, in order to see their college, and printing office. . . . We followed a road which we supposed was the right one, but went full half an hour out of the way, and would have gone still further, had not a negro who met us, and of whom we inquired, disabused us of our mistake. . . . We reached Cambridge, about eight o'clock. It is not a large village, and the houses stand very much apart. The college building is the most conspicuous among them. We went to it, expecting to see something curious, as it is the only college, or would-be academy of the Protestants in all America, but we found ourselves mistaken. In approaching the house, we neither heard nor saw any thing mentionable; but, going to the other side of the building, we heard noise enough in an upper room, to lead my comrade to suppose they were engaged in disputation. We entered, and went up stairs, when a person met us, and requested us to walk in, which we did. We found there, eight or ten young fellows, sitting around, smoking tobacco, with the smoke of which the room was so full, that you could hardly see; and the whole house smelt so strong of it, that when I was going up stairs, I said, this is certainly a tavern. We excused ourselves, that we could speak English only a little, but understood Dutch or French, which they did not. However, we spoke as well as we could. We inquired how many professors there were, and they replied not one, that there was no money to support one. We asked how many students there were. They said at first, thirty, and then came down to twenty; I afterwards understood there are probably not ten. They could hardly speak a word of Latin, so that my comrade could not converse with them.

Jasper Dankers, Journal of a Voyage to New York, *1680, in Hart, ed.,* American History, *vol. 1, pp. 498–99.*

Now for the Planter's late Objections against this work, as I have heard them represented. . . .

That it would make them [*slaves*] less governable; the contrary to which is experimentally known amongst their Neighbors, both French and Spaniards in those parts. Now 'twould be too great a blemish to the Reformation, to suppose that Popery only makes its Converts better, but Protestancy worse; as this Allegation being admitted, it must be granted. And to prevent any fond conceit in them of Liberty, (an especial branch of the same Article,) if there be any such danger, let two or three of each great Family be first baptized; whereby the rest seeing them continued as they were, that Opinion would soon vanish. . . .

As to their (alike pretended) Stupidity, there is as little truth therein: divers of them being known and confessed by their Owners, to be extraordinary Ingenious, and even to exceed many of the English. As for the rest, they were much the same with other People, destitute of the means of knowledge, and wanting Education.

Virginia reverend Morgan Godwyn, "Proposals for the Carrying on of the Negro's Christianity," 1681, in Hart, ed., American History, *vol. 1, p. 300.*

The Maryland mission flourishes; the seed which our Fathers sowed there is growing up into a copious crop and promises an abundant harvest hereafter. Four years ago they opened, in the midst of barbarism, a school of humane letters, conducted by two of them, and the [*Indian*] youths born there, unusually devoted to letters, are making good progress. This new-born school has sent to St. Omer two students, who are surpassed in intelligence by few Europeans and strive for the palm with the foremost of their class. Hence we infer that these lands, undeservedly called barbarous, are most prolific, not alone of gold and silver and other products of the earth, but also of men made for virtue and the higher education. . . .

All this year there has been a great contention about property. The enemies of the Society have enviously spread the report that it possessed immense wealth, almost enough to sustain an army, thus turning to the injury of the Society the very beneficence of our Fathers, who to those who have had recourse to them have administered the desired aid promptly, and in proportion to their slender resources generously; and yet it is certain that those who speak thus are either deceived or deceiving, for whatever Ours possess in

[*Maryland*] would hardly suffice to support a hundred. And if we take account of what is lost through the ignorance of those in charge of it, of what is lost through the avarice of rustics [*tenant farmers*] withholding the annual revenues, of what is spent on lawyers that the estate itself be not filched away, it suffices for far fewer, unless they aid themselves by their own labor.

Annual letter of Maryland Jesuits, 1681, in Hall, ed., Narratives, *p. 143.*

The Method laid down for Sale and Division of the Country of West-Jersey, is by Proprieties, (that is to say) One Propriety contains the Hundredth Part of the Whole Country: Of which Proprieties, many are already Sold, and disposed of to Purchasers; and several of the same remains yet to be Sold. In each of these Hundred Parts or Proprieties, the Quantity of Acres, cannot be absolutely Ascertained; but its generally judged to be Twenty Thousand Acres, and up-wards; but some have accounted each Propriety to contain much more. And if any Person be not minded to deal for a Whole Propriety; Two, Four, Six, Eight, or more, may join in the Purchase thereof; There being Land enough in one of these Proprieties for many Families.

"The Present State of West Jersey," 1681, in Myers, ed., Narratives, *pp. 193–94.*

Our further will and pleasure is, that a transcript of Duplicate of all laws which shall be so as aforesaid, made and published within the said province, shall within five years after the making thereof, be transmitted and delivered to the privy Council . . . ; And if any of the said Laws within the space of six months, after that they shall be so transmitted and delivered, be declared by us . . . in our . . . privy Council, inconsistent with the sovereignty or lawful prerogative of us, . . . or contrary to the faith and allegiance due by [to] the legal Government of this realm, from the said William Penn . . . or of the Planters and Inhabitants of the said province; and that thereupon any of the said Laws shall be adjudged and declared to be void. . . .

Charter of Pennsylvania, March 1681, in Macdonald, ed., Documentary Source Book, *p. 82.*

Claes Jansen brings in the ear mark for his cattle and hogs and desires that the same may be recorded. . . .

Justice Otto Ernest Coch acquaints the Court, that he has bought and paid of the Indian proprietors a certain swampy or marshy island called by the Indians

Quistconck lying at the upper end of Tinnachkonck Island in the river opposite Andrews Boone's Creek; and desires the Court's approbation. The Court having well informed themselves about the premises, do allow thereof. . . .

Upon complaint made by the overseers of the highways; the Court have and do hereby condemn John Champion to pay a fine of twenty and five gilders, for his not working upon the highway when due warning was given him. . . .

Benck Salung sworn in Court sayeth that Hendrick Colman told him that he heard Moens Staeckst say that all the Court were Rogues. . . .

Upon an information of William Coyles Constable at the falls against Gilbert Wheeler at the said falls, for selling of strong liquors by retail to the Indians contrary to the laws. . . . The Court have and do hereby condemn the said Gilbert Wheeler to pay a fine the sum of four pounds. . . .

County Court Records, Upland, Pennsylvania, June 1681, in Hart, ed., American History, *vol. 2, pp. 206–08.*

This great God has written his law in our hearts, by which we are taught and commanded to love, and to help, and to do good to one another. Now this great God hath been pleased to make me concerned in your part of the world; and the King of the country where I live hath given me a great province therein; but I desire to enjoy it with your love and consent, that we may always live together as neighbors and friends. . . . Now, I would have you well observe, that I am very sensible to the unkindness and injustice which have been too much exercised toward you by the people of these parts of the world, who have sought themselves to make great advantages by you, rather than to be examples of justice and goodness unto you. This I hear has been a matter of trouble to you, and caused great grudging and animosities, sometimes to the shedding of blood, which hath made the great God angry. I have a great love and regard toward you, and desire to win and gain your love and friendship by a kind, just and peaceable life; and the people I send are of the same mind, and in all things behave themselves accordingly; and if in any thing any shall offend you or your people, you shall have a full and speedy satisfaction for the same, by an equal number of just men on both sides. . . .

William Penn's letter to Pennsylvania Indians, August 1681, quoted in Wallower, Colonial Pennsylvania, *p. 52.*

This Day I again spent in secret Humiliations and Supplications before the Lord.

Matters of Humiliation, were, My old and new Sins. My exceeding Want of *Grace.* And my wonderful Unprofitableness in every Relation.

Matters of Supplication, were, That God would be reconciled unto me; and that the Mediation of the Lord Jesus Christ, might rescue me from the Dangers whereto my Sins exposed me. . . .

The Lord helped me, in the morning of this Day, to bewail my own Vileness, before Him, with many Tears, and with much Abasement, and Confusion of Spirit.

When I came to seek *Reconciliation,* the Lord put Arguments into my Mouth; I pleaded, Jer. 3. 12 and at last, I concluded, "Lord, What wilt thou have me to do? Am I to confess my Sin? I have done it; Oh! do thou now forgive the Iniquity thereof. Am I to renounce my Sin? I do so, I do it; it is an evil, bitter, hateful Thing unto me. Thou art my only Portion. . . . Am I to go unto the Lord Jesus Christ? He only can make Satisfaction for my Sins, and purchase my Reconciliation. To Him I would go. Lord, Help me; for tho' I hear Him calling, *look and be saved! and come and have Rest.* Yet, except the Father draw me, I cannot look, I cannot come.

The Reverend Cotton Mather, September 3, 1681, Diary, *pp. 26–27.*

. . . in the purchase of those Negroes I requested you to buy for me . . . five or six, whereof three or four to be boys, a man and woman or men and women, the boys from eight to seventeen or eighteen, the rest as young as you can procure them. . . .

The Plantation where I now live contains a thousand acres, at least 700 acres of it being rich thicket, the remainder good hearty plantable land, without any waste either by marshes or great swamps the commodiousness, conveniency and pleasantness yourself well knows, upon it there is three quarters well furnished with all necessary houses; grounds and fencing, together with a choice crew of negroes at each plantation, most of them this Country born, the remainder as likely as most in Virginia, there being twenty-nine in all, with stocks of cattle and hogs at each quarter, upon the same land, is our Dwelling house furnished with all accommodations for a comfortable and gentile living . . . four good Cellars, a Dairy, Dovecot, Stable, Barn, Henhouse, Kitchen and all other conveniencys and all in a manner new, a large Orchard, of about 2500

Malvern Hill, Henrico County, Virginia, built late 17th century
(Historic American Building Survey)

Apple trees most grafted, well fenced with a Locust fence, which is as durable as most brick walls, a Garden, a hundred foot square, well paled in, a Yard wherein is most of the foresaid necessary houses, pallizado'd in with locust Puncheons....

> *Letter of Colonel William Fitzhugh, Virginia planter, 1681–86, in Hart, ed.,* American History, *vol. 1, pp. 303–06.*

Ashley-River, about seven Miles in from the Sea, divides it self into two Branches; the Southernmost retaining the name of *Ashley-River,* the North Branch is called *Cooper-River.* In May, 1680 the Lords Proprietors sent their Orders to the Government there, appointing the Port-Town for these two Rivers to be Built on the Point of Land that divides them, and to be called *Charles* Town, since which time about an hundred Houses are there Built, and more are Building daily by the Persons of all sorts that come there to Inhabit, from the more Northern English Colonies, and the Sugar Islands, *England and Ireland;* and many Persons who went to *Carolina* Servants, being Industrious since they came out of their times with their Masters, at whose charge they were Transported, have gotten good Stocks of Cattle, and Servants of their own; have here also Built Houses, and exercise their Trades: And many that went thither in that condition, are now worth several Hundreds of Pounds, and live in a very plentiful condition, and their Estates still increasing.

> *Samuel Wilson,* An Account of the Province of Carolina, *1682, in Hart, ed.,* American History, *vol. 1, p. 284.*

Concerning the Laws Given by William Penn

Firstly, no one shall be disturbed on account of his belief, but freedom of conscience shall be granted to all inhabitants of the province, so that every nation may build and conduct churches and schools according to their desires.

2. Sunday shall be consecrated to the public worship of God. The teaching of God shall be so zealously carried on that its purity can be recognized in each listener from the fruits which arise from it....

4. The sessions of the court shall be held publicly, at appointed times, so that everyone may attend them....

6. Cursing, blasphemy, misuse of the name of God, quarreling, cheating, drunkenness, shall be punished with the pillory.

7. All workmen shall be content with their definite stipulated wages.

8. Each child, that is twelve years of age, shall be put to some handicraft or other honorable trade.

> *Francis Pastorius, 1682,* Geographical Description of Pennsylvania, *in Myers, ed.,* Narratives, *pp. 379–80.*

The 30th of July came an Indian to our Governor and told him that 800 Spaniards were upon their march coming from St. Augustine. (a place . . . about 150 miles to the South of us, where the Spaniards are seated and have a pretty strong Town) to fall upon the English, upon which the Council met three times and ordered 20 great Guns . . . to be brought to Charles Town, and sent Scouts at a good distance (knowing which way they must come) to discover their strength and the truth of it, which if they had seen anything were to return with all speed, and 700 men were to have met them, which were to lay in Ambuscade in a Cave, swam to where the Spaniards were to come, through a Marsh, that every step they would be up to their middle. Our people were so far from being afraid that they mightily rejoiced at the news of it, wishing that they might have some just cause of War with the Spaniards, that they might grant commissions to Privateers, and themselves fall on them at St. Augustine....

> *Letter of Thomas Newe, May 29, 1682, in Salley, ed.,* Narratives, *pp. 185–86.*

On October 24, [*1683*] I, Francis Daniel Pastorius, with the good will of the governor, laid out another new city, of the name of Germantown or Germanopolis, at a distance of two hour's walk from Philadelphia, where there are a good black fertile soil, and many fresh wholesome springs of water, many oak, walnut, and chestnut trees, and also good pasturage for cattle. The first settlement consisted of only twelve families of forty-one persons, the greater part High German mechanics and weavers, because I had ascertained that linen cloth would be indispensable. . . . Before this, I had also built a little house in Philadelphia, thirty feet long and fifteen wide. Because of the scarcity of glass the windows were of oiled paper. Over the house-door I had written:

Parva Domus, sed amica Bonis, procul est profani [A little house but a friend to the good; remain at a distance, ye profane], Whereat our Governor, when he visited me, burst into laughter, and encouraged me to keep on building.

Francis Pastorius, 1683, in Hart, ed.,
American History, *vol. 1, p. 560.*

Their order is thus: The king sits in the middle of an half-moon, and has his council, the old and wise, on each hand. Behind them, or at a little distance, sit the younger fry in the same figure. Having consulted and resolved their business, the king ordered one of them to speak to me. He stood up, came to me, and in the name of the king saluted me, then took me by the hand, and told me that he was ordered by his king to speak to me, and that now it was not he but the king who spoke, because what he should say was the king's mind. He first prayed me to excuse them, that they had not complied with me the last time. He feared there might be some fault in the interpreter, being neither Indian nor English. Besides, it was the Indian custom to deliberate and take up much time in council before they resolved; and that, if the young people and owners of the land had been as ready as he, I had not met with so much delay. Having thus introduced his matter, he fell to the bounds of the land they had agreed to dispose of, and the price; which now is little and dear, that which would have bought twenty miles not buying now two. During the time that this person spoke, not a man of them was observed to whisper or smile—the old grave, the young reverent, in their deportment. They speak little, but fervently, and with elegance. I have never seen more natural sagacity . . . and he will deserve the name of wise who outwits them in any treaty about a thing they understand.

William Penn's treaty with the Delaware, 1683, in Hart, ed., American History, vol. 1, p. 558.

Sir you knew that the church and people of Natick about two years and a half since, made their application and gave a Call by a general vote to the Reverend Mr. Gookin, Minister of Sherborn . . . that he would please to preach a Lecture to us at Natick; which invitation of ours, God inclined his heart to accept. . . . Tis true he preacheth to us in the English tongue, which all do not fully understand, but some learn a little and desire to know more of it, but their being a well spoken and Intelligent interpreter of our own Countrymen, who being the day before instructed and informed by Mr. Gookin in the matter to be delivered, is prompt and ready to interpret and communicate unto us in our own language, which practice as we understand is approved of in Scripture in the primitive times as in 1. Corinthians. 14. 27., 28. that if one speak in an unknown tongue another should interpret. Unto this Lecture many Englishmen and women of the neighborhood do resort, who by their example and communion with us in the worship of God it tendeth (as is evident) to promote not only Religion but Civility amongst us.

Letter to the Reverend John Eliot from Indians of Natick, Massachusetts, March 1683, in Company for Propagation, Some Correspondence, *pp. 74–75.*

There be people of several sorts of religions, but few very zealous; the people, being mostly New-England men, do mostly incline to their way; and in every town there is a meetinghouse, where they worship publicly every week: They have no public laws in the country for maintaining public teachers, but the towns that have them, make way within themselves to maintain them; we know none that have a settled preacher, that follows no other employment, save one town, Newark. . . .

The richest Planters have not above 8 or 10 Servants; they will have some of them, 1 Dozen of Cows, yea some 20 or 30; 8 or 10 Oxen, horses more than they know themselves, for they keep breeding Mares, and keep no more horses at home than they have occasion to work; The rest they let run in the wood both Winter and Summer, and take them as they have occasion to use them. Swine they have in great flocks in the wood, and Sheep in flocks also, but they let them not run in the woods for fear of being destroyed by wolves. Their profit arises from the Improvement of their Land, and Increase of their Bestial.

There will be in most of the Towns already settled at least 100 Houses, but they are not built so regular as the Towns in our Country.... Every house in the Town hath a Lot Of 4 Acres lying to it: so that every one building upon his own Lot makes the town Irregular and scattering. Their Streets are laid out too large, and the Sheep in the Towns are mostly maintained in them: They are so large that they need not trouble to pave them.

David Barclay describes East Jersey, 1684, in Hart, ed., American History, *vol. 1, pp. 570–71.*

As for your Enquiry, By what means they came to be deprived of their Charters, Rights and Liberties; please to understand, that in the year 1683, a Quo Warranto was issued out against them, and with the notification thereof by the then King's Order there was a Declaration published, enjoining those few particular Persons mentioned in the Quo Warranto, to make their defense at their own particular Charge, without any help by a public Stock: By this it was easy to see that some Persons were resolved to have the Charters condemned. ... But tho they had not sufficient time given them to make their Defense, yet judgment was entered against them for Default in not appearing; when it was impossible, considering the remote distance of New England from Westminster-hall, that they should appear in the time allowed.

Thus illegally was the Charter of the Massachusetts Colony wrested from them....

Increase Mather, 1684, "A Brief Relation of the State of New England," in Hart, ed., American History, *vol. 1, pp. 462–63.*

For eight months we had suffered from the contribution and the quartering of the soldiers, on account of religion, enduring many inconveniencies. We therefore resolved on quitting France at night ... and abandoning the house with its furniture.... We were detained in London for three months, waiting for a vessel ready to sail for Carolina. Once embarked, we were miserably off indeed. The scarlet fever broke out in our ship, and many died, among them our aged mother.... Our vessel put in for repairs, having been badly injured in a severe storm. Our captain ... was thrown into prison, and the ship was seized. It was with the great difficulty that we secured our passage in another ship, for all our money had been spent. After our arrival in Carolina [*in 1685*], we suffered all sorts of evils. Our eldest brother died of a fever, eighteen months after arriving coming here.... We ourselves have been exposed, since leaving France, to all kinds of afflictions, in the forms of sickness, pestilence, famine, poverty, and the roughest labor. I have been for six months at a time in this county without tasting bread, laboring meanwhile like a slave in tilling the ground. Indeed, I have spent three or four years without knowing what it was to eat bread whenever I wanted it.

Letter of Huguenot Judith Giton Manigault, to her brother in Germany, describing events from about 1684 to 1690, in Baird, ed., History, *vol. 2, pp. 112–14, 182–83.*

I believe for these 7 years last past, there has not come over into this province [*New York*], twenty English Scotch or Irish families. But on the contrary on Long Island the people increase so fast that they complain for want of land and many remove from thence into the neighboring province. But of French there have been since my coming here several families come both from St. Christopher's and England and a great many more are expected as also from Holland are come several Dutch families which is another great argument of the necessity of adding to this Government the Neighboring English Colonies, that a more equal balance may be kept, between his Majesty's natural born subjects and foreigners....

Every Town ought to have a Minister. New York has first a Chaplain belonging to the Fort of the Church of England; Secondly, a Dutch Calvinist, thirdly a French Calvinist, fourthly a Dutch Lutheran—Here, be not many of the Church of England; few Roman Catholics; abundance of Quakers preachers men and Women especially; Singing Quakers, Ranting Quakers, Sabbatarians; Antisabbatarians; Some Anabaptists some Independents; some Jews; in short of all sorts of opinions there are some, and the most part of none at all.... It is the endeavor of all Persons here to bring up their children and servants in that opinion which themselves, profess, but this I observe that they take no care of the conversion of their Slaves.

New York governor Thomas Dongan, 1687, in Hart, ed., American History, *vol. 1, p. 543.*

These are the reasons why we are against the traffic of mens-body....

In Europe there are many oppressed for conscience sake; and here there are those oppressed which are of a black color. And we, who know that men must not commit adultery, some do commit adultery in others,

View of New Amsterdam (in fact renamed New York after 1664), from a 1685 map by Nicolaes Visscher *(Library of Congress)*

separating wives from their husbands and giving them to others, and some sell the children of those poor creatures to other men. Oh! do consider well this thing, you who do it, if you would be done at this manner, and if it is done according [to] Christianity? ...

Pray! What thing in the world can be done worse toward us than if men should rob or steal us away and sell us for slaves to strange countries, separating husbands from their wives and children.... And we who profess that it is not lawful to steal must likewise avoid to purchase such things as are stolen, but rather help to stop this robbing and stealing if possible and such men ought to be delivered out of the hands of the robbers and set free as well as in Europe. Then is Pennsylvania to have a good report; instead it has now a bad one for this sake in other countries. Especially whereas the Europeans are desirous to know in what manner the Quakers do rule in their province, and most of them do look upon us with an envious eye. But if this is done well, what shall we say is done evil?

If once these slaves (which they say are so wicked and stubborn men) should join themselves, fight for their freedom and handle their masters and mistresses as they did handle them before, will these masters and mistresses take the sword at hand and war against these poor slaves, like we are able to believe some will not refuse to do? Or have these Negroes not as much right to fight for their freedom as you have to keep them slaves?

Francis Pastorius and others to the Germantown Quakers, February 1688, in Hart, ed., American History, *vol. 2, pp. 291–92.*

... if his Majesty ... was resolved to annex us to some other government, we then desired that (inasmuch as Boston had been our old correspondents and a people whose principles and manners we had been acquainted with), we might be annexed rather to Sir Edmund Andros his government than to Col. Dongan's; which choice of ours was taken for a resignation of our Government, though that was never intended by us for such, nor had it the formalities in law to make it a resignation as we humbly conceive. Yet Sir Edmund Andros was commissioned by his Majesty to take us under his government. Pursuant to which, about the end of October, 1687, he with a company of Gentlemen and Grenadiers to the number of sixty or upwards came to Hartford (the chief seat of this Government) caused his commission to be read and declared our government to be dissolved, and put into commission both civil and military officers through out our Colony as he pleased when he passed through the principal parts thereof.

Connecticut governor Robert Treat to the king, 1689, in Hart, ed., American History, *vol. 1, p. 424.*

It's now 14 weeks since the revolution of the government here [*i.e., overthrow of the Dominion of New England*] . . . future consequences we are ignorant of, yet we know that, at present, we are eased of those great oppressions that we groaned under, by the exercise of an arbitrary and illegal commission. . . . The business was acted by the soldiers that came armed into Boston from all parts, to the great amazement of all beholders, being greatly animated by the Prince's declarations, which about that time came into the country, and heightened by the oppressions of the governor, judges, and the most wicked extortion of their debauched officers. The ancient magistrates and elders, although they had strenuously advised to further waiting for orders from England, and discouraged any attempts of that nature so far as they had opportunity, yet were they now compelled to assist with their presence and counsels for the prevention of bloodshed, which had most certainly been the issue if prudent counsels had not been given to both parties. . . . Sir Edmond Andros . . . forthwith came and surrendered himself. The same day, about 30 more of the principal persons of that knot were secured. . . . Mr. Dudley in a peculiar manner is the object of the people's displeasure, even throughout all the colonies where he hath sat judge, they deeply resent his correspondency with that wicked man Mr. Randolph for the overturning the government. . . .

Thomas Danforth, deputy-governor of Massachusetts, 1689, in Hart, ed., American History, *vol. 1, pp. 463–64.*

But against Expectation, it soon happened, that on the last day of said Month of May, Capt. Leysler having a Vessel . . . for which he refused to pay the Duty, did in a Seditious manner stir up the meanest sort of the Inhabitants (affirming *That King James being fled the Kingdom, all manner of Government was fallen in this Province*) to rise in Arms, and forcibly possess themselves of the Fort and Stores, which accordingly was effected whitest the Lieut. Governor and Council, with the Convention, were met at the City Hall to consult what might be proper for the common Good and Safety; where a party of Armed Men came from the Fort, and forced the Lieut. Governor to deliver them the Keys; and seized also in his Chamber a Chest with Seven Hundred Seventy Three Pounds, Twelve Shillings in Money of the Government. And though Col. Bayard, with some others appointed by the Convention, used all endeavors to prevent those Disorders, all proved

vain; for most of those that appeared in Arms were Drunk, and cried out, *They disown'd all manner of Government*. Whereupon, by Capt. Leysler's persuasion, they proclaimed him to be their Commander, there being then no other Commission Officer amongst them.

Capt. Leysler, being in this manner possessed of the Fort, took some Persons to his Assistance, which he call'd, The Committee of Safety. And the Lieut. Governor, Francis Nicollson being in this manner forced out of his Command, for the safety of his Person, which was daily threatened, withdrew out of the Province. . . .

"Letter from a Gentleman of New York," 1689, in Hart, ed., American History, *vol. 1, p. 545.*

It was with great dread known, that the late King James was bound in Conscience to endeavor to Damn the English Nation to Popery and Slavery, and therefore no wonder . . . that he took a particular care of this province, of which he was the Proprietor, and at one jump leapt over all the bounds, and Law of English Right and Government; and appointed a Governor [*Thomas Dongan*] of this Province of New York, who . . . gave active Obedience to his Prince without reserve; and accepted a Commission . . . giving him power with consent of any Seven of his Council to make Laws and to raise Taxes (as the French King doth) without consent of the People, (for the Council are no body, but whom [he] pleases to name, and therefore could represent nothing but the King's pleasure). . . . And this Governor and Council were the tools to enslave their Country, who pursuant to their Commission did make Laws and Assessed Taxes accordingly, without any Representative of the people, as appears by the Records of the Council book. . . .

This was the condition of New York, the Slavery and Popery that it lay under, until the Hand of Heaven sent the glorious King William to break those chains. . . . And these were the reasons that moved the Gentlemen concerned in the Revolution of New York [*Leisler's Rebellion*] to be early in shaking off their Tyrants, and declaring for their Deliverer.

Anonymous, 1689, "Loyalty Vindicated," in Andrews, ed., Narratives, *pp. 375–76.*

In the next place, Churches and Chapels (which by the said Charter should be Built and Consecrated recording to the Ecclesiastical Laws of the Kingdom of England) to our great regret and Discouragement of our Religion are erected and converted to the use of Popish Idolatry and Superstition. and Seminary Priests are the only Incumbents (for which there is a Supply provided by sending our Popish Youth be Educated at St. Omers) as also the chief Advisers and Councilors in Affairs of Government, and the Richest and most Fertile land set apart for their Use and Maintenance, while other lands that are piously intended, and given for the Maintenance of the Protestant Ministry, become Escheat, and are taken as Forfeit, the Ministers themselves discouraged and no care taken for their Subsistence.

The Power to Enact Laws is another branch of his Lordship's Authority; but how well that has been Executed and Circumstanced is too notorious. His present lordship upon the Death of his Father, in order thereunto, sent out Writs for Four (as was ever the usage) for each County to serve as Representatives of the People; but when Elected, there were Two only of each Respective Four pick'd out and summoned to that Convention, Whereby many Laws were made, and greatest Levy yet known, laid upon the Inhabitants.

"Declaration of Protestant Subjects in Maryland," 1689, *in Andrews, ed.,* Narratives, *p. 307.*

After the Indians had thus laid waste Pemmaquid, they moved us to New Harbor, about two miles east of Pemmaquid, a cove frequented by fishermen. At this place, there were, before the war, about twelve houses. These the inhabitants deserted soon as the rumor of war reached the place. When we turned our backs on the town, my heart was ready to break! I saw my mother. She spoke to me, but I could not answer her. That night we tarried at New Harbor, and the next day went in their canoes for Penobscot. About noon, the canoe in which my mother was, and that in which I was, came side by side; whether accidently or by my mother's desire I cannot say. She asked me how I did. I think I said "pretty well," but my heart was so full of grief I scarcely knew whether audible to her. Then she said, "O, my child! . . . Poor babe, we are going into the wilderness, the Lord knows where!" . . .

Captivity narrative of John Gyles, August 1689, in VanDerBeets, Held Captive, *p. 97.*

This General Court having information from England that the colony of Plymouth had been joined to the government of New York, but at the same time was prevented by the Reverend Mr. Mather, who gave an account . . . how little service it would be to their majesties, and how great dissatisfaction and inconvenience it would be to the people; we are also informed that after that we were like to be annexed to Boston . . . being also informed there is a possibility that we may obtain a charter for ourselves if we speedily address to their majesties employ a suitable person to manage and raise sufficient moneys to carry the same end; this Court thinking it their duty to inform the several inhabitants in the several towns in this colony thereof . . .—it is therefore ordered, that the magistrates or deputies in each town forth with order the constables to warn the inhabitants of the towns to assemble, and give notice to them of the occasion, and that they there have the information above mentioned, that they may consider thereof, and draw up their minds therein, and that the same be signified to the adjournment of this Court; and in particular that it be known whether it be their minds we should sit still and fall into the hands of those that can catch us, without using means to procure that which may be for our good, or prevent that which may be our inconvenience. . . .

General Court of Plymouth, 1690, in Hart, ed., American History, *vol. 1, pp. 363–64.*

8

The English Colonies Enter the 18th Century
1690–1730

COLONIAL POLICY AND IMPERIAL CONTROL

After King William's War began in 1690, imperial officials were briefly distracted from management of colonial affairs. In 1696, attention to the colonies was renewed. In response to loud complaints from merchants in England about colonial trade violations, Parliament passed the Navigation Act of 1696. The new act restated now-familiar provisions but also enacted new mechanisms for enforcement. Colonial governors could be removed from office for nonenforcement; a regular and organized customs service was established; and special admiralty courts, separate from the regular court system of the colonies, were appointed to try all cases involving trade violations. The act also required foreigners and noncitizens to obtain permission before purchasing colonial land, to prevent them from establishing trading bases. After 1705, Parliament also lengthened the list of enumerated articles, or exports that could be sold only to England. Added were beaver skins and other furs, rice (South Carolina's main export), and naval stores (the lumber, pitch, tar, and turpentine exported by several colonies).

After Parliament passed the Navigation Act of 1696, King William feared that it intended to usurp all control of colonial policy, traditionally a royal prerogative. Within months, he replaced the Lords of Trade with the Board of Commissioners for Trade and Plantations, or the Board of Trade. No longer a subcommittee of the Privy Council, the Board of Trade was an independent group of officials charged with gathering information, examining colonial law, and recommending colonial policy. Unlike the Lords of Trade, members were not all noblemen and included representatives from Parliament. Long-standing imperial goals, however, remained the same: more centralized management and increased colonial subservience to the crown.

Part of the effort to establish control over the colonies was the movement to "royalize" them, which had begun in the 1680s. In royal colonies, the crown appointed the governor, the council, and other officials and reviewed all laws passed by the assembly. In 1701, Parliament proposed the Reunification Act to make all existing North American colonies royal. Opposition to the bill was organized by William Penn, proprietor of Pennsylvania, and it was defeated. Many colonists supported royal control, however, sometimes in the hope that it might replace a disorderly local government, provide more religious toleration, or offer more military protection. New Jersey became a royal colony in 1702. In 1719, Carolinians revolted in favor of royal government, although royalization did not occur until 1729.

Queen Anne, the successor to King William and Queen Mary, died in 1714 without a living heir. She was succeeded by George I, great-grandson of James I and the first English king from the German House of Hanover. George I spoke almost no English and had little interest in active governing. Under his reign, powerful Whigs, as the Parliamentarian party was now called, dominated government. Sir Robert Walpole, the chief Whig advisor to the king, believed that colonies should be allowed to develop with as little interference as possible. This approach was called "salutary neglect." The influence of the Board of Trade was lessened; Parliament itself, however, passed more than 80 colonial regulatory acts by the middle of the 18th century.

Colonial Government in the Early 18th Century

After 1690, no centralized administration existed among the English colonies, although at times more than one colony shared a royal governor. Nor did colonies conform to a single type. Connecticut and Rhode Island were charter colonies, in which governmental power belonged to the political community defined by the charter itself. They were permitted to choose all their own officials and make their own laws. Massachusetts (and Maine, which it governed) was a blend of charter and royal colony; the governor was appointed by the Crown, and the laws were subject to royal veto. In proprietary colonies, both land and governmental oversight were delegated to an individual or group of individuals by the Crown. By 1730, only Pennsylvania and Maryland remained full proprietary colonies, although both became royal briefly during the period. The remaining colonies were royal.

Regardless of their status as royal, charter, or proprietary, all of the colonies had similar governmental institutions. The council, called the assistants or magistrates in some colonies, usually served as the upper house of the assembly but was also an executive body, an advisory group for the governor, and a high court of appeal. Most councils were appointed (a few were elected) from among well-established and wealthy citizens. By 1700, all colonies also had an official known as the colonial agent, sometimes an Englishman and sometimes a colonist, who was stationed in London to represent their point of view to the Crown.

The colonial assemblies, called by different names in different colonies, were composed of representatives elected by freemen; until an assembly became bicameral, the council usually sat with the representatives as well and sometimes restricted their actions. In New England, representatives were sent from towns or townships; in the other colonies, they were sent from counties. After 1690, the colonial assemblies gradually became more powerful. Most could levy or approve all taxes and appropriations, giving them considerable influence over the governor and sometimes even over the Crown. They were not democratic in the modern sense, however, because all colonies restricted the franchise. For white men, the primary requirement by 1700 was ownership of a certain amount of land or other wealth, rather than church membership or "good character." Catholic and Jewish men were often restricted from voting, however. Free black men were barred from voting rights by law or custom, although historians believe there were some exceptions. All women were barred from voting in all places. Although white male suffrage was not universal, a higher proportion of white men in the colonies were entitled to vote than in England at the time.

Colonial courts had several levels. The justice of the peace, usually appointed by the governor, tried minor offenses. The county courts and courts of quarter session were composed of area justices and had jurisdiction over more serious criminal offenses or civil disputes. The general and circuit courts had judges or magistrates appointed by the Crown or governor and council; they heard appeals from lower courts and tried serious criminal offenses. Their decisions could be appealed to the governor and council; in royal colonies, the council's decisions could be appealed to the Crown. In all colonies, citizens were entitled to the "rights of Englishmen," which included trial by jury, writ of habeas corpus (the right not to be imprisoned without knowing the offense and without being brought to trial), and the right to face accusers and to call witnesses. Colonists nonetheless complained frequently about favoritism shown by appointed judges.

At the local level, government was carried out by towns or townships in New England and by counties in other areas. In New England, colonists attended town meetings and chose selectmen to administer local affairs. Elsewhere, county courts also performed administrative activities. As the population grew, many new, specialized local officials developed such as prosecuting attorneys, coroners, and registrars. As cities grew, they often obtained municipal charters from the governor or the assembly. Municipal charters empowered cities to govern themselves with officials similar to those of a colony: a mayor and a council, sometimes known as aldermen.

Imperial Wars

Beginning in the second half of the 17th century, the major European nations conducted a long series of wars of realignment, sometimes called the Second Hundred Years' War. Almost all had repercussions in the colonies. When Europeans declared war, English, French, and Spanish colonists took the opportunity to do battle over rivalries and local issues. Many of the European wars were called by different names in North America.

Shortly after William and Mary jointly took the throne in 1689, the War of the League of Augsburg began. England allied with Spain, the Netherlands, and some German princes against its most important enemy, France. In North America, hostilities erupted in Acadia, northern New England, and northern New York and became known as King William's War. Since 1685, conflict over the fur trade in those areas had been intensifying between the English-Iroquois alliance and the French-Algonquian alliance. In 1690, the French and Indians attacked and destroyed Schenectady, near the English fur-trading center of Albany. Equally destructive attacks were soon made on settlements in Maine. Under the leadership of Massachusetts governor Sir William Phips, the English captured Port Royal in Acadia, but a campaign to attack Quebec was not successful.

King William's War dragged on for seven years, during which the French-Indian alliance recaptured Port Royal and intermittently destroyed frontier villages in northern New England. The English Crown requisitioned colonial militias and sent military leaders to mount united intercolonial actions. The Crown's efforts met with little success, however. The colonists balked at cooperating with either the Crown or each other, except when their own settlements and interests were immediately endangered.

On September 30, 1697, the Treaty of Ryswick was signed in Europe, returning all areas in North America to their prewar colonial rulers. In America, the war had wreaked great destruction on the northern frontier, and England's Iroquois allies had suffered the loss of over half their warriors. In addition, the enmity and rivalry between French and English colonials had intensified greatly. After the war, the French began the fortification and settlement of the Mississippi River valley, completing their western encirclement of the English colonies from the St. Lawrence and Great Lakes to the Gulf of Mexico. The English Crown sent Richard Coote, earl of Bellomont to unify New England and New York and increase colonial military strength. Individual colonial assemblies, however, still had little inclination to cooperate. None saw its interests as identical to those of other colonies; each still thought of itself as a separate province of the empire in competition with other provinces for trade and settlers. After the conclusion of King William's War, New York even established illicit but profitable trade with Montreal.

In 1702, under the new British monarch, Queen Anne, England entered the War of the Spanish Succession. In Europe, England allied with many of its earlier partners to thwart a French-Spanish union. In North America, where hostilities were called Queen Anne's War, fighting began almost immediately. French-allied Abenaki attacked settlements in Maine and Massachusetts, killing or enslaving settlers and destroying villages. The Deerfield, Massachusetts, massacre of 1704 was the most severe; more than 100 English captives were marched to Canada. New Englanders, unable to interest other colonies in aiding them, attacked Acadia. Hostilities spread to the south. Carolinians attacked Spanish Florida twice, in 1702 and 1704; in retaliation, the Spanish unsuccessfully attacked Charleston in 1706. In the north, another invasion of Quebec was planned, but once again it failed.

In 1713, the Treaty of Utrecht ended the war in Europe. England received Hudson's Bay, Newfoundland, and Acadia (soon renamed Nova Scotia); it also received permission to carry slaves to Spanish colonies. After 1713, another European war did not break out on English colonial soil for 30 years. However, the War of the Quadruple Alliance (1719–21) had repercussions in the southern colonies. The French were now allied with the English against the Spanish, destabilizing former alliances with and among Native American groups.

NORTHERN NEW ENGLAND: MAINE AND NEW HAMPSHIRE

Maine's northeastern frontier was also the ill-defined boundary between French Acadia and New England. During King William's War, every settlement in Maine was exposed to French and Abenaki raids, and many were leveled. More than 700 settlers were killed or taken as captives to Canada. By the end of the war, all settlements in Maine had been abandoned except those near the modern New Hampshire border.

Massachusetts began to view Maine, over which it had jurisdiction, as a frontier buffer zone to protect more populous colonies against French incursions. In July 1701, the Massachusetts General Court passed an act forbidding inhabitants of 21 border towns in Maine to relocate without permission. Inspired by Boston minister Cotton Mather, a group of young Puritan missionaries, most of them Harvard graduates, migrated to the area, where they helped to reestablish and maintain communities in Maine and New Hampshire. During Queen Anne's War the settlements were again attacked. From Maine's perspective, the award of Acadia to the English in 1714 was a particularly welcome development.

After Queen Anne's War, the Massachusetts General Court actively encouraged development in Maine. Grants were made to several proprietors in the areas of present-day Portland and Casco Bay; the new proprietors were required to build schoolhouses, meeting houses, mills, and roads. This development, of course, again encroached on Indian lands, and intermittent guerrilla warfare continued for a decade. In 1722, Abenaki attacked the Brunswick area and Massachusetts declared war (sometimes called Dummer's War) on the Eastern Indians, as the Maine tribes were collectively known. In August 1724, soldiers from York, a frequently attacked Maine settlement, descended on the Indian village and mission at Norridgewoc, murdering its Jesuit priest, Father Sebastian Rale. (New England colonists long believed that French Jesuits encouraged Indians to attack English border settlements.) A year later a fierce battle at Lovewell's Pond resulted in serious losses for both the Pequawket (an Abenaki band) and the English. In 1725, the Treaty of Casco Bay, or Dummer's Treaty, was signed. After that date, Indian warfare ended in Maine; the power of the Abenaki was broken in the area and most fled to Canada.

In New Hampshire, no charter and no effective colonywide administration existed when the Dominion of New England ended in 1689. New Hampshire officially resumed its status and organization as a royal colony. Shortly afterward, the colony was hit by surprise Indian attacks, led by the Pennacook, and many colonists were convinced of the need to reunite with Massachusetts for protection. In March 1690, Massachusetts accepted a petition for reannexation, signed by more than 350 New Hampshire freemen. The English Crown demurred, however, unwilling to increase the power of Massachusetts. In addition, the current English heirs and owners of the Mason proprietorship, (which the Crown had granted on New Hampshire land in 1623), also objected.

The New Hampshire assembly again petitioned the Crown for annexation to Massachusetts in 1693, and the controversy dragged on for several years. In 1699, the Crown finally reached a compromise: New Hampshire would share a governor with Massachusetts, primarily to coordinate military defense. In other respects the colony would be separate from Massachusetts, with its own royally appointed council and its own assembly of representatives from each town. By 1715, the claims of the Mason proprietors were also put to rest. Colonists convinced Crown officials to vacate the old proprietorship using a well-executed forgery of an Indian deed called the Wheelwright patent. The forgery, illicitly entered into the colony's records, showed that a group of colonists had a legal title to the land before John Mason did. Historians did not uncover the ruse for almost 200 years.

During these years, New Hampshire residents suffered from continuing French and Indian hostilities. Hampton and Exeter were struck again and again. By 1700, the colony had developed a system of garrison houses—fortified homes or dwellings in each settlement. Women assumed new responsibilities, because almost every one of the 1,000 adult males of the colony served on militia duty at some time. Hannah Dustin of Massachusetts became a heroine to colonists in 1697 after killing and escaping from 10 French-allied Indians; they had captured her and several others, killed her six-day-old baby girl, Martha, by bashing her against a tree; and forced the captives to march to New Hampshire. As the Indians slept, Dustin, another woman, and a boy used stolen hatchets to kill them. She later went back and scalped them to prove what she had done.

In 1713, the so-called Eastern Indians of Maine met in Portsmouth to sign a peace treaty with the English. The costs of a quarter-century of intermittent warfare in New Hampshire, however, had been high. In 1717, John Wentworth was appointed governor, and the fortunes of the struggling colony began to rise. Wentworth, the first of a family political dynasty, served in office until 1728. He reduced the political factionalism in the colony and oversaw significant economic development. By 1730, settlements had spread as far as 50 miles inland, and the population had increased to more than 10,000.

WITCHCRAFT IN NEW ENGLAND

By the time the Massachusetts Charter was renewed in 1691, fewer and fewer of its citizens embraced the notion of a unified biblical commonwealth. Ministers had interpreted King Philip's War, a smallpox epidemic, and even the loss of the charter as evidence of God's displeasure. In 1679–80, a ministerial synod warned that an even greater sign of divine wrath was yet possible. In 1692, that sign seemed to appear in Salem Village (modern Danvers). In January, a group of teenage girls began to behave strangely, suffering from fits and hallucinations. The doctor and local ministers agreed that they had been afflicted by the devil, working through local witches.

Belief in witchcraft was almost universal in the 16th and 17th centuries among the well educated and prominent as well as the illiterate and lowly. In Europe, thousands were accused and hundreds executed; in New England, too, some accused witches had been put to death before the 1690s. The Salem girls claimed to have been bewitched by Tituba, a West Indian black slave owned by the Reverend Samuel Parris, and by two older women of the community, Sarah Good and Sarah Osbourn. Magistrates examined the girls and committed the women to prison. Soon panic broke out; neighbor was accusing neighbor of casting spells, not only in Salem but in many other New England villages. Before the hysteria ended, even prominent people had been accused, including at least one minister and the wife of Governor Phips.

Witchcraft trials began in Salem in June 1692. Nineteen women and men were executed in that town alone, including one man crushed to death by weights, the punishment for those who would not confess. (Those who did confess were hanged.) At least 150 more were jailed on suspicion. When Governor Phips returned to the colony from a military campaign in Acadia, however, he stopped the trials. By spring 1693, ministers and community leaders openly expressed grave doubts about the proceedings. Few questioned that the devil had caused the visions, called spectral evidence, and other symptoms suffered by the accusers. Many, however, began to doubt that the accused were in league with the powers of evil.

Soon colonists began to realize the horror of the acts they had committed. Some of the girls who made the original accusations recanted and said they had lied. At least one judge, Samuel Sewall, and one minister, the Reverend John Hale, confessed to errors in judgment and apologized for their participation. In 1697, the Massachusetts General Court declared a day of penitence; in 1711, the surviving accused had their civil rights restored and the families of those executed were voted compensation.

Many theories have been advanced to explain the witchcraft proceedings in New England. Immediately after the event, many colonists blamed the Indians, whose rituals were commonly believed to be satanic. Today a few historians argue that witchcraft probably was really practiced, given universal belief in its power, and probably did have psychogenic effects on susceptible people. Theories exist that Salem was afflicted with ergot poisoning (a fungus that affects grain and causes hallucinations) or a mosquito-borne disease. Most modern historians, however, credit the stress caused by long-term social change and Indian warfare. Once the accusations began, they opened floodgates of long-standing local quarrels and personal grievances. Most historians also agree that generational hostility was important. All of the original accusers were young women under the age of 20 (who had little power in Puritan society), and all the accused were women between 40 and 60. Not coincidentally, the girls chose older women who were all slightly marginal to the community and therefore vulnerable. To the girls, they were probably convenient scapegoats for female *and* male authority figures who were far too powerful to attack openly. In any case, the life-and-death power

Jethro Coffin House, Nantucket, built 1686; an original Cape Cod house *(Historic American Building Survey)*

that the young women gained by their accusations depended on the willing participation of those same authority figures. Their later recantations were of little use to the executed or those whose lives were ruined by the trials.

The witchcraft episode had lasting repercussions on religion in New England. Its excesses strengthened the position of those who disliked the church's exclusiveness and its influence in political affairs. In 1699, for example, a group of wealthy merchants and other citizens broke away from the established Congregational church in Boston to found the Brattle Street Church. The new church took the Half-Way Covenant several steps further, admitting any professed Christian to full membership. Many others called for oversight of individual churches and ministers. In 1708, the Congregational churches of Connecticut adopted the Saybrook Platform, creating councils, or synods, to set doctrine and appoint ministers for the formerly independent Congregational churches of the area.

OTHER DEVELOPMENTS IN SOUTHERN NEW ENGLAND

Prior to 1713, Indian warfare retarded growth in southern as well as northern New England. After 1713, however, expansion occurred rapidly. The back country began to fill in, peopled both by new immigrants and by the children of older residents who could not afford land in settled communities. In Massachusetts alone, the 1690 population of almost 50,000 had more than doubled by 1730.

The new Massachusetts Charter, partly negotiated by the Reverend Increase Mather and granted by the Crown in 1691, disallowed church membership as a qualification for the franchise. Congregational churches remained entitled to tax support, however, and religious toleration gained only slow and grudging acceptance in Massachusetts. Sir William Phips was appointed the first royal governor. Phips, born in poverty in Maine and one of 26 children, had risen to become the first American knighted by the British government. He and the eight governors who followed him by 1730, however, all quarreled with the Massachusetts General Court. The court slowly gained in power during the period and also passed a statute restoring power to town governments, which had been curtailed during the Dominion of New England.

Connecticut resumed government under the terms of its 1662 charter after the Dominion of New England ended, although the crown did not officially confirm its right to do so. (According to tradition, the charter had never been surrendered, having been hidden in an oak tree.) In 1693, New York governor Benjamin Fletcher arrived to take control of the Connecticut militia. Because the charter gave control of the militia to the colony itself, Connecticut drummers were ordered to drown Fletcher out when he tried to read his royal commission. Afterward, Connecticut officials quickly sought confirmation of the charter's legitimacy, which the crown eventually granted.

Connecticut remained a colony of small diversified farmers. No powerful mercantile group like that of Massachusetts or New York had yet developed, although a shipbuilding industry was well established by 1730. After 1700, both Baptist and Anglican congregations were founded in the formerly orthodox Puritan colony; by 1730, their adherents as well as Quakers were exempted from paying taxes to support Congregational churches. Records indicate, however, that the law was not always followed, and religious toleration was never warmly embraced.

In 1700, the Connecticut Assembly passed a law requiring towns with at least 70 families to tax residents for the support of schools. If the assessment proved insufficient, the town was required to make up half the remainder itself and charge parents the rest. If a town failed to establish a school, the funds were taken for the colony treasury. This method of financing schools lasted for the remainder of the colonial period. In 1701, the assembly formally established the Collegiate School, known after 1718 as Yale. The third colonial college (after Harvard and the College of William and Mary), Yale had 10 Congregational ministers as trustees. The shocking conversion of Rector Timothy Culter and two students to Anglicanism in 1722 was followed by many years of stricter ministerial control over the faculty. The college did not receive an independent charter until 1745 and was forced to rely on yearly grants from the assembly.

Between 1690 and 1730, Rhode Island transformed itself from a small outpost of religious dissenters into a flourishing agricultural colony, with a prominent port and center of trade at Newport. The 1690s opened with confusion over the colony's status. The five towns of Rhode Island guarded their auton-

Quaker meetinghouse at Newport, Rhode Island, built 1699
(Courtesy The Newport Historical Society, P1779)

omy, little colonywide administration existed, and political factionalism was rife. In 1694, Queen Mary confirmed that the Rhode Island Charter of 1663 was still legitimate. In 1696, the assembly agreed to rotate its meetings among the five towns, and five separate capitol buildings were eventually built. The assembly also became bicameral.

In 1697, Governor Samuel Cranston took office, serving until his death in 1727. Under his leadership, colonywide government was strengthened and cooperation with imperial authorities improved, especially in regard to enforcement of the Navigation Acts. In 1703, a final boundary agreement with Connecticut was reached. In 1719, the first compilation of law and tax policy was completed; it was published in 1727 when James Franklin (Benjamin's brother) brought the first printing press to Newport. As order increased, the population did as well. The colony sponsored the development of roads, ferries, and bridges to enable farmers to transport goods to Newport. The shipbuilding industry grew. Ship owners developed a highly successful carrying trade, or business transporting goods from one port to another. By 1730, the colony had grown from about 5,000 subsistence farmers to a diversified population of 17,000.

In Rhode Island, where Roger Williams is often credited with founding the first Baptist church in America, that denomination continued to grow steadily, but by 1730 two Congregational churches also existed and Anglicanism had spread. The Quakers' Yearly Meeting, or annual regional convention, at Newport was the largest and most important in New England. New Jewish immigrants began arriving after the turn of the century as well. By 1730, blacks probably comprised about five percent of the population and legislation had been passed requiring owners who manumitted (freed) their slaves to post bonds. Slaves were concentrated in larger towns and on the large estates of the Narragansett area.

NEW EUROPEAN IMMIGRATION

Between 1690 and 1730 the non-Indian population in the English North American colonies almost tripled, from slightly more than 200,000 to more than 600,000. In part, the increase was due to a high rate of natural increase. Equally important was a new flood of immigrants. The largest group arrived as slaves, involuntarily transported from Africa. But many Europeans arrived as well, the majority of whom were not English.

By 1700, probably about 20 percent of the white population in the English colonies was of non-English descent. After 1713, non-English people began emigrating in larger numbers, easily recruited by colonial promoters. In continental Europe, land was scarce, wars were frequent, and religious persecution and political discrimination were rampant. Officials in England, on the other hand, discouraged the emigration of anyone except convicts, who once again were sent to the colonies in significant numbers.

The earliest European group to arrive in large numbers was the Huguenots (French Calvinist Protestants). Historians disagree on the number, but between 2,000 and 12,000 Huguenots emigrated after 1685, when France ended religious toleration. Most Huguenots were educated and middle class, and as a group they prospered exceptionally well. The largest Huguenot settlement was in South Carolina, where many became wealthy planters. Well-known colonial names such as Revere, Bowdoin, Vassar, Gallaudet, and Faneuil were of Huguenot descent.

A second large group, composed almost entirely of German speakers, arrived from modern Germany, France, and Switzerland. At the time, most German-speaking people lived in small principalities where each new ruler forced his religious preferences on his subjects. In addition, the French military continually conducted brutal raids in the Rhine River valley. In 1707, refugees began arriving in London and Parliament began a resettlement program in Ireland and North America.

By 1727, about 15,000 Germans and Swiss belonging to various small ethnic groups had arrived; eventually, more than 100,000 immigrated. Most disembarked in Pennsylvania, although some also went to French Louisiana and others to Canada. At the time, they were called Rhinelanders, Palatines, or "Dutch" (from the English pronunciation of *Deutsche*, or German); later, they were commonly called "Pennsylvania Dutch." The so-called plain people such as the Mennonites and Amish established separate communities. The majority, however, were "church people"—Lutheran and Reformed plus a few Catholics and Protestant sectarians. They entered the economic and political mainstream, although many kept their language and culture for some time. By 1730, many Germans had begun moving into the back country of Maryland and Virginia.

Immigrants from the Rhine River valley often arrived under an indenture called the redemption agreement. Redemptioners, also called free-willers, were transported without charge to America, usually in family groups. Once their ship arrived, they were not permitted to disembark until the captain had sold their services. Redemptioners usually did not come from backgrounds as distressed as the early English indentured servants. Many had been established farmers or craftsmen before emigrating.

A third white group, traditionally called the Scotch-Irish, also arrived in large numbers. The Scotch-Irish were not an ethnic mixture of Scots and Irish; rather, they were a distinct geographical group—primarily Lowland Scots who had emigrated to northern Ireland or Ulster in the early 1600s. The Scotch-Irish were strongly attached to the Presbyterian Church, and more than 90 percent are believed to have been literate. In 1717, when "rack renting" began in Ulster (high rents almost equal to the value of the property), the first group of 5,000 Scotch-Irish debarked for New England. They were not warmly welcomed, and they in turn disliked being required to support established Congregational churches. Some Scotch-Irish settled on the New England frontier, but most moved to Pennsylvania, spreading from there into the backcountry of Maryland and Virginia. In the 18th century, they were usually called Ulstermen or Irish; in the 19th century, when many Catholic Irish immigrated to North America, the term Scotch-Irish arose to distinguish the groups. Today, some historians prefer the designation Ulster Scots.

THE MIDDLE COLONIES: NEW YORK AND NEW JERSEY

After Leisler's Rebellion in 1689, English officials began to standardize the varied local institutions left in place in New York after the surrender of New Amsterdam. In April 1691, a new assembly met and passed the Judiciary Act, which instituted a new legal and judicial system based on English common law and "the rights of Englishmen." Newcomers who were not citizens of England or its possessions had to acquire the franchise to apply for trading privileges. The Ministry Act of 1693 established the Anglican Church in four downriver counties, although the Dutch Reformed Church remained entitled to support by local option. Laws began to be printed after Quaker William Bradford arrived in 1693, converted to Anglicanism, and became the official public printer.

In 1707, Edward Hyde, Lord Cornbury, the governor of New York, arrested the well-known Scottish dissenter Francis Makemie for preaching without a license (which Cornbury had refused to give him). Makemie, considered the founder of the Presbyterian Church in America, became a *cause célèbre* in the traditionally tolerant colony. He stood trial and won with the help of three Anglican lawyers. As a direct result, the assembly outlawed assessing acquitted parties for expenses as had been done to Makemie. On the whole, however, the most serious religious battles in New York occurred within, not among, denominations, reflecting the colony's complicated and long-standing divisions.

The Hudson Valley, Long Island, and New York City all had very different economies. Animosity continued between small, antimonopoly landowners and the Anglo-Dutch merchant elite—the old Leislerian and anti-Leislerian groups. Even the threat to the colony's physical security during King William's War and Queen Anne's War could not bring them to an agreement. Although the province was directly threatened, fur-trading interests centered in Albany wanted to prevent disrupting trading alliances at all costs and lobbied for "defensive neutrality." From 1713 through 1730, however, New York enjoyed a period of commercial growth that tied the entire colony closer together and closer to English interests. Early political parties began to develop, actually reducing the divisions of earlier years.

Ackerman House, Hackensack, New Jersey, built 1704, in a Flemish variant of Dutch colonial style *(Historic American Building Survey)*

Over all, the non-Indian population of New York grew from about 18,000 in 1690 to more than 50,000 in 1730. Some Scotch-Irish and Germans began to populate the rural areas; however, immigrants did not find the colony a particularly attractive destination. Land could not be obtained easily, because the owners of large tracts wanted to rent rather than sell. Taxes were high, and established monopolies discouraged the enterprising. New York did, however, remain the largest importer of slaves in the North. The black population grew from about 10 percent of the population in 1700 to 15 percent by 1730. Some slaves worked the large farms in the Hudson Valley, but most were attached individually to households in the city.

In both East and West Jersey, colonists entered the 1690s still dissatisfied with proprietary rule. Civil disorders occurred with increasing frequency. In 1701, the Board of Trade recommended that East and West Jersey be combined as one royal colony. The proprietors surrendered their rights to rule but not to collect quitrents. In 1702, the colony of New Jersey was established; it shared a governor with New York until 1738. The transition to royal rule did not begin smoothly under Governor Cornbury, a particularly venal official also known for walking about New York in women's clothing rumored to belong to his cousin, Queen Anne. After 1710, however, the New Jersey assembly began to force concessions from sitting governors by withholding financial appropriations.

When the Jerseys were combined, the total non-Indian population was about 10,000—7,500 in the east and 2,500 in the west. About 300 were slaves or free blacks. The west was primarily a Quaker community, the east more ethnically and religiously diverse. Some large estates existed in Monmouth County, but as a whole the colony was relatively poor. By 1730, the population had increased to more than 30,000.

THE MIDDLE COLONIES: PENNSYLVANIA AND DELAWARE

In summer 1690, William Penn was arrested in England, one of 18 men whom the crown feared might start a rebellion in favor of the former king, James II. Although soon released, Penn was arrested again in January 1691 for preaching the funeral sermon of George Fox, the great Quaker leader. Meanwhile, in his proprietary colony, the Lower Counties of Delaware refused to participate in the Pennsylvania Assembly, and the assembly quarreled with the council. They also failed to submit laws for royal approval or to enforce the Navigation Acts. In October 1692, King William, concerned in part that Pennsylvania would be easy prey for the French in the ongoing war, put New York governor Benjamin Fletcher in control to organize defenses. The Quaker-dominated assembly, however, refused either to appropriate money for its own defense during King William's War or to aid other colonies, pleading religious grounds.

In 1693, Penn was exonerated in England; the following year, his proprietary rights were restored and he appointed William Markham governor. In 1696, the assembly passed Markham's Frame, or the Third Frame of Government, which increased the assembly's power.

In December 1699, Penn and his second wife, Hannah Collowhill Penn, arrived in the colony and took up residence at Pennsbury. The economy was flourishing, and Philadelphia had grown to 5,000. However, merchants still disregarded the Navigation Acts and tolerated pirates in Delaware Bay. Anglicans and Quakers were quarreling, and the Quakers were split among themselves— divisions that were reflected in politics. Confusion reigned over which constitution was in force, and the assembly was unable to agree on a new one. Penn removed Markham and ruled the colony himself for a year without a constitution. In late 1701, Penn returned to London to fight against the Reunification Act, Parliament's unsuccessful attempt to make all existing colonies royal. Before his departure, the assembly finally passed a new (and fourth) constitution, the Charter of Privileges, known as the most liberal of all colonial constitutions. Under the charter, the separation between the legislative, executive, and judicial branches of government increased. The appointed council lost all legislative power and became advisory. The assembly, composed of men from each county elected annually by freemen, gained independence and had the right to set its own sessions, initiate legislation, and nominate county officials. The Charter of Privileges also codified freedom of conscience and other individual rights. Partly influenced by Pennsylvania's Quaker legacy, it also evidenced Penn's willingness to permit his proprietary colony to govern itself.

On October 25, 1704, representatives from the Three Lower Counties of Delaware met as a separate assembly at New Castle, with the approval of Governor John Evans. Evans, a non-Quaker, convinced the Lower Counties Assembly to pass a militia act in 1705, but he was less successful in Pennsylvania. Evans staged a mock invasion meant to highlight the colony's lack of preparation for Queen Anne's War; the Quaker-dominated assembly was so scandalized that it again refused even to aid other colonies. Fortunately, Penn continued to manage Indian relations so successfully that Pennsylvania was the only colony in which no hostilities occurred between 1690 and 1730.

Unfortunately, Penn's finances had been badly mismanaged; he was deeply in debt and briefly imprisoned in England because of it. Seeing no alternative, he drew up papers to make Pennsylvania a royal colony but suffered a stroke before signing them. Hannah Penn successfully took over direction of the colony during his illness and continued after his death in 1718. After Hannah's death in 1727, her surviving sons inherited the proprietary title.

Between 1690 and 1730, Pennsylvania received a larger variety of immigrants than any other colony. Before 1710, most were English, with a few Dutch and Welsh. After 1710, Germans and Swiss began to arrive. Waves of Scotch-Irish came in 1718–19 and again in 1725–29; by 1730, Philadelphia alone had 13 Presbyterian churches. It also had a resident Catholic priest. Other groups included Huguenots, Scots, and Jews as well as African slaves. In 1700, the population was less than 20,000; by 1730, it was more than 50,000, including about 4,000 slaves, and growing quickly. Although slavery was never actually written into law in Pennsylvania, a statute of 1700 acknowledged its existence and established separate courts and punishments for slaves. An act of 1725 restricted slaves' mobility and punished miscegenation. Many Quakers objected to slavery, however, and after 1705 the assembly passed a series of large duties to discourage additional slave trading. All were disallowed by the Board of Trade.

In 1723, 17-year-old Benjamin Franklin arrived from Boston to obtain a job as a printer and begin his remarkable career. In 1728, he became the 22-year-old proprietor of his own printing business, publishing the weekly *Pennsylvania Gazette,* eventually one of colonial America's prominent newspapers.

AFRICAN ARRIVALS AND THE GROWTH OF SLAVERY

The shift to an unfree labor force composed primarily of African slaves began in England's North American colonies after 1680. After 1700, the large-scale importation of slaves grew rapidly. Although no entirely reliable statistics of slave population are available, there were probably fewer than 30,000 in 1700 and possibly as many as 100,000 by 1730. Between 1690 and 1730, the number of blacks (both slave and free) grew from about 5 percent of the total colonial population to more than 15 percent. Slaves lived in every colony. By the early 18th century, however, some three-quarters of the total slave population lived in Maryland or south of there. By 1710, slaves were a majority of the population in South Carolina.[1]

Since the founding of the English colonies in the early 1600s, unfree but primarily white labor had been purchased to exploit the opportunities of commercial agriculture. A colonist could become very wealthy if crops in demand abroad could be grown cheaply and on a large scale. Although it is very difficult to comprehend today, in the early colonial era, everyone, including religious leaders, accepted without question the existence of servitude among the "lower orders." Few people even questioned the necessity of brutal physical punishment. The modern concept of individual human rights did not exist, and the concept of exploitation was not recognized. Actual slavery was somewhat less universally accepted, even though forms of slavery existed in most parts of the known world, including Africa itself, and among many Indian tribes. However, in the New World slavery eventually developed distinct characteristics that did not exist elsewhere. The most prominent was its dependence on racial difference.

In 1700, the number of white indentured servants and black slaves in the colonies was approximately equal. Shortly thereafter, slaves became a majority of unfree laborers. The shift occurred for several reasons. The number of whites willing to emigrate as indentured servants decreased; at the same time, the demand for labor escalated, especially in the southern and middle colonies. Planters wanted to cultivate more tobacco because its price was rising. Rice cultivation, introduced into Carolina in the 1690s, required even more laborers than tobacco. In 1698, the Crown gave up its royal monopoly on the slave trade and opened it to all English traders, which made it easier for colonists to purchase slaves. Last but not least, planters were becoming increasingly dissatisfied with white servants, finding them difficult to manage and threatening to the public order once freed. African slaves, on the other hand, were defined as chattel, or property; an owner could treat slaves as he wished with little interference from the law or the courts. Unlike white indentured servants, slaves need never be freed, and their skin color made it more difficult for them to avoid detection if they escaped. Slaves also offered planters the possibility of a self-perpetuating labor force, since children born to female slaves were slaves as well.

For all of these reasons, colonial planters began to prefer slaves, although it was more expensive to purchase a slave than to purchase the indenture of a white servant. The wealthiest planters made the switch first. Colonial legislatures contributed by passing slave codes, or groups of laws that regulated the behavior and restricted the rights of black people.

Most slaves imported to America came from the west coast of Africa, which white colonists called Guinea. The slaves belonged to many distinct societies and ethnic groups and spoke different languages, just as Europeans did. From Senegambia came people often called Gambians. From locations farther down the coast came the Mandinga, the Koromanti, and others; from the Bights (coastline curves or bays) of Benin and Biafra came the Benin and the Igbo. From farther south beyond the Gulf of Guinea came the Angola and Kongo. Today the names of these and many other African ethnic groups are far less widely known that those of European immigrants arriving at the same time; in the early 18th century, however, slave owners were quite knowledgeable about them. Planters strongly preferred slaves from one group or another (although probably because of stereotypes like those held about various European groups). In the late 17th and early 18th century, about three-quarters of the slaves brought to the Chesapeake were Senegambian or Igbo. In the Carolinas, a similar percentage were Angolan.[2]

The slave trade operated from a series of European factories, or forts, built along the west coast of Africa, headed by an official called a factor. In the early years, some African rulers and merchants participated as well, also amassing great profits. War captives and other dependent groups, as well as kidnap victims, were marched in chains to the factories. There they awaited ships called slavers. They were crammed into inhumanly designed holds, often only three feet high, for the notorious Middle Passage to the West Indies. Along the way they endured bad weather, pirates, epidemic illness, and almost unimaginably unsanitary conditions. Those who arrived alive were sold at auction. Under this system, at least 10 million slaves arrived in the New World. (Some historians estimate that an equal number died between their native villages and the New World.) Only about 5 percent came to North America, however; 95 percent went to Spanish or other European colonies in the islands, South, or Central America.

Although slaves lived in every North American colony, they were not spread out evenly within them. In the northern and middle colonies, most slaves lived in urban areas. Few slaveowners had more than one or two slaves; most slaves worked and usually lived in close proximity to whites. Exceptions occurred in the Hudson Valley, the Narragansett area of Rhode Island, and parts of Connecticut where large agricultural and livestock holdings existed. In New England, many slaves experienced "family slavery," incorporated to some extent into Puritan household governance as white servants were.[3] From the Chesapeake south, most slaves lived on large plantations, where they worked together in large groups; increasingly, however, many smaller farmers also owned a few slaves. Not all blacks were agricultural workers, although both men and women were assigned to fieldwork on large plantations. In 1700 probably about 15 percent were skilled craftsmen or women, general laborers, domestic workers, or "jacks of all trade," and the percentage increased as the century progressed.

Free blacks lived in all colonies as well. Some were descendants of indentured blacks. Some purchased their freedom. Some had been manumitted, or freed, for special service like military duty, by a slaveowner's will, or because they had become too old to work. Other free blacks were born to white mothers and black fathers (since a child born to a free mother was free). Children born to Indian mothers and black fathers, called "mustees," were also usually free. As white colonials increasingly identified slave status with race, however, free blacks were increasingly restricted by law and were always in danger of needing to prove their freedom should it be questioned.

The most frequent and effective rebellion against slavery (as well as white servitude) was to run away, as the many colonial newspaper advertisements for runaways attest. Some blacks escaped to Indian tribes (although other Indian groups were slave bounty hunters). Some communities of runaways, called maroons, are known to have existed in the backcountry. One such group was discovered, attacked, and dispersed in the Blue Ridge Mountains of Virginia in 1729.

As larger numbers of Africans arrived in the colonies, organized attempts to obtain freedom became more common. In 1709, for example, an insurrection was organized by blacks and Indians in two counties in Virginia. An informant revealed the plot, however, and the leaders were hanged, drawn, and quartered; the slave informant was given his freedom. In 1712, a rebellion of about two dozen well-armed slaves in New York City resulted in the deaths of 14 whites. During the following two weeks, more than 70 men and women were jailed and 27 condemned to die by hanging or burning. At least three conspiracies were discovered in South Carolina before 1720; in that year, several slaves were executed or deported for planning to attack Charleston.

Prior to 1730, the acceptance of Christianity did not make great headway among slaves and free blacks. Some masters resisted the conversion of their slaves, fearing it would lead them to expect better treatment or even encourage them to demand freedom (Christians traditionally were forbidden to enslave other Christians). Missionary efforts began in the late 17th century, however. Cotton Mather himself wrote a *Catechism for Negroes* and the English Anglican Society for the Propagation of the Gospel (SPG) sent missionaries who were instructed to teach as well as preach; Elias Neau in New York established one of the best-known "schools" in 1704. In New England as well as other places, slaves sometimes attended church with their masters, sitting in specially designated sections.

THE CHESAPEAKE: VIRGINIA

In 1690, Francis Nicholson was appointed governor of Virginia. He arrived with instructions from the Lords of Trade to quiet the colonists' complaints about the autocratic governors sent in the wake of Bacon's Rebellion (1676). Despite Nicholson's previous unhappy experience as lieutenant governor of New York, he worked successfully with the Burgesses and the council in Virginia until his transfer to Maryland in 1694. He returned as governor of Virginia from 1698 to 1704.

In 1691, during Nicholson's tenure, the General Assembly petitioned the Crown to establish a college in Virginia. On February 8, 1693, a royal charter was issued to the College of William and Mary, the second colonial college (after Harvard). Foundations were laid in August 1695 at Middle Plantation (later Williamsburg), using plans drawn by the famous English architect Christopher Wren. The Reverend James Blair, the Anglican commissary, or representative of the bishop of London, was appointed rector and became a powerful figure in Virginia life and politics. Although the College of William and Mary probably did not immediately offer a full 18th-century college curriculum, it quickly assumed an influential role among the colony's elite. In 1700, the first commencement generated great interest. Wealthy planters, small farmers, and Indians all attended the ceremonies. After Jamestown burned to the ground in 1698, the General

Assembly was convinced (after hearing five well-coached student speeches) to build the new capitol near the college. At Williamsburg, named in honor of the king, the college and the capitol faced each other at opposite ends of a broad and imposing street. In 1717, the first theater in the English colonies was built there.

By the turn of the 18th century, the non-Indian population of Virginia, the largest colony, approached 70,000, including about 20,000 blacks. Individual settlers had begun to enter the Piedmont region through the river valleys, although officially the colony encouraged only "societies," or groups of settlers, to migrate west. In 1700, French Huguenots settled Manakin Town near modern Richmond. After 1718, convicts again began to be transported to Virginia by a new act of Parliament. In 1722, the assembly attempted to evade the act by making ship captains responsible for the behavior of those they transported; the crown overruled the measure. During the remainder of the 18th century, as many as 20,000 English convicts were transported to the Chesapeake. Most were indentured and sold to planters. A few were free, having been banished to the colonies for Jacobite activity (a movement to restore the descendants of King James II and his second wife to the throne).

In 1710, Colonel Alexander Spotswood, a vigorous former military officer, arrived as governor. Spotswood actively managed Indian relations, increasing trade and maintaining peace. During the Tuscarora War in North Carolina, he negotiated treaties with groups who did not join the fighting. When the Carolina Tuscarora were defeated in 1713 and driven north into Virginia, Spotswood sent tributary Indians to negotiate a treaty with them as well. In 1713–14, he developed Indian settlements, or reservations, in crucial areas to defend the colony's frontiers. Spotswood also founded Germanna in 1714, a settlement of Swiss and German emigrants on the northwestern frontier. Using the expertise of the immigrant miners and artisans (and ignoring mercantile policy), he established a successful ironworks that produced finished goods for sale in the colony as well as pig iron to ship to London. In 1716, Spotswood led an expedition beyond the Blue Ridge Mountains that became legendary as the symbolic opening of the Virginia west to white settlement. He was not successful, however, at curbing the power of the council and interlocked wealthy planter families, who monopolized colony offices and held large, speculative tracts of land. Spotswood also quarreled with the burgesses, who often perceived matters of taxation and Indian relations quite differently than he did. He was removed from office in 1722 but stayed on in Virginia as a planter himself.

When Sir William Gooch assumed residence at the governor's palace in Williamsburg in 1727, the so-called golden age of the plantation in Virginia began. Tobacco prices rose to new heights, and great wealth was created with the extensive use of slave labor. The largest planter, Robert "King" Carter, owned more than 300,000 acres of land and 1,000 slaves. Another prominent planter was William Byrd II; in 1728 he and other commissioners ran a long-disputed boundary line between Virginia and North Carolina. By that date, dissension between large planters and the vastly more numerous small farmers of Virginia had eased considerably. Many historians believe that they were united by the increasingly common fact of slaveownership and accompanying fears of slave insurrections. In 1723, a year after an unsuccessful insurrection was discovered, the assembly passed a high duty on the importation of slaves from Africa, but merchants protested and the Crown disallowed it. By 1730, the colony had a non-Indian population of more than 100,000 people, about 40,000 of them slaves.

THE CHESAPEAKE: MARYLAND

Maryland officially became a royal colony in 1692. Until Governor Francis Nicholson was transferred from Virginia to Maryland in 1694, politics remained turbulent. Upon his arrival, Nicholson almost immediately moved the capital from St. Marys, the symbol of Calvert and Catholic power, to a new city on the Severn, the old Puritan stronghold. It was soon named Annapolis in honor of Queen Anne. Nicholson, an amateur architect, helped design the distinctive circles, radial streets, and residential squares of the town. He also oversaw the chartering in 1696 of a free school, King William's School (later St. John's College).

Under royal government, religious toleration was greatly reduced in Maryland. In 1692, the Church of England became the established church, and a poll (or head) tax of 40 pounds of tobacco was established to support it. Prominent Quakers in the assembly resigned when required to swear an oath and resisted demands that they join the militia. Presbyterians resisted the poll tax. The 600–700 Catholic laity, eight priests, and three brothers in the colony were forbidden to worship freely. In 1704, Catholics were forbidden to establish schools or make converts; in 1718, an "oath of abhorrency"—a stronger form of the oath of supremacy—was required to obtain the franchise. (The oath of supremacy was an acknowledgment of the English Crown as head of the church as well as the state.)

Under royal control, the Calvert proprietors continued to receive quitrents and other income from the colony, although they were stripped of governmental rights. In 1715, Benedict Leonard Calvert abandoned Catholicism, converted himself and his children to Anglicanism, and petitioned the crown to have full proprietary rights restored. He died soon afterward, but his minor son Charles, the fifth Lord Baltimore, was restored to full proprietary rights. The Maryland Assembly, however, having gained strength under royal control, did not relinquish its new powers upon the return of proprietary government.

Between 1690 and 1730, a new pattern of larger landholdings and agriculture based on slave labor emerged in Maryland. About 1700, the non-Indian population as a whole began to grow significantly. The first census, in 1701, listed 32,258 persons; by 1730, there were 82,000, probably more than 20 percent of them black. The Tidewater region (the level coastal plains) filled in, and settlers began moving into the Piedmont (the area west of the coastal plains but east of the Appalacian Mountains). In 1700, printer Thomas Reading brought out *A Complete Body of the Laws of Maryland,* and in 1704 he began updating them after each session of the assembly. Previously, judges had relied on handwritten copies. In 1726 another printer, William Parks, arrived in Annapolis, beginning the first newspaper of the southern colonies, the *Maryland Gazette,* on September 12, 1727.

INDIAN WARS IN THE CAROLINAS

In 1702, when Queen Anne's War began in Europe, South Carolinians believed themselves to be directly threatened by both the French and the Spanish in

North America. The triangular-shaped territory between Spanish Florida, French Louisiana, and South Carolina was disputed land, and South Carolina traders had increasingly ventured into it. James Moore, elected governor by the council in 1700, led white and Creek forces to attack St. Augustine in 1702. Although the English devastated the town, the large fortress guarding the town, the Castillo de San Marcos, held. Before retreating overland, Moore burned his own ships to prevent the Spanish from seizing them. Upon his return, angry shipowners forced him from office. A year later, he personally financed an expedition to northwestern Florida, called Apalache province. Moore and combined white-Indian troops destroyed the Catholic mission system in the area, confiscated church property, and captured about 1,000 Apalachee, whom they sold as slaves to the West Indies. The Spanish retaliated in 1706 by sending Spanish and French warships to Charleston. Charleston residents, however, won an impressive victory. For several years thereafter, the French, Spanish, and English all intrigued against each other, drawing southern Indian nations—primarily the Creek, Choctaw, and Chickasaw—to one side or the other and creating instability.

In Albemarle, or North Carolina, expansion began in earnest during the 1690s. In 1710, under the leadership of Baron Christoph von Graffenreid, more than 400 Swiss established the town of New Bern in the back country. Indian relations were already uneasy there, not only between whites and Indians but also among hostile tribes. Some 7,000 Tuscarora lived in the area; they were angry at white encroachment and unfair trading practices and were also suffering from Susquehannock and Seneca raiding. In September 1711, the Tuscarora, allied with several smaller local tribes, captured surveyor John Lawson, his black slave, and Graffenreid. They killed Lawson and the following day conducted well-organized raids on outlying farms and villages, killing more than 130 white and black colonists, about half of them Swiss or German, and taking many captives. Carolinians retaliated by leading some 500 Yamasee warriors against the Tuscarora, and the Tuscarora War began.

A peace was negotiated, but it did not hold. The colonists seized and enslaved Indians, and Indians began raids again in 1712. North Carolina, ravaged by a yellow fever epidemic, called on South Carolina for help. In March 1713, Colonel James Moore, Jr. (son of the ex-governor), led South Carolina forces and a larger group of Creek, Cherokee, and Catawba against the Tuscarora. By the time a preliminary treaty was signed later in the year, about 1,400 Tuscarora had been killed and another 1,000 enslaved; 2,000 survivors fled north to join the Iroquois Confederacy, also called the Five Nations. Whites confiscated most tribal lands. The final peace did not come until February 1715, when the remaining bands agreed to live on reserved lands. The northern Tuscarora, however, part of what was now called the Six Nations, continued to visit the area and to seek revenge against the Catawba and Creek.

A mere two months after the final peace in the Tuscarora War, the Yamasee War began in South Carolina. The Yamasee—many of whom had recently fought with South Carolinians against the Spanish—attacked a group of white traders and several frontier settlements. The Yamasee were, with good cause, angry over unscrupulous trading practices and slave taking. Other tribes soon allied with them, including the Creek, Catawba, and remnants of the Guale and other southern tribes. Raids approached within 12 miles of Charleston.

South Carolina, with a population of about 5,000 whites and 8,000 blacks, organized a paid militia; some slaves were even armed. Massachusetts and Virginia provided aid. Although military actions made little progress, negotiations were more successful. The Cherokee were convinced to abandon their neutrality and begin a war with the Creek; the Catawba and Creek withdrew from the Yamasee alliance. Although the English and Yamasee made peace in 1717, sporadic raiding on the frontier dragged on until 1727, when the Cherokee-Creek hostilities ended. In South Carolina, more than 400 settlers had been killed. Frontiers were emptied, trade was disrupted, and as much as half the cultivated land in the colony was temporarily abandoned. Both the French and Spanish gained from increased anti-English sentiment among the Indians. The remaining Yamasee moved south and allied with the Spanish.

THE CAROLINAS SEPARATE

As the 1690s opened in the Carolinas, political dissension continued in the colony—between older and newer counties, Anglicans and dissenters, the proprietors and the colonists. In 1691, the proprietors appointed Philip Ludwell of Virginia the new governor at Charleston. They instructed him to appoint a deputy for the settlements north of Cape Fear. From that date, North Carolina and South Carolina were effectively separate. South Carolina had grown into a society of large landholders, with a thriving urban center and port at Charleston. Indian slavery there was more extensive than in any other English colony, although quickly being replaced by black slavery, and Indian trade was important to the economy. North Carolina, on the other hand, lacked a major port and remained primarily a colony of small farmers. Its staple, like that of Chesapeake, was tobacco, although grains and cattle were also exported.

After 1691, North Carolina's politics were less chaotic but still contentious. In 1701 and again in 1705, the assembly passed Vestry Acts in an attempt to establish the Church of England. Quakers, Calvinists, and Baptists protested so vehemently that the proprietors disallowed the first act and the second was never enforced. Between 1707 and 1710, a confusing dispute between Anglican and dissenting factions, known as Cary's Rebellion occurred, during which Quakers and others joined one deposed governor in trying to depose his successor. In 1710, the proprietors, hoping to reestablish order, appointed Edward Hyde (not to be confused with Edward Hyde, Lord Cornbury, to whom he was related), as governor. On May 9, 1712, the colony was officially divided.

By 1715, North Carolina had acquired an unsavory reputation as a particular haven for pirates. Small, fast pirate ships could hide easily in the Outer Banks; the colony's government was too weak and unstable to oppose them; the colonists, long accustomed to smuggling tobacco themselves, were content to avoid the higher prices charged by legitimate traders. Other colonies and the crown, however, were increasingly unhappy with the disruption to trade. In 1717, King George issued a proclamation of amnesty to pirates who retired; many of them—formerly commissioned privateers for Queen Anne—agreed to do so. During fall 1718, almost 50 others were captured and executed in North Carolina. In November, Governor Spotswood of Virginia sent an expedition to capture the notorious Edward Teach, better known as Blackbeard. After Teach's death, the hold of pirates on the colony was broken.

St. James Church (Anglican), Goose
Creek, South Carolina, built 1711
(Historic American Building Survey)

In South Carolina, the colonists continued to quarrel with each other and
the proprietors; they were particular unhappy with the proprietors' lack of support during the Indian wars. Many sought to become a royal colony. In 1717,
they sent the Crown a petition signed by about half the free white men of the
colony; in 1719, an outright rebellion against the proprietors occurred. Acting
on rumors of an attack by the Spanish, the Commons (as the South Carolina
Assembly was now called) deposed the proprietary governor and sent an agent
to England to ask once again for royal control. The Crown sent a provisional
governor; for the next decade, the situation remained confused, and the legal status of the colony unclear. In 1729, the proprietors finally reached an agreement
with the Crown. The Crown bought out seven of the shares; the eighth, a
Carteret heir, refused to sell proprietary land rights, a situation that troubled the
colony until the American Revolution. North and South Carolina thus became
two separate royal colonies.

The most important event in South Carolina, however, was the spread of rice
cultivation in the 1690s, which some historians believe was introduced by slaves
from rice-growing areas of Africa. By 1730, rice had reached an annual export of
18 million pounds. Extremely large plantations had arisen to finance the costly
irrigation systems rice required; each plantation, in turn, required large numbers
of slaves. In 1730, the estimated population of each of the Carolinas had reached
30,000. While slaves were probably less than 20 percent of the population of
North Carolina, more than 70 percent of South Carolina's population was
enslaved.

CHRONICLE OF EVENTS

1690

King William's War (the War of the League of Augsburg) opens in America. French and Indian attacks on New York, Maine, and New Hampshire soon follow.

Massachusetts accepts a petition from the royal province of New Hampshire to be reannexed; it is disallowed by the Crown.

In the Carolinas, rice cultivation begins to increase.

May: The English, under Sir William Phips, capture Port Royal, Acadia.

1691

The French retake Port Royal.

Massachusetts receives a new charter and becomes a semiroyal colony. Maine and Plymouth are consolidated with Massachusetts Bay; Plymouth ends its life as a separate colony. Massachusetts is no longer permitted to use church membership as a qualification for the franchise.

In New York, Jacob Leisler, leader of the 1689 rebellion, is hanged.

Carolina proprietors instruct the governor in Charleston to appoint a deputy governor for the northern settlements (modern North Carolina).

1692

In Massachusetts, Sir William Phips becomes the first royal governor; he is also the first colonial knighted by the Crown. Massachusetts reinstates the power of town government, weakened under the Dominion of New England.

In Pennsylvania, the royal governor of New York takes control of the colony.

Maryland officially becomes a royal colony and the Anglican Church is established; religious toleration is greatly reduced.

June: Witchcraft trials begin in Salem. The first "witch," Bridget Bishop, is executed.

September: Some 25 witches have been executed in New England and another 150 accused are in jail in Salem.

1693

New Hampshire petitions the Crown to reannex it to Massachusetts; the controversy will drag on until 1699.

Connecticut successfully requests confirmation of its independent charter from the Crown.

New York establishes the Anglican Church in certain counties. The first printing press is established in the colony.

Virginia receives a royal charter for the College of William and Mary, the second colonial college.

1694

William Penn has his proprietary rights to the colony of Pennsylvania restored.

Queen Mary confirms that Rhode Island retains its pre-Dominion charter, granted in 1663.

In Maryland, Governor Francis Nicholson moves the capital from St. Marys to Annapolis.

1696

Parliament passes the Navigation Act of 1696, with several provisions for enforcement.

King William replaces the Lords of Trade with the Board of Trade, an independent group with representatives from Parliament.

In Pennsylvania, the assembly passes Markham's Frame, or the Third Frame of Government.

1697

The Treaty of Ryswick ends King William's War. All conquered lands in America are returned to their former claimants. The French will now work to complete their fortified "crescent" from the St. Lawrence down the Mississippi River to the Gulf of Mexico.

The Massachusetts General Court declares a day of penitence for the witchcraft proceedings.

1698

The Crown opens the slave trade to any Englishman; after this date, the large-scale importation of black slaves will increase rapidly in the North American colonies.

In Virginia, Jamestown burns to the ground and a new capital is built at Williamsburg.

1699

The Crown announces that New Hampshire is to retain its own assembly and council but will share a governor with Massachusetts.

William Penn and his second wife, Hannah, return to Pennsylvania. Penn rules the colony himself, without a constitution, for more than a year.

1700

Connecticut passes a law requiring towns to tax citizens for the support of schools.

In Maryland, the complete laws of the colony are printed for the first time.

In Virginia, French Huguenots settle Manakin Town, near modern Richmond.

The non-Indian population of the English colonies is about 250,000, about 30,000 of whom are black slaves. About 80 percent of the white population is of English background and 20 percent other European. The number of white servants and black slaves in the colonies is approximately equal, but blacks will soon become a majority of unfree laborers.

1701

Parliament proposes the Reunification Act to "royalize" all the colonies. William Penn organizes efforts to defeat it. From now until the American Revolution, the colonies will be no more uniform or centralized than they are as of this date.

In Connecticut, the assembly establishes the Collegiate School, later called Yale, the third colonial college.

The Pennsylvania Assembly passes the Charter of Privileges, the colony's fourth constitution. It is a progressive document that separates legislative, judicial, and executive branches of government.

1702

Queen Anne (Mary's sister) ascends the English throne. Queen Anne's War (the War of the Spanish Succession) begins. France and Spain are allied against England. In America, the French and Abenaki begin attacks on Maine and Massachusetts.

East and West Jersey are united as the royal colony of New Jersey.

Governor James Moore of South Carolina leads an attack on St. Augustine. English forces destroy the town but fail to capture the fort.

1703

Rhode Island and Connecticut agree on their border.

Former governor Moore of South Carolina attacks Spanish missions in the Apalache area of northwestern Florida.

1704

The English attack Acadia. The French and Indians massacre colonists at Deerfield, Massachusetts.

The Three Lower Counties of Delaware convene a separate assembly, with the consent of Pennsylvania.

1705

Parliament lengthens the list of enumerated articles (those that can be traded only to England) to include furs, rice, and naval stores.

1706

August: French and Spanish forces attack Charleston but are driven away.

1707

England and Scotland unite under the Act of Union.

1708

The Saybrook Platform is adopted by Connecticut churches, establishing some oversight of ministers and congregations.

New York prosecutes Presbyterian minister Francis Makemie for preaching without a license; he stands trial and is acquitted.

1709

In Virginia, a conspiracy of slaves and Indians is discovered; its leaders are executed.

1710

The English capture Port Royal; it is renamed Annapolis Royal.

German and Swiss migrants begin a large migration to North America.

In Virginia, a conspiracy of slaves and Indians is discovered.

In North Carolina, Swiss colonists establish the town of New Bern.

By this date, black slaves are a majority of the non-Indian population in South Carolina.

1711

In Massachusetts, still-living persons accused of witchcraft in 1692 have their civil rights restored; the survivors of those executed receive monetary compensation.

The Tuscarora War begins in the Carolinas.

1712

In New York City, a slave rebellion occurs; 14 whites are killed. About two dozen armed blacks take part, but many more are executed in the aftermath.

Letitia Street House, Philadelphia, built 1703–15; a small merchant's or skilled artisan's house *(Historic American Building Survey)*

May 9: North and South Carolina are officially separated.

1713

The Treaty of Utrecht ends Queen Anne's War. Britain receives Newfoundland and Acadia (renamed Nova Scotia) as well as permission to carry slaves to Spain's New World colonies.

Eastern Indian nations meet in Portsmouth and sign a peace treaty. After this, growth occurs rapidly in most of New England.

The Tuscarora War effectively ends, although the final treaty is not signed until 1715. Many Tuscarora flee to the north and join the Iroquois Confederacy or Five Nations, now known as the Six Nations.

1714

Queen Anne dies without an heir; King George I of the German House of Hanover ascends the throne of England. The Parliamentarian party, now called the Whigs, dominates the government. George's chief adviser, Sir Robert Walpole, favors "salutary neglect" for the colonies.

1715

Leonard Calvert converts to Anglicanism. His son Charles, the fifth Lord Baltimore, receives full restoration of proprietary rights.

In South Carolina, the Yamasee War begins. The Cherokee begin a war with the Creek that will last until 1727; sporadic raiding occurs on the frontiers of Carolina until that date.

1716

Governor Alexander Spotswood of Virginia leads an expedition over the Blue Ridge Mountains; it symbolizes opening the west to white settlement.

1717

The Crown offers to pardon pirates who give up their trade.

"Rack renting" begins in Ulster, Ireland, and large-scale Scotch-Irish emigration to North America begins.

In South Carolina, the Yamasee War ends. The Yamasee ally again with the Spanish.

1718

Parliament passes new legislation encouraging the shipment of convicts to the colonies; as many as 20,000 will be sent by the end of the 18th century despite Virginia's attempts to resist.

The French found New Orleans.

William Penn dies; his widow, Hannah, continues management of the colony.

1719

The War of the Quadruple Alliance begins in Europe, lasting until 1721. It has repercussions in the American south as France, Spain, and England compete for Indian alliances.

In Rhode Island, laws are codified and published.

In the Carolinas, a revolt occurs in favor of royal government.

1720

A slave rebellion is uncovered in Charleston; its leaders are executed.

1721

A smallpox epidemic breaks out in Boston; the first inoculations against the disease are given.

1722

The Abenaki attack Brunswick; the Massachusetts General Court declares war on the Eastern Indians.

1724

August: Soldiers from York, Maine, attack the Indian mission village of Norwidgewock and murder the French Jesuit priest.

1725

The Treaty of Casco Bay, sometimes called Dummer's Treaty, ends the Indian war in northern New England. After this date, many Kennebec tribes flee to Canada; few additional hostilities will occur in the area.

1727

Hannah Penn dies, and the sons of William and Hannah inherit the proprietorship of Pennsylvania.

The Maryland Gazette, the first newspaper in the southern colonies, is established.

Southern Indian wars finally end; settlement will slowly be reestablished in South Carolina.

1728

A Virginia commission headed by William Byrd II leads a survey expedition to run a boundary line on the long-disputed Carolina-Virginia border.

Benjamin Franklin becomes publisher of the *Pennsylvania Gazette.*

1729

A community of escaped slaves is attacked and dispersed in the Blue Ridge Mountains of Virginia.

The Carolina proprietors finally reach an agreement with the Crown; North and South Carolina become royal colonies.

1730

The non-Indian population of the colonies is more than 625,000; between 15 and 20 percent of the population is black.

EYEWITNESS TESTIMONY

The women in the garrison [*Wells, Maine*] on this occasion took up the Amazonian stroke, and not only brought ammunition to the men, but also with manly resolution fired several times upon the enemy.

The Reverend Cotton Mather, ca. 1690, Magnalia, *vol. 2, p. 534.*

And forasmuch as great inconveniences may happen to this country by the setting of negroes and mulattoes free, by their either entertaining negro slaves from their masters' service, or receiving stolen goods, or being grown old bringing a charge upon the country; for prevention thereof, Be it enacted ... That no negro or mulatto be after the end of this present session of assembly set free by any person or persons whatsoever, unless such person or persons, their heirs, executors or administrators pay for the transportation of such negro or negroes out of the country within six months after such setting them free, upon penalty of paying of ten pounds sterling to the Church wardens of the parish where such person shall dwell with, which money, or so much thereof as shall be necessary, the said Church wardens are to cause the said negro or mulatto to be transported out of the country....

. . . . .

That if any English woman being free shall have a bastard child by any negro or mulatto, she pay the sum of fifteen pounds sterling, within one month after such bastard child be born, to the Church wardens of the parish where she shall be delivered of such child, and in default of such payment she shall be taken into the possession of the said Church wardens and disposed of [*indentured*] for five years ... and that such bastard child be bound out as a servant by the said Church wardens until he or she shall attain the age of thirty years....

Virginia statutes, 1691, Hening, Statutes, *vol. 3, pp. 87–88.*

But the winter must not pass over without a storm of blood! The Popish Indians, after long silence and repose in their inaccessible kennels, which made our frontier towns a little remit of their tired vigilance, did, January 25, 1691, set upon the town of York where the inhabitants were in their unguarded houses here and there scattered, quiet and secure. Upon the firing of a gun by the Indians, which was their signal, the inhabitants looked out but unto their amazement, found their houses to be invested with horrid savages who immediately kill'd many of those unprovided inhabitants, and more they took prisoners. This body of Indians consisting of divers hundreds, then sent in their summons to some of the garrison's houses; and those garrisons, whereof some had no more than two or three men in them, yet being so well manned, as to reply, that they would spend their blood unto the last drop, e'er they would surrender; these cowardly miscreants had not mettle enough to meddle with 'em. So they retired into their howling thicket, having first murdered about fifty, and captivated near a hundred of that unhappy people. In this calamity great was the share that fell to the family of Mr. Shubael Dummer, the pastor of the little flock they prey'd upon; those bloodhounds, being set on by some Romish missionaries, had long been wishing that they might embrue their hand in the blood of some New-English Minister; and in this action they had their diabolical satisfaction.

The Reverend Cotton Mather, describing events of January 25, 1691, Magnalia, *vol. 2, pp. 530–31.*

The German-Town of which I spoke before,
Which is, at least, in length one Mile and More,
Where lives High-German People, and Low-
 Dutch,
Whose Trade in weaving Linen Cloth is much,
There grows the Flax, as also you may know,
That from the same they do divide the Tow;
Their Trade fits well within this Habitation,
We find Convenience for their Occupation.
One Trade brings in employment for another,
So that we may suppose each Trade a Brother;
From Linen Rags good Paper doth derive,
The first Trade keeps the second Trade alive....

Richard Frame, "A Short Description of Pennsylvania," 1692, in Myers, Narratives, *pp. 304–05.*

What's that? Must the Younger Women, do ye say, hearken to the Elder?—They must be another Sort of Elder Women than You then! They must not be Elder Witches, I am sure, Pray, do you for once Hearken to me.—What a dreadful sight are You! An Old Woman, an Old Servant of the Devil! You, that should instruct such poor, young, Foolish Creatures as I am to serve the Lord Jesus Christ, come and urge me to serve the Devil! ...

Memorandum: T'was an ordinary thing for the Devil to persecute her with Stories of what this and that Body in the Town spoke against her. The Unjust and Absurd Reflections cast upon her by Rash People in the coffee-houses or elsewhere, We discerned that the Devil Reported such Passages unto her in her Fits, to discourage her. . . .

But when she had so much Release from the captivating Impressions of the Wretches that haunted her, as to be able to see and hear the Good People about her in the Room, She underwent another sort of plague, which I don't Remember that ever I observed in more than One or Two Bewitched persons beside her. Her Tortures were turned into Frolics; and She became as extravagant as a Wildcat. . . . She would sometimes have diverse of these Fits in a Day, and she was always excessively Witty in them; never downright Profane, but yet sufficiently Insolent and Abusive to such as were about her. And in these Fits also she took an extraordinary Liberty . . . to amnidivert upon all. . . .

"Demonic possession" of Mercy Short, 1692, reported by The Reverend Cotton Mather, A Brand Plucked Out of the Burning, in Burr, ed., Narratives, pp. 268–71.

The examination of Sarah Good before the worshipful Assts. John Harthorn [*and*] Jonathan Curran

(H.) Sarah Good what evil Spirit have you familiarity with?

(S.G.) None.

(H) Have you made no contract with the devil? Good answered no.

(H) Why do you hurt these children?

(g) I do not hurt them. I scorn it.

(H) Who do you employ then to do it?

(g) I employ no body.

(H) What creature do you employ them?

(g) No creature but I am falsely accused.

(H) Why did you go away muttering from Mr. Parris his house

(g) I did not mutter but I thanked him for what he gave my child.

(H) Have you made no contract with the devil?

(g) No.

Examination of Sarah Good, March 1, 1692, in Hart, ed., American History, vol. 2, pp. 41–42.

16 July 1692. Ann Foster Examined conffesed that it was Goody Carier that made her a witch that she came to her in person about Six yeares agoe & told her if she would not be awitch the divill should tare her in peices and Cary her away at w'ch. time she promised to Serve the divill, that she had bewitched a hog of John Lovjoyes to Death & that she had hurt Some persons in Salem Vilage that goody Carier came to her & would have her bewitch two children of Andrew Allins & that she had then two popets made and stuck pins in them to bewitch the said Children by which one of them dyed the other very sick, that she was at the meeting of the witches at Salem Villiage that Goody Carier came & told her of the meeting & would have her goe, so they gat upon Sticks & went said Jorny & being ther did see mr Burroughs the minister who spake to them all. . . .

Trial transcript, in Boyer and Nissenbaum, eds., "Salem Witchcraft," pp. 342–43.

First, as to the method which the Salem Justices do take in their examinations, it is truly this: A warrant being issued out to apprehend the persons that are charged and complained of by the afflicted children, (as they are called); said persons are brought before the Justices, (the afflicted being present.) The Justices ask the apprehended why they afflict those poor children; to which the apprehended answer, they do not afflict them. The Justices order the apprehended to look upon the said children, which accordingly they do; and at the time of that look, (I dare not say by that look, as the Salem Gentlemen do) the afflicted are cast into a fit. The apprehended are then blinded, and ordered to touch the afflicted; and at that touch, tho' not by the touch, (as above) the afflicted ordinarily do come out of their fits. The afflicted persons then declare and affirm, that the apprehended have afflicted them; upon which the apprehended persons, tho' of never so good repute, are forthwith committed to prison, on suspicion for witchcraft. . . .

Boston merchant Thomas Brattle to a clergyman, October 1692, in Burr, ed., Narratives, pp. 170–71.

. . . when I came home I found many persons in a strange ferment of dissatisfaction which was increased by some hot Spirits that blew up the flame on enquiring into the matter I found that the Devil had taken upon him the name and shape of several persons who were doubtless innocent and to my certain knowledge of good reputation for which cause I have now forbidden the committing of any more that shall be accused without unavoidable necessity, and those that have been committed I would shelter from any Proceedings against them wherein there may be the least suspicion of any wrong to be done unto the Innocent. I would also wait for any particular directions or commands if their Majesties please to give me any for the fuller ordering this perplexed affair. I have also put a stop to the printing of any discourses one way or other, that may increase the needless disputes of people upon this occasion, because I saw a likely-hood of kindling an inextinguishable flame if I should admit any public and open Contests. . . .

Governor William Phips to the crown, October 12, 1692, in Burr, ed., Narratives, *pp. 196–97.*

White-Newbold House, Perquimans County, North Carolina, built early 18th century; a small plantation or farm house *(Historic American Building Survey)*

Mrs. Durant enters for her two Grand Children a young sorrel mare with a star in her forehead Called Bonne the same mare and her increase and increases to Ann and Elizabeth Waller to them and their heirs for ever. . . .

Hannah Gosby has entered nine Rights [*headrights*] John Gosby, John Anderson, John Kinsey, Richard Waterlow, Kathrine Kinsey, Jean Anderson and 3 hands from John Northcoate, Joseph Hepworth, Jeremiah White and Henry Clay senior in all nine Rights. . . .

[November 6]. A Bill of enditem was Brought against William Shreenes and presented to the Grand jury the Grand jury finds Billa vera [*true*] a Petty jury was sent out and found the prisoner guilty of Petty Larceny and so returned the Bill whereupon he was ordered by the Court to have 30 lashes upon his naked back stripped to his waist and severely Whipped and be bound to serve for his Fees one year and half from this day . . . to his Master John Hatton besides his former Indenture of five years. . . .

Perquimans Precinct Court, North Carolina, 1694, in Hart, ed., American History, *vol. 2, pp. 191–92.*

As to their religion, they are very much divided; few of them intelligent and sincere, but the most part ignorant and conceited, fickle and regardless. As to their wealth and disposition thereto, the Dutch are rich and sparing; the English neither very rich, nor too great husbands; the French are poor, and therefore forced to be penurious. As to their way of trade and dealing, they are all generally cunning and crafty, but many of them not so just to their words as they should be.

John Miller, Description of the Province of New York. . . . 1695, *quoted in Kammen,* Colonial New York, *p. 150.*

And We do hereby further Authorize and empower you Our said Commissioners, to examine into and weigh such Acts of the Assemblies of the Plantations respectively as shall from time to time be sent or transmitted hither for Our Approbation; And to set down and represent as aforesaid the Usefulness or Mischief thereof to Our Crown, and to Our said Kingdom of England, or to the Plantations themselves, in case the same should be established for Laws there; And also to consider what matters may be recommended as fit to be passed in the Assemblies there, To hear complaints of Oppressions and maladministrations, in Our Plantations, in order to represent as aforesaid what you in your Discretions shall think proper; And also to require an Account of all Monies given for Public uses by the Assemblies in Our Plantations, and how the same are and have been expended or laid out.

King William creates the Board of Trade, 1696, in Hart, ed., American History, *vol. 2, pp. 130–31.*

... servants are not so willing to go there [*Virginia*] as formerly because the members of Council and others who make an interest in the Government have from time to time procured grants of very large tracts of land, so that for many years there has been no waste land to be taken up by those who bring with them servants, or by servants who have served their time....

Edward Randolph to the Board of Trade, 1696, quoted in Robinson, Southern, *p. 134.*

Samuel Sewall, sensible of the reiterated strokes of God upon himself and family; and being sensible, that as to the Guilt contracted upon ... at Salem (to which the order for this Day relates) [*the witchcraft trials*] he is, upon many accounts, more concerned than any that he knows of, Desires to take the Blame and shame of it, Asking pardon of men, And especially desiring prayers that God, who has an Unlimited Authority, would pardon that sin and all other his sins; personal and Relative: And according to his infinite Benignity, and Sovereignty, Not Visit the sin of him, or of any other, upon himself or any of his, nor upon the Land. But that He would powerfully defend him against all Temptations to Sin, for the future, and vouchsafe him the efficacious, saving Conduct of his Word and Spirit.

Judge Samuel Sewall, 1697, in Hart, ed., American History, *vol. 2, p. 49.*

Poor People both men and Women, will get near three times more Wages for their Labour in this country, than they can earn either in England or Wales.... I shall instance in a few, which may serve.... The first was a Black-Smith (my next Neighbour), who himself and one Negro man he had, got Fifty Shillings in one Day, by working up a Hundred Pound Weight of Iron....

I shall add another Reason why Women's Wages are so exorbitant; they are not yet very numerous, which makes them stand upon high Terms for their several Services, in Seamstering, Washing, Spinning, Knitting, Sewing, and in all the other parts of their Employments.... [M]oreover they are usually Marry'd before they are Twenty Years of Age, and when once in

that Noose, are for the most part a little uneasy, and make their Husbands so too, till they procure them a Maid Servant to bear the burden of the Work, as also in some measure to wait on them too.

Gabriel Thomas, Historical ... Account of Pennsylvania *[1698], in Myers, ed.,* Narratives, *pp. 319, 326–27.*

No less than ten years have rolled away since we have been plunged into the distresses of a War with a barbarous enemy. In this war we have seen the fruitful land of almost one whole province [*Maine*], and another whole county [*New Hampshire*], turned into barrenness; doubtless not without the provocations of wickedness in them who dwelt herein; men had sown fields there along the shore in settlement for an hundred miles together, and had multiplied greatly into a cluster of towns ... but in this war we have seen them diminished again, and brought low, through oppression, affliction, and sorrow. I am to lead you this day thro' a spacious country, which had been on many accounts the most charming part of New-England; and I must herewithal say, *come, behold the words of the Lord, what desolations he had made in that land....* Let us all then enquire, what may have been those provoking evils, for which the holy and blessed God hath given the sword a commission so dreadful to devour us?

The Reverend Cotton Mather, 1698, Magnalia, *vol. 2, p. 373.*

... I find that those Pirates that have given the greatest disturbance in the East Indies and Red Sea, have been either fitted from New York or Rhode Island, and mann'd from New York. The ships commanded by Mason, Tew, Glover and Hore, had their commissions from the Governor of New York. The three last from [*former Governor*] Fletcher and although these Commissions (which are on record here) appear to be given only against the King's enemies; yet it was known to all the inhabitants of this City that they were bound to the Indies and the Red Sea, it being openly declared by the said Commanders, whereby they raised men and were quickly able to proceed, and so notoriously public that it was generally believed that they had assurance from Col. Fletcher, that they may return with the spoil to New York and be protected.... And Captain Tew that had been before a most notorious pirate (complained of by the East India Company) on his return from the Indies with great riches made a visit to New

York, where (although a man of most mean and infamous character) he was received and caressed by Col. Fletcher, dined and supped often with him, and appeared publically in his coach with him, and they exchanged presents, as gold watches etc. one another, all this is known to most of the City. . . .

Richard, earl of Bellomont to the Board of Trade, 1698,
in Hart, ed., American History, *vol. 2, pp. 244–45.*

Relations are Rattle with Brattle and Brattle,
Lord Bro'r mayn't command,
But Mather and Mather had rather and rather
The good old way should stand.
Saints Cotton and Hooker, Oh look down and
    look here, . . .
Our churches turn genteel,
Our Parsons grow trim and trig with Wealth
    Wine and Wig
And their heads are covered with meal.

Nailed to the door of the Brattle Street Church, 1699,
quoted in Miller, New England Mind, *p. 244.*

There are in itt [*Annapolis, Maryland*] about fourty dwelling houses . . . seven or eight whereof cann afford good lodging and accommodations for strangers. There is alsoe a State house and a free schoole built with bricke which make a great shew among a parcell of wooden houses, and the foundations of a church laid, the only bricke church in Maryland. They have two market daies in the week.

An unidentified observer, 1699, quoted in Land,
Colonial Maryland, *p. 96.*

I find the Inhabitants [*of Carolina*] greatly alarmed upon the news that the French continue their resolution to make a settling at Messasipi [*Mississippi*] River, from [whence] they may come over land to the head of Ashley River without opposition, 'tis not yet known what care the Lords Proprietors intend to take for their preservation. . . . But 'tis apparent that all the time of this French war they never sent them one barrel of powder or a pound of lead to help them. They conclude they have no reason to depend upon them for assistance, and are resolved to forsake this Country betimes, if they find the French are settled at Meschasipi, or if upon the death of the King of Spain these Countries fall into the hands of the French as inevitably they will. . . .

Edward Randolph to the Board of Trade, March 1699,
in Salley, ed., Narratives, *pp. 204, 206.*

The Province of East Jersey has in it Ten Towns. . . . These Towns are not like the towns in England, the houses built close together on a small spot of ground, but they include large portions of the Country Of 4, 5, 8, 10, 12, 15 miles in length, and as much in breadth, and all the Settlements within such State and bounds is said to be within such a Township. . . . Those towns and the whole province was peopl'd mostly from the adjacent colonies of New York and New England, and generally by Those of very narrow fortunes, and such as could not well subsist in the places they left. . . .

Bergen, and the out Plantations are most Dutch, and were settled from New York and the United Provinces they are pretty equally divided into Calvinist and Lutheran, they have one pretty little Church, and are a sober people, there are a few English Dissenters mixt among them.

Aqueckenonck was peopled from New York also, they are Dutch mostly and generally Calvinist. Elizabeth Town and Newark, were peopled from New England, are generally Independents. . . . Woodbridge was settled from New England. . . . There was a number of Scots Presbyterians amongst them. . . . Piscattaway was settled from New England, and is called the Anabaptist Town. . . . Perth Amboy the Capital City was settled from Europe . . . and when all the Churchmen [*Anglicans*] in the Province are got together, we make up about twelve Communicants. . . .

Freehold was settled from Scotland . . . and about the one half of it are Scotch Presbyterians, and a sober people, the other part of it was settled by People . . . who are generally speaking of no religion. . . . Middletown was settled from New York and New England, it is a large Township, there is no such thing as Church or Religion amongst them, they are perhaps the most ignorant and wicked People in the world, their meetings on Sundays is at the Public house, where they get their fill of Rum, and go to fighting and running of races which are Practices much in use that day all the Province over. Shrewsbury settled from New England, Rhode Island and New York, there is in it about thirty Quakers of both Sexes. . . .

Governor Lewis Morris, 1700 in Hart, ed.,
American History, *vol. 2, pp. 276–78.*

The Design of founding a College in the Colony of Connecticut, was first conceived by the ministers. . . . The first Plan was very formal and minute drawn up by some Gentleman in Imitation of the Protestant

Colleges and Universities in France, founded by their general Synods. In which it was proposed, "That a College should be erected by a general Synod of the consociated Churches in the Colony of Connecticut. . . . That the Synod should agree upon a Confession of Faith to be consented to by the President, Inspectors and Tutors." . . . [I]n the mean Time, in the lesser Conventions of Ministers in Associations and Councils, and in private Conversation, ten of the principal Ministers in the Colony, were nominated and agreed upon by a general Consent both of the Ministers and People, to stand as Trustees or Undertakers to found, erect and govern a College. . . .

The Ministers so nominated . . . brought a Number of Books and presented them to the Body; and laying them on the Table, said these Words, or to this Effect; "*I give these Books for the founding* [of] *a College in this Colony.*"

The Reverend Thomas Clap, ca. 1700, The History of Yale-College *[1766], in Hart, ed.,* American History, *vol. 2, pp. 255–56.*

The numerousness of slaves at this day in the province, and the uneasiness of them under their slavery, has put many upon thinking whether the foundation of it be firmly and well laid, so as to sustain the vast weight that is built upon it. It is most certain that all men, as they are the sons of Adam, are coheirs, and have equal right unto liberty, and all other outward comforts of life. "God hath given the earth (with all its commodities) unto the sons of Adam" (Ps. 1 15:16). . . .

. . . through the indulgence of God to our first parents after the Fall, the outward estate of all and every of their children remains the same as to one another; so that, originally and naturally, there is no such thing as slavery. Joseph was rightfully no more a slave to his brethren than they were to him; and they had no more authority to sell him than they had to slay him. And if they had nothing to do to sell him, the Ishmaelites bargaining with them and paying down twenty pieces of silver, could not make a title. Neither could Potiphar have any better interest in him than the Ishmaelites had (Gen. 37:20, 27, 28); for he that shall in this case plead alteration of property seems to have forfeited a great part of his own claim to humanity. There is no proportion between twenty pieces of silver and liberty. . . .

Massachusetts judge Samuel Sewall, The Selling of Joseph, *1700, in Adler, ed.,* Negro, *vol. 3, pp. 438–39.*

It is . . . ordered that the Constables shall take their turns on the Sabbath day to prevent drawing of strong drink in tippling houses, and breaking the Sabbath day, and whosoever shall be found drawing of any strong liquor in said houses to any person, shall forfeit the sum of twenty shillings for each offence. . . .

May 16, 1700—Whereas Peter Jedon and John Pettitt and family, both French, from Sopus, appear desiring liberty to pass to Canada, and that a man or two may be allowed to carry them thither, which is permitted, and thought convenient that the Persons that carry them thither shall enter into bonds that they shall transport no horses or mares to Canada as the late proclamation requires. . . .

[Sept 3—] The Churchwardens of Schenectady do make application to the Mayor, Recorder, Aldermen and Common Council, desiring two persons to be allowed and appointed to go Round by the Inhabitants of the City, to see if they can obtain any Contribution to make up the salary due to there Minister. . . .

It is concluded that a warrant be issued to the fire masters to visit the Chimneys and fire places within this City every three weeks, beginning the 2d of December next and so continuing during the time of three months. . . .

City council meeting, Albany, New York May 1700, in Hart, ed., American History, *vol. 2, pp. 208–11.*

. . . Two Thousand Pounds were raised to equip his Honour [*Governor Moore of South Carolina*] and his Comrades out for their beloved Exercise of Plundering, and Slave-catching. This they performed well enough, but carrying on the Pretence too far, and coming to sit down before the strong Castle of St. Augustin, while they were sending their Plunder to Jamaica by their trusty Officers, under Colour of seeking Supplies, sending for Bombs and Mortars, in the midst of all their Riot and Misrule, they were alarm'd by the coming of Four Vessels into the Harbour, in which were (they say) 200 Enemies. At first, being encouraged by Wine up to a Height above performing any Thing, the General Moore resolves bravely to put on Board his Eight Vessels then riding in the Harbour, all their Goods and Plunder, and with his few Men about 500, Fight thro' the Enemy, and so come Home. But the Pillow which often lets out Heat to make way for Caution, changed this his Resolution; So the next Day, having destroyed as many of his own Ships, and as much of his War Stores and Provisions as the haste they were in would allow, he retreats with such Caution and Dispatch, that he lost not one Man by the Enemy.

John Ash, 1702, The Present State of Affairs in Carolina, in Salley, ed., Narratives, pp. 272–73.

That notwithstanding your Lordships repeated Commands to your Deputies, to procure a good regulation of the Indian Trade, on which our friendly Correspondence with all our neighbouring Indians, and the Peace and Safety of this Colony chiefly depends, yet the said late Governor Moore has been by his Artifices, the Chief (if not the Only) Occasion of obstructing the same, designing nothing less than ingrossing the same for himself and Accomplices; having already almost utterly ruin'd the Trade for Skins and Furs (whereby we held our chief Correspondence with England) and turn'd it into a Trade of Indian or Slave-making, whereby the Indians to the South and West of us are already involv'd in Blood and Confusion, a Trade so odious and abominable, that every other Colony in America (altho' they have equal temptation) abhor to follow.

South Carolinians to the proprietors, 1703, in Salley, ed., Narratives, p. 240.

For as much as great inconveniences may arise, by the liberty of printing in our said province, you are to provide by all necessary orders, that no person keep any press for printing, nor that any book, pamphlet or other matters whatsoever be printed without your especial leave and license first obtained.

Queen Anne to New Jersey governor Lord Cornbury, 1703, quoted in Cunningham, New Jersey, p. 88.

They give the title of merchant to every trader; who Rate their Goods according to the time and specie they pay in: viz. Pay, money, Pay as money, and trusting. *Pay* is Grain, Pork, Beef, &c. at the prices set by the General Court that Year; *money* is pieces of Eight, Reals, or Boston or Bay shillings (as they call them,) or Good hard money, as sometimes silver coin is termed by them; also Wampum, viz. Indian beads which serves for change. *Pay as money* is provisions, as aforesaid, one Third cheaper then as the Assembly or General Court sets it; and *Trust* as they and the merchant agree for time.

Now, when the buyer comes to ask for a commodity, sometimes before the merchant answers that he has it, he says, *is Your pay ready?* Perhaps the Chap Replies Yes: what do You pay in? says the merchant. The buyer having answered, then the price is set; as suppose he wants a sixpenny knife, in *pay* it is 12d—in *pay as money* eight pence, and hard money its own price, viz. 6d. It seems a very Intricate way of trade. . . .

Journal of Sarah Kemble Knight's journey to Connecticut, 1704, in Hart, ed., American History, vol. 2, pp. 228–29.

Cambridge, October 29. About 11 of the Clock in the morning, there happened a Fire in Harvard Collage occasioned by a foul chimney. . . . 2 of the Students putting their backs to the Scuttle, forced it open, and threw water briskly, so that they quickly extinguished the Fire, which otherwise had been of very ill consequence. . . .

Piscataqua, November 2. On Monday the 30th last about break of say, the House of the Rev. Mr. Nathaniel Rogers, minister of Portsmouth, was burnt to the Ground in a few minutes, his youngest Child, and a Negro Woman of Mrs. Elatson's his Mother-in-law, consumed in the flames. . . . Mrs. Elatson saved the eldest Child by throwing him out of a Chamber Window into his Father's Arms. . . . None can tell how this Fire came, most probably it began in their Kitchen. . . .

Philadelphia, October 27. On the 22nd arrived here a Sloop from Carolina, Robert Wright Master, says, That a Flag of Truce was returned from St. Augustine. . . .

An Act is past in Maryland for prohibiting the Importation of Bread, Beer, Flour, Malt, Wheat or other English or Indian Grains or Meal, Horses, Mares, Colts, or Fillies, or Tobacco from Pennsylvania. . . .

Advertisement. A Negro Woman Slave about 22 years of Age, to be Sold by Mr. Nicholas Boone Bookseller, and to be seen at the London Coffee House, next door to the Post-Office, in Boston.

Boston News-Letter, November 6, 1704, in Weeks and Bacon, eds., Historical Digest, pp. 140–41.

. . . popish recusants, convict, negroes, mulattoes and Indian servants, and others, not being christians, shall be deemed and taken to be persons incapable in law, to be witnesses in any cases whatsoever.

. . . . .

And for a further christian care and usage of all christian servants . . . if any negro, mulatto, or Indian, Jew, Moor, Mahometan, or other infidel . . . shall, notwithstanding, purchase any christian white servant, the said servant shall, ipso facto, become free and acquit from any service then due. . . .

Virginia Assembly, 1705, in Hening, Statutes, *vol. 3, pp. 298, 458.*

New-York, May 20. This day arrived a Sloop from St. Thomas in 20 days, who brings News that the French gave out there, that they designed . . . for New-York, which has caused us to make all possible provision to give them a warm reception; All persons having provided themselves with and Ammunition, and all hands are employed upon Fortifying this City, which in a short time will be put in a good posture of defense; Our inhabitants having voluntarily advanced large Sums of Money for the procuring of Materials, until such time our Assembly Sits, which will be on the 24th Instant. A great many new carriages are already made for the Mounting of our Cannon, and a great number of Stockadoes and Plank brought to Town, for the making of Platforms, breast-works, etc. . . .

Hartford, May 20. This day a Woman was Condemned to Die for Murdering her Husband, which as done by throwing a pair of Tailor's Shears at him, which hitting him on the head, in a few days it prov'd fatal to him.

Boston News-Letter, May 27, 1706, in Weeks and Bacon, eds., Historical Digest, *pp. 327–28.*

New-port, Rhode Island, June 7 . . . there came to our Governour one John Walker (Master of a Sloop bound to Boston from Connecticut, loaden with 78 barrels of Pork, 7 of Beef, 700 Bushels of Wheat and Indian Corn) who gave his Honour this Account, That on Saturday last in the afternoon he had been Chased in the Sound by a French Privateer Sloop, and to avoid being taken, he and his men got into their small boat, and left their sloop to the mercy of the Privateer who took her, and they getting on shore at Watch-Hill, Alarmed the people all along the Narragensett shore and Stonington, where it was Lined with near 1000 men in Arms. . . . Our Governour immediately issued forth a Proclamation for Volunteers, and in less than 2 hours time, we had 2 Sloops fitted out with 100 and odd men well armed, under Command of Major William Wanton and Capt. Thomas Payne, who Sailed from hence about 10 a Clock in the morning, and about 2 a Clock in the afternoon made themselves Masters of the Privateer and her Prize about 3 leagues

to the Southward of Block-Island. . . . She was bound for Port-Royal, in order to Cruise this Summer on the New-England Coast.

Advertisements. Ran-away at Boston on the 26th of December last, Samuel Downs, a Man-Servant, aged about 25 years, a spare man, middle Stature, light brown Hair, speaketh broad English; he was in May last at work in Sea-brook in Connecticut Colony. . . . Whoever will take up and secure the said Run-away, so that he may be delivered unto Mr. John Colman Merchant in Boston, shall be immediately paid Five Pounds, and Charges.

Boston News-Letter, June 10, 1706, in Weeks and Bacon, eds., Historical Digest, *pp. 338–41, 347.*

Jan ye 16, 1707. My company killed a yearling whale made 27 barrels. Feb ye 4, Indian Harry with his boat struck a whale and called for my boat to help him. I had but a third which was 4 barrels. Feb 22, my two boats and my sons and Floyds boats killed a yearling whale of which I had half—made 36 barrels, my share 18 barrels. Feb 24 my company killed a school whale which made 35 barrels. March 13, my company killed a small yearling made 30 barrels. March 17, my company killed two yearlings in one day; one made 27, the other 14 barrels.

Journal of whaling captain Mrs. Martha Smith, 1707, quoted in Earle, Colonial Dames, *pp. 74–75.*

This government has consisted of two parts; the Province of Pennsylvania, and the Three Lower Counties of Delaware. To the first the proprietor [*William Penn*] has a most clear and undoubted right, both for soil and government, by the King's letters patent or royal charter; for the latter he has much less to show. . . . After his first arrival, however, in these parts, he prevailed with the people both of the province and those counties to join in one government under him . . . and so they continued, not without many fractions, till after the time of his last departure, when some disaffected persons took advantage of a clause, which he had unhappily inserted in a charter he gave the people, and broke off entirely from those lower counties; since which time we have had two assemblies. . . . Last fall the assembly of those counties [*Delaware*] took occasion to inquire into their own powers, upon a design to set new measures on foot, and have sent home an address by one of their members . . . who is to negotiate the matter with the Lords of Trade and the ministry, to obtain powers to some person or other, who the Queen may think fit . . . to discharge all the necessary duties of government over them. . . .

Pennsylvanian James Logan to an English Quaker, 1709, in Hart, ed., American History, *vol. 2, pp. 72–73.*

[*June*] 9 . . . I ate mutton and sallet for dinner. My Eugene ran away for no reason but because he had not done anything yesterday. I sent my people after him but in vain. The sloop came from Falling Creek with copper, timber, and planks. In the evening Captain Keeling came to see us to account with me for the quitrents of New Kent. . . .

10 . . . George B-th brought home my boy Eugene. . . . The Captain and I had some discourse about the philosopher's stone which he is following with great diligence. . . . Eugene was whipped for running away and had the bit put on him. . . .

[*August*] 13 . . . Twelve Pamunkey Indians came over. We gave them some victuals and some rum and put them over the river. I danced my dance. I removed more books into the library. I read some geometry and walked to see the people at work. I ate fish for dinner. . . . In the evening John Blackman came from the Falls and brought me word some of my people were sick and that my coaler was sick at the coal mine. I scolded with him about the little work he had done this summer.

[*September*] 2 . . . Notwithstanding the rain Mrs. Ware came to desire me to take tobacco for her debt to me but I refused because tobacco was good for nothing. . . .

15 . . . I wrote a letter to England to make interest for the government of Maryland; God send good success. Jenny was whipped for abundance of faults. I ate fresh beef for dinner.

William Byrd, excerpt from his secret diary, 1709, Great American, *pp. 26, 34, 39.*

Philadelphia . . . is a noble, large, and populous City. . . . It is built square in Form of a Chess-Board, which each Front facing one of the Rivers. . . . There are several Coves and Docks where large Ships are built; and by a moderate Computation, there has been launch'd from the Stocks of this City in forty Year, near 300 Sail of Ships, besides Small-Craft, which may in some sort give us an Idea of the Opulency of the Place. Many of their Merchants keep their Coaches, and the Tradesmens Shops and Streets are well frequented. All Religions are tolerated here, which is one Means to increase the Riches of the Place. . . . Mr. Badcock's Brewhouse is a noble, large Building, and has in it one single Vessel that will hold eight Ton of Liquor. . . . There are three Fairs in the Year, and every Week two Markets. In time of the Fairs the City is so throng'd, as well as the adjacent Plantations, that it is hard to find a Lodging. . . .

There is a Post-Office lately erected, which goes to Boston in New-England, Charles-town in Carolina, and the other neighbouring Places. The uncultivated Ground, which is not grubb'd, sells for ten times the Value it did at first; though there is none of that sort within ten Miles round the City: And that within the Neighbourhood that was sold for ten Pound at first will fetch above three hundred now.

"Richard Castleman, Gent.," 1710, in Hart, ed., American History, *vol. 2, pp. 74–76.*

The jurors are not here [*in South Carolina*] returned by the Sheriffs, but the Names of all the best qualified Persons in the Country are agreed upon and settled by Act of Assembly, and put together into a Ballot-Box. At the End of every Court this is set upon the Table, before the judge and Bench, and after it is shaken, a little Child draws Out 48 Names, which are read, and a List of them taken by the Sheriff, that he may know whom to summons. These 48 are put in the second Division of the Ballot-Box, out of which, at the opening of the next Court, another Child draws 12, who are to serve as jurors; and if any just Exception be made, he draws others, until the jury be full. . . .

The Ballot-Box hath three Locks and Keys, kept by three several Persons appointed by the General Assembly, whereof the judge of the Court is one; neither can the Box be opened without the Presence of those three.

The Reason of all this Precaution in returning jurors is, for the better and more effectual Preservation of the Lives and Estates of the Inhabitants. For the Sheriffs, Marshals, and all other such Officers, being appointed by the Governor, and keeping their Places only during his Pleasure, if the returning of Juries lay in their Power, 'tis more than probable, they might at some time or other, pack such Instruments as would be ready to gratify him, to the Ruin of any Person against whom he had conceiv'd Malice or Displeasure.

"A Swiss Gentleman," 1710, in Hart, ed., American History, *vol. 2, pp. 188–89.*

You, S: do now, in the Presence of God, and these Witnesses, take R: to be your *Wife,* Promising that so far as shall be consistent with the relation which you now sustain, as a Servant, you will Perform the part of a *Husband* towards her; And in particular you Promise that you will *Love* her; and that, as you shall have the Opportunity and Ability, you will take a proper *Care* of her in Sickness and Health, in Prosperity and Adversity: And that you will be True and *Faithful* to her, and will Cleave to her *only, so long* as God, in his Providence, shall continue your and her abode in Such Place (or Places) as that you can conveniently come together. . . .

I then agreeable to your Request, and with the Consent of your Masters and Mistresses, do Declare, that you have License given you to be conversant and familiar together, as *Husband and Wife,* so long as God shall continue your Places of abode as aforesaid; and so long as you shall behave yourselves as it becometh Servants to do: For you must both of you bear in mind that you Remain Still as really and truly as ever, your Master's Property, and therefore it will be justly expected, both by God and Man, that you behave and conduct yourselves, as Obedient and faithful Servants towards your respective Masters and Mistresses for the Time being.

> *Marriage ceremony for slaves, Massachusetts, ca. 1710, quoted in Howard,* History, *pp. 225–26.*

The Case of the Palatines, and others Germans, in the Province of New York. . . .

That, in the year 1709, The Palatines and other Germans, being invited to come into England about Four Thousand of them were sent into New York in America, of which about 1700 Died on Board. . . .

That on their landing they were quartered in Tents, and divided into six companies, having each a Captain of their own. . . .

That afterwards, they were removed on Lands belonging to Mr. Livingstone, where they erected small Houses for shelter during the winter season.

That in the Spring following they were ordered into the woods, to make Pitch and Tar, where they lived about two years; But the country not being fit to raise any considerable quality of Naval Stores, They were commanded to Build, to clear, and improve the ground, belonging to a private person.

That the Indians have yielded to Her late Majesty of pious memory a small Tract of Land called Schorie for the use of the Palatines, they in fifteen days cleared a way of fifteen miles through the woods and settled fifty Families therein.

That in the following Spring the remainder of the said Palatines joined the said fifty families so settled therein. . . . But that country being too small for their increasing families, they were constrained to purchase some Neighboring land of the Indians. . . .

And after having built small Houses, and Huts, there about one year after the said purchase some gentlemen of Albany, declared to the Palatines, that themselves having purchased the said country of Schorie of the Governor of New York they would not permit them to live there, unless an agreement were also made with those of Albany; But that the Palatines having refused to enter into such an agreement, a Sheriff and some officers were sent. . . .

> *Conrad Weiser, describing the events of 1709–10, in Hart, ed.,* American History, *vol. 2, pp. 77–79.*

And if any come [*to Long Island*] from *New York* [*city*] with Vessels and Goods, and the People would deal with them, the Trader would set the Price on his Goods, and also on what the People had of the Growth of the Countrey . . . so that they were Compelled to take what they were proffered or keep their Goods by them. *Southold* people being much Oppressed, as they informed me: Wheat then selling at *Boston Five Shillings and Six-pence* per bushel, and at *New York but Three Shillings and Four-pence;* they had not liberty to carry or

Hendrick de Bries House, East Greenbush, New York, built 1723; a rural Dutch colonial farmhouse *(Historic American Building Survey)*

send it to *Boston:* Nor any Vessel suffer'd to come at them from thence; and not coming to them from New York, their Wheat and Grain lay by them, until the Vermin Eat and Spoil'd it; and they were much Impoverished thereby.

Samuel Mulford to the New York Assembly, 1714, quoted in Kammen, Colonial New York, p. 164.

The Women are the most industrious Sex in that Place, and by their good Housewifery, make a great deal of Cloath of their own Cotton, Wool, and Flax; Some of them keeping their Families, (though large) very decently appareled, both the Linnens and Woollens, so that they have no occasion to run into the Merchants Debt, or lay their money out on Stores for Cloathing. ... They marry very young, some at Thirteen or Fourteen; and She that stays till Twenty is reckoned a stale Maid, which is a very indifferent Character in that warm country. The Women are very fruitful, most Houses being full of Little Ones. ... Many of the women are very handy in Canoes and will manage them with great Dexterity and Skill, which they become accustomed to in this watery Country. They are ready to help their Husbands in any servile Work, as Planting, when the Season or the Weather requires Expedition; Pride seldom banishing good Housewifery. The girls are not bred up to the Wheel and Sewing only, but the Dairy, and affairs of the House they are very well acquainted withal; so that you shall see them whilst very young, manage their Business with a great deal of Conduct and Alacrity.

John Lawson, History of North Carolina, 1714, pp. 85–86.

I was informed that the English Inhabitants of Groton had lately divided among themselves a neck of Land lying by the Sea side a neck of Land lying by the Sea side, which the Indians claim as belonging of Right unto them; and that the Indians having pulled up and removed some fence that the English had made there, were sued for it, and damages and charges recovered of them to the value of seven or eight pounds; that for this, execution had been lately brought upon the Estate of the two Sachems, and that one of the Sachems being something of a Dealer in Smithery had by the officers, his Anvil and some of his tools taken from him....

Journal of the Reverend Experience Mayhew, October 1714, in Company for Propagation, Some Correspondence, pp. 113–14.

Whereas we the Sagamores of Penacook, Pentucket, Squamsquot, and Nuchawanick, are Inclined to have the English inhabit amongst us, as they are amongst our countrymen in the Massachusetts bay, by such means we hope in time to be strengthened against our enemies, the Tarratens, who yearly doth us damage, likewise being persuaded that it will be for the good of us and our posterity. ... Know all men by these presents that we ... for a competent valuation in goods already received in coats, shirts, and victuals and also for the considerations aforesaid do ... give, grant, bargain, sell, Release, Ratify, and Confirm unto John Wheelwright of the Massachusetts bay Late of England ... Augustin Story, Thomas Wite., William Wentworth, and Thomas Levitt ... all that part of the mainland bounded by the River of Piscataqua and the River of Merrimack.... In witness whereof, we have hereunto set our hands and seals the Seventeenth Day of May, 1629.

Entered and recorded According to the original, the 20th May, 1714.

The Wheelwright Patent, May 20, 1714 (a forgery dated 1629), in New Hampshire, Provincial Papers, vol. 1, pp. 56–60.

Aug 5th. [*1714*] Fast for Rain at the Lecture.... Note. about 2. p. m. Hannah was coming hastily down the new Stairs, fell, and broke the Pan of her Right Knee in two; one part went upward, the other downward. I got her down and set her in my chair, sent for Dr. Cutler: who told us how it was; we led her up into her Chamber: Neighbour Hamilton and others came in and got her to bed, then Dr. Cutler bathed it, with spirits of Wine, put on a large Plaister, then with bolsters and large Swathing bound it up tite to bring the broken pieces together, and Unite them. Madam Davenport sent for him before he had done....

Lord's-day, Aug. 29. Beard arrives, who brings the Act of Parliament against Dissenters keeping School; which ordains that no Catechism shall be taught in Schools, but that in the Common prayer Book [*i.e., Anglican*]....

[*October*] 11th [*1715*] ... At Natick the Indians of the Committee executed the Parchment Dead for the Land at Magunkaquog: and paid the Proprietors Three pounds apiece.

[*October*] 12. Solomon Thomas acquaints me that Isaac Nehemiah [a Natick Indian], one of the Committee, had hang'd himself.

Lord's Day, January 15 [*1716*]. An Extraordinary Cold Storm of Wind and Snow. . . . Bread was frozen at the Lord's Table: Mr. Pemberton administered. . . . Though was so Cold, yet John Tuckerman was baptised. At six a-clock my ink freezes so that I can hardly write by a good fire in my Wive's Chamber. . . .

Samuel Sewall, 1714–16, Diary,
pp. 142, 148–50.

We walked about the town [*Germanna, Virginia*] which is palisaded with stakes stuck in the ground, and laid close the one to the other, and of substance to bear out a musket-shot. There are but nine families, and they have nine houses, built all in a line; and before every house, about twenty feet distant from it, they have small sheds built for their hogs and hens, so that the hog-sties and houses make a street. The place that is paled in is a pentagon, very regularly laid out; and in the very centre there is a blockhouse, made with five sides, which answer to the five sides of the great inclosure; there are loop-holes through it, from which you may see all the inside of the inclosure. This was intended for a retreat for the people, in case they were not able to defend the palisadoes, if attacked by the Indians.

They made use of this block-house for divine service. They go to prayers constantly once a day, and have two sermons on Sunday . . . in their own language. . . .

John Fontaine, 1715, quoted in Robinson,
Southern, pp. 128–29.

. . . many months before I mett with any Intimations of treating ye Small-Pox with ye Methods of Inoculation, any where in *Europe,* I had from a Servant of my own, an Account of its being practiced in *Africa.* Enquiring of my Negro-Man *Onesimus,* who is a pretty Intelligent Fellow, Whether he ever had ye Small-Pox, he answered *Yes, and No;* and then told me that he had undergone an Operation, which had given him something of ye Small-Pox, and would forever preserve him from it, adding, That it was often used among ye *Guaramantese* [Coromantees], and whoever had ye Courage to use it, was forever free from ye Fear of the Contagion. He described ye Operation to me, and showed me in his Arm ye Scar.

Cotton Mather to the English Royal Society, 1716,
quoted in Wood, "Impact of
Smallpox," p. 24.

By . . . the forts they [*the French*] have already built, the British Plantations are in a manner Surrounded by their [*the French's*] Commerce with the numerous Nations of Indians seated on both sides of the Lakes; they may not only Engross the whole Skin Trade, but may, when they please, Send out such Bodies of Indians on the back of these Plantations as may greatly distress his Majesty's's Subjects here, And should they multiply their Settlements along these Lakes, so as to join their Dominions of Canada to their new Colony of Louisiana, they might even possess themselves of any of these Plantations they pleased. Nature, 'tis true, has formed a Barrier for us by that long Chain of Mountains which run from the back of South Carolina as far as New York, and which are only passable in some few places, but even that Natural Defense may prove rather destructive to us, if they are not possessed by us before they are known to them. To prevent the dangers which Threaten his Majesty's Dominions here from the growing power of these Neighbors, nothing seems to me of more consequence than that now while the Nations are at peace, and while the French are yet incapable of possessing all that vast Tract which lies on the back of these Plantations, we should attempt to make some Settlements on the Lakes, and at the same time possess our selves of those passes of the great Mountains, which are necessary to preserve a Communication with such Settlements.

Governor Alexander Spotswood, 1718, in Hart, ed.,
American History, vol. 2, pp. 317–18.

Be it enacted That where any mariners or others are gone, or hereafter shall go to sea, leaving their wives at shopkeeping, or to work for their livelihood at any other trade in this province, all such wives shall be deemed, adjudged and taken, and are hereby declared to be, as feme sole traders, and shall have ability and are by this act enabled, to sue and be sued, plead and be impleaded at law, in any court or court in this province, during their husbands' natural lives, without naming their husbands in such suits, plea or actions. . . .

II. And be it further enacted, That if any of the said absent husbands being owners of lands, tenements, or other estate . . . shall hereafter give, grant mortgage or alienate, from his wife and children, any of his said lands, tenements or estate, without making an equivalent provision for their maintenance in lieu thereof, every such gift, grant, mortgage or alienation shall be de adjudged and taken to be null and void.

IV. But if such absent husband, having his health and liberty, stays away so long from his wife and children, without making such provision for their maintenance before or after his going away, till they are like to become chargeable to the town or place where they inhabit [*i.e., need charitable assistance*]; or in case such husband doth live or shall live in adultery, or cohabit unlawfully with another woman . . . the lands tenements and estate belonging to such husbands, shall be and are hereby made liable and subject to be seized and taken in execution, to satisfy any sums or sums of money which the wives of such husbands, or guardians of their children, shall necessarily expend or lay out for their support or maintenance. . . .

Pennsylvania feme sole trader act, 1718, Laws of the Commonwealth, *vol. 1, pp. 100–01.*

. . . I was generally a leader among the boys, and sometimes led them into scrapes, of which I will mention one instance, as it shows an early projecting public spirit, though not then justly conducted.

There was a salt marsh that bounded part of the mill pond, on the edge of which at high water, we used to stand to fish for minnows. By much trampling, we had made it a mere quagmire. My proposal was to build a wharf there fit for us to stand upon, and I showed my comrades a large heap of stones which were intended for a new house near the marsh, and which would very well suit our purpose. Accordingly in the evening when the workmen were gone, I assembled a number of my playfellows, and working with them diligently like so many emmets [*ants*], sometimes two or three to a stone, we brought them all away and built our little wharf. The next morning the workmen were surprised at missing the stones; which were found in our wharf. Inquiry was made after the removers; we were discovered and complained of; several of us were corrected by our fathers; and though I pleaded the usefulness of the work, mine convinced me that nothing was useful which was not honest.

Benjamin Franklin, ca. 1718, Autobiography, *pp. 11–12.*

There is one Thing more I have heard often urg'd against the Charter Colonies, and . . . I can see neither Reason nor Colour for it. 'Tis said, that their increasing Numbers and Wealth join'd to their great Distance from Britain will give them an Opportunity in the Course of some Years to throw off their Dependance on the Nation, and declare themselves a free State, if not curbed in Time by being made entirely subject to the Crown. Whereas in Truth there's no Body tho' but little acquainted with these or any of the Northern Plantations, who does not know and confess, that their Poverty and the declining State of their Trade is so great at present, that there's far more Danger of their sinking, without some extraordinary Support from the Crown, than of their ever revolting from it. So that I may say without being ludicrous, that it would not be more absurd to place two of His Majesty's Beef-Eaters to watch an Infant in the Cradle that it don't rise and cut its Father's Throat, than to guard these weak Infant Colonies to prevent their shaking off the British Yoke. Besides, they are so distinct from one another in their Forms of Government, in their Religious Rites, in their Emulation of Trade, and consequently in their Affections, that they can never be suppos'd to unite in so dangerous an Enterprise.

Jeremiah Dummer, Massachusetts agent, 1721, in Hart, American History, *vol. 2, p. 134.*

It is voted and ordered that from and after the first day of April next No Geese shall be Let go upon the Common or in the highways nor in the water with in this Township of Providence or with in the jurisdiction there of nor upon any other persons Land . . . on the penalty of the forfeiture of all such Geese that are so found.

It is voted and ordered that Hemdens Lane and the highway that Leads from thence to Pautuckett may be fenced for the space of five years . . . provided there be sufficient Gates set up and maintained in said Lane and highway that may be Convenient for both horse men and Carts to pass through. . . .

It is also voted and ordered that Each free holder with in this Township of Providence shall from and after this day have two pence per head for every head of a Gray Squirrel that shall be by them brought before the Town's Treasurer. . . . And the said Treasurer shall be Careful to accept of no squirrels heads but such as are killed within this Township. . . .

For as much as Mr. James Browne hath Positively Refused to serve in the place of a Town Council man: where upon Cap. James Olney is Chosen in his Room and also Mr. Edward Smith hath positively Refused to serve in the place and office of a Town Councilman where upon Mr Phillip Tillinghast is Chosen in his Room.

Town meeting, Providence, January 1721, in Hart, ed., American History, *vol. 2, pp, 214–15.*

It is to be noted, as I am well informed, that just before the meeting of that Assembly [*1723*], there had been a conspiracy discovered amongst the negroes to cutt off the English, wherein the free negroes and mulattos were much suspected to have been concerned (which will forever be the case) and tho' there could be no legal proof, so as to convict them, yet such was the insolence of the free negroes at that time, that the next Assembly thought it necessary, not only to make the meeting of slaves very penal, but to fix a perpetual brand upon free negroes and mulattos by excluding them from that great priviledge of a Freeman [*the fran-chise*], well knowing they always did, and ever will adhere to and favor the slaves . . . and to preserve a decent distinction between them and their betters. . . .

Virginia governor William Gooch to the Board of Trade,
1723, quoted in Aptheker, American, *p. 178.*

Publick Notice is hereby given That there is arrived in this city one Mrs. Rodes who will teach any young ladies or Gentlewomen to read and speak French to perfection. She will give constant Attendance at her Dwelling-House in the Second Street in the Alley next door to Dr. Owens. She likewise teaches to flourish on Muslin after the most expeditious way, and at very reasonable Prices. She likewise draws all Manner of Patterns for Flourishing on Muslin, and those in Fashion of Lace, which is very pretty and quickly learned. She likewise draws Patterns for Embroidering and Petticoats, etc. And those who have a Mind to learn, she will teach very reasonable. She hath very good Orange-Oyl to dispose of by the Quarter of a Pound or Ounce; the said Oyl being very good for the Wind-Cholick and Stomach, and fit for many other Things. And likewise Sweet-Meats, as Lemon and Orange-Peel, very made; it will be disposed by the Pound, Half-pound, or Quarter, very cheap.

N.B. She gives attendance from Nine in the Morning till Twelve, and in the Afternoon, if any Gentlewomen require it, at their Houses. As she is but a New-Comer to this Place, all persons, who have a mind to know more, may inquire at Mrs. Rachel Renier in Chestnut-street, and she will inform them.

American Mercury, *Philadelphia, May 1723, quoted in*
Dexter, *Colonial Women, pp. 88–89.*

. . . two of these barbarous savages came in upon us, next eleven more . . . and killed one child immediately as soon as they had entered the door, thinking thereby to strike in us the greater terror. . . . They next go rifling through the house in a great hurry . . . and packed up some linen, woolen, and what other things pleased them best. And when they had done what they would, they turned out of the house immediately and being at the door, two of my younger children, one six and other four years old, came in sight, and being under a great surprise, cried aloud, upon which one of the Indians, running to them, takes one under each arm and brings them to us. My maid prevailed with the biggest to be quiet and still but the other could by no means be prevailed with but continued screeching and crying very much in the fright, and the Indians, to ease themselves of the noise and to prevent danger of a discovery that might arise from it, immediate before my face knocked its brains out. I bore this as well as I could, not daring to appear disturbed. . . .

Now having killed two of my children, they scalped them . . . and then put forward to leave the house in great haste . . . taking what they had packed together with myself and the little babe fourteen days old, the boy six, and two daughters, the one about fourteen and the other about sixteen years [and] my servant girl. . . .

Captivity narrative of Elizabeth Hanson, 1724, in
Vaughan and Clark, eds., Puritans, *pp. 231–32.*

And now, my kinsman, I will give you an account of the life and fortunes of my dear father, from the time he left Wales to the day of his death. . . . Three weeks to the time when he first heard tell of Pennsylvania . . . he took leave of his neighbors and relatives. . . . During this long voyage he learned to speak and read English tolerably well. . . . They now came . . . to the place where Philadelphia is at present situated. At the time there was, as the Welsh say, *na thy nac ymogor,* (neither house nor shelter), but the wild woods. . . . He longed very much at this time for milk. During his wanderings he met with a drunken old man, who understood neither Welsh nor English, and who, noticing the stranger, invited him to his dwelling. . . . They were Swedes. Here he made his home, till he had a habitation of his own. . . .

In the autumn of this year [*1682*] several from Wales arrived here [*Pennsylvania*]: Edward ab Rhys, Edward Jones of Bala, William ab Edward, and many others. By this time there was a kind of neighborhood here, although as neighbors they could little benefit each other. They were sometimes employed in making huts beneath some cliff, or under the hollow banks of rivulets, thus sheltering themselves where their fancy dictated. There were neither cows nor horses to be had at any price. . . .

At this time my father, Thomas Sion Evan, was living with the Swedes . . . and intending daily to return to Wales; but as time advanced, the country improved. In the course of three years several were beginning to obtain a pretty good livelihood, and my father determined to remain with them. . . . Everything was agreeable to these innocent people; although in want of some present necessaries, yet they were peaceable and friendly to each other. In process of time, however, the little which he had prospered, so that he became possessed of horses, cows, and everything else that was necessary for him or even that he wished; indeed he never coveted much. During the latter years of his life, he kept twelve milk cows. About the end of July [1707] . . . he departed this life, leaving a small farm each for my brother and myself, a corresponding portion for my sister, and a fair dower for my mother.

John Jones to a relative in Wales, 1725, in Myers, ed.,
Narratives, *pp. 455–58.*

[*August 12, 1725*] Some time before my departure from Terriquo Arrived there three Chickasaws from their own Nation with a Message. . . .

That they were Sent to the Cherokees by their head men to give them an Account that they heard by way of the Toomes (a settlement of the French Indians) that the Creeks had Concluded on a talk to cut off Terriquo Town last Year.

That the Chicasaws have made a peace with the Choctaws but for no Longer time than they can have an Opportunity of Cutting a Number of The Choctaws off as they Served the Chickasaws some time ago. . . . They also give an Account that the Broad river is full of Canoes with French Indians in them and that they are all about in these parts. . . .
[*August 26 1725*] Arrived here two Chickasaws from the Savannah Town who came with a Message to the Cherokees to give them an Account that the Cowetas were gone in a body against the Yamassees and that the Upper Creeks designed to come up against the Upper Settlements of this Nation. . . .

Journal of Colonel Richard Chicken, South Carolina, in
Mereness, ed., Travels, *pp. 121–22, 133.*

A weighty Concern coming upon many ffaithful ffriends [*Quakers*] at this Meeting in Relation to divers undue Liberties that are too frequently taken by some . . . Tenderly to Caution and Advise ffriends against those things which we think Inconsistent with our Ancient Christian Testimony of Plainness. . . .

As first, That Immodest ffashion of hooped Petty-coats. . . .

And also That None of S[ai]d ffriends Accustom themselves to wear their Gowns with Superfluous ffolds behind, but plain and Decent. Nor to go without Aprons. . . .

And that ffriends are careful to avoid Wearing of Stript Shoos, or Red or White heel'd Shoos. . . .

Also that ffriends Avoid ye Unnecessary use of ffans in Meetings. . . .

And also That ffriends do not Accustom themselves to go in bare Breasts or bare Necks.

There is Likewise a Tender Concern upon our minds to recommend unto all ffriends, the Constant use of ye plain Language. . . .

Dear Sisters, These Things we Solidly recommend. . . . That we might be unto ye Lord, a Chosen Generation, A Royal Priesthood, An Holy Nation, a Peculiar People. . . .

Signed on behalf & by ord[er] of ye s[ai]d meeting By Hannah Hill.

Yearly Meeting of Women Quakers, Burlington,
New Jersey, September 1726, in Berkin and Norton, eds.,
Women of America, *pp. 134–36.*

There are three things which the founders of this college proposed to themselves, to which all its statutes should be directed. The first is that the youth of Virginia should be well educated to learning and good morals. The second is, that the churches of America, especially Virginia, should be supplied with good ministers after the doctrine and government of the Church of England; and that the college should be a constant seminary for this purpose. The third is, that the Indians of America should be instructed in the Christian religion, and that some of the Indian youth that are well-behaved and well-inclined, being first well prepared in the divinity school, may be sent out to preach the gospel to their countrymen in their own tongue, after they have duly been put in orders of deacons and priests. . . .

There are two sorts of scholars; one of them who are maintained at their own charge, and pay school wages in the schools where the masters are allowed to take wages as above; the other sort is of those who are maintained at the college's charge.

Statutes of William and Mary, 1727, in Knight, ed.,
Documentary History, *vol. 1, pp. 509, 521.*

[*March 6, 1728*] . . . we were told that on the South Shore, not far from the Inlet, dwelt a Marooner, that Modestly called himself a Hermit, tho' he forfeited that Name by Suffering a wanton Female to cohabit with Him.

His Habitation was a Bower, covered with Bark after the Indian Fashion, which in that mild Situation protected him pretty well from the Weather. Like the Ravens, he neither plow'd nor sow'd, but insisted chiefly upon Oysters, which his Hand-maid made a Shift to gather from the Adjacent Rocks. Sometimes, too, for Change of Diet, he sent her to drive up the Neighbour's Cows, to Moisten their Mouths with a little Milk. But as for raiment, he depended mostly upon his Length of Beard, and She upon her Length of Hair, part which she brought decently forward, and the rest dangled behind quite down to her Rump, like one Of Herodotus's East Indian Pygmies.

Thus did these Wretches live in a dirty State of Nature, and were mere Adamites, Innocence only excepted.

7. This morning the Surveyors began to run the Diving line from Cedar Post we had driven into the Sand. . . .

William Byrd, 1728, "History of the Dividing Line,"
in Writings, *pp. 36–37.*

[*March 11, 1728*] We had encamped so early, that we found time in the Evening to walk near half a Mile into the Woods. There we came Upon a Family of Mulattoes that call'd themselves free, tho' by the Shy-

Brafferton Hall (the Indian School), College of William and Mary, built 1723 *(Historic American Building Survey)*

ness of the Master of the House, who took care to Keep least in Sight, their Freedom seem'd a little Doubtful. It is certain many Slaves Shelter themselves in this Obscure Part of the World, nor will any of their righteous Neighbors discover them. On the Contrary, they find their Account in Settling such Fugitives on some out-of-the-way-corner of their Land, to raise Stocks for a mean and inconsiderable Share, well knowing their Condition makes it necessary for them to Submit to any Terms.

Nor were these worthy Borderers [*residents of the disputed border territory*] content to Shelter Runaway Slaves, but Debtors and Criminals have often met with the like Indulgence. But if the Government of North Carolina has encourag'd this unneighborly Policy in order to increase their People, it is no more than what Ancient Rome did before them, which was made a City of Refuge for all Debtors and Fugitives, and from that wretched Beginning grew up in time to be Mistress of a great Part of the World.

William Byrd, 1728, "History,"
in Writings, *p. 47.*

9

The English Colonies at the Middle of the 18th Century
1730–1750

IMPERIAL POLICY

Under King George II, who ascended the British throne in 1727, the tenets of mercantilism continued as the basis of British imperial policy. Sir Robert Walpole, a Whig who was now called by the new term *prime minister,* continued to exert power over colonial affairs, aided by the secretary of state, Thomas Pelham-Holles, duke of Newcastle. They continued salutary neglect of the colonies, although they did carefully select royal governors and other officials. Meanwhile, Parliament continued its attempts to exert economic control. The Hat Act of 1732 suppressed the growing manufacture of beaver-skin headgear in Rhode Island and New England. The Molasses Act of 1733 placed a prohibitively heavy duty on sugar imported from the French West Indies to force colonists to buy sugar from the British West Indies for their important rum industry. The Iron Act of 1750 attempted to restrict the colonial manufacture of metal items like plows, kettles, and nails and to encourage the shipment of all "pigs" (large unfinished bars of iron) to Britain. By 1750, nonetheless, every colony from Virginia through to New England had established ironworks or "iron plantations"; Pennsylvania alone had 73. Although the trade acts were rarely enforced with success, they were much resented by colonists.

In 1740, Parliament passed an act to systematize laws for naturalizing immigrants from foreign nations to any colony of England's colonial empire. (People who were born in either Britain or any of its colonies, of course, were already British citizens and did not need to be naturalized.) Prior to 1740, each colony set its own requirements for naturalization; because colonies wanted settlers, local requirements were usually easy to meet. From the Crown's standpoint, however, this system caused difficulties, especially when naturalized citizens of one colony (a Holland-born New Yorker, for example) moved to another colony. After 1740, a citizen of another nation could become a naturalized British citizen with rights in all of England's colonies if he or she resided in any one colony for seven years; took an oath or affirmation of loyalty; and was either a member of a Protestant congregation, a Quaker, or a Jew (the latter two groups were exempted from repeating the words "upon the true faith of a Christian" when taking the oath). (Catholic immigrants could not become naturalized citizens without disavowing their religious beliefs, although there were, of course, British Catholics who were citizens by right of birth.) Most colonies continued to grant their own colony-specific local citizenship on the basis of far shorter residence requirements although it did not make a person a naturalized citizen of Britain.

However, becoming a naturalized citizen, whether of Britain or of one specific colony, remained different from obtaining colonial voting rights. Each colony was still a separate "province," and controlled admission to its own franchise. Only free white men could obtain voting rights, and to do so they were required to own real property or other wealth, the amount varying from colony to colony. Catholic and Jewish men were restricted from voting in most colonies in the mid-18th century regardless of citizenship. Requirements for voting in local elections, however, were often less restrictive.

THE FOUNDING OF GEORGIA

The last of England's 13 American colonies to be founded, Georgia was conceived as a solution to two entirely different problems: the plight of English debtors and the English-Spanish rivalry in the so-called "debatable land" between South Carolina and Florida. As the population of South Carolina increased, turbulence in the debatable land was an increasing concern to English colonial officials. In response, James Oglethorpe, a member of Parliament who once headed an inquiry into debtors' prisons, developed a plan to establish a buffer colony that would also be a philanthropic project, peopled by the poor. In 1732, Oglethorpe and 21 other trustees received a charter for land between the Savannah and Altamaha Rivers. Georgia, named for the king, was to function as a proprietary colony for 21 years, after which it would revert to Crown control. Although the charter gave extensive powers to the trustees, none was permitted to own land in the colony or to hold any office from which he might profit financially. No specific provision was made for representative government in the colony itself (and no assembly met until 1751); instead, it was to be governed from England by a Common Council of 15 members. Otherwise, colonists were to have the usual "rights of Englishmen," and religious liberty was granted to all "except Papists" (Catholics).

Unfortunately, most of the philanthropist trustees had far more interest in designing the colony than in its practical government. They established many regulations, codified in the Rules of 1735, but only three laws: the creation of an Indian commissioner to license traders and fix all prices; the prohibition of "strong waters," or hard liquor (but not wines, ales, and beers), especially as items of Indian trade; and the prohibition of human slavery. Trustees did not even appoint a governor until 1743. In the absence of a governor, Oglethorpe assumed the role, accompanying the first colonists to America and personally shepherding the colony during its early years.

The Georgia project developed an enthusiastic following in England. Churches collected money, clergymen donated moral and religious tracts, ordinary citizens contributed seeds and farming implements, the Bank of England made a large contribution, and Parliament appropriated a sizable sum—the first such appropriation for founding a colony in England's history. The colony was advertised and promoted widely, but the trustees screened all prospective settlers. Only the industrious, sober, and moral—the "worthy poor"—were accepted. The first colonists were primarily unemployed laborers, craftsmen, or small tradesmen. During the entire trusteeship, fewer than a dozen people actually released from debtors' prisons ever arrived in Georgia.

In January 1733, Oglethorpe landed in South Carolina with 35 families, then headed for the Savannah River. There, in February, he negotiated a treaty with Tomochichi, *mico* (chief) of the small Yamacraw band of Creek living nearby. Oglethorpe obtained land rights with the translating and negotiating help of Mary Musgrove or Coosaponakeesa, the half-Creek wife of a South Carolina trader who maintained a very successful post and large cattle farm in the area. In summer 1734, Oglethorpe took Chief Tomochichi, several other Yamacraw, and John Musgrove to London to ratify the treaty. The group attracted much comment and attention for the Georgia colony.

Oglethorpe laid out a settlement at modern Savannah, with six public squares each surrounded by house lots of 60 by 90 feet. At the edge of town were garden plots and farming acreage. In July 1733, land, livestock, and supplies were distributed to the colonists. Land grants to male charity colonists were 50 acres; noncharity emigrants were entitled to additional headrights for servants. No grant, however, could exceed 500 acres. Land was granted in trust rather than in freehold; it reverted to the trustees if the male owner had no son to inherit it at his death. Although the land system quickly proved unpopular and unworkable, its purpose in the trustees' minds was twofold: to guarantee the presence of an armed man on each nearby farm for defense and to prevent the formation of large estates. At the time the land was divided, a court was established; magistrates as well as other minor officials were chosen from among the colonists. No other formal governmental institutions were organized.

In summer 1733, 42 Jewish settlers arrived in Savannah, some of them also "worthy poor" selected and funded by the Jewish community in London.

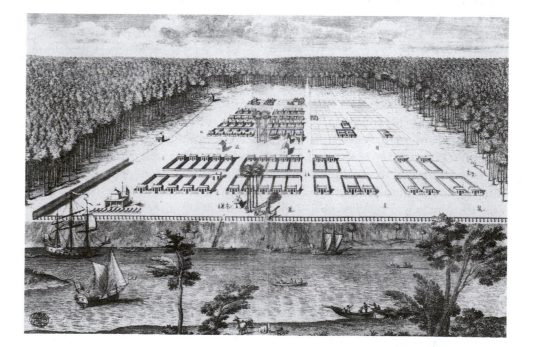

View of Savannah, Georgia, 1734
(Library of Congress)

Fortunately, they were accompanied by Dr. Samuel Nunis, who cared for colonists suffering from the usual "seasoning" illnesses after the doctor who accompanied Oglethorpe succumbed himself. In March 1734, German Protestants expelled from Salzburg arrived and founded the community of Ebenezer; by 1741, more than 1,200 Salzburgers had immigrated. German-speaking pacifist Moravians also arrived in 1734 but soon migrated to Pennsylvania. Lowland Scots arrived in 1734 and Highland Scots in 1736, the latter settling at Darien on the Altamaha River. In 1735, Oglethorpe purchased a shipload of Irish convicts to perform farm work for fatherless families, but convict labor proved no more popular in Georgia than in Virginia. The trustees also continued to send additional English colonists "on the charity" until about 1738. After that date, they sent primarily indentured servants, who worked on public works projects or in the common farmlands maintained to ensure an adequate food supply. The trustees, who had adopted the silkworm on their official seal, also attempted to establish silk culture. They required 100 mulberry trees to be planted for each 10 acres cleared, and in May 1733 they sent two families of Italian silkgrowers. Eventually the colony exported silk, although never without the assistance of subsidies.

The care of orphans became a concern in Georgia as early as the colony's first summer, when many settlers died. In 1737, the Ebenezer group founded an orphanage, which was visited by Great Awakening evangelist George Whitefield on his first trip to America. In 1740, Whitefield returned to Georgia to found Bethesda, a widely publicized orphanage, which housed children from several colonies.

The Georgia Project Undergoes Changes

In 1734, Georgia's trustees, dissatisfied with Oglethorpe's failure to keep written records, sent William Stephens to the colony to act as secretary. After nine years of service, he became the first governor, or "president," of the colony in 1743, serving until 1751, when he resigned at age 80. In the intervening years, the trustees made many changes to their original plan and regulations. In 1739, land policies were altered to allow women to inherit from their husbands or fathers. In 1742, the prohibition on rum was ended. The law that caused the most controversy, however, was the prohibition of slavery. In 1739, a disgruntled proslavery group left Georgia for Charleston, where they published a scathing polemic against Oglethorpe and his project. Both pro- and antislavery factions continued to petition the trustees. In fact, some slaves were present in Georgia from its earliest years, brought by settlers who had migrated from other colonies. In 1750, the trustees gave in to arguments that the colony could not prosper without slave labor and consented to the unrestricted importation of black slaves. In the same year, they increased maximum land holdings to 2,000 acres.

Throughout his tenure in Georgia, Oglethorpe took quite seriously the goal of making Georgia a defensive buffer colony. In 1736, he established more than 100 colonists at Fort Frederica on St. Simons Island. Although lacking any official appointment or authorization, he built additional military forts between Frederica and the St. Johns River, much to the displeasure of the Spanish and eventually of Sir Robert Walpole. In August 1736, Oglethorpe agreed to allow officials in London and Madrid to establish the boundary between Georgia and

Florida. A year later, with English-Spanish relations growing more strained, he sailed to London to secure a commission as military commander of the colony; thereafter, he was called General Oglethorpe, having never received the title governor. In 1738, he returned with a contingent of more than 600 English soldiers. After five years of hostilities with the Spanish (the War of Jenkins's Ear), Oglethorpe was called back to London in 1743 to answer charges that he had mismanaged the war. Although he was completely exonerated, his interest in Georgia ended, and he never returned to the colony.

After Oglethorpe's departure, Mary Musgrove demanded compensation for her long-time services to Georgia. For many years, she and her late husband John had provided meat and other food to the colony, for which they had not received adequate payment. More important, Mary Musgrove, who had been educated among whites in South Carolina, had worked loyally as an interpreter and very successful Indian agent. At Oglethorpe's request she had even established a new post, on the Altamaha River to gather intelligence about the Spanish and their Indian allies. Nonetheless, the English had grown increasingly unwilling to recognize her large and growing land claims, obtained through her own agreements with the Creek. In July 1747, under the influence of her third husband, a renegade Anglican missionary named Thomas Bosomworth, she led an armed party of Creek to Savannah. The militia was called out to keep order, and by mid-August the Creek dispersed. The Bosomworths eventually resorted to the London courts; by 1760, they were awarded a cash settlement and title to St. Catharine's Island. Mary died three or four years later, however, and her hard-earned possessions passed by English law to Bosomworth rather than to her matrilineal relatives, as was the Creek custom.

By 1750 Georgia had established itself economically. In 1737, a fort was settled at Augusta and developed into an important Indian trading center. By 1750, the non-Indian population stood at about 3,000.

THE WAR OF JENKINS'S EAR AND KING GEORGE'S WAR

By 1738, an undeclared war between England and Spain existed in the seas of the Spanish Indies. English ships legally transporting slaves also indulged in widespread smuggling, and Spanish ships patrolling the coasts treated captured smugglers harshly. In June 1739, British smuggler Thomas Jenkins was captured near Florida and had his ear cut off. According to Jenkins, the Spanish captain ordered him to carry his ear "home to the King, your master, whom, if he were present, I would serve in like fashion." English public opinion was inflamed, and in October the Anglo-Spanish War was officially declared; it became known popularly as the War of Jenkins's Ear.

On the English-Spanish border in Georgia, General Oglethorpe used personal diplomacy to strengthen the frontier. With the assistance of Mary Musgrove, he secured the loyalty of the Creek and negotiated with Chickasaw and Cherokee chiefs to alleviate their complaints about trading practices. In 1740, with aid from South Carolina, Oglethorpe led a combined English-Indian force against Spanish St. Augustine. Oglethorpe laid siege to the Castillo de San Marcos for 38 days but failed to capture it. Spain retaliated in 1742, sending 2,000 troops from Cuba to attack St. Simons Island. They were ambushed at the Battle of Bloody Marsh, however, and retreated.

In 1740, the War of the Austrian Succession began in Europe with France now an ally of Spain. Hostilities soon spread to the colonies, where they blended into the War of Jenkins's Ear and took the name King George's War after 1744. Additional raiding continued in the south until 1748, including a second colonial attempt to invade St. Augustine in March 1743, but none was conclusive. The major battles, however, moved north. France unsuccessfully attacked sites in Acadia. In 1744, New England officials decided to mount an expedition against Louisbourg, the strongest fortress in North America. Louisbourg, located on Cape Breton Island, defended the entrance to the St. Lawrence River and served as the main port for New France; New Englanders believed it also served as a base for French privateers. The Louisbourg campaign was planned entirely by colonials; Governor William Shirley (a lawyer) organized more than 4,000 relatively untrained volunteers, to be commanded by William Pepperell (a merchant from Kittery, Maine). Other colonies sent aid, and even Quaker Pennsylvania contributed supplies. In March 1745, more than 90 ships, mostly merchant and fishing vessels, sailed from Boston. They were joined en route by a small British war fleet. On June 28, after 46 days of constant cannon bombardment, Louisbourg surrendered to the New England forces. Although the French later sent two fleets to revenge the attack, neither arrived in North America successfully.

After 1745, the French and their Indian allies began attacks on frontier settlements in Maine, New York, and New England that continued for the remainder of the war. In New York and Pennsylvania, Indian agents used personal diplomacy to stabilize frontiers, convincing some members of the powerful Iroquois Confederacy to counterattack the French. The colonial unity that had preceded the siege of Louisbourg dissipated, however, and a plan to launch another major attack on Canada in 1747 was never carried out. In 1748, the Treaty of Aix-la-Chapelle returned all conquered North American territories to their prewar colonial rulers. Much to the displeasure of the victorious New Englanders, Louisbourg was returned to France.

Neither the war nor the peace ended disputes between the English and French colonies. The fur trade was still contested in two arenas—the Hudson Bay–Lake Champlain area and the Great Lakes region—and Acadian boundaries were still unsettled.

THE OHIO VALLEY AND THE BACKCOUNTRY

While the English held Louisbourg from 1745 to 1748, few trade goods reached New France. Very quickly, English traders from western New York and Pennsylvania made great inroads into previously French trading territory in the Ohio River basin. The Miami even moved east from Illinois, founding Pickawillany trading center (in modern southwestern Ohio). In 1748, at Logstown, a trading center on the Ohio River (modern Pennsylvania), an important trade agreement was negotiated by Conrad Weiser, a German emigré, Indian trader, and agent. Many Ohio Valley tribes formally agreed to trade with the English. In 1747, the Ohio Company was organized by London merchants and Virginia planters; in 1749, the Crown, eager to see the area settled, granted the company 200,000 acres west of the Monongahela River.

The French, too, however, viewed the Ohio Valley as extremely important territory, not only for trade but for its waterways, which formed the shortest route from New France to the Mississippi. In 1749, Canadien captain Pierre Céloron de Bienville led a force of French and Indians into the valley. Bienville planted lead plates at the mouths of streams emptying into the Allegheny and Ohio Rivers, claiming all territory they drained for France. French officials hoped the display would impress the Ohio Valley tribes, but it did not successfully convince them to restrict their trading to the French alone.

Although white settlement had not yet moved into the Ohio Valley by 1750, settlement had become continuous in the backcountry, or Piedmont region, as far south as North Carolina. The Piedmont, the area between the fall line and the Appalachian Mountains, stretched from Pennsylvania to Georgia. Colonists traversed it over Great Wagon Road, which began in Philadelphia, ran west to York, Pennsylvania, then turned south. By the mid-1730s, it continued into the Shenandoah River valley of Virginia and by 1750 to Wachovia, North Carolina, and points south. By the time the road pushed the entire way into Georgia in the 1760s, it was more than 700 miles long with villages dotting its length. The majority of settlers who followed the road were new Scotch-Irish and German immigrants. Others were older settlers who traveled westward from the Tidewater region (the level coastal plains from Maryland southward) in search of cheaper or better land.

Farms in the Piedmont usually were small and worked without the use of slaves or servants. The backcountry quickly acquired a reputation among "easterners" and travelers as a crude, uncultured, and disorderly society. For a time, formal government as well as religion and education lagged behind settlement. Ready-made leaders and institutions did not travel with the individual 18th-century backcountry settlers as they had with the colonizing groups that arrived in the 17th century. Nonetheless, the vast majority of backcountry farmers were hardworking and law-abiding—although it was true that a less orderly element also developed. On the other hand, an elite slowly began to develop as well. Like the earliest new elites of the seaboard settlements, it was defined by wealth, aggressively accumulated.

All of the colonies struggled with the incorporation of new backcountry communities into existing colonial governments, whose seats were located on the seaboard and in some cases on the other side of mountains. Colonies from Pennsylvania south generally formed new counties in the backcountry, but their representation in assemblies was not proportional. In turn, few backcountry migrants felt as closely tied to one specific colony as seaboard colonists did.

THE GREAT AWAKENING

In the early decades of the 18th century, a decline in church membership, relative to population, occurred throughout the colonies. Indifference to religion was widespread. Colonial colleges educated more and more young men who did not intend to enter the ministry. Ministers and religiously observant elites struggled to retain their intellectual and social authority. Some intellectuals embraced outright rationalism, which questioned the active involvement of God in everyday human affairs.

After 1740, a religious revival known as the Great Awakening swept the colonies, influenced by a revival that occurred in all of Protestant Europe. Portents of the movement had arisen in the 1720s, when Theodore Frelinghuyson "awakened" the Dutch Reformed Church in New Jersey and Gilbert Tennent the Presbyterian Church in Pennsylvania. In 1734, the Reverend Jonathan Edwards began a major revival in his Congregational church at Northampton, Massachusetts. Edwards believed that the emotions had to be engaged before conversion could occur and upright behavior could have meaning. He avoided traditional "plain-style" Puritan preaching, which appealed to logic; his most famous sermon, "Sinners in the Hands of an Angry God" (1741), described the horrors of hell so vividly that many congregants collapsed before he finished. Edwards, a graduate of Yale, remained the preeminent theologian of the revival movement.

The Great Awakening proper began with the arrival of George Whitefield (pronounced Whit-field) in the colonies in 1739. An Englishman and ordained Anglican minister, he traveled from New Hampshire to Georgia and back, reportedly preaching to audiences of up to 20,000. Whitefield simplified Protestant belief, ignoring denominational, doctrinal differences and referring to conventional ministers as "dead men." Instead, he focused on an emotional conversion experience. Whitefield and his fellow itinerant revivalists, called exhorters, often induced an experience of conversion so powerful that it caused weeping, fainting, and other physical manifestations. Their detractors mocked these effects at length.

Although exhorters were usually ordained in established churches, they also encouraged unordained and often uneducated volunteers to preach. This challenge to church authority, along with a flamboyant preaching style, led to a split among both Congregationalists (called Old Lights and New Lights) and Presbyterians. Old Lights believed that the exhorters were encouraging animal passion, not spiritual ecstasy. In some places, they passed laws against the itinerants and persecuted their followers. In 1742, for example, President Thomas Clap of Yale attempted to force student David Brainerd to confess and publicly renounce New Light sympathies. (Brainerd had made a remark in private that was overheard, repeated to a local citizen, and reported back to the college president—who then cross-examined all of the student's friends, compelling them to become informers.) When Brainerd refused, he was expelled.[1]

Although the revival proper ended by 1744, it brought about long-term changes in American religion. Church membership increased dramatically. Many of the "awakened" joined the Baptists, who had always emphasized regenerative conversion experiences. As a result, the number of Baptist congregations grew from fewer than 20 in 1740 to more than 500 by the time of the American Revolution. The Great Awakening also made Protestant Christianity acceptable for the first time to significant numbers of free blacks and slaves. The newly inclusive theology and its reduced emphasis on literacy was partly responsible, since few slaves were permitted to learn to read. In addition, the exhorters' style was more akin to African religious traditions, which emphasized the emotional participation of the group and the experience of spirit possession.

Many historians believe that the Great Awakening encouraged broader social and political changes as well. The exhorters were not involved in politics, but their religious message was both unifying and democratic. Ordinary people in all 13 colonies participated in the same revival experience, without denominational exclusiveness. They heard exhorters preach that God spoke directly to all, even the most common of people, without the assistance of literate elites and authorities. In most churches, the new sense of religious inclusiveness also encouraged various social reform efforts. After the Great Awakening, for example, slave owners were prevailed upon to provide religious instruction for their slaves and even to treat them in a more "Christian" manner.

The revival also had a strong impact on higher education, the primary purpose of which was still to provide an educated ministry. Many new private "academies" were founded to train New Light ministers, some of which offered college work. The forerunner of these was begun by Presbyterian minister William Tennent (father of Gilbert) in Neshaminy, Pennsylvania, sometime in the 1730s. Opponents derisively named it the "Log College" because its first building was a log house. In 1746, Presbyterians in New York—some of them graduates of the Log College—established the College of New Jersey, later renamed Princeton. In the following two decades, revived religious interest inspired the founding of King's College (later Columbia), Brown, Queen's College (later Rutgers), and Dartmouth. Alone among the colonial colleges, the Academy (later University) of Pennsylvania was founded by an ecumenical group with partially secular aims.

THE INFLUENCE OF THE ENLIGHTENMENT

Although emotional revivalism engaged many colonists in the middle decades of the 18th century, the intellectual movement called the Enlightenment (or Age of Reason) appealed to many others. It was inspired by the idea, propounded by English mathematician and scientist Isaac Newton (1642–1727), that God had created immutable laws to govern the universe. Enlightenment thinkers believed these laws could be discovered through the use of human reason, if one relied on experience and observation rather than tradition. They believed, furthermore, that once "natural laws" were known, human beings could and should reorganize their institutions and activities to live in better harmony with God's design. Thus, Enlightenment thinking encouraged social reform, political reform, and the belief in human progress.

Enlightenment ideas also encouraged science, which was usually called natural philosophy in the 18th century. Natural philosophy included the fields today called physics, chemistry, mathematics, and astronomy as well as "natural history" (botany, zoology, and geology). Scientific activity became both prestigious and popular, although there were few "professional" scientists. Most scientific activity was carried on by men of affairs—doctors, lawyers, merchants, and skilled craftsmen like Benjamin Franklin. Some women like Jane Colden participated as well.

Most American clergymen supported the pursuit of scientific knowledge in the 18th century, although many European clerics did not. American theologians believed that science was another way to understand God and his works and expected it to reinforce orthodox religion. Even two of the most famous Puritan ministers, Cotton and Increase Mather, engaged in scientific observation. One branch of Enlightenment thinking, however, developed heretical religious ideas called Deism. Deists accepted the ideas of Johannes Kepler, a German mathematician and astronomer. Kepler compared the universe to a clock and God to the clockmaker, who had built the universe and set it in motion but intervened no further in its workings. Deists rejected orthodox beliefs like divine revelation. Many European Deists openly rejected the church as well; in America, however, most Deists publicly supported the institutions and values of Christianity.

COLONIAL CATHOLICS

In 1734, the first urban Catholic church in America, St. Joseph's, was opened in Philadelphia. It was headed by a Jesuit priest, Father Joseph Greaton, who had migrated from Maryland. The majority of Catholics in Pennsylvania were German immigrants. In 1741, German Jesuits began to arrive to establish congregations in rural areas of Pennsylvania, New Jersey, and eventually New York (where a 1700 law banished priests and disenfranchised Catholic freemen). Although Pennsylvania was the most religiously tolerant colony, the largest number of Catholics continued to reside in Maryland, where they were probably about 10 percent of the total population. Under Maryland law, tolerance was extended to religious services conducted in private homes. Many wealthy planters who were Catholics maintained private chapels on their grounds, where local communicants also worshiped, and Maryland Jesuits traveled to conduct services in scattered congregations. Since the 1640s, Jesuits had intermittently conducted a school at Newton Manor. In the 1740s, they established a second at Bohemia Manor (left to them by the descendants of Augustine Hermann, the Prague-born negotiator and cartographer to whom Philip Calvert gave a large estate in the 17th century). Maryland Jesuits were regulated by the colonial government; they continued to maintain large, slave-worked plantations, but no longer did missionary work among Native Americans.

Colonial Catholics experienced intermittent hostility from both colonial officials and varying Protestant groups. They were often suspected of being "internal enemies" who would support military attacks on the English colonies by Catholic France or Spain. In some cases, Catholics were forbidden by statute from serving in colonial militias, had their arms and ammunition confiscated, and were required to pay extra taxes. The Jesuits came under particular suspicion because of the order's activities among the French-allied Indians in Acadia.

SLAVE UNREST AND WHITE RESPONSES

The mid–18th century was one of the most active periods of slave unrest in the history of the English North American colonies. It was marked by extensive fear among white citizens, the discovery of numerous insurrection plots, and ruthless suppression. Although slave owners exerted sufficient control to compel day-to-day obedience, they had no illusions that their slaves were universally content. In 1730, for example, a rumor spread among blacks in Virginia that the Crown had ordered the freeing of Christian slaves. When officials denied it, groups formed to plan an insurrection. The plot was discovered and the leaders executed. A similar event occurred in New Jersey in 1734. The fear of such uprisings was never far from slave owners' minds, particularly in light of the far more numerous and violent insurrections in the West Indies and South American colonies.

"Saltwater" Africans—those newly arrived in the colonies—often offered overt resistance, sometimes attempting to escape in groups. The second and subsequent generations of "country-born" slaves engaged in more subtle forms of resistance to overwork and to slavery itself—for instance, working at a slow pace, breaking tools, feigning ignorance or illness, or temporarily disappearing. Some developed extensive underground market systems of goods taken from their masters. Others engaged in the more consequential acts of arson and poisoning, the latter drawn from African herbal medicine. Although whites fears of arson and poisoning may have been exaggerated, both were made felony crimes in most slave codes of the early 18th century. In slave-dominant South Carolina, slave patrols began scouring the countryside in 1721. In 1734, a formal patrol was established in each militia district in the colony, with the power to question any black person, search any home, confiscate any weapon, and kill any black person who resisted.

Since the late 17th century, slaves in the southernmost settlements occasionally escaped to Spanish Florida. In 1733, King Philip V of Spain issued a new edict reiterating the 1693 royal decree of freedom for English slaves who reached St. Augustine and accepted Catholicism. As the news spread, escape attempts increased. After war between England and Spain was declared in 1739, a group of about 20 blacks, most of them Angolans, met at dawn on September 9 at the Stono River about 20 miles from Charleston. Led by a slave named Jemmy, they captured a store where guns and ammunition were sold, murdered two white shopkeepers, and began a march into Georgia, with Florida as their ultimate destination. At every home or plantation on the Pon Pon Road, they stopped to collect blacks (some eager, some reluctant) and to murder whites. By late afternoon, white colonists had assembled and defeated the rebels, who numbered as many as 100. Some 20 whites and 30 blacks were dead. In the following weeks, 60 more blacks were executed, and an extensive manhunt was launched to track down escapees. After the Stono Rebellion, the South Carolina Assembly passed some measures designed to improve the treatment of slaves (although they also offered a new bounty on the scalps of runaways). Nonetheless, new plots were discovered in Charleston in December 1739 and summer 1740, which resulted in the hanging of 50 alleged conspirators. In fall 1740, a planned insurrection was discovered in Annapolis, Maryland. The following spring, the rebellions moved north.

It is clear from the historical record that slaves often considered, and occasionally attempted, rebellion against bondage. It is also clear, however, that whites—gripped by fear—did not always distinguish between real and imagined conspiracies. New York, which had the largest slave population in the north, passed a harsh slave code in the 1730s after fear of a rebellion swept the colony. In 1740, two slaves were hanged for barn-burning in New Jersey, and rumors again swept New York that slaves were plotting to poison the water supply. In spring 1741, following a hard winter that caused much suffering among the poor, New York City was gripped by hysteria that came to resemble the New England witchcraft trials. A series of thefts and fires occurred, which whites feared was the work of a slave conspiracy. Under some duress, a 16-year-old white indentured servant, Mary Burton, provided information about a possible plot masterminded by her employer, a white tavern keeper and fence named John Hughson. On the testimony of a white prison inmate, two black habitués of Hughson's tavern, named Caesar and Prince, were executed and many others were jailed. Soon New York took on the psychology of Salem in 1692. The gov-

Slave quarters built in the 1730s at the Isaac Royall mansion, Medford, Massachusetts *(Historic American Building Survey)*

ernor of New York offered to spare the life of any accused conspirator who would "confess" and name others involved in the plot. Not surprisingly, many did. Extremely irregular legal proceedings followed, under the direction of Judge Daniel Horsmanden and others. In June, New York officials received a letter from General Oglethorpe of Georgia claiming that the Catholic Spanish were infiltrating the northern colonies to instigate black rebellions as a war tactic. Officials promptly added Catholics to the roster of suspects. In August, John Ury, a white Latin teacher, was executed as a priest and spy. Although some New Yorkers began to question to proceedings, additional conspirators continued to be named. After Mary Burton began to hint that prominent persons might be involved, however, the trials were brought to a quick conclusion. Twenty-two men and women had been hanged (four of them white), another 13 blacks were burned at the stake, and 70 slaves were sold and deported to the West Indies. More than 150 blacks and 25 whites remained in jail. Mary Burton vanished, granted freedom from her indenture, as did all remaining members of the Hughson family, who had been imprisoned without trial. The actual nature of the conspiracy, if any, has never been determined.

THE ROLE AND STATUS OF COLONIAL WOMEN

The majority of free women in the 18th century were farm wives, most of whose time was spent performing the vital labor of "housewifery." Historians use the term *domestic* (or *household*) *production* to describe their work, which was very different from modern household care. Women grew vegetables and herbs, milked cows, and bred and raised poultry in addition to churning, baking, cooking, and preserving food. They made candles, brooms, soap, and starch; heated water and laundered by hand; and sewed, knitted, and quilted all linens and clothing, spinning the thread and weaving the cloth as well. Usually they also engaged in some kind of barter or marketing, exchanging small surpluses produced in their households with other households or with traders. By 1750, women who lived in larger towns could purchase cloth, thread, and some other items, but no colonial woman could avoid domestic work entirely. Wealthy women organized and oversaw domestic production for their entire household of workers, servants, and slaves. Women who headed large households were also expected to learn practical medicine and function as nurses and healers, and some other women specialized as healers. Even women who were not wealthy usually did not work in isolation; they worked alongside female children, relatives, neighbors, or servants, who were employed in about one-third of all households. Women who worked for wages and slave women had to find ways to produce their household's needs in addition to all of their other tasks. The demands of frequent pregnancies and the responsibilities of child rearing were added to the tasks of domestic production. Throughout the colonial period, infant and maternal mortality rates remained very high.

In urban areas, as many as 10 percent of adult women worked at businesses and trades. Wives of artisans sometimes assisted their husbands, and it was not unusual for a widow to continue a business after her husband's death. A number entered the publishing business. In 1735, for example, Anne Smith Franklin (Benjamin's sister-in-law) inherited her husband's printing press and business in Newport, Rhode Island. She and her daughters continued to run the business and served as the colony's official printers until 1748, when her son James took over. Although women printers are the best-documented colonial businesswomen (because their names appear on everything they produced), it was more common for women to work at trades or run shops related to domestic labor such as millinery, dry goods, or groceries. Others owned and managed taverns, coffeehouses, or boardinghouses; women held a majority of the liquor licenses in many towns. Some women also kept fee-based schools for very young children or for older girls, who were usually excluded from public grammar schools. The crucial profession of midwife, existing in every town, was entirely female.

A few women distinguished themselves in more unusual pursuits. In the early 18th century, for example, Long Islander Martha Tunstall Smith took over the large whaling business of her late husband, averaging 20 whales per year and sometimes commanding her own ship. In Newport, Temperance Talmage Grant, the wife of merchant and privateer Sueton Grant, successfully continued his business after his death in 1744; she managed European agents and privateer contracts during King George's War, even on occasion arguing her own interests in courts of law. In New York, Jane Colden, daughter of Governor Cadwallader Colden, became an accomplished botanist, identifying many native plants.

The best-known woman of the era was South Carolinian Eliza Lucas Pinckney. In 1739, when her father was called to royal service in Antigua, he left 17-year-old Eliza in charge of the family plantations as well as three younger siblings and their invalid mother. Eliza took complete managerial control of overseers and slaves as well as finances, record keeping, and trade. She experimented with crops and in 1741 successfully grew indigo from seeds sent by her father. Within three years, she was distributing seeds to fellow planters; within a decade, indigo had joined rice as a successful Carolinian staple and export. After her marriage, Eliza continued agricultural experiments, successfully (although not profitably) producing silk.

Throughout the colonial era, the English colonies followed the common law principle called coverture. Women lost their legal or civil identity when they married. A single women had the legal status of *feme sole*. She could earn and keep wages; make contracts; sue or be sued; buy, own, and sell property; and will her possessions to her chosen heirs. When she married, however, her legal status changed to *feme covert*. Under coverture, her legal identity was "covered" by that of her husband. Her wages, personal property, children, and person all belonged to him. She could no longer enter into contracts, sue, or own property. Husbands were, however, generally prohibited by law from disposing of property a wife brought into the marriage, called a dowry. Upon the death of her husband, a woman regained the status of feme sole. Although she had not actually "owned" any part of her husband's estate during his lifetime, a widow was legally entitled to a dower right—the use (but not the ownership) of a one-third share of her late husband's property during her lifetime. On her death or remarriage, the property reverted to his legal heirs or to the heirs he had chosen in his will. A husband could also appoint someone other than his wife to be the guardian of her own children upon his death.

In the day-to-day reality of routine legal practice, the principles of coverture were sometimes disregarded. Some colonies also passed statutes that eased certain legal restrictions on women in the 18th century. Pennsylvania, for example, passed a "feme sole trader" act in 1718. It enabled deserted wives, or wives whose husbands were away as soldiers, to assume some of the rights of single women when entering the work force. South Carolina passed a "Feme Covert Sole Trader" act in 1744 to enable married women who engaged in trade to conduct business more reliably—making contracts to purchase goods or pay wages and assuming liability for their own debts. The difficulties of widows were always a particular concern, especially after several decades of continual war. (In Boston between 1725 and 1750, for example, widows composed up to 30 percent of the female population.) Exceptions to the inheritance laws were sometimes made to enable a widow to continue a farm or business. Neither individual rulings nor new laws were made for the purpose of increasing women's rights, however. Instead, they were made to solve practical community problems—particularly the number of women in need of charitable support—and were based on the practical value and social necessity of women's labor.

Several common practices also modified the letter of coverture property law. To protect family property, wealthy fathers sometimes wrote trusts or prenuptial contracts for their daughters' dowries. Although daughters usually did not inherit as much as sons, some fathers did make large bequests to them, written to enable them to retain control of the property whether they married or not. A husband could also bequeath his wife complete ownership of all his property if he chose, and some did. Because of these practices, by the 18th century some women in every colony controlled large estates.

Nonetheless, in the pre-Revolutionary years, women continued to be considered inferior to men in abilities and intellect, and "weaker vessels" in character or moral will. Colonial beliefs about women were very different from the later Victorian notion that women were inherently "good." Colonists were far more inclined to think of women as sinful, sexual, and even aggressive, as opposed to the later Victorian view of them as pure, spiritual, and passive. The lives of colonial women were circumscribed by law and by the dangers of frontier life, the demands of hard work, and the rigors of childbearing. The right to advance their own interests in the political world was denied to them, even if they were large property holders. Except among Quakers, participation in church governance was also denied.

THE URBAN SCENE

By 1750, the five major towns of the English colonies had grown into full commercial centers. In 1743, Boston had a population of more than 16,000; Philadelphia 13,000; New York 11,000; Charleston 6,800; and Newport 6,200. With the exception of Boston, which faced new commercial competition from the other four, all were growing rapidly.[2]

Town political institutions changed little during the period, although New York received a more liberal charter in 1731. Boston and Newport continued to be governed by town meetings and were the only two cities that had the power to tax for local improvements. (Rhode Island used the slave import duty for this purpose.) New York and Philadelphia were governed according to the terms of municipal charters. In Charleston, no separate city government existed. The city was governed by the assembly and thus controlled by the wealthy planters who dominated colony government. In the other cities the gentry also dominated the powerful offices and maintained political control.

In all the towns, real estate values rose and housing became more compact. In New York and Boston, multifamily homes or apartment buildings, called tenements, began to appear. Mansions for the rich and imposing new public build-

Judge Pringle House, built mid–18th century in the long, narrow style popular with wealthy Charleston residents *(Historic American Building Survey)*

ings were built, usually in the Georgian style also popular in London; Philadelphia's State House (later called Independence Hall), begun in 1736 and finished in 1750, was the largest. At the other extreme, the poor were an increasing urban concern. All the towns and some private charitable groups increased their activities and facilities for poor relief. Most was "home relief," the payment of small stipends to the poor or housing them with private families. Nonetheless, Philadelphia built an almshouse in 1732, New York in 1735, Charleston in 1736, and Boston in 1739.

Increasing population density also brought increasing problems of public health and safety. When Boston offered a bounty for rats in 1741, for example, almost 8,500 were caught within a year. Smallpox epidemics struck Philadelphia in 1730, 1732, and 1736; Charleston in 1733 and 1738; New York in 1731 and 1738; Boston in 1738; and Newport in 1739. Charleston suffered yellow fever epidemics in 1732, 1739, and 1745. Other diseases like measles and diphtheria also struck occasionally. Inoculation for smallpox was generally accepted after 1730, although not before it caused a great controversy. A form of smallpox inoculation was well known to Africans. The Reverend Cotton Mather's slave demonstrated it to him in 1721, about the same time European physicians were learning of the method. Mather publicized it to Boston physicians, most of whom opposed it. The perseverance of Mather and Dr. Zabdiel Boylston of Boston, and the success of the method itself, gradually overcame resistance and led many to seek treatment there.

Preventing and managing fires in the crowded and mostly wood-built towns led to the founding of volunteer fire companies and the purchase of new "engines" to pump water. In 1736, Benjamin Franklin and other leading citizens founded the Union Fire Company in Philadelphia, which became a model for many other organizations. Charleston suffered the most disastrous fire of any city to date in 1740. By 1750, all of the towns also had crime problems: robbery, violence, child murderers, confidence (or "con") men and women, prostitution's "bawdy houses," and roving gangs. Frequent mob disorders occurred; some were mere brawls, but others were politically motivated, such as the anti-impressment (or naval draft) riots in Boston, the most serious in 1747. Night watches existed in all cities, requiring citizen participation under appointed or elected constables. Most crimes were still punished by fine or publicly administered physical punishment. Except in Philadelphia, jails were inadequate and escapes alarmingly common.

By 1750, the colonial cities had many retail shops. Artisans like jewelers, silversmiths, and watchmakers prospered. In all towns except Charleston, where slaves or free blacks also held markets, only freemen or officially registered "inhabitants" were allowed to conduct trade. Itinerant peddlers were expelled from New York in 1731 and again in 1739, but in the countryside their business flourished. Town markets, where food from the countryside was sold, began to be regulated by city officials. In Boston, farmers objected vehemently and destroyed the first market building in 1737. In 1740, Peter Faneuil (who had grown wealthy in the slave trade) offered to build a new market house, which was opened in 1742 with a large public meeting room on the top floor.

The focus of town life was the "public house," an urban institution that continued to grow in importance. Taverns offered liquor, food, and sometimes lodging; coffeehouses offered only drinks, including liquor. Much like an urban hotel today, taverns were the sites of meetings for social or political organizations, business transactions, fashionable events, and casual recreation. In many places, councils and even assemblies that lacked official facilities met there. Other taverns catered to laborers and servants.

COLONIAL NEWSPAPERS AND LIBRARIES

By 1732, each of the five major colonial towns had at least one newspaper. Published weekly, they usually contained four pages of local and European news, ship arrivals, official edicts and speeches, essays (some original, some freely copied from elsewhere), and much advertising—for books, consumer goods, medical nostrums, and runaway servants, slaves, and spouses. Opinion and gossip were freely inserted into news items. Most newspapers were written, edited, and published by one person; often, the newspaper editor was also the postmaster, public or government printer, and bookseller. Almanacs were also widely printed, outsold only by the Bible. They contained calendars and information about the weather and farming methods, as well as poems, bits of historical or scientific information, and clever sayings. Benjamin Franklin's *Poor Richard's Almanack* (1732–57) is the best remembered, although the almanacs of Nathaniel Ames and his son (published 1725–75) outsold it.

In 1734–35, the resolution of a significant libel case greatly encouraged freedom of the colonial press. John Peter Zenger, a German immigrant and publisher of the *New York Weekly Journal,* was arrested by the colonial council for his paper's little-disguised attacks on royal governor William Cosby. The *Journal* was written not by Zenger but by a group of merchants and lawyers who opposed Cosby's corrupt and very unpopular administration. They secured Andrew Hamilton of Philadelphia, a well-known trial lawyer, to defend the case.

In libel trials at the time, the only role of the jury was to decide if an offending article had actually been published. The appointed judges then determined if it was libelous. "Libel" meant to expose a (usually prominent) person to public ridicule or to damage his or her reputation, thus encouraging political or social disorder. Truth was not a defense; in fact, judges often assumed that accurate statements were the most libelous.

Lawyer Hamilton took the astonishing approach of conceding to the jury that Zenger had indeed published the articles. He then asked the jury to determine *themselves* whether the articles were libelous, and furthermore, to acquit Zenger if they found the articles to be true. The jury unanimously freed Zenger. The worried judges allowed the verdict to stand, and most colonies soon followed the precedent. To be sure, colonial officials and even assemblies continued to arrest or shut down editors who criticized them. Nonetheless, after the Zenger case, newspapers were increasingly vocal on political issues.

By the middle of the 18th century, the first public libraries has been founded in the colonies, although they were not usually free of charge to users. The first had been authorized in 1698 by the South Carolina Legislature and opened in 1700 with the Anglican minister as librarian. In 1730, New York City also organized a library, opened to the public in 1746. Both remained small, however, until they were reorganized as subscription libraries (requiring a paid membership) in Charleston in 1748 and New York in 1754. In 1731, Benjamin Franklin founded

Connecticut Hall at Yale, built 1750–52 *(Historic American Building Survey)*

the Library Company of Philadelphia, a subscription library for works of scientific interest; it soon became the largest in the colonies. By the time of the Revolution, subscription libraries had also been founded in many smaller towns. Libraries were usually organized by professionals or middle-class artisans, while the very wealthy amassed their own private libraries.

CHRONICLE OF EVENTS

1730

King George II reigns in England, having succeeded his father George I in 1727.

Philadelphia suffers a smallpox epidemic; after this date, inoculation for smallpox is generally accepted.

A yellow fever epidemic sweeps through Charleston.

In Virginia, a suspected slave conspiracy is discovered.

1731

New York receives a new municipal charter. The city suffers a smallpox epidemic.

Benjamin Franklin founds the Library Company of Philadelphia.

1732

Benjamin Franklin's *Poor Richard's Almanack* begins publication.

A smallpox epidemic hits Philadelphia; yellow fever strikes Charleston.

James Oglethorpe and other philanthropist trustees receive a charter to land between the Savannah and Altamaha Rivers to found Georgia as a buffer colony and haven for the "worthy poor" of England. Trustees fail to establish extensive governmental institutions or appoint a governor. In the breech, Oglethorpe himself will lead the colony.

1733

The Molasses Act places a prohibitively heavy duty on sugar imported from French West Indies; it is largely unenforced.

Charleston suffers a smallpox epidemic.

King Philip V of Spain issues a new edict reiterating the 1693 promise of freedom for any English slave who reaches St. Augustine and accepts Catholicism.

January: Oglethorpe lands in South Carolina with 35 families bound for Georgia.

February: James Oglethorpe negotiates a treaty with the Yamacraw Creek, aided by Mary Musgrove, and lays out the site of Savannah.

1734

The Reverend Jonathan Edwards begins a revival in Massachusetts.

The first urban Catholic church in America, St. Joseph's, opens in Philadelphia.

John Peter Zenger, publisher of the *New York Weekly Journal,* is arrested for libel against New York governor William Cosby.

In New Jersey, a suspected slave conspiracy is discovered. In South Carolina, a formal slave patrol is established in each militia district, with the power to kill any blacks who resist.

June: James Oglethorpe visits London with Chief Tomochichi and several other Yamacraw; they generate much interest in the Georgia project.

1735

In a precedent-setting decision, a New York jury unanimously acquits John Peter Zenger of libel, although they are not legally entitled to do so; judges allow the irregular verdict to stand. After the decision, colonial newspapers are increasingly vocal on political issues.

Georgia trustees prohibit human slavery; the law will occasion a 15-year controversy before being nullified.

1736

Benjamin Franklin founds the volunteer Union Fire Company in Philadelphia. The city suffers a smallpox epidemic.

1737

Farmers destroy the first Boston market building.

1738

Lewis Morris is appointed royal governor of New Jersey alone; prior to this date the colony shared a governor with New York.

Smallpox epidemics strike Boston, New York, and Charleston.

Oglethorpe, now commissioned as a general, returns to Georgia from England with more than 600 English soldiers.

The all-black town of Fort Mose is founded near St. Augustine; many of its residents are escaped slaves from the English colonies.

1739

Evangelist George Whitefield arrives in the colonies, preaching up and down the Atlantic coast. He simplifies Protestant doctrine and focuses on an emotional conversion experience.

A smallpox epidemic spreads through Newport; yellow fever hits Charleston.

September 9: Approximately 20 black slaves begin the Stono Rebellion about 20 miles from Charleston, marching toward Georgia. By evening the rebels, now numbering about 100, are attacked and defeated by white colonists. About 20 whites and 30 blacks have been killed; 60 more blacks are executed in the following weeks.

October: The Anglo-Spanish War, or the War of Jenkins's Ear, is officially declared. It will blend into King George's War in 1744.

December: A slave conspiracy to revolt is discovered in Charleston.

1740

The War of the Austrian Succession begins, with France an ally of Spain against England.

Parliament passes a colonial naturalization act, by which any non-British citizen can become a naturalized citizen with rights in all of the colonies.

Imperial officials fix the boundaries of New Hampshire with Maine and Massachusetts, settling a long-standing controversy.

The Great Awakening sweeps the colonies, lasting until about 1744.

Two slaves are hanged for barn-burning in New Jersey; rumors of a conspiracy sweep New York. A slave conspiracy is discovered in Annapolis and Charleston, where more than 50 conspirators are hanged in 1739–40.

Charleston experiences the most disastrous fire of any colonial city to date.

The Reverend Whitefield founds Bethesda in Georgia, an orphanage housing children from several colonies.

General Oglethorpe leads a combined English-Indian force against St. Augustine. He lays siege to the Castillo for 38 days but fails to capture it.

1741

The northern colonies experience a severe winter, causing great hardship among the poor due to high fuel prices.

New York is gripped by fears of a slave conspiracy. Public hysteria grows, arrests mushroom, and Catholics are added to the list of possible conspirators. By fall, when the trials are stopped, 22 men and women have been hanged (four of them white) and

13 blacks burned at the stake, with 70 slaves deported. More than 150 blacks and 25 whites remain in jail.

Eliza Lucas Pinckney, who took over management of the family plantations in 1739 at age 17, successfully grows indigo from seed. Within a decade, indigo will become a new staple crop in South Carolina.

1742

A new city market house opens in Boston, the gift of merchant Peter Faneuil.

Spanish troops from Cuba numbering at least 2,000 counterattack Georgia forces at St. Simons Island; they are ambushed at the Battle of Bloody Marsh and retreat.

1743

The War of the Austrian Succession (called King George's War in America) begins, with France an ally of Spain against England. Some hostilities will continue on the southern frontiers until 1748, but most of the war will be conducted in the northern colonies and Acadia.

Oglethorpe is called back to London to answer charges that he mismanaged the war with the Spanish. He is exonerated but never returns to Georgia.

William Stephens becomes the first "president," or governor, of Georgia.

The population of Boston is more than 16,000; Philadelphia 13,000; New York 11,000; Charleston 6,800; and Newport 6,200.

1744

King George's War, the American front of the War of the Austrian Succession, begins.

Civil disorders begin in New Jersey; they will last until 1748.

South Carolina passes a "Feme Covert Sole Trader" act to enable married businesswomen to conduct trade more easily.

1745

French and Indian parties begin attacks on settlements in northern colonies, which will continue until 1748.

A yellow fever epidemic strikes Charleston.

June 28: New England forces led by William Pepperell capture French Fort Louisbourg; the expedition is planned and executed entirely by colonials.

1746

New Side Presbyterians establish the College of New Jersey, later renamed Princeton.

New York City opens its library (founded in 1730) to the public.

1747

The Ohio Company is organized by London merchants and Virginia planters.

A naval draft riot occurs in Boston.

1748

The peace of Aix-la-Chapelle ends King George's War and returns all conquered North American territories to their prewar owners. Louisbourg is returned to France. Many French and English disputes in North America remain unsettled.

Conrad Weiser negotiates an important trade agreement at Logstown, Pennsylvania. Tribes formerly allied with France agreed to trade with the English.

Charleston's library, founded 1700, is opened to public subscription.

1749

The English Crown grants the Ohio Company 200,000 acres west of the Monongahela River

Canadien captain Pierre Céloron de Bienville leads troops through the Ohio Valley, planting lead plates at the mouths of streams emptying into the Allegheny and Ohio Rivers.

Mary Musgrove Bosomworth and her husband lead a party of Creek to Savannah to demand compensation for her long-time services to Georgia as an Indian negotiator. The militia keeps the peace; in London courts award her land and compensation.

1750

The Iron Act attempts to restrict the colonial manufacture of metal items; it is the least successful of all English trade acts.

By this date, settlement in the Piedmont is continuous to North Carolina. The Great Wagon Road runs through North Carolina.

Philadelphia's State House (later called Independence Hall), begun in 1736, is completed.

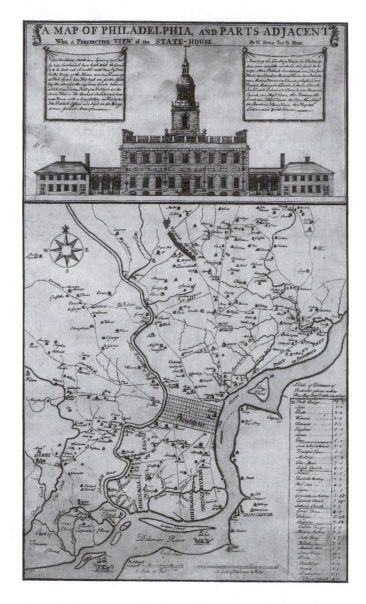

Philadelphia and its new State House, 1752, a map by Nicholas Scull *(Library of Congress)*

Georgia trustees abandon the prohibition on slavery and end the colony's land trust policies; after this date, large plantations will form.

The non-Indian population of the 13 English Colonies is about 1,200,000; about 20 percent of the population is black, more than 95 percent of them enslaved.

EYEWITNESS TESTIMONY

TO RECOVER VENISON WHEN IT STINKS: Take as much cold water in a tub as will cover it a handful over, and put in good store of salt, and let it lie three or four hours. Then take your venison out, and let it lie in as much hot water and salt, and let it lie as long as before. Then have your crust in readiness, and take it out and dry it very well, and season it with pepper and salt pretty high, and put it in your pastry. Do not use the bones of your venison for gravy, but get fresh beef or other bones.

The Compleat Housewife, 1730, quoted in Booth, Hung, p. 90.

We have no neighboring Spaniards, or other Europeans, except the French, who, according to the best intelligence we can get, are extremely numerous and strong both at Canada and Cape-Breton.

The effect which the French settlements have on this province is, that the Indians are frequently instigated and influenced by them to disturb the peace and quiet of this province, we having been often put to a vast expense both of blood and treasure, to defend ourselves against their cruel outrages.

New Hampshire governor John Wentworth to the Board of Trade, 1731, in Hart, ed., American History, *vol. 2, pp. 56–57.*

Here I arrived about three a'clock, and found only Mrs. Spotswood [*wife of the Virginia governor*] at Home, who receiv'd her Old acquaintance with many a gracious Smile. I was carry'd into a Room elegantly set off with Pier Glasses, the largest of which came soon after to an odd Misfortune. Amongst other favourite Animals that cheer'd this Lady's Solitude, a Brace of Tame Deer ran familiarly about the House, and one of them came to stare at me as a Stranger. But unluckily Spying his own Figure in the Glass, he made a spring over the Tea Table that stood under it, and shatter'd the Glass to pieces, and falling back upon the Tea Table, made a terrible Fracas among the China. This Exploit was so sudden, and accompany'd with such a Noise, that it surpriz'd me, and perfectly frighten'd Mrs. Spotswood. But twas worth all the Damage to shew the Moderation and good humour with which she bore this disaster.

William Byrd, "A Progress to the Mines," 1732, Writings, *pp. 356–57.*

The Colonel [*Governor Spotswood*] . . . carry'd us directly to his Air Furnace, which is a very ingenious and profitable contrivance. The use of it is to melt his Sow Iron, in Order to cast it into sundry Utensils, such as Backs for Chimneys, Andirons, Fenders, Plates for Hearths, Pots, Mortars, Rollers for Gardeners, Skillets, Boxes for Cart Wheels; and many other things . . . much better than those which come from England. . . . Mr. Flowry is the Artist that directed the Building of this Ingenious Structure, which is contrived after this Manner. There is an Opening about a foot Square for the fresh Air to pass thro' from without. This leads up to an Iron Grate that holds about half a Bushel of Sea Coal, and is about 6 foot higher than the opening. When the Fire is kindled, it rarefies the Air in such a Manner as to make a very strong Draught from without. About two foot above the Grate is a hole that leads into a kind of Oven, the Floor of which is laid Shelving towards the Mouth. In the Middle of this Oven, on one Side, is another hole that leads into the Funnel of a Chimney, about 40 foot high. The Smoke mounts up this way, drawing the Flame after it with so much force, that in less than an hour it melts the Sows of Iron that are thrust towards the upper end of the Oven. As the Metal melts it runs towards the Mouth into a hollow place, out of which the Potter lades it in Iron. Ladles, in order to pour it into the Several Molds just by. The Mouth of the Oven is Stopped close with a Moveable stone Shutter, which he removes so soon as he perceives, thro' the peep holes, that the Iron is melted.

William Byrd, 1732, Writings, *pp. 375–77.*

We were accustomed to look upon, what were called *gentle folks,* as beings of a superior order. For my part, I was quite shy of them, and kept off at a humble distance. A *perriwig,* in those days, was a distinguishing badge of *gentle folk*—and when I saw a man riding the road, near our house, with a wig on, it would so alarm my fears and give me such a disagreeable feeling, that, I dare say, I would run off, as for my life. Such ideas of the differences between *gentle* and *simple,* were, I believe, universal among all of my rank and age. . . .

My parents neither sought nor expected any titles, honors, or great things, whether for themselves or children. Their highest ambition was to teach their children to read, write and understand the fundamental rules of arithmetic. I remember also that they taught us short prayers, and made us very perfect in repeating the *Church Catechism.* They wished us all to be brought up in some honest calling, that we might earn our bread, by the sweat of our brows, as they did.

Devereaux Jarrett, Virginia carpenter, born 1732,
"Autobiography," p. 361.

. . . if there be any Poor, who do not, or cannot add to the Riches of their Country by Labour, they must lie a dead Weight on the Publick; and as every wise Government, like the Bees, should not suffer any Drones in the State, these Poor should be situated in such Places, where they might be easy themselves, and useful to the Commonwealth.

If this can be done by transplanting such as are necessitous and starving here, and consequently unnecessary; it is incumbent on us . . . to promote and enlarge our Settlements abroad with unusual Industry. . . . The *French* are continually undermining us both in the *East* and *West-Indies*. . . . *Portugal* owes her Riches chiefly to her Plantations; *Sweden, Denmark,* and *Germany* find themselves poor, because they have not any at present, tho' they abound with laborious Men. The Colonies of *Spain* supply the want of Industry in her Natives, and Trade in her Towns: . . . the Scarcity [*poverty*] of her People at home . . . is evidently owing to the Nature of her Government, her Religion, and its Inquisition: As may be seen by *Italy,* who has no colonies, yet is thin of Inhabitants, especially in the *Pope's* Dominions: And tho' of as rich a Soil as any in the World, yet her People are poor, and the Country in many Places uncultivated, by shutting up those, who would serve their Maker in a better Manner by being industrious, and would be more useful Members of Society as Plowmen than as Monks.

Benjamin Martyn, "Reasons for Establishing the Colony
of Georgia," 1733, in Reese, Most Delightful,
pp. 199–200.

I fixed upon a healthy situation, about Ten Miles from the Sea. The River here forms an Half-moon, along the South side of which the Banks are about Forty Feet high, and on the Top a Flat, which they call a Bluff. The plain High ground extends into the Country Five or Six Miles, and along the River-side about a mile. Ships that draw Twelve Feet Water can ride within Ten Yards of the Bank. Upon the River-side, in the Centre of this Plain, I have laid out the Town, opposite to which is an Island of very rich Pasturage, which I think should be kept for the Trustees Cattle. The River is pretty wide, the Water fresh, and from the Key of the Town you see its whole Course to the Sea. . . . The Landskip is very agreeable, the Stream being wide, and bordered with high Woods on both sides. . . . I have marked out the Town and Common; half of the former is already cleared, and the first House was begun Yesterday in the Afternoon. A little Indian Nation, the only one within Fifty Miles, is not only at Amity, but desirous to be Subjects to his Majesty King George, to have Lands given them among us, and to breed their Children at our Schools. Their Chief and his beloved Man, who is the Second Man in the Nation, desire to be instructed in the Christian Religion.

James Oglethorpe to the Georgia Trustees, 1733, quoted in
Jones, History, *vol. 1, pp. 122–23.*

We, the widdows of this city, have had a Meeting, and as our case is something Deplorable, we beg . . . that we may be Relieved, it is as follows.

We are the House keepers, Pay our Taxes, carry on Trade, and most of us are She Merchants [*business-women*], and as we in some measure contribute to the Support of Government, we ought to be Intituled to some of the Sweets of it; but we find ourselves intirely neglected, While the Husbands that live in our Neighbourhood are daily invited to dine at Court: we have the Vanity to think we can be full as Entertaining, and make as brave a Defense in case of an Invasion, and perhaps not turn Taile so soon as some of them. . . .

Letter to New York Journal, *1733, quoted in Dexter,*
Colonial Women, *p. 18.*

VOTED that there be a Slave Bought by the Parish to be Imployed for the use of said Parish in Labouring for the Rev. Mr. Samuel Moody VOTED that Samuel Cane Esqr, Elder Richard Milberry and Mr. Joseph Holt be Imployed as agents for the Parish to purchase a Slave for said Parish.

Town meeting, York, Maine, January 1733,
quoted in Banks, History, *p. 98.*

I met with many trials in my lying in, it being an extreme cold season. My child was born on Oct. 27, 1732. The next spring, my husband returned home; but went to sea again, and died abroad in November, 1733. I was then in my twentieth year. The news of my husband's death came to me on the first of the next April. . . . But God appeared wonderfully for my support. I saw his hand, and was enabled to submit with patience to his will. I daily looked round me, to see how much heavier the hand of God was laid on some others, than it was on me. . . .

I could see no way in which I could get a living. All doors seemed to be shut. But I verily believed that God would point out a way for me. And accordingly, the very day I came to a resolution to move as soon as I could, a stranger to my case, who kept a school a little way off, came to me, and told me that she only waited for a fair wind to go to Carolina; and, if it would suit me, I should have her chamber and schollars; which I joyfully accepted. Thus the widow's God remarkably provided for me. This was on Nov. 19, 1734. I was then placed in a family, who discovered a great deal of affection for me; and in all respects used me as tenderly as if I had been a near relation.

Newport resident Sarah Osbourn, in Hopkins, ed., Memoirs, *pp. 18–21.*

The Choctaws are down according to your request. They say they like the English better than the French, and that they will stand by the English as long as they have one left alive. This was more than Carolina could ever do. . . . Hope all are in good health including my husband—I beg your Honor, to take care of him, he being in a strange place and not able to take care of himself, and to send him home as soon as possible.

Letter of Mary Musgrove to James Oglethorpe in London, July 17, 1734, quoted in Todd, Mary Musgrove, *p. 49.*

We hear from Chester County, that last Week at a Vendue held there, a Man being unreasonably abusive to his Wife upon some trifling Occasion, the Women form'd themselves into a Court, and order'd him to be apprehended by their Officers and brought to Tryal: Being found guilty he was condemn'd to be duck'd 3 times in a neighbouring Pond, and to have one half cut off, of his Hair and Beard (which it seems he wore at full length) and the Sentence was accordingly executed, to the great Diversion of the Spectators.

Benjamin Franklin, in his Pennsylvania Gazette, *April 17, 1735, in Franklin,* Writings, *p. 261.*

The question before the court and you, gentlemen of the jury, is not of small nor private concern. It is not the cause of the poor printer, nor of New York alone, which you are now trying. No! It may in its consequences affect every freeman that lives under a British government on the main of America. It is the best cause. It is the cause of liberty, and I make no doubt but

your upright conduct this day will not only entitle you to the love and esteem of your fellow citizens, but every man who prefers freedom to a life of slavery will bless and honor you as men who have baffled the attempt of tyranny, and by an impartial and uncorrupt verdict have laid a noble foundation for securing to ourselves, our posterity and our neighbors that to which nature and the laws of our country have given us a right—the liberty—both of exposing and opposing arbitrary power . . . by speaking and writing—truth.

Andrew Hamilton's summation, Zenger case, August 1735, quoted in Tebbel, Compact History, *p. 29.*

After meeting [*in Rahway, New Jersey*] a certain person was dissatisfied about women's public speaking in religious meetings; Rose Tibbets having publicly exhorted them in this meeting to be religious and to fear God, and having prayed to God for us all, and praised his holy name, the said person desired we would endeavor to satisfy him about it. . . . To which it was answered, that the apostle Paul only forbade, or did not permit forward or busy women to speak or ask questions in the church; but advised them to ask their husbands at home, and that doubtless he never intended to debar such godly women who had a real necessity laid on them, and were concerned by the Almighty to speak unto or pray for the people, else he would not have showed them how they ought to behave themselves in the service. For if he had any design to hinder such, whom the Almighty should call to this work, then he must have contradicted himself, where he shows how they must behave themselves in their duty of speaking or praying; and he would likewise thereby have opposed the apostle Peter, who said, Now is fulfilled the prophecy of the prophet Joel that in the latter days sons and daughters should prophesy. So that it is clear and plain, they who would limit or silence those who have a gift from God to preach or pray in public, from the words of the apostle Paul, oppose him to himself, and to the apostle Peter, and also to the prophet Joel.

Quaker Thomas Chalkley, 1737, Journal, *pp. 372–73.*

Fare you well Davis, your Prisoners are fled,
Your Prison's broke open while you are in Bed.

On the floor of Newport prison, March 1737, quoted in Bridenbaugh, Cities in the Wilderness, *p. 386.*

That many Idle and lazy Straglers [*peddlers*], who have no Families to maintain, who pay neither Lot nor Scot, nor do any Duty in the Service of their King or Country, yet are suffered to wander from House to House, and from Place to Place, to dispose of all manner of Wares and Merchandize, to the ruin of Trade, and is a great hurt to the Traders and Shopkeepers.

New York Gazette, 1738, quoted in Bridenbaugh,
Cities in the Wilderness, *p. 336.*

It happens very providentially that Mr. Tennant and his brethren are appointed to be a presbytery by the synod, so that they intend breeding up gracious youths, and sending them out from time to time into our Lord's vineyard. The place wherein the young men study now is, in contempt, called the college. It is a log house, about twenty feet long, and nearby as many broad; and, to me, it seemed to resemble the schools of the old prophets. That their habitations were mean, and that they sought not great things for themselves, is plain from that passage of Scripture, wherein we are told, that at the feast of the sons of the prophets, one of them put on the pot, whilst the others went to fetch some herbs out of the field. From this despised place seven or eight worthy ministers of Jesus have lately been sent forth; more are almost ready to be sent; and a foundation is now laying for the instruction of many others.

Journal of Rev. George Whitefield, 1739, quoted in
Cremin, American Education, *pp. 322–23.*

Septr. 20th . . . A Negro came to the General and told him that what was said of the Negroes Rising in Carolina was true and that they had marched to Stono Bridge where they had Murdered two Storekeepers Cut their Heads off and Set them on the Stairs Robbed the stores of what they wanted and went on killing what Men, Women and Children they met, Burning of Houses and Committing other Outrages, and that One hundred Planters who had assembled themselves together pursued them and found them in an open Field. . . . [A]bout fifty of these Villains attempted to go home but were taken by the Planters who Cut off their heads and set them up at every Mile Post they came to.

"A Ranger's Report," 1739, in Mereness, ed., Travels,
pp. 222–23.

VERSES written by a young Lady. . . .
How wretched is a *Woman's* Fate,
No happy Change her Fortune knows,
Subject to Man in Every State.

How can she then be free from Woes? . . .
  REPLY to Ladies Complaint
Dear Miss, of Custom you complain,
It seems to me you languish,
For some dear, simply homely Swain,
To ease you of some Anguish. . . .

South Carolina Gazette, ca. 1740, quoted in
Hudak, Early American, *pp. 138–39.*

Thursday, October 9 . . . When I came near the meeting-house [*in Boston*], I found it much impressed upon my heart, that I should preach upon our Lord's conference with Nicodemus. When I got into the pulpit, I saw a great number of ministers sitting around and before me. Coming to these words, "art thou a master in Israel, and knowest not these things?" the Lord enabled me to open my mouth boldly against unconverted ministers; for, I am persuaded, the generality of preachers talk of an unknown and unfelt Christ. The reason why congregations have been so dead is, because they had dead men preaching to them. O that the Lord may quicken and revive them! How can dead men beget living children? It is true, indeed, that God may convert people by the devil, if He chooses; and so He may by unconverted ministers; but I believe, He seldom makes use of either of them for this purpose.

Whitefield's journal, 1740, in Bushman, ed.,
Great Awakening, *p. 30.*

And now my Brethren! . . . If you have been thus awaken'd out of your carnal Security, you have the Testimony of *the Spirit himself,* that he has begun a good Work in you. It is true, that this is no certain Evidence of a sanctifying Change. Many have been brought thus far, that have worn off these Impressions; and return'd to Folly, like *a Dog to his Vomit, and like the Sow that was washed to her wallowing in the Mire.* . . . But if the Spirit of God carry on his Work to purpose, he will bring the convinced Sinner to see the infinite Defect of all his Performances and of all his Attainments, of all his Duties, Reformations, Promises, religious Frames, and moral Carriages, and of all he does or can do, to render him acceptable to God. He will bring him to see, that he is undone, and cannot help himself; and that he is utterly unworthy that God should help him. He will bring him to see, that it is a wonder of God's Patience that he is out of Hell; and that it will be a Wonder indeed of sovereign free Grace, if such a polluted guilty Rebel finally escapes eternal Ruin. He will bring him to lie at God's Footstool, as a guilty condemned Malefactor with the Halter about his Neck, having nothing to plead in his own Favour, nothing to depend upon, but abused and forfeited Grace and Mercy.

The Reverend Jonathan Dickinson, sermon, 1740, in Heimert and Miller, eds., Great Awakening, *pp. 102–03.*

Some of you have seen buildings on fire; imagine therefore with yourselves, what a poor hand you would make at fighting with the flames, if you were in the midst of so great and fierce a fire. You have often seen a spider, or some other noisome insect, when thrown into the midst of a fierce fire, and have observed how immediately it yields to the force of the flames. There is no long struggle, no fighting against the fire, no strength exerted to oppose the heat, or to fly from it; but it immediately stretches forth itself and yields; and the fire takes possession of it, and at once it becomes full of fire; and is burned into a bright coal. Here is a little image of what you will be the subjects of in hell, except you repent and fly to Christ. However you may think that you will fortify yourselves, and bear as well as you can; the first moment you shall be cast into hell, all your strength will sink and be utterly abolished. To encourage yourselves, that you will set yourself to bear hell torments as well as you can, is just as if a worm, that is about to be thrown into a glowing furnace, should swell and fortify itself, and prepare itself to fight the flames. . . . You who now . . . sit here in these seats so easy and quiet, and go away so careless; by and by will shake, and tremble, and cry out, and shriek, and gnash your teeth. . . .

The Reverend Jonathan Edwards, "The Future Punishment of the Wicked Unavoidable and Intolerable," sermon, 1741, in Miller, ed., Major Writers, *vol. 2, pp. 154–55.*

There is a Creature here which you perhaps never heard of before. It is called an *Exhorter.* It is of both Sexes, but generally of the Male, and young. Its distinguishing qualities, are *Ignorance, Impudence, Zeal.* . . . Such of them as have good Voices do *great Execution;* they move their hearers, make them cry, faint, swoon, fall into Convulsions. . . . You may hear screaming, singing, laughing, praying, all at once; and, in other parts, they fall into Visions, Trances, Convulsions. When they come out of their Trances, they commonly tell a senseless Story of Heaven and Hell, and whom and what they saw there.

Boston resident, ca. 1741, quoted in Barck and Lefler, Colonial America, *p. 403.*

If thro' an Optick Glass
You view a spire of Grass
That in the Road is trod,
With Admiration you may gaze
On Veins that branch a thousand ways,
In nice proportion wrought.
Which truly to th' assisted Eyes are brought,
That he who is not void of common sense
Or fill'd with daring Impudence,
Must own its Maker truly to be GOD.

Nathaniel Ames's almanac, 1741, in Briggs, ed., Essays, *p. 146.*

. . . General Olgethorpe gave me my freedom last year, as I wrote you, allowed me a small quantity of provision, and a cow, a calf, a sheep, promising me some housewarming tools and a hog. . . .

To tell you plainly, I have altered my course of living, that is I am married to a high German girl, of decent, sober, godly beautiful body, one whom [I] love above all the world. The Reverend Mr. Bolzius married us, my master. I, having built a house upon our town lot, which every freeholder is obliged to do, and fence in the lot and plant it with mulberry, peach and apple trees, design to own land for planting, and to build a house to live in upon our plantation, it being six miles out of town. Our plantations are settled very regularly, they lying all along by a river called Abercorn River, so that every one of our people can go from his plantation by water, in a canoe to town, or to Georgia town or anywhere else to sell their goods. I have likewise a canoe or boat which I made myself. We make them out of great large cyprus tree. They must be hewn out all in one piece.

Henry Bishop of Ebenezer to his parents in Europe, January 1741, in Lane, ed., General, *vol. 2. pp. 532–34.*

We have some in this Neighbourhood who have a little Land and a few slaves and Cattle to give their children, that never think of making a Will till they come upon a sick bed and find it too expensive to send to town for a Lawyer. If you will not laugh too immoderately at me I'll trust you with a secret. I have made two Wills already. I know I have done no harm for I conn'd my lesson Very perfect and know how to convey by Will Estates real and personal and never forget in its proper place him and his heirs for Ever, nor that tis to be sign'd by 3 Witnesses in presence of one another but the most comfortable remembrance of all is that Doctor Wood says the Law makes great allowance for last Wills and Testaments presuming the Testator could not have Council learned in the Law. But after all what can I do if a poor creature lies a dying and the family takes it into their head that I can serve them, I cannot refuse. . . .

Eliza Lucas Pinckney, letter, June 1741, in Hart, ed.,
American History, *vol. 2, pp. 238–39.*

To Taunton Massachusetts. Preached there, Job XXVII/8 one or two cried out. Appointed another meeting in the evening, Hos. XIII/13. I believed 30 cried out; almost all the negroes in town wounded [*moved*], 3 or 4 converted. A great work in the town. . . . Col. Leonard's negro in such distress that it took 3 men to hold him. I was forced to break off my sermon before I had done, the outcry was so great.

Exhorter Reverend Eleazer Wheelock's diary,
November 1741, quoted in Piersen,
Black Yankees, *p. 70.*

John Robertson, late Bricklayer in *Frederica* in *Georgia*, maketh Oath and saith, That on or about the 9th of *August* last, being at Work on Mr. *Davison*'s House, adjoining to Mr. *Hawkins*'s, at the said *Frederica;* on which the said *Davison* was putting a new Roof, he did propose to the said Hawkins, to take up a few Shingles, and a Gutter belonging to the said *Hawkins*'s House, and put the said Gutter on the Party-Wall, to which the said *Hawkins* agreed, saying, that it would be a Benefit to him. . . . But the said *Hawkins* being out of Town, a Day or two after *General* Oglethorpe *sent to the said* Davison, *to forbid him to touch any thing belonging to the said* Hawkins's *House;* tho' the said Gutter encroached 14 Inches on the said Davison's Ground. . . . That the said *Oglethorpe* did, soon after on the same Day, stand on the Sill of the said *Hawkins*'s house . . . and *ordered* Mr. Cannon to *build the said Joice* [*joist*] *six Inches lower.* . . . And further, that the said *Oglethorpe* did then say to the said *Cannon,* if you touch a Shingle of what the Doctor (meaning *Hawkins*) has put down, I'LL SHOOT YOU, to which he added a great Oath. . . . That the said *Davison,* being thus hinder'd from finishing his House, was forced to remove his Goods from the said House (which was quite open) and *had only a Stable for his Family.* . . .

Deposition of John Robertson, November 1741, in Reese,
ed., Clamorous Malcontents, *pp. 298–99.*

. . . there was a cry among the people, *the Spanish negroes; the Spanish negroes; take up the Spanish negroes.* The occasion of this was the two fires (Thomas's and Hilton's) happening so closely together, only one day intervening, on each side of captain Sarly's house; and it being known that Sarly had purchased a Spanish negro, some time before brought into this port, among several others, in a prize [*ship*] taken by captain Lush; all which negroes were condemned as slaves, in the court of Admiralty, and sold accordingly at vendue; and that they afterwards pretending to have been free men in their own country, began to grumble at their hard usage, of being sold as slaves. . . . [A]nd he behaving himself insolently upon some people's asking him questions concerning them . . . it was told to a magistrate who was near, and he ordered him to gaol, and also gave direction to constables to commit all the rest of that cargo, in order for their safe custody and examination.

Trial records, 1741–42, Horsmanden, New York
Conspiracy, *p. 28.*

It was considered, that though there was an act of the province for trying negroes, as in other colonies, for all manner of offences by the justices, etc. in a summary way; yet as this was a scheme of villainy in which white people were confederated with them, and most probably were the first movers and seducers of the slaves; from the nature of such a conjunction, there was reason to apprehend there was a conspiracy of deeper design and more dangerous contrivance than the slaves themselves were capable of. . . .

Trial records, 1741–42, Horsmanden, New York
Conspiracy, *pp. 43–44.*

Sept. 20, 1741. Wrote to my father on plantation business. . . . Also informed my father of the alteration tis supposed there will be in the value of our money occasioned by a late Act of Parliament that Extends to all America which is to dissolve all private banks. . . . [I]nformed him of the Tyrannical Government at Georgia. . . . Nov. 11, 1741. Wrote to Mr. Murray to send down a boat load of white oak staves, bacon and salted beef for the West Indies. Sent up at the same time a barrel salt $\frac{1}{2}$ with salt peter. Some brown sugar for the bacon. Vinegar and a couple bottles Wine for Mrs. Murray and desire he will send down all the butter and hogs lard. Jan. 1742 . . . [S]hall try different soils for the Lucern grass this year. The ginger turns out but poorly. We want a supply of Indigo Seed. Sent by this Vessel a waiter of my own japaning, my first Essay [*attempt*]. Sent also the Rice and beef. Sent Governor Thomas of Philadelphia's Daughter a tea chest of my own doing. . . .

> *Journal of Eliza Lucas Pinckney, in Hart, ed.,*
> American History, *vol. 2, pp. 239–40.*

I. I shall give you some account of Enthusiasm, in its nature and influence.

II. Point you to a rule by which you may judge of persons, whether they are under the influence of Enthusiasm.

III. Say what may be proper to guard you against this unhappy turn of mind.

The whole will then be follow'd with some suitable Application. . . .

. . . the Enthusiast is one, who has a conceit of himself as a person favoured with the extraordinary presence of the Deity. He mistakes the workings of his own passions for divine communications, and fancies himself immediately inspired by the SPIRIT of GOD, when all the while, he is under no other influence than that of an over-heated imagination.

The cause of this enthusiasm is a bad temperament of the blood and spirits; 'tis properly a disease, a sort of madness. . . .

> *The Reverend Charles Chauncy, plain-style sermon,*
> *Boston, 1742, in Heimert and Miller, eds.,*
> Great Awakening, *pp. 230–31.*

July the 7th . . . The Spaniards hearing of the Fate of their first Party met with sent out another of 300 Men under the Command of Don Antonio Barbara Captain of a Company of Grenadiers; about three o' th' Clock in the afternoon the Spanish advanced up to the Place where we were Posted and some of them being Come within our Lines a Sharp Fire continued on all hands and betwixt both parties for some time. The Spaniards fell in great Numbers amongst which was Several Officers and also that Famous Captain of Grenadiers; the Number of the Spaniards was so great and their Fire so brisk, that some Platoons of ours gave way and were Retiring in Confusion but the timely presence of the General prevented their Retiring far. He immediately ordered them to Rally, riding himself up to the Place where he found Lieutt Sutherland and Lieutt Charles Mackay with the Highlanders and Rangers had Entirely defeated the Spaniards. We lost

not one Man in the two Attacks but one Mr. Maclane a Highland Gentleman who running very hard in pursuit of the Enemy spoiled the Circulation of his Blood and died Soon after he was brought to Town. The Spaniards after this never ventured out beyond their out Sentinels who were also fortified. . . .

July 15th. The Spaniards in great Confusion Quit St. Simons and go on board their Vessels and some go to Sea and Some within land to St. Andrews. . . .

> *"A Ranger's Report of Travels with General Oglethorpe,"*
> *1742, in Mereness, ed.,* Travels, *pp. 234–35.*

. . . the borderers on the lines [*between Massachusetts and New Hampshire*] live like toads under a barrow, being run into gaols on the one side and the other as often as they please to quarrel. . . . They pull down one another's houses, often wound each other, and I fear it will end in bloodshed.

> *Governor Jonathan Belcher to Board of Trade, 1733,*
> *quoted in Daniell,* Colonial New Hampshire, *p. 135.*

On the point formed by the entrance of the river, stands the fort or trading castle [*Oswego*]. It is a strong stone house, encompassed with a stone wall near 90 feet high and 120 paces round, built of large squared stones, very curious for their softness; I cut my name in it with my knife. The town consists of about 70 longhouses, of which one half are in a row near the river, the other half opposite to them. On the other side of a fair were two streets divided by a row of posts in the midst, where each *Indian* has his house to lay his goods, and where any of the traders may traffick with him. This is surely an excellent regulation for preventing the traders from imposing on the *Indians,* a practise they have been formerly too much guilty of, and which has frequently involved the *English* colonies in difficulties and constantly tended to depreciate us in the esteem of the natives. . . . a judgment I am sorry to confess that has (till lately) tended much to the making them in favour rather of the French than English. . . .

> *John Bartram, journal entry, July 1743,* Journey,
> *pp. 66–67.*

This afternoon the chiefs [of the Iroquois Confederacy] met in council, and three of them spoke for near a quarter of an hour each. Two of these, while speaking, walked backward and forward in the common passage, near two-thirds of its length, with a slow, even pace and much composure and gravity in the countenance. The other delivered what he had to say sitting in the middle, in a graceful tone exhorting them to a close, indissoluble amity and unanimity; for it was by this perfect union their forefathers had conquered their enemies, were respected by their allies, and honored by the world; that they were now met according to their ancient custom, tho' several imminent dangers stood in their way, mountains, rivers, snakes and evil spirits, but that by the assistance of the great Spirit they now saw each other's faces according to appointment.

This the interpreter told me was the opening of the diet, and was in the opinion of these people abundantly sufficient for one day, since there is nothing they hold in contempt so much as a precipitation in public councils. Indeed they esteem it at all times a mark of much levity in anyone to return an immediate answer to a serious question, however obvious, and they consequently spin out a treaty, where many points are to be moved, to a great length of time. . . .

John Bartram's journal, July 1743, in Cruickshank, ed.,
John and William, p. 43.

Friday, June 8 . . . I dined att a taveren [*in Philadelphia*] with a very mixed company of different nations and religions. There were Scots, English, Dutch, Germans, and Irish; there were Roman Catholicks, Churchmen, Presbyterians, Quakers, Newlightmen, Methodists, Seventh day men, Moravians, Anabaptists, and one Jew. The whole company consisted of 25 planted round an oblong table in a great hall well stoked with flys. The company divided into comittees in conversation; the prevailing topick was politicks and conjectures of a French war. A knott of Quakers there talked only about selling of flower [*flour*] and the low price it bore. The[y] touched a little upon religion, and high words arose among some of the sectaries, but their blood was not hot enough to quarrell. . . . Att 6 a'clock I went to the coffee house and drank a dish of coffee with Mr. H[asel]l.

After staying there an hour or two, I was introduced by Dr. Phineas Bond into the Governour's Club, a society of gentlemen that met at a taveren every night and converse on various subjects. The Governour gives them his presence once a week, which is generally upon Wednesday, . . . so that I did not see him there. Our conversation was entertaining; the subject was the English poets and some of the foreign writers. . . .

Tuesday, August 7 . . . Att night I went to the Scots' Quarterly Society which met att the Sun Tavern [*Boston*]. This is a charitable society and act for the relief of the poor of their nation. . . .

Dr. Alexander Hamilton, journal entry, 1744,
Gentleman's Progress, pp. 20–21, 133.

And whereas feme coverts in this Province who are sole traders do sometimes contract debts in this Province, with design to defraud the persons with whom they contract such debts, by sheltering and defending themselves from any suit brought against them, by reason of their coverture, whereby several persons may be defrauded of their just dues; and feme coverts, sole traders, are often under difficulties in recovering payment of debts contracted with them, by reason of the absence of their husbands, in whose name they are obliged to sue for all debts due to them, sometimes not being able to produce any power or authority from their husbands, *Be it therefore enacted* by the authority aforesaid, That any feme covert, being a sole trader, in this Province, shall be liable to any suit or action to be brought against her for any debt contracted as a sole trader, and shall also have full power and authority to sue for and recover . . . and that all proceedings to judgment and execution by or against such feme covert, being a sole trader, shall be as if such woman was sole, and not under coverture. . . .

South Carolina act, 1744, in Cooper, ed.,
Statutes, p. 620.

If a "talk" was to be held with the Indians at Frederika, Savannah, or any other point, nothing could be done without the important aid of Mary [*Musgrove*]. If warriors were required for the defense of the colony, it was through Mary's influence that they were obtained. Did disaffection, leaning on French intrigue or Spanish guile, hold aloft the "bloody stick" and threaten the massacre of the inhabitants, her power became conspicuous in the soothing of asperated feelings, and in the recall of half-alienated affections.

Journal of William Stephens, president of Georgia colony,
ca. 1745, quoted in Todd, Mary Musgrove, p. 88.

. . . as to their general Usage of them, 'tis monstrous, and shocking. To be sure, a *new Negro*, if he must be broke, either from Obstinacy, or, which I am more apt to suppose, from Greatness of Soul, will require . . . hard discipline. . . . You would really be surpiz'd at their

Perseverance . . . and they often die before they can be conquer'd.

Anonymous traveler, London Magazine, *1745–46, quoted in Wood,* Black Majority, *p. 287n.*

On the 15th of Jan. 1745 . . . great Numbers of People came together in a riotous & tumultuous manner in the Town of Newark, that they pay'd no Regard to the Commands of the Magistrates to disperse, or to the Proclamation made to them in the King's Name. . . .

It appears that one Amos Roberts, a principal leading Man among these Common Disturbers, at that Time, mounted his Horse, & called out, *Those who are upon my List follow me,* Which all . . . did, being then about 300 in Number. It appears that, the said Roberts & his Accomplices, met & armed, as before, came to the Gaol in a violent Manner, & having beat & broke thro' the Guard, & struck the Sheriff several Blows, they broke open the Gaol Doors, & took from thence . . . Prisoners . . . confined for Debt. . . .

. . . May 3rd and 8th 1746, It appears that the Infection of the Riots was spreading into West Jersey; For that the People settled on that Hundred thousand Acre Tract, in the County of Hunterdon, belonging to those Proprietors in & about London, called the West New Jersey Society, within a fortnight then last past, had two great Meetings, in Order to stand by One Another in Defence of their Possessions against the said Proprietors. . . .

Council of New Jersey, in Hart, ed., American History, *vol. 2, pp. 80–82.*

Camp before Louisburg [Louisbourg], *May 6* [1745]: We have got possession of the grand Battery; the French departed from it three days ago; they spiked all the guns, but we have got seven of them clear, and five of them are continually playing upon the town. Our soldiers are all in good heart, and I doubt not in a few days we shall have the town. We have taken a great number of prisoners. . . .

Camp before Louisburg, *May 26.* Commodore Warren has taken the Vigilante, a 64 gun ship from France, coming with ammunition for this garrison. She was manned with five hundred men, had five hundred barrels gunpowder on board: she lost thirty men before she struck. . . . This has given new life to all our officers and soldiers. . . .

Capt. Fletcher has had the misfortune to lose ten men by the Indians; seven killed, and three taken prisoners. They went ashore ten miles above where we lay to get wood, and keeping no guard, were beset by the Indians and cut off.

Camp before Louisburg, *June 2d.* We have made an attempt upon the Island battery, and failed. Abbot, a townsman of mine, was wounded in the leg, and I fear he will lose his life. An hundred men are missing, and we are in hopes they are taken, as two boats laden with men were seen going into the town after the attack, when the French gave three hurrahs. Young Gray is dead, and three of Capt. Grant's men are missing, all of Salem. Our scouts have had an engagement with a number of French and Indians which we routed; killed thirty and wounded forty; we lost but six killed; among them is the brave Capt. Dimmock, of Barnstable, and twenty wounded, some very dangerously. Our men got under the very walls before the French fired a gun.

Louisburg, *June 7th, 1745.* The Governor, aware of our preparations for a general assault, thought it best to capitulate, and has just surrendered the city to our arms.

Captain Samuel Curwen's journal, 1745, in Hart, ed., American History, *vol. 2, pp. 347–49.*

From the granting of the charter until 1747, the Governor and Deputy Governor were chosen and declared to be chosen, as well as the Assistants, if they had more votes for the office than any other person, but now some active men that were given to change fomented an opinion that the Governor nor Deputy Governor were not chosen unless they had more votes then all that were scattered among other persons. These men were of such activity and influence that in 1749 neither the Governor nor Deputy Governor could be declared chosen because not according to this standard, but since neither of them wanted but a few votes the Assembly elected them. Thus they were not blown down tho' much shaken at the root. The freemen being acquainted by this that the greater part did not vote for the present Governor and Deputy Governor were prone to mischief. . . .

Connecticut Governor Roger Wolcott, in Hart, ed., American History, *vol. 2, p. 59.*

Sat. 16th [*August 1745*]. Early on the Morn began our march again; Harness'd with 3. Days provisions at each of our Backs; when we had Traveled about an hour a voiolent Flux Siezed me which oblidged me to throw all my provissions away to keep up with the Company; for here was no Mincing the Matter, we must Either March or be left to perish in the Wild Desert or fall a

A Chesapeake tobacco wharf, detail from a 1752 map by Fry and Jefferson *(Library of Congress)*

prey to the more mercieless Savages; this Day we Travelled 9 miles e're we came to one Drop of water the weather very hot and Sultry however we came at last to a pond where many of Our Company laid themselves down on their Bellies near the Brink and Lap'd the water like So many Doggs. . . .

[*Tues.* 19th] . . . about 25 Leagues Distant from Anopoliss Royall . . . here was about 700 [*French*] Soldiers Encamp'd. . . . Here the French gave us Shoes made of a red Leather Some were of Scal Skins but they had neither heels nor Soales which they and the Indians Call Mogazins; they then Ordered us to prepare for our March Tomorrow. . . .

Fri., 29th of August. at Day break we saw come by us about 50 [*Canadian*] men women and Children upon horses and Mules who had been routed from the Island St. John's by Admiral Warren; they came to our Tents and Cursed us. . . . [W]e asked them wether our Circumstances in their Opinion was not worse then theirs, Since they were amongst their friends and in a State of Freedom we were Prisoners and going to a Place where we had great reason to Expect never to return at; Least till the Conclusion of a Peace. . . .

"Journal of a Captive, 1745–1748," in Calder, ed.,
Colonial Captivities, *pp. 22–23.*

When I eat drank and lodged free cost with people who lived in Ease on the hard toil of their slaves I felt uneasy, and as my mind was inward to the Lord, I found, from place to place, this uneasiness return upon me at times through the whole visit [*through Virginia and Maryland*]. Where the masters bore a good share of burthen, and lived frugally, so that their Servants were well provided for, and their labour moderate, I felt more easy; but where they lived in a costly way, and laid heavy burthens on their slaves, my exercise was often great, and I frequently had conversations with them in private concerning it. Secondly, This trade of importing [*slaves*] from [their native country] being much Encouraged amongst them, and the white people and their children so generally living without much labour was frequently the subject of my serious thought, and I Saw in these Southern Provinces, so many Vices and Corruptions increased by this trade and way of life, that it appeared to me as a dark gloominess hanging over the land, and though now many willingly run into it, yet in the future the Consequence will be grievous to posterity.

Quaker John Woolman, 1746, Journal, p. 167.

When the well's dry, we know the Worth of Water.
It is wise not to seek a Secret, and Honest not to reveal it.
Lost time is never found again.
He that's secure is not safe.
Pardoning the Bad, is injuring the Good.
He is not well-bred, that cannot bear Ill-Breeding in others.
If *Passion* drives, let *Reason* hold the reigns.
Drink does not drown *Care,* but waters it, and makes it grow faster.
If your head is wax, don't walk in the sun.
Having been poor is no shame, but being ashamed of it, is.
9 Men in 10 are suicides.

Benjamin Franklin, sayings from his almanacs, 1746–49, Writings, *pp. 1237–54, passim.*

Your kind present of an electric tube, with directions for using it, has put several of us on making electrical experiments, in which we have observed some particular phaenomena that we look upon to be new. . . . [T]hough possibly, they may not be new to you, as among the numbers daily employed in those experi-ments on your side the water, 'tis probable some one or other has hit on the same observations. For my own part, I never was before engaged in any study that so totally engrossed my attention and my time as this has lately done; for what with making experiments when I can be alone, and repeating them to my Friends and Acquaintance, who, from the novelty of the thing, come continually in crouds to see them, I have, during some months past, had little leisure for any thing else.

Benjamin Franklin to Londoner Peter Collison, March 1747, in Labaree and Bell, eds., Mr. Franklin, *p. 5.*

Muschitoes, or *Musketoes,* a little venomous fly, so light that perhaps 50 of them, before they've fill'd their bellies, scarce weigh a grain, yet each has all the parts necessary to life, motion, digestion, generation, &c. as veins, arteries, muscles, &c. each has in his little body room for the five senses of hearing, feeling, smelling, tasting: How inconceivably small must their organs be! How inexpressibly fine the workmanship! And yet there are little animals discovered by the micro-scope, to whom a *Musketo* is an *Elephant!* In a scarce summer any citizen may provide Musketoes suffi-cient for his family, by leaving tubs of rain-water uncover'd in his yard for in such water they lay their eggs, which when hatch'd, become first little fish, afterwards put forth legs and leave the water, and fly into your windows.

Benjamin Franklin, Poor Richard's Almanack, *1748, in* Writings, *p. 1248.*

Philadelphia, April 14. 1748. Run away from Samuel Lippincott of Northampton in the country of Burling-ton, an Irish servant Maid, named Mary Muckleroy, of a middle Stature: Had on when she went away, a blue and white striped gown, of large and small stripes, cuffed with blue, a white muslin handkerchief, an old blue quilt, a new Persian black bonnet, a new pair of calf-skin shoes, a fine Holland cap, with a cambrick border, an old black short cloak lined with Bengal, blue worsted stockings, with white clocks, a very good fine shirt, and a very good white apron. She took with her a sorrel horse, about 14 hands high, shod before, and paces very well. It is supposed there is an Irishman gone with her. Whoever takes up and secures the said woman and horse, so that they may be had again, shall have Three Pounds reward, and reasonable charges. . . .

Pennsylvania Gazette, 1748, in Hart, ed., American History, *vol. 2, p. 301.*

For an Inward Fever make a Whey of Boyld Milk with a Large head of house Leek Boyld in it. pound or bruise the house Leek first & putt it into a pint of Boyling hot milk & Lett it Simmer a few minutes over the fire ... then Strain it & drink halfe a pint Every Night when you Go to Bed. I advised my Neighbour Vernon to Give this to her Eldest Son, who was Reduced that he Could Scarce Creep 200 foot with a stick to Support him & this quickly Coold & abated the Inward Fever & Cured him, tho' the Docter Could not help him & it has Cured Henry Hartleys wife & Severall others.

Notebook of Elizabeth Coates Paschall, ca. 1749, quoted in Gartrell, "Woman Healers," p. 15.

... the people [*German emigrants*] are packed densely, like herrings so to say, in the large sea-vessels. One person receives a place of scarcely 2 feet width and 6 feet length in the bedstead, while many a ship carries four to six hundred souls.... [D]uring the voyage there is on board these ships terrible misery, stench, fumes, horror, vomiting, many kinds of sea-sickness, fever, dysentery, headache, heat, constipation, boils, scurvy, cancer, mouth-rot, and the like, all of which come from old and sharply salted food and meat, also from very bad and foul water, so that many die miserably.... [T]he lice abound so frightfully, especially on sick people, that they can be scraped off the body. The misery reaches the climax when a gale rages for 2 or 3 nights and days,

so that every one believes that the ship will go to the bottom with all human beings on board. In such a visitation the people cry and pray most piteously.... [T]he sea rages and surges, so that the waves rise often like high mountains one above the other, and often tumble over the ship ... no one can either walk, or sit, or lie, and the closely packed people in the berths are thereby tumbled over each other, both the sick and the well....

No one can have an idea of the sufferings which women in confinement [*pregnant*] have to bear with their innocent children on board these ships. Few in this class escape with their lives; many a mother is cast into the water with her child as soon as she is dead.... Children from 1 to 7 years rarely survive the voyage.... I witnessed such misery in no less than 32 children in our ship, all of whom were thrown into the sea.

Gottlieb Mittelberger, 1750, Journey, pp. 18–23.

When some one has died ... the time appointed for the funeral is always indicated only to the 4 nearest neighbors; each of these in his turn notifies his own nearest neighbor. In this manner such an invitation to a funeral is made known more than fifty English miles around in 24 hours.... While the people are coming in, good cake cut into pieces is handed around on a large tin platter to those present; each person receives then in a goblet, a hot West India Rum punch, into which lemon, sugar and juniper berries are put, which give it a delicious taste. After this, hot and sweetened cider is served.... When the people have nearly all assembled, and the time for the burial has come, the dead body is carried to the general burial-place, or where that is too far away, the deceased is buried in his own field. The assembled people ride all in silence behind the coffin, and sometimes one can count from 100 to 500 persons on horseback. The coffins are all made of fine walnut wood and stained brown with a shining varnish. Well-to-do people have four finely-wrought brass handles attached to the coffin, by which the latter is held and carried to the grave. If the deceased person was a young man, the body is carried to the grave by four maidens, while that of a deceased maiden is carried by four unmarried men.

Gottlieb Mittelberger, 1750, Journey, pp. 57–58.

Müller House and Mill, Millbach, Pennsylvania, built 1752 by prosperous Pennsylvania Germans *(Unknown Photographer, Millbach House and Mill, Courtesy the Philadelphia Museum of Art)*

Seed Box, a globular Berry, a little flatten'd, with a Navel on its top composed of the Styles, containing 10 Cells, & each Cell, one rounish Seed, flattened & one edge much thinner than the other. The Stalk is thick &

smooth, of a red colour, branchd out alternately, from the corners of the Leaf Stalk, the Leaves stand single with long Foot Stalks, set alternately on the Stalk, & Branches they are large & smooth, ovally shaped, broadest near the bottom & a little sharpen'd, at the top more sharpen'd, the edges are intire, and they have a thick Rib along the midle, with fibers on each side of it, branching out towards the edges of the Leaf....

NB. The Phytolacca Root [*Pokeweed*] is very useful in the treatment of cancirs
some curious persons in England have endeavoured to propogate this plant by the Seed braigth from America, but could not produce any plant from the Seed.

The propagation from this plant is maket in America in the Dung of birds. For this reason it may be necessary, to give in Europe the berries to birds, & to plant the Seeds with the Dung of the fowls, through which they pass intire.

Jane Colden, "Flora of New York," ca. 1750,
Botanic Manuscript, *p. 83.*

The hatters of England have prevailed to obtain an Act in their own favor restraining that manufacture in America, in order to oblige the Americans to send their beaver to England to be manufactured, and purchase back the hats, loaded with the charges of a double transportation. In the same manner have a few nail-makers, and a still smaller body of steelmakers (perhaps there are not half a dozen of these in England), pre-vailed totally to forbid by an Act of Parliament the erection of slitting-mills, or steel furnaces, in America; that the Americans may be obliged to take all their nails for their buildings, and steel for their tools, from these artificers, under the same disadvantages.

Benjamin Franklin, ca. 1750, quoted in Barck and Lefler,
Colonial America, *p. 233.*

Besides the different sects of Christians, many Jews have settled in New York.... They have a synagogue, own their dwelling-houses, possess large country-seats and are allowed to keep shops in town. They have likewise several ships, which they load and send out with their own goods.... I was in their synagogue last evening for the first time, and to-day at noon I visited it again.... A young rabbi read the divine service, which was partly in Hebrew and partly in the Rabbinical dialect....

The streets [in New York] do not run so straight as those of Philadelphia, and sometimes are quite crooked; however, they are very spacious and well built, and most of them are paved, except in high places, where it has been found useless. In the chief streets there are trees planted, which in summer give them a fine appearance, and during the excessive heat at that time afford a cooling shade. I found it extremely pleasant to walk in the town, for it seemed like a garden....

Peter Kalm, November 1750, Peter Kalm's Travels,
vol. 1, pp. 129–32.

PART IV

A New Nation Takes Shape
1750 to 1776

10

The Realignment of North America
1750–1776

CONFLICT LOOMS BETWEEN THE FRENCH AND ENGLISH

Many North American issues were left unsettled by the Treaty of Aix-la-Chapelle (1748), which ended King George's War. Long-standing commercial and fishing rivalries continued between New France and the English colonies. The Great Lakes and the Hudson Bay–Lake Champlain fur-trading areas remained disputed. The boundaries of Acadia remained unclear. After signing the treaty, both France and England increased their efforts to maintain control of the northern seaboard. The French enlarged the garrison at Louisbourg and increased Catholic missionary work in the area. The British founded Halifax in 1749, transporting 1,500 German and Swiss Protestants to Nova Scotia in 1750–51 and establishing the first Protestant church in Canada. Migrants from New England soon followed; in 1752, one of them, John Bushell, established Canada's first newspaper, the *Halifax Gazette*. Within a decade Halifax was an important military base.

Despite the unresolved issues, however, the final North American war between the French and English did not begin in Canada. Instead, it ignited in the Ohio Valley—the triangle of land drained by the Ohio River (from western Pennsylvania and modern West Virginia) to the Mississippi River. The area was claimed by both New France and the English colonies—as well as by Native Americans. The French wanted to protect their Indian trade and their water route from Canada to the Mississippi. The English, on the other hand, possessed colonial charters that granted sea-to-sea land rights (although no one understood the actual distance that described). English traders were quickly expanding westward; the Ohio Land Company was eager to do business with land-hungry farmers. The Iroquois Confederacy considered the valley its hunting grounds and wanted to keep western Algonquian tribes out of the area. They also knew that they benefitted in trade negotiations when neither France nor England had a monopoly on the area. The Lenni Lenape and Shawnee, who were Iroquois tributaries, had recently been pushed into the area from the east. Mingo, Iroquois Confederacy members sometimes known as the western Seneca had also settled there, overseeing negotiations for all other tribes.

Captain Snow's map of the Ohio Valley, 1754 *(Library of Congress)*

A showdown was inevitable. It began with private rather than official acts. In spring 1752, the Ohio Land Company convened an Indian conference at Logstown. They obtained the approval of Iroquois Mingo chief Tanaghrisson to construct a trading house at the forks of the Ohio, where the Monongahela and Allegheny Rivers meet (modern Pittsburgh). In New France, as officials fretted but took no action, French-Ottawa trader Charles de Langlade independently gathered a force of French and western Indians, primarily Ottawa and Ojibway. On June 21, he led them from Detroit to Pickawillany, the large Miami trading town (present-day western Ohio). After leveling the town, they practiced ritual cannibalism on a trader and a Miami chief. The English failed to aid their Miami trading partners, who subsequently returned westward and reallied with the French. English trade in the area almost ceased.

Shortly thereafter official actions began. A new governor-general of Canada, Ange Duquesne de Menneville, marquis de Duquesne, arrived with instructions to oust the English from the Ohio Valley. In June 1753, he sent more than 2,000 French and Indians to construct a string of four forts from Lake Erie to the forks of the Ohio. The expedition was overworked and ill-supplied, probably due to profiteering by the venal intendant, François Bigot; more than 400 men died en route. Nevertheless, an immediate drop in English trade occurred in western Pennsylvania. British officials soon authorized Virginia governor Robert Dinwiddie, an investor in the Ohio Company, to demand that the French depart the Ohio Valley. In November 1753, Dinwiddie commissioned 21-year-old George Washington to carry the message. Washington and his small party were received courteously by the French at Fort Le Boeuf (in the northwest corner of modern Pennsylvania). They were informed, however, that the French intended to remain and to continue constructing forts.

Dinwiddie responded by dispatching workmen to the forks to build a fort before the French arrived. In March, he dispatched troops led by Washington to protect them. Before Washington reached the forks, however, the French arrived. Under the command of Pierre de Contrecoeur, they drove the English workers out and began building Fort Duquesne. Washington, alerted by Chief Tanaghrisson, met a small party of French soldiers near Great Meadows (southwestern Pennsylvania). On May 28, 1754, English and Indian forces killed 10 French soldiers, including their leader, Coulon de Jumonville. In the following weeks, while Washington parleyed with the Lenape and Shawnee, who refused to join him, his militia built the realistically named but ill-constructed Fort Necessity. There, on July 3, Washington's militia of about 150 men was attacked by 900 French and Indians. After nine hours, Washington surrendered Fort Necessity in what turned out to be the first battle of the French and Indian War.

In England, imperial officials had become concerned about French incursions as well as relations with the Iroquois. They also recognized that military defense was impeded by the colonies' failure to cooperate. The Board of Trade ordered colonial governors to a meeting in Albany. (By the time it convened in June 1754, Washington was already in Pennsylvania.) At Albany, delegates first heard the grievances of 150 Iroquois chiefs, who refused to join an alliance against the French because they were disgruntled at English military ineffectiveness. The Albany delegation then turned to the issue of intercolonial military cooperation. Pennsylvania representative Benjamin Franklin and others drafted a proposal called the Albany Plan of Union. It provided for an elected intercolonial assembly, with power to levy taxes for a common defense. Delegates approved the plan, but it was subsequently rejected by every colonial assembly as well as by English officials. The colonies saw themselves as separate and independent provinces of the greater British nation. Even Washington's recent defeat could not move them to voluntary mutual cooperation.

THE FRENCH AND INDIAN WAR

Despite the lack of colonial cooperation, British authorities continued planning a military campaign to stop the French advance in North America. In April 1755, General Edward Braddock arrived in Virginia with two British regiments. The French sent 3,000 French soldiers and 27 warships to Canada. Braddock, Washington, and the regiments set out for Fort Duquesne, hacking a road through mountainous forests to transport heavy cannon, a supply train, and a herd of cattle. On July 9, about eight miles from Fort Duquesne, they were ambushed by Contrecoeur's French and Indian forces. The traditionally trained British troops were badly defeated by the French, who employed Indian wilderness or guerrilla warfare techniques. Braddock (who had five horses shot from beneath him) was mortally wounded, as were 900 of his men. Impressed by the French victory at the Battle of the Wilderness, the Lenape, Shawnee, and Mingo allied with England's enemy.

Elsewhere, the war also went badly for the English. The back country of Pennsylvania, Maryland, and Virginia suffered continuing Indian raids. In Nova Scotia, Micmac continued to harass English settlers. The French recruited

Acadians, or French neutrals who lived under British rule. When Colonel Robert Monckton's troops captured Fort Beauséjour in June 1755, 300 Acadians were found in the enemy forces. Although the Acts of Capitulation required their pardon, the British ordered the expulsion of all Acadians from the area.

War was not formally declared in Europe until May 1756, where it was called the Seven Years' War and eventually spread to colonies in India, Africa, the Philippines, and the West Indies. In Canada, Louis-Joseph, the marquis de Montcalm, arrived in 1756 as the new military commander. Montcalm chose to focus on the protection of Quebec, Montreal, and the St. Lawrence Valley. The traditionally trained Montcalm rarely saw eye-to-eye with the new governor-general Philipe de Rigaud, the marquis de Vaudreuil, who was a Canadien, son of a former governor-general, and past governor of French Louisiana. Nonetheless, by 1757 the French were clearly winning the war. In the north, French forces, relying on wilderness warfare techniques, captured Fort Oswego (the English port of entry to the Great Lakes) and Fort William Henry (safeguarding the route to Lake Champlain). To the south, Governor Louis Billouart de Kerlérec of French Louisiana employed personal diplomacy to maintain French alliances with the Creek and Choctaw. In 1759, partly at his instigation, the Cherokee attacked South Carolina, beginning hostilities that lasted until 1761.

In Europe, early battles also went badly for the British. Late in 1757, William Pitt became secretary of state and prime minister. Pitt assumed control of the war, developing new strategies for all fronts. In North America, he laid plans to conquer New France. He encouraged the colonies—several of which had experienced serious draft resistance riots in 1756—to raise both funds and troops. He reinforced the Navigation Acts to prevent illicit colonial trade with New France. Finally, he sent new military leaders and instructed them to take the offensive.

Under Pitt's leadership, the tide began to turn. In Acadia, General Jeffrey Amherst besieged Louisbourg with a fleet of 150 warships, obtaining its surrender in July 26, 1758. In the Ohio Valley, General John Forbes cut a road across Pennsylvania to Fort Duquesne. He captured it in November (although the French destroyed the structure before surrendering) and renamed the site Fort Pitt. The Iroquois, somewhat mollified, met at Easton and convinced the Lenape to end their alliance with the French. In 1759, the English captured Forts Carillon (Ticonderoga), St. Frederic (Crown Point), and Niagara in upper New York.

In June 1759, British forces gathered at Louisbourg and sailed up the St. Lawrence, led by General James Wolfe. After keeping the city of Quebec under constant bombardment for three months, Wolfe landed his troops in September, and they scaled the cliffs under cover of night. On September 13, they attacked Quebec from the Plains of Abraham, an undefended plateau above the city. In a battle lasting about 15 minutes, the British were victorious, though both Wolfe and Montcalm lost their lives. On September 17, the city officially surrendered. The fall of Quebec determined the outcome of the war, although fighting continued for two more years. Montreal, the last important French stronghold, surrendered to Amherst on September 8, 1760. By the end of 1761, Detroit and other French posts in the west had surrendered. In September 1762, the last encounter between French and British troops occurred in Acadia.

The treaty ending the war, signed in Paris on February 10, 1763, redrew the map of North America. France surrendered Canada, including Acadia and St. John's and Cape Breton Islands to Britain. (Some British officials did not want to accept Canada, foreseeing that the removal of the French would greatly increase the power of the thirteen colonies to the south.) France also ceded all Louisiana territory east of the Mississippi River to the English, excepting the city of New Orleans. France ceded New Orleans and all of Louisiana territory west of the Mississippi to Spain. Spain, which had fought as an ally of France, ceded Florida to the English. Both Britain and Spain received navigational rights on the Mississippi River.

Although France retained several small islands and fishing rights in Newfoundland, the French empire in North America was at an end. After 1763, Spain was England's only rival in North America.

THE FATE OF THE ACADIANS

In 1755, the peaceful farming and fishing population of French Acadians numbered between 10 and 12 thousand. Neutral since 1710, they consistently refused to take the oath of allegiance to Britain, required of all other colonial subjects. After Acadians were discovered at Fort Beauséjour in June, Colonel Charles Lawrence, the acting governor of Nova Scotia, convened Acadian representatives and demanded that they take the loyalty oath. When they refused, Lawrence jailed them. New representatives were convened. They also refused the oath, unless Acadians were exempted from bearing arms. To British military officers, all Acadians—who viewed themselves as blameless and unthreatening—were potential traitors. In July, the Council of Nova Scotia unanimously passed an act of deportation. Merchant ships in the colony's harbors were immediately hired and supplied. Although some English officials were reluctant, *le grand dérangement,* or immediate expulsion, from Acadia—began in August.

Acadians were forced from their homes by soldiers with only the belongings they could carry and put on ships bound for various British colonies elsewhere. At least one-quarter died before reaching their destination. About 7,000 had been deported by the end of 1756, and as many as 3,000 more before deportation officially ended in 1762. About 1,500 fled to Ile St. Jean (St. John's), the St. Lawrence Valley, and the French islands of Miquelon and St. Pierre off Newfoundland. Many extended families, central to the Acadian social order, were separated forever. Most emptied villages were burned.

Deportees were deposited in almost every major English seaport from New England to Georgia. No colony was eager to receive them, suspicious of their Catholicism and determination to preserve their cultural identity. New England and Pennsylvania tried to parcel them out to towns. In Maryland, philanthropists tried to place them in private homes. Virginia refused to accept them; the burgesses paid to transport them to other British ports, which sent them on to France. In South Carolina and Georgia, many died in the seasoning year. Most who survived headed west to Louisiana or north to reclaim their homes.

In 1764, about 3,000 Acadians returned to Nova Scotia with British permission. Returnees almost always found their fertile, dyked farmlands had been claimed by new, English-speaking settlers; they were forced to move on to unclaimed areas. In 1765, Acadians living in France were permitted to return to

North America. Most went to Louisiana, their passage paid by the Spanish crown. As many as 3,000 Acadians settled there permanently, where their descendants shorted "Acadian" to "Cajun."

CANADA UNDER BRITISH RULE

After the Treaty of Paris in 1763, the British holdings in North America included the 13 colonies; Florida; Hudson's Bay, or Rupert's Land; Acadia, including Nova Scotia, modern New Brunswick, Cape Breton, and St. John's (modern Prince Edward) Islands; and Newfoundland, including Labrador and the Magdalen and Anticosti Islands. It also included New France, now renamed the Province of Quebec, whose citizens had an entirely different language, culture, and religious tradition. With these and holdings elsewhere in the world, the British Empire had become a dominant power.

The new British Canada had a population of less than 100,000, exclusive of Native Americans. Over half lived in Quebec, including 3,500 slaves, both Africans and *panis,* or Indians. Some slaves and a few free blacks lived throughout the eastern seaboard settlements as well. The Métis, a distinct people of mixed Indian and French ancestry, probably numbered 2,000. British Canada was also home to at least 200,000 independent indigenous people, members of at least five significantly different culture groups. To the west and north of the Great Lakes, Native Americans still lived traditionally, although some had limited contact with Europeans. In contrast, tribes in the St. Lawrence and Great Lakes areas, whose numbers had been greatly reduced by epidemic disease, were economically interdependent with white civilization.

Rupert's Land remained relatively unexplored; the only European settlements there were trading bases of the Hudson's Bay Company. In Newfoundland, the year-round population was about 10,000, although it doubled in the summer. Official colonization and governmental institutions were still restricted due to pressure from commercial fishing interests, and lawlessness was widespread. Settlers victimized the native Beothuk without restraint. About 9,000 people lived in Acadia. In 1758, the first representative government and assembly in Canada was established in Nova Scotia. Throughout the 1760s, many settlers from New England arrived in the maritime provinces, usually migrating in groups. After 1764, returning Acadians began resettling in modern New Brunswick. In 1767, St. John's was divided into large land grants for British military officials and other Englishmen, on the condition that they send settlers. Few did, but 2,000 Ulster Scots (called Scotch-Irish in America) and Scots emigrated to St. John's and Cape Breton Islands. In 1769, St. John's became a separate colony, and in 1773 representative government was established there. On Cape Breton, the fort at Louisbourg was dismantled and the town fell into decay. Halifax, with a population of about 3,000, replaced it as the most important port north of New England.

On September 20, 1760, three years before the Treaty of Paris was signed, the province of Quebec was placed under British military rule. Quebec had suffered greatly in the war. More than 2,000 of the French elite had returned to France, and the bishop of Quebec had died shortly before the surrender. Under British general Jeffery Amherst, however, the interim military administration of the colony was reasonably successful. Although the terms of surrender did not guarantee the continuance of French institutions, Amherst avoided major changes. Neither property rights nor free exercise of religion was disrupted.

Principles of government for the new British Province of Quebec were finally set out in the Proclamation of 1763, announced by George III on October 7. Property rights and freedom of worship were officially guaranteed, although Catholics were forbidden by British law from holding office. In August 1764, civil government was officially established. General James Murray was appointed governor by the Crown; he was to be assisted by a council until an elected assembly could be established. Unfortunately, under British law only the tiny minority of Protestants in the colony was eligible to be council members, legislators, or justices of the peace. Murray wisely improvised, retaining some elements of French civil law, allowing Catholics to serve as jurors, and convincing the British government to allow the appointment of a new Catholic bishop, Jean Briand, in 1766.

The Treaty of Paris, like Vaudreuil's articles of capitulation, contained a clause protecting slavery in New France and guaranteeing that slave owners could instruct their slaves as Catholics. Although neither the Canadian clergy nor citizens objected to the institution of slavery, it did not expand and the French Code Noir had never been adopted.[1] Most slaves were domestic servants. Nonetheless, records indicate that many attempted to escape, blacks far more often than panis.

Ambitious English merchants and traders soon migrated to Quebec and Montreal. Because of their English contacts, they quickly dominated commerce. British officials hoped that other aspects of life in the former New France could be transformed in a similar manner by large-scale migration from other English colonies. They immediately ended the French prohibition on both Protestant and Jewish immigration to Quebec; the first Jews to arrive accompanied the British army in 1760. Officials also attempted to redirect restless American colonists to head north by prohibiting settlement west of the Alleghenies in 1763. This prohibition proved unenforceable, however, and failed to achieve its

A view of Montreal, 1762 *(New York Public Library, Phelps Stokes Collection Before 1760 B-73, D. 111, Print Collection, Miriam and Ira D. Wallach Division of Art, Prints, and Photographs, Astor, Lenox, and Tilden Foundations)*

intended effect. At the same time, the birth rate of French Catholic Canada rose to the highest of any colonial people of European origin. By the end of the 1770s, the French-speaking population had increased to more than 90,000. Nonetheless, many vacated Quebec seigneuries were granted to Englishmen.

THE QUEBEC ACT AND AMERICAN REBELLION

The French-Canadian clergy and elite were generally pleased with Governor Murray's accommodations to their traditional, authoritarian, and aristocratic culture. English visitors to the new British province romanticized its order and stability. English Canadian merchants, however, complained constantly. Quebec soon experienced the same clash of values that had occurred earlier in Massachusetts between the merchants and the Puritan elite. Merchants viewed Murray as an aristocrat who retarded the growth of the economy and blocked representative government. Due to their pressure, he was replaced by Sir Guy Carleton in June 1766. However, Carleton also proved to be a traditionalist, one who suspected merchants of supporting the growing colonial rebellion to the south. On the other hand, he viewed the French elite and the province's deferential habitants as dedicated royalists, and he believed they would transfer their allegiance to the British monarchy if the British respected their culture.

Partly on Carleton's advice, in 1774 the British government replaced the Proclamation of 1763 with the Quebec Act. This act established a system of government for Quebec unique among British colonies. It officially ended the attempt to establish representative government in the province and reinstituted French civil law, although English criminal law and its guarantees for the accused were retained. The Quebec Act also granted Catholics more rights and opened up membership in the governor's council. The right of the Catholic Church to collect tithes and the traditional powers of seigneurs were also legally reinstituted.

From the perspective of the American colonies to the south, the Quebec Act had one other provision that was far more important: Quebec province was given governmental authority over the Ohio Valley. Supposedly, the provision was intended to facilitate the fur trade. American colonists, however, viewed Quebec's enlargement with alarm. It extended an unrepresentative and authoritarian government into territory they believed was theirs and wanted to settle. American colonists classified the Quebec Act with the so-called British Intolerable Acts that directly preceded the American Revolution.

By 1775, American revolutionary literature was circulating widely in Quebec province. Most ordinary Canadians, however, were indifferent to the issues that inflamed Americans and unwilling to jeopardize their special religious and political accommodations. Even the English merchants, who disliked the Quebec Act, were reluctant to jeopardize their economic success within the British empire. Because so few Canadians supported the Revolutionary cause, Americans feared that Quebec would be used as a base for British military operations. In fall 1775, American troops attacked the province, capturing Montreal in November and invading Quebec on December 31. Governor Carleton quickly learned that the habitants did not intend to fight for the British Crown any more than they intended to join the American rebels. They refused to join the militia even when urged by priests, seigneurs, and officials; the few who did support the British were called *vendus,* or sellouts. The Americans were not forced to retreat until May 1776, when 10,000 British troops arrived in Canada.

Even in Nova Scotia, support for the American cause was scant, despite the close ties many settlers had to New England. Few were affected by the tax acts that enraged the Americans and fewer still were interested in the Ohio Valley. Many were economically dependent on the British garrison and naval base of Halifax. Ordinary Nova Scotians reacted like their counterparts in Quebec. "Neutral Yankees," like repatriated Acadians and local Indians, avoided joining either the British imperial cause or the Revolution and continued to trade with both sides whenever possible.

SPANISH FLORIDA BECOMES BRITISH

Prior to 1763, Spanish Florida continued to struggle, remaining dependent on illicit trade with the French and English. Indian relations were not well managed, and the fear of attack was constant. To increase the protection of St. Augustine, Governor Fulgencio García de Solís reestablished Fort Mose north of the city in 1752. Former residents of the free black settlement, who now lived in St. Augustine, moved back to the frontier with great reluctance. On orders from the Spanish Crown, Fort Mose continued to welcome escaped slaves from the English colonies. In 1759, Spanish officials sent Father Juan Joseph de Solana to investigate conditions in Florida. He reported many problems, and in 1762 officials sent a new governor, Melchor Feliú, with instructions to solve them. Instead, a year later, Feliú found himself presiding over the colony's evacuation.

Spanish Florida had survived 200 years of neglect, poverty, and military attacks. In 1763, it finally fell to the English with one stroke of a European diplomatic pen. The Treaty of Paris ended Florida's First Spanish Period and ushered in two decades of British rule (in 1783 the colony was returned for a time to Spanish control). By terms of the treaty, the Florida colony was extended west to the Mississippi River, encompassing part of modern Alabama, Mississippi, and Louisiana. It included the French settlements of Mobile (with a population of about 350), Biloxi, and Natchez. On October 7, 1763, the English split Florida into two colonies, divided by the Apalachicola River. West Florida reached north to the 32nd parallel; its capital was Pensacola. The northern border of East

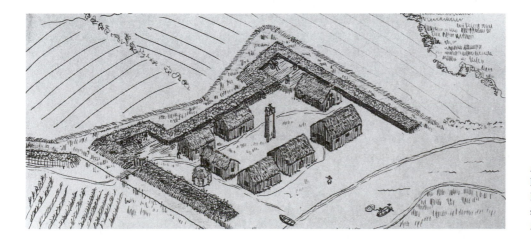

A modern drawing based on historical research of Fort Mose, Florida, 1760, the first all-black settlement *(Courtesy St. Augustine Historical Society)*

Florida extended from the confluence of the Chattahoochee and Flint Rivers to the St. Marys (the modern boundary between Florida and Georgia). The capital of East Florida was St. Augustine.

The Treaty of Paris permitted Spanish residents to remain in Florida, retain their property, and practice Catholicism freely. Only a few stayed, however, since most were dependent on the situado, or Spanish government subsidy. Almost the entire East Florida population of 3,046 left for Cuba, including whites, blacks, and Christian Indians; King Charles III of Spain provided free transportation and resettlement subsidies. The Franciscans left as well, and most church-related structures became English public buildings. Unsold private property was left in the hands of Jesse Fish, a Florida resident and agent of the Walton Exporting Company of New York. In West Florida, almost all of the 800 residents evacuated to Vera Cruz, Mexico, in September 1763. English entrepreneur James Noble purchased most of their property. He also purchased 1 million acres from the Yamasee, later disallowed by the British Crown.

The British integrated the Florida colonies into their empire, introducing changes in government, Indian relations, land policies, and economic policies. In East Florida, the first British governor was James Grant, who arrived in August 1764 and served until 1774. A South Carolinian of Scottish descent, Grant established a colonial council but never called an assembly, hoping to avoid the political turmoil occurring in the 13 older colonies. In West Florida, the first British governor was George Johnstone. In November 1766, he called the first Florida assembly. Johnstone disliked his post, however, and had already abandoned the colony when he was recalled in February 1767. His replacement, Montfort Browne, concentrated primarily on efforts to establish his own proprietary colony and was replaced by Peter Chester in 1770.

East Florida governor James Grant had experience in Indian diplomacy. He and Indian Commissioner John Stuart immediately worked to establish good relations with local tribes, most of whom were former French allies. They held numerous conferences and distributed gifts widely. Despite these efforts, Indian relations remained troubled throughout the British period for reasons that were, by now, standard. Colonists continually confiscated land, and traders engaged in unfair practices, often plying Indians with rum in order to obtain their goods for little or nothing in exchange. In an attempt to address Indian complaints, Florida officials licensed traders. Although complaints continued, negotiators managed to prevent Florida Indians from supporting the American Revolution.

Anxious to attract settlers to Florida, British officials offered two types of land grants. Privy Council grants of up to 20,000 acres were available for wealthy entrepreneurs if they settled one white Protestant per 100 acres. These grants were popular in England; 242 were made in East Florida prior to 1776. Only 22 were actually settled, however; most were held for speculation and thus actually discouraged settlement. A second type of land grant was available to families. Head rights were 100 acres for the family head and 50 acres for each additional person, white or black. With this offer, 576 family grants were made. Wealthy settlers from the Carolinas brought slaves and established large plantations along the St. Johns River. In 1765, Denys Rolle imported debtors, vagrants, prostitutes, and other unfortunates from Britain to found Rollestown on the St. Johns. In the late 1760s, Dr. Andrew Turnbull and other wealthy Englishmen founded a settlement in East Florida named New Smyrna. The Board of Trade encouraged the project, hoping for the establishment of Mediterranean agriculture and silk culture. Turnbull purchased black slaves from Georgia and Carolina to prepare the land. He then recruited 200 Greeks, 100 Italians (although he could find no silk growers), and more than 1,000 Spanish-speaking Catholics from Minorca, who brought their own priest. Unfortunately, food supplies were inadequate, disease swept the colony, and colonists quickly came to resent the plantation overseers. By 1773, almost 900 New Smyrna settlers had died. The colony ceased to exist, although the surviving settlers remained in Florida.

Unlike England's other North American colonies, Florida's civil and military establishment was supported by the crown, as it had been by the Spanish. Four regular British regiments were stationed there; St. Augustine became a garrison town and soon acquired a reputation for disorder and debauchery. Anglican ministers and schoolmasters were sent by the Society for the Propagation of the Gospel, but their influence was never great. Although British Florida was not self-supporting, East Florida exported oranges and West Florida exported skins, along with lumber products, naval stores, and some crops. West Floridians also engaged in profitable if illicit trade in Spanish-controlled New Orleans.

By 1776, the combined white and black population of Florida was about 6,000. In that same year, the estimated Indian population in West Florida alone was more than 26,000. In the two Floridas the Seminole alone numbered about 15,000. The Seminole (a word meaning "wild ones" or "runaways") were former Creek Confederacy members who incorporated remnants of several other southern tribes, moving into depopulated areas of Florida. By the early 1770s, they had established nine flourishing agricultural and ranching towns in the central Florida grasslands. Near to these towns, escaped black slaves began to form communities, which the Seminole accepted and protected as tributaries. After the Revolutionary War began, slave escapes became more common, and the so-called Black Seminole communities grew quickly—as did Florida's population of whites and still-enslaved blacks. Because the Floridas did not join the Revolution, they became a refuge for southern Loyalists, who brought as many of their slaves as they could.

THE LAST YEARS OF FRENCH LOUISIANA

After 1750, Louisiana was again threatened by Chickasaw hostilities, a recurring problem throughout the previous decade. In 1752, when raids occurred near New Orleans, Louisiana governor Philippe Vaudreuil mobilized French troops and compelled a formal surrender. Soon after, Vaudreuil requested reassignment to his native Canada, where the office of governor-general was vacant. He served as the last governor of New France, forced to surrender it to the British at the end of the French and Indian war.

In February 1753, Louis Billouart, chevalier de Kerlérec, arrived in New Orleans as the new governor of Louisiana. Although no fighting occurred in Louisiana during the French and Indian War, the next decade was economically difficult for the colony. Trade was cut off with France and the island colonies; no supplies, immigrants, or slaves arrived, although Kerlérec did settle Louisiana's first Acadians. Within the colony, government officials once again began quarreling. In addition, the Capuchins (who oversaw the southern part of the colony) struggled for power with the Jesuits (who oversaw northern territories). The Capuchins prevailed in 1764 when the Jesuits left Louisiana.

French Louisiana had many similarities to English colonies in which slavery was very important, and its white citizens exhibited similar social mores. Black slaves remained the majority of the population, and the existence of black slavery united whites as it did in the southernmost English colonies. Although the last Louisiana slave rebellion occurred in 1731, in 1751 a systematic black code was passed by the Superior Council. The Regulations of 1751 forbade slaves to hold social gatherings or to leave home after sundown. More significantly, the regulations authorized all whites actively to police blacks, giving them power to stop, question, and in certain circumstances beat or shoot blacks in situations they considered suspicious. The regulations also attempted to curtail the considerable independent economic activity of slaves, although with little success.

Like slaves in the English colonies, Louisiana slaves were divided by ethnicity. The majority in the mid–18th century, however, were of Bambara descent (from the upper Senegal River in Senegambia), a group known for its military tradition. Under both the French and the Spanish, Louisiana slaves served in militia units. The colony itself held a large number of slaves, at the crown's expense, on what was known as the King's Plantation. These slaves, sometimes trained in special skills, provided labor for various public works. The Catholic Church and three of its religious orders (Jesuit, Capuchin, and Ursuline) were also large slaveholders. In addition, by the mid-1760s, about 200 free blacks lived in the colony; free blacks could hold property, make contracts, and exercise other rights. A few Indians were permanent slaves as well, although most Indian captives were traded to the West Indies.

Parlange Plantation, Pointe Coupée Parish, Louisiana, built ca. 1750 in the French colonial style *(Historical American Building Survey)*

After 1731, the arrival of new slaves virtually ceased for 40 years. Louisiana planters were forced to improve living conditions and lessen workloads to make it easier for slaves to form families and give birth to children. By the end of the French period, most blacks were native-born. A distinct culture began to form, fusing African, Caribbean, French, and even some Native American traditions. A distinctive African-influenced French language developed. Alternative religious rites with African and Caribbean roots developed and were practiced alongside Catholicism, much to the disapproval of church officials.

Catholicism was the established religion in Louisiana, although by 1750 about 10 percent of the population was probably Protestant. After 1750, some Jews also arrived. Only Catholics could worship publically, however, and people of other faiths could marry only if they embraced Catholic rites. Because white women remained scarce in the colony, girls often married very early in their teenage years. In many other ways, women's positions and roles were similar to those in the English colonies. Women occasionally engaged in commercial activities, often upon the death of a spouse. Courts protected them from egregious spousal abuse and in a few cases ordered separate maintenance, although divorce was impossible. French-based law, however, recognized community property—at marriage all property of both spouses was joined—and widows were always entitled to one-half of their husband's estate.[2]

FRENCH LOUISIANA BECOMES A SPANISH COLONY

On November 3, 1762, France ceded Louisiana to its ally Spain by the secret Treaty of Fontainebleau. The change was confirmed by the Treaty of Paris a year later. News of the Spanish takeover did not reach the colony, however, until October 1764. Residents reacted with dismay, fear, and outright protest. In New Orleans, a large group of residents assembled and sent leading citizens to France to plead for reconsideration; King Louis XV did not grant them an audience. The Spanish, however, showed little eagerness to take over their new colony. The first Spanish governor did not arrive until 1766 and did not assume full control until August 1767. In the interim, the French flag continued to fly, everyday affairs proceeded more or less as usual—and the colonists' independence grew. When French governor Jean-Jacques d'Abbadie died in February 1765, Charles Philippe Aubry, the military commander of the colony, took control, and the Superior Council enlarged its proper functions.

In July 1765, King Charles III of Spain appointed Antonio de Ulloa to be the first Spanish governor of Louisiana. A renowned scientist and respected naval officer, Ulloa was fluent in French but unfortunately had few political instincts and little interest in protocol. His intellectualism was unappreciated by the French colonists, and his preference for a modest life was incomprehensible. He arrived March 5, 1766, at the Balize, a port outpost at the mouth of the Mississippi River, with an unimpressive contingent of fewer than 100 soldiers. After a brief inspection tour of the province, he returned to the Balize to live. There, on January 20, 1767, he finally took official possession of Louisiana for Spain. The king had instructed Ulloa to make as few changes as possible. He therefore permitted the French flag to continue flying and entered into an unusual agreement with military commander Aubry to share governance of the colony.

Ulloa had to cope with several difficulties, including an inadequate budget. His attempts to enforce Spanish trade regulations in 1766–67 seriously threatened Louisiana's powerful commercial community. Spanish regulations limited legal trade to Spanish goods, ships, and a very few designated ports. Louisiana merchants, however, had well-developed trade networks in France and other French colonies; they were also accustomed to conducting illicit trade with the nearby British. When Ulloa forbade the importation even of French wines, outraged citizens petitioned the Superior Council, although unsuccessfully.

Ulloa did improve Indian relations and establish good relations with the governor of British West Florida. But public opposition to the governor grew. In late October 1768, open rebellion occurred when French, Acadian, and German colonists gathered in New Orleans. More than 560 signed a petition protesting Ulloa's policies, and the Superior Council drew up formal charges of maladministration. The council remained in session throughout the night, and the crowd grew. The Superior Council ordered the governor to leave the colony. Ulloa took refuge on a French ship with his family, advisers, and priests. They cast off for Cuba in early November; some believe that a mob cut the mooring cables.

The Superior Council ruled the colony in a kind of default independence for almost a year, during which time they sought not self-government but the reestablishment of French royal control. They sent a delegation to Paris, but the French crown reaffirmed Spanish sovereignty—and instructed military commander Aubry to provide the names of all those involved in the Insurrection of 1768. Meanwhile, Ulloa dispatched his own report.

King Charles III soon ordered a large Spanish military detachment to reestablish control in Louisiana. They were led by General Alejandro O'Reilly, an Irishman who had distinguished himself in the military service of Spain. O'Reilly's armada arrived from Cuba on August 28, 1769. It numbered more than 2,000 Spanish soldiers in 24 ships; the total population of New Orleans at the time was about 3,000. Eventually, O'Reilly made a dramatic entrance into New Orleans, preceded by a grand military parade. He ceremoniously lowered the French flag and raised the Spanish, then proceeded to the Church of St. Louis for a mass. Soon after the formalities ended, he began his investigation of the insurrection. Within two days, the decisive general had arrested 13 leaders of the insurrection, without notice, and then proclaimed amnesty to all other participants. Three days later, citizens throughout the province were required to swear an oath of loyalty to Spain. The 13 accused, who included leading citizens and a nephew of former governor Jean-Baptiste Le Moyne, sieur de Bienville, were charged with treason and ordered to stand trial. The trials were conducted under Spanish principles, with no jury and O'Reilly himself as judge. On October 24, he pardoned one man, a printer who had merely published the orders of the Superior Council. He sentenced six to prison in Cuba and the remaining six to death (although one had already died in custody). On October 25, they were executed by a military firing squad. All 12 had their extensive property confiscated and their families turned out penniless. Shocked by the harshness of the punishments, the citizens of Louisiana nicknamed the general "Bloody O'Reilly."

O'Reilly was a man of great administrative talent and astonishing energy. He remained in Louisiana only seven months but firmly established Spanish control, reorganizing the militia and strengthening fortifications throughout the colony. He also revamped the judiciary and the civil government, instituted a new legal code based on the Spanish Law of the Indies, and made Castilian Spanish the official language of the government. In New Orleans, he established the Spanish institution of the *cabildo* (town council) in place of the French Superior Council, to make municipal regulations and serve as a court of law. He divided the rest of the huge Louisiana territory into districts, each under a commandant who served as civil, judicial, and military leader. The districts were divided into smaller areas supervised by a *syndic* (comparable to the English justice of the peace). O'Reilly appointed surveyors to determine property boundaries and establish clear land titles, then issued a new ordinance offering grants to encourage colonization. He created 21 ecclesiastical parishes and had them placed under the bishop of Santiago de Cuba instead of the bishop of Quebec. He also attempted to lessen the trade disruptions caused by Spanish regulations. He met with powerful Indian chiefs, entertaining them lavishly, and licensed French traders, using them for Indian diplomacy and control. O'Reilly also ordered a census of the province. It counted more than 13,538 people, at least half of whom were slaves. The New Orleans population was 3,190, including 1,225 slaves and 100 free persons of color.

In March 1770, O'Reilly returned to Cuba with his troops and was succeeded by Governor Luís de Unzaga y Amezaga. Unzaga won the goodwill of the French when he turned a blind eye to illicit trade with British West Florida. Because the Peace of Paris allowed British ships to dock on the Mississippi River, ships were used as floating trading posts where merchandise was bought and sold. Most were docked near Bayou Manchac, and "going to Manchac" became a stock phrase for illicit trade.

After 1770, Louisiana entered a period of great population growth and prosperity, partially subsidized and encouraged by the Spanish Crown. The colony was never truly Hispanicized, however, and few Spanish settlers arrived. Spanish officials often married French wives and were absorbed into the French elite. French Acadians continued to arrive, eventually spreading out both below and above New Orleans. The slave trade resumed, although large numbers of Africans did not arrive prior to 1776. The Spanish also encouraged the growth of a free black population, from which they hoped to obtain volunteers for the militia. More manumissions occurred in the first decade of Spanish rule than in the entire French period; the majority, however, were women and children, over three-quarters of mixed race. As in all Spanish colonies, Catholicism was the established religion, and freedom of conscience did not exist. Spain never attempted large-scale missionary work among the Indians of Louisiana, however, as it did in the Southwest.

While Spain was in the process of subduing Louisiana, events in the English colonies were leading to the American Revolution. The Spanish Crown did not officially favor colonial rebellion but welcomed a war that might weaken England. Soon after the opening battles, the Spanish secretly began to support the rebels. In 1776, Captain George Gibson of Virginia visited Unzaga with a letter from General Charles Lee requesting a supply route up the Mississippi and Ohio Rivers to Fort Pitt. The supply route was established with the assistance of American trader Oliver Pollock (who had emigrated from northern Ireland to Pennsylvania, then set up businesses in Havana and later New Orleans). Through the port of New Orleans, Spain supplied the rebels with arms, uniforms, medicine, and other goods.

THE UPPER MISSISSIPPI AND THE FOUNDING OF ST. LOUIS

The vast majority of colonists in the French province of Louisiana lived on the lower Mississippi River, between Pointe Coupée and New Orleans. The extensive Louisiana territory, however, also included land to the east and west of the Mississippi as far north as the Great Lakes. When the Peace of Paris was signed in 1763, small French forts and trading settlements dotted the Mississippi and Missouri Rivers, reaching to the lower Red River (modern North Dakota). The Illinois District east of the Mississippi was also attached to Louisiana. Since 1700, French Jesuits had worked in the upper Mississippi and Illinois District, which were also frequented by French trappers. Small settlements had grown around missions to the Kaskaskia and Cahokia Indians of the Illinois confederation on the east bank of the Mississippi across from modern St. Louis. Nearby, French settlers built Prairie de Roche and Fort Chartres, also on the east bank. On the Mississippi's west bank, Ste. Genevieve was founded in 1735, and nearby lead mines were worked by black slaves.

In 1763, before Louisiana learned of the Treaty of Paris, Gilbert Antoine Maxent was granted the monopoly for Indian trade on the Missouri River and the west bank of the Mississippi. Maxent, a New Orleans merchant, commissioned Pierre Liguest Laclède to establish a post in the area. Laclède, the younger son of an old French family, packed his 200-book library and headed to the Missouri wilderness. In December 1763, he and his 13-year-old clerk and assistant, Auguste Chouteau, selected a promising site near the mouth of the Missouri. Workmen began constructing a planned settlement, which included an impressive stone building to serve as company headquarters. In April 1764, Laclède named the site St. Louis, in honor of French King Louis XV's patron saint.

By a stroke of timing fortunate for Laclède, nearby French settlers soon learned that all land east of the Mississippi had been ceded to Britain. By the end of 1764, many French families in east-bank settlements moved to Laclède's St. Louis. Late in 1765, when the new British commander took over Fort Chartres, the small remaining French garrison relocated to St. Louis as well. The new town prospered immediately and quickly became the center of trade in the region. Each spring, Indians from the upper Mississippi and Missouri valleys arrived with furs. The settlement had little agriculture, however, and was nicknamed Paincourt—"short of bread"—because it had to import much of its food. Eventually Laclède bought out Maxent and made Chouteau his partner. Chouteau remained in St. Louis as its most prominent trader and citizen until his death in 1829.

By 1776, the town's total population was about 650, of whom about 30 percent were black slaves.[3] In 1775, Spanish officials began a subsidized effort to attract French and other Catholic settlers to Spanish Missouri from Canada. Some English settlers also migrated from the east, although Spain was not anxious to receive them. British and Spanish-licensed Louisiana traders frequently crossed the Mississippi into each other's territory, despite the prohibitions and protests of both governments. On occasion, both attempted to involve Indian tribes in the controversy. Some of these British traders were from the American colonies, but others were French Canadians—now, of course, legally British traders—who were continuing to work in their old, familiar territory.

THE SPANISH SOUTHWEST BEFORE 1763

In 1750, northern Pimería Alta (modern Arizona) had no official Spanish towns. Jesuit missions existed, however, and Hispanic settlers from Sonora (modern Mexico) had moved north to fertile lands along the Santa Cruz River. In November 1751, the Jesuits at Saríc were attacked by the northern Akimel O'odham (Pima) led by Luis Oacpicagigua. Hostilities soon spread up the Santa Cruz River valley, where two priests and more than 100 Hispanic settlers lost their Lives. In March 1752, in a negotiated settlement, Oacpicagigua surrendered to Governor Diego Ortiz Parilla. When Spanish officials inquired into the causes of the Pima Revolt, the Jesuits blamed the military, while Governor Parilla blamed the Jesuits. As a result of the insurrection, a new presidio, or garrison town, of professional soldiers was established at Tubac in 1752. Many families abandoned their outlying ranches and moved closer to the fort. Tubac became the first formally founded Spanish community in modern Arizona.

By 1752, New Mexico was home to 3,402 Hispanic settlers. Most lived along the Rio Grande and the Chama, close to either Santa Fe, La Cañada, or Albuquerque. The three towns were no longer compact villas, despite occasional orders by the governor to consolidate for defense. At Santa Fe, the defensive wall had been removed and residents lived out near their fields. At Albuquerque, smaller settlements grew around the town where residents could obtain better land. Communities of *genízaros,* or detribalized Hispanicized Indians, lived near the towns in separate communities. Usually poor and of low social standing, few owned land, and most worked as servants to the Spanish.

In Texas, San Antonio continued to grow, and the East Texas settlements survived. Elsewhere in the interior, however, no new missions or civilian settlements were successfully established. In 1755, the San Gabriel River missions ended when two priests were murdered. The culprits were probably Spanish soldiers; friars had excommunicated the entire garrison for scandalous sexual behavior. The San Sabá area mission was destroyed by Comanche and other northern tribes in March 1758; southern Trinity River missions were abandoned by 1770. On the coast of Texas, however, Spain had more success. In the late 1740s, a new Gulf coast province, Costa del Seno Mexicano, was established from Matagorda Bay south to Tampico (in modern Mexico). In 1750, José Vázquez Borrego established Nuestra Señora de los Dolores, and in 1755 Tomás Sánchez established Laredo, both within modern Texas.

Throughout the 1750s and 1760s, all across the Spanish Southwest, Apache and other nomadic tribes increased their violent and costly depredations. The Apache, pushed south by the Comanche and northern tribes, now formed a band across northern Arizona, New Mexico, and Texas. In Arizona, they continually plundered the more sedentary Akimel O'odham (Pima) as well as the Spanish, attacking from the north. In New Mexico, the Apache, Ute, Navajo, and Comanche all swooped down from the north and west, stealing livestock and taking captives from the sedentary, agricultural Pueblo and the Spanish. In interior Texas, the Apache and Comanche were hostile to each other as well as to Spanish missions and settlements.

In Arizona and Texas, the Spanish military was almost completely ineffective at stopping Apache raids, partly because they did not understand that Apache were organized into small local groups who acted independently. Apache sometimes allied to conduct war, but treaties made with one group did not extend to all others. In any case, the Apache did not consider most of their raiding to be warfare, which they usually conducted only for blood revenge, although sometimes they attacked the Spanish to avenge mistreatment or protect their liberty. But much Apache raiding was a kind of economic activity, the means by which they obtained food and trade items.

In New Mexico, the Spanish military was more successful, because they developed an alliance with Pueblo Indians to fight their common enemy. Pueblo sometimes carried on independent campaigns against the nomadic tribes as well, which were often more successful than Spanish campaigns.[4]

Despite the constant unrest, a universal truce was called each year for the New Mexico trade fairs. The largest were those at Taos, held in the summer; and Pecos, held in the fall. Large groups of the fiercest nomadic bands attended. They brought skins, mules, horses, and, most importantly, the captives taken from other tribes to sell as servants. In exchange, nomadic Indians got Pueblo textiles and agricultural products as well as Spanish metal goods.

THE REFORMS OF KING CHARLES III

At the end of the Seven Years' War in 1763, Spain badly needed to rejuvenate its imperial power and its military defenses in New Spain. Britain now controlled land as far west as the Mississippi River. All across the American Southwest, nomadic Indians threatened New Spain's northern frontier. On the Pacific coast, Russia's ships advanced further southward each year. All these threats indicated that Spain's valuable silver-producing colonies in Mexico might soon be vulnerable.

In 1759, the energetic and innovative King Charles III came to the Spanish throne. When the war ended, he embarked on a sweeping program of modernization. Charles intended to end economic stagnation and colonial corruption, increase trade and commerce, streamline colonial administration, and make his expanded empire more profitable. In 1765, he sent José de Gálvez to New Spain as *visitador general,* to inspect and overhaul colonial administration and policy. To evaluate military defense on the northern frontier, he sent Don Cayetano María Pignatelli Rubí Corbera y San Climent, the Marqués de Rubí. In 1766, Rubí began a two-year, 7,500-mile tour. He found the military ill-trained, underfunded, inefficient, uncoordinated, and headed by profiteering officers. Rubí recommended reorganizing military administration and repositioning all presidios in a cordon or line, stretching from the Gulf of California to the Gulf of Mexico. He also recommended conducting a war of extermination against the Apache. Rubí's recommendations were put into effect in the new Reglamento (regulations) of 1772. For the first time since reaching the New World, the Spanish defined the *indios bárbaros* (barbarous, or non-Christian Indians) as an enemy rather than as subjects for pacification and conversion.

The reorganization of the presidios was carried out by Hugo O'Conor, appointed *commandante inspector* in 1771. The red-haired O'Conor, called El Capitán Colorado (Captain Red) by the Indians, relocated some presidios and closed many others. Unfortunately, O'Conor's changes made little immediate difference. In the 1770s, Hispanic loss of life and property in Indian hostilities actually rose. In 1776, Charles III created the *Provincias Internas* (interior provinces). Northern New Spain, including the American Southwest, became a separate administrative unit under the direct supervision of the Crown. At its head was a *commandante general,* responsible for both civil and military affairs. The first was Teodoro de Croix, appointed in 1776. Overall, Charles's reforms de-emphasized religious institutions as a means of "pacifying" the frontier and strengthened military institutions.

As part of King Charles's economic reforms, he wanted to create a frontier society on the French or even English model. Neither of those nations segregated Indians from Europeans. In fact, the free trade between the two groups created great wealth for their colonies. Jesuit missions in New Spain, on the other hand, held extensive lands, controlled all trade with Indians converts, and isolated them from secular society. In 1767, Charles expelled the Jesuits from Spain and its empire. In Arizona and elsewhere in New Spain, Jesuit missionaries were required to lock the doors of their missions, leaving keys in the hands of nearby presidio military officials. They were marched across Mexico to Vera Cruz, then transported to Europe on a Swedish ship. In August 1768, José de Gálvez issued instructions to convert Jesuit missions to civilian settlements. Indians received individual grants of formerly communal Jesuit land. They were also given the freedom to conduct trade and decide their own leaders.

However, the Crown did not abandon the religious life of its Indian subjects. In 1768, Franciscans arrived in Arizona, joining others of their order in New Mexico and Texas. The Arizona Franciscans were given small royal stipends and forbidden to use the missions as an economic resource. Under the new arrangements, the Indians' submission to church authority immediately lessened; few were as Hispanicized as officials had presumed. The Franciscan missions survived, although they never attained the power held by the Jesuits.

THE SPANISH SOUTHWEST AFTER 1763

In Arizona, almost the entire Hispanic population was concentrated around Tubac in 1763. A 1767 census counted about 200 persons in 34 civilian households and 300 more in military households. In late 1775, O'Connor decided to relocate the Tubac garrison 40 miles north, to the Akimal O'odham mission village of San Agustín de Tucson. He hoped it would increase defenses against the Apache and guard the new overland route to California. Most of the Hispanic population of Tubac moved, led by Lieutenant Juan María de Oliva. They reached Tucson in 1776, where they built a compact village surrounded by a defensive wall. Homes, fields, and grazing lands lay beyond.

In New Mexico, the old hope of finding precious metals revived. In 1765, a Ute arrived in Santa Rosa y Santo Tomás de Abiquiu, a frontier outpost, with a small nugget of silver. Rumors spread that its source was to the northwest. Two different search expeditions were sent by Governor Tomás Vélez Cachupín. They found the ruins of the Anasazi civilization and crossed into modern Utah, taking possession of it for Spain. Neither located silver deposits, although they did exist in the area.

In Texas, the population of San Antonio grew slowly, from about 600 in 1763 to 1,300 by 1776. In 1769, Juan María, barón de Ripperdá, became governor. He moved to San Antonio, then ordered the evacuation of Los Adaes, the nominal capital, as well as nearby missions and the 500 settlers in East Texas. Many did not survive the three-month march to San Antonio; those who did were discontented. In 1774, they were permitted to return to East Texas, where they founded Nuestra Señora del Pilar de Bucareli. Bucareli soon became a thriving center of illicit trade with the Indians and Louisiana. In 1779, the settlement was reestablished at Nacogdoches.

After 1763, overland trade from Spanish Louisiana to the Spanish Southwest increased greatly, although yearly trade caravans to Mexico continued. Former French traders were licensed as Spanish traders. Spain's new frontier policy also called for using the traders as Indian agents to win the allegiance of the Comanche and northern tribes, or *Norteños,* as the Spanish called the Wichita and other tribes. Spain employed French-born Athanase de Mézières as a main agent and diplomat. (Mézières was the son-in-law of Louis Saint-Denis, the intrepid Frenchman who founded Natchitoches and opened trade with New Spain in 1716.) In 1769, Mézières became governor of Natchitoches and negotiated treaties with many of the northern tribes.

Between 1750 and 1776, the Hispanic-surnamed population grew slowly but steadily throughout northern New Spain. Very little documented Spanish immigration occurred but people of Spanish descent continued to intermarry with people of Indian, African, or mixed ethnic descent. New Spain's elaborate racial classifications were still important, and relations among different groups were not always harmonious. By 1776, however, many Hispanic settlers had multiethnic ancestry.[5]

THE FIRST SETTLEMENT OF CALIFORNIA

One of Visitador General José de Gálvez's top priorities for northern New Spain was the occupation of Alta California (Upper California, the modern U.S. state of California). More than 150 years earlier, in 1602–03, the Pacific coast had been explored for Spain by Sebastián Vizcaíno; the crown continued to consider it Spanish territory. Russian hunting ships had begun visiting the coast, however, after the explorations of Vitus Bering in 1728 and 1741—a threat well publicized by 18th-century Spanish writers. Gálvez decided to send an expedition northward from Baja California (Lower California in modern Mexico) to occupy the bays of San Diego and Monterey. No overland trail existed, and sea travel northward from Baja California was extremely difficult due to currents and prevailing winds. To increase the expedition's chance of success, Gálvez divided it into four groups. Two were to travel by land and two by sea. To head the project he selected Gaspar de Portolá and Fray Junípero Serra. Portolá was a dedicated military officer; Serra, despite his ill-health and mature age, was a Franciscan friar of great tenacity.

The two groups traveling by ship reached San Diego in April, their crews suffering severely from scurvy and other illnesses. A third supply ship was lost at sea. The first overland group of 25 soldiers, 42 Christian Indians, and 200 head of cattle arrived in May. In June, the overland party of Portolá and Serra arrived. They found a tentlike hospital constructed from the ships' sails. Of the 300 men who set out in the four groups, over a third did not survive, and half of those still alive were ill.

Portolá sent one ship back to Baja California for supplies and continued north with a small group. They experienced several earthquakes en route and passed Monterey Bay without recognizing it. In November, they reached the previously undiscovered and uncharted San Francisco Bay. Ships had passed its entrance for over a century, but none had noticed the best harbor on the Pacific coast. Portolá himself did not recognize its value immediately. Short of provisions (the party survived by eating its pack mules), he returned to San Diego discouraged by his failure to locate the bay he had been sent to occupy.

Meanwhile, on July 16, 1769, Fray Serra founded the mission of San Diego de Alcala. The men there continued to suffer from illness and inadequate food. Deaths continued. The Ipai Indians were initially welcoming but quickly grew less friendly; they finally attacked, killing one of the mission party. Only 20 members of the expedition remained alive in January 1770 when Portolá returned. The supply ship had not yet appeared. Fray Serra wanted to stay, but Portolá set a deadline for departure. The supply ship finally arrived at the last moment—according to legend, on the last day of Fray Serra's novena, or nine-day Catholic prayer ritual. The group remained in California.

In June, Portolá made a second expedition to Monterey, this time identifying it correctly. He founded a presidio there, which remained the capital of Alta California during the era of Spanish occupation. Its mission, San Carlos Borroméo, was located at Carmel Bay. Missions at San Gabriel and San Antonio were founded in 1771, San Luis Obispo in 1772, and San Juan Capistrano in 1776. Although in later years the California missions developed a distinctive architectural style, the early buildings were made only of wood and thatch.

To the Catholic missionaries, the coastal Indian groups of California appeared to offer a promising field for their work. The Indians, who had extremely varied cultures, had no political confederations, little tradition of organized warfare, and no guns. Nonetheless, missionaries made few converts in the early years. Both the missionaries and the soldiers seem to have treated the Indians harshly, although they blamed each other for the difficulties. Indians were quickly provoked to hostilities, particularly because of soldiers' extensive sexual violence against Indian women. (Historians are unsure if it was more prevalent or simply better documented in California.) By 1775, the first Indian revolt occurred; Ipai burned the mission at San Diego and killed the priest.

California settlements remained small and very isolated in their first decade. Spanish settlers were unable to immediately adjust their agricultural habits to the land and climate, despite its fertility. In 1774, the Hispanic population increased to 180 when the first women and children arrived by sea. But a land route was desperately needed to make immigration and supply easier. A 2,200-mile overland trail was finally opened from Tubac, Arizona, by Franciscan fray Francisco Garcés and military officer Juan Bautista de Anza. Setting out in March 1774, they established friendly relations with the Indians through whose lands they passed (although relations later soured disastrously). In October 1775, Anza made a second trip with 240 persons. Most were impoverished recruits from northern New Spain, the majority of them women and children. They traveled across both a desert and snow-covered mountains, accompanied by 400 cattle, 700 horses, and many supplies. One woman died in childbirth along the way, but no other deaths occurred, and several children were born en route. Anza arrived in San Gabriel in January 1776, his party actually larger than when it left Arizona. Some settled in Monterey; others continued north to San Francisco Bay, where the presidio of San Francisco de Asís was formally established on September 17, 1776. Meanwhile, Fray Garcés had attempted to open a route eastward from Monterrey to Santa Fe. On July 4, 1776—at the same time the Declaration of Independence was being adopted in Philadelphia—he was forced to turn back to California by hostile Hopi.

CHRONICLE OF EVENTS

1750

The non-Indian population of the English colonies is about 1,200,000; the population of New France is about 55,000.

The British transport 1,500 German and Swiss Protestants to Nova Scotia; they are the first German-speaking people in Canada.

France, England, and the Iroquois Confederacy all claim the Ohio Valley.

1751

In Halifax, the first Protestant church in Canada is established.

November: The Pima Revolt begins in northern Pimería Alta (modern Arizona). It will end in a negotiated peace in March 1752.

1752

Canada's first newspaper, the *Halifax Gazette,* is established.

The Ohio Land Company convenes an Indian conference at Logstown; Indians agree to a trading house at the forks of the Ohio River (modern Pittsburgh).

The free black town of Fort Mose is reestablished near St. Augustine.

Chickasaw attack settlers near New Orleans; Louisiana governor Philippe de Rigaud Vaudreuil sends French troops and compels a formal surrender.

A presidio is established at Tubac, the first official villa, or town, in modern Arizona.

June 21: Charles de Langlade leads French and western Indian troops from Detroit to the destroy the Miami town of Pickawillany. The Miami re-ally with the French.

1753

Louis Billouart de Kerlérec arrives in New Orleans as the new Louisiana governor.

June: Marquis Duquesne de Menneville, the governor-general of Canada, sends an expedition to construct a string of four forts connecting Lake Erie to the forks of the Ohio River.

November: Virginia governor Robert Dinwiddie sends George Washington to demand that the French depart the Ohio Valley. Washington is received courteously but informed that the French will remain.

1754

Governor Dinwiddie sends workers to the forks of the Ohio to build a fort before the French arrive; he sends Washington with militia troops to protect the workers. Before Washington arrives, the French drive the English workers out and begin building Fort Duquesne.

May 28: Near Great Meadows, Pennsylvania, Washington and Indian forces attack a small French scouting party, killing their leader, Coulon de Jumonville, and others.

June: Colonial governors meet at Albany to consider Iroquois grievances and intercolonial cooperation. They fail to secure Indian support against the French; the Albany Plan of Union, drafted by Benjamin Franklin, is later rejected by every colonial assembly.

July 3: Washington and his force of 150 are attacked by 900 French and Indians at Fort Necessity. After nine hours, Washington surrenders; it is the first battle of the French and Indian War.

1755

In Texas, missions and settlements in the San Gabriel River area end when two priests are murdered. Laredo is founded.

April: General Edward Braddock arrives in Virginia with two British regiments. The French send 3,000 French soldiers and 27 warships to Canada.

June: British troops capture Fort Beauséjour and find 300 Acadians among the enemy. All Acadians are asked to take a loyalty oath but refuse.

July: The Council of Nova Scotia passes an act to deport all Acadians.

July 9: Braddock and Washington are ambushed by French and Indians about eight miles from Fort Duquesne and are badly defeated at the Battle of the Wilderness. Braddock is mortally wounded.

August: Le grand dérangement—the expulsion of Acadians from Nova Scotia—begins. About 7,000 are deported by the end of the year, and up to 3,000 more before deportation officially ends.

1756

Louis-Joseph, Marquis de Montcalm, arrives in New France as the new military commander.

May: The Seven Years' War (called the French and Indian War in America) is formally declared in Europe; it will spread to many locations around the world.

1757

William Pitt assumes control of war strategy in Britain. He lays plans to conquer New France. Although the French have been victorious to date, the tide will soon turn in favor of the English.

1758

An elected assembly is established in Nova Scotia, the first representative government in Canada. For the next decade, settlers will arrive from New England.

In Texas, Comanche destroy the San Sabá mission.

July: General Jeffery Amherst captures Louisbourg.

November: General John Forbes captures Fort Duquesne, renaming it Fort Pitt. The Iroquois Confederacy convinces the Lenape to break its alliance with the French.

1759

Charles III ascends the throne of Spain.

The British capture Carillon (Ticonderoga), St. Frederic (Crown Point), and Niagara in upper New York.

The Cherokee attack South Carolina, beginning a war that will last until 1761.

June: British forces led by General James Wolfe sail up the St. Lawrence. They will keep the city of Quebec under constant bombardment for three months.

September 13: Wolfe attacks Quebec from the Plains of Abraham. Both Wolfe and French commander Montcalm lose their lives.

September 17: Quebec surrenders to the British.

Old Barracks, Trenton, New Jersey, built 1759 to house British soldiers during the French and Indian War *(Historic American Building Survey)*

1760

September 8: Montreal, the last important French stronghold, surrenders to General Jeffrey Amherst.

September 20: Amherst places Quebec under military rule.

1761

Detroit and other western French posts surrender to Britain.

1762

September: The last encounter between French and British troops occurs in Acadia.

November 3: Louisiana is ceded to France's ally Spain by the secret Treaty of Fontainebleau.

1763

February: The Treaty of Paris is signed, ending the Seven Years' War (the French and Indian War). France cedes Canada and all Louisiana territory east of the Mississippi River except New Orleans to the British and all of Louisiana territory west of the Mississippi including New Orleans to Spain. Spain cedes Florida to the British. The French empire in North America ends; Spain and Britain divide the continent.

October: The Proclamation of 1763 sets out British policies for governing the province of Quebec. General James Murray is appointed the first governor; he bends many rules to accommodate French institutions and Catholic traditions in Quebec.

October 7: The English split Florida into two separate colonies, East and West Florida, divided by the Apalachicola River. West Florida extends to the Mississippi River and includes Biloxi and Mobile. Most Hispanic residents of East Florida evacuate to Cuba; most residents of West Florida to Vera Cruz.

December: Pierre Liguest Laclède selects a site near the mouth of the Missouri River to establish a trading settlement (the future St. Louis); workmen being construction.

1764

Acadians are permitted to return to Canada. About 3,000 settle in New Brunswick.

April: Pierre Laclède names his Missouri settlement St. Louis. Soon thereafter, word reaches upper Mississippi French settlers that territory east of the Mississippi has been ceded to Britain; many move to St. Louis.

October: News of the Spanish takeover of Louisiana finally reaches New Orleans. Residents react in disbelief and send a delegation to France to plead for reconsideration.

1765

Acadians living in France are permitted to return to North America. Most go to Louisiana, becoming the ancestors of modern Cajuns.

Governors of English Florida hold a series of conferences with local Indian groups. Relations will remain difficult throughout the English period.

When Louisiana governor Jean-Jacques d'Abbadie dies in February, Charles Philippe Aubry, the military commander of the colony, takes control; the Superior Council takes on more functions.

José de Gálvez arrives to inspect and reform administration in New Spain as *visitador general.*

Expeditions search northwestern New Mexico for silver deposits; silver is not located, but modern Utah in entered and claimed for Spain.

July: King Charles III of Spain appoints Antonio de Ulloa the first Spanish governor of Louisiana.

1766

Don Cayetano María Pignatelli Rubí Corbera y San Climent, the Marqués de Rubí, begins his two-year tour of New Spain's northern frontier to evaluate military defenses.

1767

The Jesuit order is expelled from the Spanish empire and forced to leave Arizona.

January 20: Governor Ulloa finally takes possession of Louisiana for Spain, although he permits the French flag to continue flying at New Orleans. Charles Aubrey continues to share power.

1768

Franciscans replace Jesuit missionaries in Pimería Alta (modern Arizona).

October: The Louisiana Insurrection of 1768 occurs. Colonists gather in New Orleans to protest Ulloa's policies; the Superior Council draws up formal charges of maladministration.

November: Governor Antonio de Ulloa leaves Louisiana. Charles Aubrey remains in charge, and the Superior Council rules the colony for almost a year. A delegation is sent to Paris to convince the king to reclaim Louisiana; they are not successful.

1769

St. John's Island (modern Prince Edward Island) becomes a separate colony.

Juan María baron de Ripperdá becomes governor of Texas; he moves to San Antonio rather than Los Adaes and orders the evacuation of East Texas.

José de Gálvez sends an expedition to occupy and settle Alta California. Two land and two sea expeditions leave Baja California. In June, the fourth and last expedition reaches San Diego.

July 16: Father Junípero Serra founds the mission of San Diego de Alcala.

August 28: General Alejandro O'Reilly arrives to reestablish order in Louisiana with more than 2,000 Spanish soldiers in 24 ships.

October: O'Reilly sentences six leaders of the Louisiana insurrection to prison in Cuba and six to death; the condemned are shot by a firing squad the following day. The family property of all 12 is confiscated.

November: Gaspar de Portolá reaches the previously undiscovered and uncharted San Francisco Bay.

1770

March: General O'Reilly relinquishes Louisiana to Governor Luís de Unzaga and returns to Cuba with the remaining Spanish troops. During seven months in Louisiana, O'Reilly has placed the colony firmly under Spanish control and made many organizational and administrative changes.

June: A presidio is founded at Monterey, California.

1771

Hugo O'Conor, *commandante inspector,* begins to reorganize presidios in the Spanish Southwest.

1772

The Reglamento, or new regulations, are decreed to reorganize New Spain's northern frontier, based on the Marqués de Rubí's recommendations.

1773

Representative government is established at St. John's Island.

1774

The British government replaces the Proclamation of 1763 with the Quebec Act. The act opens certain offices to Catholics; restores seigneurial rights and the right of the Catholic Church to collect tithes; reinstitutes French civil law; and extends the southern boundary of Quebec province to include the Ohio Valley. The latter provision is extremely unpopular in the 13 colonies.

Capitan Juan Bautista de Anza and Father Francisco Garcés open a trail from Arizona to Monterey. The first Hispanic women and children arrive in California by ship.

Settlers forced to move to San Antonio are permitted to return to East Texas, where they found the settlement of Bucareli (later moved to Nacogdoches).

1775

Ipai Indians conduct the first mission revolt in California, at San Diego.

October: Capitan Anza leads a group of 240 colonists overland from Tubac to Monterey, then on to San Francisco.

November: The American colonial army attacks Quebec Province, capturing Montreal.

December 31: Quebec city is invaded by the American army, but Governor Guy Carleton and his militia of about 1,000 men hold the city.

1776

The Provincias Internas of New Spain (interior provinces, including Texas, New Mexico, modern Arizona, and California, plus northern Mexico) become a separate administrative unit under direct supervision of the Spanish Crown. Military occupation replaces mission building as Spain's dominant method of securing the frontier.

The garrison at Tubac is moved north, and the civil settlement of Tucson is founded.

March: Capitan Anza's group of about 250 Hispanic settlers arrives in Monterey.

May: British reinforcements numbering 10,000 arrive in Canada, forcing American Revolutionaries to retreat.

July 4: Father Francisco Garcés, attempting to open a route eastward from Monterey to Santa Fe, is forced to turn back by hostile Hopi.

September 17: The presidio of San Francisco is founded.

EYEWITNESS TESTIMONY

We cannot deny that this colony [*Canada*] has always been a burden to France and that it will probably continue to be so for a very long time to come. But it is also the most powerful obstacle we can use to check English ambitions. The only proof of this I need give are the many attempts the English have made against this colony over more than a century. . . . Canada alone can enable us to wage war on the English possessions in continental America. . . . [I]f we do not build up a counterweight that is capable of containing them within their present limits and of forcing them to remain on the defensive, they will soon acquire . . . great facility for making formidable preparations for war in continental America. . . . As an aftermath, France would lose the hegemony that she must claim in Europe. . . . We should not deceive ourselves into thinking that we can have a navy that can compare to theirs for many years. Our only recourse is to attack them in their overseas possessions. . . .

French official Marquis de la Galissonière, "Mémoire sur les colonies," 1750, in Mackirdy et al., eds., Changing Perspectives, *pp. 9–10.*

The settlers of Albuquerque wish to have a soldier for every cow and horse they pasture so that they would have nothing to worry about and could live in slovenly indifference. I have tried to accustom them to the idea that each one should take care of the defense of his own hacienda. The number of settlers in that area is sufficient to do so. Besides, they are well trained and experienced in war.

New Mexico governor Tomás Vélez Cachupín, ca. 1750, quoted in Simmons, Albuquerque, *p. 100.*

The trade that the French are developing with the Comanches by means of the Jumanos will in time result in grave injury to this Province [*New Mexico*]. Although the Comanche nation carries on a like trade with us, coming to the pueblo of Taos, where they hold their fairs and trade in skins and Indians of various nations, whom they enslave in their wars, for horses, mares, mules hunting knives, and other trifles, always, whenever the occasion offers for stealing horses or attacking the pueblos of Pecos and Galisteo, they do not pass it up. . . . They have such a grudge against these two pueblos that I find it necessary to garrison them with thirty presidial soldiers and to keep scouts out, so that by detecting them in time they can warn me and sally to meet them. . . . I have fortified these two pueblos of Pecos and Galisteo with earthworks and towers at the gates capable of defending them against these enemies, since the presidio cannot always keep the garrison there because it has many places to cover.

Governor Cachupín to the viceroy, March 1750, quoted in Kessel, Kiva, *p. 357.*

It appears from a letter of the Marquis de la Jonquiere, that the efforts the English are making, and the expenses they incur, to gain over the Indians, are not without success among several Nations. . . .

The River Ohio, otherwise called the Beautiful river, and its tributaries belong indisputably to France, by virtue of its discovery by Sieur de la Salle; of the trading posts the French have had there since, and of possession. . . . It is only within a few years that the English have undertaken to trade there; and now they pretend to exclude us from it.

They have not, up to the present time, however, maintained that these rivers belong to them; they pretend only that the Iroquois are masters of them and being the Sovereigns of these Indians, that they can exercise their rights. But 'tis certain that these Indians have none, and that, besides, the pretended sovereignty of the English over them is a chimera.

Meanwhile 'tis of the greatest importance to arrest the progress of the pretensions and expeditions of the English in that quarter. Should they succeed there, they would cut off the communication between the two Colonies of Canada and Louisiana, and would be in a position to trouble them, and to ruin both the one and the other, independent of the advantages they would at once experience in their trade to the prejudice of ours. . . .

. . . 'tis considered proper to direct M. Duquesne to lay down henceforward in Canada a different system that always followed hitherto in regard to wars among the Indians. With a view to occupy and weaken them, the principle has been to excite and foment these sorts of wars. That was of advantage in the infancy of the settlement of Canada. But in the condition to which these Nations are now reduced, and in their present dispositions generally, it is in every respect more useful that the French perform between them the part of protectors and pacificators. . . . Cases, however, may occur in which it will be proper to excite war against certain Nations attached to the English.

French Royal Ministerial minutes, 1752, in Hart, ed.,
American History, *vol. 2, pp. 354–56.*

At the instigation of the English, the Piankashaws and the Weas planned to wipe out completely five French villages which were established among the Illinois. . . . I was in Kaskaskia territory where Monsieur de Montcharvaux was in command. He did not know exactly what the Indians were up to, but, remembering the Natchez massacre, he suspected them of some treachery because of their great show of affection during their too frequent visits to the homes of the French.

. . . It was my opinion that the best way to find out what the Indians were plotting was to remain on the defensive without giving any indication of our suspicions. I suggested that we send out several colonists, mounted on their horses and armed with rifles as though they were going hunting. After roaming about for a while, they were to come galloping back to the settlement as though they had discovered something new. All we would have to do then, in the midst of this general alarm, would be to observe the Indians carefully; the expressions on their faces would betray them. My advice was taken, and the Indians thought that the French had discovered their plot. The massacre was to have taken place on Christmas Day right after High Mass. The Indians had found out when Christmas would be by asking on what day the Great Spirit's Son had been born.

When they thought their plot had been discovered, they tried to flee. We opened fire and killed twenty-two of them.

French officer Jean-Bernard Bossu, 1752,
Travels, *pp. 69–70.*

. . . there was no possibility of sending out the foreign Settlers [*German immigrants*] this year to any places distant from Halifax there being no Provisions for that purpose in Store, for as the Season is so far advanced I could not do it without sending with them nine months Provisions at the same time, and it is my sincere opinion that . . . a further supply of fifteen Months more, will be absolutely necessary to be allowed them. This I should think they cannot possibly do without, for as most of them are poor Wretches that have scarce a farthing of Money among them. . . . [T]he People in

general who were sent over this year by Mr. Dick complain of his having persuaded them at their embarking to sell off every thing even the little Bedding they had, by which means they have lain on the bare Decks and Platforms during their Voyage and are still destitute of all kind of bedding. This has caused the death of many both on the Passage and here ashore since they were landed; what Mr. Dick could mean by persuading these poor wretches to dispose of all their Bedding and little Necessarys in the manner as they have represented to me, I really cannot say, but to me it looks as if it was done to give room for crowding in a greater number of People into the Ships. . . .

Halifax official to Board of Trade, 1752, in Clark,
Social Development, *pp. 122–23.*

I find as appropriate and necessary for the reduction of Upper Pimería . . . two forts. . . . One should be put in the place . . . named *Tucuson* inasmuch as [it is] abundant in water and pasture for the remount herds and cattle as well as the population. With such a garrison the subjugation and reduction of the most heathen, which embraces the Northern and Eastern part of said Pimería, would be achieved. Not only that part of the Northern Piman Indians which inhabits the banks of the Rio Xila, but also the rancherias of the apostate Apaches farther upstream and in the nearby mountains would be curbed. Such a garrison would cover the territory and give a hand to the Post of San Phelipe de Guebavi at Terrenate, enabling their captains zealously to comply with the civil and politic orders of His Majesty for the education of the Indians.

Jesuit Philip Segesser to the governor, May 1752,
quoted *in Dobyns,* Spanish *pp. 12–13.*

So many deserters, so much trouble in the provinces Washington traversed, so much discord among these troops of different provinces [*the 13 colonies*] that claim to be independent! It is that which convinces me that we will always defeat such forces, as badly organized as they are unwarlike.

Marquis Duquesne, 1754, quoted in Eccles, Canadian
Frontier, *p. 165.*

Denis Kaninguen, who deserted from the English army camp yesterday morning, arrived at the camp of Fort Duquesne today, 30 June. . . . He reports that . . . Monsieur de Jumonville had been killed by an English detachment which surprised him. . . . Monsieur de

Jumonville having been wounded and having fallen, Thaninhison [Tanaghrisson], a savage, came up to him and had said, Thou art not yet dead, my father, and struck several hatchet blows with which he killed him.

Deposition taken by Captain Pierre de Contrecoeur, June 1754, quoted in Anderson, Crucible, *p. 57.*

... they then, from every little rising, tree, stump, Stone, and bush kept up a constant galding fire upon us; which was returned in the beset manner we could till late in the Afternn. when their fell the most tremendous rain that can be conceived, filled our trenches with Water, Wet not only the Ammunition in the Cartouch boxes and firelocks, but that which was in a small temporary Stockade in the middle of the Intrenchment called Fort Necessity erected for the sole purpose of its security, and that of the few stores we had; and left us nothing but a few (for all were not provided with them) Bayonets for defence.

Colonel George Washington, June 1754, in Fitzpatrick, ed., Writings, *vol. 39, p. 40.*

There was at this place a Small Stocade Fort [*Necessity*] made in a circular form round a Small House that stood in the middle of it to keep our provisions and ammunition in, and was covered with Bark and some Skins and might be about fourteen feet Square and the Walls of the Fort might be eight feet distance from the said house all round. The French were at that time so near that Severall of our people were wounded by the splinters beat off by the Bulletts from the said House.

Deposition of Private John Shaw, June 1754, in Cleland, George Washington, *p. 98.*

One of that party, *Monceau* by name, a *Canadian*, made his Escape and tells us that they [*Washington's forces*] had built themselves Cabbins, in a low Bottom [*Great Meadows*], where they sheltered themselves, as it rained hard. About seven o'Clock the next Morning, they saw themselves surrounded by the *English* on one Side and the *Indians* on the Other. The *English* gave them two Volleys, but the *Indians* did not fire. Mr. *de Jumonville*, by his Interpreter, told them to desist, that he had something to tell them. Upon which they ceased firing. Then Mr. *de Jumonville* ordered the Summons which I had sent them to retire, to be read. ... The aforesaid *Monceau*, saw all our *Frenchmen* coming up close to Mr. *de Jumonville*, whilst they were reading the Summons,

so that they were all in Platoons, between the *English* and the *Indians*. ...

Captain Pierre de Contrecoeur to Marquis Duquesne, June 2, 1754, quoted in Anderson, Crucible, *pp. 53–54.*

The English do not intend to hurt you, or any of your allies; this news, we know, must have been forged by the French, who are constantly treacherous, asserting the greatest falsehoods whenever they think they will turn out to their advantage; they speak well, promise fine things, but all from the lips only; whilst their heart is corrupt and full of the poison of the serpent. You have been their children, and they would have done every thing for you, but they no sooner thought themselves strong enough, than they returned to their natural pride and drove you off from your lands, declaring you had no right on the Ohio. The English, your real friends, are too generous to think of using the Six Nations, their faithful allies, in such manner. ... [T]hey (at your repeated request) sent an army to maintain your rights to put you again in possession of your lands, and to take care of your wives and children, to dispossess the French, to support your prerogatives and to secure that whole country to you. ... [W]e cannot reasonably doubt of being joined by the rest of your forces to oppose the common enemy.

George Washington to an Indian council, July 1754, in Washington, Journal, *pp. 110–11.*

Whereas I think, for the good of this island in general, that gallows should be erected in the several districts in order to deter (frequent robberies that are committed by) a parcel of villains, who think that they can do what they please with impunity. You are therefore hereby required and directed to cause gallows to be erected in the most public places in your several districts, and cause all such persons as are guilty of robbery, felony, or the like crimes, to be sent round to this place in order to take their trial at the annual assizes held here, as I am determined to proceed against all such with the utmost severity of the law. Given ... at St. John's [*Newfoundland*], the 12th of October, 1754.

Order of Governor Hugh Bonfoy, quoted in Pedley, History, *p. 97.*

As the French Inhabitants of this Province have never yet, at any time, taken the oath of allegiance to His Majesty, unqualified, I thought it my duty to avail

Blockhouse at Winslow, Maine, built 1754 *(Historic American Building Survey)*

myself of the present occasion, to propose it to them. . . . [T]he oath was proposed to them. They endeavoured, as much as possible, to evade it, and at last desired to return home and consult the rest of the Inhabitants, that they might either accept or refuse the oath in a body; but they were informed that we expected every man upon this occasion to answer for himself. . . . The next morning, they appeared and refused to take the oath without the old reserve of not being obliged to bear arms, upon which they were acquainted, that they refused to become English subjects, we could no longer look upon them in that light; that we should send them to France by the first opportunity, and till then, they were ordered to be kept prisoners at George's Island, where they were immediately conducted.

Colonel Charles Lawrence to Board of Trade, 1755, quoted in Murdoch, History, *pp. 283–84.*

M. De Contrecoeur, Captain of Infantry, Commandant of Fort Duquesne . . . detached M. de Beaujou . . . together with 20 Cadets, 100 Soldiers, 100 Canadians and 600 Indians, with orders to lie in ambush at a favorable spot, which he had reconnoitered the previous evening. The detachment, before it could reach its place of destination, found itself in presence of the enemy within three leagues of that fort. M. de Beaujeu, finding his ambush had failed, decided on an attack. This he made with so much vigor as to astonish the enemy, who were waiting for us in the best possible order; but their artillery, loaded with grape, having opened its fire, our men gave way in turn. The Indians, also, frightened by the report of the cannon rather than by any damage it could inflict, began to yield, when M. de Beaujeu was killed. M. Dumas began to encourage his detachment. He ordered the officers in command of the Indians to spread themselves along the wings so as to take the enemy in flank, whilst he, M. de Lignery and the other officers who led the French, were attacking them in front. This order was executed so promptly that the enemy, who were already shouting their "Long live the King," thought now only of defending themselves. The fight was obstinate on both sides and success long doubtful; but the enemy at last gave way. Efforts were made, in vain, to introduce some sort of order in their retreat. The whoop of the Indians, which echoed through the forest, struck terror into the heart of the entire enemy. The rout was complete. . . . They have lost . . . their General, whose name was Mr. Braddock, and almost all their officers.

Anonymous Frenchman, 1755, in Hart, ed., American History, *vol. 2, pp. 365–67.*

1755, Sept. 5 . . . Delivered them [*the Acadians*] by Interpreters the King's orders In the following words:

. . . your Lands and Tenements, Cattle . . . and Live Stock of all Sorts are Forfeited to the Crown with all your other Effects Saving your Money and Household Goods and you your selves to be removed from this . . . Province.

That it is Peremptorily his Majesty's orders That the whole French Inhabitants of these Districts, be removed, and I am Through his Majesty's Goodness Directed to allow you Liberty to Carry of your money and Household Goods as Many as you Can without Discommoding the Vessels you Go in. I shall do Everything in my Power that all Those Goods be Secured to you and that you are Not Molested in Carrying of them of and also that whole Families Shall go in the Same Vessel, and make this remove which I am Sensible must give you a great Deal of Trouble as Easy as his Majesty's Service will admit and hope that in what Ever part of the world you may Fall you may be Faithful Subjects, a Peaceable and happy People.

I Must also inform you That it is his Majesty's Pleasure that you remain in Security under the Inspection and Direction of the Troops that I have the Honor to Command.

Sept. 10 . . . as there was Five Transports Idle which Came from Boston, it would be for the Good of his Majesty's service and that it Tended to the Better Security of the whole, that fifty men of the French Inhabitants be Embarked on Board Each of the five Vessels, taking First all their young men. . . . I Sent for Father Landrey Their Principal Speaker who Talks English and Told him, the Time was Come for part of the Inhabitants to Embark and that the Number Concluded for this Day was 250 and that we Should begin with the young men and Desired he would Inform his brethern of it. He was greatly Surprised. I Told him it must be Done and that I Should order the whole Prisoners to be Drawn up Six Deep, their young men on the Left, and as the Tide in a Very Little time Favoured my Design Could not Give them above an Hour to Prepare for going on Board. . . . The whole of the French Inhabitants where Drawn together In one Body their young men as Directed on the Left. . . . I then ordered Capt Adams . . . to Draw of from the main Body to Guard the young men of the French amounting to 141 Men to the Transports and order the Prisoners to March. They all answered they would Not go without their Fathers. I Told them that was a word I did not understand for that the King's Command was to me absolute & Should be absolutely obeyed & That I Did not Love to use Harsh Means but that the time Did not admit of Parleys or Delays and Then ordered the whole Troops to Fix their Bayonets and advance Towards the French, and Bid the 4 right hand Files of the Prisoners Consisting of 24 men . . . one of whom I Took hold on (who opposed the Marching) and bid March. He obeyed & the rest followed though Slowly, and went of Praying, Singing & Crying being Met by the women & Children all the way (which is $1\frac{1}{2}$ mile) with Great Lamentations upon their Knees praying &c.

Colonel John Winslow's journal, in Hart, ed.,
American History, vol. 2,
pp. 362–65.

When the assembly [*an Abenaki war-feast*] has been organized, the Orator of the Tribe begins to speak, and solemnly addresses the guests. . . . I have more than once heard addresses which would not have been disavowed by our finest minds in France. An eloquence drawn wholly from nature does not cause any one to regret the help of art.

When the speech is finished, they proceed to name the Captains who are to command the [war] party. As soon as one is named, he rises from his place and proceeds to seize the head of one of the animals which are to make the principle part of the feast. He raises it high enough to be seen by the whole assembly, crying aloud: *Behold the head of the enemy.* Shouts of joy and applause are then raised on every side, and announce the satisfaction of the assembly. The Captain, with the head of the animal still in his hand, foes through the lines singing his war-song, in which he exerts all his force in boasting and insulting defiance of the enemy, and in the exaggerated eulogies which he lavishes upon himself. To hear them extolling themselves in these moments of military enthusiasm, you might believe them all to be Heroes who are able to carry off all, crush all, vanquish all. As he passes in review before the Savages, these latter answer his chant by hollow cries, broken, drawn from the pit of the stomach. . . . He afterwards resumes his place, where he is no sooner seated, than perhaps there is put on his head a pot of hot ashes; but this is an act of friendship. . . .

Unnamed Jesuit, annual letter, 1757, in Thwaites, ed.,
Jesuit Relations, *vol. 90, pp. 98–101.*

That a house of representatives of the inhabitants of this province be the Civil Legislature thereof, in conjunction with H.M. governor or commander-in chief for the time being, and his majesty's council of the said province.

The first House to be elected and convened in the following manner, and to be styled the General Assembly, viz.,

That there shall be elected for the province at large, until the same shall be divided into counties, sixteen members; for the township of Halifax, four; for the township of Lunenburgh, two. . . .

That when fifty qualified electors shall be settled at . . . any other townships which may hereafter be erected, each of the said townships so settled shall, for their encouragement, be entitled to send two representatives to the General Assembly. . . .

That the house shall always consist of at least eleven members present, besides the speaker, before they enter upon business.

That no person shall be chosen as a member of the said house, or shall have a right of voting in the elect of any member of the said house, who shall be a Popish recusant, or shall be under the age of twenty-one years, or who shall not, at the time of such election, be possessed in his own right, of a freehold estate within the district for which he shall be elected. . . .

Council of Nova Scotia, 1757, quoted in Murdoch,
History, vol. 2, pp. 334–35.

. . . The Sieur de Montcalm died late last night; when his wound was dressed, and he settled in bed, the Surgeons who attended him were desired to acquaint him ingenuously with their sentiments of him, and, being answered that his wound was mortal, he calmly replied, "he was glad of it:" his Excellency then demanded, "whether he could survive it long, and how long?" He was told, "about a dozen hours, perhaps more, peradventure less." "So much the better," rejoined this eminent warrior; "I am happy I shall not live to see the surrender of Quebec." . . .

After our late worthy General [*Wolfe*], of renowned memory, was carried off wounded, to the rear of the front line, he desired those who were about him to lay him down; being asked if he would have a Surgeon? he replied, "It is needless; it is all over with me." One of them then cried out, "They run, see how they run." "Who runs!" demanded our hero, with great earnestness, like a person roused from sleep? The Officer answered, "The enemy, Sir; Egad they give way everywhere." Thereupon the General rejoined, "Go one of you, my lads, to Colonel Burton—; tell him to march Webb's regiment with all speed down to Charles's river, to cut off the retreat of the fugitives from the bridge." Then, turning on his side, he added, "Now, God be praised, I will die in peace:" and thus expired.

Captain John Knox, 1759, Historical Journal of the
Campaigns in North America, in Hart, ed.,
American History, vol. 2, p. 372.

The whole being under the Command of Brigadiers Monckton & Murray were put into the Flat Bottom'd Boats & after some Movement of the Ships made by Admiral Holmes to draw the attention of the Enemy above, The Boats fell down with the Tide & Landed on the North Shore [of Quebec] within a League of Cape Diamond an Hour before Day Break. The rapidity of the Tide of Ebb carried them a little below the intended place of attack—which obliged the Light Infantry to Scramble up a woody precipice in order to secure the landing the Troops by dislodging a Captains

Post which defended the small intrench'd Path the Troops were to ascend—after a little Firing the Light Infantry gained the top of the Precipice. . . .

I immediately made Brig. Murray being detached with Anstruther's Battalion to attack the 4 Gun Battery upon the left, was recall'd by the General who now saw the French Army crossing the River St. Charles. General Wolfe thereupon began to form his Line. . . . [H]is rear & left was protected by Col. Howe's Light Infantry, who was return'd from the 4 Gun Battery before mention'd, which was soon abandon'd to him, where he found 4 Guns of General Montcalm having collected the whole of his Force from the Beauport side, & advancing upon shew'd his Intention to flank our left. . . . The Enemy lined the Bushes in their Front with 1500 Indians & Canadians & I dare say had placed most of their best Marksmen there, who kept up a very galling tho' irregular fire upon our whole Line, who bore it with the greatest patience and good Order; reserving their fire for the Main body now advancing. . . .

My attention to the left will not permit me to be very exact with regard to every Circumstance which passed in the Center, much less to the right, but it is most certain that the Enemy form'd in good Order, & that their attack was very brisk & animated on that side, our Troops reserved their Fire till within 40 Yards which was so well continued that the Enemy everywhere gave way. T'was there our General [*Wolfe*] fell at the Head of Braggs & the Louisbourg Grenadiers, advancing with their Bayonets, about the same time B. General Monkton received his wound at the head of Lascelles; In the front of the opposite Battalions fell also Mons. Montcalm, & his Second in Command since died of his wounds on board our ship. . . .

The 17th [*September*] at noon before we had any Battery erected or could have had any for 2 or 3 days, A Flagg of Truce came out with proposals of Capitulation, which I sent back again to Town allowing them 4 Hours to capitulate or no farther Treaty. The Admiral had at this time brought up his large ships as intending to attack the Town. The French Officer returned at Night with Terms of Capitulation which with the Admiral were considered, agreed to, and signed, at 8 in the morning the 18th Instant. . . .

General George Townshend, to William Pitt describing
the fall of Quebec, September 1759, in Pitt,
Correspondence, vol. 2, pp. 165–68.

The Bishop's House, Quebec, in 1781 *(Courtesy National Archives of Canada/C 000352)*

I do myself the Honour of acquainting you that it has pleased God to crown His Majesty's Arms with Success over all His Enemies upon the Ohio, by my having obliged the Enemy to burn and abandon Fort Du Quesne, which they effectuated on the 25th [*November 1758*], and of which I took possession next day, the Enemy having made their Escape down the River towards the Mississippi in their Boats, being abandoned by their Indians, whom I had previously engaged to leave them, and who now seem all willing and ready to implore His Majesty's most Gracious Protection. So give me leave to congratulate you upon this great Event, of having totally expelled the French from this prodigious tract of Country, and of having reconciled the various tribes of Indians inhabiting it to His Majesty's Government. . . . I have used the freedom of giving your name to Fort Du Quesne [*i.e., Fort Pitt*]. . . .

General John Forbes to William Pitt, November 1759,
in Pitt, Correspondence,
pp. 406–09.

. . . the repeated warnings which I had now received, of sure destruction at Michilimackinac, could not but oppress my mind. I could not even yield myself, without danger, to the course suggested by my fears; for my provisions were nearly exhausted, and to return, was, therefore, almost impracticable.

The hostility of the Indians was exclusively against the English. Between them, and my Canadian attendants, there appeared the most cordial good will. This circumstance suggested one means of escape, of which, by the advice of my friend, Campion, I resolved to attempt availing myself, and which was, that of putting on the dress, usually worn by such of the Canadians as pursue the trade into which I had entered, and assimilating myself, as much as I was able, to their appearance and manners. To this end, I laid aside my English clothes, and covered myself only with a cloth, passed about the middle; a shirt, hanging loose; a molton, or blanket coat; and a large, red, milled worsted cap. The next thing was to smear my face and hands with dirt, and grease; and, this done, I took the, place of one of my men, and, when Indians approached, used the paddle, with as much skill as I possessed. I had the satisfaction to find, that my disguise enabled me to pass several canoes, without attracting the smallest notice.

Alexander Henry, 1760, Travels and Adventures, *pp. 34–35.*

. . . I have postponed until now to give you, my Lord, an account of a new product and of a new commerce now presenting itself. I am referring to sugar cane growing, the success of which, after repeated trials, is now promising well. As early as 1742, the Jesuits of New Orleans were growing in boxes a few feeble plants. . . . These plants grew in summer and lived through the winter, thanks to the care taken to put them in hot houses, but they remained languishing; the stem being thin and not very long, they did not ripen and gave no syrup. These weak plants, however, sprouted with time. Several inhabitants asked the Jesuits for some and transplanted them in their field; those who took the greatest care of them, but above all, those who ventured to plant them in free soil (en pleine terre), and in the open, and did not let their cattle pasture in the patches, proved that these creoles sprouts were giving very high hopes. These trials went on, on a small scale, as late as 1757, when M. du Bremil, one of the more well-to-do settlers of this colony . . . undertook to begin sugar cane growing on a grand scale.

Louisiana ordonnateur Rochemore to a French official, *1760, quoted in Delanglez,* French Jesuits, *pp. 390–91.*

. . . I was using my utmost endeavours to engage the Creek Indians in a war with the Cherokees which I am still employed in, tho' it proves a Work of much difficulty as the French and Cherokees have great Influence in that Nation. But whilst I am negotiating Publically I am working in private with the Straggling parties of Creeks that occasionally visit me in hopes by their means to embroil their Nation insensibly and as it were against its inclination. We have already prevailed on different gangs to go against the Cherokees, and I have this day had the Satisfaction of seeing one party return with the Scalps of three of them. I shall to the utmost of my power improve this earnest of success, but as nothing is to be effected with the Savages without distributing of considerable Presents, and treating the head Men and Warriors as well as subsisting their Wives and Children in their Absence when they go to war there is

a necessity that I should be amply supplied with Goods and Money for such purposes.—It is of the last importance that the Creeks should be induced to assist us for otherwise the War with the Cherokees may be a very tedious and Expensive one.

Henry Ellis, lieutenant governor of Georgia, to William Pitt, April 1760, in Pitt, Correspondence, *vol. 2, p. 277.*

19th [*September 1760*]. Mons & Madame Vaudreuil made me a visit in the afternoon; were very civil. As the Quebec garrison was all gone Governor Murray is to set out for Quebec tomorrow. I ordered all the Militia of the town & suburbs to be out and deliver up their Arms & take the Oath of Allegiance, so soon as the Marquis is gone. . . .

21st. I had information of several of our deserters & sent partys after them. . . .

22nd . . . I gave Gen Gage his instructions, and gave out a Proclamation of my having appointed him Governor, & several things that I imagined right to be made publick. I went into town to Mons Vaudreuils house as I had delivered to Sr Wm Johnson as many things for the Indians out of the stores as he thought necessary, and (to see) that every thing was settled with the French Indians who delivered up all prisoners.

I ordered our Indians home. The priest of Asquisashna came to me in the evening. The inhabitants of Crown Point wanted to go back, but I would not permit them. If Canada should be restored they will be dangerous English subjects. . . .

25th. I went to visit Les Soers [*Sisters*] Religieuses and les Soers de la Congregation. The first take charge and care of all our sick & are very good nurses. I never saw any sick better attended. I sent them a present of 200 Crowns and two dozen of Madeira, as they told me they had no wine. I likewise paid a visit to the Superior of the Church.

Jeffrey Amherst, 1760, Journal, *pp. 253–55.*

Father Alphonsus Espinosa is the Minister of San Xavier [*Arizona*], and he has to attend to more people then there are in all the other Missions. Many of the old people are new in the Faith, and he has to work hard with them to instruct them and keep in obedience; for such is their character that the Opatas, when they are advised by the priest to be obedient and gentle, say: "Are we perhaps Papagos?"

Anonymous [Juan Nentuig], Rudo Ensayo [*1762–63*], *quoted in Wagoner,* Early Arizona, *p. 109.*

. . . [*Pierre Laclède*] examined all the ground from the Fort de Chartres to the Missouri. He was delighted to see the situation (where St. Louis at present stands); he did not hesitate a moment to form there the establishment that he proposed. Besides the beauty of the site, he found there all the advantages that one could desire to found a settlement which might become very considerable hereafter. After having examined all thoroughly, he fixed upon the place where he wished to form his settlement, marked with his own hand some trees. . . . [H]e said, with enthusiasm, . . . that he had found a situation where he was going to form a settlement, which might become, hereafter, one of the finest cities of America—so many advantages were embraced in this site, by its locality and its central position. . . . He occupied himself with his settlement, fixed the place where he wished to build his house, laid a plan of the village he wished to found (and named it Saint Louis, in honor of Louis XV, whose subject he expected to remain, for a long time;—he never imagined he was a subject of the King of Spain); and ordered me to follow the plan exactly. . . .

Auguste Chouteau's journal, 1764, in McDermott, ed.,
Early Histories, *pp. 48–49.*

. . . all the Missouris went away, to go up the Missouri and return to their ancient village—having remained here fifteen days, in the course of which I had the cellar of the house, which we were to build, dug by the women and children. I gave them, in payment, vermilion, awls and verdigris. They dug the largest part of it, and carried the earth in wooden platters and baskets, which they bore upon their heads.

Auguste Chouteau's journal, 1764, in McDermott, ed.,
Early Histories, *pp. 51–52.*

1. That no Indian trader [*in British Florida*] . . . shall sell or give to any Indian any spirituous liquor of any kind whatsoever. . . .

3. That no trader shall employ any person or clerk, packhorseman or factor in their service before any agreement is first entered into in writing between them specifying the time, and condition of service, and also his or their names indorsed on the back of the licence which may be given to such trader whereby the principal trader shall then be deem'd answerable for his or their conduct. . . .

5. That no Indian trader shall employ any Negro or Indian or half breed, who from his manner of life

shall in the conscience of a jury be considered as living under the Indian government as a factor or deputy to trade in any town or village on account of the said trader. . . .

9. That no Indian trader . . . shall sell any swann shott or riffled guns to the Indians. . . .

13. That no Indian trader by himself substitute or servant shall propagate any false report or reports among the Indians, or convene any meetings with them or deliver any messages to them without the concurrence of the commissary first obtained in writing. . . .

Regulations of Florida governors John Stuart and George Johnstone, 1764, quoted in Alden, John Stuart,
pp. 259–62.

The Women here [*French Canada*] affect dress very much, and resemble in their manners, conversation and behavior, those of their Mother Country such as style themselves Noblesse, scarce hold any correspondence but with one another, despising all others, and calling them des Bourgeois. . . . The people in general, and even the most sensible of them, are prodigiously fond of their ancient manner of Government, and have not yet found out, the advantages attending a free Inquest by juries. Time only can open their Eyes in this matter, and many others, where the Scale will always appear to a cool and Sensible Man, to be of our Side. . . .

Upon the whole I think they were too suddenly adopted into our Government, at a time [when] there was no proper people of our Religion and Language to be made Magistrates, and before the Natives could have any Idea of our Laws and Forms of Justice, which are ever prolix and very expensive. In former days all their Suits were determined in a short time and at scarce any expense, at present the case is diametrically opposite, and therefore it is no wonder they complain of the Change.

The British Inhabitants as yet settled in Canada are the Scum of the Earth . . . and from want of knowing what our Constitution is, and judging only from the bad behavior of such fellows as are set over them, they are with great reason apt to think ill of such people, and to condemn the whole System.

Journal of Lord Adam Gordon, British officer, 1764, in Mereness, ed., Travels, *pp. 432–33, 440–41.*

Resolved, That to prevent an abuse frequently complained of, that of killing the cattle of other persons and selling the carcasses at Mercates, that for the future all persons who shall expose any beef for sale, shall be obliged to hang out the green hide with the hair out, on his stockade fronting the street for four hours in the day.

Resolution of West Florida Council, Mobile, December 1764, quoted in Johnson, British West Indies, *p. 28.*

Upon their [*indentured servants*] landing they are immediately seized with the pride which every man is possessed of who wears a white face in America, and they say they won't be slaves and so they make their escape.

East Florida governor James Grant, ca. 1765, quoted in Landers, Black Society, *p. 67.*

It is to be feared that the arrival of the Spaniards which we are expecting every day will cause a revolution very favorable to the English. All the nations of the continent know by hearsay about the cruelties which the Spaniards have practiced elsewhere in America and detest them generally. . . . It is certain that if the Spaniards try to act in the same way in Louisiana all will be lost. In the first war, the English will have legions of savages at their orders who, with arms and munitions and joined to the old enemies of the Spaniards, will penetrate easily as far as the mines, which are not three hundred leagues from the Mississippi and will destroy the source of the Spanish riches on some future day.

Charles Philippe Aubry to French officials, February 1765, quoted in Moore, Revolt, *p. 85.*

I have resolved that in this new acquisition [*Louisiana*] no innovation will be made in the government and no law or custom prevailing in the Indies will be applied, it being considered as a separate colony. . . . [I]t is my will that with complete independence of the minister of the Indies, the council, and other associated tribunals all matters be referred to the minister of state, who alone will keep me informed of whatever occurs relative to your commission, and by this route you will receive your orders, instructions pertaining to the government and policy of that new, independent domain. . . .

King Charles III of Spain to Antonio de Ulloa, May 1, 1765, quoted in Moore, Revolt, *p. 43.*

He has sent me . . . 8 or 9 [Acadians] . . . and order'd them to be Landed [*housed*] on me; which will subject me to the expense of at least 12 a week, beside making me liable to a great deal of Danger by their corrupting mine & other Negroe Slaves on this River, of which there is at least the num: of 300 that may be call'd Roman Catholicks: who, being, by some very late practices and declarations, dangerous in themselves . . . because some of my Slaves have lately said, They expect that the French . . . wou'd soon set them Free.

Maryland planter Colonel Edward Lloyd, ca. 1756, quoted in Brasseaux, Founding, *p. 41.*

On Entering the Fort [*at Pensacola*] I was Astonished to see the poor Huts that are in it; but much more so when viewing the Condition of them, and that of the Poor Soldiers who inhabit here. Their Barracks are covered with Bark on the Sides and Roof, which naturally Shrivels in a short time the heat of the Sun, which was the case now. The Firmament appeared thro' the Top and on all sides, The men were walking About like Ghosts on a damp Sandy Floor, that is near a Foot under the Level. . . . Some of the Officers Huts were Similar, only the difference of a few Boards laid over the sand to tread on. . . . The Hospital has only the distinction of always being first Covered, and the Provision Stores that of being the last. . . .

It is high Time to fix the Necessary Garrison for this place, and as soon as that is done, to Erect proper Barracks for them. The Rooms should be raised at least 5 feet above the Ground. . . . In the furnishing of them, Attention Should be had in those Parts to prevent the Men from being Tormented in their Beds by the Muskitos, being open to them as they now are, Exposes them like the Beasts of the Field, to the Sting of these Venomous Insect or Fly, only there is not so many out of Doors, as Inside. . . .

Journal of Captain Harry Gordon, chief engineer of British forces, 1766, in Mereness, ed., Travels, *p. 486.*

[*Cahokia*] is . . . the uppermost Settlement on our Side [*of the Mississippi*]. In the Route we pass Le Petit Village . . . a place formerly Inhabited by 12 Families, now only by one since our Possession. The Abandoned houses most of them well built and left in good Order, the Grounds are favorable near the Village for Grain, particularly Wheat; and Extensive cleared Land, Sufficient for the labor of 100 to Cultivate. . . . [*In Cahokia*] are 43 Families of French who live well, and so might three times the Number, as there is a great Quantity of Arable clear land of the best soil near it; There is likewise 20 Cabins [of the] Peoria Indians left here, the rest and best part are moved to the French side, 2 Miles below Pain Court [*i.e., St. Louis*]. It is reckoned the Wheat thrives better here than at Kaskaskias. . . .

The Village of Pain Court . . . has already 50 families . . . and seems flourish very quick. At this place Mr. Le Chef [*Pierre Laclède*] the principal Indian Trader resides, who takes so good Measures, that the whole Trade of the Missouri, that of the Mississippi Northwards, and that of the Nations near La Baye, Michigan [*modern Green Bay, Wisconsin*], and St. Joseph's, by the Illinois River is entirely brought to him. He appears to be sensible, Clever, and has been very well Educated; is very Active, and will give us some trouble before we get the parts of this Trade that belong to us, out of his Hands.

Our possession of the Illinois is only useful at present in one respect, it Shows the Indian Nations our Superiority over the French. . . . The French carry on the Trade all round us by Land and by Water; 1st up the Mississippi, and to the Lakes . . .; 2ndly up the Ohio to the Wabash Indians, and even the small Quantity of Skins or Furs that the Kaskaskias and Peoria's (who are on our side) get by hunting is Carried under our Nose to Misere and Pain Court.

Captain Harry Gordon's journal, 1766, in Mereness, ed., Travels, *pp. 474–76.*

. . . it ever has been a practice allowed of, to enclose spots for gardens and potato grounds, so far back as where no fishing works can be made, but no governor or other person having ever been empowered to parcel out and divide lands, or to pass patents or grants for lands in this country, the whole must be deemed according to the Fishing Act a public common, and free to all persons to cut wood for the uses of the fishery, for fuel, &c., or to turn cattle upon, or to cut grass, and every one may take away what they cut.

Governor Sir Hugh Palliser of Newfoundland, July 1766, quoted in Pedley, History, *p. 119.*

Since all the inhabitants, from the most exalted to the most abject, from the richest to the poorest, are devoted disciples and zealous partisans of the said Society [of Jesus], you will easily understand that I took care not to trust any of them to carry out the King's orders [*to expel the Jesuits*]. The secret would surely have transpired, which was in no way appropriate. Therefore I determined to divulge it to no one but Señor Gálvez,

the minister who is here by order of the King, and to your son. [Teodoro de Croix]. As a result, among the three of us we made all the necessary arrangements, writing in our own hand the orders for its execution, which I dispatched immediately by special couriers in order that on the same day at the same hour the King's will might be done.

Viceroy Teodor de Croix to his brother, June 30, 1767, quoted in Kessell, Friars, *p. 11.*

A group of Acadians arrived [at New Orleans] in the month of July or August 1767. We destined them for Fort St. Gabriel, but, as they put it into their heads [that we] must permit [some of] them to remain vagrants in the city [and allow] the others to occupy lands contiguous to those of the other Acadians who were established opposite the Cabannocé coast, we had all of the trouble in the world to subject them to our arrangements. It was necessary to tell them that, if they did not wish to take themselves there, it would be necessary to expel them from the colony, as it [their intransigence] was unprecedented, for His Majesty, who satisfied all of the needs of a destitute nation, must be allowed to prescribe these conditions [of settlement].

Antonio de Ulloa's memoirs, quoted in Brasseaux, Founding, *p. 81.*

The greatest number of the Pous live about St. Joseph, and are still much in the French Interest, and by the Intrigues of a Runaway Set [*i.e., coureurs du bois*] of the latter at this place, and Miami, prevent any English Traders settling in that quarter. . . . Upon the Wabash where it falls into the Ohio, is still a French Settlement called St. Vincelle [*modern Vincennes*] said to Consist of about 150 families. They are mostly run away Traders; they are under no Command, as we have no Fort or Commanding Officer at that place; they are reckoned to be entirely devoted to the French Interest. They are supplied with their Goods by French Traders from Detroit, who steal out in the night time, without the Knowledge of the Commanding Officer. The Indians settled about the Islands of Sandusky, are a branch of the Hurons, The Traders on the Illinois brought in accounts that the Spaniards had built a Fort on our side of the Mississippi, a good way up at a place called Ouisconsin [*Wisconsin*] at a River which Communicates with the West side of Lake Michigan; and likewise, that they have built another, at a place called Pilowitimi, near the Confluence of the Illinois with the

Mississippi; on our side of that River; as also that they take great pains by presents etc. to gain the Friendship of all the Indians in that quarter.

. . . [Detroit] is reckoned able to raise betwixt 250 and 300 Men, able to bear Arms, it supplies almost all the Forts a great way round, with Flour and Indian corn of which they have always very plentifull Crops, and what is never known to fail; they use at this place, in lieu of Oil the fat of the Bear, melted down, which the Indians bring them in a kind of flask, made of Deer Skin; it was pretty palatable, and does not eat so strong as might be Imagined. . . .

British merchant John Lees of Quebec, 1768,
Journal, pp. 40–41.

Having told the Pimas that they were the absolute owners of the missions' goods *[after the expulsion of the Jesuits]* and that as such they might dispose of them as they saw fit, he handed over to them the keys to the granaries. That was the end of the maize. In just a few days they must have consumed at Tumacácori more than fifty *fanegas* without accounting for it. . . . The same thing was happening with the horses, cattle, etc. Everything would have been finished off within a few days. For this reason on my own initiative I have taken back the keys, leaving out enough provisions for their normal needs . . . until such time as the *comisario* appears, when I shall warn him not to proceed in such a disorganized manner.

Lieutenant Juan Bautista de Anza to Governor Juan
Claudio de Pineda, Sept. 1767, quoted in Kessell,
Mission, pp. 189–90.

Having maturely weighed all this, I require in behalf of the King: . . .

That M. Ulloa be declared to have violated our laws, forms and customs, and the orders of His Catholic Majesty, in relation to the act of cession, as it appears by his letter, dated from Havana, on the 10th of July, 1765.

That he be declared usurper of illegal authority, by causing subjects of France to be punished, and oppressed, without having previously complied with the laws, forms, and customs, in having his powers, titles, and provisions registered by the Supreme Council, with the copy of the act of cession.

That M. Ulloa, Commissioner of His Catholic Majesty, be enjoined to leave the colony in the frigate in which he came, without delay, to avoid accidents or new clamors, and to go and give an account of his con-

duct to His Catholic Majesty; and, with regard to the different posts established by the said M. Ulloa, that he be desired to leave in writing such orders as he shall think necessary; and that he be declared responsible for all the events which he might have foreseen; and that Mess. Aubry and Foucault [*the ordonnateur*] be requested, and even summoned, in the name of our Sovereign Lord, the King, to continue to govern and administer the colony as heretofore.

Chauvin de La Frénière, Louisiana attorney general,
to the Superior Council, October 1768,
quoted in Gayarré, History, vol. 2, p. 381.

Leaving the sick under a hut of poles which I had erected [*in San Diego*], I gathered the small portion of food which had not been spoiled in the ships and went on by land with that small company of . . . skeletons, who had been spared by scurvy, hunger, and thirst.

Letter of Gaspar de Portolá, July 1769, quoted in Rolle,
California, p. 51.

Having great confidence in your well known zeal and activity in behalf of my Royal Service, I have decided to send you to America with several missions. Since the most important is to take formal possession of the Colony of Louisiana, which my most worthy Christian and beloved Cousin has ceded to me, I have decided that as soon as you reach the island of Cuba you must obtain the proper number of soldiers and ammunition and other supplies which you feel are necessary, and that after having then taken possession of it in my Royal Name, you must make formal charges and punish according to the law the instigators and accomplices of the uprising which occurred in New Orleans. . . . So that you may carry out my instructions fully, I give you today such power and jurisdiction as shall be necessary for handling each matter, case, and incident. . . .

King Charles III of Spain to Alejandro O'Reilly,
April 1769, quoted in Texada, Alejandro, p. 26.

Our troops in the center of the Plaza [in New Orleans] occupied three sides of a square and the French soldiers closed the square. The General [*Alejandro O'Reilly*] disembarked at 5:30 P.M. and came to the center of the Plaza, where he presented to M. Aubry that which he was waiting for, namely the order of His Catholic Majesty. Immediately, the latter placed at his feet the keys of the city. At the same time Spanish flags were run up in various parts of the city, and the artillery and the troops on the Plaza fired a general salute. After this, our General, with the French commander and all the officers, whose duties permitted them, entered the church, where a Te Deum was sung as an act of Thanksgiving.

Spanish lieutenant colonel Francisco Bouligny, August 1769, quoted in Texada, Alejandro, p. 33.

The alternate actions of this nation [*Comanche*] at the same time, now peace, now war, demonstrate their accustomed faithlessness, either because of a premeditated principle of the entire nation or because their captains do not enjoy the superiority necessary to impose obedience and each individual does what he pleases, accommodating himself to enter in peace whenever he deems it advantageous and making war whenever his barbarous nature dictates.

Since it is impossible to reduce them to obedience to one or more captains or to limit their freedom so that they do not do as they fancy, I have adopted the policy of admitting them to peace whenever they ask for it and come with their trade goods and of waging war whenever they assault our frontiers and commit plunder. From war alone, all that results is loss of life and property, but from the alternate this poor citizenry gains some good, as occurred at the last two fairs, or *rescates,* of which I have spoken. Indeed at little cost they bought nearly 200 horses and mules, 12 muskets with ammunition, and a considerable number of buffalo hides . . . as well as some Indian captives who are added to the body of our Holy Faith.

New Mexico governor Pedro Mendinueta, 1771, quoted in Kessel, Kiva, p. 393.

. . . there is tuo french Gentlemen, that wrote me Concerning Some runaway Slaves that they have About your place the one: is Monsr. Trenonay; that lives at point Coupie; he has 2 Negro man Has Run away from his plantation some time ago; which he has been Informed keeps about Mr. John Murrays plantation with his Negros Or at least they has been Seen there Some time ago; he says he don't Value What Expencess there may Arise for having them taken and we Secur'd; with Irons &c, and that they may be sent by the first oppertuny, to the Address of Mrnsr. Bonrepaux in New Orleans. . . .—the Other is one Monsr. Daniel fagot that has been a french Officer here to fore; and is now at the Illinois; a Gentleman that Used me with the Greatest politeness when the Indians Gave me up at the Illinois in 1764. . . . [I]f it is possible to git him his

Molato man that run away from the Illinois about 21 months aGo And is now in the Chicasaw Nation; with some of the Traders. . . .

Manchac merchant John Fitzpatrick to Mobile trader Peter Swanson, September 1771, in Dalrymple, ed., Merchant, pp. 110–11.

The manners and way of life of the white people in Florida, differ very greatly from those in other provinces of America, particularly in respect of clothing; they are very plain, their dress consists of a slight waistcoat of stripped cotton, and a pair of trousers of the same, and often no coat; if any it is a short one of some light stuff; in winter a kind of surtout, made of a blanket, and a pair of Indian boots is all the addition; the women also dress light and are not very expensive. . . .

. . . [St. Augustine] is very ill built, the streets being all except crooked and narrow. The date on one of the houses I remember to be 1571; these are of stone, mostly flat roofed, heavy and look badly. Till the arrival of the English neither glass windows nor chimneys were known here, the lower windows all had a projecting frame of wooden rails before them. On the 3rd of January 1766, a frost destroyed all the tropical productions in the country except the oranges; the Spaniards called this a judgement on the place, for being become the property of Heretics, as they never had experienced the like.

Bernard Romans, 1773, Concise Natural History, *pp. 112, 262–66.*

We do not ask you, by this address, to commence hostilities against the government of our common sovereign.

The Spanish Governor's House, St. Augustine, painted 1764 *(Courtesy St. Augustine Historical Society)*

We only invite you to consult your own glory and welfare, and not to suffer yourselves to be inveigled or intimidated by infamous ministers so far as to become the instruments of their cruelty and despotism, but to unite with us in one social compact, formed on the generous principles of equal liberty, and cemented by such an exchange of beneficial and endearing offices as to render it perpetual. In order to complete this highly desirable union, we submit it to your consideration, whether it may not be expedient for you to meet together in your several towns and districts, and elect deputies, who after meeting in a provincial congress, may choose delegates, to represent your province in the continental congress, to be held at Philadelphia, on the tenth day of May, 1775.

In this present congress . . . it has been with universal pleasure, and a unanimous vote, resolved, that we should consider the violation of your rights, by the act [*the Quebec Act*] for altering the government of your province as a violation of our own; and that you should be invited to accede to our confederation, which has no other objects than the perfect security of the natural and civil rights of all the constituent members, according to their respective circumstances, and the preservation of a happy and lasting connection with Great Britain. . . .

First Continental Congress to inhabitants of Quebec,
October 1774, quoted in Christie, History,
vol. 1, pp. 24–25.

These Indians [*in Florida*] have large handsome canoes, which they form out of the trunks of Cypress trees (Cupressus distieba) some of them commodious enough to accommodate twenty or thirty warriors. In these large canoes they descend the river on trading and hunting expeditions on the sea coast, neighbouring islands and keys, quite to the point of Florida, and sometimes cross the gulph, extending their navigations to the Bahama islands and even to Cuba: a crew of these adventurers had just arrived, having returned from Cuba but a few days before our arrival, with a cargo of spirituous liquors, Coffee, Sugar and Tobacco.

Naturalist William Bartram, ca. 1774–76,
Travels of William, p. 226.

Came to again, at an old deserted plantation [*in East Florida*], the property of a British gentleman, but some years since vacated. A very spacious frame building was settling to the ground and mouldering to earth; here are very extensive old fields, where were growing the West-Indian or perennial Cotton and Indigo, which had been cultivated here, and some scattered remains of the ancient Orange groves, which had been left standing at the clearing of the Plantation.

I have often been affected with extreme regret, at beholding the destruction and devastation which has been committed, or indiscreetly exercised on those extensive, fruitful Orange groves, on the banks of St. Juan [*St. Johns River*], by the new planters under the British government, some hundred acres of which, at a single plantation, has been entirely destroyed to make room for the Indigo, Cotton, Corn, Batatas, &e. or as they say, to extirpate the mosquitoes, alleging that groves near their dwellings are haunts and shelters for those persecuting insects; some plantations have not a single tree standing, and where any have been left, it is only a small coppice or clump, nakedly exposed and destitute; perhaps fifty or an hundred trees standing near the dwelling-bouse, having no lofty cool grove of expansive Live Oaks, Laurel Magnolias and Palms to shade and protect them. . . .

Naturalist William Bartram, ca. 1774–77,
Travels Through, p. 160.

The city of Mobile is situated on the easy ascent of a rising bank, extending near half a mile back on the level plain above; it has been near a mile in length, though now chiefly in ruins, many houses vacant and mouldering to earth; yet there are a few good buildings inhabited by French gentlemen, English, Scotch, and Irish, and emigrants from the Northern British colonies. Messrs. Swanson and M'Gillivary who have the management of the Indian trade, carried on to the Chicasaws, Chactaws, Upper and Lower Creeks, &c. have made here very extraordinary improvements in buildings. . . . The principal French buildings are constructed of brick, and are of one story, but on an extensive scale, four square, encompassing on three sides a large area or court yard, the principal apartment is on the side fronting the street; they seem in some degree to have copied after the Creek habitation in the general plan; those of the poorer class are constructed of a strong frame of Cypress, filled in with brick, plaistered and white-washed inside and out.

Naturalist William Bartram, ca. 1774–77,
Travels of William, p. 404.

To be sold. A likely well made Negro boy, about sixteen years old. Enquire of the printer.

Nova Scotia Gazette, *March 1775, quoted in Murdoch,*
History, *vol. 2, p. 546.*

Sunday, April 16, 1775 . . . Crossed Turtle Creek. Dined at Myer's Ordinary. After dinner took a man to conduct us to the place where General Braddock was defeated by the French and Indians the 9th July 1755. It is on the Banks of the Mon-in-ga-ha-ly River. Found great numbers of bones, both men and horses. The trees are injured, I suppose by the Artillery. . . . We could not find one whole skull, all of them broke to pieces in the upper part, some of them had holes broken in them about an inch diameter, suppose it to be done with a Pipe Tomahawk. I am told the wounded were all massacred by the Indians. Got to Fort Pitt in the evening. . . .

Nicholas Cresswell, English visitor, Journal, *p. 64.*

Our inhabitants of Passamaquoddy and Saint John's river are wholly from New England, as are the greatest part of the inhabitants of Annapolis river, and those of the townships of Cornwallis, Horton, Falmouth and Newport, some of which are not forty miles from this town; that by reason of their connection with the people of New England, little or no dependance can be placed on the militia there, to make any resistance against them [*American Revolutionaries*]; that many in this town are disaffected, on which, likewise, I can have no great dependency; that should such an attempt be made, I dread the consequences. . . . [T]he buildings in the navy yard have been set on fire, but timely discovered and extinguished,—and from the place it happened, where no fire is ever carried, and near the magazine of powder, it is certain, without all doubt, a malicious design to destroy that yard. The perpetrators have not yet been discovered. . . . I would propose to your lordship, that a regiment of 1000 men be raised for the defense of this province, to be composed of Germans, Neutrals, and Irish, without regard to their religion—and were such troops to be placed under my directions, I think I could be answerable for the preservation of this province from being subverted by the *rebels.* . . .

Governor Francis Legge of Nova Scotia to British secretary of state, July 1775, quoted in Murdoch,
History, *vol. 2, pp. 550–51.*

I certify: that having carried out the examination which . . . the New Royal Regulation of Presidios issued by His Majesty on the tenth of September of 1772 prescribes for the removal of the company of San Ygnacio de Tubac in the Province of Sonora, I chose and marked out, in the presence of the Reverend Father Friar Francisco Garcés and Lieutenant Don Juan de Carmona, for the new situation of said presidio, with the denomination of San Agustin de Toixon [*Tucson*], the place of this name situated at a distance of eighteen leagues from that of Tubac, because the requisite conditions of water, pasture, and wood occur, as well as a perfect closing of the Apache frontier.

Hugo O'Conor, August 1775, quoted in Dobyns,
Spanish, *p. 58.*

All the bay, which is called the round bay (Bahia Redondo), though it is not shaped that way, is surrounded with steep hills, without trees, excepting two spots on the slopes fronting the two harbors to the southwest. The rest of it is arid, rugged, and of a melancholic aspect. . . . Standing in the cañon, which is to the northeast, there is a channel a mile and a half wide, deep and clear. East of its entrance there is a rancheria of about four hundred souls. I had dealings with them, but did not buy anything, though I presented them with beads, which you had given me for that purpose, and some old clothing of mine. Their acquaintance was useful to my men and to me, as they presented us with exquisite fishes (amongst them salmon), seeds, and pinole. I had the opportunity of visiting them four times and found them always as friendly as the first time . . . without being impertinent, as are many others I have seen during the conquest. This Indian village has some scows or canoes, made of tule, so well constructed and woven that they caused me great admiration. Four men get in them to go fishing, pushing with two-ended oars with such speed that I found they went faster than the launch.

Pilot Don José de Canizares's notes on San Francisco Bay, September, 1775, in Eldredge, March, *pp. 66–67.*

MASS. The bell is rung at sunrise. The married men enter, each one with his wife, and they kneel together in a row on each side of the nave of the church. Each couple has its own place designated in accordance with the census list. When there are many, the married couples make two rows on each side, the two men in the middle and the women at the sides. This may seem a superficial matter, but it is not, for experience has taught me that when these women are together they spend all the time dedicated to prayer and Mass in gossip. . . .

The widowers and widows form another row, the widows on the Gospel side and the widowers on the Epistle side. . . . From the pulpit to the altar on the Epistle side are seated in order the boys receiving instructions in doctrine. . . . The girls are on the Gospel side. Beside them are the two fiscales mayores and their subordinates, six in number, so that they may not permit them to play games and laugh. . . .

The petty governor and his lieutenant have their places at the door so that the people may not leave during the hour of prayer and Mass.

When all are in their places, the fiscal mayor notifies the father, who comes down with his census lists and takes attendance to see whether everyone is there. . . . If anyone is missing, the petty governor goes to fetch him. . . . If the truant is a woman, her husband is sent to fetch her.

Fray Joaquín de Jesús Ruiz, "Observations on . . . New Mexico Missions," 1776, in Dominguez, Missions, *pp. 308–09.*

On the 17th day of June, 1776, about two in the afternoon, the company of soldiers and families from Sonora set out from Monterey [*to found San Francisco*]. It was composed of its commander, Lieutenant Don José Joaquín Moraga, a sergeant, two corporals, and ten soldiers, all with their wives and families except the commander, who had left his in Sonora. In addition there were seven families of settlers, rationed and provisioned by the king; other persons attached to the soldiers and their families; five servant boys, muleteers and vaqueros, who conducted about two hundred of the king's cattle and some belonging to individuals, and the mule train which carried the provisions and utensils

necessary for the road. . . . [W]e two ministers, Father Fray Pedro Benito Cambón and I, went with two servants who conducted the loads, and three unmarried Indian neophytes, two of them from Old California and the other from the mission of Carmelo, who drove the cattle for the mission, numbering eighty-six head, which were incorporated with those for the presidio. . . .

On the 27th day of June the expedition arrived in the neighborhood of the harbor, and the commander ordered the camp halted on the bank of a lagoon called by Señor Anza Nuestra Señora de los Dolores. . . . [E]verything progressed so well that by the middle of September the soldiers had their houses already made of logs, all with flat roofs; the lieutenant had his government house; and a warehouse was finished of the same material, large enough to store all the provisions brought by the bark.

Fray Francisco Palou, Historical Memoirs, *vol. 4, pp. 118–19.*

The great trouble and difficulty I meet with in keeping good order amongst the fishers in a part of this government [*Labrador*] is occasioned chiefly by a number of disorderly people from your Province. . . . The last year whilst a tribe of four to five hundred of the Esquemeaux's savages were with me at Pitt's Harbour (and by means of interpreters) I made a peace with them and sent them away extremely well satisfied, without the least offensive thing happening. I am well informed some New England vessels contrary to the orders I have published went to the Northward, and robbed, plundered, and murdered some of their old men, women, and children, who they left at home, so I expect some mischief will happen this year; revenge being their declared principle.

Newfoundland governor Sir Hugh Palliser to Massachusetts governor Francis Bernard, August 1776, in Prowse, History, *pp. 327–28.*

11

The Road to Revolution in the English Colonies
1750–1776

INDIAN COMMISSIONERS

As a result of Indian complaints at the Albany Conference of 1754, the British Crown instructed General Edward Braddock to appoint Indian commissioners, or superintendents, in 1755. These appointments placed Indian diplomacy, formerly managed by individual colonies, under control of the Crown. One purpose of the new system was to prevent Indian attacks on frontier settlements, often made in retaliation for unfair trading practices. Such practices were a persistent and forceful Indian complaint. Many traders provided excessive liquor to Indian hunters and traders, then took their goods for little or no compensation. Although liquor originally had a ceremonial function in negotiations between Indians and whites, by the middle of the 18th century, both supplying and drinking it were widely abused.

William Johnson, a respected negotiator whose large estate was in the Mohawk Valley of New York, was appointed Indian superintendent of the Northern Department. His assistant was George Croghan of Pennsylvania. In 1758, while the French and Indian War raged, they held a major conference with the Iroquois at Easton, Pennsylvania. It was attended by the governor and entire colonial council of Pennsylvania, the governor of New Jersey, and many military officials. Iroquois tributaries agreed to withdraw from French alliances; in return, the English agreed to withdraw all settlement west of the Appalachian Mountains. The Treaty of Easton was ratified by the English Crown. Unfortunately, individual settlers violated it almost immediately, especially in Pennsylvania, where significant trans-Appalachian settlement already existed.

Indian agents frequently suggested that a clear policy of Indian rights should be developed. They repeatedly urged that no grants, settlements, or government organization should be made in new areas without their approval. In December 1761, the Crown instructed colonial governors to follow these recommendations. Unfortunately, they were little enforced.

PONTIAC'S WAR

Although North American hostilities in the French and Indian War ended in 1761, the Treaty of Paris was not officially signed until March 1763. Before the

British Crown could issue policies for its newly gained lands, a new Indian-English war erupted on the western frontiers.

General Jeffrey Amherst, who had successfully managed the military occupation of Quebec, badly mismanaged Indian relations in former French territories. Amherst was personally contemptuous of Indians. He referred to them as "pernicious vermin," infamously proposing to send them smallpox-infected blankets. Even had he not despised Indians, however, his authoritarian decisiveness was ill-suited to a task requiring slow negotiation and cross-cultural understanding. During 1761 and 1762, before the Seven Years' War had ended in Europe, he ordered British troops to begin occupying French forts in the upper Mississippi Valley. The French-allied Indians resisted acknowledging the English takeover (as did many French settlers). Amherst added to the problems by delivering a diplomatic insult. Ignoring the emphatic advice of Indian Commissioners Johnson and Croghan, he refused to continue the French policy of providing diplomatic gifts. The insult was doubly resented because the western Indians were unusually short of supplies, due to wartime interruptions of trade.

Eastern tribes, alarmed that British promises made at Easton had been disregarded, knew that the English would continue to demand larger tracts of land. Those Indian leaders who chose to accommodate Europeans lost much of their influence. Many tribes were undergoing a spiritual renewal, hoping to return to traditional ways and end dependence on European goods. The pan-Indian movement originated in the Susquehanna River valley. The most charismatic of its leaders was Neolin, who became known as the Delaware Prophet. In the early 1760s, he spread his message throughout the whole Ohio River valley and Great Lakes area.

From this widespread Indian dissatisfaction and ferment, a powerful political leader emerged: Pontiac, an Ottawa chief. Upon learning of the final French defeat in North America, Pontiac coordinated an Indian alliance to strike before the English recovered from the long war. Indian leaders hoped to oust the English from the Mississippi and Ohio River valleys and contain settlement east of the Appalachian Mountains. Their plans were little detected by non-Indians and completely discounted by ranking British officers.

On May 7, 1763, Pontiac laid siege to Fort Detroit. Although Major Henry Gladwin and 150 fighting men withstood it, other western tribes soon attacked every other major English-occupied fort west and north of Fort Pitt. One after another fell, often by means of skillfully executed Indian military subterfuge. By the end of June, the only western forts remaining under English control were Fort Detroit, Fort Niagara, and Fort Pitt. In August, the Lenni Lenape (Delaware) struck at Stewart's Crossing, about 25 miles south of Fort Pitt, and soon laid siege to Fort Pitt itself. Amherst finally grasped the seriousness of the war. He dispatched Colonel Henry Bouquet to aid Captain Simeon Ecuyer at Pittsburgh. En route, Bouquet achieved a costly but important victory over a force of Lenni Lenape, Mingo, and Shawnee at the Battle of Bushy Run. Nonetheless, Indian bands continued to raid vulnerable settlements in the backcountry of Pennsylvania, Maryland, and Virginia. As many as 2,000 settlers and traders were killed or captured, and many more driven from their homes.

Meanwhile, the British sent three expeditions to relieve the ongoing siege of Detroit. The first was defeated en route by Pontiac's forces; the second reached the fort but was defeated at the Battle of Bloody Run on July 31. The third left

Niagara in summer 1764, but by that time Pontiac himself had ended the siege. His Indian alliance was disintegrating. Some groups were dissatisfied with the war's progress and others accepted Britain's Proclamation of 1763, which forbade English settlers to move west of the Ohio. In October 1764, Pontiac entered peace negotiations.

During Pontiac's War, the Indian alliance had been large and not entirely unified. Peace negotiations were correspondingly long and complicated. General Thomas Gage, who had replaced Jeffrey Amherst as North American commander, ordered severe punishment for the Indians. His officers and Indian agents wisely followed a milder course. Indian Commissioner William Johnson spent nearly a year in negotiations, slowly regaining forts and captives for the English. In August 1765, Pontiac and representatives of many other tribes accepted peace terms at a Detroit council. In July 1766, a great council of eastern as well as western tribes concluded a treaty with Johnson at Oswego. Peace prevailed until the American Revolution, although Pontiac himself was killed by a Peoria Indian at Cahokia in 1769.

THE PROCLAMATION LINES

American colonists fought the French and Indian War primarily to gain control of the Ohio Valley, the triangle of land formed by the Ohio and Mississippi Rivers. Some wanted only to control trade with Native American groups residing there. Many others, however, wanted to open the valley to white settlement. Even before the war ended, several land companies began petitioning British officials for huge grants. Many individuals simply moved into the region, especially in western Pennsylvania. Some were traders or speculators representing larger organizations, but most were individual settlers seeking land.

As the French and Indian War drew to a close, imperial officials began considering future policies for trans–Appalachian settlement. The completed plan was included in the Proclamation of 1763, issued by King George III on October 7. It declared land west of the Appalachian Mountains to be Indian territory and prohibited white settlement there. The so-called Proclamation Line ran from Canada to Florida along the crest of the Appalachian range, clearly defined by geographical landmarks. West of the line, the Indian territory was placed under military jurisdiction, with no provision for civil government. Land grants were prohibited, previous purchases were declared void, and existing settlers were ordered to leave. Traders were required to obtain a special licence. The Plan for the Future Management of Indian Affairs (or Plan of 1764) formalized Indian commissioners' power in the territory and decreed a tax on trade.

British officials drew the Proclamation Line primarily because the Crown wanted to prevent new hostilities with the Indians. Some officials saw diplomatic if not ethical considerations in simply confiscating more Indian land. They planned, however, slowly and peacefully to move the line westward by concluding treaties with various Indian tribes.

The Proclamation Line was immediately and extremely unpopular with colonists. Many simply disregarded the law and squatted on desirable lands. Officials in Virginia and Pennsylvania not only ignored the squatters but improved the roads they used to travel west. Western trade boomed, but the wealth it generated for the few licensed merchants, traders, and hunters increased the resentment of many others. British officials soon realized that their plan would never be effective. They could afford neither to enforce it, thanks to Britain's tremendous war debt, nor to establish an imperial department of Indian affairs as the Indian commissioners recommended. In March 1768, officials announced a modified plan for the Indian territory. It specifically authorized the movement of the Proclamation Line westward by means of land treaties or purchases. Indian superintendents were to oversee all acquisitions and retained the power to settle disputes. The control of trade, however, was returned to individual colonies.

Numerous land companies soon formed in hopes of obtaining large grants. None was ultimately successful, but their lobbying speeded the treaty-making process to establish a new Proclamation Line. In the north, the Treaty of Fort Stanwix was concluded by Indian commissioners with the Iroquois Confederacy in 1768. It extended colonial control to trans-Appalachian land east of the Ohio River as far south as the Tennessee River. Superintendent of the Southern Department John Stuart negotiated the Treaty of Hard Labor (1768) and the Treaty of Lochaber (1770) with Cherokee and Creek, extending the line west in Virginia through Georgia.

By 1776, about 25,000 colonists lived beyond the Appalachian Mountains in the "new west." Although the new Proclamation Line treaties had opened extensive areas to white settlement, they made no formal provisions for civil government there. Neither did they require Native Americans to vacate the land. From Pennsylvania northward, the Iroquois remained to the west of the Appalachian barrier; south of modern Tennessee, Cherokee, Creek, and other southern tribes continued to inhabit the "new west." North of the Ohio River lived western tribes as well as the Seneca, who were angry at being excluded from negotiations by both the Iroquois and the southern tribes. Much early trans-Appalachian white settlement, therefore, was concentrated in relatively unoccupied land between the Ohio and Tennessee Rivers (most of modern Kentucky and Tennessee). This land was contested by Indians to the north and south but was not permanently inhabited by either.

DISCONTENT IN THE BACKCOUNTRY

Between 1750 and 1776, the non-Indian population grew to a quarter-million in the backcountry, the area west of the fall line but east of the Appalachian Mountains. Discontent among its residents multiplied as well. The backcountry had been granted very little representation in the colonial assemblies, although most white male settlers were landowners and qualified for the franchise. Few institutions of civil government existed, because assemblies had not established them. Colonial governments were dominated by urban, wealthy seaboard elites—commercial men in the northeast and slaveholding planters in the south. They had little interest in enlarging the relative power of backcountry farmers. Like other eastern colonists, they understood little about frontier life and could easily dismiss its problems. Although assemblies resisted spending money to solve the backcountry's problems, they spent freely to maintain their own "lawful authority" when the backcountry erupted in civil disorder.

One major cause of dissatisfaction in the backcountry was the lack of roads, schools, and other improvements, which settlers believed should be built by the colonial government. Another was the lack of local courts and administrative offices. To participate in a trial, obtain necessary services, or even exercise the right to vote, backcountry residents had to travel great distances. Such journeys were usually prohibitive and always expensive. The greatest source of dissatisfaction, however, was the lack of law enforcement and adequate defense. Residents believed that they suffered disproportionately from both Indian hostilities and unchecked criminal activity.

During the French and Indian War, the backcountry was ravaged by Indian *petite guerre*—sudden, unprovoked hit-and-run attacks. From New York through South Carolina, colonists suffered loss of life, destruction of property, and subsequent poverty. In Pennsylvania, the situation became so desperate that it ended 75 years of unified Quaker domination in the assembly. Under pressure from enraged citizens and alarmed British officials, the War Quakers split from the Principled Quakers and passed a Militia Bill in 1755. The new militia companies soon built a chain of forts and blockhouses from Easton to Mercersberg. Although the forts did not stop Indian raiding, they did provide Pennsylvania backcountry settlers with a safe retreat and reassurance. Indian raids in Pennsylvania began again during Pontiac's War. This time the assembly failed to act, partly from Quaker scruples and partly to defy the Penn proprietors, with whom colony officials were struggling for power. Pennsylvania frontier refugees poured into Carlisle and other defended settlements, their possessions gone and their plight desperate.

Pennsylvania backcountry frustrations increased. Finally, they erupted violently against blameless Indians who were under the protection of the colonial government. On December 14, 1763, a group called the Paxton Boys (from the town of Paxton, near Lancaster) murdered 20 Moravian-converted Conestoga Susquehannock—men, women, and children. The local coroner's jury claimed it could not identify the assailants. In January 1764, about 600 Paxton Boys marched toward Philadelphia, claiming to seek an audience with the governor

The Moravian settlement of Bethlehem, Pennsylvania, in 1757 *(New York Public Library Print Collection, D. 107, Print Collection, Miriam and Ira Wallach Division of Art, Prints and Photographs, Astor, Lenox, and Tilden Foundations)*

but rumored to be bent on murdering nearby Lenni Lenape Indians. The Pennsylvania Assembly quickly appropriated funds to fortify Philadelphia. Some Quakers even joined the hastily formed militia. Benjamin Franklin led a delegation out to meet the Paxton Boys and persuaded them to return home without incident. A few stayed to address the assembly, but they were put off and finally dismissed. The Paxton episode reunified Presbyterians, who had many congregations on the frontier, and made them a new political force in the Quaker-dominated colony.

The most serious backcountry protest occurred in the Carolinas and was known as the Regulator movement (the name developed because they wanted to "regulate" the backcountry). North and South Carolina Regulators were not formally connected but had the same underlying complaints. In North Carolina, backcountry residents especially resented their lack of control over local officials. These officials were appointed by the distant colonial government and were usually newcomers to the community, with little investment in its welfare. Offices were often sold to the highest bidder. The selling of offices was customary in the colonial era and was not in itself considered corrupt; however, in the sparsely settled backcountry, it created distinct ills. Officials often purchased multiple offices—sheriff and justice of the peace, for example—leaving dissatisfied citizens no avenue of complaint. In lieu of a salary, officials collected fees from the people who used their services. Backcountry residents greatly resented paying fees for law enforcement. They universally viewed local officials as greedy and corrupt.

Tension increased in 1766, when the North Carolina Assembly funded a new governor's mansion at New Bern—from monies intended for public schools. In August, the first Regulator meeting was held, attended by respectable backcountry farmers large and small, numbering well in the thousands. Militia officers were appointed to drive outlaws from the communities and to pressure corrupt officials into mending their ways. Regulation Advertisement Number One, detailing grievances, was sent to the assembly. It was ignored, as were the others that followed. In 1768, the "Regulation" was formally organized. In response, North Carolina governor William Tyron ordered the arrest of Regulators for vigilante acts. After the first arrests, civil disorders occurred in several places. In September 1770, Hillsborough Regulators took over the court, expelling the judge. In January 1771, the North Carolina Assembly passed the Johnston Riot Act, aimed at suppressing the movement. Instead, it increased the Regulation's membership. The backcountry was in turmoil, and the east was in panic. Governor Tyron called out the militia. In May 1771, the militia defeated 2,000 poorly prepared Regulators at Great Alamance Creek, also called the Regulator War. In the aftermath, six Regulators were hanged for treason; more than 6,000 were pardoned by the governor. As many as 1,500 families, however, moved out of North Carolina into modern Tennessee.

In South Carolina, Regulators focused on the issue of criminal activity in backcountry communities. After the Cherokee War ended in 1761, gangs of roving men (most former hardscrabble soldiers) terrorized the settlers. In the winter of 1760–61, many residents took refuge in forts. In 1763, the end of Pontiac's War unleashed a new wave of decommissioned soldiers and a new wave of serious crimes against persons and property as well as sexual violence against women.

Unfortunately, the only courts in South Carolina were located at Charleston. Transporting prisoners, witnesses, and evidence there from the backcountry was almost impossible. Although South Carolina officials were more sympathetic than their counterparts in North Carolina, early backcountry efforts to obtain local county courts came to nothing. Many assembly members did not understand the severity of the problem, and many Charleston residents stood to lose financially if courts were decentralized. In 1767, a number of backcountry outlaws were finally caught and convicted of horse thieving—but pardoned by a new governor, Charles Montagu. After the pardon, a group of settlers took justice in their own hands, attacking and burning the houses of suspected criminals. The assembly worried about the threat of civil disorder (fearing that South Carolina's slave majority might join in) and ordered the arrest of the vigilantes.

In June 1768, a Plan of Regulation was drawn up by backcountry property owners, angered that Regulators were arrested while the outlaws went free. The colony agreed to commission troops of rangers; almost all were Regulator members. As rangers, they began legally to bring outlaw activity under control. In 1770 and 1771, Lieutenant Governor William Bull pardoned many Regulators convicted of vigilante activities. In 1772, local courts opened, authorized by the Circuit Court Act of 1769. The Regulator movement virtually ended in South Carolina, with sectional relations in the colony much improved. Nonetheless, in both Carolinas backcountry residents remained notoriously unsympathetic to the growing Revolutionary cause. Many perceived a strong whiff of hypocrisy in easterners' complaints of "taxation without representation" and unfair treatment by the British government.

THE NEW WEST

Adventurous settlers began crossing the Appalachian Mountains well before the Proclamation of 1763 forbade it. Thomas Cresap reached the forks of the Ohio River in 1750. William Stewart founded Stewart's Crossing nearby in 1753. Settlers arrived shortly after the English captured Fort Pitt in 1758 and Forts Oswego and Niagara in 1759. After the Proclamation Line was moved in the late 1760s, settlement in the "new west" began in earnest. Virginians established settlements in modern West Virginia in 1769. In 1768, Virginians and Carolinians settled in the Watauga River area (the northeastern "point" of modern Tennessee). In 1772, under the leadership of North Carolinian James Robertson, they founded the first government west of the Appalachians, "by consent of the people," on land leased from the Cherokee. The Watauga Association agreed on a written document, elected a court to legislate and adjudicate, and appointed other officials. In 1775, they united with settlers on the Nolichucky River to the south, forming the Washington District. In 1776, the district petitioned for and received representation in the Provincial Congress of North Carolina. The following year it became Washington County (now in Tennessee).

Settlement of modern Kentucky also began. In 1774, James Harrod led 31 men from Pennsylvania to found Harrodsburg. In 1775, Richard Henderson of North Carolina, founder of the Transylvania Company, concluded the Treaty of Sycamore Shoals with the Cherokee, purchasing land between the Cumberland and Kentucky Rivers. According to tradition, Cherokee chief Dragging Canoe warned the negotiators that land farther south would be "dark and bloody ground"—hostile and difficult to settle. The phrase stuck to eastern Kentucky and Tennessee.

Meanwhile, Daniel Boone blazed a trail through the Cumberland Gap to the Kentucky River for the Transylvania Company. Boone was the most famous of the colonial frontiersmen and long hunters. (Long hunters made trips into the wilderness lasting at least one entire season, seeking animal skins and furs.) In April 1775, he founded the town of Boonesborough. Its first female residents, who accompanied the expedition, were Boone's 14-year-old married daughter Susannah Hays and a slave woman who worked as the cook (her name is not recorded). Henderson opened a land office nearby. Although both North Carolina and Virginia declared Boone's purchase under the Sycamore Shoals treaty void, about 300 settlers had arrived by May. Delegates from the four existing settlements met and established courts and laws. In October, Transylvania Company officials attended the First Continental Congress, unsuccessfully seeking recognition for "Transylvania" as the 14th colony. In June 1776, they appealed for recognition to the Virginia council and assembly. On December 31, Virginia officially recognized Kentucky County, Virginia (with approximately the same boundaries as the modern state) and gave it representation in the assembly.

The westernmost of all English settlements was Detroit, acquired from the French. English troops arrived from Quebec to take possession on November 29, 1760. The first English traders began arriving in January 1761 from Pennsylvania and New York. Detroit's commander, Captain Donald Campbell, established good relations with the mostly French-speaking settlers. White and métis population was probably close to 2,000 by 1776.

THE UPPER OHIO VALLEY, LORD DUNMORE'S WAR, AND THE MASON-DIXON LINE

Although the 1758 Treaty of Easton outlawed settlement in trans-Appalachian Pennsylvania, by 1763 Pittsburgh—at the gateway to the Ohio Valley—had 630 residents. At the conclusion of Pontiac's War, two large Philadelphia trading firms established themselves there. By 1768, when the Treaty of Fort Stanwix made settlement legal, an estimated 2,000 colonists already lived nearby. In 1769 the Penn proprietors opened a land office in Pittsburgh. On the first day, almost 2,800 new applicants filed for the three-hundred-acre land grants offered in the nearby river valleys.

Despite the Penn's land office, however, the fertile valleys of the upper Ohio River, also continued to be claimed by Virginia—who had, after all, sent young George Washington to order the French out in 1754. Settlers arrived in the area not only via Forbes Road, leading west from Carlisle, Pennsylvania, but also via Braddock's Road, leading north from Virginia (both cut during the French and Indian War). The area was also home to Shawnee, Mingo, and Lenni Lenape claimants. As always, increasing white settlement led to frequent skirmishes and the threat of greater Indian hostilities. In early 1774, Virginia governor John Murray, Lord Dunmore, sent the Virginia militia to seize Fort Pitt, which had been abandoned as a British military installation the previous year. He promptly renamed it Fort Dunmore, drew up an organizational plan for Pittsburgh and the upper Ohio Valley, and appointed officials. He then used the fort as a base from which to attack the Shawnee at the mouth of the Kanawha River. On October

10, Dunmore's forces forced the Shawnee into retreat at the Battle of Point Pleasant, after which Dunmore negotiated a peace which greatly facilitated future white settlement. Virginia appeared to have won jurisdiction in the upper Ohio Valley.

Revolutionary events, however, soon distracted both Pennsylvania officials and Lord Dunmore from continuing what has come to be called Lord Dunmore's War. In 1776, by which time the ardent Loyalist Dunmore had been forced to flee Virginia, settlers took the issue into their own hands. Shortly after independence was declared, residents of the Ohio River Valley in modern Ohio, West Virginia, and western Pennsylvania asked Congress for recognition as "Westsylvania," the 14th colony. Their request was not granted.

In the years following the French and Indian War, Pennsylvania officials had more success settling a boundary dispute to the east. In 1760, Maryland's Calvert proprietors and the Penn proprietors proceeded to mark a boundary ordered by British courts a decade earlier. They hired two English mathematicians and astronomers, Charles Mason and Jeremiah Dixon, to determine a line. Mason and Dixon had begun in the east and reached the westernmost point of Maryland's boundary with Pennsylvania by 1767. In 1779, their line was extended west to put the Pennsylvania-Virginia (modern West Virginia) boundary dispute to rest as well. The Mason-Dixon line soon became the symbolic dividing point between North and South in the new American nation.

THE DEVELOPMENT OF AFRICAN-AMERICAN CULTURE

New African slaves continued to arrive in the colonies, but American-born blacks became a majority after 1750. Although descended from different African ethnic and national groups, they began to forge a shared culture and a new social structure, with some variations from region to region. More important, the new African-American culture was constrained by the inescapable limitations of slavery.

Newly arrived Africans spoke many mutually unintelligible languages, but not English. They slowly blended English vocabulary with shared African speech patterns. In turn, African-American speech influenced white language, especially in the south. After 1750, many white visitors began to comment—unfavorably—on this influence. It was most pronounced among the white elite, who used black house servants and caregivers for their children, and among white servants who worked closely with blacks. In isolated areas of the lower south, a distinctive black language called Gullah developed.

A more serious problem than language for newly arrived slaves was the loss of family, both immediate and the extended kinship networks that controlled social relationships in Africa. By 1750, new black families and a new system of kin and respected elders had formed. White slave owners had also become more interested in preserving slave families, and public opinion encouraged their efforts. Historical evidence indicates that slaves valued marriage and the family very highly. They developed their own marriage ceremonies and defended their families against tremendous odds. The slave family had no legal status, however, and the threat of separation hung constantly over the heads of parents, children, and marriage partners. Family life was also complicated because parents could not protect their children from mistreatment nor husbands their wives from sexual abuse or from overwork during pregnancy. Many couples lived apart after marriage at the residences of different masters. Despite these difficulties, historians believe that a majority of slave households were nuclear families at the end of the colonial period, although other family patterns existed as well.[1]

After 1750, African-American slaves increasingly embraced Christianity, particularly evangelical Protestantism. In the aftermath of the Great Awakening, the resistance of slave owners to religious activities among their slaves lessened. White missionaries worked among them, and in many areas whites and blacks attended services together. Black preachers also began to appear, emphasizing aspects of Christian theology that were relevant to African-American experiences and spiritual traditions. (In more than one recorded instance, preachers had to hurry out of town after mentioning the escape of the Israelites from Egypt.) As the colonial period ended, African Americans began to form and lead separate black congregations in Georgia, Virginia, and elsewhere. They also began to adapt white rituals to African traditions; for example, they held "double" funerals, which included both grieving and celebration.

Between 1750 and the American Revolution, annual celebrations of several days' length, similar to the Louisiana Mardi Gras, became part of African-American colonial culture. The celebrations honored black leaders, satirized the white community, and included parades, feasting, and dancing. In the northern and middle colonies, black kings or governors were elected. They served as a extra-legal authorities within the black community for the following year, settling disputes and enforcing standards. In New England, the festival was called Negro Election Day; in the middle colonies, the celebrations occurred during Pinkster (the Dutch word for Pentecost, a post-Easter Christian celebration) or Militia Day, when white colonists observed yearly training. In the South, the election of black governors was forbidden, but other aspects of the yearly holiday were observed.

THE DEBATE OVER SLAVERY

In the decades preceding the Revolution, the first extended consideration of human slavery began in the American colonies. Prior to 1750, only a few people questioned slavery's morality or even usefulness in the social order. Discussion stirred when Georgia, the only colony in which slavery was originally illegal, lifted its ban and legalized it in 1750. After 1763, when white colonists began to debate their own oppression by Britain, slavery became a more public topic. Some began to question its morality. Some began to think it contradictory to a belief in "natural rights" and liberties that, they argued, no government could legitimately curtail. Some even thought slavery violated sound economic theory, encouraging laziness in slave owners and unprofitable work habits in slaves themselves. Not surprisingly, many people vigorously defended slavery, especially those whose wealth and social position depended on it. Because slaves were defined as *chattel,* or material property, some argued that there was no contradiction between Revolutionary liberty and slave ownership. Indeed, the right to own and control "property" was central to the English concept of liberty. Even many who upheld slavery, however, came to believe that the treatment of slaves should be improved.

Quakers took the lead in opposing slavery. Before the Revolution, they disciplined members who participated in the slave trade and organized the first official antislavery society. Also pre-Revolution, prohibitive laws against the trade were passed in the New England states, and a prohibitive duty enacted in Pennsylvania. People such as New Jersey Quaker John Woolman, Pennsylvanian Anthony Benezet (who established a school for blacks in Philadelphia in 1770), and even Benjamin Franklin quietly wrote protests. Reformers publicized slaves of exceptional accomplishment, like the poet Phillis Wheatley. Wheatley had been kidnapped, brought to America, and sold into a Boston family at the age of seven. In 1773, she became the first African American to publish a book of poetry, earning an international reputation after *Poems on Various Subjects, Religious and Moral,* was published in England.

Slaves themselves understood the parallels between their own lives and political events in the pre-Revolutionary era, as their actions clearly showed. In the north, where blacks usually lived in close proximity to whites, many heard discussions in which the words *slavery* and *tyranny* were constantly used to describe the colonies' relationship to Britain. Beginning in the late 1760s, "freedom cases" appeared in New England courts. Black individuals sued their masters using similar arguments, and they often won. In January 1773, a group of slaves petitioned the General Court of Massachusetts for freedom on the basis of "natural rights." Other such petitions followed. In the South, blacks who embraced pre-Revolutionary ideas were less successful. In 1766, Charleston blacks created panic when they marched through the streets chanting "Liberty! Liberty!" Southern slaves, however, quickly grasped that political events were dividing slave owners and thus weakening their authority. As early as the Stamp Act crisis in 1765, escape attempts began to increase in the southern colonies. The number of slaves who escaped between then and the end of the Revolution cannot be accurately established, but historians estimate it to be many tens of thousands.

THE FOUNDING FATHERS

In the decades before the American Revolution, intellectual activity became a common and popular avocation among many colonists. Influenced by Enlightenment thinking, they believed that new political and social ideas could be developed and could bring about great human progress. Many educated and wealthy colonists in particular took the deliberation of such ideas very seriously. They corresponded extensively with international acquaintances as well as with each other. From this intellectual ferment a remarkable group of men emerged, who would be called the Founding Fathers by later generations. Primarily members of the colonial elite, most (but not all) were formally educated. In the north there were lawyers like John and Samuel Adams and James Otis, merchants like John Hancock, and self-made men like Benjamin

Phillis Wheatley, as pictured in her 1773 *Poems (National Portrait Gallery, Smithsonian Institution, NPG.77.2)*

Franklin. In the south, most were wealthy planters, and all were slave owners—George Washington, Thomas Jefferson, Patrick Henry, and many others. They questioned slavery, along with all other political arrangements, although it was far too entrenched in the South's economy to be outlawed by an uncertain new colonial union. Statesmen in individual New England and the Middle Atlantic colonies, however, continued questioning the institution; in 1780 they would begin to pass colony-by-colony laws to end it.

Through their deliberations, the Founding Fathers gave voice to a revolutionary new ideology, based in a belief in natural rights, political liberty, and equality under law. When events precipitated an irreconcilable break with Britain, they led (and sometimes instigated) the movement for American independence. They created (and later dominated) new institutions for the new republic. In doing so, they created a new and enduring political system. Perhaps more remarkably, they justified it with a vocabulary of high ethical purpose that enabled later generations to correct the deficiencies of the very system they created.

CONTROVERSY OVER SUGAR AND STAMPS

As imperial authorities were aware, American merchants and shippers had a long tradition of evading British trade and navigation acts. During the French and Indian War, imperial authorities attempted to enforce the laws more strictly, primarily to cut off trade with the enemy. In 1755, the Crown permitted the use of writs of assistance, or blanket search warrants with no specifically stated object. In 1761, King George III renewed the writs, and protests erupted in Massachusetts. Soon after, however, North American hostilities ended, and colonists resumed their customary technique of evasion.

In April 1763, a month after the Treaty of Paris was signed, George Grenville became the Crown's chief adviser. He immediately developed plans to reduce England's unprecedented national debt and to balance future budgets. Grenville was determined to require colonists to finance part of their own administration and defense. The colonists were in fact among the lowest-taxed people in the Western world. Historians estimate that for every one shilling colonists paid in taxes, citizens residing in England paid over 25.

In March 1764, Parliament passed the Revenue Act of 1764, or Sugar Act. It renewed the provisions of the 1733 Molasses Act, which taxed sugar products imported to the colonies for the manufacture of rum. (Rum was extremely important, because it was used in the complex triangular slave trade and in all Indian trade.) The Sugar Act was more restrictive than the earlier Molasses Act, however. It enumerated many new items, required ship captains to list all cargo and post bonds, and moved the juryless admiralty courts to Halifax. It also established, for the first time, regulations and duties for short-distance trade among the colonies themselves, which was usually conducted by numerous small, local shippers. At the same time the Crown ordered all customs officials to man their posts at once, and the British navy was ordered to assist them. Most importantly for future events, the Sugar Act clearly established Parliament's right to enact taxes in the colonies, solely for the purpose of raising revenue. All previous Navigation Acts, in contrast, had been enacted solely to regulate trade.

When colonists learned of the Sugar Act in May, strong protests followed. In public meetings, Samuel Adams, James Otis, and others objected because the colonies were being subjected to taxes not of their own making or consent. The loudest protests came from large merchants and the many small local traders, both of whom were directly affected. They argued that a decline in business would worsen the postwar depression, which was already causing great distress among large numbers of ordinary people. Every colony lodged some manner of complaint with imperial authorities. Several assemblies passed formal protests. Even in Virginia, where the governor Lord Dunmore prevented the assembly from convening, the council and the burgesses met on their own to compose a protest. Private organizations of merchants and other citizens sent memorials and petitions. Colonial agents were instructed to lobby against the act. Committees formed in several colonies to keep in touch with their fellows elsewhere, especially since a stamp act was also rumored to be under consideration.

Grenville, who was also facing violent tax protests at home in England, did nothing more for a year. Supposedly, he wanted to give the colonists a chance to suggest a different method of raising revenue to pay for their own military defense. No suggestions were forthcoming. In March 1765, Parliament passed the Revenue Act of 1765, or Stamp Act, to take effect in November. All revenue from the Stamp Act was to be used to maintain an anticipated 10,000 British troops in America. Soon after, the Quartering Act was passed to require all colonies to house and supply troops if existing military barracks proved insufficient. Although colonists living on the frontiers always sought additional military protection, colonists on the seaboard had little desire for royal troops to be stationed among them. Many suspected that the soldiers would be used for imperial oversight rather than defense.

The Stamp Act levied a tax on everyday commercial and business activities within the colonies. It required the use of paper that was "stamped," or embossed with an official seal, for all manner of documents and paper products. Included were newspapers, pamphlets, almanacs, all legal documents, land documents, contracts of any kind, advertisements or handbills, diplomas, receipts or bills for shipping and other business transactions, dice and playing cards, even tavern licenses. The Stamp Act also—and oddly—taxed all documents drawn up in "ecclesiastical courts." These two words caused tremendous apprehension among American colonists, to whom religious and civil tyranny were always closely related. No Anglican bishop had ever been appointed for the colonies, despite lobbying by Anglican clerics, and therefore no ecclesiastical courts existed. Many worried that the Stamp Act hinted at additional plans to establish the Church of England in the colonies.

The Stamp Act unleashed a fury of protest in the colonies, to the surprise of British officials. The two colonial groups who were particularly affected by the act were also well-positioned to lead a vocal campaign: lawyers and publishers. They had little difficulty finding sympathizers, because most ordinary citizens were affected as well. Small shopkeepers, artisans, and other working people, still suffering from the economic depression, began to support the protests. They also began to discuss and debate the larger political issues raised by the act. Newspapers aided the debate by publishing formal protests prepared by colonial assemblies and circulating them widely from colony to colony.

On May 29, the fiery young Patrick Henry introduced seven resolutions to the Virginia Assembly. The first four forcefully restated the historic rights of Englishmen and Virginians. The last three directly challenged British authority, declaring that the Virginia assembly alone had power to tax the colony—and labeling anyone who disagreed a traitor to the colony. After acrimonious debate, the Virginia burgesses passed the first four. All seven of the Virginia Resolves, however, circulated widely in newspapers. Many colonists considered them far too extreme. The resolves did, however, clearly state the logical outcome of the current debate and provided a new frame for public discussion. After they appeared, leaders of more radical persuasion gained a more prominent voice.

Massachusetts officials responded to the Stamp Act by inviting colonies to send representatives to New York City "to draw up a united, dutiful, loyal and humble" petition to the Crown. Representatives from nine colonies met in October. (The royal governors of New Hampshire, Virginia, North Carolina, and Georgia refused to convene their assemblies or otherwise select representatives, although the assemblies themselves sent word that they would agree to the decisions of the meeting.) The Stamp Act Congress, as the meeting came to be called, produced a Declaration of Rights and Grievances and addressed a petition to the king and a memorial to Parliament. The documents affirmed loyalty to the king and "all due subordination" to Parliament. They argued, however, that the "rights of Englishmen" entitled colonists to be taxed only by a body in which they had representation. Since distance prohibited their representation in Parliament, only colonial assemblies had the power to tax. Although agreement on the

Baltimore in 1752 *(New York Public Library Phelps Stokes Collection 1752 B-70, D. 98, Print Collection, Miriam and Ira Wallach Division of Art, Prints and Photographs, Astor, Lenox, and Tilden Foundations)*

documents was not unanimous, the Stamp Act Congress was significant. It was the first extensive display of political agreement and voluntary cooperation among the usually fractious colonies.

Meanwhile, reasoned and principled arguments against the British course of action began to appear in newspaper and pamphlets throughout the colonies. Daniel Dulany, an English-trained Maryland lawyer and council member, wrote one of the most influential and widely circulated of these publications. Entitled *Considerations upon the Propriety of Imposing Taxes in the British Colonies,* it appeared first in the *Maryland Gazette,* whose publisher printed a skull and crossbones where the tax stamp should appear. Dulany clearly explained the principle of "no taxation without representation" by comparing the very different English and American ideas of "representation." In England, representation was virtual, because suffrage was very limited and many members were elected from districts that had little correspondence to actual population or geography. Every member of Parliament was thought to represent the interests of the nation as a whole, but no member represented any one specific, identifiable group of people within it. Dulany called virtual representation "a mere cob-web, spread to catch the unwary." In the colonies, representation was direct. Every assembly member was clearly elected to represent the interests of a specific geographical site and the specific property owners who lived there.

Other forms of opposition to the stamp tax developed. The idea of substituting American-made products for imported British goods was soon taken up as a cause by many groups—housewives and ordinary citizens as well as political leaders. The earliest Revolutionary women's association formed at Providence in 1766. Vowing to replace imported fabrics with homespun, 17 women met at the home of Deacon Ephraim Bowen to spin all day. Their second meeting was so large that it was held in the courthouse, and "spinning bees" soon became popular throughout the colonies. Shortly before the Stamp Act was to take effect, merchants in New York, Boston, Philadelphia, and many smaller towns formally adopted nonimportation and nonconsumption agreements, refusing to import or sell British goods. Ministers, particularly in Congregational and Presbyterian churches, began to preach sermons supporting the protests. They reminded congregations of the tyranny their 17th-century forebearers had suffered at the hands of William Land, archbishop of Canterbury, and King Charles I (who, as listeners remembered, were eventually beheaded). Ministers also began to use what politicians would later call committees of correspondence, to keep each other informed of violations to non-Anglican Protestant religious liberty.

Organizations called the Sons of Liberty formed in Connecticut and quickly spread, with the goal of making collection of the stamp tax impossible. ("Sons of Liberty" was a phrase coined by a sympathetic member of Parliament, Isaac Barré.) The leaders and spokesmen of the Sons of Liberty were usually merchants, lawyers, large planters, or even clergy. Most members, however, were small farmers in rural areas and, in towns, small shopkeepers, working people, and seamen. In many places, Sons of Liberty protests erupted into riots and caused much damage. But they forced most stamp tax agents to resign—or flee for their own safety. Merchants and shippers destroyed or "embargoed" stamped paper. By November 1, 1765, when the Stamp Act was to take effect, no major colonial seaport had a supply of stamped paper or an agent to sell it. The legal conduct of almost any business or court transaction was impossible. Most officials had no choice but to ignore the use of unstamped paper. In New York and a few other places, enforcement attempts were met with violent disorders.

In England, meanwhile, George Grenville had been replaced by Charles Watson-Wentworth, the marquis of Rockingham. Rockingham favored repealing Grenville's Stamp Act. British manufacturers and merchants had been seriously hurt by nonimportation agreements and the campaign to do without British goods. But Rockingham also thought it crucial for Parliament to uphold its right to tax the colonies, regardless of their protests. Parliament therefore repealed the Stamp Act on the grounds that it hurt British trade. The king signed the measure on March 18, 1766. On the same day, however, Parliament passed the Declaratory Act, which declared Parliament's right to make laws for the colonies, including tax laws, and to void any colonial statutes that restricted its power.

In America, colonists were so overjoyed at the repeal of the Stamp Act that they paid little attention to the Declaratory Act. Funds were collected to erect statues to King George III and new towns were named for William Pitt, who had shepherded the measure through the House of Commons. Trade and importation resumed. In Britain, however, anticolonial sentiment ran high. Many British now believed that the colonies would demand independence—although few colonists themselves had yet accepted that idea.

NEW CONTROVERSY OVER THE TOWNSHEND ACTS

Unfortunately, appeasing the American colonists worsened Britain's financial problems. In England, taxes were increased and much turmoil resulted, both among the people and within government. Politicians fought among themselves, and the various ministers were unable to do their jobs effectively. By 1767, Parliament was forced to lower English taxes, and another budget shortfall soon loomed. Chancellor of the Exchequer Charles Townshend proposed a multipart plan to tax the colonies and to strengthen imperial control over them. The Revenue Act of 1767 imposed a series of small customs duties on a large number of items Americans imported from Britain, such as glass, lead, paper, and tea. All money collected was to be used by Britain to pay royal governors, judges, and other officials—whose salaries had been previously controlled by colonial assemblies. Separate measures reorganized the customs service and legalized writs of assistance, or blanket search warrants. Another act suspended the New York Assembly, which had refused to comply with the 1765 Quartering Act. (Quartering Acts required communities to house and feed soldiers when necessary; New York's refusal was significant because it was the headquarters of British troops in America.) Together, these measures were called the Townshend Acts.

News of the Townshend Acts reached the colonies in September 1767. At first the reaction, while unfavorable, was moderate. The New York Assembly agreed (by one vote) to provide funds to quarter the British troops. Public debate resumed, however, and more pointedly questioned the relationship of the colonies to Britain. In December 1767, John Dickinson, an English-trained Pennsylvania attorney and farmer, published the first of 12 influential *Letters from a Farmer in Pennsylvania*. Dickinson rejected abstract political theories that attempted to define the proper relationship between England and the colonies. Instead, he spoke in favor of liberty, freedom, and especially colonial union. The colonies "form *one* political body," wrote Dickinson, "of which *each colony* is a *member.*" Easy to understand, the *Letters* were widely reprinted in newspapers and pamphlets in both America and Europe. They provided a new frame for public discussion.

In February 1768, the Massachusetts General Court approved a circular letter, moderate in tone, and forwarded it to all other colonial legislatures. Primarily drafted by Samuel Adams, it argued that colonies had a right to be taxed only by elected representatives and that colonial judges and governors should be paid only with funds controlled by the colonists themselves. Although the letter urged united action by the colonies, it closed by denying a desire for independence. Unfortunately, newly appointed British officials Lord Frederick North (exchequer) and Wills Hill, Lord Hillsborough (secretary of state for the colonies) reacted angrily. Massachusetts governor Francis Bernard was instructed to dissolve the assembly unless it rescinded the letter. Other governors were instructed to dissolve their assemblies if they attempted to read it in session. In June, the Massachusetts General Court, already at loggerheads with Governor Bernard, overwhelmingly refused to rescind, upon which he dissolved the court. Imperial officials, further angered, threatened to transport any colonist suspected of treason to England for trial. They also sent the warship *Romney* to Boston to back up the headquarters of the customs service.

Parliament had established severe penalties for trade violations, including seizure and sale of ships and cargoes. The spoils were divided equally among customs officials, the governor, and the British treasury. Not surprisingly, this policy encouraged both aggressiveness and greed among the customs commissioners. It also hurt common seamen as well as shipowners and merchants, since seamen often imported small items to sell privately for profit. On June 10, customs officials ordered the seizure of wealthy merchant John Hancock's ship *Liberty* for, they claimed, forcibly refusing inspection. Three days later, the officials were forced by a rioting mob to take refuge on the *Romney.* Imperial officials dispatched royal troops to Boston from England and from the military base in Halifax.

Boston immediately convened a town meeting. Since the colonial assembly was forbidden to meet, Boston called for other towns to send representatives to a "convention" in September. Ninety-six towns did so. The Massachusetts Convention of 1768 met for six days and formulated a statement of grievances. In May 1769, the Virginia House of Burgesses passed resolutions restating the principle of "no taxation without representation" and the right to local jury trial. The burgesses also resolved that the colonies had the right to collaborate. To underline the point, they sent the resolutions to other colonies for agreement. The Virginia governor promptly dissolved the assembly. Ironically, in the same month, Lord Hillsborough agreed to permit the Massachusetts Assembly to resume meeting. It met in July and immediately passed a resolution reaffirming its sole right to tax the colony.

Meanwhile, to protest the Townshend Acts, Massachusetts merchants once again attempted to organize boycotts of British imports and popularize reliance on American-made alternatives. In other northern colonies, merchants dragged their feet until the Massachusetts Assembly was dissolved; they then began to renew nonconsumption and nonimportation agreements. The southern colonies, similarly, did not participate widely until the Virginia assembly was dissolved. After that event, the burgesses met as a convention and endorsed a nonimportation agreement, including a refusal to import slaves. Almost every major planter signed it, and it was soon accepted throughout the south. Despite the agreements, however, some merchants continued to trade with Britain. To force their cooperation, the Sons of Liberty were revived. On many occasions, mobs dragged suspected backsliders to "liberty trees" or "liberty poles" erected in public places, where the merchants were forced to agree to the boycott.

Royal troops had reached Boston in September 1768, but no immediate violence occurred. Indeed, in summer 1769, two of the four regiments were sent back to Halifax. As months passed, however, antagonism increased. Bostonians continually baited the soldiers, calling them "red coats," "lobster backs," and the more profane "bloody backs." Several serious incidents occurred, including the accidental killing of an 11-year-old boy by soldiers. On the night of March 5, 1770, the tension erupted. Snowball-throwing escalated, and a mob surrounded sentries at the customhouse. Reinforcements arrived, and in the confusion, soldiers fired. Five Bostonians were killed and six wounded. Several British soldiers were tried for the deaths and very skillfully defended by Son of Liberty John Adams. Two were convicted of manslaughter, branded on their thumbs, and released. The Boston Massacre, as the event was called, was reported in the colonies as the cold-blooded murder of unoffending citizens. The facts, however, have never been conclusively established. Many historians see Adams's defense as a matter of principle, but some speculate it was undertaken to prevent the involvement of colonial radicals from coming to light.

While the Boston Massacre was occurring, back in England Parliament was rescinding the Townshend Acts, with one exception: the duty on tea. Once again British trade had been hurt by boycotts, and English merchants feared that the colonies might permanently increase their manufacturing capacity. Unlike most other imports, however, tea could not be manufactured in America. Used by all social classes, it was, in addition, the heart of an important social ritual among the genteel. The tax would daily remind the colonists of Parliament's supremacy. Although some colonial activists wanted to continue the boycotts until even the tea duty was repealed, most citizens did not. Instead, many merchants took the time-honored approach of evading the duty by smuggling tea from Holland and elsewhere.

New Trouble over Tea

On the surface, the relationship between England and its American colonies was calm for over two years after the repeal of the Townshend Acts. Although some colonial governors continued to behave arbitrarily, prosperity resumed and even flourished in the colonies. Under the surface, however, divisions were hardening among the colonists. Conservatives—called Tories, or Loyalists—were willing to accept the recent compromises. They had no desire to break with Britain, and they opposed the extension of democracy. Moderates and radicals—called Whigs and, later, Patriots—remained suspicious of Britain. Radicals, in addition, wanted to broaden the rights of ordinary people. Their foremost spokesman, Sam Adams, was a master of organization and propaganda. Local Sons of Liberty were again organized, and members began to promote the extension of democratic rights.

In June 1772, the surface calm ended when the Crown announced that it would henceforth pay the salaries of the governors and judges. Colonists objected strongly. They understood that their ability to set salaries helped them restrain the governor and secure the loyalty of judges to colonial interests. In November, Massachusetts held a town meeting at which a formal Committee of Correspondence was established, under the guidance of Sam Adams. Within three months, 80 more standing committees had been formed in smaller towns of the colony, much to the displeasure of Governor Thomas Hutchinson, who had not inherited from his ancestor Anne Hutchinson a taste for dissent. The purpose of the committees of correspondence—in an age with few means of long-distance communication—was to state local beliefs about political principles and colonial rights, to document violations, and to disseminate the information to other towns and colonies. Like modern special interest groups, committees also began to influence public opinion by providing information about their ideas to the press and public.

In January 1773, Governor Hutchinson denounced the committee movement to the assembly. He was answered with a paper drafted by Sam Adams and revised by John Adams, arguing that the colony owed allegiance only to the Crown, not to Parliament. The distinction soon gained great popularity. Soon after, Benjamin Franklin, still in London, obtained letters written by Governor Hutchinson to British officials, in which the governor advised them to restrict "English liberties" in the colonies. The letters were, of course, widely published.

At the same time, a royal commission was busy in Rhode Island investigating the 1772 burning of a grounded British warship, the *Gaspée,* by angry colonists. The ship had been used to capture colonial smugglers. Colonists were fearful that accused citizens would be transported to England, but none were indicted, because the colonists refused to testify or name suspects. The *Gaspée* incident was publicized widely, if not always objectively, by the Massachusetts Committees of Correspondence. It prompted the Virginia Assembly to form its own committee in March 1773 and to send a circular letter recommending that other colonies do the same. The Virginia governor once again dissolved the assembly. Within a year, however, every colony except Pennsylvania had joined the committee movement.

Meanwhile, an event was occurring in England that would soon have great repercussions in the colonies. The giant East India Tea Company, in operation for well over a century and a half, was nearly bankrupt. In an attempt to ameliorate its problems, Lord North shepherded the Tea Act of 1773 through Parliament. The act permitted the company to import tea directly to the colonies, eliminating all British middlemen. It would, Lord North believed, not only increase the company's profits but lower tea prices in the colonies as well; by lowering prices, it would eliminate colonial smuggling and increase revenue from the tea duty. Unfortunately, company officials unwisely bypassed established colonial tea merchants and chose "agents" from among Loyalists who had opposed the old non-importation agreements. Merchants who sold smuggled tea were already unhappy, and the selection of agents angered most others. Old arguments against tea duties were resurrected, but a new argument against monopoly also developed. Merchants warned that tea was only the entering wedge. Soon, they claimed, all British products would be sold only through approved agents. Mass meetings were held in port cities, their instigators determined to force the agents out of business.

Soon the first ships loaded with East India Company tea began to arrive in colonial ports. Charleston locked it in a cellar warehouse. New York and Philadelphia kept the ships far out at harbor. But in Boston, Governor Hutchinson ordered the docking of the ships, determined to force the issue. On December 16, a group of about 50 men in Mohawk costume boarded the ships and dumped 45 tons of tea overboard. From dockside, large groups watched the Boston Tea Party. Although colonial reaction was not uniformly favorable, the event was a turning point in England. Lord North, King George, Parliament, and every other official now saw the issue as a very simple one: whether Britain could maintain supremacy over its own colonies. They embargoed Boston.

Women's groups throughout the colonies, who often called themselves Daughters of Liberty, vowed to give up tea. They developed substitutes such as Liberty Tea from the herb loose-strife and Labrador Tea from raspberries. In October 1774, Edenton, North Carolina, hosted one of the most famous women's Tea Parties—that is, a gathering of women to publically renounce tea-drinking. In the colonial era, women did not ordinarily form associations even for charitable or church work, let alone to speak out on political issues. Women's Tea Parties attracted much comment on both sides of the Atlantic.

THE INTOLERABLE ACTS

Following the Boston Tea Party, the king insisted on a severe response. Lord North developed an extensive program to regain Britain's control over the colonies, and Parliament soon began passing it into law. In March 1774, the Boston Port Bill closed the port until the East India Company was reimbursed. The news arrived in May, shocking all with its harshness. Boston's Committee of Correspondence sent Paul Revere throughout nearby colonies with a copy of the act. The Virginia Assembly, at the urging of Thomas Jefferson, declared a day of fasting and prayer. The governor dissolved the assembly, which reassembled as an "association." On June 1, all colonies commemorated the Port Bill, as Virginia had suggested, with church services and flags at half-mast. Many sent food to Boston to prevent Britain from starving the city into submission.

In May and June 1774, Parliament passed three acts that, along with the Port Act, came to be called the Intolerable, or Coercive, Acts in the colonies. The first was the Act for Better Regulating the Government of Massachusetts. The "regulating act" curtailed Massachusetts's charter rights, greatly enlarging the power of the king and royal governor and reducing that of the General Court and town meetings. The second was the Administration of Justice Act (the "murdering act" to colonists), which provided trials in England for soldiers and officials accused of capital crimes in the colonies. The third was a renewed Quartering Act. Colonists also considered the Quebec Act, passed in June 1774, as one of the Intolerable Acts, although it was not intended as part of North's punitive program. It gave Britain's new Quebec Province control over the Ohio Valley, extending unrepresentative government and a semiestablished Catholic Church into territory that several colonies claimed and many colonists were anxious to settle.

North's final action was to replace Massachusetts governor Hutchinson with General Thomas Gage, commander in chief of British forces in America. Gage was a competent man with an American wife, but he was nonetheless convinced that only a firm line would preserve Britain's North American colonies.

THE FIRST CONTINENTAL CONGRESS

By summer 1774, in response to a Massachusetts circular letter, all of the colonies except Georgia had selected delegates, to attend a meeting. By late August, most had arrived in Philadelphia. The majority of the delegates were lawyers, and almost all were experienced politicians, although the best known colonial statesman in the world, Benjamin Franklin, remained in London where for some years he had represented colonial views to Parliament. Every existing colonial college was represented by at least one alumnus. Although delegates were divided between radicals favoring resistance and moderates favoring compromise, most still believed that reconciliation with Great Britain was possible.

The meeting of more than 50 delegates assembled in Carpenter's Hall on September 5, choosing Peyton Randolph of Virginia the president of the congress. (Although the meeting was called a congress, it was not a legislative group like the modern U.S. Congress.) After much discussion, delegates agreed that each colony, regardless of size, would have one vote. Most delegates had been clearly instructed by their colonies to "consult" only and to seek ways to reconcile their differences with Britain. They formed committees to list American rights and their violations. They discussed in great detail the colonies' different legal practices and the principles from which the practices derived. They referred to works of philosophy from the library. Soon, however, they abandoned the strict definition of "consultation." On October 14, they approved a Declaration of Rights and Resolves, written primarily by John Adams. The 10 resolutions appealed to both "natural rights" and the historic "rights of Englishmen." Delegates also wrote an address to the king. They composed open letters to citizens of Quebec and other Canadian colonies, the two Florida colonies, and the American public. On October 20, they adopted the "Association," a nonimportation, nonconsumption, and nonexportation agreement to become effective on December 1. They established Association committees in every colony to oversee and enforce the agreements. At the last session, held October 26, the delegates agreed to meet again in May 1775 if all their grievances had not been settled by that date.

THE SHOTS HEARD ROUND THE WORLD

King George III, who had a solid majority of supporters in a newly elected Parliament, declared the colonies to be in rebellion. In November, Parliament endorsed the king's position. In January 1775, Parliament rejected several conciliation plans proposed by William Pitt. The Crown issued orders to all colonial governors to prohibit the election of delegates to a Second Continental Congress. In February, Parliament agreed to offer Lord North's compromise plan to the colonies. The plan exempted colonies from imposed imperial taxation if they agreed to tax themselves and remit the monies to the imperial authorities. In the same month, however, the Crown ordered troops and three generals to

America. In March, Parliament passed the New England Restraining Act, which prohibited fishing off Newfoundland and trade with nations other than Britain. By April, other colonies were included.

As door after door slammed shut on reconciliation, the colonies increased their preparations for war and independent government. By the end of 1774, 10 colonies had extralegal "congresses." Eleven colonies formally adopted the Association, or nonimportation agreements, which had an immediate economic effect on England's exporters. New York and Georgia did not formally join the Association, but local committees of correspondence enforced its provisions in many locales. Military preparations took place. Nonetheless, dissension among colonists increased as the possibility of war became more certain. The Whigs strongly opposed Britain and its current policies, but only a small group of radical Whigs completely favored independence. The Tories favored loyalty to the king or to British policy, but only a small group among them was anxious to take up arms against their fellow colonists. A third large group was still neutral in 1774. Some were simply indifferent to political issues, while some rejected violence for religious or other reasons. Many others feared social upheaval far more than they fear British oppression. They adopted the antidemocratic argument that tyranny by a king or established ruling class was far preferable to tyranny by the masses of ordinary people. Over the next two years neutrals declined in number, and differences within the Whig and Tory groups lessened, while lines between them hardened.

In Boston, turmoil continued, as did harassment of the British troops. Colonists resisted the "regulating act" by preventing newly and royally appointed councillors and judges from meeting. They formed an extralegal colonial congress and appointed a Committee of Safety to oversee militia operations. Throughout the colony, "committees of observation" formed to keep watch on the British troops. General and Governor Thomas Gage was forced to import workers and materials from Nova Scotia to build barracks for his troops when local workers refused. Outside Boston, the colonists formed militia companies called Minutemen (because they could fight on a minute's notice) and gathered ammunition and other supplies.

In spring 1775, Gage received instructions from Lord Dartmouth, secretary of war, to imprison the leaders of the local resistance. Although Gage himself doubted the wisdom of the order, he prepared to accomplish it by first secretly marching from Boston to Concord to capture the stockpile of weapons. The plan was immediately discovered by the committees of observation. Paul Revere and William Dawes rode off to warn others. Throughout the night of April 18, as Major John Pitcairn's troops passed through each small village, church bells rang out to signal their approach. At dawn, they reached Lexington, where 70 American minutemen awaited them on the green. When Pitcairn demanded that the colonials disperse, their captain gave the order to withdraw. But a shot rang out—no one knows which side fired it—and in the confusion, a battle began. Eight colonials were killed.

The British immediately continued their advance to Concord, six miles away. Near the town, a small party of British troops met the colonial militia at North Bridge; here, the British did fire first. The Concord battle lasted five minutes—and was later immortalized as "the shot heard round the world" in an 1837 poem by Ralph Waldo Emerson. As British troops started back to Boston, enraged colonials sniped at them the entire way from behind houses, barns, and fence walls. By the time the troops reached Lexington, they were panicked, with 70 men killed and another 165 wounded. In the afternoon, they were rescued by 1,200 British troops from Boston, who escorted the survivors back to the city. Altogether, the British lost more than 350 men.

The Lexington and Concord battles were immediately publicized throughout the colonies. All began to arm, raise troops, and prepare for war. In Virginia, Patrick Henry led an armed group to Williamsburg in early May, after Governor Dunmore confiscated the gunpowder stored there. Shortly thereafter, the burgesses appeared at the assembly in arms and the governor fled the colony. In New England, militiamen occupied Breed's Hill overlooking Boston to await the outcome of the Second Continental Congress.

THE SECOND CONTINENTAL CONGRESS

On May 10, 1775, the Second Continental Congress began to assemble in Philadelphia. Within a week, at least one delegate from all 13 colonies had arrived. Many of the former delegates returned, augmented by newcomers John Hancock, the Boston merchant (and smuggler), who replaced Peyton Randolph as president; Benjamin Franklin, just home from England; and Thomas Jefferson, a young Virginian whose political writings had won him notice. George Washington arrived in his militia uniform. Delegates met in the Pennsylvania Statehouse. They had little real power and were dependent on extralegal colonial congresses to accept and ratify their decisions. Moderates still dominated, although all were aware that they were in a state of war.

A week after the meeting began, delegates received the unexpected and not entirely welcome report that two eager young men from Connecticut, Ethan Allen and Benedict Arnold, had led troops to capture Fort Ticonderoga from the British. Congress had intended to fight only battles that appeared defensive, for both political and practical reasons. Now it had little choice but to take responsibly for directing the war and the soldiers gathering in Massachusetts. Naming them the Continental army, the congress worked to raise funds, provide equipment, and organize troops. On June 15, they selected George Washington as commander in chief. The choice was unanimous, despite the fact that Washington's military record to date was less than encouraging. However, he was a southerner, which reassured the South that the war was not just New England's; and he was wealthy, which reassured conservative colonists that the war's goal was not social revolution. By month's end, the congress had approved 69 articles of war. Washington and his staff headed for Boston. There, the colonial militia had recently lost the Battle of Bunker Hill but were greatly encouraged to have inflicted twice as many losses on the well-trained British regulars than they had suffered themselves.

Back in Philadelphia, the Second Continental Congress continued its work. Delegates composed a series of addresses. The first, approved July 8 and authored by Pennsylvania's John Dickinson, was the Olive Branch Petition to King George. In humble rhetoric it begged the king to intercede for his beleaguered subjects with an overbearing Parliament. The second was a Declaration of Causes of Taking Up Arms, to be published in Boston by General Washington. The third was an Address to the Inhabitants of Great Britain, an attempt to

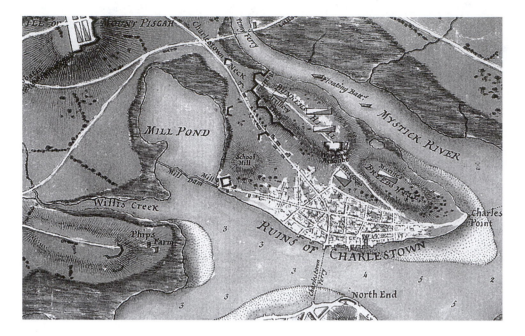

Charlestown (Boston), 1776, after the battle of Bunker and Breed's Hill, a map by Sir Thomas Page *(Library of Congress)*

influence public opinion by warning residents of England that the war would be expensive. Delegates also wrote to colonies in Canada, inviting them to join the resistance.

The next acts of Congress dealt with issues within the colonies. An Indian Department was set up and commissioners appointed. Money was appropriated to make treaties with Indians in the west and to assure them that the war with Britain was a "family quarrel" that did not require their participation. (Many tribes eventually divided over the war and fought on both sides.) Congress also recommended that colonies appoint safety committees to serve as their temporary executive branches, with power to oversee military activities. At the end of July, Benjamin Franklin presented Articles of Confederation and Perpetual Union. Moderates prevented approval, still hoping for reconciliation with Britain. They also blocked a declaration of open trade. Before adjourning for the month of August, Congress established a postal system and a military hospital— and rejected Lord North's compromise proposal to permit the colonists to decide themselves how to raise tax monies.

In September, Congress readjourned. Slowly and cautiously over the next 10 months, the delegates began to inch closer to independence. Throughout the autumn, moderates retained control and separation from Britain was an issue little discussed and publically denied. Ten of the colonies established "provisional" or "temporary" new governments.

While Congress inched along, General Washington strode vigorously into the lead. In September 1775, he reversed the defensive posture preferred by Congress and attacked Canada. By October, he had a small navy of six vessels in operation against British supply and troop ships, despite the fact that Congress had voted against creating a naval branch the previous spring. (Congress formally authorized a navy by December.) Throughout New England, Washington encouraged local leaders who favored resistance. With the assistance of General John Sullivan in New Hampshire, he issued the first order for seizure of Crown officials or Loyalists "acting as enemies of the their county." Soon New Hampshire called a constitutional convention and became the first colony to establish an independent constitutional government with authority drawn from the consent of the governed. With Washington's encouragement, Connecticut and Rhode Island soon wrote laws defining treason and demanded loyally oaths of their citizens.

On November 9, Congress received the news that King George III had refused their Olive Branch Petition and had dispatched more than 20,000 troops to the colonies for an all-out attack. They also received King George's August 23 proclamation declaring the colonies in open rebellion and declaring all who aided or abetted the effort to be engaging in treason. The declaration of treason, of course, covered all congressional activities and all representatives, both moderate and radical. Men in both groups now had only two options: winning the war or facing possible execution as traitors. While Congress debated its next act, General Richard Montgomery captured Montreal for the colonials, and Benedict Arnold planned an attack on Quebec. Despite the active fighting, in all official documents Congress continued to acknowledge allegiance to the king. In December, Congress learned that the king (in an October 26 speech) had accused the colonies of seeking independence. The colonies themselves had never yet officially used that term, claiming only that they sought to defend their legitimate "rights as Englishmen."

SLAVES AND THE IMPENDING WAR

Some royal officials in the colonies, and some Englishmen at home, put forth numerous proposals to arm, incite, recruit, or organize troops of black slaves and white indentured servants to fight the American rebels. In October 1774, a bill to free all slaves was introduced in Parliament's House of Commons, with the express purpose of frightening white colonists into submission. Like other such proposals, it drew harsh criticism from many English people and was defeated. Nonetheless, the British military developed a "southern strategy" of encouraging slaves to flee their masters and join the British forces. In November 1775, Virginia governor Lord Dunmore offered freedom to slaves and indentured servants who joined his troops; close to 1,000 did so.

Slaves themselves shared a widely held belief that in the event of war a British victory would give them freedom. Most knew that slavery had been declared illegal in England in 1772, although the judicial decision did not affect the rest of Britain's Colonial empire. In places like Sullivan's Island, South Carolina, runaways began gathering to join the British. Many white colonists believed that the British were actively instigating slave insurrections. In spring 1775, a plot was discovered in Charleston. Insurrections also occurred in Georgia and North Carolina in the winter and spring of 1774–75. Their effect, of course, was to increase the support of white southerners for independence from Britain.

Nonetheless, many slaves, escaped slaves, and free blacks became Patriots. The first man to die in the Boston Massacre, Crispus Attucks, was an escaped slave and doubtless understood the value of liberty. But as a common seaman of many years experience, he also understood the effects of the trade and navigation acts. In May 1775, the Committee of Safety of the Continental Congress approved the enlistment of free blacks (but not slaves) in colonial militias.

Evidence indicates, however, that slaves as well as free blacks fought in the earliest battles—Lexington, Concord, Bunker Hill, and others. In January 1776, the Continental Congress approved the enlistment of free blacks in the Continental army. Before the war's end, both Congress and many states offered slaves freedom to enlist. Blacks eventually fought in the forces of all colonies except South Carolina and Georgia.

PUBLIC OPINION IN 1776

Events in the fall and winter of 1775–76 inflamed resentment against British policies. In October 1775, British warships attacked and burned Falmouth (modern Portland) to the ground. On January 1, 1776, Virginia governor Lord Dunmore ordered the burning of Norfolk. On January 9, a pamphlet appeared in Philadelphia by a recent English immigrant named Thomas Paine. Entitled *Common Sense,* it provided the first popular and unqualified rationale for independence. Paine argued that American liberties derived from the "natural rights of man," not the British constitution. The pamphlet also contained the first open and public attack on the king, whom Paine called the "sullen-tempered Pharaoh of England." *Common Sense* was very widely distributed and discussed. Translated into German and other languages for Americans who did not read English, it met a receptive readership and had an immediate effect, crystalizing public opinion. Those neutral colonists who had been undecided began to talk familiarly of independence. Those moderates who still preferred reconciliation with Britain urged the Second Continental Congress to prepare a statement of intention regarding "independency." For two months, various documents were drafted, discussed, debated, and tabled, but representatives were unable to agree on any formal action.

Nonetheless, the colonists were far from unanimous in their support of independence in 1776. New England and Virginia were strongly dominated by Patriots. Virginia had been completely alienated by Governor Dunmore's actions; New Englanders by the trade acts, the customs commissioners, and the soldiers. In New York, however, Loyalists were so strong that the congress declared Queen's County to be outside the colonial government for its Loyalist activity. Loyalists were also strong in Pennsylvania, where both Quaker pacifists and some German groups opposed the war. Maryland, Delaware, and New Jersey supported the Patriots by only slim margins. The remaining southern colonies were divided, although increasing British naval activity along the coasts convinced many to join the cause. Throughout the colonies, religious affiliations also influenced political leanings. Anglicans in the north were usually solidly Tory, although in the south they were divided. Congregationalists, Presbyterians, and Baptists opposed the Anglican establishment—and its Loyalist sympathies. Catholics, probably about one percent of the colonial population, were divided; several were prominent Patriots, including Maryland planter Charles Carroll, an eventual signer of the Declaration of Independence.

Among the many ordinary people who were usually uninvolved in politics, loyalty to the king and Britain was the accepted and normal state of affairs. As activist Patriots organized and perfected methods of influencing public opinion, however, many ordinary people were won over to the Revo-

Old Drawyers Presbyterian Church, Delaware, built 1773 *(Historic American Building Survey)*

lutionary cause. Loyalists, on the other hand, rarely organized among themselves or attempted to influence public opinion, although they did form bands to cooperate with British troops. After the battles of Lexington and Concord, however, they experienced widespread public persecution. Tarring and feathering, ducking, the suppression of free speech and press, and even arrest of Loyalists became common.

THE COLONIES DECLARE INDEPENDENCE

On February 27, 1776, Congress received a copy of the Prohibitory Act (passed by Parliament on December 22, 1775). It clearly defined colonial actions as treasonous, embargoed all trade, and authorized the seizure of colonial ships. Moderates were astonished at its severity. Everyone was stunned by the unofficial report that Britain was even then in the process of hiring German mercenary troops. Mercenaries indicated to the colonies that Britain intended to crush them. Since soldiers who fought for profit claimed the spoils of war, little distinction would be made between colonists of different political persuasions as towns were looted and prisoners taken.

Recent news from the front had not been encouraging. General Montgomery had been killed at Quebec, but the town had not fallen. At the end of March, however, the embargo of Boston was lifted. On April 6, radicals prevailed upon the Continental Congress to open American ports to free trade with the world. Although the die was now clearly cast, a large group of moderates continued to hold out against declaring independence and to await the arrival of rumored "peace commissioners" from England.

Individual colonies moved toward independence. All in New England solidly supported it. By spring 1776, a constitutional convention was assembling in Virginia. South Carolina adopted a constitution in March. In April, North

Carolina instructed its delegates in Congress to agree to any joint decision of independence, the first colony to do so. The middle colonies of New York, New Jersey, Pennsylvania, and Maryland remained the centers of the strongest opposition. Pennsylvania, the geographical center of the colonies, was particularly crucial. On May 20, a meeting of Philadelphians—carefully arranged by radical Patriots—voted to oust the colony's duly elected moderate assembly and install a new one.

On June 7, 1776, Richard Henry Lee of Virginia presented a resolution to Congress, as he had been empowered to do by the Virginia convention. It read in part:

> That these United Colonies are, and of right ought to be, free and independent States, that they are absolved from all allegiance to the British crown and that all political connection between them and the state of Great Britain is, and ought to be totally dissolved. . . .
>
> That a plan of confederation be prepared and transmitted to the respective colonies for their consideration and approbation.

For two days, Congress debated the Lee resolution. In order to allow more negotiation with the middle colonies, a three-week hiatus was called. During that time, a five-man committee met to compose a document. Its members were Robert Livingston of New York, Roger Sherman of Connecticut, Benjamin Franklin of Pennsylvania, John Adams of Massachusetts, and Thomas Jefferson of Virginia, the chairman.

On July 1 and 2, Congress convened for its final debates on the question of independence. In the afternoon of the second day, the vote was taken. The colonies unanimously declared independence—that is, no negative votes were cast. Three Pennsylvania moderates who continued to opposed separation did not attend the vote, and the New York delegation abstained, claiming it lacked clear instructions from its colony. In fact, both colonies' delegates chose to allow the vote for independence to be recorded as unanimous. On July 3 and 4, Congress edited the Declaration of Independence that Jefferson had written, cutting its length by a third. (The cuts included a section that blamed the king of England for the existence of slavery in America.) The Declaration of Independence did not contain principles that were new or surprising to the congressional delegates. All the ideas had been debated during the 10 months of meetings of the Second Continental Congress, although Jefferson articulated them with exceptional power and grace. The declaration addressed itself to the king and did not even acknowledge the existence of Parliament. Drawing on the idea of social compact, it argued that governments were formed by the "consent of the governed." Maintaining that people possessed natural rights which government did not have the authority take away (Jefferson called them "unalienable rights"), it justified the colonial revolt.

By the end of the day on July 4, 1776, the Second Continental Congress had delivered to a printer a document entitled "The Unanimous Declaration of the Thirteen United States of America." On July 8, the declaration was read to a crowd gathered outside at the Pennsylvania Statehouse (later renamed Independence Hall). The king's arms were torn from over the door, church bells rang in unison with the large bell in the tower (later renamed the

Liberty Bell), and the celebration continued into the night. The colonial era in the 13 colonies was at an end.

THE SPIRIT OF 1776

In 1776, the 13 colonies were remarkably vigorous. In the quarter century since 1750, the French had been chased from North America, and the Spanish contained beyond the Mississippi. The "new west" had opened for settlement. Since 1750, the non-Indian population had doubled to more than 2.5 million, about 500,000 enslaved. Immigrants had surged into the colonies, most of them headed for vacant lands on the frontiers. New waves of Scotch-Irish and Palatine Germans and Swiss had arrived, as well as at least 30,000 English and 40,000 Scots. They were joined by many new African slaves, more than 80,000 of whom arrived after 1760 alone. Both coastal and interior travel had become easier; roads and postal services were developing. Economic ties among the colonies had increased. A larger proportion of people owned land than in any other nation of the world—between 50 and 75 percent of white family units (historians have not successfully established a more exact figure). In settled areas, basic education was widely available. While the economic distance between rich and poor was pronounced, the political submission and social deference of ordinary people had declined significantly since the 17th century.

As part of the British empire, the colonies were obviously flourishing. What, then, ultimately led them to seek independence? When offering answers to that question, historians divide into two broad camps. One side emphasizes ideas and commitment to principle as the motive force. The other emphasizes economic interest and social change. Yet on both sides, many historians also acknowledge that the Revolution remains, from some perspectives, a surprising event that defies easy explanation. A mere 15 years earlier, each colony resisted cooperating with the others in even small matters, and most white colonists were proud of their identify as citizens of the British empire. Apart from that identity, they were deeply divided—by wealth, religious affiliations, ethnic identity, regional experiences, and, in some cases, language. Yet by 1776 they had come to believe that they shared enough common interests and values to consider themselves "Americans."

They declared themselves a separate nation—and braved war with the most powerful military forces in Europe.

CHRONICLE OF EVENTS

1750

The non-Indian population of the English colonies is about 1.2 million; about 20 percent are enslaved.

Slavery is legalized in Georgia, the only colony where it was formerly forbidden.

By this date, a majority of slaves are American-born.

1754

July: The French and Indian War begins. Throughout the war, the back country will suffer Indian raids.

August: At the Albany Conference, Benjamin Franklin presents a plan of union for intercolonial defense. It is rejected by all 13 colonies.

1755

The Crown authorizes Indian commissioners for northern and southern districts, removing Indian relations from the control of individual colonies.

After great pressure by colonists, the Pennsylvania Assembly passes a Militia Bill to defend its frontier.

1766

May: The Seven Years' War (the French and Indian War) is formally declared in Europe.

1758

Indian Commissioner William Johnson concludes a major treaty with the Iroquois at Easton. The English agree to withdraw all settlements west of the Appalachian Mountains, but settlers quickly disregard it, particularly in Pennsylvania.

1759

The Cherokee War begins in South Carolina.

1760

George III becomes king of England upon the death of George II.

English troops take possession of French Fort Detroit.

Charles Mason and Jeremiah Dixon begin surveying a boundary line between Pennsylvania and Maryland; the Mason-Dixon Line will become the symbolic divide between north and south.

1761

Although the Seven Years' War has not officially ended in Europe, British troops begin occupying French forts throughout the upper Mississippi Valley.

The Cherokee War ends; bands of roving outlaws begin to terrorize back-country settlers in the Carolinas. During the winter, many South Carolina residents take refuge in forts.

The renewal of writs of assistance, or search warrants for smuggled goods, arouses opposition in Massachusetts and elsewhere.

1763

March: The Treaty of Paris is signed, ending the Seven Years' War (the French and Indian War). France cedes Canada and Louisiana territory east of the Mississippi to Britain and territory west of the Mississippi, including New Orleans, to Spain. Spain cedes Florida to Britain.

April: George Grenville becomes prime minister of England; he is determined to reduce the war debt and require colonists to bear the costs of their own defense.

May 7: Pontiac's War opens when Pontiac, an Ottawa chief, attacks the British at Fort Detroit. Other Western Tribes soon attack and capture almost every major English-occupied fort west of Fort Pitt.

June: The only western forts remaining under English control are Fort Detroit, Fort Niagra, and Fort Pitt.

August: The Delaware strike at Stewart's Crossing, then attack Fort Pitt. Colonel Henry Bouquet, en route to Fort Pitt, defeats the Lenni Lenape at the Battle of Bushy Run.

October: Chief Pontiac enters peace negotiations. The end of Pontiac's War unleashes a new wave of serious crimes by roving outlaw bands in the backcountry of the Carolinas.

October 7: George III issues the Proclamation of 1763. It declares the Ohio Valley and land west of the Appalachian Mountains to be Indian territory, reserved to their use and prohibited for white settlement. Indian territory is under military command and outside the jurisdiction of the colonies. Settlers in the area are ordered to leave. The Proclamation Line is set, running from Canada to Florida along the crest of the Appalachian Mountain range.

December 14: Anger over lack of defense in the backcountry erupts in Pennsylvania. The Paxton Boys murder 20 peaceful Conestoga Susquehannock men, women, and children. The local coroner's jury claims to be unable to identify the assailants.

1764

The Plan for the Future Management of Indian Affairs formalizes Indian commissioners' power and taxes trade in Indian territory.

January: Angered over the Pennsylvania Assembly's inaction on frontier defense, 600 Paxton Boys march toward Philadelphia. The assembly fortifies Philadelphia; some Quakers even join the militia. Benjamin Franklin persuades the Paxton Boys to return home without incident.

March: Parliament passes the Sugar Act; it clearly states that Britain has the right to tax colonists directly.

1765

As colonists debate violations of their rights by Britain, debate over human slavery in the colonies also increases.

March: Parliament passes the Stamp Act, to take effect November 1. It requires the use of paper that is "stamped," or embossed with an official seal, for all manner of documents and paper products, affecting the vast majority of colonists. Consequently, groups called the Sons of Liberty begin to form. In many places, their demonstrations against the Stamp Act turn into riots.

May 29: The Virginia House of Burgesses passes four of Patrick Henry's Virginia Resolves.

August: Pontiac and representatives of many other tribes accept peace terms at a Detroit council.

October 7–25: The Stamp Act Congress meets in New York.

November 1: On the day the Stamp Act is to take effect, no major colonial seaport has a supply of stamped paper or an agent to sell it, thanks to colonial opposition.

1766

Women form an association in Providence, Rhode Island, to promote the use of American-made fabrics. Similar associations are formed, often called Daughters of Liberty.

March 18: King George III signs the repeal of the Stamp Act; Parliament passes the Declaratory Act, stating its right to make laws for the colonies.

July: Eastern and western tribes conclude the final treaty of Pontiac's War at Oswego.

August: North Carolina Regulators hold their first meeting to address backcountry complaints. Attendance is in the thousands.

1767

June to July: Parliament passes the Townshend Acts, a series of small customs duties on a large number of items Americans imported from Britain; it also suspends the New York Assembly for refusing to comply with the 1765 Quartering Act.

In South Carolina, convicted backcountry outlaws are pardoned by the new governor. Settlers take justice into their own hands, attacking and burning the houses of suspected criminals. The assembly orders the arrest of the vigilantes.

1768

Virginians and Carolinians establish settlements in the Watauga River area of modern Tennessee.

In South Carolina, a Plan of Regulation is drawn up by backcountry property owners to deal with criminal activity. As a result the colony commissions troops of rangers, almost all Regulator members, to bring outlaw activity under control.

The North Carolina Regulators formally organize.

The Proclamation Line is extended west by the Treaty of Fort Stanwix in the north and the Treaty of Hard Labor in the south.

February: The Massachusetts Assembly approves a circular letter urging united action against the Townshend Acts.

March: Imperial officials announce a new plan for the Indian territories. Movement of the Proclamation Line is authorized and control of Indian trade is returned to the individual colonies.

June: Governor Francis Barnard dissolves the Massachusetts Assembly for refusing to rescind its circular letter. Boston customs officials seize John Hancock's ship *Liberty;* a mob forces the commissioners to take refuge offshore. Royal troops are dispatched to Boston. Boston calls for towns to send representatives to a "convention."

September: The extralegal Massachusetts Convention of 1768 convenes. Many northern colonies sign nonimportation and nonconsumption agreements.

1769

Ottawa chief Pontiac is killed by a Peoria Indian of the Illinois confederation at Cahokia.

The Penn proprietors open a land office in Pittsburgh, at the gateway to the desirable Ohio valley. The first day, 2,800 settlers file land claims.

May: The Virginia House of Burgesses passes resolutions supporting the principle of "no taxation without representation." The Virginia governor dissolves them; they meet as a "convention" and endorse a nonimportation agreement that includes a refusal to import slaves. The agreement is soon accepted throughout the south.

July: The Massachusetts Assembly passes a new resolution reaffirming its sole right to tax colonists.

1770

In South Carolina, the governor pardons many Regulators convicted for vigilante activity.

In the South, the Treaty of Lochaber with Cherokee and Creek completes a new Proclamation Line extending legal settlement west of the Appalachian Mountains.

March 5: A snowball fight between soldiers and Bostonians escalates. In the confusion, shots are fired into the crowd; five Bostonians are killed. Parliament rescinds the Townshend Acts, with the exception of the duty on tea, most colonial boycotts end, after the colonists receive the news, although smuggling of tea is extensive.

September: Hillsborough, North Carolina, Regulators take over court, expelling the judge and other officials.

1771

January: The North Carolina assembly passes the Johnston Riot Act to suppress the Regulators. The movement's membership increases; the backcountry is in turmoil.

May: The North Carolina militia defeats 2,000 Regulators at Great Alamance Creek. Six Regulators are hanged for treason. More than 6,000 accept the governor's offer of pardon.

1772

In England, a judicial decision declares slavery illegal.

In South Carolina, circuit courts formally open and the Regulator movement virtually ends.

In modern Tennessee, Watauga River settlers form the first civil government west of the Appalachian Mountains, called the Watauga Association.

June: The Crown announces it will henceforth pay the salaries of colonial governors and judges.

Colonists object, because they fear loss of control over officials.

November: At a Massachusetts town meeting, a formal Committee of Correspondence is formed under the guidance of Sam Adams. Within three months, so more are formed in smaller towns, and the movement soon spreads to other colonies.

1773

January: Sam Adams and John Adams draft a paper renouncing allegiance to Parliament and arguing that the colony owes allegiance only to the Crown.

June: The first freedom petition by slaves to the Massachusetts General Court is received; it draws on the language of liberty and natural rights.

May: Parliament passes the Tea Act of 1773 in an attempt to keep the East India Tea Company out of bankruptcy.

December 16: Men disguised as Mohawk Indians board tea ships in the Boston Harbor and dump 45 tons of tea overboard. From the docks, large groups watch the Boston Tea Party.

1774

James Harrod leads 31 Pennsylvanians to found Harrodsburg, Kentucky.

Both Pennsylvania and Virginia claim the upper Ohio Valley. Lord Dunmore, governor of Virginia, sends troops to occupy Fort Pitt at Pittsburgh, no longer used as a military post. Lord Dunmore's War begins; it involves a political contest between the two colonies and open hostilities with the Shawnee and other Indians. It will dissipate as the Revolution begins.

March: Parliament passes the Boston Port Bill, closing the port until the East India Company is reimbursed for its tea.

May and June: Parliament passes a Quartering Act, the Administration of Justice Act, the Regulating Act, and the Quebec Act. Colonists name these four acts the Intolerable, or Coercive, Acts. Massachusetts governor Thomas Hutchinson is replaced by General Thomas Gage, also commander in chief of British forces in America.

June 1: All colonies commemorate the closing of Boston with church services and flags at half-mast. Many send food to the town.

September 5: The First Continental Congress assembles in Carpenter's Hall, Philadelphia, choosing Virginian Peyton Randolph president. They approve a Declaration of Rights and Resolves.

October: To frighten the colonists into submission, Parliament introduces a bill to free all slaves. It is defeated. In Edenton, North Carolina, women hold a Tea Party, or meeting to publically renounce the drinking of tea. Many other women's tea parties are held elsewhere.

October 20: The Continental Congress resolves to form an association in every colony to oversee and enforce nonimportation, nonexportation, and nonconsumption agreements.

October 26: The last session of the First Continental Congress meets. Delegates agree to meet again in May 1775.

December: By the end of the year, 10 colonies have extralegal congresses; 11 colonies have adopted the association.

winter 1774–75: Slave insurrections occur in Georgia and North Carolina. White colonists believe that the British are attempting to instigate slave rebellions throughout the colonies.

1775

The Watauga Association joins settlers in the Nolichucky River, forming the Washington District.

The Transylvania Company concludes the Treaty of Sycamore Shoals with the Cherokee, for land between the Cumberland and Kentucky Rivers. Meanwhile, Daniel Boone blazes a trail for the company through the Cumberland Gap.

February: British troops and three generals are sent to America. Lord North proposes a compromise requiring the colonies to tax themselves.

April: Daniel Boone founds the town of Boonesborough, Kentucky.

April 18: The British plan a march to Concord, Massachusetts, to destroy arms and take colonial leaders prisoner. Colonists are warned by Paul Revere and others.

April 19: Colonists meet the British at Lexington and Concord, the first battles of the Revolutionary War.

May: In modern Kentucky, settlers establish a plan of government.

May 5: The Continental Congress approves the enlistment of free blacks in militias. Slaves are also known to have fought in early battles.

May 10: The Second Continental Congress assembles and learns that Ethan Allen and Benedict Arnold have captured Fort Ticonderoga. The delegates take responsibly for directing the war and organize the Continental army.

June 15: George Washington is unanimously selected commander in chief by the Continental Congress.

July: Congress addresses the Olive Branch Petition to King George III and writes a Declaration of Causes of Taking Up Arms. Benjamin Franklin presents articles of confederation; they are rejected.

August: The congress rejects Lord North's compromise regarding taxation. Congress also establishes a postal service, headed by Franklin.

August 23: King George III declares the colonies in open rebellion and all participants to be treasonous. (The colonists do not receive the news until November.)

September: Washington attacks Canada and makes plans to convert merchant ships into a navy.

October: British warships attack and burn Falmouth (modern Portland, Maine). In Kentucky, settlers petition the Continental Congress to be admitted as the 14th colony, Transylvania; they are refused.

November: In Virginia, loyalist governor Lord Dunmore offers to free any slave or indentured servant who will join his troops. Up to 1,000 do so. Slaves widely believe that a British victory will mean freedom, and many attempt to escape to join the British.

1776

The 13 colonies have a non–Indian population of 2.5 million (doubled since 1750); 500,000 are slaves. Approximately 250,000 colonists live in the backcountry; about 25,000 live beyond the Appalachian Mountains in the "new west."

Colonists do not unanimously support independence, but Patriots and radicals are well organized to influence public opinion. Persecution of Loyalists is widespread.

By this date, African Americans have organized their first independent Protestant congregations in Georgia and Virginia. Quakers have disciplined members who participate in the slave trade and have formed the first antislavery societies. The slave trade has been outlawed in much of New England, and a prohibitive duty enacted in Pennsylvania.

The Washington District in modern Tennessee receives representation in the North Carolina Assembly.

After independence is declared, Ohio Valley settlers request recognition as the 14th colony, named Westsylvania; approval is denied.

January: The Continental Congress approves the enlistment of free blacks in the Continental army.

January 1: In Virginia, Lord Dunmore orders the burning of Norfolk.

January 9: Thomas Paine's pamphlet *Common Sense* appears. The first unqualified argument for independence, it is very widely read and has great influence.

February: The Continental Congress receives the Prohibitory Act (passed by Parliament December 1775). It embargoes trade and authorizes the seizure of all colonial ships. The congress also learns that Britain is hiring German mercenary soldiers. Both indicate that the British intend to crush the colonies.

April: The Continental Congress declares its ports open to free trade with the world, in direct contradiction of British policy. North Carolina becomes the first colony to instruct its congressional representatives to approve any joint declaration of independence.

June: Kentucky settlements appeal for organization as a county of Virginia. The request is approved in December.

June 7: Richard Henry Lee of Virginia presents a resolution for independence to the Continental Congress. The congress calls a 3-week adjournment and appoints a committee, headed by Thomas Jefferson, to compose a declaration of independence.

July 1: The Continental Congress begins its last debates on independence.

July 2: The Lee resolution passes unanimously, although New York abstains, claiming lack of directions from its colonial assembly.

July 3: The congress begins considering Jefferson's Declaration of Independence. Its ideas have already been widely debated in Congress.

July 4: The congress cuts Jefferson's declaration by one-third, passes it, and takes it to a printer.

July 8: The Declaration of Independence is read from the steps of the Pennsylvania Statehouse in Philadelphia (later Independence Hall). Church bells ring, along with the tower bell (later called the Liberty Bell), and the celebration continues into the night.

EYEWITNESS TESTIMONY

The Parnasim [*presidents of the congregation*] & Elders having received undouted Testimony That severall of our Bretheren, that reside in the Country [*i.e., back-country*] have and do dayly violate the principles [*of*] our holy religion, such as Trading on the Sabath, Eating of forbidden Meats, & other Henious Crimes, and as our Holy Law injoins us to reprove one Another agreeable to the Commandments in Liviticus . . . thou shalt surely reprove thy Neighbour and not suffer sin upon him, the consideration of this Divine Precept has Induced the Parnasim & Elders to come to the following resolution in order to check the above mentioned growing evil, and as our *Hachamim* observe . . . That is no one is to be Punished unless First admonished, therefore whosoever for the future continues to act contrary to our Holy Law by breacking any of the principles command will not be deem'd a member of our Congregation. . . . [B]ut those that repent & obey the precepts of the Almighty, We beseech the Divine goodness to open to them the Gates of Mercy. . . .

Minute book, Congregation Shearith Israel, New York City, September 1757, in "Earliest Extant," pp. 256–57.

All these things will contribute, directly or indirectly, to facilitate what we must ever pray and labour for, till we obtain it, the establishment of Bishops of our Church [*Anglican*] in America. This I have long had at heart: and not only said but written a great deal in favor of it to such as I hoped might be brought off from their prejudices, either wholly or in some measure. Nor, unsuccessful as the attempts have been shall I ever abandon the scheme, as long as I live. But pushing it openly at present would certainly prove both fruitless and detrimental. . . . The powerful objection made at home against our proposal, is, that the Dissenters abroad have terrible apprehensions of being injured by it. And in proportion as their remonstrances are vehement, our endeavours will be unpromising. Therefore the principal point is to convince them, that whatever the Bishops were, from whom their ancestors fled into the New World, those of the present age are, and have always been, most sincere patrons of extensive toleration. . . .

Thomas Seeker, archbishop of Canterbury, 1758, in Hart, ed., American History, *vol. 2, pp. 289–90.*

Their amusements are chiefly dancing in the winter, and in the summer forming parties of pleasure upon the Schuilkill [*Schuylkill River*], and in the country. There is a society of sixteen ladies and as many gentlemen called The fishing company, who meet once a fortnight upon the Schuilkill. They have a very pleasant room erected in a romantic situation upon the banks of that river where they generally dine and drink tea. There are several pretty walks about it, and some wild and rugged rocks which together with the water and fine groves that adorn the banks, from a most beautiful and picturesque scene. There are boats and fishing tackle of all sorts, and the company divert themselves with walking, fishing, going up the water, dancing, singing, conversing, or just as they please. The ladies wear an uniform and appear with great ease and advantage from the neatness and simplicity of it. The first and most distinguished people of the colony are of this society. . . .

English visitor to Philadelphia, 1759, quoted in Earle, Colonial Dames, *pp. 217–18.*

Touro Synagogue, Newport, built 1759–63 (*Historic American Building Survey*)

Great reliance was placed upon the powers of nature, and critical days were expected with solicitude, in order to observe the discharge of the morbid cause of fevers from the system. This matter was looked for chiefly in the urine, and glasses to retain it were a necessary part of the furniture of every sick room. . . . The medicines to promote sweats were generally of feeble nature. The spiritus mindereri, and the spirit of sweet nitre were in daily use for that purpose. In dangerous cases, saffron and Virginia snake root were added to them.

Blood-letting was used plentifully in pleurisies and rheumatisms, but sparingly in all other diseases. Blood was often drawn from the feet, in order to excite a revulsion of disease from the superior parts of the body. . . .

The use of opium was confined chiefly to ease pain, to compose a cough, and to restrain preternatural discharges from the body. . . .

Dr. Benjamin Rush. "Comparative State of Medicine in Philadelphia Between the Years 1760 and 1766 . . . ,"
in Wood, Rising, *pp. 223–25.*

Placing on Men the ignominious Title, SLAVE, dressing them in uncomely Garments, keeping them to servile Labour, in which they are often dirty, tends gradually to fix a Notion in the Mind, that they are a Sort of People below us in Nature, and leads us to consider them as such in all our Conclusions about them. And, moreover, a Person which in our Esteem is mean and contemptible, if their Language or Behaviour toward us is or disrespectful, it excites Wrath more powerfully than the like Conduct in one we accounted our Equal or Superior: and where this happens to be the Case, it disqualifies for candid Judgment; for it is unfit for a Person to sit as judge in a Case where his own personal Resentments are stirred up; and, as Members of Society in a well framed Government, we are mutually dependent. Present Interest incites to Duty, and makes each Man attentive to the Convenience of others: but he whose Will is a Law to others, and can enforce Obedience by Punishment; he whose Wants are supplied without feeling any Obligation to make equal Returns to his Benefactor, his irregular Appetites find an open Field for Motion, and he is in Danger of growing hard, and inattentive to their Convenience who labour for his Support; and so loses that Disposition in which alone Men are fit to govern.

John Woolman, "Considerations on the Keeping of
Negroes," 1760, Journal, *p. 363.*

I will to my dying day oppose with all the powers and faculties God has given men, all such instruments of slavery on the one hand, and villainy on the other, as this writ of assistance is. It appears to me the worst instrument of arbitrary power, the most destructive of English liberty and the fundamental principles of law, that ever was found in an English law-book. . . .

. . . In the first place, the writ is universal, being directed to all and singular justices, Sheriffs, Constables, and all other officers and subjects; so, that, in short, it is directed to every subject in the King's dominions. Every one with this writ may be a tyrant; if this commission be legal, a tyrant in a legal manner also may control, imprison, or murder any one within the realm. In the next place, it is perpetual; there is no return. A man is accountable to no person for his doings. Every man may reign secure in his petty tyranny, and spread terror and desolation around him. In the third place, a person with this writ, in the daytime, may enter all houses, shops, &c, at will, and command all to assist him. Fourthly, by this writ not only deputies, &c., but even their menial servants, are allowed to lord it over us. Now one of the most essential branches of English liberty is the freedom of one's house. A man's house is his castle; and whilst he is quiet, he is as well guarded as a prince in his castle. This writ, if it should be declared legal, would totally annihilate this privilege. Custom-house officers may enter our houses, when they please; we are commanded to permit their entry. Their menial servants may enter, may break locks, bars, and every thing in their way; and whether they break through malice or revenge, no man, no court, can inquire.

James Otis to the Massachusetts General Court, 1761,
in Hart, American History, *vol. 2, pp. 375–77.*

Septr. 23 [1762] Received a Letter this Evening-from Samuel Emlen junr. intimating his Wife's indisposition, went there about 9 o'clock & stay'd till near 3 in the morning, when H. D. [*Henry Drinker, her husband*] came to inform of Sal's being Saucy, so came Home, about 5 in the morning (the 24th) E. Emlen was delivered of a fine Boy Joshua junr.

Octor. 11: 1762 My little Sally taken unwell with a vomitting and Purging, Doctors Redman and Evans tended her, seems now recover'd, the 26th. . . .

A Negro of Patty Craddocks, dead at Abel James's of the Small Pox, it proves Mortal to Many. Octor 26: 1762.

Decemr. 24 Sally Fisher dead of the Small-Pox, her Brother Johny bury'd last Week of the same disorder.

Febry. 6: 1763—First-Day Afternoon very unwell, Miscarried; Sally, Inoculated, last sixth-Day.

8 Weeks gone, when it happn'd. . . .

June 20, 1763, little Joshua Emlen was this Afternoon buried, he dyed the 19 of a vomitting purging and cutting Teeth &c. . . .

Sepr. the 19: 1763; Busy all Day: Cleaning House, went this Evening to see Catty Howell, who, Miscarried last seventh Day, and has been very ill. . . .

May 19 a Vessel from Pool brought the Account of the Repeal of the Stamp Act, the 20th. The Town [*Philadelphia*] illuminated upon the occasion.

May the 25. H.D. and M.S. went to Darby, to the Burial of Sarah Fordham, who dyed of a Cancer in her Breast.

Elizabeth Drinker, Philadelphia Quaker,
Diary, *pp. 27–30, 36.*

About the commencement of the Indian war in 1763, a trading Jew [*i.e., a Jewish trader*], named Chapman, who was going up the Detroit river with a batteau-load of goods which he had brought from Albany, was taken by some Indians of the Chippeway nation, and destined to be put to death. A Frenchman impelled by motives of friendship and humanity, found means to steal the prisoner, and kept him so concealed for some time, that although the most diligent search was made, the place of his confinement could not be discovered. At last, however, the unfortunate man was betrayed by some false friend, and again fell into the power of the Indians who took him across the river to be burned and tortured. Tied to the stake and the fire burning by his side, his thirst from the great heat, became intolerable, and he begged that some drink might be given to him. It is a custom with the Indians, previous to a prisoner being put to death, to give him what they call his last meal; a bowl of pottage or broth was therefore brought to him for that purpose. Eager to quench his thirst, he put the bowl immediately to his lips, and the liquor being very hot, he was dreadfully scalded. Being a man of very quick temper, the moment he felt his mouth burned, he threw the bowl with its contents full in the face of the man who handed it to him. "He is mad! He is mad" resounded from all quarters. The bystanders considered his conduct as an act of insanity, and immediately untied the cords with which he was bound, and let him go where he pleased.

British major Roberts, "Diary of the Siege of Detroit,"
1763, quoted in Heineman, "Startling Experience,"
pp. 33–34.

They planted by your care? No! Your oppressions planted 'em in America. They fled your tyranny to a then uncultivated and inhospitable country—where they exposed themselves to all the hardships to which

human nature is liable, and among others to the cruelties of a savage foe. . . .

They nourished by your indulgence? They grew by your neglect of 'em: as soon as you began to care about 'em, that care was exercised by sending persons to rule over 'em in one department or another, who were . . . sent to spy out their liberty, to misrepresent their actions and to prey upon 'em: men whose behavior on many occasions has caused the blood of these sons of liberty to recoil within them. . . . Remember I this day told you so, that same spirit of freedom which actuated these people at first, will accompany them still. . . .

Isaac Barré to Parliament, 1763, quoted in
Fleming, Liberty!, *p. 51.*

. . . we have marked, described, and perpetuated the said west line, by setting up and erecting therein stones at the end of every mile, from the place of beginning to the distance of one hundred and thirty-two miles, near the foot of a hill, called and known by the name of Sideling hill; every five mile stone having on the side facing the north, the arms of the said Thomas Penn and Richard Penn graved thereon, and on the side facing the south, the arms of Frederick Lord Baltimore graved thereon, and the other intermediate stones are graved with the letter P on the north side, and the letter M on the south side. . . .

Commissioners of the Mason-Dixon Line, ca. 1763,
in Hart, ed., American History, *vol. 2, p. 109.*

Their [*the Indians'*] punishment must [therefore] be previous to the treating with them, and when that shall happen, all they can expect is forgiveness, and a Trade, under proper regulations, opened to them. But as to *presents,* it would certainly be the highest presumption in them to expect any. Justice they shall have, but no more; for they can never be considered by us as a people to whom we owe *rewards;* and it would be madness, to the highest degree, ever to bestow favors on a race who have so treacherously, and without any provocation on our side, attacked our Posts, and butchered our Garrisons. Presents should be given only to those who remain our firm friends.

General Jeffrey Amherst to Indian Commissioner William
Johnson, September 1763, quoted in Anderson,
Crucible, *pp. 543–44.*

Go on, good Christians, never spare
To give your Indians Clothes to wear;

Send 'em good Beef, and Pork, and Bread,
Guns, Powder, Flints, and Store of Lead,
To Shoot Your Neighbors through the Head. . . .
Paxton Boy poem, 1763, quoted in Kelly,
Pennsylvania, p. 492.

I am to acquaint your Honour that between two and three of the clock this afternoon, upwards of a hundred armed men, from the Westward, rode very fast into Town [*Lancaster, Pennsylvania*], turned their Horses into Mr. Slough's (an Inn-keeper) Yard, and proceeded with the greatest Precipitation to the Work House, stove open the door and killed all the Indians, and then took to their horses and rode off, all their business was done, and they were returning to their horses before I could get half way down to the Work-House; the Sheriff and Coroner, however, & several others, got down as soon as the Rioters, but could not prevail with them to stop their hands; some people say they heard them declare they would proceed to the Province Island, and destroy the Indians there.

Mayor Edward Shippen to Thomas Penn,
December 1763, quoted in Kelly,
Pennsylvania, pp. 490–91.

The storm which had been so long gathering has at length exploded. Had Government removed the Indians from Conestoga, which had frequently been urged without success, this painful catastrophe might have been avoided. What could I do with men heated to madness? All that I could do was done; I expostulated; but *life* and *reason* were set at defiance. And yet the men [*Paxton Boys*] in private life are virtuous and respectable; not cruel, but mild and merciful.

The Reverend John Elder to Thomas Penn,
December 1763, quoted in Kelly, Pennsylvania, p. 491.

I was informed by Mr. LeGrand and Monsiuer Dirris-seaux that before Canada was taken Pondiac [*Pontiac*] and some Chiefs from Detroit . . . had gone down to Fort Pitt . . . enquiring the treatment they would have should the English succeed, to which was answered first of all the Rivers would run in Rum, that presents from this Great King were to be unlimited, that all sorts of goods were to be in the utmost plenty and so cheap as a Blanket for two Beavers, 4 Raccoons taken for a Beaver, with many other fair promises. . . . That in about a year after Pondiac in particular had been heared to complain and say the English were liars,

which opinion became so general, that a long time before they openly declared themselves in arms, a general discontent was amongst all the Nations. . . .

Indian commissioner James Grant describes events
proceeding 1761, quoted in Goodrich,
First, pp. 120–21.

In purity and wholesomeness of air, and richness of soil, [Detroit] may be said to equal, if not excel any, even the best parts of America. Every European grain flourishes here in the utmost perfection; and hemp and flax, in particular, might be raised to the greatest advantage. The woods are everywhere filled with vines of spontaneous growth; and their grape yields a juice equal in flavour to the most excellent burgundy. The country around it appears like a great park stocked with buffaloes, deer, pheasants, wild turkies, and partridges. Domestic animals and fowls are here in the utmost perfection. Aquatic birds of every species are in the greatest plenty, and of the highest flavour, and the rivers afford an astonishing variety of the most delicious fish. The soil and climate are so favorable to vegetation, that every vegetable is to be procured with the smallest trouble. . . .

British lieutenant Thomas Mante, 1764, quoted in Russell,
British Régime, pp. 99–100.

But none of the means of information are more sacred, or have been cherished with more tenderness and care by the settlers of America, than the press. Care has been taken that the art of printing should be encouraged, and that it should be easy and cheap and safe for any person to communicate his thoughts to the public. And you, Messieurs printers, whatever the tyrants of the earth may say of your paper, have done important service to your country by your readiness and freedom in publishing the speculations of the curious . . . for the jaws of power are always opened to devour, and her arm is always stretched out, if possible, to destroy the freedom of thinking, speaking, and writing. . . .

Be not intimidated, therefore, by any terrors, from publishing with the utmost freedom, whatever can be warranted by the laws of your country; nor suffer yourselves to be wheedled out of your liberty by any pretences of politeness, delicacy, or decency. These, as they are often used, are but three different names for hypocrisy, chicanery, and cowardice.

John Adams, "Dissertation on the Feudal and Canon
Law," 1765, in Works, *vol. 3, 456–57.*

The members of this Congress, sincerely devoted, with the warmest sentiments of affection and duty to his majesty's person and government, inviolably attached to the present happy establishment of the protestant succession. . . . [E]steem it our indispensable duty to make the following declarations, of our humble opinion respecting the most essential rights and liberties of the colonists, and of the grievances under which they labor, by reason of several late acts of parliament.

1st. That his majesty's subjects in these colonies owe the same allegiance to the crown of Great Britain, that is owing from his subjects born within the realm, and all due subordination to that august body, the parliament of Great Britain.

2nd. That his majesty's liege subjects in these colonies are entitled to all the inherent rights and privileges of his natural born subjects within the kingdom of Great Britain.

3rd. That it is inseparably essential to the freedom of a people, and the undoubted rights of Englishmen, that no taxes should be imposed on them, but with their own consent, given personally, or by their representatives.

4th. That the people of these colonies are not, and from their local circumstances, cannot be, represented in the house of commons in Great Britain.

5th. That the only representatives of the people of these colonies, are persons chosen therein, by themselves; and that no taxes ever have been, or can be constitutionally imposed on them, but by their respective legislatures. . . .

Stamp Act Congress, "Declaration of Rights and Grievances," 1765, in Hart, ed., American History, vol. 2, pp. 402–03.

The populace of Boston, about a week since, had given a very notable instance of their detestation of the above unconstitutional [Stamp] Act, and had sufficiently shown in what light they viewed the man who would under take to be the stamp distributor. But, not content with this, the last night they again assembled in King's Street; where, after having kindled a fire, they proceeded, in two separate bodies, to attack the houses of two gentlemen of distinction, who, it had been suggested, were accessories to the present burthens; and did great damage in destroying their houses, furniture, &c., and irreparable damage in destroying their papers. Both parties, who before had

acted separately, then unitedly proceeded to the Chief-justice's [*later, Governor Thomas Hutchinson's*] house. . . . In this situation, all his family, it is said, abandoned the house, but himself and his eldest daughter, whom he repeatedly begged to depart; but as he found all ineffectual, and her resolution fixed to stay and share his fate, with a tumult of passions only to be imagined, he took her in his arms, and carried her to a place of safety, just before the incensed mob arrived. . . . They beset the house on all sides, and soon destroyed every thing of value. . . . The destruction was really amazing; for it was equal to the fury of the onset. But what above all is to be lamented is the loss of some of the most valuable records of the country, and other ancient papers. . . .

Josiah Quincy, Jr., August 1765, in Hart, ed., American History, vol. 2, p. 398.

Herewith I have the pleasure of transmitting to you copies of two Acts of Parliament just passed. The first [*the Declaratory Act*] for securing the dependency of the Colonies on the Mother Country; the second for the repeal of the [Stamp] Act. . . .

The moderation, the forbearance, the unexampled lenity and tenderness of Parliament towards the Colonies, which are so signally displayed in those Acts, cannot but dispose the province, committed to your care, to that return of cheerful obedience to the Laws and Legislative authority of Great Britain and to those sentiments of respectful gratitude to the Mother Country, which are the natural, and, I trust, will be the certain effects of so much grace and condescension, so remarkably manifested on the part of his Majesty and of the Parliament; and the future happiness and prosperity of the Colonies will very much depend on the testimonies, they shall now give of these dispositions.

British secretary of state to colonial governors, 1766, in Hart, American History, vol. 2, p. 411.

We arrived at the Mingo Town, which by our Reckoning is 71 miles below Fort Pitt; The Country between broken, with very high Ridges, the Valleys Narrow, and the Course of the River plunged from many high Grounds which compose its Banks. . . . The 23rd came to the Mouth of the Muskingum . . . a very large River 250 Yards Wide at its Confluence with the Ohio. . . . Our Indians killed several Buffalo, between the Mingo Town and the Muskingum; We first met with a herd of this kind of Animal, about 100 miles below Fort Pitt. . . .

British captain Harry Gordon, journal, 1766,
in Mereness, ed., Travels, *pp. 474–76.*

Whereas several of the houses of representatives in his Majesty's colonies and plantations in America, have of late, against law, claimed to themselves, or to the general assemblies of the same, the sole and exclusive right of imposing duties and taxes upon his Majesty's subjects in the said colonies and Plantations; and have, in pursuance of such claim, passed certain votes, resolutions, and orders, derogatory to the legislative authority of parliament, and inconsistent with the dependency of the said colonies and plantations upon the crown of Great Britain: . . . be it declared. . . . That the said colonies and plantations in America have been, are, and of right ought to be, subordinate unto, and dependent upon the imperial crown and parliament of Great Britain; and that the King's majesty, by and with the advice and consent of the lords spiritual and temporal, and commons of Great Britain, in parliament assembled, had, hath, and of right ought to have, full power and authority to make laws and statutes of sufficient force and validity to bind the colonies and people of America, subjects of the crown of Great Britain, in all cases whatsoever.

The Declaratory Act, March 1766, in Macdonald, ed.,
Documentary, *p. 140.*

We have an excellent prince [*King*], in whose good dispositions towards us we may confide. We have a generous, sensible, and humane nation, to whom we may apply. They may be deceived: they may, by artful men, be provoked to anger against us; but I cannot yet believe they will be cruel or unjust; or that their anger will be implacable. Let us behave like dutiful children, who have received unmerited blows from a beloved parent. Let us complain to our parents; but let our complaints speak at the same time, the language of affliction and veneration.

John Dickinson, Letters from a Farmer, *no. 3, 1767,*
in Hart, ed., American History, *vol. 2, pp. 426–27.*

When Fanning first to Orange came,
He looked both pale and wan:
An old patch'd coat upon his back,
An old mare he rode on.
Both man and mare wa'nt worth five pounds,

As I've been often told;
But by his civil robberies,
He's laced his coat with gold,

Rednap Howell, North Carolina Regulator ballad about
hated official Edward Fanning, 1768, quoted in Lefler
and Powell, Colonial North Carolina, *p. 169.*

1768, January 1. Preached at Granny Quarter Creek [*South Carolina backcountry*] to a mix'd Multitude of People from various Quarters—But no bringing of this Tribe into any Order. They are the lowest Pack of Wretches my Eyes ever saw, or that I have met with in these Woods—As wild as the very deer—No making of them sit still during Service—but they will be in and out—forward and backward the whole Time (Women especially) as Bees to and fro to their Hives—All this must be born with at the beginning of Things—Nor can be mended till churches are built, and the Country reduc'd to some Form. How would the Polite People of London stare, to see the Females (many very pretty) come to Service in their Shifts and a short petticoat only, barefooted and Bare legged—Without Caps or Handkerchiefs—dress'd only in their Hair, Quite in a State of Nature for Nakedness is counted as Nothing—as they sleep altogether in Common in one Room, and shift and dress openly without Ceremony—The Men appear in Frocks or Shirts and long Trousers—No Shoes or Stockings—But I should remember that I am talking of . . . Religious Matters, Not the Custom of the Country.

Anglican missionary Charles Woodmason,
journal entry, Carolina, *pp. 31–32.*

. . . his Majesty's American subjects, who acknowledge themselves bound by the ties of allegiance, have an equitable claim to the full enjoyment of the fundamental rules of the British constitution; that it is an essential, unalterable right, in nature, engrafted into the British constitution, as a fundamental law, and ever held sacred and irrevocable by the subjects within the realm, that what a man has honestly acquired is absolutely his own, which he may freely give, but it cannot be taken from him without his consent; that the American subjects may, therefore, exclusive of any consideration of charter rights, with a decent firmness, adapted to the character of free men and subjects, assert this natural and constitutional right.

Massachusetts Circular letter, February 1768,
in Macdonald, Documentary, *p. 148.*

Many of the common people have been in a frenzy, and talk'd of dying in defense of their liberties, and have spoke and printed what is highly criminal, and too many of rank above the vulgar, and some in *public posts* have countenanced and encouraged them until they increased so much in their numbers and in their opinion of their importance as to submit to government no further than they thought proper. The legislative powers have been influenced by them, and the executive powers entirely lost their force. . . . The government has been so long in the hands of the populace that it must come out of them by degrees, at least it will be a work of time to bring the people back to just notions of the nature of government. . . . There must be an abridgment of what are called English liberties. . . .

I must beg the favor of you to keep secret every thing I write, until we are in a more settled state. . . .

Letter of Massachusetts Chief Justice (soon governor) Thomas Hutchinson to a British friend, 1768–69, in Hart, American History, *vol. 2, pp. 421–23.*

1769. Sept. 13.—Took my first Degree at Yale College. By the appointment of my Class, I delivered the Valedictory Oration previous to our departure to prepare for the Commencement. Defended a Latin Syllogistic Thesis, at the Commencement. About this time, the Colonies came into a non-importation agreement of goods from Great Britain in consequence of the Stamp Act & other arbitrary acts of the British parliament. The Class agreed with 3 or 4 dissensients, to appear in home made clothes at the Commencement. We were put to some difficulty to obtain all the articles, of American manufacture. Inspired with a patriotic spirit, we took pride in our plain coarse republican dress, & were applauded by the friends of Liberty.

The Reverend David McClure, future Presbyterian missionary, Diary, *p. 19.*

Bring no Dogs with You—they are very troublesome. . . . [D]o not practice that unseemly, rude, indecent Custom of Chewing or of spitting, which is very ridiculous and absurd in Pubic, especially in Women and in God's House.

The Reverend Charles Woodmason, "On Correct Behavior in Church," 1770, in Carolina, *pp. 88–89.*

At a time when our invaluable Rights and Privileges are attacked in an unconstitutional and most alarming Manner, and as we find we are reproached for not being so ready as could be desired, to lend our Assistance, we think it our Duty perfectly to concur with the true Friends of Liberty in all Measures they have taken to save this abused Country from Ruin and Slavery. And particularly, we join with the very respectable Body of Merchants and other Inhabitants of this Town, who met in Faneuil Hall the 23d of this Instant, in their Resolutions, totally to abstain from the Use of Tea; And as the greatest Part of the Revenue arising by Virtue of the late Acts, is produced from the Duty paid upon Tea, which Revenue is wholly expended to support the American Board of Commissioners; We, the Subscribers, do strictly engage, that we will totally abstain from the Use of that Article, (Sickness excepted) not only in our respective Families, but that we will absolutely refuse it, if it should be offered to us upon any Occasion whatsoever. This Agreement we cheerfully come into, as we believe the very distressed Situation of our Country requires it, and we do hereby oblige ourselves religiously to observe it, till the late Revenue Acts are repealed.

Agreement of 300 women, Boston Evening Post, *February 1770, quoted in Earle,* Colonial Dames, *pp. 245–46.*

This unhappy affair began by Some Boys & young fellows throwing Snow Balls at the sentry placed at the Customhouse Door. On which 8 or 9 Solders Came to his assistance. Soon after a Number of people collected, when the Capt. commanded the Soldiers to fire, which they did and 3 Men were Kil'd on the Spot & several Mortally Wounded, one of which died next morning. The Capt. soon drew off his Soldiers up to the Main Guard, or the Consequences might have been terrible, for on the Guns firing the people were alarmed & set the Bells a Ringing as if for Fire, which drew Multitudes to the place of action. Governor Hutchinson, who was commander in Chief, was sent for & Came to the Council Chamber, where some of the Magistrates attended. The Governor desired the Multitude about 10 o'clock to separate & go home peaceable & he would do all in his power that justice should be done &e. The 29th Regiment being then under Arms on the south side of the Townhouse, but the people insisted that the Soldiers should be ordered to their Barracks first before they would separate, Which being done the people separated about 1 o'clock. Capt. Preston was take up by a warrant given to the high Sherif by justice Dania & Tudor and came under Examination about 2 o'clock & we sent him to Jail soon after 3, having Evidence sufficient, to commit him, on his ordering the soldiers to fire: So about 4 o'clock the Town became quiet. The next forenoon the 8 Soldiers that fired on the inhabitants was also sent to Jail.

Boston merchant John Tudor, March 1770, in Hart, ed.,
American History, *vol. 2, p. 429.*

[*Captured slaves*] Brought to the Workhouse,

Two Negroe fellows, brought from the Creek nation, cannot speak English to tell their own or their master's names; one of them is a stout able fellow, about 6 feet high, aged about 28 years, has his country marks thus:)) on each side of his face, and holes in his ears; the other is about 5 feet 9 inches high, aged 22 years, of a yellow complexion with holes in his ears. December 7, 1769.

A Negroe fellow, who says his name is Bostos, but cannot tell his master's name; he is about 5 feet 10 inches high, and about 20 years of age; taken up near the Alatamaha. December 11, 1769.

A New Negroe fellow, can't speak English so as to tell his master's or his own name, about five feet one inch high, about 20 years of age . . . taken up at Great-Ogachoe, 80 miles from town. 21st January 1720.

Georgia Gazette, March 28, 1770, quoted in Davis,
Fledgling Province, *p. 136.*

A number of thirty-three respectable ladies of the town [*Rowley, Massachusetts*] met at sunrise with their wheels to spend the day at the house of the Rev'd Jedidiah Jewell in the laudable design of a spinning match. At an hour before sunset, the ladies then appearing neatly dressed, principally in homespun, a polite and generous repast of American production was set for their entertainment, after which being present many spectators of both sexes, Mr. Jewell delivered a profitable discourse from Romans xii. 2: Not slothful in business, fervent in spirit, serving the Lord.

Boston Newsletter, July 1770, quoted in Earle,
Colonial Dames, *p. 242.*

On Monday last being the second day of Hillsborough [*North Carolina*] Superior Court, early in the morning the Town was filled with a great number of these people shouting, hallooing & making a considerable tumult in the streets. At about 11 o'clock the Court was opened, and immediately the House filled as close as one man could stand by another, some with clubs

others with whips and switches, few or none without some weapon. When the House had become so crowded that no more could well get in, one of them (whose name I think is called Fields) came forward and told me he had something to say before I proceeded to business. The accounts I had previously received together with the manner and appearance of these men and the abruptness of their address rendered my situation extremely uneasy. Upon my informing Fields that he might speak on he proceeded to let me know that he spoke for the whole Body of the People called Regulators. That they understood that I would not try their causes, and their determination was to have them

Chowan County Court House, Edenton, North Carolina, built 1767 (*Historic American Building Survey*)

tried, for they had come down to see justice done and justice they will have, and if I would proceed to try those causes it might prevent much mischief. . . . Thus I found myself under a necessity of attempting to soften and turn away the fury of this mad people, in the best manner in my power, and as much as could well be, pacify their rage and at the same time preserve the little remaining dignity of the Court. The consequence of which was that after spending upwards of half an hour in this disagreeable situation the mob cried out "Retire, retire, and let the Court go on." Upon which most of the regulators went out and seemed to be in consultation in a party by themselves.

The little hopes of peace derived from this piece of behaviour were very transient, for in a few minutes Mr. Williams an Attorney of that Court was coming in and had advanced near the door when they fell on him in a most furious manner with Clubs and sticks of enormous size and it was with great difficulty he saved his life by taking shelter in a neighboring Store House. Mr. Fanning was next the object of their fury, him they seized and took with a degree of violence not to be described from off the bench where he had retired for protection and assistance and with hideous shouts of barbarian cruelty dragged him by the heels out of doors, while others engaged in dealing out blows. . . .

Judge Richard Henderson, September 1770, in Hart, ed., American History, *vol. 2, pp. 426–27.*

It was on the first of May, in the year 1769, that I resigned my domestic happiness for a time, and left my family and peaceable habitation on the Yadkin River, in North-Carolina, to wander through the wilderness of America, in quest of the country of Kentucke. . . . [A]fter a long and fatiguing journey through a mountainous wilderness, in a westward direction, on the seventh day of June following, we found ourselves on Red-River, where John Finley had formerly been trading with the Indians, and, from the top of an eminence, saw with pleasure the beautiful level of Kentucke. . . . In this forest, the habitation of beasts of every kind natural to America, we practised hunting with great success until the twenty-second day of December following. . . . In the decline of the day, near Kentucke river, as we ascended the brow of a small hill, a number of Indians rushed out of a thick cane-brake upon us, and made us prisoners. The time of our sorrow was now arrived, and the scene fully opened. The Indians plundered us of what we had, and kept us in confinement seven days,

treating us with common savage usage. During this time we discovered no uneasiness or desire to escape, which made them less suspicious of us; but in the dead of night, as we lay in a thick cane-brake by a large fire, when sleep had locked up their senses, my situation not disposing me for rest, I touched my companion and gently awoke him. We improved this favourable opportunity, and departed, leaving them to take their rest, and speedily directed our course towards our old camp, but found it plundered, and the company dispersed and gone home. . . . [W]e left this place, not thinking it safe to stay there longer, and proceeded to Cumberland river, reconnoitering that part of the country until March, 1771, and giving names to the different waters. . . . Soon after, I returned home to my family with a determination to bring them as soon as possible to live in Kentucke, which I esteemed a second paradise, at the risk of my life and fortune.

Daniel Boone's autobiography [1784], in Hart, American History, *vol. 2, pp. 383–84.*

. . . last Thursday I purchas'd with my aunt Deming's leave, a very beautiful white feather hat, that is, the out side, which is a bit of white hollond with the feathers sew'd on in a most curious manner white & unsullyed as the falling snow, this hat I have long been saving my money to procure for which I have let your kind allowance, Papa, lay in my aunt's hands till this hat which I spoke for was brought home. As I am (as we say) a daughter of liberty I chuse to wear as much of our own manufactory as possible.

Anna Green Winslow, age 11, February 21, 1771, Diary, *pp. 31–32.*

Dear mamma, I suppose that you would be glad to hear that Betty Smith who has given you so much trouble, is well & behaves herself well & I should be glad if I could write you so. But the truth is, no sooner was the 29th Regiment encamp'd upon the common but miss Betty took herself among them (as the Irish say) & there she stay'd with Bill Pinchion & awhile. The next news of her was, that she was got into gaol for stealing: from whence she was taken to the publick whipping post. The next adventure was to the Castle, after the soldier's were remov'd there, for the murder of the 5th March last [*the Boston Massacre*]. When they turn'd her away from there, she came up to town again, and soon got into the workhouse for new misdemeanours, she soon ran away from there and set up her old trade of pilfering again, for which she was put a second time into gaol, there she still remains. About two months agone (as well as I can remember) she & a number of her wretched companions set the gaol on fire, in order to get out, but the fire was extinguished. . . . I heard somebody say that as she has some connections with the army no doubt but she would be cleared, and perhaps, have a pension in the bargain.

Anna Green Winslow, age 11, February 25, 1771,
Diary, pp. 36–37.

The roads through this Indian country are no more than a single horse path, among the trees. For a wilderness the traveling was pleasant, as there was no underbrush & the trees do not grow very closely together. We traveled diligently all day. I was apprehensive that we had missed the path. Robert was a great smoker of tobacco, & frequently lighted his pipe, by striking fire, as he sat on his horse, & often in the course of the day, exclaimed in his jargon, "Ding me, but this path will take us somewhere." At sun setting we arrived at Kuskuskoong [*western Pennsylvania*] & found my Interpreter Joseph there. . . . It was a neat Moravian village, consisting of one street & houses pretty compact, on each side, with gardens, back. There was a convenient Log church, with a small bell, in which the Indians assembled for morning & evening prayer. The village was full, as their brethren the Susquehanna Indians had arrived. . . . The Missionaries have their wives & families with them. . . . At the sound of the bell, the Indians assembled in the church for evening prayer. It was lighted with candles around the walls, on which hung some common paintings of Jesus in the manger of Bethlehem with Joseph & Mary; Jesus on the Cross, & the Resurrection &c. On one side set the elderly men & the boys by themselves, & on the other the women & girls. The evening exercise consisted of devout hymns in the Indian language. . . . After singing . . . the missionary addressed them, in a short exhortation in the Indian language. . . .

The Reverend David McClure, September 5, 1772,
Diary, pp. 47–49.

Sesamen or oily grain . . . was introduced by some of the Negroes from the coast of Africa, into Carolina, and is the best thing yet known for extracting a fine esculent oil; it will grow in any sandy ground, even luxuriantly, and yields more oil than any thing we have as yet any knowledge of: Capt. P M'Kay of Sunbury in Geor-

gia, told me that a quantity of this seed sent to Philadelphia, yielded him twelve quarts per bushel; incredible as this may appear, I have the greatest reason to believe him; the first run of this oil is always transparent, the second expression, which is procured by the addition of hot water, is muddy, but on standing it will deposit a white sediment, and become as limpid as the first; this oil is at first of a slightly pungent taste, but soon loses that and will never grow rancid even if left exposed to the air; the Negroes use it as food either raw, toasted, or boiled in their soups and are very fond of it, they call it *Benni.*

Bernard Romans, 1773, Concise History, *pp. 130–31.*

Should you, my lord, while you peruse my song,
Wonder from whence my love of Freedom
    sprung,
Whence flow these wishes for the common good,
By feeling hearts along best understood,
I, young in life, by seeming cruel fare,
Was snatched from Afric's fancied happy seat:
What pangs excruciating must molest,
What sorrows labour in my parents' breast?
Steeled was that soul and by no misery moved
That from a father seized his babe beloved:
Such, such my case. And can I then but pray
Others may never feel tyrannic sway?

Phillis Wheatley, "To the Right Honourable William,
Earl of Dartmouth," 1773, in Gilbert and Gubar, eds.,
Norton Anthology, *p. 134.*

They mustered, I'm told, upon Fort Hill, to the number of about two hundred, and proceeded, two by two, to Griffin's wharf, where Hall, Bruce, and Coffin lay, each with 114 chests of the ill-fated article on board; the two former with only that article, but the latter arrived at the wharf only the day before, was freighted with a large quantity of other goods, which they took the greatest care not to injure in the least, and before nine o'clock in the evening, every chest from on board the three vessels was knocked to pieces and flung over the sides. They say the actors were Indians from Narragansett. Whether they were or not, to a transient observer they appeared as such, being clothed in Blankets with the heads muffled, and copper colored countenances, being each armed with a hatchet or axe and pair pistols . . . their jargon was unintelligible to any but themselves. Not the least insult was offered to any person, save one, Captain Conner, a letter of horses in this place, not many years since removed from dear Ireland, who had ripped up the lining of his coat and waistcoat under the arms, and watching his opportunity had nearly filled 'em with tea, but being detected, was handled pretty roughly. They not only stripped him of his clothes, but gave him a coat of mud, with a severe bruising into the bargain; and nothing but their utter aversion to make any disturbance prevented his being tarred and feathered.

John Andrews, 1773, in Hart, ed., American History, *vol. 2, p. 433.*

The Indians, as they were then called, repaired to the wharf, where the ships lay that had the tea on board. They were followed by hundreds of people to see the event of the transactions of those who made so grotesque an appearance.

The Indians immediately repaired on board Captain Hall's ship, where they hoisted out the chests of tea. When on deck they stove them and emptied the tea overboard.

Having cleared this ship they proceeded to Captain Bruce's, and then to Captain Coffin's brig. They applied themselves so dexterously to the destruction of this commodity, that in the space of three hours they broke up three hundred and forty-two chests, which was the whole number of these vessels, and poured their contents into the harbor.

When the tide rose it floated the broken chests and the tea. The surface of the water was filled therewith a considerable way from the south part of the town to Dorchester Neck and lodged on the shores.

Massachusetts Gazette, *1773, in Hart, ed.,* Camps, *p. 163.*

The Petition of us the subscribers in behalf of all those who by divine Permission are held in a state of slavery, within the bowels of a free Country, Humbly sheweth,—

That your petitioners apprehend they have in common with other men a natural right to be free and without molestation to enjoy such property as they may acquire by their industry. . . .

Slave petition to Massachusetts General Court, June 1773, Massachusetts Historical Society, *Collections, 5th ser., no. 3., (1877), p. 432.*

Land was the object which invited the greater number of these people to cross the mountain, for as the saying then was, "It was to be had here for taking up." . . . My father with a small number of his neighbors made their settlement in the spring of 1773. . . .

The furniture for the table, for several years after the settlement of this country [*western Virginia*], consisted of a few pewter dishes, plates, and spoons; but mostly of wooden bowls, trenchers and noggins. If these last were scarce, gourds and hard shelled squashes made up the deficiency.

The iron pots, knives, and forks were brought from the east side of the mountains along with the salt, and iron on pack horses.

These articles of furniture, corresponded very well with the articles of diet, on which they were employed. "Hog and hominy" were proverbial for the dish of which they were the component parts. Jonny cake and pone were at the outset of the settlements of the country, the only forms of bread in use for breakfast and dinner. At supper, milk and mush were the standard dish. When milk was not plenty, which was often the case, owing to the scarcity of cattle, or the want of proper pasture for them, the substantial dish of hominy had to supply the place of them; mush was frequently eaten with sweetened water, molasses, bears oil, or the gravy of fried meat. . . .

The Reverend Joseph Doddrrige describing conditions in 1773, in Hart, ed., American History, *vol. 2, pp. 387–91.*

. . . your Petitioners apprehend we have in common with all other men a natural right to our freedoms without Being depriv'd of them by our fellow men as we . . . have never forfeited this blessing by any compact or agreement whatever. But we were unjustly dragged by the cruel hand of power . . . from a Populous and Pleasant and plentiful country and Brought hither to be made slaves for Life in a Christian land. . . . The endearing ties of husband and wife we are strangers to for we are no longer man and wife than our masters and mistresses think proper married or unmarried. Our children are also taken from us by force and sent many miles from us where we seldom or ever see them again there to be made slaves of for life which sometimes is very short by reason of being dragged from their mother's breast. Thus our lives are embittered to us on these accounts. By our deplorable situation we are rendered incapable of showing our obedience to almighty God. How can a slave perform the duties of a husband to a wife or parent to his child? How can a husband leave master and work and cleave to his wife? How can the wife submit themselves to their husbands in all things? How can the child obey their parents in all things?

Slave petition to Massachusetts General Court, May 25, 1774 in Massachusetts Historical Society, Collections, 5th ser., no. 3 (1877), p. 433.

Blush ye pretended votaries for freedom! ye trifling patriots! who are making a vain parade of being advocated for the liberties of mankind, who are thus making a mockery of your profession by trampling on the sacred natural rights and privileges of Africans; for while you are fasting, praying, nonimporting, nonexporting, remonstrating, resolving, and pleading for a restoration of your charter rights, you at the same time are continuing this lawless, cruel, inhuman, and abominable practice of enslaving your fellow creatures. . . .

Baptist preacher John Allen, The Watchman's Alarm, 1774, quoted in Bailyn, Ideological Origins, p. 240.

Absented from on board the ship *Mary,* Capt. James Walden, lying at the subscribers's wharf, Six Indented Men Servants, viz.,

John Humphries, about 20 years old, 5 feet 4 inches high, with short black hair and a swarthy complexion, had on when he eloped a suit of black broadcloth, born in London.

Michael Herring, aged 27 years, 5 feet 6 inches high, short hair, a dark complexion, had on a sailor's frock and trousers, born in Ireland.

Robert Cock, aged 24 years, about 5 feet high, in a seaman's dress, curled hair, with a dark complexion, born in London.

Richard Owen, a tailor by trade, aged about 40 years, 5 feet 6 or 7 inches high, had on a blue coat and light colored waistcoat, born in Wales.

John Grant, aged 37 years, about 5 feet 7 inches high, had on when he went away a soldier's coat, born in Scotland.

Edward Granville, by trade a barber, aged 29 years, about 5 feet 7 inches high, with tied hair, pitted with the smallpox, had on a brown coat and breeches, with a white waistcoat, born in London.

Whoever will apprehend and deliver any of the above servants to the subscribers, or to the Keeper of the Jail in Savannah, shall have twenty shilling sterling for each, with reasonable charges; and all persons are hereby forbid harboring them, as they will, upon conviction, be prosecuted to the utmost rigor of the law.

Georgia Gazette, May 25, 1774, quoted in Davis, Fledgling Province, p. 151.

[Our] uniform generally was a hunting shirt dyed as fancy pointed, and the youths of the schools and colleges in Philadelphia formed themselves in companies distinguished by different colors, armed with guns and trained to military exercises. In the month of September, 1774, these companies were all collected, and in the rear of the Rifle or Frock men marched to Frankford, about five miles from Philadelphia, for the purpose of escorting the delegates to town. They were on horseback, two and two, and with their military escort formed a long procession. The road was lined with people and resounded with huzzas, drums, etc., and exhibited a lively scene. In the humble office of sergeant I had thus the honor of escorting into Philadelphia the First American Congress.

Jacob Mordecai describes events when he was 12, September 1774, in Mordecai, "Notice," p. 41.

He mentioned particularly the method of voting, whether it should be by Colonies, or by the poll, or by interests.

Mr. [Patrick] Henry then arose, and said, this was the first General Congress which had ever happened; that no former Congress could be a precedent; that we should have occasion for more general congresses, and therefore that a precedent ought to be established now; that it would be great injustice if a little Colony should have the same weight in the councils of America as a great one. . . . Major Sullivan observed that a little Colony had its all at stake as well as a great one. . . .

Mr. Henry. Government is dissolved. Fleets and armies and the present state of things show that government is dissolved. Where are your landmarks, your boundaries of Colonies? We are in a state of nature, sir. I did propose that a scale should be laid down; that part of North America which was once Massachusetts Bay, and that part which was once Virginia, ought to be considered as having a weight. Will not people complain? Ten thousand Virginians have not out weighed one thousand others. I will submit, however; I am determined to submit, if I am over-ruled. . . . The distinctions between Virginians, Pennsylvanians, New Yorkers, and New Englanders, are no more. I am not a Virginian, but an American. Slaves are to be thrown out of the question, and if the freemen can be represented according to their numbers, I am satisfied.

Mr. Lynch. I differ in one point from the gentleman from Virginia, that is, in thinking that numbers only ought to determine the weight of Colonies. I think that property ought to be considered, and that it ought to be a compound of numbers and property that should determine the weight of the Colonies.

John Adams, September 5, 1774, diary of the First Continental Congress, in Hart, ed., American History, *vol. 2, pp. 434–36.*

The good people of the several colonies . . . justly alarmed at these arbitrary proceedings of parliament and administration, have severally elected, constituted, and appointed deputies to meet, and sit in general Congress, in the city of Philadelphia, in order to obtain such establishment, as that their religion, laws, and liberties, may not be subverted: Whereupon the deputies so appointed being now assembled, in a full and free representation of these colonies, taking into their most serious consideration, the best means of attaining the ends aforesaid, do . . . DECLARE.

That the inhabitants of the English colonies in North-America, by the immutable laws of nature, the principles of the English constitution, and the several charters or compacts, have the following RIGHTS:

Resolved, 1. That they are entitled to life, liberty and property: and they have never ceded to any foreign power whatever, a right to dispose of either without their consent.

Resolved, 2. That our ancestors, who first settled these colonies, were at the time of their emigration from the mother country, entitled to all the rights, liberties, and immunities of free and natural-born subjects, within the realm of England.

Resolved, 3. That by such emigration they by no means forfeited, surrendered, or lost any of those rights. . . .

Resolved, 4. That the foundation of English liberty, and of all free government, is a right in the people to participate in their legislative council: and as the English colonists are not represented, and from their local and other circumstances, cannot properly be represented in the British parliament, they are entitled to a free and exclusive power of legislation in their several provinces. . . .

Declaration and Resolves, First Continental Congress, October 1774, in Macdonald, ed., Documentary, *p. 164.*

We, His Majesty's loyal subjects. . . . To obtain redress of these grievances, which threaten destruction to the lives, liberty, and property of his majesty's subjects, in North America, we are of opinion, that a non-importation, non-consumption, and non-exportation agreement, faithfully adhered to, will prove the most speedy, effectual, and peaceable measure: And, therefore, we do, for ourselves, and the inhabitants of the several colonies, whom we represent, firmly agree and associate, under the sacred ties of virtue, honour and love of our country, as follows:

First, That from and after the first day of December next, we will not import, into British America, from Great Britain or Ireland, any goods, wares, or merchandise whatsoever, or from any other place, any such goods, wares, or merchandise, as shall have been exported from Great Britain or Ireland; nor will we, after that day, import any East-India tea from any part of the world; nor any molasses, syrups, paneles, coffee, or pimento, from the British plantations or from Dominica; nor wines from Madeira, or the Western Islands; nor foreign indigo.

Second, We will neither import nor purchase, any slave imported after the first day of December next; after which time, we will wholly discontinue the slave trade, and will neither be concerned in it ourselves, nor will we hire our vessels, nor sell our commodities or manufactures to those who are concerned in it.

Third, As a non-consumption agreement; strictly adhered to, will be an effectual security for the observation of the non-importation, we, as above, solemnly agree and associate, that from this day, we will not purchase or use any tea, imported on account of the East India Company. . . .

The "Association," First Continental Congress, October 1774, in Macdonald, ed., Documentary, *pp. 166–68.*

Alexandria, Virginia . . . Thursday, December 15, 1774. Nothing but Committees and Politics, which puts everything in confusion. . . . *Saturday, December 24th, 1774.* Great quantities of Hogs killed in town. They salt the Pork and export it to the West Indies. It makes a considerable branch of commerce. . . . *Sunday, December 25th, 1774.* Christmas Day. But little regarded here. . . .

Sunday, January 1st, 1775. The Parson is drunk and can't perform the duties of his office. This is the first day of the New Year, which seems to be big with matters of great consequence. . . .

English visitor Nicholas Cresswell, Journal, *pp. 51–52.*

Every body of fashion both from the town and round the country were invited [*to the funeral*], but the Solemnity was greatly hurt by a set of Volunteers [*country people*], who, I thought, must have fallen from the moon; above a hundred of whom (of both sexes) arrived in canoes, just as the clergyman was going to begin the service, and made such a noise, it was hardly to be heard. A hogshead of rum and broth and vast quantities of pork, beef and cornbread were set forth for the entertainment of these gentry. But as they observed the tables already covered for the guests after the funeral, they took care to be first back from it, and before any one got to the hall, were placed at the tables, and those that had not room to sit carried off the dishes to another room, so that an elegant entertainment that had been provided went for nothing. At last they got into their canoes, and I saw them row thro' the creeks, and suppose they have little spots of ground up the woods, which afford them corn and pork, and that on such occasions they flock down like crows to a carrion.

They were no sooner gone than the Negroes assembled to perform their part of the funeral rites, which they did by running, jumping, crying and various exercises. They are a noble troop, the best in all the country. . . .

Scottish visitor to North Carolinia Janet Schaw, 1775, in Schaw, Journal, p. 171.

Saturday, January 7th, 1775. Last night I went to the Ball. It seems this is one of their annual Balls supported in the following manner: A large rich cake is provided and cut into small pieces and handed round to the company, who at the same time draws a ticket out of a Hat with something merry wrote on it. He that draws the King has the Honor of treating the company with a Ball the next year. . . . The Lady that draws the Queen has the trouble of making the cake. Here was about 37 ladies dressed and powdered to some of them very handsome and as much vanity as is necessary. All of them fond of dancing, but I do not think they perform it with the greatest elegance. Betwixt the Country dances they have what I call everlasting jigs. A couple gets up and begins to dance a jig (to some Negro tune) others comes and cuts them out, and these dances last as long as the Fiddler can play. This is sociable, but I think it looks more like a Bacchanalian dance than one in a polite assembly. Old Women, Young wives with children in the lap, widows, maids and girls come promiscuously to these assemblies which generally

continue till morning. A cold supper, Punch, Wines, Coffee and Chocolate, but no Tea. This is a forbidden herb. . . .

Tuesday, January 10, 1775. These three days I have spent in making enquiries about the nature and situation of the Land in the Illinois Country. . . . The lands are exceedingly rich, produce Tobacco, Indigo, and Wheat. . . . It likewise abounds with Lead and mines of Copper, but very few inhabitants and those French. I am told by these gentlemen that there will be some risk in going down the Ohio River. The Indians often cut the White people off, in their passage down to the Mississippi. I think I have a prospect of making it worth while and will hazard the passage.

English visitor Nicholas Cresswell, Journal, pp. 53–55.

[*Jan. 14, 1775*] As our Regiment is quartered on a Wharf which projects into part of the [Boston] harbour, and there is a very considerable range without any obstruction, we have fixed figures of men as large as life, made of thin boards, on small stages, which are anchored at a proper distance from the end of the Wharf, at which the men fire. Objects afloat, which move up and down with the tide, are frequently pointed out for them to fire at, and Premiums are sometimes given for the best Shots, by which means some of our men have become excellent marksmen.

British officer Frederick Mackenzie, diary entry, British Fusilier, pp. 28–29.

We came down in the morning in time for the review [*of the North Carolina militia*] which the heat made as terrible to the spectators as to the soldiers, or what you please to call them. They had certainly fainted under it, had not the constant draughts of grog supported them. Their exercise was that of bush-fighting, but it appeared so confused and so perfectly different from any thing I ever saw, I cannot say whether they performed it well or not; but this I know that they were heated with rum till capable of committing the most shocking outrages. . . . I must really laugh while I recollect their figures: 2000 men in their shirts and trousers, preceded by a very ill beat-drum and a fiddler, who was also in his shirt with a long sword and a cue at his hair, who played with all his might. They made indeed a most unmartial appearance. But the worst figure there can shoot from behind a bush and kill even a General Wolfe.

Scottish visitor Janet Schaw, spring 1775, Journal, pp. 189–90.

Richard Clark, Esq., a consignee of the tea, was obliged to retire from Salem to Boston, as an asylum; and his son Isaac went to Plymouth to collect debts, but in the night was assaulted by a mob and obliged to get out of town at midnight. Jesse Dunbar, of Halifax, in Plymouth county, bought some fat cattle of Mr. Thomas the councillor, and drove them to Plymouth for sale; one of the oxen being skinned and hung up, the committee came to him, and finding he bought it of Mr. Thomas, they put the ox into a cart, and fixing Dunbar in his belly, carted him four miles, and there made him pay a dollar, after taking three more cattle and a horse from him. The Plymouth mob delivered him to the Kingston mob, which carted him four miles further, and forced from him another dollar, then delivered him to the Duxborough mob, who abused him by throwing the tripe in his face, and endeavoring to cover him with it to the endangering his life. They then threw dirt at him, and after other abuses carried him to said Thomas's house, and made him pay another sum of money, and he not taking the beef, they flung it in the road and quitted him. Daniel Dunbar, of Halifax, an ensign of militia there, had his colors demanded by the mob, some of the selectmen being the chief actors. He refused; they broke into his house, took him out, forced him upon a rail, and after keeping him for two or three hours in such abuses, he was forced to give his colors up to save his life. . . . In February, at Plymouth, a number of ladies attempted to divert themselves at their assembly room, but the mob collected, (the committee having met previous thereto,) and flung stones which broke the shutters and windows, and endangered their lives. They were forced to get out of the hall, and were pelted and abused to their own homes.

Anonymous newspaper article describing harassment of Loyalists, March 1775, in Hart, ed., American History, *vol. 2, 460–61.*

Monday, April 17th, 1775 . . . In the afternoon, viewing the town and Fort [Pitt]. It is pleasantly situated at the conjunction of the Moningahaley and Allegany Rivers. . . . The town is small, about 30 houses, the people chiefly in Indian trade. The Fort is some distance from the town close in the forks of the Rivers. . . . Deserted and demolished by own troops about three years ago, but repaired last summer by the Virginians [*i.e., Lord Dunmore*] and has now a small garrison in it. It is a pentagonal form. Three of the Bastions and two of the curtains faced with brick, the rest picketed. Bar-

racks for a considerable number of men, and there is the remains of a genteel house for the Governor, but now in ruins, as well as the Gardens which are beautifully situated on the Banks of the Allegany well planted with Apple and Peach trees. . . . Spent the evening at Mr. Gambel's, an Indian Trader in town. . . .

Sunday, April 30, 1775 . . . The Land from the foot of the Laurel Mountain to Fort Pitt is rich beyond conception. Walnut and Cherry trees grow to an amazing size. . . . Great plenty of Wild Plums Trees and a Species of the Pimento, these are small Bushes. . . . I have seen stratums of Coal 14 feet thick equal in quality to the English Coal. . . . Very thinly inhabited. The few there are in general great rascals.

Yaughagany River, Virginia [Pennsylvania]—Monday, May 1st 1775 . . . Crossed several Fish pots. These fish pots are made by throwing up the small stones and gravel something like a mill weir, beginning at the side of the River and proceeding in a diagonal line, till they meet in the middle of the stream, where they fix a thing like the body of a cart, contracted where the water flows in just to admit the fish, but so contrived as to prevent their return or escape.

English visitor Nicholas Cresswell, 1775,
Journal, *pp. 64–69.*

. . . I was sent for by Doc. Joseph Warren, of said Boston, on the evening of the 18th of April, about 10 o'Clock; when he desired me "to go to Lexington, and inform Mr. Samuel Adams, and the Hon [orable] John Hancock Esqr. that there was a number of Soldiers, composed of Light troops, & Grenadiers, marching to the bottom of the Common, where was a number of Boats to receive them; it was supposed, that they were going to Lexington, by the way of Cambridge River, to take *them* or go to Concord, to distroy the Colony Stores." I proceeded immediately, and was put across Charles River, and landed near Charlestown Battery, went in town, and there got a Horse. . . . I set off, it was then about 11 o'Clock, the Moon shone bright. I had got almost over Charlestown Common, towards Cambridge, when I saw two Officers on Horse back, standing under the shade of a Tree, in a narrow part of the roade. I was near enough to see their Holsters, & cockades. One of them Started his horse towards me. . . . I turned my horse short about, and rid upon a full Gallop for Mistick Road, he followed me about 300 yardes, and finding he could not catch me, returned. I proceeded to Lexington, thro Mistick, and alarmed Mr.

Adams & Col. Hancock. After I had been there about half an hour Mr. Daws arrived, who came from Boston, over the neck; we set off for Concord. . . .

Paul Revere's deposition, 1775, in Nineteenth of April, *[not paginated].*

Upon this our men [*at Lexington*] dispersed—but many of them not so speedily as they might have done, not having the most distant idea of such brutal barbarity and more than savage cruelty, from the troops of a British King, as they immediately experienced. For, no sooner did they come in sight of our company but one of them, supposed to be an officer of rank, was heard to say to the troops, "Damn them, we will have them!" Upon which the troops shouted aloud, huzza'd, and rushed furiously towards our men. About the same time, three officers (supposed to be Colonel Smith, Major Pitcairn, and another officer) advanced on horse back to the front of the body, and coming within five or six rods of the militia, one of them cried out, "Ye villains, ye rebels, disperse! Damn you, disperse!"—or words to this effect. . . . The second of these officers about this time fired a pistol towards the militia as they were dispersing. The foremost, who was within a few yards of our men, brandishing his sword and then pointing towards them, with a loud voice said to the troops, "Fire! By God, fire!"—which was instantly followed by a discharge of arms from the said troops, succeeded by a very heavy and close fire upon our dispersing party, so long as any of them were within reach.

Narrative of the Reverend Jonas Clark, April 19, 1775, in Dorson, ed., American Rebels, *pp. 22–23.*

[*Apr. 19, 1775, from Lexington through Charlestown*] Our men had very few opportunities of getting good shots at the Rebels, as they hardly ever fired but under cover of a Stone wall, from behind a tree, or out of a house; and the moment they had fired they lay down out of sight until they had loaded again, or the Column had passed. In the road indeed in our rear, they were most numerous, and came on pretty close, frequently calling out, "*King Hancock forever.*" Many of them were killed in the houses on the road side from whence they fired; in some of them 7 or 8 men were destroyed. Some houses were forced open in which no person could be discovered, but when the Column had passed, numbers sallied out from some place in which they had lain concealed, fired at the rear Guard, and augmented

the numbers which followed us. If we had had time to set fire to those houses many Rebels must have perished in them. . . . Many houses were plundered by the Soldiers, notwithstanding the efforts of the Officers to prevent it. I have no doubt this inflamed the Rebels, and made many of them follow us farther than they would otherwise have done.

British officer Frederick Mackenzie, diary entry, British Fusilier, *pp. 57–58.*

Hamnah Adams, wife of Deacon Joseph Adams, of the second precinct in Cambridge, testifieth and saith, that on the nineteenth day of April last past, upon the return of the king's troops front Concord, divers of them entered our house, by bursting open the doors, and three of the soldiers broke into the room in which I then was, laid on my bed, being scarcely able to walk from my bed to the fire, not having been to my chamber door from my being delivered in childbirth to that time. One of said soldiers immediately opened my curtains with his bayonet fixed, pointing the same to my breast. I immediately cried out, "for the Lord's sake do not kill me;" he replied, "damn you." One that stood near said, "we will not hurt the woman, if she will go out of the house, but we will surely burn it." I immediately arose, threw a blanket over me, went out and crawled into a corn-house near the door, with my infant in my arms, where I remained until they were gone. They immediately set the house on fire, in which I had left five children, and no other person; but the fire was happily extinguished, when the house was in the utmost danger of being utterly consumed.

Deposition on events of April 19, 1775, in Journals of Each Provincial Congress, *p. 677.*

Last night advice was received from Virginia that the powder and stores in the magazine at Williamsburg were taken from thence by some marines belonging to one of His Majesty's vessels on that station, by order of His Excellency Lord Dunmore.

This intelligence has given an additional alarm to our patriotic party; and accordingly some gentlemen were deputed by the convention to wait on the governor, soliciting him to give directions that the arms, powder, and stores belonging to the province should be delivered into their possession, apprehensions being entertained "That some ship of war may arrive in the harbor of Annapolis whose commander might probably have instructions to seize the same." The deputation was received with respect, and the governor promised to consult his council with all possible dispatch. This answer has given satisfaction for the present; and the militia, who were assembled to enforce submission, are departed quietly to their habitations.

To prevent riot and confusion, the governor and council have thought it advisable to comply with the requisition of the convention, on condition that the colonels of the militia in the respective counties under the ancient establishment solicit for the delivery of the arms, powder, and stores. . . . In these turbulent times something must be yielded to the clamor of an infatuated multitude.

English visitor William Eddis, April 27–28, 1775,
Letters, pp. 108–09.

. . . directions were privately sent to me from the then colony (now state) of Connecticut to raise the Green Mountain Boys, and, if possible, with them to surprise and take the fortress of Ticonderoga. This enterprise I cheerfully undertook; . . . and arrived at the lake opposite to Ticonderoga on the evening of the ninth day of May, 1775, with two hundred and thirty valiant Green Mountain Boys, and it was with the utmost difficulty that I procured boats to cross the lake. . . .

The garrison being asleep, except the sentries, we gave three huzzas which greatly surprised them. One of the sentries made a pass at one of my officers with a charged bayonet, and slightly wounded him. My first thought was to kill him with my sword; but, in an instant, I altered the design and fury of the blow to a slight cut on the side of the head; upon which he dropped his gun and asked quarter, which I readily granted him, and demanded of him the place where the commanding officer kept. He showed me a pair of stairs in the front of a barrack, on the west part of the garrison, which led up to a second story in said barrack, to which I immediately repaired, and ordered the commander, Captain De la Place, to come forth instantly, or I would sacrifice the whole garrison; at which the Captain came immediately to the door, with his breeches in his hand, when I ordered him to deliver me the fort instantly.

He asked me by what authority I demanded it.

I answered him, "In the name of the great Jehovah, and the Continental Congress."

Colonel Ethan Allen, May 1775,
Narrative, pp. 12–14.

Tho' I am truly sensible of the high Honour done me in this Appointment, yet I feel great distress from a consciousness that my abilities and Military experience may not be equal to the extensive and important Trust: However, as the Congress desires I will enter upon the momentous duty, and exert every power I Possess In their Service for the support of the glorious Cause: I beg they will accept my most cordial thanks for this distinguished testimony of their Approbation.

But lest some unlucky event should happen unfavourable to my reputation, I beg it may be remembered by every Gent[lema]n in the room, that I this day declare with the utmost sincerity, I do not think my self equal to the Command I am honoured with.

Sir, I beg leave to Assure the Congress that as no pecuniary Consideration could have tempted me to have accepted this Arduous employment [at the expence of my domestic ease and happiness] I do not wish to make any proffit from it: I will keep an exact Account of my expences; those I doubt not they will discharge and that is all I desire.

George Washington to John Hancock, president of the
Continental Congress, June 16, 1775, in Washington,
Basic Writings, p. 111.

Philadelphia, June 18, 1775. My Dearest: I am now set down to write to you on a subject, which fills me with inexpressible concern, and this concern is greatly aggravated and increased, when I reflect upon the uneasiness I know it will give you. It has been determined in Congress, that the whole army raised for the defence of the American cause shall be put under my care, and that it is necessary for me to proceed immediately to Boston to take upon me the command of it. You may believe me, my dear Patsy, when I assure you, in the most solemn manner that, so far from seeking this appointment, I have used every endeavor in my power to avoid it, not only from my unwillingness to part with you and the family, but from a consciousness of its being a trust too great for my capacity, and that I should enjoy more real happiness in one month with you at home, than I have the most distant prospect of finding abroad, if my stay were to be seven times seven years. But as it has been a kind of destiny, that has thrown me upon this service, I shall hope that my undertaking it is designed to answer some good purpose. . . .

As life is always uncertain, and common prudence dictates to every man the necessity of settling his temporal concerns, while it is in his power, and while the mind is calm and undisturbed, I have . . . got Colonel Pendleton to draft a will for me. . . .

George Washington to his wife, Affectionately Yours, *pp. 54–55.*

If it was possible for men, who exercise their reason to believe, that the divine Author of our existence intended a part of the human race to hold an absolute property in, and an unbounded power over others, marked out by his infinite goodness and wisdom as the objects of a legal domination never rightfully resistible, however severe and oppressive, the inhabitants of these colonies might at least require from the parliament of Great Britain some evidence, that this dreadful authority over them, has been granted to that body. But a reverence for our great Creator, principles of humanity, and the dictates of common sense, must convince all those who reflect upon the subject, that government was instituted to promote the welfare of mankind, and ought to be administered for the attainment of that end. . . .

Our cause is just. Our union is perfect. Our internal resources are great. . . . We gratefully acknowledge, as signal instances of the Divine favour towards us, that his Providence would not permit us to be called into this severe controversy, until we were grown up to our present strength, had been previously exercised in warlike operation, and possessed of the means of defending ourselves. With hearts fortified with these animating reflections, we most solemnly, before God and the world, declare, that, exerting the utmost energy of those powers, which our Beneficent Creator hath gracious bestowed upon us, the arms we have been compelled by our enemies to assume, we will, in defiance of every hazard, with unabating firmness and perseverance, employ for the preservation of our liberties; being with one mind resolved to die freemen rather than to live slaves. . . .

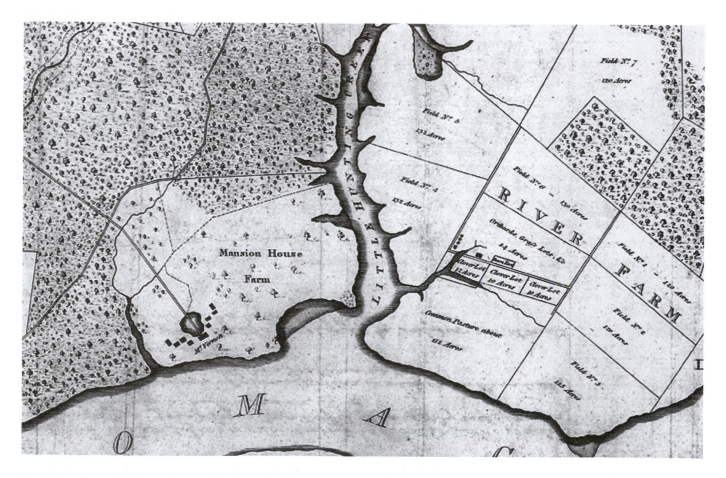

Detail from George Washington's map of his plantation, Mount Vernon, Virginia *(Library of Congress)*

. . . We have not raised armies with ambitious designs of separating from Great Britain, and establishing independent states. We fight not for glory or for conquest. We exhibit to man ind the remarkable spectacle of a people attacked by unprovoked enemies, without any imputation or even suspicion of offence. . . . In our own native land, in defense of the freedom that is our birth-right, and which we ever enjoyed till the late violation of it—for the protection of our property, acquired solely by the honest industry of our forefathers and ourselves, against violence actually offered, we have taken up arms. We shall lay them down when hostilities shall cease on the part of the aggressors, and all danger of their being renewed shall be removed, and not before.

Second Continental Congress, "Declaration of the Causes of Taking Up Arms," July 1775, in Macdonald, ed., Documentary, pp. 177–79.

Whereas many of our subjects in divers parts of our Colonies and Plantations in North America, misled by dangerous and ill designing men, and forgetting the allegiance which they owe to the power that has protected and supported them; after various disorderly acts committed in disturbance of the public peace, to the obstruction of lawful commerce, and to the oppression of our loyal subjects carrying on the same; have at length proceeded to open and avowed rebellion, by arraying themselves in a hostile manner, to withstand the execution of the law, and traitorously preparing, ordering and levying war against us. . . .

King George III, Proclamation of Rebellion, August 23, 1775, in Macdonald, ed., Documentary, p. 189.

[*Nov. 2, 1775*] Traveled four miles; I shot a small bird called a sedee and a squirrel, which I lived upon this day. About noon we met some Frenchmen with cattle for our army, and some meal in a canoe. I had a small piece of meat and bread given me; yesterday my messmates gave away victuals to strangers, but refused me, though they knew I had mine stolen from me. This evening, to our great joy, we arrived at the first French house, where was provisions ready for us. The first victuals I got was boiled rice, which I bought of the Indians, giving one shilling and four pence for about a pint and a half. Here we were joined by about seventy or eighty Indians, all finely ornamented, in their way, with broaches, bracelets and other trinkets, and their faces painted. I had gone barefoot these two or three days, and wore my feet sore.

3—Snowed all day; marched about nine miles, when we drawed provisions.

4—Marched about thirteen miles.

Nov. 5. Sunday—Marched about twelve miles. Our Colonel went forward and got beef killed for us every ten or twelve miles, and served us potatoes instead of bread. I stood sentry over one Flood, who was whipped for stealing Captain Dearborn's pocketbook. This was at St. Mary's.

6. Marched twenty miles; very bad traveling, as it was all the way to Quebec. Twelve miles was through woods, in the night, midleg in mud and snow. I traveled the whole day without eating, and could not get any house to lay in, but lodged in a barn all night.

Private James Melvin, writing about Arnold's expedition,
Journal, *pp. 53–55.*

. . . I do hereby further declare all indented servants, Negroes, or others . . . free, that are able and willing to bear arms, they joining his Majesty's troops, as soon as may be, for the more speedily reducing the Colony to a proper sense of their duty, to His Majesty's crown and dignity.

Virginia governor Lord Dunmore, November 7, 1775, quoted in Quarles, Negro, p. 25.

America is only a secondary object in the system of British politics. England consults the good of this country no farther than it answers her own purpose. Wherefore her own interest leads her to suppress the growth of ours in every case which doth not promote her ad vantage, or in the least interferes with it. A pretty state we should soon be in, under such a second hand government, considering what has happened Men do not change from enemies to friends by the alteration of a name: And in order to shew that reconciliation now is a dangerous doctrine, I affirm, that it would be policy in the King at this time, to repeal the acts for the sake of reinstating himself in the government of the provinces; In order that HE MAY ACCOMPLISH BY CRAFT AND SUBTLETY, IN THE LONG RUN, WHAT HE CANNOT DO BY FORCE AND VIOLENCE IN THE SHORT ONE. Reconciliation and ruin are nearly related. . . .

But where, say some, is the King of America? I'll tell you, Friend, he reigns above, and doth not make havoc of mankind like the Royal Brute of Great Britain. Yet that we may not appear to be defective even in earthly honours, let a day be solemnly set apart for proclaiming the Charter; let it be brought forth placed on the Divine Law, the word of God; let a crown be placed thereon, by which the world may know, that so far as we approve of monarchy, that in America THE LAW IS KING.

Thomas Paine, Common Sense, *January 1776, in Hart, ed.,* American History, *vol. 2, pp. 530–33.*

January 1, 1776—Grant us help in this day of trouble; a very remarkable year past; the most that I ever saw—unnatural war, great sickness, and remarkable drought. 100 years ago we were in a struggle with the Indians, who rose up in rebellion and designed the ruin of the country, but God preserved us. In this year past the leaders of our nation have sent troops to subdue and bring us under in this country, to submit to their arbitrary and tyrannical measures. Much blood has been shed—towns destroyed. . . .

5—By post we have the king's speech to Parliament and observe that he seems resolutely set to bring the Americans under. —O Lord, be pleased to restrain the wrath of man and cause it to praise thee. . . .

July 24—A number of people gathered together, some dressed like Indians with blankets, and manifested uneasiness with those that trade in rum, molasses, sugar, etc. I understand that a number went to Merchant Colton's and have again taken away his goods. I don't see the justice or equity of it. Many don't approve of it, but have not resolution enough to interpose and endeavour redress. I am fearful of special troubles in this place, not only on account of Samuel Colton's goods, but also because several of our people are going into service in Connecticut, and so our quota will be deficient, and possibly men may be drafted.

August 11—This day I read publicly, being required thereto by the Provincial Council, the Declaration of the Continental Congress for Independency. . . .

Diary of the Reverend Stephen Williams, Longmeadow, Massachusetts, in Hart, ed., American History, *vol. 2, pp. 455–56.*

. . . I have sometimes been ready to think that the passion for liberty cannot be equally strong in the breasts of those who have been accustomed to deprive their fellow creatures of theirs. Of this I am certain, that it is not founded upon that generous and Christian principle of doing to others as we would that other do unto us. . . .

. . . I long to hear that you have declared an independency—and by the way, in the new Code of Laws which I suppose it will be necessary for you to make I desire you would Remember the Ladies, and be more generous and favorable to them than your ancestors. Do not put such unlimited power into the hands of the Husbands. Remember, all Men would be tyrants if they could. If particular care and attention is not paid to the Ladies we are determined to foment a Rebellion, and will not hold ourselves bound by any Laws in which we have no voice or Representation.

That your sex are Naturally Tyrannical is a Truth so thoroughly established as to admit of no dispute, but such of you as wish to be happy willingly give up the harsh title of Master for the more tender and endearing one of friend.

Abigail Adams to her husband John Adams, March 31, 1776, in Wortman, ed., Women, *p. 81.*

As to your extraordinary Code of Laws, I cannot but laugh. We have been told that our struggle has loosened the bands of Government everywhere; that Children and Apprentices were disobedient—that schools and Colledges were grown turbulent—that Indians slighted their Guardians and Negroes grew insolent to their masters, But your Letter was the first Intimation that another Tribe more numerous and powerfull that all the rest were grown discontented. . . . Depend upon it, We know better than to repeal our Masculine systems.

John Adams replies to Abigail, April 14, 1776, quoted in Hoff, Law, *p. 60.*

It is certain, in theory, that the only moral foundation of government is, the consent of the people. But to what an extent shall we carry this principle? Shall we say that every individual of the community, old and young, male and female, as well as rich and poor, must consent, expressly, to every act of legislation? No, you will say, this is impossible. How, then, does the right arise in the majority to govern the minority, against their will? Whence arises the right of the men to govern the women, without their consent? Whence the right of the old to bind the young, without theirs? . . .

. . . Is it not equally true, that Men in general in every Society, who are wholly destitute of Property, are also too little acquainted with public affairs to form a Right Judgment, and too dependent upon other Men to have a Will of their own? If this is a Fact, if you give to every man, who has no Property, a Vote, will you not make a fine encouraging Provision for Corruption by your fundamental Law? Such is the Frailty of the human Heart, that very few Men, who have no Property, have any Judgment of their own. . . .

Depend upon it, Sir, it is dangerous to open so fruitful a source of controversy and altercation as would be opened by attempting to alter the qualifications of voters; there will be no end of it. New claims will arise; women will demand a vote; lads from twelve to twenty-one will think their rights not enough attended to; and every man who has not a farthing, will demand an equal voice with any other, in all acts of state. It tends to confound and destroy all distinctions, and prostrate all ranks to one common level.

John Adams to John Sullivan, May 1776, in Adams,
Works, vol. 9, pp. 376–79.

In Congress, Friday, June 7, 1776. The delegates from Virginia moved in obedience to instructions from their constituents that the Congress should declare that these United colonies are & of right ought to be free & independent states. . . .

It appearing in the course of these debates that the colonies of N. York, New Jersey, Pennsylvania, Delaware, Maryland, and South Carolina were not yet matured for falling from the parent stem, but that they were fast advancing to that state, it was thought most prudent to wait a while for them, and to postpone the final decision to July 1. . . . On Monday, the 1st of July the house . . . resumed the consideration of the original motion made by the delegates of Virginia, which being again debated through the day, was carried in the affirmative by the votes of N. Hampshire, Connecticut, Massachusetts, Rhode Island, N. Jersey, Maryland, Virginia, N. Carolina, & Georgia. S. Carolina and Pennsylvania voted against it. Delaware having but two members present, they were divided. The delegates for New York declared they were for it themselves & were assured their constituents were for it, but that their instructions having been drawn near a twelve month before, when reconciliation was still the general object, they were enjoined by them to do nothing which should impede that object. They therefore thought themselves not justifiable in voting on either side, and asked leave to withdraw from the question, which was given them. The committee rose & reported their resolution to the house. Mr. Edward Rutledge of S. Carolina then requested the determination might be put off to the next day, as he believed his colleagues, tho' they disapproved of the resolution, would then join in

it for the sake of unanimity. [It] . . . was accordingly postponed to the next day, when it was again moved and S. Carolina concurred in voting for it. In the meantime a third member had come post from the Delaware counties and turned the vote of that colony in favour of the resolution. Members of a different sentiment attending that morning from Pennsylvania also, their vote was changed, so that the whole 12 colonies who were authorized to vote at all, gave their voices for it; and within a few days, the convention of N. York approved of it and thus supplied the void occasioned by the withdrawing of her delegates from the vote.

Thomas Jefferson, 1776, in Hart, ed., American
History, *vol. 2, pp. 537–39.*

26 Wednesday, June 1776. Last night after going to bed, Moses my son's man, Joe, Billy, Postillion, John, Mulatto, Peter, Tom, Panticove, Manuel & Lancaster Sam ran away, to be sure, to Ld. Dunmore, for they got privately into Beale's room before dark & took out my son's gun & one I had there, took out of his drawer in my passage all his ammunition furniture, Landon's bag of bullets and all the Powder, and went off in my Petty Augur [*piragua or pirogue, a dugout canoe*] new trimmed, and it is supposed that Mr. Robinson's People are gone with them, for a skow they came down in is, it seems, at my landing.

Virginia planter Landon Carter's diary, quoted in
Quarles, *Negro, p. 27.*

Congress proceeded [*July 2*] . . . to consider the declaration of Independence. . . . The pusillanimous idea that we had friends in England worth keeping terms with, still haunted the minds of many. For this reason those passages which conveyed censures on the people of England were struck out, lest they should give them offence. The clause too, reprobating the enslaving the inhabitants of Africa, was struck out in complaisance to South Carolina and Georgia, who had never attempted to restrain the importation of slaves, and who on the contrary still wished to continue it. Our northern brethren also I believe felt a little tender under those censures; for tho' their people have very few slaves themselves yet they had been pretty considerable carriers of them to others. The debates having taken up the greater parts of the 2d 3d & 4th days of July were, in the evening of the last, closed the declaration was reported by the commee, agreed to by the house and signed by every member present except Mr.

Dickinson. . . . [T]he sentiments of men are known not only by what they receive, but what they reject also. . . .

Thomas Jefferson, 1776, in Hart, ed., American History, *vol. 2, pp. 537–39.*

He [*King George*] has waged cruel war against human nature itself, violating its most sacred rights of life and liberty in the persons of a distant people who never offended him [*i.e., Africans*], captivating and carrying them into slavery in another hemisphere, or to incur miserable death in their transportation thither. . . . [H]e is now exciting those very people to rise in arms against us, and to purchase that liberty of which *he* has deprived them by murdering the people upon whom *he* also obtruded them: thus paying off former crimes committed against the *liberties* of one people, with crimes which he urges them to commit against the *lives* of another.

Passage removed from Jefferson's draft of the Declaration, in Jefferson, Writings, *vol. 2, pp. 52–54.*

You and I, my dear friend, have been sent into life at a time when the greatest lawgivers of antiquity would have wished to live. How few of the human race have ever enjoyed an opportunity of making an election of government. . . . When! before the present epocha, had

three millions of people full power and a fair opportunity to form and establish the wisest and happiest government that human wisdom can contrive?

John Adams, Thoughts on Government, *1776, quoted in Bailyn,* Ideological Origins, *pp. 272–73.*

The second day of July, 1776, will be the most memorable epoch in the history of America. I am apt to believe that it will be celebrated by succeeding generations as the great anniversary festival. It ought to be commemorated, as the day of deliverance, by solemn acts of devotion to God Almighty. It ought to be solemnized with pomp and parade, with shows, games, sports, guns, bells, bonfires, and illuminations, from one end of this continent to the other, from this time forward, forevermore.

You will think me transported with enthusiasm, but I am not. I am well aware of the toil, and blood, and treasure, that it will cost to maintain this declaration, and support and defend these States. Yet, through all the gloom, I can see the rays of ravishing light and glory. I can see that the end is more than worth all the means, and that posterity will triumph in that day's transaction. . . .

John Adams to Abigail Adams, July 3, 1776, in Hart, ed., Camps, *pp. 174–75.*

APPENDIX A
Documents

1. THE FIRST ENGLISH COLONIAL CHARTER, 1578

The Letters Patents granted by her Majesty to Sir Humphrey Gilbert, Knight, for the inhabiting and planting of our people in America.

I. Elizabeth by the grace of God Queen of England, &c. To all people to which presents shall come, greeting. Know ye that of our especial grace, certain science and mere motion, we have given and granted, and by these presents for us, our heirs and successors, do give and grant to our trustee and well beloved servant Sir Humphrey Gilbert of Compton, in our County of Devonshire knight, and to his heirs and assignees for ever, free liberty and license from time to time and at all times for ever hereafter, to discover, find, search out, and view such remote, heathen and barbarous lands, countries and territories not actually possessed of any Christian prince or people, as to him, his heirs & assignees, and to every or any of them, shall seem good. . . . And we do likewise by these presents, . . . give full authority and power to the said Sir Humphrey, his heirs and assignees . . . [that he shall] have, take, and lead in the same voyages, to travel thitherward, and to inhabit there with him . . . so many of our subjects as shall willingly accompany him . . . with sufficient shipping and furniture for their transportations,—so that none of the same persons . . . be such as hereafter shall be specially restrained by us. . . . And further, that he the said Humphrey, his heirs and assignees . . . shall have, hold, occupy and enjoy . . . all the soil of all such lands, countries, and territories to be discovered or possessed as aforesaid, and of all Cities, Castles, Towns and Villages, and places in the same . . . to be had or used with full power to dispose thereof, & of every part therefore in fee simple or otherwise, according to the order of the laws of England . . . paying unto us for all services, duties and demands, the fifth part of all the ore of gold and silver, that from time to time, and at all times after such discovery, subduing and possessing shall be there gotten. . . .

II. And moreover, we do by these presents . . . give and grant license to the said sir Humphrey, his heirs and assignees Gilbert, his heirs and assignees . . . [that he shall] for his and their defense, encounter, expel, repel, and resist, as by sea as by land, and by all other ways whatsoever, all . . . as without the special license and liking of the said Sir Humphrey, his heirs and assignees . . . shall attempt to inhabit within the said countries . . . or that shall enterprise or attempt at any time hereafter unlawfully to annoy either by Sea or land, the said Sir Humphrey, his heirs and assignees, or any of them.

III. . . . And we do grant to the said Sir Humphrey . . . and to all and every other person and persons, being of our allegiance, whose names shall be noted or entered in some of our courts of Record, within this our Realm of England . . . [that] shall travel to such lands, countries, and territories as aforesaid . . . may have, and enjoy all the privilege of free denizens and persons native of England, and within our allegiance: any law, custom, or usage to the contrary notwithstanding.

IV. And forasmuch as upon the finding out, discovering and inhabiting of such remote lands, countries, and territories as aforesaid, it shall be necessary for the safety of all men that shall adventure themselves in those journeys and voyages, to determine to live together in Christian peace and civil quietness each with other, whereby every one many with more pleasure and profit enjoy that whereunto they shall attain with great pain and peril; we, for us, our heirs and successors, are likewise please and contented, and by these presents do give and grant to the said sir Humphrey . . . full and mere power and authority to correct, punish, pardon, govern and rule by . . . good discretions and policies, as well in causes capital or criminal, as civil, both marine and other, all such our subjects and others . . . that shall abide within two hundred leagues of any of the said place or places . . . so always that the said statutes, laws and ordinances may be as near as conveniently may, agreeable to the form of the laws and policy of England: and also, that they be not against the true Christian faith or religion now professed in the church of England, nor in any wise to withdraw any of the subjects or people of those lands or places from the allegiance of us, our heirs or successors, as their immediate Sovereigns under God. . . .

V. Provided always, and our will and pleasure is, and we do hereby declare to all Christian Kings, princes and states, that if the said sir Humphrey . . . shall at any time or times hereafter rob or spoil by Sea or land, or do any act of unjust and unlawful hostility to . . . any of the Subjects of any King . . . being then in perfect league and amity with us . . . and that upon such injury . . . [we] shall make open proclamation . . . that the said Sir Humphrey . . . make full restitution and satisfaction of all such injuries done. . . .

Witness ourself at Westminister the 11 day of June, the twentieth year of our reign. Anno Domini 1578.

2. SECOND CHARTER OF VIRGINIA, 1609

James, by the grace of God King of England, Scotland, France and Ireland, defender of the faith, etc. To all to whom these presents shall come, greeting.

Whereas, at the humble suit and request of sundry our loving and well disposed subjects intending to deduce a colony and to make habitation and plantation of sundry of our people in that part of America commonly called Virginia, and other part and territories in America either appertaining unto us or which are not actually possessed of any Christian prince or people within certain bound and regions, we have formerly, by our letters patents bearing date the tenth of April in the fourth year of our reign of England, France, and Ireland, and the nine and thirtieth of Scotland, granted to Sir Thomas Gates, Sir George Somers and others, for the more speedy accomplishment of the said plantation and habitation, that they should divide themselves into two colonies the one consisting of divers Knights, gentlemen, merchants and others of our city of London, called the First Colony; and the other of sundry Knights, gentlemen and others of the cities of Bristol, Exeter, the town of Plymouth, and other places, called the Second Colony and have yielded and granted main and sundry privileges and liberties to each Colony for their quiet settling and good government therein, as by the said letters patents more at large appeareth.

Now, forasmuch as divers and sundry of our loving subjects, as well adventurers as planters, of the said First Colony (which have already engaged them selves in furthering the business of the said plantation and do further intend by the assistance of Almighty God to prosecute the same to a happy end) have of late been humble suitors unto us that, in respect of their great charges and the adventure of many of their lives which they have hazarded in the said discovery and plantation of the said country, we would be pleased to grant them a further enlargement and explanation of the said grant, privilege and liberties, and that such councilors and other officers may be appointed amongst them to manage and direct their affairs as are willing and ready to adventure with them; as also whose dwellings are not so far remote from the city of London but that they may at convenient times be ready at hand to give advice and assistance upon all occasions requisite.

We, greatly affecting the effectual prosecution and happy success of the said plantation and commending their good desires therein, for their further encouragement in accomplishing so excellent a work, much pleasing to God and profitable to our Kingdoms, do, of our special grace and certain knowledge and mere motion, for us, our heirs and successors, give, grant and confirm to our trusty and well beloved subjects,

And to such and so many as they do or shall hereafter admit to be joined with them, in form hereafter in this presents expressed, whether they go in their persons to be planters there in the said plantation, or whether they go not, but do adventure their moneys, goods or chattels, that they shall be one body or commonalty perpetual and shall have perpetual succession and one common seal to serve for the said body or commonalty; and that they and their successors shall be known, called and incorporated by the name of The Treasurer and Company of Adventurers and Planters of the City of London for the First Colony in Virginia.

And that they and their successors shall be from henceforth, forever enabled to take, acquire and purchase, by the name aforesaid (license for the same from us, our heirs or successors first had and obtained) any manner of lands, tenements and hereditaments, goods and chattels, within our realm of England and dominion of Wales; and that they and their successors shall be likewise enabled, by the name aforesaid, to plead and to be impleaded before any of our judges or justices, in any our courts, and in any actions or suits whatsoever.

And we do also, of our said special grace, certain knowledge and mere motion, give, grant and confirm unto the said Treasurer and Company, and their successors, under the reservations, limitations and declarations hereafter expressed, all those lands, countries and territories situate, lying and being in that place of America called Virginia, from the point of land called Cape or Point Comfort all along the seacoast to the northward two hundred miles and from the said point of Cape Comfort all along the sea coast to the southward two hundred miles; and all that space and circuit of land lying from the sea coast of the precinct aforesaid up unto the land, throughout, from sea to sea, west and northwest; and also all the island being within one hundred miles along the coast of both seas of the precinct aforesaid; together with all the soils, grounds, havens and ports, mines, as well royal mines of gold and silver as other minerals, pearls and precious stones, quarries, woods, rivers, waters, fishings, commodities, jurisdictions, royalties, privileges, franchises and preeminences within the said territory and the precincts thereof whatsoever; and thereto or there abouts, both by sea and land, being or in any sort belonging or appertaining, and which we by our letters patents may or can grant; and in as ample manner and sort as we or any our noble progenitors have heretofore granted to any company, body politic or corporate, or to any adventurer or adventurers, undertaker or undertakers, of any discoveries, plantation or traffic of, in, or into any foreign parts whatsoever; and in as large and ample manner as if the same were herein particularly mentioned and expressed: to have, hold, possess and enjoy all and singular the said lands, countries and territories with all and singular other the premises heretofore by this presents granted or mentioned to be granted, to them, the said Treasurer and Company, their successors and assigns, forever; to the sole and proper use of them, the said Treasurer and Company, their successors and assigns forever, to be holden of us, our heirs and successors, as of our manor of East Greenwich, in free and common socage and not in capite; yielding and paying, therefore, to us, our heirs and successors, the fifth part Only of all ore of gold and silver that from time to time, and at all times hereafter, shall be there gotten, had and obtained, for all manner of service.

And, nevertheless, our will and pleasure is, and we do by this presents charge, command, warrant and authorize, that the said Treasurer and Company and their successors, or the major part of them which shall be present and assembled for that purpose, shall from time to time under their common seal distribute, convey, assign and set over such particular portions of lands, tenements and hereditaments, by these presents formerly granted, unto such our loving subjects naturally born of denizens, or others, as well adventurers as planters, as by the said Company, upon a commission of survey and distribution executed and returned for that purpose, shall be named, appointed and allowed, wherein our will and pleasure is, that respect be had as well of the proportion of the adventurer as to the special service, hazard, exploit or merit of any person so as to be recompensed, advanced or rewarded.

And for as much as the good and prosperous success of the said plantation cannot but chiefly depend, next under the blessing of God and the support of our royal authority, upon the provident and good direction of the whole enterprise by a careful and understanding Council, and that it is not convenient that all the adventurers shall be so often drawn to meet and assemble as shall be requisite for them to have meetings and conference about their affairs, therefore we do ordain, establish and confirm that there shall be perpetually one Council here resident, according to the tenor of our former letters patents, which Council shall have a seal for the better government and administration of the said plantation besides the legal seal of the Company or Corporation, as in our former letters patents is also expressed.

And further we established and ordain that Henry, Earl of Southampton, William, Earl of Pembrooke, [and fifty others] shall be our Council for the said Company of Adventurers and Planters in Virginia.

And the said Sir Thomas Smith we ordain to be Treasurer of the said Company, which Treasurer shall have authority to give order for the warning of the Council and summoning the Company to their courts and meetings.

And the said Council and Treasurer or any of them shall be from henceforth nominated, chosen, continued, displaced, changed, altered and supplied, as death or other several occasions shall require, out of the Company of the said adventurers by the voice of the greater part of the said Council and adventurers in their assembly for that purpose; provided always that every Councillor so newly elected shall be presented to the Lord Chancellor of England, or to the Lord High Treasurer of England, or the Lord Chamberlain of the household of us, our heirs and successors, for the time being to take his oath of a Councilor to us, our heirs and successors, for the said Company and Colony in Virginia.

And we do by this presents, of our especial grace, certain knowledge and mere motion, for us, our heirs and successors, grant unto the said Treasurer and Company and their successors, that if it happen at any time or times the Treasurer for the time being to be sick, or to have any such cause of absent from the city of London as shall be allowed by the said Council or the greater part of them assembled, so as he cannot attend the affairs of that Company, in every such case it shall and may be lawful for such Treasurer for the time being to assign, constitute and appoint one of the Council for Company to be likewise allowed by the Council or the greater part of them assembled to be the deputy Treasurer for the said Company; which Deputy shall have power to do and execute all things which belong to the said Treasurer during such time as such Treasurer shall be sick or otherwise absent, upon cause allowed of by the said Council or the major part of them as aforesaid, so fully and wholly and in as large and ample manner and form and to all intents and purposes as the said Treasurer if he were present himself may or might do and execute the same.

And further of our especial grace, certain knowledge and mere motion, for us, our heirs and successors, we do by this presents give and grant full power and authority to our said Council here resident as well at this present time as hereafter, from time to time, to nominate, make, constitute, ordain and confirm by such name or names, style or styles as to them shall seem good, and likewise to revoke, discharge, change and alter as well all and singular governors, officers and ministers which already hath been made, as also which hereafter shall be by them thought fit and needful to be made or used for the government of the said Colony and plantation.

And also to make, ordain and establish all manner of orders, laws, directions, instructions, forms and ceremonies of government and magistracy, fit and necessary, for and concerning the government of the said Colony and plantation; and the same at all times hereafter to abrogate, revoke or change, not only within the precincts of the said Colony but also upon the seas in going and coming to and from the said Colony, as they in their good discretions shall think to be fittest for the good of the adventurers and inhibitors there.

And we do also declare that for divers reasons and considerations us thereunto especially moving, our will and pleasure is and we do hereby ordain that immediately from and after such time as any such governor or principal officer so to be nominated and appointed by our said Council for the government of the said Colony, as aforesaid, shall arrive in Virginia and give notice unto the Colony there resident of our pleasure in this behalf, the government, power and authority of the President and Council, heretofore by our former letters patents there established, and all laws and constitutions by them formerly made, shall utterly cease and be determined; and all officers, governors and ministers formerly constituted or appointed shall be discharged, any thing in our said former letters patents concerning the said plantation contained in aeneaus to the contrary

notwithstanding; straightly charging and commanding the President and Council now resident in the said Colony upon their allegiance after knowledge given unto them of our will and pleasure by this presents signified and declared, that they forth with be obedient to such governor or governors as by our said Council here resident shall be named and appointed as aforesaid; and to all directions, orders and commandments which they shall receive from them, as well in the present resigning and giving up of their authority, offices, charge and places, as in all other attendance as shall be by them from time to time required.

And we do further by this presents ordain and establish that the said Treasurer and Council here resident, and their successors or any four of them assembled (the Treasurer being one), shall from time to time have full power and authority to admit and receive any other person into their company, corporation and freedom; and further, in a general assembly of the adventurers, with the consent of the greater part upon good cause, to disfranchise and putt out any person or persons out of the said freedom and Company.

And we do also grant and confirm for us, our heirs and successors that it shall be lawful for the said Treasurer and Company and their successors, by directions of the Governors there, to dig and to search for all manner of mines of gold, silver, copper, iron, lead, tin and other minerals as well within the precincts aforesaid as within any part of the main land not formerly granted to any other; and to have and enjoy the gold, silver, copper, iron, lead, and tin, and all other minerals to be gotten thereby, to the use and behoove of the said Company of Planters and Adventurers, yielding therefore and paying yearly unto us, our heirs and successors, as aforesaid.

And we do further of our special grace, certain knowledge and mere motion, for us, our heirs and successors, grant, by this presents to and with the said Treasurer and Company and their successors, that it shall be lawful and free for them and their assigns at all and every time and times here after, out of our realm of England and out of all other our dominions, to take and lead into the said voyage, and for and towards the said plantation, and to travel thitherwards and to abide and inhabit therein the said Colony and plantation, all such and so many of our loving subjects, or any other strangers that will become our loving subjects and live under our allegiance, as shall willingly accompany them in the said voyage and plantation with sufficient shipping armor, weapons, ordinance, munition, powder, shot, victuals, and such merchandise or wares as are esteemed by the wild people in those parts, clothing, implements, furniture, cattle, horses and mares, and all other things necessary for the said plantation and for their use and defense and trade with the people there, and in passing and returning to and from without yielding or paying subsidy, custom, imposition, or any other tax or duties to us, our heirs or successors, for the space of seven years from the date of this presents; provided, that none of the said persons be such as shall be hereafter by special name restrained by us, our heirs or successors.

And for their further encouragement, of our special grace and favor, we do by these presents for us, our heirs and successors, yield and grant to and with the said Treasurer and Company and their successors and every of them, their factors and assigns, that they and every of them shall be free and quiet of all subsides and customs in Virginia for the space of one and twenty years, and from all taxes and impositions for ever, upon any goods or merchandises at any time or times hereafter, either upon importation thither or exportation from thence into our realm of England or into any other of our realms or dominions, by the said Treasurer and Company and their successors, their deputies, factors or assigns or any of them, except only the five pound per centum due for custom upon all such good and merchandises as shall be brought or imported into our realm of England or any other of this our dominions according to the ancient trade of merchants, which five pounds per centum only being paid, it shall be thenceforth lawful and free for the said Adventurers the same goods and merchandises to export and carry out of our said dominions into foreign parts without any custom, tax or other duty to be paid to us our heirs or successors or to any other our officers or deputies; provided, that the said goods and merchandises be shipped out within thirteen months after their first landing within any part of those dominions.

And we do also confirm and grant to the said Treasurer and Company, and their successors, as also to all and every such governor or other officers and ministers as by our said Council shall be appointed, to have power and authority of government and command in or over the said Colony or plantation; that they and every of them shall and lawfully may from time to time and at all times forever hereafter, for their several defense and safety, encounter, expulse, repel and resist by force and arms, as well by sea as by land, and all ways and means whatsoever, all and every such person and persons whatsoever as without the special license of the said Treasurer and Company and their successors shall attempt to inhabit within the said several precincts and limits of the said Colony and plantation; and also, all and every such person and persons whatsoever as shall enterprise, or attempt at any time hereafter, destruction, invasion, hurt, detriment or annoyance to the said Colony and plantation, as is likewise specified in the said former grant.

And that it shall be lawful for the said Treasurer and Company, and their successors and every of them, from time to time and at all times hereafter, and they shall have full power and authority, to take and surprise by all ways and means whatsoever all and every person and persons whatsoever, with their ships, goods and other furniture, trafficking in any harbor, creek or place within the limits or precincts of the said Colony and plantation, not being allowed by the said Company to be adventurers or planters of the said Colony, until such time as they being of any realms or dominions under our obedience shall pay or agree to pay, to the hands of the Treasurer or of some other officer deputed by the said governors in Virginia (over and above such subsidy and custom as the said Company is or here after shall be to pay) five pounds per centum upon all goods and merchandises so brought in thither, and also five per centum upon all goods by them shipped out from thence; and being strangers and not under our obedience until they have payed (over and above such subsidy and custom as the same Treasurer and Company and their successors is or hereafter shall be to pay) ten pounds per centum upon all such goods, likewise carried in and out, any thing in the former letters patents to the contrary not withstanding; and the same sums of money and benefit as aforesaid for and during the space of one and twenty years shall be wholly employed to the benefit and behoove of the said Colony and plantation; and after the said one and twenty years ended, the same shall be taken to the use of us, our heirs or successors, by such officer and minister as by us, our heirs or successors, shall be thereunto assigned and appointed, as is specified in the said former letters patents.

Also we do, for us, our heirs and successors, declare by this presents, that all and every the persons being our subjects which shall go and inhabit within the said Colony and plantation, and every of their children and posterity which shall happen to be born within any the limits thereof, shall have and enjoy all liberties, franchises and immunities of free denizens and natural subjects within any of our other dominions to all intents and purposes as if they had been abiding and born within this our kingdom of England or in any other of our dominions.

And forasmuch as it shall be necessary for all such our loving subjects as shall inhabit within the said precincts of Virginia aforesaid to determine to live together in the fear and true worship of Almighty God, Christian peace and civil quietness, each with other, whereby every one may with more safety, pleasure and profit enjoy that where unto they shall attain with great pain and peril, we, for us, our heirs and successors, are likewise pleased and contented and by this presents do give and grant unto the said Treasurer and Company and their successors and to such governors, officers and ministers as shall be, by our said Council, constituted and appointed, according to the natures and limits of their offices and places respectively, that they shall and may from time to time for ever hereafter, within the said precincts of Virginia or in the way by the seas thither and from thence, have full and absolute power and authority to correct, punish, pardon, govern and rule all such the subjects of us, our heirs and successors as shall from time to time adventure themselves in any voyage thither or that shall at any time hereafter inhabit in the precincts and territory of the said Colony as aforesaid, according to such order, ordinances, constitution, directions and instruction as by our said Council, as aforesaid, shall be established; and in defect thereof, in case of necessity according to the good discretions of the said governors and officers respectively, as well in cases capital and criminal as civil, both marine and other, so always as the said statues, ordinances and proceedings as near as conveniently may be, be agreeable to the laws, statutes, government and policy of this our realm of England.

And we do further of our special grace, certain knowledge and mere motion, grant, declare and ordain that such principal governor as from time to time shall duly and lawfully be authorized and appointed, in manner and forms in this presents heretofore expressed, shall have full power and authority to use and exercise martial law in cases of rebellion or mutiny in as large and ample manner as our lieutenant in our counties within our realm of England have or ought to have by force of their commissions of lieutenancy.

And furthermore, if any person or persons, adventurers or planters, of the said Colony, or any other at any time or times hereafter, shall transport any money, goods or merchandises out of any of our kingdoms with a pretense or purpose to land, sell or otherwise dispose the same within the limits and bounds of the said Colony, and yet nevertheless being at sea or after he hath landed within any part of the said Colony shall carry the same into any other foreign Country, with a purpose there to sell and dispose there of that, then all the goods and chattels of the said person or persons so offending and transported, together with the ship or vessel wherein such transportation was made, shall be forfeited to us, our heirs and successors.

And further, our will and pleasure is, that in all questions and doubts that shall arise upon any difficulty of construction or interpretation of any thing contained either in this or in our said former letters patents, the same shall be taken and interpreted in most ample and beneficial manner for the said Treasurer and Company and their successors and every member there of.

And further, we do by this presents ratify and confirm unto the said Treasurer and Company and their successors all privileges, franchises, liberties and immunities granted in our said former letters patents and not in this our letters patents revoked, altered, changed or abridged.

And finally, our will and pleasure is and we do further hereby for us, our heirs and successors grant and agree, to and with the said Treasurer and Company and their successors, that all and singular person and persons which shall at any time or times hereafter adventure any Sum or sums of money in and towards the said plantation of the said Colony in Virginia and shall be admitted by the said Council and Company as adventurers of the said Colony, in form aforesaid, and shall be enrolled in the book or record of the adventurers of the said Company, shall and may be accompted, accepted, taken, held and reputed Adventurers of the said Colony and shall and may enjoy all and singular grants, privileges, liberties, benefits, profits, commodities and immunities, advantages and emoluments whatsoever as fully, largely, amply and absolutely as if they and every of them had been precisely, plainly, singularly and distinctly named and inserted in this our letters patents.

And lastly, because the principal effect which we can desire or expect of this action is the conversion and reduction of the people in those parts unto the true worships of God and Christian religion, in which respect we would be loath that any person should be permitted to pass that we suspected to affect the superstitions of the Church of Rome, we do hereby declare that it is our will and pleasure that none be permitted to pass in any voyage from time to time to be made into the said country but such as first shall have taken the oath of supremacy, for which purpose we do by this presents give full power and authority to the Treasurer for the time being, and any three of the Council, to tender and exhibit the said oath to all such persons as shall at any time be sent and employed in the said voyage.

Although express mention of the true yearly value or certainty of the premises, or any of them, or of any other gifts or grants, by us or any of our progenitors or predecessors, to the aforesaid Treasurer and Company heretofore made, in these presents is not made; or any act, statute, ordinance, provision, proclamation, or restraint, to the contrary hereof had, made, ordained, or provided, or any other thing, cause, or matter, whatsoever, in any wise notwithstanding. In witness whereof we have caused these our letters to be made patent. Witness ourself at Westminster, the 23d day of May [*1609*] in the seventh year of our reign of England, France, and Ireland, and of Scotland the [*blank*]

Per ipsum Regem exactum.

3. THE MAYFLOWER COMPACT, 1620

In the name of God, Amen. We, whose names are underwritten, the Loyal Subjects of our dread Sovereign Lord King James, by the grace of God, of Great Britain, France, and Ireland, King, *Defender of the faith,* and &. Having undertaken for the Glory of God, and Advancement of the Christian Faith; and the Honor of our King and Country, a Voyage to plant the first colony in the northern Parts of Virginia; Do by these Presents, solemnly and mutually in the Presence of God and one another, covenant and combine ourselves together into a civil Body Politic, for our better Ordering and Preservation, and Furtherance of the Ends aforesaid; And by the Virtue hereof do enact, constitute, and frame, such just and equal Laws, Ordinances, Acts, Constitutions, and Offices, from time to time, as shall be though most meet and convenient for the general Good of the colony; unto which we

promise all due Submission and Obedience. In witness whereof we have hereunder subscribed our names at Cape Cod the 11 of November, in the year of the reign of our sovereign lord, King James, of England, France, and Ireland the eighteenth, and of Scotland the fifty-fourth. Anno Domini, 1620.

4. FUNDAMENTAL ORDERS OF CONNECTICUT, 1639

For as much as it hath pleased Almighty God by the wise disposition of his divine providence so to order and dispose of things that we the Inhabitants and Residents of Windsor, Hartford and Wethersfield are now cohabiting and dwelling in and upon the River of Connecticut and the lands thereunto adjoining; and well knowing where a people are gathered together the word of God requires that to maintain the peace and union of such a people there should be an orderly and decent Government established according to God, to order and dispose of the affairs of the people at all seasons as occasion shall require; do therefore associate and conjoin ourselves to be as one Public State or Commonwealth; and do for ourselves and our successors and such as shall be adjoined to us at any time hereafter, enter into Combination and Confederation together, to maintain and preserve the liberty and purity of the Gospel of our Lord Jesus which we now profess, as also, the discipline of the Churches, which according to the truth of the said Gospel is now practiced amongst us; as also in our civil affairs to be guided and governed according to such Laws, Rules, Orders and Decrees as shall be made, ordered, and decreed as followeth:

1. It is Ordered, sentenced, and decreed, that there shall be yearly two General Assemblies or Courts, the one the second Thursday in April, the other the second Thursday in September following; the first shall be called the Court of Election, wherein shall be yearly chosen from time to time, so many Magistrates and other public Officers as shall be found requisite: Whereof one to be chosen Governor for the year ensuing and until another be chosen, and no other Magistrate to be chosen for more than one year: provided always there be six chosen besides the Governor, which being chosen and sworn according to an Oath recorded for that purpose, shall have the power to administer justice according to the Laws here established, and for want thereof, according to the Rule of

the Word of God; which choice shall be made by all that are admitted freemen and have taken the Oath of Fidelity, and do cohabit within this Jurisdiction having been admitted Inhabitants by the major part of the Town wherein they live or the major part of such as shall be then present.

2. It is Ordered, sentenced, and decreed, that the election of the aforesaid Magistrates shall be in this manner: every person present and qualified for choice shall bring in (to the person deputed to receive them) one single paper with the name of him written in it whom he desires to have Governor, and that he that hath the greatest number of papers shall be Governor for that year. And the rest of the Magistrates or public officers to be chosen in this manner: the Secretary for the time being shall first read the names of all that are to be put to choice and then shall severally nominate them distinctly, and every one that would have the person nominated to be chosen shall bring in one single paper written upon, and he that would not have him chosen shall bring in a blank; and every one that hath more written papers than blanks shall be a Magistrate for that year; which papers shall be received and told by one or more that shall be then chosen by the court and sworn to be faithful therein; but in case there should not be six chosen as aforesaid, besides the Governor, out of those which are nominated, than he or they which have the most written papers shall be a Magistrate or Magistrates for the ensuing year, to make up the aforesaid number.

3. It is Ordered, sentenced, and decreed, that the Secretary shall not nominate any person, nor shall any person be chosen newly into the Magistracy which was not propounded in some General Court before, to be nominated the next election; and to that end it shall be lawful for each of the Towns aforesaid by their deputies to nominate any two whom they conceive fit to be put to election; and the Court may add so many more as they judge requisite.

4. It is Ordered, sentenced, and decreed, that no person be chosen Governor above once in two years, and that the Governor be always a member of some approved Congregation, and formerly of the Magistracy within this Jurisdiction; and that all the Magistrates, Freemen of this Commonwealth; and that no Magistrate or other public officer shall execute any part of his or their office before they are severally sworn, which shall be done in the face of the court

if they be present, and in case of absence by some deputed for that purpose.

5. It is Ordered, sentenced, and decreed, that to the aforesaid Court of Election the several Towns shall send their deputies, and when the Elections are ended they may proceed in any public service as at other Courts. Also the other General Court in September shall be for making of laws, and any other public occasion, which concerns the good of the Commonwealth.

6. It is Ordered, sentenced, and decreed, that the Governor shall, either by himself or by the Secretary, send out summons to the Constables of every Town for the calling of these two standing Courts one month at least before their several times: And also if the Governor and the greatest part of the Magistrates see cause upon any special occasion to call a General Court, they may give order to the Secretary so to do within fourteen days' warning: And if urgent necessity so required, upon a shorter notice, giving sufficient grounds for it to the deputies when they meet, or else be questioned for the same; And if the Governor and major part of Magistrates shall either neglect or refuse to call the two General standing Courts or either of them, as also at other times when the occasions of the Commonwealth require, the Freemen thereof, or the major part of them, shall petition to them so to do; if then it be either denied or neglected, the said Freemen, or the major part of them, shall have the power to give order to the Constables of the several Towns to do the same, and so may meet together, and choose to themselves a Moderator, and may proceed to do any act of power which any other General Courts may.

7. It is Ordered, sentenced, and decreed, that after there are warrants given out for any of the said General Courts, the Constable or Constables of each Town, shall forthwith give notice distinctly to the inhabitants of the same, in some public assembly or by going or sending from house to house, that at a place and time by him or them limited and set, they meet and assemble themselves together to elect and choose certain deputies to be at the General Court then following to agitate the affairs of the Commonwealth; which said deputies shall be chosen by all that are admitted Inhabitants in the several Towns and have taken the oath of fidelity; provided that none be chosen a Deputy for any General Court which is not a Freeman of this Commonwealth.

The aforesaid deputies shall be chosen in manner following: every person that is present and qualified as before expressed, shall bring the names of such, written in several papers, as they desire to have chosen for that employment, and these three or four, more or less, being the number agreed on to be chosen for that time, that have the greatest number of papers written for them shall be deputies for that Court; whose names shall be endorsed on the back side of the warrant and returned into the Court, with the Constable or Constables' hand unto the same.

8. It is Ordered, sentenced, and decreed, that Windsor, Hartford, and Wethersfield shall have power, each Town, to send four of their Freemen as their deputies to every General Court; and Whatsoever other Town shall be hereafter added to this Jurisdiction, they shall send so many deputies as the Court shall judge meet, a reasonable proportion to the number of Freemen that are in the said Towns being to be attended therein; which deputies shall have the power of the whole Town to give their votes and allowance to all such laws and orders as may be for the public good, and unto which the said Towns are to be found.

9. It is Ordered, sentenced, and decreed, that the deputies thus chosen shall have power and liberty to appoint a time and a place of meeting together before any General Court, to advise and consult of all such things as may concern the good of the public, as also to examine their own Elections, whether according to the order, and if they or the greatest part of them find any election to be illegal they may seclude such for present from their meeting, and return the same and their reasons to the Court; and if it be proved true, the Court may fine the party or parties so intruding, and the Town, if they see cause, and give out a warrant to go to a new election in a legal way, either in part or in whole. Also the said deputies shall have power to fine any that shall be disorderly at their meetings, or for not coming in due time or place according to appointment; and they may return the said fines into the Court if it be refused to be paid, and the Treasurer to take notice of it, and to escheat or levy the same as he does other fines.

10. It is Ordered, sentenced, and decreed, that every General Court, except such as through neglect of the Governor and the greatest part of the Magistrates and Freemen themselves do call, shall consist of the Governor, or some one chosen to moderate the Court, and four other Magistrates at least, with the major part of the deputies of the several Towns legally chosen; and in case the Freemen, or major part of them, through neglect or refusal of the Governor and major part of the Magistrates, shall call a Court, it shall consist of the major part of Freemen that are present or their deputies, with a Moderator chosen by them: In which said General Courts shall consist the supreme power of the Commonwealth, and they only shall have power to make laws or repeal them, to grant levies, to admit of Freemen, dispose of lands undisposed of, to several Towns or persons, and also shall have power to call either Court or Magistrate or any other person whatsoever into question for any misdemeanor, and may for just causes displace or deal otherwise according to the nature of the offense; and also may deal in any other matter that concerns the good of this Commonwealth, except election of Magistrates, which shall be done by the whole body of Freemen.

In which Court the Governor or Moderator shall have power to order the Court, to give liberty of speech, and silence unseasonable and disorderly speakings, to put all things to vote, and in case the vote be equal to have the casting voice. But none of these Courts shall be adjourned or dissolved without the consent of the major part of the Court.

11. It is Ordered, sentenced, and decreed, that when any General Court upon the occasions of the Commonwealth have agreed upon any sum, or sums of money to be levied upon the several Towns within this Jurisdiction, that a committee be chosen to set out and appoint what shall be the proportion of every Town to pay of the said levy, provided the committee be made up of an equal number out of each Town.

14th January 1639 the 11 Orders above said are voted.

5. MASSACHUSETTS BODY OF LIBERTIES, 1641

The Liberties of the Massachusetts Colony in New England
The free fruition of such liberties Immunities and privileges as humanity, Civility, and Christianity call for as due to every man in his place and proportion without impeachment and Infringement hath ever bene and ever will be the tranquility and Stability of Churches and Commonwealths. And the denial or deprival thereof, the disturbance if not the ruin of both.

We hold it therefore our duty and safety whilst we are about the further establishing of this Government to collect and express all such freedoms as for present we foresee may concern us, and our posterity after us, And to ratify them with our solemn consent.

We do therefore this day religiously and unanimously decree and confirm these following Rites, liberties and privileges concerning our Churches, and Civil State to be respectively impartially and inviolably enjoyed and observed throughout our Jurisdiction for ever.

1. No man's life shall be taken away, no man's honor or good name shall be stained, no man's person shall be arrested, restrained, banished, dismembered, nor any ways punished, no man shall be deprived of his wife or children, no man's goods or estate shall be taken away from him, nor any way endamaged under color of law or Countenance of Authority, unless it be by virtues or equity of some express law of the Country warranting the same, established by a general Court and sufficiently published, or in case of the defect of a law in any particular case by the word of God. And in Capital cases, or in cases concerning dismembering or banishment according to that word to be judged by the General Court.

2. Every person within this Jurisdiction, whether Inhabitant or foreigner shall enjoy the same justice and law, that is general for the plantation, which we constitute and execute one towards another without partiality or delay.

3. No man shall be urged to take any oath or subscribe any articles, covenants or remonstrance, of a public and Civil nature, but such as the General Court hath considered, allowed and required.

4. No man shall be punished for not appearing at or before any Civil Assembly, Court, Council, Magistrate, or Officer, nor for the omission of any office or service, if he shall be necessarily hindered by any apparent Act or providence of God, which he could neither foresee nor avoid. Provided that this law shall not prejudice any person of his just cost or damage, in any civil action.

5. No man shall be compelled to any public work or service unless the press be grounded upon some act of the general Court, and have reasonable allowance therefore.

6. No man shall be pressed in person to any office, work, wars or other public service, that is necessarily and sufficiently exempted by any natural or personal impediment, as by want of years, greatness of age, defect of mind, failing of senses, or impotence of Limbs.

7. No man shall be compelled to go out of the limits of this plantation upon any offensive wars which this Commonwealth or any of our friends or confederates shall voluntarily undertake. But only upon such vindictive and defensive wars in our own behalf or the behalf of our friends and confederates as shall be enterprised by the Counsel and consent of a Court general, or by authority derived from the same.

8. No man's Cattle or goods of what kind soever shall be pressed or taken for any public use or service, unless it be by warrant grounded upon some act of the general Court, nor without such reasonable prices and hire as the ordinary rates of the Country do afford. And if his Cattle or goods shall perish or suffer damage in such service, the owner shall be sufficiently recompensed.

9. No monopolies shall be granted or allowed amongst us, but of such new Inventions that are profitable to the Country, and that for a short time.

10. All our lands and heritages shall be free from all fines and licenses upon Alienations, and from all hariotts, wardships, Liveries, Primer-seisins, year day and wast, Escheats, and forfeitures, upon the deaths of parents or Ancestors, be they natural, casual or Judicial.

11. All persons which are of the age of 21 years, and of right understanding and memories, whether excommunicate or condemned shall have full power and liberty to make their wills and testaments, and other lawful alienations of their lands and estates.

12. Every man whether Inhabitant or foreigner, free or not free shall have liberty to come to any public Court, Council, or Town meeting, and either by speech or writing to move any lawful, seasonable, and material question, or to present any necessary motion, complaint, petition, Bill or information, whereof that meeting hath proper cognizance, so it be done in convenient time, due order, and respective manner.

13. No man shall be rated here for any estate or revenue he hath in England, or in any foreign partes till it be transported hither.

14. Any Conveyance or Alienation of land or other estate what so ever, made by any woman that is married, any child under age, Idiot or distracted person, shall be good if it be passed and ratified by the consent of a general Court.

15. All Covenous of fraudulent Alienations or Conveyances of lands, tenements, or any heriditaments, shall be of no validity to defeat any man from due

debts or legacies, or from any just title, claim or possession, of that which is so fraudulently conveyed.

16. Every Inhabitant that is an house holder shall have free fishing and fowling in any great ponds and Bays, Coves and Rivers, so far as the sea ebbs and flows within the precincts of the town where they dwell, unless the freemen of the same Town or the General Court have otherwise appropriated them, provided that this shall not be extended to give leave to any man to come upon others property without their leave.

17. Every man of or within this Jurisdiction shall have free liberty, notwithstanding any Civil power to remove both himself, and his family at their pleasure out of the same, provided there be no legal impediment to the contrary.

Rites Rules and Liberties Concerning Judicial Proceedings

18. No man's person shall be restrained or imprisoned by any authority whatsoever, before the law hath sentenced him thereto, if he can put in sufficient security, bail or mainprize, for his appearance, and good behavior in the mean time, unless it be in Crimes Capital, and Contempts in open Court, and in such cases where some express act of Court doth allow it.

19. If in a general Court any miscarriage shall be amongst the Assistants when they are by themselves that may deserve an Admonition or fine under 20 sh. it shall be examined and sentenced amongst themselves, If amongst the Deputies when they are by themselves, it shall be examined and sentenced amongst themselves, If it be when the whole Court is together, it shall be judged by the whole Court, and not severally as before.

20. If any which are to sit as Judges in any other Court shall demean themselves offensively in the Court, The rest of the Judges present shall have power to censure him for it, if the cause be of a high nature it shall be presented to and censured at the next superior Court.

21. In all cases where the first summons are not served six days before the Court, and the cause briefly specified in the warrant, where appearance is to be made by the party summoned, it shall be at his liberty whether he will appear or no, except all cases that are to be handled in Courts suddenly called, upon extraordinary occasions, In all cases where there appears present and urgent cause any assistant or officer appointed shall have power to make out attachments for the first summons.

22. No man in any suit or action against an other shall falsely pretend great debts or damages to vex his adversary, if it shall appear any doth so, The Court shall have power to set a reasonable fine on his head.

23. No man shall be adjudged to pay for detaining any debt from any Creditor above eight pounds in the hundred for one year, And not above that rate proportionable for all sums what so ever, neither shall this be a color or countenance to allow any usury amongst us contrary to the law of god.

24. In all Trespasses or damages done to any man or men, If it can be proved to be done by the mere default of him or them to whom the trespass is done, It shall be judged no trespass, nor any damage given for it.

25. No Summons pleading Judgement, or any kind of proceeding in Court or course of Justice shall be abated, arrested or reversed upon any kind of circumstantial errors or mistakes, If the person and cause be rightly understood and intended by the Court.

26. Every man that findeth himself unfit to plead his own cause in any Court shall have Liberty to employ any man against whom the Court doth no except, to help him, Provided he give him no fee or reward for his pains. This shall not exempt the party him self from Answering such Questions in person as the Court shall think meet to demand of him.

27. If any plaintiff shall give into any Court a declaration of his cause in writing, The defendant shall also have liberty and time to give in his answer in writing, And so in all further proceedings between party and party, So it doth not further hinder the dispatch of Justice then the Court shall be willing unto.

28. The plaintiff in all Actions brought in any Court shall have liberty to withdraw his Action, or to be nonsuited before the Jury hath given in their verdict, in which case he shall always pay full cost and charges to the defendant, and may afterwards renew his suit at another Court if he please.

29. In all actions at law it shall be the liberty of the plaintiff and defendant by mutual consent to choose whether they will be tried by the Bench or by a Jury, unless it be where the law upon just reason hath otherwise determined. The like liberty shall be granted to all persons in Criminal cases.

30. It shall be in the liberty both of plaintiff and defendant, and likewise every delinquent (to be judged by a Jury) to challenge any of the Jurors. And if his

challenge be found just and reasonable by the Bench, or the rest of the Jury, as the challenger shall choose it shall be allowed him, and tales de cercumstantibus impaneled in their room.

31. In all cases where evidences is so obscure or defective that the Jury cannot clearly and safely give a positive verdict, whether it be a grand or petit Jury, It shall have liberty to give a non Liquit, or a special verdict, in which last, that is in a special verdict, the Judgement of the cause shall be left to the Court, And all Jurors shall have liberty in matters of fact if they cannot find the main issue, yet to find and present in their verdict so much as they can, If the Bench and Jurors shall so suffer at any time about their verdict that either of them cannot proceed with peace of conscience the case shall be referred to the General Court, who shall take the question from both and determine it.

32. Every man shall have liberty to replevy his Cattle or goods impounded, distreined, seized, or extended, unless it be upon execution after Judgment, and in payment of fines. Provided he puts in good security to prosecute his replevin, And to satisfy such demands as his Adversary shall recover against him in Law.

33. No man's person shall be arrested, or imprisoned upon execution or judgment for any debt or fine, If the law can find competent means of satisfaction otherwise from his estate, and if not his person may be arrested and imprisoned where he shall be kept at his own charge, not the plaintiff's till satisfaction be made, unless the Court that had cognizance of the cause or some superior Court shall otherwise provide.

34. If any man shall be proved and Judged a common Barrator vexing others with unjust frequent and endless suites, It shall be in the power of Courts both to Deny him the benefit of the law, and to punish him for his Barratry.

35. No man's corn nor hay that is in the field or upon the Cart, nor his garden stuff, nor any thing subject to present decay, shall be taken in any distress, unless he that takes it doth presently bestow it where it may not be embezzled nor suffer spoil or decay, or give security to satisfy the worth thereof if it comes to any harm.

36. It shall be in the liberty of every man cast condemned or sentenced in any cause in any Inferior Court, to make their appeal to the Court of Assistants, provided they tender their appeal and put in security to prosecute it, before the Court be ended wherein they were condemned, And within six days next ensuing put

in good security before some Assistant to satisfy what his Adversary shall recover against him; And if the cause be of a Criminal nature for his good behavior, and appearance, And every man shall have liberty to complain to the General Court of any Injustice done him in any Court of Assistants or other.

37. In all cases where it appears to the Court that the plaintiff hath willingly and wittingly done wrong to the defendant in commencing and prosecuting an action or complaint against him, They shall have power to impose upon him a proportionable fine to the use of the defendant or accused person, for his false complaint or clamor.

38. Every man shall have liberty to Record in the public Rolls of any Court any Testimony given upon oath in the same Court, or before two Assistants, or any deed or evidence legally confirmed there to remain in perpetuam rei memoriam, that is for perpetual memorial or evidence upon occasion.

39. In all actions both real and personal between party and party, the Court shall have power to respite execution for a convenient time, when in their prudence they see just cause so to do.

40. No Conveyance, Deed, or promise whatsoever shall be of validity, If it be gotten by Illegal violence, imprisonment, threatening, or any kind of forcible compulsion called Dures.

41. Every man that is to Answer for any criminal cause, whether he be in prison or under bail, his cause shall be heard and determined at the next Court that hath proper Cognizance thereof, And may be done without prejudice of Justice.

42. No man shall be twice sentenced by Civil Justice for one and the same Crime, offence, or Trespass.

43. No man shall be beaten with above 40 stripes, nor shall any true gentleman, nor any man equal to a gentleman be punished with whipping, unless his crime be very shameful, and his course of life vicious and profligate.

44. No man condemned to die shall be put to death within four days next after his condemnation, unless the Court see special cause to the contrary, or in case of martial law, nor shall the body of any man so put to death be unburied 12 hours unless it be in case of Anatomy.

45. No man shall be forced by Torture to confess any Crime against himself nor any other unless it be in some Capital case, where he is first fully convicted by clear and sufficient evidence to be guilty, After which

if the cause be of that nature, That it is very apparent there be other conspirators, or confederates with him, Then he may be tortured, yet not with such Tortures as be Barbarous and inhumane.

46. For bodily punishments we allow amongst us none that are inhumane Barbarous or cruel.

47. No man shall be put to death without the testimony of two or three witnesses or that which is equivalent thereunto.

48. Every Inhabitant of the Country shall have free liberty to search and view any Rules, Records, or Registers of any Court or office except the Council, And to have a transcript or exemplification thereof written examined, and signed by the hand of the officer of the office paying the appointed fees therefore.

49. No free man shall be compelled to serve upon Juries above two Courts in a year, except grand Jury men, who shall hold two Courts together at the least.

50. All Jurors shall be chosen continually by the freemen of the Town where they dwell.

51. All Associates selected at any time to Assist the Assistants in Inferior Courts, shall be nominated by the Towns belonging to that Court, by orderly agreement among themselves.

52. Children, Idiots, Distracted persons, and all that are strangers, or new comers to our plantation, shall have such allowances and dispensations in any cause whether Criminal or other as religion and reason require.

53. The age of discretion for passing away of lands or such kind of herediments, or for giving, of votes, verdicts or Sentence in any Civil Courts or causes, shall be one and twenty years.

54. Whensoever any thing is to be put to vote, any sentence to be pronounced, or any other matter to be proposed, or read in any Court or Assembly, If the president or moderator thereof shall refuse to perform it, the Major parte of the members of that Court or Assembly shall have power to appoint any other meet man of them to do it, And if there be just cause to punish him that should and would not.

55. In all suits or Actions in any Court, the plaintiff shall have liberty to make all the titles and claims to that he sues for he can. And the Defendant shall have liberty to plead all the pleas he can in answer to them, and the Court shall judge according to the entire evidence of all.

56. If any man shall behave himself offensively at any Town meeting, the rest of the freemen then pre-sent, shall have power to sentence him for his offence. So be it the mulct or penalty exceed not twenty shillings.

57. Whensoever any person shall come to any very sudden untimely and unnatural death, Some assistant, or the Constables of that Town shall forthwith summon a Jury of twelve freemen to inquire of the cause and manner of their death, and shall present a true verdict thereof to some near Assistant, or the next Court to be held for that Town upon their oath.

Liberties More Peculiarly Concerning the Freemen

58. Civil Authority hath power and liberty to see the peace, ordinances and Rules of Christ observed in every church according to his word. So it be done in a Civil and not in an Ecclesiastical way.

59. Civil Authority hath power and liberty to deal with any Church member in a way of Civil Justice, notwithstanding any Church relation, office or interest.

60. No church censure shall degrade or depose any man from any Civil dignity, office, or Authority he shall have in the Commonwealth.

61. No Magistrate, Juror, Officer, or other man shall be bound to inform present or reveal any private crime or offence, wherein there is no peril or danger to this plantation or any member thereof, when any necessary tie of conscience binds him to secrecy grounded upon the word of god, unless it be in case of testimony lawfully required.

62. Any Shire or Town shall have liberty to choose their Deputies whom and where they please for the General Court. So be it they be freemen, and have taken their oath of fealty, and Inhabiting in this Jurisdiction.

63. No Governor, Deputy Governor, Assistant, Associate, or grand Jury man at any Court, nor any Deputy for the General Court, shall at any time bear his own charges at any Court, but their necessary expenses shall be defrayed either by the Town or Shire on whose service they are, or by the Country in general.

64. Every Action between party and party, and proceedings against delinquents in Criminal causes shall be briefly and distinctly entered on the Rolls of every Court by the Recorder thereof. That such actions be not afterwards brought again to the vexation of any man.

65. No custom or prescription shall ever prevail amongst us in any moral cause, our meaning is main-

tain anything that can be proved to be morally sinful by the word of god.

66. The Freemen of every Township shall have power to make such by laws and constitutions as may concern the welfare of their Town, provided they be not of a Criminal, but only of a prudential nature, And that their penalties exceed not 20 sh. for one offence. And that they be not repugnant to the public laws and orders of the Country. And if any Inhabitant shall neglect or refuse to observe them, they shall have power to levy the appointed penalties by distress.

67. It is the constant liberty of the freemen of this plantation to choose yearly at the Court of Election out of the freemen all the General officers of this Jurisdiction. If they please to discharge them at the day of Election by way of vote. They may do it without showing cause. But if at any other general Court, we hold it due justice, that the reasons thereof be alleged and proved. By general officers we mean, our Governor, Deputy Governor, Assistants, Treasurer, General of our wars. And our Admiral at Sea, and such as are or hereafter may be of the like general nature.

68. It is the liberty of the freemen to choose such deputies for the General Court out of themselves, either in their own Towns or elsewhere as they judge fittest. And because we cannot foresee what variety and weight of occasions may fall into future consideration, And what counsels we may stand in need of, we decree. That the Deputies (to attend the General Court in the behalf of the Country) shall not any time be stated or enacted, but from Court to Court, or at the most but for one year, that the Country may have an Annual liberty to do in that case what is most behooveful for the best welfare thereof.

69. No General Court shall be dissolved or adjourned without the consent of the Major part thereof.

70. All Freemen called to give any advice, vote, verdict, or sentence in any Court, Council, or Civil Assembly, shall have full freedoms to do it according to their true Judgments and Consciences, So it be done orderly and inoffensively for the manner.

71. The Governor shall have a casting voice whensoever an Equi vote shall fall out in the Court of Assistants, or general assembly, So shall the president or moderator have in all Civil Courts or Assemblies.

72. The Governor and Deputy Governor Jointly consenting or any three Assistants concurring in consent shall have power out of Court to reprieve a condemned malefactor, till the next quarter or general Court. The general Court only shall have power to pardon a condemned malefactor.

73. The General Court hath liberty and Authority to send out any member of this Commonwealth of what quality, condition or office whatsoever into foreign parts about any public message or Negotiation. Provided the party sent be acquainted with the affair he goeth about, and be willing to undertake the service.

74. The freemen of every Town or Township, shall have full power to choose yearly or for less time out of themselves a convenient number of fit men to order the planting or prudential occasions of that Town, according to Instructions given them in writing, Provided nothing be done by them contrary to the public laws and orders of the Country, provided also the number of such select persons be not above nine.

75. It is and shall be the liberty of any member or members of any Court Council or Civil Assembly in cases of making or executing any order or law, that properly concern religion, or any cause capital, or wars, or Subscription to any public Articles or Remonstrance, in case they cannot in Judgement and conscience consent to that way the Major vote or suffrage goes, to make their contra Remonstrance or protestation in speech or writing, and upon request to have their dissent recorded in the Rolls of that Court. So it be done Christianly and respectively for the manner. And their dissent only be entered without the reasons thereof, for the avoiding of tediousness.

76. Whensoever any Jury of trials or Jurors are not clear in their Judgments or consciences concerning any cause wherein they are to give their verdict, They shall have liberty in open Court to advise with any man they think fit to resolve or direct them, before they give in their verdict.

77. In all cases wherein any freeman is to give his vote, be it in point of Election, making constitutions and orders or passing sentence in any case of Judicature or the like, if he cannot see reason to give it positively one way or an other, he shall have liberty to be silent, and not pressed to a determined vote.

78. The General or public Treasury or any part thereof shall never be expended but by the appointment of a General Court, nor any Shire Treasury, but by the appointment of the freemen thereof, nor any Town Treasury but by the freemen of that Township.

Liberties of Women

79. If any man at his death shall not leave his wife a competent portion of his estate, upon just complaint made to the General Court she shall be relieved.

80. Every married woman shall be free from bodily correction or stripes by her husband, unless it be in his own defense upon her assault. If there be any just cause of correction complaint shall be made to Authority assembled in some Court, from which only she shall receive it.

Liberties of Children

81. When parents die intestate, the Elder son shall have a double portion of his whole estate real and personal, unless the General Court upon just cause alleged shall judge otherwise.

82. When parents die intestate having no heirs males of their bodies their Daughters shall inherit as Copartners, unless the General Court upon just reason shall judge otherwise.

83. If any parents shall wilfully and unreasonably deny any child timely or convenient marriage, or shall exercise any unnatural severity towards them, such children shall have free liberty to complain to Authority for redress.

84. No Orphan during their minority which was not committed to tuition or service by the parents in their life time, shall afterwards be absolutely disposed of by any kindred, friend, Executor, Township, or Church, nor by themselves without the consent of some Court, wherein two Assistants at least shall be present.

Liberties of Servants

85. If any servants shall flee from the Tyranny and cruelty of their masters to the house of any freeman of the same Town, they shall be there protected and sustained till due order be taken for their relief. Provided due notice thereof be speedily given to their masters from whom they fled. And the next Assistant or Constable where the party flying is harbored.

86. No servant shall be put off for above a year to any other neither in the life time of their master nor after their death by their Executors or Administrators unless it be by consent of Authority assembled in some Court or two Assistants.

87. If any man smite out the eye or tooth of his man-servant, or maid servant, or otherwise maim or much disfigure him, unless it be by mere casualty, he shall let them go free from his service. And shall have such further recompense as the Court shall allow him.

88. Servants that have served diligently and faithfully to the benefit of their masters seven years, shall not be sent away empty. And if any have been unfaithful, negligent or unprofitable in their service, notwithstanding the good usage of their masters, they shall not be dismissed till they have made satisfaction according to the Judgment of Authority.

Liberties of Foreigners and Strangers

89. If any people of other Nations professing the true Christian Religion shall flee to us from the Tyranny or oppression of their persecutors, or from famine, wars, or the like necessary and compulsory cause, They shall be entertained and succored amongst us, according to that power and prudence, god shall give us.

90. If any ships or other vessels, be it friend or enemy, shall suffer shipwreck upon our Coast, there shall be no violence or wrong offered to their persons or goods. But their persons shall be harbored, and relieved, and their goods preserved in safety till Authority may be certified thereof, and shall take further order therein.

91. There shall never be any bond slavery, villainage or Captivity amongst us unless it be lawful Captives taken in just wars, and such strangers as willingly sell themselves or are sold to us. And these shall have all the liberties and Christian usages which the law of god established in Israel concerning such persons doth morally require. This exempts none from servitude who shall be Judged thereto by Authority.

Of the Brute Creature

92. No man shall exercise any Tyranny or Cruelty towards any brute Creature which are usually kept for man's use.

93. If any man shall have occasion to lead or drive Cattle from place to place that is far of, so that they be weary, or hungry, or fall sick, or lamb, It shall be lawful to rest or refresh them, for competent time, in any open place that is not Corn, meadow, or inclosed for some peculiar use.

94. *Capital Laws.*

1. (Deut. 13. 6, 10. Deut. 17. 2, 6. Ex. 22.20) If any man after legal conviction shall have or worship any other god, but the lord god, he shall be put to death.

2. (Ex. 22. 18. Lev. 20. 27. Deut. 18. 10.) If any man or woman be a witch, (that is hath or consulteth with a familiar spirit,) They shall be put to death.

3. (Lev. 24. 15, 16.) If any person shall Blaspheme the name of god, the father, Son or Holy Ghost, with direct, express, presumptuous or high handed blasphemy, or shall curse god in the like manner, he shall be put to death.

4. (Ex. 21. 12. Numb. 35. 13, 14, 30, 31.) If any person commit any wilful murder, which is manslaughter, committed upon premeditated malice, hatred, or Cruelty, not in a man's necessary and just defense, nor by mere casualty against his will, he shall be put to death.

5. (Numb. 25, 20, 21. Lev. 24. 17) If any person slayeth an other suddenly in his anger or Cruelty of passion, he shall be put to death.

6. (Ex. 21. 14.) If any person shall slay an other through guile, either by poisoning or other such devilish practice, he shall be put to death.

7. (Lev. 20. 15, 16.) If any man or woman shall lie with any beast or brute creature by Carnal Copulation, They shall surely be put to death. And the beast shall be slain, and buried and not eaten.

8. (Lev. 20. 13.) If any man lieth with mankind as he lieth with a woman, both of them have committed abomination, they both shall surely be put to death.

9. (Lev. 20. 19. and 18, 20. Deut. 22. 23, 24.) If any person committeth Adultery with a married or espoused wife, the Adulterer and Adulteress shall surely be put to death.

10. (Ex. 21. 16.) If any man stealeth a man or mankind, he shall surely be put to death.

11. (Deut. 19. 16, 18, 19.) If any man rise up by false witness, wittingly and of purpose to take away any man's life, he shall be put to death.

12. If any man shall conspire and attempt any invasion, insurrection, or public rebellion against our commonwealth, or shall endeavor to surprise any Town or Towns, fort or forts therein, or shall treacherously and perfidiously attempt the alteration and subversion of our frame of polity or Government fundamentally, he shall be put to death.

95. *A Declaration of the Liberties the Lord Jesus hath given to the Churches.*

1. All the people of god within this Jurisdiction who are not in a church way, and be orthodox in Judgment, and not scandalous in life, shall have full liberty to gather themselves into a Church Estate. Provided they do it in a Christian way, with due observation of the rules of Christ revealed in his word.

2. Every Church hath full liberty to exercise all the ordinances of god, according to the rules of scripture.

3. Every Church hath free liberty of Election and ordination of all their officers from time to time, provided they be able, pious and orthodox.

4. Every Church hath free liberty of Admission, Recommendation, Dismission, and Expulsion, or deposal of their officers, and members, upon due cause, with free exercise of the Discipline and Censures of Christ according to the rules of his word.

5. No Injunctions are to be put upon any Church, Church officers or member in point of Doctrine, worship or Discipline, whether for substance or circumstance besides the Institutions of the lord.

6. Every Church of Christ hath freedoms to celebrate days of fasting and prayer, and of thanksgiving according to the word of god.

7. The Elders of Churches have free liberty to meet monthly, Quarterly, or otherwise, in convenient numbers and places, for conferences, and consultations about Christian and Church questions and occasions.

8. All Churches have liberty to deal with any of their members in a church way that are in the hand of Justice. So it be not to retard or hinder the course thereof.

9. Every Church hath liberty to deal with any magistrate, Deputy of Court or other officer what so ever that is a member in a church way in case of apparent and just offence given in their places, so it be done with due observance and respect.

10. We allow private meetings for edification in religion amongst Christians of all sorts of people. So it be without just offence for number, time, place, and other circumstances.

11. For the preventing and removing of error and offence that may grow and spread in any of the Churches in this Jurisdiction, And for the preserving of truth and peace in the several churches within themselves, and for the maintenance and exercise of brotherly communion, amongst all the churches in the Country, It is allowed and ratified, by the Authority of this General Court as a lawful liberty of the Churches of Christ. That once in every month of the year (when the season will bear it) It shall be lawful for the ministers and Elders, of the Churches near adjoining together, with any other of the brethren

with the consent of the churches to assemble by course in each several Church one after an other. To the intent after the preaching of the word by such a minister as shall be requested thereto by the Elders of the church where the Assembly is held, The rest of the day may be spent in public Christian Conference about the discussing and resolving of any such doubts and cases of conscience concerning matter of doctrine or worship or government of the church as shall be propounded by any of the Brethern of that church, will leave also to any other Brother to propound his objections or answers for further satisfaction according to the word of god. Provided that the whole action be guided and moderated by the Elders of the Church where the Assembly is held, or by such others as they shall appoint. And that no thing be concluded and imposed by way of Authority from one or more churches upon an other, but only by way of Brotherly conference and consultations. That the truth may be searched out to the satisfying of every man's conscience in the sight of god according his word. And because such an Assembly and the work thereof can not be duly attended to if other lectures be held in the same week. It is therefore agreed with the consent of the Churches. That in that week such an Assembly is held, All the lectures in all the neighboring Churches for that week shall be forborne. That so the public service of Christ in this more solemn Assembly may be transacted with greater diligence and attention.

96. Howsoever these above specified rites, freedoms Immunities, Authorities and privileges, both Civil and Ecclesiastical are expressed only under the name and title of Liberties, and not in the exact form of Laws or Statutes, yet we do with one consent fully Authorize, and earnestly entreat all that are and shall be in Authority to consider them as laws, and not to fail to inflict condign and proportionable punishments upon every man impartially, that shall infringe or violate any of them.

97. We likewise give full power and liberty to any person that shall at any time be denied or deprived of any of them, to commence and prosecute their suit, Complaint or action against any man that shall so do in any Court that hath proper Cognizance or judicature thereof.

98. Lastly because our duty and desire is to do nothing suddenly which fundamentally concern us, we decree that these rites and liberties, shall be Audibly read and deliberately weighed at every General Court that shall be held, within three years next ensuing, And such of them as shall not be altered or repealed they shall stand so ratified, That no man shall infringe them without due punishment.

And if any General Court within these next three years shall fail or forget to read and consider them as abovesaid. The Governor and Deputy Governor for the time being, and every Assistant present at such Courts, shall forfeit 20sh. a man, and every Deputy 10sh. a man for each neglect, which shall be paid out of their proper estate, and not by the Country or the Towns which choose them, and whensoever there shall arise any question in any Court among the Assistants and Associates thereof about the explanation of these Rites and liberties, The General Court only shall have power to interpret them.

6. NEW ENGLAND CONFEDERATION, 1643

The Articles of Confederation between the Plantations under the Government of the Massachusetts, the Plantations under the Government of New Plymouth, the Plantations under the Government of Connecticut, and the Government of New Haven with the Plantations in Combination therewith:

Whereas we all came into these parts of America with one and the same end and aim, namely, to advance the Kingdom of our Lord Jesus Christ and to enjoy the liberties of the Gospel in purity with peace; and whereas in our settling (by a wise providence of God) we are further dispersed upon the sea coasts and rivers than was at first intended, so that we can not according to our desire with convenience communicate in one government and jurisdiction; and whereas we live encompassed with people of several nations and strange languages which hereafter may prove injurious to us or our posterity. And forasmuch as the natives have formerly committed sundry Insolence and outrages upon several Plantations of the English and have of late combined themselves against us: and seeing by reason of those sad distractions in England which they have heard of, and by which they know vie are hindered from that humble way of seeking advice, or reaping those comfortable fruits of protection, which at other times we might well expect. We therefore do conceive it our bounden duty, without delay to enter into a present Consociation amongst ourselves, for mutual help and strength in all our future concernments: That, as in nation and religion, so in other respects, we be and continue one according to the tenor and true meaning of the ensuing articles: Wherefore it is fully agreed and concluded by and between the parties or Jurisdictions above named, and they jointly and severally do by these presents agree and conclude that they all be and henceforth be called by the name of the United Colonies of New England.

2. The said United Colonies for themselves and their posterities do jointly and severally hereby enter into a firm and perpetual league of friendship and amity for offence and defense, mutual advice and succor upon all just occasions both for preserving and propagating the truth and liberties of the Gospel and for their own mutual safety and welfare.

3. It is further agreed that the Plantations which at present are or hereafter shall be settled within the limits of the Massachusetts shall be forever under the Massachusetts and shall have peculiar jurisdiction among themselves in all cases as an entire body, and that Plymouth, Connecticut, and New Heaven shall each of them have like peculiar jurisdiction and government within their limits; and in reference to the Plantations which already are settled, or shall hereafter be erected, or shall settle within their limits respectively; provided no other Jurisdiction shall hereafter be taken in as a distinct head or member of this Confederation, nor shall any other Plantation or Jurisdiction in present being, and not already in combination or under the jurisdiction of any of these Confederates, be received by any of them; nor shall any two of the Confederates join in one Jurisdiction without consent of the rest, which consent to be interpreted as is expressed in the sixth article ensuing.

4. It is by these Confederates agreed that the charge of all just wars, whether offensive or defensive, upon what part or member of this Confederation soever they fall, shall both in men, provisions and all other disbursements be borne by all the parts of this Confederation in different proportions according to their different ability in manner following, namely, that the Commissioners for each Jurisdiction from time to time, as there shall be occasion, bring a true account and number of all their males in every Plantation, or any way belonging to or under their several Jurisdictions, of what quality or condition soever they be, from sixteen years old to threescore, being inhabitants there. And that according to the different numbers which from time to time shall be found in each Jurisdiction upon a true and just account, the service of men and all charges of the war be borne by the poll: each Jurisdiction or Plantation being left to their own just course and custom of rating themselves and people according to their different estates with due respects to their qualities and exemptions amongst themselves though the Confederation take no notice of any such privilege: and that according to their different charge of each Jurisdiction and Plantation the whole advantage of the war (if it please God so to bless their endeavors) whether it be in lands, goods, or persons, shall be proportionately divided among the said Confederates.

5. It is further agreed, that if any of these Jurisdictions or any Plantation under or in combination with them, be invaded by any enemy whomsoever, upon notice and request of any three magistrates of that Jurisdiction so invaded, the rest of the Confederates without any further meeting or expostulation shall forthwith send aid to the Confederate in danger but in different proportions; namely, the Massachusetts an hundred men sufficiently armed and provided for such a service and journey, and each of the rest, forty-five so armed and provided, or any less number, if less be required according to this proportion. But if such Confederate in danger may be supplied by their next Confederates, not exceeding the number hereby agreed, they may crave help there, and seek no further for the present: the charge to be borne as in this article is expressed: and at the return to be victualled and supplied with powder and shot for their journey (if there be need) by that Jurisdiction which employed or sent for them; but none of the Jurisdictions to exceed these numbers until by a meeting of the Commissioners for this Confederation a greater aid appear necessary. And this proportion to continue till upon knowledge of greater numbers in each Jurisdiction which shall be brought to the next meeting, some other proportion be ordered. But in any such case of sending men for present aid, whether before or after such order or alteration, it is agreed that at the meeting of the Commissioners for this Confederation, the cause of such war or invasion be duly considered: and if it appear that the fault lay in the parties so invaded then that Jurisdiction or Plantation make just satisfaction, both to the invaders whom they have injured, and bear all the charges of the war themselves, without requiring any allowance from the rest of the Confederates towards the same. And further that if any Jurisdiction see any danger of invasion approaching, and there be

time for a meeting, that in such a case three magistrates of the Jurisdiction may summon a meeting at such convenient place as themselves shall think meet, to consider and provide against the threatened danger; provided when they are met they may remove to what place they please; only whilst any of these four Confederates have but three magistrates in their Jurisdiction, their requests, or summons, from any two of them shall be accounted of equal force with the three mentioned in both the clauses of this article, till there be an increase of magistrates there.

6. It is also agreed, that for the managing and concluding of all Affairs and concerning the whole Confederation two Commissioners shall be chosen by and out of each of these four Jurisdictions: namely, two for the Massachusetts, two for Plymouth, two for Connecticut, and two for New Haven, being all in Church-fellowship with us, which shall bring full power from their several General Courts respectively to hear, examine, weigh, and determine all affairs of our war, or peace, leagues, aids, charges, and numbers of men for war, division of spoils and whatsoever is gotten by conquest, receiving of more Confederates for Plantations into combination with any of the Confederates, and all things of like nature, which are the proper concomitants or consequents of such a Confederation for amity, offense, and defense: not intermeddling with the government of any of the Jurisdictions, which by the third article is preserved entirely to themselves. But if these eight Commissioners when they meet shall not all agree yet it [is] concluded that any six of the eight agreeing shall have power to settle and determine the business in question. But if six do not agree, that then such propositions with their reasons so far as they have been debated, be sent and referred to the four General Courts; namely, the Massachusetts, Plymouth, Connecticut, and New Haven; and if at all the said General Courts the business so referred be concluded, then to be prosecuted by the Confederates and all their members. It is further agreed that these eight Commissioners shall meet once every year besides extraordinary meetings (according to the fifth article) to consider, treat, and conclude of all affairs belonging to this Confederation, which meeting shall ever be the first Thursday in September. And that the next meeting after the date of these presents, which shall be accounted the second meeting, shall be at Boston in the Massachusetts, the third at Hartford, the fourth at New Haven, the fifth at Plymouth, the sixth and seventh at Boston; and then Hartford, New Haven, and Plymouth, and so in course successively, if in the meantime some middle place be not found out and agreed on, which may be commodious for all the Jurisdictions.

7. It is further agreed that at each meeting of these eight Commissioners, whether ordinary or extraordinary, they or six of then agreeing as before, may choose their President out of themselves whose office work shall be to take care and direct for order and a comely carrying on of all proceedings in the present meeting: but he shall be invested with no such power or respect, as by which he shall hinder the propounding or progress of any business, or any way cast the scales otherwise than in the precedent article is agreed.

8. It is also agreed that the Commissioners for this Confederation hereafter at their meetings, whether ordinary or extraordinary, as they may have commission or opportunity, do endeavor to frame and establish agreements and orders in general cases of a civil nature, wherein all the Plantations are interested, for preserving of peace among themselves, for preventing as much as may be all occasion of war or differences with others, as about the free and speedy passage of justice in every Jurisdiction, to all the Confederates equally as to their own, receiving those that remove from one Plantation to another without due certificate, how all the Jurisdictions may carry it towards the Indians, that they neither grow insolent nor be injured without due satisfaction, lest war break in upon the Confederates through such miscarriages. It is also agreed that if any servant run away from his master into any other of these confederated Jurisdictions, that in such case, upon the certificate of one magistrate in the Jurisdiction out of which the said servant fled, or upon other due proof, the said servant shall be delivered, either to his master, or any other that pursues and brings such certificate or proof. And that upon the escape of any prisoner whatsoever, or fugitive for any criminal cause, whether breaking prison, or getting from the officer, or otherwise escaping, upon the certificate of two magistrates of the Jurisdiction out of which the escape is made, that he was a prisoner, or such an offender at the time of the escape, the magistrates, or some of them of that Jurisdiction where for the present the said prisoner or fugitive abideth, shall forthwith grant such a warrant as the case will bear, for the apprehending of any such person, and the delivery of him into the hands of the officer or other person who pursues him. And if there be help

required, for the safe returning of any such offender, then it shall be granted to him that craves the same, he paying the charges thereof.

9. And for that the justest wars may be of dangerous consequence, especially to the smaller Plantations in these United Colonies, it is agreed that neither the Massachusetts, Plymouth, Connecticut, nor New Haven, nor any of the members of them, shall at any time hereafter begin, undertake, or engage themselves, or this Confederation, or any part thereof in any war whatsoever (sudden exigencies, with the necessary consequents thereof excepted), which are also to be moderated as much as the case will permit, without the consent and agreement of the forementioned eight Commissioners, or at least six of them, as in the sixth article is provided: and that no charge be required of any of the Confederates, in case of a defensive war, till the said Commissioners have met, and approved the justice of the war, and have agreed upon the sum of money to be levied, which sum is then to be paid by the several Confederates in proportion according to the fourth article.

10. That in extraordinary occasions, when meetings are summoned by three magistrates of any Jurisdiction, or two as in the fifth article, any of the Commissioners come not, due warning being given or sent, it is agreed that four of the Commissioners shall have power to direct a war which cannot be delayed, and to send for due proportions of men out of each Jurisdiction, as well as six might do if all met; but not less than six shall determine the justice of the war, or allow the demands or bills of charges, or cause any levies to be made for the same.

11. It is further agreed that if any of the Confederates shall hereafter break any of these present articles, or be any other ways injurious to any one of the other Jurisdictions; such breach of agreement or injury shall be duly considered and ordered by the Commissioners for the other Jurisdictions, that both peace and this present Confederation may be entirely preserved without violation.

12. Lastly, this perpetual Confederation, and the several articles and agreements thereof being read and seriously considered, both by the General Court for the Massachusetts, and by the Commissioners for Plymouth, Connecticut, and New Haven, were fully allowed and confirmed by three of the forenamed Confederates, namely, the Massachusetts, Connecticut, and New Haven; only the Commissioners for Plymouth having no commission to concludes desired respite until they might advise with their General Court; whereupon it was agreed and concluded by the said Court of the Massachusetts, and the Commissioners for the other two Confederates, that, if Plymouth consent, then the whole treaty as it stands in these present articles is, and shall continue, firm and stable without alteration: but if Plymouth come not in yet the other three Confederates do by these presents confirm the whole Confederation, and all the articles thereof; only in September next when the second meeting of the Commissioners is to be at Boston, new consideration may be taken of the sixth article, which concerns number of Commissioners for meeting and concluding the affairs of this Confederation to the satisfaction of the Court of the Massachusetts, and the Commissioners for the other two Confederates, but the rest to stand unquestioned.

In testimony whereof, the General Court of the Massachusetts by their Secretary, and the Commissioners for Connecticut and New Haven, have subscribed these present articles of this nineteenth of the third* month, commonly called May, Anno Domini 1643.

At a meeting of the Commissioners for the Confederation held at Boston the 7th of September, it appearing that the General Court of New Plymouth and the several townships thereof have read, considered, and approved these Articles of Confederation, as appeareth by commission of their General Court bearing date the 29th of August, 1643, to Mr. Edward Winslow and Mr. William Collier to ratify and confirm the same on their behalf: we therefore, the Commissioners for the Massachusetts, Connecticut, and New Haven, do also from our several Governments subscribe unto them.

7. The Maryland Toleration Act, 1649

An Act Concerning Religion

Forasmuch as in a well governed and Christian Common Wealth matters concerning Religion and the honor of God ought in the first place to be taken into serious consideration and endeavored to be settled, Be it therefore ordered and enacted by the Right Honorable Cecilius Lord Baron of Baltimore absolute Lord

---

* Until 1750, when England adopted the "new style" calendar, March was the first month of the year.

and Proprietary of this Province with the advice and consent of this General Assembly:

That whatsoever person or persons within this Province and the Islands thereunto belonging shall from henceforth blaspheme God, that is Curse him, or deny our Savior Jesus Christ to be the son of God, or shall deny the holy Trinity the father son and holy Ghost, or the Godhead of any of the said Three persons of the Trinity or the Unity of the Godhead, or shall use or utter any reproachful Speeches, words or language concerning the said Holy Trinity, or any of the said three persons thereof, shall be punished with death and confiscation or forfeiture of all his or her lands and goods to the Lord Proprietary and his heirs. And be it also Enacted by the Authority and with the advise and assent aforesaid, That whatsoever person or persons shall from henceforth use or utter any reproachful words or Speeches concerning the blessed Virgin Mary the Mother of our Savior or the holy Apostles or Evangelists or any of them shall in such case for the first offence forfeit to the said Lord Proprietary and his heirs Lords and Proprietaries of this Province the sum of five pound Sterling or the value thereof to be Levied on the goods and chattels of every such person so offending, but in case such Offender or Offenders, shall not then have goods and chattels sufficient for the satisfying of such forfeiture, or that the same be not otherwise speedily satisfied that then such Offender or Offenders shall be publically whipped and be imprisoned during the pleasure of the Lord Proprietary or the Lieutenant or chief Governor of this Province for the time being. And that every such Offender or Offenders for every second offence shall forfeit ten pound sterling or the value thereof to be levied as aforesaid, or in case such offender or Offenders shall not then have goods and chattels within this Province sufficient for that purpose then to be publically and severely whipped and imprisoned as before is expressed. And that every person or persons before mentioned offending herein the third time, shall for such third Offence forfeit all his lands and Goods and be for ever banished and expelled out of this Province.

And be it also further Enacted by the same authority advise and assent that whatsoever person or persons shall from henceforth upon any occasion of Offence or otherwise in a reproachful manner or Way declare call or denominate any person or persons whatsoever inhabiting, residing, trafficking, trading or commercing within this Province or within any the Ports, Harbors, Creeks or Havens to the same belonging an heretic, Schismatic, Idolater, puritan, Independent, Presbyterian, popish priest, Jesuit, Jesuited papist, Lutheran, Calvinist, Anabaptist, Brownist, Antinomian, Barrowist, Roundhead, Separatist, or any other name or term in a reproachful manner relating to matter of Religion shall for every such Offence forfeit and loose the sum of ten shillings sterling or the value thereof to be levied on the goods and chattels of every such Offender and Offenders, the one half thereof to be forfeited and paid unto the person and persons of whom such reproachful words are or shall be spoken or uttered, and the other half thereof to the Lord Proprietary and his heirs Lords and Proprietaries of this Province. But if such person or persons who shall at any time utter or speak any such reproachful words or Language shall not have Goods or Chattels sufficient and overt within this Province to be taken to satisfy the penalty aforesaid or that the same be not otherwise speedily satisfied, that then the person or persons so offending shall be publically whipped, and shall suffer imprisonment without bail or mainprize [bail] until he, she or they respectively shall satisfy the party so offended or grieved by such reproachful Language by asking him or her respectively forgiveness publically for such his Offence before the Magistrate of chief Officer or Officers of the Town or place where such Offence shall be given.

And be it further likewise Enacted by the Authority and consent aforesaid That every person and persons within this Province that shall at any time hereafter profane the Sabbath or Lord's day called Sunday by frequent swearing, drunkenness or by any uncivil or disorderly recreation, or by working on that day when absolute necessity doth not require it shall for every such first offence forfeit 2s 6d sterling or the value thereof, and for the second offence 5s sterling or the value thereof, and for the third offence and so for every time he shall offend in like manner afterwards 10s sterling or the value thereof. And in case such offender and offenders shall not have sufficient goods or chattels within this Province to satisfy any of the said Penalties respectively hereby imposed for profaning the Sabbath or Lords day called Sunday as aforesaid, That in Every such case the party so offending shall for the first and second offence in that kind be imprisoned till he or she shall publically in open Court before the chief Commander Judge or Magistrate, of that County Town or precinct where such offence shall be committed acknowledge the Scandal and offence he hath in that respect given against God and the good and civil Government of this Province, And for the third offence and for every time after shall also be publically whipped.

And whereas the enforcing of the conscience in matters of Religion hath frequently fallen out to be of dangerous Consequence in those commonwealths where it hath been practiced, And for the more quiet and peaceable government of this Province, and the better to preserve mutual Love and amity amongst the Inhabitants thereof, Be it Therefore also by the Lord Proprietary with the advise and consent of this Assembly Ordained and enacted (except as in this present Act is before Declared and set forth) that no person or persons whatsoever within this Province, or the Islands, Ports, Harbors, Creeks, or havens thereunto belonging professing to believe in Jesus Christ, shall from henceforth be any ways troubled, Molested or discountenanced for or in respect of his or her religion nor in the free exercise thereof within this Province or the Islands thereunto belonging nor any way compelled to the belief or exercise of any other Religion against his or her consent, so as they be not unfaithful to the Lord Proprietary, or molest or conspire against the civil Government established or to be established in this Province under him or his heirs. And that all and every person and persons that shall presume Contrary to this Act and the true intent and meaning thereof directly or indirectly either in person or estate willfully to wrong disturb trouble or molest any person whatsoever within this Province professing to believe in Jesus Christ for or in respect of his or her religion or the free exercise thereof within this Province other than is provided for in this Act that such person or persons so offending, shall be compelled to pay treble damages to the party so wronged or molested, and for every such offence shall also forfeit 20s sterling in money or the value thereof, half thereof for the use of the Lord Proprietary, and his heirs Lords and Proprietaries of this Province, and the other half for the use of the party so wronged or molested as aforesaid, Or if the party so offending as aforesaid shall refuse or be unable to recompense the party so wronged, or to satisfy such fine or forfeiture, then such Offender shall be severely punished by public whipping and imprisonment during the pleasure of the Lord Proprietary, or his Lieutenant or chief Governor of this

Province for the time being without bail or mainprize.

And be it further also Enacted by the authority and consent aforesaid That the Sheriff or other Officer or Officers from time to time to be appointed and authorized for that purpose, of the County Town or precinct where every particular offence in this present Act contained shall happen at any time to be committed and whereupon there is hereby a forfeiture fine or penalty imposed shall from time to time distrain and seize the goods and estate of every such person so offending as aforesaid against this present Act or any part thereof, and sell the same or any part thereof for the full satisfaction of such forfeiture, fine, or penalty as aforesaid, Restoring unto the party so offending the Remainder or overplus of the said goods or estate after such satisfaction so made as aforesaid.

The freemen have assented.

8. Pennsylvania Charter of Privileges, 1701

Charter of Privileges Granted by William Penn, esq. to the Inhabitants of Pennsylvania and Territories, October 28, 1701

WILLIAM PENN, Proprietary and Governor of the Province of Pennsylvania and Territories thereunto belonging, To all to whom these Presents shall come, sendeth Greeting. WHEREAS King CHARLES the Second, by His Letters Patents, under the Great Seal of England, bearing Date the Fourth Day of March in the Year One Thousand Six Hundred and Eighty-one, was graciously pleased to give and grant unto me, and my Heirs and Assigns for ever, this Province of Pennsylvania, with divers great Powers and Jurisdictions for the well Government thereof.

AND WHEREAS the King's dearest Brother, JAMES Duke of YORK and ALBANY, &c. by his Deeds of Feoffment, under his Hand and Seal duly perfected, bearing Date the Twenty-Fourth Day of August, One Thousand Six Hundred Eighty and Two, did grant unto me, my Heirs and Assigns, all that Tract of Land, now called the Territories of Pennsylvania, together with Powers and Jurisdictions for the good Government thereof.

AND WHEREAS for the Encouragement of all the Freemen and Planters, that might be concerned in the said Province and Territories, and for the good Government thereof, I the said WILLIAM PENN, in the Year One Thousand Six Hundred Eighty and Three, for me, my Heirs and Assigns, did grant and confirm unto all the Freemen Planters and Adventurers therein, divers Liberties, Franchises and Properties, as by the said Grant, entitled, The FRAME of the Government of the Province of Pennsylvania, and Territories thereunto belonging, in America, may appear; which Charter or Frame being found in some Parts of it, not so suitable to the present Circumstances of the Inhabitants, was in the Third Month, in the Year One Thousand Seven Hundred, delivered up to me, by Six Parts of Seven of the Freemen of this Province and Territories, in General Assembly met, Provision being made in the said Charter, for that End and Purpose.

AND WHEREAS I was then pleased to promise, That I would restore the said Charter to them again, with necessary Alterations, or in lieu thereof, give them another, better adapted to answer the present Circumstances and Conditions of the said Inhabitants; which they have now, by their Representatives in General Assembly met at Philadelphia, requested me to grant.

KNOW YE THEREFORE, That for the further Well-being and good Government of the said Province, and Territories; and in Pursuance of the Rights and Powers before-mentioned, I the said William Penn do declare, grant and confirm, unto all the Freemen, Planters and Adventurers, and other Inhabitants of this Province and Territories, these following Liberties, Franchises and Privileges, so far as in me lieth, to be held, enjoyed and kept, by the Freemen, Planters and Adventurers, and other Inhabitants of and in the said Province and Territories hereunto annexed, for ever.

First

BECAUSE no People can be truly happy, though under the greatest Enjoyment of Civil Liberties, if abridged of the Freedom of their Consciences, as to their Religious Profession and Worship: And Almighty God being the only Lord of Conscience, Father of Lights and Spirits; and the Author as well as Object of all divine Knowledge, Faith and Worship, who only [can] enlighten the Minds, and persuade and convince the Understandings of People, I do hereby grant and declare, That no Person or Persons, inhabiting in this Province or Territories, who shall confess and acknowledge One almighty God, the Creator, Upholder and Ruler of the World; and profess him or themselves obliged to live quietly under the Civil Government, shall be in any Case molested or prejudiced, in his or their Person or Estate, because of his or their conscientious Persuasion or Practice, nor be compelled to frequent or maintain any religious Worship, Place or Ministry, contrary to his or their Mind, or to do or suffer any other Act or Thing, contrary to their religious Persuasion.

AND that all Persons who also profess to believe in Jesus Christ, the Savior of the World, shall be capable (notwithstanding their other Persuasions and Practices in Point of Conscience and Religion) to serve this Government in any Capacity, both legislatively and executively, he or they solemnly promising, when lawfully required, Allegiance to the King as Sovereign, and Fidelity to the Proprietary and Governor, and taking the Attests as now established by the Law made at New-Castle, in the Year One Thousand and Seven Hundred, entitled, An Act directing the Attests of several Officers and Ministers, as now amended and confirmed this present Assembly.

II

FOR the well governing of this Province and Territories, there shall be an Assembly yearly chosen, by the Freemen thereof, to consist of Four Persons out of each County, of most Note for Virtue, Wisdom and Ability, (or of a greater number at any Time, as the Governor and Assembly shall agree) upon the First Day of October for ever; and shall sit on the Fourteenth Day of the same Month, at Philadelphia, unless the Governor and Council for the Time being, shall see Cause to appoint another Place within the said Province or Territories: Which Assembly shall have Power to chose a Speaker and other their Officers; and shall be Judges of the Qualifications and Elections of their own Members; sit upon their own Adjournment; appoint committees; prepare Bills in order to pass into Laws; impeach Criminals, and redress Grievances; and shall have all other Powers and Privileges of an Assembly, according to the Rights of the free-born Subjects of England, and as is usual in any of the King's Plantations in America.

AND if any County or Counties, shall refuse or neglect to chose their respective Representatives as aforesaid, or if chosen, do not meet to serve in Assembly, those who are so chosen and met, shall have the full Power of an Assembly, in as ample Manner as if all the

Representatives had been chosen and met, provided they are not less than Two Thirds of the whole Number that ought to meet.

AND that the Qualifications of Electors and Elected, and all other Matters and Things relating to Elections of Representatives to serve in Assemblies, though not herein particularly expressed, shall be and remain as by a Law of this Government, made at New-Castle in the Year One Thousand Seven Hundred, entitled, An Act to ascertain the Number of Members of Assembly, and to regulate the Elections.

III

THAT the Freemen in each respective County at the Time and Place of Meeting for Electing their Representatives to serve in Assembly, may as often as there shall be Occasion, chose a double Number of Persons to present to the Governor for Sheriffs and Coroners to serve for Three Years, if so long they behave themselves well; out of which respective Elections and Presentments, the Governor shall nominate and commissionate one for each of the said Offices, the Third Day after such Presentment, or else the First named in such Presentment, for each Office as aforesaid, shall stand and serve in that Office for the Time before respectively limited; and in Case of Death or Default, such Vacancies shall be supplied by the Governor, to serve to the End of the said Term.

PROVIDED ALWAYS, That if the said Freemen shall at any Time neglect or decline to chose a Person or Persons for either or both the aforesaid Offices then and in such Case, the Persons that are or shall be in the respective Offices of Sheriffs or Coroners, at the Time of Election, shall remain therein, until they shall be removed by another Election as aforesaid.

AND that the Justices of the respective Counties shall or may nominate and present to the Governor Three Persons, to serve for Clerk of the Peace for the said County, when there is a Vacancy, one of which the Governor shall commissionate within Ten Days after such Presentment, or else the First nominated shall serve in the said Office during good Behavior.

IV

THAT the Laws of this Government shall be in this Style, viz. By the Governor, with the Consent and Approbations of the Freemen in General Assembly Met; and shall be, after Confirmation by the Governor, forthwith recorded in the Rolls Office, and kept at Philadelphia, unless the Governor and Assembly shall agree to appoint another Place.

V

THAT all Criminals shall have the same Privileges of Witnesses and Council as their Prosecutors.

VI

THAT no Person or Persons shall or may, at any Time hereafter, be obliged to answer any Complaint, Matter or Thing whatsoever, relating to Property, before the Governor and Council, or in any other Place, but in ordinary Course of Justice, unless Appeals thereunto shall be hereafter by Law appointed.

VII

THAT no Person within this Government, shall be licensed by the Governor to keep an Ordinary, Tavern or House of Public Entertainment, but such who are first recommended to him, under the Hands of the Justices of the respective Counties, signed in open Court; which Justices are and shall be hereby empowered, to suppress and forbid any Person, keeping such Public-House as aforesaid, upon their Misbehavior, on such Penalties as the Law cloth or shall direct; and to recommend others from time to time, as they shall see Occasion.

VIII

IF any person, through Temptation or Melancholy, shall destroy himself; his Estate, real and personal, shall notwithstanding descend to his Wife and Children, or Relations, as if he had died a natural Death; and if any Person shall be destroyed or killed by Casualty or Accident, there shall be no Forfeiture to the Governor by reason thereof.

AND no Act, Law or Ordinance whatsoever, shall at any Time hereafter, be made or done, to alter, change or diminish the Form or Effect of this Charter, or of any Part or Clause therein, contrary to the true Intent and Meaning thereof, without the Consent of the Governor for the Time being, and Six Parts of Seven of the Assembly met.

BUT because the Happiness of Mankind depends so much upon the Enjoying of Liberty of their Consciences as aforesaid, I do hereby solemnly declare, promise and grant, for me, my Heirs and Assigns, That the First Article of this Charter relating to Liberty of Conscience, and every Part and Clause therein, according to the true Intent and Meaning thereof, shall be kept and remain, without any alteration, inviolably for ever.

AND LASTLY, I the said William Penn, Proprietary and Governor of the Province of Pennsylvania, and Territories thereunto belonging, for myself, my Heirs and Assigns, have solemnly declared, granted and confirmed, and do hereby solemnly declare, grant and confirm, That neither I, my Heirs or Assigns, shall procure or do any Thing or Things whereby the Liberties In this Charter contained and expressed, nor any Part thereof, shall be infringed or broken: And if any thing shall be procured or done, by any Person or Persons, contrary to these Presents, it shall be held of no Force or Effect.

IN WITNESS whereof, I the said William Penn, at Philadelphia in Pennsylvania, have unto this present Charter of Liberties, set my Hand and broad Seal, this Twenty-Eighth Day of October, in the Year of Our Lord One Thousand Seven Hundred and One, being the Thirteenth Year of the Reign of King William the Third, over England, Scotland, France and Ireland, &c. and the Twenty-First Year of my Government.

AND NOTWITHSTANDING the Closure and Test of this present Charter as aforesaid, I think fit to add this following Proviso thereunto, as Part of the same, That is to say, That notwithstanding any Clause or Clauses in the above-mentioned Charter, obliging the Province and Territories to join together in Legislation, I am content, and do hereby declare, that if the Representatives of the Province and Territories shall not hereafter agree to join together in Legislation, and that the same shall be signified unto me, or my Deputy, in open Assembly, or otherwise from under the Hands and Seals of the Representatives, for the Time being, of the Province and Territories, or the major Part of either of them, at any Time within Three Years from the Date hereof, that in such Case, the Inhabitants of each of the Three Counties of this Province, shall not have less than Eight Persons to represent them in Assembly, for the Province; and the Inhabitants of the Town of Philadelphia (when the said Town is incorporated) Two Persons to represent them in Assembly; and the Inhabitants of each County in the Territories, shall have as many Persons to represent them in a distinct Assembly for the Territories, as shall be by them requested as aforesaid.

NOTWITHSTANDING which Separation of the Province and Territories, in Respect of Legislation, I do hereby promise, grant and declare, That the Inhabitants of both Province and Territories, shall separately enjoy all other Liberties, Privileges and Benefits, granted jointly to them in this Charter, any Law, Usage or Custom of this Government heretofore made and practiced, or any Law made and passed by this General Assembly, to the Contrary hereof, notwithstanding.

WILLIAM PENN.

9. ALBANY PLAN OF UNION, 1754

It is proposed that humble application be made for an act of Parliament of Great Britain, by virtue of which one general government may be formed in America, including all the said colonies, within and under which government each colony may retain its present constitution, except in the particulars wherein a change may be directed by the said act, as hereafter follows.

1. That the said general government be administered by a President-General, to be appointed and supported by the crown; and a Grand Council, to be chosen by the representatives of the people of the several Colonies met in their respective assemblies.

2. That within—months after the passing [of] such [an] act, the House of Representatives that happen to be sitting within that time, or that shall especially for that purpose convened, may and shall choose members for the Grand Council, in the following proportion, that is to say,

Massachusetts Bay	7
New Hampshire	2
Connecticut	5
Rhode Island	2
New York	4
New Jersey	3
Pennsylvania	6
Maryland	4
Virginia	7
North Carolina	4
South Carolina	4
	48

3. —who shall meet for the first time at the city of Philadelphia, being called by the President-General as soon as conveniently may be after his appointment.

4. That there shall be a new election of the members of the Grand Council every three years; and, on the death or resignation of any member, his place

should be supplied by a new choice at the next sitting of the Assembly of the Colony he represented.

5. That after the first three years, when the proportion of money arising out of each Colony to the general treasury can be known, the number of members to be chosen for each Colony shall, from time to time, in all ensuing elections, be regulated by that proportion, yet so as that the number to be chosen by any one Province be not more than seven, nor less than two.

6. That the Grand Council shall meet once in every year, and oftener if occasion require, at such time and place as they shall adjourn to at the last preceding meeting, or as they shall be called to meet at by the President-General on any emergency; he having first obtained in writing the consent of seven of the members to such call, and sent duly and timely notice to the whole.

7. That the Grand Council have power to choose their speaker; and shall neither be dissolved, prorogued, nor continued sitting longer than six weeks at one time, without their own consent or the special command of the crown.

8. That the members of the Grand Council shall be allowed for their service ten shillings sterling per diem, during their session and journey to and from the place of meeting; twenty miles to be reckoned a day's journey.

9. That the assent of the President-General be requisite to all acts of the Grand Council, and that it be his office and duty to cause them to be carried into execution.

10. That the President-General, with the advice of the Grand Council, hold or direct all Indian treaties, in which the general interest of the Colonies may be concerned; and make peace or declare war with Indian nations.

11. That they make such laws as they judge necessary for regulating all Indian trade.

12. That they make all purchases from Indians, for the crown, of lands not now within the bounds of particular Colonies, or that shall not be within their bounds when some of them are reduced to more convenient dimensions.

13. That they make new settlements on such purchases, by granting lands in the King's name, reserving a quitrent to the crown for the use of the general treasury.

14. That they make laws for regulating and governing such new settlements, till the crown shall think fit to form them into particular governments.

15. That they raise and pay soldiers and build forts for the defense of any of the Colonies, and equip vessels of force to guard the coasts and protect the trade on the ocean, lakes, or great rivers; but they shall not impress men in any Colony, without the consent of the Legislature.

16. That for these purposes they have power to make laws, and lay and levy such general duties, imposts, or taxes, as to them shall appear most equal and just (considering the ability and other circumstances of the inhabitants in the several Colonies), and such as may be collected with the least inconvenience to the people; rather discouraging luxury, than loading industry with unnecessary burdens.

17. That they may appoint a General Treasurer and Particular Treasurer in each government when necessary; and, from time to time, may order the sums in the treasuries of each government into the general treasury; or draw on them for special payments, as they find most convenient.

18. Yet no money to issue but by joint orders of the President-General and Grand Council; except where sums have been appropriated to particular purposes, and the President-General is previously empowered by an act to draw such sums.

19. That the general accounts shall be yearly settled and reported to the several Assemblies.

20. That a quorum of the Grand Council, empowered to act with the President-General, do consist of twenty-five members; among whom there shall be one or more from a majority of the Colonies.

21. That the laws made by them for the purposes aforesaid shall not be repugnant, but, as near as may be, agreeable to the laws of England, and shall be transmitted to the King in Council for approbation, as soon as may be after their passing; and if not disapproved within three years after presentation, to remain in force.

22. That, in case of the death of the President-General, the Speaker of the Grand Council for the time being shall succeed, and be vested with the same powers and authorities, to continue till the King's pleasure be known.

23. That all military commission officers, whether for land or sea service, to act under this general constitution, shall be nominated by the President-General; but the approbation of the Grand Council is to be obtained, before they receive their commissions. And all civil officers are to be nominated by the Grand

Council, and to receive the President-General's approbation before they officiate.

24. But, in case of vacancy by death or removal of any officer, civil or military, under this constitution, the Governor of the Province in which such vacancy happens may appoint, till the pleasure of the President-General and Grand Council can be known.

25. That the particular military as well as civil establishments in each Colony remain in their present state, the general constitution notwithstanding; and that on sudden emergencies any Colony may defend itself, and lay the accounts of expense thence arising before the President-General and General Council, who may allow and order payment of the same, as far as they judge such accounts just and reasonable.

10. TREATY OF PARIS, 1763

The definitive Treaty of Peace and Friendship between his Britannic Majesty, the Most Christian King, and the King of Spain. Concluded at Paris the 10th day of February, 1763. To which the King of Portugal acceded on the same day.

In the Name of the Most Holy and Undivided Trinity, Father, Son, and Holy Ghost. So be it. Be it known to all those whom it shall, or may, in any manner, belong,

It has pleased the Most High to diffuse the spirit of union and concord among the Princes, whose divisions had spread troubles in the four parts of the world, and to inspire them with the inclination to cause the comforts of peace to succeed to the misfortunes of a long and bloody war, which having arisen between England and France during the reign of the Most Serene and Most Potent Prince, George the Second, by the grace of God, King of Great Britain, of glorious memory, continued under the reign of the Most Serene and Most Potent Prince, George the Third, his successor, and, in its progress, communicated itself to Spain and Portugal: Consequently, the Most Serene and Most Potent Prince, George the Third, by the grace of God, King of Great Britain, France, and Ireland, Duke of Brunswick and Lunenbourg, Arch Treasurer and Elector of the Holy Roman Empire; the Most Serene and Most Potent Prince, Lewis the Fifteenth, by the grace of God, Most Christian King; and the Most Serene and Most Potent Prince, Charles the Third, by the grace of God, King of Spain and of the Indies, after having laid the foundations of peace in the preliminaries signed at Fontainebleau the third of November last; and the

Most Serene and Most Potent Prince, Don Joseph the First, by the grace of God, King of Portugal and of the Algarves, after having acceded thereto, determined to complete, without delay, this great and important work. For this purpose, the high contracting parties have named and appointed their respective Ambassadors Extraordinary and Ministers Plenipotentiary [*the names of the ambassadors follow*]. . . .

Who, after having duly communicated to each other their full powers, in good form, copies whereof are transcribed at the end of the present treaty of peace, have agreed upon the articles, the tenor of which is as follows:

Article I.

There shall be a Christian, universal, and perpetual peace, as well as by sea as by land, and a sincere and constant friendship shall be re established between their Britannic, Most Christian, Catholic, and Most Faithful Majesties, and between their heirs and successors, kingdoms, dominions, provinces, countries, subjects, and vassals, of what quality or condition so ever they be, without exceptions of places or of persons: So that the high contracting parties shall give the greatest attention to maintain between themselves and their said dominions and subjects this reciprocal friendship and correspondence, without permitting, on either side, any kind of hostilities, by sea or by land, to be committed from henceforth, for any cause, or under any pretense whatsoever, and every thing shall be carefully avoided which might hereafter prejudice the union happily re-established, applying themselves, on the contrary, on every occasion, to procure for each other whatever may contribute to their mutual glory, interests, and advantages, without giving any assistance or protection, directly or indirectly, to those who would cause any prejudice to either of the high contracting parties: there shall be a general oblivion of every thing that may have been done or committed before or since the commencement of the war which is just ended.

II.

The treaties of Westphalia of 1648; those of Madrid between the Crowns of Great Britain and Spain of 1661, and 1670; the treaties of peace of Nimeguen of 1678, and 1679; of Ryswick of 1697; those of peace and of commerce of Utrecht of 1713; that of

Baden of 1714; the treaty of the triple alliance of the Hague of 1717; that of the quadruple alliance of London of 1718; the treaty of peace of Vienna of 1738; the definitive treaty of Aix la Chapelle of 1748; and that of Madrid, between the Crowns of Great Britain and Spain of 1750: as well as the treaties between the Crowns of Spain and Portugal of the 13th of February, 1668; of the 6th of February, 1715; and of the 12th of February, 1761; and that of the 11th of April, 1713, between France and Portugal with the guaranties of Great Britain, serve as a basis and foundation to the peace, and to the present treaty: and for this purpose they are all renewed and confirmed in the best form, as well as all the general, which subsisted between the high contracting parties before the war, as if they were inserted here word for word, so that they are to be exactly observed, for the future, in their whole tenor, and religiously executed on all sides, in all their points, which shall not be derogated from by the present treaty, notwithstanding all that may have been stipulated to the contrary by any of the high contracting parties: and all the said parties declare, that they will not suffer any privilege, favor, or indulgence to subsist, contrary to the treaties above confirmed, except what shall have been agreed and stipulated by the present treaty.

III.

All the prisoners made, on all sides, as well by land as by sea, and the hostages carried away or given during the war, and to this day, shall be restored, without ransom, six weeks, at least, to be computed from the day of the exchange of the ratification of the present treaty, each crown respectively paying the advances which shall have been made for the subsistence and maintenance of their prisoners by the Sovereign of the country where they shall have been detained, according to the attested receipts and estimates and other authentic vouchers which shall be furnished on one side and the other. And securities shall be reciprocally given for the payment of the debts which the prisoners shall have contracted in the countries where they have been detained until their entire liberty. And all the ships of war and merchant vessels which shall have been taken since the expiration of the terms agreed upon for the cessation of hostilities by sea shall likewise be restored, *bone fide*, with all their crews and cargoes: and the execution of this article shall be proceeded upon immediately after the exchange of the ratifications of this treaty.

IV.

His Most Christian Majesty [*of France*] renounces all pretensions which he has heretofore formed or might have formed to Nova Scotia or Acadia in all its parts, and guaranties the whole of it, and with all its dependencies, to the King of Great Britain: Moreover, his Most Christian Majesty cedes and guaranties to his said Britannic Majesty, in full right, Canada, with all its dependencies, as well as the island of Cape Breton, and all the other islands and coasts in the Gulf and river of St. Lawrence, and in general, every thing that depends on the said countries, lands, islands, and coasts, with the sovereignty, property, possession, and all rights acquired by treaty, or otherwise, which the Most Christian King and the Crown of France have had till now over the said countries, lands, islands, places, coasts, and their inhabitants, so that the Most Christian King cedes and makes over the whole to the said King, and to the Crown of Great Britain, and that in the most ample manner and form, without restriction, and without any liberty to depart from the said cession and guaranty under any pretense, or to disturb Great Britain in the possessions above mentioned. His Britannic Majesty, on his side, agrees to grant the liberty of the Catholic religion to the inhabitants of Canada: he will, in consequence, give the most precise and most effectual orders, that his new Roman Catholic subjects may profess the worship of their religion according to the rites of the Romish church, as far as the laws of Great Britain permit. His Britannic Majesty farther agrees, that the French inhabitants, or others who had been subjects of the Most Christian King in Canada, may retire with all safety and freedom wherever they shall think proper, and may sell their estates, provided it be to the subjects of his Britannic Majesty, and bring away their effects as well as their persons, without being restrained in their emigration, under any pretense whatsoever, except that of debts or of criminal prosecutions: The term limited for this emigration shall be fixed to the space of eighteen months, to be computed from the day of the exchange of the ratification of the present treaty.

V.

The subjects of France shall have the liberty of fishing and drying on a part of the coasts of the island of Newfoundland, such as it is specified in the XIIIth article of the treaty of Utrecht; which article is renewed and confirmed by the present treaty, (except what relates to the island of Cape Breton, as well as to the other islands and coasts in the mouth and in the Gulf of St. Lawrence:) And his Britannic Majesty consents to leave to the subjects of the Most Christian King the liberty of fishing in the Gulf of St. Lawrence, on condition that the subjects of France do not exercise the said fishery but at the distance of three leagues from all the coasts belonging to Great Britain, as well those of the continent as those of the islands situated in the said Gulf of St. Lawrence. And as to what relates to the fishery on the coasts of the island of Cape Breton, out of the said Gulf, the subjects of the Most Christian King shall not be permitted to exercise the said fishery but at the distance of fifteen leagues from the coasts of the island of Cape Breton; and the fishery on the coasts of Nova Scotia or Acadia, and every where else out of the said Gulf, shall remain on the foot of former treaties.

VI.

The King of Great Britain cedes the islands of St. Pierre and Macquelon, in full right, to his Most Christian Majesty, to serve as a shelter to the French fishermen; and his said Most Christian Majesty engages not to fortify the said islands; to erect no buildings upon them but merely for the conveniency of the fishery; and to keep upon them a guard of fifty men only for the police.

VII.

In order to re-establish peace on solid and durable foundations, and to remove for ever all subject of dispute with regard to the limits of the British and French territories on the continent of America; it is agreed, that, for the future, the confines between the dominions of his Britannic Majesty and those of his Most Christian Majesty, in that part of the world, shall be fixed irrevocably by a line drawn along the middle of the River Mississippi, from its source to the river Iberville, and from thence, by a line drawn along the middle of this river, and the lakes Maurepas and Pontchartrain to the sea; and for this purpose, the Most Christian King cedes in full right, and guaranties to his Britannic Majesty the river and port of the Mobile, and every thing which he possesses, or ought to possess, on the left side of the river Mississippi, except the town of New Orleans and the island in which it is situated, which shall remain to France, provided that the navigation of the river Mississippi shall be equally free, as well to the subjects of Great Britain as to those of France, in its whole breadth and length, from its source

to the sea, and expressly that part which is between the said island of New Orleans and the right bank of that river, as well as the passage both in and out of its mouth: It is farther stipulated, that the vessels belonging to the subjects of either nation shall not be stopped, visited, or subjected to the payment of any duty whatsoever. The stipulations inserted in the IVth article, in favor of the inhabitants of Canada shall also take place with regard to the inhabitants of the countries ceded by this article.

VIII.

The King of Great Britain shall restore to France the islands of Guadeloupe, of Mariegalante, of Desirade, of Martinico, and of Belleisle; and the fortresses of these islands shall be restored in the same condition they were in when they were conquered by the British arms, provided that his Britannic Majesty's subjects, who shall have settled in the said islands, or those who shall have any commercial affairs to settle there or in other places restored to France by the present treaty, shall have liberty to sell their lands and their estates, to settle their affairs, to recover their debts, and to bring away their effects as well as their persons, on board vessels, which they shall be permitted to send to the said islands and other places restored as above, and which shall serve for this use only, without being restrained on account of their religion, or under any other pretense whatsoever, except that of debts or of criminal prosecutions: and for this purpose, the term of eighteen months is allowed to his Britannic Majesty's subjects, to be computed from the day of the exchange of the ratifications of the present treaty; but, as the liberty granted to his Britannic Majesty's subjects, to bring away their persons and their effects, in vessels of their nation, may be liable to abuses if precautions were not taken to prevent them; it has been expressly agreed between his Britannic Majesty and his Most Christian Majesty, that the number of English vessels which have leave to go to the said islands and places restored to France, shall be limited, as well as the number of tons of each one; that they shall go in ballast; shall set sail at a fixed time; and shall make one voyage only; all the effects belonging to the English being to be embarked at the same time. It has been farther agreed, that his Most Christian Majesty shall cause the necessary passports to be given to the said vessels; that, for the greater security, it shall be allowed to place two French clerks or guards in each of the said vessels, which shall be visited in the landing places and ports of the said islands and places restored to France, and that the merchandise which shall be found therein shall be confiscated.

IX.

The Most Christian King cedes and guaranties to his Britannic Majesty, in full right, the islands of Grenada, and the Grenadines, with the same stipulations in favor of the inhabitants of this colony, inserted in the IVth article for those of Canada: And the partition of the islands called neutral, is agreed and fixed, so that those of St. Vincent, Dominico, and Tobago, shall remain in full right to Great Britain, and that of St. Lucia shall be delivered to France, to enjoy the same likewise in full right, and the high contracting parties guaranty the partition so stipulated.

X.

His Britannic Majesty shall restore to France the island of Goree in the condition it was in when conquered: and his Most Christian Majesty cedes, in full right, and guaranties to the King of Great Britain the river Senegal, with the forts and factories of St. Lewis, Podor, and Galam, and with all the rights and dependencies of the said river Senegal.

XI.

In the East Indies Great Britain shall restore to France, in the condition they are now in, the different factories which that Crown possessed, as well as on the coast of Coromandel and Orixa as on that of Malabar, as also in Bengal, at the beginning of the year 1749. And his Most Christian Majesty renounces all pretension to the acquisitions which he has made on the coast of Coromandel and Orixa since the said beginning of the year 1749. His Most Christian Majesty shall restore, on his side, all that he may have conquered from Great Britain in the East Indies during the present war; and will expressly cause Nattal and Tapanoully, in the island of Sumatra, to be restored; he engages farther, not to erect fortifications, or to keep troops in any part of the dominions of the Subah of Bengal. And in order to preserve future peace on the coast of Coromandel and Orixa, the English and French shall acknowledge Mahomet Ally Khan for lawful Nabob of the Carnatick, and Salabat Jing for lawful Subah of the Decan; and both parties shall renounce all demands and pretensions of satisfaction with which they might charge each other, or their Indian allies, for the depredations or pil-

lage committed on the one side or on the other during the war.

XII.

The island of Minorca shall be restored to his Britannic Majesty, as well as Fort St. Philip, in the same condition they were in when conquered by the arms of the Most Christian King; and with the artillery which was there when the said island and the said fort were taken.

XIII.

The town and port of Dunkirk shall be put into the state fixed by the last treaty of Aix la Chapelle, and by former treaties. The Cunette shall be destroyed immediately after the exchange of the ratifications of the present treaty, as well as the forts and batteries which defend the entrance on the side of the sea; and provision shall be made at the same time for the wholesomeness of the air, and for the health of the inhabitants, by some other means, to the satisfaction of the King of Great Britain.

XIV.

France shall restore all the countries belonging to the Electorate of Hanover, to the Landgrave of Hesse, to the Duke of Brunswick, and to the Count of La Lippe Buckebourg, which are or shall be occupied by his Most Christian Majesty's arms: the fortresses of these different countries shall be restored in the same condition they were in when conquered by the French arms; and the pieces of artillery, which shall have been carried elsewhere, shall be replaced by the same number, of the same bore, weight and metal.

XV.

In case the stipulations contained in the XIIIth article of the preliminaries should not be completed at the time of the signature of the present treaty, as well with regard to the evacuations to be made by the armies of France of the fortresses of Cleves, Wezel, Guelders, and of all the countries belonging to the King of Prussia, as with regard to the evacuations to be made by the British and French armies of the countries which they occupy in Westphalia, Lower Saxony, on the Lower Rhine, the Upper Rhine, and in all the empire; and to the retreat of the troops into the dominions of their respective Sovereigns: their Britannic and Most Christian Majesties promise to proceed, *bone fide,* with all the dispatch the case will permit of to the said evacuations, the entire completion whereof they stipulate before the 15th of March next, or sooner if it can be done; and their Britannic and Most Christian Majesties farther engage and promise to each other, not to furnish any succors of any kind to their respective allies who shall continue engaged in the war in Germany.

XVI.

The decision of the prizes made in time of peace by the subjects of Great Britain, on the Spaniards, shall be referred to the Courts of Justice of the Admiralty of Great Britain, conformably to the rules established among all nations, so that the validity of the said prizes, between the British and Spanish nations, shall be decided and judged, according to the law of nations, and according to treaties, in the Courts of Justice of the nation who shall have made the capture.

XVII.

His Britannic Majesty shall cause to be demolished all the fortifications which his subjects shall have erected in the bay of Honduras, and other places of the territory of Spain in that part of the world, four months after the ratification of the present treaty; and his Catholic Majesty [*of Spain*] shall not permit his Britannic Majesty's subjects, or their workmen, to be disturbed or molested under any pretense whatsoever in the said places, in their occupation of cutting, loading, and carrying away log-wood; and for this purpose, they may build, without hindrance, and occupy, without interruption, the houses and magazines necessary for them, for their families, and for their effects; and his Catholic Majesty assures to them, by this article, the full enjoyment of those advantages and powers on the Spanish coasts and territories, as above stipulated, immediately after the ratification of the present treaty.

XVIII.

His Catholic Majesty desists, as well for himself as for his successors, from all pretension which he may have formed in favor of the Guipuscoans, and other his subjects, to the right of fishing in the neighborhood of the island of Newfoundland.

XIX.

The King of Great Britain shall restore to Spain all the territory which he has conquered in the island of Cuba, with the fortress of the Havana; and this fortress, as well as all the other fortresses of the said island, shall be restored in the same condition they were in when conquered by his Britannic Majesty's arms, provided that his Britannic Majesty's subjects who shall have settled in the said island, restored to Spain by the present treaty, or those who shall have any commercial affairs to settle there, shall have liberty to sell their lands and their estates, to settle their affairs, recover their debts, and to bring away their effects, as well as their persons, on board vessels which they shall be permitted to send to the said island restored as above, and which shall serve for that use only, without being restrained on account of their religion, or under any other pretense whatsoever, except that of debts or of criminal prosecutions: And for this purpose, the term of eighteen months is allowed to his Britannic Majesty's subjects, to be computed from the day of the exchange of the ratifications of the present treaty: but as the liberty granted to his Britannic Majesty's subjects, to bring away their persons and their effects, in vessels of their nation, may be liable to abuses if precautions were not taken to prevent them; it has been expressly agreed between his Britannic Majesty and his Catholic Majesty, that the number of English vessels which shall have leave to go to the said island restored to Spain shall be limited, as well as the number of tons of each one; that they shall go in ballast; shall set sail at a fixed time; and shall make one voyage only; all the effects belonging to the English being to be embarked at the same time: it has been farther agreed, that his Catholic Majesty shall cause the necessary passports to be given to the said vessels; that for the greater security, it shall be allowed to place two Spanish clerks or guards in each of the said vessels, which shall be visited in the landing places and ports of the said island restored to Spain, and that the merchandise which shall be found therein shall be confiscated.

XX.

In consequence of the restitution stipulated in the preceding article, his Catholic Majesty cedes and guaranties, in full right, to his Britannic Majesty, Florida, with Fort St. Augustin, and the Bay of Pensacola, as well as all that Spain possesses on the continent of North America, to the East or to the South East of the river Mississippi. And, in general, every thing that depends on the said countries and lands, with the sovereignty, property, possession, and all rights, acquired by treaties or otherwise, which the Catholic King and the Crown of Spain have had till now over the said countries, lands, places, and their inhabitants; so that the Catholic King cedes and makes over the whole to the said King and to the Crown of Great Britain, and that in the most ample manner and form. His Britannic Majesty agrees, on his side, to grant to the inhabitants of the countries above ceded, the liberty of the Catholic religion; he will, consequently, give the most express and the most effectual orders that his new Roman Catholic subjects may profess the worship of their religion according to the rites of the Romish church, as far as the laws of Great Britain permit. His Britannic Majesty farther agrees, that the Spanish inhabitants, or others who had been subjects of the Catholic King in the said countries, may retire, with all safety and freedom, wherever they think proper; and may sell their estates, provided it be to his Britannic Majesty's subjects, and bring away their effects, as well as their persons without being restrained in their emigration, under any pretense whatsoever, except that of debts, or of criminal prosecutions: the term limited for this emigration being fixed to the space of eighteen months, to be computed from the day of the exchange of the ratifications of the present treaty. It is moreover stipulated, that his Catholic Majesty shall have power to cause all the effects that may belong to him, to be brought away, whether it be artillery or other things.

XXI.

The French and Spanish troops shall evacuate all the territories, lands, towns, places, and castles, of his Most faithful Majesty [*of Portugal*] in Europe, without any reserve, which shall have been conquered by the armies of France and Spain, and shall restore them in the same condition they were in when conquered, with the same artillery and ammunition, which were found there: And with regard to the Portuguese Colonies in America, Africa, or in the East Indies, if any change shall have happened there, all things shall be restored on the same footing they were in, and conformably to the preceding treaties which subsisted between the Courts of France, Spain, and Portugal, before the present war.

XXII.

All the papers, letters, documents, and archives, which were found in the countries, territories, towns and places that are restored, and those belonging to the countries ceded, shall be, respectively and *bone fide,* delivered, or furnished at the same time, if possible, that possession is taken, or, at latest, four months after the exchange of the ratifications of the present treaty, in whatever places the said papers or documents may be found.

XXIII.

All the countries and territories, which may have been conquered, in whatsoever part of the world, by the arms of their Britannic and Most Faithful Majesties, as well as by those of their Most Christian and Catholic Majesties, which are not included in the present treaty, either under the title of cessions, or under the title of restitutions, shall be restored without difficulty, and without requiring any compensations.

XXIV.

As it is necessary to assign a fixed epoch for the restitutions and the evacuati ons, to be made by each of the high contracting parties, it is agreed, that the British and French troops shall complete, before the 15th of March next, all that shall remain to be executed of the XIIth and XIIIth articles of the preliminaries, signed the 3d day of November last, with regard to the evacuation to be made in the Empire, or elsewhere. The island of Belleisle shall be evacuated six weeks after the exchange of the ratifications of the present treaty, or sooner if it can be done. Guadeloupe, Desirade, Mariegalante Martinico, and St. Lucia, three months after the exchange of the ratifications of the present treaty, or sooner if it can be done. Great Britain shall likewise, at the end of three months after the exchange of the ratifications of the present treaty, or sooner if it can be done, enter into possession of the river and port of the Mobile, and of all that is to form the limits of the territory of Great Britain, on the side of the river Mississippi, as they are specified in the VIIth article. The island of Goree shall be evacuated by Great Britain, three months after the exchange of the ratifications of the present treaty; and the island of Minorca by France, at the same epoch, or sooner if it can be done: And according to the conditions of the VIth article, France shall likewise enter into possession of the islands of St Peter, and of Miquelon, at the end of three months after the exchange of the ratifications of the present treaty. The Factories in the East Indies shall be restored six months after the exchange of the ratifications of the present treaty, or sooner if it can be done. The fortress of the Havana, with all that has been conquered in the island of Cuba, shall be restored three months after the exchange of the ratifications of the present treaty, or sooner if it can be done: And, at the same time, Great Britain shall enter into possession of the country ceded by Spain according to the XXth article. All the places and countries of his most Faithful Majesty, in Europe, shall be restored immediately after the exchange of the ratification of the present treaty: And the Portuguese colonies, which may have been conquered, shall be restored in the space of three months in the West Indies, and of six months in the East Indies, after the exchange of the ratifications of the present treaty, or sooner if it can be done. All the fortresses, the restitution whereof is stipulated above, shall be restored with the artillery and ammunition, which were found there at the time of the conquest. In consequence whereof, the necessary orders shall be sent by each of the high contracting parties, with reciprocal passports for the ships that shall carry them, immediately after the exchange of the ratifications of the present treaty.

XXV.

His Britannic Majesty, as Elector of Brunswick Lunenbourg, as well for himself as for his heirs and successors, and all the dominions and possessions of his said Majesty in Germany, are included and guarantied by the present treaty of peace.

XXVI.

Their sacred Britannic, Most Christian, Catholic, and Most Faithful Majesties, promise to observe sincerely and *bone fide,* all the articles contained and settled in the present treaty; and they will not suffer the same to be infringed, directly or indirectly, by their respective subjects; and the said high contracting parties, generally and reciprocally, guaranty to each other all the stipulations of the present treaty.

XXVII.

The solemn ratifications of the present treaty, expedited in good and due form, shall be exchanged in this city of Paris, between the high contracting parties, in the space of a month, or sooner if possible, to be computed from the day of the signature of the present treaty.

11. THE PROCLAMATION OF 1763

BY THE KING. A PROCLAMATION. GEORGE R.
Whereas We have taken into Our Royal Consideration the extensive and valuable Acquisitions in America, secured to our Crown by the late Definitive Treaty of Peace, concluded at Paris the 10th Day of February last; and being desirous that all Our loving Subjects, as well of our Kingdom as of our Colonies in America, may avail themselves with all convenient Speed, of the great Benefits and Advantages which must accrue therefrom to their Commerce, Manufactures, and Navigation, We have thought fit, with the Advice of our Privy Council. to issue this our Royal Proclamation, hereby to publish and declare to all our loving Subjects, that we have, with the Advice of our Said Privy Council, granted our Letters Patent, under our Great Seal of Great Britain, to erect, within the Countries and Islands ceded and confirmed to Us by the said Treaty, Four distinct and separate Governments, styled and called by the names of Quebec, East Florida, West Florida and Grenada, and limited and bounded as follows, viz.

First—The Government of Quebec bounded on the Labrador Coast by the River St. John, and from thence by a Line drawn from the Head of that River through the Lake St. John, to the South end of the Lake Nipissim; from whence the said Line, crossing the River St. Lawrence, and the Lake Champlain, in 45. Degrees of North Latitude, passes along the High Lands which divide the Rivers that empty themselves into the said River St. Lawrence from those which fall into the Sea; and also along the North Coast of the Baye des Chaleurs, and the Coast of the Gulf of St. Lawrence to Cape Rosieres, and from thence crossing the Mouth of the River St. Lawrence by the West End of the Island of Anticosti, terminates at the aforesaid River of St. John.

Secondly—The Government of East Florida. bounded to the Westward by the Gulf of Mexico and the Apalachicola River; to the Northward by a Line drawn from that part of the said River where the Chatahouchee and Flint Rivers meet, to the source of St. Mary's River. and by the course of the said River to the Atlantic Ocean; and to the Eastward and Southward by the Atlantic Ocean and the Gulf of Florida, including all Islands within Six Leagues of the Sea Coast.

Thirdly—The Government of West Florida. bounded to the Southward by the Gulf of Mexico. including all Islands within Six Leagues of the Coast. from the River Apalachicola to Lake Pontchartrain; to the Westward by the said Lake, the Lake Maurepas, and the River Mississippi; to the Northward by a Line drawn due East from that part of the River Mississippi which lies in 31 Degrees North Latitude. to the River Apalachicola or Chatahouchee; and to the Eastward by the said River.

Fourthly—The Government of Grenada, comprehending the Island of that name, together with the Grenadines, and the Islands of Dominico, St. Vincent's and Tobago. And to the end that the open and free Fishery of our Subjects may be extended to and carried on upon the Coast of Labrador, and the adjacent Islands. We have thought fit. with the advice of our said Privy Council to put all that Coast, from the River St. John's to Hudson's Straits, together with the Islands of Anticosti and Madelaine, and all other smaller Islands Lying upon the said Coast, under the care and Inspection of our Governor of Newfoundland.

We have also, with the advice of our Privy Council, thought fit to annex the Islands of St. John's and Cape Breton, or Isle Royale, with the lesser Islands adjacent thereto, to our Government of Nova Scotia.

We have also, with the advice of our Privy Council aforesaid, annexed to our Province of Georgia all the Lands Lying between the Rivers Alatamaha and St. Mary's.

And whereas it will greatly contribute to the speedy settling of our said new Governments, that our loving Subjects should be informed of our Paternal care, for the security of the Liberties and Properties of those who are and shall become Inhabitants thereof, We have thought fit to publish and declare, by this Our Proclamation, that We have, in the Letters Patent under our Great Seal of Great Britain, by which the said Governments are constituted, given express Power and Direction to our Governors of our Said Colonies respectively, that so soon as the state and circumstances of the said Colonies will admit thereof, they shall, with the Advice and Consent of the Members of our Council, summon and call General Assemblies within the said Governments respectively, in such Manner and Form as is used and directed in those Colonies and Provinces in America which are under our immediate Government: And We have also given Power to the said Governors, with the consent of our Said Councils, and the Representatives of the People so to be summoned as aforesaid, to make, constitute, and ordain Laws, Statutes, and Ordinances for the Public Peace, Welfare, and good Government of our said Colonies, and of the People and Inhabitants thereof, as near as may be agreeable to the Laws of England, and under such Regulations and Restrictions as are used in other Colonies;

and in the mean Time, and until such Assemblies can be called as aforesaid, all Persons Inhabiting in or resorting to our Said Colonies may confide in our Royal Protection for the Enjoyment of the Benefit of the Laws of our Realm of England; for which Purpose We have given Power under our Great Seal to the Governors of our said Colonies respectively to erect and constitute, with the Advice of our said Councils respectively, Courts of Judicature and public Justice within our Said Colonies for hearing and determining all Causes, as well Criminal as Civil, according to Law and Equity, and as near as may be agreeable to the Laws of England, with Liberty to all Perssons who may think themselves aggrieved by the Sentences of such Courts, in all Civil Cases, to appeal, under the usual Limitations and Restrictions, to Us in our Privy Council.

We have also thought fit, with the advice of our Privy Council as aforesaid, to give unto the Governors and Councils of our said Three new Colonies, upon the Continent full Power and Authority to settle and agree with the Inhabitants of our said new Colonies or with any other Persons who shall resort thereto, for such Lands, Tenements and Hereditaments, as are now or hereafter shall be in our Power to dispose of; and them to grant to any such Person or Persons upon such Terms, and under such moderate Quit-Rents, Services and Acknowledgments, as have been appointed and settled in our other Colonies, and under such other Conditions as shall appear to us to be necessary and expedient for the Advantage of the Grantees, and the Improvement and settlement of our said Colonies.

And Whereas, We are desirous, upon all occasions, to testify our Royal Sense and Approbation of the Conduct and bravery of the Officers and Soldiers of our Armies, and to reward the same, We do hereby command and empower our Governors of our said Three new Colonies, and all other our Governors of our several Provinces on the Continent of North America, to grant without Fee or Reward, to such reduced Officers as have served in North America during the late War, and to such Private Soldiers as have been or shall be disbanded in America, and are actually residing there, and shall personally apply for the same, the following Quantities of Lands, subject, at the Expiration of Ten Years, to the same Quit-Rents as other Lands are subject to in the Province within which they are granted, as also subject to the same Conditions of Cultivation and Improvement; viz.

To every Person having the Rank of a Field Officer—5,000 Acres.

To every Captain—3,000 Acres.

To every Subaltern or Staff Officer,—2,000 Acres.

To every Non-Commission Officer,—200 Acres.

To every Private Man—50 Acres.

We do likewise authorize and require the Governors and Commanders in Chief of all our said Colonies upon the Continent of North America to grant the like Quantities of Land, and upon the same conditions, to such reduced Officers of our Navy of like Rank as served on board our Ships of War in North America at the times of the Reduction of Louisbourg and Quebec in the late War, and who shall personally apply to our respective Governors for such Grants.

And whereas it is just and reasonable, and essential to our Interest, and the Security of our Colonies, that the several Nations or Tribes of Indians with whom We are connected, and who live under our Protection, should not be molested or disturbed in the Possession of such Parts of Our Dominions and Territories as, not having been ceded to or purchased by Us, are reserved to them, or any of them, as their Hunting Grounds.—We do therefore, with the Advice of our Privy Council, declare it to be our Royal Will and Pleasure, that no Governor or Commander in Chief in any of our Colonies of Quebec, East Florida, or West Florida, do presume, upon any Pretense whatever, to grant Warrants of Survey, or pass any Patents for Lands beyond the Bounds of their respective Governments, as described in their Commissions: as also that no Governor or Commander in Chief in any of our other Colonies or Plantations in America do presume for the present, and until our further Pleasure be known, to grant Warrants of Survey, or pass patents for any lands beyond the heads or sources of any of the rivers which fall into the Atlantic Ocean from the west or northwest; or upon any lands whatever, which, not having been ceded to or purchased by us, as aforesaid, are reserved to the said Indians, or any of them.

And We do further declare it to be Our Royal Will and Pleasure, for the present as aforesaid, to reserve under our Sovereignty, Protection, and Dominion, for the use of the said Indians, all the Lands and Territories not included within the Limits of Our said Three new Governments, or within the Limits of the Territory granted to the Hudson's Bay Company, as also all the Lands and Territories lying to the Westward of the Sources of the Rivers which fall into the Sea from the West and North West as aforesaid.

And We do hereby strictly forbid, on Pain of our Displeasure, all our loving Subjects from making any Purchases or Settlements whatever, or taking Possession of any of the Lands above reserved. without our especial leave and Licence for that Purpose first obtained.

And We do further strictly enjoin and require all Persons whatever who have either wilfully or inadvertently seated themselves upon any Lands within the Countries above described or upon any other Lands which, not having been ceded to or purchased by Us, are still reserved to the said Indians as aforesaid, forthwith to remove themselves from such Settlements.

And whereas great Frauds and Abuses have been committed in purchasing Lands of the Indians, to the great Prejudice of our Interests. and to the great Dissatisfaction of the said Indians: In order, therefore, to prevent such Irregularities for the future, and to the end that the Indians may be convinced of our Justice and determined Resolution to remove all reasonable Cause of Discontent, We do with the Advice of our Privy Council strictly enjoin and require that no private Person do presume to make any purchase from the said Indians of any Lands reserved to the said Indians, within those parts of our Colonies where We have thought proper to allow Settlement: but that, if at any Time any of the Said Indians should be inclined to dispose of the said Lands, the same shall be Purchased only for Us, in our Name, at some public Meeting or Assembly of the said Indians, to be held for that Purpose by the Governor or Commander in Chief of our Colony respectively within which they shall lie: and in case they shall lie within the limits of any proprietary government, they shall be purchased only for the use and in the name of such proprietaries, conformable to such directions and instructions as we or they shall think proper to give for that purpose. And we do, by the advice of our Privy Council, declare and enjoin, that the trade with the said Indians shall be free and open to all our subjects whatever, provided that every person who may incline to trade with the said Indians do take out a license for carrying on such trade, from the Governor or commander in chief of any of our colonies respectively where such person shall reside, and also give security to observe such regulations as we shall at any time think fit, by ourselves or commissaries to be appointed for this purpose, to direct and appoint for the benefit of the said trade.

And we do hereby authorize, enjoin, and require the Governors and Commanders in Chief of all our Colonies respectively, as well those under Our immediate Government as those under the Government and Direction of Proprietaries, to grant such Licences without Fee or Reward, taking especial Care to insert therein a Condition, that such Licence shall be void, and the Security forfeited in case the Person to whom the same is granted shall refuse or neglect to observe such Regulations as We shall think proper to prescribe as aforesaid.

And we do further expressly conjoin and require all Officers whatever, as well Military as those Employed in the Management and Direction of Indian Affairs, within the Territories reserved as aforesaid for the use of the said Indians, to seize and apprehend all Persons whatever who, standing charged with Treason, Misprisions of Treason, Murders, or other Felonies or Misdemeanors shall fly from Justice and take Refuge in the said Territory, and to send them under a proper guard to the Colony where the Crime was committed of which they, stand accused, in order to take their Trial for the same.

Given at our Court at St. James's the 7th Day of October 1763. in the Third Year of our Reign.

GOD SAVE THE KING

12. THE QUEBEC ACT, 1774

An act for making more effectual provisions for the government of the province of Quebec in North America

WHEREAS his Majesty, by his royal proclamation, bearing date the seventh day of October, in the third year of his reign, thought fit to declare the provisions which have been made in respect to certain countries, territories, and islands in America, ceded to his Majesty by the definitive treaty of peace, concluded at Paris on the tenth day of February, one thousand seven hundred and sixty-three: and whereas, by the arrangements made by the said royal proclamation, a very large extent of country, within which there were several colonies and settlements of the subjects of France, who claimed to remain therein under the faith of the said treaty, was left, without any provisions being made for the administration of civil government therein; and certain parts of the territory of Canada, where sedentary fisheries had been established and carried on by the subjects of France, inhabitants of the said province of Canada, under grants and concessions from the government thereof, were annexed to

the government of Newfoundland, and thereby regulations inconsistent with the nature of such fisheries: may it therefore please your most excellent Majesty that it may be enacted; and be it enacted by the King's most excellent majesty, by and with the advice and consent of the lords spiritual and temporal, and commons, in this present parliament assembled, and by the authority of the same, That all the territories, islands, and countries in *North America,* belonging to the crown of *Great Britain,* bounded on the south by a line from the bay of *Chaleurs,* along the high lands which divide the rivers that empty themselves into the river *Saint Lawrence* from those which fall into the sea, to a point in forty-five degrees of northern latitude, on the eastern bank of the river *Connecticut,* keeping the same latitude directly west, through the lake *Champlain,* until, in the same latitude, it meets the river *Saint Lawrence;* from thence up the eastern bank of the said river to the lake *Ontario;* thence through the lake *Ontario,* and the river commonly called *Niagara;* and thence along by the eastern and south-eastern bank of lake *Erie,* following the said bank, until the same shall be intersected by the northern boundary, granted by the charter of the province of *Pennsylvania,* in case the same shall be so intersected; and from thence along the said northern and western boundaries of the said province, until the said western boundary strike the *Ohio:* but in case the said bank of the said lake shall not be found to be so intersected, then following the said bank until it shall arrive at that point of the said bank which shall be nearest to the north-western angle of the said province of *Pennsylvania;* and thence, by a right line, to the said north-western angle of the said province; and thence along the western boundary of the said province, until it strike the river *Ohio;* and along the bank of the said river, westward, to the banks of the *Mississippi,* and northward to the southern boundary of the territory granted to the merchants adventurers of *England,* trading to *Hudson's Bay;* and also all such territories, islands, and countries, which have since the tenth of *February,* one thousand seven hundred and sixty-three, been made part of the government of *Newfoundland,* be, and they are hereby, during his Majesty's pleasure, annexed to, and made part and parcel of the province of *Quebec,* as created and established by the said royal proclamation of the seventh of *October,* one thousand seven hundred and sixty-three.

II. Provided always, That nothing herein contained, relative to the boundary of the province of *Quebec,* shall in anywise affect the boundaries of any other colony.

III. Provided always, and be it enacted, That nothing in this act contained shall extend, or be construed to extend, to make void, or to vary or alter any right, title, or possession, derived under any grant, conveyance, or otherwise howsoever, of or to any lands within the said province, or the provinces thereto adjoining; but that the same shall remain and be in force, and have effect, as if this act had never been made.

IV. And whereas the provisions, made by the said proclamation in respect to this civil government of the said province of Quebec and the powers and authorities given to the governor and other civil officers of the said province, by the grants and commissions issued in consequence thereof, have been found, upon experience, to be inapplicable to the state and circumstances of the said province, the inhabitants whereof amounted, at the conquest, to above sixty five thousand persons professing the religion of the church of Rome, and enjoying an established form of constitution and system of laws, by which their persons and property had been protected, governed, and ordered, for a long series of years, from the first establishment of the said province of Canada; be it therefore further enacted by the authority aforesaid, That the said proclamation as it relates to the said province of *Quebec,* and the commission under the authority whereof the government of the said province is at present administered, and all and every the ordinance and ordinances made by the governor and council of *Quebec* for the time being, relative to the civil government and administration of justice in the said province, and all commissions to judges and other officers thereof, be, and the same are hereby revoked, annulled, and made void, from and after the first day of *May,* one thousand seven hundred and seventy-five.

V. And, for the more perfect security and ease of the minds of the inhabitants of the said province, it is hereby declared, That his Majesty's subjects, professing the religion of the church of *Rome* of and in the said province of *Quebec,* may have, hold, and enjoy the free exercise of the religion of the church of *Rome,* subject to the King's supremacy, declared and established by an act, made in the first year of the reign of Queen *Elizabeth,* over all the dominions and countries which then did, or thereafter should belong, to the imperial crown of this realm; and that the clergy of the said church may hold, receive, and enjoy, their accustomed dues and rights, with respect to such persons only as shall profess the said religion.

VI. Provided nevertheless, That it shall be lawful for his Majesty, his heirs or successors, to make such provision out of the rest of the said accustomed dues and rights, for the encouragement of the protestant religion, and for the maintenance and support of a protestant clergy within the said province, as he or they shall, from time to time, think necessary and expedient.

VII. Provided always, and be it enacted, That no person, professing the religion of the church of *Rome,* and residing in the said province, shall be obliged to take the oath required by the said statute passed in the first year of the reign of Queen *Elizabeth,* or any other oaths substituted by any other act in the place thereof; but that every such person who, by the said statute is required to take the oath therein mentioned, shall be obliged, and is hereby required, to take and subscribe the following oath before the governor, or such other person in such court of record as his Majesty shall appoint, who are hereby authorized to administer the same; *videlicet.*

I A. B. do sincerely promise and swear, That I will be faithful, and bear true allegiance to his majesty King George, and him will defend to the utmost of my power, against all traitorous conspiracies, and attempts whatsoever, which shall be made against his person, crown, and dignity; and I will do my utmost endeavor to disclose and make known to his majesty; his heirs and successors, all treasons, and traitorous conspiracies, and attempts, which I shall know to be against him, or any of them; and all this I do swear without any equivocation, mental evasion, or secret reservation, and renouncing all pardons and dispensations from any power or person whomsoever to the contrary. So help me GOD.

And every such person, who shall neglect or refuse to take the said oath before mentioned, shall incur and be liable to the same penalties, forfeitures, disabilities, and incapacities, as he would have incurred and been liable to for neglecting or refusing to take the oath required by the said statute passed in the first year of the reign of Queen *Elizabeth.*

VIII. And be it further enacted by the authority aforesaid, That his Majesty's *Canadian* subjects, within the province of *Quebec,* the religious orders and communities only excepted, may also hold and enjoy their property and possessions, together with all customs and usages relative thereto, and all other their civil rights, in as large, ample, and beneficial manner, as if the said proclamation, commissions, ordinances, and other acts and instruments, had not been made, and as may consist with their allegiance to his Majesty, and subjection to the crown and parliament of *Great Britain;* and that in all matters of controversy, relative to property and civil rights, resort shall be had to the laws of *Canada,* as the rule for the decision of the same; and all causes that shall hereafter be instituted in any of the courts of justice to be appointed within and for the said province, by his Majesty, his heirs and successors, shall, with respect to such property and rights, be determined agreeably to the said laws and customs of *Canada,* until they shall be varied or altered by any ordinances that shall, from time to time, be passed in the said province by the governor, lieutenant governor, or commander in chief, for the time being, by and with the advice and consent of the legislative council of the same, to be appointed in manner herein after mentioned.

IX. Provided always, That nothing in this act contained shall extend, or be construed to extend, to any lands that have been granted by his Majesty, or shall hereafter be granted by his Majesty, his heirs and successors, to be holden in free and common socage.

X. Provided also, That it shall and may be lawful to and for every person that is owner of any lands, goods, or credits, in the said province, and that has a right to alienate the said lands, goods, or credits, in his or her life-time, by deed of sale, gift, or otherwise, to devise or bequeath the same at his or her death, by his or her last will and testament; any law, usage, or custom, heretofore or now prevailing in the province, to the contrary hereof in anywise notwithstanding; such will being executed, either according to the laws of *Canada,* or according to the forms prescribed by the laws of *England.*

XI. And whereas the certainty and lenity of the criminal law of England, and the benefits and advantages resulting for the use of it, have been sensibly felt by the inhabitants, from an experience of more than nine years, during which it has been uniformly administered; be it therefore further enacted by the authority aforesaid, That the same shall continue to be administered, and shall be observed as law in the province of *Quebec,* as well in the description and quality of the offence as in the method of prosecution and trial; and the punishments and forfeitures thereby inflicted to the exclusion of every other rule of criminal law, or mode of proceeding thereon, which did or might prevail in the said province before the year of our Lord one thousand seven hundred and sixty-four; any thing in this act to the contrary thereof in any respect notwithstanding; subject nevertheless to such alterations and amendments as the governor, lieutenant-governor, or commander in chief for the time being, by and with the advice and consent of the legislative council of the said province, hereafter to be appointed, shall, from time to time, cause to be made therein, in manner herein-after directed.

XII. And whereas it may be necessary to ordain many regulations for the future welfare and good government of the province of Quebec, the occasions of which cannot now be foreseen, nor, without much delay and inconvenience, be provided for, without instructing that authority, for a certain time, and under proper restrictions, to persons resident there: and whereas it is at present inexpedient to call an assembly; be it therefore enacted by the authority aforesaid, That it shall and may be lawful for his Majesty, his heirs and successors, by warrant under his or their signet or sign manual, and with the advice of the privy council, to constitute and appoint a council for the affairs of the province of *Quebec,* to consist of such persons resident there, not exceeding twenty-three, nor less than seventeen, as his Majesty, his heirs and successors, shall be pleased to appoint; and, upon the death, removal, or absence of any of the members of the said council, in like manner to constitute and appoint such and so many other person or persons as shall be necessary to supply the vacancy or vacancies; which council, so appointed and nominated, or the major part thereof, shall have power and authority to make ordinances for the peace, welfare, and good government, of the said province, with the consent of his Majesty's governor, or, in his absence, of the lieutenant-governor, or commander in chief for the time being.

XIII. Provided always, That nothing in this act contained shall extend to authorize or empower the said legislative council to lay any taxes or duties within the said province, such rates and taxes only excepted as the inhabitants of any town or district within the said province may be authorized by the said council to assess, levy, and apply, within the said town or district, for the purpose of making roads, erecting and repairing the local convenience and economy of such town or district.

XIV. Provided also, and be it enacted by the authority aforesaid, That every ordinance so to be made, shall, within six months, be transmitted by the governor, or, in his absence, by the lieutenant-governor, or commander in chief for the time being, and laid before his Majesty for his royal approbation; and if his Majesty shall think fit to disallow thereof, the same shall cease and be void from the time that his Majesty's order in council thereupon shall be promulgated at *Quebec.*

XV. Provided also, That no ordinance touching religion, or by which any punishment may be inflicted greater than fine or imprisonment for three months, shall be of any force or effect, until the same shall have received his Majesty's approbation.

XVI. Provided also, That no ordinance shall be passed at any meeting of the council where less than a majority of the whole council is present, or at any time except between the first day of *January* and the first day of *May,* unless upon some urgent occasion, in which case every member thereof resident at *Quebec,* or within fifty miles thereof, shall be personally summoned by the governor, or, in his absence, by his lieutenant-governor or commander in chief for the time being, to attend the same.

XVII. And be it further enacted by the authority aforesaid, That nothing herein contained shall extend, or be construed to extend, to prevent or hinder his Majesty, his heirs and successors, by his or their letters patent under the great seal of *Great Britain,* from erecting, constituting, and appointing, such courts of criminal, civil, and ecclesiastical jurisdiction within and for the said province of *Quebec,* and appointing, from time to time, the judges and officers thereof, as his Majesty, his heirs and successors, shall think necessary and proper for the circumstances of the said province.

XVIII. Provided always, and it is hereby enacted, That nothing in this act contained shall extend, or be construed to extend, to repeal or make void, within the said province of *Quebec,* any act or acts of the parliament of *Great Britain* heretofore made, for prohibiting, restraining, or regulating, the trade or commerce of his Majesty's colonies and plantations in *America;* but that all and every the said acts, and also all acts of parliament heretofore made concerning or respecting the said colonies and plantations, shall be, and are hereby declared to be, in force, within the said province of *Quebec,* and every part thereof.

13. THE DECLARATION OF INDEPENDENCE, 1776

The Declaration of Independence of the Thirteen Colonies In CONGRESS, *July 4, 1776*
THE UNANIMOUS DECLARATION OF THE THIRTEEN UNITED STATES OF AMERICA.

When in the Course of human events, it becomes necessary for one people to dissolve the political bonds which have connected them with another, and to assume among the powers of the earth, the separate and equal station to which the Laws of Nature and of Nature's God entitle them, a decent respect to the opinions of mankind requires that they should declare the causes which impel them to the separation.

We hold these truths to be self-evident, that all men are created equal, that they are endowed by their Creator with certain unalienable Rights, that among these are Life, Liberty, and the pursuit of Happiness. That to secure these rights, Governments are instituted among Men, deriving their just powers from the consent of the governed. That whenever any Form of Government becomes destructive of these ends, it is the Right of the People to alter or to abolish it, and to institute new Government, laying its foundation on such principles and organizing its powers in such form, as to them shall seem most likely to effect their Safety and Happiness. Prudence, indeed, will dictate that Governments long established should not be changed for light and transient causes; and accordingly all experience hath shown, that mankind are more disposed to suffer, while evils are sufferable, than to right themselves by abolishing the forms to which they are accustomed. But when a long train of abuses and usurpations, pursuing invariably the same object, evinces a design to reduce them under absolute Despotism, it is their right, it is their duty, to throw off such Government, and to provide new Guards for their future security.

Such has been the patient sufferance of these Colonies; and such is now the necessity which constrains them to alter their former Systems of Government. The history of the present King of Great Britain is a history of repeated injuries and usurpations, all having in direct object the establishment of an absolute Tyranny over these States. To prove this, let Facts be submitted to a candid world.

He has refused his Assent to Laws, the most wholesome and necessary for the public good.

He has forbidden his Governors to pass Laws of immediate and pressing importance, unless suspended in their operation till his Assent should be obtained, and when so suspended, he has utterly neglected to attend to them.

He has refused to pass other Laws for the accommodation of large districts of people, unless those people would relinquish the right of Representation in the Legislature, a right inestimable to them and formidable to tyrants only.

He has called together legislative bodies at places unusual, uncomfortable, and distant from the depository of their public Records, for the sole purpose of fatiguing them into compliance with his measures.

He has dissolved Representative Houses repeatedly, for opposing with manly firmness his invasions on the rights of the people.

He has refused for a long time, after such dissolutions, to cause others to be elected; whereby the Legislative powers, incapable of Annihilation, have returned to the People at large for their exercise; the State remaining in the meantime exposed to all the dangers of invasion from without, and convulsions within.

He has endeavoured to prevent the population of these States; for that purpose obstructing the Laws for Naturalization of Foreigners; refusing to pass others to encourage their migrations hither, and raising the conditions of new Appropriations of Lands.

He has obstructed the Administration of Justice, by refusing his Assent to Laws for establishing Judiciary powers.

He has made Judges dependent on his Will alone, for the tenure of their offices, and the amount and payment of their salaries.

He has erected a multitude of New Offices, and sent hither swarms of Officers to harass our people, and eat out their substance.

He has kept among us, in times of peace, Standing Armies, without the consent of our legislatures.

He has affected to render the Military independent of and superior to the Civil power.

He has combined with others to subject us to a jurisdiction foreign to our constitution and unacknowledged by our laws; giving his Assent to their Acts of pretended Legislation:

For quartering large bodies of armed troops among us:

For protecting them by a mock Trial from punishment for any Murders which they should commit on the Inhabitants of these States:

For cutting off our Trade with all parts of the world:

For imposing Taxes on us without our Consent:

For depriving us in many cases of the benefits of Trial by Jury:

For transporting us beyond Seas to be tried for pretended offences:

For abolishing the free System of English Laws in a neighbouring Province [*Quebec*], establishing therein an Arbitrary government, and enlarging its Boundaries so as to render it at once an example and fit instrument for introducing the same absolute rule into these Colonies:

For taking away our Charters, abolishing our most valuable Laws and altering fundamentally the Forms of our Governments:

For suspending our own Legislatures, and declaring themselves invested with power to legislate for us in all cases whatsoever.

He has abdicated Government here by declaring us out of his Protection and waging War against us.

He has plundered our seas, ravaged our Coasts, burnt our towns, and destroyed the lives of our people.

He is at this time transporting large Armies of foreign Mercenaries to complete the works of death, desolation and tyranny, already begun with circumstances of cruelty and perfidy scarcely paralleled in the most barbarous ages, and totally unworthy the Head of a civilized nation.

He has constrained our fellow Citizens taken Captive on the high Seas to bear Arms against their Country, to become the executioners of their friends and Brethren, or to fall themselves by their Hands.

He has excited domestic insurrections amongst us, and has endeavoured to bring on the inhabitants of our frontiers, the merciless Indian Savages, whose known rule of warfare is an undistinguished destruction of all ages, sexes and conditions.

In every stage of these Oppressions We have Petitioned for Redress in the most humble terms. Our repeated Petitions have been answered only by repeated injury. A Prince, whose character is thus marked by every act which may define a Tyrant, is unfit to be the ruler of a free people.

Nor have We been wanting in attentions to our British brethren.

We have warned them from time to time of attempts by their legislature to extend an unwarrantable jurisdiction over us.

We have reminded them of the circumstances of our emigration and settlement here.

We have appealed to their native justice and magnanimity, and we have conjured them by the ties of our common kindred to disavow these usurpations, which would inevitably interrupt our connections and correspondence.

They too have been deaf to the voice of justice and of consanguinity. We must, therefore, acquiesce in the necessity, which denounces our Separation, and hold them, as we hold the rest of mankind, Enemies in War, in Peace Friends.

We, therefore, the Representatives of the United States of America, in General Congress, Assembled, appealing to the Supreme Judge of the world for the rectitude of our intentions, do, in the Name, and by the authority of the good People of these Colonies, solemnly publish and declare.

That these United Colonies are, and of Right ought to be Free and Independent States; that they are Absolved from all Allegiance to the British Crown, and that all political connection between them and the State of Great Britain is and ought to be totally dissolved; and that as Free and Independent States, they have full Power to levy War, conclude Peace, contract Alliances, establish Commerce, and to do all other Acts and Things which Independent States may of right do.

And for the support of this Declaration, with a firm reliance on the protection of Divine Providence, we mutually pledge to each other our Lives, our Fortunes, and our sacred Honor.

John Hancock

New Hampshire: Josiah Bartlett, William Whipple, Matthew Thornton

Massachusetts: Samuel Adams, John Adams, Robert Treat Paine, Elbridge Gerry

Rhode Island: Stephen Hopkins, William Ellery

Connecticut: Roger Sherman, Samuel Huntington, William Williams, Oliver Wolcott

New York: William Floyd, Philip Livingston, Francis Lewis, Lewis Morris

New Jersey: Richard Stockton, John Witherspoon, Francis Hopkinson, John Hart, Abraham Clark

Pennsylvania: Robert Morris, Benjamin Rush, Benjamin Franklin, John Morton, George Clymer, James Smith, George Taylor, James Wilson, George Ross

Delaware: Caesar Rodney, George Read, Thomas McKean

Maryland: Samuel Chase, William Paca, Thomas Stone, Charles Carroll of Carrollton

Virginia: George Wythe, Richard Henry Lee, Thomas Jefferson, Benjamin Harrison, Thomas Nelson, Jr., Francis Lightfoot Lee, Carter Braxton

North Carolina: William Hooper, Joseph Hewes, John Penn

South Carolina: Edward Rutledge, Thomas Heyward, Jr., Thomas Lynch, Jr., Arthur Middleton

Georgia: Button Gwinnett, Lyman Hall, George Walton

APPENDIX B
Biographies of Major Personalities

Adams, Abigail Smith (1744–1818) *wife of John Adams, second first lady of the United States*
Born in Massachusetts, Abigail Adams married John in 1764; the couple had five children. Although she had no formal education, she was widely read and highly intelligent. She is remembered for the many perceptive letters she exchanged with her husband, friends, and children over four decades, which comment on the events of the Revolutionary era and provide extensive detail about everyday life. She consistently urged her husband to consider the rights of women and slaves while developing a new nation. For a decade after 1774, Abigail managed the family farm while her husband participated in Revolutionary activities. In November, 1800, the couple became the first occupants of the newly built White House in Washington, D.C., for the last few months of John's presidency. The couple's son, John Quincy Adams, later became the sixth president of the United States.

Adams, John (1735–1826) *Revolutionary leader, second president of the United States*
Born in Quincy, Massachusetts, Adams was a Harvard graduate and a lawyer. After 1770, he was one of the most active Revolutionary leaders. He served as a delegate to the First and Second Continental Congress, nominating George Washington to be commander in chief of the Continental army. He served on the five-man committee in charge of preparing the Declaration of Independence and was a signer of the final document. During the war, he served as a foreign diplomat and later helped negotiate the peace treaty with Britain. He then served two terms as the first vice president of the United States (elected 1788, 1792) and one term as its second president (1796–1800). During his presidency, he lost popular favor and was defeated for a second term by Thomas Jefferson. Embittered, he retired to private life in Massachusetts, although he later reconciled with Jefferson.

Adams's best-known writing is his correspondence with Jefferson and with his wife Abigail, although he published political works as well. Both Jefferson and Adams died on July 4, 1826—the 50th anniversary of the Declaration of Independence.

Adams, Samuel (1722–1803) *radical Revolutionary leader, writer, publicist, organizer*
Born in Boston, Samuel Adams attended Harvard and was a second cousin of John Adams. Unsuccessful at business, for a time he served as tax collector. He was among the most radical of Patriots after the passage of the Sugar Act, and by 1770 he was committed to the idea of independence. As a member of the Massachusetts General Court, he wrote many of the documents issued by that body after 1764. He organized the first official Committee of Correspondence and urged the formation of more such committees throughout Massachusetts. He also helped organize the Sons of Liberty. Adams served as a delegate to the Continental Congresses and signed the Declaration of Independence. After the war, he became lieutenant governor (1789–93) and governor of Massachusetts (1794–97). Adams was the most active and effective propagandist and mobilizer of public opinion for the Revolutionary cause, often able to unite colonists of different social classes. He organized or led much of the opposition to acts passed by Parliament after 1763, including the Boston Tea Party. He created a steady stream of publicity for the independence movement, in the press and via the committees of correspondence. As political parties began to form after the Revolution, he allied with the Jeffersonian Democrats rather than the Federalists.

Aguayo, marqués de (1677–1734) *Spanish military and colonial official*
After the French captured Pensacola from the Spanish in 1719, Aguayo led Spanish forces to Texas from

Mexico at his own expense. He strengthened Spanish establishments in Texas and forced the French to abandon the area. After 1722, he returned to Spain.

Alexander, William (earl of Stirling)
(1567–1640) *colonizer, poet*
Born in Scotland, Alexander was a courtier who became a favorite of King James I. He was chosen as one of the committee who prepared the King James version of the Bible. He received a grant to settle "New Scotland" (modern Nova Scotia) in 1621; it was confirmed in 1625, despite rival French claims. Attempts to establish a colony did not succeed, and land rights were restored to the French in 1629 via treaty. Alexander died in debt in London.

Allen, Ethan (1738–1789) *Revolutionary hero, Vermont leader*
Born in Connecticut, Allen served in the French and Indian War, then became colonel of the Great Mountain Boys (the Vermont militia). With Benedict Arnold he organized a successful surprise attack on Fort Ticonderoga in 1775. Allen went on to attack Montreal, where he was captured by the French and held prisoner until 1778. After his release, he served as a militia general and resumed his long-time efforts to gain recognition for Vermont as a separate state.

Amherst, Jeffrey (1717–1797) *British commander in chief in North America*
Born in England, Amherst commanded the forces in America during the French and Indian War. Before the final peace was signed, he successfully oversaw the military occupation of New France after the fall of Quebec (1760–73). Amherst mismanaged Indian relations in the former French territories of upper Louisiana, however, contributing to the outbreak of Pontiac's War.

Andros, Sir Edmund (1637–1714) *British colonial governor*
Originally an appointee of the duke of York, Andros (pronounced Andrews) was an aristocrat who served as a military officer. He was appointed governor of New York in 1674. In 1686, he was appointed governor over the entire Dominion of New England, a union of the northern colonies established by British imperial officials who hoped it would improve colonial defense. His autocratic style of governing, as well as his militant Anglicanism, was greatly resented in New England. He stripped the Massachusetts assembly of many powers, including land distribution, and imposed quitrents which affected every land-owning citizen. In the wake of England's Glorious Revolution of 1688, colonial leaders seized Andros and sent him back to England. In 1692, however, Crown officials returned him to the colonies as governor of Virginia, where he served until 1697.

Anne (1665–1714) *queen of England (reigned 1702–14)*
The second daughter of James II, Anne succeeded King William and Queen Mary, her sister. The Act of Union, which united England and Scotland in 1707, changed her title to queen of Great Britain. She was the last monarch of the Stuart line and was succeeded by George I.

Anza, Juan Bastista de (1735–1788) *soldier, explorer in the Spanish Southwest*
Born in Mexico, Anza served as captain at the presidio of Tubac. In 1774, he blazed an overland trail to Monterey, and in 1776 he led expedition that founded San Francisco. He became governor of New Mexico in 1777; he resigned in 1788 and died soon after in Mexico. Anza was the son of another Spanish frontier soldier of the same name who was active in Arizona in the 1720s.

Argall, Samuel (ca. 1572–ca. 1626) *English privateer*
Born in Bristol, Argall was commissioned as admiral by the Virginia Company of London to protect the Jamestown venture. In 1613, he abducted the Pamunkey princess Pocahontas to force her father Powhatan to negotiate with the colonists. In 1613–14, he attacked and destroyed the French settlement at St. Saveur and Port Royal, Acadia. He returned to England and was later knighted by James I. It was Argall who in 1610 gave the name Delaware (for Lord De La Warr) to the bay, river, and surrounding area.

Arnold, Benedict (1741–1801) *Revolutionary military hero, traitor*
Born in Connecticut, Arnold was apprenticed by his parents and became a successful merchant. He and Ethan Allen led a successful attack on Fort Ticonderoga in 1775 and Arnold led a march to Quebec later in the year. Arnold, a brilliant tactician, compiled a masterful military record for the Patriots in the first years of the Revolutionary War. In 1777, he was placed in command of Philadelphia. Court-martialed in 1779 for using his troops for private purposes, he began

traitorous correspondence with the British commander, plotting to turn over West Point. The plot was discovered; the British officer was captured by Americans and hanged. Arnold fled to a British ship but later returned to lead raids on his former countrymen. After the war, he lived in England.

Attucks, Crispus (ca. 1723–1770) *Patriot*

Attucks, who may have been of both African and Indian descent, is believed to have escaped from slavery in Framingham, Massachusetts. An imposing man, he worked for more than 20 years as a seaman out of Boston. In 1770, he was the first casualty at the Boston Massacre; some accounts credit him with leading the civilian group that attacked the British soldiers.

Aubry, Charles Philippe (unknown–1768) *military commander of French Louisiana*

Aubry was the virtual head of the Louisiana colony following the death of the last French governor, Jean-Jacques d'Abbadie, in 1765. After the arrival of the first Spanish governor, Antonio de Ulloa, in 1766, Aubry continued to share governance of the colony in an unusual arrangement. He earned the anger of his fellow French colonists when he provided names of French insurrectionists to Spain, under orders of the French Crown. He died in a shipwreck on his return journey to France.

Aulnay de Charnisay, sieur d' (Charles de Menou) (1604–1650) *Acadian governor*

Born in France, d'Aulnay arrived in Acadia in 1632 and served as governor from 1635 to 1650. He engaged in many years of conflict with Charles de la Tour over official control of the area, finally defeating de la Tour in 1645. D'Aulnay drowned in the Annapolis River when his canoe overturned.

Ayllón, Lucas Vázquez de (ca. 1475–1526) *colonizer, official in New Spain*

Born in Spain, Ayllón arrived in Hispaniola in 1502, where he served as a judge. In 1526, he financed and accompanied an expedition of over 500 colonists and slaves to the Carolina coast, probably the earliest Spanish attempt to found a permanent colony in North America. The expedition was disastrous. Struck by malaria, Ayllón and a large majority of his colonists died. The remainder returned to Santo Domingo or blended into Guale Indian society.

Bacon, Nathaniel (1647–1676) *Virginia councillor, rebel*

Born in England to a prominent family, Bacon migrated to Virginia with his young wife, who had been disinherited because her father disapproved of their marriage. He purchased two plantations along the James River and soon after became a member of Governor William Berkeley's council. In defiance of Berkeley's orders, he led expeditions against Indians who threatened frontier settlements. Berkeley declared him a rebel, and in 1676 he led a full-scale popular revolt, called Bacon's Rebellion, capturing and burning Jamestown. Shortly thereafter, Bacon died, probably of dysentery, and the rebellion ended.

Bartram, John (1699–1777) *botanist*

Born to a Quaker family in Pennsylvania, Bartram acquired worldwide fame for the botanical garden he established on his farm near Philadelphia. He exchanged correspondence, plants, and seeds with many European botanists and conducted the first American experiments in hybridization. He traveled widely to gather specimens, often accompanied by his son William. He was appointed Royal Botanist in 1765. Bartram was largely self-educated.

Bartram, William (1739–1823) *naturalist*

Born in Pennsylvania, William was the son of John Bartram. He continued his father's botanical work and began extensive observation and cataloging of native American birds. He traveled widely in the southern colonies immediately before the Revolution, writing about his experiences in his influential *Travels* (published 1791).

Benavides, Father Alonso de (ca. 1580–1635) *Spanish Franciscan; custodian in New Mexico, 1625–29*

During Father Benavides appointment in New Mexico, he authored two reports that, while promotional, are important sources of information about the Spanish colonies in North America in the early 17th century.

Berkeley, Sir William (1606–1677) *royal governor of colonial Virginia*

Appointed governor in 1641, Berkeley held office until 1676, with a brief interruption. During his first term, he administered the colony well and was a popular figure. Berkeley was a staunch royalist who promoted careful relations with the Indians, although his policies were never popular with settlers on the Virginia frontiers. He was forced out of office when the English Commonwealth was established in 1652, but he remained in the colony. After the Restoration, he resumed office. During his second term, Indian hostilities, economic problems, and Berkeley's own increasingly dictatorial style led to Bacon's Rebellion (1676). Although the Rebellion was quelled, he was recalled to England, where he died.

Biencourt, Charles de (baron de Saint-Just) (1592–1624) *colonizer of Acadia*

Born in France, Biencourt traveled to Port Royal, Acadia, in 1606 with his father, Jean de Biencourt de Poutrincourt, and returned in 1610 when the colony was reestablished. When Poutrincourt returned to France in 1611, he placed Port Royal under his son's authority. During his absence the Jesuits created difficulties and the British privateer Samuel Argall destroyed the settlement. Poutrincourt returned only briefly, transferring his holdings to his son. Biencourt and a few colonists conducted fishing and fur-trading but the settlement did not thrive. He lived among the Indians in the years preceding his death.

Biencourt de Poutrincourt, Jean de See POUTRINCOURT.

Bienville, sieur de (Jean-Baptiste Le Moyne) (1680–1767) *explorer of French Louisiana, founder of New Orleans*

Born in Montreal to a prominent fur-trading family, Bienville accompanied his brother Pierre Le Moyne, sieur d'Iberville to explore the lower Mississippi Valley in 1698–99. They established the first settlements in Louisiana's gulf territory. Bienville assumed control of the project when his brother left to command a naval fleet, continuing exploration and colonization in the area. He served three terms as governor of Louisiana: 1701–02, 1718–26, and 1733–43. In 1718, he established the town of New Orleans, making it the capital of Louisiana in 1721. He resigned his office in 1743 and returned to France, where he died.

Bienville, Pierre Céleron de (Pierre Céleron de Blainville) (1693–1759) *soldier*

Born in Montreal, Bienville commanded several fur trade posts. In 1749, because of increasing English influence in the Ohio Valley, he was assigned to tour the area and take possession of it for France. He buried lead plates stating France's claim at the mouth of tributaries along the Ohio, but he did not successfully convince many Indian groups to renounce trade with the English. He spent the remainder of his life in New France. His journal of the Ohio Valley mission was later published in Paris.

Bigot, François (1703–ca. 1777) *last intendant of New France*

Born in France, Bigot was trained as a lawyer before entering the civil service. He was appointed commissary of Louisbourg in 1739; its fall to the English in 1744 is believed to be partially due to his financial malfeasance, which left the fort ill-supplied. In 1748, officials sent him back to New France as the intendant, a powerful office. His astoundingly widespread profiteering and corruption weakened the colony economically and contributed significantly to its conquest by Britain in 1759. Bigot was returned to France and imprisoned in the Bastille before being banished from the kingdom. His place of death is not known, although he probably remained in Europe.

Billouart, Louis See KERLÉREC.

Blair, James (1655–1743) *first president of the College of William and Mary*

Blair, an Anglican clergyman, arrived in Virginia in 1685 and married into a well-connected family. At the center of many political intrigues during his lifetime, he nonetheless proposed and worked tirelessly to establish a college in the colony. After William and Mary was chartered in 1693, he held the office of president until his death 50 years later. He also served as acting governor in 1740–41.

Boone, Daniel (1734–1820) *legendary colonial frontiersman, Kentucky pioneer*

Born in Pennsylvania, Boone moved with his family to the North Carolina back country in 1750. A hunter and trapper by trade, he often worked in modern Kentucky, one of the first colonists to explore that area. While in the employ of the Transylvania Company, he blazed a trail through the Cumberland Gap later known as the Wilderness Road and led settlers to the region in 1775. He founded Boonesborough in the same year. During the Revolutionary War, he became a hero for fighting western Indians allied with the British. Captured by Indians in 1778 and taken to Detroit, he escaped, returned to Kentucky territory, and defended Boonesborough when it was besieged. Despite his services to Kentucky and the country, his land claims were declared invalid. He moved to Missouri (which was under Spanish control), where he obtained a land grant in 1799. Boone never achieved wealth. For the last 20 years of his life, he continued his work as a hunter and trapper in Missouri, amid a large extended family. In 1784, his "autobiography" was put in literary form by John Filson. *Discovery, Settlement, and Present State of Kentucky* subsequently brought Boone national fame.

Braddock, Edward (1695–1755) *commander of British forces in America*
Braddock, a Scot with long service as a military officer, was sent to America as the French and Indian War loomed. He organized an expedition from Virginia to Fort Duquesne (modern Pittsburgh); en route, his troops arduously hacked a road through the wilderness from Cumberland, Maryland, across the Allegheny Mountains. Braddock insisted that his troops follow traditional European military tactics. At the Battle of the Wilderness (July 13, 1755), they were badly routed by a much smaller group of French and Indians using the tactics of wilderness warfare. Braddock was killed in battle and his aide, Lieutenant Colonel George Washington, commanded the retreat. The soldiers buried Braddock in the roadway, then marched over his grave to disguise it from the enemy. The road they had cut from Maryland was later used by settlers traveling to the Ohio Valley and was known as Braddock's Road.

Bradford, William (1590–1657) *leader of the Pilgrims, governor of Plymouth Colony*
Born in England, Bradford helped organize and lead a group of Separatists, or radical dissenters from the Church of England, who became known as the Pilgrims. The group emigrated first to Holland, then to Massachusetts aboard the *Mayflower* in 1620. Before disembarking, Bradford helped write the Mayflower Compact, a voluntary agreement to form a government. Bradford was elected governor 30 times between 1621 and 1656. He was a practical and skilled leader who welcomed nonconformists of varying beliefs, managed Indian relations reasonably well, and managed to keep Plymouth

autonomous from the much larger Massachusetts Bay Colony. He was a member of the Undertakers, the group that assumed the colony's debt to free it from London investors. His history *"Of Plimouth Plantation,"* first published in 1856, gave the name *pilgrims* to the Plymouth Separatists and is an indispensable source of information about early Massachusetts.

Bradford, William (1663–1752) *founder of a family of prominent colonial printers*
Bradford was the first printer in Pennsylvania. In 1693 he became New York colony's official printer and in 1725 started New York's first newspaper, the weekly *New-York Gazette*.

Bradstreet, Anne Dudley (ca. 1612–1672) *colonial author, first American to publish a book of poems*
Born in England, Bradstreet arrived in Massachusetts in 1630 as part of the Great Migration. A brother-in-law had her poems published in England in 1650 as *The Tenth Muse Lately Sprung Up in America;* additional work was published posthumously. Although her poetry shows she knew classical models for literature, some of her best works deal with her family and everyday life. Bradstreet, who often suffered from ill health, was the mother of eight children. She held a prominent place in her community; both her father Thomas Dudley and her husband Simon Bradstreet served as colonial governors of Massachusetts.

Brent, Margaret (ca. 1600–1671) *first American woman to demand a vote*
Born in England, Brent emigrated to Maryland in 1638 with her adult brothers and sister. Because she also transported many servants, she claimed a large land grant and became the first female landowner in the colony. Her remarkable business and legal sense and her personal friendship with Lord Baltimore eventually made her one of the largest landholders of the colony. During the 1644 dispute over jurisdiction of Kent Island she personally raised a group of armed militiamen to defend his interests and later negotiated a settlement with colony soldiers over back pay. In 1647, when Governor Leonard Calvert died, she was appointed executor of his estate. The following year she requested two votes in the assembly, one for herself as a landowner and another as Calvert's representative. They were denied, and Lord Baltimore himself expressed his displeasure at her

actions. Brent later moved to Virginia, where she spent the remainder of her life.

Byrd, William II (1674–1744) *planter, writer in colonial Virginia*

Born in Virginia, Byrd was sent to England to be educated. Upon his father's death in 1704, he inherited the large estate and fortune the elder William Byrd (1652–1704) had amassed as a frontier planter and Indian trader. William Byrd II was a lawyer who served the colony in several official capacities, including council president. Dubbed "the Great American Gentleman" by one scholar, he indulged in science as a hobby and amassed the largest private library in the colonies at Westover, his plantation. His urbane writings provide much information on the social history of his day. His "secret" diary, written in shorthand code, was not discovered and translated until the 1940s; it is the most extensive known journal of the era by a southerner.

Cabeza de Vaca, Álvar Núñez (1490–1557) *Spanish explorer, soldier*

Cabeza de Vaca, born in Castile, joined the 1527 expedition of Pánfilo de Narváez to Florida. After that expedition met with disaster, he was one of four survivors who reached Mexico after wandering through the American Southwest for eight years. His famous *Relation* was published in 1542; some of the tales he repeated inspired continuing Spanish belief in the existence of fabulously rich civilizations somewhere north of Mexico. He later served as an official and explorer in Central and South America, but he returned to Spain under accusations of malfeasance.

Cabot, John (Giovanni Caboto) (1450–1499) *navigator, explorer*

Born Giovanni Caboto in Italy, John Cabot moved to England and sailed to the New World for King Henry VII in 1497. His landfall was possibly at Newfoundland. On his second voyage, begun in 1498, he was lost at sea. Cabot's voyages and discoveries were later used as the basis for the English claim to North America. His son Sebastian Cabot (ca. 1483–1557) carried on his explorations.

Cadillac, sieur de (Antoine de la Mothe) (1656–1730) *French colonial official, founder of Detroit*

Cadillac arrived in Canada in 1683. While military commander of Michilimackinac, an important fur-trading post, he received a grant of land in modern Michigan. In 1701, he established a colony at Detroit, serving as its governor for a decade. He served as governor of Louisiana from 1713 to 1717, after which he returned to France.

Calvert, Benedict Leonard (unknown–1715) *fourth baron Baltimore*

Benedict Calvert, who spent his entire life in England, converted from Catholicism to Anglicanism to assure the restoration of full proprietary rights in Maryland. The rights were confirmed a month before his death in April 1715. He was succeeded by his son Charles.

Calvert, Cecilius (Cecil Calvert) (1605–1675) *second baron Baltimore, founder of Maryland*

Cecilius (or Cecil), the official recipient of the Maryland grant on the death of his father George, developed policies and organized the colonizing expeditions to Maryland in 1633. He himself never visited the colony, entrusting its governance to his younger brother Leonard.

Calvert, Charles (1637–1715) *third baron Baltimore, governor and proprietor of Maryland*

Born in England, Charles became the governor of Maryland in 1661; he became proprietor as well after the death of his father Cecilius in 1675. Charles returned to England after the Coode Rebellion of 1688–89 and was deprived of proprietary rights of governance, largely because of his status as a Catholic. His son Benedict Leonard converted to Anglicanism, and his grandson Charles assumed full proprietary rights in 1715.

Calvert, Charles (1699–1751) *fifth baron Baltimore*

Born in England, Charles was confirmed an Anglican. At the age of 16, he became Lord Baltimore and proprietor of Maryland upon the death of his father Benedict Leonard.

Calvert, George (1579–1632) *first baron Baltimore, English statesman, colonizer*

A well-connected Oxford graduate, member of Parliament, and secretary of state, George Calvert resigned his posts when he converted to Catholicism in 1625. To reward him for his many services, however, King James elevated him to Baron of Baltimore and gave him large Irish land grants. In 1623, Calvert received a grant to found a colony in Newfoundland, but it was unsuccessful; he and his family visited it in 1628, and then migrated to Virginia in 1629, but officials there feared their religious affiliation. In 1632, George received a grant for Maryland territory to found a colony where Catholics might worship freely, but he died before the grant became official. His son Cecilius founded the colony he had planned.

Calvert, Leonard   (1606–1647) *first governor of Maryland*

Leonard was the son of George and younger brother of Cecelius, the first and second barons Baltimore. He served as governor from 1634 to 1644 and 1646 to 1647. During his terms, he summoned the first assembly and later granted it the power to initiate legislation. In 1638, he captured Kent Island from Virginian William Claiborne, who joined with Maryland Protestants in a rebellion against the governor in 1644. Leonard fled to Virginia but returned in 1646 with armed troops and regained control of the colony, where he died shortly thereafter.

Carleton, Sir Guy   (1724–1808) *governor of British Canada*

Born in Ireland, Carleton was a military officer who accompanied General James Wolfe's forces to Quebec. During his service as governor (1768–78), he encouraged the policy of conciliation with the French Canadian civil and religious elite, although he postponed the establishment of representative government. His advice strongly influenced Britain's Quebec Act of 1774, which extended Quebec's control into the Ohio Valley and angered the American colonists. Carleton returned to North America in 1782 as the British military commander to oversee the evacuation of British forces from New York. He served again as governor from 1786 to 1796, after which he retired permanently to England.

Carteret, Philip   (1639–1682) *first governor of colonial New Jersey*

Philip was born on the Isle of Jersey in England's Channel Islands, home of the Carteret family. His father Sir George was a proprietor of both Carolina and New Jersey. He served as governor of New Jersey from 1664 to 1682, when he resigned in a dispute with both New York and his colonists.

Cartier, Jacques   (1491–1557) *explorer who claimed modern Canada for France*

Cartier explored the Gulf and the River St. Lawrence on two voyages in 1534 and 1535–36. On the second trip, he reached the site of modern Montreal and wintered at the site of Quebec, during which his men suffered terribly. On a third voyage in 1541–42, he again wintered near Quebec, developing bad relations with the Indians. In the spring he returned to France, abandoning the newly arrived colonists whom he had been commissioned to accompany. He most likely remained in France for the rest of his life. France based its claims to North America on Cartier's explorations. His writings helped popularize the idea of North American exploration, settlement, and missionary work.

Champlain, Samuel de   (ca. 1567–1635) *French explorer who founded Quebec*

Champlain was an explorer and mapmaker for France who held the title of Royal Geographer. During his lifetime, he explored the Great Lakes and northern New York areas as well as the northeastern seaboard. After several exploratory voyages he accompanied the Sieur de Monts' attempt to found Port Royal in 1604. In 1608, Champlain arrived with 27 men to build the Habitation at Quebec, later serving as its governor. He allied himself with the Huron and other Algonquian Indians and joined them to fight the Iroquois in 1609, using European firearms. Champlain's devotion to the fortunes of his colony through almost three decades earned him the title Father of New France. When Quebec (the first permanent French settlement in New France) was captured by the British in 1629, he went back to France but returned to rebuild Quebec in 1734; he was buried there on his death a year later. He left several volumes of writings as well as maps and drawings.

Charles I   (1600–1649) *king of England (reigned 1625–49)*

The son of James I, Charles continued his father's assertion of the divine right and absolute authority of kings, in addition to encouraging Archbishop William Laud's campaigns to suppress religious nonconformists. During Charles's reign, the Great Migration of Puritans to America occurred. From 1629 to 1640, he refused to convene Parliament, precipitating events that led to the English Civil Wars. The royalist supporters of the king were defeated by the Parliamentarians under the leadership of Oliver Cromwell. Charles was tried and beheaded in 1649, beginning the Commonwealth period during which England had no king.

Charles II (1630–1685) *king of England (reigned 1660–85)*

Son of Charles I, Charles II fled England when his father was deposed. He regained the throne in 1660, however, and promised religious tolerance. This event ushered in the historical period called the Restoration, noted for the return of lavish display as well as low moral and ethical standards. Charles left no legitimate heir. He was succeeded by his brother, the duke of York (James II), to whom he had previously made a large North American grant.

Charles II (Carlos) (1661–1700) *king of Spain (reigned 1665–1700)*

Until Charles II came of age, Spain was controlled by a regency. During the remainder of his ineffective reign, Charles earned the sobriquet "Carlos el Hechizado" (Charles the Mad), and Spain's international power declined significantly. Charles left no heirs and was the last of the Habsburg dynasty. He appointed Philip of Anjou, a Bourbon and the grandson of Louis XIV of France, to succeed him. The appointment precipitated the War of Spanish Succession.

Charles III (Don Carlos) (1716–1788) *king of Spain (reigned 1759–88)*

Charles, son of Philip V, succeeded his half-brother Ferdinand VI on the throne of Spain in 1759, after having ruled as the duke of Parma and king of Naples (by right of his mother, Isabella of Parma) for 25 years. Charles undertook extensive reforms both domestically and within the Spanish Empire in America to reestablish Spain as an international power. He appointed men of high competence to official positions and applied modern, Enlightenment principles to the management of government. To increase the control of the Spanish state over its national Catholic Church, he expelled the Jesuits from Spain and its empire in 1767 and limited the power of the Inquisition. He secretly provided aid to the American revolutionaries after 1776, although he never officially recognized the new nation. He gradually did away with many restrictions on trade. He proved a highly competent ruler, effecting an economic and cultural revival by the end of his reign.

Charles IX (1550–1574) *king of France (reigned 1560–74)*

Charles IX succeeded to the throne at the age of 10; his mother Catherine de' Medici acted as regent until he came of age. Charles's reign was marked by the fierce French civil and religious wars between Catholics and Huguenots (French Protestants). During his regency, the crown permitted and sponsored several attempts to establish French Huguenot colonies in the New World, including one at Fort Caroline in Florida in 1564. Under his mother's influence, Charles ordered the St. Bartholomew's Day Massacre of 1572, in which thousands of Huguenots, including Admiral Gaspard de Coligny, were slain.

Chouteau, René Auguste (1749–1829) *trader, colonizer*

Born in New Orleans, Chouteau accompanied Pierre Laclède to found St. Louis while still a teenager. He remained in the new settlement, becoming one of its leading citizens. Both before and after the purchase of Louisiana by the United States in 1804, he served in many official capacities, including judge, militia commander, Indian agent, and chairman of the town's board of directors.

Claiborne, William (ca. 1587–1677) *political figure in early Virginia and Maryland*

Claiborne was born in England and settled in Virginia in 1621. He established a trading post on Kent Island, which he claimed for Virginia. He later waged a battle with Maryland for jurisdiction of the island, and in 1652 he was instrumental in driving the Calverts temporarily out of their colony. Claiborne helped rule Maryland from 1652 to 1657.

Colbert, Jean-Baptiste (1619–1683) *powerful French statesman under King Louis XIV*

Colbert, a proponent of mercantilism, controlled or influenced almost all aspects of French government after 1661, including colonial policy. He had a direct role in converting New France from a proprietary to a royal colony. Officially, he held the titles controller of finance and secretary of state for the navy. Under his influence, France became the dominant power in Europe.

Colden, Jane (1724–1766) *botanist*

Born in New York, Jane was the daughter of Cadwallader Colden, a scientist and governor of New York

(1761–76). Educated by her father as a botanist, by 1757 she had catalogued more than 300 native North American plants, using the Linnaean system. She corresponded with European scientists and discovered and named the gardenia. In 1759, she married Dr. William Farquhar; the remaining years of her life were spent in domestic duties. Her work on plant classification was published posthumously in 1770.

Contrecoeur, sieur de (Claude Pierre Pécaudy) (1706–1775) *soldier*

Born in New France, Contrecoeur was the commanding officer at Fort Duquesne during the French and Indian War until it fell to the British. He died in Montreal.

Coronado, Francisco Vásquez de (1510–1554) *Spanish conquistador, explorer*

Born in Spain, Coronado arrived in New Spain in 1535 with Antonio de Mendoza, viceroy of Mexico, and assumed several offices there. In 1540–41, he led an expedition throughout the American Southwest as far east as Kansas establishing Spain's claim to the area. He was tried and fined for mismanagement of the expedition. He died in Mexico.

Cortés, Hernán (Hernán Cortéz) (1485–1547) *Spanish conquistador*

Born in Spain, Cortés participated in the 1511 conquest of Cuba. In 1518, he led an expedition to the mainland, conquering the Aztec Empire of Mexico for Spain. In 1528, he became captain-general of New Spain. He later returned to Seville, where he died.

Cotton, Reverend John (1584–1652) *Puritan clergyman*

A graduate of Cambridge, Cotton became one of the most prominent spiritual and intellectual leaders of early Massachusetts Bay Colony. In 1633, he emigrated from England to Massachusetts, where he became the influential minister of the First Church of Boston. He upheld Puritan orthodoxy and theocracy, helping to banish Roger Williams and bring Anne Hutchinson to trial for heresy. Cotton published many religious writings. His daughter married Increase Mather; his grandson was Cotton Mather.

Croghan, George (ca. 1720–1782) *Indian negotiator, Indian agent*

Born in Ireland, Croghan emigrated in 1741 to Carlisle, Pennsylvania on the edge of the western frontier. He slowly built an Indian trade network throughout the Ohio Valley, learning many Indian languages as he did so. He was appointed Indian agent for Pennsylvania in the late 1740s, negotiating many treaties and slowly winning Indian allegiance from the French. After the start of the French and Indian War, his trading network in the Valley was seriously disrupted. In 1756, he was appointed deputy superintendent of Indian affairs for the northern district, serving until 1772. He played an important role in negotiations settling Pontiac's War. He assisted the Patriots during the Revolution but died with few financial resources.

Cromwell, Oliver (1599–1658) *leading figure in England's Puritan Revolution and its Commonwealth period of 1649–60*

Cromwell was a member of Parliament and leader of the opposition to King Charles I. He led forces that won several important military victories in the English Civil Wars of 1642–51. From 1653 to 1659, he exercised extensive powers as Lord Protector of England. Offered the throne in 1657, he refused. Upon his death in 1658, he was succeeded by his far less competent son Richard for a brief period before Charles II was restored to the throne.

Culpeper, John (fl. 1675–85) *leader of Culpeper's Rebellion*

A South Carolina settler who move to North Carolina, Culpeper led the 1677 revolt in protest of enforcement of duties on tobacco, which colonists were accustomed to exporting illegally. After the revolt succeeded, he was elected governor, serving until 1783. He was later tried for treason in England but pardoned by the intervention of the Carolina proprietors.

Culpeper, Lord Thomas (1635–1689) *colonial governor of Virginia*

In 1673, Culpeper received a large proprietary grant of lands in Virginia from King Charles II. In 1675, he was appointed governor "for life" to replace Berkeley, but he was nonetheless removed by British officials in 1684. He appointed deputies to administer the colony on orders of the Crown and spent only short periods there in 1680 and 1683. He pardoned participants in Bacon's Rebellion but hanged some planters who destroyed tobacco crops in the 1680s and also dissolved the assembly.

Dartmouth, Lord (William Legge) (1731–1801)
British statesman in the pre-Revolutionary years
Born in London, Dartmouth was the stepbrother of Lord North. He served as British secretary of state for the colonies (1772–75) at first attempting conciliation but later trying to strictly enforce Parliamentary authority. He resigned his secretariat position because he did not want to wage war against the colonists, although he retained other official positions in Britain. Dartmouth, a devout Anglican, served as president of an English group who supported an Indian school founded by Connecticut minister Eleazar Wheelock. In 1769, when the school was moved to New Hampshire and chartered as a college, it was named Dartmouth in his honor.

Dickinson, John (1732–1808) *Pennsylvania statesman, writer*
Born in Maryland, Dickinson became a prominent member of the Philadelphia bar. His *Letters from a Farmer in Pennsylvania* (1767–68), widely read and very influential, protested the Townsend Acts and argued in favor of colonial union. Dickinson was a representative to the first and second Continental Congresses. However, he opposed declaring independence. He abstained from the final vote by absenting himself from the meeting, which enabled Pennsylvania delegates to support independence unanimously. He was later a delegate to the Constitutional Convention (1787) and wrote another series of letters that helped secure the new constitution's approval.

Dinwiddie, Robert (1693–1770) *colonial governor of Virginia*
Born in Scotland, Dinwiddie entered colonial service and served as southern surveyor-general before being appointed governor in Virginia. He was also a major investor in the Ohio Land Company of Virginia. In 1753 he sent George Washington to the Ohio Valley to investigate French advances in the territory, which led to the French and Indian War. In 1758, he returned to England at his own request and retired.

Dongan, Thomas (1634–1715) *colonial governor of New York*
Born to a royalist family in Ireland, Dongan joined an Irish regiment of the French army after the establishment of the English Commonwealth. He was recalled to England's colonial service in 1677. He served as New York's governor from 1682 to 1688, becoming the first Catholic to hold a major office in the English colonies outside of Maryland. While governor, he called New York's first representative assembly and allied with the Iroquois confederacy against the French. He returned to England in 1691 and succeeded his older brother as earl of Limerick in 1698.

Dragging Canoe (ca. 1730–1792) *Cherokee chief*
Leader of the Cherokee Chickamunga band, Dragging Canoe helped negotiate the Treaty of Sycamore Shoals, selling land in eastern Kentucky to the Transylvania Company. He reputedly told negotiators that the remaining land in modern Kentucky and Tennessee would be "dark and bloody ground," a phrase which stuck to the area. The Cherokee supported the British during the Revolution. After 1776, Dragging Canoe led forces against settlers on the trans-Appalachian North Carolina frontier, setting off raids by other southern tribes throughout the south. Whites retaliated with severity and broke Cherokee power in 1777.

Drake, Sir Francis (1543–1596) *English pirate, privateer, explorer*
A member of John Hawkins's originating slave-trading expedition for the English in 1567, Drake soon led English efforts to break into the Spanish monopoly on the slave trade. In the 1560s and 1570s, he conducted violent and lucrative raids against Spanish ports and ships in the Carribean. In 1577–80, he circumnavigated the globe, the second person to do so. He resumed raids in New Spain in the 1580s, which contributed to King Philip II's decision to launch the Spanish Armada against England. Drake helped command the English maritime defeat of the Armada. He died of dysentery while in the Gulf of Mexico.

Dudley, Joseph (1647–1720) *colonial governor in Massachusetts*
Dudley served as governor of Massachusetts and allied smaller colonies until relieved by Governor Andros in 1696. Dudley served on Andros's council and as a superior court judge but was instrumental in the governor's overthrow in 1689. He was tried in England for his role but returned to Massachusetts as governor from 1702 to 1715, during which time he became extremely unpopular among the colonists. He also served the New York colony as head of the council.

Dulany, Daniel (1722–1797) *colonial lawyer, writer*
Born in Annapolis, Dulany was a lawyer and prominent politician. His *Considerations upon the Propriety of Imposing Taxes in the British Colonies,* which became a best selling pamphlet, clearly explained the concept of "taxation without representation." During the Revolution, Dulany remained a Loyalist and had little further influence.

Dunmore, Earl of (John Murray) (1732–1809) *royal colonial governor*
Born to an aristocratic family in Scotland, Lord Dunmore served as the governor of New York (1770) and Virginia (1771–1775). In 1774, he waged "Lord Dunmore's War," taking possession of Fort Pitt, establishing an organizational plan for the upper Ohio Valley, and defeating nearby Indian tribes who threatened English settlement. As the Revolution approached, his harsh actions helped to arouse the Patriots' support in Virginia. He dissolved the assembly three times for its activities, and in 1775 he confiscated the ammunition stored at Williamsburg. Forced for safety's sake to live and govern from an anchored warship, in November 1775 he offered freedom to slaves and indentured servants who would join his militia (close to 1,000 did). He declared martial law in Virginia and bombarded Norfolk in January 1776, setting the town on fire. His troops were defeated, however, and he was forced to return to England. He later served as governor of Bermuda; he died in England.

Dunster, Henry (1609–1659) *first president of Harvard University*
Born in England, Dunster attended Cambridge and arrived in Massachusetts in 1640 to be installed as Harvard's first official president. The school, open for only one year, was in disarray. Dunster revived and reestablished it on a sound academic and financial basis. His decision to become a Baptist in 1653 scandalized the Congregationalists who controlled the school, and he was removed from the presidency and publically admonished. He remained in Massachusetts, preaching until his death.

Duston, Hannah (Hannah Dustin, Hannah Durston) (1657–ca. 1736) *colonial heroine of Indian wars*
Born in Haverhill, Massachusetts, Duston, a farmer's wife, was taken captive by Indians in 1697. Her six-day old child was murdered before her eyes. She, another white woman, and a young boy were marched over 100 miles to central New Hampshire, where she was to reside with her Indian master's family. However, she and her companions killed and scalped 10 of their Indian captors (including six children) with a hatchet, enabling them to escape. The Massachusetts General Court granted her a bounty for the scalps. She raised nine other children to maturity.

Duquesne Michel Ange (marquis de Menneville) (1701–1778) *governor of New France (1752–55)*
Duquesne ordered French forces to occupy the Ohio Valley in 1753, helping to ignite the French and Indian War. He returned permanently to France in 1755.

Edwards, Jonathan (1703–1758) *clergyman, theologian*
Born in Connecticut, Edwards graduated from Yale. His preaching, which drew on the emotions as well as reason, led to a revival in his Northampton church in the 1730s that presaged the Great Awakening of the 1740s. He later became a missionary to the Indians and, in 1757, president of the College of New Jersey (later Princeton University), although he died of smallpox shortly thereafter. The best theologian of the mid-18th century evangelical revival, Edwards authored many sermons and treatises, some of which are still considered contributions to theology.

Eliot, Reverend John (1604–1690) *Puritan clergyman and missionary to Indians*
Eliot arrived in Roxbury from England in 1631, serving its church for close to 60 years. In 1646, he begin work among the Indians, and in 1651 he founded the first "Praying Town" at Natick, where Indians were gathered to live in the kind of community Puritans believed to be necessary to their religious faith. Eliot learned many Indian languages. He wrote a catechism in Algonquian; in 1654, he published a partial translation of the Bible which was completed in 1663. The "Indian Bible" was the first Bible of any kind printed in North America.

Elizabeth I (1533–1603) *queen of England (reigned 1558–1603)*
The daughter of Henry VIII, Elizabeth I was the last of the Tudor monarchs. She defended Protestantism and was forced to execute her Catholic half-sister Mary, queen of

Scots, to secure her own throne. Elizabeth's reign was relatively peaceful. English prosperity in commerce and industry were combined with unparalleled literary and artistic production, including the works of William Shakespeare. During her reign, English exploration and colonization in North America began. In 1578, she issued the first English colonial charter to Sir Humphrey Gilbert to found a colony in modern Canada.

Estéban (Estevanico) (ca. 1500–1539) *African-Spanish explorer*
Estéban, a slave from Morocco, joined his Spanish master on the ill-fated 1527 expedition of Pánfilo de Narváez to Florida. He was one of four survivors who reached Mexico after wandering through the American Southwest for eight years. In 1539, he reentered the American Southwest as a guide to an expedition, but he was killed by Pueblo Indians.

Fletcher, Benjamin (1640–1703) *colonial governor*
A military officer, Fletcher was appointed governor of New York (1692–97) and Pennsylvania (1692) to prepare and organize the colonies for King William's War. He used the offices to enrich himself, even consorting with pirates, and was removed in 1697 under arrest for corruption.

Forbes, John (1710–1759) *British general*
Born in Scotland, Forbes was called from his posting at Halifax in 1758 to lead the second advance against Fort Duquesne (modern Pittsburgh) in the French and Indian War. He chose not to use Braddock's Road but had his troops cut a new path west from Carlisle, Pennsylvania. His mission was successful; the French evacuated and burned Duquesne, and Forbes built Fort Pitt on the site. Like Braddock's Road, Forbes's Road was used after the war by settlers traveling to the Ohio Valley.

Francis I (1494–1547) *king of France (reigned 1515–47)*
Anxious to defy Spain's claim to sovereignty of the entire New World, Francis I probably commissioned the voyage of Giovanni de Verrazano in 1524, which established a French claim to North America. In 1533, Francis persuaded Pope Clement VII that the papal bull *Inter Caetera* gave Spain a claim only to territory explored prior to 1493. A year later, he began commissioning Cartier's voyages of exploration for France. He also commissioned Jean-François Roberval's unsuccessful attempt to establish a colony in modern Canada in 1541–42. Francis was sympathetic to Protestantism, which appeared in France in the 1520s. Subsequent religious persecution began under his son and successor, Henry II.

Franklin, Anne Smith (1696–1763) *printer*
Born in Boston, Anne married James Franklin, a printer, in 1723 as his brother Benjamin ended his term as an apprentice. The couple moved their printing business to Newport in 1727. When James died at age 38, Anne took over and ran the business for 13 years, training her daughters Elizabeth (called Sarah) and Mary to set type. In 1736, she became the official colony printer. After her son James came of age, he assumed the business, but Anne probably continued to share the work. In 1762, James died, and Anne again ran the business and the newspaper he had founded until her death the following year. She was the second woman to own a printing business in the English colonies and the first who actually continued the business on her own for an extended time.

Franklin, Benjamin (1706–1790) *colonial writer, moral and political philosopher, scientist, inventor, official, statesman*
Born in Boston, to a Puritan family of modest means, Franklin was apprenticed as a printer at the age of 12. He educated himself by lifelong omnivorous reading. He arrived in Philadelphia in 1723 and purchased the *Pennsylvania Gazette* in 1729. He enjoyed great success with *Poor Richard's Almanack,* a compendium of historical, scientific, and agricultural information whose shrewd, pithy proverbs became famous. Franklin organized the first circulating library, the American Philosophical Association, and an early fire company. He invented a famous and widely manufactured stove and conducted scientific experiments, especially in electricity, which earned him election to the British Royal Society and an honorary doctorate from the University of Edinburgh, after which he was often called Dr. Franklin. He had an international reputation and corresponded many others interested in the new sciences. Franklin was instrumental in organizing a colonial postal service, serving as postmaster for many years before as well as after the colonies became independent. He was also instrumental in founding an academy in Philadelphia which offered a more practical curriculum than

Latin and Greek literature; it became the University of Pennsylvania. In 1751, he was first elected to the Pennsylvania Assembly. He served as a representative to the Albany Congress, where he presented a plan for colonial union. (It was passed by the congress but rejected by the individual colonies.) He served as a long-time colonial agent in England, appearing before the House of Commons to explain American protests of the Stamp Act. His fondness for England ended as the Revolution approached, at which time he was undoubtedly the best known "American" in the world. He returned to the colonies in 1775, in time to serve as a representative to the Second Continental Congress and a member of the five-man committee that drafted the Declaration of Independence. After the Revolutionary War, he helped negotiate the peace treaty and served as a delegate to the Constitutional Convention at the age of 83. The plain style, common sense, optimism, and shrewd pragmatism of his writings have come to represent an important component of Americanism. Franklin's autobiography is considered one of the great nonfiction works of early American literature.

Frontenac, comte de (Louis de Baude) (1622–1698) *military leader, governor-general of New France*
Frontenac was appointed governor by Louis XIV, serving from 1672 to 1682 and again from 1689 to his death in 1698. Although his administrations were marked by continual quarreling with *intendants* and church officials, he was an exceptionally talented military commander and is the most prominent of New France's governors. Frontenac was also very successful at diplomacy with the Indians, who called him "Great Onontio," or patriarch. Personally involved in the fur trade, he supported its expansion; he also supported explorations like those of René-Robert Cavelier La Salle.

Gage, Thomas (1721–1787) *British military commander, royal governor*
After serving in the French and Indian War, Gage was governor of Montreal during the British military occupation. In 1763, he was appointed commander in chief of the British forces in North America, which were headquartered in New York, one of the most influential posts in the colonies. As colonial protests deepened in 1774, he was appointed royal governor of Massachusetts with the expectation that he could reenforce British authority. Although Gage performed most of his duties with competence, he underestimated the movement for independence. He constantly recommended authoritarian and usually inflammatory measures. He ordered the British march to Lexington and Concord that began the Revolutionary War, in execution of Lord North's order to seize ammunition and probably to arrest Sam Adams and John Hancock. After the Battle of Bunker Hill in June 1775, he was recalled to England.

Gálvez, José de (1720–1787) *visitador general (inspector) of New Spain*
Born in Spain, Gálvez was sent to New Spain by Charles III in 1765 to initiate reforms. In North America, Gálvez ordered the reorganization of defenses, the occupation of Alta California, and the administrative separation of the Provincias Internas (interior provinces, including the American Southwest) from the viceroyalty of Mexico. He returned to Spain in 1771 and later became head of the Council of the Indies, Spain's primary body for colonial oversight.

Garcés, Father Francisco (1738–1781) *Franciscan missionary, explorer*
Based at San Xavier del Bac, Garcés made four journeys throughout Arizona. In 1774, he joined Juan Bastista de Anza's overland expedition from Tubac to California. In 1776, he attempted to open a route back from Monterey to Arizona but was turned back by hostile Hopi. He was killed in the Yuma Uprising of 1781.

Gilbert, Sir Humphrey (1539–1583) *English soldier, explorer*
A tireless promoter of British colonization for many years, Gilbert obtained the first British charter to found a colony in North America; he sailed to Newfoundland and claimed it for the crown on August 3, 1583. His ship was lost on the return voyage to England later that month. Gilbert was Sir Walter Raleigh's half-brother.

George I (1660–1727) *king of England (reigned 1714–1727)*
George I, who succeeded Queen Anne, was the first monarch from the German House of Hanover; his mother was the granddaughter of James I. He spoke little English and evidenced little interest in governing Britain. As a result, the Whigs and Sir Robert Walpole, the chief minister, gained in power.

George II (1683–1760) *king of England (reigned 1727–1760)*
Son of George I, George II had little more interest in governing than his father, although Britain prospered during his reign. Sir Robert Walpole continued in power for the first half of George II's reign.

George III (1738–1820) *king of England (reigned 1760–1820)*
Grandson of George II, George III was thoroughly Anglicized. Beginning in 1765, he suffered intermittent bouts of insanity, now believed to be caused by a rare genetic disorder called porphyria. During his reign, Britain lost the American colonies as a result of the Revolutionary War.

Gorges, Sir Ferdinando (ca. 1568–1647) *English colonial promoter*
The youngest son of an aristocratic family, Gorges was a member of the Virginia Company of Plymouth and organized the 1607 expedition to Sagadahoc (modern Maine), one of the earliest English colonization attempts. Later a member of the Council of New England, in 1622 he and John Mason secured a patent to much of Maine; along with the Mason grant in New Hampshire, it caused years of controversy with settlers and with the government of Massachusetts. In 1677, his grandson finally released his Maine claim to Massachusetts.

Grenville, George (1712–1770) *British politician*
Grenville served as First Lord of the Treasury, or prime minister, following the Seven Years' War, from 1763 to 1765. He embarked on a plan to reduce the English national debt that eventually led to the American Revolution. He introduced the Sugar Act (1764) and Stamp Act (1765) but left office during the crisis that followed when he fell out of favor with King George III.

Hamilton, Andrew (ca. 1676–1741) *lawyer*
Born in Scotland, Hamilton arrived in Virginia before 1700 as an indentured servant. He was admitted to the bar and purchased a large land holding in Maryland, where he served in the assembly. After further legal studies in England, he settled in Philadelphia, where he became well known as a trial lawyer and served as the colony's attorney general, colonial agent, speaker of the house, and judge. He also donated the land on which the State House (later Independence Hall) was built. In 1734, he was engaged by the owners of the *New York Weekly Journal* to defend its publisher, John Peter Zenger, against charges of libel. Hamilton used an unorthodox defense and won the case. The decision was important in the establishment of freedom of the press in the colonies.

Hancock, John (1737–1793) *Revolutionary statesman, merchant*
Born in Massachusetts, Hancock attended Harvard. He inherited a large mercantile business in the 1760s, which he enlarged by smuggling, defying the English trade laws. He led merchants in protests of the Stamp Act and other British legislation, often working closely with Samuel Adams, and served in the Massachusetts General Court from 1769 to 1774. He was president of the Second Continental Congress and served as the first governor of the state of Massachusetts (1780–85 and 1787–93). Hancock was the first delegate to sign the Declaration of Independence; his extra-large writing gave rise to the American use of "John Hancock" as slang for *signature*.

Harvard, John (1607–1638) *benefactor of Harvard College*
Born in England, Harvard attended Cambridge and migrated to Massachusetts in 1637, serving as assistant minister at the First Church of Charleston. When he died a year later, he left £800 (half his estate) and his library to the new college at Cambridge, Massachusetts, a significant gift at the time and one which enabled its continuation. In 1639, the Massachusetts General Court named the college after him in gratitude.

Hébert, Louis (unknown–1627) *colonist called the First Farmer of New France*
Born in Paris, Hébert was apothecary to the king when he accompanied Samuel Champlain and De Monts to Port Royal in 1604. That colony was abandoned in 1607, but in 1617 Hébert and his family returned to Samuel de Champlain's Quebec, where he continued his skillful cultivation of herbs and crops. He received a land grant there in 1623. He and his family are honored as the first agricultural settlers of New France.

Henderson, Richard (1735–1785) *colonizer in Kentucky and Tennessee*
Born in Virginia, Henderson organized the Transylvania Company while an official in North Carolina. He

hired Daniel Boone as a scout and trailblazer for Kentucky land he purchased from the Cherokee via the Treaty of Sycamore Shoals in 1775. In 1779–80, he promoted the settlement of French Lick, Tennessee (modern Nashville).

Hennepin, Louis (ca. 1640–ca. 1701) *Franciscan missionary, explorer*

Born in Belgium, Hennepin accompanied René-Robert Cavelier La Salle to Canada in 1675 and explored the Great Lakes region. In 1680, they reached and established Fort Crèvecoeur (modern Peoria, Illinois). Hennepin continued to explore the upper Mississippi Valley. He was captured by Sioux (Dakota, Lakota, Nakota), with whom he reached and named the Falls of St. Anthony (site of modern Minneapolis). He was released in 1681 and returned to France in 1682, publishing the first description of the area and an account of his adventures a year later. In 1697, he revised it, falsely claiming to have reached the mouth of the Mississippi. His final years were probably spent in a monastery in Rome.

Henry, Patrick (1736–1799) *Revolutionary statesman, orator*

Henry was born on a frontier plantation in Virginia. His father was a Scots emigrant who served as a justice of the county court. He attended a local school and was then tutored by his father, who was well-educated in the classics. Henry failed at storekeeping and farming but quickly succeeded at study of the law; he was admitted to the bar in 1760. He led the Virginia radicals in the pre-Revolutionary years and with Thomas Jefferson and Richard Henry Lee established a committee of correspondence in the colony. As a Virginia burgess and representative to the Continental Congresses, he lent his brilliant and eloquent oratory to the colonial cause, gaining a wide reputation. However, at the First Continental Congress, he opposed seeking complete independence from Britain, a stance that limited his leadership as future events unfolded. Henry served as governor of Virginia (1776–79 and 1784–86) and took a prominent role in the state legislature (1780–84 and 1787–90). He declined to attend the Constitutional Convention, however, and opposed ratification of the document, apparently because he believed it gave too much power to the federal government. Later in his life, he came to support the Federalist position, running for the state legislature on their platform in 1799. He

won but died before taking his seat. Few original versions of Henry's speeches are known to exist; most have been preserved in writing by those who heard him, including his 1775 speech to the Second Virginia Convention which contains his famous phrase, "Give me liberty, or give me death!"

Henry II (1519–1559) *king of France (reigned 1547–1559)*

The son of Francis I, Henry II began the persecution of the Huguenots, who were led by Gaspard de Coligny, admiral of France. He married the strong-willed Catherine de Médici, and three of their children came to the throne: Francis II (1559–60), Charles IX (1560–74), and Henry III (1574–89).

Henry III (1551–1589) *king of France (reigned 1574–1589)*

The third son of Henry II and Catherine de' Medici, Henry led forces against the Huguenots and helped his mother plan the 1572 Saint Bartholomew's Day Massacre of leading Huguenots. He was assassinated in the course of the religious wars and succeeded by Henry of Navarre.

Henry IV (Henry of Navarre) (1553–1610) *king of France (reigned 1589–1610)*

Raised a Protestant, Henry of Navarre eventually assumed leadership of the Huguenots in the French Religious Wars of 1560–98. Upon ascending the French throne, however, he officially embraced Catholicism and ended the fighting. He remained privately sympathetic to Protestants and in 1598 issued the Edict of Nantes, which extended limited religious toleration to Huguenots. (The edict was revoked in 1685 by Louis XIV, spurring Huguenot immigration to America.)

Herrman, Augustine (ca. 1605–1686) *trader, cartographer*

Born in Prague, Bohemia, Hermann arrived in New Amsterdam as an employee of the Dutch West Indies Company in 1643. He developed an Indian trade and extensive tobacco export business. A member of Governor Willem Kieft's Twelve Men, the first representative advisory group in the colony's history, and Stuyvesant's similar Nine Men, he fell out of favor briefly for signing the remonstrance of the latter group. In 1660, Stuyvesant sent him to Maryland to negotiate the long-standing boundary dispute over Delaware territory. He so impressed the Calvert proprietors that they gave him Maryland citizenship and a large land grant in (later) Cecil County, where he built Bohemia Manor. Herrman published *Virginia and Maryland as it was Planted and Inhabited in this Present Year 1670,* a ten-year-long cartographical project considered one of the finest maps of the New World, which he undertook for the Calverts and which proved invaluable in helping them with numerous boundary disputes. His descendants gave Bohemia Manor to the Jesuits, who opened a school there in the 1740s.

Hooker, Reverend Thomas (1586–1647) *Puritan clergyman who helped found Connecticut*

Hooker emigrated from England to Cambridge with John Cotton in 1633. A powerful preacher, he disagreed with the leaders of Massachusetts Bay on many issues, and in 1636 he received permission to move with his congregation to the Connecticut Valley, where they founded Hartford. Hooker helped author the Fundamental Orders, Connecticut's first constitution.

Hudson, Henry (ca. 1550–ca. 1611) *explorer*

In 1609, Hudson sailed in the employ of the Dutch East India Company to search for the Northwest Passage. He explored the North Atlantic coast, the Delaware Bay, and the Hudson River as far as Albany. His activities established the basis of the Dutch claim to North America as well as a Dutch relationship with the Iroquois, whom he met and entertained. In 1610, Hudson sailed again, this time for the English, and was trapped in Hudson's Bay, Canada, by the onset of winter. His crew mutinied and set him, his son, and seven other men adrift in a small boat in 1611; they are presumed to have perished.

Hutchinson, Anne Marbury (1591–1643) *spiritual leader banished from Massachusetts Bay*

Hutchinson emigrated from England to Boston in 1634 with her 12 children; a 13th was born in 1636. She herself was a skilled midwife; her husband was a prosperous landowner and merchant. Originally a disciple of Reverend John Cotton, she led discussion groups in her home, where she preached that people were saved by their personal, inate awareness of divine grace rather than their upright behavior. Hutchinson's religious ideas challenged the authority of the male clergy. In 1637, she was tried for theological heresy and "traducing the ministers" in the colony's first major battle over orthodoxy. Hutchinson was banished and excommunicated. She migrated to Rhode Island with her followers, establishing Portsmouth on Aquidneck. There she became pregnant again, but when the badly deformed baby was stillborn, her Puritan adversaries interpreted the event as divine punishment. She later moved to Long Island, where she and five of her six youngest children were killed in an Indian attack. Hutchinson left no writings of her own; her ideas are known from the transcripts of her civil and church trials.

Hutchinson, Thomas (1711–1780) *loyalist, royal governor of Massachusetts*

Born in Boston, Hutchinson was the great-grandson of Anne Hutchinson's eldest son Edward. He attended Harvard and became a successful merchant before entering a long political career. He served in the Massachusetts assembly (1737–49), council (1749–66), chief justice of the superior court (1760–69), lieutenant governor (1758–57), and royal governor (1770–74). His support of British authority made him increasingly unpopular in the colony. In 1765, his home was destroyed by a mob protesting the Stamp Act, and his attempts to enforce the Tea Act led directly to the Boston Tea Party. After his letters advising the restriction of colonial rights were obtained by Benjamin Franklin and published, he was recalled. He left for England in 1774 and remained there until his death. Hutchinson is also noted for his three-volume *History of the Colony and Province of Massachusetts-Bay.*

Iberville, sieur d' (Pierre Le Moyne) (1661–1706) *French-Canadian naval officer, explorer*

Born in Quebec to a prominent fur-trading family, Iberville became a naval officer and led several successful attacks on England's Hudson's Bay posts in the 1680s and 1690s. In 1698–99, he led an expedition to the Gulf and Mississippi Delta, founding the first French settlements in lower Louisiana Territory. In 1700, he established Biloxi. With the outbreak of the War of the Spanish Succession, he took command of the French fleet in the West Indies; he left his younger brother Jean Baptiste Bienville to continue the colonization of Louisiana. Iberville died unexpectedly in Havana while on a naval assignment.

James I (1566–1625) *king of England (reigned 1603–25)*
James I, who ascended to the throne on the death of Queen Elizabeth, was the first Stuart king. He supported the Anglican church and establishment, beginning persecution of Separatists and Puritans as well as Catholics. In 1611, he oversaw the publication of the King James Version of the Bible. Under James the first permanent English colony at Jamestown was founded. He was succeeded by his son Charles I.

James II (1633–1701) *king of England (reigned 1685–1688)*
Son of Charles I and brother of Charles II, James was titled the duke of York and Albany. After his brother's restoration to the throne he became Lord High Admiral and received a huge land grant in North America. In 1664, he sent forces to seize New Netherland from the Dutch; it was renamed New York and integrated into the British colonial empire. After the death of his first wife in 1672, he publicly converted to Catholicism. On the death of Charles II in 1685, James became king. In 1688, his second wife gave birth to a son, raising the possibility of a Catholic succession to the throne of England. (James' first wife had borne only daughters.) This event precipitated the Glorious Revolution and the ascent of William and Mary. James subsequently fled to France. With the aid of King Louis XIV, he landed in Ireland in 1690 in an attempt to regain his throne, but his troops were defeated. He returned to France, where he remained until his death.

Jefferson, Thomas (1743–1826) *Revolutionary statesman, third president of the United States*
Born in Virginia, Jefferson attended William and Mary and was admitted to the bar, earning a reputation as a serious young man with a formidable command of legal scholarship. He served in the House of Burgesses and in 1774 wrote "A Summary View of the Rights of British America." It argued that the colonies were bound to the king only voluntarily and brought him immediate repute as an advocate of independence. He was soon appointed a delegate to the Second Continental Congress. Personally shy, he took little part in the debates but played a significant role as a drafter of written resolutions. In June 1776, he was appointed to head a committee to propose a Declaration of Independence. John Adams asked him to prepare a draft, which he did in a few days. The second and longest section of the document repeats old grievances against King George (and was significantly edited and shortened by other committee members). The opening two paragraphs, however, were not changed and have come to be regarded as America's original statement of political belief. He returned to Virginia, beginning a revision of the legal code and educational system and serving as governor (1779–81). In 1782, his wife died in childbirth, leaving him with two young daughters. After the war, he served as minister to France, secretary of state, and vice president under Adams. Jefferson continued to uphold the an antifederalist point of view. He, James Madison, and others formed a partylike opposition called the Democratic-Republicans, which opposed the centralization of power in the federal government and supported individual liberties. In 1800, he was elected president (1801–09) in a bitterly contested battle that was ultimately given to the House of Representatives to decide. While president, he arranged the Louisiana Purchase, prohibited the further importation of slaves, and supported exploration of the West, organizing the Lewis and Clark expedition. He retired to his plantation, Monticello, and helped design and found the University of Virginia in 1819. Both Jefferson and John Adams died on July 4, 1826—the 50th anniversary of the Declaration of Independence. Jefferson was deeply in debt when he died (several million dollars in today's terms), due primarily to his lavish lifestyle. His home, Monticello, and its furnishings were auctioned off by creditors. Today, Jefferson is considered one of America's most paradoxical geniuses. He was a powerful and eloquent proponent of liberty and equality and denounced slavery far more extensively than most Americans of his day. Yet he had large slave holdings throughout his life, believed blacks to be innately inferior to whites, and maintained a long-time liaison with an enslaved woman, Sally Hemings, with whom he probably had at least one child. At his death, he freed only five slaves, all of them Hemings's children.

Johnson, William (1715–1774) *Indian agent, negotiator*
Born in Ireland, Johnson emigrated to the Mohawk Valley of New York in 1738, eventually becoming one of the largest landholders and wealthiest settlers in the colony. The colorful Johnson's estate became the cen-

ter of Indian trade in the area, and his second and third wives were Mohawk women; one of them was Molly Brant, sister of Indian leader Joseph Brant. Johnson had great skill as an Indian diplomat and successfully kept the Iroquois loyal to the British, for which he was knighted. He serves as northern Indian superintendent from 1755 until his death in 1774.

Jumonville, sieur de (Joseph Coulon de Villiers) (1718–1754) *soldier*
Born in New France, Jumonville was an experienced Indian negotiator. In 1754, he was sent from Fort Duquesne to scout an approaching company of Virginians, led by Colonel George Washington. Washington and his men attacked and killed Jumonville and several of his men, an incident that led directly to the opening battle of the French and Indian War.

Kerlérec, chevalier de (Louis Billouart) (fl. 1753–1763) *governor of Louisiana*
Kerlérec first visited Louisiana with French troops after the 1729 Natchez massacre. He returned in 1763 as governor and was recalled in 1763, after Louisiana had been ceded to Spain. He oversaw the colony during the Seven Years' War, expending much energy in Indian diplomacy, and made arrangements to receive the first Acadians to arrive in Louisiana.

Kieft, Willem (1597–1647) *director-general of New Netherland*
Sent to North America in 1637, Kieft served until 1645. His governorship was marred by an ill-advised Indian policy that caused disastrous hostilities. In 1641, he established the Twelve Men, the first representative advisory council in the colony. He dissolved the group for disagreeing with his policies but reconvened Eight Men in 1643. Kieft died in a shipwreck in 1647, on his return voyage to the Netherlands.

Kino, Father Eusebio Francisco (1645–1711) *explorer, mapmaker, missionary*
Born in Italy and educated in Germany, Kino arrived in Mexico in 1665 as a Jesuit missionary. He explored the entire Southwest as far as the California coast, making about 40 separate expeditions. He established the first Catholic missions in modern Arizona and expended tremendous energy winning the loyalty of the Native Americans there.

Knight, Sarah Kemble (1666–1727) *teacher, businesswoman, diarist*
Born in Boston, Knight kept a dame school; according to an unsubstantiated tradition Benjamin Franklin was her pupil as a child. She assumed many of her father's and husband's business responsibilities upon the latter's death in 1706. In 1704, she made a difficult and dangerous horseback journey from her home in Boston through Connecticut to New York. She kept a vivid diary of the journey, published as *The Journal of Madame Knight*.

Laclède, Pierre Liguest (ca. 1724–1778) *founder of St. Louis*
Born in France, Laclède was commissioned by a New Orleans trading company to establish a trading post on the upper Mississippi. In late 1763, he selected the site of his planned settlement, which he named St. Louis. The settlement quickly prospered, but in 1778 Laclède died on a journey returning from New Orleans.

Lane, Ralph (1530–1603) *English military officer*
A courtier to Elizabeth I and a military officer in Ireland, Lane accompanied George Grenville on his 1585 Grenville expedition to Roanoke, North Carolina, and remained in charge of the group over the winter. Before the struggling garrison was rescued and returned to England in 1586 by Francis Drake, Lane had led the earliest English hostilities against Native Americans in North America. Lane returned to live in Ireland and resumed military service there.

Langlade, Charles de (1729–1801) *fur trader*
Langlade, who was born in Michilimackinac, was the son of a French nobleman and an Ottawa mother. He was educated by the Jesuits and also spent time living among the Ottawa. He earned great respect among the western Indians as a soldier-chief and led them in the French and Indian War. After the war, he settled in Green Bay with his father, where their trading post was the earliest colonial settlement. During the Revolution, he supported the British, providing assistance with the Indians.

La Peltrie, Madame Marie-Madelaine de (1603–1671) *founder of the first convent in Canada*
Born in France, Madame de la Peltrie felt called to a religious life but was forced to marry by her family. She

was widowed in 1625, and in 1639 she journeyed to New France, using her personal fortune to endow and help found an Ursuline convent and school for Indian and French girls in Quebec. In 1642, she joined the new Montreal colonists, helping to found and operate a hospital there despite continuing Iroquois attacks. In 1646, she herself joined the Ursuline order. She died in Quebec.

La Salle, sieur de (René-Robert Cavelier)
(1643–1687) *explorer who claimed the Mississippi Valley for France*

Born in France, La Salle was trained as a Jesuit but left the order. Arriving in Canada as a young man, he searched for the Northwest Passage and explored the Great Lakes and Ohio River Valley. In 1682, he and his assistant Henri de Tonti descended the Illinois River to the Mississippi and its mouth at the Gulf of Mexico. They claimed the entire area for France and named it Louisiana after King Louis XIV. La Salle and Tonti then retraced their route and established the first fur trading post on the Illinois River. Along with Governor Louis de Baude Frontenac, La Salle envisioned a vast commercial system throughout the Louisiana Territory, anchored by settlements. He returned to France to obtain support to found a colony. In 1686, his colonizing voyage, headed for the mouth of the Mississippi, landed on the coast of Texas in Spanish-claimed territory. A year later, in 1687, LaSalle was murdered by his own men. The remaining colonists in Texas were later discovered by the Spanish and taken to Mexico.

LaTour, Charles de Saint-Etienne de
(1593–1666) *French governor of Acadia*

LaTour accompanied his father on Jean de Biencourt de Poutrincourt's expedition to found Port Royal in 1604. On the death of Poutrincourt's son Pierre Céleron de Biencourt, LaTour assumed the land rights and remained in Acadia. He engaged in a long-term battle with Charles d'Aulney for control of the area. He remained in Acadia for the remainder of his life, even after it passed into English hands.

Laud, William (1573–1645) *archbishop of Canterbury (1633–1645)*

Laud, royal chaplain after 1611 and a close adviser to Charles I, was an uncompromising opponent of Puritans. He believed that the power of the state and the established church were inseparable. He was appointed bishop of London in 1629 and archbishop of Canterbury in 1633, but his influence exercised through less official channels was widespread long before those dates. He attempted to revive Anglicanism throughout England by enforcing the letter of religious law and insisted that dissenters conform to orthodoxy. In many cases he supported ruthless persecution and imprisonment. Many Puritans and other Separatists and some Catholics left England, many eventually emigrating to North America. In 1639, the so-called Bishop's Wars began in Scotland, provoked by his attempts to force Anglicanism on the largely Presbyterian Scots. By the time the English Civil Wars began, Laud had provoked extensive popular hatred. In 1644, he was tried by Parliament for high treason and beheaded in 1645.

Laudonnière, René (fl. 1562–1582) *colonizer*

Laudonnière accompanied Jean Ribaud on his 1562 voyage to North America, which failed to found a permanent French Huguenot colony. In 1564, Laudonnière headed a second attempt, founding Fort Caroline in Florida. When the colony was destroyed by the Spanish in 1565, he escaped and returned to France. His account of the events, *L'Histoire notable de la Floride,* was published posthumously in 1586.

Laval, Bishop (François-Xavier Montmorency Laval) (1623–1708) *first bishop of Quebec*

Born to a prominent aristocratic French family, Laval arrived in New France in 1659 to head the Catholic church in the colony. In 1674, he received the title Bishop of Quebec, which oversaw all French territories in America and reported directly to the pope. Until his official retirement in 1688, the domineering, quarrelsome, but personally upright Laval exercised great influence on the civil as well as spiritual life of the colony. He conducted a campaign to end the sale of liquor to the Indians and founded the Seminary of Quebec (later Laval University), where he died.

Law, John (1671–1729) *financier who helped develop Louisiana territory*

Born in Scotland, Law authored well-known works on money and banking before emigrating to France to attempt financial reforms. He founded a state bank and created a stock market boom. His promotion of French Louisiana created tremendous interest and huge investments. After the scheme collapsed, it was known as the Mississippi Bubble. Law fled France in 1720, dying bankrupt in Venice.

Lawrence, Charles (1709–1760) *British governor of Nova Scotia (1756–1760)*
Born in England, Lawrence ordered the deportation of all Acadians in 1755 while acting military governor. He became a general and governor and died in Nova Scotia.

Lawson, John (unknown–1711) *explorer, writer*
Lawson arrived in the Carolinas from Great Britain in the early 18th century, eventually serving as Carolina's Surveyor-General. His much-reprinted travel writings, *A History of Carolina,* (1709)—written mainly to encourage immigration—treated the Indians sympathetically and argued for better treatment of them. While surveying land for a Swiss settlement in the colony, he was captured, tried under tribal law (probably for his surveying of Indian lands to be encroached by white settlers), and executed by Tuscarora Indians.

Lee, Richard Henry (1732–1794) *Revolutionary statesman who introduced the resolution for independence*
Born in Virginia, Lee was sent to England to be educated. A burgess who worked with Jefferson and Henry to establish a Virginia committee of correspondence, Lee became a delegate to the Continental Congresses. On June 7, 1776, he introduced the Lee Resolution proposing independence. A signer of the Declaration of Independence, he later served as a senator from Virginia.

Leisler, Jacob (1640–1691) *leader of Leisler's Rebellion in New York*
A German emigrant, Leisler married into the Dutch colonial elite. In 1689, when the colonies received word of England's Glorious Revolution, he led an insurrection to seize control of the colony from the Anglo-Dutch merchant alliance, who were opposed by both the older Dutch elite and many small farmers. Leisler ruled the colony until 1691. In that year, a new English governor, Henry Sloughter, arrived accompanied by a regiment. He declared Leisler a traitor and hanged him. Leisler was pardoned posthumously by Parliament.

Le Moyne, Jean-Baptiste See BIENVILLE.

Le Moyne, Pierre See IBERVILLE.

Lescarbot, Marc (fl. 1570–1642) *lawyer, writer*
Born in France, Lescarbot spent 1606–07 at Jean de Biencourt de Poutrincourt's colony of Port Royal. He returned to France and published *Histoire de la nouvelle France* in 1609, which provided extensive information about the Port Royal venture.

Louis XIII (1601–1643) *king of France (reigned 1610–43)*
The son of Henry VI, Louis XIII ascended to the throne at the age of nine. At the age of 16, he exiled his mother, Marie de' Medici, to end her regency. For the remainder of his reign, he was strongly influenced by the powerful Cardinal Richelieu. Together, they increased royal power within France and the power of France against Spain in Europe. In 1627, Richelieu developed an interest in Champlain's Quebec colony and formed the Company of the 100 Associates to develop it. Although Quebec was forced to surrender to the English in 1629 while England was supporting Huguenot rebellions in France, the treaty of Saint-Germain-en-Laye (1631) returned France's North American settlements.

Louis XIV (1638–1715) *king of France (reigned 1643–1715)*
Louis XIV, who ascended the throne at the age of four, began his direct rule in 1661. Eventually he became known as the Sun King, ruling over one of France's most notable periods as the quintessential absolute monarch. He kept an extravagant court at his palace in Versailles, but chose ministers of great talent like Jean-Baptiste Colbert. He spent enormous sums to extend France's power in Europe through a series of wars between 1667 and 1697, then precipitated the War of the Spanish Succession (1701–14) to put his grandson on the throne of Spain. In 1663, Louis made New France a royal colony and provided generous financing, and New France entered a period of growth. In 1685, he revoked the Edict of Nantes and revived persecution of Protestants, spurring Huguenot immigration to America.

Louis XV (1710–1774) *king of France (reigned 1715–1774)*
The great-grandson of Louis XIV, Louis ascended to the throne at age five; until 1723, the duc d'Orléans was regent. Louis reigned over a period of declining French empire and disastrous wars. At the Treaty of Paris concluding the Seven Years' War in 1763, he agreed to cede

Canada to the English and Louisiana Territory west of the Mississippi, including New Orleans, to Spain. By his death, royal authority in France was in decline.

Maisonneuve, sieur de (Paul de Chomedy) (1612–1672) *founder of Montreal*

Born in France, Maisonneuve was a successful military officer before being appointed leader of a 1642 expedition of colonists, sponsored by the Société of Notre-Dame de Montréal. He served as governor of the colony for 22 years. He returned to France and died in obscurity.

Makemie, Reverend Francis (1658–1708) *founder of the Presbyterian church in America*

Born in Ireland, Makemie came to America in 1683 and spent the remainder of his life as a traveling preacher, primarily in Maryland and Virginia. In 1707, he was arrested in New York on orders of Governor Cornbury; the case became a cause célèbre, and Makemie's acquittal reinforced religious tolerance in the colony. Makemie never shied away from religious controversy and left many polemical writings.

Manteo (fl. late 16th century) *Indian translator*

A member of the Hatteras Croatoan people, Manteo was probably born near Albemarle Sound. He served as an interpreter and guide for the first Roanoke settlers, making trips to England in 1584 and 1586. He accompanied the John White voyage back to Roanoke in 1587. In that same year, the English held a ceremony to crown him "Lord of Roanoke," an attempt to make him and his people tributaries to the English crown.

María de Jésus de Agreda (María Coronel) (1602–1665) *nun, religious mystic who inspired the American southwestern legend of the Lady in Blue*

Born in Agreda, Spain, María became a cloistered Franciscan nun and abbess (1627), an office which she held until her death. Although her mystical writings were controversial within the church, and King Philip IV of Spain visited and corresponded with her. María claimed to have experienced mystical bilocation during which she "visited" the American Southwest. At the same time, several southwestern Indian tribes repeated stories to missionary priests of visits by a mysterious white woman in blue robes who urged them to seek conversion to Christianity. María provided details about

a land and people she had never actually visited, and some religious authorities accepted her claims.

Marie of the Incarnation (1599–1672) *first superior of the Ursuline convent at Quebec*

Born in France, Marie was widowed at the age of 20. When her infant son reached the age of 12 she entered the convent. In 1639, she accompanied Madame de la Peltrie to Canada, where they founded a convent; Marie served as superior until her death. She learned several Indian languages and composed catechisms and dictionaries, which have not survived, in Huron and other Algonquian languages. Her letters to her son and other writings, however, have been published and offer a unique viewpoint on life in early New France.

Mary II (1662–1694) *queen of England (reigned 1689–94)*

Mary was the eldest daughter of James II. Although her father converted to Catholicism, Mary was a Protestant. When James was driven from the throne in the Glorious Revolution of 1688–89, Parliament invited Mary and her Dutch husband, William III of Orange, to assume the throne.

Mason, John (1586–1635) *English colonizer*

A well-connected Englishman, Mason served as the governor of Newfoundland (1615–21). In 1622, he received a patent to modern Maine with Ferdinando Gorges. In 1629, he received a patent to territory he named New Hampshire. He established a settlement there and is considered a founder of the modern state. Mason's heirs fought colonists over rights to the land until 1715.

Massasoit (ca. 1580–1661) *Wampanoag leader*

Massasoit welcomed the Pilgrims when they arrived in 1620, sold them land, traded with them, and encouraged his tribe to teach them about native crops and agricultural methods. He signed a treaty with Plymouth Colony in 1621, partially to strengthen his own position against the Narragansett. He became disenchanted with the English as time progressed, however, and his son Philip (Metacom) went to war with them in 1675.

Mather, Cotton (1663–1728) *Puritan clergyman, theologian, intellectual, writer*

Born in Boston, Cotton Mather was the son of Increase Mather and the grandson of Reverend John

Cotton and Reverend Richard Mather. After attending Harvard, he eventually succeeded his father as minister of the Second Church of Boston. Together, the two controlled the pulpit from 1664 to 1728. During his lifetime, Mather engaged in many quarrels—personal, theological, and political, including the revolt against Governor Edmund Andros in 1692. He wrote about witchcraft (*Wonders of the Invisible World*), but he later denounced the Salem trials. In 1721, he took a strong stand in favor of smallpox inoculation, despite powerful opposition. He wrote over 450 works on scientific and historical as well as religious and ethical subjects. Mather was a controversial but extremely influential figure who consistently supported the established Puritan order in New England. His most important work is *Magnalia Christi Americana,* an elaborately embellished history of the region. He married three times and was the father of 15 children, only two of whom survived him.

Mather, Increase (1639–1723) *Puritan clergyman, leader*
Born in Massachusetts, Increase Mather became the minister at the Second Church of Boston in 1664 after preaching briefly in England. After Massachusetts's charter was revoked in 1688, he journeyed back to England. Through his efforts, a new charter and governor were obtained for the colony. From 1685 to 1701, he served as president of his alma mater, Harvard College. Although not a fanatical thinker, his personality drew him into many controversies. He left over 130 written works.

Mather, Richard (1596–1669) *Puritan clergyman, church leader*
Born in England, Richard attended Oxford. He arrived in Massachusetts in 1635. He exerted considerable influence on the early Massachusetts church and was one of the main translators who produced the *Bay Psalm Book*. He is the father of Increase Mather.

Membertou (unknown–1611) *Micmac chief*
Membertou befriended Jean de Biencourt de Poutrincourt's colony at Port Royal and guarded the settlement when it was temporarily abandoned by the French (1607–10). After 1610, Membertou permitted Port Royal's new priest, Father Jessé Fléché, to baptize him and his family. When he died the following year, Jesuits in the colony insisted that he be buried in sanctified ground and refused to return his body to his people, creating much bad feeling.

Menéndez, Francisco (fl. 1715–1763) *military and political leader of Fort Mose*
Possibly born in Africa, Menéndez escaped to the Yamasee Indians from slavery in South Carolina, fighting with them in the Yamasee War of 1715. In 1724, he arrived in St. Augustine with a group of escaped slaves, seeking asylum. In 1729, Florida officials sold the group at auction within the colony. Soon after, Menéndez was appointed head of the slave militia and was freed in 1738 to help found Fort Mose. After the fort was destroyed and abandoned in 1740, he worked on a privateering vessel. In 1741, he was captured by the English and returned to slavery in the Bahamas, but by 1752, when Fort Mose was reestablished, he was once again living in Florida. He accompanied Florida evacuees to Cuba in 1763.

Menéndez de Avilés, Pedro (1519–1574) *Spanish naval officer, founder of Saint Augustine*
Menéndez was born in Spain to a family of landed gentry and went to sea as a young teenager. While captain of the Spanish fleet in the Indies, Menéndez was commissioned by King Philip II to expel the French Huguenot colony at Fort Caroline, Florida. In 1565, he established a colony at Saint Augustine, the first permanent Spanish settlement in North America, and massacred all French inhabitants who did not escape. He later explored the Atlantic and Gulf coasts and established forts throughout the area. Recalled to Spain in 1567, he died while organizing a Spanish fleet to sail against the English.

Metacom (Metacomet, Philip, King Philip) (ca. 1640–1676) *Wampanoag leader*
Son of Massasoit, Metacom became sachem, or leader, of the Wampanoag in 1662 after his older brother Alexander died in English custody. He became increasingly disaffected with the Puritan settlers. He resisted their attempts to convert his people and refused to sell them the additional land they desired. In 1675, he led an uprising against the English known as King Philip's War. Although his warriors inflicted great destruction on the English, they were defeated in 1676. Philip himself was killed in Rhode Island by an informer during

the war. His body was beheaded and quartered; his head was displayed on a pike for 25 years at Plymouth.

Minuit, Peter (1580–1638) *director-general (governor) of New Netherland*

Minuit, a Dutch-speaking Walloon born in Germany, arrived in New Amsterdam in 1626. He gained lasting fame by purchasing the island of Manhattan from the local Indians for 60 guilders. Although he developed the small port town and established trading relations with New England, he was recalled in 1631. In 1637, under the auspices of a Swedish colonizing company, he returned to the New World with settlers for the small colony of New Sweden, on the banks of the Delaware. He was lost at sea near the West Indies on a trading voyage in 1638.

Montcalm, marquis de (Louis Joseph Montcalm) (1712–1759) *commander of the French forces in Canada (1756–59)*

Born in France, Montcalm joined the military at age 12 and inherited his title in 1735. In 1756, he became commander in North America. He was noted for his successful military leadership but was hampered in New France by the division of authority with Vaudreuil, the governor-general. He died from wounds suffered at the Battle of Quebec on September 14, 1759, the day before the city was officially surrendered to the English.

Monts, sieur du (Pierre du Gua de Monts, Pierre Guast De Monts) (ca. 1560–1628) *French colonizer of Acadia*

In 1603, de Monts, an ally of Henry IV, received a fur-trade monopoly and land grant in Acadia, where he, Champlain, and Poutrincourt established the colony of Port Royal. De Monts returned to France permanently in 1606. After regaining his monopoly in 1608, he sponsored Samuel de Champlain's expedition to found Quebec.

Moore, James (unknown–1706) *trader, colonial official*

Born in Ireland, Moore migrated to South Carolina in 1675, establishing himself in the Indian trade. He served as governor of the colony from 1700 to 1703. During Queen Anne's War, he led an official expedition against St. Augustine as well as an independent raid of the Apalache area of Florida. He also participated in extensive Indian slave raiding.

Morton, Thomas (ca. 1575–ca. 1647) *trader, Puritan opponent*

Morton, a well-connected English Anglican, arrived in Massachusetts in 1622 and founded an all-male trading colony at Merry Mount (modern Quincy), known for its licentious lifestyle. Morton angered his Puritan neighbors by selling guns to the Indians, consorting with Indian women, and erecting a maypole, which they viewed as a celebration of paganism. He was exiled to England in 1627, returned to the colony by 1630, was exiled again, returned by 1643, and went to Maine, where lived the remainder of his life. While in England, he wrote *New England Canaan* (1637), a work very critical of the Puritans and their colonies in Massachusetts.

Murray, Sir James (1721–1794) *first English governor of Quebec (1760–68)*

Born in Scotland and a military officer under General James Wolfe, Murray inherited command of English forces at the Battle of Quebec after the general's death. Murray served first as the military governor of Quebec city and was appointed the first civil governor of Quebec Province in 1764. He followed a policy of conciliation with the elites of New France, which earned him the emnity of the English merchants. He was recalled but cleared of any wrongdoing and later served as colonial governor of Minorca. He died in England.

Musgrove, Mary (Mary Bosomworth, Coosaponakeesa) (ca. 1700–1763) *Creek interpreter, negotiator, trader*

Mary, or Coosaponakeesa, was born in Coweta, modern Alabama, to a Creek mother and a white father. After her marriage to John Musgrove, the couple operated very successful trading posts at Yamacraw Bluff and later Alamahatma, modern Georgia. Mary Musgrove's interpreting and negotiating skills were pivotal to the success of James Oglethorpe's new colony. Musgrove continued her work after the death of both John Musgrove and her second husband. Her third husband, Thomas Bosomworth, a renegade English Anglican chaplain, influenced her to pursue less successful activities. She sought the title of "empress" of the Creek people (they recognized no such office) and led warriors to Savannah in 1747 to force the English to recognize her land claims. In 1759 or 1760, she was awarded some compensation for her long services by

London courts. She died on St. Catherine's Island, to which she held title. None of her children survived her.

Neolin (Delaware Prophet, "The Enlightened One") (fl. 1760s) *Lenni Lenape (Delaware) spiritual leader*

Neolin was born and lived in Lenni Lenape (Delaware) territory near Lake Erie. Around 1760, he became prominent among many Indian groups for his prophecies based in a mystical experience. He preached that the Great Spirit would help Indians drive the whites from their lands, providing they renounced white goods and customs and returned to their previous way of life. His prophecies were influential in inspiring the cooperation of many Indian groups in Pontiac's Rebellion (1763), which he had predicted. After the conclusion of the war, Neolin lost most of his influence and eventually disappeared from the historical record.

Nicholson, Francis (1655–1728) *English colonial governor*

Born in England, Nicholson was once of the most successful career colonial administrators. He served as lieutenant governor of New York (appointed 1686) and governor of Virginia (1690–94 and 1698–1704), Maryland (1694–98), and Nova Scotia (1713–15), after which he returned to England. He was appointed titular governor of South Carolina in 1719, but he did not personally assume the office. In New York, Nicholson was caught in events surrounding the Glorious Revolution in England and Leisler's Rebellion in the colony, and he fled back to England. In Virginia, however, he mended political relations still raw from Bacon's Rebellion; he also oversaw the chartering of the College of William and Mary and the reseating of the capital at Williamsburg. In Maryland, he ended political turmoil and reseated the capital at Baltimore. In 1710, during Queen Anne's War, he led the successful English capture of Acadia.

North, Lord (Frederick North, earl of Guilford) (1732–1792) *English prime minister during the American Revolution*

Lord North was elected to Parliament at the age of 22 and served for almost four decades. He was a member of the Privy Council before becoming prime minister in 1770. He underestimated the discontent and determination of the colonists in Amer-

ica. Early in his term, he attempted to both conciliate the colonists and maintain imperial and Parliamentary authority. After the war began, he did not give it his wholehearted personal support but maintained his office in opposition to the Whig opponents of George III and the Tories. He resigned in 1782, after British troops had surrendered. The following year, he formed a coalition with the Whigs but retired from politics a few years later. In 1790, he succeeded to his father's title, Earl of Guilford.

Oacpicagigua, Luis (fl. 1750s) *Akimel O'odham (Pima) leader*

Born in Mexico, Oacpicagigua hoped to drive Europeans from traditional Akimel O'odham territory. In November 1751, he led an attack on Jesuits at Saríc, which expanded into the Pima Revolt of 1751–52. He surrendered in a negotiated settlement.

O'Conor, Hugo (Hugo O'Connor, Hugo Oconor) (fl. 1765–1777) *Spanish military leader*

Born in Dublin, O'Conor joined the Spanish army and arrived in New Spain in 1765 to join Lieutenant General Juan de Villalba, head of the military team sent to new Spain by Charles III to reorganize colonial frontier defenses. He held several frontier posts, including acting governor of Texas in 1767–70. His red hair earned him the nickname "capitán colorado" (Captain Red) among the Indians. In 1772, he was promoted to colonel and inspector of the interior provinces. Responsible for defense of the frontier, he continued the reorganization of presidios and oversaw military actions against the Apache. In 1773, he evacuated East Texas settlers to San Antonio, although they later convinced the viceroy to overrule his orders. In 1776, on his orders, the settlement at Tubac, Arizona, was relocated to Tucson and the first Hispanic settlement established there. He resigned in 1777, probably disappointed at not having received the position of first commandante general of the new Interior Provinces.

Oglethorpe, James Edward (1696–1785) *founder of Georgia*

Born in London, Oglethorpe was a member of Parliament and part of a group of philanthropists who sought to found a colony where the poor might make a fresh start. Oglethorpe accompanied the first colonists to North America in 1732. He successfully established the colony of Georgia, although he had no official title there until he became general in 1738. In 1743, he was recalled to London to answer charges that he had mismanaged hostilities with the Spanish. He was exonerated but did not return to America and exhibited little additional interest in the colony he had founded and overseen for a decade.

Oñate, Don Juan de (ca. 1549–ca. 1624) *Spanish explorer, founder of New Mexico*
Born to a wealthy family in Mexico, Oñate contracted in 1595 to lead a party of colonists, at his own expense, to found a Spanish colony to the north. He conquered much of the area of modern New Mexico and founded a settlement at San Gabriel. He also explored throughout western America from modern Kansas to the Gulf of California. His colony suffered in his absence, however, and he was recalled in 1607 and replaced as governor in 1608.

Opechancanough (ca. 1545–1646) *leader of the Powhatan Confederacy*
A brother of Powhatan, Opechancanough assumed leadership of the Powhatan Confederacy after the older chief's death. On March 22, 1622, he led an uprising against the Virginians that killed a quarter of the colonial population. In 1644, when he was close to 100, he led another called Opechancanough's War. Captured by the colonists, he was murdered by a guard while in a Virginia jail.

O'Reilly, Alejandro (1722–1794) *Spanish general*
Born in Ireland, O'Reilly distinguished himself in the Spanish military. In 1769, he was ordered to Louisiana to quell the revolt of French citizens against Ulloa, the colony's first Spanish governor. He won the nickname Bloody O'Reilly for his decisive punishment of the rebels. Although he spent less than a year in the colony, he effected widespread administrative reorganizations and policy change, which remained in place to the end of the Spanish period. In 1771, he was made a Spanish count.

Otis, James (1725–1783) *Revolutionary Patriot*
Born in Massachusetts, Otis attended Harvard and practiced law in Boston. When the king reapproved writs of assistance in 1761, Otis held the position of royal advocate general (similar to state attorney general). He resigned the position to take up the defense of

the merchants who resisted and protested the writs. In several important speeches and writings, he used the principles of natural rights and natural law to defend the colonial cause. In the early years of the independence movement, Otis was one of its most prominent leaders, much quoted and much reviled by opponents; he apparently coined the phrase "taxation without representation is tyranny." He became head of the Massachusetts Committee of Correspondence. He suffered from intermittent insanity, however, which virtually incapacitated him after he was beaten by a British officer in a brawl in 1769. He died after being struck by lightning.

Paine, Thomas (1737–1809) *radical political thinker, writer*
Born in England, Paine left school at age 13. He worked for a time as a tax collector but was dismissed after writing a proposal to end corruption in the tax service. Benjamin Franklin advised him to emigrate. He arrived in the colonies in 1774 and obtained a position as an editor of *Pennsylvania Magazine* in Philadelphia; his first piece was a scathing indictment entitled "African Slavery in America." In 1776, he published the extremely influential 50-page pamphlet *Common Sense,* which attacked the king and argued for immediate declaration of independence from Britain. Over 50,000 copies were printed within a few months. Paine then began publishing a series of sixteen influential pamphlets entitled *The Crisis* (1776–83). The first began with the famous words, "These are the times that try men's souls"; Washington had it read to his troops suffering through the terrible winter at Valley Forge. Although Paine was poor his whole life, he refused to accept royalties, allowing his works to be published and circulate freely. After the war, the state of Pennsylvania provided a small pension and the state of New York deeded him a small farm in New Rochelle. He continued to write radical political philosophy; among other things, he proposed a social security system, a progressive income tax, and a world peace organization. In 1787, he returned to Europe and became embroiled in the violently divided opinion about the French Revolution, publishing *The Rights of Man* in 1791–92. Driven out of England, he was warmly received in France as a member of the constitutional convention but was imprisoned when he courageously decried the excesses of the revolution. His last major work, *The Age of Reason*

(1794–1796), earned him bitter attacks because it was believed to propound deism, although Paine thought of himself as a Quaker throughout his life. He returned to the United States in 1802, but he died ostracized and in poverty. In 1819, a visiting English journalist dug up his coffin, intending to give him a hero's burial in England. The project met with opposition there, however, and what happened to Paine's bones in England remains unknown to this day.

Pastorius, Francis Daniel (1651–1720) *land agent in colonial Pennsylvania*

Born in Germany, Pastorius immigrated to Pennsylvania on behalf of a German Quaker group, where he arranged and established the settlement of Germantown in 1683. He continued to serve as an agent for Mennonites and other Pietists. In 1688, he authored the first known protest against slavery by a white colonist.

Penn, Hannah Collowhill (1671–1726) *acting proprietor of Pennsylvania*

Born in England to a prosperous Quaker family, Hannah became William Penn's second wife in 1696, when she was 25 and he was a 52-year-old widower with teenaged children. During their marriage, she gave birth to eight children. She made only one trip to William's proprietary colony of Pennsylvania, in 1699–1701. After her husband's incapacitating stroke in 1712, however, she took over management of his affairs as well as her large household, her deceased parents' estate, and a troublesome stepson. On William's death, she became the sole executor of his will and estate; she continued management of the colony until her death despite political opposition there and a long-running contest of his will in England. At her death, her sons survived her as proprietors of the colony.

Penn, William (1644–1718) *founder and proprietor of Pennsylvania*

Born in London to a prominent admiral and his wife, Penn was converted to Quakerism as a young man. Although he retained his identity as a courtier, he became a Quaker activist and was imprisoned several times because of it. Penn took a role in the establishment of the colony of West Jersey (later part of New Jersey). In 1681, he received a large grant to lands named Pennsylvania (in honor of his father; the grant

was intended to release the king from a large debt owed Admiral Penn). William Penn, who became an outstanding colonial leader, gave freedom of worship to all, including Catholics and Indians. He was noted for his honest dealings with the Native Americans who inhabited the land he had been granted, which he conscientiously purchased. Penn's policies soon turned Pennsylvania and Philadelphia into the fastest-growing colony and city in North America. Before returning to England in 1701, he approved a liberal new constitution for his colony, which separated the legislative, judicial, and executive branches and gave wide powers to the legislature. Unfortunately, his personal finances had been dishonestly managed by his agent in England, and Penn was imprisoned briefly for debt. Penn believed he had no alternative but to turn his colony over to the Crown. He suffered a debilitating stroke in 1712. His wife Hannah assumed management of the proprietorship until her own death, when it passed to their three sons.

Pepperell, Sir William (1696–1759) *merchant, military officer*

Born in Maine, Pepperell became a successful merchant as well as council member and judge of Massachusetts colony, which administered Maine. With Governor Shirley, he organized the 1745 attack and capture of Louisbourg from the French. For his efforts, he was created a baronet (the lowest hereditary English title) in 1746, the first American-born colonist to be so honored.

Peralta, Pedro de (ca. 1584–1666) *founder of Santa Fe*

A Spanish official in New Spain, Peralta replaced Don Juan de Oñate as governor of New Mexico in 1609 and founded its capital at Santa Fe. His term was marked after 1612 by sometimes violent conflict with the Franciscans in the colony. He was recalled in 1614 and later served in Acapulco and Caracas. He retired to Spain in 1652.

Philip, King See METACOM.

Philip II (1527–1598) *king of Spain (reigned 1556–98)*

Philip II championed both the power of Spain and interests of the Catholic faith; often, in his mind the two were identical. He reigned at the height of Spain's influence and geographical extension as a world power, although the revolt of the Protestant Netherlands began and the Spanish Armada was defeated while attempting to invade England in 1588. His political opponents, particularly in Protestant nations, inaccurately portrayed him as bigoted and cruel. Philip was, however, frequently suspicious of his own advisors and capable of tyranny in defense of the Counter-Reformation, which he believed he had been appointed by God to defend. He personally involved himself in all details of governance, famously requiring every event and issue to be presented and evaluated in writing. This innovation greatly slowed the wheels of government (although it has provided much information for historians). During his reign, the first Spanish settlement in North America was founded at St. Augustine, and Don Juan de Oñate took possession of New Mexico for Spain.

Philip III (1578–1621) *king of Spain (reigned 1598–1621)*

The son and far less capable successor of Philip II, Philip III took little personal interest in governing. Spanish power began to decline, and the economic problems he ignored and compounded created great difficulties for his successor, Philip IV. During his reign, settlement began in New Mexico and Santa Fe was founded.

Philip IV (1605–1665) *king of Spain (reigned 1621–65)*

Philip IV's reign marked a decline in Spain's political and commercial power. He engaged in costly wars with France, Germany, and the Netherlands, weakening his empire with military defeats, economic distress, and social turmoil. He was succeeded by his son Charles II.

Philip V (1683–1746) *king of Spain (reigned 1700–46)*

The ascension of Philip, grandson of Louis XIV of France, provoked the War of Spanish Succession. By the Treaty of Utrecht, which ended the war in 1713, Philip kept the throne of Spain but gave up claim to the throne of France. Philip began the Bourbon dynasty, noted for its modernizing, administrative reforms of Spanish government. During his reign, Spain regained some of its international stature. He was succeeded by his son Ferdinand VI (reigned 1746–59), whose reign was relatively uneventful.

Phips, Sir William (1650–1695) *colonial governor*

Phips was born in very modest circumstances in Maine and began his career working on a fishing ship. In 1687, he recovered a sunken Spanish treasure ship off Haiti; as a result, he was the first native-born American to be knighted (the honorary English title of knight is not hereditary). During King William's War, he led forces to capture Port Royal, Nova Scotia, from the French. By 1690, he was a member of the Mathers' Second Church of Boston. In 1692, he was appointed governor of Massachusetts, in which capacity he put an end to the witchcraft trials in Salem.

Pinckney, Elizabeth Lucas (Eliza Pinckney) (1722–1793) *plantation manager*

Born in Antigua, British West Indies, Eliza Lucas was educated in England before arriving in South Carolina in 1738 with her family. When her father was recalled to active service a year later, he left 17-year-old Eliza her in charge of her ailing mother, her siblings, and the family plantations. A remarkably multitalented and active woman, in 1741 she began experimenting with difficult indigo cultivation, which had been tried and abandoned early in South Carolina history. By 1744, she had produced and shipped a successful harvest and was distributing seeds to other planters; by 1750, it had become a staple export of the colony. In 1744 she married Charles Pinckney, a childless widower, and spent 1753–78 in London with him. She continued her experiments, adding silk culture, and assuming complete management of their plantations after his death. The couple had three children. Her sons Charles and Thomas were both Patriots who served the new nation in various offices. Her daughter, Harriet Horry, also became a successful plantation manager upon the death of her husband. George Washington, at his own request, served as a pall bearer at Pinckney's funeral.

Pitt, William (Pitt the Elder) (1708–1778) *prime minister of Great Britain (1766–68)*

Pitt entered the House of Commons in 1735 from a borough controlled by his wealthy and distinguished family. A powerful orator, he led the opposition to Walpole and served as secretary of state. Appointed prime minister in 1756 amid British military disasters in the Seven Years' War, the able and energetic Pitt led Britain to victory. He resigned his office in 1761 after a disagreement with the young King George III. Tremendously popular in both Britain and the colonies, Pitt was known as the Great Commoner. He was required to enter the House of Lords in 1768, however, when he was created the first Earl of Chatham. He defended colonial resistance to the Stamp Act; his main concern, however, was always the strength of the British empire. In 1766, at the request of the king, he once again took office but was unable to form a successful ministry amid the unstable political factions. In 1778, he collapsed in Parliament while delivering a speech urging leniency to the colonies but opposing independence; he died shortly thereafter. His son William Pitt the Younger also became a distinguished prime minister of Britain.

Pocahontas (ca. 1596–1617) *daughter of Powhatan legendary for her association with the Jamestown, Virginia settlement*
Pocahontas was the daughter of Powhatan, chief of the Powhatan Confederacy in Virginia when the first settlers arrived at Jamestown in 1607. According to Captain James Smith's *History of Virginia,* she saved his life when he was captured by the Indians, although many historians doubt the accuracy of his tale. However, there is no doubt that she was later taken hostage by the colonists to force negotiations with Powhatan. While a captive, she was converted to Christianity, took the name Rebecca, and married John Rolfe in 1614. She accompanied him to England in 1616, where she was presented to the king, sat for her portrait, and became a celebrity. She died the following year in England, probably of smallpox; she was survived by a son, Thomas Rolfe, born in 1615.

Ponce de León, Juan (1460–1521) *Spanish conquistadore who established Spanish claim to Florida*
Born in Spain, Ponce de León accompanied Columbus on his second voyage. He led the conquest of Puerto Rico for Spain in 1508 and became its governor. In 1513, he landed near modern St. Augustine while on an Indian slave raid, naming the territory La Florida. While on a second expedition in 1521, he was fatally wounded in Indian hostilities on Florida's west coast; he died after reaching Havana.

Pontiac (ca. 1720–1769) *Ottawa leader*
Probably born in the territory of modern Ohio, Pontiac was a tall, eloquent man who became a respected Ottawa leader. Influenced by Neolin and other prophets of spiritual renewal, he developed a determination to contain the Europeans east of the Ohio River. In early 1763, he coordinated a pan-Indian attack to occur while the English and French were still weakened by the long French and Indian War. After the conclusion of Pontiac's War, his influence waned. In 1769, he was killed by a Peoria Indian at Cahokia, Illinois.

Popé (ca. 1630–ca. 1690) *Tewa leader in the Pueblo Rebellion*
Popé, a medicineman from the San Juan pueblo, opposed white missionary work and settlement among the Pueblo. After 1675, when the Spanish began to arrest and punish Indian spiritual leaders, his influence grew. After being arrested and publicly flogged three times, he sequestered himself at distant Taos pueblo, where he planned and coordinated the Pueblo Revolt of 1680. After the Spanish were driven out of New Mexico, his personal rule was not successful and his influence waned. Popé remains the only Indian leader to successfully expel Europeans from Indian lands where they had founded settlements.

Portolá, Gaspar de (ca. 1723–1786) *military officer, founder of California settlements*
Portolá was born in Spain to an aristocratic family. While serving as the governor of Baja California, he was selected as the military head of Gálvez's expedition to secure Spain's claim in Alta California. Portolá oversaw the founding of the first California mission settlement at San Diego in 1769, also discovered San Francisco Bay (although he did not recognize its value at first sight) and founded a settlement at Monterey in 1770. He returned to Spain in 1784.

Poutrincourt, Jean de Biencourt de (1557–1615) *colonizer of Acadia*
Born in France, Poutrincourt accompanied Samuel de Champlain and Pierre de Monts to Acadia in 1604 and contributed many years of effort to the establishment of a colony at Port Royal. Appointed governor in 1606, he closed the settlement in 1607 as ordered but returned with new financing in 1610 to reestablish it. After a power struggle with the Jesuits, Poutrincourt made a visit to France but was imprisoned briefly there. By the time he returned to Acadia in 1613, his colony had been destroyed by English privateer Samuel Argall. The defeated Poutrincourt made his final return to France, although his son Charles Biencourt remained in Acadia.

Powhatan (Wahunsonakok) (ca. 1547–1618) *head of the Powhatan Confederacy*
When the first settlers arrived at Jamestown, Powhatan controlled the expanding Powhatan Confederacy in eastern Virginia, numbering about 32 bands in over 125 villages. Although he did not immediately welcome the Englishmen, he negotiated a truce after his daughter Pocahontas married John Rolfe in 1614.

Printz, Johan Björnsson (1592–1663) *governor of New Sweden (1643–53)*
Son of a Lutheran pastor, Printz studied theology briefly before entering the military. In 1642, he was appointed governor of Sweden's colony on the Delaware. He energetically revived the small settlement but returned to Sweden in 1653, where he served as governor of his home district.

Radisson, Pierre-Esprit (1636–1710) *explorer, fur trader*
Born in France, Radisson arrived in Canada in 1651 and spent two years living among the Iroquois. After 1654, he and his brother-in-law Médard Chouart de Grosselliers explored and traded in the Great Lakes and Upper Mississippi region for six years. In 1663, the government of New France confiscated their furs and fined them for failing to obtain a license. As a result, they offered their services to the English, exploring Hudson's Bay and inspiring the formation of the Hudson's Bay Company in 1670. Radisson took up residence in Quebec in the 1680s, but later returned to the employ of the Hudson's Bay Company and probably died in England.

Raleigh, Sir Walter (1554–1618) *English soldier and courtier who tirelessly supported colonization in North America*
The half-brother of Sir Humphrey Gilbert, Raleigh was for many years a great favorite of Queen Elizabeth. In 1584, he received a charter to found a colony in the New World. It included a huge stretch of land from Newfoundland to Florida. Raleigh received permission from his benefactress to name it "Virginia," in her honor as the Virgin (unmarried) Queen. In 1585, he sent explorers to Roanoke Island, followed by a group of colonists in 1587. When a supply ship finally reached the small colony in 1590, all of the settlers had vanished. Raleigh continued to invest his time and personal fortune in various colonization schemes and helped introduce tobacco into England. He eventually lost favor at court when King James I ascended the throne, and was beheaded. Raleigh was also a successful poet and wrote prose works describing his explorations.

Randolph, Edward (1632–1703) *royal colonial official*
Born in England, Randolph was introduced to the colonies when he arrived in 1676 to investigate Massachusetts for violations of imperial policy. In 1678, he became surveyor (collector) of customs for New England, headquartered in Boston. The virulent opposition he met led him to lobby extensively for the revocation of Massachusetts' charter. After the charter was revoked in 1684, he served in various offices of the Dominion of New England. He was imprisoned by colonials when they overthrew the Dominion but was sent back to England on the king's orders. In 1691, he was returned to the colonies as surveyor general of customs for all North America and in that office continued to press for increased royal control. He died in Virginia.

Randolph, Peyton (1721–1775) *colonial statesman*
Born in Virginia, Randolph attended the College of William and Mary and studied law in England. He was one of the most prominent leaders of colonial cause in Virginia in the pre-Revolutionary years and was elected first president of the First Continental Congress. He suffered a stroke in shortly after the convention opened, however, and died in Philadelphia.

Revere, Paul (1735–1818) *Patriot, engraver, silversmith*
Born in Boston, Revere learned the engraver's trade from his French Huguenot father. He fought in the French and Indian War and took an active part in many radical pre-Revolutionary activities, including the Sons of Liberty, Boston Tea Party, and Committees of Correspondence. His drawings and engravings publicizing events like the Boston Massacre were widely circulated in the colonies. He served as a courier for revolutionary groups and achieved the status of folk hero with his rides from Boston to Lexington and Concord in 1775. On April 16 that year, he rode to warn Samuel Adams and John Hancock of British plans to arrest them, arranging for a signal system of lanterns to be hung in church steeples. On April 18, he rode with

two other men to warn citizens of approaching British troops (popularized in Henry Wadsworth Longfellow's poem "The Midnight Ride of Paul Revere," 1863). He was captured by the British on that night but released. His brief career as a military officer in the Revolutionary War was not successful; in 1782, he was court-martialed for unsoldierly conduct but was acquitted. Revere was also a foundry owner and a prominent silversmith. He designed the first Continental money and the seals of the colonies; his foundry equipped the U.S.S. *Constitution* (Old Ironsides).

Ribaud, Jean (Jean Ribault) (ca. 1520–1565) *sea captain, colonizer*
Born in France, Ribaud became a respected naval officer. In 1562, he led a French Huguenot expedition to Florida, establishing the short-lived settlement Charlesfort in modern South Carolina. He sailed to England for supplies but was briefly imprisoned there, where he wrote his memoirs. In 1565, he returned to Florida to relieve Laudonnière's settlement at Fort Caroline. His fleet was destroyed in a hurricane while sailing to meet the Spanish expedition of Menéndez de Avilés, sent to drive out the French. Ribaud and his surviving soldiers were captured and executed by the Spanish.

Robertson, James (1742–1814) *frontiersman, colonizer*
Born in Virginia, Robertson moved to North Carolina and by 1770 was living west of the Appalachians. He was a leader of the Watauga settlements (modern Tennessee) and a founder of Nashville. He was leader in western participation in the Revolution and afterwards worked as an Indian and land agent. After the war, the Tennessee settlements were ceded to the federal government by North Carolina, leaving them in effect with no legitimate civil government until 1790, when the Southwest Territory was created. During the interim, Robertson served as governor of the east Tennessee settlements and a leader in their unsuccessful attempt to gain recognition as the state of Franklin (later Tennessee).

Roberval, sieur de (Jean-François de la Roque) (ca. 1500–1560) *colonizer*
In 1541, King Francis I of France appointed Roberval, a courtier, Huguenot, and pirate, as "lieutenant general of Canada." Directed to establish a French colony, Roberval founded Charlesbourg Royal near modern Quebec. In 1543, surviving colonists including Roberval were

rescued and returned to France, but Roberval's colony helped to secure a French claim to North America.

Rolfe, John (1585–1622) *Jamestown colonist who introduced tobacco cultivation*
Born in England, Rolfe joined the Jamestown colony in 1610. In 1612, he successfully cultivated West Indian tobacco in Virginia, assuring the survival of the colony. He married the Powhatan princess Pocahontas in 1614. After her death during their visit to England in 1616–17, Rolfe returned to Virginia and is assumed to have perished in the Powhatan Massacre of 1622, when his farm was completely destroyed.

Rowlandson, Mary White (ca. 1635–after 1678) *author of the first American captivity narrative*
Wife of a Lancaster, Massachusetts minister, Rowlandson and her three children were taken captive by Indians during King Philip's War. She was marched and enslaved for over seven weeks, during which time her young daughter died in her arms. After her ransom, her husband took a pulpit in Wethersfield, Connecticut, in 1677, where she spent the remainder of her life. *The Narrative of the Captivity and Restoration of Mrs. Mary Rowlandson* (1682), written after she was ransomed, became extremely popular and ran through over 30 editions. It detailed her sufferings while providing sharp pictures of the life and personalities of her Indian captors; it also drew parallels between her captivity and the Christian religious experience of sin and salvation. Rowlandson's work established a new genre or type of American literature; many more such works followed by other Indian captives.

Rubí, marqués de (fl. 1765–1767) *Spanish officer*
Sent by King Charles III to inspect the military defenses of New Spain in 1765, Rubí traveled over 7,500 miles in 1766–67. He recommended rearranging the presidios on the northern frontier of New Spain in a line (the line very roughly approximates the modern boundary between Mexico and the United States) and a policy of exterminating the Apaches. Both policies were adopted in the new Spanish Reglamento (regulations) of 1772.

Saint-Denis, Louis Juchereau de (1676–1744) *explorer, trader, trade negotiator*
Born in Quebec, Saint-Denis migrated to the lower Mississippi Louisiana settlements. In 1714, he estab-

lished a small garrison at Natchitoches, the first permanent settlement in modern Louisiana and for many years the westernmost French trading outpost. In 1716, he reached the New Mexican presidio of San Juan Bautista, hoping to establish French trade there (illegal under Spanish law). He was imprisoned, however, and Spanish colonists were organized to establish a defensive settlement in East Texas. While in New Spain, St.-Denis married the granddaughter of the presidio's captain and became a Spanish subject, then accompanied Spanish colonists to East Texas. St.-Denis and his wife eventually returned to Louisiana, where he remained an important trade negotiator. His son-in-law, Athanase de Mézières, also served the Spanish as an Indian trade negotiator and diplomat after 1763.

Serra, Father Junípero (1713–1784) *Franciscan missionary, founder of California missions*
Born in Spain, Serra abandoned a promising career in the Catholic church hierarchy to become a missionary in New Spain. Chosen the religious head of Gálvez's colonizing project in Alta California, he founded the first California mission at San Diego on July 16, 1769, as well as eight later missions. He frequently battled secular and military officials over treatment of the California Indians. Already middle-aged in the 1760s, he suffered from ill health but walked thousands of miles throughout California visiting missions. He died near Monterey.

Sewall, Samuel (1652–1730) *colonial judge*
Born in England, Sewall arrived in Massachusetts as a child in 1661. A lawyer, he served as a Massachusetts council member from 1684 to 1725. He served on the Massachusetts Superior Court from 1692 to 1728, from 1718 as the Chief Justice. During that time, he presided over the witchcraft trials at Salem. In 1697, he publically confessed error in those proceedings and recanted, the only judge to do so. Among his important writings are a long-term diary of life in Massachusetts and an early protest against slavery, "The Selling of Joseph" (1700).

Shirley, William (1694–1771) *colonial governor of Massachusetts*
Born in England, Shirley emigrated to Boston in 1731 to assume a position as Admiralty Court judge, where he generally upheld the official British point of view. He served as governor from 1741 to 1749 and 1753 to 1756. During King George's War, he organized the successful 1745 attack and capture of Louisbourg from the French. He briefly served as commander of British forces during the French and Indian War and as British governor of the Bahamas, 1761–67, before returning to Massachusetts.

Sosa, Gaspar Castano de (fl. 1590) *official in New Spain*
In 1590, Sosa, lieutenant governor of Nuevo Leon, a Mexican province, led the first colonizing expedition into New Mexico. His activities were not authorized by the crown, however, and he was forcibly returned to Mexico.

Smith, Captain John (1580–1631) *explorer, colonizer, cartographer*
Smith was born and died in England. A soldier of fortune before he joined the Jamestown expedition, he was captured and sold into slavery in Turkey but managed to escape. He became president of the Jamestown colony in 1608, imposing forceful discipline on the disorganized and starving men. He is credited with saving the settlement, thus insuring its survival. In 1609, he lost his position and returned to England. He made additional voyages and explorations from 1614 to 1617, giving the name "New England" to the northern seaboard of North America. During the remainder of his life, he published many writings that described the natural abundance of North America and promoted English colonization. He also wrote a history of the Virginia settlement and published several early maps of North America.

Squanto (Tisquantum) (ca. 1590–1622) *Wampanoag of the Patuxet band, interpreter for and friend of the Pilgrims*
Squanto, or Tisquantum, was captured by English exploratory voyages at least once and possibly twice, both times spending time in England before managing to return to his native Massachusetts for good in 1619. In 1620, when the Pilgrims arrived at the site of his former village (which had been destroyed by epidemic illness), he became the interpreter and negotiator in their dealings with Massasoit, the Wampanoag chief. He also helped teach the colonists how to hunt and cultivate crops using Indian techniques. Squanto, who was probably a sachem among the Patuxet, died of smallpox.

Stuyvesant, Peter (1592–1672) *Dutch director-general (governor) of New Netherland (1646–64)*
Stuyvesant arrived in the New World to a trading port and colony in disorder and decline. He proceeded to impose strict regulations, hoping to attract more families, and rebuilt New Amsterdam. The temperamental and authoritarian governor less wisely continued to oppose the introduction of a representative assembly in New Netherland. In 1655, he captured New Sweden, bringing that small colony under Dutch control. In 1664, when an English war fleet arrived, he was unable to secure the support of citizens, among whom he was not popular. He was obliged to surrender the colony. Stuyvesant himself remained in New Netherland (New York) until his death. He was known for his silver-decorated wooden leg, which replaced a limb lost in a military battle before arriving in New Amsterdam.

Spotswood, Alexander (1676–1740) *colonial governor of Virginia*
Born in Tangier, Africa, Spotswood was governor of Virginia from 1710 to 1722 and deputy postmaster general of colonies from 1730 to 1739. He is noted for his active management of Indian relations, for developing an iron industry in Virginia, and especially for foreseeing the value of the western frontier. In 1716, Spotswood led the first expedition of white men to cross beyond the Blue Ridge Mountains into the Shenandoah Valley. His attempts at land reform were not successful, but he remained in Virginia as a planter after being removed from office.

Tanaghrisson (Tanacharison, Half-King) (ca. 1700–1754) *Mingo ally of British in French and Indian war*
Born a Catawba, Tanaghrisson was adopted into the Seneca and became a Western Seneca or Mingo chief in the eastern Ohio Valley. Often called the Half-King, because he was an intermediatary official between the Iroquois confederacy and its Ohio Valley tributary tribes, he participated in negotiations for numerous treaties. In 1752–53, he negotiated with George Washington and accompanied his troops in the 1754 attack on Jumonville. He died near modern Harrisburg, Pennsylvania.

Teach, Edward (Blackbeard) (ca. 1680–1718) *English pirate*
Probably born in Bristol, Teach is believed to have acted as a privateer during Queen Anne's War. He was widely known and feared for his atrocities throughout the West Indies and along the coast of the Carolinas. After 1718, he established a base in North Carolina and made an prize-sharing agreement with the governor, Charles Eden. At the request of angry citizens, Governor Alexander Spotswood of Virginia dispatched two British ships with troops which attacked and killed him. The famous pirate and his supposed buried treasure, never discovered, passed into folklore.

Tennent, Gilbert (1703–1764) *Presbyterian minister*
Son of William Tennent, Gilbert attended Yale and served pulpits in New Jersey and the middle colonies. He became a prominent figure in the Great Awakening, supporting evangelical "New Side" or "New Light" religious beliefs and practices. He later worked to reunite the Presbyterian church.

Tennent, William (1673–1746) *Presbyterian minister*
Born in Ireland, William Tennent attended the University of Edinburgh. He migrated to Pennsylvania in 1718 among the Scotch-Irish, serving pulpits in New York and Pennsylvania. In 1735, he built a school in Neshaminy, Pennsylvania, to tutor his four sons and other young men preparing for the ministry. As the Great Awakening swept the country, the school stressed evangelical beliefs and was dubbed the Log College by detractors of the movement.

Townshend, Charles (1725–1767) *British chancellor of the exchequer*
An official with experience on the Board of Trade and other offices, Townshend assumed the central role in the short second ministry of an ailing William Pitt. "Champagne Charlie," as he was called for his notorious lifestyle, was charged with balancing the budget. He passed a series of four colonial tax measures that directly threatened to end colonial control over the governor's and judges' salaries. He died soon after, at the age of 41.

Ulloa, Antonio de (1716–1795) *Spanish naval officer, scientist, governor of Louisiana*
Ulloa served the Spanish Crown in a number of capacities in his life. In 1734–35, he undertook a scientific expedition to New Spain; his account of the journey, *A Voyage to South America* (1748) established his worldwide scientific reputation. He served as governor of Peru before his appointment to Louisiana, where his

tenure was unsuccessful and resulted in the Rebellion of 1768. Forced to leave the province, he returned to Spain. He established the first museum of natural history and metallurgical lab in his native country.

Vargas, Don Diego de (ca. 1643–1704) *governor of New Mexico*

Born in Spain, Vargas was a minor nobleman who journeyed to New Spain in 1672 to seek his fortune. In 1691, he was appointed governor of New Mexico, which was then in the hands of Pueblo who had retaken it from the Spanish in the Revolt of 1690. In 1693, he reconquered New Mexico, a feat greatly celebrated in Mexico and Spain. In 1704, he was killed in hostilities with the Apache.

Vaudreuil-Cavagnal, marquis de (Pierre de Rigaud) (1698–1778) *last governor of New France*

Born in Quebec, Vaudreuil was the son of Canadian governor-general Philippe de Rigaud (1643–1725), appointed in 1703. Vaudreuil served as governor of Louisiana from 1743 to 1753, when he requested and received appointment as governor-general of Canada shortly before the start of the French and Indian War. He disagreed with Louis Joseph Montcalm about conduct of the war and failed to countermand the destructive self-enrichment of Intendant Bigot. In 1759, he surrendered the city of Quebec to the English after Montcalm's death. He returned to France, where he was tried and acquitted for maladministration. He spent the remainder of his life in France.

Verrazzano, Giovanni de (ca. 1485–1528) *explorer*

Born in Italy, Verrazzano explored the Atlantic coast of North America in 1524 for private French interests, during the reign of King Francis I. He established the existence of a continuous land mass from Canada to Florida and also discovered the mouth of the Hudson River and anchored in New York Bay between Manhattan and Staten Island (now Verrazzano Narrows). During his second voyage in 1528, he was killed by indigenous people in the West Indies. His voyage and discoveries were later used as the basis for the French claim to North America and "Acadia," which he named.

Walpole, Sir Robert (1676–1745) *British statesman*

Walpole is generally regarded as the first prime minister of England, although he himself disliked the title. Serving as a Whig Member of Parliament continually from 1700, his goals were low taxes in Britain and peace abroad. He greatly influenced colonial policy in the first half of the 18th century, maintaining a policy termed "benign neglect" to allow the colonies to develop freely.

Ward, Reverend Nathaniel (ca. 1578–ca. 1652) *Puritan clergyman known for his popular writings denouncing religious tolerance*

Ward, excommunicated by Bishop Laud in 1633, arrived in the Massachusetts Bay colony shortly thereafter and took the pulpit in Agawam (modern Ipswich). He was the primary writer of the Massachusetts Bodies of Liberties, the colony's first legal code. Adopted in 1641, it recognized certain fundamental human rights and legal guarantees. His most popular work, however, was *The Simple Cobbler of Agawam* (1645), which used the persona of a shoemaker to denounce religious tolerance (never popular among Puritans) and other issues in the name of "common sense."

Washington, George (1732–1799) *commander of the Continental Army, first president of the United States*

Washington was born in Virginia. His father died when he was 11 years old, leaving the most valuable family properties to George's older half-brothers. Washington was privately educated and did not attend college. He learned surveying and earned both significant remuneration and official approval for his service in the unsettled west of Virginia, modern West Virginia, and Pennsylvania. In 1752, his older brother Lawrence died and George acquired a lifetime lease to Mount Vernon. At the age of 21, he obtained Lawrence's former position in the Virginia militia and volunteered for a mission to scout the French. His journal of the trip, published in 1754, increased his public recognition. His first military command against the French at Fort Necessity in the Ohio Valley met with defeat, but during the ensuing French and Indian War, Washington gained experience, knowledge, and the high regard of the British commanders under whom he served. In 1759, he married the wealthy widow Martha Custis and became the guardian of her two children and their estates; the couple had no children together. Now among the wealthiest of the Virginia planters, he devoted time after the war to the development of his plantations and the management of the enslaved work force. Washington was elected to the House of Burgesses in 1758, serving until 1774. He was also a county court judge for many years as well as a delegate to the First and Second Continental Congresses. In June 1775, he was appointed commander in chief of the colonial army still in the process of formation. He faced the formidable task of transforming disorganized and inexperienced volunteers into a disciplined army with capable officers. He held the army together through the winter at Valley Forge (1777–78) despite inadequate assistance, lack of public interest, and the difficulty of obtaining long term recruits. After that date, French assistance enabled him mount new offensives, finally defeating the British under Lord Cornwallis at Yorktown, Virginia, in 1781. After the peace in 1783, Washington attempted to retire to private life at Mount Vernon but soon became instrumental in calling the Constitutional Convention of 1787. Although he was a delegate, he had little role in the actual composition of the Constitution. He lent his prestige and influence to its ratification in 1788, however, and was unanimously elected the first President of the new union. During his first term, he planned a new national capital city on the Potomac from his quarters in the temporary capital at New York. By the end of his first term, antagonism had grown significantly between the supporters of Alexander Hamilton (who championed federalism and commercial development) and of Thomas Jefferson and James Madison (who championed states' rights and agricultural interests). Believing his leadership remained necessary, he accepted a second term in 1792. During that term many difficulties developed and Washington, no longer unanimously revered, was subjected to attacks by his political opponents. He refused to seek a third term and was succeeded by his vice president, John Adams. His famous Farewell Address (1796) argued for a strong union, reconciliation of party conflict, and non-participation in European political struggles. In 1798, Adams reappointed Washington as commander in chief when war with France threatened, but the crisis dissipated. Washington spent his last two years in private life at Mount Vernon. He died in December 1799, probably of a streptococcus infection complicated by the common medical treatment of blood-letting. According to the terms of his will, his slaves were not freed upon his death but were to be freed upon the death of his wife. Through a lifetime of dignified public service, Washington earned the nickname "father of his country."

Weiser, Johann Conrad (1696–1760) *Indian negotiator, Indian agent*

Born in Germany, Weiser emigrated to New York in 1710. He became conversant with the Mohawk language and culture by living among the Indians as a young man and subsequently acted as an interpreter for other settlers. In 1729, he and his family moved to Pennsylvania and began working as an Indian agent and negotiator there, in an official capacity after 1740. He helped to negotiate several important treaties and secure the allegiance of the Iroquois during the French and Indian War. Weiser was also a musician and a religious evangelist after 1735, when he underwent a conversion. He helped found a German language press and the town of Reading, Pennsylvania, and held several offices there in his later life.

Wheatley, Phillis (ca. 1754–1784) *poet*

Born in Gambia, West Africa, Wheatley was captured and sold into slavery in 1761 at the age of seven. The Boston Wheatley family that purchased her educated her and encouraged the development of her poetic gift. She became the first African American to publish a book of poetry when her *Poems on Various Subjects, Religious and Moral,* was published in England in 1773. Freed after its publication, she married a free black, John Peters, in 1778 and gave birth to three children, all of whom died. Although Wheatley earned an international reputation and was used by white antislavery advocates as proof of the intellectual capacities of Africans, she was never able to obtain a publisher for a second book. She died in poverty and obscurity.

Wheelwright, Reverend John (1592–1679) *religious rebel*

Born in England, Wheelwright attended Cambridge and arrived in New England in 1636. In 1637, he was banished for his support of Anne Hutchinson. He and his followers founded Exeter, New Hampshire; after that colony became part of Massachusetts in 1643, he moved to Maine and established a new settlement there. He later returned to New Hampshire.

White, Father Andrew (1579–1656) *Jesuit missionary*

Born in London and educated in France, White served (illegally) as a Jesuit missionary in England. He was banished to the Netherlands but returned in 1629, accompanying the first Calvert expedition to Maryland in 1634. For a decade, he worked among the colonists and Indians. In 1644, he was arrested during the Claiborne Protestant uprising and sent to England, and again banished to the Netherlands. He risked execution to return to England again as a missionary.

White, John (fl. 1577–1593) *artist, governor of the short-lived Roanoke colony*
White accompanied George Grenville on his early voyage to Roanoke, producing detailed drawings and watercolors of Native Americans as well as plant and animal life. (The drawing were published in altered form in the 16th century; the unaltered originals were not rediscovered until the 20th century.) In 1597, White, holding the title *governor,* returned to Roanoke with settlers; it was the first English attempt at a permanent colony within the modern United States. He sailed back to England for supplies, leaving his daughter and new granddaughter, the first child of English parents whose birth in America is recorded. When he returned to Roanoke in 1591, the colony had disappeared. White returned to England and retired in Ireland, writing the account of his final voyage in the last year of his life.

Whitefield, George (1715–1770) *itinerant minister, most prominent figure of the Great Awakening*
Born in England, Whitefield (pronounced Whitfield) was an Oxford graduate ordained in the Anglican church. A powerful speaker, he became a leading Methodist minister, preaching emotional sermons urging spiritual regeneration. Between 1738 and 1770, he visited America seven times. He preached up and down the coast from New England to Georgia, reportedly attracting crowds of up to 20,000. In 1740, he founded a much-publicized orphanage in Georgia. He died in Massachusetts.

Wigglesworth, Michael (1631–1705) *minister, poet*
Born in England, Wigglesworth emigrated to Massachusetts in 1638 with his parents, later attending Harvard. Despite suffering frequent illness, he married three times, fathered eight children, and became a respected minister and Harvard faculty member. He is remembered primarily as a popular poet, however, who penned popular verse designed to inspire his readers to Puritan holiness. His most famous work was *Day of Doom,* 1662.

William and Mary See WILLIAM III; MARY II.

William III of Orange (1650–1702) *king of England (reigned 1689–1702)*
Son of Prince William of Orange, William III succeeded his father as ruler of the Netherlands in 1672. He married Mary, daughter of King James II of England. Both William and Mary were Protestants, and in 1689 they replaced her Catholic father on the throne of England at invitation of Parliament following the Glorious Revolution. Until Mary's death in 1694, they ruled England jointly. During their reign, the English Bill of Rights was passed (1689).

Williams, Roger (1603–1683) *radical dissenting minister, founder of Rhode Island*
Born in England, Williams attended Cambridge and arrived in Massachusetts Bay Colony in 1630. He was a favorite of John Winthrop, although he passionately championed religious tolerance and the separation of church and state. In 1636, he was banished from the strict Puritan colony for his unorthodox religious views. He lived in both Plymouth and Salem; later he and his followers founded a settlement at Providence which allowed freedom of conscience and kept religious and civil affairs separated. In 1644, he traveled to England, successfully obtaining a legal charter for the colony; he went again in 1651–54 to have it re-confirmed. Williams believed that any land not purchased from the Indians was in fact stolen, regardless of any royal grant. He served the New England colonists many times as a peacemaker with the Narragansett and other tribes, maintaining respect and influence among them until King Philip's War. Among his writings is an English-Indian lexicon, *Key into the Languages of America.* The Baptist denomination in America claims Williams as its founder.

Winslow, John (1703–1774) *military officer*
Born in Massachusetts, Winslow held several local offices and participated in many military battles, including the War of Jenkins's Ear. In 1755, he was assigned to Acadia, where he directed the deportation of the Acadians under the orders of Governor Charles Lawrence. He retired from the military in 1757 and

returned to Massachusetts, serving in the General Court in 1757–58 and 1761–65.

Winthrop, John (1587–1649) *a founder and first governor of Massachusetts Bay colony*

Winthrop, a member of the English gentry, attended Cambridge and studied law. Before leaving England he took a central role in plans to found a Puritan colony in the New World. He was elected governor before the group sailed. Arriving in 1630, he led the colony almost continuously until 1645, chosen 12 times at yearly elections. Winthrop was an able leader, although he opposed modern ideas of democracy and could be sanctimonious on occasion. He helped organize the New England Confederation and served as its first president. His writings include "A Model of Christian Charity," written aboard ship, which urged the colonists to found a utopian community, in covenant with each other and with God. His journal (also titled *The History of New England*), first published in 1825, is one of the most important sources of information about the early years of the colony. Winthrop was married four times and had a total of 16 children.

Winthrop, John (Winthrop the Younger) (1606–1676) *colonial governor of Connecticut*

The son of John Winthrop, he arrived in Boston in 1631. In 1633, he helped found Agawam (modern Ipswich), and in 1643 he organized investors to found the first integrated ironworks in America at Saugus. He served several terms on the Massachusetts governor's council, then became a Connecticut magistrate (1651), lieutenant governor (1657), and governor (1659 until his death). He traveled to England to obtain the charter uniting Connecticut and New Haven colonies in 1662. Winthrop was one of the first Americans elected to the Royal Society in England.

Wolfe, James (1727–1759) *British general who captured Quebec*

Born in England, Wolfe entered the army at the age of 14. During the French and Indian War, he became second in command to Jeffrey Amherst, British commander in North America, and was promoted to major

general after capturing Louisbourg in 1758. In June 1759, Wolfe sailed his troops up the Saint Lawrence River, encamping above Quebec. On the night of September 12, they landed and scaled a steep cliff to the Plains of Abraham above the city. The following morning, British troops defeated the French in a brief battle, and Quebec fell. Wolfe was killed in the battle, and the French commander Louis Joseph Montcalm died of his wounds the next day.

Woodmason, Charles (ca. 1720–after 1776) *Anglican cleric*

Born in England, Woodmason moved to South Carolina in 1752 without his family, accumulating land and slaves and holding minor official positions including tax collector. In 1765, he became an itinerant Anglican minister to the backwoods settlements, where he became a supporter and writer for the Regulator movement. He left vivid journals of his seven years on the frontier. After 1772, he moved to Virginia and Maryland. A Loyalist, he returned to England in 1774.

Woolman, John (1720–1772) *Quaker leader, abolitionist*

Born in New Jersey, Woolman was a devout Quaker who traveled and preached throughout the eastern seaboard. Because Quaker faith did not have an official paid ministry, he supported himself as a tailor. He was particularly noted for his early and outspoken opposition to slavery, publishing many tracts. His *Journal and Essays,* begun when he was 36 and published in 1774, is a major work of spiritual experience and antislavery thinking.

Zenger, John Peter (1697–1746) *printer, publisher*

Born in Germany, Zenger migrated to New York in 1710, where he was apprenticed to printer William Bradford. By 1733, he was printing the *New York Weekly Journal,* the mouthpiece of a group of merchants and lawyers who opposed royal governor Cosby's corrupt administration. He was arrested and tried for libel in 1734 but acquitted by the jury. The Zenger decision is considered a landmark in establishing a free press in America.

APPENDIX C
Maps

1. North American Indian Groups in the 16th Century
2. Acadia and Gulf of St. Lawrence
3. English Colonial Grants, 1609–1620
4. Colonial Grants, 1621–1650
5. Colonial Grants, 1662–1732
6. European Claims in North America, 1750
7. English Possessions and Proclamation Lines after 1763
8. Spanish and French Settlements in the American Interior to 1776

NORTH AMERICAN INDIAN GROUPS IN THE 16TH CENTURY

Arctic Ocean

Inuit
Koyukon
Athapascan
Ingalik
Tanana
Tanaina
Inuit
Hare
Inuit
Aleut
Han
Ahtena
Kutchin
Yellowknife
Tlingit
Tutchone
Mountain
Dogrib
Nahane
(Kaska,
Tagish, Tahltan)
Slave
Haida
Sekani
Chipewyan
Tsimshian
Beaver
Hudson Bay
Bella Bella
Carrier
Cree
Naskapi
Nootka
Bella Coola
Sarcee
Montagnais
Beothuk
Cowichan
Kwakiutl
Lillooet
Shuswap
Clallam
Stalo
Songish
Columbia
Blackfeet
Ojibway
Algonkin
Micmac
Malecite
Puyallup
Spokane
Kalispel
Assiniboine
Anishinabe
(Chippewa)
Nipissing
Passamaquoddy
Yakama
Pend D'Oreille
Chinook
Coeur D'Alene
Gros Ventre (Atsina)
Menominee
See inset
Puyallup
Cayuse
Nez Perce
Blood
Crow
Hidatsa
Winnebago
Tillamook
Klamath
Mandan
Fox
Neutral
Yurok
Modoc
Bannock
Arikara
Sauk
Potawatomi
Wintun
Shoshone
Sioux (Lakota)
Kickapoo
Monacan
Pomo
Maidu
Northern
Paiute
Cheyenne
Ponca
Omaha
Miami
Illinois
Powhatan Confederacy
Miwok
Arapaho
Iowa
Missouri
Shawnee
Roanoke
Castano
Washoe
Ute
Pawnee
Otoe
Osage
Tuscarora
Chesapeake
Yokuts
Paiute
Kansa
Cuitoa
Quapaw
Yuchi
Meherrin
Croatan
Chumash
Havasupai
Hopi
Cherokee
Cusabo
Luiseño
Cahuilla
Hualapai
Tiwa
Wichita
Chickasaw
Catawba
Guale
Mojave
Tewa
Alabama
Creek
Halchidhoma
Navajo
Zuni
Keres
Kiowa
Tacatacura
Yavapai
Piro
Comanche
Caddo
Choctaw
Apalachee
Tunica
Yuma
Maricopa
Kadohadacho
Natchez
Mobile
Ais
Kohuana
Cocopah
Tohono O'odham
Hasanai
Atakapa
Timucua
Akimel O'odham
Apache
Seri
Jumano
Karankawa
Calusa
Yaqui
Coahuiltec
Gulf of Mexico
Atlantic Ocean
Arawak (Taino)
Totonac
Tarascan
Carib
Aztec
Maya
Caribbean Sea
Cuna

Pacific Ocean

N

Inset:

* During the 16th century, the Mohegan were subsumed in the Abenaki.

Ottawa
Penobscot
Abenaki
Huron
Lake Ontario
Massachuset
Mohawk
Mahican
Oneida
Pequot
Mohegan*
Onondaga
Wampanoag
Cayuga
Wappinger
Narragansett
Lake Erie
Seneca
Montauk
Lenni Lenape
Susquehannock
Atlantic Ocean

Cuna

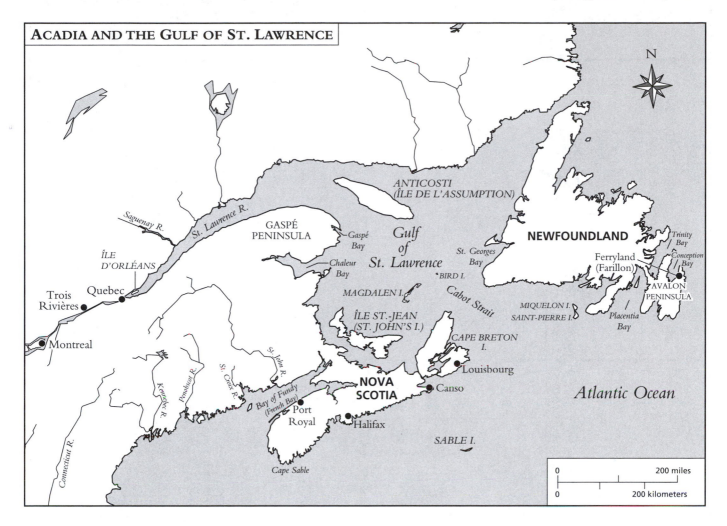

ACADIA AND THE GULF OF ST. LAWRENCE

N

Saguenay R.

St. Lawrence R.

ÎLE
D'ORLÉANS

GASPÉ
PENINSULA

*Gaspé
Bay*

*Chaleur
Bay*

*Gulf
of
St. Lawrence*

ANTICOSTI
(ÎLE DE L'ASSUMPTION)

NEWFOUNDLAND

*Trinity
Bay*

*St. Georges
Bay*

*Conception
Bay*

Ferryland
(Farillon)

AVALON
PENINSULA

BIRD I.

Trois
Rivières

Quebec

Montreal

MAGDALEN I.

ÎLE ST.-JEAN
(ST. JOHN'S I.)

Cabot Strait

MIQUELON I.

SAINT-PIERRE I.

*Placentia
Bay*

Penobscot R.

Kennebec R.

St. Croix R.

St. John R.

CAPE BRETON
I.

Louisbourg

**NOVA
SCOTIA**

Canso

*Bay of Fundy
(French Bay)*

Port
Royal

Halifax

Atlantic Ocean

Connecticut R.

Cape Sable

SABLE I.

| 0 | | 200 miles |
| 0 | | 200 kilometers |

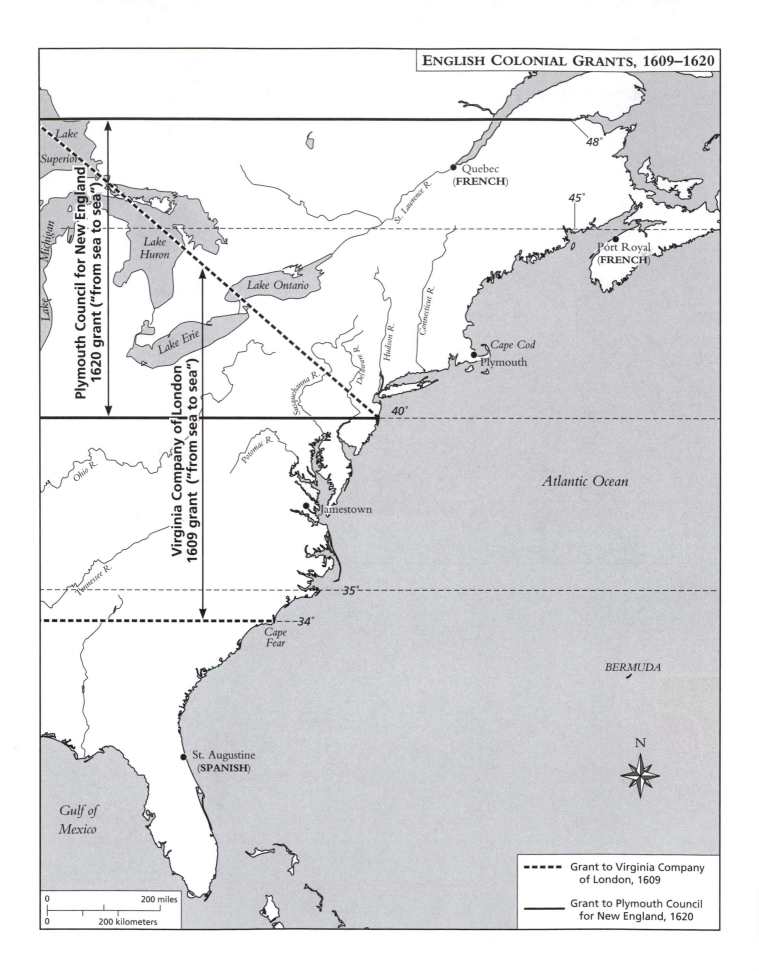

ENGLISH COLONIAL GRANTS, 1609–1620

Lake Superior

Lake Michigan

Lake Huron

Lake Erie

Lake Ontario

48°

45°

40°

35°

34°

Quebec (**FRENCH**)

St. Lawrence R.

Port Royal (**FRENCH**)

Connecticut R.

Hudson R.

Delaware R.

Susquehanna R.

Cape Cod
Plymouth

Ohio R.

Potomac R.

Tennessee R.

Jamestown

Cape Fear

Atlantic Ocean

BERMUDA

N

St. Augustine (**SPANISH**)

Gulf of Mexico

Plymouth Council for New England 1620 grant ("from sea to sea")

Virginia Company of London 1609 grant ("from sea to sea")

0   200 miles

0   200 kilometers

- - - - - Grant to Virginia Company of London, 1609

————— Grant to Plymouth Council for New England, 1620

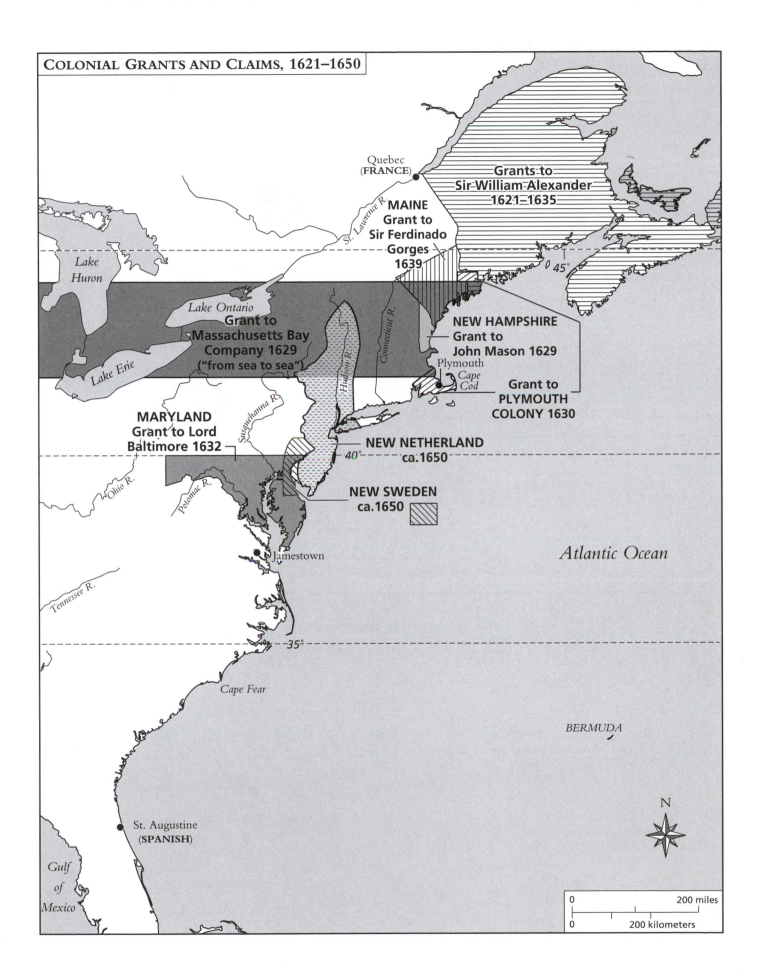

COLONIAL GRANTS AND CLAIMS, 1621–1650

Grants to
Sir William Alexander
1621–1635

Quebec
(FRANCE)

MAINE
Grant to
Sir Ferdinado
Gorges
1639

45°

NEW HAMPSHIRE
Grant to
John Mason 1629

Lake Huron

Lake Ontario
Grant to
Massachusetts Bay
Company 1629
("from sea to sea")

Lake Erie

Plymouth
Cape Cod

Grant to
PLYMOUTH
COLONY 1630

MARYLAND
Grant to Lord
Baltimore 1632

Susquehanna R.

Hudson R.

Connecticut R.

St. Lawrence R.

NEW NETHERLAND
ca. 1650

40°

Ohio R.

Potomac R.

NEW SWEDEN
ca. 1650

Atlantic Ocean

Jamestown

Tennessee R.

35°

Cape Fear

BERMUDA

St. Augustine
(SPANISH)

Gulf
of
Mexico

N

0   200 miles
0   200 kilometers

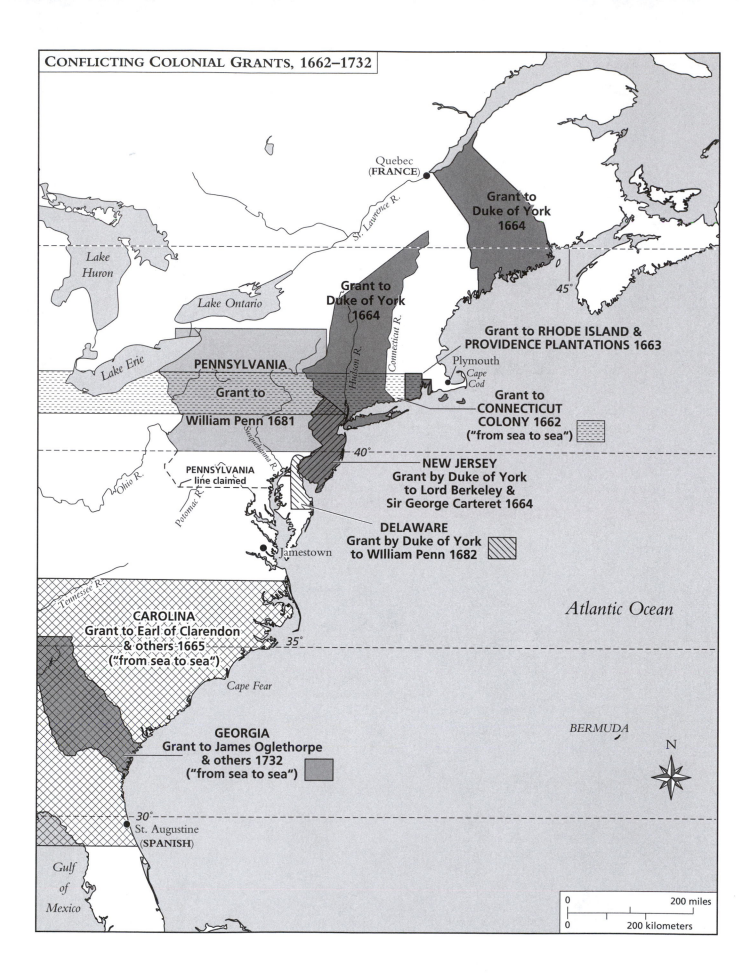

CONFLICTING COLONIAL GRANTS, 1662–1732

Quebec
(FRANCE)

Grant to Duke of York 1664

Lake Huron

Lake Ontario

Grant to Duke of York 1664

Grant to RHODE ISLAND & PROVIDENCE PLANTATIONS 1663

Lake Erie

PENNSYLVANIA

Grant to William Penn 1681

Plymouth
Cape Cod

Grant to CONNECTICUT COLONY 1662 ("from sea to sea")

45°

St. Lawrence R.

Hudson R.

Connecticut R.

PENNSYLVANIA line claimed

Ohio R.

Susquehanna R.

Potomac R.

40°

NEW JERSEY Grant by Duke of York to Lord Berkeley & Sir George Carteret 1664

DELAWARE Grant by Duke of York to WIlliam Penn 1682

Jamestown

Tennessee R.

CAROLINA Grant to Earl of Clarendon & others 1665 ("from sea to sea")

35°

Cape Fear

Atlantic Ocean

GEORGIA Grant to James Oglethorpe & others 1732 ("from sea to sea")

BERMUDA

N

30°

St. Augustine
(SPANISH)

Gulf of Mexico

| 0 | | 200 miles |
| 0 | | 200 kilometers |

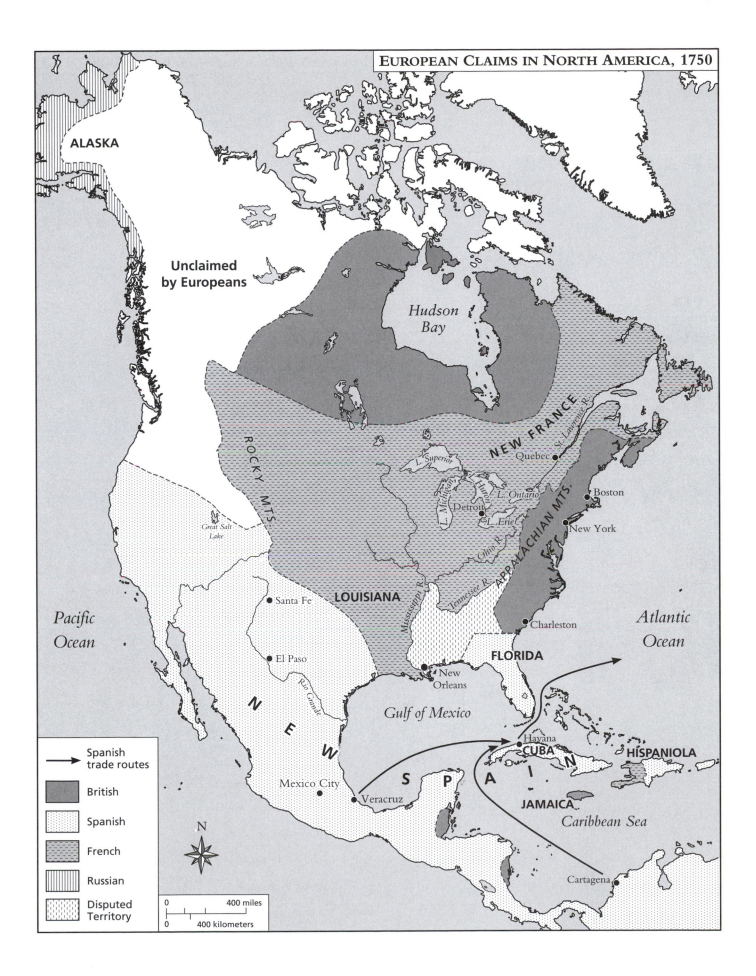

EUROPEAN CLAIMS IN NORTH AMERICA, 1750

ALASKA

Unclaimed
by Europeans

Hudson
Bay

NEW FRANCE

Quebec

St. Lawrence R.

L. Superior

ROCKY MTS.

L. Michigan

L. Huron

L. Ontario

Detroit

L. Erie

Boston

New York

Great Salt
Lake

APPALACHIAN MTS.

Ohio R.

Santa Fe

LOUISIANA

Mississippi R.

Tennessee R.

Charleston

Pacific
Ocean

El Paso

FLORIDA

Atlantic
Ocean

Rio Grande

New
Orleans

N E W

Gulf of Mexico

Havana

CUBA

HISPANIOLA

Spanish
trade routes

S P A I N

British

Mexico City

Veracruz

JAMAICA

Caribbean Sea

Spanish

French

N

Russian

Cartagena

Disputed
Territory

0   400 miles

0   400 kilometers

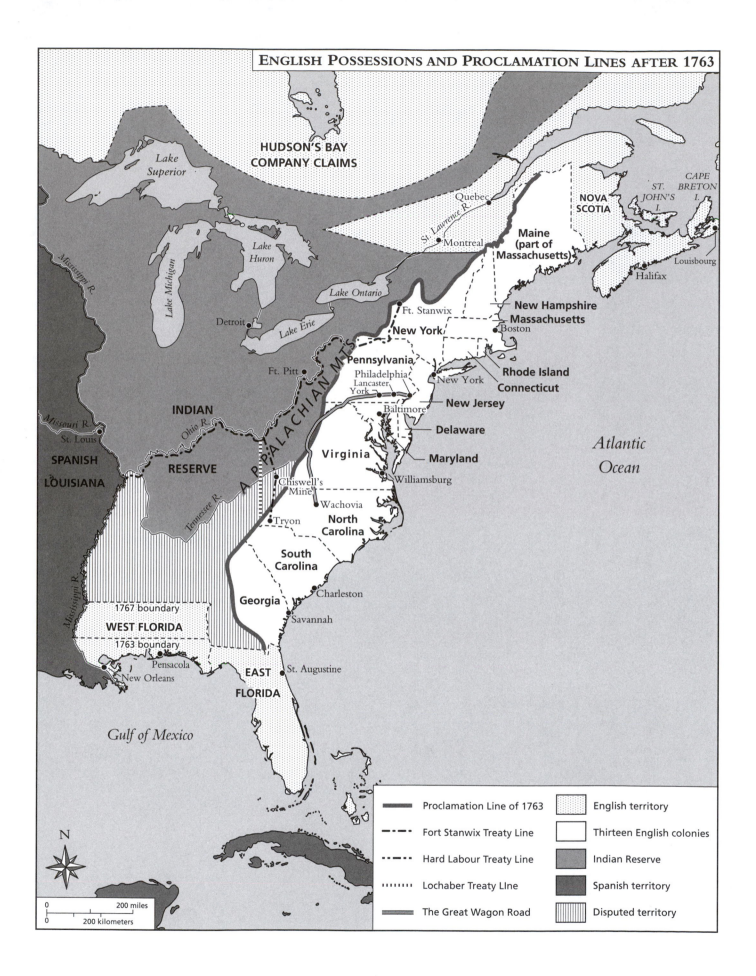

ENGLISH POSSESSIONS AND PROCLAMATION LINES AFTER 1763

HUDSON'S BAY
COMPANY CLAIMS

Lake Superior

Lake Michigan

Lake Huron

Detroit

Lake Erie

Lake Ontario

Missouri R.

Mississippi R.

Quebec

St. Lawrence R.

Montreal

NOVA
SCOTIA

ST. JOHN'S I.

CAPE BRETON I.

Louisbourg

Maine
(part of
Massachusetts)

Halifax

Ft. Stanwix

New York

New Hampshire
Massachusetts
Boston

Ft. Pitt

APPALACHIAN MTS

INDIAN

RESERVE

Ohio R.

Pennsylvania

Philadelphia
Lancaster
York

Baltimore

New York

Rhode Island
Connecticut

New Jersey

Delaware

SPANISH

LOUISIANA

St. Louis

Tennessee R.

Chiswell's
Mine

Wachovia

Tryon

Virginia

Williamsburg

Maryland

North
Carolina

South
Carolina

Georgia

Charleston

1767 boundary

WEST FLORIDA

1763 boundary

Mississippi R.

Savannah

Pensacola

New Orleans

EAST

FLORIDA

St. Augustine

Gulf of Mexico

*Atlantic
Ocean*

N

—— Proclamation Line of 1763	▦ English territory	
– · – Fort Stanwix Treaty Line	☐ Thirteen English colonies	
– ·· – Hard Labour Treaty Line	▓ Indian Reserve	
······· Lochaber Treaty LIne	▓ Spanish territory	
═══ The Great Wagon Road	▥ Disputed territory	

0   200 miles

0   200 kilometers

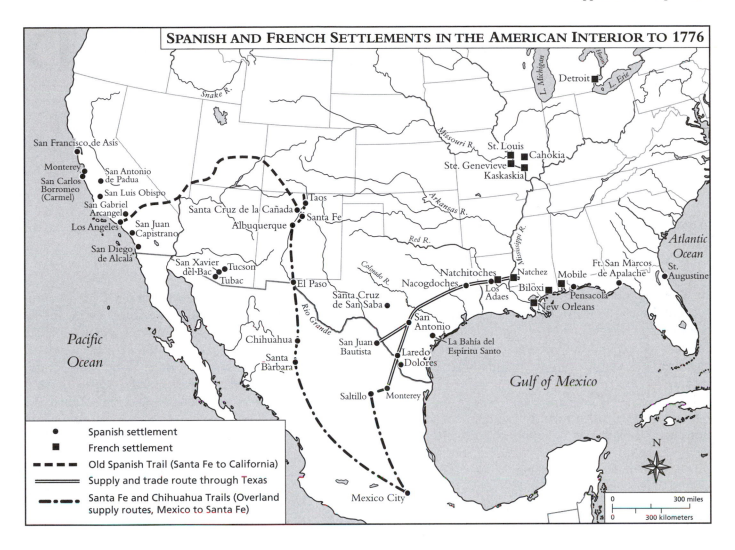

SPANISH AND FRENCH SETTLEMENTS IN THE AMERICAN INTERIOR TO 1776

Legend:
- ● Spanish settlement
- ■ French settlement
- – – – Old Spanish Trail (Santa Fe to California)
- ═══ Supply and trade route through Texas
- –·–· Santa Fe and Chihuahua Trails (Overland supply routes, Mexico to Santa Fe)

Labels on map:

Snake R.

Detroit

L. Michigan · *L. Erie* · *L. Huron*

San Francisco de Asís
Monterey
San Carlos Borromeo (Carmel)
San Antonio de Padua
San Luis Obispo
San Gabriel Arcangel
Los Angeles
San Juan Capistrano
San Diego de Alcalá
San Xavier del Bac
Tucson
Tubac

Santa Cruz de la Cañada
Taos
Albuquerque
Santa Fe
El Paso

St. Louis · Cahokia
Ste. Genevieve
Kaskaskia

Missouri R.
Arkansas R.
Red R.
Colorado R.
Rio Grande
Mississippi R.

Natchitoches
Nacogdoches
Natchez
Mobile
Ft. San Marcos de Apalache
St. Augustine
Los Adaes
Biloxi
Pensacola
New Orleans

Atlantic Ocean

Santa Cruz de San Saba
San Antonio
Chihuahua
San Juan Bautista
Laredo
Dolores
Santa Bárbara
La Bahía del Espíritu Santo

Pacific Ocean

Gulf of Mexico

Saltillo
Monterey
Mexico City

N

0   300 miles
0   300 kilometers

APPENDIX D

Glossary

Acadia   Territory that today is the Canadian provinces of Nova Scotia, Prince Edward Island, and New Brunswick, plus part of the state of Maine. Acadia's boundaries were never precisely established; the French and English fought over them until 1763. Originally the name was used on maps to identify the French claim to the North American coast, established by Giovanni de Verrazzano in 1524. He called the area "Arcadia," which mapmakers altered to Acadia.

adelantado   Spanish term for a person with a royal contract for exploration, conquest, and/or settlement of a region in New Spain. An *adelantado* was usually given some military support and the assistance of clergy at the expense of the Crown. He was required to pay other costs of exploration or settlement by himself. In return, he expected to generate income and achieve a higher status for himself and his descendants. Usually, his contract gave him the authority to govern the settlement he founded.

Admiralty courts   Special English courts, separate from the regular court system of the colonies, which tried all cases involving trade or other maritime violations. The courts operated without local juries under judges appointed by the Crown.

adventurer   An investor in a colonization venture. During the era when colonization began, to "adventure" meant to invest in a business or commercial speculation with the hope of future profits. Early colonization schemes had adventurers or investors and planters or colonists.

agent, colonial   A representative of one or more colonies, stationed in London to represent the interests and positions of his clients to the Crown.

alcalde   A mayor or magistrate. An alcade was an official appointed to govern a district within a colonized territory.

apprenticeship   A contract under which a young person was bound to a skilled person for a period of years or until age 21, in order to learn a craft or other skills. The apprentice worked for maintenance and very low or no wages. Both girls and boys were bound, the girls usually to learn domestic skills. Apprenticeship was considered a form of education in the colonial era. In most of the English colonies, masters were obligated to teach their apprentices to read.

assistants   Another name for members of the council in an English colony, used especially in early New England. The board members of the **joint-stock companies** that founded some colonies were also called assistants.

backcountry   In the English colonies, the settlements west of the established seaboard and Tidewater settlements and east of the Appalachians.

black code   See **slave code; Code Noir.**

Board of Trade (Board of Commissioners for Trade and Plantations)   An independent group of officials established by King William in 1696 to gather information about British colonies, examine colonial law, and recommend colonial policy. The recommendations required the approval of the king, but they carried great weight. The Board of Trade replaced the Lords of Trade; unlike the Lords, Board of Trade members were not all noblemen. It lost power during the American Revolution and disbanded in 1782.

bouwries   The Dutch term for farms.

burgher   The Dutch term for a (male) resident of a town who made his living by some means other than farming, especially one who had voting rights. A *burgher government* was an independent or chartered municipal government. A *burgomaster* was a municipal official similar to a mayor.

cabildo   Spanish for a town or municipal council.

casas reales   Spanish for government buildings.

Cavaliers   The name given to royalists or supporters of Charles I during the English Civil Wars (1641–49). The Cavaliers' opponents, many of whom were Puritans, were called Roundheads or Parliamentarians. Some Cavaliers eventually immigrated to the Chesapeake colonies.

charter   A written grant from the crown that specifies rights and institutions of government in a defined location, delegates them to a stated group of people, and defines the relationship between the future colony and the Crown/founding nation itself.

chartered colony   A colony possessing a **charter** from the Crown that establishes the institutions of self-government. It includes instructions for the ongoing selection of the colony's governing bodies by its citizens. The term *chartered colony* is used to distinguish a colony that is neither a **royal colony** nor a **proprietary colony**, although the latter was usually established by the granting of a charter (in its general sense) to a person or group of people.

chattel slavery   A form of slavery in which human slaves are legally defined as the material possessions of the slave owner; that is, as "moveable" property, like a piece of furniture or a head of cattle. The fact that slaves in colonial America were defined as *chattels* made it possible for some white owners to argue that there was no contradiction between Revolutionary "liberty" and slave ownership, because the English concept of liberty included the right to own and control property.

Chesapeake colonies   Maryland and Virginia, the colonies with an eastern coastline on the Chesapeake Bay.

Code Noir   French for Black Code. The code was a series of laws specifically regulating the behavior of slaves, setting penalties for crimes and offenses, requiring their instruction in the Catholic faith, and regulating their treatment by slave owners. The first Code Noir was designed by Jean-Baptiste Colbert and passed in 1685 for use in France's colonies outside of North America. The Code was never officially adopted in New France. In 1724, an adaptation of the Code was adopted in Louisiana, where it also expelled Jews from the colony.

commissary   The business manager of a colony, responsible among other things for arranging for its supplies. In the French colonies, the office of **intendant** later incorporated these responsibilities. When applied to an official of a religious order, the term refers to the head administrator in an area who serves as the bishop's direct representative. See also *custodio.*

Committee for Trade and Plantations   See **Lords of Trade.**

committees of correspondence   Bodies formed in the English colonies after 1764 to correspond with each other about British violations of colonial rights in their locales. They also composed statements of what they believed colonial rights to be. The committees disseminated information to sources such as newspapers and submitted it to other towns and colonies, thus influencing public opinion. They had an important role in establishing a shared sense of colonial identity as well as actual intercolonial cooperation. The first official committee of correspondence began in Boston in 1772 under the leadership of Samuel Adams. Informal committees existed before that time among religious leaders (who feared the violation of religious rights by the Anglican establishment) as well as political leaders.

conform   The term used to describe the strict adherence of ministers and churches to the established beliefs and procedures of the English Anglican church.

conquistadores   Spanish explorers and conquerors of South, Central, and North America and the island nations of the West Indies in the 16th century. By that date, Spain had a long tradition of *hidalgos,* or minor aristocrats, whose sole occupation was a military (and religious) crusade against the Muslim Moors of Africa who had ruled Spain and Portugal since 718. In 1492–coincidentally the same year that Columbus landed in the New World—Catholic Spain succeeded in expelling the Moors. Jews were also expelled if they would not convert to Christianity. With no remaining enemies at home, many Spanish men of military background turned their attention to the newly found lands across the ocean. Conquistadores gained a deserved reputation for extensive brutality, although few gained the riches they sought in the New World. They did, however, establish Spanish rule and the Catholic faith among the indigenous peoples they found and usually enslaved there.

convent   The home of either men (friars, brothers, or priests) or women (nuns) in Catholic religious orders.

council, colonial   In the English colonies, a group of appointed officials who assisted the governor. Members were usually appointed by the crown or the governor himself from among the colony's prominent citizens and usually represented the interests of the well-established and wealthy. In a few places, members were elected. For much of the colonial era, most councils functioned like an upper legislative house, often with veto power over the elected assembly. By the mid-18th century in some colonies, the council functioned more like a modern cabinet of advisors to the governor.

country-born   Term applied to slaves of African descent who were born in America. Compare **saltwater Africans.**

coureurs de bois   French for independent fur traders (literally, runners or couriers of the woods) who traveled far into Indian territories to obtain and trade for furs. Often, they lived among Indians for a period of time to learn their languages and culture. Their activity was an alternative to the usual trading pattern of established posts or rendevous points to which Indian traders themselves transported their goods to the French. Coureurs de bois operated without official permission or license. Compare **voyageurs.**

Covenant Chain   A trade and military alliance formed by the Iroquois with many other less powerful Indian nations, at the urging of the British. The Iro-

quois conducted trade, land, and military negotiations for nations whom they conquered or controlled and established intermediary chiefs who represented the interests of the associated tribes to confederacy councils. Tanaghrisson, the Mingo Half-King, was such a representative. The associated tribes had no real power in the confederacy, however. The British supported the concept to regulate Indian relations and make negotiations easier.

coverture   The legal principle under which women, upon marriage, were "covered" by their husband's identity. In other words, a married woman, or *feme covert,* lost her own civil and legal identity; and could not own property, enter into contracts, sue in court, claim her own wages, or determine the fate of her own children. Under coverture, an unmarried woman, or *feme sole,* did possess those rights to some measure. Coverture, which developed from English common law, remained the legal principle in America until the mid-19th century.

criollos   Residents of New Spain who were born in the New World. Compare **peninsulares.**

custodio   The Spanish term applied to the head Franciscan administrator in a defined area of missions, where he serves as the direct representative of the bishop. The term is usually translated into English as *custodian* but sometimes as *commissary.*

dame school   A school kept by a woman in her home to teach young children the rudiments of literacy, especially reading. Parents paid a small fee to send their children to dame schools.

Daughters of Liberty   The name taken by groups of women who organized in support of the Patriot cause in the pre-Revolutionary era. One of their main activities was the spinning bee, to produce homespun fabric as a substitute for imported cloth. The Daughters encouraged housewives to support nonimportation agreements, including that on tea, and earned much publicity in newspapers of the day. They were not organizationally connected to the Sons of Liberty.

debatable land   The territory between modern South Carolina and Florida. It was contested by the English and Spanish from the founding of the Carolinas until 1763, in alliance with shifting combinations of the southern Indian tribes who were its traditional occupants.

director-general   The term for a Dutch colonial governor.

Dominion of New England   The administrative combination of all the New England colonies plus New York and New Jersey, created by King James II in 1685. It was governed by one royally appointed governor (Sir Edmund Andros) and a council. Individual colonial assemblies lost their power. Designed to increase and centralize royal control, the Dominion was widely disliked by the colonists and contributed to the rebellions that occurred in the wake of the Glorious Revolution in England. The Dominion of New England was overthrown by colonists in Massachusetts in 1688.

dower right   The right of a widow, under the principles of coverture, to the use (but not the ownership) of a one-third share of her late husband's property during her lifetime. Despite the fact that she had not actually "owned" any part of her husband's estate during his lifetime, she could not be completely disinherited. On her death or remarriage, the property reverted to her husband's legal heirs. In the French colonies, which recognized community property, the dower right was one-half.

dowry   The property a colonial wife brought into a marriage. Most colonies prohibited husbands from disposing of dowry property without their wives' consent. See also **coverture.**

election, the elect   Terms used by Puritans to describe salvation (*election*) and those people who were believed to have been chosen for salvation (*the elect*) by God. The Puritans believed that election was solely by God's grace and could not be influenced by human effort.

Election Day   The day (usually in May or June) in Massachusetts and other New England colonies when annual civil elections were held for governor and other offices. It was a kind of holiday, marked by special sermons, speeches, and other events. *Negro Election Day* was a holiday and festival for slaves and free blacks, held primarily in New England, when the black community elected kings or governors to serve as extra-legal authorities within the black community.

encomendero   Spanish term for a person who is granted ownership of an *encomienda.* In return for the grant, he is obliged to render military service to the king if it is needed.

encomienda   Spanish term for a grant by the king of a large area of land in which all the residents owe to the grantee, or *encomendero,* a certain amount of labor or goods. They were designed primarily to enable Spanish colonists to exploit the labor of indigenous people in the New World. Technically, an encomienda is not actually a grant of land ownership, although in early New Spain the distinction was sometimes blurred. By the time Florida was established as a Spanish colony, the number of *encomiendas* granted by the crown had already begun to decline because of widespread abuses. Never well established in Florida, encomiendas were used more widely in New Mexico but discontinued entirely after the Pueblo Revolt of 1680.

engagé   French for a worker transported to New France under contract to work for a certain period of time, in exchange for lodging, food, and usually some salary. Engagés were similar to indentured servants but were less likely to be unskilled agricultural workers, because New France had little commercial agriculture. They were also more likely to return to Europe when their indentures ended.

enumerated goods   Items that could be exported from the colonies only to England or another colonial province, instead of being sold on the open international market for the highest possible price. Enumerated goods were listed by name in trade and navigation acts passed by Parliament.

established church   A church supported by government funds and recognized by the government as an institution connected to the civil colony or nation. Usually an established church and a government support the acquiescence of citizens to the authority of the other.

fall line   In geographical terms, the point along waterways marked by many falls and rapids, indicating the change from a more elevated area to plains. In colonial history, the fall line usually refers to the north-south running line that divides the Piedmont plateau from the Tidewater or other coastal plains.

Five Nations, League of   See **Iroquois Confederacy.**

freehold   Land owned absolutely and without restriction "in fee simple." It can be sold or passed on to one's descendants.

freeman   In the most general sense, men who owned a freehold in the colonial period; often used as a synonym for "voter." In order to vote in colonial elections or otherwise participate in the government of the colony, a man had to first be a landowner. However, being a landowner was not necessarily sufficient. In early New England, acceptance as a freeman-voter had to be granted by the existing body of freemen-voters. Acceptance required church membership in the early years, and later, a more general proof of good conduct. Later still, New England joined the other colonies in requiring a total estate of a certain value or ownership of a certain number of acres in order to vote. (In many places, less strict requirements existed for local elections.) In the city of New York, the classification of freeman had an economic as well as political meaning. Merchants and craftsmen could not engage in business until duly registered as a freeman (and paying a fee) with a local magistrate. With perhaps a few exceptions in the very early colonial era, only white freeholders were eligible to vote.

free school   A primary school established by a local government in the English colonies. Free schools were public schools, but they were not, in fact, usually free. In general, parents were charged a modest fee, although poor children might be educated at the community's expense.

General Court   The assembly or legislature of colonial Massachusetts. Originally, the General Court functioned judicially in important matters (like a modern supreme court) in addition to passing legislation.

genizaros   Spanish term for detribalized and usually Hispanicized Indians. The term is not applied to the Pueblo.

gente de razón   A Spanish term used to distinguish Hispanic or European people from unconverted Indians who maintained their traditional culture. The term sometimes includes Hispanicized Christian Indians as well. Literally, it means "people of reason."

gentry   During the colonial era, people ranking below the titled nobility but of prominent birth or established social status, significant financial resources, and landownership. The possession of a university education also usually qualified a man (primarily clergy) to be considered part of the gentry. Male members of the gentry were referred to as *gentlemen*. Sometimes, however, the term *gentleman* is used to describe a man who does not work for income because he is independently wealthy.

governor-general   The term for the governor of New France. The governor was responsible for diplomatic relations, military affairs, and the waging of war. Compare **intendant.**

grammar school   Originally, a school in which boys learned the rudiments of classical languages in order to prepare for the classical curriculum of a colonial college. Before being admitted to an early colonial grammar school, a student would have already attended a primary or free school or would know how to read and write well.

Great Migration   The migration of 20,000 Puritans and other dissenting Protestants from England to New England, occurring between 1630 and 1642. The Great Migration began when a group of Puritans bought out the charter of the Massachusetts Bay Company (1629); it ended with the beginning of the English Civil War.

habitant   French term for a settler in New France who is a farmer. It also implies he is part of a distinctive rural, French, and Catholic culture.

halfway covenant   A plan of partial church membership adopted in most New England Puritan congregations after 1662. The children of full church members could join the church without proof of a conversion experience if they lived upright lives and professed belief. They could not receive the sacrament of communion nor participate in church governance, although they could have their children baptized. Probably more importantly, they became eligible for civil voting privileges, because only church members were permitted to vote in many places in New England. By the opening of the 18th century, the distinction between full and halfway members had disappeared.

headright A grant of land, usually 50 acres per head, to any man (and sometimes woman) who paid the cost of passage to the colonies for himself or for any other person. It was most commonly used in the southern colonies in conjunction with the importation of indentured servants or slaves. Headright was eventually discontinued in the 18th century because so many people (especially ship captains) abused it, attempting to claim new rights every time they journeyed in and out of the colony.

hidalgo Spanish term for "gentleman"; the lowest rank of Spanish aristocracy. Supposedly, a *hidalgo* could prove he had no Jewish or African Muslim ancestors (both groups were expelled from Spain in 1492) and did not engage in trade. In Spain prior to the 16th century, the hildago was a kind of knight or military man who fought against the Moors, conquerers of Spain and Portugal in 718. In New Spain, the title was often used an honorary title more equivalent to an English gentleman or member of the gentry.

Huguenots French Calvinist Protestants. Huguenots had been subject to persecution at various times in France since the 16th century and figured in the earliest French attempts to found colonies in North America. After the revocation of the Edict of Nantes in 1695, which had granted them toleration in France, many Huguenots emigrated to the English colonies.

indentured servitude A form of unfree labor widely used in colonial America, begun by the Virginia Company to provide workers for their colony at Jamestown. In exchange for their passage to America and maintenance during servitude, indentured servants signed a contract for a certain term, commonly seven years for adults but as few as two when workers were in heavy demand. Children usually served until age 21. While indentured, they could not marry or own property. Upon completing their indentures, most were entitled to "freedom dues," which usually included some clothing, tools, and land. Most servants were

imported to do unskilled agricultural labor or domestic work, but very skilled craftsmen, some teachers, and others also came on indentures. Until the 18th century, indentured servants were cheaper than slaves and suffered many of the same difficulties, including poor food, clothing, and facilities, cruel treatment, sexual exploitation, high mortality rates, and severe penalties for misbehavior. The term *indenture* comes from the sheet of paper on which the contract was written. It was divided along an "indented" or irregular edge. One half was kept by the servant himself; the indented halves prevented the dishonest forging of a contract by either master or servant. Between one-half and two-thirds of all European immigrants to North America in the colonial era were indentured servants. The institution lasted into the 19th century, although it was not significant after the 18th.

indigo A high quality, natural blue dye, native to India.

intendant The head administrator of a French colony. The intendant oversaw public order, justice, and—probably most importantly—the colony's finances. His role was separate from that of the governor, which was restricted to military and diplomatic relations. In practice, governors and intendants often struggled for power and quarreled over specific issues. In the 18th century, the Spanish adopted the intendant system for their colonies as well.

Inter Caetera A papal bull, or official decree, issued in 1493 by Pope Alexander VI, which divided recently discovered lands between the nations of Spain and Portugal. It confirmed Spain's claim to most of the New World, which Columbus reached by sailing west; Portugal was awarded lands reached by sailing south and east around Africa. The bull instructs the crowns to appoint religious representatives to convert the indigenous people of these lands to Catholicism. In 1494, Spain and Portugal agreed to the Treaty of Tordesillas, based on *Inter Caetera,* dividing the New World between them along a longitudinal line 370 leagues west of the Cape Verde Islands. This line gave part of Brazil to Portugal, the remainder of North and South America to Spain.

Intolerable Acts Name given by English colonists to a series of five acts passed by Britain in 1774; also called the Coercive Acts. They included the Boston Port Act, closing Boston; the "regulating act," which curtailed Massachusetts charter rights; the Administration of Justice Act, which provided trials in England for officials accused in the colonies; a renewed Quartering Act, which required colonies to house and feed soldiers; and the Quebec Act, which gave British Canada jurisdiction over the Ohio Valley.

Iroquois Confederacy (Iroquois League, League of Five Nations, League of Six Nations, Haudenasaunee)   The largest and most powerful Indian alliance or association in colonial North America, based in upstate New York. The original nations, also known as the Five Nations were the Mohawk, Oneida, Onondaga, Cayuga, and Seneca. After 1711, the Tuscarora migrated northward and joined them, the group then becoming known as the Six Nations.

joint-stock company   An association of stockholders or investors who pooled their capital (and thus limited their individual risk) to engage in trading ventures and colonization ventures in the New World. Joint-stock companies developed in England and elsewhere in Europe in the 16th century, as new maritime explorations and discoveries made increased international trade a possibility. They were semi-private organizations, organized to undertake a specific venture for which they were chartered by the crown. Usually they were granted monopoly rights to develop, rule, and trade in an area. The Dutch West India Company and the London Company are examples.

justice of the peace   A local judge and law enforcement officer who handled minor criminal and civil offenses and had the power to detain and punish local offenders with fines or jail terms after conducting very informal proceedings. Deriving from English common law, the office was widely used during the colonial era, especially in thinly populated areas. Justices were usually prominent local people who charged fees for their services.

kiva   Underground sites for traditional ceremonial and religious activities among southwestern Indian groups.

Law of the Indies   The special body of law developed by Spain to deal with its colonial possessions in the New World.

Lords of Trade (Committee of the Privy Council for Trade and Plantations)   A permanent subcommittee of the Privy Council. Established in 1674, the Lords of Trade collected information about the colonies and developed policy for them. Under Charles II, they had the power to enforce as well as make decisions; under James II, they functioned in an advisory capacity and power over the colonies returned to the whole Privy Council. All members were noblemen. The Lords replaced the advisory joint Council for Foreign Plantations and Council of Trade, established in 1660 by Charles II (reorganized as the Joint Council for Trade and Plantations in 1672).

Loyalists   Colonists who opposed separation from Britain during the Revolutionary era, also called Tories. Loyalists faced great suppression and even persection as the Revolution approached. Nonetheless, probably about one-fifth of the colonists remained loyal to the crown throughout the war, and many of those fought for the British army. After the war was over, 50,000 fled the new nation, emigrating to Canada, England, or the British West Indies. Many received compensation from the British government. Their American property was confiscated by the new government and sold.

maroons   Residents of a concealed community of fugitive former slaves, especially in the Caribbean.

mercantilism   An economic doctrine followed in many countries of Europe from the 16th to the 18th centuries. It held that national interests demanded government protection of home manufacturing and industries by means of tariffs, and of merchants by means of monopolies. International trade was held to be important, but the goal was a positive balance of exports over imports to enable the nation to accumulate bullion or precious metals. Colonies were believed to be important as the suppliers of raw materials (enabling the nation to be more independent from foreign nations) and as the consumers of manufactured goods. Colonial trade was therefore strictly regulated under the policies of mercantilism.

Métis   A distinct people or ethnic group in Canada, who combined French and Indian heritage and traditions into a new and distinct culture. The Métis originally developed from the children of marriages between Indian women and French fur traders and woodsmen.

monopoly   The exclusive right to produce, supply, or market a certain commodity. In the colonial era, the imperial nations often granted national monopolies on certain commodities of trade, such as furs or tobacco, to groups or individuals as a way of encouraging economic development or colonization in the New World. Such a monopoly meant that all individual suppliers would have to sell their goods to the monopolist, who had the sole right to resell them in Europe or elsewhere.

naval stores   Products such as pitch, tar, resin, turpentine, lumber, tall white pine tree trunks (used for masts). These products were vital in the 17th and 18th centuries, when England's navy and merchant marine ruled the seas in ships constructed of wood.

Navigation Acts   A series of acts passed between 1651 and 1767 designed to regulate colonial trade for the benefit of England and prevent colonies from developing independent economies. They enacted duties and specified items that could be shipped and sold only to Britain or its other colonies. Significant acts were passed in 1651 (the First Navigation Act); 1660 (the Staple Act or Second Navigation Act); 1673 (the Plantation Duties, or Third Navigation Act); and 1696 (the Navigation Act of 1696). During the 18th century, modifications or supplements to the 17th century acts were passed, as well as the new Revenue Act of 1767 (one of the Townshend Acts). Until 1760, colonists were widely able to evade the acts. After that time, England focused more on enforcement, because the Crown desired to generate revenue as well as regulate trade. The resistance and anger of the colonists over the new policies started a chain of events that ended in the American Revolution.

New West   Term used in the Revolutionary era to describe territory west of the Appalachian Mountains and east of the Mississippi. It was officially opened to English colonists in the late 1760s when the so-called Proclamation Line was extended westward by a series of treaties with the Indians.

Northwest Passage   The name given to a sought-for passage by water across North America from the Atlantic to the Pacific. From the 1500s to the 1800s, countless European explorers searched for it, hoping to find a shorter route to the rich trading markets of eastern Asia. The route explorers sought through North America, of course, does not exist. In the 1850s, a sea route around North America by way of the Arctic Ocean was finally charted, although it was not actually traversed until the early 20th century.

Old Light/New Light   Terms used to describe the rift in the Congregational and other Protestant denominations, caused by the religious revival called the Great Awakening. Old Lights were traditionalists; New Lights were adherents of a more inclusive, evangelical theology and a more emotional style of preaching. In the Presbyterian Church, the two camps were called Old Side and New Side.

pacification   The term substituted by the Spanish for the conquest of lands and indigenous peoples in the New World. It was introduced in Philip II's Comprehensive Orders for New Discoveries (1573). The change was part of the crown's attempt to end the violence and abuses committed by the earliest conquistadores and settlers. Pacification increased the role of Catholic missionaries in securing the loyalty of Indians to Spain and decreased that of the military.

patent (letters patent)   A patent, sometimes called letters patent, was a document from the Crown granting certain rights and/or territories to its holder.

Patriots   Colonists who actively supported the cause of American independence. Compare **Loyalists.**

patroon, patroonship   Terms describing a form of land ownership. In New Netherland, the patroonship was a large grant of land to an individual or several individuals, called patroons, who were required to establish settlers there. Settlers in turn were granted or sold plots of land, which they held in perpetual leases rather than owning as freeholds. The patroon had the rights to establish and control the institutions of local government, including courts, and to collect quitrents or other forms of yearly payment from settlers. In New Netherland, only one patroonship was ultimately successful, that of Rensselaerswyck. Settlers much preferred to own land outright in freehold, as it was possible to do in the nearby English colonies.

peninsulares Spanish term for residents of colonies in New Spain who were born in Spain. Compare **criollos.**

petite guerre A French term for a style of Indian warfare, new to Europeans when they arrived in North America. *Petite guerre* was conducted in a series of relatively small-scale, sudden, unexpected attacks on undefended settlements or isolated farmsteads. During the attacks, the settlement or farm would be destroyed, crops burned, and settlers killed or taken prisoner. It was used by the Iroquois against the French in the middle of the 17th century and also figured prominently in French and Indian attacks in New England in the late 17th and early 18th century. See also **wilderness warfare.**

Piedmont The hilly area east of the Appalachian Mountains and west of the coastal plains (or Tidewater). In colonial history, the term usually refers specifically to Maryland, Virginia, and North Carolina. In geographical terms, however, the Piedmont stretches from modern New York to Alabama.

plantation In the 16th century, often a synonym for an entire settlement—e.g., Plymouth Plantation. The term *plantation* was also used to describe any smaller community or establishment that functioned as an economic unit; early iron manufacturing operations were called plantations, as were some mining operations. Particularly in the southern and island colonies, it was primarily used to describe an agricultural operation whose purpose was to produce staples for the export market. Through much of the colonial era, a plantation in the Chesapeake and southern colonies could be a small or a large farm that produced for the market, usually using some hired, indentured, or slave labor. By the 19th century, the term had come to be associated with very large, slave-worked land holdings.

planter At the opening of the colonial era, any settler who emigrated to "plant" a new European colony; as opposed to an adventurer or an investor who speculated on the venture but did not personally or permanently emigrate. Especially in the southern colonies, the term soon came to be used as a synonym for a farmer who produced crops for the export market, whether the farm was large or small. By the 19th cen-

tury the term had become associated primarily with owners of very large plantations with many slaves.

poll tax A head tax, or tax per person. When a poll tax was levied, freemen could be refused the right to vote if they did not pay it. Heads of households were assessed not only for themselves but for their dependents and slaves at some proportion of the whole number.

Praying Indian/Praying Town Terms describing Christianized Indians in New England who lived in settlements established by PURITAN missionaries. The first Praying Town was established in Natick, Massachusetts, in 1651; at their height in 1674, there were fourteen villages with over 4,000 converts. The Puritans' faith demanded a community of literate believers; Praying Towns were an attempt to establish such communities among New England Indians, where they could be schooled in literacy as well as doctrine. They were also taught crafts or other means of supporting themselves in settled communities.

presidio Spanish term, now adopted into English, for a fort or military installation in New Spain, in contrast to both *villas* or civil towns/civilian settlements and missions or religious settlements controlled by clergy.

privateering Piracy committed against ships of a foreign and enemy nation. Privateering increased after Spain began transporting silver and gold back to Europe from its colonies in Central and South America. England and other enemies of Spain chose to think of privateering as a political and patriotic act, although individual investors often financed the operation and shared in its profit. Technically, a privateer operated under license of the Crown in times of international hostilities or when issued a "letter of reprisal" to revenge piracy by another nation. In reality, those requirements were often disregarded. In times of actual war, privateers sometimes acted as a privately chartered navy.

Privy Council Group of advisers to the British Crown, personally selected by the monarch. The council, in whole or in small committees, performed many of the functions of government. It began to decline in power in the 18th century, as Parliament assumed more governing power and the British cabinet system of ministers came into being.

Proclamation Line(s)   The Proclamation Line was the westward boundary of officially permissible English colonization, first established in the Proclamation of 1763. At that time, it ran along the crest of the Appalachian chain; land to its west was officially Indian territory. The line was extremely unpopular and widely ignored by settlers. After 1768, the crown officially authorized movement of the line westward as soon as appropriate Indian treaties could be concluded. The treaties of Fort Stanwix (1768), Hard Labor (1768), and Lochaber (1770) demarcated new lines.

proprietary colony   A colony founded and controlled by a private organization for commercial profit or by a private individual for profit, status, and other reasons. The group or individual in possession of a grant, charter, patent, or contract from the Crown used its own resources to settle and develop the colony, in hope of future returns. Proprietors were delegated authority from the Crown to oversee the establishment and management of civil government in their colonies. The Jamestown colony was a proprietary venture by a joint-stock company hoping to extract valuable minerals or establish commercial agriculture. Maryland and Pennsylvania were colonies founded by individual proprietors who hoped to establish religious havens as well as increase their personal wealth.

proprietor, proprietorship   The term *proprietor* is used in several ways in colonial history. Usually, it means a person or persons in possession of a grant, charter, patent, or contract from the Crown to found and control a colony. Alternatively, it can mean a person in possession of a grant of certain rights to land in a existing civil jurisdiction, on which **quitrents** can be collected from the settlers who have purchased or been granted land there, but over which the proprietor exercises little formal control. A proprietorship is based on the idea that ultimate ownership of the land rests with the Crown; in effect, the Crown delegates certain of its rights to a private individual.

proprietors, town   In early New England, the original group of men approved by the colonial assembly to found a new town or settlement. Ownership of the new town's land grant was vested in the proprietors in exchange for an agreement to secure a minister and establish institutions of governance.

pueblo   Spanish term, literally, for a small town. Spanish explorers applied the name to a large group of Indians living in modern New Mexico because they lived in permanent villages. The term has come to mean those multistoried adobe structures inhabited by the Pueblo Indians as well as the collective names for these tribes (Tiwa, Tewa, Towa, Keres, Zuni, Hopi).

Puritans   Originally, a group of reformers within the English Anglican Church during the reign of Queen Elizabeth (d. 1603). They desired to make the church more consistently Protestant and Calvinist, and less akin to Catholicism, in its ritual, practices, and structure. They also wanted to weed out long-term abuses such as unfit clergy. During the succeeding reigns of James I and Charles I, Puritans continued their efforts to reform the English church but were increasingly persecuted by Crown and church officials. Some Puritans were primarily reformists; they considered themselves right-thinking Anglicans and were not necessarily opposed to an established church. Others were Separatists; they believed that the Anglican church was beyond reform and wished to separate from it entirely. The Pilgrims who arrived in Plymouth in 1620 were Separatists; the migration of English people to Massachusetts that began in 1630 was composed largely of reformist Puritans. The congregations they founded exercised almost complete independence and self-government; they eventually became known as the Congregational denomination.

quitrent   A yearly payment that landowners were required to make to proprietors. Quitrents existed throughout proprietary colonies, and anywhere else individuals had been awarded proprietary land grants by the Crown. The roots of the colonial quitrent were in the feudal system. Originally feudal tenants owed their lord a part of their produce and some military service; eventually, a monetary payment was substituted for those obligations. By the time the colonies were established, the quitrent functioned like a property tax, with one important exception. Its sole purpose was to provide income to those who held proprietary grants; it was not reinvested in public services of any kind as a government-levied tax would have been.

redemption agreement, redemptioner Terms describing a form of immigration. A redemption agreement was a form of indentured labor, which developed with the Palatine or German migrants to America after the late 17th century. The redemptioner agreed to pay his or her passage upon arrival in America. Some were "redeemed" by a friend or relative in the colonies. Most contracted to sell their labor once they had docked in an American port, in order to satisfy their debt.

reduction Translation of Spanish term (*reduccion*) for the act of settling converted Indians within a mission or village.

regidor Spanish term for a member of a cabildo or municipal council.

repartimiento Spanish for a limited term of forced labor by rotating groups of Indians. It was designed to accomplish public works projects in Spanish settlements but was often badly abused by private settlers.

Requerimiento A statement that summarized Spanish Catholic theology, demanded that its hearers accept the authority of the Spanish Crown and the pope, and warned of the consequences if they did not. Conquistadores and explorers were required to read it to the indigenous people whenever they entered a new part of the New World. It was almost always read in Spanish rather than the native language to Indians who comprehended little if any of its meaning.

rights of Englishmen Usually identified with rights established in English common law, and especially with the English system of courts and trial by jury. English colonists were entitled to the "rights of Englishmen" since the first colonial charter was granted to Sir Humphrey Gilbert—that is, to the same freedoms and protections possessed by native-born residents of England. After the Glorious Revolution in England (1688), colonists increasingly identified the rights of Englishmen with the ideas that the king and Parliament, as well as individuals, were subject to laws passed by representative bodies.

royal colony A colony under the direct control of a nation's Crown. The Crown sets policy for the colony; selects officials to govern it (often sending men who would return to Europe after their tour of duty); establishes or regulates the procedures under which it is administered; and provides support, especially military. Royal colonies can also have some institutions of self-government, such as assemblies. However, the Crown has authority to review (and reject) any law passed in the colony.

saltwater Africans Term applied to slaves born in Africa. Compare **country-born**.

salutary neglect An unofficial name for the policy of permitting colonies to develop with little imperial interference. Prior to 1660, it was the de facto policy for the English colonies and was specifically preferred by Sir Robert Walpole and some other officials in the early 18th century.

schout In the Dutch system of government, a local official who served as a combined sheriff and prosecuting attorney.

schpens In the Dutch system of government, a local official who served as a combined alderman and magistrate, with both judicial and administrative authority.

seasoning (seasoning year) The first year or more of residence in the New World. During that period, newcomers adjusted to the new climate and culture, often contracting diseases to which they had no resistance. Seasoning was considered more difficult in southern climates.

seigneur, seigneurie French terms describing a form of land ownership. In New France, the *seigneurie* was a large grant of land to a wealthy or prominent individual or to the church. The grantee was called the *seigneur* and was required to establish settlers on the land. Settlers in turn were granted plots of land called *rotures,* which they held in perpetual leases rather than owning as **freeholds.** The seigneur was required to see that land was cleared and planted within a specified time, establish a mill, develop roads or other necessary improvements, and establish a court of law over which he had jurisdiction. Settlers on the land owed him yearly *cens et rentes* ("dues" or tribute, often a certain portion of what they produced) and some yearly service for public works. The seigneurial system, which began after 1627, was used as a means of organizing and accomplishing settlement as well as establishing an elite for New France.

Separatists   Reformist English Protestants in the early 17th century who believed that the Anglican church was beyond reform and wished to separate from it. Separatists were one kind of Puritan, but not all Puritans were Separatists.

situado   Spanish term for a financial subsidy sent to a colony and used to pay its officials, soldiers, and religious personnel.

Six Nations, League of   See **Iroquois Confederacy.**

slave code   A series of laws specifically regulating the behavior of slaves and free black people and setting penalties for various crimes and offenses. In the English colonies, slave codes began to be passed in the early 18th century.

Sons of Liberty   Colonial organizations formed to protest against British policies in the pre-Revolutionary era. The first group was founded in Boston in 1765 and participated in both the Boston Massacre and the Boston Tea Party. The Sons published and circulated anti-British propaganda. They also held public demonstrations and protests, many of which involved violence or persecution of political opponents. Although Sons of Liberty leaders were usually people of some prominence, many members were ordinary farmers or working people.

spirit, spiriting   A spirit was a kidnapper, and spiriting was the act of kidnapping. The terms were applied to persons who kidnapped British citizens and transported them to America as indentured servants against their will.

starving time   A period of suffering endured during the first year of settlement in many colonies, when transported supplies ran short before the first crops could be successfully harvested.

Tidewater   The coastal plains of Virginia and Maryland, east of the fall line.

Tories   The name colonial revolutionaries gave to Loyalists who opposed separation from Britain. In Britain after 1689, the Tories were one of two major political parties (the other was the Whigs). The British Tories were conservatives, both politically and religiously. The party developed among those who supported absolute royalism and "legitimate" kings. They opposed a powerful representative Parliament, the deposing of Charles I, and the later ascension of King William and Queen Mary at the invitation of Parliament.

town proprietors   See **proprietors, town.**

triangular trade   A pattern of colonial commerce involving a series of exchanges between Americas, Africa, and Europe. The best-known triangular trade was the slave trade: rum and other goods were sent from Europe to Africa and exchanged for slaves; the slaves were taken to the Indies or North America and exchanged for sugar or tobacco; the sugar and tobacco were sent to Europe and exchanged for manufactured goods. Other important triangular-trade routes existed that did not deal in human beings. Although *trade* followed the triangular pattern, *individual ships* very rarely did; almost all individual voyages were round trips between two ports.

tribute   A regular payment, usually in goods, from one group to another to acknowledge dependence, the desire for military protection, or subjugation. In some cases, the payment is merely a token; in other cases, it is a significant means of increasing the wealth of the dominant group. A *tributary* is a group that makes such a payment and is therefore under the protection of a stronger group. In the colonial era, many Indian tribes were tributaries of stronger tribes or of a European power.

villa   Spanish term for a formally established and incorporated town.

visita   Spanish term for a small or distant Catholic mission with no resident priest; it received occasional visits from a missionary.

visitador   Spanish term for inspector.

voyageur   French term for professional fur traders and woodsmen who traveled deep into the Canadian wilderness in a manner similar to the **coureurs de** bois. However, unlike the coureurs de bois, the voyageurs were legal traders. They were officially licensed by the government of New France (by means of permits called *congés,* first issued in 1681) and were usually employees of fur trading companies. Also unlike the coureurs de bois, who often worked alone, voyageurs usually worked and traveled in groups, using distinctive, large, six-man canoes. They were especially skilled in navigating waterways into and throughout the wilderness, and a colorful tradition grew around their lifestyle. By the end of the 18th century, the distinction between the coureurs de bois and the voyagers had become unimportant.

Walloon   Protestants native to French-speaking Belgium and bordering areas of France.

Whigs   One of two major political parties in England during the 18th to mid-19th centuries (the other was the Tories). The Whigs favored reform and parliamentary rights. During the Revolutionary period, American colonists who supported separation from Britain were sometimes called Whigs. In the mid-19th century, an American political party called (American) Whigs developed, marked by a dislike and distrust of a strong executive government.

wilderness warfare (Indian guerrilla warfare)   A military tactic. Wilderness warfare was a fighting style new to Europeans when they arrived in the colonies. Indian warriors concealed themselves behind trees or other obstacles as they moved into place and fired at their opponents, often ambushing them. Wilderness warfare was very different from the formation and line-based European tactics, in which uniformed soldiers often marched toward each other in full sight, firing at clearly visible opponents. Although colonial militias became very adept at wilderness warfare, European commanders sent to North America consistently found it difficult to accept. See also *petite guerre.*

NOTES

1. EUROPEAN SETTLEMENT OF NORTH AMERICA TO 1607

1. Historical and anthropological research on the Spanish experience in colonial Florida is ongoing. For details of life in St. Augustine, see Eugene Lyon, "Settlement and Survival," pp. 40–61; for information on ethnicity see Amy Turner Bushnell, "Republic of Spaniards, Republic of Indians," pp. 62–77. Both essays appear in *New History of Florida,* ed. M. Gannon (Gainesville: University Press of Florida, 1996).

2. NEW SPAIN, NEW FRANCE, AND ACADIA, 1607–1670

1. See David J. Weber, *The Spanish Frontier in North America* (New Haven: Yale University Press, 1992), p. 125.
2. On European diseases and their effect on the Indians of Spanish Florida, see Henry F. Dobyns, "The Invasion of Florida: Disease and the Indians of Florida," in *Spanish Pathways in Florida,* ed. A. Henderson and G. Mormino (Sarasota: Pineapple Press, 1991), pp. 58–77.
3. For details about 17th century life in St. Augustine, see Amy Bushnell, *The King's Coffer* (Gainesville: University Press of Florida, 1981), especially chapter 2.

3. THE FOUNDING OF VIRGINIA, NEW ENGLAND, AND NEW NETHERLAND, 1607–1630

1. W. Stitt Robinson, *The Southern Colonial Frontier* (Albuquerque: University of New Mexico Press, 1979), p. 23.
2. On Powhatan, see Ian Steele, *Warpaths: Invasions of North America* (New York: Oxford University Press, 1994), pp. 37–38.
3. On the treatment of indentured servants in America, see Edmund Morgan, *American Slavery, American Freedom* (New York: Norton, 1975), pp. 123–30.

4. Robinson, *Southern,* pp. 30–32.

4. SETTLEMENT SPREADS IN NEW ENGLAND, THE CHESAPEAKE, AND THE MIDDLE ATLANTIC, 1630–1642

1. See Samuel Eliot Morison, *The Founding of Harvard College* (Cambridge: Harvard University Press, 1935).
2. Today literacy usually refers to the ability to read and write. In the colonial era, however, the teaching of *writing* was separate from (and not as common as) the teaching of *reading*. Historians believe that many more colonists could read than could write and that the difference was especially pronounced among the female population.
3. Population statistics from Ellen Lloyd Trover, ed., *Chronology and Documentary Handbook of the State of Virginia* (Dobbs Ferry, N.Y.: Oceana Publications, 1978).
4. On indentured servants, see Robinson, *Southern, 1607–1763,* pp. 52–53.
5. Architectural historians point out that every immigrant to America did not learn log construction from the Swedish. Immigrants from forested areas of Europe such as Germany, Switzerland, and elsewhere were also familiar with the building method before their arrival in America. The British, Irish, Scots, French, or Spanish, however, were not. For details about life in New Sweden, see the works of Amandus Johnson, such as *Swedish Settlements on the Delaware,* 1911 (Reprint Baltimore: Genealogical Publishing Company, 1969).

5. THE ENGLISH COLONIES MEET IN THE MIDDLE, 1642–1670

1. The information on colonial urban life in this section is indebted to Carl Bridenbaugh, *Cities in the Wilderness* (New York: Ronald Press, 1938).

[CHAPTER 6: NO NOTES]

7. EXPANSION, MISRULE, AND REBELLION IN THE ENGLISH COLONIES, 1670–1691

1. Population statistics are taken primarily from the series *Chronology and Documentary Handbooks* for the individual colony in question.

8. THE ENGLISH COLONIES ENTER THE 18TH CENTURY, 1691–1730

1. Historical research on American slavery during the colonial era is ongoing, and many areas of disagreement continue to exist. Works focusing on the colonial era that were helpful in the preparation of this section are: for an overview, Peter Kolchin, *American Slavery, 1619–1817* (New York: Hill and Wang, 1993); the more detailed work of Ira Berlin, *Many Thousands Gone* (Cambridge, MA: Belknap, Harvard University Press, 1998); and works limited to specific areas such as Peter H. Wood, *The Black Majority* (New York: Knopf, 1974) and those cited below.

2. On the ethnicity of African slaves in North America, see Philip D. Morgan, *Slave Counterpoint* (Chapel Hill: University of North Carolina Press, 1998), p. 62 ff.

3. On slavery in New England, see William D. Piersen, *Black Yankees* (Amherst: University of Massachusetts Press, 1988).

9. THE ENGLISH COLONIES AT THE MIDDLE OF THE 18TH CENTURY, 1730–1750

1. Richard Hofstadter, *Academic Freedom in the Age of the College* (New York: Columbia University Press, 1955, 1961), pp. 168–69.

2. Carl Bridenbaugh, *Cities in Revolt* (New York: Knopf, 1955), p. 5. Information in this section is indebted to that volume.

10. THE REALIGNMENT OF NORTH AMERICA, 1750–1776

1. On slavery in colonial Canada, see Robin Winks, *The Blacks in Canada* (Montreal: McGill-Queen's University Press, 1971), chapters 1 and 2. Statistics above, cited by Winks, are from the work of Marcel Trudel, *L'esclavage au Canada français.*

2. Information on Louisiana society in this section is drawn from Thomas N. Ingersoll, *Mammon and Manon in Early New Orleans* (Knoxville: University of Tennessee Press, 1999), chapters 1–5. On slavery in Louisiana, see also Berlin, *Many Thousands Gone,* chapters 4 and 8.

3. Selwyn K. Troen and Glen E. Holt, eds., *St. Louis* (New York: New Viewpoints, Franklin Watts, 1977), chapter 2.

4. For information on Spanish-Pueblo military alliances, see Donald Cutter and Iris Engstrand, *Quest for Empire: Spanish Settlement in the Southwest* (Golden, Colo.: Fulcrum, 1996), chapter 8.

5. Donald Chipman, *Spanish Texas* (Austin: University of Texas Press, 1992), p. 188ff.

11. THE ROAD TO REVOLUTION IN THE ENGLISH COLONIES, 1750–1776

1. On the formation of a new African-American culture, see Berlin, *Many Thousands Gone,* chapters 5 to 7; and Kolchin, *American Slavery,* chapters 2 and 3.

BIBLIOGRAPHY

In an effort to help maintain accessibility to the general reader, this bibliography contains full references only for sources of Eyewitness Testimony, supplemented by a small group of works that were consulted extensively in the preparation of this book. It omits many additional historical studies that were consulted on specific topics but not directly referenced or quoted. Since it is not possible to list these studies individually, this note must serve as a general acknowledgment of many additional historians whose work has made available a great pool of research on colonial North America.

Adams, John. *Works of John Adams, Second President of the United States.* Edited by C. Adams. 10 vols. Boston: 1850–56.

Adler, Mortimer, ed. *The Negro in American History.* Vol. 3, *Slaves and Masters, 1567–1854.* N.p.: Encyclopaedia Britannica Educational Corp., 1969.

AJHSP [*American Jewish Historical Society Publications*]. New York: Vols. 1–50, 1893–June 1961.

Alden, John R. *John Stuart and the Southern Colonial Frontier: A Study of Indian Relations, War, Trade, and Land Problems in the Southern Wilderness, 1754–1775.* Ann Arbor: University of Michigan Press, 1944.

Allen, Ethan. A *Narrative of Col. Ethan Allen's Captivity, Written by Himself.* 4th ed. Burlington, Vt.: Goodrich, 1846.

Amherst, Jeffery. *Journal of Jeffery Amherst.* Edited by J.C. Webster. Canadian Historical Studies. Edited by L. Pierce. Toronto: Ryerson Press, 1931.

Anderson, Fred. *Crucible of War: The Seven Years' War and the Fate of Empire in British North America, 1754–1766.* New York: Alfred A. Knopf, 2000.

Andrews, Charles M., ed. *Narratives of the Insurrections, 1675–1690.* Original Narratives of Early American History. New York: Scribner, 1915.

Andrews, William L., ed. *Journeys in New Worlds: Early American Women's Narratives.* Madison: University of Wisconsin Press, 1990.

Aptheker, Herbert. *American Negro Slave Revolts.* New York: International Publishers, 1943, 1983.

————, ed. *Documentary History of the Negro People in the United States.* Vol. 1, *Colonial Times through the Civil War.* New York: Carol Publishing Group, 1951, 1990.

Bailyn, Bernard. *Ideological Origins of the American Revolution.* Cambridge: Harvard University Press, Belknap, 1967.

————. *New England Merchants in the Seventeenth Century.* New York: Harper and Row, Torchbooks, 1955.

Baird, Charles W. *History of the Huguenot Emigration to America.* 2 vols. New York: Dodd, Mead, 1885.

Banks, Ronald F. *A History of Maine.* Dubuque, Iowa: Kendall/Hunt Publishing, 1969.

Barck, Oscar T., Jr., and Hugh T. Lefler. *Colonial America.* 2nd ed. New York: Macmillan, 1968.

Bartram, John. *A Journey from Pennsylvania to Onondaga in 1743, by John Bartram, Lewis Evans, [and] Conrad Weiser.* Barre, Mass.: Imprint Society, 1973.

Bartram, William. *Travels of William Bartram.* Edited by Mark Van Doren. New York: Macy-Masius, 1928.

————. *Travels Through North and South Carolina, Georgia, East and West Florida.* Salt Lake City, Utah: Peregrine Smith, 1980.

The Bay Psalm Book, Being a Facsimile of the 1st Edition, Printed by Stephen Day at Cambridge in New England, 1640. Introduced by W. Eames. New York: Dodd Mead, 1903.

Benavides, Fray Alonso de. *Revised Memorial of 1634.* Edited by F. Hodge, G. Hammond, and A. Rey. Albuquerque: University of New Mexico Press, 1945.

Bercovitch, Sacvan. *American Jeremiad.* Madison: University of Wisconsin Press, 1978.

Berkin, Carol Ruth, and Mary Beth Norton, eds. *Women of America: A History.* Boston, Mass.: Houghton Mifflin, 1979.

Berlin, Ira. *Many Thousands Gone: The First Two Centuries of Slavery in North America.* Cambridge, Mass.: Harvard University Press, Belknap, 1998.

Billings, Warren M. *The Old Dominion in the Seventeenth Century: A Documentary History of Virginia, 1606–1689.* Documentary Problems in Early American History. Chapel Hill: University of North Carolina Press for the Institute of Early American Culture, 1975.

Blau, Joseph L., ed. *Cornerstones of Religious Freedom in America.* Boston: Beacon Press, 1949.

Booth, Sally Smith. *Hung, Strung, and Potted: A History of Eating in Colonial America.* New York: Clarshank, Potter, 1971.

Bossu Jean-Bernard. *Travels in the Interior of North America, 1751–1762.* Translated and edited by S. Feiler. Norman: University of Oklahoma Press, 1962.

Boucher, Pierre. *Canada in the Seventeenth Century.* Translated by E. Montizambert. 1664. Reprint, Montreal: George E. Desbarats, 1883. [Original title *True and Genuine Description of New France, Commonly Called Canada.*]

Boyd, Mark F., Hale G. Smith, and John W. Griffin, eds. *Here Once They Stood: The Tragic End of the Apalachee Missions.* Gainesville: University of Florida Press, 1951.

Boyer, Paul, and Stephen Nissenbaum, eds. "The Salem Witchcraft Papers: Verbatim Transcripts of the Legal Documents of the Salem Witchcraft Outbreak of 1692, Compiled and Transcribed in 1938 by the WPA under the Supervision of Archie N. Frost." URL: etext.lib.virginia.edu.

Bradford, William. *Bradford's History "Of Plimouth Plantation."* Boston, Mass.: Wright and Potter, 1898.

Bradstreet, Anne. *Works of Anne Bradstreet.* Edited by J. Hensley. Cambridge, Mass.: Harvard University Press, Belknap, 1967.

Brasseaux, Carl A. *The Founding of New Acadia: The Beginnings of Acadian Life in Louisiana, 1765–1803.* Baton Rouge: Louisiana State University Press, 1987.

Bridenbaugh, Carl. *Cities in Revolt: Urban Life in America, 1743–1776.* New York: Alfred A. Knopf, 1955.

———. *Cities in the Wilderness: The First Century of Urban Life in America, 1625–1742.* New York: Ronald Press, 1938.

———. *Jamestown: 1544–1699.* New York: Oxford University Press, 1980.

Briggs, Sam, ed. *Essays, Humor, and Poems of Nathaniel Ames.* Cleveland, Ohio: Short and Forman, 1891.

Brodhead, John Romeyn. *Documents Relative to the Colonial History of the State of New York.* 15 vols. Edited by F. O'Callaghan. Albany, N.Y.: Weed, Parsons, 1853–87.

———. *History of the State of New York.* New York: Harper and Brothers, 1853–71.

Brownlee, W. Elliot, and Mary M. Brownlee, eds. *Women in the American Economy: A Documentary History, 1675–1929.* New Haven, Conn.: Yale University Press, 1976.

Brugger, Robert J. *Maryland, A Middle Temperament: 1634–1980.* Baltimore: Johns Hopkins University Press for the Maryland Historical Society, 1988.

Burr, George Lincoln, ed. *Narratives of the Witchcraft Cases, 1648–1706.* Original Narratives of Early American History. New York: Barnes, 1914.

Burrage, Henry F., ed. *Early English and French Voyages, Chiefly from Hakluyt, 1534–1608.* New York: Scribner, 1906.

Bushman, Richard L., ed. *The Great Awakening: Documents on the Revival of Religion, 1740–1745.* Documentary Problems in Early American History. New York: Atheneum for the Institute of Early American History and Culture, 1970.

Bushnell, Amy. *The King's Coffer: Proprietors of the Spanish Florida Treasury, 1565–1702.* Gainesville: University Presses of Florida, 1981.

———. "Republic of Spaniards, Republic of Indians." In *New History of Florida.* Edited by M. Gannon. Gainesville: University Presses of Florida, 1996.

Bustamante, Adrian H. "Españoles, Castas, y Labradores: Santa Fe Society in the Eighteenth Century." In *Santa Fe: History of an Ancient City.* Edited by D. Noble, Santa Fe, New Mexico: School of American Research Press, 1989.

Byrd, William. *The Great American Gentleman: The Secret Diary of William Byrd of Westover, 1709–1712.* Edited by L. Wright and M. Tinling. New York: Capricorn Books, 1963.

———. *Writings of Colonel William Byrd of Westover, Esquire.* Edited by J. Bassett. New York: Doubleday, Page, 1901.

Calder, Isabel M., ed. *Colonial Captivities, Marches, and Journeys.* New York: Macmillan, 1935.

Caldwell, Howard Walter, and Clark Edmund Persinger. *A Source History of the United States: From Discovery 1492 to End of Reconstruction 1877.* Chicago: Ainsworth and Company, 1909.

Caruso, John Anthony. *The Southern Frontier.* Indianapolis, Ind.: Bobbs Merrill, 1963.

Céliz, Fray Francisco. *Diary of the Alarcon Expedition into Texas, 1718–1719.* Translated by F. Hoffman. Los Angeles, Calif.: Quivera Society, 1935.

Chalkley, Thomas. *Journal.* Philadelphia, Penn.: Friends Bookstore, n.d.

Champlain, Samuel de. *Voyages of Samuel Champlain, 1604–1635.* Edited by W. Grant. New York: Scribner, 1907.

Chapin, Howard M. *Documentary History of Rhode Island.* Providence, R.I.: Preston and Rounds, 1916.

Charlevoix, Pierre-Francois-Xavier, S.J. *Journal of a Voyage to North America, Undertaken by Order of the French King.* 1744. 2 vols. London: R. and J. Dodsley, 1771.

Charters and General Laws of the Colony and Province of Massachusetts Bay. Boston, Mass.: T.B. Wait, 1814.

Chipman, Donald E. *Spanish Texas, 1519–1821.* Austin: University of Texas Press, 1992.

Christie, Robert. *A History of the Late Province of Lower Canada, Parliamentary and Political.* 6 vols. Montreal: Richard Worthington, 1866.

Chronology and Documentary Handbook Series. Dobbs Ferry, N.Y.: Oceana Publications, 1973–78.

Clark, S. D. *The Social Development of Canada.* Toronto: University of Toronto Press, 1942.

Cleland, Hugh. *George Washington in the Ohio Valley.* Pittsburgh, Penn.: University of Pittsburgh Press, 1955.

Colden, Jane. *Botanic Manuscript of Jane Colden.* Edited by H. Rickertt. New York: Chanticleer Press for the Garden Club of Orange and Duchess Counties, 1973.

Coleman, Kenneth. *Colonial Georgia: A History.* History of the American Colonies. Edited by M. Klein. New York: Scribner, 1976.

Colonial Laws of New York from the Year 1664 to the Revolution. 5 vols. Albany: J.B. Lyon, State Printer, 1894.

Company for Propagation of the Gospel in New England. *Some Correspondence Between the Governors and Treasurers of the New England Company in London and the Commissioners of the United Colonies in America.* London: Spottswood and Company, 1896.

Cooper, Thomas, ed. *Statutes at Large of South Carolina.* Vol. 3. Columbia, S.C.: 1838.

Cott, Nancy, ed. *Root of Bitterness: Documents of the Social History of American Women.* New York: Dutton, 1972.

Cremin, Lawrence A. *American Education: The Colonial Experience 1607–1783.* New York: Harper and Row, 1970.

Cresswell, Nicholas. *Journal of Nicholas Cresswell.* New York: Dial Press, 1924.

Cruickshank, Helen Gere, ed. *John and William Bartram's America: Selections from the Writings of the Philadelphia Naturalists.* American Naturalist Series. Edited by F. Wiley. New York: Devin-Adair Company, 1957.

Cunningham, John T. *New Jersey.* Colonial Histories. New York: Thomas Nelson, 1971.

Cutter, Donald, and Engstrand, Iris. *Quest for Empire: Spanish Settlement in the Southwest* Golden, Colo.: Fulcrum, 1996.

Daniell, Jere R. *Colonial New Hampshire: A History.* History of the American Colonies. Edited by Klein and J. Cooke Millwood, N.Y.: KTO Press, 1981.

Davis, Harold E. *The Fledgling Province: Social and Cultural Life in Colonial Georgia, 1733–1776.* Chapel Hill: University of North Carolina Press for the Institute of Early American History and Culture, Williamsburg, 1976.

Delanglez, Jean, S.J. *The French Jesuits in Lower Louisiana, 1700–1763.* Catholic University Studies in American Church History, Vol. 21. Washington, D.C.: Catholic University of America, 1935.

Dexter, Elisabeth Anthony. *Colonial Women of Affairs: A Study of Women in Business and the Professions in America Before 1776.* Boston, Mass.: Houghton Mifflin, 1924.

Dobyns, Henry F. *Spanish Colonial Tucson: A Demographic History.* Tucson: University of Arizona Press, 1976.

———. "The Invasion of Florida: Disease and the Indians of Florida." In *Spanish Pathways in Florida, 1492–1992.* Edited by A. Henderson and G. Mormino. Sarasota, Fla.: Pineapple Press, 1991.

Dollier de Casson, François. *A History of Montreal 1640–1672.* Edited and translated by R. Flenley. London: J.M. Dent and Sons, 1928.

Dominguez, Fray Francisco Ananasio. *The Missions of New Mexico, 1776.* Translated by E. Adams and Father A. Chavez. Albuquerque: University of New Mexico Press, 1956.

Dorson, Richard M., ed. *American Rebels: Narratives of the Patriots.* New York: Pantheon Books, 1953.

Drinker, Elizabeth. *The Diary of Elizabeth Drinker: The Life Cycle of an Eighteenth Century Women.* Edited by E. Crane. Boston, Mass.: Northeastern University Press, 1994.

Earle, Alice Morse. *Colonial Dames and Good Wives.* Boston, Mass.: Houghton, Mifflin, 1895.

"The Earliest Extant Minute Books of the Spanish and Portuguese Congregation Shearith Israel in New York, 1728–1786." In *The Jewish Experience in America.* Edited by A. Karp. Vol. 1, *The Colonial Period.* Waltham, Mass.: American Jewish Historical Society, 1969.

Eccles, W. J. *The Canadian Frontier, 1534–1760*. Rev. ed. Histories of the American Frontier. Edited by R. Billington. Albuquerque: University of New Mexico Press, 1983.

Eddis, William. *Letters from America*. Edited by A. Land. Cambridge, Mass.: Harvard University Press, Belknap, 1969.

Edmonds, Walter D. *The Musket and the Cross*. Boston, Mass.: Little Brown, 1968.

Eldredge, Zoeth S. *The March of Portolá and the Discovery of the Bay of San Francisco*. San Francisco: California Promotion Committee, 1909.

Emerson, Everett, ed. *Letters from New England: The Massachusetts Bay Colony, 1629–1638*. Amherst: University of Massachusetts Press, 1976.

Espinosa, J. Manuel, trans. *First Expedition of Vargas into New Mexico, 1692*. Albuquerque: University of New Mexico Press, 1940.

Finegan, Thomas E. *Free Schools: A Documentary History of the Free School Movement in New York State*. Albany: University of the State of New York, 1921.

Firth, C. H., ed. *American Garland, being a Collection of Ballads Relating to America, 1563–1739*. Oxford, England: B. H. Blackwell, 1915.

Fitzpatrick, John. *The Merchant of Manchac: The Letterbooks of John Fitzpatrick, 1768–1790*. Edited by M. Dalrymple. Baton Rouge: Louisiana State University Press, 1978.

Fleming, Thomas. *Liberty! The American Revolution*. New York: Viking, 1997.

Franklin, Benjamin. *The Autobiography of Benjamin Franklin*. Boston, Mass.: Houghton Mifflin, Riverside Press, 1923.

———. *Writings*. Edited by J. A. L. LeMay. New York: Library of America, 1987.

French, B. F., ed. *Historical Collections of Louisiana and Florida*. New York: Albert Mason, 1875.

———. *Historical Memoirs of Louisiana*. Vol. 5. New York: Lampert, Blakeman, and Law, 1833.

Gannon, Michael. *The Cross in the Sand*. Gainesville: University Presses of Florida, 1993.

———, ed. *New History of Florida*. Gainesville: University Presses of Florida, 1996.

Gartrell, Ellen G. "Women Healers and Domestic Remedies in 18th Century America: The Recipe Book of Elizabeth Coates Paschall." In *Early American*

Medicine: A Symposium. Edited by R. Goler and P. Imperato. New York: Fraunces Tavern Museum, 1987.

Gaudet, Placide. "Acadian Genealogy and Notes." In *Report Concerning Canadian Archives for the Year 1905.* Appendix A of Vol. 2. Ottawa: E.S. Dawson, 1906.

Gayarré, Charles. *History of Louisiana.* 4 vols. New York: Redfield, 1854–56.

Gilbert, Sandra M., and Susan Gubar. *Norton Anthology of Literature by Women: The Tradition in English.* New York: Norton, 1985.

Goodrich, Calvin. *The First Michigan Frontier.* Ann Arbor: University of Michigan Press, 1940.

Hackett, Charles Wilson, ed. *Historical Documents Relating to New Mexico, Nueva Vizcaya, and Approaches Thereto, to 1773.* Vol. 3. Washington, D.C.: Carnegie Institution, 1937.

———. *Revolt of the Pueblo Indians of New Mexico and Otermín's Attempted Reconquest, 1680–1682.* 2 vols. Albuquerque: University of New Mexico Press, 1942.

Hakluyt, Richard. *Principal Navigations, Voyages, Traffiques and Discoveries of the English Nation.* 12 vols. Glasgow: J. MacLehose and Sons, 1903–05.

Hall, Clayton Colman, ed. *Narratives of Early Maryland, 1633–1684.* New York: Scribner, 1910.

Hamilton, Alexander. *Gentleman's Progress: The Itinerarium of Dr. Alexander Hamilton, 1744.* Ed. C. Bridenbaugh. Chapel Hill: University of North Carolina Press, 1948.

Hammond, George P., and Agipto Rey, eds. *Don Juan de Oñate, Colonizer of New Mexico, 1595–1628.* 2 vols. Albuquerque: University of New Mexico Press, 1953.

Hart, Albert Bushnell, ed. *American History as Told By Contemporaries.* Vol. 1, *Era of Colonization, 1492–1689.* New York: Macmillan, 1897.

———. *American History as Told By Contemporaries.* Vol. 2, *Building of the Republic, 1689–1788.* New York: Macmillan, 1898.

———. *Camps and Firesides of the American Revolution.* New York: Macmillan, 1922.

Hawke, David. *The Colonial Experience.* Indianapolis: Bobbs-Merrill Education Publishing, 1966.

Hazen-Hammond, Susan. *A Short History of Santa Fe.* San Francisco, Calif.: Lexikos, 1988.

Heimert, Alan, and Perry Miller, eds. *The Great Awakening: Documents Illustrating the Crisis and Its Consequences.* Indianapolis, Ind.: Bobbs Merrill, 1967.

Heineman, Hon. David E. "The Startling Experience of a Jewish Trader During Pontiac's Siege of Detroit in 1763." *AJHSP* 23 (1915): 31–35.

Henderson, Ann, and Gary R. Mormino, eds. *Spanish Pathways in Florida, 1492–1992.* Sarasota, Fla.: Pineapple Press, 1991.

Hening, William Waller, comp. *The Statutes at Large, Being a Collection of all the Laws of Virginia.* 13 vols. New York: Bartow, 1823.

Hennepin, Father Louis. *Description of Louisiana, Newly Discovered to the Southwest of New France by Order of the King.* 1683. Translated by M. Cross. Minneapolis: University of Minnesota Press, 1938.

Henry, Alexander. *Travels and Adventures in Canada and the Indian Territories Between the Years 1760 and 1776.* Edited by J. Bain. Rutland, Vt.: Charles E. Tuttle Co., 1969.

Hoff, Joan. *Law, Gender, and Injustice: A Legal History of U.S. Women.* New York: New York University Press, 1991.

Hofstadter, Richard. *Academic Freedom in the Age of the College.* New York: Columbia University Press, 1955, 1961.

Holli, Melvin G., ed. *Detroit.* Documentary History of American Cities. Edited by T. Hareven and S. Thernstrom. New York: Franklin Watts, New Viewpoints, 1976.

Horsmanden, Daniel. *The New York Conspiracy.* 1744. Edited by T.J. Davis. Boston, Mass.: Beacon Press, 1971.

Howard, George Elliot. *History of Matrimonial Institutions: Chiefly in England and the United States.* Vol. 2. Chicago, Ill.: University of Chicago Press, 1904.

Hudak, Leona M. *Early American Women Printers and Publishers, 1639–1820.* Metuchen, N.J.: Scarecrow Press, 1978.

Hutchinson, Thomas. *History of the Colony and Province of Massachusetts-Bay.* 1760. Reprint, Cambridge, Mass.: Harvard University Press, 1936.

Illick, Joseph E. *Colonial Pennsylvania: A History.* New York: Scribner, 1976.

Ingersoll, Thomas N. *Mammon and Manon in Early New Orleans: The First Slave Society in the Deep South, 1718–1819.* Knoxville: University of Tennessee Press, 1999.

James, Sydney V. *Colonial Rhode Island: A History.* History of the American Colonies. Edited by M. Klein and J. Cooke. New York: Scribner 1975.

Jarrett, Devereaux. "The Autobiography of Devereaux Jarrett." *William and Mary Quarterly,* 3rd series, vol. 10 (1952): 361.

Jefferson, Thomas. *Writings of Thomas Jefferson.* Vol. 2. Edited by P. Ford. New York: Putnam, 1893.

Jogues, Father Isaac. *Narrative of a Captivity among the Mohawk Indians and a Description of New Netherland in 1642–43.* New York: Edward Dunigan and Brother, 1856.

Johnson, Amandus. *Swedish Settlements on the Delaware.* 1911. Reprint, Baltimore, Md.: Genealogical Publishing Company, 1969.

———. *Instruction for Johan Printz, Governor of New Sweden.* Philadelphia, Penn.: Swedish Colonial Society, 1930.

Johnson, Cecil. *British West Indies, 1763–1783.* New Haven, Conn.: Yale University Press, 1943.

Johnson, Edward. *Johnson's Wonder-Working Providence, 1628–1651.* Edited by J. Franklin Jameson. New York: Scribner, 1910.

Jones, Charles C. Jr. *History of Georgia.* 2 vols. Boston, Mass.: Houghton, Mifflin, 1883.

Jones, Elizabeth. *Gentlemen and Jesuits: Quests for Glory and Adventure in the Early Days of New France.* Toronto: University of Toronto Press, 1986.

Journals of Each Provincial Congress of Massachusetts in 1774 and 1775, and of the Committee of Safety, with an Appendix. . . . Boston: Dutton and Wentworth, Printers to the State, 1838.

Joutel, Henri. *Journal of LaSalle's Last Voyage.* London, 1714. Reprint, New York: Corinth Books, 1962.

Kalm, Pehr [Peter]. *Travels into North America.* 2nd ed. 2 vols. 1749, London: T. Lowndes, 1761.

Kalm, Peter. *Peter Kalm's Travels in North America.* Edited by A. Benson. New York: Wilson-Erickson, 1937.

Kammen, Michael. *Colonial New York: A History.* History of the American Colonies. Edited by M. Klein and J. Cooke. New York: Scribner, 1975.

Kelley, Joseph J., Jr. *Pennsylvania, The Colonial Years, 1681–1776.* Garden City, N.Y.: Doubleday, 1980.

Kessell, John L. *Friars, Soldiers, and Reformers: Hispanic Arizona and the Sonora Mission Frontier, 1767–1856.* Tucson: University of Arizona Press, 1976.

————. *Kiva, Cross, and Crown: The Pecos Indians and New Mexico, 1540–1840.* Washington, D.C.: National Park Service, 1979.

————. *Mission of Sorrows: Jesuit Guevavi and the Pimas, 1891–1767.* Tucson: University of Arizona Press, 1970.

Kingsbury, Susan Myra, ed. *Records of the Virginia Company of London.* 4 vols. Washington, D.C.: GPO, 1906–35.

Klein, Philip S., and Ari Hoogenboom. *A History of Pennsylvania.* 2nd ed. University Park: Pennsylvania State University Press, 1980.

Knight, Edgar Wallace. *Documentary History of Education in the South before 1860.* 5 vols. Chapel Hill: University of North Carolina Press, 1949–53.

Kolchin, Peter. *American Slavery, 1619–1817.* New York: Hill and Wang, 1993.

Kupperman, Karen Ordahl. *Roanoke: The Abandoned Colony.* Totowa, N.J.: Rowman and Allanheld, 1984.

Labaree, Benjamin W. *Colonial Massachusetts: A History.* History of the American Colonies. Edited by M. Klein and J. Cooke. Millwood, N.Y.: KTO Press, 1979.

Lahontan, Baron de. *New Voyages to North America.* 2 vols. 1703. Edited by R. Thwaites. Chicago, Ill.: A. C. McClurg, 1905.

LaMontagne, Leopold, ed. *Royal Fort Frontenac.* Trans. R. Preston. Toronto: Champlain Society, 1958.

Land, Aubrey C. *Colonial Maryland: A History.* History of the American Colonies. Edited by M. Klein and J. Cooke. Millwood, N.Y.: KTO Press, 1981.

Landers, Jane. *Black Society in Spanish Florida.* Urbana: University of Illinois Press, 1999.

Lane, Mills, ed. *General Oglethorpe's Georgia: Colonial Letters 1733–1743.* 2 vols. Savannah: Beehive Press, 1975.

Labaree, Leonard W., and Whitfield J. Bell, Jr., eds. *Mr. Franklin: A Selection from his Personal Letters.* New Haven, Conn.: Yale University Press, 1956.

Langdon, George D., Jr. *Pilgrim Colony: A History of New Plymouth 1620–1691.* New Haven, Conn.: Yale University Press, 1966.

Laws of the Commonwealth of Pennsylvania, from the 14th Day of October 1700 to [April 1822]. 7 vols. Philadelphia: J. Bioren, 1810–1822.

Lawson, John. *History of North Carolina.* 1714. Richmond, Va.: Garrett and Massie, 1937.

Lees, John. *Journal of J.L. of Quebec, Merchant.* Detroit: Society of Colonial Wars of the State of Michigan, 1911.

Lefler, Hugh T., and William S. Powell. *Colonial North Carolina: A History.* History of the American Colonies. Edited by M. Klein and J. Cooke. New York: Scribner, 1973.

Le Moyne, Pierre, Sieur d'Iberville. *Iberville's Gulf Journals.* Translated and edited by R. McWilliams. University, Ala.: University of Alabama Press, 1981.

Leonard, Irving Albert, trans. *The Mercurio Volante of Don Carlos de Sigüenza y Góngora: An Account of the First Expedition of Don Diego de Vargas into New Mexico in 1692.* Los Angeles, Calif.: Quivera Society, 1932.

———. *Spanish Approach to Pensacola, 1689–1693.* Albuquerque, N. Mex.: Quivira Society, 1939.

Lerner, Gerda, ed. *The Female Experience: An American Documentary.* Indianapolis, Ind.: Bobbs Merrill, 1977.

Lescarbot, Marc. *Nova Francia: A Description of Acadia, 1606.* Translated by P. Erondelle. 1609. New York: Harper and Brothers, 1928.

Levermore, Charles Herbert, ed. *Forerunners and Competitors of the Pilgrims and Puritans.* Vol. 2. Brooklyn: New England Society of Brooklyn, 1912.

Locke, John. *Fundamental Constitutions of Carolina.* 1669. Avalon Project. URL yale.edu/lawweb/avalon.

Lorant, Stefan, ed. *The New World: The First Pictures of America.* New York: Duell, Sloan, and Pearce, 1946.

———. *Pittsburgh: The Story of an American City.* Updated ed. Lenox, Mass.: Authors Editions, Inc., 1974.

Lyon, Eugene. "Settlement and Survival." In *New History of Florida.* Edited by M. Gannon. Gainesville: University Presses of Florida, 1996.

Macdonald, William, ed. *Documentary Source Book of American History.* New York: Macmillan, 1908.

Mackenzie, Frederick. *A British Fusilier in Revolutionary Boston.* Edited by A. French. Cambridge, Mass.: Harvard University Press, 1926.

———. *Diary of Frederick Mackenzie.* Vol. 1. Cambridge, Mass.: Harvard University Press, 1926.

MacKirdy, Kenneth, John S. Moir, and Yves, F. Zoltvany. *Changing Perspectives in Canadian History.* Notre Dame: University of Notre Dame Press, 1967.

Mahaffie, Charles D., Jr. *A Land of Discord Always: Acadia from Its Beginning to the Expulsion of its People, 1604–1755*. Camden, Maine: Down East Books, 1995.

Marcus, Jacob Rader. *The Jew in the American World: A Sourcebook*. Detroit, Mich.: Wayne State University Press, 1966.

Marie de l'Incarnation, mère. *Marie of the Incarnation: Selected Writings*. Edited and translated by Irene Mahoney, O.S.U. New York: Paulist Press, 1989.

Mather, Cotton. *Diary of Cotton Mather, 1681–1708*. Boston: Massachusetts Historical Society, 1911.

———. *Magnalia Christi Americana, or, the Ecclesiastical History of New England*. 1702. Vol. 2. Hartford, Conn.: Silas Andrus, 1820.

Massachusetts Historical Society *Collections*. 70 vols. comprising series 1 to 7. Boston: Massachusetts Historical Society, 1792–.

Massachusetts Historical Society *Proceedings*. 109 Vols. Boston: Massachusetts Historical Society, 1879–1997.

McClure, David. *Diary of David McClure, Doctor of Divinity*. New York: Knickerbocker Press, 1899.

McDermott, John Francis, ed. *The Early Histories of St. Louis*. St. Louis: St. Louis Historical Documents Fund, 1952.

Melvin, James. *Journal of James Melvin, Private Soldier in Arnold's Expedition Against Quebec in the Year 1775*. Edited by A. Melvin. Portland, Maine: Hubbard W. Bryant, 1902.

Mereness, Newton D., ed. *Travels in the American Colonies*. New York: Macmillan, 1916.

Merrens, H. Roy, ed. *The Colonial South Carolina Scene: Contemporary Views, 1697–1774*. Columbia: University of South Carolina Press, 1977.

Miller, Perry. *New England Mind, From Colony to Province*. Cambridge, Mass.: Harvard University Press, 1953.

———. *Major Writers of America*. 2 vols. New York: Harcourt, Brace and World, 1962.

Mittelberger, Gottlieb, *Journey to Pennsylvania in the Year 1750*. Translated by C. Eben, Philadelphia, Penn.: John Joseph McVey, 1898.

Moore, John Preston. *Revolt in Louisiana: The Spanish Occupation, 1766–1770*. Baton Rouge: Louisiana State University Press, 1976.

Mordecai, Gratz. "Notice of Jacob Mordecai, Founder and Proprietor from 1809 to 1818 of the Warrenton (N.C.) Female Seminary." *AJHSP* 6 (1897): 39–48.

Morgan, Edmund S. *American Slavery, American Freedom: The Ordeal of Colonial Virginia.* New York: Norton, 1975.

Morgan, Philip D. *Slave Counterpoint: Black Culture in the Eighteenth-Century Chesapeake and Lowcountry.* Chapel Hill: University of North Carolina Press for the Omohundro Institute of Early American History and Culture, 1998.

Morison, Samuel Eliot. *Builders of the Bay Colony.* 2nd ed. Boston: Houghton Mifflin, 1958.

———. *The Founding of Harvard College.* Cambridge, Mass.: Harvard University Press, 1935.

———. *Samuel de Champlain, Father of New France.* Boston, Mass.: Little Brown, 1972.

Morton, Richard L. *Colonial Virginia.* 2 vols. Chapel Hill: University of North Carolina Press for the Virginia Historical Society, 1960.

Morton, Thomas. *New English Canaan.* Amsterdam: Jacob Frederick Stam, 1637. Reprint, New York: Da Capo, 1969.

Muhlenberg, Henry Melchior. *Journals.* Translated by T. Tappert and J. Doberstein, Vol. 1. Philadelphia, Penn.: Muhlenberg Press, 1942.

Munroe, John A. *Colonial Delaware: A History.* History of the American Colonies. Edited by M. Klein and J. Cooke. Millwood, N.Y.: KTO Press, 1978.

Murdoch, Beamish. *A History of Nova-Scotia or Acadie.* Vol. 1. Halifax: James Barnes, 1865.

Myers, Albert, ed. *Narratives of Early Pennsylvania, West New Jersey, and Delaware, 1630–1707.* Original Narratives of Early American History. New York: Scribner, 1912.

Nash, Gary. *Red, White, and Black: The Peoples of Early North America.* 4th ed. Upper Saddle River, N.J.: Prentice Hall, 2000.

New Hampshire. *Provincial Papers: Documents and Records Relating to the Province of New Hampshire, from the Earliest Period of its Settlement: 1623–[1776].* 5 vols. Edited by N. Bouton. Concord, N.H.: G.E. Jenks, State Printer, 1867–73.

Nineteenth of April, 1775: A Collection of First-Hand Accounts. Lincoln, Mass.: Sawtells of Somerset, 1968.

Norman, Charles. *Discovers of America: A Wilderness Continent Seen Through the Eyes of the First Explorers.* New York: Crowell, 1968.

NYSL (New York State Library). *Van Rensselaer Bowier Manuscripts.* Ed. and trans. by A. J. F. van Laer. Albany: University of the State of New York, 1908.

O'Callaghan, E. B. *Documentary History of the State of New York.* 4 vols. Albany: Weed, Parsons, 1849–51.

Osborn, Sarah. *Memoirs of the Life of Mrs. Sarah Osborn.* Edited by S. Hopkins. Worcester, Mass.: Leonard Worcester, 1799.

Palou, Fray Francisco, O.F.M. *Historical Memoirs of New California.* 4 vols. Edited by H. Bolton. Berkeley: University of California Press, 1926.

Parkman, Francis. *The Old Regime in Canada.* Vol. 1. In *France and England in North America.* Edited by D. Levin. New York: Viking, Literary Classics of the United States, 1983.

Pedley, Charles. *The History of Newfoundland.* London: Longman Green, 1863.

Piersen, William D. *Black Yankees: The Development of an Afro-American Subculture in Eighteenth-Century New England.* Amherst: University of Massachusetts Press, 1988.

———. *From Africa to America: African American History from the Colonial Era to the Early Republic, 1526–1790.* New York: Twayne Publishers, 1996.

Pitt, William. *Correspondence of William Pitt When Secretary of State with Colonial Governors and Military and Naval Commissioners in America.* 2 vols. Edited by G. Kimball. New York: Macmillan, 1906.

Pomfret, John E. *Colonial New Jersey: A History.* History of the American Colonies. Edited by M. Klein and J. Cooke. New York: Scribner, 1973.

Poore, Benjamin Perley, ed. *Federal and State Constitutions, Colonial Charters, and Other Organic Laws of the United States.* 2 vols. Washington, D.C.: GPO, 1878.

Preston, Howard W., ed. *Documents Illustrative of American History, 1606–1863.* New York: Putnam, 1907.

Prowse, D. W. *History of Newfoundland from the English, Colonial, and Foreign Records.* London: Macmillan, 1895.

Quarles, Benjamin. *The Negro in the American Revolution.* Williamsburg, Va.: Institute of Early American History and Culture, University of North Carolina Press, 1961, 1996.

Quebec English Schools Network [database online]. "Some Missing Pages: The Black Community in the History of Quebec and Canada." Rev. 1996. URL:qesn.meq.gouv.qc.ca.

Quinn, David B. *North America from Earliest Discovery to First Settlements: The Norse Voyages–1612.* New York: Harper and Row, 1977.

————. *North American Discovery, Circa 1000–1612.* Documentary History of the United States. New York: Harper and Row, 1971.

Quinn, David B., and Allison Quinn, eds. *New American World: A Documentary History.* Vol. 5, *Extension of Settlement in Florida, Virginia, and the Spanish Southwest.* New York: Arno Press, 1979.

Radisson, Pierre Espirit. *Explorations of Pierre Esprit Radisson.* Edited by A. Adams. Minneapolis, Minn.: Ross and Haines, 1961.

Reese, Trevor R., ed. *The Most Delightful Country of the Universe: Promotional Literature of the Colony of Georgia, 1717–1734.* Savannah: Beehive Press, 1972.

————. *Clamorous Malcontents: Criticisms and Defenses of the Colony of Georgia, 1741–1743.* Savannah, Ga.: Beehive Press, 1973.

"Remonstrance of the Inhabitants of the Town of Flushing." 1657. Long Island: Our Story. URL: lihistory.com.

Riendeau, Roger, *Brief History of Canada.* Markham, Ontario: Fitzhenry and Whiteside, 2000.

Rink, Oliver A. *Holland on the Hudson: An Economic and Social History of Dutch New York.* Ithaca, N.Y.: Cornell University Press, 1989.

Robinson, W. Stitt. *The Southern Colonial Frontier, 1607–1763.* Albuquerque: University of New Mexico Press, 1979.

Rogers, Alan. *Empire and Liberty: American Resistance to British Authority, 1755–1763.* Berkeley: University of California Press, 1974.

Rolle, Andrew P. *California: A History.* 4th ed. Arlington Heights, Ill.: Harlan Davidson, 1987.

Romans, Bernard. *A Concise Natural History of East and West Florida.* Vol. 1. New York: [printed for the author], 1775.

Rowe, Frederick W. *A History of Newfoundland and Labrador.* Toronto: McGraw Hill Ryerson, 1980.

Russell, Nelson Vance. *The British Régime in the Old Northwest, 1760–1796.* Northfield, Minn.: Carleton College, 1939.

Salley, Alexander S., ed. *Narratives of Early Carolina, 1650–1708.* Original Narratives of Early American History. New York: Scribner, 1911.

Santos, Richard G., trans. *Aguayo Expedition into Texas, 1721.* Austin, Texas: Jenkins Publishing, 1981.

Schaw, Janet. *Journal of a Lady of Quality, Being a Narrative of a Journey from Scotland to the West Indies, North Carolina, and Portugal, in the Years 1774 to 1776.* Edited by E. Andrews. New Haven, Conn.: Yale University Press, 1921.

Scholes, Frances V. "The First Decade of the Inquisition in New Mexico." *New Mexico Historical Review* 19 (1935): 195–241.

————. *Church and State in New Mexico, 1610–1650.* Albuquerque: Historical Society of New Mexico, 1937.

————. *Troublous Times in New Mexico, 1659–1670.* Albuquerque: Historical Society of New Mexico, 1942.

Sewall, Samuel. *Diary of Samuel Sewall.* Edited by H. Wish. New York: Capricorn, 1967.

Shurtleff, Nathaniel B. *Records of the Governor and Company of the Massachusetts Bay in New England.* 5 vols. Boston, Mass.: W. White, 1853–54.

Silverman, Kenneth, ed. *Colonial American Poetry.* New York: Hafner, 1968.

Simmons, Marc. *Albuquerque, A Narrative History.* Albuquerque: University of New Mexico Press, 1982.

Spruill, Julia C. *Women's Life and Work in the Southern Colonies.* Chapel Hill: University of North Carolina Press, 1938.

Steele, Ian K. *Warpaths: Invasions of North America.* New York: Oxford University Press, 1994.

Strachey, William, comp. *For the Colony in Virginea Britannia.* 1612. Reprint, London: W. Burre, 1900.

Streeter, Sebastian F., ed. *Papers Relating to the Early History of Maryland.* Baltimore: Maryland Historical Society, 1876.

Taylor, Robert J. *Colonial Connecticut: A History.* History of the American Colonies. Edited by M. Klein and J. Cooke. Millwood, N.Y.: KTO Press, 1979.

Tebbel, John. *Compact History of the American Newspaper.* Rev. ed. New York: Hawthorn Books, 1969.

Texada, David K. *Alejandro O'Reilly and the New Orleans Rebels.* Lafayette: University of Southwestern Louisiana History Series, 2, 1970.

Thorpe, Francis Newton, ed. *The Federal and State Constitutions, Colonial Charters, and Other Organic Laws of the States, Territories, and Colonies Now or Heretofore Forming the United States of America.* Vol. 1. Washington, D.C.: GPO, 1909.

Thwaites, Reuben G., ed. *Jesuit Relations and Allied Documents.* 73 vols. Cleveland, Ohio: Burrows Brothers, 1896–1901.

Todd, Helen. *Mary Musgrove, Georgia Indian Princess.* Chicago: Seven Oaks, 1981.

Troen, Selwyn K., and Glen E. Holt, eds. *St. Louis.* Documentary History of American Cities. Edited by T. Hareven and S. Thernstrom. New York: New Viewpoints, Franklin Watts, 1977.

Tyler, Lyon Gardiner, ed. *Narratives of Early Virginia, 1606–1625. Original Narratives of Early American History.* New York: Scribner, 1907.

Tyrrell, Joseph Burr, ed. *Documents Relating to the Early History of Hudson's Bay.* Toronto: Champlain Society, 1931.

VanDerBeets, Richard, ed. *Held Captive by Indians: Selected Narratives 1642–1836.* Knoxville: University of Tennessee Press, 1973.

Vaughan, Alden T., and Edward W. Clark, eds. *Puritans Among the Indians: Accounts of Captivity and Redemption, 1676–1724.* Cambridge, Mass.: Harvard University Press, Belknap, 1981.

Virginia Magazine of History and Biography. Richmond: Virginia Historical Society. V, 1–; July 1893–.

Wagoner, Jay J. *Early Arizona: Prehistory to Civil War.* Tucson: University of Arizona Press, 1995.

Wallower, Lucille. *Colonial Pennsylvania.* N.p.: Thomas Nelson and Sons, 1969.

Washington, George. *Affectionately Yours, George Washington: A Self-Portrait in Letters of Friendship.* Edited by T. Fleming. New York: W. W. Norton, 1967.

———. *Basic Writings of George Washington.* Edited by Saxe Commins. New York: Random House, 1948.

———. *Journal of Colonel George Washington.* Edited by J. Toner. Albany, N.Y.: Joel Munsell's Sons, 1893.

———. *The Writings of George Washington from the Original Manuscript Sources, 1745–1799.* Edited by J. Fitzpatrick. Vol. 10. Washington D.C.: Government Printing Office, 1931–44.

Weber, David J. *The Spanish Frontier in North America.* New Haven, Conn.: Yale University Press, 1992.

Weeks, Lyman Horace, and Edwin M. Bacon, eds. *An Historical Digest of the Provincial Press.* Vol. 1. Boston, Mass.: Society for Americana, Inc., 1911.

Weir, Robert M. *Colonial South Carolina: A History.* History of the American Colonies. Edited by M. Klein and J. Cooke. Millwood, N.Y.: KTO Press, 1983.

West, Willis Mason, ed. *Source Book in American History to 1787.* Boston: Allyn and Bacon, 1913.

William and Mary Quarterly. 2nd series, vols. 1–23 (January 1921–October 1943.)

Williams, Roger. *Letters of Roger Williams.* Edited by J. Bartlett. Providence, R.I.: Narragansett Club, 1874.

Winks, Robin. *The Blacks in Canada: A History.* Montreal: McGill-Queen's University Press, 1971.

Winslow, Anna Green. *Diary of Anna Green Winslow, a Boston School Girl of 1771.* Edited by A. Earle. Boston, Mass.: Houghton Mifflin, 1894.

Winthrop, John. *History of New England from 1630 to 1649.* 2 vols. Edited by J. Savage. Boston, Mass.: Little Brown, 1853.

———. *Journal of John Winthrop, 1630–1649.* Abridged ed. Edited by R. Dunn and L. Yeandle. Cambridge, Mass.: Harvard University Press, Belknap, 1996.

———. *Winthrop Papers.* Boston, Mass.: Massachusetts Historical Society, 1929–.

Wood, Gordon S., ed. *The Rising Glory of America, 1760–1820.* New York: Braziller, 1971.

Wood, Peter H. *The Black Majority: Negroes in Colonial South Carolina from 1670 through the Stono Rebellion.* New York: Alfred A. Knopf, 1974.

———. "The Impact of Smallpox on the Native Population of the 18th-Century South." In *Early American Medicine: A Symposium.* Edited by R. Goler and P. Imperato. New York: Fraunces Tavern Museum, 1987.

Woodcock, George. *The Canadians.* Cambridge, Mass.: Harvard University Press, 1979.

Woodmason, Charles. *The Carolina Backcountry on the Eve of the Revolution: The Journal and other Writings of Charles Woodmason, Anglican Itinerant.* Edited by R. Hooker. Chapel Hill: University of North Carolina Press for the Institute of Early American Culture, Williamsburg, 1953.

Woolman, John. *Journal and Essays.* Edited by A. Gummere. New York: Macmillan, 1922.

Wortman, Marlene Stein, ed. *Women in American Law.* Vol. 1, *From Colonial Times to the New Deal.* New York: Holmes & Meier, 1985.

Young, Alexander, ed. *Chronicles of the First Planters of the Colony of Massachusetts Bay, from 1623–1636*. Boston, Mass.: Charles C. Little and James Brown, 1846.

Zoltvany, Yves F., ed. *The French Tradition in America*. Documentary History of the United States. New York: Harper and Row, 1969.

INDEX

Page locators in **boldface** indicate main entries.
Page locators in *italic* indicate illustrations. Page locators followed by an *m* indicate maps.

A

Abbadie, Jean-Jacques 349, 361
Abenaki Indians 261, 262, 281, 283
Academy of Pennsylvania 308
Acadia 20. *See also* Port Royal, Acadia
  before 1607 5, 17–18
  from 1607 to 1670 56
  from 1670 to 1750 194, 195, 211, 261, 281, 282, 305, 319
  from 1750 to 1776 340–342, 359–361
  chronicle of events, 1607–1670 **56–59**
  eyewitness testimony, 1607–1670 **60–63, 68, 71**
  fur trade in 16–18
  historical context, 1607–1670 **53–54**
  and King William's War 260
  St. Croix 17–18, 21
  and Treaty of Utrecht 261
Acadia and the Gulf of St. Lawrence 515*m*
Ackerman House (New Jersey) *269*
Acoma Indians 12
Acoma Pueblo *11*, 21
Acre, Louis-Armand de Lom d' *See* Lahontan, baron de
Act for Better Regulating the Government of Massachusetts 397
Act of Union 281
Acts of Capitulation 340
Adams, Abigail Smith 432, **477**
Adams, John 410, 424, 432–433, **477**
  and colony's allegiance 397
  and Declaration of Independence 406
  and Declaration of Rights and Resolves 399
  at First Continental Congress 424–425
  as Founding Father 389
  as Son of Liberty 396
  from *Works* 416
Adams, Samuel 389, 391, 395–397, 410, **477**
Adam Thoroughgood House (Virginia) *126*

Address to the Inhabitants of Great Britain 401–402
adelantados 8, 11
Administration of Justice Act 339, 397
adobe architecture 44
Affectionately Yours (Washington) 429–430
Africa xiv–xv, 272–273
African-American culture 349, 387–388
Africans xiv–xvi, 5, 79. *See also* blacks; slavery
Age of Reason 308
agriculture. *See* farming
Aguayo, marqués de 205–206, **477–478**
Aguayo Expedition (Santos) 222
Aguilar, Alfonso Rael de 221
Aguilera, Teresa de 43
Akimel O'odham (Pima) Indians 204, 353
Alarcón, Martín de 205
Albany 236, 241, 244, 339
  city council meeting in 289
  fur trade in 269
  from 1670 to 1691 244
  from 1750 to 1776 359
Albany Conference 408
Albany Plan of Union, 1754 339, 359, 460–462
Albemarle 234, 242, *242m,* 244. *See also* North Carolina
Albuquerque 204, 211, 353
Albuquerque (Simmons) 363
alcaldes 42
Alden, John 84
aldermen 260
Alejandro (Texada) 374–375
Alexander, William (earl of Stirling) 53, 57, 82, 150–155, **478**
Alexander VI (pope) 5, 19
Algonkin Indians 48
Algonquian Indians 79, 85, 89, 157, 171, 233
Allen, Ethan 401, 411, 429, **478**
Allen, John 424
Allerton, Issac 86, 93
almanacs 316

Alsop, George 187–188
Alta California 356, 357, 361
Altamirano, Don Juan Cabezas 10, 22, 36
Altman, Father John 123
Amandas, Philip 13–14
America, map of, 1562 *4m*
American Education (Cremin) 324
American Garland (Firth) 175
American History (Hart)
  from 1607 to 1630 106
  from 1630 to 1642 135, 139–142, 145
  from 1642 to 1670 176–181, 183–188
  from 1670 to 1691 (English colonies) 246–257
  from 1670 to 1750 (New France, New Spain) 215, 218, 223–224
  from 1690 to 1730 (English colonies) 285–293, 295, 296
  from 1730 to 1750 (English colonies) 321, 325–327, 329, 331
  from 1750 to 1776 339, 363–364, 366–368, 413–415, 417–425, 427, 431–434
American Jeremiad (Bercovitch) 189
American Mercury 297
American Negro Slave Revolts (Aptheker) 297
American Rebels (Dorson) 428
American Revolution. *See* Revolutionary War
America (Theodore De Bry) 15
Ames, Nathaniel 316, 325
Amherst, Jeffrey 340, 342–343, 360, 370, 380, 415, **478**
Amish 267
Andrews, John 422–423
Andros, Sir Edmund 235, 236, 239–240, 243, 245, **478**
Anglican Church. *See* Church of England
Anglo-Dutch Wars 162
Anglo-Spanish War 208, 304, 319
Angola 273
Annapolis, Maryland 276, 280, 310, 319

Annapolis Royal 281
Anne (queen of England) 259, 261, 281, 282, 290, **478**
antinomian movement 115
Anza, Juan Bautista de 357–358, 362, 374, **478**
Apache Indians 202–205, 353, 354
Apalachee Indians 57, 58
  Moore's capture of 277
  rebellions by 46
  in St. Augustine 44, 208, 209
  sold into slavery 211
Appalachian Mountains 381, 382, 385
Aquidneck 115
Arcadia 5. *See also* Acadia
Archdale, John 217
Argall, Samuel 53, 57, 76, 78, 80, 91, **478**
Arizona 204–205
  from 1670 to 1750 211, 212
  from 1750 to 1776 353–355, 359, 361, 362
Arizonac 205, 212
Ark (ship) 122, 130
Arlington, Lord (Henry Bennet) 229, 243
Arnold, Benedict 401, 403, 411, **478–479**
arpents 52
Arriola, Andrés de 206
arson 310
Arte (ship) 122
articles of confederation 411
Articles of Confederation and Perpetual Union 402
Ash, John 289–290
Asia, trade routes to xiii–xv
assemblies, colonial 259–260. *See also specific colonies*
assistants 259
Association (agreement) 399, 400, 411, 425
Atlantic coast, exploration of xv, 87
Attucks, Crispus 403, **479**
Aubry, Charles Philippe 349, 350, 361, 372, **479**

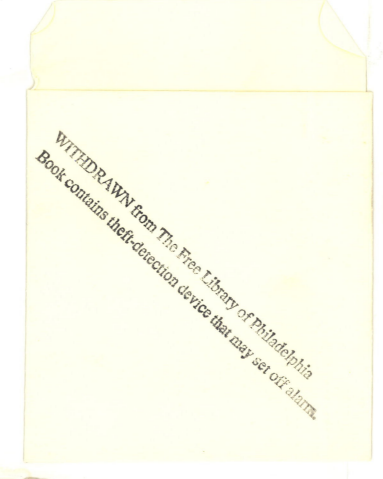